Halliday
WINE COMPANION

ESTABLISHED 1986 · WINECOMPANION.COM.AU

2024

THE BESTSELLING AND DEFINITIVE GUIDE TO AUSTRALIAN WINE
EDITED BY CAMPBELL MATTINSON

Hardie Grant

BOOKS

Published in 2023 by Hardie Grant Books,
an imprint of Hardie Grant Publishing

Hardie Grant Books (Melbourne)
Wurundjeri Country
Building 1, 658 Church Street
Richmond, Victoria 3121

Hardie Grant Books (London)
5th & 6th Floors
52–54 Southwark Street
London SE1 1UN

hardiegrant.com/books

The *Halliday Wine Companion* is a joint venture between James Halliday and
HGX Pty Ltd.

The map in this publication incorporates data copyright © Commonwealth of
Australia (Geoscience Australia) 2004. Geoscience Australia has not evaluated
the data as altered and incorporated within this publication and therefore gives
no warranty regarding accuracy, completeness, currency or suitability for any
particular purpose.

Australian wine zones and wine regions data copyright © Wine Australia

Halliday Wine Companion 2024
ISBN 978 1 76145 003 7

Cover design by Pidgeon Ward
Cover art by Ka Mo
Photography by Briony Hardinge
Typeset by Megan Ellis
Edited by Nola James
Printed in Australia by McPherson's Printing Group, Maryborough, Victoria

Printed in Australia by Griffin Press, an Accredited ISO AS/NZS 14001
Environmental Management System printer.

The paper this book is printed on is certified against the Forest
Stewardship Council® Standards. Griffin Press holds FSC® chain
of custody certification SCS-COC-001185. FSC® promotes
environmentally responsible, socially beneficial and economically
viable management of the world's forests.

Hardie Grant acknowledges the Traditional Owners of the country on which we
work, the Wurundjeri people of the Kulin nation and the Gadigal people of the
Eora nation, and recognises their continuing connection to the land, waters and
culture. We pay our respects to their Elders past and present.

Contents

The tasting team

James Halliday

Respected wine critic and vigneron James Halliday is the founder of the *Halliday Wine Companion*. With a wine career spanning over 50 years, he was one of the founders of Brokenwood in the Hunter Valley, and later, Coldstream Hills in the Yarra Valley. James is an unmatched authority on all aspects of the wine industry, and for more than 30 years, was among the most senior and active wine judges in Australia. He has won a clutch of awards for his contributions, including the Australian wine industry's ultimate accolade, the Maurice O'Shea Award. In 2010 he was made of Member of the Order of Australia for his services to the wine industry. James has written or contributed to over 80 books on wine since 1970 and has written a weekly wine column for Australian newspapers since 1978.

Regional focus: Hunter Valley, NSW; Langhorne Creek, SA

Campbell Mattinson

Campbell Mattinson fell in love with wine in the mid-1990s and no (good) wine, ever since, has been safe. He started *The WineFront* in 2002, produced three editions of *The Big Red Wine Book* (in 2008, 2009 and 2010; published by Hardie Grant) and his book *The Wine Hunter* – which won various awards both in Australia and overseas including a prestigious Louis Roederer International Wine Writers' Award – is now onto its fourth reprint. He is the only person to have won the Australian Wine Communicator of the Year Award twice.

Campbell was also the founding editor of *Halliday* magazine in 2012, and he's been a reviewer for the *Halliday Wine Companion* since 2013.

Regional focus: Fleurieu, Limestone Coast, Riverland, Southern Flinders Ranges, Southern Eyre Peninsula, SA; Heathcote, Western Victoria, North West Victoria, VIC

Website: campbellmattinson.com | Twitter: @CBMattinson | Instagram: @campbell.mattinson

Dave Brookes

An established wine journalist, Dave contributes to a range of publications here and overseas. Originally from New Zealand, Dave lived in South Australia's Barossa for many years and has almost 30 years' experience working in the wine industry across a range of sectors; including retail, wholesale, wineries, the secondary market and brand management. Dave was awarded Dux of the prestigious Len Evans Tutorial in 2011 and is a sought-after judge and panel chair on the wine show circuit, having judged at more than 70 wine shows around Australia and internationally.

Regional focus: Barossa and Eden valleys, SA; Tasmania

Instagram: @withnailian

Jane Faulkner

Jane is a journalist by training and wine writer by vocation. A long-time contributor and columnist for *Halliday* magazine, she has been reviewing for the *Companion* since 2016. Respected for her honesty and fairness yet rigour and independence in her writing and tasting, Jane is constantly honing those skills. She started her career in newspapers, later working at *The Age/ The Sydney Morning Herald*, and also in TV and radio. She is a sought-after wine judge, locally and internationally, and chairs numerous shows. On a personal level, Jane is an Italophile, spending considerable time each year visiting its wine regions and dreams of living in Piemonte. Yet she never tires of travelling throughout the wine world in search of stories and bottles from inspirational, thoughtful producers.

Regional focus: Margaret River, WA; Mornington Peninsula, Macedon Ranges, Sunbury and Gippsland, Vic; Southern NSW including Canberra

Twitter: @winematters | Facebook: Jane Faulkner | Instagram: @winematters

Jeni Port

Jeni is a trained journalist, who was a cadet on Melbourne's *The Sun News-Pictorial* newspaper (now *Herald Sun*) when she caught the wine bug. She was working in the paper's Women's Section (yes, really) and her first story was on a woman winemaker – a subject that would become a recurring theme over her career. She wrote a weekly food market review, which quickly incorporated wine stories and that was the start of the paper's first wine column. She covered wine in *The Age* for 30 years and is an author and wine judge here and overseas, including in Germany for Mundus Vini, and Europe for Concours Mondial de Bruxelles. Jeni has served on various wine bodies, is a founding board member of the Australian Women in Wine awards and has won numerous awards for wine writing over her career. She started the first Australian women wine judges' register for Australian wine shows to make use of, retiring from Australian wine show judging in 2021 to make space for young female associate judges to move up.

Regional focus: Central Victoria (Nagambie Lakes and Strathbogie Ranges) and North East Victoria (including Beechworth, King Valley and Rutherglen).

Twitter: @jeniport | Instagram: @jeniport | Facebook: Jeni Port

Mike Bennie

When Mike Bennie isn't wandering vineyards across the globe, he is a freelance wine and drinks writer, journalist and presenter. Mike is the wine/drinks editor for Australia's leading food magazine, *delicious.*, editor-at-large and contributor to Australia's most interactive wine commentary website, *The WineFront* and his work is found in a variety of other local and international publications. Mike is also a co-founder and partner in the Sydney-based P&V Wine + Liquor Merchants, a store and education space devoted to artisan fermented, brewed and distilled products. Mike is also the drinks director of the highly-respected *WA Good Food Guide*. He is a proud co-founder and co-director of the now-retired artisan and sustainability-focused Rootstock Sydney food and wine festival. Mike is currently the chair of the Australian Organic Wine Awards. He also makes a bit of wine in Tasmania and is a regular presenter at festivals and corporate and industry events.

Regional focus: Western Australia (except Margaret River); Clare Valley, SA; Granite Belt, Qld

Twitter: @mikebennie101 | Instagram: @mikebennie101

Ned Goodwin MW

Born in London, raised in Australia and educated in Tokyo and Paris, Ned splits his time between Tokyo, where he lived for 14 years, and his beloved Sydney. Ned is a Dux of the Len Evans Tutorial, Japan's first master of wine, an educator, consultant, judge, critic and motivational speaker and presenter. He has served as wine director for one of Asia's largest restaurant groups and was also the 'wine face' for All Nippon Airways. In addition, he is an Asian-focused ambassador for a champagne house, the host of *Langton's TV*, has had his own TV wine show in Japan, is on the Wine Committee at Italy's illustrious Biondi-Santi and has his own import company, Wine Diamonds. Before Japan, Ned was a sommelier, including at Michelin-starred Veritas in New York, which had arguably the finest wine list in the world.

Regional focus: McLaren Vale, Adelaide Hills, Adelaide Plains, SA

Twitter: @rednedwine | Instagram: @NedGoodwinMW

Philip Rich

Philip has more than 25 years' experience as a wine retailer, educator, show judge and writer. In 1996, Philip joined the van Haandels at The Prince of Wales and Stokehouse in Melbourne, where he was responsible for the wine buying, developing award-winning wine lists and sommelier training. Philip also co-founded Melbourne's Prince Wine Store and Bellota Wine Bar, and wrote the monthly wine column for *The Australian Financial Review Magazine* for 17 years. Philip has chaired various wine shows, including the James Halliday Chardonnay Challenge, Yarra Valley Wine Show, Margaret River Wine Show, Mornington Peninsula Wine Show and The Australian Pinot Noir Challenge. In addition to tasting for the *Companion*, Philip is the new chair for the Limestone Coast Wine Show and divides his time between helping look after France Soir's 6000 bottle cellar and consulting to MacPhee's.

Regional focus: Yarra Valley, Geelong VIC

Twitter: @jayer78 | Instagram: @psrichebourg

Shanteh Wale

Shanteh cut her teeth at Sydney's award-winning Quay Restaurant where she worked for over a decade as a sommelier and held the position of head sommelier from 2018 until 2022. She has been nominated for the *Good Food Guide* Sommelier of the Year Award on three occasions and her experience as a Len Evans scholar in 2019 was one of the highlights of her career. Shanteh is host of her own drinks podcast *Over A Glass* with the Deep in the Weeds Network, and spends her time writing for various publications and judging at regional, state and city wine shows across the country.

Regional focus: Central Ranges, Big Rivers, South Coast, Northern Rivers, Northern Slopes, NSW

Twitter: @shanteh | Instagram: @shantehwale

Halliday
WINE COMPANION

Australia's geographical indications

Regions and subregions marked with an asterisk are not registered but are in common usage.

NEW SOUTH WALES

WINE ZONE		WINE REGION		SUBREGION
Big Rivers	(A)	Murray Darling	1	
		Perricoota	2	
		Riverina	3	
		Swan Hill	4	
Central Ranges	(B)	Cowra	5	
		Mudgee	6	
		Orange	7	
Hunter Valley	(C)	Hunter	8	Broke Fordwich Pokolbin Upper Hunter
Northern Rivers	(D)	Hastings River	9	
Northern Slopes	(E)	New England Australia	10	
South Coast	(F)	Shoalhaven Coast	11	
		Southern Highlands	12	
Southern New South Wales	(G)	Canberra District	13	
		Gundagai	14	
		Hilltops	15	
		Tumbarumba	16	
Western Plains	(H)			

SOUTH AUSTRALIA

WINE ZONE		WINE REGION		SUBREGION
Adelaide Super Zone includes Mount Lofty Ranges, Fleurieu and Barossa wine regions				
Barossa		Barossa Valley	17	
		Eden Valley	18	High Eden
Fleurieu	(J)	Currency Creek	19	
		Kangaroo Island	20	
		Langhorne Creek	21	
		McLaren Vale	22	
		Southern Fleurieu	23	
Mount Lofty Ranges		Adelaide Hills	24	Lenswood Piccadilly Valley
		Adelaide Plains	25	
		Clare Valley	26	Polish River* Watervale*
Far North	(K)	Southern Flinders Ranges	27	
Limestone Coast	(L)	Coonawarra	28	
		Mount Benson	29	
		Mount Gambier	30	
		Padthaway	31	
		Robe	32	
		Wrattonbully	33	
Lower Murray	(M)	Riverland	34	
The Peninsulas	(N)	Southern Eyre Peninsula*	35	

AUSTRALIAN CAPITAL TERRITORY

WINE ZONE	WINE REGION	SUBREGION

NORTHERN TERRITORY

WINE ZONE	WINE REGION	SUBREGION

VICTORIA

WINE ZONE		WINE REGION		SUBREGION
Central Victoria	(P)	Bendigo	36	
		Goulburn Valley	37	Nagambie Lakes
		Heathcote	38	
		Strathbogie Ranges	39	
		Upper Goulburn	40	
Gippsland	(Q)			
North East Victoria	(R)	Alpine Valleys	41	
		Beechworth	42	
		Glenrowan	43	
		King Valley	44	
		Rutherglen	45	
North West Victoria	(S)	Murray Darling	46	
		Swan Hill	47	
Port Phillip	(T)	Geelong	48	
		Macedon Ranges	49	
		Mornington Peninsula	50	
		Sunbury	51	
		Yarra Valley	52	
Western Victoria	(U)	Ballarat*	53	
		Grampians	54	Great Western
		Henty	55	
		Pyrenees	56	

WESTERN AUSTRALIA

WINE ZONE		WINE REGION		SUBREGION
Central Western Australia	(V)			
Eastern Plains, Inland and North of Western Australia	(W)			
Greater Perth	(X)	Peel	57	
		Perth Hills	58	
		Swan District	59	Swan Valley
South West Australia	(Y)	Blackwood Valley	60	
		Geographe	61	
		Great Southern	62	Albany Denmark Frankland River Mount Barker Porongurup
		Manjimup	63	
		Margaret River	64	
		Pemberton	65	
West Australian South East Coastal	(Z)			

QUEENSLAND

WINE ZONE	WINE REGION		SUBREGION
Queensland	Granite Belt	66	
	South Burnett	67	

TASMANIA

WINE ZONE	WINE REGION		SUBREGION
Tasmania	Northern Tasmania*	68	
	Southern Tasmania*	69	
	East Coast Tasmania*	70	

N

0   500 km

Timor Sea

130°
10°

D.

120°

TANAMI
DESERT

GREAT SANDY

DESERT

INDIAN

HAMMERSLEY RA.

GIBSON

DESERT

20°

Tropic of Capricorn

WESTERN

OCEAN

W

AUSTRALIA

GREAT VICTORIA
DESERT

PLA

30°

NULLARBOR

X

Great Au

59 58

Perth ●

Z

57 V

61

60

64

63 62

Y

65

SOUTHERN

130°

120°

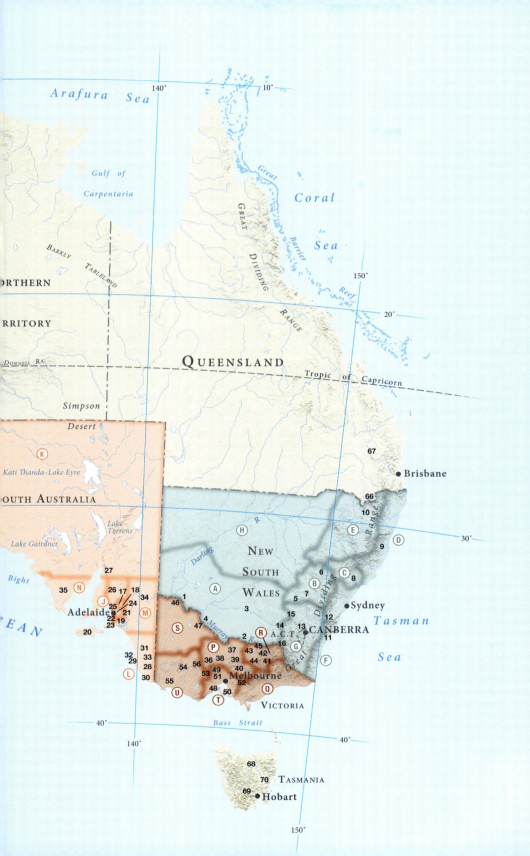

Arafura Sea

Gulf of Carpentaria

Coral

Sea

BARKLY TABLELAND

GREAT DIVIDING RANGE

Great Barrier Reef

NORTHERN
TERRITORY

DONNELL RA.

Simpson Desert

QUEENSLAND

Tropic of Capricorn

K

Kati Thanda–Lake Eyre

SOUTH AUSTRALIA

Lake Torrens

Lake Gairdner

Bight

67

● Brisbane

66

10

9 D

30°

H

Darling

NEW

SOUTH

WALES

E

Range

35 N

27

26 17 18

J 25 24 34

Adelaide ● 22 21

23 19

20

M

A

1

46

3

6

B

7

5

C

8

15

Sydney ●

12

CANBERRA ●

11

Tasman

Sea

S

47

4

Murray

2

R A.C.T.

14 13

16

G

Great

F

P

31

37

38 39

43 45

42

44 41

L

32 29

33

28

30

54 56

36

53 51

49

40

55

48

Melbourne ●

52

50

U

T

Q

VICTORIA

40°

Bass Strait

40°

68

70 TASMANIA

69 ● Hobart

150°

Introduction

Cometh the moment, cometh the book. It wasn't stage-managed in any way – all the wines were tasted blind – but when the wraps were taken off the winning wines at our annual Halliday Wine Companion Awards judging this year, we were all struck by the value we had revealed. Our Wine of the Year (and Red Wine of the Year) has a recommended retail price of under $50. Our Chardonnay of the Year is under $40. Our Shiraz Cabernet winner is $32. Our Shiraz of the Year (which retails at $48) was pitted unwittingly against wines with retail prices five, 10 and over 20 *times* its price, and it won. Our Riesling of the Year is under $50, while the winner of (our new category) Pinot Gris of the Year is under $35.

It's an impossible call to make definitively but at a time when there's a great deal of emphasis on the cost of living, we may well have produced one of, if not the, best-value *Halliday* guides ever.

There are 2770 wines in this guide that are marked as Special Value for their price and quality. Langhorne Creek, Padthaway, McLaren Vale and the Yarra Valley provided the value high points in terms of Award winners, but the regions that really drove these value numbers might surprise you; those with the most Special Value wines were Margaret River (277), Yarra Valley (212) and McLaren Vale (195).

Value never hurts but, unswervingly, our whole process is designed to find the best of the best, regardless of price. For this edition the team tasted through 8468 wines, up 3.3% on last year. It's almost de rigueur to say, at this point, something along the lines of *now is a great time to buy Australian wine*. The greater truth is that it's always a great time to buy Australian wine. We're a big country. Our wine regions are far flung. There's always a bunch of delicious grapes hanging out there somewhere, a fretful winemaker nearby, waiting for the perfect moment to pick and nurture it into wine.

It's our job to find this wine, to identify it, and to share it. We're confident that we've done just that; in this edition, we've unearthed some beauties.

One of the things I've always admired about our friend, mentor and founder, James Halliday, is his steadfast refusal to shirk the hard yakka. He rose to the top of his profession as a lawyer, and to the top as a vigneron, and to the top as a wine writer, publisher and communicator. But never once throughout has he shown any desire to step away from the coalface. In this edition he rolled up his sleeves and added the Hunter Valley to his scope of regions covered, though his influence extends far beyond the list of regions to which he's assigned. I don't work in the same office as James, but I'm pretty certain that he has sat and frowned at every single page and made sure, to the best of his abilities, that what it says is correct.

The *Halliday Wine Companion* is what it is because of James, and his input on a day-to-day level remains immense.

This of course is not to diminish the work of the tasting panel, every member of which has invested themselves greatly in the production of this book. I look at this edition, for instance, and see what great value the addition of Dave Brookes has been for this guide. Dave no longer lives in the Barossa or Eden valleys but he did for a long time, and his knowledge of these regions and its people in particular has really borne fruit this year. In short, he knows where to look and who to ask, and as a result he's brought home the bacon. The Barossa now has more 5-star wineries than any other Australian region.

Of course Jane Faulkner, Mike Bennie, Jeni Port, Philip Rich, Shanteh Wale and Ned Goodwin MW have done exactly the same for their own respective regions, and uncovered their own gems.

Something I noticed, as the panel (double) blind-tasted its way through wine after gorgeous wine at the annual judging, was the deep pool of love everyone on the tasting team has for wine. This might sound like the bleeding obvious, but this team has vast experience behind them. At no point does it ever seem to have become *just a job*. Every class of wines at the judging was strong, as you'd expect, but if you'd been an onlooker as the chardonnay, shiraz and grenache classes — all of which were shimmeringly beautiful — were judged, you would have called the waiter over and said, 'I'll have what they're having.'

The one thing you never want to receive is a wine recommendation from someone who is a bit jaded and over it. No one on the Halliday team falls into that category. We love Australian wine, deep down and true. That's why we're so keen to share the best of them with you.

With that, it's over to the real heroes: the wines.

Campbell Mattinson
Chief Editor, *Halliday Wine Companion 2024*
May 2023

We are of the view at the *Halliday Wine Companion* that the fresh and the new are the lifeblood of our wonderful wine landscape. That the championship of new names, new styles and new approaches is both the way forward, and the way the wine lives of us all are expanded. There are few things we enjoy more than the uncovering of a new (potentially great) producer, variety or style. But history and the making of it is vital and important, and should never be left behind. Classic is classic for a reason. With that in mind we are chuffed to launch, with this edition, the Halliday Hall of Fame, and to announce two of the most incredibly worthy inductees.

How to use this book

Wineries

Bleasdale Vineyards

1640 Langhorne Creek Road, Langhorne Creek, SA 5255 **Region** Langhorne Creek
T (08) 8537 4000 **www**.bleasdale.com.au **Open** 7 days 10–5 **Winemaker** Paul Hotker,
Matt Laube **Viticulturist** Sarah Keough **Est.** 1850 **Dozens** 70 000 **Vyds** 45ha
Not only one of the most historic wineries in Australia, with over 170 years of continuous
winemaking by the direct descendants of the founding Potts family, but one of the leading
quality producers in the land. Not so long before the start of the 21st century, its vineyards
were flooded every winter by diversion of the Bremer River, which provided moisture
throughout the dry, cool, growing season. In the new millennium, every drop of water is
counted. The vineyards have been significantly upgraded and refocused: shiraz accounts for
45% of plantings, supported by 7 other proven varieties; sauvignon blanc, pinot gris and
chardonnay are sourced from the Adelaide Hills. Bleasdale Vineyards is the *Halliday Wine
Companion 2024* Winery of the Year.

Bleasdale Vineyards

The producer name appearing on the front label is used throughout the book.

★★★★★

We look at the ratings for this year and the previous year; if the wines tasted this
year justify a higher rating than last year, that higher rating has been given. If, on
the other hand, the wines are of lesser quality, the winery rating will drop half a star.
Where no wines were submitted by a well-rated winery with a reliable track record
of providing samples, we may roll over last year's rating; these wineries can be found
on www.winecompanion.com.au. Only wineries who submitted wines for review
this year are in this edition.

Some may think the ratings are too generous, but of the more than 3000 wineries
on www.winecompanion.com.au, 1132 submitted wines for review this year. Space
constraints dictate that not every review and score can be printed in this book, which
means that star ratings are best understood in that context.

The number at the end of each rating below notes the number of wineries in that
category in this year's edition, and the percentage is taken from the total number of
wineries who submitted wines this year.

In total, 41% of wineries awarded a star rating this year have achieved the coveted
5-star status.

Outstanding winery regularly producing wines of exemplary quality and typicity. Will have at least two wines rated at 95 points or above, and has typically held a 5-star rating for the previous three years. 90 wineries, 8%

Where the winery name itself is printed in red, it is a winery generally acknowledged to have held a long track record of excellence, typically having held a 5-star rating for 10 years. Truly the best of the best. 167 wineries, 14.8%

 Outstanding winery capable of producing wines of very high quality, and did so this year. Will have at least two wines rated at 95 points or above. 205 wineries, 18.1%

 Excellent winery able to produce wines of high to very high quality, knocking on the door of a 5-star rating. Will have one wine rated at 95 or above, two (or more) at 90 or above, and others 86–89. 145 wineries, 12.8%

 Very good producer of wines with class and character. Will have two (or more) wines rated at 90 or above (or possibly one at 95 or above). 378 wineries, 33.4%

 A solid, usually reliable, maker of good, sometimes very good, wines. Will have one wine rated at 90 points or above, others 86–89. 96 wineries, 8.5%

 A typically good winery, but often has a few lesser wines. Will have wines rated at 86–89 points. 43 wineries, 3.8%

NR The NR rating mainly appears on www.winecompanion.com.au. The rating is given in a range of circumstances: where there have been no tastings in the 12-month period; where there have been tastings, but with no wines scoring more than 85 points; or where the tastings have, for one reason or another, proved not to fairly reflect the reputation of a winery with a track record of success. 8 wineries, 0.7%

 The vine leaf symbol indicates the 55 wineries that are new entries in this year's *Wine Companion*.

1640 Langhorne Creek Road, Langhorne Creek, SA 5255

Contact details are usually those of the winery and cellar door, but in a few instances may simply be a postal address; this occurs when the wine is made at another winery or wineries, and is sold only through the website and/or retail.

Region Langhorne Creek

A full list of zones, regions and subregions appears on page 9. Occasionally you will see 'various', meaning the winery sources grapes from a number of regions, often without a vineyard of its own, or a cellar door.

www.bleasdale.com.au

An important reference point, normally containing material not found (for space reasons) in this book.

Open 7 days 10–5

Although a winery might be listed as not open or only open on weekends, many may in fact be prepared to open by appointment. A telephone call will establish whether this is possible or not. For space reasons we have simplified the open hours listed; where the hours vary each day or for holidays, we simply refer the reader to the website.

Winemaker Paul Hotker, Matt Laube

In all but the smallest producers, the winemaker is simply the head of a team; there may be many executive winemakers actually responsible for specific wines in the medium to large companies (80 000 dozens and upwards). Once again, space constraints mean usually only one or two winemakers are named, even if they are part of a larger team.

Viticulturist Sarah Keough

Viticulturists have long been the unsung heroes of Australian wine – every winemaker will tell you they can't make great wine without great fruit. As for the winemaker, we acknowledge that in many instances the viticulturist heads a team, and while we honour everyone, we regret that space constraints preclude the opportunity to name them all.

Est. 1850

Keep in mind that some makers consider the year in which they purchased the land to be the year of establishment, others the year in which they first planted grapes, others the year they first made wine, and so on. There may also be minor complications where there has been a change of ownership or break in production.

Dozens 70 000

This figure (representing the number of 9L/12-bottle cases produced each year) is merely an indication of the size of the operation. Some winery entries do not feature a production figure: this is typically because the winery (principally, but not exclusively, the large companies) regards this information as confidential.

Vyds 45ha

The hectares of vineyard/s owned by the winery.

Not only one of the most historic wineries in Australia, with over 170 years of continuous winemaking by the direct descendants of the founding Potts family, but one of the leading quality producers in the land. Not so long before the start of the 21st century, its vineyards were flooded every winter by diversion of the Bremer River, which provided moisture (…)

Winery summaries have been written by the Halliday team.

Tasting notes

ᵱᵱᵱᵱᵱ **The Iron Duke Cabernet Sauvignon 2021, Langhorne Creek** Cabernet
Sauvignon of the Year. A best-barrel selection, and oh my, it's a beautifully
structured and textured cabernet sauvignon. Here cassis has the purity and sparkle
of wine which you could drink tonight or in 30 years time. Screw cap. 13.5% alc.
RATING 98 **DRINK** 2023–2051 $89 JH ✪ ❤

The inadequacies of reducing the complexities of a wine to a number are patently
apparent, but nonetheless we persist with the international 100-point system because
it is universally understood. Space constraints dictate that only the top wines for each
winery are printed in full in this book, with points, drinking windows and prices
included for wines scoring 90 points and above. Tasting notes for wines that are
95 points and over are printed in red. Tasting notes for all wines receiving 84 points
or above appear on www.winecompanion.com.au.

97–99	G O L D	ᵱᵱᵱᵱᵱ	**Exceptional** Wines of major trophy standard in important wine shows.
95–96		ᵱᵱᵱᵱᵱ	**Outstanding** Wines of gold medal standard, usually with a great pedigree.
94	S I L V E R	ᵱᵱᵱᵱᵱ	Wines on the cusp of gold medal status.
90–93		ᵱᵱᵱᵱᵱ	**Highly recommended** Wines of silver medal standard, demonstrating great quality, style and character, and worthy of a place in any cellar.
89	B R O N Z E	ᵱᵱᵱᵱ	**Recommended** Wines on the cusp of silver medal standard.
86–88		ᵱᵱᵱᵱ	Wines of bronze medal standard; well-produced, flavoursome wines, usually not requiring cellaring.
84–85		ᵱᵱᵱᵱ	**Acceptable** Wines of good commercial quality, free from significant fault.
80–83		ᵱᵱᵱ	**Over to you** Everyday wines, without much character, and/or somewhat faulty.
75–79		ᵱᵱᵱ	**Not recommended** Wines with one or more significant winemaking faults.

✪   **Special Value** Wines considered to offer special value for money
within the context of their glass symbol status. This can apply at any
pricepoint, and for consistency a basic algorithm is applied to take into
account the price of a wine and the points it is awarded. A value rosette
is given, for instance, to $25 wines scoring 90 or more, $30 wines
scoring 92 points or more, $40 wines of 94 points or more, $75 wines
of 96 points or more and $150 wines scoring 98 points or more.

❤   **Shortlisted for 2024 Awards** Nominated by the tasting panel as the
best example of this variety/style in its region.

The Iron Duke Cabernet Sauvignon 2021, Langhorne Creek Cabernet Sauvignon of the Year. A best-barrel selection, and oh my, it's a beautifully structured and textured cabernet sauvignon. (...) Screw cap. 13.5% alc. **RATING** 98 **DRINK** 2023-2051 $89 JH ✪ ♥

In most cases, space constraints do not permit viticultural and winemaking details for each wine to be included in the book, but you can find the full details at the start of the note for most wines at www.winecompanion.com.au.

This tasting note will usually have been made within the 12 months prior to publication. Even that is a long time, and during the life of this book the wine will almost certainly change. More than this, remember that tasting is a highly subjective and imperfect art.

The initials JH, CM, DB, JF, JP, MB, NG, PR or SW appearing at the end of the note signify that James Halliday, Campbell Mattinson, Dave Brookes, Jane Faulkner, Jeni Port, Mike Bennie, Ned Goodwin MW, Philip Rich or Shanteh Wale tasted the wine and provided the tasting note and rating. Biographies for each member of the tasting team and their regional focuses can be found on pages 4–7. Where the initials PD appear, the score attributed to that wine was a Panel Decision at the annual Awards judging.

Screw cap

The closures in use for the wines tasted are (in descending order): screw cap 88.6% (last year 90.7%), Diam 5.7% (last year 3.9%), one-piece natural cork 4% (last year 4.1%) and crown seal 1%. The remaining 0.7% (in descending order of importance) are Vinolok, agglomerate, cans, stoppers and swing top.

13.5% alc.

This piece of information is in one sense self-explanatory. What is less obvious is the increasing concern of many Australian winemakers about the rise in levels of alcohol, and much research and practical experimentation (for example picking earlier, or higher fermentation temperatures in open fermenters) is occurring. Reverse osmosis and yeast selection are two of the options available to decrease higher-than-desirable alcohol levels. Recent changes to domestic and export labelling mean the stated alcohol will be within a maximum of 0.5% difference to that obtained by analysis.

DRINK 2023-2051

The optimal time to drink a wine is of course subjective; some of us love young wines and others old. This is as personal to the taster as their review and their score. We have proposed dates according to when we would most love to drink this wine, and we commend these to you as a reference for managing your cellar and when to drink each bottle.

$89

Prices are provided by the winery, and should be regarded as a guide, particularly if purchased retail.

Winery of the Year

Bleasdale Vineyards Langhorne Creek

There's an argument to say that the Bleasdale winery, both historically and most certainly at the hand of winemaker Paul Hotker, should be regarded as every Australian wine lover's best friend. It's probably best known as a value producer, thanks to the fact – as James Halliday so aptly puts it – that there's 'value across the board', but it's become abundantly apparent in recent years that Bleasdale is a whole lot more than that. This is best illustrated by the fact that we've thrown the full might of Australian cabernet sauvignon against Bleasdale's Iron Duke in the past two years, and assessed them all blind, and in consecutive years, for consecutive vintages, it has come out on top. When we say 'the full might', we mean Margaret River royalty, and Coonawarra royalty, and Yarra Valley royalty. And it still won.

As Bleasdale itself proclaims, whether one of its wines is $12 or $70, it is determined that every wine in its range 'conveys a story in the glass that substantiates its history, diversity and increasingly, its pedigree'.

There was no doubt a great foundation and culture to build on, in vineyards and growers, people and history, but the work of Bleasdale's head winemaker Paul Hotker cannot be underestimated. He and his team are relentless in their determination to work magic, and we will never tire of celebrating it.

To wit: Bleasdale is our Winery of the Year because at our annual (blind) judging it won two major awards: Best Cabernet Sauvignon (Iron Duke Cabernet 2021) and Best Cabernet Shiraz (Wellington Road Cabernet Shiraz 2021). Quite remarkably, it has 22 wines ranked at 90 or higher in this guide, including no less than 16 at 95 points or higher. Three of these wines went right to the top, scoring 97 or higher. To qualify as a 5-star winery in the *Halliday Wine Companion* a winery needs a minimum of two 95+ wines. Bleasdale qualified as a 5-star winery eight times over. Most commonly, it did so with wines that most would consider as well-priced. Yet more: it achieved all this across a range of different styles, from full-bodied reds to cool-climate-ish chardonnay, from sparkling shiraz to riesling, from tempranillo through to spicy syrah, tempranillo and grenache blends. It kicked goals, too at sparkling blanc de blancs and pinot gris.

Bleasdale, this year's winner of our Winery of the Year, has won this award in the most emphatic fashion.

Runners-up

Oakridge Wines Yarra Valley

Every year, new owners or old, Oakridge mounts a compelling case for itself. If you want evidence, then seven wines in this guide with a score of 97 or higher is probably all that you need, though a further eight wines with a score of 95 or 96 is very thick icing. This means that Oakridge has a staggering 15 wines with a score of 95 or higher in this guide. It is one of Australia and the Yarra Valley's most pre-eminent producers, and while it's long-standing and ongoing specialty is chardonnay, it has for quite some time now completely outgrown this definition. It is also a wonderful producer of Yarra Valley cabernet sauvignon, and a star of pinot noir, sauvignon blanc, shiraz, pinot meunier and even at times riesling. That it has also, on top of all this overwhelming quality, won this year's Best Value Winery almost beggar's belief. If in doubt, buy Oakridge.

Pepper Tree Wines Hunter Valley

The remarkable thing, when you look at Pepper Tree's list of high-rating wines this year, is how many of them are ultra-fresh new releases, but also how many are held-back releases with a decade already under their belt. What is more, Pepper Tree Wines has been putting on this kind of performance every year for a long time now (Pepper Tree has achieved 5-star winery status in 17 out of the past 18 editions). Pepper Tree's wines taste great now, and they age incredibly well, demonstrably so, there's no guess-work about it. Indeed you can try them for yourself: these aged wines are available as museum releases. Chardonnay, shiraz and semillon are no doubt the winery's stars, as they should be for a Hunter Valley producer, but cabernet sauvignon, merlot and riesling (from Orange) also excel.

Yangarra Estate Vineyard McLaren Vale

It's the name that just keeps popping up, every year, all the time. It does for all the right reasons. Great vineyards, great management, great winemaking, great wines. Everything here, on both the land and in the cellar, is treated with respect, with care, with thought and with good reason. Critically, over and over, it shows in the glass. Nine of its wines scored 95 or higher, and its Old Vine Grenache – with a retail price below $50 – beat all-comers to win both our Red Wine of the Year and Wine of the Year. Yangarra doesn't deal with a great deal of different varieties, but it fundamentally lays down the law on grenache, shiraz, roussanne and various Rhône-inspired reds and whites.

Leogate Estate Hunter Valley

This Hunter Valley producer has put up a truly remarkable performance this year; it gave the Winery of the Year award a real shake. Eighteen wines submitted, every one of them scoring in the 90s, 10 of them scoring 95 or above, with four of these wines at the rarefied 97 point mark. Leogate Estate does the regional specialties of semillon and shiraz exceptionally well, as it does chardonnay, the latter of particular note after a decade in the cellar.

Giant Steps Yarra Valley

One step forward for this leading Yarra Valley winery is one giant step forward for Australian wine. The championship of a host of single-vineyard sites by this producer over the past 25 years has been as inspiring as it has been uniformly delicious, and the march forward in this quality–obsessed, land-driven focus continues at pace. The addition of the (outstanding) 1986-planted Bastard Hill vineyard to the Giant Steps fold in 2023 was yet another coup, as has been the addition of head winemaker Melanie Chester. Former head winemaker (and current consultant) Steve Flamsteed's words that Giant Steps is about 'beautiful ingredients, carefully made', couldn't be more apt.

All Saints Estate **Rutherglen**

All Saints Estate is a winery that demands to be celebrated. It has no less than 17 wines with a score in the 90s in this edition, with nine of those wines at 95 points or higher, including two (fortifieds) at 100. It won the Best Fortified category; its range of fortified wines is nothing short of magnificent. But there is also of course more to All Saints Estate than fortified wine; it had one of the top-scoring durifs, and its cabernet sauvignon, sangiovese and blends of the two all scored well.

Yalumba **Eden Valley**

Yalumba's history is as rich or richer than any other producer in Australian wine, and still its current-release wines remain stellar. Yalumba simply never takes its foot off the quality pedal. Nineteen wines with a score of 90 or higher shows the incredible depth of its portfolio, while two wines at 98 and another two at 97 shows that when Yalumba goes all-out at quality, its wines are the rival of anyone, anywhere.

Penley Estate **Coonawarra**

Penley Estate is not a new name and yet its wine range right now is as fresh as it is exciting. Indeed few (if any) wineries can match Penley Estate in the way it combines traditional, cellar-worthy wine styles with newer, fresher ways of thinking and drinking. Winemaker Kate Goodman is the driving force here, though she's clearly been uncommonly well enabled by the estate's owners, and supported by clever marketing and label-redesign. The critical factor is always the wine in the glass: 15 wines submitted, all attracting a score above 90, with nine wines earning a score of 94 or higher. Penley Estate has always been a good producer but in recent years it has elevated its standing considerably.

First Creek Wines **Hunter Valley**

Any producer who can make a 97-point vermentino is a producer worth following. When this wine is surrounded in its range by various other 95, 96 and 97 point wines (for semillon, shiraz, fiano and chardonnay) then it's clear that we have a producer of the highest repute. The Silkmans (Liz, Greg and Shaun) sure know how to produce great wine. In this guide First Creek, in the Hunter Valley, has 11 wines with a score of 95 or higher. First Creek Wines is, in short, a champion of the Hunter Valley.

Previous Winery of the Year recipients were Paringa Estate (2007), Balnaves of Coonawarra (2008), Brookland Valley (2009), Tyrrell's (2010), Larry Cherubino Wines (2011), Port Phillip Estate/Kooyong (2012), Kilikanoon (2013), Penfolds (2014), Hentley Farm Wines (2015), Tahbilk (2016), Mount Pleasant (2017), Mount Mary (2018), Seville Estate (2019), Jim Barry Wines (2020), Henschke (2021), Yarra Yering (2022) and Pooley Wines (2023).

Winemaker of the Year

Winemaker of the Year is all about 'best winemaking practice' but it's also about significance, and importance, of the stamp the person has or is making on the Australian wine landscape.

Kate Goodman, Penley Estate Coonawarra

One of the first things Ang and Bec Tolley – owners of Penley Estate – did when their winemaking brother, Kym, retired was to appoint gun winemaker Kate Goodman to the post. It turns out to have been one of the best decisions they've ever made. Ang and Bec took over the running of the business outright in 2015, appointed Goodman in 2016, and she almost immediately set about a grand re-think of every wine the estate did (or didn't) make.

We hesitate to mention this, given that it has nothing to do with Goodman's winemaking, but in 2017 she was diagnosed with a life-threatening illness, and so what she has since achieved is in the context of an intense and lengthy personal health battle.

And oh my, what she has achieved. First and foremost, she has elevated the estate's traditional cabernet sauvignon (and cabernet-based) wines, so that they now stand toe-to-toe with Coonawarra's best. These wines will mature magnificently. This award may well be her due on the strength of these wines alone, but then the energy, excitement and vigour she has built into the Penley range as a complement to its traditional base is, quite simply, a glory to behold.

Preservative-free cabernet sauvignon, whole-bunch shiraz, whole-bunch cabernet, assorted field blends, concrete egg-fermented (and matured) cabernet, chardonnay raised in amphorae, varietal cabernet franc, wine released in 2L casks, and wine bottled in lightweight glass. Put all these developments to the Penley range together and it amounts to a ground-breaking shift for both the estate and for the Coonawarra region.

But then, Kate Goodman is one of those people who is passionate about the job at hand, or she's not doing it. She puts her heart and soul into every wine she makes. She's done this at Wirra Wirra, Tim Knappstein, Seppelt and Punt Road in the past, as well as with her personal winemaking projects. But it's at Penley that she's taken wine by the scruff of the neck and given it an almighty shake.

Runners-up

Jim Chatto, Pepper Tree Wines Hunter Valley

Everywhere Jim Chatto goes, ultra-fine wine follows. He's recently returned as a consultant winemaker to Pepper Tree Wines in the Hunter Valley (13 wines scoring 95 or above in this edition) though of course he's best known for the superb Tasmanian pinot noir he produces under his own name (all six Chatto wines in this edition scored 93 or high, the top two wines 96 and 97).

Mark Messenger, Juniper Estate Margaret River

Mark Messenger is the kind of quiet achiever that we all should be making a fuss about. Every year, year after year, he creates finely crafted wines out of Juniper

Estate in Margaret River, where he's been winemaker since 1999. The proof of his prowess, in the glass, is stellar: 10 wines in this guide with a score in the 90s, seven of them (remarkably) at 95 or higher.

Paul Dahlenburg, Eldorado Road & Baileys of Glenrowan Glenrowan/ Beechworth

The heart of North East Victoria's winegrowing district resides in this man. He makes wines out of Glenrowan (for both his own label, and at Baileys of Glenrowan), Beechworth and Rutherglen, as well as from various spots in-between, including from his home at Eldorado. He has the deepest of respect for the history of what he does, where it comes from, and or its people. And yet he makes modern wines, rich in flavour, friendly, huggable, bright. Dahlenburg is a gem of the Australian wine landscape.

Colin McBryde, Adelina Clare Valley

What Colin McBryde is doing out of Adelina in the Clare Valley is nothing short of mesmerising. He's brilliantly modern and steadfastly traditional all at once; we'd go so far as to say that he's a keeper of the Clare Valley faith, in many ways. His rieslings are exquisite; his red wines are alive with character and charm.

Michael Downer, Murdoch Hill Adelaide Hills

You don't produce the Shiraz of the Year without really knowing what you're doing, both in the cellar and in the vineyard. Michael Downer has proven his credentials over and over again but his 2021 releases place him once again in 'best winemaker in the land' discussions.

Sam Middleton, Mount Mary Yarra Valley

It's hard to stop raving about Sam Middleton. He stepped into the role of winemaker at Mount Mary on a hiding to nothing, following in the footsteps of the legendary Dr John as he was, and yet he has somehow made the range his own, seamlessly, magically, wonderfully.

Samantha Connew, Stargazer Tasmania

Last year Samantha Connew's Stargazer was nominated for our Winery of the Year; this year she came close to winning Winemaker of the Year. Connew is clearly doing a lot of things right and consistently so, as most obviously evidenced by the four wines she has in this guide with a score of 96 or higher.

Gerald Naef, Patina Wines Orange

Anyone who submits six wines to this guide and takes away an average score of 95+ is worthy of Winemaker of the Year considerations. This is 'every egg, a bird' territory. Gerald Naef has been making wine at Orange for over 20 years and, along the way, has become the deep thinker of the region; the person to whom everyone goes to for advice. It makes celebrating Gerald Naef seem as natural as waking up in the morning.

Previous Winemaker of the Year recipients were Robert Diletti (2015), Peter Fraser (2016), Sarah Crowe (2017), Paul Hotker (2018), Julian Langworthy (2019), Vanya Cullen (2020), Brett Grocke (2021), Michael Dhillon (2022) and Glen Goodall (2023).

Viticulturist of the Year

There isn't a winemaker alive who doesn't know that unless all is right in the vineyard there's only so much that the winemaker can do. The viticulturists – the people who grow the grapes – are therefore a, if not *the*, crucial part of the puzzle. This award celebrates the people who grow the wines that we love.

Mark Walpole, Fighting Gully Road Beechworth

Mark Walpole isn't afraid to get his hands dirty. He lives and breathes vineyards; it's as if his very blood runs in straight, varietal rows. His influence in North East Victoria extends back to his time at Brown Brothers, where he was a pioneer of 'alternative varieties', though his work with all manner of both obscure and classic varieties at his Whorouly vineyard (in the Alpine Valleys region); at his Fighting Gully Road vineyard (in the Beechworth region); previously at Greenstone (at Heathcote) and at the old Smith's vineyard, to name just a few of his key areas of influence, is at every turn both inspiring and significant. Mark Walpole is a viticulturist's viticulturist; he is the real deal. His great love is sangiovese, of which he is arguably the chief Australian authority, but in truth Mark Walpole is an authority on viticulture, full stop.

   Not that he would ever put such a label on himself. What Walpole mostly is, though, is curious. At the heart of every great viticulturist is a relentless desire to experiment, and every day that is indeed what Mark Walpole does. He trials things. He puts wonder to work. His pursuit of a better way, a different way, a more appropriate way, is relentless. It's what makes him one of the Australian wine industry's greatest assets; it's what makes him so overwhelmingly deserving of this award.

Runners-up

Liz Riley, Mistletoe Wines & Scarborough Wine Co Hunter Valley

Liz Riley is one of the most highly regarded (and awarded) viticulturists in Australia. She could be nominated for this award every year and she'd get close to winning it every time. The proof of her good work is overwhelmingly in the pudding at both Scarborough and Mistletoe in the Hunter Valley, though her influence as a consultant extends throughout the region and across New South Wales generally.

Dr Dylan Grigg, Consultant Various

There's a secret weapon in modern Australian wine and his name is Dr Dylan Grigg. Indeed, if you were to make a list of the producers who have excelled over the past decade there would be a quite incredible crossover with Dr Grigg's client list. Gentle Folk, Murdoch Hill, Mac Forbes, Ngeringa, Adelina, Spinifex, and Tapanappa Foggy Hill (to name a few) have all benefited from Dr Grigg's knowledge. His specialty is old vines and what makes them so special – he then applies these learnings to younger vines. Our wine industry would be much the lesser without him.

Bart Molony, Vasse Felix Margaret River

As Halliday Panel member Jane Faulkner says, Bart Malony is 'the one tasting the fruit saying, "Virginia, it's time to come and check this out".' Virginia in this case is Virginia Willcock, famed chief winemaker at Vasse Felix in Margaret River, and maker of scores of fabulous wines. The implication is of course that Malony, who has been integral to the running of Vasse Felix's vineyards since 2004, is a key part of this picture. We reckon he just might be. He's planted vineyards, he's expanded vineyards and he's massaged established vineyards to the best form of their life. In short, he's done (and is doing) it all.

Rhys Thomas, Swinney Frankland River

Rhys Thomas has a passion for bush vines and for sustainable agriculture both. He's only been at Swinney a short time – having taken over from noted viticulturist Lee Haselgrove – but, as panel member Mike Bennie says, '[the] Swinney [property] is about a custodianship, and I wanted to talk about viticulturists as custodians. For me, Swinney and their wines are some of the best in Western Australia, and so recognition of custodianship over a certain vineyard is important.' In short, Rhys Thomas brings a wealth of experience and attention to detail to the table as he builds on both a significant foundation, and a significant patch of land.

Stuart Proud, Thousand Candles Yarra Valley

There are a lot of winemakers who kick the trunk of the odd vine every now and then and call themselves viticulturists. Stuart Proud is the opposite. A true-blue, bona-fide, long term viticulturist who has slowly and organically moved to the winemaking side of things; he makes the wines from the ground up. He's still the vineyard guy, we should emphasise, and a great one at that. He's just managed to complete the loop, so that every step in the growing and making process leads logically on from the last. The proof of Proud's work is not only in the wines of Thousand Candles, though it most certainly is there, but also in the clamber of elite winemakers from around the valley keen to secure some of the Proud-grown grapes.

Michael Lane, Yangarra Estate Vineyard & Hickinbotham Clarendon Vineyard McLaren Vale

There's something about Michael Lane. He manages both the Yangarra Estate vineyards and the Hickinbotham Clarendon vineyard, and given that Yangarra produced the Wine of the Year and that so many of the Yangarra wines scored over 95 points, and that the 5-star Hickinbotham also produced its own suite of 95 point wines, it's pretty clear that Lane has the McLaren Vale vineyards under his charge absolutely singing.

Jacob Stein, Robert Stein Vineyard Mudgee

Whatever Jacob Stein is doing in his region of Mudgee, it's working. Most of the awards he's won over the past decade or more have been winemaking awards, but he's also a trained viticulturist and in that space, in the words of panel member Shanteh Wale, 'he has elevated the region, kept New South Wales really pushing forward, and with the new Blue Hen series [of wines], which is a little bit more experimental, what he's doing is exciting.' All 11 wines submitted for this edition scored 90 or higher. He grows elite grapes.

Previous Viticulturist of the Year recipients were Vanya Cullen (2022) and Tom Carson (2023).

Best Value Winery

The Best Value awards are arguably the most important in the book. They're also the most difficult to judge. The reason is that there are several different ways to look at value, and each of these ways is valid. A simple search for high-scoring wines under $25 or $30 may well be the easiest way, but then (very) high scoring wines at $50 or $60 can easily be justified as high in value (especially when they beat wines in their category at three or more times their price). Just to complicate matters further: if the most expensive new-release wines in the world can cost several thousand dollars each, then even a wine at $250 can be deemed Special Value if its quality is the equal of such wines. At the *Halliday Wine Companion*, we are champions of quality in its purest form, and have no desire to become part of the race to the bottom. If the wine is excellent, we'll celebrate it. In this context, we have approached value this year from several different angles.

In individual wine terms, the Best Value wines at various pricepoints are:

Under $20 Amelia Park Trellis Chardonnay 2021, 94 points, $18

Under $30 Mistletoe Wines Home Vineyard Shiraz 2021, 97 points, $25

Under $40 Castle Rock Estate Diletti Riesling 2021, 98 points, $36
Honourable mention: Landaire at Padthaway Estate Chardonnay 2021, 98 points, $37

Under $50 Lake Breeze Wines Arthur's Reserve Cabernet Sauvignon Malbec Petit Verdot 2020, 98 points, $48

At $50 Serrat Shiraz Viognier 2022, 98 points and
Yalumba The Virgilius Viognier 2021, 98 points

Wine of the Year Yangarra Old Vine Grenache 2021, 99 points, $45

The Best Value wineries are:

Oakridge Wines Yarra Valley

You get the feeling when you look at the Oakridge range that this producer respects its customers as much as it does the quality of its wines. This is perhaps best illustrated by the fact that, of Oakridge's 15 wines in this guide to have scored 95 or above, every single one of them qualified as Special Value in its category. It's also pleasing to note that 10 of Oakridge's absolute top-scoring wines (it went close to winning Winery of the Year) are priced at under $50. Indeed, both of its outstanding sub-$50 single vineyard Willowlake 2021 releases, pinot noir and chardonnay, scored 97 points. This is one of a number of areas where Oakridge shines: at consistently getting the very top-end of quality into value considerations. When we were discussing potential winners of this Best Value Winery award, the words 'Oakridge wins in a canter' were used. Oakridge proves that to drink the very best, you don't need to break the bank.

Runners-up

Bremerton Langhorne Creek

When you delve into the *2024 Halliday Wine Companion* database and do a simple search for 'most number of Special Value wines under $50', Bremerton produces the largest number of results. Needless to say, it came within a whisker of winning this award. No less than 23 of its wines qualify as Special Value and every one of them is under $50. This includes wines that have scored in the high 80s (with RRPs below $20) but if you push the parameters to wines that have scored 94 or higher, Bremerton still racks up an impressive 11 Special Value wines (all under $50). This makes the Bremerton range one of the happiest hunting grounds on the Australian market today, with all manner of tastes catered for: from shiraz and cabernet to verdelho, fiano, lagrein, malbec, tempranillo-graciano and more.

Bleasdale Langhorne Creek

Bleasdale has become a quality juggernaut, but Special Value wines are the kind of bread and butter it knows more about than most. It has 21 wines in this edition priced under $50 that have scored 94 points or higher, including two wines at 97 points and one at 98 points. Rarely, if ever, does a Winery of the Year also offer such mesmerising value for money, but the simple fact is that these wines stack up no matter which way you look at them. This kind of performance isn't new for Bleasdale; this is what it does.

De Bortoli Yarra Valley

De Bortoli makes top-end wine but along the way it makes sure that everyone is kept happy. Indeed it didn't seem to matter what criteria we set as we scoured the database for the Best Value wines, the De Bortoli name kept coming up. That's not unexpected when you consider that De Bortoli's Yarra Valley arm notched 19 wines under $50 with a Special Value rating. This includes 14 wines at or below $25, which is no feat in itself, though to put a cherry on top it also includes five wines under $50 that have scored 94 points or higher. The stars of De Bortoli's range this year were made with chardonnay, pinot noir, gamay noir and syrah, but name a variety or style and there's every chance that De Bortoli has nailed it, at a fair price.

Bondar Wines McLaren Vale

Bondar's Violet Hour Shiraz 2021 is, at $32 and 97 points, not only a beautiful McLaren Vale shiraz but a contender for the Best Value wine of the year. It's an insight into the stunning consumer-friendly story that is Bondar. In this guide Bondar has six wines under $40 with a score of 95 or higher. It has nine Special Value wines under $50, most of which score near the very top end of the scale. Shiraz, grenache, monastrell, a GSM blend, nero d'avola, rosé and (Adelaide Hills) chardonnay – all excel.

Billy Button Wines Alpine Valleys

Billy Button is the brand of the ultra-talented Jo Marsh who, with Eleana Anderson, also took out the Dark Horse of the Year award this year. At Billy Button she makes a large and eclectic range of wines that, as soon as you taste one, you just want to settle down and drink. It's lucky then that so many of the wines here are well priced – 17 of the Billy Button wines earned the Special Value rosette.

Briar Ridge Vineyard Hunter Valley

Ten of Briar Ridge's wines were awarded Special Value status; all of these wines scored 94 or higher and, of these wines, eight are priced at or below $50. This

Hunter Valley producer (also sourcing grapes from Wrattonbully) has both its value and quality cylinders firing across a range of varieties and styles: fiano, shiraz, chardonnay, semillon and albariño among them.

Mordrelle Wines **Adelaide Hills**

A couple of years ago we uncovered Mordrelle, and it's been a great pleasure to ride its swift progress since. Over the past three editions its winery status has gone from 4-stars to 4.5, to its now 5-star status. Amid this quality rise, value remains paramount, especially among its Langhorne Creek releases (Mordrelle's base is at Hahndorf in the Adelaide Hills). From Langhorne Creek we find six red wines priced at or under $50, all of which (this isn't a typo) are scored at 96 or higher. If you haven't yet cottoned on to Mordrelle, now's the time.

Two Hands Wines **Barossa Valley**

Sexy Beast Barossa Cabernet Sauvignon 2021: $32, 94 points. Twelftree Seaview Grenache Mourvedre 2020: $35, 95 points. These two wines from this multi-regional producer illustrate that while Two Hands often operates at the very top end of town, there's still ample – and outstanding – value to be found in this range, emphasised again by the seven wines it has in this guide, priced below $50, with scores of 94 and higher.

Xanadu Wines **Margaret River**

If someone asked you for the name of a single winery, and you knew that both quality and value were important to them but you had no idea of their personal wine preferences, then Xanadu would be a perfect choice. It makes such an outstanding range of wines and styles, all with their fruit flavours presented bell clear. Sauvignon blanc, nouveau syrah, semillon, cabernet sauvignon, graciano shiraz, chardonnay, cabernet franc, viognier and more – all these varieties scored (very) high in this edition, and earned value rosettes.

Carillion Wines **Hunter Valley**

Ten wines with a Special Value rosette, nine of them at or below $50, and of these nine there are six wines with a rating of 95 or higher. When we are looking at value we always, of course, place an emphasis on price, but there's always an extra weighting to producers whose 'value' wines are scored in the thin air of 95 points plus. That's Carillion; very high-scored wines, often at very reasonable prices.

Dappled Wines **Yarra Valley**

Yarra Valley producer Dappled isn't here for the volume of its Special Value wines. It's here because of its sheer outstanding consistency. It submitted six wines for this guide; every one of them was awarded the Special Value rosette, the lowest score was 94, and four of them scored 96. Job well done.

Previous Best Value Winery recipients were Hoddles Creek Estate (2015), West Cape Howe (2016), Larry Cherubino Wines (2017), Grosset (2018), Provenance (2019), Domaine Naturaliste (2020), Best's (2021), Lake Breeze Wines (2022) and Deep Woods Estate (2023).

Best New Winery

Any one of the wineries listed here could, in any other year, have won the award for Best New Winery. The standard this year was that high. This award recognises the best of the wineries that are new to the *Halliday Wine Companion.*

Joshua Cooper Wines Victoria

We have Josh Cooper here in the Best New Winery category, but he could easily have been placed in the open Winery of the Year section and won it. Such is the incredible quality of his wines, and its consistency. He submitted six wines to us, and the lowest score was 95. We would say that the numbers speak for themselves, but of course it's not the numbers speaking, it's the wines.

Josh Cooper, who makes wines mostly out of central Victoria up to Macedon, grew up at the noted Cobaw Ridge winery (he's the son of Alan and Nellie Cooper) and it's fair to say that his knowledge and respect for what makes quality wine runs deep. There's an authenticity to his wines, a command, and a life. He is a great Best New Winery winner.

Runners-up

Gentle Folk Adelaide Hills

Gentle Folk wines are interesting, individual, lovingly crafted and just plain delicious. This Adelaide Hills producer is the work of Gareth and Rainbo Belton, both of whom are marine scientists, specialising in marine plants (seaweeds). The wines here are deep-down good; try the syrah or the barrel- fermented sauvignon blanc and tell us that we're wrong.

Fleet Wines Gippsland

This will not be the last you hear of Fleet. Indeed, if we had a rocket symbol we would place it beside this name. It's the work of noted wine professionals Lisa and Justin Jenkins, and although being a comparatively small outfit, they somehow managed to produce 12 wines this year that have been rated at 90 points or higher, with three of them rated at 95. The wines come from established vineyards in the Yarra Valley, Gippsland and Mornington Peninsula regions, though Fleet has also put down its own roots at Leongatha (Gippsland). The world is at this producer's feet.

Neldner Road Barossa Valley

This is the new name of famed Barossa winemaker Dave Powell, formerly of Powell & Son and, before that, of Torbreck. All of the wines, which showcase the best of both the Barossa and the Eden valleys, are nothing if not powerful, but even so there are signs of restraint at every turn, not to mention nuance. Indeed there's an argument to say that Dave Powell, right now, is at the peak of his winemaking powers; that his wines are the best they have been.

Entropy Wines Gippsland

Nothing is guaranteed in life but we'd be very surprised if, one day, Entropy doesn't take out a major award in this guide. It has already obtained the coveted 5-star winery rating, and yet in terms of its own (high-density) vineyard at Leongatha in the Gippsland region of Victoria, its story has only just begun. Ryan Ponsford, the man behind the label, is characterised by deep thought, hard work and an artistic flair; it's little wonder that he's turning out outstanding pinot noir and syrah, among other varieties. Remarkably, Entropy has seven wines in this edition with a score of 95 or higher.

Winmark Wines Hunter Valley

Karin Adcock isn't the winemaker but she's the driver behind this outstanding new estate in the Hunter Valley. By new we mean both rejuvenated – the estate was formerly known as Poole's Rock – and new to this guide, though we hope to follow every step from here. All four wines submitted this year were chardonnay, all scored above 90 points, and two scored 95 or higher. The net result: instant 5-star winery status.

MMAD McLaren Vale

Two masters of wine and two of the most highly regarded winemakers: that's the team behind MMAD. The names respectively are no less than Martin Shaw, Michael Hill Smith, Adam Wadewitz and David LeMire. There are three wines in the range – shiraz, grenache and chenin blanc – all from Blewitt Springs in McLaren Vale. All are outstanding. They scored 97, 97 and 95 respectively, which by any standard is an incredible debut (not to mention strike-rate).

Nightfall Wines Coonawarra

New names out of Coonawarra are relatively uncommon and they are especially so at this quality level. The Nightfall wines – made with cabernet sauvignon, cabernet franc and merlot – are from an established single vineyard and are the creation of Sam Brand, who (as you can tell by his surname) has a long winemaking history behind him (four generations, stretching back to 1852). The first releases could hardly be more impressive.

Terrason Wines Victoria

Terrason has a knack for sourcing excellent-quality grapes from both the King and Yarra valleys and then, with minimal intervention between times, turning out characterful wines of real interest. Chardonnay and pinot noir from the Yarra Valley were the stars of this year's tastings.

Gaffy & Neal Mornington Peninsula

To qualify as a 5-star producer you need to have received two reviews, for two separate wines, of 95 or higher. (Darrin) Gaffy and (Doug) Neal only submitted two wines – two chardonnays from near Merricks on the Mornington Peninsula – and both qualified. Says it all, really.

Previous Best New Winery recipients were Rob Dolan Wines (2014), Flowstone (2015), Bicknell fc (2016), Bondar Wines (2017), Dappled (2018), Mewstone (2019), Shy Susan (2020), Varney Wines (2021), Place of Changing Winds (2022) and Living Roots (2023).

Dark Horses

This is the award we give to a winery who has made it to the hallowed territory of 5-star winery status. It's an exciting moment for them, and for all of us.

Anderson & Marsh Alpine Valleys

Three wines, two star winemakers, one label. It turns out that it's a killer combination. The people involved are Eleana Anderson (of Mayford) and Jo Marsh (of Billy Button), two near-neighbours in the Alpine Valleys in North East Victoria with an enormous feel for grapes, the way they are grown, and the various ways they can be turned into wine. Of course Marsh and Anderson individually have been turning out fantastic wines for a long time now, which is why this pairing is such dream territory. Anderson & Marsh entered three wines for this edition; their average score was 95.

Runners-up

Emilian Yarra Valley

If you see the wines of this Yarra Valley producer, you should pounce. The quantities are small but the produce is excellent. There's an understatement to these wines; they're not taxing, they're charming. This label has only existed since 2016 but, step by subtle step, it's gotten better and better.

Mount Eyre Vineyards Hunter Valley

Mount Eyre in the Hunter Valley has been under its current ownership since 1999, but both the families involved have been around wine for a lot longer than that – indeed for centuries. Mount Eyre grows a range of varieties across three vineyards but it's no real surprise, given history, that their rating has skyrocketed off the back of dry, food-friendly, high-quality white wines, in particular semillon and fiano.

Topper's Mountain Wines New England

Topper's Mountain is an innovator, not a follower. As a result it's one of Australia's most interesting producers. Located in the New England region, it focuses on a wide range of road-less-travelled varieties, often in highly successful fashion, as perhaps best illustrated by the fact that its rating is built off the back of a duo of outstanding releases made with the gros manseng variety. Yes, gros manseng. Topper's Mountain is the first winery from the New England region to achieve a 5-star winery rating since the 2009 edition.

Curator Wine Company Barossa Valley

Full-bodied red wine, grown and made in the Barossa Valley, often designed to highlight and champion sub-regional differences. Curator's estate vineyard is at Marananga but wines are also made to showcase Greenock and Vine Vale, amongst others. This is a winery where shiraz, cabernet and grenache rule the roost here, the net result – in this edition – 9 wines with a score of 92 or higher.

Wine of the Year

You could have blown us over with a feather. The same grape variety, from the same producer, has somehow managed to win our Wine of the Year for the second time in the space of only a few years. We taste over 8000 wines each year. When we sit down the judge the Awards, we have no idea what the wines are, from start to finish. The chances therefore of a grenache from the same estate in McLaren Vale making it through all the various stages and discussions to come out on top, twice; well, they're somewhere between Buckley's and none. And yet Yangarra Estate has done just that. Its High Sands Grenache 2016 took out the Wine of the Year in 2020; this year its Old Vine Grenache 2021 has achieved the same feat. On top of that, the voting in favour of this year's winner was emphatic.

Yangarra Estate Vineyard Old Vine Grenache 2021, McLaren Vale

It's a giant killer. It's not the top wine in Yangarra Estate's own grenache hierarchy and yet in an independent review, against wines at all price levels, it reigned supreme. It was grown on bush vines that have been doing their thing in the Blewitt Springs sub-region since they went into the ground in 1946. James Halliday, when he first put the wine near his nose, said 'I'm gone for all money without even tasting it'. This wine has it all: scent, fruit, savouriness and structure. It is rock solid, rolled gold, quality.

Sparkling Wine of the Year

Sittella Wines Grand Prestige Late Disgorged 2010, Pemberton

This wine has been causing a stir around the traps for all the right reasons. It's a knockout style but it's also 100% convincing; it jumped out of our line-up for the heady, powerful display that it puts on; as panel member Mike Bennie writes, it's 'profound'. It's not just a (sparkling) wine, it's an experience.

White Wine of the Year

Landaire at Padthaway Estate Chardonnay 2021, Padthaway

Against the highest of high class fields, this wine won the chardonnay category, and it then went on to win White Wine of the Year. Padthaway chardonnay, take a bow. This is a beautiful wine, complex and neat at once, like a hotel bed, tucked in ultra-tight but with cushions, pillows and layers aplenty.

Red Wine of the Year

Yangarra Estate Vineyard Old Vine Grenache 2021, McLaren Vale

Hall of Fame

James Halliday Hall of Fame: Wine

An eligible wine will have won its category in this guide on five occasions or more. Inductees to the James Halliday Hall of Fame: Wine are expected to be roughly as rare as its first recipient.

Seppeltsfield 100 Year Old Para Vintage Tawny 1923, Barossa Valley

We are proud to announce the Seppeltsfield 100 Year Old Para Vintage Tawny, in this case 1923, as the first inductee into the James Halliday Hall of Fame: Wine. James Halliday, in describing the current release's 100-point grading, wrote that 'It is the one and only wine whose history, past, and future demands it.' He could also be describing its entry into the Hall of Fame. The simple fact that you can buy a 100-year-old wine is incredible; as is the wine's 144 year consecutive lineage, as is – if you're ever lucky enough to enjoy a drop – the truly wondrous, life-enhancing, overwhelming taste of it. The importance and quality of this wine is beyond refute; it is a gift from generations past, a wine altar on which we worship, an ode in a bottle to Australian wine history.

James Halliday Hall of Fame: Australian Wine Industry

This is the highest honour of any bestowed by the *Halliday Wine Companion*, on an individual or an aspect of the Australian wine industry deemed to be of the highest regard and significance.

Prue Henschke

If the Hill of Grace vineyard could talk, you'd reckon that it would thank the world and perhaps even the Lord for bestowing the force-of-nature that is Prue Henschke upon it. The same applies to all of the Eden and Barossa valley vineyards under Henschke's care, as it does to the family's orchard-turned-vineyard at Lenswood in the Adelaide Hills. Prue Henschke graduated from Adelaide University in 1973, having studied zoology and botany. For the past 50 years she has set about improving both the environment of her vines and the environment of her regions. The aim, at all times, has been to grow better-tasting grapes via healthier vines in an improved landscape. Prue Henschke is someone who could easily have won Viticulturist of the Year, in any 'competition' around the world, every year. She could because every year she leaves her world that little bit healthier, and that little bit better. It goes without saying that intellectual rigour is a key to her renown, as is determination and hard work. But there's more to Prue Henschke than the sum of these parts. It's doubtful that Prue Henschke has ever walked past a problem without stopping first to put it to rights. Her footsteps at all times are feather-light; her impact, at all times, profound. Prue Henschke is the inaugural inductee into the James Halliday Hall of Fame: Australian Wine Industry. On the basis of 50 years of proof, we cannot think of a better person to prepare the ground for those who follow.

Top rated by variety

The following list represent the 617 top-scoring wines in this edition. Price is not a factor in these lists; quality is the only consideration. These lists work best as a quick reference though. As always, the note and accompanying information beneath each winery entry (in the body of the book) is the best guide as to whether the wine is for you.

Given that we review over 8000 wines each year, space in this book is fiercely contested. The number of wines in each category listed here is limited by a rating cut-off that reflects the strength of its class. Chardonnay, semillon, pinot noir and shiraz again stand tall here, besting all other categories for sheer volume of outstanding wines, with cabernet sauvignon snapping at the heels of these categories.

The winner of each category was determined collaboratively by the full Halliday tasting panel, save for Ned Goodwin MW who was absent from the judging due to an international commitment. Wines submitted for the final judging were nominated by each taster, courtesy of them being the top-scoring wine in their category, from the regions each taster covers. This year we allowed each taster two 'wild card' wines (one red and one white) in case any taster had a particular regard or affection for an additional wine. All wines at the judging were then tasted blind, all the way through. For the first time, the identity of all wines tasted at the annual judging were kept completely hidden until all results had been finalised.

Some wine names in the lists here have been shortened for space reasons. Full tasting notes (and names) can of course be found in the body of the book, below each winery entry.

Sparkling Wine

Accepted wisdom is that Tasmania rules the sparkling wine roost, and while as a general statement this remains true it's also evident that at the very top end, competition is on for young and old. A sparkling wine from Pemberton won the category this year (it was a runaway victor at the judging), with wines from Tasmania, the Yarra Valley, Orange and the King Valley also figuring prominently. In the past two years we have run separate red/white/rosé sparkling classes , but this year it was one class combined. The winner of this class now is the true sparkling crown-holder of the year.

Sparkling Wine of the Year: Sittella Wines Grand Prestige Late Disgorged 2010, Pemberton

Rating	Wine	Region
97	House of Arras Rosé 2014	Tasmania
97	Gembrook Hill Blanc de Blancs 2017	Yarra Valley
97	Gilbert Family Wines Blancs de Blancs #2 Chardonnay 2016	Orange
97	House of Arras EJ Carr Late Disgorged 2007	Tasmania
97	Brown Brothers Patricia Extended Lees Pinot Noir Chardonnay 2010	King Valley
96	Delamere Vineyards Non Vintage Rosé NV	Tasmania
96	Bellebonne Natalie Fryar Vintage Rosé 2020	Tasmania
96	Coldstream Hills Blanc de Blancs 2017	Yarra Valley
96	Centennial Vineyards Blanc de Blancs NV	Southern Highlands

96	Delamere Vineyards Blanc de Blancs 2015	Tasmania
96	Delamere Vineyards Blanc de Blancs 2016	Tasmania
96	House of Arras Grand Vintage 2014	Tasmania
96	Printhie Wines Swift Cuvée Brut #10 NV	Orange
96	Printhie Wines Swift Vintage Brut 2015	Orange
96	Stefano Lubiana Late Disgorged 2008	Tasmania
96	Stefano Lubiana Grande Vintage 2011	Tasmania
96	Pirie Tasmania Late Disgorged Chardonnay Pinot Noir 2011	Tasmania
96	Rob Hall Wines Harriet's Vineyard Blanc de Noir Pinot Noir 2019	Yarra Valley
96	Seppelt Salinger Vintage Cuvée Méthode Traditionnelle 2017	Henty
95	Teusner MC Sparkling Shiraz Late Disgorgement 2005	Barossa Valley
95	Bleasdale Vineyards Sparkling Shiraz NV	Langhorne Creek
95	Bremerton Wines CHW Traditional Method Sparkling Shiraz 2020	Langhorne Creek
95	Billy Button Wines The Cherished Sparkling Shiraz 2022	Alpine Valleys
95	Charles Melton Wines Sparkling Red NV	Barossa Valley
95	Lark Hill Roxanne! Petillant Naturel 2021	Canberra District
95	Bellebonne Bis Rosé NV	Tasmania
95	Pipers Brook Vineyard Kreglinger Brut Rosé NV	Tasmania
95	Mandala Gathering LD Blanc de Blancs Chardonnay 1995	Yarra Valley
95	Philip Shaw Wines No.10 Méthode Traditionnelle Chardonnay 2010	Orange
95	Deviation Road Beltana Blanc de Blancs 2016	Adelaide Hills
95	House of Arras Blanc de Blancs 2014	Tasmania
95	Clover Hill Cuvée Prestige Blanc de Blancs 2010	Tasmania
95	Lobethal Road Wines Maja Late Disgorged 2017	Adelaide Hills
95	Kellybrook Blanc de Blancs 2019	Yarra Valley
95	Coombe Yarra Valley Tribute Series Nellie Melba Blanc de Blancs 2019	Yarra Valley
95	Bangor Vineyard Late Disgorged Blanc de Blanc Chardonnay 2016	Tasmania
95	Oakdene Kristen Sparkling Blanc de Blancs 2018	Geelong
95	Colmar Estate Chardonnay Pinot Noir 2015	Orange
95	Freycinet Vineyard R3 Radenti Chardonnay Pinot Noir NV	Tasmania
95	Bellebonne Natalie Fryar Vintage Cuvée 2019	Tasmania
95	Mitchell Harris Wines Sabre 2019	Macedon Ranges/ Pyrenees/Ballarat
95	Portsea Estate Brut Vintage Méthode Traditionnelle 2018	Mornington Peninsula
95	Mount Majura Vineyard The Silurian Late Disgorged Chardonnay Pinot Noir 2010	Canberra District
95	Gilbert Family Wines Methode Traditionelle #2 2016	Orange
95	Apogee Deluxe Vintage Brut 2019	Tasmania
95	Ashton Hills Vineyard Pinot Noir Vintage Rosé 2019	Adelaide Hills
95	Colmar Estate Brut 2017	Orange
95	Longview Vineyard Wagtail Pinot Noir Chardonnay Brut 2018	Adelaide Hills
95	Printhie Wines Swift Cuvée Brut #11 Pinot Noir Chardonnay NV	Orange
95	Pirie Tasmania Vintage Pinot Noir Chardonnay 2018	Tasmania
95	Coldstream Hills Pinot Noir Chardonnay 2017	Yarra Valley
95	Brown Brothers Patricia Pinot Noir Chardonnay Brut 2016	King Valley
95	Risky Business Wines Prosecco NV	King Valley
95	Dal Zotto Wines L'Immigrante Prosecco 2021	King Valley

| 95 | Dal Zotto Wines Pucino VP Prosecco 2022 | King Valley |
| 95 | Dal Zotto Wines Pucino Col Fondo Prosecco 2021 | King Valley |

Riesling

So much for retirement. Neil 'limefinger' Pike is renowned as a master of Clare Valley riesling, but his legend should be even better known than it is. He's a master of both the Watervale and Polish Hill River sub-regions, the latter – part of Pike's 'retirement project' – responsible for this year's Riesling of the Year. Interestingly, at this year's blind judging ATR Chockstone Grampians Riesling 2022 (not listed below but top rated for its region) was neck-and-neck with the limefinger after the first round of judging, which says a lot about the quality of the Chockstone, and even more about how fortunate we are to have so many great Australian riesling regions.

Riesling of the Year: limefinger Solace Riesling 2022, Clare Valley

Rating	Wine	Region
98	Castle Rock Estate Diletti Riesling 2021	Porongurup
97	Nick O'Leary Wines White Rocks Riesling 2022	Canberra District
97	Pepper Tree Wines Stone Mountain Single Vineyard Premium Reserve Riesling 2022	Orange
97	Henschke Julius Riesling 2022	Eden Valley
97	Seppelt Drumborg Vineyard Riesling 2022	Henty
97	Pewsey Vale Vineyard 10 Years Cellar Aged The Contours Museum Reserve Single Vineyard Estate Riesling 2013	Eden Valley
97	Holm Oak Riesling 2022	Tasmania
97	Stargazer Wine Palisander Vineyard Riesling 2021	Tasmania
96	Jim Barry Wines The Florita Riesling 2022	Clare Valley
96	Carillion Wines Museum Release Riesling 2015	Orange
96	Robert Stein Vineyard Reserve Riesling 2022	Mudgee
96	Robert Stein Vineyard Half Dry RS 15 Riesling 2022	Orange
96	Crawford River Wines Reserve Riesling 2018	Henty
96	Nick O'Leary Wines Heywood Riesling 2022	Canberra District
96	West Cape Howe Wines Riesling 2022	Porongurup
96	Forest Hill Vineyard Block 1 Riesling 2022	Mount Barker
96	Mac Forbes RS15 Riesling 2022	Strathbogie Ranges
96	Ministry of Clouds Riesling 2022	Clare Valley
96	Orlando Steingarten Riesling 2022	Eden Valley
96	Pipers Brook Vineyard Riesling 2022	Tasmania
96	Leo Buring DW Z20 Leopold Riesling 2022	Tasmania
96	Granite Hills Knight Riesling 2022	Macedon Ranges
96	Mitchell McNicol Riesling 2013	Clare Valley
96	Pikes The Merle Riesling 2017	Clare Valley
96	Grosset G110 2022	Clare Valley
96	Pooley Wines Butcher's Hill Riesling 2022	Tasmania
96	Frankland Estate Isolation Ridge Riesling 2022	Frankland River
96	Pooley Wines Cooinda Vale Riesling 2022	Tasmania
96	Forest Hill Vineyard Riesling 2022	Mount Barker
96	Mount Horrocks Watervale Riesling 2022	Clare Valley
96	Dandelion Vineyards Wonderland of the Eden Valley Riesling 2022	Eden Valley
96	Gilbert Family Wines gilbert Museum Release Riesling 2016	Orange
96	Kerrigan + Berry Riesling 2022	Mount Barker
96	Stargazer Wine Coal River Valley Riesling 2022	Tasmania
96	Rieslingfreak No. 1 Riesling 2020	Clare Valley

96	Rieslingfreak No. 2 Riesling 2022	Clare Valley
96	Tar & Roses Lewis Riesling 2022	Central Victoria
96	Adelina Wines Polish Hill River Riesling 2022	Clare Valley
96	Coates Wines The Riesling 2022	Adelaide Hills

Chardonnay

Chardonnay is at a crackerjack point in its history and the chardonnay category this year was an electrifying bracket to judge. There is now no reason to drink any Australian chardonnay other than a world-class one. The Padthaway region has a proud history of great chardonnay growing but even so, the achievement here of Landaire at Padthaway Estate cannot be underestimated. This category is a smorgasbord of riches and the Landaire chardonnay is a pearler. The wine to go within a whisker of the Landaire (in the final of three rounds of judging) was Hoddles Creek Estate 1er Chardonnay 2021, though Oakridge's 864 Single Block Release was the clubhouse leader at the end of the first round. The judging of this category was so tight, that it was tense. Many chardonnays this year would have made worthy winners.

Chardonnay of the Year: Landaire at Padthaway Estate Chardonnay 2021, Padthaway

Rating	Wine	Region
98	Giant Steps Applejack Vineyard Chardonnay 2022	Yarra Valley
98	Hoddles Creek Estate 1er Chardonnay 2021	Yarra Valley
98	Vasse Felix Heytesbury Chardonnay 2021	Margaret River
98	Penfolds Yattarna Bin 144 Chardonnay 2020	Tasmania/Ad. Hills
98	Oakridge Wines 864 Single Block Release Drive Block Funder & Diamond Vineyard Chardonnay 2021	Yarra Valley Yarra Valley
98	Giaconda Estate Vineyard Chardonnay 2021	Beechworth
98	Tolpuddle Vineyard Chardonnay 2021	Tasmania
98	Seville Estate Chardonnay 2022	Yarra Valley
97	Coldstream Hills Reserve Chardonnay 2021	Yarra Valley
97	Cherubino Cherubino Chardonnay 2021	Margaret River
97	Scotchmans Hill Cornelius Sutton Vineyard Chardonnay 2020	Geelong
97	Xanadu Wines Stevens Road Chardonnay 2021	Margaret River
97	Xanadu Wines Reserve Chardonnay 2021	Margaret River
97	Tapanappa Tiers Vineyard Chardonnay 2022	Piccadilly Valley
97	Dominique Portet Single Vineyard Chardonnay 2021	Yarra Valley
97	Domaine Naturaliste Purus Chardonnay 2021	Margaret River
97	Juniper Cornerstone Wilyabrup Chardonnay 2021	Margaret River
97	Lowestoft La Meilleure Chardonnay 2021	Tasmania
97	Geoff Weaver Aged Release Chardonnay 2013	Lenswood
97	BK Wines Ma Fleur Chardonnay 2008	Piccadilly Valley
97	Delamere Vineyards Block 3 Chardonnay 2021	Tasmania
97	Mayer Chardonnay 2022	Yarra Valley
97	Oakridge Wines Vineyard Series Willowlake Chardonnay 2021	Yarra Valley
97	Leeuwin Estate Prelude Vineyards Chardonnay 2021	Margaret River
97	Wantirna Estate Isabella Chardonnay 2021	Yarra Valley
97	Denton Chardonnay 2021	Yarra Valley
97	Battles Wine The Burnside Chardonnay 2022	Margaret River
97	Leeuwin Estate Art Series Chardonnay 2020	Margaret River
97	Whispering Brook Vintage Release Limited Release Chardonnay 2017	Hunter Valley

97	Helen's Hill Estate Breachley Block Single Vineyard Chardonnay 2021	Yarra Valley
97	Stella Bella Wines Luminosa Chardonnay 2021	Margaret River
97	Bird on a Wire Wines Chardonnay 2021	Yarra Valley
97	Grosset Piccadilly Chardonnay 2021	Adelaide Hills
97	Patrick Sullivan Wines Ada River Chardonnay 2022	Gippsland
97	Sidewood Estate Owen's Chardonnay 2021	Adelaide Hills
97	Bass Phillip Premium Old Vines Chardonnay 2021	Gippsland
97	Tyrrell's Wines HVD Chardonnay 2022	Hunter Valley
97	Tyrrell's Wines Single Vineyard Belford Chardonnay 2021	Hunter Valley
97	Toolangi F Block Chardonnay 2021	Yarra Valley
97	Penfolds Reserve Bin A Chardonnay 2021	Adelaide Hills
97	Cullen Wines Kevin John Wilyabrup 2021	Margaret River
97	Leogate Estate Wines Museum Release Creek Bed Reserve Chardonnay 2013	Hunter Valley
97	Gilbert Family Wines gilbert Museum Release Chardonnay 2016	Orange
97	Medhurst Estate Vineyard Chardonnay 2022	Yarra Valley
97	Yarra Yering Carrodus Chardonnay 2021	Yarra Valley
97	Mount Terrible Chardonnay 2022	Central Victoria
97	Giant Steps Tarraford Vineyard Chardonnay 2022	Yarra Valley
97	Windows Estate Petit Lot Chardonnay 2021	Margaret River
97	Dirty Three Wines All The Dirts Chardonnay 2022	Gippsland
97	Cobaw Ridge Chardonnay 2021	Macedon Ranges
97	Deep Woods Estate Reserve Chardonnay 2021	Margaret River
97	Bindi Wines Quartz Chardonnay 2021	Macedon Ranges
97	Shaw + Smith M3 Chardonnay 2021	Adelaide Hills

Semillon

It's impossible to look at the list of top-scoring wines in this category without once again concluding that the region-variety match of the Hunter Valley and semillon is one of the genuine wonders of the world. The time to make a fuss over Hunter Valley semillon is yesterday, today and tomorrow.

Semillon of the Year: Pepper Tree Wines Museum Release Limited Release Tallawanta Single Vineyard Semillon 2013, Hunter Valley

Rating	Wine	Region
98	Whispering Brook Vintage Release Single Vineyard Limited Release Semillon 2017	Hunter Valley
98	Tyrrell's Wines Vat 1 Winemaker's Selection Semillon 2022	Hunter Valley
98	Brokenwood ILR Reserve Semillon 2017	Hunter Valley
98	Mistletoe Wines Museum Release Reserve Semillon 2009	Hunter Valley
97	Audrey Wilkinson Museum Release The Ridge Semillon 2013	Hunter Valley
97	First Creek Wines Museum Release Winemaker's Reserve Semillon 2013	Hunter Valley
97	First Creek Wines Winemaker's Reserve Semillon 2022	Hunter Valley
97	De Iuliis Aged Release Single Vineyard 2017	Hunter Valley
97	Audrey Wilkinson Museum Release The Ridge Reserve Semillon 2010	Hunter Valley
97	Bimbadgen Museum Release Signature Semillon 2014	Hunter Valley
97	Pepper Tree Wines Museum Release Alluvius Single Vineyard Reserve Semillon 2013	Hunter Valley
97	Thomas Wines Braemore Cellar Reserve Semillon 2017	Hunter Valley
97	Silkman Wines Reserve Semillon 2022	Hunter Valley

97	Leogate Estate Wines Museum Release Reserve Semillon 2010	Hunter Valley
97	Mount Pleasant Lovedale Semillon 2022	Hunter Valley
96	Charteris Wines The Bellevue Vineyard Semillon 2022	Hunter Valley
96	McLeish Estate Wines Cellar Reserve Semillon 2016	Hunter Valley
96	McLeish Estate Wines Reserve Semillon 2022	Hunter Valley
96	Margan Wines Aged Release Francis John Semillon 2018	Hunter Valley
96	First Creek Wines Oakey Creek Vineyard Semillon 2022	Hunter Valley
96	First Creek Wines Museum Release Winemaker's Reserve Semillon 2017	Hunter Valley
96	Whispering Brook Single Vineyard Limited Release Semillon 2022	Hunter Valley
96	First Creek Wines Single Vineyard Murphy Vineyard Semillon 2022	Hunter Valley
96	First Creek Wines Museum Release Murphy Vineyard Semillon 2017	Hunter Valley
96	Audrey Wilkinson The Ridge Semillon 2022	Hunter Valley
96	Bimbadgen Museum Release Signature Palmers Lane Semillon 2014	Hunter Valley
96	Peter Lehmann Margaret Semillon 2016	Barossa
96	Glenguin Estate Aged Release Glenguin Vineyard Semillon 2017	Hunter Valley
96	Mount Eyre Vineyards Honeytree Semillon 2022	Hunter Valley
96	Silkman Wines Single Vineyard Blackberry Semillon 2022	Hunter Valley
96	Silkman Wines Museum Release Reserve Semillon 2017	Hunter Valley
96	Carillion Wines Origins Old Grafts Semillon 2022	Hunter Valley
96	Pepper Tree Wines Single Vineyard Alluvius Semillon 2022	Hunter Valley
96	Keith Tulloch Wine Latara Vineyard Semillon 2022	Hunter Valley
96	Mistletoe Wines Reserve Semillon 2021	Hunter Valley
96	Coates Wines Vin d'Or Semillon 2021	Adelaide Hills

Sauvignon Blanc

Last year's winner of this category was from Margaret River (Flowstone), but the Adelaide Hills had the most top-scoring wines. This year Margaret River takes the honours from both angles. The top three wines at our Awards judging were from Margaret River, Margaret River and the Pyrenees, respectively. Wines (including the winner) with judicious wood ageing performed well in this category.

Sauvignon Blanc of the Year: Domaine Naturaliste Sauvage Sauvignon Blanc 2021, Margaret River

Rating	Wine	Region
96	Squitchy Lane Vineyard SQL Sauvignon Blanc 2019	Yarra Valley
96	Jericho Wines Kuitpo Lockett Vineyard Fumé Blanc 2021	Adelaide Hills
96	McHenry Hohnen Vintners Sauvignon Blanc 2022	Margaret River
96	Windows Estate Petit Lot La Terre 2021	Margaret River
96	Flametree S.R.S. Karridale Sauvignon Blanc 2021	Margaret River
96	Domaine A Lady A Sauvignon Blanc 2019	Tasmania
95	Josef Chromy Wines Sauvignon Blanc 2022	Tasmania
95	Rahona Valley Sauvignon Blanc 2022	Mornington Peninsula
95	Trait Wines Sauvignon Blanc 2022	Margaret River
95	Terre à Terre Crayères Vineyard Sauvignon Blanc 2022	Wrattonbully
95	Flowstone Wines Sauvignon Blanc 2021	Margaret River
95	Gembrook Hill Sauvignon Blanc 2021	Yarra Valley
95	Vasse Felix Sauvignon Blanc 2021	Margaret River
95	Oakridge Wines Sauvignon 2021	Yarra Valley

95	Michael Hall Wines Sauvignon Blanc 2022	Adelaide Hills
95	Mitchell Harris Wines Sauvignon Blanc Fumé 2022	Pyrenees
95	Driftwood Estate Artifacts Fumé Blanc 2022	Margaret River
95	Sidewood Estate Sauvignon Blanc 2022	Adelaide Hills
95	Gentle Folk Blanc 2022	Adelaide Hills
95	Clyde Park Vineyard Sauvignon Blanc 2022	Geelong
95	Mulline Curlewis Sauvignon Blanc 2022	Geelong
95	Mulline Sauvignon Blanc 2022	Geelong
95	Gilbert Family Wines gilbert Sauvignon Blanc 2022	Orange
95	Moss Wood Ribbon Vale Elsa 2021	Margaret River
95	Higher Plane Led Astray Fumé Blanc 2022	Margaret River
95	Flametree S.R.S. Karridale Sauvignon Blanc 2022	Margaret River
95	Fermoy Estate Coldfire Fumé Blanc 2022	Margaret River
95	Deep Woods Estate Sauvignon Blanc 2022	Margaret River

Pinot Gris/Grigio

We are pleased to announce, at long last, a stand-alone category for pinot gris and pinot grigio. Mayer Bloody Hill PG is a very fine inaugural winner, with Bleasdale and Yabby Lake both going close to claiming the chocolates. Pinot gris/grigio wines make up around 10% of all the white wines tasted for this guide, outnumbering both sauvignon blanc and semillon. It's a significant variety with, in the best examples, the quality (and texture) to match.

Pinot Gris/Grigio of the Year: Mayer Bloody Hill Villages Healesville Pinot Gris 2022, Yarra Valley

Rating	Wine	Region
95	Scorpo Wines Bestia Pinot Grigio Tradizionale 2021	Mornington Peninsula
95	Trofeo Estate ESC Pinot Gris Terracotta Amphora Wine 2021	Mornington Peninsula
95	Moorooduc Estate Pinot Gris On Skins 2022	Mornington Peninsula
95	Quealy Winemakers Feri Maris Single Block Pinot Grigio 2022	Mornington Peninsula
95	La Prova Pinot Grigio 2022	Adelaide Hills
95	Coombe Yarra Valley Pinot Gris 2022	Yarra Valley
95	Shadowfax Winery Pinot Gris 2022	Macedon Ranges
95	Crittenden Estate Pinot Gris 2022	Mornington Peninsula
95	Cooks Lot Allotment No. 666 Pinot Gris 2022	Central Ranges
95	Rahona Valley Abel Pinot Gris 2022	Tasmania
95	Carlei Estate | Carlei Green Vineyards Green Vineyards Cardinia Ranges Pinot Gris 2021	Victoria
95	Ocean Eight Vineyard & Winery Pinot Gris 2022	Mornington Peninsula
95	Quealy Winemakers Tussie Mussie Pinot Gris 2022	Mornington Peninsula
95	Bleasdale Vineyards Pinot Gris 2022	Adelaide Hills
95	Stilvi Jungle Freak Single Vineyard Pinot Gris 2022	Mornington Peninsula
95	Indigo Vineyard Pinot Grigio 2021	Beechworth
95	Delatite Pinot Gris 2022	Upper Goulburn
95	Garagiste Merricks Pinot Gris 2022	Mornington Peninsula
95	Clyde Park Vineyard Pinot Gris 2022	Geelong
95	Rouleur Pinot Gris et al 2022	Yarra Valley
95	Apogee Alto Pinot Gris 2022	Tasmania
95	Yabby Lake Vineyard Single Vineyard Pinot Gris 2022	Mornington Peninsula
95	Fleet Wines Lichen Pinot Gris 2022	Mornington Peninsula
95	Eden Road Wines The Long Road Pinot Gris 2022	Southern NSW

Other Whites & Blends

This was one of the most exciting categories to judge. Other Whites & Blends is an uninspiring name but there are simply so many great wines to drink here. Indeed, of all the categories, this was the one that provoked the most discussion, off the back of the fact that the wines themselves had us all sitting up straighter. Mount Mary can count itself incredibly unlucky not to have come out on top here, so close was the scoring, but the John Kosovich Chenin is a beautiful and personality-laden wine, as are many of the wines here.

Other Whites & Blends of the Year: John Kosovich Wines Bottle Aged Reserve Chenin Blanc 2018, Swan Valley

Rating	Wine	Region
98	Mount Mary Triolet 2021	Yarra Valley
98	Yalumba The Virgilius Viognier 2021	Eden Valley
97	Yeringberg Marsanne Roussanne 2021	Yarra Valley
97	Yangarra Estate Vineyard Roux Beaute Roussanne 2021	McLaren Vale
97	Crittenden Estate Cri de Coeur Sous Voile Savagnin 2018	Mornington Peninsula
97	First Creek Wines Limited Release Small Batch Vermentino 2022	Hunter Valley
97	Yalumba The Virgilius Viognier 2020	Eden Valley
96	Windows Estate Petit Lot Chenin Blanc 2021	Margaret River
96	L.A.S. Vino CBDB Chenin Blanc Dynamic Blend 2021	Margaret River
96	Eldorado Road Dreamfields Fiano 2022	Alpine Valleys
96	La Prova Uno Fiano 2021	Adelaide Hills
96	Flowstone Wines Gewürztraminer 2021	Margaret River
96	Hahndorf Hill Winery GRU Grüner Veltliner 2022	Adelaide Hills
96	Sinapius Single Vineyard Close Planted Grüner Veltliner 2021	Tasmania
96	Stargazer Wine Tupelo 2022	Tasmania
96	Brash Higgins R/SM Saddlebags Hill Vineyard Riesling Semillon 2021	McLaren Vale
96	Entropy Wines Warragul Vineyard Sauvignon Blanc Semillon 2022	Gippsland
96	Yarra Yering Dry White Wine No. 1 2021	Yarra Valley
96	Sutton Grange Winery Estate Viognier 2021	Bendigo

Rosé

It was telling just how many of the wines at the annual Awards judging were either pale crimson or copper in colour, and how few were bright crimson and/or fuschsia-pink. The 'rosé revolution' of the past decade (and longer) is now dominated 'pale and dry' styles.

Rosé of the Year: Sutton Grange Winery Fairbank Rosé 2022 Central Victoria Zone

Rating	Wine	Region
97	Charles Melton Wines Rosé of Virginia 2022	Barossa Valley
96	Yeringberg Rosé Cabernet Shiraz 2022	Yarra Valley
96	Giant Steps Rosé 2022	Yarra Valley
96	Pooley Wines Cooinda Vale Rosé Pinot Noir 2021	Tasmania
96	Eastern Peake Taché 2021	Ballarat
96	Dominique Portet Single Vineyard Rosé 2022	Yarra Valley
96	Cobaw Ridge Il Pinko Rosé 2021	Macedon Ranges

95	Paringa Estate Estate Rosé 2022	Mornington Peninsula
95	Bondar Wines Grenache Cinsault Rosé 2022	McLaren Vale
95	Medhurst Estate Vineyard Rosé 2022	Yarra Valley
95	La Prova Aglianico Rosato 2022	Adelaide Hills
95	tripe.Iscariot Aspic Grenache Rosé 2022	Margaret River
95	Aravina Estate Grenache Rosé Limited Release 2022	Margaret River
95	Bindi Wines Dhillon Col Mountain Vineyard Rosé Grenache 2022	Heathcote
95	Tahbilk Grenache Mourvèdre Rosé 2022	Nagambie Lakes
95	Vanguardist Wines Grenache Mourvèdre Rosé 2022	McLaren Vale
95	Marchand & Burch Rosé 2022	Western Australia
95	McHenry Hohnen Vintners Chloé 2022	Margaret River
95	Emilian Single Vineyard Nebbiolo Rosé 2022	Yarra Valley
95	La Kooki Wines Rosé Blonde 2022	Margaret River
95	Kerri Greens Sage Phoque 2021	Mornington Peninsula
95	Trofeo Estate Amphora Terracotta Rosé 2022	Mornington Peninsula
95	Montalto Estate Rosé 2022	Mornington Peninsula
95	Thompson Estate Four Chambers Pinot Noir Rosé 2022	Margaret River
95	Garagiste Merricks Rosé 2022	Mornington Peninsula
95	L.A.S. Vino Albino PNO Rosé 2021	Margaret River
95	Foxeys Hangout Rosé 2022	Mornington Peninsula
95	Denton Shed Rosé 2022	Yarra Valley
95	Patina Orange Rosé 2021	Orange
95	Collector Wines Shoreline Sangiovese Rosé 2022	Gundagai/ Canberra District
95	Vinea Marson Rosato 2021	Heathcote
95	Nocturne Wines Carbunup SR Sangiovese Tempranillo 2022	Margaret River
95	Howard Park Miamup Rosé 2022	Margaret River
95	Hay Shed Hill Wines KP Naturally Rosé 2022	Geographe
95	Deep Woods Estate Rosé 2022	Margaret River

Pinot Noir

Pinot noir in Australia has come a very long way. Every year now there are many gorgeous examples of this variety produced from a fairly narrow (but remarkably reliable) band of regions. The Yarra Valley in particular has hit a stunning patch of form, as the list below clearly shows. Giant Steps' Applejack Vineyard Pinot Noir from 2022 is a ripping wine, and was a clear winner at the Awards judging.

Pinot Noir of the Year: Giant Steps Applejack Vineyard Pinot Noir 2022, Yarra Valley

Rating	Wine	Region
98	Coldstream Hills Deer Farm Vineyard Block E Pinot Noir 2021	Yarra Valley
98	Place of Changing Winds High Density Pinot Noir 2021	Macedon Ranges
98	Place of Changing Winds Between Two Mountains Pinot Noir 2021	Macedon Ranges
98	Oakridge Wines 864 Single Block Release Aqueduct Block Henk Vineyard Pinot Noir 2021	Yarra Valley
98	Delamere Vineyards Pinot Noir 2021	Tasmania
98	Giaconda Estate Vineyard Pinot Noir 2021	Beechworth
98	Bindi Wines Block 8 Pinot Noir 2021	Macedon Ranges
97	Coldstream Hills Deer Farm Vineyard Block D Pinot Noir 2021	Yarra Valley
97	Carillion Wines Origins Six Clones Pinot Noir 2022	Orange

97	Chatto Isle Pinot Noir 2021	Tasmania
97	Scorpo Wines Old Cherry Orchard 10K Pinot Noir 2021	Mornington Peninsula
97	Giant Steps Primavera Vineyard Pinot Noir 2022	Yarra Valley
97	Mewstone Wines Pinot Noir 2021	Tasmania
97	Hoddles Creek Estate 1er Pinot Noir 2021	Yarra Valley
97	Hoddles Creek Estate PSB Pinot Noir 2021	Yarra Valley
97	Gembrook Hill I.J.M. Pinot Noir 2021	Yarra Valley
97	Wantirna Estate Lily Yarra Valley Pinot Noir 2020	Yarra Valley
97	Pooley Wines Jack Denis Pooley Pinot Noir 2021	Tasmania
97	Seville Estate Pinot Noir 2022	Yarra Valley
97	Punch Lance's Vineyard Pinot Noir 2020	Yarra Valley
97	Savaterre Pinot Noir 2019	Beechworth
97	Oakridge Wines Vineyard Series Willowlake Pinot Noir 2021	Yarra Valley
97	De Bortoli Lusatia Yarra Valley Pinot Noir 2021	Yarra Valley
97	Bass Phillip Reserve Pinot Noir 2020	Gippsland
97	Bass Phillip Reserve Pinot Noir 2021	Gippsland
97	Castle Rock Estate Diletti Pinot Noir 2021	Porongurup
97	Medhurst Reserve Pinot Noir 2021	Yarra Valley
97	Serrat Pinot Noir 2022	Yarra Valley
97	Mount Mary Pinot Noir 2021	Yarra Valley
97	Seville Estate Dr McMahon Pinot Noir 2021	Yarra Valley
97	Mulline Single Vineyard Sutherlands Creek Pinot Noir 2022	Geelong
97	Bellbrae Estate Tetaz Pinot Noir 2020	Geelong
97	Yarra Yering Carrodus Pinot Noir 2021	Yarra Valley
97	Yarra Yering Pinot Noir 2021	Yarra Valley
97	Stargazer Wine Palisander Vineyard Pinot Noir 2021	Tasmania
97	Yabby Lake Vineyard Single Block Release Block 2 Pinot Noir 2022	Mornington Peninsula
97	Holm Oak The Wizard Pinot Noir 2020	Tasmania
97	Yering Station Scarlett Pinot Noir 2021	Yarra Valley
97	Bindi Wines Block 5 Pinot Noir 2021	Macedon Ranges

Grenache and blends

There were four stand-out brackets – or five if you include Fortified – at our Awards judging. Chardonnay for the sheer number of terrific wines; Other Whites & Blends for the high interest factor; Shiraz for its diversity; and Grenache for its ability to sweep tasters off their feet and to then send them into raptures. It hasn't happened overnight and we've sung this song (from the rooftops) before, but grenache has well and truly arrived as a star of our great wine country. Go deep. Go long.

Grenache & Blends of ther Year: Yangarra Estate Vineyard Old Vine Grenache 2021, McLaren Vale

Rating	Wine	Region
98	Alkina Wine Estate Polygon No.5 Grenache 2019	Barossa Valley
97	Mandoon Estate Discovery Series Bush Vine Grenache 2021	Swan Valley
97	Spinifex Sol Solice Grenache 2022	Barossa
97	Bondar Wines Vestige Grenache 2021	McLaren Vale
97	MMAD Vineyard Blewitt Springs Grenache 2021	McLaren Vale
97	Wirra Wirra Vineyards The Absconder Grenache 2021	McLaren Vale
97	Thistledown Wines This Charming Man Grenache 2022	McLaren Vale
97	Alkina Wine Estate Polygon No. 3 Grenache 2019	Barossa Valley
97	Yangarra Estate Vineyard High Sands Grenache 2020	McLaren Vale

97	Charles Melton Wines Nine Popes 2019	Barossa
97	Yangarra Estate Vineyard GSM 2021	McLaren Vale
96	Aphelion Wine Hickinbotham Single Vineyard Grenache 2022	McLaren Vale
96	Chapel Hill 1952 Vines Grenache 2021	McLaren Vale
96	Turkey Flat Grenache 2021	Barossa Valley
96	Juxtaposed Wait Vineyard Grenache 2021	McLaren Vale
96	Vanguardist Wines Grenache 2021	McLaren Vale
96	Hentley Farm Wines The Old Legend Grenache 2021	Barossa Valley
96	Bondar Wines Higher Springs Grenache 2021	McLaren Vale
96	Peter Lehmann The Barossan Grenache 2021	Barossa
96	HEAD Wines Old Vine Grenache 2021	Barossa
96	Two Hands Wines Twelftree Schuller Grenache 2020	McLaren Vale
96	Two Hands Wines Twelftree Chaffeys Road Grenache 2021	McLaren Vale
96	Two Hands Wines Twelftree Adams Road Grenache 2021	McLaren Vale
96	Torbreck Vintners Les Amis Grenache 2020	Barossa Valley
96	Serrat Grenache Noir 2022	Yarra Valley
96	Brash Higgins Smart Vineyard Grenache 2021	McLaren Vale
96	Thistledown Wines Sands of Time Grenache 2022	McLaren Vale
96	Thistledown Wines The Vagabond Old Vine Grenache 2022	McLaren Vale
96	Yangarra Estate Vineyard Ovitelli Grenache 2021	McLaren Vale
96	Arila Gardens Sand Garden Grenache 2021	Barossa Valley
96	Henschke Johann's Garden 2021	Barossa Valley
96	Hayes Family Wines Three Kings 2021	Barossa Valley
96	Alkina Wine Estate Old Quarter Single Vineyard GSM 2021	Barossa Valley
96	Tscharke Gnadenfrei Red I Grenache Shiraz Mourvèdre 2021	Barossa Valley
96	Bondar Wines Junto GSM 2021	McLaren Vale

Shiraz

It's worth running your eyes down this list and just, for a second, thinking of both the style of, and the regional impact on, each wine. Every wine here is a beautiful example of its type and yet there are so many fine and different types. One of the (many) great strengths of shiraz is that there's a high level of transparency in the way its region shows through. Murdoch Hill's The Landau Syrah is both the perfect example, and an absolute belter of a wine.

Shiraz of the Year: Murdoch Hill The Landau Single Vineyard Oakbank Syrah 2021, Adelaide Hills

Rating	Wine	Region
99	Henschke Hill of Grace 2018	Eden Valley
99	Tyrrell's Wines Old Patch Shiraz 2021	Hunter Valley
98	Henschke Mount Edelstone 2018	Eden Valley
98	Serrat Shiraz Viognier 2022	Yarra Valley
98	Pepper Tree Wines Museum Release Tallawanta Single Heritage Vineyard Shiraz 2013	Hunter Valley
98	Brokenwood Graveyard Vineyard Shiraz 2021	Hunter Valley
98	Meerea Park Cellar Release BLACK Shiraz 2018	Hunter Valley
98	Tyrrell's Wines Johnno's Shiraz 2021	Hunter Valley
98	Torbreck Vintners The Laird 2018	Barossa Valley
98	Amelia Park Wines Reserve Shiraz 2020	Frankland River
98	Mount Pleasant 1921 Vines Old Paddock Vineyard Shiraz 2021	Hunter Valley
98	Mount Pleasant 1880 Vines Old Hill Vineyard Shiraz 2021	Hunter Valley
98	Yarra Yering Underhill 2021	Yarra Valley

98	Pepper Tree Wines Museum Release Single Vineyard Reserve Coquun Shiraz 2013	Hunter Valley
98	Oakridge Wines 864 Single Block Release Close Planted Block Oakridge Vineyard Syrah 2021	Yarra Valley
97	Nick O'Leary Wines Bolaro Shiraz 2021	Canberra District
97	Chris Ringland Hoffmann Vineyard Shiraz 2015	Barossa
97	Spinifex La Maline 2021	Eden Valley
97	Tahbilk 1860 Vines Shiraz 2019	Nagambie Lakes
97	Dalwhinnie The Pinnacle Shiraz 2020	Pyrenees
97	Koomilya JC Block Shiraz 2019	McLaren Vale
97	Wolf Blass Platinum Label Medlands Vineyard Shiraz 2019	Barossa Valley
97	Wolf Blass Platinum Label Shiraz 2019	Barossa Valley
97	Pyren Vineyard Reserve Syrah 2021	Pyrenees
97	Audrey Wilkinson Museum Release The Lake Shiraz 2014	Hunter Valley
97	Eldorado Road Perseverance Old Vine Shiraz 2021	Glenrowan
97	Mayer Syrah 2022	Yarra Valley
97	Pepper Tree Wines Museum Release Limited Release Tallavera Single Vineyard Shiraz 2013	Hunter Valley
97	Henschke Hill of Roses 2018	Eden Valley
97	Seville Estate Dr McMahon Shiraz 2020	Yarra Valley
97	Penfolds RWT Bin 798 Shiraz 2020	Barossa Valley
97	Hentley Farm Wines Clos Otto Shiraz 2020	Barossa Valley
97	Bondar Wines Rayner Vineyard Shiraz 2021	McLaren Vale
97	Bondar Wines Violet Hour Shiraz 2021	McLaren Vale
97	Greenock Creek Wines Roennfeldt Road Shiraz 2018	Barossa Valley
97	HEAD Wines Wilton Hill Barossa Ranges Shiraz 2020	Eden Valley
97	Mistletoe Wines Home Vineyard Shiraz 2021	Hunter Valley
97	Tyrrell's Wines 8 Acres Shiraz 2021	Hunter Valley
97	Seville Estate Old Vine Reserve Shiraz 2021	Yarra Valley
97	Maverick Wines Ahrens' Creek Ancestor Vine Shiraz 2020	Barossa Valley
97	Forest Hill Vineyard Block 9 Shiraz 2021	Mount Barker
97	Torbreck Vintners RunRig 2020	Barossa Valley
97	Pooles Rock Cellar Release Post Office Shiraz 2014	Hunter Valley
97	Pooles Rock Cellar Release Post Office Shiraz 2011	Hunter Valley
97	MMAD Vineyard Blewitt Springs Shiraz 2021	McLaren Vale
97	Brokenwood Tallawanta Vineyard Shiraz 2021	Hunter Valley
97	Leogate Estate Wines Museum Release Malabar Reserve Shiraz 2014	Hunter Valley
97	Thomas Wines Kiss Limited Release Shiraz 2021	Hunter Valley
97	Leogate Estate Wines Cellar Release The Basin Reserve Shiraz 2018	Hunter Valley
97	Mulline Single Vineyard Bannockburn Syrah 2022	Geelong
97	Mount Pleasant O.P. & O.H. Single Vineyard Shiraz 2021	Hunter Valley
97	Mount Pleasant Mountain D Full Bodied Dry Red 2021	Hunter Valley
97	Mount Pleasant Rosehill Vineyard Shiraz 2021	Hunter Valley
97	Penfolds Magill Estate Shiraz 2020	Adelaide
97	Syrahmi La La Shiraz 2017	Heathcote
97	Yangarra Estate Vineyard Shiraz 2021	McLaren Vale
97	Yalumba The Octavius Old Vine Shiraz 2018	Barossa
97	Gentle Folk Village Syrah 2022	Adelaide Hills
97	Paul Nelson Wines Loam Syrah 2022	Frankland River
97	Windows Estate Petit Lot Basket Pressed Syrah 2019	Margaret River
97	Yering Station Reserve Shiraz Viognier 2021	Yarra Valley

Cabernet Shiraz Blends

As we note in the introduction to this edition, classics are classics for a reason. There's more to the list of wines here than blends of cabernet and shiraz but this classic combination is the backbone here. Bleasdale has been on an amazing run of good form in recent years and, again here, it's ripped out another beauty.

Cabernet Shiraz Blend of the Year: Bleasdale Vineyards Wellington Road Shiraz Cabernet 2021, Langhorne Creek

Rating	Wine	Region
98	Yalumba The Caley Cabernet Shiraz 2018	Coonawarra/ Barossa Valley
97	Lake Breeze Wines The Drake Cabernet Sauvignon Shiraz 2018	Langhorne Creek
96	Terre à Terre Crayères Vineyard Cabernet Sauvignon Shiraz 2020	Wrattonbully
96	Howard Park ASW Cabernet Sauvignon Shiraz 2020	Margaret River
96	Yalumba The Signature Cabernet Sauvignon Shiraz 2019	Barossa
96	Taltarni The Patron Pyrenees Cabernet Shiraz 2017	Pyrenees
96	Penley Estate Eos Cabernet Shiraz 2020	Coonawarra
96	Hardys The Eight (VIII) Cabernet Shiraz 2016	Frankland River/ McLaren Vale/ Coonawarra
96	St Hugo Black Shiraz Cabernet 2018	Barossa/Coonawarra
96	Penley Estate Eos Shiraz Cabernet Sauvignon 2021	Coonawarra
96	Maverick Wines The Maverick Shiraz Cabernet Sauvignon 2020	Barossa
96	Bremerton Wines B.O.V. 2019	Langhorne Creek
95	Majella The Malleea 2018	Coonawarra
95	Redman The Redman 2019	Coonawarra
95	Tapanappa Whalebone Vineyard Cabernet Shiraz 2019	Wrattonbully
95	Pepper Tree Wines Museum Release Single Vineyard Strandlines Reserve Cabernet Shiraz 2013	Wrattonbully
95	Penfolds Bin 389 Cabernet Shiraz 2020	South Australia
95	Hickinbotham Clarendon Vineyard The Peake Cabernet Shiraz 2021	McLaren Vale
95	Yalumba FDR1A Cabernet Shiraz 2018	Barossa
95	Sweetwater Wines Single Estate Shiraz Cabernet 2021	Hunter Valley
95	Thomas St Vincent Blewitt Springs Septentrionale Rouge 2020	Fleurieu
95	Glaetzer Wines Anaperenna 2021	Barossa Valley
95	Ponting 366 Shiraz Cabernet Sauvignon 2019	McLaren Vale/ Coonawarra
95	Henschke Apple Tree Bench 2019	Barossa Valley

Cabernet Sauvignon

This is a feat that won't be repeated too often. Bleasdale The Iron Duke has taken out the Cabernet Sauvignon category for the second year running, beating off a quality field by a convincing margin (on the first round of judging), and then withstanding an onslaught of support for Xanadu Reserve Cabernet Sauvignon 2020. Underestimate both Bleasdale and Langhorne Creek at your peril.

Cabernet Sauvignon of the Year: Bleasdale Vineyards The Iron Duke Cabernet Sauvignon 2021, Langhorne Creek

Rating	Wine	Region
98	Cherubino Cherubino Budworth Riversdale Vineyard Cabernet Sauvignon 2019	Frankland River
97	Cherubino Cherubino Cabernet Sauvignon 2020	Margaret River
97	Xanadu Wines Reserve Cabernet Sauvignon 2020	Margaret River
97	Mandoon Estate Reserve Research Station Cabernet Sauvignon 2018	Margaret River
97	Juniper Cornerstone Wilyabrup Cabernet Sauvignon 2016	Margaret River
97	Oakridge Wines Original Vineyard Cabernet Sauvignon 2021	Yarra Valley
97	De Iuliis Cabernet Sauvignon 2021	Hilltops
97	HOOSEGG Double Happy Cabernet Sauvignon 2019	Orange
97	Leeuwin Estate Art Series Cabernet Sauvignon 2019	Margaret River
97	Pepper Tree Wines Museum Release Block 21A Single Vineyard Reserve Cabernet Sauvignon 2013	Wrattonbully
97	Penfolds Bin 169 Cabernet Sauvignon 2019	Coonawarra
97	Parker Coonawarra Estate First Growth 2019	Coonawarra
97	Woodlands Ruby Jane Cabernet Sauvignon 2019	Margaret River
97	Punt Road Napoleone Vineyard Block 3 Cabernet Sauvignon 2021	Yarra Valley
97	Brand & Sons Sanctuary Cabernet Sauvignon 2019	Coonawarra
97	Oakridge Wines 864 Single Block Release Winery Block Oakridge Vineyard Cabernet Sauvignon 2021	Yarra Valley
97	Thompson Estate The Specialist Cabernet Sauvignon 2019	Margaret River
97	Flametree S.R.S. Wilyabrup Cabernet Sauvignon 2019	Margaret River
97	Joshua Cooper Wines Balgownie Vineyard 1970 Block Cabernet Sauvignon 2021	Bendigo
97	Yarra Yering Carrodus Cabernet Sauvignon 2021	Yarra Valley
97	Deep Woods Estate Single Vineyard G2 Cabernet Sauvignon 2020	Margaret River
97	Deep Woods Estate Reserve Cabernet Sauvignon 2020	Margaret River
96	Rochford Wines Isabella's Single Vineyard Cabernet Sauvignon 2021	Yarra Valley
96	Nocturne Wines Sheoak Single Vineyard Cabernet Sauvignon 2021	Margaret River
96	Xanadu Wines Stevens Road Cabernet Sauvignon 2020	Margaret River
96	Tahbilk Eric Stevens Purbrick Cabernet Sauvignon 2019	Nagambie Lakes
96	Dalwhinnie Moonambel Cabernet 2020	Pyrenees
96	Wynns Coonawarra Estate John Riddoch Limited Release Cabernet Sauvignon 2020	Coonawarra
96	Wynns Coonawarra Estate Black Label Cabernet Sauvignon 2021	Coonawarra
96	Wynns Coonawarra Estate Glengyle Single Vineyard Cabernet Sauvignon 2021	Coonawarra
96	Mandala The Mandala Butterfly Cabernet Sauvignon 2021	Yarra Valley
96	Juniper Cornerstone Wilyabrup Cabernet Sauvignon 2018	Margaret River
96	St Huberts Reserve Cabernet Sauvignon 2021	Yarra Valley
96	Blue Pyrenees Estate Richardson Reserve Cabernet Sauvignon 2019	Pyrenees
96	Balnaves of Coonawarra Cabernet Sauvignon 2020	Coonawarra
96	Penley Estate Helios Cabernet Sauvignon 2021	Coonawarra
96	Penfolds Bin 407 Cabernet Sauvignon 2020	South Australia
96	Penley Estate Steyning Cabernet Sauvignon 2020	Coonawarra
96	Penley Estate Steyning Cabernet Sauvignon 2021	Coonawarra
96	Lindeman's Coonawarra Trio St George Vineyard Cabernet Sauvignon 2021	Coonawarra
96	Pierro VR Cabernet Sauvignon 2018	Margaret River

96	Stella Bella Wines Luminosa Cabernet Sauvignon 2020	Margaret River
96	Punt Road Napoleone Vineyard Block 11 Cabernet Sauvignon 2021	Yarra Valley
96	Greenock Creek Wines Roennfeldt Road Cabernet Sauvignon 2018	Barossa Valley
96	Henschke Cyril Henschke 2018	Eden Valley
96	De Bortoli Melba Amphora Cabernet Sauvignon 2022	Yarra Valley
96	Brokenwood Wildwood Road Cabernet Sauvignon 2021	Margaret River
96	Tokar Estate Coldstream Vineyard Cabernet Sauvignon 2021	Yarra Valley
96	Singlefile Wines The Philip Adrian Cabernet Sauvignon 2019	Frankland River
96	Briar Ridge Vineyard Big Bully Stonefields Vineyard Cabernet Sauvignon 2021	Wrattonbully
96	Vasse Felix Cabernet Sauvignon 2020	Margaret River
96	Cullen Wines Vanya Full Moon Fruit Day Cabernet Sauvignon 2019	Margaret River
96	Brand's Laira Coonawarra 171 Cabernet Sauvignon 2019	Coonawarra
96	Maverick Wines Ahrens' Creek Cabernet Sauvignon 2020	Barossa Valley
96	Thompson Estate The Specialist Cabernet Sauvignon 2020	Margaret River
96	Yering Station Reserve Cabernet Sauvignon 2021	Yarra Valley
96	Hay Shed Hill Wines Cabernet Sauvignon 2020	Margaret River
96	Mordrelle Wines Basket Press Cabernet Sauvignon 2019	Langhorne Creek
96	Flametree S.R.S. Wilyabrup Cabernet Sauvignon 2020	Margaret River

Cabernet & Family

This is a category for 'Bordeaux' varieties, blends or varietal wines, excluding wines made of cabernet sauvignon only (which has its own category). Houghton C. W. Ferguson Cabernet Malbec 2020, from Frankland River, won the category for its sheer undeniable, plush loveliness, though Grosset's exquisitely elegant Gaia 2020 (not in the list below), come a very close second. The wines listed below often don't attract a lot of fuss (with exceptions), but true beauty resides here.

Cabernet & Family of the Year: Houghton C.W. Ferguson Cabernet Malbec 2020, Frankland River

Rating	Wine	Region
98	Yeringberg Yeringberg 2021	Yarra Valley
98	Vasse Felix Tom Cullity Cabernet Sauvignon Malbec 2019	Margaret River
98	Lake Breeze Wines Arthur's Reserve Cabernet Sauvignon Malbec Petit Verdot 2020	Langhorne Creek
98	Mount Mary Quintet 2021	Yarra Valley
98	Yarra Yering Dry Red Wine No. 1 2021	Yarra Valley
97	Bleasdale Vineyards Frank Potts 2021	Langhorne Creek
97	Cullen Wines Diana Madeline Wilyabrup 2021	Margaret River
97	Parker Coonawarra Estate 95 Block 2020	Coonawarra
97	Warramunda Estate Liv Zak Malbec 2021	Yarra Valley
97	Mordrelle Wines The Gaucho Ltd Edition Reserva Malbec 2020	Langhorne Creek
96	Rob Hall Wines Cabernets 2022	Yarra Valley
96	Woodlands Margaret 2019	Margaret River
96	Ross Hill Wines Pinnacle Series Griffin Road Vineyard Cabernet Franc 2021	Orange
96	HOOSEGG Jade Moon Cabernet Franc 2019	Orange
96	Frankland Estate Olmo's Reward 2020	Frankland River
96	McHenry Hohnen Vintners Rolling Stone 2019	Margaret River
96	Yarra Yering Agincourt Cabernet Malbec 2021	Yarra Valley

96	Deep Woods Estate Single Vineyard Cabernet Malbec 2021	Margaret River
96	Carillion Wines Origins Arbitrage Cabernet Merlot Shiraz 2019	Wrattonbully
96	Squitchy Lane Vineyard Cabernet Sauvignon Cabernet Franc Merlot 2019	Yarra Valley
96	Yarra Edge Edward Single Vineyard Cabernet Sauvignon Cabernet Franc Merlot 2021	Yarra Valley
96	Dominique Portet Single Vineyard Cabernet Sauvignon Malbec 2021	Yarra Valley
96	Lindeman's Coonawarra Trio Pyrus Cabernet Sauvignon Merlot Malbec 2021	Coonawarra
96	Mordrelle Wines The Gaucho Malbec 2021	Langhorne Creek
96	Mordrelle Wines Cellar Release The Gaucho Basket Press Malbec 2017	Langhorne Creek
96	Serengale Vineyard Merlot Cabernet 2019	Beechworth
96	Tapanappa Whalebone Vineyard Merlot Cabernet Franc 2019	Wrattonbully

Other Reds & Blends

Of all categories, other than perhaps grenache, this was the one where there was the most agreement. All the wines were served blind and yet the iconic Yarra Yering Dry Red No. 3 streeted the field. There was also, quite rightly, strong support for Swinney Farvie Mourvèdre 2021, the latter producer going close to winning this category last year as well.

Other Reds & Blends of the Year: Yarra Yering Dry Red Wine No. 3 2021, Yarra Valley

Rating	Wine	Region
97	Mordrelle Wines Malbec Lagrein Cabernet Sauvignon Shiraz 2021	Langhorne Creek
97	Domenica Wines Nebbiolo 2019	Beechworth
97	Hewitson Barrel 1853 Shiraz Mourvèdre 2020	Barossa Valley
96	Mordrelle Wines Basket Press Barbera 2020	Langhorne Creek
96	Sinapius Esme 2021	Tasmania
96	Cobaw Ridge Lagrein 2021	Macedon Ranges
96	John Duval Wines Annexus Mataro 2021	Barossa Valley
96	Neldner Road Kleinig Mataro 2017	Barossa Valley
96	Bondar Wines Monastrell 2021	McLaren Vale
96	Mitolo Wines Masso Montepulciano 2021	McLaren Vale
96	Swinney Farvie Mourvèdre 2021	Frankland River
96	Hewitson Old Garden Vineyard Mourvèdre 2020	Barossa Valley
96	Frankland Estate Isolation Ridge Mourvèdre 2021	Frankland River
96	Mayer Nebbiolo 2022	Yarra Valley
96	Pizzini Coronamento Nebbiolo 2018	King Valley
96	Pipan Steel IX Nebbiolo 2018	Alpine Valleys
96	Giaconda Nebbiolo 2019	Beechworth
96	Eldorado Road Riserva Nero d'Avola 2021	Beechworth
96	Emilian L'assemblage Rouge 2022	Yarra Valley
96	Yarra Yering Light Dry Red Pinot Shiraz 2022	Yarra Valley
96	Charles Melton Wines La Belle Mère GSR 2019	Barossa
96	Thomas St Vincent Blewitt Springs Provencale Rouge 2020	Fleurieu
96	Bremerton Wines Bâtonnage Shiraz Malbec 2021	Langhorne Creek
96	Thousand Candles Gathering Field Shiraz Malbec 2021	Yarra Valley
96	Yarra Yering Dry Red Wine No. 2 2021	Yarra Valley
96	Hewitson Barrel 1853 Shiraz Mourvèdre 2019	Barossa Valley

96	Bekkers Syrah Grenache 2021	McLaren Vale
96	Mayford Wines Porepunkah Tempranillo 2021	Alpine Valleys
96	Anderson & Marsh Parell Tempranillo 2021	Alpine Valleys
96	Mordrelle Wines Basket Press Tempranillo 2021	Langhorne Creek
96	Seppeltsfield No. EC3 Tinta Cão Tinta Amarela Touriga 2021	Barossa

Sweet

The wines below are easy to drink, but difficult to judge, most particularly as a class. Stark differences in sweetness level and style means it's difficult to compare apples with apples, which leaves us instead judging cumquats with mandarins. That said, in a rich style, De Bortoli's Noble One 2020 was a clear winner at this year's judging.

Sweet Wine of the Year: De Bortoli (Riverina) Noble One Botrytis Semillon 2020, Riverina

Rating	Wine	Region
96	Rieslingfreak No. 8 Riesling 2022	Clare Valley
95	Hahndorf Hill Winery Green Angel Late Harvest Grüner Veltliner 2021	Adelaide Hills
95	Delatite Late Harvest Riesling 2022	Upper Goulburn
95	De Beaurepaire Wines Coeur d'Or Botrytis Semillon 2021	Central Ranges
95	R. Paulazzo F-1833 Botrytis Semillon 2019	Riverina
95	Pizzini Per gli Angeli 2013	King Valley
95	Lillypilly Estate Museum Release Noble Blend 1st Rendition 2008	Riverina
94	Pooley Wines Butcher's Hill Cane Cut Riesling 2022	Tasmania

Fortified

Seppeltsfield 100 Year Old Para Vintage Tawny has been elevated to the James Halliday Hall of Fame, courtesy of the fact that it has won this category a minimum of five times (it's won on nine occasions). The All Saints Museum Muscat was not only magnificent in its rich, decadent flavour, but also had a level of sheer drinkability that had us all draining our glasses. This nectar should never be wasted.

Fortified Wine of the Year: All Saints Estate Museum Muscat NV, Rutherglen

Rating	Wine	Region
100	Seppeltsfield 100 Year Old Para Vintage Tawny 1923	Barossa Valley
100	All Saints Estate Museum Muscadelle NV	Rutherglen
99	Campbells Merchant Prince Rare Muscat NV	Rutherglen
98	Chambers Rosewood Rare Muscat NV	Rutherglen
98	Morris Old Premium Rare Muscat NV	Rutherglen
98	All Saints Estate Rare Muscat NV	Rutherglen
98	McWilliam's Hanwood Very Rare Tawny Aged 30 Years NV	Riverina
98	Campbells Isabella Rare Topaque NV	Rutherglen
98	Morris Old Premium Rare Topaque NV	Rutherglen

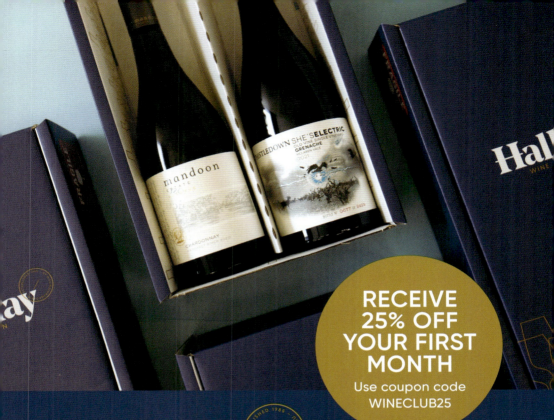

Halliday Wine Club

Gold medal
wines only
(95+ points)

Australia's
leading authority
on wine

Curated wine selections
from over 9,000
wines tasted

Delivering the
stories behind
the wine

Join now to continue your wine journey with us.

For more information visit
winecompanion.com.au/wineclub
or scan the QR code.

Best wineries by region

This is the full roll call of 5-star wineries of the year arranged by region. This encompasses a three-tier classification (fully explained on page 15). The winery names printed in red denote the best of the best with a long track record of excellence, typically upholding a 5-star rating for 10 years. Five red stars are awarded to wineries who have typically upheld 5-star ratings for at least four years. Wineries with 5 black stars have achieved excellence this year (and sometimes longer). With 462 wineries qualifying this year, this heroic list is your quick reference guide to the finest estates in the country.

ADELAIDE

Hewitson ★★★★★
Patritti Wines ★★★★★

ADELAIDE HILLS

Ashton Hills Vineyard ★★★★★
BK Wines ★★★★★
Coates Wines ★★★★★
CRFT Wines ★★★★★
Deviation Road ★★★★★
Gentle Folk ★★★★★
Geoff Weaver ★★★★★
Hahndorf Hill Winery ★★★★★
Howard Vineyard ★★★★★
Jericho Wines ★★★★★
Karrawatta ★★★★★
La Prova ★★★★★
Longview Vineyard ★★★★★
Mordrelle Wines ★★★★★
Murdoch Hill ★★★★★
Petaluma ★★★★★
Pike & Joyce ★★★★★
Riposte Wines ★★★★★
Shaw + Smith ★★★★★
Sidewood Estate ★★★★★
The Lane Vineyard ★★★★★

ALPINE VALLEYS

Anderson & Marsh ★★★★★
Billy Button Wines ★★★★★
Mayford Wines ★★★★★
Pipan Steel ★★★★★

BALLARAT

Eastern Peake ★★★★★

BAROSSA VALLEY

Alkina Wine Estate ★★★★★
Arila Gardens ★★★★★
Bethany Wines ★★★★★
Brothers at War ★★★★★
Charles Melton Wines ★★★★★
Château Tanunda ★★★★★
Chris Ringland ★★★★★
Curator Wine Company ★★★★★
Elderton ★★★★★
Eperosa ★★★★★
Gibson ★★★★★
Glaetzer Wines ★★★★★
Greenock Creek Wines ★★★★★
Groom ★★★★★
Hayes Family Wines ★★★★★
HEAD Wines ★★★★★
Hentley Farm Wines ★★★★★
Hobbs Barossa Ranges ★★★★★
JJ Hahn ★★★★★
John Duval Wines ★★★★★
Kaesler Wines ★★★★★
Kalleske ★★★★★
Langmeil Winery ★★★★★
Laughing Jack ★★★★★
Maverick Wines ★★★★★
Neldner Road ★★★★★
Orlando ★★★★★
Otherness ★★★★★
Penfolds ★★★★★
Peter Lehmann ★★★★★
Purple Hands Wines ★★★★★
Quin Wines ★★★★★
St Hugo ★★★★★
Saltram ★★★★★

Seabrook Wines ★★★★★
Seppeltsfield ★★★★★
Sons of Eden ★★★★★
Soul Growers ★★★★★
Spinifex ★★★★★
Teusner ★★★★★
Thorn-Clarke Wines ★★★★★
Torbreck Vintners ★★★★★
Tscharke ★★★★★
Turkey Flat ★★★★★
Two Hands Wines ★★★★★
Utopos ★★★★★
Vanguardist Wines ★★★★★
Vindana Wines ★★★★★
Wolf Blass ★★★★★
Z Wine ★★★★★

BEECHWORTH

A. Rodda Wines ★★★★★
Domenica Wines ★★★★★
Eldorado Road ★★★★★
Fighting Gully Road ★★★★★
Giaconda ★★★★★
Savaterre ★★★★★
Valhalla Wines ★★★★★
Vignerons Schmölzer & Brown ★★★★★

BENDIGO

Balgownie Estate ★★★★★
Sutton Grange Winery ★★★★★

CANBERRRA DISTRICT

Clonakilla ★★★★★
Collector Wines ★★★★★
Eden Road Wines ★★★★★
Helm ★★★★★
Lark Hill ★★★★★
Mount Majura Vineyard ★★★★★
Nick O'Leary Wines ★★★★★
Ravensworth ★★★★★

CENTRAL RANGES

De Beaurepaire Wines ★★★★★
Gilbert Family Wines ★★★★★
Mount Terrible ★★★★★

CLARE VALLEY

Adelina Wines ★★★★★
Gaelic Cemetery Vineyard ★★★★★
Grosset ★★★★★
Jim Barry Wines ★★★★★

Kilikanoon Wines ★★★★★
Koerner Wine ★★★★★
limefinger ★★★★★
Mount Horrocks ★★★★★
O'Leary Walker Wines ★★★★★
Pikes ★★★★★
Rieslingfreak ★★★★★
Sevenhill Cellars ★★★★★
Taylors ★★★★★
Vickery ★★★★★

COONAWARRA

Balnaves of Coonawarra ★★★★★
Brand & Sons ★★★★★
Leconfield ★★★★★
Lindeman's ★★★★★
Nightfall Wines ★★★★★
Parker Coonawarra Estate ★★★★★
Penley Estate ★★★★★
Reschke Wines ★★★★★
Wynns Coonawarra Estate ★★★★★

DENMARK

Paul Nelson Wines ★★★★★

EDEN VALLEY

Flaxman Wines ★★★★★
Heathvale ★★★★★
Henschke ★★★★★
Max & Me ★★★★★
mesh ★★★★★
Mountadam Vineyards ★★★★★
Pewsey Vale Vineyard ★★★★★
Poonawatta ★★★★★
Yalumba ★★★★★

FRANKLAND RIVER

Alkoomi ★★★★★
Frankland Estate ★★★★★
Swinney ★★★★★

GEELONG

Banks Road ★★★★★
Bannockburn Vineyards ★★★★★
Bellbrae Estate ★★★★★
Clyde Park Vineyard ★★★★★
Mulline ★★★★★
Oakdene ★★★★★
Provenance Wines ★★★★★
Scotchmans Hill ★★★★★

GEOGRAPHE

Capel Vale ★★★★★
Ironcloud Wines ★★★★★
Willow Bridge Estate ★★★★★

GIPPSLAND

Bass Phillip ★★★★★
Blue Gables ★★★★★
Dirty Three Wines ★★★★★
Entropy Wines ★★★★★
Fleet Wines ★★★★★
Lightfoot Wines ★★★★★
Narkoojee ★★★★★
Patrick Sullivan Wines ★★★★★
William Downie ★★★★★

GLENROWAN

Baileys of Glenrowan ★★★★★

GRAMPIANS

Clarnette Wines ★★★★★
Fallen Giants ★★★★★
Mount Langi Ghiran Vineyards ★★★★★
The Story Wines ★★★★★

GREAT SOUTHERN

Castelli Estate ★★★★★
Forest Hill Vineyard ★★★★★
Harewood Estate ★★★★★
Singlefile Wines ★★★★★

GREAT WESTERN

ATR Wines ★★★★★
Best's Wines ★★★★★
Seppelt ★★★★★

HEATHCOTE

Ellis Wines ★★★★★
Jasper Hill ★★★★★
Paul Osicka ★★★★★
Sanguine Estate ★★★★★
Syrahmi ★★★★★
Tellurian ★★★★★

HENTY

Crawford River Wines ★★★★★
Hochkirch Wines ★★★★★

HUNTER VALLEY

Audrey Wilkinson ★★★★★
Bimbadgen ★★★★★
Briar Ridge Vineyard ★★★★★
Brokenwood ★★★★★
Carillion Wines ★★★★★
Charteris Wines ★★★★★
David Hook Wines ★★★★★
De Iuliis ★★★★★
First Creek Wines ★★★★★
Glenguin Estate ★★★★★
Gundog Estate ★★★★★
Keith Tulloch Wine ★★★★★
Leogate Estate Wines ★★★★★
McLeish Estate Wines ★★★★★
Margan Wines ★★★★★
Meerea Park ★★★★★
Mercer Wines ★★★★★
Mistletoe Wines ★★★★★
Mount Eyre Vineyards ★★★★★
Mount Pleasant ★★★★★
Pepper Tree Wines ★★★★★
Peter Drayton Wines ★★★★★
Pooles Rock ★★★★★
RidgeView Wines ★★★★★
Scarborough Wine Co ★★★★★
Silkman Wines ★★★★★
Stomp Wines ★★★★★
Thomas Wines ★★★★★
Tinklers Vineyard ★★★★★
Tyrrell's Wines ★★★★★
Usher Tinkler Wines ★★★★★
Whispering Brook ★★★★★
Winmark Wines ★★★★★

KANGAROO ISLAND

The Islander Estate Vineyards ★★★★★

KING VALLEY

Brown Brothers ★★★★★
Dal Zotto Wines ★★★★★
Pizzini ★★★★★

LANGHORNE CREEK

Bleasdale Vineyards ★★★★★
Bremerton Wines ★★★★★
Kimbolton Wines ★★★★★
Lake Breeze Wines ★★★★★
Metala ★★★★★

LENSWOOD

Mt Lofty Ranges Vineyard ★★★★★

MACEDON RANGES

Bindi Wines ★★★★★
Cobaw Ridge ★★★★★
Curly Flat ★★★★★
Granite Hills ★★★★★
Lyons Will Estate ★★★★★
Passing Clouds ★★★★★
Place of Changing Winds ★★★★★

MARGARET RIVER

Amelia Park Wines ★★★★★
Aravina Estate ★★★★★
Arlewood Estate ★★★★★
Cape Mentelle ★★★★★
Cherubino ★★★★★
Clairault Streicker Wines ★★★★★
Cullen Wines ★★★★★
Deep Woods Estate ★★★★★
Domaine Naturaliste ★★★★★
Driftwood Estate ★★★★★
Evans & Tate ★★★★★
Evoi Wines ★★★★★
Fermoy Estate ★★★★★
Flametree ★★★★★
Flowstone Wines ★★★★★
Fraser Gallop Estate ★★★★★
Hay Shed Hill Wines ★★★★★
Higher Plane ★★★★★
Howard Park ★★★★★
Juniper ★★★★★
L.A.S. Vino ★★★★★
Leeuwin Estate ★★★★★
McHenry Hohnen Vintners ★★★★★
Miles from Nowhere ★★★★★
Moss Wood ★★★★★
Nocturne Wines ★★★★★
Peccavi Wines ★★★★★
Pierro ★★★★★
Snake + Herring ★★★★★
Stella Bella Wines ★★★★★
Thompson Estate ★★★★★
Trait Wines ★★★★★
tripe.Iscariot ★★★★★
Vasse Felix ★★★★★
Victory Point Wines ★★★★★
Voyager Estate ★★★★★
Wills Domain ★★★★★
Windows Estate ★★★★★

Wise Wine ★★★★★
Woodlands ★★★★★
Xanadu Wines ★★★★★

MCLAREN VALE

Angove Family Winemakers ★★★★★
Aphelion Wine ★★★★★
Bekkers ★★★★★
Bondar Wines ★★★★★
Brash Higgins ★★★★★
Chalk Hill ★★★★★
Chapel Hill ★★★★★
Clarendon Hills ★★★★★
Coriole ★★★★★
Dune Wine ★★★★★
Gemtree Wines ★★★★★
Grounded Cru ★★★★★
Hardys ★★★★★
Haselgrove Wines ★★★★★
Hickinbotham Clarendon Vineyard
   ★★★★★
Hugh Hamilton Wines ★★★★★
Inkwell ★★★★★
Juxtaposed ★★★★★
Kay Brothers ★★★★★
Koomilya ★★★★★
Ministry of Clouds ★★★★★
Mr Riggs Wine Company ★★★★★
Mitolo Wines ★★★★★
MMAD Vineyard ★★★★★
Oliver's Taranga Vineyards ★★★★★
Paralian Wines ★★★★★
Primo Estate ★★★★★
SC Pannell ★★★★★
Serafino Wines ★★★★★
Smidge Wines ★★★★★
Thomas St Vincent ★★★★★
Varney Wines ★★★★★
Wirra Wirra Vineyards ★★★★★
Yangarra Estate Vineyard ★★★★★

MORNINGTON PENINSULA

Crittenden Estate ★★★★★
Dexter Wines ★★★★★
Eldridge Estate of Red Hill ★★★★★
Foxeys Hangout ★★★★★
Gaffy & Neal ★★★★★
Garagiste ★★★★★
Hurley Vineyard ★★★★★
Kerri Greens ★★★★★
Kooyong ★★★★★

Lindenderry Estate ★★★★★
Main Ridge Estate ★★★★★
Montalto ★★★★★
Moorooduc Estate ★★★★★
Ocean Eight Vineyard & Winery
★★★★★
Paringa Estate ★★★★★
Port Phillip Estate ★★★★★
Principia ★★★★★
Quealy Winemakers ★★★★★
Rahona Valley ★★★★★
Rare Hare ★★★★★
Scorpo Wines ★★★★★
Stonier Wines ★★★★★
Ten Minutes by Tractor ★★★★★
Trofeo Estate ★★★★★
Yabby Lake Vineyard ★★★★★

MOUNT BARKER

3 Drops ★★★★★
Plantagenet Wines ★★★★★
West Cape Howe Wines ★★★★★

MOUNT LOFTY RANGES

Michael Hall Wines ★★★★★

MUDGEE

Logan Wines ★★★★★
Robert Oatley Vineyards ★★★★★
Robert Stein Vineyard ★★★★★

NAGAMBIE LAKES

Mitchelton ★★★★★
Tahbilk ★★★★★
Tar & Roses ★★★★★

NEW ENGLAND

Topper's Mountain Wines ★★★★★

ORANGE

Bloodwood ★★★★★
Brangayne of Orange ★★★★★
Colmar Estate ★★★★★
Cooks Lot ★★★★★
HOOSEGG ★★★★★
Patina ★★★★★
Philip Shaw Wines ★★★★★
Printhie Wines ★★★★★
Ross Hill Wines ★★★★★
Swinging Bridge ★★★★★

PERTH HILLS

Millbrook Winery ★★★★★

PICCADILLY VALLEY

Tapanappa ★★★★★
Terre à Terre ★★★★★

PORONGURUP

Castle Rock Estate ★★★★★
Duke's Vineyard ★★★★★

PORT PHILIP

Shadowfax Winery ★★★★★

PYRENEES

Blue Pyrenees Estate ★★★★★
Dalwhinnie ★★★★★
DogRock Winery ★★★★★
Glenlofty Estate ★★★★★
Mitchell Harris Wines ★★★★★
Pyren Vineyard ★★★★★
Taltarni ★★★★★

RIVERINA

Calabria Family Wines ★★★★★
De Bortoli (Riverina) ★★★★★
McWilliam's ★★★★★

RUTHERGLEN

All Saints Estate ★★★★★
Buller Wines ★★★★★
Campbells ★★★★★
Chambers Rosewood ★★★★★
Jones Winery & Vineyard ★★★★★
Morris ★★★★★
Pfeiffer Wines ★★★★★
Stanton & Killeen Wines ★★★★★

SHOALHAVEN COAST

Cupitt's Estate ★★★★★

SOUTH AUSTRALIA

Dandelion Vineyards ★★★★★
Heirloom Vineyards ★★★★★
Thistledown Wines ★★★★★

SOUTH WEST AUSTRALIA

Kerrigan + Berry ★★★★★

STRATHBOGIE RANGES

Maygars Hill Winery ★★★★★

SUNBURY

Craiglee ★★★★★

SWAN DISTRICT

Mandoon Estate ★★★★★

SWAN VALLEY

Corymbia ★★★★★
Houghton ★★★★★
Sandalford ★★★★★
Sittella Wines ★★★★★

TASMANIA

Apogee ★★★★★
Bellebonne ★★★★★
Chatto ★★★★★
Craigow ★★★★★
Dalrymple Vineyards ★★★★★
Delamere Vineyards ★★★★★
Domaine A ★★★★★
Dr Edge ★★★★★
Freycinet Vineyard ★★★★★
Holm Oak ★★★★★
Home Hill ★★★★★
House of Arras ★★★★★
Jansz Tasmania ★★★★★
Lowestoft ★★★★★
Meadowbank Wines ★★★★★
Merriworth ★★★★★
Mewstone Wines ★★★★★
Moorilla Estate ★★★★★
Ossa Wines ★★★★★
Pipers Brook Vineyard ★★★★★
Pirie Tasmania ★★★★★
Pooley Wines ★★★★★
Sailor Seeks Horse ★★★★★
Sinapius ★★★★★
Stargazer Wine ★★★★★
Stefano Lubiana ★★★★★
Tolpuddle Vineyard ★★★★★
Wellington & Wolfe ★★★★★

UPPER GOULBURN

Delatite ★★★★★
Mr Hugh Wines ★★★★★

VARIOUS

Handpicked Wines ★★★★★
M. Chapoutier Australia ★★★★★
Rouleur ★★★★★

VICTORIA

Diletto ★★★★★
Joshua Cooper Wines ★★★★★
Terrason Wines ★★★★★
The Happy Winemaker ★★★★★

WESTERN AUSTRALIA

Battles Wine ★★★★★
Byron & Harold ★★★★★

YARRA VALLEY

Bicknell fc ★★★★★
Burton McMahon ★★★★★
Centare ★★★★★
Chandon Australia ★★★★★
Coldstream Hills ★★★★★
Coombe Yarra Valley ★★★★★
Dappled Wines ★★★★★
De Bortoli ★★★★★
Denton ★★★★★
Dominique Portet ★★★★★
Emilian ★★★★★
Fetherston Vintners ★★★★★
Gembrook Hill ★★★★★
Giant Steps ★★★★★
Helen's Hill Estate ★★★★★
Hoddles Creek Estate ★★★★★
Mac Forbes ★★★★★
Mandala ★★★★★
Mayer ★★★★★
Medhurst ★★★★★
Mount Mary ★★★★★
Oakridge Wines ★★★★★
Payne's Rise ★★★★★
Punt Road ★★★★★
Rob Hall Wines ★★★★★
Rochford Wines ★★★★★
Salo Wines ★★★★★
Serrat ★★★★★
Seville Estate ★★★★★
SOUMAH ★★★★★
Squitchy Lane Vineyard ★★★★★
TarraWarra Estate ★★★★★
The Wanderer ★★★★★
Thousand Candles ★★★★★
Tokar Estate ★★★★★
Toolangi ★★★★★
Wantirna Estate ★★★★★
Warramunda Estate ★★★★★
Yering Station ★★★★★
Yeringberg ★★★★★

Australian vintage charts

Each number represents a rating out of 10 for the quality of vintages in each region. As always, these ratings are volunteered by key winemakers in their regions. As each variety and vineyard is unique, these numbers should thus be regarded as indicative rather than prescriptive.

Red wine   White wine   Fortified

	2018	2019	2020	2021	2022
NSW					
Hunter Valley	9	8	–	7	9
	8	9	–	8	8
Mudgee	9	7	–	8	7
	8	7	–	7	8
Orange	9	8	–	7	7
	8	9	–	8	8
Canberra District	9	9	–	8	8
	8	9	–	9	9
Hilltops	9	9	–	8	8
	8	8	–	8	9
Southern Highlands	8	7	–	7	6
	8	8	–	7	7
Tumbarumba	9	8	–	7	8
	9	8	–	8	8
Riverina/Griffith	8	8	7	8	7
	8	8	7	8	7
Shoalhaven	8	7	–	7	6
	8	8	–	7	7

	2018	2019	2020	2021	2022
SA					
Barossa Valley	9	9	8	9	9
	7	7	7	8	8
Eden Valley	9	9	7	9	8
	9	9	8	10	9
Clare Valley	7	8	6	8	8
	7	9	8	9	9
Adelaide Hills	8	9	8	8	9
	7	8	9	8	9
McLaren Vale	8	8	8	9	9
	7	7	9	8	9
Southern Fleurieu	10	8	9	9	8
	8	7	9	9	7
Langhorne Creek	9	9	8	10	10
	7	7	7	6	7
Kangaroo Island	9	8	–	9	7
	9	9	–	9	8
Adelaide Plains	–	–	9	9	–
	–	–	9	9	–

	2018	2019	2020	2021	2022
Coonawarra	9	10	8	9	9
	8	8	8	8	9
Wrattonbully	9	10	10	10	9
	9	10	10	10	9
Padthaway	–	10	10	9	9
	–	9	9	10	9
Mount Benson & Robe	9	8	8	9	9
	9	9	9	9	9
Riverland	8	8	7	9	7
	8	8	8	9	8
VIC					
Yarra Valley	7	9	8	10	9
	7	8	8	10	10
Mornington Peninsula	9	8	7	10	9
	8	9	8	9	9
Geelong	8	10	5	7	9
	7	8	7	8	8
Macedon Ranges	9	8	8	8	8
	7	7	10	9	9

	2018	2019	2020	2021	2022
Sunbury	–	7	7	8	–
	–	8	8	8	–
Gippsland	9	9	9	10	7
	9	9	10	10	9
Bendigo	8	9	9	10	10
	8	8	8	9	9
Heathcote	8	9	9	8	9
	7	6	7	7	7
Grampians	8	9	8	7	8
	8	9	7	7	6
Pyrenees	10	8	8	8	8
	8	8	7	8	8
Henty	10	9	6	9	10
	10	8	8	9	10
Beechworth	8	8	–	9	8
	8	9	–	9	9
Nagambie Lakes	9	9	8	8	8
	7	7	7	8	9
Upper Goulburn	9	8	8	9	9
	8	9	8	9	9
Strathbogie Ranges	9	8	8	–	6
	9	8	7	–	8
King Valley	9	9	–	7	8
	9	7	–	9	9
Alpine Valleys	9	7	–	9	8
	10	9	–	10	8

	2018	2019	2020	2021	2022
Glenrowan	8	9	–	8	7
	7	7	–	7	6
Rutherglen	9	8	–	8	8
	9	8	–	7	7
Murray Darling	7	8	8	–	8
	8	8	8	–	8

WA

	2018	2019	2020	2021	2022
Margaret River	9	8	9	8	9
	9	9	9	8	9
Great Southern	10	8	8	–	7
	9	8	8	–	8
Manjimup	8	7	8	7	8
	9	8	8	8	8
Pemberton	9	10	9	9	9
	9	9	8	9	8
Geographe	8	8	9	8	7
	8	8	8	7	7
Perth Hills	8	8	9	8	7
	9	7	7	8	7
Swan Valley	9	8	9	8	8
	8	10	8	10	8

QLD

	2018	2019	2020	2021	2022
Granite Belt	10	8	–	7	8
	9	8	–	8	9
South Burnett	9	9	7	8	7
	9	8	9	10	9

TAS

	2018	2019	2020	2021	2022
Northern Tasmania	8	9	7	9	9
	8	9	6	9	8
Southern Tasmania	8	9	8	8	8
	9	8	9	9	8
East Coast Tasmania	–	–	–	8	8
	–	–	–	9	8

Australian vintage 2023: a snapshot

Australia's vignerons are used to drought and heat, knowing that droughts are always ended by floods. They are emphatically not used to rain and cold winds prevailing through an entire spring and summer, and red wine baumes closer to 11.5 than 14.5 degrees (or higher). Given the wailing wall of vintage 2023, expectations are low, but here and there are hints of secret hope that finesse, freshness and purity may reward those who didn't despair. We are a resilient nation, and there are ways and means provided by clever pieces of equipment – optical sorters of individual berries, peristaltic pumps, and so forth – that make better wine. The most striking aspects of the summer that went AWOL were the failure of the forest of weather apps on your smartphone to get La Niña right, and how weirdly similar weather patterns thousands of kilometres apart took shape.

New South Wales

The **Hunter Valley** formed a unity ticket with South Australia. La Niña provided Pokolbin the wettest year on record: 1365mm of rain with 97 rain days, making downy mildew an unrelenting threat. Play it again, Sam, with access to vineyards and bogged tractors and spray carts finally restoring calm over the last two months of the year. Even then, the start of harvest was delayed until the first week of February, low yields the order of the day. The **Hunter** is as the Hunter does, even a hailstorm along the way only a hiccup, giving birth to excellent shiraz (great colour, lovely fruit flavours), followed by semillon. **Mudgee** waited until January and February for warm and dry weather, rain reappearing in the lead up to Easter. A hurried finish to harvest saw low yields of high-quality fruit. The **Canberra District** had the third coolest vintage in 50 years (two days of light frosts in mid-December) plus floods, hail and rain, but warm, dry weather started in January and continued to the late finish. Riesling excelled with incredible flavours, crisp acid and perfect balance. Shiraz split opinions, the patience of Job paid off for one reporter who finished harvest on 28 April, plus some excellent viognier. **Orange** writhed in the grip of La Niña with, and I quote one local winemaker,, 'the added annoyance of a series of nasty, localised hailstorms'. A vintage for sparkling and pink wines, but not for shiraz or cabernet sauvignon. Riesling and chardonnay will run the saviour mission, should there be one. The **Southern Highlands** region was facing disaster, three to four weeks behind, but warmer weather in February, drier in March, resulted in good pinot noir, chardonnay and pinot meunier for the sparkling wine pot. **Hilltops** had the same weather as the Highlands, but started with a warmer matrix and pleasing white (fiano, prosecco and pinot grigio) and red wines (cabernet sauvignon and nebbiolo). **Shoalhaven Coast** lost well over 50% of its harvest to La Niña, the one solace was ripe flavours across the board. **Riverina** enjoyed late winter and spring rains until constant rain took the gloss off, and a mild summer meant the latest start of vintage for over 20 years.

South Australia

La Niña screamed its pretty little head off throughout spring, epitomised in the **Barossa Valley** by a wet lead up in October, which seemed almost dry once November's rain measured 150mm+ compared to an average of 35mm. Vines assumed triffid-like proportions, with vast canopies and large crops. A dry December produced relief, but these conditions meant preventative sprays against downy mildew and the threat of botrytis. Nature provided a welcome measure of crop thinning for grenache: the adroit viticulturists ended up with good yields of aromatic – indeed, perfumed grenache – but cabernet sauvignon was the star, always doing best in cool vintages. Says one winemaker: 'We will be picking in May on the Valley floor. A long time since that's happened.' **Eden Valley** started dry and warm, but then the season changed, cool and moist, riesling in its element, shiraz the best of the reds. **Clare Valley**'s season was very late by recent standards – similar to the late '80s. Riesling had the best of both worlds in the cool conditions, and low to moderate yields; although, at the time of publication, it was not easy to characterise the reds. The **Adelaide Hills** was marked by notable rain right through the growing season, temperatures cool to cold, the coolest for 11 years. Flowering was impacted by rain, with pinot noir and chardonnay hard hit, invoking low yields. Sauvignon blanc yields were moderate, some shiraz blocks high. **McLaren Vale** fared better than most in the lottery draw. Mild early summer, warmer January to March, only one day over 40 degrees, though below average yields. Even this had a good side, with red varieties led by shiraz offering colour and varietal intensity, and excellent density – a rare commodity for the vintage, shiraz the star. **Southern Fleurieu** was hit hard by record winter and spring rain that continued through flowering and into what should have been summer, yields commensurately low. **Coonawarra** had a mixed broth, with disease control paying handsome dividends when rain events in March turned into a distinctly wet April. One reporter enjoyed brilliant purple colours, dark blackberry, blueberry and mulberry fruits, baumes 13 degrees to 14 degrees, similar to 2017, another had variable results, cabernet lighter and leafier. **Langhorne Creek** knew there would be challenges ahead when October tripled the average rainfall, and November quadrupled it. A week of sunny weather coincided with rapid flowering and fruit-set. But, notwithstanding the promise, yields of shiraz and cabernet were below average. When the rain returned at the end of March, sleep went out the window and one-third of the crop was harvested in three days. Another surprise was the quality of the grenache, cabernet and malbec, only a shade behind the great '21 and '22 vintages. **Wrattonbully** gave exceptional sauvignon blanc, cabernet sauvignon and cabernet franc for those who controlled yields and opened canopies. **Padthaway**'s weather ran counter to so many other regions it was testing reality, rain close to average for months on end, and there were no extended periods of hot weather. White varieties, with chardonnay in the lead, were all very good. **Kangaroo Island** joined the gang dealing with poor flowering and fruit-set followed by downy mildew, but selective picking helped (poor fruit left on the ground, ditto with late season botrytis). Low yields and clean fruit produced excellent cabernet franc, semillon, malbec and sauvignon blanc. **Mount Benson** and **Robe** followed suit with one excited winery reporting 'all varieties stood out'. The **Riverland** recorded its highest flood levels since 1956 and vintage was delayed by three to four weeks, which was made to measure for the white varieties, providing fresh acidity and bright flavours, although most of the reds were still on the vine in April.

Victoria

The **Yarra Valley** had the wettest August and October on record, and La Niña made sure September and November didn't let up until Christmas was approaching. High rainfall, warm nights and high humidity lead to very high downy mildew pressure and resultant significant crop losses. But more was to come. Wind and rain upset flowering and low bud fruitfulness (a legacy of a year ago) all contributing to low bunch weights at harvest. But the new year heralded a total change in the weather: blue skies, low humidity, 25°C daytime temperatures and no heat spikes gave birth to grapes with modest baumes, perfect acidity and high concentration of varietal flavour. One respondent suggests that pinot noir and chardonnay could rival the great '22 and '21 vintages. For later ripening varieties it will be a year of perfume and elegance. The **Mornington Peninsula** pointed to the third La Niña in a row reducing yields by 50%, yet harvest didn't start until three to four weeks later than the new normal. Pinot noir is the standout with lovely depth of flavour and of intensity. **Geelong** reported one item of good news: the vineyard dam was full for the first time since 2011! Pinot noir produced 40% of average yields, chardonnay 70%, and quality was described as good across the board rather than great. **Ballarat**, **Henty** and reprise of Geelong from one reporter with fruit sources elicited the comment: 'For the third season in a row significantly cool conditions have led to a waiting game whilst we rolled the botrytis dice,' with yields all over the place and also 'a miserable year for pine mushrooms in Ballarat!' Chardonnay is the standout variety, he continues, 'While the wines will be ethereal rather than concentrated in style, they will fully translate the growing season and country they were grown in.' Henty was a ritual slaughterhouse for all except riesling. **Gippsland** had the patented 2023 climate outcome of two halves and a Delphic comment 'excellent for the fruit picked' of chardonnay, pinot noir and shiraz. The **Grampians** had a subvariant of weather, most notably most varieties having greater yields than '22, and the best quality rosette going to riesling, pinot noir and pinot meunier. **Beechworth** was cool and wet all the way, low to moderate yields, chardonnay and pinot noir the standout varieties; others not picked as at mid-April. **Upper Goulburn**'s wet, cold spring smashed fruit-set, but mid-summer surprised with warm and even ripening conditions and high quality riesling, pinot gris and gewürztraminer. The **Alpine Valleys** and **King Valley** had many things in common: a very late start to vintage (La Niña); dreadful weather until December; good from February onwards; yields all down – the only question which suffered least; quality also variable, but highlights different. The Alpine Valleys standouts were sparkling pinot noir, chardonnay (all purposes), shiraz, albariño and cabernet sauvignon. The King Valley highlights red wines (cool nights, sunny days, perfect ripening) and extremely high quality prosecco (high natural acidity, moderate yields). The **Macedon Ranges** had marvellous weather after a chaotic spring. Yields were normal, and chardonnay has fine acidity, pinot noir with excellent colour and phenolic ripeness. Finesse and latent power are the watch words. **Nagambie Lakes**, however, had an even more horrific time of it. Tahbilk's property is 1215ha, and of the 195ha that is vineyard, 93ha was submerged by the flooding of the Goulburn River (including the 32ha of vines planted between 1860 and 1969). The farmer in Alister Purbrick says, 'overall, we are extremely happy with the result despite the volumes being quite low. We estimate that vineyard yields will be around 60-70% below normal expectations.' The **Strathbogie Ranges** is home to Fowles Wines, which sits on top of a hill in the region, and even it was flooded. One of its irrigation dams burst and the Fowles team had to repair the breach within five days before the next bout of forecast rain. Bogging of tractors became routine, keeping stress levels all too high. After December, still cold and wet, there were heavy localised rain events, but overall conditions were sufficiently dry to ripen the white varieties and pinot noir, the fuller-bodied reds not picked until the very end of April. 'A cracking sauvignon blanc, chardonnay, riesling and vermentino year, with great fruit intensity.' And, most surprisingly, yields in line with historical average. **Bendigo** followed the mainstream: miserable weather, yields low to very low, growers losing 30–100% of their crop, the bright spot – shiraz. Overall quality was described by one reporter as, 'what hit the winery deck was great. There was just very little of it.' **Heathcote** conformed with attention to detail in the weather taking on a new meaning, but one distinguished winemaker said the wines 'look very promising at this early stage, quite elegant and finely balanced with lovely detail and presence, reminiscent of '17 and '14; shiraz the standout.' In the **Pyrenees** a supposed end to La Niña set the expectations of a return to warm and dry weather, but instead it was cold and wet, which delayed ripening by many weeks. The reds were close to average yield, but the whites were well below, the standout varieties being arinto, chardonnay and pinot noir. **Glenrowan**'s vintage intake was delayed by three weeks; the cool, wet season creating higher disease pressure, impacting on a lower than average yield. A respected winemaker says, 'shiraz, which is the region's signature variety, clearly demonstrates how insightful our forebears were'. The well-publicised flooding through the Murray River system meant access was lost to vineyards in **Rutherglen**, some parts totally underwater for weeks. Harvest started on 1 March, but took some time to gain momentum and still going on into May. Yields were impacted accordingly, down 30–90%. Quality is, of course, variable, however there are gems such as chardonnay, shiraz and muscat, picked just before the Easter rain.

Western Australia

Margaret River had a cool spring that delayed flowering by one to three weeks across different varieties, creating a slow and steady growing season. Very dry summer conditions (no rainfall across the December to February period), but temperatures in line with long term averages, cool night times and no heatwaves, ensuring good acid retention and fruit vibrancy. The moderate, dry conditions through March and April also set the reds up well with excellent tannin, colour and flavour development. The only major issue was bird pressure and some isolated damage due to the lack of marri blossom. The standout varieties are chardonnay, sauvignon blanc and cabernet sauvignon, with excellent quality overall. The **Great Southern** had high winter/spring rainfall giving the vines a good, albeit two weeks late, head start. Mild conditions lead to a slow, even ripening; late March rain held up the reds, but a hot spell towards the end of April saw them finish off nicely. Riesling, chardonnay, pinot noir and cabernet were the standouts of a very late and prolonged, but overall successful, vintage. **Pemberton** had plenty of winter rainfall which filled up the dams; spring bringing drier weather, temperatures warm but not too hot. Cool nights before harvest started in March, the yields moderate. Sauvignon blanc and chardonnay were the standouts, with very good overall quality. **Geographe** had warm and dry conditions leading up to harvest, with moderate to higher yields across all varieties. Shiraz, malbec and chardonnay stood out in a pleasant vintage where yields and quality were both good. Very good late winter rains and warm day time temperatures at the start of spring meant early season growth in the **Swan Valley**, the mild spring temperatures continuing to late November. No rain from mid-November until the end of March meant disease pressure was non-existent. A relatively mild summer (only two days with temperatures over 40°C), and heat spikes were shorter and lower than normal. Fruit ripened slowly and evenly, the harvest dates matching the past 25-year average, the table wine grapes picked at slightly lower baumes than usual with intensely flavoured fruit. Chenin blanc, verdelho, grenache and tempranillo are the standouts of and excellent vintage.

Tasmania

A cool wet spring but without the intense rainfall of the mainland. La Niña impacted significantly, with cool and wet conditions in summer delayed flowering and poor fruit-set, the ultimate yields low to very low. Poor yields to one side, the overall quality was very good to high, the standouts riesling, chardonnay and pinot noir (the latter two for both table wines and sparkling).

Queensland

After a wet start to spring in the **Granite Belt**, November and December then turned exceptionally dry, leading to a delayed start to vintage. Colour and flavour in the reds was exceptional; the standouts including shiraz, cabernet sauvignon, tempranillo, sangiovese and saperavi. Expectations are high for exceptional wines with depth of colour and flavour. **South Burnett** had a reasonable amount of rain leading up to harvest and early budburst. A cooler than average spring and a later start to summer slowed down the ripening season considerably, around two to three weeks later than average. According to one winemaker, the tempranillo 'looks stunning this year, as do many of the reds, even the Bordeaux varieties benefited from the slower growing season'. Verdelho and viognier are the pick of the whites from a vintage with excellent quality overall.

Australian wineries
and wines

A. Rodda Wines

PO Box 589, Beechworth, Vic 3747 **Region** Beechworth
T 0400 350 135 **www**.aroddawines.com.au **Open** Not **Winemaker** Adrian Rodda
Est. 2010 **Dozens** 800 **Vyds** 2ha

Adrian Rodda has been winemaking since '98. Originally working with David Bicknell at
Oakridge, he was involved in the development of the superb Oakridge 864 Chardonnay, his
final contribution was in '09. At the start of '10 he and wife Christie, a doctor, moved to
Beechworth and co-leased Smiths vineyard, planted to chardonnay in '79, with Mark Walpole
of Fighting Gully Road. He makes 2 additional single-vineyard chardonnays: Willowlake,
with fruit sourced from the Yarra Valley vineyard of the same name, and Baxendale from a
site in Whitlands at 560-620m elevation.

🍷🍷🍷🍷🍷 **Smiths Vineyard Chardonnay 2021, Beechworth** Cool-climate acidity is
like an electrical current pulsing through this wine. Stone fruit, grapefruit, quince,
almond skin and nougat. Impressive line and integrity with a literal lick of stony
minerality. And oak? It's there, but happy in its role as a quiet support player.
Screw cap. 13% alc. **RATING** 96 **DRINK** 2023-2034 $55 JP ✪
Triangle Block Smith's Vineyard Chardonnay 2021, Beechworth
Consistently a stand-out wine revealing deep concentration and precision.
A study in cool-climate beauty, of spring blossoms, citrus and white peach,
lightly spiced and dressed in a nutty, leesy complexity. Runs deep and long,
and oh-so beautifully in balance. A delight. Screw cap. 13% alc. **RATING** 96
DRINK 2023-2032 $90 JP
Baxendale Vineyard Whitlands Chardonnay 2021, King Valley At 600m
elevation, fruit from the Baxendale vineyard always shows impressive acidity and
energy. In a great vintage such as '21, it brings a tight linear presence, balanced
and beautifully integrated, providing an ideal launching pad for bright citrus, stone
fruits and aromatic florals. A busy, racy youngster with a big future ahead. Screw
cap. 13% alc. **RATING** 95 **DRINK** 2023-2031 $48 JP ✪
Aquila Audax Vineyard Tempranillo 2021, Beechworth Yes, that's a high
price for tempranillo. Yes, it's worth it. Quality fruit gets the VIP treatment,
producing a serious, seamless tempranillo that highlights the grape's cherry and
cassis fruits beautifully. Acacia, bracken, wild herbs and autumnal notes weave
between spiced dark berries. Fine tannins carry the wine long, accompanied by
some cherry stone crunch and verve. Deceptively elegant, but there's a power
surging underneath. Screw cap. 14% alc. **RATING** 95 **DRINK** 2023-2030 $40 JP ✪

🍷🍷🍷🍷🍷 **Cuvée de Chais Cabernets 2021, Beechworth RATING** 93
DRINK 2023-2028 $40 JP
Willow Lake Vineyard Chardonnay 2021, Yarra Valley RATING 93
DRINK 2023-2031 $55 JP

Acres Wilde

1185 Glenrowan-Boweya Road, Taminick, Vic 3675 (postal) **Region** North East Victoria
T 0427 701 017 **www**.acreswilde.com.au **Open** Not **Winemaker** Chris Beach
Est. 2011 **Dozens** 260

Chris Beach made his way into the wine industry after various farming pursuits, including
dairy, orchards and tractor driving. Along the way there was overseas travel and stints at snow
resorts and in the building industry. However, the past 15 years or so have been spent in the
vineyards and wineries of North East Victoria. He is currently working as a cellar hand at
a Glenrowan winery, making his own wine under his own label in his down time. At first,
Chris' 'winery' was a brick garage, but he has since moved up in the world and is utilising a
large tin shed. He prefers to follow a minimal approach as much as possible.

🍷🍷🍷🍷🍷 **VP Durif Shiraz 2018, King Valley** Durif with shiraz in support, in a fortified
style. Retains the freshness of youth – it is a youngster still at 5yo – with layers
of sweet black fruits, blueberry, licorice, spice and chocolate. Nice intensity on

display with brandy spirit warmth. 500ml. Screw cap. 17.3% alc. **RATING** 92 **DRINK** 2023–2028 $18 JP ✪

Adelina Wines   ★★★★★

PO Box 75, Sevenhill, SA 5453 **Region** Clare Valley
T (08) 8842 1549 **www**.adelina.com.au **Open** Not **Winemaker** Colin McBryde,
Michael Maloney **Est.** 2002 **Dozens** 4000 **Vyds** 6ha
Established by Jennie Gardner and Col McBryde. The winery and vineyard are set in the Springfarm Valley, just south of the Clare township. The old vineyard, part dating back to 1910, is divided into 1ha each of shiraz and grenache. There's also a further 1ha of bush-vine mataro, 0.5ha of malbec and 2.2ha of shiraz, with a field blend (grafted in '15 onto 0.22ha of '76-planted cabernet) covering off shiraz, grenache, mataro, carignan, ugni blanc and roussanne. The winery is a simple shed with the basic requisites to process the grapes and make wine. Most is estate-grown, but some fruit, including riesling, comes from a few sites in the Clare Valley and Adelaide Hills.

ŶŶŶŶŶ **Polish Hill River Riesling 2022, Clare Valley** A ballistically good expression of the Clare Valley staple. Compact, taut, lengthy and oh-so precise. A flourish of lemon/lime citrus, green apple, fennel seeds and wet slate. Mouth-watering acidity a sluice around fine, powdery texture and that superb, persistent finish. Stellar drinking now, all refreshing, vibrant, crystalline, and yet you can see a very long cellar life, too. Screw cap. 10.9% alc. **RATING** 96 **DRINK** 2022–2040 $28 MB ✪ ♥
Ruchioch Riesling 2022, Clare Valley A slate and pumice-like mineral character stutters through the wine, chalkiness and chew in texture alongside. Scents are set to lime, anise, white pepper and faint blackcurrant, the palate a wash of lime, that minerally/stony quality and touches of fennel. The finish is juicy and lavish yet refreshing. Layers to this riesling, and all up very good. Screw cap. 11.2% alc. **RATING** 95 **DRINK** 2022–2035 $33 MB ✪

ŶŶŶŶŶ **Arneis 2022, Adelaide Hills RATING** 93 **DRINK** 2022–2025 $28 MB ✪
Watervale Riesling 2022, Clare Valley RATING 92 **DRINK** 2022–2035 $28 MB ✪

After Hours Wine   ★★★☆

455 North Jindong Road, Carbunup, WA 6285 **Region** Margaret River
T 0414 420 670 **www**.afterhourswine.com.au **Open** 7 days 10–4, or by appt
Winemaker Phil Potter **Est.** 2006 **Dozens** 2500 **Vyds** 8.6ha
Warwick and Cherylyn Mathews acquired the long-established Hopelands Vineyard in '05, planted to cabernet sauvignon (2.6ha), shiraz (1.6ha), merlot, semillon, sauvignon blanc and chardonnay (1.1ha each). The first wine was made in '06, after which they decided to completely rework the vineyard. The vines were retrained, with a consequent reduction in yield.

ŶŶŶŶŶ **Chardonnay 2021, Margaret River** Packed with flavour from toasty oak, stone fruit, citrus and layers of spices, plus there's a richness from some creamy lees influence. Yet the upfront acidity keeps everything on a tight leash and thus, the palate is tightly coiled. Time will allow it to unfurl. Screw cap. 13.5% alc. **RATING** 90 **DRINK** 2023–2029 $37 JF

Alkina Wine Estate   ★★★★★

41 Victor Road, Greenock, SA 5360 **Region** Barossa Valley
T (08) 8562 8246 **www**.alkinawine.com **Open** 7 days 11–5 **Winemaker** Amelia Nolan,
Alberto Antonini **Viticulturist** Johnny Schuster **Est.** 2015 **Dozens** 3000 **Vyds** 43ha
Alkina was born in '15 when Argentinian vintner Alejandro Bulgheroni purchased his Greenock property with its 1950s-planted vineyard. The front 40ha of the farm has been certified organic and biodynamic since '18. The organically farmed back block, formerly

the Owens vineyard, was added in '17 and was certified in '22. In '17, the addition of terroir expert Pedro Parra to the team led to the Polygon mapping project; a deep dive into what makes the unique terroir of the property tick. Think traditional western Barossa grape varieties with wild yeasts, some with a little skin contact, whole-bunch ferments, concrete eggs and fermenters, Italian clay amphorae, Georgian qvevri and older large-format oak and you're on the right track.

🍷🍷🍷🍷🍷 **Polygon No. 5 Grenache 2019, Barossa Valley** This is a beauty. A little more wild-eyed than its Polygon No. 3 sibling, with savoury dark cherries and red plums intertwined with ironstone, souk-like spices, pressed flowers, gingerbread, cola, white blossom, pomegranate and dried raspberries. Supple, svelte and sinewy with a nervous, vital disposition and a fine, graceful exit bathed in red-fruits, compact fine tannin and spice. Superb! Cork. 14% alc. **RATING** 98 **DRINK** 2023–2036 $295 DB ♥

Polygon No. 3 Grenache 2019, Barossa Valley I've been blown away by the grenache from Alkina – we're edging towards the Australian version of Rayas here. Airy, detailed and ethereal with clarity of both aromatics and fruit. Plums, ironstone, rose petals, fine spices, gingerbread, rhubarb, sage and earth; tannins powdery and acidity fine and precise. Just beautiful drinking and it will only improve. Cork. 13.6% alc. **RATING** 97 **DRINK** 2023–2038 $295 DB

🍷🍷🍷🍷🍷 **Old Quarter Single Vineyard Grenache Shiraz Mataro 2021, Barossa Valley** A serious blend that's deep in colour and bursting with ripe blood plum, boysenberry and black cherry fruits with hints of exotic spices, violets, raspberry coulis, light amaro herbs, earth, iodine and sea spray. There is a beautiful sense of composure and self-assuredness, everything in its place. It's a ripper. Screw cap. 14% alc. **RATING** 96 **DRINK** 2023–2035 $100 DB

Spice Garden Single Vineyard Shiraz 2021, Barossa Valley A beautiful vivid crimson with characters of ripe plums, blackberry and boysenberry with hints of spice, roasting meats, almond blossom, earth, iodine and licorice. Snappy limestone acid drive and chewy, ripe tannins to a savoury, pure and long finish. Great stuff. Cork. 13.9% alc. **RATING** 95 **DRINK** 2023–2038 $100 DB

🍷🍷🍷🍷🍷 **Kin Rosé 2022, Barossa Valley** **RATING** 93 **DRINK** 2023–2026 $35 DB ✪
Kin Semillon 2022, Barossa Valley **RATING** 93 **DRINK** 2023–2026 $35 DB ✪
Kin Grenache 2022, Barossa Valley **RATING** 93 **DRINK** 2023–2027 $36 DB
Kin Shiraz 2022, Barossa Valley **RATING** 93 **DRINK** 2023–2029 $36 DB
Night Sky Grenache Shiraz Mataro 2021, Barossa Valley **RATING** 92 **DRINK** 2023–2028 $47 DB

Alkoomi   ★★★★★

1411 Wingebellup Road, Frankland River, WA 6396 **Region** Frankland River **T** (08) 9855 2229 www.alkoomiwines.com.au **Open** Mon–Sat 10–4.30 Frankland River, Mon–Sat 11–5 Albany **Winemaker** Marelize Russouw **Viticulturist** Tim Penniment **Est.** 1971 **Dozens** 60 000 **Vyds** 105ha

Established in '71 by Merv and Judy Lange, Alkoomi has grown from 1ha to one of WA's largest family-owned and -operated wineries. Now owned by daughter Sandy Hallett and her husband Rod, Alkoomi continues the tradition of producing high-quality wines that showcase the Frankland River region. Alkoomi is actively reducing its environmental footprint; future plans will see the introduction of new varietals. A second cellar door is located in Albany.

🍷🍷🍷🍷🍷 **Jarrah Shiraz 2017, Frankland River** A wine in its comfort zone. Plush, mellow and medium weight with lively perfume, some toasty, sweet spice savouriness lending character. A shiraz that's in a great place, still bright enough with forest berry fruitiness, but showing the savouriness of ageing, too. The balance is spot-on. It tastes great, drinks a charm, and delivers a sense of elegance. Screw cap. 14.5% alc. **RATING** 94 **DRINK** 2023–2035 $45 MB

Blackbutt Cabernet Blend 2016, Frankland River A soft and supple expression, deeply flavoured but with levity and some residual freshness on its side, notwithstanding a beautiful swish of enlivening tannin, sinewy and graphite-laced and cool. It's an elegant wine despite the gentle decay in dried fruits and nuts among raspberry and cassis fruit. It feels raring to go, wine in its prime, beautiful and deep. Screw cap. 14.5% alc. RATING 94 DRINK 2023–2030 $62 MB

♥♥♥♥♀ **Blackbutt Cabernet Blend 2017, Frankland River** RATING 93
DRINK 2026–2035 $62 MB
Wandoo 2017, Frankland River RATING 93 DRINK 2023–2035 $40 MB
Alkoomi Collection Chardonnay 2022, Frankland River RATING 91
DRINK 2023–2028 $28 MB ✪
Jarrah Shiraz 2016, Frankland River RATING 91 DRINK 2023–2026 $45 MB

All Saints Estate

205 All Saints Road, Wahgunyah, Vic 3687 **Region** Rutherglen
T 1800 021 621 www.allsaintswine.com.au **Open** 7 days 10–5 & public hols 11–5
Winemaker Nick Brown **Viticulturist** Will Stephen **Est.** 1864 **Dozens** 22 000
Vyds 47.9ha
All Saints' National Trust–listed property, with its towering castle centrepiece, is a must-stop for any visitor to the region. All Saints and St Leonards are owned and managed by 4th-generation Brown family members Eliza, Angela and Nick. Eliza is an energetic and highly intelligent leader, wise beyond her years, and highly regarded by the wine industry. The winery rating reflects the fortified wines, including the unique releases of Museum Muscat and Muscadelle, each with an average age of more than 100 years.

♥♥♥♥♥ **Museum Muscadelle NV, Rutherglen** With an average age of 100+ years, your senses are alight. Dark walnut in colour with an olive green edge. Muscadelle-deep intensity in swirling aromas of dried fruits, panforte, malt, orange peel, prune, caramel and grilled almonds. So deeply complex to taste, and yet so fresh through the just-so addition of neutral clean spirit. A true taste of history. 375ml. Screw cap. 18% alc. RATING 100 $1200 JP
Museum Muscat NV, Rutherglen Fortified Wine of the Year. That perfume, so ethereal, aromatic and lasting. The concentrated intensity of mature parcels of wine and the brightness of youth in treacle, soused raisins, dried fig, butterscotch toffee, honey-drizzled sticky pudding and nutty nougat. The blender's hand is foremost in the use of neutral fortifying spirit to bring everything to a wonderful culmination. Sit back and drink it all in, figuratively and literally. 500ml. Screw cap. 18% alc. RATING 100 $1200 JP ♥
Rare Muscat NV, Rutherglen Not many Australian fortified producers can deliver a wine with an average age of 45 years. The taste of Rare Muscat is a taste of history. Rich, luxurious in texture and complex in flavour; layered in malt extract, toffee, fruitcake, dusty walnut, honey-drenched dried fruits and still so fresh. Maintains a rare elegance. Finishes long and fine. A special treat. 375ml. Vinolok. 18% alc. RATING 98 $130 JP ✪
Grand Muscat NV, Rutherglen The step up from Classic to Grand is a big one. Immediately, the colour turns dark walnut, the perfume astonishes with its beauty, and flavour intensity becomes a marathon in length. And, all the while, you register so much with each sip. There's treacle, nutty rancio and leather, raisin, vanilla caramel, dried fig and more. Behold the art of the blender. 375ml. Vinolok. 18% alc. RATING 97 $80 JP ✪
Grand Tawny NV, Rutherglen Too often, Rutherglen tawny misses out on the fortified spotlight. Hopefully, this magical release can grab some of that recognition. Mahogany/tawny tones reveal the kind of flavour intensity that makes aged tawny so special: brandied fig, caramel, toffee, vanilla, soused dried fruits. All up, generously raisiny against a background of aged rancio nuttiness. Resonates clean and long. 375ml. Vinolok. 18% alc. RATING 97 $80 JP ✪

🍷🍷🍷🍷🍷 **Rare Muscadelle NV, Rutherglen** Muscadelle or Topaque, the extraordinary tasting experience that the Rare Classification brings to the glass remains. Singularly complex and deeply impressive. Honey-drizzled fruitcake, malt, gingerbread, nutty toffee, salted caramel and so much more as the sticky lusciousness of it all coats the tongue and the memory bank. Gets the freshness of spirit just right. 375ml. Vinolok. 18% alc. **RATING** 96 $130 JP

Durif 2021, Rutherglen From the inky, impenetrable purple hues to the sweet-hearted mid-palate all aromatic and lively (you don't normally see that for durif), the grape shines. The maker brings out the herbal/florals of the grape in violet, pepper and dried rosemary with dark fruits, forest floor, dusty cocoa and woodsy spice. Tannins behave while bringing a firm structure and potential for serious ageing. Scared of durif? Think again. Screw cap. 14.5% alc. **RATING** 95 **DRINK** 2023-2032 $35 JP ✪

Classic Muscat NV, Rutherglen The house Muscat style pursues a floral-led elegance highlighted and enhanced by a scintillating fresh spirit. There's an energy here, a brightness, whether it's the bouquet of rose petals, nougat, panforte, orange peel and malt extract, or the manner in which the spirit cleanly slices through the sweet richness of the palate. Great taste, great price. 375ml. Vinolok. 18% alc. **RATING** 95 $45 JP ✪

Grand Muscadelle NV, Rutherglen All Saints Estate has the stocks on hand to produce a Grand Muscadelle with an average age of 25 years. Here, it offers the essential muscadelle personality, albeit amplified by age. Butterscotch, cold tea, dried fruits, raisin, buttery toffee and malt bring forth an extraordinary resonance and lasting length of flavour. And yet so fresh and lively. That's where the blender can take a bow. 375ml. Vinolok. 18% alc. **RATING** 95 $80 JP

🍷🍷🍷🍷 **Classic Muscadelle NV, Rutherglen** **RATING** 93 $45 JP
Rosa 2022, Alpine Valleys Rutherglen **RATING** 91 **DRINK** 2023-2026 $35 JP
Shiraz 2021, Rutherglen **RATING** 91 **DRINK** 2023-2030 $35 JP
Muscadelle NV, Rutherglen **RATING** 91 $30 JP
Sangiovese Cabernet 2022, Rutherglen **RATING** 90 **DRINK** 2023-2026 $30 JP
Grenache Shiraz Mourvèdre 2021, Rutherglen **RATING** 90 **DRINK** 2023-2028 $45 JP
Cabernet Sauvignon 2021, Rutherglen **RATING** 90 **DRINK** 2023-2029 $30 JP
Muscat NV, Rutherglen **RATING** 90 $30 JP

Allegiance Wines ★★★★

3446 Jingellic Road, Tumbarumba, NSW 2653 **Region** Various
T 0434 561 718 **www**.allegiancewines.com.au **Open** By appt **Winemaker** Renae Hirsch **Viticulturist** Mick Doughty **Est.** 2009 **Dozens** 30 000 **Vyds** 8ha

When Tim Cox established Allegiance Wines in '09 he had the decided advantage of having worked in the Australian wine industry across many facets for almost 30 years. He worked on both the sales and marketing side, and also on the supplier side with Southcorp. Having started out as a virtual wine business, Allegiance now has its own vineyards with 8ha under vine in Tumbarumba, planted to 5.5ha pinot gris and 2.5ha chardonnay. It also purchases fruit from the Barossa, Coonawarra, Margaret River and Tumbarumba.

🍷🍷🍷🍷🍷 **Unity Cabernet Sauvignon 2021, Coonawarra** Bands of dark fruit meet sizeable ribs of tannin. This is a substantial wine, and a well-controlled one. Blackcurrant, red licorice and boysenberry flavours come infused with coffee, vanilla, bay leaf and twiggy herbs. There's an ashen, slightly bitter note to the aftertaste, which should mellow in time, but if you're patient there's a lot of fruit power here. Screw cap. 14.5% alc. **RATING** 94 **DRINK** 2028-2043 $100 CM

The Artisan Reserve Cabernet Sauvignon 2021, Coonawarra Blackcurrant, mint, roasted coffee and redcurrant flavours flow gradually into dark chocolate territory. It's juicy, it's powerful, it's plush and it's convincing. Screw cap. 14.5% alc. **RATING** 94 **DRINK** 2027-2037 $60 CM

🍷🍷🍷🍷🍷 Unity Chardonnay 2021, Tumbarumba RATING 93 DRINK 2022–2029 $60 JF
The Artisan Reserve Shiraz 2021, Barossa Valley RATING 91
DRINK 2023–2030 $60 DB
The Artisan Grenache 2021, South Australia RATING 90 DRINK 2023–2027
$40 CM

Altus Rise

10 North Street, Mount Lawley, WA 6050 (postal) **Region** Margaret River
T 0400 532 805 **www.altusrise.com.au Open** Not **Winemaker** Laura Bowler
Viticulturist Chris Credaro **Est.** 2019
Altus Rise was founded by friends Chris Credaro, Kim O'Hara and Jan Skrapac. All have
abundant experience in the wine industry. Chris is a highly experienced viticulturist and
member of the Credaro family and its extensive vineyard holdings. Kim O'Hara has 20 years
of wine sales and marketing experience, while Jan Skrapac has a wealth of financial and
management expertise.

🍷🍷🍷🍷🍷 Ascension Shiraz 2021, Margaret River Packed to the rafters with sweet, rich
fruit yet tempered by lots of savoury inputs. The warming spices, the cedary oak,
bresaola and pepper all add to its pleasure. Fuller bodied yet not too weighty with
starchy tannins and decent length plus everything spread with refreshing acidity.
Screw cap. 13% alc. RATING 93 DRINK 2022–2031 $45 JF
Ascension Cabernet Sauvignon 2021, Margaret River This comes across as
cool and cooling – as in the flavours of cassis and mulberries taste slightly chilled,
intriguing and appealing. There's also mint and eucalyptus plus nori. The tannins
are a little raspy and the acidity is really leading the show but this comes into its
own with food. Screw cap. 14% alc. RATING 90 DRINK 2023–2031 $45 JF

Amelia Park Wines

3857 Caves Road, Wilyabrup, WA 6280 **Region** Margaret River
T (08) 9755 6747 **www.ameliaparkwines.com.au Open** 7 days 10–5 **Winemaker** Jeremy
Gordon **Est.** 2009 **Dozens** 25 000 **Vyds** 9.6ha
Jeremy Gordon's winemaking career started with Evans & Tate, and Houghton thereafter,
before moving to the eastern states to broaden his experience. He eventually returned to
Margaret River, and after several years founded Amelia Park Wines with his wife Daniela
Gordon and business partner Peter Walsh. They later purchased the Moss Brothers site in
Wilyabrup, allowing the construction of a winery and cellar door.

🍷🍷🍷🍷🍷 Reserve Shiraz 2020, Frankland River Black pepper and spice beat a drum
under the luscious black cherry and plum fruit that surges out of the glass. The
contribution of French oak is positive, joining hands with the velvety tannins. Power
with elegance. Screw cap. 14.5% alc. RATING 98 DRINK 2023–2050 $70 JH ✪

🍷🍷🍷🍷🍷 Semillon Sauvignon Blanc 2022, Margaret River A small portion wild-yeast
fermented in steel barrels has added a dimension of complexity to a wine that has
a blend of herbal and tropical fruits that fit hand in glove. Margaret River does it
again. Screw cap. 12.5% alc. RATING 95 DRINK 2023–2026 $25 JH ✪
Trellis Chardonnay 2021, Margaret River What's the catch, other than a
plenitude of Margaret River chardonnay? It's varietal, it's balanced and it's long.
Fantastic value. Screw cap. 12.5% alc. RATING 94 DRINK 2023–2026 $18 JH ✪

🍷🍷🍷🍷🍷 Cabernet Merlot 2021, Margaret River RATING 92 DRINK 2024–2034 $35 JF
Trellis Rosé 2022, Frankland River RATING 91 DRINK 2022–2024 $18 JF ✪
Shiraz 2021, Frankland River RATING 91 DRINK 2023–2030 $35 JH
Trellis Cabernet Merlot 2021, Margaret River RATING 90 DRINK 2022–2026
$18 JF ✪

Anderson

1619 Chiltern Road, Rutherglen, Vic 3685 **Region** Rutherglen
T (02) 6032 8111 **www**.andersonwinery.com.au **Open** Mon–Sat 10–4
Winemaker Howard and Christobelle Anderson **Est.** 1992 **Dozens** 2000 **Vyds** 8.8ha
Having notched up a winemaking career spanning over 55 years, including a stint at Seppelt
Great Western, Howard Anderson and family started their winery with a focus on sparkling
wine before extending across all table wine styles. Daughter Christobelle graduated from the
University of Adelaide in '03 and has worked in Alsace, Champagne and Burgundy either
side of joining her father full-time in '05. The original estate plantings of shiraz, durif and
petit verdot (6ha) have evolved, now standing at 2.5ha durif, 2ha shiraz, 1ha petit verdot,
1ha saperavi, 1ha muscat, 0.5ha each of tempranillo and chenin blanc and 0.3ha of viognier.

🍷🍷🍷🍷🍷 **Cellar Block Durif 2017, Rutherglen** Intended for extended ageing, but with
enough aromatic fruit intensity and overall tannic power to make you consider
firing up the barbie. Lasting bramble, cassis, violet, briar, turned earth and anise
aromas. Meets the palate with major concentration and force, generous inky
tannins, spice, a wealth of black-berried flavour and lots more. Complexity lives
here. Screw cap. 14.5% alc. **RATING** 95 **DRINK** 2022-2037 $50 JP ❂

Verrier Basket Press Durif Shiraz 2017, Rutherglen Durif brings structure
and firm tannin to this blend, while shiraz contributes sweetness of fruit and
open-hearted generosity. The result is immediate drinkability. While alcohol is on
the high side, it's not obvious, such is the wine's overall aromatic and fruit power.
Plum, blackberry, lively spice, violet and subtle vanillin oak integration mesh
cleanly and evenly with even-handed tannins. Screw cap. 14.8% alc. **RATING** 94
DRINK 2022-2030 $35 JP ❂

🍷🍷🍷🍷🍷 **Storyteller Durif 2017, Rutherglen RATING** 93 **DRINK** 2022-2033 $35 JP
Cellar Block Petit Verdot 2017, Rutherglen RATING 92 **DRINK** 2022-2032
$50 JP
Cellar Block Saperavi 2017, Rutherglen RATING 90 **DRINK** 2022-2034 $50 JP

Anderson & Marsh

6815 Great Alpine Road, Porepunkah, Vic 3740 (postal) **Region** Alpine Valleys
T 0419 984 982 **Winemaker** Eleana Anderson, Jo Marsh **Est.** 2014 **Dozens** 60
A joint project between Alpine Valleys winemakers Eleana Anderson (of Mayford Wines) and
Jo Marsh (of Billy Button). Close friends and neighbours, they set out to produce the style
of sparkling wines they love to drink – crisp and tight – from the town where they both live,
Porepunkah. A local parcel of albariño became available in '18, which they were both very
interested in, so they decided to make it together under their new label. Tempranillo was an
obvious choice to partner with the albariño (parell is Spanish for pair). Wines are available to
taste at the Billy Button cellar doors (see separate listing). Anderson & Marsh is the *Halliday
Wine Companion 2024* Dark Horse of the Year.

🍷🍷🍷🍷🍷 **Parell Tempranillo 2021, Alpine Valleys** Spain meets Alpine Valleys and it's
fireworks all around. The result is an impressive wine of power and elegance. Intense
scents of wet earth, dark berries, alpine herbs and licorice spice with gentle savoury
overtones. The palate lifts, the aromatics rise and elegance and poise rule with
tannins fine and nimble. A top year brings tempranillo into its own in this part of
the world. Bravo! Screw cap. 14.3% alc. **RATING** 96 **DRINK** 2022-2027 $45 JP ❂

Parell Albariño 2022, Alpine Valleys The major white grape of Spain brings
both energy and warmth to the glass with a touch of savouriness. Layers of
grapefruit, lemon peel, apple, preserved lemon and beeswax build and build in
the mouth. The mix of tart bite and mealy softness talks to the grape's noted
natural acidity. Tasted 6 months before release, but easily on track for a big future.
Screw cap. 13% alc. **RATING** 95 **DRINK** 2023-2027 $35 JP ❂

Catani Blanc de Blancs 2017, Alpine Valleys With extended time on lees,
this presents a complex and powerful sparkling take on Alpine Valleys chardonnay

with baked apple, grilled pineapple, honeyed fig aromas and flavours and an overriding warm nuttiness. Smooth across the mid-palate with a lovely spiciness to close. Worth the wait. Crown, 11% alc. **RATING** 94 **DRINK** 2023-2029 $65 JP

Anderson Hill ★★★★

407 Croft Road, Lenswood, SA 5240 **Region** Lenswood
T 0407 070 295 **www**.andersonhill.com.au **Open** 7 days 11–5 **Winemaker** Ben Anderson **Viticulturist** Ben Anderson **Est.** 1994 **Dozens** 4000 **Vyds** 9ha
Ben and Clare Anderson planted their vineyard at 600m elevation in Lenswood, in the Adelaide Hills, in '94. A small part of the grape production is sold (Hardys and Penfolds have been top-end purchasers of the chardonnay), but most is retained for their own wines. The cellar door has panoramic views.

ㅇㅇㅇㅇㅇ **O Series Shiraz 2021, Adelaide Hills** A fine nose of varietal fidelity with camphor, iodine, blueberry and white pepper. Clove and smoked meat, too. Long and plush, if not a bit hot. The tannins corral, refine and pummel the palate with an impression of savouriness. Good gear. A winner. Screw cap. 14.7% alc. **RATING** 93 **DRINK** 2022-2029 $50 NG
O Series Chardonnay 2021, Lenswood This is a lean style, eschewing the softening effects of mlf while riding a rail of tension imparted by lees work and well-nestled oak. Riffs on green apple, honeydew melon and white fig carouse about a core of creamed cashew and nougatine. A bit shrill, but will settle with a few years of patience. Screw cap. 13.5% alc. **RATING** 92 **DRINK** 2022-2027 $45 NG
Single Vineyard Reserve Shiraz 2021, Adelaide Hills Mottled dark fruits, clove and blackstrap licorice are bolstered by toasty oak and a sluice of iodine for lift. This is a sweet, full-weighted and traditional expression. Not much finesse, but plenty of punch. Screw cap. 14.7% alc. **RATING** 91 **DRINK** 2022-2032 $95 NG
Margo Chardonnay 2021, Lenswood Taut, linear and tensile, this mid-weighted expression rides a febrile line of high acidity melded with a curb of gentle oak. All while splaying stone fruits, spiced apple and quince accents to good effect. Nicely done. Screw cap. 13.5% alc. **RATING** 90 **DRINK** 2022-2026 $30 NG
O Series Pinot Noir 2021, Lenswood Sappy red-fruit allusions, a whiff of ume plum, brine and campfire scents skitter along lithe, twiggy tannins. Could use some stuffing, but a perfectly pleasant pinot with a waft of Adelaide Hills sassafras across the finish. Screw cap. 13.5% alc. **RATING** 90 **DRINK** 2022-2027 $45 NG

Andrew Peace Wines ★★★★

Murray Valley Highway, Piangil, Vic 3597 **Region** Swan Hill
T (03) 5030 5291 **www**.apwines.com **Open** Mon–Fri 9–5, Sat 12–4
Winemaker Andrew Peace **Est.** 1995 **Dozens** 300 000 **Vyds** 1000ha
The Peace family has been a major Swan Hill grapegrower since '80, moving into winemaking with the opening of a $3 million winery in '96. Varieties planted include chardonnay, colombard, grenache, malbec, mataro, merlot, pinot gris, riesling, sangiovese, sauvignon blanc, semillon, tempranillo and viognier. The winery was an early adopter of sagrantino in Australia.

ㅇㅇㅇㅇㅇ **Australia Felix Sagrantino 2020, Victoria** Brine and saltbush characters merge into juicy red and black cherry. This wine is both a bit different and familiar, the combination of salty/rusty tang and sweet, berried fruit most appealing. Sagrantino is invariably tannic but this rendition keeps things relatively modest in that regard, though it has good shape. It's a lighter style and a good package all around. Screw cap. 14.5% alc. **RATING** 92 **DRINK** 2023-2029 $32 CM
Full Moon Shiraz Sagrantino 2021, Victoria It's not thick or concentrated but it does have a good deal of personality. Sweet-sour cherries and roasted nut flavours blend with orange oil and fragrant herbs. It's juicy, a little tonic-like, and a good option if you're in the mood for something a bit different. Screw cap. 14.5% alc. **RATING** 90 **DRINK** 2023-2028 $22 CM

Angas & Bremer ★★★★

8 The Parade West, Kent Town, SA 5067 (postal) **Region** Langhorne Creek
T (08) 8537 0600 **www**.angasandbremer.com.au **Open** Not **Winemaker** Peter Pollard
Est. 2017 **Dozens** 7500

Langhorne Creek's climate is profoundly driven by the Southern Ocean and its average altitude of 20m, lower than that of any other region on the mainland. You might expect ample rainfall, but its growing season total of just 169mm makes irrigation essential. The net outcome is generous yields with a lower-than-average need for sprays and lower overall cost per tonne of grapes. Thus most growers have organic accreditation, Angas & Bremer included. It has a registered compost area for vintage waste, and sprays winery waste water on a native eucalyptus woodlot. (JH)

🍷🍷🍷🍷🍷 **Touriga Nacional 2021, Langhorne Creek** Unexpectedly a mouthful of luscious plum and blackberry fruit plus soft tannins. Screw cap. 14% alc. **RATING** 92 **DRINK** 2023–2028 $25 JH ✪
Shiraz 2021, Langhorne Creek Good depth and hue. It has above-average depth and structure, and its best years are still to come as its fruit softens and the oak backs off. Screw cap. 14.8% alc. **RATING** 91 **DRINK** 2024–2029 $25 JH ✪
The Creek 2021, Langhorne Creek Grenache/touriga/malbec, with a little graciano and shiraz. Reflects the vintage; despite all, no sign of the orange blossom or apricot mentioned on its back label. Screw cap. 14.5% alc. **RATING** 90 **DRINK** 2023–2025 $20 JH ✪

Angove Family Winemakers ★★★★★

Bookmark Avenue, Renmark, SA 5341 **Region** McLaren Vale
T (08) 8580 3100 **www**.angove.com.au **Open** Mon–Fri 10–5, Sat 10–4, Sun & public hols 10–3 **Winemaker** Tony Ingle, Paul Kernich, Ben Horley, Amelia Anspach **Viticulturist** Nick Bakkum **Est.** 1886 **Dozens** 500 000 **Vyds** 300ha

Founded in 1886, Angove Family Winemakers is one of Australia's most successful wine businesses, a 5th-generation family company with a tradition of excellence and an eye for the future. Angove includes The Medhyk, Warboys Vineyard, Family Crest, Organics and Wild Olive Organic brands. The McLaren Vale cellar door is nestled in the family's certified organic and biodynamic Warboys vineyard on Chalk Hill Road, and the Renmark cellar door on Bookmark Avenue. In early '19, Angove acquired Primo Estate's 12.7ha Angel Gully vineyard and renamed the site Angels Rise. Angove is committed to remaining privately owned.

🍷🍷🍷🍷🍷 **Angels Rise Shiraz 2020, McLaren Vale** While this is rather oaky to kick off, the flirt of redder fruits, musk, lavender and rosehip meshed with the frisk of palpably natural acidity, elevated and pure, is a far more pleasant approach than the repetition of reduction. This is joyous, floral and alive! Screw cap. 14.5% alc. **RATING** 95 **DRINK** 2022–2028 $75 NG
Warboys Vineyard Shiraz Grenache 2020, McLaren Vale A blend with the heft and richer fruit of shiraz playing rhythm to grenache's more intricate, vibrato lead. This just holds its own, despite the implacable sweetness of shiraz teeming across the edges of restraint. The oak, used to beautiful effect. Boysenberry, raspberry bonbon, clove, pastis and cedar. Screw cap. 14% alc. **RATING** 95 **DRINK** 2022–2032 $75 NG
Warboys Vineyard Grenache 2020, McLaren Vale A lovely wine that's refined, pure and long, despite an element of oak that merely serves to dry out the finish while suggesting excessive ageing. Kirsch, bergamot, rosehip and cranberry. The time on skins feels adequate, yet a little more courage will elevate this into the regional pantheon. Screw cap. 14% alc. **RATING** 95 **DRINK** 2022–2028 $75 NG
The Medhyk Shiraz 2019, McLaren Vale Sweetness of fruit, sexy oak cladding, dutiful freshness and ample flavour without excessive reduction. Quelle miracle! Loosely knit without overdoing it. Licorice root, clove, cardamom and sappy kirsch to a blue fruited punch. For those in the market for stylised shiraz, this is very good. Screw cap. 14.5% alc. **RATING** 94 **DRINK** 2022–2028 $65 NG

ŢŢŢŢ♀ **Warboys Vineyard Shiraz 2020, McLaren Vale** RATING 93 DRINK 2022-2030
$75 NG
Grenache 2022, McLaren Vale RATING 92 DRINK 2022-2026 $25 NG
Shiraz 2020, McLaren Vale RATING 91 DRINK 2022-2030 $25 NG ✪
Tempranillo 2021, McLaren Vale RATING 90 DRINK 2022-2026 $25 NG ✪

Angus the Bull ★★★☆

2/14 Sydney Road, Manly, NSW 2095 (postal) **Region** Central Victoria
T (02) 8966 9020 **www**.angusthebull.com **Open** Not **Winemaker** Hamish MacGowan
Est. 2002 **Dozens** 20 000
Hamish MacGowan took the virtual winery idea to its ultimate conclusion with a single
steak-friendly wine (Angus the Bull Cabernet Sauvignon). The range has since been
extended to include the Wee Angus Merlot and a single-vineyard Heathcote wine called
Black Angus. Each year parcels of grapes are selected from several sites across Central Victoria
in a multi-regional blending approach designed to minimise vintage variation.

ŢŢŢŢ♀ **Black Angus Cabernet Sauvignon 2019, Heathcote** A minty red wine
with bold fruit flavour at the heart of it, complemented by a general softness.
If you're in the mood for a hearty red, this is an easy wine to like. Blackberry,
leather, hay and cedarwood characters sweep confidently through the palate,
before chewy tannin steps in to help shape the finish. Cork. 14% alc. RATING 93
DRINK 2022-2030 $60 CM

Anim Wine ★★★★

PO Box 65, Tas 7052 **Region** Southern Tasmania
T 0400 203 865 **www**.animwine.com **Open** By appt **Winemaker** Max Marriott
Viticulturist Max Marriott **Est.** 2018 **Dozens** 500
The production may be small, but the story of owners Max and Siobhan Marriott is anything
but. Max earned a bachelor of viticulture and oenology from Lincoln University in NZ. He
then managed vineyards in Central Otago and worked vintages in the Mosel, Oregon and
Burgundy. After a few years in Oregon, the pair repatriated to Tasmania. Max is involved
with Clarence House and also leases the Tinderbox vineyard, with grapes sourced from both.
Anim is named after their children Audrey, Niamh and Imogen.

ŢŢŢŢŢ **Field Fizz 2022, Tasmania** A fizzy, wild-eyed blend of pinot noir/chardonnay/
pinot blanc/merlot/cabernet sauvignon/tempranillo/muscat. It smells of blood
oranges, grapefruit, watermelon and nectarine with hints of spent yeast, cider,
redcurrant jelly and pressed flowers. Clean and dry, it finishes with a fine,
energetic spritz and gentle, softly spiced red fruits. One of the best Aussie pét-nats
I've seen. Crown. 13% alc. RATING 94 DRINK 2023-2025 $35 DB ✪
Tinderbox Pinot Noir 2021, Tasmania A lovely wine awash with gamey
nuance, wild mountain and amaro-herb notes and a core of wild-eyed
macerated strawberry, dark cherry and plum fruits. Silky, savoury and spicy
with just the right amount of funk in its trunk. Screw cap. 13% alc. RATING 94
DRINK 2023-2027 $50 DB
Windrush Pinot Noir 2021, Tasmania The lightest, most finely poised of
Anim's pinot noirs. Zingy cherry and plum fruits mesh with fine spice, forest
floor notes and mushroom broth, with fine-grained tannins and a wonderful sapid
acid line adding propulsion across the palate. Screw cap. 13.5% alc. RATING 94
DRINK 2023-2028 $50 DB

ŢŢŢŢ♀ **Pinot Blanc 2022, Tasmania** RATING 93 DRINK 2023-2026 $35 DB
Clarence Pinot Noir 2021, Tasmania RATING 93 DRINK 2023-2027 $50 DB
Sauvignon 2022, Tasmania RATING 92 DRINK 2023-2026 $40 DB
Anima Pinot Noir 2020, Tasmania RATING 92 DRINK 2023-2028 $85 DB
Hop Nat 2022, Tasmania RATING 90 DRINK 2023-2025 $35 DB
Field Blend 2021, Tasmania RATING 90 DRINK 2023-2025 $32 DB

Anvers ★★★★

633 Razorback Road, Kangarilla, SA 5157 **Region** Adelaide Hills
T (08) 7085 0615 **www.anvers.com.au Open** Thurs–Sun 11.30–5 **Winemaker** Kym
Milne MW **Viticulturist** Mark Vella (Vitiworks) **Est.** 1998 **Dozens** 8000 **Vyds** 16ha
Anvers is a family-owned estate at Kangarilla in the Adelaide Hills, established by Myriam and
Wayne Keoghan. The name is a nod to Myriam's Belgian origins in Antwerp. The vineyard
is planted to 16ha of sauvignon blanc, chardonnay, shiraz, barbera and gamay; cabernet
sauvignon is sourced from Langhorne Creek. Winemaker Kym Milne MW has 30 years of
experience, including a stint as chief winemaker for Villa Maria in NZ. An old dairy, built in
1949, has been converted into a cellar door.

🍷🍷🍷🍷🍷 **Barbera 2022, Adelaide Hills** Bright acidity, nicely wrought oak and
blueberry, anise, creosote and alpine notes, a waft of mint and pine across the
crunchy finish. Not a great deal of grape tannin, but that is the varietal personality.
Delicious and thirst-slaking and ready for instantaneous satiation. Screw cap.
14% alc. **RATING** 93 **DRINK** 2023-2027 $35 NG ✪
Gamay 2022, Adelaide Hills Possibly the finest gamay I've tasted in Australia
after the mighty Sorrenberg. Reminiscent of fine cru beaujolais. Mid-weighted,
juicy and so energetic that it sets the palate up with mottled blue fruits, damson
plum and sour cherry before delivering a savoury thread of verdant astringency.
Wines as beautiful as this should not be taken for granted. Screw cap. 13.5% alc.
RATING 93 **DRINK** 2023–2028 $35 NG ✪
Kingsway Shiraz 2020, Adelaide Hills A rich wine that manages to coax
the palate into interest, rather than bludgeoning it into submission, splaying
boysenberry, dark cherry and notes of iodine, nori and lilac into all the right spots
without the clutch of reduction pushed too far. The oak, an addendum rather
than a shriek, directs the flavours toward a spurt of juicy freshness that punctuates
the solid finish. Screw cap. 14.5% alc. **RATING** 92 **DRINK** 2022-2028 $35 NG
Block 7 Syrah 2021, Adelaide Hills A stark departure from the 'shiraz' sibling,
reliant more on reduction and a dollop of whole-cluster-derived mezcal, dill,
exotic spice and fibrous tannins, thrown into the mix. Full bodied, with blue fruits
aplenty, too. It all works fairly well, although the greenness of the stems rides the
bony tannins to a jittery, slightly acerbic finish. Interesting to taste, perhaps, in a
couple of years. Screw cap. 14% alc. **RATING** 91 **DRINK** 2022-2027 $35 NG
Razorback Road Sauvignon Blanc 2022, Adelaide Hills To style, with more
herbal accents, optimally ripe mid-palate and propulsion of tropical fruit tones
than many. Guava, greengage, nashi pear, apple skin and a whiff of sugar snap pea
and fennel. This pulls few surprises but is made with a certain grace. Screw cap.
13% alc. **RATING** 90 **DRINK** 2022-2023 $25 NG ✪
Kingsway Chardonnay 2021, Adelaide Hills Fine aromas, expressing a
demure restraint as much as subtle stone fruits and truffled lees accents. A billow of
oak defines the cushy, mid-weighted palate. The finish, of modest length, pinched
by the oak tannins. Screw cap. 13% alc. **RATING** 90 **DRINK** 2022-2027 $35 NG
Fortified Shiraz 2021, Adelaide Hills Rustic and old-school. Date, toffee and
molasses. Avuncular gear in need of a creased armchair and an open mind as the
spirit sticks out from the fray to sear the finish. Screw cap. 16% alc. **RATING** 90
DRINK 2022-2035 $45 NG

Aphelion Wine ★★★★★

18 St Andrews Terrace, Willunga, SA 5172 **Region** McLaren Vale
T 0404 390 840 **www.aphelionwine.com.au Open** By appt **Winemaker** Rob Mack
Est. 2014 **Dozens** 2500
When you consider the credentials of winemaker Rob Mack and co-founder Louise Rhodes
Mack, great art comes to mind. Rob accumulated 2 degrees in accounting and management
in '07, and wine science from CSU in '16; he is also part-way through his MW studies. He
scaled the heights of direct marketing as wine buyer and planner for Laithwaites Wine People
and spent the next 18 months as production manager for Direct Wines in McLaren Vale. He

has worked with 5 wineries, 4 in McLaren Vale. Rob was voted Young Gun of Wine '18 and Aphelion won Best Small Producer at the McLaren Vale Wine Show in '19.

🍷🍷🍷🍷🍷 **Hickinbotham Single Vineyard Grenache 2022, McLaren Vale** By far the best single-vineyard iteration of this range. Ferrous. Bloodstone, damson plum, crushed mint, raspberry coulis and dried thyme. Such vivacity, drive and length, positioned between a compact framework of tannins extracted with such exactitude and confidence. Compression and release manifest as brilliance. Screw cap. 14% alc. RATING 96 DRINK 2023–2030 $70 NG ✪

Wait Single Vineyard Grenache 2022, McLaren Vale Exotic and frisky and gorgeous. This is a thoroughbred, suggestive of Indian spices and carnal corners. Clove, bergamot, kirsch, cinnamon spice and a waft of optimism, manifest in the most long-limbed reach of tannic bristle and maritime freshness that it brings a tear. Screw cap. 14.3% alc. RATING 95 DRINK 2023–2030 $70 NG

Affinity GM 2021, McLaren Vale A delicious grenache/mourvèdre blend of considerable structure and serious depth, juxtaposed against an effortless drinkability promoted by a whole-berry, whole-bunchy friskiness. Best, the strata of tannins that underlie a stream of cranberry, rosehip, fecund strawberry and heather, with a saline spurt of acidity pulsing long. Screw cap. 14.2% alc. RATING 95 DRINK 2022–2027 $38 NG ✪

Rapture Grenache 2022, McLaren Vale This pushes the margins of ripeness and whole bunches to the limits. Yet with aplomb. Dill pickle and jitters of mezcal ride shotgun to sweet cherry, bergamot, clove and raspberry bonbon. This is contemporary grenache of the highest order, if not a bit abstemious. I look forward to seeing this with just a little age, should it make it. Screw cap. 14.3% alc. RATING 94 DRINK 2022–2027 $100 NG

🍷🍷🍷🍷🍷 **The Confluence Grenache 2022, McLaren Vale** RATING 93 DRINK 2023–2028 $38 NG

Welkin Rosé 2022, McLaren Vale RATING 93 DRINK 2022–2024 $28 NG ✪

Brini Single Vineyard Grenache 2022, McLaren Vale RATING 92 DRINK 2023–2028 $70 NG

Welkin Grenache 2022, McLaren Vale RATING 92 DRINK 2022–2025 $28 NG ✪

Welkin Nero d'Avola 2022, McLaren Vale RATING 92 DRINK 2022–2024 $28 NG ✪

Pir Blewitt Springs Chenin Blanc 2022, McLaren Vale RATING 91 DRINK 2023–2030 $38 NG

Welkin Chenin Blanc 2022, Adelaide Hills RATING 90 DRINK 2022–2025 $28 NG

Emergent Mataro 2020, McLaren Vale RATING 90 DRINK 2023–2026 $38 NG

Apogee   ★★★★★

1083 Golconda Road, Lebrina, Tas 7254 **Region** Northern Tasmania **T** (02) 6395 6358 www.apogeetasmania.com **Open** By appt **Winemaker** Andrew Pirie **Viticulturist** Andrew Pirie **Est.** 2007 **Dozens** 1000 **Vyds** 2ha

Dr Andrew Pirie AM has stood tall among those who have sought to understand and exploit Tasmania's terroir and climate over the past 40 years, though he is quietly spoken and humble. His vision almost 50 years ago – longer still on some measures – saw the establishment of Pipers Brook Vineyard in '74, using the detailed studies of Tasmania's regional climates. In '77 he became the first (and last) person to complete study for his doctorate in viticulture from the University of Sydney. While making some of the best table wines from Tasmania in the last quarter of the 20th century, his focus shifted to sparkling wine in '99. In 2007 he acquired a 2ha site near Lebrina in the Pipers River district, planting pinot noir (62%), chardonnay (16%) and a little pinot meunier (2%) for sparkling wine, as well as pinot gris (20%) for table wine. Apogee's historic farm cottage is now an intimate cellar door where (by appointment) visitors can observe a hand disgorging demonstration. Pinot gris and pinot noir are made under the Alto label.

ŸŸŸŸŸ **Deluxe Vintage Brut 2019, Tasmania** Andrew Pirie has crafted a wonderful sparkling wine that's expansive yet displays tension and vitality. Notes of baked apple, fresh brioche, white flowers and stone with wafts of redcurrant, soft spice, almond paste and biscuity notes. There's a swell of dosage on the finish along with autolysis notes. The wine finishes long and pure with apple and pastry at the fore. Diam. 12.9% alc. **RATING** 95 **DRINK** 2023–2030 $70 DB

Alto Pinot Gris 2022, Tasmania Textural sway, slinky almost, with characters of pear, citrus, white flowers, lanolin, rose petal, crushed river stone and lighter notes of marzipan. It's got that richness of flavour you'd expect, with plenty of mid-palate fat tempered by mineral-laden Tassie acidity, finishing long and true. Screw cap. 13.5% alc. **RATING** 95 **DRINK** 2023–2028 $40 DB ✿ ♥

Vintage Deluxe Rosé 2019, Tasmania Salmon pink in the glass with a fine, energetic bead and notes of redcurrant, red apple, blood orange, grapefruit and a liminal waft of wild strawberries. Some fresh pastry characters flow in on the palate, which shows fine, lacy acidity, a light tug of textural skin tannins and a lovely cadence as it sweeps off the palate with a vapour trail of red fruits, stone and soft spice. Diam. 13.2% alc. **RATING** 94 **DRINK** 2023–2030 $89 DB

Alto Pinot Noir 2021, Tasmania Deep cherry red in the glass with a sense of latent power to its aromatic profile. Cherry, strawberry and red plum tones mesh with an underbrush of soft spice, leaf litter, shiitake mushroom, game meats and French oak nuance. Fine tannins and a porcelain line of acidity provide ample cadence and drive as the wine powers to a persistent finish. Screw cap. 14% alc. **RATING** 94 **DRINK** 2023–2030 $70 DB

Alto Pinot Noir 2020, Tasmania Super colour. Has the thumbprint of naked varietal power, with luscious red fruits and Asian spices threaded through the palate. Fine tannins underwrite a high-quality pinot that will richly repay cellaring for 10+ years. Screw cap. 13% alc. **RATING** 94 **DRINK** 2023–2035 $65 JH

Aravina Estate   ★★★★★

61 Thornton Road, Yallingup, WA 6282 **Region** Margaret River
T (08) 9750 1111 **www**.aravinaestate.com **Open** 7 days 11–5 **Winemaker** Ryan Aggiss
Est. 2010 **Dozens** 10 000 **Vyds** 29.6ha
In '10, Steve Tobin and family acquired the winery and vineyard of Amberley Estate from Accolade, renaming it Aravina Estate. The family have almost 30ha under vine, including semillon, sauvignon blanc, chenin blanc, chardonnay, cabernet, merlot, shiraz, tempranillo and malbec; touriga nacional was planted in '19. All wines have been vinified on the estate since '18. Winemaker Ryan Aggiss was formerly winemaker at Houghton's Nannup site.

ŸŸŸŸŸ **Limited Release Grenache Rosé 2022, Margaret River** Grenache makes brilliant rosé because of its flavour profile, acidity and general all-around goodness. Pastel pink shot with bronze. Fragrant with florals, red licorice, Pink Lady apples and a hint of baking spices. Fabulous palate: textural with a smidge of lemon cream, a light tannin pull to the finish and refreshing acidity all the way through. Screw cap. 12% alc. **RATING** 95 **DRINK** 2023–2025 $30 JF ✿

Limited Release Arinto 2022, Margaret River The only arinto in Margaret River and the first vintage. With its high acidity and heady aromas, this Portuguese white seems right at home. The pitch-perfect and very refreshing palate is full of sliced lemon and briny oyster shell tang. Juicy and savoury, it's not a fruit-bomb wine, yippee! Screw cap. 11.5% alc. **RATING** 95 **DRINK** 2023–2027 $35 JF ✿

Wildwood Ridge Reserve Chardonnay 2022, Margaret River It stays in a savoury zone, although bursts of citrus and white nectarine pop out from time to time. Toasty oak leaves a thumbprint, but it's thankfully not dominating. Refreshing, zesty and tangy, a slip of phenolics all add to the enjoyment. Screw cap. 12.3% alc. **RATING** 95 **DRINK** 2023–2030 $60 JF

Wildwood Ridge Reserve Cabernet Sauvignon 2021, Margaret River I'm a sucker for the regional aromas and flavours of Margaret River cabernet sauvignon: all the mulberries, cassis, Aussie bush, nori and in this, soy sauce, yet a lot of restraint, too. The tannins are neatly placed and approachable, the palate beautifully modulated and fine and the acidity leads out long and persistent on the finish. Screw cap. 14% alc. RATING 95 DRINK 2024–2038 $60 JF

Wildwood Ridge Reserve Stella BDX 2020, Margaret River A barrel selection of cabernet sauvignon/merlot/malbec/cabernet franc/petit verdot. It is excellent. Fuller bodied but not weighty, with shapely, elongated tannins, fine acidity and a core of perfectly managed fruit and savoury flavours. Yep, a stellar wine. Screw cap. 14% alc. RATING 95 DRINK 2024–2038 $100 JF

Single Vineyard Block 4 Chenin Blanc 2022, Margaret River Highly strung with acidity cinching all the flavours. Occasionally it loosens up to allow some chamomile, citrus, quince and red apple skin to emerge with an appealing lemon/briny character. A smidge of texture, presumably from time in barrel, and a neat phenolic pull all add to this good wine. Screw cap. 12% alc. RATING 94 DRINK 2023–2030 $38 JF ✪

♈♈♈♈♀ **Single Vineyard Shiraz 2022, Margaret River** RATING 93 DRINK 2024–2034 $35 JF ✪

The A Collection Cabernet Merlot Malbec 2022, Margaret River RATING 92 DRINK 2023–2028 $25 JF ✪

Limited Release Tempranillo 2022, Margaret River RATING 91 DRINK 2023–2028 $35 JF

Wildwood Ridge Reserve Merlot 2021, Margaret River RATING 90 DRINK 2023–2031 $60 JF

Arila Gardens ★★★★★

103 Moppa Rd, Nuriootpa, SA 5355 **Region** Barossa Valley
T 0411 244 429 **www**.arilagardens.com **Open** By appt **Winemaker** Adam Clay
Viticulturist Adam Clay **Est.** 2018 **Dozens** 1000 **Vyds** 7ha

Adam and Marie Clay purchased 8ha in Moppa (Arila Gardens) in '18, after overseas harvests and a decade as a winemaker at Penfolds in the Barossa. Arila, an Indigenous word for 'sand, land and earth', is split into 3 distinct terroirs: Sand Garden, Quartz Garden and Ironstone Garden, with grenache vines planted in 1900 and shiraz in the '40s. The Gardens of Moppa wines are regional expressions, blended across the estate vineyards. The Garden Selection wines are crafted from the best individual rows and sections of each terroir, exploring the nuance of site. These are wines that sing clearly of their subregional soils, have snappy packaging and a very bright future.

♈♈♈♈♈ **Sand Garden Grenache 2021, Barossa Valley** From a 1900-planted vineyard. Notes of raspberry, red plum, tobacco, gingerbread, grilled watermelon, cola and almond blossom. Calm, composed and savoury with a lovely fruit presence, briny, lipsmacking acid drive and a supple, kinetic structure that bodes well for the future. Screw cap. 14.5% alc. RATING 96 DRINK 2023–2033 $85 DB

Ironstone & Quartz Gardens Shiraz 2021, Barossa Bright purple red in the glass with violet-dusted satsuma plum and blackberry fruits cut with baking spices, earth, licorice, rum and raisin chocolate, charcuterie, espresso and warm earth. The tannins are compact, perhaps lacking the resolution of last year's release but this will rectify with time in bottle. Another great release. Screw cap. 14.5% alc. RATING 95 DRINK 2023–2036 $85 DB

Gardens of Moppa Shiraz 2021, Barossa Valley Purple crimson in the glass and bursting at the seams with juicy plum, mulberry, boysenberry, baking spices, dark chocolate, cocoa powder, earth and orange blossom. A velvety, pure fruit flow with fine, gypsum-like tannins and a rich chocolatey sheen to the black fruits on the finish. Screw cap. 14.5% alc. RATING 94 DRINK 2023–2032 $40 DB ✪

♈♈♈♈♀ **Gardens of Moppa GSM 2021, Barossa Valley** RATING 93 DRINK 2023–2029 $40 DB

Arlewood Estate

679 Calgardup Road West, Forest Grove, WA 6286 **Region** Margaret River
T (08) 9757 6676 **www**.arlewood.com.au **Open** Fri 11–5, Sat 10–5 or by appt
Winemaker Cath Oates **Viticulturist** Adrian Gosatti, Jordan Gosatti, Colin Bell
Est. 1988 **Dozens** 2500 **Vyds** 6.08ha

Arlewood Estate was planted in '99 by the then Xanadu winemaker Jurg Muggli. Garry Gosatti purchased the run-down, close-planted vineyard in '08. His involvement in its resurrection was hands-on, and the cool site in the south of Margaret River remains his obsession. Garry's sons Jordan and Adrian now work in the vineyard and Garry drives down every weekend from Perth, clearly believing that the owner's footsteps make the best fertiliser.

Chardonnay 2022, Margaret River Packed with flavour. This is so driven by racing-car fast acidity, with flavours following in its wake. Grapefruit, lemon-infused baked apple with creamed honey and moreish creamy, nutty lees, too, with slinky oak and its spice notes. No surprise the finish is persistent and uplifting. Screw cap. 13% alc. **RATING** 95 **DRINK** 2022–2032 $50 JF ✪

Cabernet Sauvignon 2020, Margaret River At the time of tasting, this was still a year away from its release. It wants to strut its regional stuff now. The mulberries, the cassis, the whiff of the ocean and the beautiful fine tannins. It spends 22 months in French oak, and the wine has taken everything in (even if it would have perhaps a tad more vitality with less time in oak). Still, this has elegance and delights as a result. Screw cap. 14% alc. **RATING** 95 **DRINK** 2023–2035 $95 JF

La Bratta Bianco 2020, Margaret River La Bratta is all chardonnay this vintage, and it's very good. Rich and ripe, full of stone fruit and citrus with freshness and complexity, depth and detail. Creamy, nutty lees and fruit infused with oak, but it's all so well integrated offering a spicy, savoury edge before the palate fleshes out to a lingering finish. Screw cap. 13.5% alc. **RATING** 95 **DRINK** 2022–2030 $60 JF

Arli Wine

2/540 Goulburn Valley Highway, Shepparton North, Vic 3531 (postal)
Region Goulburn Valley
T 0427 529 183 **www**.arliwine.com.au **Open** Not **Winemaker** John Kremor **Est.** 2021
Dozens 300

Raised on his parents' vineyard in Merbein, John Kremor was destined for a life in wine. His first job was at BRL Hardy in Buronga, working his way up from the laboratory and cellar into the role of assistant winemaker. During his time there, he and his partner Leanna also redeveloped a local dried-fruit property with cabernet sauvignon and chardonnay, selling the fruit to a local winery. In '21 John returned to his first love, sourcing and making small parcels of wine from the Goulburn Valley region.

Picture This Shiraz 2022, Heathcote Unfined and unfiltered. Dense, dark purple hues and a signature spice-laden array of dark berry fruits. Very Heathcote. The ripeness of fruit has easily slurped up the American oak contributing dusty, woodsy spice to the plush palate. Tannins are even and lightly savoury. Shows good depth and elegant structure. Screw cap. 14.5% alc. **RATING** 92 **DRINK** 2023–2028 $40 JP

Leggerezza Shiraz 2022, Central Victoria A Dookie Hills shiraz with plenty of personality. Bright red with a purple rim, the scent immediately rises in fresh red fruits – raspberry, cherry, plum – with attractive dried herbs, too. The palate is soft with a touch of savoury earthiness working hand in hand with red fruits. An additional spicy pepperiness brings added lift and interest. Fab drinking now. Screw cap. 12.5% alc. **RATING** 91 **DRINK** 2023–2027 $25 JP ✪

Dookie Hills Riesling 2022, Central Victoria A quick swish in the glass and this little charmer opens right up, with plenty of floral flourish in white flowers, honeysuckle and citrus. A wine of gentle grace in dusty lemon and lime with plenty of tangy acid drive to accompany it into the future. The lemony bite to close gets the tastebuds working like crazy. Delish. Screw cap. 11.3% alc. **RATING** 90 **DRINK** 2022–2028 $25 JP ✪

Armstrong Wines ★★★★

2 Abbottshall Road, Hawthorn, SA 5062 (postal) **Region** Grampians
T 0419 815 735 **www**.armstrongwines.com.au **Open** Not **Winemaker** Tony Royal
Est. 1989 **Dozens** 3000 **Vyds** 7ha
Armstrong Vineyards was established by Tony Royal, former Seppelt (Great Western) winemaker. The first 2ha of shiraz vines were planted in '89, the remaining 4.7ha in the mid-'90s. The Armstrong label is the top tier, followed by La Lutte and Royal Scribe labels.

🍷🍷🍷🍷🍷 **La Lutte Grenache 2022, Heathcote** Flow of flavour is excellent here. This is medium weight at most but the spice notes, the general feeling of control, and the clean run of flavour through the finish are all clear markers of quality. Floral aspects add a certain prettiness and from every angle this says 'drink me, drink me now'. Screw cap. 14.5% alc. **RATING** 93 **DRINK** 2023–2028 $28 CM ✪
La Lutte Nouveau Shiraz 2022, Grampians Juicy cherry-berry flavours with lashings of twiggy spice. Walnut, red liorice and smoky reductive inputs, too. Fun to drink but more than that too; it's textural, complex and refreshing all at once. Screw cap. 14.5% alc. **RATING** 91 **DRINK** 2023–2027 $24 CM ✪
La Lutte Tempranillo 2022, Heathcote It's medium weight at most but the red-berried flavours and clove-like accents, combined with juicy acidity and grainy tannin, make for a well-rounded wine. Subtle woodsmoke and chocolate characters are an attractive finishing touch. Overall balance has been well judged here. Screw cap. 14.5% alc. **RATING** 91 **DRINK** 2023–2027 $28 CM ✪

Artisans of Barossa ★★★★

24 Vine Vale Road, Tanunda SA 5352 **Region** Barossa Valley
T (08) 8563 3935 **www**.artisansofbarossa.com **Open** 7 days 8–5 **Winemaker** Various
Est. 2005 **Dozens** 3000
Artisans of Barossa is a group of winemakers that share a like-minded approach to winemaking and enjoyment of wine. They are Hobbs of Barossa Ranges, Schwarz Wine Company, John Duval Wines, Sons of Eden, Spinifex Wines, Chaffey Bros. Wine Co., Lienert Vineyards and Purple Hands. Each is highly successful in its own business, but relishes the opportunity of coming together to build on their collective winemaking skills and experience, knowledge of the vineyard landscape, and their connections through the local wine community. The latest release is Project 2021, with the makers all sourcing grenache from the Rosenzweig vineyard in Vine Vale to make 6 unique wines.

🍷🍷🍷🍷🍷 **Project 21 Schell Grenache 2021, Barossa Valley** Made by Peter Schell of Spinifex Wines. Whole bunches and whole berries (50/50%), 6 months in old French oak puncheons. Exotically spiced plum and berry fruits, orange blossom, ginger cake, cola and earth. Sandy tannins. Has the highest alcohol of the bunch but handles it well. Screw cap. 15.4% alc. **RATING** 93 **DRINK** 2023–2028 $42 DB
Project 21 Hartwig Engela Grenache 2021, Barossa Valley From the Chaffey Bros. Whole bunches (50%) for carbonic maceration, matured in old French oak puncheons for 6 months. Punchy raspberry, red plum and cherry fruits, exotic spices, light amaro notes, gingerbread and orange blossom. An all-around sense of 'I could drink a lot of this,' too. Screw cap. 14.4% alc. **RATING** 93 **DRINK** 2023–2027 $42 DB
Project 21 Stansborough Slade Grenache 2021, Barossa Valley The Purple Hands crew show their stuff: 30% whole bunches and matured in old oak puncheons for 6 months. Pinot-like hue with notes of raspberry, red cherry and plum underscored with ginger spice and purple florals. Spacious and airy in the mouth with light powdery tannins and a savoury lick at the end. Screw cap. 14.5% alc. **RATING** 92 **DRINK** 2023–2027 $42 DB

Project 21 Lienert Grenache 2021, Barossa Valley No surprises here, just a lovely, sprightly, savoury and spicy grenache. The whole-bunch component (40%) has opened the wine right up, letting the light in. It's also light on tannin with a swift acid cadence and a lipsmacking finish. Screw cap. 14.5% alc. **RATING** 92 **DRINK** 2023-2027 $42 DB

Project 21 Schwarz Grenache 2021, Barossa Valley From Jason Schwarz, 100% whole bunches (50% carbonic maceration), aged in old French puncheons for 6 months. Purple hued with a juicy, bouncy vibe and an array of ripe plum and cherry fruits cut through with exotic spices, ginger cake, purple florals and earth. More depth and texture here and a slightly wild edge that is lovely. Screw cap. 14.5% alc. **RATING** 92 **DRINK** 2023-2027 $42 DB

Project 21 Hobbs & Hobbs Grenache 2021, Barossa Valley From Hobbs of Barossa. Whole berries, hand plunged and foot stomped, matured in seasoned French oak for 6 months. A lovely vibrant colour with increasing raspberry and macerated plum aromatic heft and a little more fruit weight on the palate compared to some of its project mates. Finishes spicy and balanced with a light sandy tannin grip. Screw cap. 14.8% alc. **RATING** 92 **DRINK** 2023-2027 $42 DB

Artwine

72 Bird in Hand Road, Woodside, SA 5244 **Region** Mount Lofty Ranges
T 0411 422 450 **www.**artwine.com.au **Open** 7 days 11–5 **Winemaker** Contract
Est. 1997 **Dozens** 10 000 **Vyds** 21ha
Owned by Judy and Glen Kelly, Artwine has 3 vineyards. The Springfarm Road and Sawmill Road sites are in the Clare Valley and the 3rd vineyard is in the Adelaide Hills at Woodside, which houses their cellar door. Glen and Judy's research of climatic conditions, coupled with their love of Mediterranean wines, has resulted in eclectic mix of varieties being planted.

ꟼꟼꟼꟼꟼ **Smiling Gamay 2022, Adelaide Hills** A brilliant wine, this. Wild strawberries, thyme, orange verbena and a bone of gentle astringency tucking in the seams. A dangerously easy wine to gulp. Screw cap. 12.5% alc. **RATING** 93 **DRINK** 2022-2026 $45 NG

Saint Vincent Pinot Noir 2021, Adelaide Hills This is very well done, despite my trepidation when I glimpsed the low alcohol. Fecund strawberry, dried thyme, lavender and candied orange peel. The tannins, perky and astringent, serving as the framework. Screw cap. 12.5% alc. **RATING** 92 **DRINK** 2022-2027 $45 NG

Masterpiece Grenache Gris 2022, Clare Valley There is a lot to love here. A nose of pickled pimentos, scrubbed lemon rind and balm. The barrel and lees work imbue depth and breadth while evincing a take-over-the-palate sort of authority. If this were a degree riper, rather than picked with trepidation on acidity, it would be a very good wine. As it stands, just good. Screw cap. 12.5% alc. **RATING** 91 **DRINK** 2022-2026 $45 NG

Pack Leader Cabernet Franc 2021, Clare Valley Full bodied, sappy, floral and sweet of fruit, with boysenberry, spearmint and mulberry leaf carried along by a raft of gentle astringency. I would like to see more savouriness. Screw cap. 14.5% alc. **RATING** 90 **DRINK** 2022-2025 $45 NG

Ashbrook Estate

379 Tom Cullity Drive, Wilyabrup, WA 6280 **Region** Margaret River
T (08) 9755 6262 **www.**ashbrookwines.com.au **Open** 7 days 10–5
Winemaker Catherine Edwards, Brian Devitt **Viticulturist** Richard Devitt, Brian Devitt **Est.** 1975 **Dozens** 12 500 **Vyds** 17.4ha
This fastidious producer shuns publicity and is less known than is deserved, selling much of its wine through the cellar door and to a loyal mailing list clientele. It is very much a family affair: Brian Devitt is at the helm, winemaking is by his daughter Catherine, and viticulture by son Richard who is also a qualified winemaker. (JH)

ΨΨΨΨΨ **Reserve Cabernet Sauvignon 2017, Margaret River** Plenty of fresh mulberries and fruit compote woven throughout an ostensibly savoury wine, with wafts of tobacco, warming spices and warm earth. Fuller bodied with shapely tannins and a little drying on the finish, yet there's texture and evenness throughout. Screw cap. 14% alc. RATING 95 DRINK 2023–2030 $70 JF

ΨΨΨΨΨ **Sauvignon Blanc 2022, Margaret River** RATING 93 DRINK 2022–2025 $27 JF ✪
Riesling 2022, Margaret River RATING 92 DRINK 2023–2032 $27 JF ✪
Reserve Chardonnay 2021, Margaret River RATING 91 DRINK 2023–2028 $70 JF
Verdelho 2022, Margaret River RATING 90 DRINK 2022–2026 $27 JF
Semillon 2022, Margaret River RATING 90 DRINK 2023–2032 $27 JF
Shiraz 2020, Margaret River RATING 90 DRINK 2024–2032 $32 JF

Ashton Hills Vineyard ★★★★★

126 Tregarthen Road, Ashton, SA 5137 **Region** Adelaide Hills
T (08) 8390 1243 **www.ashtonhills.com.au Open** Fri–Mon 11–5 **Winemaker** Liam Van Pelt **Viticulturist** Anton Groffen **Est.** 1982 **Dozens** 3000 **Vyds** 3ha
The Ashton Hills winery will always be the heart and soul of the Adelaide Hills wine region. Founder Stephen George set all the benchmarks; his relentless pursuit of myriad grape clones and varieties laid the foundation for the thriving region of today. Ashton Hills has been owned by Wirra Wirra since 2015, though it speaks volumes that Stephen still lives on the property and remains involved in its operation. This has been the most respectful of handovers, best proven by the steady and continued stream of top-tier releases.

ΨΨΨΨΨ **Pinot Noir Vintage Rosé 2019, Adelaide Hills** I've always liked this wine. A gorgeous pallid coral hue. The fruit is a skittish beam of red fruits, just ripe enough, powdery and crunchy and energetic. Long and pleasing and delicious. The skill on show is knowing when lees work (1 year on this release) is sufficient to achieve the goal of nerve, flavour and etherealness. Diam. 13% alc. RATING 95 DRINK 2022–2028 $40 NG ✪
Estate Riesling 2022, Adelaide Hills This comes from 8 rows of riesling, enough to make 120 dozen – Stephen couldn't bring himself to remove it and plant more pinot noir. The voluminous blossom-filled bouquet precedes a vivid, dancing array of citrus, Granny Smith apple and glittering acidity on the long palate. Screw cap. 12% alc. RATING 95 DRINK 2023–2042 $40 JH ✪
Reserve Chardonnay 2022, Adelaide Hills Fine aromas of grated parmesan, toasted hazelnuts and truffle. Reticent. Shins and elbows. Little obvious fruit aromas, although fruit sweetness. Plenty of peat. Time will work magic here, such is the structural lattice of oak, mineral and the long-limbed cadence. Intriguing stuff. Screw cap. 12% alc. RATING 95 DRINK 2023–2030 $85 NG

ΨΨΨΨΨ **Reserve Pinot Noir 2022, Piccadilly Valley** RATING 93 DRINK 2023–2030 $80 NG
Pinot X Pinot 2022, Adelaide Hills RATING 93 DRINK 2022–2027 $40 NG
Sparkling Shiraz 2016, Clare Valley RATING 92 DRINK 2022–2028 $60 NG
Estate Pinot Noir 2022, Piccadilly Valley RATING 92 DRINK 2023–2028 $60 NG
Growers Single Vineyard Pinot Noir 2022, Piccadilly Valley RATING 90 DRINK 2023–2029 $55 NG

Atlas Wines ★★★★

PO Box 458, Clare, SA 5453 **Region** Clare Valley
T 0419 847 491 **www.atlaswines.com Open** Not **Winemaker** Adam Barton **Est.** 2007 **Dozens** 8000 **Vyds** 17ha
Adam Barton and Amy Lane established Atlas Wines in '07 with the purchase of their White Hut vineyard. They added their Leasingham vineyard in '19 and a further vineyard and

winery in the Barossa in '23. Together they farm 27ha across the Clare and Barossa valleys; shiraz dominates, but tempranillo, vermentino, fiano and pinot gris are also planted. Fruit is also sourced from other growers. Adam is winemaker, with an extensive winemaking career spanning McLaren Vale, the Barossa Valley, Coonawarra, California and the Clare Valley.

🍷🍷🍷🍷🍷 **172° Watervale Riesling 2022, Clare Valley** This drinks a treat. Tightly wound but with some pliancy and juiciness, too. Lemon, lime and green apple scents and flavours with a tidy line of granitic, minerally acidity through the core. It feels very precise and pent up with huge velocity and energy and a very long tail of puckering tang. Sheesh, this is great! Classic Clare, but on a pedestal. Screw cap. 11.5% alc. **RATING** 94 **DRINK** 2022–2040 $30 MB ✪

Vintage Project Riesling 2022, Eden Valley A textural feast. It's chewy, chalky, puckering and shows deeper, complex fruit characters among minerally elements and light, nutty savouriness. Serious expression here. Scents and flavours of lime, blackcurrant, wet slate and flint. Intense and concentrated, with bristling acidity underlying. Boom. Big impact. Compelling. Screw cap. 12.5% alc. **RATING** 94 **DRINK** 2022–2035 $30 MB ✪

🍷🍷🍷🍷♀ **Rosé 2022, Clare Valley RATING** 93 **DRINK** 2022–2024 $25 MB ✪
429° Shiraz 2021, Clare Valley RATING 93 **DRINK** 2022–2032 $45 MB
Chardonnay 2021, Adelaide Hills RATING 92 **DRINK** 2022–2028 $40 MB
Shiraz 2021, Clare Valley RATING 91 **DRINK** 2022–2030 $30 MB
The Spaniard 2021, Clare Valley RATING 91 **DRINK** 2022–2027 $30 MB

ATR Wines

103 Hard Hill Road, Armstrong, Vic 3377 (postal) **Region** Great Western
T 0457 922 400 **www.**atrwines.com.au **Open** Not **Winemaker** Adam Richardson
Est. 2005 **Dozens** 4000 **Vyds** 7.6ha

Perth-born Adam Richardson began his winemaking career in '95, working for Normans, d'Arenberg and Oakridge along the way. He has held senior winemaking roles, ultimately with TWE America before moving back to Australia with his American wife Eva and children in late '15. In '05 he put down roots in the Grampians region, establishing a vineyard with old shiraz clones from the 19th century and riesling, extending the plantings with tannat, nebbiolo, durif and viognier. At the time of writing in March '23, Adam and Eva plan to return to the US; ATR wines is up for sale. Australia's loss is Oregon's gain.

🍷🍷🍷🍷🍷 **Chockstone Riesling 2022, Grampians** Intensity of flavour is quite remarkable here. This really explodes onto the palate. Lemon, green pineapple, slate and musk characters drive straight and true, start to finish, all the way through to a (very) lengthy finish. This will mature over the long term. Screw cap. 13% alc. **RATING** 95 **DRINK** 2024–2037 $25 CM ✪ ♥

Chockstone Shiraz 2021, Grampians This is where the fun starts. Silken texture, wild flings of spice, sweet/ripe cherry-plum fruit flavour and a long finish, replete with roasted nut, ripe fruit and savoury nuances. Grade A Grampians shiraz, open, sweet-fruited and accessible but with a lot going on besides. Screw cap. 14.5% alc. **RATING** 95 **DRINK** 2023–2030 $28 CM ✪

🍷🍷🍷🍷♀ **Man Jack Shiraz 2021, Grampians RATING** 90 **DRINK** 2023–2027 $20 CM ✪
Hard Hill Road Nebbiolo 2020, Grampians RATING 90 **DRINK** 2024–2029 $50 CM

Atze's Corner Wines

451 Research Road, Nuriootpa, SA 5355 **Region** Barossa Valley
T 0407 621 989 **www.**atzes.com **Open** Fri–Sat 1–5, Sun & public hols 12.30–4.30
Winemaker Andrew Kalleske **Est.** 2005 **Dozens** 2500 **Vyds** 30ha

The Kalleske family has widespread involvement in grapegrowing and winemaking in the Barossa Valley. This venture is that of Andrew Kalleske, son of John and Barb. In 1975 they purchased the Atze vineyard, which included a small block of shiraz planted in 1912, but with additional plantings along the way, including more shiraz in 1951. There are smaller plantings of mataro, petit verdot, grenache, cabernet, tempranillo, viognier, petite sirah, graciano, montepulciano, vermentino and aglianico. The wines are all estate-grown and made onsite.

Boehm's Black Single Vineyard Shiraz 2019, Barossa Valley A deeply coloured, robust shiraz that shows plenty of deep blackberry, dark plum and black cherry fruit notes cut through with baking spices, cedar, tobacco leaf, pencil lead, salted licorice and rum and raisin chocolate. Full bodied with gobs of black fruit and a none-too-shy oak presence finishing with a powdery tannin grip and a cassis-like tail. Good stuff. Cork. 15% alc. RATING 94 DRINK 2023–2025 $80 DB

Forgotten Hero Shiraz 2019, Barossa Valley RATING 93 DRINK 2023–2033 $130 DB
Eddies Old Vine Shiraz 2019, Barossa Valley RATING 93 DRINK 2023–2033 $55 DB
John & Barb's Old Vine Grenache 2020, Barossa Valley RATING 91 DRINK 2023–2028 $60 DB
Wild Rose Vermentino 2022, Barossa Valley RATING 90 DRINK 2023–2025 $25 DB ✪

Audrey Wilkinson

750 De Beyers Road, Pokolbin, NSW 2320 **Region** Hunter Valley
T (02) 4998 1866 **www**.audreywilkinson.com.au **Open** 7 days 10–5
Winemaker Xanthe Hatcher **Est.** 1866 **Vyds** 47ha
Audrey Wilkinson is one of the most historic and beautiful properties in the Hunter Valley, known for its stunning views and pristine vineyards. It was the first vineyard planted in Pokolbin, in 1866. The property was acquired in '04 by the late Brian Agnew and has been owned and operated by his family since. The wines, made predominantly from estate-grown grapes, are released in 3 tiers: Audrey Wilkinson Series, Winemakers Selection and Reserve.

Museum Release The Lake Shiraz 2014, Hunter Valley The colour is an extraordinary bright crimson, moving into an extremely expressive bouquet of poached plum, red cherries and spices. Has just reached maturity, but the changes that the next decade will bring will result in a graceful wine that speaks of the variety and place. Screw cap. 14.5% alc. RATING 97 DRINK 2023–2034 $225 JH
Museum Release The Ridge Semillon 2013, Hunter Valley So fresh and lively that it's hard to remember this wine is 10 years old, which leaves me in a quandary. Should it be consumed before it moves into the honey/toast/ butter spectrum of most wines its age? The easy solution is to say drink now, but drink some, keep some is the better approach. Screw cap. 11% alc. RATING 97 DRINK 2023–2028 $75 JH ✪
Museum Release The Ridge Reserve Semillon 2010, Hunter Valley The bouquet is good and the palate is exquisite with its purity and perfect balance. It retains its acidity, but it's no more than a polite reminder of the variety and the skill of the winemaking team that was responsible. Flavours? Well, citrus/lime, honeysuckle, apple and grapefruit, all in lockstep and harmony of a high order. Screw cap. 11% alc. RATING 97 DRINK 2023–2025 $100 JH

The Ridge Semillon 2022, Hunter Valley The wine has still to pick up any colour, but it has a juicy element that sets it apart. Ready to enjoy now or in a decade, with progressive changes of lime/lemon on lightly browned toast, the finish with steely acidity that provides the backbone. Screw cap. 11.5% alc. RATING 96 DRINK 2023–2034 $55 JH ✪
The Oakdale Chardonnay 2022, Hunter Valley Very well made and balanced, its bouquet and palate complex but perfectly balanced, the finish likewise. Elegant, and with finesse. Screw cap. 12.5% alc. RATING 96 DRINK 2023–2032 $65 JH ✪
Museum Release The Oakdale Chardonnay 2014, Hunter Valley From a block of vines that were 40yo at vintage (thus almost 50yo now). There's a

line of grapefruit running through a challenging and complex wine with more than a hint of Burgundy in its make-up. Travelling well. Screw cap. 12.9% alc. **RATING** 96 **DRINK** 2023-2033 $120 JH

Semillon 2022, Hunter Valley This leaps out of the blocks like an Olympic sprinter at the start of a 100m race. Lemons (green and Meyer) and Granny Smith apple are lashed by razor-sharp acidity. Drink tonight or in 30 years time. Screw cap. 12% alc. **RATING** 95 **DRINK** 2023-2053 $25 JH ✪

Marsh Estate Semillon 2022, Hunter Valley Dry-grown vines approaching 50yo. The balance between the citrus-oriented flavour and its minerally acidity is first-class, immediately signalling the cool vintage. The interplay between lemon, grapefruit and Granny Smith apple is particularly attractive. Screw cap. 11.5% alc. **RATING** 95 **DRINK** 2023-2032 $45 JH ✪

Winemakers Selection Verdelho 2022, Hunter Valley It's difficult to raise expectations with verdelho. You might guess this wine is an exceptional example, and you'd be right. This is the best Hunter verdelho I can remember: a lovely cage of grapefruit zest draws you back again and again, freshening the mouthfeel as it does so. Screw cap. 12.5% alc. **RATING** 95 **DRINK** 2023-2025 $35 JH ✪

Winemakers Selection Gewürztraminer 2022, Hunter Valley Stares you down with its relentless assault of gewürztraminer. If ever a gewürztraminer can be described as medium bodied (on the back label) this is one – aromas and flavours of yellow peach, this is it, plus. Screw cap. 11.5% alc. **RATING** 95 **DRINK** 2023-2026 $35 JH ✪

Winemakers Selection Chardonnay 2022, Hunter Valley While relatively light in body, the wine is complex, and very well balanced, all the inputs harmonious. Screw cap. 12.5% alc. **RATING** 94 **DRINK** 2023-2031 $35 JH ✪

♟♟♟♟♟ **Winemakers Selection Semillon 2022, Hunter Valley** **RATING** 93 **DRINK** 2023-2032 $35 JH ✪

Rosé 2022, Hunter Valley **RATING** 92 **DRINK** 2023-2025 $25 JH ✪

Auld Family Wines   ★★★★

21 Sydenham Road, Norwood, SA 5067 (postal) **Region** Barossa Valley
T 0433 079 202 **www**.auldfamilywines.com **Open** Not **Winemaker** Simon Adams
Est. 2018 **Dozens** 7000

The Barossa-based Auld family has been involved with wine for 6 generations; the most recent, Jock and Sam Auld, founded this new brand. They rightly celebrate their family history, starting with Patrick Auld, who arrived in SA in 1842 and purchased 147ha of land at Magill, adjacent to Captain Penfold. Patrick began planting in 1845, achieving fame for Auldana's wines. In 1888, 2nd generation William Patrick Auld started a wine and spirit business in Adelaide named WP Auld and Sons. Today's wines are branded William Patrick, Strawbridge and Wilberforce – the last not the name of a family member, but a horse that Patrick rode across Australia.

♟♟♟♟♟ **Strawbridge Shiraz 2019, Barossa Valley** Deep crimson with aromas of cedar-infused blackberries and dark plums, baking spices with hints of licorice, rum and raisin, turned earth, clove, blackberry jam and poached figs. There is a solid plinth of crème de cassis-like fruit at the core of this wine, spice and licorice notes coil around it and fine, sandy tannins and sapid acidity provide the frame. Screw cap. 15% alc. **RATING** 91 **DRINK** 2023-2028 $42 DB

Wilberforce Riesling 2022, Eden Valley Pale straw in the glass with aromas of Bickford's lime cordial, orange blossom, dried herbs, crushed stone, freshly cut fennel and a waft of marzipan. Slatey and dry on the palate with a light sheen of dried herbs dusting the lime and green apple fruits, a minerally acidity tightening things up and focusing on the finish. Screw cap. 11% alc. **RATING** 90 **DRINK** 2023-2026 $35 DB

Austin's Wines

870 Steiglitz Road, Sutherlands Creek, Vic 3331 **Region** Geelong
T (03) 5281 1799 **www**.austinswines.com.au **Open** Thurs–Mon 11am–5pm
Winemaker Dwayne Cunningham **Viticulturist** Alex Demeo **Est.** 1982
Dozens 25 000 **Vyds** 61.5ha
Pamela and Richard Austin have quietly built their business from a tiny base, and it has
flourished. The vineyard has been progressively extended to just over 60ha. Son Scott and his
partner Belinda, both with a varied but successful career outside the wine industry, took over
management and ownership in '08. The quality of the wines is admirable. In '22 they opened
a new cellar door in a converted shearing shed.

ŸŸŸŸŸ **Moorabool Valley Riesling 2021, Geelong** Bright green gold. Subtle with
aromas of fresh lime, orange blossom and jasmine. Chalky textured, yet with a
lovely line of acidity running through it. The finish is refreshing with an energetic
lime twist. Screw cap. 12.2% alc. **RATING** 95 **DRINK** 2022-2033 $25 PR ❂

Moorabool Valley Riesling 2022, Geelong Bright green gold. Both
delicate and expressive with aromas of makrut lime, orange blossom, lemon oil
and jasmine. Succulent yet taut and with very bright acidity. Finishes pithy, dry
and long. A wine of considerable promise. Screw cap. 12.4% alc. **RATING** 94
DRINK 2023-2032 $35 PR ❂

Moorabool Valley Pinot Noir 2021, Geelong Bright cherry red, there's
a touch of reduction which blows off with a quick swirl to reveal attractive
raspberry fruit, a hint of Provençal herbs and some complex charcuterie notes.
Creamy textured and well weighted, this is a nicely poised and put-together wine.
Screw cap. 13.3% alc. **RATING** 94 **DRINK** 2022-2026 $50 PR

ŸŸŸŸŸ **Moorabool Valley Shiraz 2021, Geelong RATING** 93 **DRINK** 2022-2028
$49 PR
6Ft6 Rosé 2022, Geelong RATING 92 **DRINK** 2022-2024 $25 PR ❂
Moorabool Valley Chardonnay 2021, Geelong RATING 92
DRINK 2022-2026 $48 PR
6Ft6 Shiraz 2022, Geelong RATING 91 **DRINK** 2022-2024 $25 PR ❂

Aylesbury Estate ★★★★☆

72 Ratcliffe Road, Ferguson, WA 6236 (postal) **Region** Geographe
T 0427 922 755 **www**.aylesburyestate.com.au **Open** Not **Winemaker** Luke Eckersley,
Damian Hutton **Viticulturist** Ryan Gibbs **Est.** 2015 **Dozens** 6500 **Vyds** 9ha
Ryan and Narelle Gibbs are the 6th generation of the pioneering Gibbs family. When the
family first arrived in 1883, they named the farm Aylesbury, after the town in England
whence they came. For generations the family ran cattle on the 200ha property, but in 1998
they decided to plant 4.2ha of cabernet sauvignon to diversify the business. Merlot (2.5ha)
followed in '01 and sauvignon blanc (1.6ha) in '04. In '08 Ryan and Narelle took over the
business selling the grapes until '15, when they made the first Aylesbury Estate wines. Three
years later, they purchased the nearby 52 Stones vineyard, adding cooler-climate varieties
chardonnay, arneis and gamay to the Aylesbury range.

ŸŸŸŸŸ **The Pater Series Ferguson Valley Cabernet Sauvignon 2020,**
Geographe Medium- to full-weighted with cinching tannins, ebullient perfume
and an array of fruit, spice, oak and cool acidity on show. It's cassis and blackberry
jam in perfume, mint and sage leaf, white pepper and clove. The palate is rich but
controlled, tightens with twiggy tannins and finishes with a lashing of ripe fruit,
spice and herbs. It's quite the tour de force here, done well. Screw cap. 14.5% alc.
RATING 93 **DRINK** 2023-2035 $50 MB
Q05 Ferguson Valley Vermentino 2022, Geographe It's light and lithe,
but not missing glide and satiny texture. There's a great perfume of lime in tonic
water, a touch of ginger and some green tea. The palate is similarly adorned,

though the gingery element is more pronounced and the finish is very refreshing, lemony and yet a little shortbread biscuit savouriness is there, too. Really appealing and generally delightful drinking. Screw cap. 12% alc. **RATING** 92 **DRINK** 2023–2025 $35 MB

B Minor

100 Long Gully Road, Healesville, Vic 3777 (postal) **Region** Victoria
T 0433 591 617 **www**.bminor.com.au **Open** Not **Winemaker** Various **Est.** 2019
Dozens 5000
B Minor was created in '10 with a focus on fresh, creative wines specifically targeting on-premise and specialty retail venues in the US and Australia. In '20, Qiqi Fu bought out a partner in B Minor and runs the business, enlisting Best's Wines and others as contract winemakers. Qiqi Fu now principally sells B Minor wines through its website in addition to Melbourne retailers and restaurants.

🍷🍷🍷🍷 **Riesling 2022, Victoria** Fragrant florals and citrus, some white peach and apple, mark this riesling as quality all the way. Crunches its way across a taut palate in bright acidity with a crisp, chalky texture and a touch of lemon-drop sweetness to close. Screw cap. 11.5% alc. **RATING** 90 **DRINK** 2022–2028 $30 JP

Baileys of Glenrowan

779 Taminick Gap Road, Glenrowan, Vic 3675 **Region** Glenrowan
T (03) 5766 1600 **www**.baileysofglenrowan.com **Open** 7 days 10–4.30
Winemaker Paul Dahlenburg, Elizabeth Kooij **Est.** 1870 **Dozens** 25 000 **Vyds** 144ha
Paul Dahlenburg has been in charge of Baileys since 1998, overseeing an expansion in the vineyard and the construction of a 2000t capacity winery. The cellar door has a heritage museum, winery viewing deck, contemporary art gallery and landscaped grounds. Baileys has also picked up the pace with its Muscat and Topaque, reintroducing the Winemakers Selection at the top of the tree, while continuing the larger volume Founder series. Casella Family brands purchased the brand and the Glenrowan property from TWE in December '17. The vineyards and winery have been steadily undergoing conversion to organic since '11, producing the first full range of certified organic table wines from the '19 vintage.

🍷🍷🍷🍷 **Winemakers Selection Rare Old Topaque NV, Glenrowan** Deep, burnished walnut-brown hues indicate some serious average age here. The aromas confirm it with intense burnt toffee, panforte, dark chocolate, prune, malt extract and grilled hazelnuts. It's dense, sweet and complex, a mouthful of not only richness but history. Memorable. 375ml. Vinolok. 17.5% alc. **RATING** 96 $75 JP ✪
Winemakers Selection Rare Old Muscat NV, Glenrowan If this doesn't put a smile on a wine drinker's face, nothing will. An impressive amalgam of age, oak, spirit and the blender's art brings rich panforte, sticky date pudding, fig, raisin and rancio nuttiness together seamlessly, deliciously, lusciously sweet. So complex and so well priced. 375ml. Vinolok. 17.5% alc. **RATING** 95 $75 JP
VP 140 2021, Glenrowan A different take on a vintage fortified courtesy of Portuguese grape varieties. A heavy influence of dried herbs and mint, bergamot and violet florals on the raspberry and blueberry fruits. Tannins are equally pronounced but all nicely integrated through the fortifying spirit. It's early days for this VP. Give it the time it needs and deserves. Screw cap. 17.6% alc. **RATING** 94 **DRINK** 2023–2035 $30 JP ✪

🍷🍷🍷🍷 **Organic Durif 2021, Glenrowan RATING** 93 **DRINK** 2022–2034 $29 JP ✪
Founder Series Classic Topaque NV, Glenrowan RATING 93 $35 JP ✪
Founder Series Classic Muscat NV, Glenrowan RATING 93 $35 JP ✪
Organic Shiraz 2021, Glenrowan RATING 92 **DRINK** 2022–2028 $29 JP ✪
1920s Block Shiraz 2021, Glenrowan RATING 92 **DRINK** 2022–2028 $25 JP ✪
Organic Small Batch Series Fiano 2022, Glenrowan RATING 90 **DRINK** 2022–2026 $23 JP ✪

bakkheia

2718 Ferguson Road, Lowden, WA 6240 **Region** Geographe
T (08) 9732 1394 **www.**bakkheia.com.au **Open** By appt **Winemaker** Michael Edwards
Est. 2006 **Dozens** 1000 **Vyds** 3ha

This is the retirement venture of Michael and Ilonka Edwards. They moved to the Preston Valley in WA in '05 and purchased a property that had a patch of 1999-planted cabernet sauvignon. They now have 3ha of grenache, mourvèdre, graciano, tempranillo, cabernet sauvignon, shiraz and malbec; purchasing chardonnay and sauvignon blanc from a neighbour. They have an unusual approach to marketing, starting with the winery name linked to the Roman words for Bacchus and bacchanalian frenzies induced by wine, lots of wine. Wines are available through a membership system.

ㅸㅸㅸㅸㅸ **The Groszman Graciano 2021, Geographe** A delight, repping the best of the variety in tart, crunchy, red berry acidity, crisp, red plum fruit character, sour-sweet amaro-like tang and faint sea spray and alpine herb characters in the mix. Sits at just over medium weight but tannins tug the wine in line beautifully and there's structure in spades. It's a serious red, but drinkability is high. A coup. Screw cap. 14.5% alc. **RATING** 94 **DRINK** 2023–2029 $38 MB ✪

Balancing Heart

221 Old Wallangarra Road, Wyberba, Qld 4382 **Region** Granite Belt
T 1300 000 221 **www.**balancingheart.com.au **Open** Mon–Thurs 10–430, Fri–Sun 10–9
Winemaker Mike Hayes **Est.** 2020

Greg Kentish purchased the Balancing Rock vineyard in '20, renaming it Balancing Heart after a heart-shaped granite boulder in the vineyard. Assisted by famed local winemaker Mike Hayes, the project has accelerated in quality, with a focus on shiraz, chardonnay, verdelho, viognier, petit verdot and pinot gris. Balancing Heart is also a focal point for wine tourism, with accommodation and diverse cellar door offerings.

ㅸㅸㅸㅸㅸ **Energy & Grace Chardonnay 2022, Granite Belt** This has a beautiful, even texture, great flow, layers of sweet spice and gently toasted nut savouriness among briny-steely acidity, tart nectarine and cool green apple characters – the perfume and palate match such descriptors. It's a wine where fruit character and savouriness are in sync. Compelling drinking. Screw cap. 12% alc. **RATING** 94 **DRINK** 2023–2030 $39 MB ✪ ♥

ㅸㅸㅸㅸㅸ **Essence & Bloom Verdelho 2022, Granite Belt** **RATING** 93 **DRINK** 2023–2028 $33 MB ✪
Metamorphism & Texture Viognier 2022, Granite Belt **RATING** 93 **DRINK** 2023–2027 $38 MB
Small Batch Shiraz 2021, Granite Belt **RATING** 93 **DRINK** 2022–2035 $85 MB
Reserve Sagrantino 2021, Granite Belt **RATING** 93 **DRINK** 2022–2030 $100 MB
Reserve Carmenere 2021, Granite Belt **RATING** 93 **DRINK** 2022–2030 $100 MB
Verdelho 2021, Granite Belt **RATING** 93 **DRINK** 2022–2027 $33 MB ✪
Rock Shiraz 2021, Granite Belt **RATING** 93 **DRINK** 2022–2030 $75 MB
Viognier 2021, Granite Belt **RATING** 93 **DRINK** 2022–2025 $38 MB
Aphrodisia & Romanticism White Liquer Muscat 2022, Granite Belt **RATING** 93 **DRINK** 2022–2024 $33 MB ✪
High Altitude Shiraz 2021, Granite Belt **RATING** 92 **DRINK** 2022–2030 $65 MB
Wild Yeast Pinot Grigio 2021, Granite Belt **RATING** 92 **DRINK** 2022–2025 $55 MB
Museum Release Lagrein 2016, Granite Belt **RATING** 92 **DRINK** 2022–2025 $55 MB

Mineralogy & Surreal Olde Worlde Shiraz 2019, Granite Belt RATING 91
DRINK 2022-2027 $48 MB
Archaeology & Baroque Museum Release Montepulciano 2016,
Riverland RATING 90 DRINK 2022-2025 $55 MB

Balgownie Estate ★★★★★

Hermitage Road, Maiden Gully, Vic 3551 **Region** Bendigo
T (03) 5449 6222 **www.balgownieestatewines.com.au Open** 7 days 11–4
Winemaker Tony Winspear **Est.** 1969 **Dozens** 10 000 **Vyds** 35.28ha
Balgownie Estate is the senior citizen of Bendigo, its original vineyard plantings now 50 years
old. The estate also has a cellar door at 1309 Melba Hwy in the Yarra Valley, where operations
fit in neatly with the Bendigo wines. In Apr '16 a Chinese investment company purchased
the Balgownie Bendigo and Yarra Valley operations for $29 million.

ΨΨΨΨΨ **Old Vine Shiraz 2018, Bendigo** A variety of black fruits, licorice, dark
chocolate, earth, leather and a world of spice awaits. The richness of fruit is played
against a super-confident background of toasty vanillin oak still in the process
of merging. Tannins aren't shy, but they ooze class. Makes a grand statement
about shiraz from this part of the world. Screw cap. 14.5% alc. **RATING** 96
DRINK 2023-2034 $125 JP
Rock Block Shiraz 2020, Bendigo A measured shiraz constructed to reveal its
considerable charms in an almost leisurely manner. An appealing mix of earth,
spice and dark fruited aromas with underlying tapenade, chocolate and coffee
grounds. A whisper of regional bay leaf resonates without intrusion, and yet, it's
just the tip of this interesting vinous iceberg. Screw cap. 14% alc. **RATING** 95
DRINK 2022-2033 $65 JP
Centre Block Shiraz 2020, Bendigo A fine, contrasting shiraz to its Rock
Block sibling with attractive, earthy aromatics and medium-bodied style. The
result is an almost effortless balance. Briar, earth, black fruits, bay leaf and a light
pepperiness set against a firm but pleasing background of supple tannin and just-so-
toasty oak. It's a keeper. Screw cap. 14% alc. **RATING** 95 **DRINK** 2022-2032 $65 JP
Pinot Noir 2021, Yarra Valley Combines Yarra Valley elegance and red-
berried plushness in the most satisfying way. Fragrant cranberry, raspberry and
red cherry with a gentle dusting of spice. The palate delivers all of that with
an additional herbal/briar earthiness. Gathers pace as it unfolds with an almost
understated subtlety thanks to even-handed tannins and oak. Screw cap. 13.2% alc.
RATING 94 **DRINK** 2022-2027 $50 JP

ΨΨΨΨΨ **Viognier 2021, Bendigo** RATING 93 DRINK 2022-2027 $35 JP ✪
Railway Block Shiraz 2020, Bendigo RATING 93 DRINK 2022-2032 $65 JP
Shiraz 2020, Bendigo RATING 92 DRINK 2022-2030 $48 JP
Chardonnay 2019, Yarra Valley RATING 91 DRINK 2022-2027 $50 JP

Ballandean Estate Wines ★★★☆

354 Sundown Road, Ballandean, Qld 4382 **Region** Granite Belt
T (07) 4684 1226 **www.ballandeanestate.com Open** 7 days 9–5 **Winemaker** Boxi Zhen
Viticulturist Angelo Puglisi, Robyn Robertson **Est.** 1932 **Dozens** 10 000 **Vyds** 34.2ha
A rock of ages in the Granite Belt, owned by the ever-cheerful and charming Angelo and Mary
Puglisi. Ballandean Estate's cool climate, high altitude and granitic terroir deliver national and
international award-winning wines. In '23, Boxi Zhen joined the team as winemaker, taking
the reins from Dylan Rhymer, who had been with the winery for 22 vintages.

ΨΨΨΨΨ **Saperavi 2019, Granite Belt** Mellow, balanced and medium- to fuller-weight
expression done with aplomb. It's an aromatic red wine with fine, well-integrated
and firming tannins set among ripe black fruits and loaded with woody, savoury,
smoky spice. Scents of black cherry, ripe plum, smoked paprika, clove and
lavender. Flavours similar but lifted on an amaro-like tang of acidity with a sense
of refreshment with each sip. Cork. 13.2% alc. **RATING** 92 **DRINK** 2022-2030
$45 MB

Balnaves of Coonawarra

15517 Riddoch Highway, Coonawarra, SA 5263 **Region** Coonawarra
T (08) 8737 2946 **www**.balnaves.com.au **Open** Mon–Fri 9–5, w'ends 11.30–4.30
Winemaker Jacinta Jenkins, Pete Bissell **Viticulturist** Pete Balnaves **Est.** 1975
Dozens 10 000 **Vyds** 74.33ha

Grapegrower, viticultural consultant and vigneron, Doug Balnaves, and wife Annette, started in the wine industry in the early '70s. In '90 they were joined by daughter Kirsty and son Pete in what remains a family-run business. Jacinta Jenkins assumed the mantle of winemaker with Pete Bissell's retirement in '20 – who remains on a casual consulting basis. The wines are invariably excellent, often outstanding. Coonawarra at its best.

🍷🍷🍷🍷 **Cabernet Sauvignon 2020, Coonawarra** This wine is perfectly structured and flavoured. Blackcurrant, dark chocolate, bay leaf and violet flavours come threaded with tobacco and assorted fragrant herbs. It's all built on tannin, in a way, and yet the fruit flavours flood straight through, like a wave. Peer out towards the horizon, and that's where this wine's future lies. Screw cap. 14.5% alc. **RATING** 96 **DRINK** 2027–2045 $40 CM ✪

Chardonnay 2021, Coonawarra Bright, striking straw-green hue. Almost too perfect, fruit and oak as one, balanced and long in the mouth. Granny Smith apple, Meyer lemon and blanched almond marry delicacy with considerable length. Screw cap. 13% alc. **RATING** 95 **DRINK** 2023–2039 $32 JH ✪

Shiraz 2020, Coonawarra Elevated pepper spice and floral notes make for an attractive introduction. Ripe, red berried fruit flavours rush straight up in support, though a tension to both the acidity and tannin makes all this exuberance feel controlled. This is a medium-bodied wine that's been turned out impeccably. Screw cap. 14.5% alc. **RATING** 94 **DRINK** 2023–2033 $30 CM ✪

🍷🍷🍷🍷 **The Blend 2020, Coonawarra RATING** 93 **DRINK** 2024–2033 $32 CM ✪
Cabernet Merlot 2020, Coonawarra RATING 92 **DRINK** 2023–2040 $30 JH ✪

Banca Ridge

22 Caves Road, Stanthorpe, Qld 4380 **Region** Granite Belt
T (07) 4685 5050 **www**.qcwt.edu.au **Open** Tue–Sat 10.30–4 **Winemaker** Arantza Milicua Celador **Est.** 2001 **Dozens** 1500 **Vyds** 1.6ha

Banca Ridge was an initiative of the Stanthorpe State High School, which established the first commercial school winery in Queensland. Plantings have expanded from the initial marsanne and merlot to 10 varieties, including fiano, albariño, tinta cão and petit verdot. Students are involved in all stages of the grape growing and winemaking process under the direction of Arantza Milicua Celador. More recently the business has become part of the Queensland College of Wine Tourism, designed to train students in the wine, hospitality and tourism industry, and the wines produced are a credit to the school and the program.

🍷🍷🍷🍷 **Mondeuse Noire 2019, Granite Belt** This is a light and fragrant red wine shaped with silty tannins and lifted on pleasing, fresh acidity. Scents of dark cherry, blood orange, game meat and minty herbs. Flavours splashed with ripe plummy fruit characters and seasoned with clove spice. It's an appealing, savoury-leaning, slurpable red. Screw cap. 12.3% alc. **RATING** 90 **DRINK** 2022–2024 $28 MB

Bangor Vineyard

20 Blackman Bay Road, Dunalley, Tas 7177 **Region** Southern Tasmania
T 03 6253 5558 **www**.bangorshed.com.au **Open** 7 days 11–5 **Winemaker** Tasmanian Vintners **Viticulturist** Matt Dunbabin **Est.** 2010 **Dozens** 4000 **Vyds** 4ha

Bangor Vineyard is a 6200ha property on the Forestier Peninsula with 5100ha of native forest, grasslands and wetlands and 35km of coastline. Matt and Vanessa Dunbabin have PhDs in plant ecology and plant nutrition, putting beyond question their ability to protect this wonderful property – until 2000ha were burnt in the '13 bushfires that devastated their local town of Dunalley and surrounding areas. They established a cellar door in partnership with Tom and Alice Gray from Fulham Aquaculture, also badly affected by the fires, and the Bangor Vineyard Shed was born. The vineyard is planted to 1.5ha each of pinot noir and pinot gris, and 1ha of chardonnay.

Late Disgorged Blanc de Blanc Chardonnay 2016, Tasmania Pale straw with a fine, lively bead and mousse. Aromas of pure green apple and citrus fruits with hints of freshly baked biscuits, soft spice, tarte Tatin, lemon curd, buttered toast, white flowers and stone. Some lovely lemon tart and brioche notes flow in on the palate, which shows complexity, clarity, detail and a sizzling acid cadence, finishing dry and pure. Diam. 12% alc. **RATING** 95 **DRINK** 2023-2033 $110 DB

Abel Tasman Pinot Noir 2020, Tasmania A bright, light ruby in the glass with detailed aromas of red cherry, redcurrant and raspberry coulis dotted with exotic spice and hints of sous bois, mushroom broth, rhubarb, game meats, dried citrus rind and orange blossom. Such a pretty wine in the mouth with lifted red fruits, an array of spices, light amaro notes and a gamey swoosh as it sails away with a light tannin grip and bright acidity. Screw cap. 13% alc. **RATING** 94 **DRINK** 2023-2030 $55 DB

Abel Tasman Pinot Noir 2021, Tasmania **RATING** 93 **DRINK** 2023-2030 $55 DB

Méthode Traditionelle Vintage 2019, Tasmania **RATING** 92 **DRINK** 2023-2027 $55 DB

Maria Pinot Rosé 2022, Tasmania **RATING** 90 **DRINK** 2023-2025 $40 DB

Banks Road   ★★★★★

600 Banks Road, Marcus Hill, Vic 3222 **Region** Geelong
T 0455 594 391 **www.**banksroad.com.au **Open** Fri–Sun 11–5 **Winemaker** William Derham **Est.** 2001 **Dozens** 2000 **Vyds** 6ha

Banks Road is a family-owned and -operated winery on the Bellarine Peninsula. The estate vineyard is adopting biodynamic principles, eliminating the use of insecticides and moving to eliminate the use of all chemicals on the land. The winery not only processes the Banks Road grapes, but also makes wine for other small producers in the area. All in all, an impressive business.

Blanc de Blancs Chardonnay 2020, Geelong 2.5 years on lees, 5 g/L dosage. Yellow gold with green tinges. Aromas of baked apples, fresh brioche and honey can be found in this gently creamy, balanced and sparkling wine. Ready to drink, this finishes chalky and long. Cork. 12.5% alc. **RATING** 91 **DRINK** 2023-2025 $44 PR

Bellarine Shiraz 2021, Geelong A vibrant crimson red. An immediate and easygoing wine with its aromas of red and dark fruits, spice rack spices and a little cedar from the oak. Medium bodied, this is ready to drink now but there are enough fine, gently chewy and balanced tannins to ensure that this continues to improve over the next 4–5 years. Screw cap. 13.6% alc. **RATING** 91 **DRINK** 2022-2027 $40 PR

Bellarine Pinot Noir 2021, Geelong A light ruby garnet. Bright and immediate with its lifted aromatics of red fruits, spice and incense from 20% whole bunches. Juicy fruited, forward and pliant, this is ready to drink and enjoy. Screw cap. 13.2% alc. **RATING** 91 **DRINK** 2022-2026 $40 PR

Bellarine Chardonnay 2021, Geelong Bright straw with green tinges. A gentle creaminess on the bouquet together with melon and white peach and a little vanilla pod from the already well-integrated oak. The palate is similarly opulent and textural, adding to the wine's early appeal. Screw cap. 12.4% alc. **RATING** 90 **DRINK** 2022-2025 $40 PR

Bannockburn Vineyards ★★★★★

92 Kelly Lane, Bannockburn, Vic 3331 **Region** Geelong
T (03) 5281 1363 **www.**bannockburnvineyards.com **Open** By appt
Winemaker Matthew Holmes **Viticulturist** Lucas Grigsby **Est.** 1974 **Dozens** 6000
Vyds 21.2ha

The late Stuart Hooper had a deep love for the wines of Burgundy, and was able to drink the best. When he established Bannockburn, it was inevitable that pinot noir and chardonnay would form the major part of the plantings, with lesser amounts of riesling, sauvignon blanc, cabernet sauvignon, shiraz and merlot. Bannockburn is still owned by members of the Hooper family, who continue to respect Stuart's strong belief in making wines that reflect the flavours of the certified-organic vineyard.

♆♆♆♆♆ **Shiraz 2019, Geelong** Rated as a superlative red vintage. It's vibrant and light on its feet, covered with all the cool-grown epaulettes, the fruits more black than red and spices and pepper high, wide and handsome. Screw cap. 12.6% alc. **RATING** 96 **DRINK** 2023–2040 $45 JH ✪
De La Roche 2018, Geelong A deliciously supple wine, the whole bunches adding a twist of forest to the blackberry and plum fruit that illuminates both the bouquet and palate. As ready now as it will ever be. Screw cap. 13.5% alc. **RATING** 96 **DRINK** 2023–2033 $55 JH ✪

Barangaroo Boutique Wines ★★★★

928 Plush-Hannans Road, Lower Norton, Vic 3401 **Region** Western Victoria
T 0400 570 673 **www.**barangaroowines.com.au **Open** Sat–Sun 12–4.30
Winemaker Ron Snep **Viticulturist** Chris McClure **Est.** 2005 **Dozens** 600
Vyds 2.29ha

Chris and Sheila McClure established their vineyard on a ridge running north to south, which allows for morning sun, free drainage and frost protection, with soils of buckshot gravel loam. Plantings began in '05, the largest being just under 1ha of shiraz, with the first vintage made in '10.

♆♆♆♆♀ **The Cromdale Reserve Shiraz 2021, Western Victoria** Reserve wines tend to offer more of everything, whether it's needed or not, and thankfully this wine doesn't fall into that trap. It is more elegant than the standard shiraz, though it still has plenty of body, and it's more complex too. Smoked meat, saltbush, roasted plum and tomato leaf characters make for an interesting combination, and the taut control of the finish works well, too. Screw cap. 13.4% alc. **RATING** 93 **DRINK** 2024–2034 $40 CM
Shiraz 2021, Western Victoria Traditional style of Australian shiraz with plum, toast and coffee-bean flavours charging boldly through the palate. It will take time to build complexity but if you're looking for sheer, straightforward flavour, this delivers it in spades. Screw cap. 13.4% alc. **RATING** 92 **DRINK** 2023–2031 $28 CM ✪
Merlot 2021, Western Victoria The flavours run free, the texture feels soft, the tannin is served al dente. With raspberry, violets, mint and chocolate, the enjoyment factor is high. Screw cap. 14.1% alc. **RATING** 90 **DRINK** 2023–2027 $35 CM
The Cromdale Reserve Cabernet Sauvignon 2021, Western Victoria Matured in new French oak for 18 months. Oak and fruit sit slightly separate and will take time to harmonise. Smoked cedarwood and blackberry, bay leaf and fragrant herb characters make for appealing, medium-weight drinking. Screw cap. 13.7% alc. **RATING** 90 **DRINK** 2024–2031 $40 CM

Barossa Boy Wines ★★★★

Underground Barossa, 161 Murray Street, Tanunda, SA 5382 **Region** Barossa Valley
T (08) 8563 7550 **www.**barossaboywines.com.au **Open** Mon–Fri 10–4, Sat–Sun 11–5
Winemaker Trent Burge **Est.** 2016 **Dozens** 3500

Sixth-generation Barossan Trent Burge is the son of Grant and Helen Burge, and a self-styled country boy who liked nothing better than exploring the family's 356ha of vineyards. In '06 he joined the Grant Burge business, learning every facet of winemaking and marketing. In Feb '16, Accolade acquired the business, making it inevitable that Trent would strike out on his own. The slick website, high quality labelling and packaging of his Barossa Boy Wines bear witness to his marketing experience. His grapes come from vineyards in special sites across the Barossa and Eden valleys, and it's a fair bet the family vineyards play a large role in that.

ŸŸŸŸŸ **Cheeky Tilly Riesling 2022, Eden Valley** Pale straw with an inviting nose of Bickford's lime cordial, lemon and grapefruit with hints of Christmas lily and orange blossom, crushed quartz, grapefruit zest, almond paste and a peek of marzipan and fennel further back. Excellent drive and focus with a crisp, dry finish that lingers with lime and light blossom notes. Screw cap. 12% alc. **RATING** 91 **DRINK** 2023–2030 $30 DB

Young Wisdom Mataro 2020, Barossa A deeply fruited mataro. As is often the case with the variety, there is a sense of broodiness to its meaty, dark-spiced blackberry and dark plum fruits with hints of turned earth, roasting game, clove, cedar, coal dust, dried summer berry fruits and a whiff of leather in the distance. Tight, chalky tannin architecture is on display with a thick, powerful fruit flow on the finish. Diam. 15% alc. **RATING** 90 **DRINK** 2023–2029 $50 DB

Double Trouble Shiraz Cabernet Sauvignon 2020, Barossa A deeply coloured Barossa blend showing characters of blackberry and black cherry fruits with hints of licorice, five-spice, choc-mint, earth, cedar, coal dust and cocoa powder. Thick and muscular cassis-like fruit on the palate, a touch of tobacco leaf peeking through, compact, tightly packed tannin and a rolling tide of kirsch on the finish. Screw cap. 14.5% alc. **RATING** 90 **DRINK** 2023–2030 $30 DB

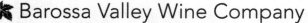

Barossa Valley Wine Company ★★★☆

275 Sir Donald Bradman Drive, Cowandilla, SA 5033 (postal) **Region** Barossa Valley **T** 1800 571 130 **www.bvwc.com.au Open** Not **Winemaker** Roxanne Kloppers **Est.** 2001
Established in '01, the Barossa Valley Wine Company produces wines that span the classic grape varieties of the region: shiraz, cabernet sauvignon and GSM blends along with a smattering of others including tempranillo and montepulciano. Based in Lyndoch in the Barossa's Southern Grounds, the wines are made by Roxanne Kloppers who has vintages under her belt from wineries across Australia along with Chateau Montelena in Napa Valley and Maison Chapoutier in the Rhône Valley.

ŸŸŸŸŸ **Stockyard Shiraz 2020, Barossa Valley** Bright crimson with aromas of vibrant blood plum and blackberry fruit underlined by hints of baking spices, licorice, dark chocolate and earth. There is a nice bright flow to the fruit profile, fine tannin grip and pure, ripe fruit and spice notes on the medium-length finish. Screw cap. 14.5% alc. **RATING** 91 **DRINK** 2023–2029 $40 DB

Barr-Eden Estate ★★★★

PO Box 117, Nuriootpa, SA 5355 **Region** Barossa Valley
T 0437 091 277 **www.loveovergold.com.au Open** Not **Winemaker** Contract **Est.** 2014
Dozens 400 **Vyds** 6.25ha
Loved by all who knew him, the late Bob McLean stood large over many parts of the SA wine industry and in '97 he purchased a block of shiraz in the Eden Valley. He was a friend of Joel Matschoss, who looked after the vineyard in the last years of Bob's life. In '14 Joel showed the fruit to Pierre-Henri Morel, newly arrived from the northern Rhône, where he had been Michel Chapoutier's right-hand man. Pierre-Henri was so impressed, he and Joel purchased the fruit, vinified it and their Love Over Gold label was born. A joint venture followed between Joel, Pierre-Henri, Michael Twelftree and Tim Hower to acquire the property with plans to grow.

ŸŸŸŸŸ **Dreams of Gold Mengler's Hill Shiraz 2021, Eden Valley** This is an attractive Eden Valley style, with spicy cherry fruit doing the heavy lifting.

It's not too oaky or extractive, all for the good of the wine. Screw cap. 14.5% alc.
RATING 92 DRINK 2023-2036 $35 JH
Avenue to Gold Mengler's Hill Shiraz 2019, Eden Valley Deep crimson
with a hint of purple and vibrant aromas of macerated plums, blueberry, cherry
and boysenberry. Hints of baking spices, sage, black pepper, licorice, violets, dark
chocolate and turned earth. Fruit rich and opulent with fine, granitic tannins and
a brisk, snappy acid line. Long of finish with a plush, earthy feel. Diam. 14.3% alc.
RATING 92 DRINK 2023-2029 $70 DB

Barrgowan Vineyard ★★★★

30 Pax Parade, Curlewis, Vic 3222 **Region** Geelong
T (03) 5250 3861 **www.**barrgowanvineyard.com.au **Open** By appt **Winemaker** Dick
Simonsen **Viticulturist** Dick Simonsen **Est.** 1993 **Dozens** 125 **Vyds** 0.2ha
Dick and Dib (Elizabeth) Simonsen began planting their shiraz (with 5 clones) in '94,
intending to make wine for their own consumption. With all clones in full production, the
Simonsens make a maximum of 200 dozen and accordingly release small quantities of shiraz,
which sell out quickly. The vines are hand pruned, the grapes hand picked, the must basket
pressed, and all wine movements are by gravity.

🍷🍷🍷🍷 **Simonsens Bellarine Peninsula Shiraz 2021, Geelong** Deeply coloured
with aromas of satsuma plum, pink peppercorns, nutmeg and just a hint of vanilla
bean. Sweetly fruited, this medium- to full-bodied wine will look even better in
another 2–3 years when the firm yet supple tannins begin to shed their winter
coat! Cork. 13.4% alc. RATING 93 DRINK 2022-2027 $40 PR

Barringwood

60 Gillams Road, Lower Barrington, Tas 7306 (postal) **Region** Northern Tasmania
T 0416 017 475 **www.**barringwood.com.au **Open** Not **Winemaker** Jeremy Dineen
Est. 1993 **Dozens** 12 000 **Vyds** 35ha
Barringwood has been producing elegant wines from the ultra-cool climate of northwest
Tasmania for over 20 years, the vines planted in '93. The vineyard is perched on a steep north-
facing slope (overlooking the Don River valley to Bass Strait), with one of the longest growing
seasons in Tasmania allowing the grapes to develop complexity while retaining acidity. Vanessa
and Neil Bagot were captivated by the property, purchasing Barringwood in '12. They
developed new vineyards at Cranbrook and Evandale, with further plantings planned.

🍷🍷🍷🍷 **Tasmanian Cuvée NV, Tasmania** Matured 17 months on lees, 6g/L dosage.
Straw in the glass with a slight blush and an energetic bead and mousse. I like the
stony focus and precision here with notes of red apple and red cherry meshing
with citrus, green apple, light dough notes, white flowers and almond paste.
It's more about a spotlight on the fruit than toasty, yeast-derived characters,
making this wine so lovely, finishing dry, vivid and moreishly delicious. Diam.
12% alc. RATING 93 $36 DB
Mill Block Pinot Noir 2021, Tasmania Seems to be a greater percentage of
whole bunches than the estate pinot, with exotic spice, amaro herbs and a struck-
flint aspect coming through on the nose; perhaps a lick more oak, too. Complex
and alluring with silken cherry fruits and hints of raspberry, shiitake, sous bois
and Chinese roast duck; tannins powdery and the line, sapid, graceful and pure.
Screw cap. 12% alc. RATING 93 DRINK 2023-2032 $70 DB
Estate Pinot Noir 2021, Tasmania A pretty-smelling wine with pinosity to
burn. Notes of spicy, juicy red cherries and strawberries with hints of orange
blossom, forest floor, game meats, fine spice notes, vanilla bean, rhubarb,
mushroom broth and charcuterie. Elegant and savoury with a fine acid line,
plenty of space and detail and an umami swirl on the finish. Good stuff.
Screw cap. 13.9% alc. RATING 92 DRINK 2023-2028 $40 DB
Riesling 2022, Tasmania Pale straw in the glass with aromas of fresh lemon,
grapefruit and lime juice with hints of tangerine rind, orange blossom and crushed

stone. The citrus fruits power along on the palate thanks to a seam of scintillating acidity and the wine finishes crisp, dry and pure with just a tweak of phenolic texture and a sapid, lipsmacking exit. Great drinking. Screw cap. 12.5% alc. **RATING** 91 **DRINK** 2023-2026 $36 DB

Grazier's Pinot Noir 2021, Tasmania A touch of whole bunches in here, methinks, with a light sheen of amaro herbs, struck flint and exotic spice flittering above elegant cherry and raspberry fruits. There is a touch of sour cherry to the acid profile and a distinctly graceful palate shape on the slowly fading finish. Screw cap. 13.5% alc. **RATING** 91 **DRINK** 2023-2029 $60 DB

Pinot Gris 2022, Tasmania Pale straw with inviting aromas of spiced pear, sherbet-edged citrus fruits and a waft of white peach. Hints of marzipan, white flowers and stone complete the picture, and the wine displays a pleasing textural slinkiness and briny acidity, finishing crisp with a plume of softly spiced pear. Screw cap. 13.9% alc. **RATING** 90 **DRINK** 2023-2024 $36 DB

Chardonnay 2021, Tasmania Light straw in the glass with aromas of white peach, citrus and nectarine fruits in creamy oak, soft spice, lemon curd, white flowers, stone and nougat. The fruit tightens and gains speed and focus on the exit. Screw cap. 13% alc. **RATING** 90 **DRINK** 2023-2025 $38 DB

Basalt Wines

1131 Princes Highway, Killarney, Vic 3283 **Region** Henty
T 0429 682 251 www.basaltwines.com **Open** Wed–Sun 10.30–5 **Winemaker** Scott Ireland **Viticulturist** Shane Clancey **Est.** 2002 **Dozens** 800 **Vyds** 2.8ha

Shane and Ali Clancey have turned a former potato paddock into a small, but very successful, wine business. In '02 Shane began planting a multi-clone pinot noir vineyard, plus a small planting of tempranillo. Basalt Wines' grape intake is supplemented by a Drumborg vineyard, including 0.4ha of 26yo MV6 pinot noir and, even more importantly, riesling of the highest quality. Shane is viticulturist, assistant winemaker, wholesaler and runs the cellar door. Ali is involved in various parts of the business, including the small flock of babydoll sheep which graze next to the winery.

ΨΨΨΨΨ **The Bream King Tempranillo 2021, Henty** This is quite beautiful. The mix of savouriness and fruitiness is tipped slightly in favour of the latter, the end result juicy and joyous with plenty of savoury chatter around the edges. Peppercorns, plums, musk and twiggy spice notes with a walnut character to the aftertaste. Very good. Screw cap. 13.5% alc. **RATING** 94 **DRINK** 2025-2033 $42 CM

ΨΨΨΨΨ **Great Ocean Road Pinot Noir 2021, Henty RATING** 93 **DRINK** 2023-2030 $45 CM
The Bream King Tempranillo 2020, Henty RATING 93 **DRINK** 2025-2032 $42 CM
Great Ocean Road Riesling 2022, Henty RATING 92 **DRINK** 2023-2030 $29 CM ✪
Shiraz 2021, Henty RATING 92 **DRINK** 2026-2033 $35 CM

Bass Phillip

16 Hunts Road, Leongatha South, Vic 3953 **Region** Gippsland
T (03) 5664 3366 www.bassphillip.com **Open** By appt **Winemaker** Jean-Marie Fourrier, John Durham **Est.** 1979 **Dozens** 1500 **Vyds** 14ha

Phillip Jones handcrafted tiny quantities of superlative pinot noir which, at its best, had no equal in Australia. Painstaking site selection, ultra-close vine spacing and the very cool climate of South Gippsland are the keys to the magic of Bass Phillip and its eerily burgundian pinots. One of Australia's greatest small producers, it's been heading down a new path since Jones sold the assets (winery, stock and 14ha of vineyards) in May '20 to a syndicate led by Burgundian winemaker Jean-Marie Fourrier (who has known Jones for 14 years) and 2 Singaporeans who already have lucrative wine businesses.

ŸŸŸŸŸ **Reserve Pinot Noir 2021, Gippsland** As complex, as detailed and as precise as you can get. Heady forest floor aromas, dark fruit, black tea, Middle Eastern spices and star anise with a dusting of cocoa. The full-bodied palate is superbly textured and coated in ripe, velvety tannins, cedary oak and refreshing acidity. I tip my hat to legendary winemaker John Durham, who came in a few years ago to help Phillip Jones finish his last vintage. Bravo. Cork. 13.8% alc. **RATING** 97 **DRINK** 2024–2040 $835 JF ♥

Premium Old Vines Chardonnay 2021, Gippsland Tightly focused with pristine fruit of sliced lemon, white peach, powdered ginger, sea spray and umami/nougatine lees, creamy, too, with the oak superbly integrated. Complex, detailed and flavoursome with chalky acidity that corrals all those flavours into obedience, finishing long and pure. What a wine. Cork. 13.4% alc. **RATING** 97 **DRINK** 2023–2035 $112 JF

Reserve Pinot Noir 2020, Gippsland Everything a reserve should be – complex, detailed, distinctive and oh-so elegant. It's heady with florals, spiced cherries, musk, woodsy spices and alluring damp forest-floor aromas. It's fuller bodied with a core of such sweet fruit, including raspberries, but it is ultimately a savoury wine. There's so much going on yet the first impression is one of lightness, before plush tannins create expansion across the palate. It builds, explodes and lingers long. Cork. 14.6% alc. **RATING** 97 **DRINK** 2022–2035 $825 JF

ŸŸŸŸŸ **Estate Old Vines Chardonnay 2021, Gippsland** While there are layers of flavour within, there's also a fine line of acidity keeping this reined in. There seems to be more detail and focus of late, even the colour is a glorious gleaming pale straw. Flavours of stone fruit, ginger spice, grapefruit and pith and fluffy creamy lees with cedary/spicy oak. Cork. 13.2% alc. **RATING** 96 **DRINK** 2023–2031 $85 JF

Premium Old Vines Pinot Noir 2021, Gippsland My, my, what a wine with its depth and structure as much as its beauty and ethereal qualities. While there are the usual dark cherries and heady aromas of baking spices, there's very much a savoury edge to this. Fuller bodied with an abundance of richness and stately raw-silk tannins. This is complex, superbly balanced and built to last a long time. But gee, it's compelling now. Cork. 14% alc. **RATING** 96 **DRINK** 2024–2037 $260 JF

Gewürztraminer 2021, Gippsland It's fabulous to be the pinot noir king and make lovely gewürztraminer on the side. It's even better when the tradition continues. As fragrant as a spring garden with roses, frangipani then musk, lychees and ginger flower chime in. The palate is a delight: textural, rich yet tempered by juicy acidity, a slip of phenolics and while it finishes dry, the upfront fruit leaves a sweet impression. Cork. 13.3% alc. **RATING** 95 **DRINK** 2022–2030 $47 JF ✪

Estate Old Vines Pinot Noir 2021, Gippsland An elegant style, almost gentle with every element from fruit and acidity to tannins neatly in place. It's a complete wine. Red cherry accents, rose petals, charred radicchio and a host of spices for good measure. It continues to unfurl beautifully in the glass. As seamless as it gets thanks to superfine tannins and a powder puff of acidity. Cork. 13.9% alc. **RATING** 95 **DRINK** 2023–2035 $105 JF

Gamay 2021, Gippsland This is gamay-licious with heady aromas and juicy flavours. It has enough seriousness to last some distance yet is irresistible now with its plushness, sweetly accented fruit with charred radicchio and woodsy spices. Medium weighted and filled out by plump if grainy tannins – refreshment guaranteed. Cork. 13.7% alc. **RATING** 95 **DRINK** 2023–2030 $67 JF

Since 1979 Pinot Noir 2021, Gippsland Good news, this is well priced in a Bass Phillip context. Sweet pulpy fruit from macerated black cherries to poached rhubarb and baking spices. Tangy and juicy with some chinotto/amaro complexity. Really good to drink today. Don't wait. Cork. 14.2% alc. **RATING** 94 **DRINK** 2023–2031 $53 JF

ŸŸŸŸŸ **North Side Block Gamay 2021, Gippsland** **RATING** 90 **DRINK** 2022–2026 $50 JF

Bass River Winery ★★★★☆

1835 Dalyston Glen Forbes Road, Glen Forbes, Vic 3990 **Region** Gippsland
T (03) 5678 8252 **www.**bassriverwinery.com **Open** Thurs–Tues 10–5
Winemaker Frank Butera **Viticulturist** Pasquale Butera, Frank Butera **Est.** 1998
Dozens 1500 **Vyds** 6ha
The Butera family's 44ha property supports grass-fed beef and olive groves as well as viticulture. Pinot noir, chardonnay, riesling, merlot and cabernet were first planted here in '98. Both the winemaking and viticulture are handled by father-and-son team Pasquale and Frank. The small production is principally sold through the cellar door, with some retailers and restaurants in the South Gippsland area.

ŸŸŸŸŸ **1835 Pinot Noir 2021, Gippsland** When a pinot is as ethereal yet as defined as this, it's time to down tools, cook dinner and let this take centre stage. While there's complexity, it has many parts coming together: cherries and pips, roses and rosehip, blood orange and zest, sumac and warming spices. All combine harmoniously across a medium-bodied palate met with fine tannins and tangy acidity. A lovely wine. Screw cap. 13% alc. **RATING** 95 **DRINK** 2022-2032 $55 JF

ŸŸŸŸŸ **Single Vineyard Rosé 2022, Gippsland RATING** 92 **DRINK** 2022-2025 $30 JF ✪
River Block Pinot Noir 2021, Gippsland RATING 91 **DRINK** 2022-2027 $40 JF

Battle of Bosworth ★★★★

92 Gaffney Road, Willunga, SA 5172 **Region** McLaren Vale
T (08) 8556 2441 **www.**battleofbosworth.com.au **Open** Mon–Sat 11–5, Sun 12–5
Winemaker Joch Bosworth, Scott McIntosh **Viticulturist** Josh McIntosh **Est.** 1970
Dozens 15 000 **Vyds** 80ha
Owned and run by Joch Bosworth (viticulture and winemaking) and partner Louise Hemsley-Smith (sales and marketing), this winery takes its name from the battle that ended the War of the Roses, fought on Bosworth Field in 1485. The vineyards were established in the early '70s in the foothills of the Mount Lofty Ranges. The vines are fully certified A-grade organic. Shiraz, cabernet sauvignon and chardonnay account for 75% of the plantings. The Spring Seed Wine Co wines are made from estate vineyards.

ŸŸŸŸŸ **Vintage Fortified Touriga 2021, McLaren Vale** Too often the fortified wine in a suite is the standout. Yet, morosely, nobody drinks it. Here is a good one. A veritable bargain, too. Sure, the spirit sticks out as a thrust of heat across the finish, yet there is depth, complexity and compelling length. All reasons to explore a meander of dark cherry, camphor, kirsch and saddle leather polished to an nth of volatile sweetness. Screw cap. 20% alc. **RATING** 93 **DRINK** 2022-2050 $25 NG ✪
Chardonnay 2022, McLaren Vale A generous chardonnay of considerable class, belying its hot-climate origins. Riffs on nougatine, creamed cashew and canned peach. The oak is sensitively applied, evincing a nudge of authority while letting further stone and tropical fruit allusions flow. The acidity, too, an honest representation of place: soft and effortless. I'd drink this very early, but with some pleasure. Screw cap. 13% alc. **RATING** 92 **DRINK** 2022-2026 $28 NG ✪
Cabernet Sauvignon 2021, McLaren Vale Maritime cabernet is a strong suit at this address. Dried sage, Murray River salt, bay leaf, currant and black olive, compressed and rolled into a long sheath by a skein of oak and grape tannins alike. Screw cap. 14.5% alc. **RATING** 92 **DRINK** 2022-2030 $28 NG ✪
Puritan Shiraz 2022, McLaren Vale This is well done. Contemporary swagger thanks to semi-carbonic fermentation, a veil of carbon dioxide and the inherent gentle maceration that is all intrinsic to a successful no-adds style. Pulpy. Fleshy. Some reductive pong to the blue fruits and licorice, but floral and contagious of energy. Drink with a brisk chill. Screw cap. 14.5% alc. **RATING** 91 **DRINK** 2022-2024 $22 NG ✪

White Boar 2021, McLaren Vale A big, fleshy, high-octane wine. Shiraz, mostly, but tastes like grenache. Kirsch, licorice strap and mocha oak. The alcohol, largely compressed and corralled by a well-applied kit of oak tannins and a slake of salty freshness, all just a bit tangy. Bereft of grape tannins. A bit of a throat burn. Given that this was a moderate and attenuated vintage, it is odd that the wine became such a behemoth. There is a fan club out there, to be sure. Screw cap. 15% alc. **RATING** 91 **DRINK** 2022-2032 $45 NG

Heretic 2021, McLaren Vale A quasi-Iberian blend of graciano/touriga/shiraz. A reductive waft of neoprene soon blows off with a swoosh, revealing scents of peony, lavender, thyme and blueberry. Pulpy and easygoing, as much as it is mid-weighted of feel, curbed by a savoury corset of well-applied oak tannins and saline, peppery freshness from the graciano. A wash of tomato leaf at the finish. Nicely done. Screw cap. 14% alc. **RATING** 91 **DRINK** 2022-2028 $28 NG ✪

Spring Seed Wine Co. Scarlet Runner Shiraz 2020, McLaren Vale Organic certified vineyards manifest as purple fruits, dried nori, lilac, lavender and a swab of tapenade across a belt of well-applied oak. This is a full-weighted wine of impressive fruit intensity, judicious handling and ample freshness, punching well above its weight with a real whiff of class. Screw cap. 14.5% alc. **RATING** 91 **DRINK** 2022-2027 $22 NG ✪

Shiraz 2021, McLaren Vale A rich shiraz with the clutch pressed firmly on the reductive mode. Like too many. The result, all floral and iodine, tightly meshed with oak of sorts, some acidity and a whiff of neoprene before a spurt of blue-fruit allusions across the clenched, meaty finish. Screw cap. 14.5% alc. **RATING** 90 **DRINK** 2022-2028 $28 NG

Battles Wine ★★★★★

77 Aitken Drive, Winthrop, WA 6150 (postal) **Region** Western Australia
T 0434 399 964 **www**.battleswine.com.au **Open** Not **Winemaker** Lance Parkin
Est. 2018 **Dozens** 850

Battles Wine was started by friends Lance Parkin (winemaker) and Kris Ambrozkiewicz (sommelier, sales). Lance was a winemaker at Houghton in the Swan Valley before the sale to the Yukich family in '19, at which point the Swan Valley-based component of the Houghton team disbanded and formed their own ventures. Battles focuses on a small collection of tiny-quantity wines from a variety of regions (at this stage, the Perth Hills, Margaret River, Great Southern and Geographe) made with great attention to detail, and vineyard provenance top of mind. Kris Ambrozkiewicz (aka Ambro) has a longstanding and intense love of wine, an impressively honed bank of wine knowledge and years of sales experience.

🍷🍷🍷🍷🍷 **The Burnside Chardonnay 2022, Margaret River** If Lance Parkin can't produce excellent chardonnay, then there's something amiss. This is exceptional. Tight, linear and pure with a certain elegance throughout. Everything is lightly applied: the spicy oak, the citrus tones, the millefeuille of creamy lees with a slight tug of phenolics as the palate shifts to overdrive for a resounding finish. Screw cap. 13% alc. **RATING** 97 **DRINK** 2023-2032 $70 JF ✪

🍷🍷🍷🍷🍷 **Blendaberg 2022, Frankland River** 43/39/18% riesling/gewürztraminer/pinot grigio. Everything about this blend(aberg) is a delight. It's fragrant with white blossom, ginger spice, musk and lemon balm. Flavours are in a similar vein, while the palate has succulence throughout and a gentle persuasion thanks to the acidity. Savoury, moreish and very satisfying. It just works. Screw cap. 12.5% alc. **RATING** 95 **DRINK** 2022-2030 $35 JF ✪

Chardonnay 2022, Margaret River This is the type of chardonnay you sit down to enjoy, let whatever day you've had dissipate, relax and take in the fine flavours. The focus is on lemon with a citrus-saline tang, the spice with oak and lees augmenting the fine palate. A really delicious drink. Screw cap. 13% alc. **RATING** 95 **DRINK** 2022-2030 $50 JF ✪

Red Blend 2021, Frankland River Geographe Mourvèdre/shiraz. The colour is ruby bright and enticing, the aromas equally appealing, all florals and sumac, red licorice and jamon. Just shy of medium bodied with delicious tangy fruit flooding the palate, yet it's savoury by and large, unencumbered by new oak and raw-silk tannins hold sway. An excellent drink now. Screw cap. 13% alc. **RATING** 95 **DRINK** 2022-2026 $38 JF ✪

Shiraz 2022, Geographe Perth Hills Outrageous purple-black hue with fruit as deeply coloured: inky, spicy, peppery, richly fruited yet reined in by acidity. A medium-bodied palate with fine tannins, though a green walnut/ cardamom character on the finish adds distracting bitterness. Not an issue when downing this with a roast. Screw cap. 13.5% alc. **RATING** 94 **DRINK** 2023-2035 $38 JF ✪

♈♈♈♈♉ **Pinot Grigio 2022, Frankland River** **RATING** 93 **DRINK** 2022-2024 $35 JF ✪
Tempranillo 2022, Margaret River **RATING** 93 **DRINK** 2023-2030 $38 JF

Bay of Fires   ★★★★☆

40 Baxters Road, Pipers River, Tas 7252 **Region** Northern Tasmania
T (03) 6382 7622 **www**.bayoffireswines.com.au **Open** Thurs–Mon 10–5 by appt
Winemaker Penny Jones **Est.** 2001
Hardys purchased its first Tasmanian grapes in '94, with the aim of further developing and refining its sparkling wines, a process that quickly gave birth to House of Arras. The next stage was the inclusion of various parcels of chardonnay from Tasmania in the '98 Eileen Hardy, then the development in '01 of the Bay of Fires brand. Under the umbrella of Accolade Wines today, Bay of Fires is home to non-vintage sparkling white and rosé, alongside impressive riesling, sauvignon blanc, pinot gris, chardonnay and pinot noir. Sourcing is focused on the Tamar, Coal and Derwent valleys and East Coast. It shares its cellar door in Pipers River with House of Arras and Eddystone Point.

♈♈♈♈♉ **Pinot Noir 2021, Tasmania** Fine, exotic spice hovers over pure cherry and macerated strawberry fruits with hints of stewed rhubarb, mushroom risotto, forest floor and light, gamey notes. Fine, lacy acidity drives things along nicely. The wine lingers endearingly, gently fading with shades of spiced cherry, pressed flowers and roasting game meats. Lots to like here. Diam. 13.5% alc. **RATING** 93 **DRINK** 2022-2028 $60 DB

Chardonnay 2021, Tasmania A pale straw hue and aromas of juicy white peach, nectarine and grapefruit. Hints of dreamy, nutty French oak, a whiff of struck-match complexity, white flowers, crushed stone and almond paste. Mouth-filling and expansive with pure, juicy stone and citrus fruits, cashew-like oak, bright acidity and a light textural tweak of phenolics on the crisp, lingering finish. Screw cap. 13.5% alc. **RATING** 93 **DRINK** 2023-2027 $55 DB

Beechworth Wine Estates   ★★★★☆

Lot 2 Diffey Road, Beechworth, Vic 3477 **Region** Beechworth
T 0419 542 845 **www**.beechworthwe.com.au **Open** By appt **Winemaker** Mark Kelly
Est. 2003 **Dozens** 3200 **Vyds** 8.6ha
John and Joanne Iwanuch describe their estate as a family-run and -owned business, with their 4 children participating in all aspects of vineyard life. Situated on the Rail Trail, 4km from Beechworth, they have planted sauvignon blanc, pinot gris, fiano, chardonnay, shiraz, cabernet sauvignon, merlot, tempranillo, sangiovese, tannat, malbec, barbera, nebbiolo and graciano.

♈♈♈♈♈ **Chardonnay 2021, Beechworth** Beechworth's signature white grape, a quality vintage and a quality maker equal one mighty exciting chardonnay. Crackles with lively fruit flavour before settling into a long, smooth palate of concentrated power. Almond, citrus, nectarine and grilled grapefruit scents. Radiates layers of ripe fruit and nougat with a distinctively regional mineral-saline intensity. Oak is well integrated and acidity is clean. Screw cap. 13.4% alc. **RATING** 95 **DRINK** 2022-2029 $38 JP ✪

ŸŸŸŸ♀ Pinot Gris 2021, Beechworth RATING 93 DRINK 2022–2025 $22 JP
Fiano 2021, Beechworth RATING 90 DRINK 2022–2025 $25 JP ✪
Shiraz 2019, Beechworth RATING 90 DRINK 2022–2025 $28 JP

Bekkers ★★★★★

212-220 Seaview Road, McLaren Vale, SA 5171 **Region** McLaren Vale
T 0408 807 568 **www**.bekkerswine.com **Open** Thurs–Sun 10–4 or by appt
Winemaker Emmanuelle Bekkers **Viticulturist** Toby Bekkers **Est.** 2010 **Dozens** 2000
Vyds 35ha
Bekkers brings together 2 high-performing, highly experienced and credentialled business
and life partners. Toby Bekkers graduated with an honours degree in applied science in
agriculture from the University of Adelaide, and over the ensuing years has had broad-
ranging responsibilities as general manager of Paxton Wines in McLaren Vale and as a leading
exponent of organic and biodynamic viticulture. Emmanuelle was born in Bandol in the
south of France and obtained 2 university degrees, in biochemistry and oenology, before
working for the Hardys in the south of France, which led her to Australia and a wide-ranging
career, including Chalk Hill.

ŸŸŸŸŸ Syrah Grenache 2021, McLaren Vale This is superb. Rich, layered and fresh,
a small portion of whole bunches imparts seasoning to a torrent of dark fruits, clove,
pepper, cinnamon, tamarind, licorice root and allspice. The trajectory, something
to behold and picking up steam with air. Beef bouillon, nourishing, at its core.
There is a lot going on here and yet this majestic wine is as cerebral or as visceral
as the moment suits. Screw cap. 14% alc. RATING 96 DRINK 2023–2035 $90 NG
Syrah 2021, McLaren Vale This is a salubriously textured, rich and powerful
wine that remains very light on its feet. Aromas of dried kelp, violet, blue
and black berries, forested pine-like riffs and raspberry bonbon, all slathered
with molten licorice. Exceptional thrust of fruit intensity and parry of tannins,
grape and oak. Built for the long haul. Screw cap. 14% alc. RATING 95
DRINK 2023–2035 $120 NG
Grenache 2021, McLaren Vale Plays a very different card to the transparent,
red-fruited pinot-like zeitgeist. Broad of texture with terracotta aromas warm
and sunny. Blood plum, clove, tamarind and souk-like exotica buffer the textural
mid-palate. The finish, long and penetrative. Despite the open-knit attack, there is
ample compression at the finish, suggesting further space to unwind in the cellar.
Excellent grenache. Screw cap. 14% alc. RATING 95 DRINK 2023–2030 $90 NG

ŸŸŸŸ♀ Tome Shiraz Greanche 2021, McLaren Vale RATING 92 DRINK 2023–2030
$55 NG

Beklyn Wines ★★★★

PO Box 802, Goolwa, SA 5214 **Region** Currency Creek
T 0405 189 363 **www**.beklynwines.com **Open** Not **Winemaker** Mark and Rebekah
Shaw **Est.** 2016 **Dozens** 600 **Vyds** 20ha
Mark and Rebekah Shaw's wine journey began while working in vineyards in McLaren
Vale in '94. In '02, they built their first home in Currency Creek on the Fleurieu Peninsula.
They planted 10ha of shiraz, and have recently planted another 10ha. Grapes for their first
wine ('16) were purchased from 3 vineyards in McLaren Vale, with grapes from their estate
plantings in play from '18. The pattern of grape growing and selling part of the production
and using the remainder to make their own wines is a sensible approach. 'Beklyn' means
'pretty brook', derived from the passage of water flowing through the estate.

ŸŸŸŸ♀ Single Vineyard Shiraz 2021, Currency Creek Most reds at this alcohol
level rely on brute force to get their message across, but this wine is different. It's
warm and gutsy, but also nuanced. Licorice, raspberry and tar flavours come laced
with aromatic herbs, twigs and general spice notes. Alcohol warmth is clear but it
brings flavour with it and, if only just, feels well balanced. Screw cap. 15.5% alc.
RATING 92 DRINK 2023–2029 $45 CM

Bellarine Estate

2270 Portarlington Road, Bellarine, Vic 3222 **Region** Geelong
T (03) 5259 3310 **www.bellarineestate.com.au Open** Thurs–Sat 12–4 **Winemaker** Julian
Kenny **Viticulturist** Julian Kenny **Est.** 1996 **Dozens** 5000 **Vyds** 10.5ha
Established in '96 by Peter and Lizette Kenny, Bellarine Estate is family run from the ground
up, with sons James and Julian the general manager and head winemaker respectively. Every
stage of the winemaking process, all the way to the final bottling, occurs onsite. The estate is
a popular meeting place, with Thirty Acres gin distillery also onsite. The vineyard is planted
to chardonnay, pinot noir, shiraz, merlot, viognier and sauvignon blanc.

 TTTTT **Two Wives Shiraz 2022, Geelong** A vibrant crimson purple. Lively on the
nose with red and blue fruits intermingled with potpourri and pink peppercorn
scents. Medium bodied, this exudes charm with its fleshy, energetic and very well-
balanced palate. The tannins are silky and long, as is the wine. Screw cap. 14% alc.
RATING 96 **DRINK** 2022–2029 $38 PR ✪

TTTTT **Phil's Pinot Noir 2022, Geelong RATING** 92 **DRINK** 2023–2027 $40 PR

Bellarmine Wines

1 Balyan Retreat, Pemberton, WA 6260 (postal) **Region** Pemberton
T 0409 687 772 **www.bellarmine.com.au Open** Not **Winemaker** Dr Diane Miller
Est. 2000 **Dozens** 5000 **Vyds** 20.2ha
This vineyard is owned by German residents Dr Willi and Gudrun Schumacher. Long-term
wine lovers, the Schumachers decided to establish a vineyard and winery of their own,
choosing Australia partly because of its stable political climate. The vineyard is planted to
riesling, pinot noir, chardonnay, shiraz, sauvignon blanc and petit verdot. The flagship wines
are 3 styles of riesling – dry, off-dry and sweet.

TTTTT **Shiraz 2021, Pemberton** Big plum, big spice. A lavish shiraz of potency, supple
texture, depth and richness but with decent lift and a touch of smoky paprika
spice. It's a lovely red from all angles, generous but well balanced, a great extension
of flavour and a good deal of regional character in tow. It feels pure of fruit, gently
seasoned and wonderfully drinkable. Utter charm. Screw cap. 14% alc. **RATING** 94
DRINK 2023–2030 $29 MB ✪

TTTTT **Chardonnay 2022, Pemberton RATING** 92 **DRINK** 2023–2030 $27 MB ✪

Bellbrae Estate

520 Great Ocean Road, Bellbrae, Vic 3228 **Region** Geelong
T (03) 5264 8480 **www.bellbraeestate.com.au Open** By appt **Winemaker** David
Crawford **Est.** 1999 **Dozens** 4000 **Vyds** 8ha
The Surf Coast area of Geelong enjoys a slightly milder climate overall than other areas of
the Geelong viticultural region. Being so close to Bass Strait, Bellbrae Estate experiences a
maritime influence that reduces the risk of frost in spring and provides more even temperature
ranges during summer – ideal growing conditions for producing elegant wines that retain
their natural acidity. Wines are released under the Bellbrae Estate and Longboard labels.

TTTTT **Tetaz Pinot Noir 2020, Geelong** A bright, medium ruby red. Gorgeous
aromas of dark plum and cherries, crushed rose petals and star anise. Medium
bodied, this has excellent intensity but remains light on its feet. Impeccably
balanced and framed by persistent and polished tannins. Worth both the money
and the hunt. Screw cap. 13.5% alc. **RATING** 97 **DRINK** 2022–2030 $80 PR ✪

TTTTT **Bells Syrah 2021, Geelong** Deep ruby red. Displays blue and black fruits
with allspice, licorice and violets. There's a lot going on! Just as good on the
medium-bodied, seamless and long palate. I like the small amount of reduction
and as good as this is now, it's also built to last. Screw cap. 13.5% alc. **RATING** 96
DRINK 2023–2031 $47 PR ✪

ΨΨΨΨΩ Bird Rock Pinot Noir 2021, Geelong RATING 92 DRINK 2022-2028 $47 PR
Boobs Chardonnay 2021, Geelong RATING 92 DRINK 2022-2026 $42 PR
Southside Sauvignon Blanc 2020, Geelong RATING 92 DRINK 2022-2024
$35 PR
Longboard Shiraz 2021, Geelong RATING 91 DRINK 2022-2027 $30 PR
Longboard Pinot Gris 2021, Bendigo RATING 91 DRINK 2022-2024
$28 PR ✪
Longboard Rosé 2022, Geelong RATING 90 DRINK 2022-2024 $30 PR

Bellebonne   ★★★★★

3 Balfour Place, Launceston, Tas 7250 (postal) **Region** Northern Tasmania
T 0412 818 348 **www.bellebonne.wine Open** Not **Winemaker** Natalie Fryar **Est.** 2015
Dozens 600
Bellebonne is Natalie Fryar's passion project. She spent 14 years at Jansz, establishing herself
as one of Australia's top sparkling makers while gaining an intimate knowledge of Tasmania's
premium sites. She crafts her elegant and sublime Bellebonne cuvées in minuscule quantities
from pockets of grower vines in Pipers River. To finance her first solo vintage, she sold a
house, worked waitressing shifts and drove her cleaner's Ford Festiva to Tassie with her red
Kelpie on the front seat. She maintains a consulting hand in several of northern Tasmania's
best sparklings and lends blending skills to her outstanding Abel Gin.

ΨΨΨΨΨ Natalie Fryar Vintage Rosé 2020, Tasmania A beautiful salmon hue
with a fine energetic bead and mousse, stunning aromatics of redcurrant, wild
strawberries, red apple and raspberry with notes of mushroom broth, fresh
pastry, crushed river stone and light creamy notes. Savoury and pure, gentle
tannin texture from the barrel ferment and a long, harmonious finish. Gorgeous
drinking. Diam. 12% alc. RATING 96 DRINK 2023-2033 $85 DB
Natalie Fryar Vintage Cuvée 2019, Tasmania 60/40% Pipers River
chardonnay/pinot noir. Pale straw with elegant white peach, grapefruit and
green apple, underlying hints of crushed stone, almond blossom, brioche, enoki
mushroom broth and a gentle wisp of freshly cut fennel bulb. Seamless with
stunning tension, clarity and a sense of filigreed grace. Plenty of subtlety, plenty
of awesome. Diam. 12% alc. RATING 95 DRINK 2023-2033 $78 DB
Bis Rosé NV, Tasmania Pretty salmon colour and superfine bubbles. A beautiful
detailed bouquet of red berries, gentle spice and crème fraîche, almond blossom
and light pastry notes. Great mineral energy with pitch-perfect balance and a
composed sense of calm and harmony on the finish. Lovely. Diam. 12% alc.
RATING 95 $45 DB ✪

Ben Murray Wines   ★★★★

PO Box 781, Tanunda, SA 5352 **Region** Barossa Valley
T 0438 824 493 **www.benmurraywines.com Open** By appt **Winemaker** Dan Eggleton
Viticulturist Johanns Find Viticulture **Est.** 2016 **Dozens** 2000 **Vyds** 1ha
Ben Murray doesn't exist, but owners Dan Eggleton and Craig Thompson do. Each has
years of experience in various facets of the wine business. Dan brings 25 years working for
businesses ranging from major corporates to boutique enterprises. Craig brings a 1ha old-vine
grenache vineyard at Lyndoch into the venture, plus experience as a wine importer.

ΨΨΨΨΩ Casa Rossa Vineyard Anima Reserve Grenache 2021, Barossa Valley
An impressive grenache that shows excellent fruit depth and purity with a fine-
grained structure. It's a bigger style with deep plum and cherry fruits cut with
spice, gingerbread, gentle cedar, purple flowers and earth. The tannin architecture
shows some grunt and the acidity is bright and true, propelling the dark fruits
forwards. Diam. 14.5% alc. RATING 92 DRINK 2023-2029 $40 DB
Shiraz 2021, Barossa Valley Deep crimson in the glass with broody blood
plum, black cherry and boysenberry top notes with an understory of baking
spices, dark chocolate, roasting meats, olive tapenade, cedar and earth. Plenty

of depth and western Barossa fruit intensity and spice on the palate with some ferrous-edged tannin grip and a deep cassis and kirsch volley on the finish. Screw cap. 14.5% alc. **RATING** 92 **DRINK** 2023–2030 $35 DB

Rosé 2022, McLaren Vale Rosé produced from mataro. Deep salmon pink with aromas of crunchy red cherry, redcurrant and red plum fruits with hints of citrus blossom, soft spice, red licorice, dried herbs and stone. Fruit forward and crunchy with a crisp, vivid acid line and a swell of red cherry and raspberry fruits with just a slink of texture. Screw cap. 12% alc. **RATING** 91 **DRINK** 2023–2025 $25 DB ✪

Marananga Grenache 2021, Barossa Valley Ripe red and dark plum fruits underscored with hints of spice, gingerbread, cola, purple flowers, earth, Cherry Ripe and some fairly softly spoken oak notes. I say fairly, as oak often pokes out a bit in grenache, but in this case, the fruit on the palate saves the day: savoury, spicy and red-fruited with fine, sandy tannins and a sweep of morello cherries on the finish. Screw cap. 14% alc. **RATING** 91 **DRINK** 2023–2028 $25 DB ✪

Sevenhill Vineyard Riesling 2022, Clare Valley Freshly squeezed lime and citrus blossom, as you would expect from the Clare, with hints of crushed stone, white flowers, celery and the lightest whiff of lanolin. Some good velocity thanks to a porcelain line of acidity and a nice display of precision on the palate. Screw cap. 11% alc. **RATING** 90 **DRINK** 2023–2027 $25 DB ✪

Sapidity White Blend 2021, Eden Valley A skin-contact blend of 50/50% semillon/sauvignon blanc. Yellow straw in the glass with aromas of pawpaw, Meyer lemon, custard apple and grapefruit. Hints of souk-like spices, lemon curd, citrus blossom, dried grass, lantana, chicken stock, struck flint and stone. Sapidity by name, sapidity by nature with a lipsmacking acid line, a gentle squeak of phenolics and a lemony finish that shows some glimpses of umami. Screw cap. 12.5% alc. **RATING** 90 **DRINK** 2023–2026 $25 DB ✪

Marananga Grenache 2020, Barossa Valley Dark satsuma plum, red apple and red cherry fruits cut with baking spices, earth, purple flowers, ginger cake, oak spice and red licorice. There's an open, loose-knit feel to the red fruits on the palate with a super-spicy vibe, a touch of tobacco leaf, a whiff of cedary oak and an earthy, savoury line on the exit. Screw cap. 14% alc. **RATING** 90 **DRINK** 2023–2028 $25 DB ✪

Ben Potts Wines   ★★★★☆

The Winehouse,1509 Langhorne Creek Road, Langhorne Creek, SA 5255
Region Langhorne Creek
T (08) 8537 3029 **www**.thewinehouse.com.au **Open** 7 days 10–4 **Winemaker** Ben Potts **Est.** 2002
Ben Potts is the 6th generation to be involved in grapegrowing and winemaking in Langhorne Creek, the first being Frank Potts, founder of Bleasdale Vineyards. Ben completed an oenology degree at Charles Sturt University, venturing into winemaking on a commercial scale in '02 (aged 25). Fiddle's Block Shiraz is named after great-grandfather Henry Fiddle, Lenny's Block Cabernet Sauvignon Malbec after grandfather Len and Bill's Block Malbec after father Bill.

🍷🍷🍷🍷🍷 **Fiddle's Block Shiraz 2021, Langhorne Creek** Shiraz from 50–80yo estate vines. The wine is deeply coloured but a fraction turbid. It is unabashedly full bodied, but the Langhorne Creek climate and soil produce a rich and velvety wine with a complex tapestry of black cherry and berry fruits, spices and dark chocolate, the tannins softly spicy. Lovely wine. Screw cap. 14.5% alc. **RATING** 96 **DRINK** 2023–2031 $40 JH ✪

🍷🍷🍷🍷🍷 **Lenny's Block Cabernet Sauvignon 2021, Langhorne Creek** **RATING** 91 **DRINK** 2023–2041 $40 JH

Bended Knee Vineyard

PO Box 334, Buninyong, Vic 3357 **Region** Ballarat
T (03) 5341 8437 **www.**bendedknee.com.au **Open** Not **Winemaker** Peter Roche
Viticulturist Peter Roche, Molly Wheatland **Est.** 1999 **Dozens** 250 **Vyds** 1.5ha
Peter and Pauline Roche have 0.5ha each of chardonnay and pinot noir planted at moderately
high density, and 0.25ha of ultra-close-planted pinot noir comprising clones 114, 115, G5V15
and 777. The Roches say, 'We are committed to sustainable viticulture and aim to leave
the planet in better shape than we found it'. Ducks, guinea fowl and chooks are vineyard
custodians, and all canopy management is done by hand, including pruning and picking.
Although production is tiny, Bended Knee wines can be found at some of Melbourne's
best restaurants.

Chardonnay 2020, Ballarat Sweet, minty, cedar characters sit over the top
of nectarine, apple and citrus-driven fruit. The various components sit in layers
for now, not having fully integrated, but the length is excellent. If extra time in
bottle brings harmony, this will be very good. Screw cap. 12% alc. **RATING** 90
DRINK 2025-2032 $45 CM

Bendooley Estate

3020 Old Hume Highway, Berrima, NSW 2577 **Region** Southern Highlands
T (02) 4877 2235 **www.**bendooleyestate.com.au **Open** 7 days 10–5
Winemaker Jonathan Holgate **Est.** 2008 **Dozens** 4000 **Vyds** 4ha
Paul Berkelouw is a 6th-generation antiquarian book dealer, a name known to just about
everyone in Australia who has any interest in such things. He and his wife, Katja, live and
work at the historic Bendooley Estate with their 3 children. Here they make wine, sell books,
host weddings and events and offer accommodation.

Reserve Pinot Gris 2019, Southern Highlands Poached peach, ripe apricot
and honeysuckle burst from the glass with ginger syrup and freshly picked loquats.
Slippery across the palate, but full of the dense weight of pinot gris, this wine
is full of complexities and charm. The heat of gingersnap cookies and grated
nutmeg continues long after you've set down your glass. Screw cap. 12.9% alc.
RATING 93 **DRINK** 2022-2030 $55 SW
Rosé 2021, Southern Highlands A hue of pretty peach tones in the glass.
Reminiscent of pink grapefruit skin and Royal Gala apple curls. Hints of
watermelon and orange bitters, the wine is even more surprising on the palate
with tart lilly pillies, red cranberries and candied orange zest. A thoughtful
wisp of tannic grip adds another dimension. Screw cap. 13% alc. **RATING** 90
DRINK 2022-2030 $28 SW
Reserve Pinot Noir 2019, Southern Highlands The '19 is a spirited pinot
noir full of brooding black cherries, blackcurrant and juniper. Elements of sage
leaf, licorice and allspice come through, while a lingering note of black tea sits
in the background. Blackberries join the mix on the palate and the wine finishes
with a hint of bitterness and firm but integrated tannins. Screw cap. 12.5% alc.
RATING 90 **DRINK** 2022-2038 $55 SW
Reserve Chardonnay 2019, Southern Highlands Ripe fuzzy peach and
pawpaw open with churned butter and popcorn kernels. Winemaker Jonathan
Holgate is considering his chardonnay fans with this full-bodied style, which has
a generous creamy mouthfeel and nutty praline nuances on the finish. Screw cap.
13% alc. **RATING** 90 **DRINK** 2022-2035 $55 SW

Bent Road

535 Bents Road, Ballandean, Qld 5382 **Region** Granite Belt
T 0418 190 104 **www.**bentroadwine.com.au **Open** By appt **Winemaker** Glen Robert
Viticulturist Robert Richter **Est.** 2004 **Dozens** 2500 **Vyds** 4ha
Bent Road is owned by winemaker Glen Robert and vineyard manager Robert Richter.
Glen is a former medical research chemist, but moved into winemaking simply because

he (and Robert) fell under the spell of wine around '00. Robert is focused on the organic management of the vineyard, which is planted to tempranillo, shiraz, merlot, marsanne, semillon and verdelho. Chardonnay and cabernet sauvignon are purchased from local growers. La Petite Mort is their low-intervention experimental range, unfined and unfiltered.

La Petite Mort Qvevri VMR 2021, Granite Belt A hugely aromatic viognier/marsanne/roussanne blend with quince, preserved lemon, ginger and frangipani characters on show. The palate is strong and firm with chalky tannins. Delivers ginger-lemon tea freshness and piquancy with faint stone fruit characters. A serious orange wine here, with texture, grip, power and concentration, but freshness and vigour too. Diam. 13.9% alc. RATING 93 DRINK 2023-2028 $35 MB

La Petite Mort Crianza Tempranillo 2018, South Eastern Australia This falls into lush territory. Dark cherries, kirsch and cola, clove spice and some brambly, earthy elements, almost truffle umami notes and licks of cedary woodiness. It's got concentration, lift and a sense of pure, rich fruit with layers of seasoning and spice. Finishes a little ferrous and earthy but feels right in the style. An excellent, savoury rendition of the variety. Diam. 13.3% alc. RATING 93 DRINK 2022-2028 $45 MB

La Petite Mort Pét-Nat 2022, Granite Belt Bottle-fermented gros manseng. Hazy in the glass. Bright and vibrant with cloudy apple juice sensibilities. Lots of vigorous, tight bubbles, some lemon squeezed into green apple characters, some oatmeal and light spice elements, too. A well-judged style that's interesting, quietly complex and generally appealing to drink. Crown. 13% alc. RATING 92 DRINK 2022-2024 $35 MB

Wilhelm Scream Tempranillo 2019, South Eastern Australia Medium bodied, rich in a way, slippery textured and a bit of extra freshness to finish. It's a pleasing, well-balanced tempranillo with hallmark sarsaparilla, cola, black cherry and sweet spice characters in abundance. The texture is smooth and lush, the wine a warming, generous mouthful with each sip. Lots of pleasure here. Screw cap. 13% alc. RATING 90 DRINK 2022-2024 $23 MB ✪

La Petite Mort Cellar Aged Marsanne 2005, Granite Belt This shows some cracked yeast characters and honeycomb, rice cracker and preserved lemon notes with the bouquet and palate in similar modes. It's a mellow, succulent white wine, medium bodied now, toasty and in a phase of attractive decay. A curio in some respects, but with faint freshness licking at the heels of the mature characters and overall general appeal. Diam. 13.5% alc. RATING 90 DRINK 2022-2025 $45 MB

Beresford Wines   ★★★★

252 Blewitt Springs Road, McLaren Flat, SA 5171 **Region** McLaren Vale
T (08) 8383 0362 **www.**beresfordwines.com.au **Open** 7 days 10-5 **Winemaker** Chris Dix
Est. 1985 **Dozens** 9000 **Vyds** 28ha
Beresford Wines is a partnership with Vale Brewing Taphouse. As well as wine and beer tasting, it offers accommodation and a wedding venue. The estate's 28ha are planted to shiraz, cabernet sauvignon, chardonnay and 6yo bush-vine grenache. Some of the wines offer excellent value.

Limited Release Cabernet Sauvignon 2020, McLaren Vale A smoother patina of structural attributes than the lower-tier expressions. Blackcurrant, molten rock, graphite, clove and a sachet of herbs strewn across the slightly sweet finish. This is a full-bodied wine that remains savoury and relatively light on its feet. Screw cap. 14.3% alc. RATING 91 DRINK 2022-2030 $80 NG

Berrigan Wines   ★★★★

165 Jeffrey Street, Nairne, SA 5252 **Region** Adelaide Hills
T 0409 665 013 **www.**berriganwines.com.au **Open** By appt **Winemaker** Dan Berrigan
Viticulturist Dan Berrigan **Est.** 2002 **Dozens** 500 **Vyds** 23ha

Berrigan Wines began in '02 in WA's Swan District, where the Berrigan family, headed by Thomas John Berrigan, planted verdelho, shiraz, cabernet sauvignon and merlot. Thomas stopped making wines in '06; in '15, son Dan Berrigan and partner Wendi decided to bring the family brand name back to life. Everything else is new, including their South Australian location. The duo started out with 8ha in Mount Benson, on the Limestone Coast, before purchasing the 15ha Shining Rock vineyard (planted by Brian Croser in '00) in the Adelaide Hills in '20. The low-yielding site supplies shiraz, sangiovese and grüner veltliner, with merlot, cabernet sauvignon, chardonnay and sauvignon blanc sourced from Mount Benson.

ƔƔƔƔƔ **Shiraz 2020, Mount Benson** Mouth-filling shiraz. Indeed, the flavours here are almost falling over themselves to please, so generous are they, so open. It tastes of black cherry, mint and plum with woodsy spice and cedar, though a kind of jubey fruit lusciousness lifts up from the wine as it breathes. There's enough tannin here to suggest that it will cellar but really, it's ready to rip now. Screw cap. 14.5% alc. **RATING** 91 **DRINK** 2022-2027 $25 CM ✪

Sangiovese 2021, Adelaide Hills A handy sangiovese. A flick of red fruits, vanilla, dried thyme and sandalwood, edging its way over a carriage of perky freshness and edgy tannins. A versatile, everyday guzzler. Screw cap. 14% alc. **RATING** 90 **DRINK** 2022-2025 $35 NG

Merlot 2020, Mount Benson Boysenberry, mint and plum flavours put on a very pleasant show. This is a medium-weight wine offering a good amount of fruit and just enough cedar oak. It's fresh and buoyant, energetic even, and refreshing in the context of flavour. Screw cap. 14% alc. **RATING** 90 **DRINK** 2022-2027 $20 CM ✪

Berton Vineyard ★★★☆

55 Mirrool Avenue, Yenda, NSW 2681 **Region** Riverina
T (02) 6968 1600 www.bertonvineyards.com.au **Open** Mon–Fri 10–4, Sat 11–4
Winemaker James Ceccato, Matthew Santos, Kia Millis, Daren Owers **Est.** 1996
Dozens 1.3 million **Vyds** 105ha
The Berton Vineyard partners – Bob and Cherie Berton, James Ceccato and Jamie Bennett – have over 100 years' combined experience in winemaking, viticulture, finance, production and marketing. The estate vineyard sits at 450m above sea level in the High Eden subregion of the Eden Valley, but the winery is located in Riverina, from where they source fruit from a variety of growers for their various labels. The Bonsai label is named for the appearance of the struggling young estate vines in the early days.

ƔƔƔƔƔ **The Bonsai 2019, High Eden** 77/23% shiraz/cabernet sauvignon. Berton Vineyard's flagship wine invokes zavarka, the Russian practice of steeping black cherries in concentrated tea. Pure blackberries, blackcurrant and sweet cherries with fine-grained, powdery tannins and a heady mix of clove, juniper and allspice. Linear and concentrated with a lasting black pepper spice. Screw cap. 14% alc. **RATING** 90 **DRINK** 2022-2028 $50 SW

Best's Wines ★★★★★

111 Best's Road, Great Western, Vic 3377 **Region** Great Western
T (03) 5356 2250 www.bestswines.com **Open** Mon–Sat 10–5, Sun 11–4
Winemaker Simon Fennell, Jacob Parton **Viticulturist** Ben Thomson **Est.** 1866
Dozens 25 000 **Vyds** 147ha
Best's winery and vineyards date back to 1866. One of the vines planted in the Nursery Block has defied identification and is thought to exist nowhere else in the world. The Thomson family has owned the property since 1920. Best's consistently produces elegant, supple wines; the Bin No. 0 is a classic, the Thomson Family Shiraz is magnificent. Very occasionally a unique pinot meunier (with 15% pinot noir) is made solely from 1868 plantings of those 2 varieties. Best's were awarded Wine of the Year in '17 and '23, and Best Value Winery '21.

🍷🍷🍷🍷🍷 **Foudre Ferment Riesling 2022, Great Western** There's a gorgeousness to these wines. A touch of sweetness to the lime- and orange-driven fruit, a modest textural element, an impression of exquisite purity throughout. It feels and tastes lovely, first sip to the last. The acidity feels daring but it's flavour-drenched, and that's the crucial point. In short, everything is in excellent order here. Screw cap. 12% alc. RATING 95 DRINK 2023–2033 $35 CM ✪

Cabernet Franc 2021, Great Western This has 'peak vintage' written all over it. It's a nutty, spicy, herb-flecked wine with boysenberry, red cherry and mulberry flavours rippling throughout. Juicy fruit, complex savoury notes and exquisite finesse. The words 'gloriously medium weight' spring to mind. This is what it's all about. Screw cap. 13.5% alc. RATING 95 DRINK 2023–2030 $45 CM ✪

Cabernet Sauvignon 2021, Great Western An exquisitely well-mannered wine. Ultrafine tannin, perfectly ripened fruit, the line of acidity placed just so. Even the oak wraps smokily around the herb notes, as if to ensure that they don't appear too loud. This mid-weight cabernet would make the perfect butler to the finest of meals. Screw cap. 14% alc. RATING 95 DRINK 2024–2034 $25 CM ✪

Riesling 2022, Henty What a delicious riesling. Lime and slate flavours burst onto the palate and soar on through the finish. It's intense, it's moreish and it's persistent. You can't ask for much more. Screw cap. 11% alc. RATING 94 DRINK 2022–2034 $35 CM ✪

Old Vine Pinot Meunier 2022, Great Western It's structured and herbal, cool and complex, and yet there's a brightness to this, and a perfume. It's a lovely wine. Boysenberry, roasted nuts, forest berries and mint, with woodsy spice and sweet cedar in support. The fresh, persistent, complex quality of this is quite something. Screw cap. 12% alc. RATING 94 DRINK 2026–2035 $45 CM

Riesling 2022, Great Western Filled to the brim with lime and lemon fruit from the first whiff to aftertaste. So juicy, with some fruit sweetness. Screw cap. 12% alc. RATING 94 DRINK 2023–2032 $25 JH ✪

Bin No. 1 Shiraz 2021, Great Western This release is on song. Black pepper and peppercorn characters float through cherry and plum fruit flavour. It's lively, it has enough depth, it finishes well and it charms throughout. The fine-grained, savoury aspect of the tannin here is of particular note. If you like the Great Western style, you can buy this with confidence. Screw cap. 14% alc. RATING 94 DRINK 2023–2033 $27 CM ✪

LSV Shiraz 2021, Great Western Oak adds coffee and cedar notes, arguably a little too keenly, but this will settle in time. The fruit flavours are pretty gorgeous: boysenberry and redcurrant infused with florals, the aftertaste adding tonic-like herb and twig notes. It's plush upfront, savoury through the finish, almost like a reverse mullet. The net effect is that it's lovely to drink. Screw cap. 13.5% alc. RATING 94 DRINK 2024–2033 $35 CM ✪

🍷🍷🍷🍷🍷 **Young Vine Pinot Meunier 2022, Great Western** RATING 93 DRINK 2025–2033 $125 CM

Pinot Noir 2022, Great Western RATING 91 DRINK 2025–2033 $27 CM ✪

Bethany Wines   ★★★★★

378 Bethany Road, Tanunda, SA 5352 **Region** Barossa Valley
T (08) 8563 2086 **www**.bethany.com.au **Open** Mon–Sat 10–5, Sun 1–5
Winemaker Alex MacClelland **Est.** 1981 **Dozens** 18 000 **Vyds** 38ha
The Schrapel family has been growing grapes in the Barossa Valley for over 140 years, their winery nestled high on a hillside on the site of an old bluestone quarry. Geoff and Rob Schrapel produce a range of consistently well made and attractively packaged wines. Bethany has vineyards in the Barossa and Eden valleys.

🍷🍷🍷🍷🍷 **GR Reserve Shiraz 2020, Barossa Valley** Deep, purple-flecked magenta in the glass with aromas of plush satsuma plum, blackberry and blueberry fruits cut with hints of baking spices, violets, jasmine, licorice, dark chocolate and earth. Full bodied, plush with ripe fruit, balanced and long of finish with super-ripe, fine tannin support and plenty of vitality and verve. Cork. 14.5% alc. **RATING** 95 **DRINK** 2023–2036 $125 DB

East Grounds Shiraz 2020, Barossa Valley Deep magenta with opulent blackberry, black cherry and macerated plum fruits. Hints of dark chocolate, jasmine, roasting meats, olive tapenade, licorice, graphite and earth. Plenty of concentration and depth but with the floral top-notes that come from the wines of the eastern grounds. Superfine gypsum-like tannins and lacy acidity provide the structure and if someone seeks a classic Barossa shiraz, this ticks all the boxes. It could be from nowhere else. Screw cap. 14.5% alc. **RATING** 95 **DRINK** 2023–2033 $55 DB

LE Shiraz 2020, Barossa Deep magenta in the glass and showing plush fruit characters of blackberry, black cherry and plum with hints of licorice, dark chocolate, baking spices and lighter wafts of eucalyptus, bay leaf and crème de cassis. Full bodied with a powdery tannin structure, black fruits are joined by hints of cedar, mint and violets on the palate, finishing long and true with excellent acid drive. Very good indeed. Cork. 14.5% alc. **RATING** 94 **DRINK** 2023–2033 $75 DB

ΥΥΥΥΥ **First Village GSM 2021, Barossa Valley** **RATING** 93 **DRINK** 2023–2028 $29 DB ✪

Blue Quarry Barrel Select Cabernet Sauvignon 2020, Barossa Valley **RATING** 93 **DRINK** 2023–2033 $45 DB

Blue Quarry Barrel Select Shiraz 2020, Barossa Valley **RATING** 93 **DRINK** 2023–2030 $45 DB

First Village Riesling 2022, Eden Valley **RATING** 92 **DRINK** 2023–2028 $28 DB ✪

Blue Quarry Single Vineyard Riesling 2022, Eden Valley **RATING** 92 **DRINK** 2023–2027 $40 DB

Blue Quarry Grenache 2021, Barossa Valley **RATING** 92 **DRINK** 2023–2028 $45 DB

First Village Shiraz 2020, Barossa Valley **RATING** 92 **DRINK** 2023–2028 $32 DB

First Village Grenache 2021, Barossa Valley **RATING** 91 **DRINK** 2023–2029 $32 DB

Bicknell fc ★★★★★

41 St Margarets Road, Healesville, Vic 3777 (postal) **Region** Yarra Valley
T 0488 678 427 **www**.bicknellfc.com **Open** Not **Winemaker** David Bicknell
Viticulturist Nicky Harris **Est.** 2011 **Dozens** 7600 **Vyds** 2.5ha
This is the busman's holiday for Oakridge chief winemaker David Bicknell and viticulturist Nicky Harris. It is focused purely on chardonnay and pinot noir, with no present intention of broadening the range nor the volume of production. The fruit comes from Val Stewart's close-planted vineyard at Gladysdale, planted in '88. The wines are labelled Applecross, the name of the highest mountain pass in Scotland, a place that David Bicknell's father was very fond of.

ΥΥΥΥΥ **Applecross Pinot Noir 2021, Yarra Valley** A bright, light–medium crimson red. From a great year, there's an extra degree of oomph in the '21 pinot compared to '20. Strawberries, redcurrant and a little whole-bunch derived rose petal lead onto the palate, which is ripe, bright, crunchy and long. An excellent effort from this very cool Upper Yarra site. Only 97 dozen made. Screw cap. 12.7% alc. **RATING** 96 **DRINK** 2023–2027 $58 PR ✪

Applecross Chardonnay 2021, Yarra Valley Aromas of red apples and just-ripened orchard fruits with a little flint. Fans out nicely on the palate. Gently savoury and with a touch of grip on the long, saline finish. Screw cap. 12.7% alc. **RATING** 96 **DRINK** 2022–2028 $58 PR ✪

Billy Button Wines   ★★★★★

11 Camp Street, Bright, Vic 3741 and 61 Myrtle St, Myrtleford, Vic 3737
Region Alpine Valleys
T (03) 5755 1569 **www.billybuttonwines.com.au Open** Wed 12–6, Thurs 12–8,
Sun 12–5 **Winemaker** Jo Marsh, Glenn James **Est.** 2014 **Dozens** 6000

Jo Marsh makes light of the numerous awards she won while studying for her degree in agricultural science (oenology) at the University of Adelaide. She then won a contested position in Southcorp's Graduate Recruitment Program; in '03, she was appointed assistant winemaker at Seppelt Great Western. By '08 she had been promoted to acting senior winemaker, responsible for all wines made onsite. After Seppelt, Jo became winemaker at Feathertop, stepping out on her own in '14 after 2 happy years. She has set up a grower network in the Alpine Valleys and makes a string of excellent wines. Glenn James joined as winemaker in '15 and the 2 later married in '16.

🍷🍷🍷🍷 **The Cherished Sparkling Shiraz 2022, Alpine Valleys** There are those who dismiss sparkling shiraz. You won't see Jo Marsh among them. Here, she combines freshness, verve and sparkle with equally delicious bright fruit intensity and the requisite spice. Dark berries, plum, sarsaparilla, chocolate and earth with the merest suggestion of sweetness. Yum. Crown. 13.5% alc. **RATING** 95 **DRINK** 2023–2030 $40 JP ✪

The Affable Barbera 2022, Alpine Valleys A lipsmacking, purple-hued, spice-filled, soft-hearted young red that rocks. The expressive, energetic joy of the barbera grape is laid bare. Licorice, dried herbs, vanilla and plum with a splash of sour cherry tartness show the grape at its youthful best. So much to see, smell and enjoy. Screw cap. 14% alc. **RATING** 95 **DRINK** 2023–2028 $32 JP ✪

Flame Robin Durif 2019, Alpine Valleys Flame Robin is the name given to a standalone Billy Button–quality red from any particular vintage. In '19, it was durif. Arrives in intense inky, dark purple hues. Takes command in the glass with a strong, black fruit tannin presence laced liberally with rosemary, pepper, dark chocolate, tapenade and spice. Seriously complex and polished. Give it the time it deserves. Screw cap. 14% alc. **RATING** 95 **DRINK** 2023–2032 $50 JP ✪

Ancestrale Prosecco 2022, Alpine Valleys This méthode ancestrale-style prosecco brings its own world of intense flavour to the glass, one that is savoury and layered and, make no mistake, dry. Citrus is re-interpreted in preserved lemon and grilled grapefruit and peel with a quince-like tartness to close. Lots of bubbly personality, too. Crown. 10.5% alc. **RATING** 94 **DRINK** 2022–2026 $32 JP ✪

The Alluring Tempranillo 2022, Alpine Valleys The Alpine Valleys and tempranillo suit each other's temperament, tempranillo responding to the cooler clime by producing a firm tannin base upon which to build a dark and brooding wine. Blackberries, dried herbs, bramble, spice and earth. Tight as a drum but give it time. Screw cap. 13.5% alc. **RATING** 94 **DRINK** 2023–2030 $32 JP ✪

The Rustic Sangiovese 2022, Alpine Valleys Upfront, honest and so very drinkable, The Rustic combines the earthy charm of the grape with the most delectable red berry fruits and anise spiciness. Keeps an Italian feel going with a firm, fine tannin presence throughout and a dry finish. Screw cap. 13.5% alc. **RATING** 94 **DRINK** 2023–2027 $32 JP ✪

🍷🍷🍷🍷🍷 **The Socialite Prosecco 2022, Alpine Valleys RATING** 93 **DRINK** 2023–2026 $32 JP ✪

The Classic Chardonnay 2022, Alpine Valleys RATING 93 **DRINK** 2023–2029 $32 JP ✪

The Renegade Refrosco 2022, Alpine Valleys RATING 93 **DRINK** 2023–2027 $32 JP ✪

The Surreptitious Schioppettino 2022, Alpine Valleys RATING 93 **DRINK** 2023–2028 $32 JP ✪

The Groovy Grüner Veltliner 2022, Alpine Valleys RATING 93 **DRINK** 2022–2027 $27 JP ✪

The Honest Fiano 2022, Alpine Valleys RATING 93 DRINK 2022–2026 $27 JP ✪

Silver Xenica Verduzzo 2021, Alpine Valleys RATING 93 DRINK 2023–2028 $40 JP

The Graceful Sparkling Pinot Rosé 2021, Alpine Valleys RATING 92 DRINK 2022–2026 $40 JP

The Little Rascal Arneis 2022, Alpine Valleys RATING 92 DRINK 2022–2026 $27 JP ✪

The Happy Gewürztraminer 2022, Alpine Valleys RATING 92 DRINK 2022–2027 $27 JP ✪

The Dapper Durif 2021, Alpine Valleys RATING 92 DRINK 2023–2029 $32 JP

The Beloved Shiraz 2021, Alpine Valleys RATING 92 DRINK 2022–2027 $32 JP

Zero Dosage Prosecco 2022, Alpine Valleys RATING 91 DRINK 2023–2027 $32 JP

The Versatile Vermentino 2022, Alpine Valleys RATING 91 DRINK 2023–2027 $27 JP ✪

Prosecco NV, King Valley Alpine Valleys RATING 90 $22 JP ✪

Silver Xenica Pecorino 2022, Alpine Valleys RATING 90 DRINK 2023–2028 $40 JP

The Mysterious Malvasia 2022, Alpine Valleys RATING 90 DRINK 2022–2026 $27 JP

Rosato 2022, Alpine Valleys RATING 90 DRINK 2022–2025 $20 JP ✪

The Delinquent Verduzzo 2022, Alpine Valleys RATING 90 DRINK 2023–2028 $27 JP

The Unexpected Aglianico 2021, Alpine Valleys RATING 90 DRINK 2022–2025 $32 JP

Bimbadgen ★★★★★

790 McDonalds Road, Pokolbin, NSW 2320 **Region** Hunter Valley
T (02) 4998 4600 **www**.bimbadgen.com.au **Open** Mon–Sat 10–4, Sun 11–3
Winemaker Richard Done **Viticulturist** Liz Riley **Est.** 1968 **Dozens** 30 000 **Vyds** 26ha
Bimbadgen's Palmers Lane vineyard was planted in 1968 and the McDonalds Road vineyard shortly thereafter. Both sites provide old-vine semillon, shiraz and chardonnay, with tempranillo a more recent addition. Since assuming ownership in '97, the Lee family has applied the same level of care and attention to cultivating Bimbadgen as they have to other properties in their portfolio. The small but impressive production is consumed largely by the owner's luxury hotel assets, with limited quantities available in the Sydney market.

♟♟♟♟ **Museum Release Signature Semillon 2014, Hunter Valley** This is by far the best of a trio of vintages ('19, '17 and '14) received as museum releases, not just because it's the oldest. It has significantly more complexity to savoury nuances running alongside herb and citrus notes, acidity the ever-present reminder that this is – after all – semillon. Screw cap. 12% alc. RATING 97 DRINK 2023–2028 $65 JH ✪

♟♟♟♟ **Museum Release Signature Palmers Lane Semillon 2014, Hunter Valley** An exceptionally youthful wine, with acidity and unsweetened lemon fused so tightly together it may live for decades to come. Whether a Peter Pan life span is unambiguously desirable/great is a question that can generate a spread of answers. My points are a fence-sitting answer. Screw cap. 12% alc. RATING 96 DRINK 2023–2028 $65 JH ✪

Aged Release Signature Shiraz 2017, Hunter Valley Sourced from a blend of Palmers Lane and McDonalds Road Vineyards. The best of Bimbadgen's 3 releases of '17 shiraz, with power, depth and length. Just embarking on a long life. Screw cap. 14.3% alc. RATING 95 DRINK 2023–2043 $110 JH

Museum Release Signature Palmers Lane Semillon 2017, Hunter Valley This wine still has years in front of it. This vintage wine is elegant and has

excellent line and length, the fruit still in the ascendant. Screw cap. 11.9% alc.
RATING 95 DRINK 2023–2032 $65 JH
Growers Vermentino 2022, Hunter Valley Historically widely grown in
Sardinia and Corsica, noted there (and now here) for its excellent acid retention
which underwrites the vibrancy and a blend of grapefruit and lemon fruits.
Its length on the finish and aftertaste is another virtue. Screw cap. 12.3% alc.
RATING 94 DRINK 2023–2028 $28 JH ✪
Aged Release McDonalds Road Shiraz 2017, Hunter Valley The first of a
run of 3 excellent consecutive vintages for the Hunter Valley. Excellent retention
of colour; a wine with good drive and length, with many years in front of it.
Screw cap. 14% alc. RATING 94 DRINK 2023–2038 $65 JH

ΨΨΨΨ♀ **Signature Semillon 2022, Hunter Valley** RATING 93 DRINK 2023–2028
$65 JH
Museum Release Signature Semillon 2019, Hunter Valley RATING 93
DRINK 2023–2034 $65 JH
Single Vineyard Palmers Lane Semillon 2022, Hunter Valley RATING 92
DRINK 2023–2027 $45 JH
Single Vineyard McDonalds Road Semillon 2022, Hunter Valley
RATING 91 DRINK 2023–2027 $45 JH
Sparkling Blanc de Blancs 2021, Hunter Valley RATING 90
DRINK 2023–2029 $50 JH

Bindi Wines ★★★★★

343 Melton Road, Gisborne, Vic 3437 (postal) **Region** Macedon Ranges
T (03) 5428 2564 **www.**bindiwines.com.au **Open** Not **Winemaker** Michael Dhillon,
Stuart Anderson (Consultant) **Est.** 1988 **Dozens** 2000 **Vyds** 7ha
The Bindi farm spans 170ha but only 7ha is planted to vines. This simple fact is an insight
into the care and respect the Dhillon family has for its land, its heritage and its future. There
are only 2 varieties planted (pinot noir and chardonnay) on the home vineyard, both long-
established for their stellar quality. Bindi is without question among a select few at the top
echelon of Australian wine and essentially has been ever since its '88 plantings first hit their
straps. Of genuine excitement is the addition of high-density pinot noir (11 300 vines/ha,
planted in '14 and '16), which is destined to add yet more lustre.

ΨΨΨΨΨ **Block 8 Pinot Noir 2021, Macedon Ranges** Rarely does a new wine make
my heart skip a beat. You don't simply taste this – you feel. A core of excellent
fruit, all dark cherries, maraschino and spice with a little amaro lift, the oak a light
flutter throughout. Fuller bodied and supple with stunning tannins all silky and
ethereal with fine acidity. It lingers long. It's thought-provoking. It's extraordinary,
more so, knowing the block was planted in '16. Respect, Michael Dhillon.
Respect. Diam. 13% alc. RATING 98 DRINK 2023–2035 $170 JF ♥
Block 5 Pinot Noir 2021, Macedon Ranges Bindi's '92-planted Block 5 and
'16-planted Block 8 are adjacent. I wonder what they 'talk about' via their root
systems. Block 5 might say: I'm older and my wine reveals a depth. In response,
Block 8 might add: Wait until you see what I'm going to become. The result is
stunning. Perfect fruit flavours, a richness yet not weighty, layers of spice, cedary
oak, complexity and detail. The tannins are textural, raw silk-like and pure.
Screw cap. 13.5% alc. RATING 97 DRINK 2023–2035 $170 JF
Quartz Chardonnay 2021, Macedon Ranges So contemplative, complex
and exquisite, this demands respect and time. It unfurls in a savoury manner with
smokin' sexy sulphides and a minerally crunch to the acidity that leads to such a
long finish. Creamy miso paste and grilled cashew lees bolster the palate, there's
some lemon saline tang and so much more. Screw cap. 14% alc. RATING 97
DRINK 2022–2035 $115 JF

ΤΤΤΤΤ **Kaye Pinot Noir 2021, Macedon Ranges** This vintage, this site (the highest at Bindi), have come together to offer the finest Kaye to date. The palate is superfine and long with supple tannins, and lots of them, yet the reaffirming acidity captures everything in its wake – the dark cherries, chinotto, blood orange and zest and lots of exotic spices with licorice root. Just lovely. Screw cap. 13.5% alc. **RATING** 96 **DRINK** 2023–2033 $115 JF

Kostas Rind Chardonnay 2021, Macedon Ranges I love the story of this wine, named after Kostas Rind, teacher, mentor and friend of Michael Dhillon's father, Bill. And I love the contents within, particularly this vintage. Richly filled with stone fruit, spiced lemon, frangipane-lined lime tart, plus spices. Neat acidity keeps check of the palate, which has depth, some weight and very good length. Screw cap. 14% alc. **RATING** 96 **DRINK** 2022–2031 $75 JF ✪

Dixon Pinot Noir 2021, Macedon Ranges If you had to choose which pinot to drink today, the Dixon is it. Everything in its place and harmoniously so: the plump black cherries, the dabs of woodsy spices, the sumac and beetroot juice. The fuller-bodied palate seamless with ripe, velvety tannins, an evenness throughout and the juicy acidity closing the deal a long time later. Diam. 13.5% alc. **RATING** 96 **DRINK** 2023–2033 $75 JF ✪

Darshan Pinot Noir 2021, Macedon Ranges Named after Michael's late father and founder of Bindi, the wonderful Darshan Singh Dhillon. This is a lovely wine, heady with autumn leaves after rain, rhubarb, beetroot and pomegranate. Very savoury yet sweetly spiced and tangy with suppleness and fine tannins with some grit and grip. A fitting tribute. Diam. 12.5% alc. **RATING** 96 **DRINK** 2023–2031 $170 JF

Dhillon Col Mountain Vineyard Grenache Rosé 2022, Heathcote Grenache can morph into beautiful wine and if it's the base of rosé, well it works a treat. While this has the spice lift, Sichuan pepper and a hint of sarsaparilla, the palate fleshes out (aged on lees for 6 months in old barrels). With its light layer of crunchy watermelon and raspberries, this is refreshing. Screw cap. 13% alc. **RATING** 95 **DRINK** 2022–2026 $35 JF ✪

Pyrette Shiraz 2021, Heathcote Showing off all the charm and exuberance of the variety from this region. Floral, smoky, peppery, lots of deep, dark fruit and spices, inky, too. Full bodied yet such vibrancy of acidity and plush, detailed tannins. A fabulous drink now and it will give more in time. Diam. 14% alc. **RATING** 95 **DRINK** 2024–2036 $40 JF ✪

Original Vineyard Pinot Noir 2021, Macedon Ranges A delightful, almost lighter Original that charms with its combo of stewed rhubarb, cherry pip and forest floor aromas. Hints of fresh herbs and tangy acidity, spicy as usual and a fineness across the palate with slightly sinewy tannins. Drinking well as of now. Diam. 13.5% alc. **RATING** 95 **DRINK** 2023–2035 $100 JF

Dhillon Col Mountain Vineyard Shiraz 2017, Heathcote Youthful even with a few years under its belt and although there's a mellowing, it's relaxed. Savoury and earthy with strong ferrous aromas, sumac and dark fruit, the palate is laid out as structured and deep. The tannins are supple and ripe, plenty of them, too, and such a counterpoint to the '21 Pyrette shiraz. Diam. 14% alc. **RATING** 95 **DRINK** 2022–2030 $80 JF

Dhillon Glenhope Vineyard Ranges Rosé 2022, Macedon Ranges A new wine made from merlot and shiraz; wild-yeast fermented in old barrels and left on fine lees for about 6 months, which explains the texture. Heady with roses, ginger flowers, Old Spice and Angostura bitters. The palate is refreshing and lithe with light tannins, dry yet with a generosity of flavour. Screw cap. 13% alc. **RATING** 94 **DRINK** 2023–2026 $30 JF ✪

ΤΤΤΤΥ **Dhillon Glenhope Vineyard Riesling 2022, Macedon Ranges RATING** 93 **DRINK** 2023–2029 $35 JF ✪

Dhillon Col Mountain Vineyard Grenache 2021, Heathcote RATING 92 **DRINK** 2024–2031 $40 JF

Bird on a Wire Wines

51 Symons Street, Healesville, Vic 3777 (postal) **Region** Yarra Valley
T 0439 045 000 **www**.birdonawirewines.com.au **Open** Not **Winemaker** Caroline Mooney
Est. 2008 **Dozens** 850

This is the full-time business of winemaker Caroline Mooney. She grew up in the Yarra Valley and has had other winemaking jobs in the valley for over 10 years. The focus is on small, single-vineyard sites owned by growers committed to producing outstanding grapes. Having worked at the legendary Domaine Jean-Louis Chave in the '06 vintage, she has a special interest in shiraz and marsanne, both grown from distinct sites on a single vineyard in the Yarra Glen area.

Chardonnay 2021, Yarra Valley A very bright green gold. A wonderfully complex Upper Yarra Valley chardonnay with aromas of stone fruits, grilled nuts, a little nougat and some marine scents. Equally good on the textured and structured palate, which finishes long with a very appealing and balanced touch of grip. It's tops now, and it'll still be good in 4–6 years, if not longer. Screw cap. 13% alc. **RATING** 97 **DRINK** 2022-2027 $35 PR ✪

Marsanne 2018, Yarra Valley **RATING** 92 **DRINK** 2022-2026 $39 PR

BK Wines

Knotts Hill, Basket Range, SA 5138 **Region** Adelaide Hills
T 0410 124 674 **www**.bkwines.com.au **Open** By appt **Winemaker** Brendon Keys
Viticulturist Brendon Keys **Est.** 2007 **Dozens** 4500

BK Wines is owned by NZ-born duo Brendon and Kirstyn Keys. Brendon has packed a great deal into the past decade. He bounced between Australia and NZ before working in California with the well known Paul Hobbs; he then helped Paul set up a winery in Argentina. Brendon's tag-line is 'Wines made with love, not money', and he has not hesitated to confound the normal rules of engagement in winemaking.

Ma Fleur Chardonnay 2008, Piccadilly Valley Salty and flor-driven. Jura, the archetype. Pithy apricot, Meyer lemon, curry leaf and salt mulched into brine. The sheer intensity of this wine cannot be bridled by pithy commentary. Stunning! Knee-jerking and thrill-seeking! Screw cap. 12.5% alc. **RATING** 97 **DRINK** 2022-2032 $150 NG

Swaby Single Vineyard Chardonnay 2021, Piccadilly Valley Jura is clearly the aspiration and the drive. Comté cheese, hay, chamomile and the illusory whiff of wood-smoked river trout. A curb of tannins, saline and firm, line the cheeks. The fruit, mercifully subdued by the idyll. A wine of considerable impact, intellectual vigour and unbridled joy. Diam. 12.5% alc. **RATING** 96 **DRINK** 2022-2028 $55 NG ✪

The Fall Single Vineyard Chardonnay 2021, Adelaide Hills This is exceptional. The early picked, lees-worked style handled with aplomb. Scents of yellow plum, spiced apple, lanolin, nashi pear and chamomile. A delicious, impeccably structured wine of poise, intensity and thrumming length, not far off a contemporary Loire chenin blanc. I have tasted these wines from their first release, and they are better than ever. Get on board. Diam. 12.8% alc. **RATING** 96 **DRINK** 2022-2028 $55 NG ✪ ♥

Gin Gin Chardonnay 2021, Adelaide Hills A broader panoply of fruit accents from marmalade to white peach and nectarine. The acidity, although the wine is lower in alcohol, feels juicier and ginger crystalline. The wine at large, broader. The oak, a well-appointed framework. Lithe and saline. Crunchy length, with fruit sweetness slipping over the acid rails to impart a whisk of generosity to the maker's tensile style. Diam. 12.5% alc. **RATING** 94 **DRINK** 2022-2029 $55 NG

 ♟♟♟♟♟ Yandra Chardonnay 2021, Lenswood RATING 93 DRINK 2022–2030 $55 NG
Saignée of Pinot Noir Rosé 2022, Lenswood RATING 92 DRINK 2022–2023
$34 NG
Carte Blanche Rouge 2021, Adelaide Hills RATING 91 DRINK 2022–2025
$40 NG

Black & Ginger ★★★★

563 Sugarloaf Road, Rhymney, Vic 3374 (postal) **Region** Great Western
T 0409 964 855 **www.**blackandginger.com.au **Open** Not **Winemaker** Hadyn Black
Est. 2015 **Dozens** 1000
This is the venture of 2 friends; Hadyn Black is cellar hand and winemaker, working in the
Great Western region. Darcy Naunton (Ginger) is an entrepreneur in Melbourne. Their
common interest in wine saw them take a great leap in '15 and buy 1t of shiraz from the
renowned Malakoff vineyard in the Pyrenees, with further vintages following. Hadyn and
partner Lucy Joyce purchased a rundown vineyard in Great Western in late '16, naming
the wine Lily's Block after Hadyn's mother, who did much of the pruning and picking but
unfortunately passed away before tasting the wine.

 ♟♟♟♟♟ **L'Amante Nebbiolo 2021, Pyrenees** Enough grip, enough flavour and a
lot of style. This is a convincing nebbiolo. It mixes red cherry, leather, rose and
chocolate characters with seamless ease and completes a dry, structured finish with
confidence. It's as interesting as it is impressive. Screw cap. 14.2% alc. **RATING** 94
DRINK 2023–2031 $45 CM

 ♟♟♟♟♟ **Lorelei Gewürztraminer 2022, Henty** RATING 93 DRINK 2023–2026
$33 CM ✪
Lily's Block Hounds Run Vineyard Shiraz 2021, Great Western RATING 93
DRINK 2024–2031 $45 CM
The Gypsy Vermentino 2022, Alpine Valleys RATING 92 DRINK 2023–2026
$33 CM
Cinco Rojas 2021, Great Western RATING 92 DRINK 2023–2027 $45 CM

BlackJack Vineyards ★★★★

3379 Harmony Way, Harcourt, Vic 3453 **Region** Bendigo
T (03) 5474 2355 **www.**blackjackwines.com.au **Open** W'ends & some public hols 11–5
Winemaker Ian McKenzie, Ken Pollock **Est.** 1987 **Dozens** 3000 **Vyds** 6ha
Established by the McKenzie and Pollock families on the site of an old apple and pear orchard
in the Harcourt Valley, BlackJack is best known for very good shiraz. Despite some tough
vintage conditions, BlackJack has managed to produce supremely honest, full-flavoured and
powerful wines, all with an edge of elegance.

 ♟♟♟♟♟ **Block 6 Shiraz 2020, Bendigo** Take a deep sniff of Block 6 Shiraz and you'll
be transported to a vineyard surrounded by magnificent Australian bushland and
giant eucalypts. It's that evocative. The Aussie scent is joined by spices, lots of
them, and rich, ripe black fruits. Discreet vanillin (French) oak provides an extra
dimension on the palate. All up, it's so Victorian, so darn smooth and tasty. Enjoy.
Screw cap. 14.5% alc. **RATING** 92 **DRINK** 2023–2033 $42 JP

Bleasdale Vineyards ★★★★★

1640 Langhorne Creek Road, Langhorne Creek, SA 5255 **Region** Langhorne Creek
T (08) 8537 4000 **www.**bleasdale.com.au **Open** 7 days 10–5 **Winemaker** Paul Hotker,
Matt Laube **Viticulturist** Sarah Keough **Est.** 1850 **Dozens** 70 000 **Vyds** 45ha
Not only one of the most historic wineries in Australia, with over 170 years of continuous
winemaking by the direct descendants of the founding Potts family, but one of the leading
quality producers in the land. Not so long before the start of the 21st century, its vineyards
were flooded every winter by diversion of the Bremer River, which provided moisture
throughout the dry, cool, growing season. In the new millennium, every drop of water is

counted. The vineyards have been significantly upgraded and refocused: shiraz accounts for 45% of plantings, supported by 7 other proven varieties; sauvignon blanc, pinot gris and chardonnay are sourced from the Adelaide Hills. Bleasdale Vineyards is the *Halliday Wine Companion 2024* Winery of the Year.

ΨΨΨΨΨ **The Iron Duke Cabernet Sauvignon 2021, Langhorne Creek** Cabernet Sauvignon of the Year. A best-barrel selection, and oh my, it's a beautifully structured and textured cabernet sauvignon. Here cassis has the purity and sparkle of wine which you could drink tonight or in 30 years time. Screw cap. 13.5% alc. **RATING** 98 **DRINK** 2023-2051 $89 JH ✪ ♥

Wellington Road Shiraz Cabernet 2021, Langhorne Creek Cabernet Shiraz of the Year. Score awarded by the Halliday tasting panel at the annual Awards judging. JH writes: Winemaker Paul Hotker made full use of a brilliant growing season and harvest, with a juicy and sleek palate redolent with red and black fruits that caress every time you return to the supple mouthfeel and lingering finish. Screw cap. 13.5% alc. **RATING** 98 **DRINK** 2023-2046 $32 PD ✪ ♥

Frank Potts 2021, Langhorne Creek Cabernet sauvignon/malbec/petit verdot/merlot. Bright crimson-purple hue heralds a very complex wine that has no need of time thanks to its balance, texture and length. An outstanding achievement offering equally exceptional value for money. Screw cap. 13.5% alc. **RATING** 97 **DRINK** 2023-2041 $35 JH ✪

ΨΨΨΨΨ **Chardonnay 2022, Adelaide Hills** Brilliant quartz-green. All the inputs have been precisely managed, notably the mlf. The bouquet and palate move hand in hand, white peach/nectarine and citrusy acidity running throughout, oak a mere servant. Screw cap. 12.5% alc. **RATING** 96 **DRINK** 2023-2032 $32 JH ✪

Sparkling Shiraz NV, Langhorne Creek Includes 'a little splash of malbec'. Base wines from the '97-22 vintages. Has threaded the needle with lower dosages than usual, investing the wine with freshness and finely wrought tannins. Is there nothing outside the skills of Paul Hotker? Not to mention, value for money across the board. Diam. 13.5% alc. **RATING** 95 $24 JH ✪

Cabernet Franc 2022, Langhorne Creek The things you don't hear about: Bleasdale has been using cabernet franc in blends for over 25 years, and this wine makes a first-up solo appearance. Fascinating aromas of raspberry, candle wax and star anise. Ready for consumption. Screw cap. 12.5% alc. **RATING** 95 **DRINK** 2023-2023 $30 JH ✪

Pinot Gris 2022, Adelaide Hills The majority is fermented cool in stainless-steel tanks; 25% is fermented with high solids and ambient yeasts in used puncheons. Bingo. Easy. Except it's not – it's arcane magic, giving pinot gris substance and flavour before a long, lemony, bright finish. Screw cap. 13% alc. **RATING** 95 **DRINK** 2023-2024 $22 JH ✪ ♥

The Wild Fig Shiraz Grenache Mourvèdre 2022, Langhorne Creek On skins 12-14 days, matured for 6 months in used puncheons or tank (to retain freshness). The wine is ridiculously good, likely to cause dribbling when tasting. Screw cap. 13.5% alc. **RATING** 95 **DRINK** 2023-2028 $22 JH ✪

Grenache 2022, Langhorne Creek Destemmed grenache blended with a small percentage of whole-bunch shiraz. The perfumed bouquet offers red cherry and raspberry, the palate revelling in the low alcohol (for grenache) and its spiced, dry finish. Screw cap. 13.5% alc. **RATING** 95 **DRINK** 2023-2032 $30 JH ✪

Riesling 2022, Adelaide Hills '22 produced impressive rieslings in the Clare Valley, so no surprise with this. Excellent acidity balanced by 3.4g/L RS; bottled May 3 to guarantee freshness after a cool ferment. The bouquet has aromas of citrus, apple blossom and talc. There's nothing aggressive about the mouthfeel, just enjoyment. Everything just so. Screw cap. 12% alc. **RATING** 95 **DRINK** 2023-2032 $30 JH ✪

Broad-Side Shiraz Cabernet Sauvignon Malbec 2021, Langhorne Creek This is a slick operation. It's storybook value, impossible to beat at this price. It's a (decorous) fruit bomb with silky tannins and plums, the malbec pulling a stunt with much more to taste than its volume suggests. The score is designed to encourage as many people as possible to give it a go. Screw cap. 13.5% alc. RATING 95 DRINK 2023–2026 $22 JH ✪

Second Innings Malbec 2021, Langhorne Creek It is a seriously good malbec by normal standards, but Bleasdale is Australia's foremost maker of the variety, investing it with rich, velvety plum and blackberry fruits, supported with amiable tannins. Exceptional value. Screw cap. 13.5% alc. RATING 95 DRINK 2023–2031 $22 JH ✪

Generations Shiraz 2021, Langhorne Creek A highly fragrant and expressive bouquet leads the palate with its spice, black pepper, licorice and blackberry flavours. The tannin and oak inputs are all they should be, as are the texture, line and length. Screw cap. 13.5% alc. RATING 95 DRINK 2023–2041 $35 JH ✪

Generations Malbec 2021, Langhorne Creek It's like picking up a bunch of malbec grapes and chomping straight into them, such is the purity, the juiciness, the out-and-out grapeyness of this release. Earth, mulberry, loganberry and plum flavours swing persuasively through the palate here, the word authenticity whispered every step of the way. Stalk, violet and clove-like notes here are at one with the fruit. This wine seems unadorned in the best and most natural of ways. Screw cap. 14% alc. RATING 95 DRINK 2023–2033 $35 CM ✪

Mulberry Tree Cabernet Sauvignon 2021, Langhorne Creek Finesse and elegance are the last words expected for a young cabernet, but they describe this most attractive wine. Has won a string of silver and gold medals. Screw cap. 13.5% alc. RATING 95 DRINK 2023–2038 $22 JH ✪

Bremerview Shiraz 2021, Langhorne Creek The wine is ridiculously good value at this price, with the warming gentle palate of Langhorne Creek: plum, dark berry fruit and just enough soft tannin. Gold medals Melbourne Royal Wine Awards and Rutherglen Wine Show '22. Screw cap. 13.5% alc. RATING 95 DRINK 2023–2036 $22 JH ✪

Blanc de Blancs NV, Adelaide Hills The base wines (100% chardonnay) came from '20–22, wild-yeast ferments of full-juice solids in tank and seasoned puncheons. The result is a complex, textured wine not made by the traditional method. Diam. 12% alc. RATING 94 $30 JH ✪

Sauvignon Blanc 2022, Adelaide Hills Winemaker Paul Hotker is a clever chap. He crushes and chills the juice to add texture and ferments 10% in French puncheons (50% new). A subtly cadenced wine that could partner with food of many cuisines. Screw cap. 12% alc. RATING 94 DRINK 2023–2036 $24 JH ✪

Wellington Road GSM 2022, Langhorne Creek A serious GSM, starting with bright, clear colour and fine but firm tannins running from start to finish. While enjoyable now, its best years are in front of it. Screw cap. 13.5% alc. RATING 94 DRINK 2025–2035 $32 JH ✪

Syrah 2022, Langhorne Creek Matured in used puncheons for 9 months, with a portion retained in tank for freshness. Made for drinking now/soon, but will be around for longer if you wish. Screw cap. 13.5% alc. RATING 94 DRINK 2023–2029 $30 JH ✪

Wellington Road GSM 2021, Langhorne Creek A blend of 67/29/4% grenache/shiraz/mataro. An expressive bouquet of plum jam and red fruits, the palate enough to warm the cockles of my heart. Medium bodied with a surprise finish of authority with savoury yet silky tannins. Screw cap. 13.5% alc. RATING 94 DRINK 2023–2031 $32 JH ✪

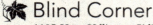 **Rosé 2022, Langhorne Creek** RATING 93 DRINK 2023–2023 $20 JH ✪

❦ Blind Corner

1105 Vasse Yallingup Siding Road, Quindalup, WA 6281 **Region** Margaret River **T** (08) 9755 1974 **www.blindcorner.com.au Open** Wed–Sat 10–4 **Winemaker** Ben Gould **Viticulturist** Ben Gould **Est.** 2005 **Dozens** 1100 **Vyds** 20ha
Ben and Naomi Gould are the dynamic duo behind this biodynamically farmed enterprise, created in '05 when they owned a site in Wilyabrup. Realising a larger vineyard was needed,

they bought a property at Quindalup in '14. Working to create the harmonious ecosystem of today, they encourage native species back onto the land, and gaps between the vines are planted with native flora or transplanted evergreen shrubs to encourage diversity. They are constantly experimenting (having two Georgian qveri buried onsite in bushland), achieving, failing, learning, and achieving again. They have chooks roaming the vineyard, bees for pollination and honey, and everything is about a holistic approach.

Sangiovese 2021, Margaret River An unusual style. Lovely to drink, just a lighter-framed example, all tangy and tart with maraschino and red cherries, kirsch and a flutter of spice. Bright acidity with Italianate tannins textural, but not overt. Surprisingly, this is made from air-dried grapes and left on skins post ferment for 100 days before 18 months in old oak. I like the outcome. Screw cap. 13% alc. **RATING** 93 **DRINK** 2022-2027 $45 JF

Nouveau Shiraz 2022, Margaret River Nouveau is a youthful shiraz off a dry-grown, certified organic/biodynamic site. It's delightfully savoury although good fruit flavours come to the fore (spiced plums and red cherries). Just a light spray of tannins, the acidity juicy and this should be served slightly chilled on a warm day. Screw cap. 12.5% alc. **RATING** 92 **DRINK** 2022-2025 $35 JF

Blanc* 2022, Margaret River A blend of sauvignon blanc and chenin blanc. On a hot day, this could slake a thirst it's so zesty, refreshing and lively. The palate is racy, with crunchy acidity to close and it is deliciously savoury. Very satisfying Screw cap. 12.5% alc. **RATING** 92 **DRINK** 2022-2024 $21 JF ✪

Orange* In Colour 2022, Margaret River A bright, mid-straw hue with wafts of woodsmoke, dried herbs and pears. It tastes a bit like poached quinces and lemon curd with refreshing citrusy flavours. The phenolics aren't over the top or bitter – more chewy and textural, and the acidity keeps this on track. Screw cap. 12.5% alc. **RATING** 90 **DRINK** 2022-2024 $21 JF ✪

Bloodwood   ★★★★★

231 Griffin Road, Orange, NSW 2800 **Region** Orange
T (02) 6362 5631 **www.**bloodwood.biz **Open** By appt **Winemaker** Stephen Doyle
Est. 1983 **Dozens** 4000 **Vyds** 8.43ha

Rhonda and Stephen Doyle are 2 of the pioneers of the Orange district; '24 will mark Bloodwood's 40th anniversary. The estate vineyards (chardonnay, riesling, merlot, cabernet sauvignon, shiraz, cabernet franc and malbec) are planted at an elevation of 810–860m, which provides a reliably cool climate. The wines are sold mainly through the cellar door and by an energetic, humorous and informatively run mailing list. Bloodwood has an impressive track record across the full gamut of wine styles, especially riesling; all of the wines have a particular elegance and grace. Very much part of the high-quality reputation of Orange.

Schubert Chardonnay 2022, Orange This chardonnay stands tall among its peers. It's a textural explosion of Meyer lemon skin, white nectarine and yellow plum. The palate coils with a python-like vice, electrifying with its perky acidity. A journey through roasted Marcona almonds, creamy vanilla bean custard and honey biscuits follows. A wine that goes from strength to strength, lingering in your memory. Screw cap. 13% alc. **RATING** 96 **DRINK** 2022-2032 $38 SW ✪

Riesling 2022, Orange Wild apple blossom, lime zest and margarita salt spring from the glass, followed by lime curd and bee pollen. With a finely chiselled sandstone-like texture, the palate is alive with nuances of mustard fruits, silt and gingernut biscuit. There is a ripeness of fruit with subtle savoury elements mixed with a high degree of shape and form that makes for a complex and considered riesling. Screw cap. 11.8% alc. **RATING** 95 **DRINK** 2022-2035 $33 SW ✪

Cabernet Sauvignon 2019, Orange Blackberries, juniper, Kalamata olive and wild thyme are quickly chased by charcoal, pepperberry and clove. Two years in bottle before release has softened tannins to a silty, powdery texture with perky acidity. This is drinking exceptionally well now and will cellar for a decade, no doubt uncovering more spices and savoury tones. A stunner of a wine at an unbeatable price. Screw cap. 13.5% alc. **RATING** 95 **DRINK** 2022-2038 $36 SW ✪

 Pinot Noir 2022, Orange RATING 93 DRINK 2022-2032 $40 SW
 Chardonnay 2021, Orange RATING 93 DRINK 2022-2032 $33 SW ✪
 Chirac 2010, Orange RATING 92 DRINK 2022-2030 $80 SW

Blue Gables ★★★★★

100 Lanigan Road, Maffra West Upper, Vic 3859 **Region** Gippsland
T (03) 5148 0372 **www.bluegables.com.au Open** Thurs–Sun 11–5 **Winemaker** Alastair
Butt, Mal Stewart (sparkling) **Viticulturist** Alistair Hicks **Est.** 2004 **Dozens** 2000
Vyds 5ha

Blue Gables is the culmination of a long-held dream for chemical engineer Alistair and
journalist wife Catherine Hicks. They purchased 8ha of a north-facing hillside slope from
Catherine's father's dairy farm and built a 2-storey gabled roof farmhouse, hence the name.
This small vineyard, nestled high above the Macalister Irrigation District in East Gippsland,
was first planted in '04, with further plantings in '05 – 0.8ha each of sauvignon blanc, pinot
gris and shiraz and 0.4ha of chardonnay. Sangiovese and pinot noir were added in '17.

 Ashton Pinot Noir 2022, Gippsland Fragrant, floral and supple, with loads
of juicy cherries and plum compote dusted with cinnamon and a whisper of
pepper. It feels light and pretty with fine tannins ensuring texture and the acidity
lengthens the palate. Screw cap. 13% alc. RATING 95 DRINK 2023-2032 $70 JF
Keith Thomas Reserve Shiraz 2021, Gippsland This will unfurl with more
complexity and detail in time. It's a gorgeous, enticing purple-red hue laden with
plums and berries, the charry oak adds flavour and drying tannins, time will sort
that out. While full bodied and rich, it has a level of precision and refreshment,
too. Screw cap. 13.2% alc. RATING 95 DRINK 2023-2038 $70 JF
Jesse Chardonnay 2021, Gippsland A very smart drink, what with its nod
to stone fruit and citrus, creamy lees and lime curd flavours across the linear palate.
It's ultra-refreshing thanks to the acidity, while the oak adds an extra dimension
both in flavour and shape. A composed Jesse and the finest to date. Screw cap.
13% alc. RATING 94 DRINK 2022-2030 $35 JF ✪

 Jesse Chardonnay 2022, Gippsland RATING 93 DRINK 2023-2030 $37 JF
 Sangiovese 2021, Gippsland RATING 93 DRINK 2022-2027 $35 JF ✪
 Pinot Gris 2022, Gippsland RATING 91 DRINK 2022-2024 $30 JF
 Hanratty Hill Shiraz 2022, Gippsland RATING 90 DRINK 2024-2034 $37 JF

Blue Poles Vineyard ★★★★☆

PO Box 34, Mount Lawley, WA 6929 **Region** Margaret River
T (08) 9757 4382 **www.bluepolesvineyard.com.au Open** Not **Winemaker** Vasse River
Wines (Sharna Kowalczuk) **Est.** 2001 **Dozens** 750 **Vyds** 6ha

Blue Poles Vineyard is named for the iconic Jackson Pollock painting *Blue Poles: Number 11,
1952*, controversially purchased by the Australian National Gallery in the '70s. The painting
came to embody the evolution of Australian's nationhood; to the owners, the name is a nod
to the 'independence and free thought' that inspires them. Their focus is merlot and cabernet
franc, but they also have shiraz, chardonnay and smaller amounts of viognier, teroldego and
marsanne planted.

 Merlot Cabernet Franc 2020, Margaret River There seems to have been
a concerted effort to keep the alcohol down here. Yet these wines often age
brilliantly, defying my conceptions. A singe of mocha oak encases Bing cherry,
sarsaparilla, chilli, vanillin cedar and a sluice of bitter chocolate, truffle and violet.
Intriguing now, but bound to grow with time in the cellar. Ridiculous value.
Screw cap. 13.5% alc. RATING 95 DRINK 2022-2035 $45 NG ✪
Chardonnay 2021, Margaret River A lean style that finds shape and fluidity
in the glass. Smart oak, and no obvious primary fruit, which I enjoy. It's more
about bones, sinew, glazed quince and a creamy core of nougatine. A broad spread
across the palate and a long drive down the gullet. Latent and unassuming now,

but time will draw this out. Screw cap. 12.6% alc. **RATING** 94 **DRINK** 2023–2031 $40 NG ✪

Allouran 2019, Margaret River A merlot/cabernet franc blend. Damson plum, redcurrant, licorice, cedar, a waft of mocha, dried tobacco and a smattering of herbs. Tannins are supple and beautifully aligned. Finishes lustrous and long without an ounce of heaviness. Could be a touch riper, but lovely all the same. Will age beautifully. Screw cap. 13.9% alc. **RATING** 94 **DRINK** 2022–2033 $30 NG ✪

🍷🍷🍷🍷🍷 **Reserve Merlot 2019, Margaret River RATING** 93 **DRINK** 2024–2032 $45 NG

Blue Pyrenees Estate   ★★★★★

656 Vinoca Road, Avoca, Vic 3467 **Region** Pyrenees
T (03) 5465 1111 **www.bluepyrenees.com.au Open** 7 days 11–5 **Winemaker** Carmel Keenan, Mel Newman **Viticulturist** Sean Howe **Est.** 1963 **Dozens** 60 000 **Vyds** 149ha
Remy Cointreau established Blue Pyrenees Estate (then known as Château Remy) in 1963, growing ugni blanc for brandy. Forty years later, the business was sold to a small group of Sydney businessmen. The core of the business is the very large estate plantings of shiraz and cabernet, most decades old, but with newer arrivals, including viognier. In '19, Blue Pyrenees Estate was purchased by Glenlofty Wines, forming the largest producer in the Pyrenees.

🍷🍷🍷🍷🍷 **Richardson Reserve Cabernet Sauvignon 2019, Pyrenees** Blackcurrant and aniseed characters blend with cedar wood, spearmint and cream. This is a wine that starts off as medium weight then builds and expands as it breathes, like the swell of a wave as it moves inshore, the result a cohesive crash of fruit, oak and tannin. It's a beauty. Cork. 14% alc. **RATING** 96 **DRINK** 2027–2045 $150 CM
Richardson Cabernet Sauvignon 2019, Pyrenees Serious but soft. Blackcurrant, mulberry, mint and coffee-cream characters flood the palate and, more importantly, impress themselves emphatically on the finish. A swagger of tannin, a powerful wash of fruit and a long finish – it's a compelling combination. Screw cap. 14% alc. **RATING** 95 **DRINK** 2026–2042 $64 CM
Richardson Shiraz 2019, Pyrenees The distinguishing feature of this wine, aside from the volume of oak, is its length. It offers cherry-plum flavours with mint, vanilla-cream and woodsy spice, but it's the combination of grainy tannin and pulsating length that really elevates it. It will be fascinating to watch this wine evolve. Diam. 14.5% alc. **RATING** 95 **DRINK** 2026–2039 $64 CM
Estate Red 2019, Pyrenees A blend of 58/32/5/5% cabernet sauvignon/ merlot/malbec/cabernet franc. Medium weight, complex and well sustained. Blackcurrant, toast, fragrant herbs and eucalyptus with cedar oak pulling it all together. This will age beautifully, thanks mostly to its balance, its harmony and its length. Screw cap. 14% alc. **RATING** 94 **DRINK** 2024–2034 $44 CM

🍷🍷🍷🍷🍷 **Champ Blanc Blend 2021, Pyrenees RATING** 93 **DRINK** 2023–2030 $37 CM
Midnight Cuvée 2020, Pyrenees RATING 92 **DRINK** 2023–2027 $37 CM
Exclusive Release Malbec 2021, Pyrenees RATING 91 **DRINK** 2023–2030 $33 CM
Section One Shiraz 2019, Pyrenees RATING 91 **DRINK** 2023–2030 $44 CM
Dry Sparkling Rosé 2021, Pyrenees RATING 90 **DRINK** 2023–2025 $33 CM
Sauvignon Blanc 2022, Pyrenees RATING 90 **DRINK** 2023–2025 $23 CM ✪

Bobar   ★★★★☆

253 Gulf Road, Yarra Glen, Vic 3775 **Region** Yarra Valley
T (03) 9730 2668 **www.bobarwines.com.au Open** By appt **Winemaker** Tom and Sally Belford **Viticulturist** Tom and Sally Belford **Est.** 2010 **Dozens** 1500 **Vyds** 5ha
Tom and Sally Belford have worked for vineyards and wineries in the cooler hilly parts of NSW, Macedon Ranges and Heathcote, and more recently in the Yarra Valley. Along the way they also managed to spend 15 months in France, dividing their time between Champagne, Beaujolais, Provence, Cahors and Sauternes. In '10 they decided to 'make a little wine for

the hell of it', and purchased shiraz from the Yarraland vineyard at Chirnside Park. It comes as close to natural wine as is possible, with whole bunches in an open fermenter, no crushing or destemming, no pigeage or pumping over, and no yeast.

ŸŸŸŸŸ **Viognier 2022, Yarra Valley** A very bright green gold. Restrained and fragrant with aromas of white peach, acacia, honey and a little spice. Just as good on the vibrant, nuanced, grapefruit pithy and long palate. Lovely wine. Diam. 11% alc. **RATING** 95 **DRINK** 2022–2026 $44 PR ✪

ŸŸŸŸŸ **85% Pinot Noir 2022, Yarra Valley RATING** 93 **DRINK** 2022–2025 $44 PR
Syrah 2022, Yarra Valley RATING 93 **DRINK** 2022–2027 $44 PR
Cabernet Franc 2022, Yarra Valley RATING 92 **DRINK** 2022–2026 $44 PR
Cabaret Cabernet Sauvignon 2020, Yarra Valley RATING 91
DRINK 2022–2025 $60 PR

Bondar Wines ★★★★★

148 McMurtrie Road, McLaren Vale, SA 5171 **Region** McLaren Vale
T 0460 898 158 **www.**bondarwines.com.au **Open** Mon–Tue 11–4, Wed–Sun 11–5
Winemaker Andre Bondar **Viticulturist** Ben Lacey **Est.** 2013 **Dozens** 3000
Vyds 13.5ha
Andre Bondar and Selina Kelly began a deliberately unhurried journey in '09, which culminated in the purchase of the celebrated Rayner Vineyard post-vintage '13. Andre had been a winemaker at Nepenthe wines for 7 years, and Selina had recently completed a law degree. They changed focus and began to look for a vineyard capable of producing great shiraz. Rayner had all the answers: a ridge bisecting the land, Blewitt Springs sand on the eastern side; and heavier clay loam soils over limestone on the western side. The vineyard has been substantially reworked and includes 10ha of shiraz, with smaller amounts of grenache, mataro, touriga, carignan, cinsault and counoise.

ŸŸŸŸŸ **Rayner Vineyard Shiraz 2021, McLaren Vale** Deep, brooding crimson purple. This is a faithful reproduction of variety and place – a meaningless statement unless I add 'of the highest quality,' which it is. It's velvet in the mouth, and mines all the black fruits, dark chocolate, licorice and spice hoped for. The tannins are polished, the oak absorbed by the fruit. Screw cap. 14% alc. **RATING** 97 **DRINK** 2023–2051 $48 JH ✪
Violet Hour Shiraz 2021, McLaren Vale Uncoils itself like a snake after a nap on a sunny afternoon, the colour rich and deep, as is every aspect of the wine on the lustrous bouquet and palate. Yet it's also a tapestry of silk and velvet, a little more than medium bodied. Bargain bonanza. Screw cap. 14% alc. **RATING** 97 **DRINK** 2023–2046 $32 JH ✪
Vestige Grenache 2021, McLaren Vale A singular story to be told. Limpid and turbid in the glass. Damson plum of hue. I can smell the puncheons on this. Diaphanous and pinotesque. The cloak of kirsch, pomelo, bergamot and pithy red cherry, underpinned by a carriage of saline freshness and bitter, gritty tannins, is something to relish with every sip. This is what I look for in Australian wine. Screw cap. 14.4% alc. **RATING** 97 **DRINK** 2022–2030 $60 NG ✪

ŸŸŸŸŸ **Junto GSM 2021, McLaren Vale** A striking wine, with a high-toned spray of flowery aromas moving into more savoury territory on the palate, bitter chocolate taking control, through to flashes of cinnamon on the finish. Sophisticated and exotic. Screw cap. 13.9% alc. **RATING** 96 **DRINK** 2023–2036 $30 JH ✪
Monastrell 2021, McLaren Vale Neither fined nor filtered. An exceptionally juicy monastrell (aka, mourvèdre), with a gentle build of texture and structure. It's a whole lot more than just another '21 fruit bomb. What a virtuoso display. Screw cap. 14% alc. **RATING** 96 **DRINK** 2023–2031 $32 JH ✪
Higher Springs Grenache 2021, McLaren Vale A bright, clear colour. Offers a tantalising bouquet, at once floral with red cherry blossom and earthy/savoury nuances. The palate is supple and very, very long, the finish is fresh and mouth-watering. Screw cap. 14.4% alc. **RATING** 96 **DRINK** 2023–2029 $60 JH ✪

Grenache Cinsault Rosé 2022, McLaren Vale The pale salmon–pink hue signals a rose petal and spice bouquet; the balance of the long palate with its wildflower/bramble is a feature, the freshness above all else. Drink anywhere, any time. Screw cap. 13% alc. **RATING** 95 **DRINK** 2023–2023 $28 JH ✪

Rayner Vineyard Grenache 2022, McLaren Vale A mid-ruby, suggestive of pinot noir. That idea shifts into a higher gear as scents of dried rose petals, kirsch, pomegranate, blood orange and dried thyme fill the space. Full and intense of flavour, yet paradoxically weightless as it shimmers across a scale of tannin from vibrato to tenor, growing in trajectory with air. An excellent, contemporary Vale grenache. Screw cap. 14% alc. **RATING** 95 **DRINK** 2023–2030 $40 NG ✪

Midnight Hour Shiraz 2021, McLaren Vale Very good. Northern Rhône glimpsed. Any sweet fruit, mercifully, knocked out by soaring aromas of violet, licorice, dried nori, ground clove and mace. Smoked meat aplenty. Some purple pastille and cherry emerge from the fray, but this is compact and taut, as much as it is jubey and generous. Lovely wine. Screw cap. 14% alc. **RATING** 95 **DRINK** 2022–2030 $48 NG ✪

Chardonnay 2021, Adelaide Hills All the bells and whistles, from a smoky, creamed cashew nose of barrel fermentation to a generous mid-palate flecked with crystalline mineral shards, pungent miso and candied cumquat. White peach and nectarine accents teem long across a juicy trail. Intense flavour, generosity and enough tension to confer sophistication. Screw cap. 12.5% alc. **RATING** 95 **DRINK** 2022–2030 $35 NG ✪

 **Nero d'Avola 2022, McLaren Vale RATING** 93 **DRINK** 2022–2025 $32 NG ✪
Higher Springs Grenache 2022, McLaren Vale RATING 93 **DRINK** 2023–2030 $60 NG
Junto GSM 2022, McLaren Vale RATING 91 **DRINK** 2023–2025 $30 NG

🍃 Boomer Creek Vineyard ★★★★

10922 Tasman Hwy, Little Swanport, Tas 7190 **Region** East Coast Tasmania
T 0423 912 360 **www.**boomercreekvineyard.com.au **Open** Wed–Sun 11–4
Winemaker Matt Wood **Viticulturist** Astrid Maurits **Est.** 2012 **Dozens** 800 **Vyds** 3ha
Boomer Creek lies in an enviable position at Little Swanport on the scenic drive up Tasmania's East Coast. The snazzy little cellar door provides views out over the water to Schouten Island at the southern tip of the Freycinet Peninsula. For the Walters family it's a third-generation, family-run operation with sheep, cattle and olives as well as vines. The 3ha Boomer Creek vineyard is planted to riesling, pinot noir and chardonnay, producing a concise range of wines that reflect the East Coast terroir nicely.

 Chardonnay 2021, Tasmania Pale straw with tight nectarine and citrus fruits underscored by hints of light cashew oak, almond blossom, soft spice and nougat. Slinky and textured with ample drive and a wash of stone and citrus fruits on the finish. Screw cap. 13% alc. **RATING** 90 **DRINK** 2023–2026 $38 DB

Pinot Noir 2018, Tasmania A light, airy cherry red in the glass with characters of bramble-edged red and dark cherry, wild strawberry and yellow plum underscored by hints of mushroom broth, earth, spice and purple floral notes. Spacious in style with delicate, spice-laden red cherry fruits, gentle tannins and a bright acid drive. Screw cap. 13.5% alc. **RATING** 90 **DRINK** 2023–2026 $40 DB

Bourke & Travers ★★★★

PO Box 457, Clare, SA 5453 **Region** Clare Valley
T 0400 745 057 **www.**bourkeandtravers.com **Open** Not **Winemaker** David Travers,
Michael Corbett **Est.** 1996 **Dozens** 250 **Vyds** 6ha
Bourke & Travers is a family project focused on 3 vineyards on a single site in the northwest of Clare Valley. Early plantings of shiraz have been joined by smaller plots of mourvèdre and bush-vine grenache. Eschewing herbicides, pesticides and insecticides, the focus is on sustainable viticulture with resulting wines reflective of such, produced with minimal

intervention. Wines have been made since '10 in a variety of styles, honouring the traditional wines of the region, with more recent releases showing a flair for innovation and more vibrant, brighter expressions.

ŸŸŸŸŸ **Single Vineyard Shiraz 2021, Clare Valley** A small amount of whole bunches in the ferment lends attractive peppery, dried herb spice to the wine. Wonderful perfume of thyme, white pepper, game meat and red berries, the palate similar, maybe some ripe plum there, too. Tightening gently on fine tannins, the extension of flavour is succulent and superb. Elegant, fresh, refined. Screw cap. 13.9% alc. RATING 94 DRINK 2022–2035 $45 MB

ŸŸŸŸŸ **Polish Hill River Riesling 2022, Clare Valley** RATING 93 DRINK 2022–2035 $26 MB ✪
Grenache Shiraz Mourvèdre 2021, Clare Valley RATING 93 DRINK 2022–2028 $35 MB ✪
Shiraz Mourvèdre 2021, Clare Valley RATING 93 DRINK 2022–2028 $35 MB ✪
Block 41 Syrah Rosé 2022, Clare Valley RATING 91 DRINK 2022–2024 $22 MB ✪

Bowen Estate   ★★★★

15459 Riddoch Highway, Coonawarra, SA 5263 **Region** Coonawarra
T (08) 8737 2229 **www**.bowenestate.com.au **Open** Mon–Fri 10–5, w'ends 10–4
Winemaker Emma Bowen **Viticulturist** Doug Bowen **Est.** 1972 **Dozens** 12 000
Vyds 33ha
Bowen Estate is a family-run business, not far off its 50th vintage. Regional veteran Doug Bowen presides over one of Coonawarra's landmarks, but he has handed over full winemaking responsibility to daughter Emma, 'retiring' to the position of viticulturist. They produce just 3 wines, a chardonnay, cabernet sauvignon and a shiraz.

ŸŸŸŸŸ **Cabernet Sauvignon 2021, Coonawarra** Firm, savoury and curranty. This is a wine for the cellar. Blackcurrant, bay leaf, sweet redcurrant and walnut characters blend with fragrant dry herbs and sweet oak. There's flavour here (and structure) but not a lot of flesh; it will grow in time. Screw cap. 14.3% alc. RATING 92 DRINK 2026–2034 $28 CM ✪
Chardonnay 2022, Coonawarra In some ways it's a simple expression of pear and nectarine-like flavour, pure and easy to enjoy. But then you see the attractive rub of cedar-and-cream oak, matched to pine and floral-like notes, and it's apparent that there's a bit more to this than first meets the eye. Screw cap. 13.5% alc. RATING 90 DRINK 2024–2028 $25 CM ✪

Box Grove Vineyard   ★★★★☆

955 Avenel-Nagambie Road, Tabilk, Vic 3607 (postal) **Region** Nagambie Lakes
T 0409 210 015 **www**.boxgrovevineyard.com.au **Open** By appt **Winemaker** Sarah Gough
Est. 1995 **Dozens** 2500 **Vyds** 28.25ha
This is the venture of the Gough family, with industry veteran (and daughter) Sarah Gough managing the vineyard, winemaking and marketing. Having started with 10ha each of shiraz and cabernet sauvignon under contract to Brown Brothers, Sarah decided to switch the focus to what could loosely be called 'Mediterranean varieties'. These days shiraz and prosecco (glera) are the main varieties, with smaller plantings of pinot gris, primitivo, vermentino, roussanne, sousão, grenache, nebbiolo, negroamaro, mourvèdre and viognier.

ŸŸŸŸŸ **Shiraz Roussanne 2021, Nagambie Lakes** A true field blend of 97/3% shiraz/roussanne. Whatever roussanne brings to the blend – aromatics? energy? texture? – long may it continue. Deep crimson hues. Lifted in scent with wild red fruits, plum, black cherry and vanilla. The palate is both juicy and textural, firmly wrapped in place by fine tannins. Such poise. A real beauty. Screw cap. 14.7% alc. RATING 95 DRINK 2023–2030 $35 JP ✪

Prosecco 2022, Nagambie Lakes Works the other side of the prosecco street, where texture comes into play together with a layer of light savouriness. The result shows a depth of fruit and taste in preserved lemon, baked apple, pear and gentle spice. Keeps its sparkling personality while delivering something extra. Crown. 11% alc. RATING 94 DRINK 2023–2026 $25 JP ✪

Roussanne 2021, Nagambie Lakes RATING 93 DRINK 2023–2026 $35 JP ✪
Negroamaro 2022, Nagambie Lakes RATING 91 DRINK 2023–2026 $30 JP

Brand & Sons

11 Mary Street, Coonawarra, SA 5263 (postal) **Region** Coonawarra
T 0488 771 046 **www**.brandandsons.com.au **Open** Not **Winemaker** Sam Brand
Viticulturist Trent Brand **Est.** 2000 **Dozens** 5000 **Vyds** 95ha
The Brand family story starts with the arrival of Eric Brand in Coonawarra in 1950. He married Nancy Redman and purchased a 24ha block from the Redman family, relinquishing his job as a baker and becoming a grapegrower. It was not until '66 that the first Brand's Laira wine was made. The family sold the Brand's Laira winery to McWilliam's Wines in '94, with Eric's son Jim Brand staying on as chief winemaker until he passed away in '05. Today Brand & Sons is run by Sam Brand, the 4th generation of this family, which has played a major role in Coonawarra for over 70 years.

Sanctuary Cabernet Sauvignon 2019, Coonawarra This takes deep-seated blackcurrant and mint flavours and injects them with long rakes of tannin. It feels profound from the first sip. Talk about impressive. The purity of the fruit, the integration of the (smoky) oak, the swagger of it; the confidence. You don't just drink this wine, you follow it. This is pretty much as good as it gets. Diam. 14.5% alc. RATING 97 DRINK 2026–2049 $150 CM ❤

Silent Partner Cabernet Sauvignon 2020, Coonawarra The coils are tight but the fruit is strong. Minted blackcurrant and boysenberry flavours blend with cedar and woodsmoke. Sizeable chains of tannin, starting from about a third of the way along the palate onwards, lock everything in place. This is a terrific wine, firm and commanding, built for the long haul. Screw cap. 14.5% alc. RATING 95 DRINK 2026–2046 $40 CM ✪
Silent Partner Cabernet Sauvignon 2018, Coonawarra This is solid, convincing, measured and neat. It's a sure bet for the cellar. Blackcurrant, mint and bay leaf flavours flow seductively throughout, with redcurrant and woodsy spice notes adding lift and spread. This isn't a huge wine, but it has very good power and is both classically styled and presented. Screw cap. 14% alc. RATING 95 DRINK 2025–2045 $40 CM ✪
Last Sunday Drive Cabernet Franc 2021, Coonawarra Firm, powerful and impressive. Blackcurrant, cocoa and eucalyptus flavours feel both rock solid and bold in the mouth (in a positive way), leading to a dry, resounding finish. You have to enjoy tannin, because there's plenty of it here, but in that context, it's very good. Screw cap. 14.5% alc. RATING 94 DRINK 2024–2033 $26 CM ✪

Old Town Single Vineyard Shiraz 2021, Coonawarra RATING 93 DRINK 2023–2038 $50 CM
Baker's Run Cabernet Sauvignon 2019, Coonawarra RATING 93 DRINK 2024–2034 $26 CM ✪
Fire & Ice Shiraz 2019, Coonawarra RATING 90 DRINK 2023–2029 $26 CM

Brand's Laira Coonawarra

14860 Riddoch Highway, Coonawarra, SA 5263 **Region** Coonawarra
T (08) 8736 3260 **www**.brandslaira.com **Open** Mon–Fri 9–4.30, w'ends & public hols 11–4 **Winemaker** Peter Weinberg, Amy Blackburn **Est.** 1966 **Dozens** 30 000 **Vyds** 278ha

Casella Family Brands purchased the historic Brand's Laira from McWilliam's in Dec '15. Over the years McWilliam's had moved from 50% to 100% ownership of Brand's and thereafter it purchased an additional 100ha of vineyards (taking Brand's to its present 278ha) and had expanded both the size, and the quality, of the winery.

ŸŸŸŸŸ **One Seven One Cabernet Sauvignon 2019, Coonawarra** A wealth of blackcurrant flavour sweeps through the palate, pushing mint and trailing tobacco, cedar, woodsmoke and fragrant dry herbs. It's firmer than the sheets in a hotel bed, though the fruit itself has softness. The wine has staying power, length, fruit and wood. And will last longer than most marriages. Screw cap. 14% alc. RATING 96 DRINK 2028–2048 $80 CM

1968 Vines Cabernet Sauvignon 2021, Coonawarra It smells of vanilla, cedar and sweet sultanas but the palate is pure Coonawarra gold, all blackcurrant and gravel, mint and tobacco. A firm, well-flavoured wine with good shape, structure and length, the tannin itself is a little forced, perhaps, but extra time in bottle will help. Screw cap. 14% alc. RATING 94 DRINK 2026–2038 $40 CM ✪

Stentiford's Old Vines Shiraz 2021, Coonawarra Volumes of plum, peppermint, redcurrant and cedar flavours flow through to a tight, grainy and tannic finish. It doesn't scream quality but suggests it strongly, thanks mainly to the concentration of fruit and the firmness of the structure. The long haul – that's what it's been built for. Screw cap. 14.5% alc. RATING 94 DRINK 2027–2046 $80 CM

ŸŸŸŸŸ **Old Station Riesling 2022, Coonawarra** RATING 90 DRINK 2023–2029 $20 CM ✪

Brangayne of Orange   ★★★★★

837 Pinnacle Road, Orange, NSW 2800 **Region** Orange
T (02) 6365 3229 **www**.brangayne.com **Open** Sun–Fri 11–4, Sat 11–5
Winemaker Simon Gilbert, Will Gilbert **Viticulturist** David Hoskins **Est.** 1994
Dozens 3500 **Vyds** 25.7ha
The Hoskins family (formerly orchardists) moved into grapegrowing in '94 and have progressively established high-quality vineyards. Brangayne produces good wines across all mainstream varieties ranging, remarkably, from pinot noir to cabernet sauvignon. It sells a substantial part of its crop to other winemakers.

ŸŸŸŸŸ **Riesling 2022, Orange** Lime candies and feijoa meet a honeysuckle and pineapple core. The elegance conjures images of river pebbles and flowing streams. The fruit sweetness is spot-on for the fluent nature of its natural acidity. Described as 'half dry' on the back label, this is a riesling for all riesling lovers – it's impossible not to love the dewy nature of this wine. Screw cap. 11% alc. RATING 95 DRINK 2022–2035 $35 SW ✪

Pinot Noir 2021, Orange Draped in baking spices, this offers a combination of red berries and black plum with cassia bark, mocha and cinnamon spice. Tanned leather, tar and wood ear mushrooms lie beneath the darker fruit spectrum. A well-considered pinot with fine tannins, sturdy shoulders and very good savoury length. Screw cap. 12.9% alc. RATING 95 DRINK 2022–2030 $42 SW ✪

ŸŸŸŸŸ **Pinot Grigio 2022, Orange** RATING 92 DRINK 2022–2030 $27 SW ✪
Sauvignon Blanc 2022, Orange RATING 90 DRINK 2022–2028 $27 SW

Brash Higgins   ★★★★★

California Road, McLaren Vale, SA 5171 **Region** McLaren Vale
T (08) 8556 4237 **www**.brashhiggins.com **Open** By appt **Winemaker** Brad Hickey
Est. 2010 **Dozens** 1000 **Vyds** 7ha
American Brad Hickey arrived in Australia to work vintage '07 in McLaren Vale, where he met his now partner Nicole Thorpe. Together they established Brash Higgins in '10. Brad has a varied background, including 10 years at some of the best New York restaurants, then a further 10 years of baking, brewing and travelling to the best-known wine regions of the

world. Nicole's 7ha Omensetter vineyard looks over the Willunga Escarpment and was planted to shiraz and cabernet sauvignon in '97. Drought prompted them to graft their first 0.5ha of shiraz to nero d'Avola in '09; they have since grown plantings to 3ha. Both the estate vineyard and the winery are certified organic.

Smart Vineyard Grenache 2021, McLaren Vale This is good, quirky and, like its winemaker, probing for secrets and answers. This is neither galumphing and heavy, nor shimmering with red-fruited pinot-esque transparency. Chinotto, tamarind, clove and kirsch, the souk-scented ferrous tannins a spicy curtail to any excess. Diam. 14.2% alc. **RATING** 96 **DRINK** 2022-2027 $85 NG

R/SM Saddlebags Hill Vineyard Riesling Semillon 2021, McLaren Vale Sublime, and among my favourite whites in the country. Lime blossom, tatami straw, porcini dashi and a luscious wave of plush, pungent and creamy lemon curd basting the mid-palate. Effusive and intense, it's a seriously delicious wine. Screw cap. 12.8% alc. **RATING** 96 **DRINK** 2022-2028 $42 NG ✪

SHZ Omensetter Vineyard 2020, McLaren Vale McLaren Vale meets northern Rhône – achieved with aplomb. Salumi, violet, white pepper grind, dried nori, blueberry, mace and clove, muddled and ground across a persistent linger defined by gritty, almost pixelated dry tannins. A stylised wine, trading in regionality as we knew it, for an aspirational zeitgeist and a remoulding of perceptions. Screw cap. 14.8% alc. **RATING** 94 **DRINK** 2022-2030 $45 NG

MRLO Lennon Vineyard Merlot 2021, McLaren Vale RATING 93 **DRINK** 2022-2027 $35 NG ✪

CRGN Carignan 2021, McLaren Vale RATING 93 **DRINK** 2022-2027 $35 NG ✪

CHN Willamba Hill Vineyard Chenin Blanc 2021, McLaren Vale RATING 93 **DRINK** 2022-2028 $42 NG

NDV Amphora Project Nero d'Avola 2021, McLaren Vale RATING 93 **DRINK** 2022-2028 $45 NG

Ripple Carbonic Omensetter Vineyard Nero d'Avola Cabernet 2022, McLaren Vale RATING 92 **DRINK** 2022-2024 $35 NG

Brave Goose Vineyard ★★★★

PO Box 852, Seymour, Vic 3660 **Region** Central Victoria
T 0417 553 225 www.bravegoosevineyard.com.au **Open** By appt **Winemaker** Nina Stocker **Est.** 1988 **Dozens** 500 **Vyds** 6.5ha
The Brave Goose vineyard was planted in 1988 by former chairman of the Grape & Wine Research and Development Corporation, Dr John Stocker, and wife Joanne. In '87 they found a property on the inside of the Great Dividing Range, near Tallarook, with north-facing slopes and shallow, weathered ironstone soils. They established 2.5ha each of shiraz and cabernet sauvignon, and 0.5ha each of merlot, viognier and gamay. The brave goose in question was the sole survivor of a flock put into the vineyard to repel cockatoos and foxes. Two decades on, Jo and John handed the operation to their winemaker daughter Nina and son-in-law John Day.

Reserve Shiraz 2021, Central Victoria Top value here. Brilliant purple hues glisten. The scent is lifted and aromatic in red flowers, spice, red licorice, black fruits, cherry, pepper and dried herbs. Complex on both the nose and the palate at this early stage, integrated, too. Tannins allow a deceptively easy, flowing ride for the fruit across the tongue, bringing effortless structure. Screw cap. 14% alc. **RATING** 94 **DRINK** 2022-2027 $28 JP ✪

Cabernet Sauvignon 2020, Central Victoria A medium-bodied red that speaks of bright, ripe fruit. The bordeaux-style blend (there's a splash of malbec and merlot) brings an elegant, expressive range of lifted black fruits, boysenberry, plum, bracken, undergrowth and eucalyptus. Good concentration, fine-edged tannins and bright fruits offer an impressive wine at a smart price. Screw cap. 14.2% alc. **RATING** 94 **DRINK** 2022-2027 $28 JP ✪

Viognier 2022, Central Victoria RATING 90 **DRINK** 2022-2025 $28 JP

Brave Souls Wine

12 Clevedon Street, Botany, NSW, 2019 (postal) **Region** Barossa Valley
T 0420 968 473 **Open** Not **Winemaker** Corey Ryan, Simon Cowham, David Fesq
Viticulturist Simon Cowham **Est.** 2017 **Dozens** 3500

Co-founder Julia Weirich travelled from Germany to Australia, where in '13 she became marketing coordinator at Fesq & Co. She later gained winemaking experience at Bass Phillip, NZ, Burgundy, Italy and South Africa, before coming back to Fesq to take the new role of European wine manager, and to Sons of Eden making Brave Souls Wine. In '20, Julia returned overseas, and the winemaking is now undertaken by Corey Ryan and Simon Cowham of Sons of Eden, alongside David Fesq. The wines are named for three men who risked their lives to rescue passengers of the SS Admella when it was shipwrecked off the South Australian coast in 1859. The tales of these 'Brave Souls' are captured within the label artwork by revered artist Bruce Goold.

🍷🍷🍷🍷🍷 **The Able Seaman GSM 2021, Barossa Valley** Last year's Able Seaman impressed me greatly. It's managed to do it again, serving up a wine of fruit purity and drinkability while being friendly on the wallet. Spicy plum and berry fruits, fine, sandy tannins and a vivid sense of freshness and detail. It's just a lovely drink. Screw cap. 14.5% alc. **RATING** 95 **DRINK** 2023–2028 $29 DB ✪

🍷🍷🍷🍷🍷 **The Whaler Shiraz 2021, Barossa RATING** 93 **DRINK** 2023–2028 $29 DB ✪

Bream Creek

Marion Bay Road, Bream Creek, Tas 7175 (postal) **Region** Southern Tasmania
T 0419 363 714 **www.**breamcreekvineyard.com.au **Open** Not **Winemaker** Liam
McElhinney **Viticulturist** Fred Peacock **Est.** 1990 **Dozens** 6500 **Vyds** 7.6ha

The Bream Creek vineyard, overlooking Marion Bay and Maria Island on Tasmania's East Coast, is one of the island state's oldest vineyards, planted in '74. The vineyard, then planted mainly to riesling and cabernet sauvignon, with smaller plantings of pinot noir, chardonnay and gewürztraminer, was purchased in '90 by renowned Tasmanian vigneron Fred Peacock, legendary for the care he bestows on the vines under his direction. As well as increasing pinot noir plantings and adding sauvignon blanc, Fred was also amongst the first in the southern hemisphere to plant schönburger.

🍷🍷🍷🍷🍷 **Reserve Chardonnay 2022, Tasmania** Pale straw. The fruit unfurls nicely with inviting white peach, nectarine, citrus and melon tones with underlying soft spice, clotted cream, wildflowers, nougat and river stone. There is some nice grapefruit-like tension and a bright cadence on the palate, impressive minerality and a finish that fades slowly with memories of creamy, softly spiced stone and citrus fruits. Limited release. Screw cap. 13.5% alc. **RATING** 94 **DRINK** 2023–2029 $48 DB

🍷🍷🍷🍷🍷 **Riesling 2022, Tasmania RATING** 93 **DRINK** 2023–2027 $22 DB ✪
Pinot Noir 2022, Tasmania RATING 92 **DRINK** 2023–2030 $45 DB
Chardonnay 2022, Tasmania RATING 92 **DRINK** 2023–2026 $36 DB
Reserve Pinot Noir 2021, Tasmania RATING 92 **DRINK** 2023–2030 $70 DB
Pinot Noir 2021, Tasmania RATING 92 **DRINK** 2023–2028 $45 DB
Late Disgorged 2011, Tasmania RATING 91 **DRINK** 2023–2026 $75 DB
Sauvignon Blanc 2022, Tasmania RATING 91 **DRINK** 2023–2026 $31 JH
Pinot Rosé 2022, Tasmania RATING 91 **DRINK** 2023–2025 $33 DB
Pinot Grigio 2022, Tasmania RATING 90 **DRINK** 2023–2025 $33 DB
Cabernet Merlot 2021, Tasmania RATING 90 **DRINK** 2023–2027 $36 DB

Bremerton Wines

14 Kent Town Road, Langhorne Creek, SA 5255 **Region** Langhorne Creek
T (08) 8537 3093 **www.**bremerton.com.au **Open** 7 days 10–5 **Winemaker** Rebecca
Willson **Est.** 1988 **Dozens** 30 000 **Vyds** 120ha

Bremerton is a family-owned winery, run by sisters Rebecca Willson (chief winemaker) and Lucy Willson (marketing manager). Previously a lucerne farm, the family experimented with grape growing in the '80s and '90s; a flood in '92 ruined the lucerne crop and led the family to switch to grape growing commercially. Today they have 120ha of premium vineyards (80% of which goes into their own labels), planted to cabernet sauvignon, shiraz, verdelho, chardonnay, sauvignon blanc, malbec, merlot, fiano, graciano and petit verdot.

ŸŸŸŸŸ **Bâtonnage Shiraz Malbec 2021, Langhorne Creek** An 83/17% blend; the malbec stirred regularly for texture and mid-palate weight. Some fermentation in French oak and maturation followed. The approach has worked very well; the blackberry of the shiraz and the plum of the malbec are seamlessly fused on the palate. It's a wine of finesse and impeccable balance. Screw cap. 14.5% alc. RATING 96 DRINK 2023–2033 $32 JH ✪

B.O.V. 2019, Langhorne Creek 90/10% shiraz/cabernet. The best 4 barrels of the vintage were selected. Oak seems to be French dominant; classy length, line and balance. Diam. 15% alc. RATING 96 DRINK 2025–2040 $85 JH

CHW Traditional Method Sparkling Shiraz 2020, Langhorne Creek The hurdle in making sparkling shiraz is to keep the sweetness under control (needed to mask the phenolics of the shiraz). This wine succeeds very well indeed. The price is right, the quality of the plum and black cherry fruit very good. Diam. 13.5% alc. RATING 95 DRINK 2023–2033 $34 JH ✪

Special Release Fiano 2022, Langhorne Creek A good example of the variety, with texture and structure achieved without new oak; the bouquet has notes of honey and beeswax. Lingers long in the mouth, and although it will benefit from a few years in bottle, many will enjoy it right now. Very good value. Screw cap. 12.5% alc. RATING 95 DRINK 2023–2028 $26 JH ✪

Special Release Grenache 2022, Langhorne Creek The colour is bright, though could be mistaken for a rosé. Wait until the finish and aftertaste are assessed – the wine packs a punch. The perfume of the bouquet is dried rose petals and spice, the palate progressively building with red cherry and white pepper. Screw cap. 13.5% alc. RATING 95 DRINK 2023–2028 $26 JH ✪

Special Release Tempranillo Graciano 2021, Langhorne Creek Lipsmackingly enjoyable. Ethereal rose petal and spice scents lead into a palate that is at once juicy and structured, its length the icing on the cake. Elegant, if you will. Screw cap. 14.5% alc. RATING 95 DRINK 2023–2028 $26 JH ✪

Special Release Malbec 2021, Langhorne Creek Don't blink or you may be floored by the intensity of this wine. Its lees were stirred regularly to add texture and mid-palate weight à la the '21 Bâtonnage Shiraz Malbec. Bremerton should open many doors with these Special Release reds. Screw cap. 14.5% alc. RATING 95 DRINK 2023–2029 $26 JH ✪

Old Adam Shiraz 2020, Langhorne Creek A supple and smooth wine with the accent on the quality fruit always dedicated to it. The balance is perfect, as is the length. Diam. 14.5% alc. RATING 95 DRINK 2023–2030 $60 JH

Walter's Reserve Cabernet 2018, Langhorne Creek Excellent colour; a powerful, full-bodied cabernet, with layers of blackcurrant and dark chocolate. Tannins, too, are powerful, nonetheless ripe and civilised. Diam. 14.5% alc. RATING 95 DRINK 2023–2033 $60 JH

Walter's Reserve Cabernet 2017, Langhorne Creek A best barrel selection made and blended for bottling, then 2 years in bottle prior to release. This was a cooler vintage than '18, and the mouthfeel more linear, the flavours encompassing cedar and cigar box. Diam. 14.5% alc. RATING 95 DRINK 2023–2035 $60 JH

Bâtonnage Chardonnay 2022, Langhorne Creek Well put together; white flesh stone fruit and melon with a breath of French oak; gentle citrusy acidity lengthens the finish; bâtonnage imparts creamy cashew. Screw cap. 13.5% alc. RATING 94 DRINK 2023–2033 $32 JH ✪

Special Release Barbera 2021, Langhorne Creek The back label says the wine was matured for 15 months in seasoned barriques so as not to mask varietal

characters. It instantly fills the mouth with flavour so dramatically fruity it's hard to see the risk. Screw cap. 14.5% alc. **RATING** 94 **DRINK** 2024–2034 $26 JH ✪
Special Release Mourvèdre 2020, Langhorne Creek The bouquet and palate move as a pair, starting with savoury/earthy notes, then the red berry subset, that runs through many of these Special Release red wines, heads towards centre stage. Screw cap. 14.5% alc. **RATING** 94 **DRINK** 2023–2029 $26 JH ✪
Bâtonnage Shiraz Malbec 2020, Langhorne Creek Decidedly adventurous winemaking for this 83/17% shiraz/malbec blend. Barrel fermented in French oak and matured with lees stirring. Satsuma plum and cherry fruit aromas and flavours hang together. Its colour is brighter than its vintage siblings. Screw cap. 14.5% alc. **RATING** 94 **DRINK** 2030–2040 $32 JH ✪
Special Release Malbec 2020, Langhorne Creek Matured for 14 months in barrel, predominantly Hungarian. A vividly coloured wine with a highly expressive bouquet. Rich in mouth-filling velvety plum, blackberry and spicy fruit. Lees stirring is unconventional with red wines, but works well here. Hard to resist at this price. Screw cap. 14% alc. **RATING** 94 **DRINK** 2025–2030 $24 JH ✪

🍷🍷🍷🍷🍷 **Special Release Vermentino 2022, Langhorne Creek RATING** 93 **DRINK** 2023–2028 $26 JH ✪
Special Release Mourvèdre 2022, Langhorne Creek RATING 93 **DRINK** 2023–2028 $26 JH ✪
Coulthard Cabernet Sauvignon 2021, Langhorne Creek RATING 93 **DRINK** 2024–2032 $22 JH ✪
Special Release Lagrein 2020, Langhorne Creek RATING 93 **DRINK** 2024–2032 $26 JH ✪
Racy Rosé 2022, Langhorne Creek RATING 92 **DRINK** 2023–2024 $19 JH ✪
Selkirk Shiraz 2021, Langhorne Creek RATING 92 **DRINK** 2023–2030 $22 JH ✪
Bâtonnage Chardonnay 2021, Langhorne Creek RATING 92 **DRINK** 2023–2033 $32 JH
Coulthard Cabernet Sauvignon 2020, Langhorne Creek RATING 92 **DRINK** 2023–2025 $22 JH ✪
Selkirk Shiraz 2020, Langhorne Creek RATING 91 **DRINK** 2023–2030 $22 JH ✪
Special Release No Added Preservatives Shiraz 2022, Langhorne Creek RATING 90 **DRINK** 2023–2025 $26 JH
Tamblyn Cabernet Shiraz Malbec Merlot 2021, Langhorne Creek RATING 90 **DRINK** 2023–2024 $19 JH ✪
Tamblyn Cabernet Shiraz Malbec Merlot 2020, Langhorne Creek RATING 90 **DRINK** 2025–2035 $18 JH ✪

Briar Ridge Vineyard ★★★★★

593 Mount View Road, Mount View, NSW 2325 **Region** Hunter Valley
T (02) 4990 3670 **www**.briarridge.com.au **Open** 7 days 10–4 **Winemaker** Alex Beckett **Est.** 1972 **Dozens** 9500 **Vyds** 39ha
Semillon and shiraz have been consistent performers here. Underlying the suitability of these varieties to the region, Briar Ridge has been a model of stability, and has the comfort of substantial estate vineyards from which it is able to select the best grapes. It hasn't hesitated to venture into other regions, either. Alex Beckett took over winemaking duties from Gwyn Olsen in '17 and he is currently part way through the master of wine program.

🍷🍷🍷🍷🍷 **Stockhausen Shiraz 2021, Hunter Valley** Superb clarity of colour is an immediate come-on to a light- to medium-bodied wine and is no false dawn. There's a multi-coloured tapestry of never-ending colours and patterns, vibrant red and black cherries, berries and spices, the freshness all-encompassing. Screw cap. 12.8% alc. **RATING** 96 **DRINK** 2025–2035 $45 JH ✪
Dairy Hill Single Vineyard Shiraz 2021, Hunter Valley Appealing full, clear crimson-purple hue. This has all the makings of a very good shiraz, and no hint of

fault: the varietal expression of plum and blackberry, ripe but not overripe – the alcohol of 12.6% is the birthmark of Hunter Valley shiraz at its peak – tannins firm but fine, acidity creates freshness, oak in balanced support. Screw cap.
RATING 96 DRINK 2025–2040 $65 JH ✪

Big Bully Stonefields Vineyard Cabernet Sauvignon 2021, Wrattonbully
Blended with 3% malbec; bottled without fining or filtration. Excellent colour through to the rim. You can't expect much more than the limitless cassis, a sprig of bay leaf, and firm tannins guaranteeing decades of life. Diam. 14.7% alc.
RATING 96 DRINK 2025–2045 $45 JH ✪

Aged Release Briar Hill Single Vineyard Chardonnay 2018, Hunter Valley Holding back Hunter chardonnay for re-release doesn't always pay a dividend, but it works well here, gliding across the tongue in fine fettle. The fruit covers the full spectrum of stone fruit and citrus, the purity and balance singing quietly in unison, the length excellent. Screw cap. 13% alc. RATING 96 DRINK 2023–2028 $64 JH ✪

Limited Release Fiano 2022, Hunter Valley Its scented bouquet is a mix of honeysuckle and citrus, the palate shares the significant savoury texture achieved without the use of oak and it develops well. I shall watch Briar Ridge's iterations with interest over the next few years. Screw cap. 12.3% alc. RATING 95 DRINK 2023–2030 $35 JH ✪

Limited Release Albariño 2022, Hunter Valley Briar Ridge's albariño is delicious, with a pleasant grip to its mix of grapefruit and white stone-fruit flavours, and mouthfeel similar to fiano. Screw cap. 12.8% alc. RATING 95 DRINK 2023–2030 $35 JH ✪

Limited Release BDX 2021, Wrattonbully A blend of barbera, cabernet franc, malbec and petit verdot, hence the bordeaux reference, yet the leading variety in the blend is barbera. Nomenclature to one side, you have high-quality estate-grown fruit, quality French oak, and a superb vintage, all coming together on a medium- to full-bodied palate. Screw cap. 13.5% alc. RATING 95 DRINK 2030–2040 $40 JH ✪

Briar Hill Single Vineyard Chardonnay 2021, Hunter Valley An attractive well-made wine. The base line is the conjunction of citrus and white stone fruit; fig, cashew and Granny Smith apple outliers at this stage, none taking centre stage. Diam is the next best thing to screw cap, but the case for using it is far less convincing here than it is with red wines. Diam. 13.5% alc. RATING 95 DRINK 2023–2029 $50 JH ✪

Museum Release Limited Release Big Bully Cabernet Sauvignon 2016, Wrattonbully A very good aged cabernet, showing all the features of this region at its best. Supple tannins and perfectly ripened fruit leave little more to be said. Screw cap. 14.2% alc. RATING 95 DRINK 2023–2036 $56 JH

Stockhausen Semillon 2022, Hunter Valley Sourced from the Dairy Hill vineyard; vinified without resorting to deliberate extraction of phenolics. Karl Stockhausen knows how to source and make Hunter Valley semillon better than most. Whole-bunch pressed and star-bright juice. Screw cap. 11.8% alc. RATING 94 DRINK 2023–2029 $38 JH ✪

Limited Release H.R.B Shiraz Pinot Noir 2021, Hunter Valley A nod to the Hunter River Burgundies of past years. This a light- to medium-bodied fresh juicy red berry wine with a burnish of superfine tannins; the contribution of 15% pinot noir has had a profound impact, the wine ready right now. Screw cap. 12.5% alc. RATING 94 DRINK 2023–2030 $40 JH ✪

Big Bully Cabernet Sauvignon 2020, Wrattonbully Wrattonbully's vignerons agreed with each other in rating the '20 vintage a 10/10 for quality (and the same for '19 and '21), a feat achieved by no other region. This estate-grown wine is medium bodied with clear-cut varietal markers thanks to the fine but persistent tannins, French oak, and cassis-filled fruit. Screw cap. 14.2% alc. RATING 94 DRINK 2023–2033 $45 JH

Museum Release Dairy Hill Single Vineyard Shiraz 2014, Hunter Valley The back label says this can be cellared carefully up to 10 years, which leaves the consumer with a life span now of only 1 year. I don't agree. It may only have 1 year before it enters the plateau of maturity, which has a 10-year lifespan as the earth and polished leather call signal appears. Screw cap. 14% alc. **RATING** 94 **DRINK** 2023-2038 $96 JH

ꟙꟙꟙꟙꟙ Hillrose Single Vineyard Shiraz 2022, Hilltops **RATING** 93 **DRINK** 2023-2032 $50 JH

Brinktop Vineyard

66 Brinktop Road, Penna, Tas 7171 **Region** Southern Tasmania
T 0407 224 543 **www**.brinktop.com.au **Open** By appt **Winemaker** Todd Goebel
Viticulturist Gill Christian **Est.** 2017 **Dozens** 1000 **Vyds** 8ha
Todd Goebel and Gillian Christian had been growing grapes and producing wine in the Coal River Valley for close to 20 years when they established Brinktop in '17. They felt a call to put their wealth of learnings to work, which began with the purchase of a house with a 1ha vineyard. This was the start of enacting a precise and deliberate vision to live onsite, manage the vines and make the wines. They adopted the name Brinktop Killara for one of the wines, Killara being the name of the property. Across the 65ha they have established 8ha of vines, chiefly selected clones of pinot noir, then chardonnay and a hectare each of shiraz and tempranillo.

ꟙꟙꟙꟙꟙ Killara Pinot Noir 2022, Tasmania A brightly coloured pinot noir that shows some lovely whole-bunch notes of amaro herbs, a whiff of Campari and exotic spices that flit around attractively over the primary fruit tones of red and dark cherry and red plum. Some nice game, sous bois and mineral salt notes waft in on the palate as the wine flows savoury smooth and true to a spicy, complex finish. Screw cap. 13.5% alc. **RATING** 92 **DRINK** 2023-2028 $55 DB
Chardonnay 2022, Tasmania Pale straw. Aromas of lemon, grapefruit, melon and peach with underlying notes of soft spice, nougat, cashew oak, white flowers, oatmeal and almond paste. Yellow fruits pop in on the palate, which shows some nice clotted cream and lemon curd tones, bright acidity and a medium-length finish of citrus, cream and stone. Screw cap. 13.5% alc. **RATING** 91 **DRINK** 2023-2027 $42 DB
Syrah 2021, Tasmania Mid-crimson with a hint of purple and aromas of juicy plum, mulberry and boysenberry fruits. Hints of exotic spices, amaro, pressed purple flowers, roasting meat and earth. A nice sense of space here with pretty plum and berry fruits, plenty of spice, chalky tannins and a twang of sour cherry in the acid profile. Screw cap. 13% alc. **RATING** 91 **DRINK** 2023-2026 $48 DB

Brokenwood

401-427 McDonalds Road, Pokolbin, NSW 2321 **Region** Hunter Valley
T (02) 4998 7559 **www**.brokenwood.com.au **Open** Mon–Fri 11–4, Sat–Sun 10–4
Winemaker Stuart Hordern, Kate Sturgess **Viticulturist** Kat Barry **Est.** 1970
Dozens 100000 **Vyds** 64ha
Brokenwood's big-selling Hunter Valley Semillon provides the volume to balance the limited quantities of the flagships ILR Reserve Semillon and Graveyard Shiraz. Brokenwood purchased the Graveyard vineyard from Hungerford Hill in '78 and has since fully rehabilitated the site. In late '22, it acquired the Oakey Creek vineyard, a long-time source of fruit for the Oakey Creek Vineyard Semillon and the aforementioned ILR. There is also a range of wines from regions including Beechworth, Orange, Central Ranges, McLaren Vale, Cowra and elsewhere. Ian Riggs had 38 vintages at the helm of Brokenwood before retiring in '20. He remains on the board of directors and is still a valued consultant; he has also contributed a great deal to various wine industry organisations.

ꟙꟙꟙꟙꟙ Graveyard Vineyard Shiraz 2021, Hunter Valley The early release of Graveyard Shiraz (along with many other Brokenwood jewels ex the '21 vintage) is presumably driven by the absence of any wines from the bushfire smoke contamination of '20, but it's a lovely wine managing to look great in this year, and doubtless will in 40 years' time too. It has a complex bouquet, with some oak nuances in the backdrop, its masterful control of tannins is one of its secrets, red fruit joining the usual black and purple to complete the tale. Screw cap. 13% alc. **RATING** 98 **DRINK** 2023–2053 $350 JH

ILR Reserve Semillon 2017, Hunter Valley From one of the masters of developed semillon, helped in this instance by the great semillon vintage. Its bouquet half suggests the use of oak – not true. It's a hypnotic wine, with Meyer lemon driving the citrus circus and the wheels of acidity. Screw cap. 11% alc. **RATING** 98 **DRINK** 2023–2042 $100 JH ✪

Tallawanta Vineyard Shiraz 2021, Hunter Valley The light, bright, clear colour causes a double take, not usual for this 102yo vineyard. However, as it were, reverse the order of assessment, and focus first on the red and black cherry finish and lingering aftertaste before rushing to judgement. This deserves the Burgundy name, with lots of whole berry. Screw cap. 13% alc. **RATING** 97 **DRINK** 2023–2033 $140 JH

ＹＹＹＹＹ **Wildwood Road Cabernet Sauvignon 2021, Margaret River** Clear and bright colour. A beautiful rendition of cassis at the precise point of the ripening cycle. It's only medium-bodied because Margaret River doesn't impose more extract, and it leaves the mouth as fresh as a spring day. Screw cap. 14% alc. **RATING** 96 **DRINK** 2024–2035 $100 JH

Rayner Vineyard Shiraz 2021, McLaren Vale This wine comes from vines planted in the early '90s, and has the comfort of the exceptional McLaren Vale '21 vintage. It's easy to see why fences around Rayner have been negotiated by Brokenwood. There's McLaren Vale dark chocolate in abundance on the bouquet, but it's the more familiar black cherry, plum and blackberry that drive the very, very long palate and aftertaste. Screw cap. 14.5% alc. **RATING** 96 **DRINK** 2024–2039 $110 JH

Oakey Creek Vineyard Chardonnay 2022, Hunter Valley The first vintage after Brokenwood purchased the vineyard from the Drayton family. There's a waft of the Brokenwood vinification before the serious business of the elegant, finely-tuned and polished palate of exemplary length. Screw cap. 12.5% alc. **RATING** 95 **DRINK** 2023–2030 $66 JH

Indigo Vineyard Chardonnay 2022, Beechworth Matured for 10 months in French puncheons (4% new). The bouquet has the carefully calibrated touch of funk used in some (though not all) of its chardonnays, translating to green grapefruit zest/pith/juice as a background for the white peach and cashew. Screw cap. 12.5% alc. **RATING** 95 **DRINK** 2023–2033 $75 JH

Verona Vineyard Shiraz 2021, Hunter Valley The '21 vintage was so-so in the Hunter, overcast or threatening to rain. There was no point trying to beef up the wines when, for example, the Graveyard had 13%. Moreover, Verona has it both ways: there's a traditional savoury element to the finish, but from start to finish there's plenty of cherry fruit to please. Screw cap. 13% alc. **RATING** 95 **DRINK** 2024–2039 $100 JH

Wade Block 2 Vineyard Shiraz 2021, McLaren Vale The vineyard is in blue ribbon territory: Blewitt Springs, and planted with a selection massale ex old vines spread through McLaren Vale. It's one for your children/grandchildren to enjoy (once they are legally permitted to do so). Blackberry, licorice and – of course – dark chocolate all fight for inclusion on the luscious palate. Screw cap. 14.5% alc. **RATING** 95 **DRINK** 2030–2040 $75 JH

Tallawanta Vineyard Semillon 2019, Hunter Valley An expressive wine from a great vineyard; a flowery bouquet is swiftly followed by an even more expressive palate, with lemon curd, lemon zest and balanced acidity. Has broken ranks with its performance at a midway point between youth and maturity, often a muffled/subdued point. Screw cap. 10.4% alc. **RATING** 95 **DRINK** 2023–2042 $66 JH

Semillon 2022, Hunter Valley Flavours of lemongrass, citrus and lanolin all contributing, this has the balance and length to transform itself over the next 5 years. Screw cap. 11% alc. **RATING** 94 **DRINK** 2023–2032 $28 JH ✪

Shiraz 2021, Hunter Valley This is the younger brother of Graveyard Shiraz, coming from young vines on the Graveyard vineyard. In other words, it's Brokenwood's entry-level Hunter shiraz. It's no lightweight wine, and the mix of plum, blackberry and black cherry fruits are swathed in ripe tannins, underwriting its future. Screw cap. 13.5% alc. **RATING** 94 **DRINK** 2026–2036 $50 JH

🍷🍷🍷🍷 **Rosato 2022, New South Wales Victoria** **RATING** 92 **DRINK** 2023–2023 $30 JH ✪

Brothers at War ★★★★★

58 Murray Street, Tanunda, SA 5252 **Region** Barossa Valley
T 0472 915 599 **www**.brothersatwar.com.au **Open** Fri–Sat 11–7, Sun–Thurs 11–5
Winemaker Angus Wardlaw **Viticulturist** Chris Alderton **Est.** 2013 **Dozens** 5000
Vyds 15ha
Brothers Angus and Sam Wardlaw are behind this exciting addition to the contemporary Barossa wine scene and, as the name suggests, they could have possibly had the odd rumble as they were growing up under the watch of their father, Barossa winemaker David Wardlaw. Established in '13 with a small intake of shiraz, the brothers gathered pace over the ensuing years, adding vigneron Chris Alderton to the mix and today the formidable trio craft a superb range of purely fruited, vibrant wines from across the Barossa and Eden Valleys. Brothers at War is a young winery with a very bright future indeed.

🍷🍷🍷🍷 **Single Vineyard Old Vine Shiraz 2020, Barossa Valley** Deep crimson with a purple edge. Vibrant satsuma plum, macerated blackberries and black cherry cut through with a dusting of baking spices, violets, licorice, amaro, dark chocolate and earth. Meaty facets come in on the palate, which is expansive with fine, supportive tannin heft, a bright acid cadence and a savoury flick to its tail. Impressive stuff. Cork. 14% alc. **RATING** 96 **DRINK** 2023–2035 $110 DB
Peace Keeper Grenache 2022, Barossa Here's a lovely grenache, airy and detailed with plentiful plum and mulberry fruits and dotted with exotic spices, gingerbread, pressed flowers, earth and cola. Fine, chalky tannin and bright acidity provide the framework while the fruit leaves a wake of ginger and purple flowers. Screw cap. 13.5% alc. **RATING** 95 **DRINK** 2023–2032 $38 DB ✪
Single Vineyard Old Vine Syrah 2020, Eden Valley Deep, purple-edged crimson in colour with notes of deep satsuma plum, blackberry and black cherry fruit underscored with fine spice, purple flowers, licorice, earth, roasting meats and kirsch. Voluminous and opulent with granitic tannins plunging down through the pure fruit, things tightening and focusing on the exit, bright acid propelling the wine off into the distance with a rooster-tail of spice and black fruits. Cork. 14% alc. **RATING** 95 **DRINK** 2023–2033 $80 DB
Single Vineyard Mataro 2020, Eden Valley Crimson in the glass with aromas of red plum and berries, a whiff of exotic spice and a liminal glance of mataro garrigue – it's an earthy, sexy, roasted game meats kind of thing. The fruit presence and flow on the palate is bang on, savoury pure and true with chalky tannin and a brisk cadence, finishing long with impressive balance. Cork. 14% alc. **RATING** 95 **DRINK** 2023–2030 $80 DB

🍷🍷🍷🍷 **Nothing in Common Riesling 2022, Eden Valley** **RATING** 93 **DRINK** 2022–2028 $38 DB
The Grape Grower Riesling 2022, Eden Valley **RATING** 93 **DRINK** 2023–2038 $28 DB ✪
The Old Man Syrah 2021, Eden Valley **RATING** 93 **DRINK** 2023–2028 $28 DB ✪
I'm Always Right Cabernet Sauvignon 2021, Eden Valley **RATING** 92 **DRINK** 2023–2029 $38 DB
Fist Fight Shiraz 2021, Barossa **RATING** 92 **DRINK** 2023–2028 $38 DB
Single Vineyard Grenache 2021, Eden Valley **RATING** 92 **DRINK** 2023–2028 $80 DB

Our Mum's Love Rosé 2022, Eden Valley RATING 91 DRINK 2023-2025
$28 DB ✪
The Darling Sister Pinot Grigio 2022, Eden Valley RATING 90
DRINK 2023-2025 $28 DB
Some Other Guy Grenache Shiraz Mataro 2021, Clare Valley Barossa
Valley RATING 90 DRINK 2023-2026 $28 DB

Brown Brothers

239 Milawa-Bobinawarrah Road, Milawa, Vic 3678 **Region** King Valley
T (03) 5720 5500 **www.brownbrothers.com.au Open** 7 days 9–5 **Winemaker** Joel
Tilbrook, Cate Looney, Geoff Alexander, Tom Canning, Simon McMillan
Viticulturist Brett McClen, Sean Dean **Est.** 1889 **Dozens** 1 million **Vyds** 570ha
Brown Brothers draws upon a considerable number of vineyards spread throughout a range of
site climates – from very warm to very cool. Known for the diversity of varieties with which it
works, the wines represent good value for money. Its cellar door receives the greatest number
of visitors in Australia. A founding member of Australia's First Families of Wine.

ŸŸŸŸŸ **Patricia Extended Lees Pinot Noir Chardonnay 2010, King Valley**
Excited by the quality of the '10 vintage, especially the acid line and length, the
makers kept a small amount aside. Boasts poise and subtle complexity in baked
apple, peach, nougat, fig, fruit mince pies, roasted almonds and spice. Filigree-fine
acidity seamlessly knits everything together across a warm, inviting palate with just
a touch of preserved lemon savouriness to close. Lasts long. A special sparkling.
Cork. 12.7% alc. RATING 97 DRINK 2023-2027 $120 JP ✪ ♥

ŸŸŸŸŸ **Patricia Pinot Noir Chardonnay Brut 2016, King Valley** An impressive
Patricia sparkling. Aromas of fresh-from-the-oven biscuits together with melon,
peach, citrus and toasted nuts. Acidity is keen and focused, a solid base for
attractive and developed lemon butter, cashew and yeast-rich flavours. This is a
most versatile sparkling. Cork. 12.5% alc. RATING 95 DRINK 2022-2028 $48 JP ✪
Patricia Chardonnay 2021, Tasmania Patricia Chardonnay is now firmly
ensconced in its new home in Tasmania, '21 imparting a coiled but focused
presence in the glass. Combines filigree-fine acidity with equally fine, subtle
fruit intensity, a lick of spice and oak-defined almond mealiness. Winemaking is
exemplary, allowing the region to star and the fruit to shine. Screw cap. 12.9% alc.
RATING 95 DRINK 2023-2031 $60 JP
Patricia Shiraz 2018, Victoria Each Patricia vintage is intrinsically, irresistibly
individual. The '18 release stands in marked difference to '17, producing a
notably savoury, earthy offering, all dark and brooding. Black is the dominant
colour – blackberry, cassis, black licorice and dark chocolate with a presiding
dark smokiness. Spices play a strong supporting role together with persistent
woody tannins. A wine for the future. Screw cap. 14.2% alc. RATING 94
DRINK 2024-2032 $70 JP

ŸŸŸŸŸ **Premium Brut Prosecco NV, King Valley** RATING 93 $27 JP ✪
Winemaker's Series Shiraz 2020, Heathcote RATING 93 DRINK 2022-2028
$25 JP ✪
Limited Release Single Vineyard Montepulciano 2022, Heathcote
RATING 91 DRINK 2023-2026 $25 JP ✪
Premium Cuvée NV, King Valley Tumbarumba RATING 90 $25 JP ✪

Brown Hill Estate

925 Rosa Brook Road, Rosa Brook, WA 6285 **Region** Margaret River
T (08) 9757 4003 **www.brownhillestate.com.au Open** 7 days 10–5 **Winemaker** Nathan
Bailey, Eddie Giles **Viticulturist** Nathan Bailey, Angélique Rouviere **Est.** 1995
Vyds 24ha
The Bailey family is involved in all stages of wine production, with minimal outside help.
Their stated aim is to produce top quality wines at affordable prices, via uncompromising

viticultural practices emphasising low yields. The vineyard is primarily planted to shiraz and cabernet, with smaller plantings of semillon, sauvignon blanc, merlot, malbec and chardonnay. The quality of the best wines in the portfolio is very good.

ΨΨΨΨΨ **Fimiston Reserve Shiraz 2020, Margaret River** An excellent dark yet bright garnet hue with a purple tinge; very aromatic with florals, an array of spices and dark fruit. Full bodied with plump tannins and while the fruit tastes quite ripe, there's freshness and lively acidity in the mix. Screw cap. 14% alc. **RATING** 93 **DRINK** 2022-2028 $55 JF

Perseverance Signature Range Cabernet Merlot 2020, Margaret River There's volume and density via fruit and oak yet also a freshness and vibrancy, too. Cassis and plum come infused with baking spices, choc-mint and a meatiness à la charcuterie. Full bodied, flexed tannins and texture, too. Screw cap. 14% alc. **RATING** 92 **DRINK** 2022-2023 $80 JF

Ivanhoe Reserve Cabernet Sauvignon 2020, Margaret River While the colour is fine and bright, this seems a touch forward on the palate. Ripe fruit moving beyond cassis into dark plums and black cherries, savoury, too, with woodsmoke and cocoa-like, ripe tannins. Full bodied, dense tending towards plushness. A weightier wine than what the region usually produces. Screw cap. 14% alc. **RATING** 90 **DRINK** 2022-2028 $55 JF

Brown Magpie Wines ★★★★

125 Larcombes Road, Modewarre, Vic 3240 (postal) **Region** Geelong **T** (03) 5266 2147 **www.**brownmagpiewines.com **Open** Not **Winemaker** Shane Breheny **Viticulturist** Robert Steel **Est.** 2002 **Dozens** 5000 **Vyds** 9ha

Shane and Loretta Breheny's 20ha property is situated predominantly on a gentle, north-facing slope, with cypress trees on the western and southern borders providing protection against the wind. Vines were planted over '01–02, with pinot noir (4ha) taking the lion's share, followed by pinot gris and shiraz (2.4ha each) and 0.1ha each of chardonnay and sauvignon blanc. Viticulture is Loretta's love; winemaking (and wine) is Shane's.

ΨΨΨΨΨ **Single Vineyard Shiraz 2021, Geelong** A medium, bright crimson red. A perfume of satsuma plums, wild strawberries, violets and mountain herbs. A medium-bodied and quite delicious wine. There's enough stuffing and fine, chalky tannins to suggest, too, that this will get even better over the next 4–6 years. Screw cap. 13.3% alc. **RATING** 93 **DRINK** 2022-2028 $45 PR

Single Vineyard Pinot Noir 2021, Geelong A medium ruby red, this offers brambly red fruits and autumnal forest floor notes as well as some bay leaf, clove and a trace of white pepper. Medium bodied, those slightly developed yet attractive forest floor notes are present on a palate that is silky textured and moderately long. Screw cap. 13.8% alc. **RATING** 91 **DRINK** 2022-2027 $45 PR

🍇 Bruno & George ★★★★

278 Golflinks Road, Rowland Flat, Barossa Valley, SA 5352 **Region** Barossa Valley **T** 0439 490 532 **www.**brunogeorgewines.com.au **Open** By appt **Winemaker** Bruce Blackwell **Est.** 2013 **Dozens** 1200

A dynamic example of the 'New Barossa' that is the brainchild of 3 mates with some serious regional pedigree. Bruce Blackwell, Christian Roediger and Josh Norman, Barossa boys through and through, source grapes from across the Barossa and Eden valleys and produce a range of wines that span the gap between 'traditional' and 'contemporary'. Regional classics such as shiraz and grenache are bolstered with Italian varieties, including an Eden Valley montepulciano. The label is set for a bright future.

ΨΨΨΨΨ **Montepulciano 2021, Eden Valley** Bright crimson with purple flashes in the glass and notes of ripe plum, red cherry and blueberry fruits along with hints of spice, almond blossom, macerated berries, cola and earth. Impressive fruit depth on a fine-tannin framework and a quite brisk acid cadence that propels it forward, finishing with a chocolatey, plummy flourish. Pretty impressive stuff. Screw cap. 13% alc. **RATING** 93 **DRINK** 2023–2028 $65 DB

Drainings Shiraz 2019, Barossa Valley Deep crimson with aromas of satsuma plum, blackberry and boysenberry with an array of spices and hints of licorice, dark chocolate, earth, purple florals and fruitcake tones. Some cedary nuance and fig notes on the palate, which is full bodied and powerful with compact tannins, bright acidity and a spicy finish showing a hint of alcohol heat. Muscular and intense. Cork. 15% alc. **RATING** 93 **DRINK** 2023–2030 $150 DB

Grenache 2020, Barossa Valley A spice-laden grenache that shows plenty of verve, with pure plum and raspberry fruits undercut with hints of earth, ginger cake, purple florals, cola and red licorice. Fine powdery tannins give a gentle frame for the fruit, finishing savoury and spicy with brisk acid drive and an affable demeanour. Screw cap. 14.5% alc. **RATING** 92 **DRINK** 2023–2026 $45 DB

Bull Lane Wine Company ★★★★

PO Box 77, Heathcote, Vic 3523 **Region** Heathcote
T 0427 970 041 **www.**bulllane.com.au **Open** Not **Winemaker** Simon Osicka
Viticulturist Alison Phillips **Est.** 2013 **Dozens** 500

After a successful career as a winemaker with what is now TWE, Simon Osicka, together with viticulturist partner Alison Phillips, returned to the eponymous family winery just within the eastern boundary of the Heathcote region in '10. Spurred on by a decade of drought impacting on the 60yo dry-grown vineyard, and a desire to create another style of shiraz, Simon and Alison spent considerable time visiting Heathcote vineyards with access to water in the lead-up to the '10 vintage. After the weather gods gave up their tricks of '11, Bull Lane was in business.

♟♟♟♟♟ **Via del Toro Nebbiolo 2019, Heathcote** While bright and clear, the tea leaf-tinged colour shows the development one expects with nebbiolo. Managing colour and the tannins must be a daunting task, one I personally have never sought. Simon Osicka and Alison Phillips have done a first-class job. Screw cap. 14% alc. **RATING** 94 **DRINK** 2023–2039 $35 JH ✪

♟♟♟♟♟ **Shiraz 2021, Heathcote RATING** 93 **DRINK** 2023–2031 $29 CM ✪

Buller Wines ★★★★★

2804 Federation Way, Rutherglen, Vic 3685 **Region** Rutherglen
T (02) 6032 9660 **www.**bullerwines.com.au **Open** 7 days 10–5 **Winemaker** Dave Whyte
Est. 1921 **Dozens** 10 000 **Vyds** 32ha

In '13, after 92 years of ownership and management by the Buller family, the business was purchased by Gerald and Mary Judd, a well-known local couple and family with extensive roots in the North East. They are hands-on in the business and have overseen major investment in the cellar, storage, operations and, importantly, vineyards. White and sparkling wines from the King Valley have been added to the range and there is a new restaurant and refurbished cellar door. Buller celebrated 100 years in '21.

♟♟♟♟♟ **Calliope Rare Topaque NV, Rutherglen** Behold the winemaker's art – in particular, the wine blender's mastery – to fuse a range of fruit parcels dating back to the '40s to combine such formidable flavour intensity with a deft, lightness of touch. The result is luscious: malt, honeyed walnuts, panforte, dried fruits, and cacao, yet with a delivery that flows effortlessly and fresh. 500ml. Screw cap. 18% alc. **RATING** 97 $250 JP

♟♟♟♟♟ **Calliope Grand Topaque NV, Rutherglen** The maker's Grand range of fortifieds boasts a 'minimum' age of 25 years. Burnished walnut in colour, complex in aromas and luscious flavours that offer the essential 'Grand' experience of cold tea, fruitcake, honey, malt and roasted almond nuttiness. The blender's skill is on display with that clean, bright flow and delivery of ambrosian flavour. The finish is long and fragrant. 500ml. Screw cap. 18% alc. **RATING** 96 $150 JP

Calliope Rare Muscat NV, Rutherglen You can count the number of Rutherglen producers able to make a Rare Muscat with an average age of 50+ years on 2 hands. Rare by name, rare by nature. Layer upon layer of flavour, sweet and luscious, a commingling of old parcels and young with fresh, clean, neutral spirit to lift the pleasure factor sky high. That's how good it is. 500ml. Screw cap. 18% alc. RATING 96 $250 JP

Calliope Grand Muscat NV, Rutherglen A stalwart Rutherglen fortified producer, Buller Wines has a rich, old solera to dip into for blending little gems such as this. Amber in colour and bringing the most delightful aromas of treacle, fruitcake, malt toffee and nuttiness to bear, it shows its Grand status on the palate with a complexity and depth of flavour that lasts and lasts. And so elegant, too. 500ml. Screw cap. 18% alc. RATING 95 $150 JP

Calliope Rare Frontignac NV, Rutherglen The base wine is from a single vineyard, 1968 vintage. With only a handful of barrels left, each year the chance to taste this wine becomes a rarer privilege. The deep olive-tawny colour and great viscosity of this fortified suggest some very old material. The bouquet confirms it in sweet toffee, dried fruits, figs, walnuts, molasses and malt. Profound and luscious, yet clean. 500ml. Screw cap. 18% alc. RATING 94 $250 JP

ŶŶŶŶŶ **Calliope Shiraz 2018, Rutherglen** RATING 91 DRINK 2022-2031 $45 JP
Balladeer Cabernet Sauvignon 2021, Rutherglen RATING 90 DRINK 2022-2028 $29 JP
Calliope Chardonnay 2021, King Valley RATING 90 DRINK 2022-2028 $32 JP
Fine Old Tawny NV, Rutherglen RATING 90 $28 JP

Bunnamagoo Estate ★★★★

603 Henry Lawson Drive, Mudgee, NSW 2850 **Region** Mudgee
T 1300 304 707 **www**.bunnamagoowines.com.au **Open** 7 days 10–4
Winemaker Robert Black **Est.** 1995 **Dozens** 100 000 **Vyds** 108ha
Bunnamagoo Estate stands on one of the first land grants in the region and is situated near the historic town of Rockley. A 6ha vineyard planted to chardonnay, merlot and cabernet sauvignon was established by Paspaley Pearls. The winery and cellar door are located at the much larger and warmer Eurunderee vineyard (102ha) at Mudgee.

ŶŶŶŶŶ **Dry Style Riesling 2022, Mudgee** Exotic citrus oils ooze from this '22 riesling. Lemon myrtle, makrut lime and lemon verbena. Shaved cucumber, green pear and apple blossom with a touch of juniper and rosemary give a sexy London Dry gin feel. The palate finishes dry but with a wisp of fruit sweetness in the middle palate. A chalky and saline finish makes for a unique little wine. Screw cap. 11% alc. RATING 93 DRINK 2022-2035 $28 SW ✪

Semillon Sauvignon Blanc 2022, Mudgee A fresh take on a classic blend. A cool ferment brings forth white pear flesh, crushed lemongrass, kiwi and pine-lime. There are hints of ginger and pineapple stem without moving too far into the tropical spectrum. Plenty of substantial flavour with a snap of acidity. Screw cap. 12.5% alc. RATING 91 DRINK 2022-2025 $28 SW ✪

Rosé 2022, Mudgee This rosé is the palest rose-petal pink in the glass and conveys the same charming aromas. Add hints of lychee, Pink Lady apples, plum and finger lime. The palate captures vivid acidity and freshness, finishing bone dry. It's as inviting as a spoonful of moreish plum sorbet. Screw cap. 12.5% alc. RATING 90 DRINK 2022-2028 $28 SW

Medium Dry Style Riesling 2022, Mudgee Pure and unadulterated riesling. A core of lemon wedge is surrounded with a posy of white florals and lime leaf with a hint of cracked river pebble. The fruit sweetness is effortless and natural acidity carries it along gracefully. A laid-back, easy-drinking style that would suit both sweet or dry palates. Screw cap. 11% alc. RATING 90 DRINK 2022-2032 $28 SW

Burge Family Winemakers ★★★★

1312 Barossa Way, Lyndoch, SA 5351 **Region** Barossa Valley
T (08) 8524 4644 **www.**burgefamily.com.au **Open** Thurs–Mon 10–5
Winemaker Derek Fitzgerald **Est.** 1928 **Dozens** 10 000 **Vyds** 10ha
In '13, Burge Family Winemakers – an iconic producer of exceptionally rich, lush and
concentrated Barossa red wines – marked 85 years of continuous winemaking by 3 generations
of the family. Burge Family was purchased by the Wilsford Group in Nov '18; the legacy of
the Burge Family has been preserved with no change in wine style. Derek Fitzgerald stepped
into Rick Burge's shoes, having made wine in the Barossa for 14 years.

Homestead Red Blend 2020, Barossa Valley A blend of 54/46% tinta cão/
souzao showing deep, resonant characters of inky macerated black fruits, dark
spices, salted licorice, cola, pressed flowers, tomato leaf and a curious waft of
spearmint. Wild-eyed, flush with spicy black fruits and cascading sandy tannins
and gesticulating wildly for some robust barbecued meat – I love it. Screw cap.
14.5% alc. **RATING** 92 **DRINK** 2023-2026 $35 DB
Zinfandel Rosé 2022, Barossa Valley Light pink in the glass and displaying a
tightly coiled aromatic profile of raspberry, red cherry and redcurrant jelly along
with hints of purple flowers, strawberry coulis, red apple and watermelon. Some
soft spice notes appear on the palate, which is crisp, clean and showing plenty
of acid drive on a finish that speeds off with notes of bright red berry fruits and
raspberry cream. Screw cap. 13% alc. **RATING** 91 **DRINK** 2023-2025 $25 DB ✪
Riesling 2022, Eden Valley Pale straw in the glass with classic Eden Valley
riesling characters of freshly squeezed lime juice, Bickford's lime cordial and
Christmas lily along with hints of crushed stone, green apple, almond paste and a
whiff of freshly cut fennel. Limey and true on the palate with some light herbal
notes joining the fray and finishing dry, clean and savoury. Screw cap. 12.5% alc.
RATING 90 **DRINK** 2023-2028 $25 DB ✪

Burke & Wills Winery ★★★★

3155 Burke & Wills Track, Mia Mia, Vic 3444 **Region** Heathcote
T (03) 5425 5400 **www.**wineandmusic.net **Open** By appt **Winemaker** Andrew Pattison,
Robert Ellis **Est.** 2003 **Dozens** 1200 **Vyds** 1.6ha
After 18 years at Lancefield Winery in the Macedon Ranges, Andrew Pattison moved his
operation a few kms north to set up Burke & Wills Winery at the southern edge of the
Heathcote region. The vineyards at Mia Mia comprise 0.6ha of shiraz, 0.6ha of bordeaux
varieties (cabernet sauvignon, petit verdot, merlot and malbec) and 0.4ha of gewürztraminer.
He still sources a small amount of Macedon Ranges fruit from his former vineyard; additional
grapes are contract-grown in Heathcote.

Vat 1 French Oak Shiraz 2019, Heathcote Grown at the southern and
coolest end of the Heathcote region. This is a warm, rich red with cedar oak laid
on thick with plenty of plum-soaked fruit nestled in behind. Oak flavour arguably
shows too keenly but then many will see that as a positive. For pure seduction
though, this wine makes a strong pitch. Screw cap. 14.5% alc. **RATING** 93
DRINK 2024-2034 $36 CM
Mia Mia Gewürztraminer 2022, Heathcote Has all the usual varietal cues,
but more refreshing than most. This is a gewürztraminer with a bit of zip. It's
driven by red apple and lychee though there are spice and rosewater aspects, too.
It's a good drink. Screw cap. 13.5% alc. **RATING** 91 **DRINK** 2023-2027 $28 CM ✪

Burton McMahon ★★★★★

101 McDonalds Road, Pokolbin, NSW 2320 **Region** Yarra Valley
T (02) 4998 6873 **www.**gundogestate.com.au **Open** 7 days 10–5 **Winemaker** Matt
Burton, Dylan McMahon **Est.** 2012 **Dozens** 2000
Burton McMahon is a collaboration between Matt Burton from Gundog Estate in the Hunter
Valley and Seville Estate winemaker Dylan McMahon (see separate entries for both). With

a shared love of chardonnay and pinot noir, the 2 friends began looking for suitable single vineyard sites to purchase fruit from in the late 2000s, making their first wines in '10. While the earlier wines came from both Gippsland and the Yarra Valley, recent releases have focused on single-vineyard chardonnay and pinot from the Upper Yarra. Made at Seville Estate, the wines are finely detailed, elegant and well priced. Available at Gundog Estate cellar door.

🍷🍷🍷🍷🍷 **D'Aloisio's Vineyard Chardonnay 2022, Yarra Valley** Multidimensional with aromas of stone fruits, lightly grilled almonds and a little spice. On the palate, this pure fruited, polished and finely tuned wine is ready to drink a little earlier than the '22 George's Vineyard Chardonnay, and I can think of worse exercises than comparing these well-priced and subtly different Upper Yarra single-vineyard wines over the years. Screw cap. 12.8% alc. **RATING** 96 **DRINK** 2023-2028 $50 PR ✪

George's Vineyard Chardonnay 2022, Yarra Valley Expressive from the first whiff with its aromas of white peaches, nectarine and lemon peel together with some white flowers and little cashew. Restrained, with mouth-watering acidity, this balanced, long and persistent wine has excellent potential. 90 dozen made. Screw cap. 12.8% alc. **RATING** 95 **DRINK** 2023-2029 $50 PR ✪

Bush Track Wines   ★★★☆

161 Myrtle Street, Myrtleford, Vic 3737 **Region** Alpine Valleys
T 0409 572 712 **www.**bushtrackwines.com.au **Open** Wed 12–6, Thurs 12–8, Sun 12–5 **Winemaker** Jo Marsh, Glenn James **Viticulturist** Bob McNamara **Est.** 1987 **Dozens** 1000 **Vyds** 8ha
Bob and Helen McNamara established the vineyard in '87, planting 11 different clones of shiraz with smaller quantities of chardonnay, cabernet sauvignon and sangiovese. They have made small volumes of wines since '06, improving vineyard practices along the way and hiring local winemakers Jo Marsh (Billy Button Wines) and Eleana Anderson (Mayford Wines). Bush Track Wines shares a cheery cellar door with Billy Button in Myrtleford.

🍷🍷🍷🍷🍷 **Ovens Valley Sparkling Shiraz 2018, Alpine Valleys** A longer time on lees and bottle age than many of its cohort, which brings forth depth and complexity. The aromas are alive in dark cherry, bramble, acacia, panforte and dark chocolate. They transfer easily onto the palate accompanied by a rich vein of spice. Combines a touch of old-school sweetness with a refreshing dry finish. Seamless in delivery. Crown. 13% alc. **RATING** 94 **DRINK** 2023-2026 $50 JP

Byrne Vineyards   ★★★★☆

PO Box 15, Kent Town BC, SA 5071 **Region** South Australia
T (08) 8132 0022 **www.**byrnevineyards.com.au **Open** Not **Winemaker** Mark Robinson, Phil Reedman MW **Est.** 1963 **Dozens** 80 000 **Vyds** 200ha
Eric and Romla Byrne purchased the property and planted a vineyard near Devlin's Pound near Waikerie in '60. Today, 3 generations are involved in the business with son Rob running the show with his daughter Petria, and grandson Will, across their vineyards in the Clare Valley and Riverland. There are a number of brands across the portfolio, including Flavabom, Sidney Wilcox, Thomson Estate, Devlin's Mount, Scotts Creek Retreat, Glamper and the Calcannia wines, mostly concentrating on the Clare Valley.

🍷🍷🍷🍷🍷 **Calcannia Sangiovese 2022, Clare Valley** A delightful drink with a strong sense of the essence of the variety in dark cherry, woody spices, fennel and cola ricocheting between the bouquet and palate. Tight tannins shape the flavours, good extension, too, with a huge dusting of sweet spice and a touch of amaro to finish. Screw cap. 14.5% alc. **RATING** 91 **DRINK** 2023-2030 $28 MB ✪

Sidney Wilcox White Field Blend 2022, South Australia Co-fermented semillon, chardonnay and riesling. It offers both flavour and grip. Apple, pear, nectarine and citrus characters burst through the palate, an apple skin-like aspect adding to the texture. There's not much in the way of aroma but the palate creates its own world, and it's a pleasing one, with a bit of difference. Screw cap. 13.5% alc. **RATING** 91 **DRINK** 2023-2026 $25 CM ✪

Byron & Harold

57 River Way, Walter Point, WA 6152 (postal) **Region** Western Australia
T 0402 010 352 **www**.byronandharold.com.au **Open** Not **Winemaker** Rory Parks
Est. 2011 **Dozens** 36000 **Vyds** 34ha
The owners of Byron & Harold make a formidable partnership, covering every aspect of winemaking, sales, marketing, business management and administration. Paul Byron and Ralph (Harold) Dunning together have more than 65 years of experience in the Australian wine trade, working at top levels for some of the most admired wineries and wine distribution companies. Andrew Lane worked for 20 years in the tourism industry, including in a senior role with Tourism Australia, leading to the formation of the Wine Tourism Export Council. More recently he developed the family vineyard (Wandering Lane).

ŶŶŶŶŶ **The Partners Cabernet Sauvignon 2020, Great Southern** Medium weight, a silky textured and refreshing expression of cabernet sauvignon. Scents of cassis, bay leaf and sea spray with faint mint/eucalyptus notes accompanied by gentle cedar spice. The palate is lush with cassis and dotted with more bay leaf, mint, chocolate and clove. So mellow, so supple, with wonderful flow and an elongated finish. Screw cap. 14.5% alc. **RATING** 94 **DRINK** 2022-2032 $60 MB

ŶŶŶŶŸ **The Partners Chardonnay 2021, Great Southern RATING** 93 **DRINK** 2022-2030 $60 MB
The Partners Riesling 2022, Great Southern RATING 92 **DRINK** 2023-2030 $40 MB
The Protocol Cabernet Sauvignon 2021, Margaret River RATING 92 **DRINK** 2024-2034 $60 JF
Rags to Riches Cabernet Sauvignon 2021, Margaret River RATING 91 **DRINK** 2023-2030 $30 JF
The Protocol Shiraz 2020, Margaret River RATING 90 **DRINK** 2023-2033 $60 JF

Cael's Gate

697 Wollombi Road, Broke, NSW 2330 (postal) **Region** Hunter Valley
T 0424 152 037 **www**.caelsgate.com.au **Open** Not **Winemaker** Chris Chew
Viticulturist Trevor Tolson **Est.** 2016 **Dozens** 250
Cael's Gate is a family-owned operation sourcing grapes from Mudgee, the Hunter and the Riverina. The Riverina may well be better known for sweet botrytised styles and large-volume expressions of a simple, fruit-forward persuasion, yet Cael's Gate defies the status quo with aplomb. All the fruit is hand picked. Extraction is judicious. Pretty good French oak is employed too.

ŶŶŶŶŸ **Handpicked Shiraz 2021, Mudgee** Attractive riffs on terracotta, mulch, tar, anise, iodine and dark cherry. There is an underbelly of verdant herb conferring savouriness before a full-weighted mid-palate expands across a lithe tannic band, exuding sweetness on either side. Charm, warmth, personality and regional fidelity in spades. Screw cap. 14% alc. **RATING** 90 **DRINK** 2022-2032 $48 NG

Calabria Family Wines

1283 Brayne Road, Griffith, NSW 2680 **Region** Riverina
T (02) 6969 0800 **www**.calabriawines.com.au **Open** Mon–Sat 10–4, Sun 11–3
Winemaker Bill Calabria AM, Emma Norbiato, Tony Steffania, Calvin Foster, Jordan Bellato **Est.** 1945 **Vyds** 100ha
Calabria Family Wines was born in Riverina, but has since cast its net wide over the Barossa Valley, too, starting with the purchase of the 100+yo William vineyard in '15. Its Three Bridges range is anchored in Riverina estate vineyards; the Saint Petri, Elisabetta, Alternato and other labels in the Barossa. The family has increased its plantings of durif and added aglianico, nero d'Avola, montepulciano and pinot bianco. There is a second, family-friendly cellar door at 284 Magnolia Road in Vine Vale in the Barossa Valley, open 11–5 daily.

ㅜㅜㅜㅜㅜ **Elisabetta Durif 2021, Barossa Valley** Deep, impenetrable inky crimson in the glass. Durif can reach some pretty heady alcohol levels – not so with this release. That's not at the expense of ripe black-fruited depth and layered spice that we know and love from the variety, either. This is an excellent example of durif with grace: balanced, fruit-pure, savoury and structured. A beautifully composed wine and a joy to drink. Screw cap. 13% alc. RATING 95 DRINK 2023–2030 $50 DB ✪

The Iconic Grand Reserve Shiraz 2020, Barossa Valley Saturated crimson in the glass with detailed fruit aromas of macerated satsuma plum, cassis and black cherry with underlying hints of baking spices, dark chocolate, light blossom tones, licorice, earth, olive tapenade, cedar and smoked meats. Full-bodied and unctuous with serious fruit depth, intensity, oak spice and earthy nuance with superfine, grainy tannins and a long finish that's flush with ripe fruit. Powerful. Screw cap. 14.5% alc. RATING 95 DRINK 2023–2043 $175 DB

ㅜㅜㅜㅜㅜ **Aged 12 Years Pedro Ximenez Semillon NV, Riverina** RATING 93 $40 SW
Three Bridges Limited Edition Botrytis Semillon NV, Riverina RATING 93 DRINK 2022–2040 $35 SW ✪
Three Bridges Durif 2021, Riverina RATING 92 DRINK 2023–2028 $25 SW ✪
Three Bridges Grenache 2021, Barossa Valley RATING 92 DRINK 2023–2027 $25 DB ✪
Three Bridges Shiraz 2021, Barossa Valley RATING 92 DRINK 2023–2028 $25 DB ✪
Alternato Malbec 2021, Barossa Valley RATING 92 DRINK 2023–2027 $45 DB
Alternato Montepulciano Nero d'Avola 2021, Barossa Valley RATING 92 DRINK 2023–2027 $45 DB
Elisabetta Shiraz 2021, Barossa Valley RATING 92 DRINK 2023–2033 $50 DB
Saint Petri Shiraz Carignan 2020, Barossa Valley RATING 92 DRINK 2023–2029 $90 DB
Alternato Sangiovese 2021, Barossa Valley RATING 91 DRINK 2023–2029 $45 DB
Bélena Pinot Grigio 2022, South Eastern Australia RATING 90 DRINK 2022–2028 $20 SW ✪
Bélena Montepulciano 2022, Riverina RATING 90 DRINK 2022–2032 $20 SW ✪
Three Bridges Mourvèdre 2021, Barossa Valley RATING 90 DRINK 2023–2029 $35 DB
Calabria Bros Grenache Shiraz Mataro 2021, Barossa Valley RATING 90 DRINK 2023–2026 $30 DB

Campbells   ★★★★★

4603 Murray Valley Highway, Rutherglen, Vic 3685 **Region** Rutherglen
T (02) 6033 6000 **www.**campbellswines.com.au **Open** 7 days 10–5 **Winemaker** Julie Campbell **Est.** 1870 **Dozens** 36 000 **Vyds** 72ha
Campbells has a long and rich history, with 5 generations of wine making. There were difficult times: phylloxera's arrival in the Bobbie Burns vineyard in 1898; the Depression of the 1930s. But the Scottish blood of founder John Campbell has ensured that the business flourished. There have been spectacular successes in unexpected quarters (white table wines, especially riesling) and expected success with Muscat and Topaque. Following the death of Colin Campbell in '19, daughters Jane and Julie Campbell are now at the helm, as managing director and head winemaker respectively. A founding member of Australia's First Families of Wine.

ㅜㅜㅜㅜㅜ **Merchant Prince Rare Muscat NV, Rutherglen** The base wine for this extraordinary fortified is more than 70 years old. It pours in slow motion, deep amber-brown in colour. It lusciously, luxuriously reveals itself slowly – it has time on its side – with an intense scent and flavour rich in coffee, caramel toffee, chocolate panforte, hazelnut, fig, quince paste and fruit peel. You are tasting history, a rare experience, indeed. 375ml. Screw cap. 17.5% alc. RATING 99 $140 JP ✪

Isabella Rare Topaque NV, Rutherglen One sip and you're transported to a world of heightened aromas and intense flavours, layers of them, almost without end, thanks to a marathon of a finish. Oak age brings rancio woody notes, caramel and burnt butter with muscadelle-rich fruitcake, honey malt biscuit sweetness, dried fruits and butterscotch. They taste immediate and fresh. Enjoy the ride. 375ml. Screw cap. 17.5% alc. RATING 98 $140 JP ✪

ΨΨΨΨΨ **Grand Muscat NV, Rutherglen** The step up in complexity with the Grand Classification is there. So, too, the freshness of spirit. Burnished walnut in colour. Resplendent in raisin, dried fruits, toffee, rancio aged characters and treacle richness. Great depth of lusciousness, skilfully blended and clean to close. 375ml. Screw cap. 17.5% alc. RATING 96 $70 JP ✪

Grand Topaque NV, Rutherglen The late Colin Campbell was a strong advocate for the change of name from Tokay to Topaque. His daughters, Julie and Jane, continue to do him proud with a seriously good rendition that explores both its rich, luscious side as well as a fresh, grapey immediacy, melded together cleanly by neutral spirit. Delicious malt-toffee, raisins, roasted nuts, honey cake, dried fruits and burnt butter. Lasts so, so long. 375ml. Screw cap. 17.5% alc. RATING 96 $70 JP ✪

Bobbie Burns Shiraz 2021, Rutherglen You have to admire not only the value for money offered by Bobbie Burns but its outstanding ability to be good drinking in its youth and age extraordinarily well. Upfront purple hues, fruit that sings in ripe blackberry, chocolate, a world of spice and the kind of intensity of flavour that lingers on and on. It's devoid of winemaking excess, just honest fruit off old vines nicely enhanced by discreet oak. Screw cap. 14.5% alc. RATING 95 DRINK 2023-2031 $26 JP ✪

Classic Topaque NV, Rutherglen An average age of 12 years. Golden amber. Penetrating aromas, fresh and raisiny, sweet cold tea, caramel toffee and orange peel. Harmonious, lush, good intensity, extra long length and the kind of freshness achieved through masterful blending and clean, neutral spirit. 500ml. Screw cap. 17.5% alc. RATING 95 $40 JP ✪

Classic Muscat NV, Rutherglen The second Classic tier of the fortified classification displays the heart and soul of Muscat with age (12 years average), a sense of raisiny youth, developing complexity and, importantly, freshness. They are all here and then some. Add the Campbells' elegant house style and you have one sublime fortified. 500ml. Screw cap. 17.5% alc. RATING 95 $40 JP ✪

ΨΨΨΨΨ **Muscat NV, Rutherglen** RATING 92 $22 JP ✪
Topaque NV, Rutherglen RATING 92 $22 JP ✪

Cape Landing ★★★★

1098 Calgardup Road, Forest Grove, WA 6286 **Region** Margaret River
T 0488 006 169 **www.**capelanding.com.au **Open** By appt **Winemaker** Bruce Dukes, Remi Guise **Viticulturist** James Harris **Est.** 1998 **Dozens** 2500 **Vyds** 14ha
The current owner, Mark Lewis, purchased the property in '16 from Cheryl and Larry de Jong, who had established the vineyard in the late '90s. For many years the vineyard supplied most of its grapes to other wineries in the area. The vineyard is planted to chardonnay, sauvignon blanc, shiraz and cabernet sauvignon. Cellar door is currently in the planning.

ΨΨΨΨΨ **Blackwood Silvereye Sauvignon Blanc 2021, Margaret River** There's lovely texture and definition with some obvious oak influence and lees bolstering all that. Refreshing and zesty with finger limes, snow peas and a hint of feijoa. Screw cap. 12.3% alc. RATING 93 DRINK 2022-2027 $38 JF

Blackwood Silvereye Chardonnay 2021, Margaret River Some slips of fruit flavour come into this, although it remains a tightly coiled, highly strung chardonnay. Tangy, crunchy acidity – and lots of it – mingle with the creamy, leesy flavouring and spicy oak. It ends up perky and refreshing and lonesome on its own; definitely in need of food as a partner. Screw cap. 12.5% alc. **RATING** 91 **DRINK** 2022-2030 $60 JF

Blackwood Chardonnay 2021, Margaret River Winemaking is making up a lot of the flavour and I have a feeling more fruit ripeness is needed here. Tightly wound with a spiral of nervy energy and mouth-watering acidity weaving flavours of creamy lees and spicy woodsy oak. This has appeal for those keen on a more linear chardonnay with some latent power. Screw cap. 11.6% alc. **RATING** 90 **DRINK** 2023-2030 $60 JF

Cape Mentelle

331 Wallcliffe Road, Margaret River, WA 6285 **Region** Margaret River
T (08) 9757 0888 **www**.capementelle.com.au **Open** 7 days 10–5 **Winemaker** Eloise Jarvis, Coralie Lewis **Viticulturist** David Moulton **Est.** 1970 **Dozens** 50 000 **Vyds** 128ha

As it turned out, '23 was a watershed moment at Cape Mentelle, a Margaret River pioneer. One of the worst-kept wine secrets came to fruition: Endeavour Group bought the business, which had been under the umbrella of Louis Vuitton Moet Hennessy for more than 30 years. But personally, we had even better news in late '22 with Eloise Jarvis coming on as senior winemaker. Why? Her first vintage job was at Cape Mentelle in '96. She loves the place. Super smart, skilled, dedicated and passionate, it bodes well. There's an excellent team working with her and great vineyards, too.

ΨΨΨΨΨ **Reserve Chardonnay 2020, Margaret River** A classy chardy enmeshed in so much flavour it constantly changes in the glass. Starts with lemon ginger herbal tea, quince paste and lemony freshness then moves into savoury territory with cashew butter, miso and creamy lees with smokin' sulphides. The cedary oak is a mere coating adding plenty of spice, too. The result, a deeply satisfying drink. Screw cap. 14% alc. **RATING** 96 **DRINK** 2023-2031 $150 JF

Shiraz 2020, Margaret River An amazing bright colour for starters, all dark purple shot with black and red. The delight continues across a fuller-bodied palate that's full of dark plums, cloves, turmeric and Sichuan pepper – a bit of excitement here. The tannins are shapely and slightly grainy and everything comes to play a harmonious chord. Screw cap. 13.9% alc. **RATING** 95 **DRINK** 2023-2033 $49 JF ✪

Cabernet Sauvignon 2020, Margaret River Lots of positive changes are afoot at Cape Mentelle, and I've a feeling it's regaining its crown in the region. A glass of this and all's well. Fragrant with mulberries, cassis, nori and baking spices, the medium-bodied palate is superfine and long with textural tannins adding to the pleasure. Screw cap. 13.7% alc. **RATING** 95 **DRINK** 2023-2038 $60 JF

Heritage Cabernet Sauvignon 2018, Margaret River From any angle, it's imposing. Obelisk in structure, rich, ripe and densely packed with excellent fruit and cedary, creamy oak plus tannins. Mulberries, cassis, dark chocolate, nori and sumac come to the fore as the full-bodied palate gives way to tooth-coating tannins, shapely if firm. Lively and vibrant yet better in time. Cork. 14.6% alc. **RATING** 95 **DRINK** 2024-2038 $110 JF

Heritage Shiraz 2018, Margaret River This is no wallflower. It's voluminous, full of ripe, plump tannins and lots of cedary oak adding to its structure and flavour. There's also a core of good fruit and layers of savouriness – tobacco, woodsmoke, beef stock and all manner of spices. It's persistent on the finish, detailed and will have a big fan base. Cork. 14.7% alc. **RATING** 95 **DRINK** 2024-2035 $110 JF

ΨΨΨΨΨ **Sauvignon Blanc 2022, Margaret River** **RATING** 93 **DRINK** 2022-2024 $26 JF ✪

Rosé 2022, Margaret River **RATING** 90 **DRINK** 2022-2024 $28 JF

Capel Vale

118 Mallokup Road, Capel, WA 6271 **Region** Geographe
T (08) 9727 1986 **www.capelvale.com.au Open** Thu–Mon 10–4.30 **Winemaker** Daniel
Hetherington **Est.** 1974 **Dozens** 21 000 **Vyds** 52ha

Established in '74 by Perth-based medical practitioner Dr Peter Pratten and Elizabeth Pratten.
The first vineyard adjacent to the winery was planted on the banks of the quiet waters of
Capel River. The viticultural empire has since expanded, spreading across Geographe (9ha),
Mount Barker (15ha) and Margaret River (28ha). There are 4 tiers in the Capel Vale portfolio:
Debut (varietals), Regional Series, Black Label Margaret River Chardonnay and Cabernet
Sauvignon and, at the top, the Single Vineyard Wines.

Single Vineyard Series Whispering Hill Riesling 2022, Mount Barker
Even in a difficult season this still comes out pure and lovely. It's lightly spiced,
touched with lemon and mandarin, and best of all, textural – it's not all racy
acidity. It's supple and delicious. Screw cap. 12% alc. **RATING** 95 **DRINK** 2023–2033
$40 JF ✪

Black Label Cabernet Sauvignon 2020, Margaret River Fruit off the
Scholar vineyard at Wilyabrup and it comes stamped with quality. An elegant
style taking the loveliest regional attributes (think mulberries, cassis and cocoa,
leafy freshness) and layering them across a medium-bodied palate replete with
fine tannins. Finishes long and satisfying. Screw cap. 14% alc. **RATING** 95
DRINK 2024–2036 $50 JF ✪

Regional Series Riesling 2022, Mount Barker RATING 93 **DRINK** 2023–2032
$27 JF ✪
Black Label Chardonnay 2022, Margaret River RATING 93
DRINK 2023–2033 $50 JF
Regional Series Cabernet Sauvignon 2021, Margaret River RATING 92
DRINK 2023–2033 $27 JF ✪
Regional Series Sauvignon Blanc 2022, Margaret River RATING 90
DRINK 2022–2024 $25 JF ✪
Debut Malbec 2022, Western Australia RATING 90 **DRINK** 2022–2025
$20 JF ✪

Capercaillie Wines

4 Londons Road, Lovedale, NSW 2325 **Region** Hunter Valley
T (02) 4990 2904 **www.capercailliewines.com.au Open** 7 days 10–4.30 **Winemaker** Lance
Mikisch **Viticulturist** Lance Mikisch **Est.** 1995 **Dozens** 5000 **Vyds** 5ha

A successful winery in terms of the quality of its wines, as well as their reach outwards
from the Hunter Valley. The Capercaillie wines have generous flavour. Its fruit sources are
spread across South Eastern Australia, although the portfolio includes wines that are 100%
Hunter Valley.

Museum Release The Ghillie 2018, Hunter Valley From the high-quality
'18 vintage, first tasted in February '20 and given 97 points. It's retained its
elegance and balance, dark cherry/plum/blackberry filling the mouth with
waves of flavour, but not intrusive tannins. Screw cap. 14% alc. **RATING** 96
DRINK 2023–2038 $70 JH ✪

Gewürztraminer 2022, Hunter Valley Only 1600 bottles made, down 60% on
average yield. It was eminently possible that the hot dry weather leading to the
drop would also strip quality. Happily, the perfumed bouquet and tropical fruits of
the palate are in full voice, balanced by the usual Hunter Valley acidity. Screw cap.
13.1% alc. **RATING** 94 **DRINK** 2023–2033 $28 JH ✪

Museum Release The Creel 2014, Hunter Valley It's not a surprise to find
this semillon priced at $100 but it is unexpected that the wine still has work to
do along the pathway to full development. Screw cap. 11.5% alc. **RATING** 94
DRINK 2023–2038 $100 JH

Chardonnay 2022, Hunter Valley RATING 91 **DRINK** 2023–2028 $35 JH

Capital Wines

13 Gladstone Street, Hall, ACT 2618 **Region** Canberra District
T (02) 6230 2022 **www.**capitalwines.com.au **Open** By appt **Winemaker** Alex McKay,
Greg Gallagher **Est.** 1986 **Dozens** 3500 **Vyds** 5ha

In early '20, Bill Mason and Colin and Kay of Jirra at Jeir Station acquired Capital Wines from
Andrew and Marion McEwin. The cellar door in Hall, less than 15 minutes from the heart
of the national capital, features the Capital Wines range, Kosciuszko wines from Tumbarumba
(owned by Bill Mason and family) and the Jirra at Jeir Station wines from Murrumbateman.
Jeir Station, halfway between Hall and Murrumbateman, supplies much of the fruit for the
Capital wines.

🍷🍷🍷🍷♀ **The Ambassador Tempranillo 2022, Riverina** Such exuberance of youth
with its juicy cherries, sarsaparilla and cherry cola flavours. There's a touch of
meaty reduction adding to a more savoury bent, refreshing acidity and slightly
grainy tannins. Not complex but a ripper red in a joven style. Screw cap.
13.2% alc. **RATING** 90 **DRINK** 2023-2025 $32 JF

Cargo Road Wines

Cargo Road, Orange, NSW 2800 **Region** Orange
T (02) 6365 6100 **www.**cargoroadwines.com **Open** By appt
Winemaker James Sweetapple **Est.** 1983 **Dozens** 3000 **Vyds** 16ha

Originally called The Midas Tree, the vineyard was planted in 1983 by Roseworthy graduate
John Swanson, who established a 2.5ha vineyard that included zinfandel – 15 years ahead of
his time. The property was acquired in '97 by Charles Lane, James Sweetapple and Brian
Walters. They have rejuvenated the original vineyard and planted more zinfandel, sauvignon
blanc, cabernet and riesling.

🍷🍷🍷🍷♀ **Riesling 2022, Orange** Margarita limes, zest and juice. White jasmine blossoms
and Granny Smith apple curls, crushed quartz and lemon sherbet. A fragrant and
linear style of riesling produced with finesse. It's a wine that flows seamlessly and
captures that lime pith texture and gentle flowing acidity. A great example of
dry Orange riesling and extremely enjoyable. Screw cap. 11.2% alc. **RATING** 93
DRINK 2022-2028 $35 SW ✪

Reserve Shiraz 2021, Orange Deeply pigmented with a beetroot hue and
filled with red tulips, rhubarb, blackcurrant and sage leaf. A savoury and weighty
mid-palate of cured meats, olive brine and chocolate-covered coffee beans.
There's energy in the acid lift and a cedar oak char just on the finish. Screw cap.
14.2% alc. **RATING** 91 **DRINK** 2022-2028 $50 SW

Gewürztraminer 2022, Orange Lychee martinis garnished with a curl of lime
zest. Musk, white lilies and pear puree. Nicely weighted with a luscious mouthfeel
and fruit that is ripe but not overtly cloying. Acidity is mindful and driving and
the wine finishes with a slate-like minerality. A very varietally true wine that feels
considered and deliberate. Screw cap. 13.5% alc. **RATING** 90 **DRINK** 2022-2026
$35 SW

Carillion Wines

749 Mount View Road, Mount View, NSW 2325 **Region** Hunter Valley
T (02) 4990 7535 **www.**carillionwines.com.au **Open** Thurs–Mon 10–5
Winemaker Andrew Ling **Viticulturist** Liz Riley, Tim Esson, Pete Balnaves **Est.** 2000
Dozens 5000 **Vyds** 148ha

In '00 the Davis family decided to select certain parcels of fruit from their 28ha Davis Family
vineyard in the Hunter Valley, along with the family's other vineyards in Orange (the 30ha
Carillion vineyard) and Wrattonbully (the 90ha Stonefields vineyard), to make wines that are
a true expression of their location. In recent years Tim Davis has taken over the reins from
his father John, and brought these wines under the Carillion banner. He also launched the
Lovable Rogue range of wines, which highlights his keen interest in alternative grape varieties
(particularly Italian), as well as exploring innovative and experimental winemaking methods.

🍷🍷🍷🍷🍷 **Origins Six Clones Pinot Noir 2022, Orange** Each clone (114, 115, 777, Abel, 667 and MV6) was hand picked and vinified separately; 30% whole bunches, wild-yeast fermentation, then pressed to third-use French puncheons for the last stage of fermentation, and 7 months' maturation in oak before blending. Vinous logistics of a high level. Transparent crimson, verging rosé, colour. The wine has a scented, perfumed bouquet and a spicy, savoury light-bodied palate. Screw cap. 13.5% alc. **RATING** 97 **DRINK** 2023-2032 $45 JH ✪

🍷🍷🍷🍷🍷 **Origins Old Grafts Semillon 2022, Hunter Valley** Tasted after a string of young rieslings, this semillon came with an extra layer of lemon and lime that pushed the boundaries of typical acidity backwards. Mind you, this is still an incisive wine of great length, qualities driven by acidity. Screw cap. 12% alc. **RATING** 96 **DRINK** 2023-2037 $35 JH ✪

Origins Saddle Block Chardonnay 2022, Hunter Valley This is the inaugural release of this wine from the estate Tallavera vineyard in Mount View. It has excellent balance and length, white stone fruit and rockmelon earning their keep. Screw cap. 13.1% alc. **RATING** 96 **DRINK** 2023-2033 $45 JH ✪

Origins Arbitrage Cabernet Merlot Shiraz 2019, Wrattonbully From a near-perfect vintage. Matured in a complex array of French oak barrel size and age. Yodels cassis on a long, very well-balanced palate and savoury notes add an extra dimension. The first of 3 exceptional/perfect Wrattonbully vintages. Screw cap. 14.2% alc. **RATING** 96 **DRINK** 2028-2038 $50 JH ✪

Museum Release Riesling 2015, Orange Hand picked in the evening, the fruit was transported to the Hunter Valley winery to be chilled and whole-bunch pressed. A flowery, perfumed bouquet leads into a beautifully balanced palate, still as fresh as a daisy. Screw cap. 12.5% alc. **RATING** 96 **DRINK** 2023-2028 $60 JH ✪

Origins GM198 Clone Riesling 2022, Orange The wine doesn't wait before delivering an orange blossom-charged bouquet that seamlessly fills the palate with more of the same before the crisp acid attack on the back palate and finish invigorates and cleanses the aftertaste. Screw cap. 12.5% alc. **RATING** 95 **DRINK** 2023-2032 $35 JH ✪

Origins Crystals Chardonnay 2021, Orange Whole-bunch pressed, the free-run juice went into new and used French oak for 12 months, stirred bi-monthly. An elegant, well-balanced chardonnay reflecting the care taken throughout its élevage. Screw cap. 13.5% alc. **RATING** 95 **DRINK** 2023-2030 $45 JH ✪

Aged Release Tallavera Grove Semillon 2015, Hunter Valley Pale straw-green; complex texture and flavour; slightly funky bouquet part of the scheme, as is the lingering finish. Screw cap. 12% alc. **RATING** 95 **DRINK** 2023-2032 $60 JH

Museum Release Stonefields Block 22 Cabernet Sauvignon 2014, Wrattonbully Poor fruit set reduced yield significantly in '14. Rich blackcurrant/cassis balanced by powerful tannins ex fruit and oak. A serious wine, demanding time. Screw cap. 13.8% alc. **RATING** 95 **DRINK** 2029-2039 $70 JH

Origins Volcanics Cabernet Sauvignon 2021, Orange This was a bounce-back vintage after 3 years of drought and the smoke-ravaged '20 vintage. Matured 18 months in French barriques (25% new). A cabernet to bring a smile to the face of a pinot noir lover. Screw cap. 14.2% alc. **RATING** 94 **DRINK** 2023-2031 $50 JH

Museum Release The Volcanics Cabernet Sauvignon 2013, Orange Hand-picked fruit from the estate vineyard at 800m elevation; thence to the Hunter Valley. Matured 18 months in French barriques (25% new). Texture is as important as structure, although tannins are also in the front row. Screw cap. 14% alc. **RATING** 94 **DRINK** 2023-2033 $70 JH

🍷🍷🍷🍷🍷 **Lovable Rogue Full Monty Montepulciano 2022, Hunter Valley** **RATING** 93 **DRINK** 2023-2029 $35 JH ✪

Lovable Rogue Moon Child Aglianico 2021, Orange **RATING** 93 **DRINK** 2029-2039 $35 JH ✪

Aged Release Tallavera Grove Fenestella Shiraz 2013, Hunter Valley **RATING** 93 **DRINK** 2023-2030 $70 JH

Ad Hoc Release Montepulciano Negro Amaro Nero d'Avola Sagrantino 2022, Hunter Valley **RATING** 91 **DRINK** 2025-2030 $35 JH

Expressions Shiraz Pinot Noir 2021, Hunter Valley Orange RATING 91 DRINK 2023–2026 $25 JH ✪
Origins Feldspars Shiraz 2021, Orange RATING 90 DRINK 2023–2028 $50 JH

Carlei Estate | Carlei Green Vineyards ★★★★☆

1 Alber Road, Upper Beaconsfield, Vic 3808 **Region** Victoria
T (03) 5944 4599 **www**.carlei.com.au **Open** W'ends 12–5 **Winemaker** Sergio Carlei, David Carlei, David Papadimitriou **Est.** 1994 **Dozens** 10 000 **Vyds** 2.25ha
Sergio Carlei has come a long way, graduating from home winemaking in a suburban garage to his own (commercial) winery in Upper Beaconsfield. Along the way, Sergio acquired a bachelor of wine science from CSU, and established a vineyard with organic and biodynamic accreditation adjacent to the Upper Beaconsfield winery, plus 7ha in Heathcote. Contract winemaking services are now a major part of the business.

🍷🍷🍷🍷🍷 **Green Vineyards Cardinia Ranges Pinot Gris 2021, Victoria** A warm and textural gris, deeply spiced, that immediately raises all manner of exciting food pairing ideas. Moves into Alsace-like territory with complex perfume and flavours rich in mango, pear, baked apple, honeysuckle, honey and exotic spice that roll smoothly in layers across the palate, finishing long. Complex and complete. Screw cap. 13.5% alc. RATING 95 DRINK 2023–2028 $29 JP ✪
Carlei Estate Nord Shiraz 2018, Heathcote It's a super-friendly wine. Dark spiced plum and blackberry aromas with licorice, chocolate and toasty oak. Plenty of sweet-fruited, concentrated ripeness flavour-wise, oak wrapping it all into shape. Dense tannins deliver an altogether polished product. Screw cap. 14.5% alc. RATING 94 DRINK 2023–2030 $59 JP
Green Vineyards Shiraz 2018, Heathcote The winemaker chose to release the '19 before the '18. A smart decision, given the upfront appeal of the '19. The '18 offers a darker intensity but boasts a similar beautiful balance. Deep perfume and flavours rich in Heathcote blackberries, cassis, pastille, bramble, wild bushland aromatics and inviting spice. Moves like a distance runner, fine tannins, firm and sleek. Screw cap. 14.5% alc. RATING 94 DRINK 2023–2032 $35 JP ✪

🍷🍷🍷🍷🍷 **Carlei Estate Sud Shiraz 2017, Heathcote** RATING 93 DRINK 2023–2030 $59 JP
Green Vineyards Cuvée Stephen Thomson Pinot Gris 2020, King Valley RATING 91 DRINK 2022–2026 $35 JP
Cosmoir Viognier 2018, Heathcote RATING 91 DRINK 2023–2027 $39 JP
Estate Chardonnay 2010, Yarra Valley RATING 91 DRINK 2023–2026 $49 JP

Casella Family Brands ★★★★

Wakely Road, Yenda, NSW 2681 (postal) **Region** Riverina
T (02) 6961 3000 **www**.casellafamilybrands.com **Open** Not **Winemaker** John Casella **Est.** 1969 **Dozens** 12.5 million **Vyds** 5000ha
Casella built a portfolio of premium and ultra-premium wines through its acquisition of Peter Lehmann in '14; and then Brand's Laira winery, cellar door and the use of the brand name from McWilliam's in '15. In Dec '17 Casella purchased Baileys of Glenrowan. Casella now has over 5000ha of vineyards spread across Australia. It is 2nd only to Treasury Wine Estates in export sales (by value), followed by Pernod Ricard and Accolade. Casella celebrated its 50th anniversary in '19.

🍷🍷🍷🍷🍷 **1919 Cabernet Sauvignon 2013, McLaren Vale** Blackcurrants, dried cherries, sage leaf and pitted olives. Christmas cake, plum jam, mocha and tobacco pouch. Tannins have softened into fine, silk-like threads and oak supports dominating fruit. Still looking vibrant and lifted. Screw cap. 13.5% alc. RATING 94 DRINK 2022–2030 $75 SW

🍷🍷🍷🍷🍷 **1919 Cabernet Sauvignon 2020, South Australia** RATING 92 DRINK 2022–2038 $75 SW

Castelli Estate

380 Mount Shadforth Road, Denmark, WA 6333 **Region** Great Southern
T (08) 9364 0400 **www.**castelliestate.com.au **Open** Wed–Sun 11–4
Winemaker Andrew Vesey **Viticulturist** Andrew Vesey **Est.** 2007 **Dozens** 20 000
Castelli Estate will cause many small winery owners to go green with envy. When Sam Castelli purchased the property in late '04, he was intending simply to use it as a family holiday destination. But because there was a partly constructed winery he decided to complete the building work and simply lock the doors. However, wine was in his blood courtesy of his father, who owned a small vineyard in Italy's south. The temptation was too much and in '07 the winery was commissioned. Fruit is sourced from some of the best sites in WA: Frankland River, Mount Barker, Pemberton and Porongurup.

🍷🍷🍷🍷🍷 **Riesling 2022, Mount Barker** A bone-dry style. And yet, despite that statement, it has lots of concentration and red apple fruitiness with a big squeeze of pink grapefruit and a sluice of saline, minerally acidity. Geez, that acidity is something else. Great perfume of citrus blossoms, lime and apple. A powerful style, too, lots of energy and depth. Serious stuff here, and done well. Should cellar for an age. Screw cap. 11.5% alc. **RATING** 94 **DRINK** 2022–2040 $27 MB ✪
Il Liris 2019, Frankland River 68/20/12% cabernet sauvignon/shiraz/malbec. A beautiful perfume laden with violets and lavender, dark cherry, faint game meat, milk chocolate and brined green olive notes. Succulent in the palate, lithe and refreshing with a web of fine tannin and a sluice of minerally acidity among choc-berry, ripe plum and clove spice. Feels loose-knit, but in all that a tour de force of quality fruit, fine tannin profile and a sense of vitality and high drinkability. Vinolok. 14.5% alc. **RATING** 94 **DRINK** 2024–2040 $80 MB

🍷🍷🍷🍷🍷 **Chardonnay 2022, Pemberton RATING** 93 **DRINK** 2023–2030 $37 MB

Castle Rock Estate

2660 Porongurup Road, Porongurup, WA 6324 **Region** Porongurup
T (08) 9853 1035 **www.**castlerockestate.com.au **Open** 7 days 10–4.30
Winemaker Robert Diletti **Est.** 1983 **Dozens** 4500 **Vyds** 11.2ha
An exceptionally well-located vineyard (riesling, pinot noir, chardonnay, sauvignon blanc, cabernet sauvignon and merlot), winery and cellar door on a 55ha property with sweeping vistas of the Porongurup Range, operated by the Diletti family. The 2-level winery, set on a natural slope, maximises gravity flow. The rieslings have always been elegant and have handsomely repaid time in bottle; the pinot noir is the most consistent performer in the region; the shiraz is a great cool-climate example; and chardonnay has joined a thoroughly impressive quartet, elegance the common link. Rob Diletti's excellent palate and sensitive winemaking mark Castle Rock as one of the superstars of WA.

🍷🍷🍷🍷🍷 **Diletti Riesling 2021, Porongurup** The bouquet gives hints that are transformed on a palate with an operatic trumpet of flavours circling the ultra-intense core of lime and lemon. One of the most spectacular young Australian rieslings I have encountered. That length, that power. Screw cap. 11% alc. **RATING** 98 **DRINK** 2023–2041 $36 JH ✪ ♥
Diletti Pinot Noir 2021, Porongurup An amazing wine, with a palate of extreme intensity and silky length. Cherries, rose petals, mouth-watering savoury tannins, all in balance and harmony. Screw cap. 13.5% alc. **RATING** 97 **DRINK** 2023–2031 $46 JH ✪

🍷🍷🍷🍷🍷 **Diletti Chardonnay 2020, Porongurup** Cloudy juice, wild fermented in French oak (20% new); part left on yeast lees after fermentation. Grapefruit zest and pith on one hand, creamy cashew on the other. The complexity coalesces to form a long, poised palate. Will mature gracefully. Screw cap. 12% alc. **RATING** 95 **DRINK** 2023–2030 $36 JH ✪
Riesling 2022, Porongurup A brittle and compact riesling of great velocity and energy. It's scented like talc, lime juice, blackcurrants, slate, smoke and warm

steel. Dive in. The palate is frisky, tightly wound and driven by pink grapefruit-like acidity. Mouth-watering with just-ripe green apple crispness. Very pent up, this is one for racy riesling enthusiasts. Screw cap. 11.5% alc. **RATING** 94 **DRINK** 2022–2030 $30 MB ✪

🍷🍷🍷🍷🍷 Skywalk Riesling 2022, Porongurup **RATING** 93 **DRINK** 2022–2030 $25 MB ✪
Pinot Noir 2021, Porongurup **RATING** 93 **DRINK** 2022–2030 $40 MB
Shiraz 2021, Porongurup **RATING** 93 **DRINK** 2022–2032 $36 MB
A&W Pinot Noir 2021, Porongurup **RATING** 93 **DRINK** 2024–2035 $52 MB
Cabernet Sauvignon 2020, Porongurup **RATING** 93 **DRINK** 2023–2033 $28 MB ✪
A&W Riesling 2022, Porongurup **RATING** 92 **DRINK** 2022–2032 $42 MB
Sauvignon Blanc 2022, Porongurup **RATING** 91 **DRINK** 2022–2025 $25 MB ✪
Grüner Veltliner 2022, Porongurup **RATING** 90 **DRINK** 2022–2025 $36 MB

Catlin Wines

Catlin on Magill, 563 Magill Road, Magill, SA 5072 **Region** Adelaide
T 0411 326 384 **www**.catlinwines.com.au **Open** Fri 4–9, Sun 12–5 **Winemaker** Darryl Catlin **Viticulturist** Darryl Catlin **Est.** 2013 **Dozens** 2000
Darryl Catlin grew up in the Barossa Valley with vineyards as his playground, picking bush-vine grenache for pocket money as a youngster. Stints with Saltram, the Australian Bottling Company and Vintner Imports followed in his 20s, before moving on to work in bottle stores while studying for a winemaking degree. Then followed a number of years at Shaw + Smith, rising from cellar hand to winemaker and eventually establishing his own business. Wines can be tasted at the urban cellar door in Adelaide, Catlin on Magill.

🍷🍷🍷🍷🍷 Tascha Chardonnay 2022, Adelaide Hills A classy chardonnay of considerable tension, a raft of stone fruit at its core all nicely corralled by vanillin oak framework that's moderately toasty with a whiff of cedar. Apricot pith, nectarine and white peach with accents of pistachio and almond meal. A bit shins and elbows at present, yet the intensity of fruit sweetness grows with air. The trajectory, long. Screw cap. 12.5% alc. **RATING** 94 **DRINK** 2022–2030 $65 NG

🍷🍷🍷🍷🍷 #4 Blanc de Traminer 2022, Adelaide Hills **RATING** 93 **DRINK** 2022–2025 $34 NG ✪
Pinot Noir 2022, Adelaide Hills **RATING** 92 **DRINK** 2022–2030 $65 NG
The Molly Mae Riesling 2022, Clare Valley **RATING** 92 **DRINK** 2022–2030 $24 NG ✪
Pudding and Pie Pinot Noir 2022, Adelaide Hills **RATING** 92 **DRINK** 2022–2027 $34 NG
The Astria Blanc de Blancs NV, Adelaide Hills **RATING** 91 $32 NG

Centare

160 Healesville – Koo Wee Rup Road, Vic 3777 (postal) **Region** Yarra Valley
T 0407 386 314 **www**.centarevineyard.com **Open** Not **Winemaker** Nicole Esdaile **Viticulturist** Cameron McIntosh **Est.** 2018 **Dozens** 2000 **Vyds** 5ha
A vineyard originally planted in 1998 on Healesville – Koo Wee Rup Road and acquired by Simon Li in '18. Nicole Esdaile from Wine Network Consulting is the winemaker/project manager and Cameron McIntosh is the consulting viticulturist, with the wines being made at the Sunshine Creek facility. New plantings at extremely high density began in Nov '20 with aspirations to produce a cabernet blend of the highest quality from the '23 vintage.

🍷🍷🍷🍷🍷 Reserve Chardonnay 2021, Yarra Valley A lovely, light bright green gold. Restrained and complex on the nose with aromas of just-picked white peach, grapefruit pith, white flowers and a hint of struck match. A very well-balanced, saline, taut and finely structured wine. 166 dozen made. Screw cap. 13% alc. **RATING** 96 **DRINK** 2022–2027 $55 PR ✪

Old Block Shiraz 2021, Yarra Valley A medium and bright crimson. The best shiraz I've tasted yet from Centare, this opens with aromas of red and blue fruits, floral notes and a little smoked meat while the oak sits discreetly in back. Just as good on the medium-bodied, vibrant and balanced palate. Screw cap. 13.5% alc. RATING 95 DRINK 2022–2027 $55 PR

ΨΨΨΨΨ **Old Block Chardonnay 2021, Yarra Valley** RATING 93 DRINK 2022–2026 $45 PR
Old Block Cabernet Sauvignon 2021, Yarra Valley RATING 91 DRINK 2023–2028 $65 PR

Centennial Vineyards   ★★★★☆

'Woodside', 252 Centennial Road, Bowral, NSW 2576 **Region** Southern Highlands **T** (02) 4861 8722 **www.centennial.net.au Open** 7 days 10–5 **Winemaker** Tony Cosgriff **Est.** 2002 **Dozens** 10 000 **Vyds** 28.65ha
Centennial Vineyards, jointly owned by wine professional John Large and investor Mark Dowling, covers 133ha of beautiful grazing land, with the vineyard planted to pinot noir (7.13ha), chardonnay (6.76ha), pinot gris (4.06ha) and smaller amounts of riesling, pinot meunier, albariño, tempranillo, grüner veltliner and gewürztraminer. Centennial purchased the 8.2ha Bridge Creek Vineyard in Orange to meet the challenge of the Southern Highlands' capricious weather.

ΨΨΨΨΨ **Blanc de Blancs NV, Southern Highlands** Oyster shell and crisp sliced fennel meets Granny Smith apple curls and hints of flint. Crushed chalk and white grapefruit juice is finely woven on a palate with lifted acidity that carries the flavour on and on. A blanc de blancs of finesse and fine-tuned energy. Sublime. Diam. 12.5% alc. RATING 96 $40 SW ✪

ΨΨΨΨΨ **Brut Rosé NV, Southern Highlands** RATING 93 $35 SW ✪
Barrel Select Sparkling Shiraz NV, Orange RATING 92 $30 SW ✪
Brut Traditionelle NV, Southern Highlands RATING 92 $35 SW
Reserve Rondinella 2022, Orange RATING 92 DRINK 2022–2025 $29 SW ✪
Reserve Single Vineyard Albariño 2021, Southern Highlands RATING 92 DRINK 2023–2026 $33 SW
Miller's Pinot NV, Southern Highlands RATING 91 $35 SW
Rosé 2022, Orange RATING 90 DRINK 2022–2025 $25 SW ✪
Shiraz 2021, Orange RATING 90 DRINK 2023–2026 $29 SW
Reserve Single Vineyard Tempranillo 2021, Orange RATING 90 DRINK 2023–2026 $35 SW

Chaffey Bros Wine Co   ★★★★

Artisans of the Barossa, 24 Vine Vale Road, Tanunda, SA 5352 **Region** Barossa **T** 0417 565 511 **www.chaffeybros.com Open** 7 days 11–5 **Winemaker** Daniel Chaffey Hartwig, Huon Fechner, Theo Engela **Est.** 2008 **Dozens** 9500
Chaffey Bros is an example of the 'New Barossa', what with their funky labels and wines that have an effortless drinkability, an intricate sense of place and a distinct feeling that they approach the winemaking in a hands-off, minimal-intervention kind of style. Eden Valley-born Daniel Chaffey Hartwig established the Chaffey Bros Wine Co in '08, before long joined by brother-in-law Theo Engela and today, the estate produces an excellent range of wines thanks to relationships with some of the Barossa's most sought-after, multi-generational grape-growing families and members of the Artisans of the Barossa collective.

ΨΨΨΨΨ **Düfte Punkt 2022, Eden Valley** A real Germanic fruit salad-esque blend here of riesling, gewürztraminer and kerner. Straw in the glass with heady aromas of lime and citrus, Turkish delight, crushed stone, white flowers, rose petals and almond paste. Textural, stony, sapid and pure, it cuts a lovely line on the palate, sashaying with a confident and delicious gait. Finishes dry and crisp, like sucking on a river pebble … if you're into that. Regardless, it's lovely. Screw cap. 12.8% alc. RATING 94 DRINK 2023–2026 $27 DB ✪

Elijah Fechner Vineyard Moculta Shiraz 2020, Eden Valley Deep, purple-splashed crimson with notes of dark blackberry and ripe dark plums. Hints of baking spices, sage, black pepper, cassis, dark chocolate and graphite. There's a cassis-like richness to the fruit flow, densely packed granitic tannins and a chocolatey tide on the deep, black-fruited finish. Screw cap. 14.5% alc. **RATING** 94 **DRINK** 2023-2030 $70 DB

Evangeline Syrah 2020, Eden Valley Abundant ripe plums and summer berry fruits, cut through with fine spice, blueberries with a whiff of vanilla and subtle, sexy French oak. There's a lovely fruit flow, some nice cool-climate crunch and a cascade of fine tannin for support. A lot to like here. Screw cap. 14.5% alc. **RATING** 94 **DRINK** 2023-2028 $38 DB ✪

🍷🍷🍷🍷🍷 **Not Your Grandma's Riesling 2022, Eden Valley** **RATING** 93 **DRINK** 2023-2028 $23 DB ✪

Not Your Grandma's Rosé 2022, Barossa Valley **RATING** 93 **DRINK** 2023-2025 $23 DB ✪

Kontrapunkt Kerner 2022, Eden Valley **RATING** 93 **DRINK** 2023-2026 $30 DB ✪

Salvis Gratia Semillon 2022, Barossa Valley **RATING** 93 **DRINK** 2023-2027 $30 DB ✪

Zeitpunkt Riesling 2021, Eden Valley **RATING** 93 **DRINK** 2023-2026 $35 DB ✪

Tripelpunkt Riesling 2022, Eden Valley **RATING** 92 **DRINK** 2023-2027 $27 DB ✪

Blühen Punkt Gewürztraminer 2022, Eden Valley **RATING** 92 **DRINK** 2023-2026 $27 DB ✪

Omnia Nova Syrah 2021, Barossa **RATING** 92 **DRINK** 2023-2025 $30 DB ✪

Lux Venit Light has Come Old Vine Rosé 2022, Barossa Valley **RATING** 91 **DRINK** 2023-2025 $30 DB

Battle for Barossa La Resistance! GSM 2021, Barossa Valley **RATING** 91 **DRINK** 2023-2026 $27 DB ✪

Not Your Grandma's Chillable Red 2021, Barossa **RATING** 91 **DRINK** 2023-2025 $23 DB ✪

Synonymous Barossa = Shiraz 2020, Barossa **RATING** 91 **DRINK** 2023-2026 $27 DB ✪

Super Barossa 2020, Barossa Valley **RATING** 91 **DRINK** 2023-2029 $38 DB

Chain of Ponds ★★★★

8 The Parade West, Kent Town, SA 5067 (postal) **Region** South Australia
T (08) 7324 3031 **www.chainofponds.com.au** **Open** Not **Winemaker** Greg Clack
Est. 1985 **Dozens** 20 000

It is years since the Chain of Ponds brand was separated from its then 200ha of estate vineyards, which were among the largest in the Adelaide Hills. It does, however, have long-term contracts with major growers. Prior to the '15 vintage, Greg Clack came onboard as full-time chief winemaker. In May '16 Chain of Ponds closed its cellar door and moved to Project Wine's small-batch processing facility at Langhorne Creek. The Single Vineyard series and estate wine are all sourced from the Adelaide Hills; the budget Novello range from further afield.

🍷🍷🍷🍷🍷 **Corkscrew Road Single Vineyard Chardonnay 2021, Adelaide Hills** Tasting across the range of chardonnay at this address is intriguing. This, the tip of the proprietary totem. Praline, nashi pear, cantaloupe, white peach and a sliver of waxy lanolin-scaped phenolics, segueing to a creamy core of nougatine and well-appointed oak. A bit tangy across the finish, but no shortage of intensity or flavour. Screw cap. 13% alc. **RATING** 93 **DRINK** 2022-2030 $35 NG ✪

Morning Star Single Vineyard Pinot Noir 2021, Adelaide Hills Lots of flavour without excessive sweetness, or the medicinal underbelly that marks pinot from climates too warm. Souk-like exotica, with riffs on tamarind, turmeric and orange peel. Sour cherry, sappy and punchy. Sandy tannins meld with a breeze of gentle freshness, framing a fun composition. Screw cap. 14% alc. **RATING** 92 **DRINK** 2022-2027 $35 NG

Unchained Tempranillo Barbera 2022, Adelaide Hills An unusual blend that works very well. Dark, palate-staining cherry riffs meld with a chord of aniseed, iodine and lilac. Mid-weighted of feel, with a firm and pithy finish, compressed by well-hewn tannins and a sluice of juicy acidity. Screw cap. 13.5% alc. **RATING** 90 **DRINK** 2022-2027 $28 NG

Chalk Hill   ★★★★★

56 Field Street, McLaren Vale **Region** McLaren Vale
T (08) 8323 6400 **www.**chalkhillwines.com.au **Open** 7 days 11–6 **Winemaker** Renae Hirsch **Viticulturist** Jock Harvey **Est.** 1973 **Dozens** 35 000 **Vyds** 89ha

The growth of Chalk Hill has accelerated after passing from parents John and Diana Harvey to grapegrowing sons Jock and Tom. Both are heavily involved in wine industry affairs. Further acquisitions mean the vineyards now span each district of McLaren Vale, planted to shiraz, cabernet sauvignon, grenache, chardonnay and barbera. The Alpha Crucis series is especially praiseworthy.

🍷🍷🍷🍷🍷 **Alpha Crucis Seaview Syrah 2021, McLaren Vale** The more ferrous and savoury of Chalk Hill's subregional syrah expressions. Subdued and reticent even, until air in the glass brings forth a growl of bloody iodine tannins, like a moat across the mouth drawing red plum, Seville orange, clove and real exotica to the palate. The tannins, a savoury forcefield. Exceptional. Screw cap. 14% alc. **RATING** 96 **DRINK** 2023-2033 $60 NG ✪

Alpha Crucis Blewitt Springs Syrah 2021, McLaren Vale Fine syrah, nudging the firmament while shifting the regional paradigm to a northern Rhône-inspired freshness. Full-weighted, yet you'd hardly know it such is the freshness and pithy, sandy tannic tension. Taut and crunchy. Bloodstone, damson plum, boysenberry, bergamot, white pepper and cardamom. Screw cap. 14% alc. **RATING** 96 **DRINK** 2023-2032 $60 NG

Alpha Crucis Limited Release Mataro Grenache 2021, McLaren Vale This is very good, boasting ample fealty to mataro's ferruginous spread as much as to grenache's effusive fruit. A savoury experience as a rivet of tannin welds itself to a burst of kirsch, dried tobacco, pepper and thyme, with salumi and a swirl of beef bouillon-umami at the core. Plenty of oak in the mix. This will cellar exceptionally well. Screw cap. 14% alc. **RATING** 95 **DRINK** 2023-3032 $60 NG

Fiano 2022, McLaren Vale Very good fiano. Peach, apricot pith and a grating of raw almond, lemon rind and shavings of pistachio impart a noble, savoury bitterness. Nicely mid-weighted, viscous and fresh, a paradoxical equation that few other varieties can match. We are getting a handle on it here. This sort of gear, the reason why. Screw cap. 13% alc. **RATING** 94 **DRINK** 2022-2027 $28 NG ✪

Alpha Crucis Blewitt Springs Grenache 2021, McLaren Vale A very good wine, yet the choice of oak detracts from a top-drawer positioning. Fine fruit, fidelitous to variety and place: kirsch, lilac, thyme and mint, ethereal and pixelated, as is the regional wont. Yet then come the tannins, too drying to let the beauty within glide. Almost there. Screw cap. 14% alc. **RATING** 94 **DRINK** 2022-2029 $60 NG

🍷🍷🍷🍷🍷 **Alpha Crucis Clarendon Syrah 2021, McLaren Vale RATING** 93 **DRINK** 2023-2033 $60 NG

Alpha Crucis Syrah 2021, McLaren Vale RATING 93 **DRINK** 2023-2032 $60 NG

Small Batch Release Montepulciano 2022, McLaren Vale RATING 92 **DRINK** 2023-2030 $40 NG

Arneis 2022, Adelaide Hills RATING 92 **DRINK** 2022-2025 $35 NG

Blewitt Springs Syrah 2021, McLaren Vale RATING 92 **DRINK** 2023-2028 $48 NG

Alpha Crucis Titan Shiraz 2021, McLaren Vale RATING 92 **DRINK** 2022-2029 $30 NG ✪

Graciano 2021, McLaren Vale RATING 92 DRINK 2022–2026 $30 NG ✪
Nebbiolo 2021, Adelaide Hills RATING 92 DRINK 2023–2028 $40 NG
Grüner Veltliner 2022, Adelaide Hills RATING 91 DRINK 2022–2024 $35 NG
Luna Cabernet Sauvignon 2021, McLaren Vale RATING 91
DRINK 2022–2025 $22 NG ✪
Syrah 2021, McLaren Vale RATING 91 DRINK 2023–2030 $30 NG
Luna Shiraz 2021, McLaren Vale RATING 91 DRINK 2022–2026 $22 NG ✪
Barbera 2021, McLaren Vale RATING 90 DRINK 2022–2024 $28 NG
Alpha Crucis Titan Cabernet Sauvignon 2021, McLaren Vale RATING 90
DRINK 2023–2027 $30 NG

Chalmers

118 Third Street, Merbein, Vic 3505 (postal) **Region** Murray Darling
T 0400 261 932 **www**.chalmers.com.au **Open** Not **Winemaker** Bart van Olphen,
Tennille Chalmers, Kim Chalmers **Viticulturist** Bruce Chalmers, Troy McInnes,
Matt Stonehouse **Est.** 1989 **Dozens** 25 000 **Vyds** 73ha

For more than a decade the Chalmers family has led the way in importing new, 'alternative'
grape varieties through its Merbein nursery and vineyard. They were prescient in seeing the
need for varieties that are suited to Australian conditions and a changing climate, pioneering
Mediterranean varieties, most recently falanghina, pecorino and ribolla gialla. With vineyards
in the Murray Darling, established in the 1980s, and Heathcote regions ('11) and through the
2nd generation Kim and Tennille Chalmers, the family produces cutting-edge wines. From
the Chalmers Project (experimental, micro-fermentation wines), the Montevecchio label
(approachable blends), Le Sorelle (a celebration of Heathcote and Murray Darling fruit), Dott.
(a tribute to viticulturist, Dr Rod Bonfiglioli) and Chalmers label (single-vineyard wines) and
more, the family excels as both growers and producers, never content with the status quo.

🍷🍷🍷🍷🍷 **Bush Vine Inzolia 2022, Murray Darling** Outstanding intensity of flavour.
Brine, nectarine, mineral, slate, nuts and florals. Sherry-like aspects, and
honeyed notes too, but simultaneously fresh and floral, not to mention lengthy.
This is absolutely out of the ordinary. Screw cap. 13.3% alc. RATING 95
DRINK 2023–2027 $53 CM ❤

Pecorino 2022, Heathcote Straight-out intensity of flavour is in a very good
place here but it's the length of the finish that seals it. White flowers, white peach,
citrus and grapefruit characters offer a seamless, sure-footed, continuous flow of
flavour. This is both elegant and concentrated; a winning combination. Screw cap.
14.2% alc. RATING 94 DRINK 2023–2027 $33 CM ✪

Fiano 2021, Heathcote So fluid, so well flavoured and so textural. Pear and
hay, roasted nuts and peach, custard apples and sweet spice notes. It was matured
in large chestnut wood and has a suggestion of sweet nuttiness to it, but the
fruit flows so convincingly and at the same time it feels so soft. Throw the word
elegant in, because it's apt, and that's the wine. Screw cap. 13.5% alc. RATING 94
DRINK 2023–2027 $39 CM ✪

🍷🍷🍷🍷🍷 **Col Fondo Aglianico 2022, Heathcote** RATING 93 DRINK 2023–2024
$35 CM ✪
Felicitas 2019, Heathcote RATING 93 DRINK 2023–2026 $53 CM
Vermentino 2022, Heathcote RATING 93 DRINK 2023–2027 $29 CM ✪
Greco 2022, Heathcote RATING 93 DRINK 2023–2028 $33 CM ✪
Falanghina 2022, Heathcote RATING 93 DRINK 2023–2026 $33 CM ✪
Bush Vine Negroamaro 2021, Murray Darling RATING 92 DRINK 2023–2027
$53 CM
Fiano 2021, Heathcote RATING 92 DRINK 2023–2026 $35 CM
Museum Release Aglianico 2013, Heathcote RATING 92 DRINK 2023–2027
$48 CM
Dott. Prosecco 2022, Victoria RATING 91 DRINK 2022–2024 $33 CM
Montevecchio Bianco Field Blend 2022, Heathcote RATING 91
DRINK 2023–2026 $25 CM ✪
Dott. Nebbiolo 2022, Heathcote RATING 91 DRINK 2024–2031 $33 CM

Montevecchio Rosso Field Blend 2022, Heathcote RATING 91
DRINK 2023-2026 $25 CM ✪
Dott. Malvasia Istriana 2022, Heathcote RATING 90 DRINK 2022-2025
$33 CM
Dott. Pavana 2022, Heathcote RATING 90 DRINK 2023-2027 $33 CM
Piedirosso 2021, Heathcote RATING 90 DRINK 2022-2026 $38 CM

ChaLou Wines

569 Emu Swamp Road, Emu Swamp, NSW 2800 **Region** Orange
T 0459 689 696 **www.chalouwines.com.au Open** Fri–Mon 11–4 **Winemaker** Nadja
Wallington, Steve Mobbs **Viticulturist** Steve Mobbs **Est.** 2020 **Dozens** 1500 **Vyds** 6ha
ChaLou is a collaborative project between winemakers Steve Mobbs and Nadja Wallington.
They met at university before gleaning ample experience in different parts of the globe.
Serendipitously, they reunited in Orange in '14 with a genuine love of farming and each
other. The proprietary vineyard is in Orange, sited at circa 900m elevation. Varieties planted
there include riesling, chardonnay, pinot noir, pinot gris, shiraz, viognier, sauvignon blanc
and arneis, with warmer-climate varieties grenache, mourvèdre, petit verdot and a bit more
viognier sourced from a Canowindra site at 400m, certified organic. The estate range is
complemented by a less expensive Dreaded Friend line. These are sassy, fresh and eminently
approachable expressions.

ŸŸŸŸŸ **Pinot Noir 2022, Orange** Red morello cherries, pomegranate, rhubarb and
smoked paper bark. Five-spice, tea leaves and dried rose petals. A wash of juicy
acidity and well-integrated, careful oak. The wine displays all the vibrant red fruit
aromatics and delicate sway of cool-climate Orange pinot noir. Beguiling without
artifice, and soulful. Screw cap. 12% alc. RATING 95 DRINK 2022-2028 $35 SW ✪

ŸŸŸŸŸ **Riesling 2022, Orange** RATING 93 DRINK 2022-2028 $35 SW ✪
The somm and the winemaker Mourvèdre 2022, Central Ranges
RATING 93 DRINK 2022-2030 $30 SW ✪
Dreaded Friend Viognier 2022, Orange RATING 93 DRINK 2022-2026
$28 SW ✪
Dreaded Friend Cabernet Franc 2022, Central Ranges RATING 92
DRINK 2022-2026 $35 SW
The somm and the winemaker Arneis 2022, Orange RATING 91
DRINK 2022-2026 $30 SW
The somm and the winemaker White Blend 2022, Central Ranges
RATING 91 DRINK 2022-2026 $30 SW
Dreaded Friend Grenache 2022, Central Ranges RATING 90
DRINK 2022-2028 $35 SW

Chambers Rosewood ★★★★★

Barkly Street, Rutherglen, Vic 3685 **Region** Rutherglen
T (02) 6032 8641 **www.chambersrosewood.com.au Open** 7 days 10–4
Winemaker Stephen Chambers **Est.** 1858 **Dozens** 5000 **Vyds** 50ha
Chambers' Rare Muscat and Rare Muscadelle (previously Topaque or Tokay) are the greatest
of all in the Rutherglen firmament and should be treated as national treasures; the other
wines in the hierarchy also magnificent. Stephen Chambers (6th generation) is winemaker,
but father Bill is seldom far away.

ŸŸŸŸŸ **Rare Muscat NV, Rutherglen** This is rarefied air by any reckoning. The
solera that brings this wine to the glass has been working its magic for 60 years.
Combines an almost whispery aromatic lift and fineness with profound intensity
and complexity. Dense and thick to pour, it releases heady treacle, toffee, raisin,
choc-caramel and honeyed sweetness, yet remains so fresh and lively. That's a
master blender at work. 375ml. Screw cap. 17.5% alc. RATING 98 $250 JP

ŸŸŸŸŸ **Grand Muscadelle NV, Rutherglen** The base wines for this fortified were laid
down in the 19th century, then added to almost every year since. In the glass,

you smell, taste and absorb history. Take in the charm and warmth of sweet plum pudding, rich prune and raisin, fruit and nut dark chocolate, honey and so much more. And so fresh and clean in spirit. Magnificent, indeed. 375ml. Screw cap. 18% alc. RATING 96 $100 JP

Old Vine Muscadelle NV, Rutherglen Equivalent to 'Classic Rutherglen Topaque' level with an average age of 6-10 years maturation. The deep amber colour indicates a move up in age and complexity. Intensity levels rise all round in rich malt, roasted nuts, toffee and raisin with a splash of savoury fish oil. A classic style of Classic, simply delicious and so moreish. 375ml. Screw cap. 18% alc. RATING 95 $30 JP ♥

ᵀᵀᵀᵀ♀ **Muscadelle NV, Rutherglen** RATING 92 $25 JP ♥
Muscat NV, Rutherglen RATING 92 $25 JP ♥
Tempranillo 2021, Rutherglen RATING 90 DRINK 2022-2032 $30 JP

Chandon Australia   ★★★★★

727 Maroondah Highway, Coldstream, Vic 3770 **Region** Yarra Valley
T (03) 9738 9200 **www**.chandon.com.au **Open** 7 days 10.30–4.30
Winemaker Dan Buckle **Est.** 1986 **Vyds** 184ha
Established by Möet & Chandon, this is one of the 2 most important wine facilities in the Yarra Valley. The tasting room has a national and international reputation, having won a number of major tourism awards in recent years. The sparkling wine product range evolved with the '94 acquisition of a substantial vineyard in the cool Strathbogie Ranges and the '14 purchase of the high-altitude vineyard established by Brown Brothers, supplementing the Yarra Valley intake with fruit from various altitudes. The high-quality standards have been maintained under the leadership of chief winemaker Dan Buckle for more than a decade.

ᵀᵀᵀᵀ♀ **Late Disgorged Special Edition Brut 2011, Yarra Valley Tasmania** A complex blend of chardonnay, pinot noir and pinot meunier predominantly from the Yarra Valley (45%) and Tasmania (24%). At the extreme end of the late-disgorged Chandon portfolio, tiraged on 14 December '11, and disgorged 4 August '21. As chardonnay from these very cool regions, the wine is still fresh and crisp, the length a Yarra Valley regional marker. Diam. 12.5% alc. RATING 93 DRINK 2023-2024 $84 JH

Chapel Hill   ★★★★★

1 Chapel Hill Road, McLaren Vale, SA 5171 **Region** McLaren Vale
T (08) 8323 8429 **www**.chapelhillwine.com.au **Open** 7 days 11–5 **Winemaker** Michael Fragos, Bryn Richards **Viticulturist** Rachel Steer **Est.** 1971 **Dozens** 70 000 **Vyds** 44ha
A leading medium-sized winery in McLaren Vale. In late '19 the business was purchased from the Swiss Thomas Schmidheiny group – which owns the respected Cuvaison winery in California and vineyards in Switzerland and Argentina – by Endeavour Drinks (part of the Woolworths group). Wine quality is unfailingly excellent. The production comes from estate plantings of shiraz, cabernet sauvignon, chardonnay and mourvèdre, plus contract-grown grapes. The red wines are made with minimal intervention, unfined and unfiltered.

ᵀᵀᵀᵀᵀ **1952 Vines Grenache 2021, McLaren Vale** A beautiful wine crafted with an assiduous sense of detail and freshness. A stellar vintage that lets this ethereal style run, threading a pinot-like scent of candied red fruits, dried thyme and lavender through the eye of a needle, so precise and granular/sandy are the tannins, so thirst slaking the freshness, so optimal the ripeness. Grenache in its glory. Screw cap. 14.5% alc. RATING 96 DRINK 2022-2028 $65 NG ♥

Gorge Block Cabernet Sauvignon 2021, McLaren Vale This is very good Vale cabernet. Broad, full and yet beautifully delineated by an escarpment of kelpy salinity, embedded oak and maritime freshness with an accent of hedgerow and mint to accentuate lift. Currant, olive and dried sage are buried amid. The finish is long and forceful, yet the signature is one of savoury refinement over sheer oomph. Screw cap. 14.5% alc. RATING 95 DRINK 2023-2033 $65 NG

Road Block Shiraz 2021, McLaren Vale Full weighted and powerful, yet there is nothing overt, jammy or caricature-like. The oak is tucked in and the fruit is dark and blue of allusion, yet doused with tapenade, mint, anise, thyme and lavender, conferring a welcome savouriness over a more typical sweetness. Fine floral lift, too, segueing to a glade of spruced tannins and saline freshness. Screw cap. 14.5% alc. RATING 95 DRINK 2022–2033 $65 NG

The Vicar Shiraz 2019, McLaren Vale Winemaking has become gentler here in recent years, shifting perceptions, mine included, in the very best way. The beef bouillon, rosemary, salami and thyme elements are evocative of fine southern Rhône. The tannins, refined, long limbed and effortlessly curbing the fray from excess. Despite the heft, there is a winning savouriness to the mould, good length and an uncanny precision. Screw cap. 14.5% alc. RATING 95 DRINK 2022–2026 $75 NG

The Parson Grenache Shiraz Mourvèdre 2021, McLaren Vale Wow. Isn't this a bargain? It's juicy, it's silky, it's beautifully balanced and so fresh on the finish. All 3 varieties have their say. You don't have to wait for it, but it will wait for you. Screw cap. 14% alc. RATING 94 DRINK 2023–2031 $18 JH ✪

ᵀᵀᵀᵀᵀ **Vermentino 2022, Fleurieu** RATING 93 DRINK 2022–2026 $22 NG ✪
The MV Shiraz 2021, McLaren Vale RATING 93 DRINK 2023–2041 $33 JH ✪
Escape Room Vermentino 2021, Fleurieu RATING 92 DRINK 2022–2024 $27 NG ✪
The Vinedresser Shiraz 2021, McLaren Vale RATING 92 DRINK 2022–2027 $25 NG ✪
The MV Mourvèdre 2021, McLaren Vale RATING 92 DRINK 2023–2028 $30 NG ✪
Escape Room Cabernet Franc 2021, Fleurieu RATING 91 DRINK 2022–2025 $27 NG ✪
Organic Small Batch #08 Shiraz 2021, McLaren Vale RATING 91 DRINK 2022–2025 $28 NG ✪
Escape Room Grenache Mourvèdre 2021, Fleurieu RATING 91 DRINK 2022–2025 $27 NG ✪
The MV Cabernet Sauvignon 2021, McLaren Vale RATING 91 DRINK 2023–2031 $33 NG
Escape Room Sauvignon Blanc 2021, Fleurieu RATING 90 DRINK 2022–2024 $27 NG
Organic Small Batch #09 Chardonnay 2021, McLaren Vale RATING 90 DRINK 2022–2026 $28 NG

Charles Melton Wines   ★★★★★

Krondorf Road, Tanunda, SA 5352 **Region** Barossa Valley
T (08) 8563 3606 **www.**charlesmeltonwines.com.au **Open** 7 days 11–5
Winemaker Charlie Melton, Sophie Melton **Est.** 1984 **Dozens** 12 000 **Vyds** 32.6ha
Charlie, one of the Barossa Valley's great characters, and wife Virginia, make some of the most eagerly sought after wines in Australia. There are 7ha of estate vineyards at Lyndoch, 9ha at Krondorf and 1.6ha at Light Pass; the lion's share shiraz and grenache, and a small planting of cabernet sauvignon. An additional 30ha property was purchased in High Eden, with 10ha of shiraz planted in '09 and a 5ha field of grenache, shiraz, mataro, carignan, cinsault, picpoul and bourboulenc planted in '10. They also source from 3 growers in Tanunda. The volume has no adverse effect on the quality of the rich, supple and harmonious wines.

ᵀᵀᵀᵀᵀ **Rosé of Virginia 2022, Barossa Valley** The vivid magenta hue is, to put it mildly, jaw-dropping. But it's far more than show; it's wondrously fruity, yet bone dry, its rainbow of small red berries enough to stop those who 'don't like rosés' in their tracks. Screw cap. 13% alc. RATING 97 DRINK 2023–2024 $32 JH ✪ ♥

Nine Popes 2019, Barossa Wonderfully fragrant red and dark plum fruits with high tones of raspberry coulis and orange blossom. Under the fruit lies layered spice and hints of red licorice, redcurrant jelly, roasting meats and earth. The fruit on the palate is pure and true, the tannins tight, powdery and fine and there is a lovely cadence to the acidity as it propels the wine forward. It's still, and always has been, a joy to drink. Screw cap. 14.5% alc. **RATING** 97 **DRINK** 2023-2035 $105 DB

La Belle Mère Barossa GSR 2019, Barossa No mataro this vintage, so a very small amount of riesling was co-fermented with grenache and shiraz. The colour isn't deep, but the riesling has performed like viognier with the still spring day brightness – as are the joyous red fruits and the sprinkle of spices on the medium-bodied palate. Screw cap. 14.5% alc. **RATING** 96 **DRINK** 2023-2031 $32 JH ✪

Sparkling Red NV, Barossa Valley Bright crimson ruby in the glass with a fine, energetic bead and bright purple mousse. Fresh, vibrant and dry with precise plum and summer berry fruits with hints of ground spice, violets and purple flowers, earth, charcuterie, light leather and mahogany tones and cherry clafoutis. Bright and vivid with great harmony and inherent drinkability. We all need to be drinking more sparkling red, yeah? Crown. 14% alc. **RATING** 95 $75 DB

Grains of Paradise Shiraz 2019, Barossa No shortage of plush blackberry, black cherry and dark plum fruits on a base of fine spice, licorice, earth, dark chocolate and roasting meats. Superfine, tightly packed tannins and bright acidity provide the frame and there is a nice sense of composure to the wine as it slowly fades away. Screw cap. 14.5% alc. **RATING** 94 **DRINK** 2023-2033 $90 DB

Voices of Angels Shiraz 2019, Adelaide Hills Crimson in the glass with aromas of bright blackberry, black cherry and dark plum fruits with hints of fine spice, black pepper, roasting meats, licorice, vanilla oak and sage. The plush fruit has soaked up that sexy oak beautifully, and the wine displays balance and composure throughout its length with tight, powdery granitic tannins and a sense of grace as it slowly trails away. Screw cap. 14.5% alc. **RATING** 94 **DRINK** 2023-2033 $90 DB

The Kirche Shiraz Cabernet Sauvignon 2019, Barossa A 60/40% blend. Powerful and full-bodied; depth and length; oak and tannins – it's all laid out for immediate attention. Very different to the normal polished Melton style. For the long haul. Screw cap. 14.5% alc. **RATING** 94 **DRINK** 2023-2044 $50 JH

Charlish & Co ★★★★

185 Tynan Rd, Kuitpo, SA 5201 **Region** Adelaide Hills
T 0405 119 075 **www**.charlishandco.com.au **Open** Sun 11–4 **Winemaker** Rebecca Stubbs, Duane Coates MW **Est.** 2021 **Dozens** 1300

Charlish & Co is a collaborative effort between real-time partners of 2 decades, chef Rebecca Stubbs and Duane Coates MW, serving as a symbiosis of culinary nous and artisanal winemaking. Stubbs' experience incorporates work in Tokyo, Shanghai and Singapore, as well as her home town of Adelaide; while Coates has worked vintages in Burgundy, the Rhône and Portugal. Stubbs is behind the assiduous fruit selection, from a small swag of trusted growers, and drives a less-is-more approach to vinification under Coates' gaze. Reducing 'wine miles' and the winery's carbon footprint is at the forefront of the brand's ethos. Natural-yeast fermentations are de rigueur and nothing is fined or filtered here.

Tinto Cabernet Sauvignon Tempranillo 2021, Langhorne Creek Adelaide Hills A modern Iberian blend with the dense fruit of Langhorne Creek. Yet this never slips into a caricature of jam or heaviness. Distinctly mid-weighted, savoury and laden with dark cherry, dried thyme, sage, aniseed and a waft of leaf conferring a moreish finish of composure, class and penetrative length. Impressive. Screw cap. 13.5% alc. **RATING** 93 **DRINK** 2022-2027 $30 NG ✪

Shiraz Viognier 2021, Langhorne Creek Adelaide Hills A stellar wine for the money, reminiscent of an expression double the price in that lifted floral and iodine-scented fashion of contemporary, medium-bodied shiraz. Blue fruits, smoked meats and tapenade, trailing long across a waft of peppery, peaty acidity, with the clutch of reduction held to perfection. Very good drinking. Screw cap. 13.5% alc. **RATING** 92 **DRINK** 2022-2026 $25 NG ✪

Rosé 2022, Adelaide Hills McLaren Vale Pinot noir/shiraz/chardonnay. Intrigue aplenty. Wild yeast-derived notes of tatami mat and porcini are evident. The oak, too, is a gingery, cinnamon film enveloping cumquat, tangerine, curry paste and loganberry. A shimmy of fruit matched to an ebb of structural latticework defines the wine's cadence across the mouth. Definitively a food wine, yet with an uncanny ageing potential. Screw cap. 12.8% alc. **RATING** 91 **DRINK** 2023-2026 $25 NG ✪

Rosso Red Blend 2021, Langhorne Creek Adelaide Hills A meld of dolcetto, barbera and sangiovese with a dollop of whole bunches care of the dolcetto. Honed in seasoned French oak to the tune of a gently mid-weighted, effusively fresh and dangerously easy wine to drink, redolent of red fruits and a twine of herbs. Drink chilled and with gusto. Delicious! Screw cap. 13% alc. **RATING** 91 **DRINK** 2022-2024 $30 NG

Viognier 2022, McLaren Vale Mid-weighted, aromatic and textural. Nothing profound, mind you. But the sort of wine one finds when lunching around the northern Rhône, the spiritual home of viognier. Apricot pith, orange blossom and ginger packed tightly amid some skinsy, chewy rims with a spurt of salinity across the finish. Generous, flavourful and fresh. Delicious drinking in the here and now. Screw cap. 13.5% alc. **RATING** 90 **DRINK** 2022-2025 $30 NG

Charlotte Dalton Wines   ★★★★☆

Factory 9, 89-91 Hill Street, Port Elliot, SA 5212 **Region** Southern Fleurieu
T 0466 541 361 **www.**charlottedaltonwines.com.au **Open** Fri 12-9, Sat-Sun 12-5
Winemaker Charlotte Hardy **Est.** 2015 **Dozens** 1200
Charlotte Hardy has been making wines for 20 years, with a star-studded career at Craggy Range (NZ), Château Giscours (Bordeaux) and David Abreu (California), but has called SA home since '07. Her winery is part of her Basket Range house, which has been through many incarnations since starting life as a pig farm in 1858. Much later it housed the Basket Range store, and at different times in the past 2 decades it has been the winery to Basket Range Wines, The Deanery Wines and now Charlotte Dalton Wines.

Fred Fiano 2022, Langhorne Creek The ever-reliable fiano delivers the goods. This spent 4 months in used barriques. Passionfruit and blood orange flavours are unusual, but enjoyable thanks to the texture. Screw cap. 12% alc. **RATING** 93 **DRINK** 2023-2034 $35 JH ✪

Grace Chardonnay 2022, Adelaide Hills This is an excellent example of a non-mlf chardonnay, coaxed from a mid-weighted neutrality by a deft touch of skin contact, judicious lees work and a minimalist approach. Pear drop, tatami straw and a trifle of aldehyde in the best sense. This is very good imminent drinking. Screw cap. 12.5% alc. **RATING** 93 **DRINK** 2022-2026 $30 NG ✪

Love Me Love You Shiraz 2022, Adelaide Hills The encroaching warmth of the region reverberates across palate-staining dark fruits as much as the cooler reductive handling and communique of dried nori, olive smear and meaty bouillon lathers the finish. A waft of Aussie menthol dries the sweet finish, saving a stray into excess. Screw cap. 13.5% alc. **RATING** 93 **DRINK** 2022-2028 $35 NG ✪

Guroo Syrah 2020, Kangaroo Island Peanut oil and black cherry, undergrowth and kirsch. This is a fluid, engaging, different-in-a-good-way red wine, juicy at heart but complex to its toes. Lots of interest here. Diam. 13.2% alc. **RATING** 93 **DRINK** 2023-2029 $50 CM

Mr Nobody Did It 2022, Adelaide Hills Semillon/riesling/fiano/chardonnay. An intriguing wine melding the piercing herbaceousness of a varietal picked early, on acidity, with a more ample, textural flow of those picked ripe. Lees-derived glycerol bolsters some skinsy ginger, tatami straw and mandarin peel, a confluence of gritty texture and umami. Lime cordial and Granny Smith apple an echo across the penetrative finish. Screw cap. 11.7% alc. **RATING** 92 **DRINK** 2022-2027 $25 NG ✪

Love You Love Me Semillon 2022, Adelaide Hills This is delicious. A variety that boasts a far broader personality than the Hunter suggests. This, a wine that exploits it with moxie. A period of skin inflection imparts ginger crystals, tamarind and mandarin chutney. Pomelo and glazed quince, too. The finish, gritty and skinsy of texture with a waft of dried tatami straw. Screw cap. 11.7% alc. RATING 92 DRINK 2022–2027 $30 NG ✪

Guroo Syrah 2021, Kangaroo Island More about savouriness than fruit, though there's certainly enough of the latter to satisfy. Game, undergrowth, snapped twigs and earth characters blend into redcurrant and sweet plum. It's medium in weight, well balanced, a touch truffly and just generally charismatic. Screw cap. 13.5% alc. RATING 91 DRINK 2023–2030 $50 CM

Charteris Wines   ★★★★★

1946 Broke Road, Pokolbin, NSW 2320 **Region** Hunter Valley
T 0412 121 319 **www**.charteriswines.com **Open** 7 days 10–5 **Winemaker** PJ Charteris
Viticulturist PJ Charteris **Est.** 2008 **Dozens** 3000 **Vyds** 1.7ha
Owners Peter James (PJ) Charteris and partner Christina Pattison met at Brokenwood in the Hunter Valley in '99. PJ was the chief executive winemaker at Brokenwood, and Christina was the marketing manager. Together they have over 3 decades of experience. For NZ-born PJ, finding a top pinot noir site in Central Otago was a spiritual homecoming (they claim to have searched both Australia and NZ for the right combination of site and variety). They also have a vineyard with the gold-plated address of Felton Road, Bannockburn, planted to clones 115 777 and Abel. PJ carries on a consultancy business in Australia, with some, though not all, of his focus being the Hunter Valley.

🍷🍷🍷🍷🍷 **The Bellevue Vineyard Semillon 2022, Hunter Valley** There's no suggestion this has had any contact with oak, but it has structure and texture beyond the norm, and the palate is delicious, with hints of the toast already apparent, but many years to come before it reaches full maturity. Screw cap. 11% alc. RATING 96 DRINK 2028–2035 $45 JH ✪

The Pokolbin Selection Chardonnay 2022, Hunter Valley A more focused wine than its sibling, the length likewise greater. Grapefruit joins the stone fruit and sibilant acidity. Screw cap. 12.5% alc. RATING 95 DRINK 2023–2035 $52 JH

Semillon 2022, Hunter Valley PJ Charteris spent the better part of a decade at Brokenwood, and tasted countless semillons, reflected in the fragrant bouquet and the juicy palate with lime and Meyer lemon nuances, the length impeccable. Screw cap. 11% alc. RATING 95 DRINK 2023–2033 $35 JH ✪

Chardonnay 2022, Hunter Valley The cooler, wetter and later vintage made vineyard vigilance a necessity; disease was kept at bay, and plush fruit was the outcome, verging on outright tropical flavours, perhaps a hint of botrytis. Screw cap. 12% alc. RATING 94 DRINK 2023–2034 $42 JH

🍷🍷🍷🍷🍸 **Shiraz 2021, Hunter Valley** RATING 93 DRINK 2026–2036 $45 JH
The Maxwell Vineyard Shiraz 2019, Hunter Valley RATING 93 DRINK 2025–2035 $60 JH
Le Fauve Rosé 2022, Hilltops RATING 91 DRINK 2023–2024 $32 JH
Le Fauve Pinot Gris 2022, Orange RATING 90 DRINK 2023–2028 $32 JH

Château Tanunda   ★★★★★

9 Basedow Road, Tanunda, SA 5352 **Region** Barossa Valley
T (08) 8563 3888 **www**.chateautanunda.com **Open** 7 days 10–5 **Winemaker** Jeremy
Ottawa, Neville Rowe **Est.** 1890 **Dozens** 150 000 **Vyds** 100ha
This is one of the most historically significant winery buildings in the Barossa Valley, built from bluestone quarried in the late 1880s and restored by the Geber family some 120 years later. Château Tanunda owns almost 100ha of vineyards in Bethany, Eden Valley, Tanunda and Vine Vale, including an impressive collection of old vines aged 50–150 years old. Additional fruit is sourced from a group of 30 growers covering the panoply of Barossa districts. The

premium wines are typically hand picked, basket pressed and neither fined nor filtered. The focus here is on old-vine wines, as well as single-district and single-vineyard wines under the Terroirs of the Barossa and The Château labels respectively. A second cellar door has opened in the Rocks, Sydney.

ΨΨΨΨΨ **100 Year Old Vines Shiraz 2020, Barossa** Deep crimson in the glass and bursting with choc-berry fruits, dark plum and mulberry notes underscored with layers of baking spices, licorice, cedar, vanillin oak and earth. Graceful with an elegant mouthfeel, plentiful tight tannins and a minerally acid cadence on its extended finish. Screw cap. 14.5% alc. **RATING** 95 **DRINK** 2023-2033 $160 DB

The Everest Shiraz 2020, Barossa Elegant aromas of blackberry, black cherry and plum are underscored by fine spice, black licorice, cedar, vanilla bean, earth, dark chocolate and panforte. A graceful palate presence with considerable fruit depth, plunging tannins and fine, lacy acidity. Finishes long and pure with a raft of spice and black fruits. One for the cellar. Cork. 14.5% alc. **RATING** 95 **DRINK** 2026-2036 $400 DB

The Everest Shiraz 2019, Barossa Valley The flagship shiraz from Château Tanunda. Deep crimson in colour with unctuous blackberry, black cherry and plum fruits cut with hints of baking spices, panforte, dark chocolate, vanillin oak, blackberry jam, clove, cedar and charcuterie. Full bodied and structured with chocolatey tannins, a vivid acid cadence and layers of elegant black fruits finishing long with a savoury, graceful air. Cork. 14.9% alc. **RATING** 95 **DRINK** 2023-2033 $330 DB

100 Year Old Vines Shiraz 2019, Barossa Valley Deep crimson. Rich blackberry and chocolate-dipped cherry notes with underlying hints of baking spices, cedar, mulberry, clove, pastis, dark chocolate and warm earth. Full bodied with a velvety flow of black and dark berry fruits, abundant spice, dried herbs, vanillin oak, cedar and licorice. Plenty of texture, extract and chalky tannin support, finishing long with a rolling swell of unctuous spiced cassis-like fruit. Cork. 14.9% alc. **RATING** 95 **DRINK** 2023-2040 $160 DB

Terroirs of the Barossa Shiraz 2020, Eden Valley Blackberry, boysenberry and dark plum characters are supported by an array of fine spice, licorice, charcuterie and dark chocolate with lighter notes of sage and wild herbs. Tight, fine tannin provides support and bright acidity the pulse. The wine lingers persistently, showing lovely fruit purity and grace. Screw cap. 14.9% alc. **RATING** 94 **DRINK** 2023-2032 $60 DB

ΨΨΨΨΨ **The Chateau Single Vineyard Cabernet Sauvignon 2021, Eden Valley** **RATING** 93 **DRINK** 2023-2030 $40 DB

Heritage Release Old Vine Shiraz 2021, Barossa **RATING** 93 **DRINK** 2023-2028 $40 DB

50 Year Old Vines Cabernet Sauvignon 2020, Barossa **RATING** 93 **DRINK** 2023-2033 $80 DB

50 Year Old Vines Shiraz 2020, Barossa **RATING** 93 **DRINK** 2023-2030 $80 DB

Terroirs of the Barossa Ebenezer District Shiraz 2020, Barossa Valley **RATING** 93 **DRINK** 2023-2030 $60 DB

The Chateau Single Vineyard Chardonnay 2021, Eden Valley **RATING** 92 **DRINK** 2023-2026 $40 DB

Grand Barossa Cabernet Sauvignon 2021, Barossa **RATING** 92 **DRINK** 2023-2027 $25 DB ✪

The Whole Dam Family 2021, Barossa **RATING** 91 **DRINK** 2023-2027 $40 DB

Grand Barossa Shiraz 2021, Barossa **RATING** 91 **DRINK** 2023-2027 $25 DB ✪

Grand Barossa Dry Riesling 2022, Barossa **RATING** 90 **DRINK** 2023-2026 $25 DB ✪

The Chateau Bethanian Single Vineyard Shiraz 2020, Barossa Valley **RATING** 90 **DRINK** 2023-2027 $40 DB

Chateau Yaldara

Hermann Thumm Drive, Lyndoch, SA 5351 **Region** Barossa Valley
T (08) 8542 0200 **www**.chateauyaldara.com.au **Open** 7 days 9–4.30 **Winemaker** Sam
Kurtz **Viticulturist** Darren Lovell **Est.** 1947 **Dozens** 50 000 **Vyds** 100ha

Tucked away in the southern subregion of Lyndoch lie the impressive old buildings of Chateau
Yaldara. Originally established in 1854 as a flour mill, it was purchased by the Adelaide Wine
Company and converted into a winery in 1891. It closed the winery in 1916 and it fell into
disrepair before Hermann Thumm purchased the property in '41. Winemaking began again
in '47, and in '67 the grand chateau was built – that is the face we see today. McGuigan Wines
purchased the estate in '99 and in '14 it was purchased by the current owners, 1847 Wines.
Traditional styles from regional classics to fortifieds are the focus at this historic estate.

🍷🍷🍷🍷🍷 **Chardonnay Pinot Noir 2015, Adelaide Hills** An impressive sparkling wine
that sports a creamy, toasty disposition and fruit notes of lemon, green apple and
grapefruit along with soft spice, brioche, crème fraîche and stone. The dosage
is bang-on, leading to a stony, savoury compressed line showing vivid drive and
length. Diam. 12% alc. **RATING** 94 **DRINK** 2023-2033 $70 DB

🍷🍷🍷🍷🍷 **Chalice Shiraz 2018, Barossa Valley RATING** 92 **DRINK** 2023-2030 $100 DB
Petit Verdot Méthode Traditionnelle 2017, Barossa Valley RATING 90
DRINK 2023-2027 $50 DB

Chatto

68 Dillons Hill Road, Glaziers Bay, Tas 7109 **Region** Southern Tasmania
T (03) 6114 2050 **www**.chattowines.com **Open** By appt **Winemaker** Jim Chatto
Viticulturist Paul Lipscombe **Est.** 2000 **Dozens** 1000 **Vyds** 1.5ha

Jim Chatto is recognised as having one of the very best palates in Australia and has proved to
be an outstanding winemaker. He and wife Daisy long wanted to get a small Tasmanian pinot
business up and running but, having moved to the Hunter Valley in '00, it took 6 years to
find a site that satisfied all of the criteria they consider ideal. It is a warm, well-drained site in
one of the coolest parts of Tasmania, looking out over Glaziers Bay. Here they have planted
8 clones of pinot noir, with a spacing of 5000 vines/ha.

🍷🍷🍷🍷🍷 **Isle Pinot Noir 2021, Tasmania** Exotic spices, with notes of game meats and
beautifully pure, dark cherry and red cherry fruits on a base of sous bois and
shiitake mushroom broth. Notes of blood plum, earth and dried roses entering the
fray on the palate. Detailed and pure with wonderful fruit depth and fine, pumice
stone tannins providing shape and support. A wine that sails long and persistent
with memories of dark cherry, wild spice, macerated strawberries, forest floor
and mountain herbs. Superb textural drinking. Screw cap. 13.4% alc. **RATING** 97
DRINK 2023-2032 $90 DB ✪

🍷🍷🍷🍷🍷 **Intrigue Pinot Noir 2021, Tasmania** A lovely Huon Valley pinot noir. Deep
cherry red in the glass showing characters of exotic spices, dark cherry and red
cherry with raspberry high notes. Hints of dried purple flowers, mushroom broth
and game meats. A beautiful fine-chalky tannin profile, porcelain acidity and a
distinctly burgundian shape to its carry. Superb drinking. Screw cap. 13% alc.
RATING 96 **DRINK** 2023-2032 $75 DB ✪

Franklinii 2021, Tasmania Fruit notes tending more towards cranberry,
raspberry and sour morello cherry. Floral top notes, fine spice and light tones
of game meats. Superfine, gypsum-like tannins support and a vivid acid line
provides the drive as the wine finishes long and pure with impressive clarity and
a nervy disposition. Lovely, delicate drinking. Screw cap. 14% alc. **RATING** 94
DRINK 2023-2028 $55 DB

Seven Inch Pinot Noir 2021, Tasmania Dark cherry and plum compote notes
dredged with exotic spice. Wafts of sarsaparilla, Chinese roast duck, mushroom
broth and beautifully judged French-oak spice. There is some sour cherry twang
to the acid profile and a lovely sense of calm and space. Finishes long with a tide

of spiced-morello cherry and macerated strawberries with gentle pumice stone tannin support. Screw cap. 13.5% alc. **RATING** 94 **DRINK** 2023-2030 $65 DB

Bird Pinot Noir 2021, Tasmania Fragrant and perfumed with plum, dark cherry and red cherry characters alongside raspberry top notes. Hints of dried rose petal, mushroom broth, stone and mountain herbs lie on a bed of fine spice and a fine, lacy acidity which lends clarity and a sense of space to the wine's shape. Sleek on the finish with a lovely cadence and wash of spiced red and dark fruits. Screw cap. 14% alc. **RATING** 94 **DRINK** 2023-2028 $65 DB

ΨΨΨΨ **Lutruwita 2021, Tasmania RATING** 93 **DRINK** 2023-2028 $45 DB

Cherry Tree Hill

12324 Hume Highway, Sutton Forest, NSW 2577 **Region** Southern Highlands
T (02) 8217 1409 **www.**cherrytreehill.com.au **Open** 7 days 10–5 **Winemaker** Anton Balog, Mark Balog **Viticulturist** Ian Evans **Est.** 2000 **Dozens** 3500 **Vyds** 13.5ha
Gabi Lorentz started Cherry Tree Hill vineyard in '00 with the planting of cabernet sauvignon and riesling, soon followed by merlot, sauvignon blanc and chardonnay. Since then, 5.5ha of the merlot and cabernet have been re-grafted to pinot noir, destined for both still and sparkling wine. Gabi's son David is now the owner and manager of the business.

ΨΨΨΨ **Hayden Reserve Pinot Noir 2019, Southern Highlands** This makes itself known from the get-go, seductive with macerated red cherries, black raspberry and pomegranate. Transportive of its place with baked red clay and fallen autumn leaves, the rolling hills of the Southern Highlands come through with cedar and ground allspice on the finish. Diam. 13.5% alc. **RATING** 95 **DRINK** 2022-2030 $110 SW

ΨΨΨΨ **Pinot Noir 2021, Mornington Peninsula RATING** 91 **DRINK** 2022-2035 $35 SW

Sauvignon Blanc 2022, South Eastern Australia RATING 90 **DRINK** 2022-2028 $18 SW ✿

Cherubino

3462 Caves Road, Wilyabrup, WA 6280 **Region** Margaret River
T (08) 9382 2379 **www.**larrycherubino.com **Open** 7 days 10–5 **Winemaker** Larry Cherubino, Andrew Siddell, Matt Buchan **Est.** 2005 **Dozens** 8000 **Vyds** 120ha
Larry Cherubino has had a particularly distinguished winemaking career, first at Hardys Tintara, then Houghton and thereafter as consultant and Flying Winemaker in Australia, NZ, South Africa, the US and Italy. He has developed numerous ranges, including Cherubino, single-vineyard range The Yard and the single-region Ad Hoc label. The range and quality of his wines is extraordinary, the prices irresistible. The runaway success of the business has seen the accumulation of 120ha of vineyards, the appointment of additional winemakers and Larry's own appointment as director of winemaking for Robert Oatley Vineyards.

ΨΨΨΨ **Cherubino Budworth Riversdale Vineyard Cabernet Sauvignon 2019, Frankland River** This fragrant, medium-bodied cabernet is something quite special. I've no doubt that Block 6 has once again provided excellent fruit (great wine is made in the vineyard, isn't it?) but skilled vinification, patience and attention to the smallest detail have made a glorious cabernet sauvignon, the palate akin to a string of shimmering, lustrous pearls. Screw cap. 13.5% alc. **RATING** 98 **DRINK** 2023-2049 $175 JH ♥

Cherubino Chardonnay 2021, Margaret River This is in a different realm to its Caves Road sibling. It is tighter, more focused and longer, grapefruit ascendant over stone fruit. It's tempting to make something of the 1% difference in alcohol, but I think a shorter time in oak (6 months, instead of 10) has also been at work. Screw cap. 13% alc. **RATING** 97 **DRINK** 2023-2036 $75 JH ✿

Cherubino Cabernet Sauvignon 2020, Margaret River Beautiful crimson-purple colour gets the wine off to a good start. It's not common to describe a 2yo cabernet as charming, but this is what you get here. There's juicy cassis fruit, quality cedary French oak and perfectly pitched tannins. I agree with the back label that the wine will gain in richness and complexity over the next 10–15 years, but I also argue the case of the wine now with its elegance and balance. Screw cap. 14.5% alc. **RATING** 97 **DRINK** 2023-2040 $75 JH ☉

ΨΨΨΨΨ **Pedestal Semillon Sauvignon Blanc 2022, Margaret River** Pedestal is all about Margaret River fruit, here an 80/20% semillon/sauvignon blanc split. It's an excellent drink offering tangy flavours, an amalgam of lime and lemon with citrusy sorbet acidity and woodsy spices. Ultra-refreshing, yet talc-like texture across the palate and a certain depth add to its classiness. Screw cap. 12% alc. **RATING** 95 **DRINK** 2022-2026 $27 JF ☉

Pedestal Shiraz 2021, Margaret River Anyone not convinced by Margaret River shiraz, try this. It's a beauty. Heady aromas of florals, spiced fruit, rusty iron and warm earth. Fleshy ripe plums and cherries on the fuller-bodied palate soak up the oak before the persistent finish kicks in. The silky tannins are something else. Impressive from first to last sip. Screw cap. 14% alc. **RATING** 95 **DRINK** 2022-2032 $27 JF ☉

Cherubino Caves Road Vineyard Chardonnay 2021, Margaret River An altogether convincing portrait of Margaret River chardonnay. Larry Cherubino has brought a span of flavours together: white and yellow peach, creamy cashew and some expensive oak add up to a wine for whenever you screw the cap off. Screw cap. 12% alc. **RATING** 95 **DRINK** 2023-2031 $55 JH

ΨΨΨΨΨ **Ad Hoc Wallflower Riesling 2022, Great Southern** **RATING** 93 **DRINK** 2023-2028 $22 MB ☉

The Yard Riversdale Vineyard Shiraz 2021, Frankland River **RATING** 93 **DRINK** 2023-2032 $35 MB ☉

Chris Ringland   ★★★★★

Franklin House, 6–8 Washington Street, Angaston, SA 5353 **Region** Barossa Valley **T** (08) 8564 3233 **www.chrisringland.com** **Open** By appt **Winemaker** Chris Ringland **Est.** 1989 **Dozens** 120 **Vyds** 2.05ha

The wines made by Chris Ringland for his eponymous brand were at the very forefront of the surge of rich, old-vine Barossa shiraz wines discovered by Robert Parker in the '80s. As a consequence of very limited production, and high-quality (albeit polarising) wine, it assumed immediate icon status. The production of 120 dozen does not include a small number of magnums, double magnums and imperials that are sold each year. The addition of 0.5ha of shiraz planted in '99, joined by 1.5ha planted in '10, has had little practical impact on availability.

ΨΨΨΨΨ **Hoffmann Vineyard Shiraz 2015, Barossa** Fruit weight, oak influence and sheer horsepower all peaking the meters in an über-intense wine. Crème de cassis and kirsch notes, tamari, seaweed paste, Dutch licorice, high-cocoa dark chocolate, clove, cedar, pencil shavings and deep, broody earth. It's a beast with thickly packed, fine tannin and leather tones flowing in on the finish. Give it a good decant and try it over a couple of days; it's quite an experience. Cork. 16.3% alc. **RATING** 97 **DRINK** 2023-2038 $550 DB

ΨΨΨΨΨ **Dimchurch Shiraz 2016, Barossa** Deep crimson with lifted aromas of satsuma plum, blackberry jam and blackberry confit dotted with purple florals, licorice, Christmas cake, oak spice, kirsch and crème de cassis. Thick and enveloping on the palate with insane fruit density, cascading, tightly packed tannins and an opulent and intense back end. Not for the faint hearted. Cork. 17.3% alc. **RATING** 96 **DRINK** 2023-2035 $176 DB

Limit Lodge Shiraz 2018, Barossa Deep crimson with aromas of blackberry jam, liquored black cherries and macerated plum with hints of Christmas cake, rum and raisin, turned earth, tobacco leaf, polished leather, prune juice and crème de cassis. Thickly proportioned with creamy, spicy oak flowing in with increased volume on the palate, which shows no shortage of horsepower, powdery tannin and a thick black-fruited swell to finish. Cork. 16.3% alc. **RATING** 95 **DRINK** 2023-2035 $125 DB

ŶŶŶŶ♀ **Reservation Shiraz 2018, Barossa Valley** RATING 93 DRINK 2023–2033 $60 DB

CR Sealed Shiraz 2021, Barossa RATING 92 DRINK 2023–2029 $35 DB

CR Shiraz 2021, Barossa RATING 92 DRINK 2023–2029 $25 DB ✪

Chrismont ★★★★

251 Upper King River Road, Cheshunt, Vic 3678 **Region** King Valley
T (03) 5729 8220 **www**.chrismont.com.au **Open** 7 days 10–5 **Winemaker** Warren Proft, Prasad Patil **Viticulturist** Arnie Pizzini, Warren Proft **Est.** 1980 **Dozens** 25 000
Vyds 100ha

Arnie and Jo Pizzini's substantial vineyards in the Cheshunt and Whitfield areas of the upper King Valley have been planted to riesling, chardonnay, pinot gris, merlot, barbera, sagrantino, marzemino, arneis, prosecco, fiano, petit manseng, tempranillo, sangiovese and nebbiolo. The La Zona range ties in the Italian heritage of the Pizzinis and is part of the intense interest in all things Italian. A feature of the cellar door is the 'floating' deck over the vineyard, which has floor-to-ceiling glass looking out over the King Valley landscape.

ŶŶŶŶ♀ **La Zona Prosecco NV, King Valley** Charmat method. Prosecco with plenty of citrusy oomph and freshness-plus. Pulsating bubbles burst in quince, green apple, citrus and white florals. Fully energised in brisk acidity on the palate, just what we love about prosecco. Crown. 11.5% alc. RATING 93 $24 JP ✪

La Zona Sagrantino 2018, King Valley Bold, dense and dark and so, so intriguing, the winemaker does this Italian grape variety proud. The inky, blackberry and bramble fruit characters are a big part of the attraction in tandem with cinnamon, allspice, leather and underbrush. Oh, and there's a warm oak presence that goes toe-to-toe with those heroic tannins. Screw cap. 14% alc. RATING 93 DRINK 2023–2030 $36 JP

La Zona Oro Dolce Late Harvest Arneis 2021, King Valley The normally cool-headed Italian white variety takes on a whole new persona as a sweet dessert wine. That eye-catching colour in bright yellow gold. The scent of fresh apricot, honey, orange peel and stewed pear. The freshness that lies ahead on the palate, so vital and clean with just a lick of dry, nutty savouriness. Delicious. 375ml. Screw cap. 11.5% alc. RATING 93 DRINK 2023–2026 $30 JP ✪

La Zona Aglianico 2021, King Valley Black cherry meets white pepper, meets truffle, meets fresh-tilled earth. Juicy, fleshy, medium bodied and savoury, there's plenty of everything set to finely tuned tannins. Downright irresistible. Screw cap. 14% alc. RATING 92 DRINK 2023–2028 $36 JP

Riesling 2022, King Valley 3–4g/L RS. Plenty of charming, fragrant King Valley character here in grapefruit, citrus and apple blossom with talc-like aromatics. Ostensibly dry with just a touch of lemon-drop fruit sweetness to close, with rounding edges. Acidity remains bright. Has immediate enjoyment written all over it. Screw cap. 12% alc. RATING 90 DRINK 2022–2026 $22 JP ✪

La Zona Arneis 2022, King Valley Gentle pear, apple and spice lead the way here in an engaging, easy-drinking wine. Impressive freshness and zing, too. The palate delivers an additional touch of honeysuckle with almond skin bite. There's a lot to like. Screw cap. 12.5% alc. RATING 90 DRINK 2022–2026 $24 JP ✪

La Zona Rosato 2022, King Valley Ticks all the rosé boxes from the subtle pink hues and summery scent to the crisp finish. The bouquet is all about fresh red berries and cherries, spice and a light leesy mealiness. Clean, crisp line of acidity moves fast across the palate. An energetic youngster that delivers. Screw cap. 13% alc. RATING 90 DRINK 2022–2025 $20 JP ✪

La Zona Barbera 2021, King Valley Definitely on the riper side, but it carries it well with lush fruit countering the alcohol weight. Black cherry to the fore with an inviting mulberry, plum, anise and sour-cherry liqueur perfume. Explores more spice on the palate as it generously, smoothly cruises to a long, satisfying finish. Screw cap. 14% alc. RATING 90 DRINK 2022–2025 $30 JP

Circe Wines

PO Box 22, Red Hill, Vic 3937 **Region** Mornington Peninsula
T 0417 328 142 **www**.circewines.com.au **Open** Not **Winemaker** Dan Buckle
Est. 2010 **Dozens** 800 **Vyds** 2.9ha

Circe Wines is the partnership of winemaker Dan Buckle and marketer Aaron Drummond, very much a weekend and holiday venture, inspired by their mutual love of pinot noir. They have a long-term lease of a vineyard in Hillcrest Road. Dan says, 'It is not far from the Buckle vineyard my dad planted in the 1980s'. Circe has 1.2ha of vines, half chardonnay and half MV6 pinot noir. They have also planted 1.7ha of pinot noir (MV6, Abel, 777, D2V5 and Bests' Old Clone) at a vineyard in William Road, Red Hill. Dan Buckle's real job is chief winemaker at Chandon Australia.

Hillcrest Road Vineyard Chardonnay 2022, Mornington Peninsula
No shortage of flavour with fine acidity reining everything in yet the finish lingers long. Beautifully composed with ginger spice and blossom, lemon and limes, lemon curd and woodsy spices, everything in balance. It's moreish, savoury and mouth-watering. Fabulous now and will garner more complexity in time. Screw cap. 13% alc. **RATING** 96 **DRINK** 2023–2032 $80 JF

Hillcrest Road Vineyard Pinot Noir 2022, Mornington Peninsula
RATING 93 **DRINK** 2023–2032 $80 JF

Clairault Streicker Wines

3277 Caves Road, Wilyabrup, WA 6280 **Region** Margaret River
T (08) 9755 6225 **www**.clairaultstreicker.com.au **Open** Wed–Sun 10–5
Winemaker Bruce Dukes **Viticulturist** Christopher Gillmore **Est.** 1976 **Dozens** 12 000
Vyds 113ha

This multifaceted business is owned by New York resident John Streicker. It began in '02 when he purchased the Yallingup Protea Farm and vineyards. This was followed by the purchase of the Ironstone vineyard in '03 and then the Bridgeland vineyard. The Ironstone vineyard is one of the oldest vineyards in Wilyabrup. In Apr '12, Streicker acquired Clairault, bringing a further 40ha of estate vines, including 12ha now over 40 years old. The 2 brands are effectively run as one venture. A large part of the grape production is sold to winemakers in the region.

Clairault Estate Chardonnay 2021, Margaret River True to form, this is in the richer, riper spectrum from fruit-to-winemaking inputs. Yet everything is well knit and complete. Stone fruit, grapefruit, and lemon zest with creamy, cashew-like lees bolster the palate as does the slinky, attractive oak. The lemon–saline flavour and talc-like texture of the acidity are a bonus that corrals all that flavour. Screw cap. 13% alc. **RATING** 95 **DRINK** 2022–2030 $50 JF ✪
Clairault Estate Cabernet Sauvignon 2019, Margaret River Luscious and immediately appealing with trademark flavours plus lashings of spices and sweet cedar oak, all of which infuse the fuller-bodied palate. Sweet fruit, too, alongside menthol, mocha, cocoa and roasted hazelnuts. It has persistence and well balances the savouriness-to-fruit ratio. Screw cap. 14% alc. **RATING** 94 **DRINK** 2023–2034 $55 JF

Streicker Ironstone Block Old Vine Chardonnay 2020, Margaret River
RATING 93 **DRINK** 2023–2028 $50 JF
Clairault Estate Cabernet Sauvignon 2020, Margaret River **RATING** 93
DRINK 2022–2030 $30 JF ✪
Streicker Ironstone Block Old Vine Cabernet Sauvignon 2018, Margaret River **RATING** 92 **DRINK** 2023–2029 $50 JF
Clairault Pinot Noir 2022, Margaret River **RATING** 90 **DRINK** 2022–2024 $24 JF ✪
Clairault Sauvignon Blanc Semillon 2022, Margaret River **RATING** 90
DRINK 2023–2025 $22 JF ✪
Clairault Chardonnay 2021, Margaret River **RATING** 90 **DRINK** 2023–2030 $28 JF

Clairault Cabernet Sauvignon Merlot 2020, Margaret River RATING 90
DRINK 2022–2028 $22 JF
Streicker Bridgeland Block Syrah 2018, Margaret River RATING 90
DRINK 2023–2028 $45 JF

Clandestine ★★★★

PO Box 501 Mount Lawley, WA 6050 **Region** Various
T 0427 482 903 **www**.clandestinevineyards.com.au **Open** Not **Winemaker** Andrew
Vessey (WA/Vic), Ben Riggs (SA) **Est.** 2020 **Dozens** 2000
Owners Nick and Trudy Stacy source fruit and winemaking in the key regions of Margaret
River, Mount Barker, Adelaide Hills and McLaren Vale. The Break Free range of Clandestine
wines is vegan-friendly and use minimal sulphites and preservatives.

🍷🍷🍷🍷 **Shiraz 2021, McLaren Vale** A bright crimson hue. Pointed aromas, slightly
reductive, of violet, blueberry, mace, clove, charcuterie and the tight cedar grain of
the wood. Florals grow with air. Few surprises here, but far less oak than is typical
of the maker. Poised, concentrated and yet, no jam or obtuse oak tannins. Stellar
value. Screw cap. 14.5% alc. RATING 92 DRINK 2022–2030 $30 NG
Break Free Little Wing Shiraz Noir Carbonic 2022, Adelaide Hills
A blend of mostly whole bunches. The inclusion of 5% pinot noir is a tacit
presence. Jubey, pulpy, mid-weighted of feel, aromatic and bouncy in the mouth.
The sort of wine poured by the glass in every cool inner-city pub. Violet,
blueberry, iodine, a smear of olive paste and a grind of pepper across the effusive
finish. Screw cap. 14.5% alc. RATING 91 DRINK 2022–2025 $30 NG
Pinot Grigio 2022, Adelaide Hills Grigio as expected. Perhaps slightly
better. Nashi pear, green apple and quince, muddled with pistachio and fennel,
are dragged to solid length by a perk of saline freshness. Screw cap. 12.5% alc.
RATING 90 DRINK 2022–2024 $25 NG

Clarence House Wines ★★★★

193 Pass Road, Cambridge, Tas 7170 (postal) **Region** Southern Tasmania
T (03) 6247 7345 **www**.chwine.com.au **Open** By appt **Winemaker** Anna Pooley, Justin
Bubb **Est.** 1998 **Dozens** 3500 **Vyds** 15ha
Clarence House was built in 1830 at Clarence Vale, Mount Rumney. The house has been
kept in great condition, and in 1998 present owner David Kilpatrick began planting vines on
a northeast-sloping block opposite the house. While pinot noir and chardonnay account for
over 8ha of the plantings, the remainder includes pinot blanc and tempranillo.

🍷🍷🍷🍷🍷 **Block 1 Pinot Noir 2021, Tasmania** Bright cherry red in the glass with aromas
of hanging game meats over the pure red and dark cherry fruits. A suggestion
of whole-bunch complexity lies below, adding nuance and interest. Silken in its
flow with layers of spice and meaty intrigue set on a framework of fine tannin
and bright acidity, finishing long, pure and true. Screw cap. 13.5% alc. RATING 94
DRINK 2023–2034 $60 DB

🍷🍷🍷🍷 **Reserve Chardonnay 2020, Tasmania** RATING 93 DRINK 2023–2026 $38 DB
Chardonnay 2021, Tasmania RATING 92 DRINK 2023–2026 $32 DB
Pinot Noir 2021, Tasmania RATING 92 DRINK 2023–2026 $38 DB
Sauvignon Blanc 2020, Tasmania RATING 91 DRINK 2023–2026 $28 DB
Pinot Blanc 2020, Tasmania RATING 90 DRINK 2023–2026 $28 DB

Clarendon Hills ★★★★★

363 The Parade, Kensington Park, 5068, SA (postal) **Region** McLaren Vale
www.clarendonhills.com.au **Open** Not **Winemaker** Roman Bratasiuk
Viticulturist Roman Bratasiuk **Est.** 1989 **Dozens** 10 000 **Vyds** 33ha
Age and experience, it would seem, have mellowed Roman Bratasiuk – and the style of
his wines. Once formidable and often rustic, they are now far more sculpted and smooth.

Roman purchased a 160ha property high in the hill country of Clarendon at an altitude close to that of the Adelaide Hills. Here he established a vineyard with single-stake trellising similar to that used on the steep slopes of Germany and Austria; it produces the Domaine Clarendon Syrah. He makes 11 wines each year, all consistently very good, a tribute to the old vines. Sons Adam and Alex have joined their father in the business – Adam in the winery, Alex managing the future direction of Clarendon Hills.

♀♀♀♀♀ **Onkaparinga Syrah 2020, McLaren Vale** In a joint like this, I seldom rate syrah higher than grenache. Yet the hand here is suited to this variety. The oak suggestive of what's to come with syrah, rather than exclamatory as is its way with grenache. Exquisite aromas of pepper-crusted salami, nori, violet and blue fruits. The mid-palate, a weld of reductive elements, the right oak, clove-crusted saline acidity and peppery tannins. A fine present and future. Diam. 13.5% alc. RATING 96 DRINK 2022-2032 $150 NG

Onkaparinga Grenache 2021, McLaren Vale Blewitt Springs fruit imbued with the sandy levity of tannin that is the signature of the region. Florals. Svelte, despite the rasp of oak. Lavender and red-fruit allusions, with a sluice of kirsch, red licorice, pomelo and bergamot. Darker settings, herbal and oak derived, juxtaposed against grenache's daintier cloth. This should age well. I await with interest. Diam. 14% alc. RATING 95 DRINK 2022-2032 $100 NG

Sandown Cabernet Sauvignon 2020, McLaren Vale This is good. Angular of tannin, the oak at the forefront with scents of smoked meat lathered with sage, dried blackcurrant and a swab of black olive paste. Yet as it sits in the glass it coalesces. A distinctly warm-climate wine that will, I believe, age well. Dense, sure, but there is freshness and poise. Should this review fail you, you can hunt me down. Diam. 14% alc. RATING 95 DRINK 2022-2035 $100 NG

Blewitt Springs Grenache 2021, McLaren Vale There's an evolution here toward fresher wines of greater exactitude and less small-oak influence. This is something I welcome. Still raspberry-mocha sweet and a little high octane. Some clove, tamarind and lavender imbuing savouriness and tang to the tannic seams, finer and more lithe than in recent years. A great vintage, too, to be sure. Diam. 14.6% alc. RATING 94 DRINK 2022-2032 $65 NG

Liandra Syrah 2020, McLaren Vale Aromatic, lithe and approachable. An ushering of fruit with gentle oak and tannins of infusion, rather than those derived from excessive extraction. Cardamom pod, clove and turmeric, with the unavoidable wash of sweet raspberry fruit ever so slightly across the mid-palate. The finish, long and well knit, with just enough tension to promote the next glass. Diam. 14% alc. RATING 94 DRINK 2022-2028 $65 NG

Domaine Clarendon BDX 2020, McLaren Vale Bouquet garni, red and blackcurrant, aniseed, dried tobacco leaf, graphite and pencil lead across a pixelated finish of precision that expands and flows long. This is really good. Laxity of oak and extraction, in the best sense. Don't get me wrong – there are tannins aplenty and this will age, rest assured. All class. Diam. 14% alc. RATING 94 DRINK 2022-2032 $45 NG

Astralis Syrah 2020, McLaren Vale Demure initially, from a gentler hand and an earlier harvest window than recent times. But there is plenty going on. Cardamom, clove, star anise, salumi, tapenade and a tinge of blue fruits. Yet this mid-weighted impresario transcends anything primary, suggesting the carnal, the ferrous. The finish is long across a peppery skein of freshness. Some drying oak tannins are the only obstacle to a higher score. Diam. 13.5% alc. RATING 94 DRINK 2022-2032 $500 NG

♀♀♀♀♀ **Old Vines Grenache 2021, McLaren Vale** RATING 93 DRINK 2022-2028 $30 NG ✪

Sandown Blewitt Springs Syrah 2020, McLaren Vale RATING 93 DRINK 2022-2032 $100 NG

Domaine Clarendon Syrah 2020, McLaren Vale RATING 92 DRINK 2022-2028 $45 NG

Clarnette Wines

270 Westgate Road, Armstrong, Vic 3377 (postal) **Region** Grampians
T 0409 083 833 **www**.clarnettewines.com.au **Open** Not **Winemaker** Leigh Clarnette
Viticulturist Andrew Toomey **Est.** 2022 **Dozens** 1200 **Vyds** 14ha
With the death of his great friend, viticulturist and business partner, Kym Ludvigsen, in '13, winemaker Leigh Clarnette took the plunge and retired their long-running wine business, Clarnette & Ludvigsen, now operating simply under Clarnette. Riesling, chardonnay, shiraz and tempranillo will continue to be sourced from the Ludvigsen family's 14ha vineyard in the heart of the Grampians. Under the new Clarnette brand, Leigh has also begun sourcing from other vineyards in the region, including the Portuguese clone of tempranillo (tinta roriz). In '21, he added pinot noir from the Pyrenees and is also keen to source grapes closer to his home in Ballarat.

🍷🍷🍷🍷 **Riesling 2022, Grampians** The fruit flavours themselves are the key here, they're just so intense and so striking, all lime and green pineapple, apple skins and lemon meringue pie. There's a textural element and a tautness, but that fruit, wow, it's a force to be reckoned with. Screw cap. 12.5% alc. **RATING** 95 **DRINK** 2023–2032 $30 CM ☻

Shiraz 2021, Grampians With 4% viognier. Clever winemaking (and growing) has resulted in a beautiful wine. Sweet plum and black cherry flavours come woven through with highly seductive roasted/woodsy spice notes. Cedar, toast, florals and black pepper notes all get a run in, the net effect delicious. You could cellar this but there's no need to. Screw cap. 14% alc. **RATING** 95 **DRINK** 2023–2030 $36 CM ☻

Viognier 2021, Pyrenees Flavour, it has plenty. Stone fruit, quartz and sweet spice/cedar notes sweep authoritatively through the palate. It feels a bit 'take no prisoners', given the volume of flavour, but then there's no alcohol warmth or oiliness. In other words, it sweeps in and wins the day in no uncertain terms. Screw cap. 13.5% alc. **RATING** 94 **DRINK** 2024–2028 $33 CM ☻

🍷🍷🍷🍷 **Rosé 2022, Grampians RATING** 93 **DRINK** 2023–2026 $25 CM ☻
Ludvigsen Chardonnay 2021, Grampians RATING 93 **DRINK** 2024–2030 $39 CM

Clay Pot Wines

Billy Button Wines, 11 Camp Street, Bright, Vic 3741 **Region** Alpine Valleys
T 0434 635 510 **www**.claypotwines.com.au **Open** 7 days 11–6
Winemaker Glenn James **Est.** 2011 **Dozens** 150
Made by Glenn James, each wine is made in a single clay amphora. Beginning life as a single wine, Pandora's Amphora in '11 (vermentino, fiano, moscato giallo), the portfolio has expanded to include Pyrrha (saperavi) and Taurian (friulano). Sourcing for Pandora moved with Glenn, beginning in Heathcote, then moving to McLaren Vale and finally finding a home in the Alpine Valleys and Tasmania.

🍷🍷🍷🍷 **Pyrrha Saperavi 2019, Alpine Valleys** A non-filtered wine made in a single amphora extolling both the virtues of the Georgian red grape and the use of terracotta jars. Saperavi, notorious for its high acidity and tannin, becomes positively elegant and fragrant revealing dried herbs, black cherry, blueberry and violets with a savoury thread of undergrowth and truffle. Trim and taut, it finishes resoundingly dry with a savoury flourish. Screw cap. 13.5% alc. **RATING** 95 **DRINK** 2023–2029 $50 JP ☻

🍷🍷🍷🍷 **Taurian Tamar Valley Friulano 2018, Tasmania RATING** 93 **DRINK** 2023–2028 $40 JP

Clayfield Wines

25 Wilde Lane, Moyston, Vic 3377 **Region** Grampians
T (03) 5354 2689 **www**.clayfieldwines.com **Open** Mon–Sat 10–5, Sun 11–4
Winemaker Simon Clayfield **Est.** 1997 **Dozens** 1000 **Vyds** 2.2ha

Former long-serving Best's winemaker Simon Clayfield and wife Kaye are now doing their own thing. They have 2ha of shiraz planted in 1997, and 0.2ha of riesling was planted in late '19. Additional grapes are purchased from local growers and, when the quality is appropriate, incorporated in the Grampians Shiraz. Production is modest, but the quality is high.

Pallah Merlot Shiraz 2015, Grampians Personality plus. Indeed this is really quite captivating. Deli meat, woodsy spice, graphite and sweet raspberry flavours flow into blueberry and orange blossoms. It's exotic in flavour, aroma and feel; ultrafine tannin essentially pulls through the entirety. This is a medium-weight wine that simply oozes character. Screw cap. 14.2% alc. **RATING** 95 **DRINK** 2022-2030 $85 CM

Moyston Ton Up Shiraz 2017, Grampians It feels warm and bold but it also shows pepper and spice notes. It's Grampians shiraz in rich, concentrated mode. Earth, toast, leather and malt flavours cruise warmly through the palate, with violet/floral characters also rising throughout. Everything here feels convincing. Screw cap. 13.9% alc. **RATING** 94 **DRINK** 2022-2032 $45 CM

Thomas Wills Shiraz 2017, Grampians RATING 93 **DRINK** 2022-2029 $40 CM

Clonakilla

3 Crisps Lane, Murrumbateman, NSW 2582 **Region** Canberra District
T (02) 6227 5877 **www**.clonakilla.com.au **Open** Mon–Fri 11–4, w'ends 10–5
Winemaker Tim Kirk, Chris Bruno **Viticulturist** Greg Mader **Est.** 1971
Dozens 20000 **Vyds** 20ha

The indefatigable Tim Kirk, with an inexhaustible thirst for knowledge, is the winemaker and manager of this family winery founded by his father, scientist Dr John Kirk. It is not at all surprising that the quality of the wines is exceptional, especially the Shiraz Viognier, which has paved the way for numerous others but remains the icon. Demand for the wines outstrips supply, even with the '98 acquisition of an adjoining 20ha property by Tim and wife Lara Kirk, planted to shiraz and viognier. In '07 the Kirk family purchased another adjoining property, planting another 1.8ha of shiraz, plus 0.4ha of grenache, mourvèdre and cinsault.

Riesling 2022, Canberra District Spring garden aromas of jasmine, lemon blossom and herbs make this vibrant riesling very enticing. The palate is a burst of juicy fresh lime and mandarin, lemongrass and grapefruit pith with tangy acidity, yet enough lemon-curd texture to flesh it out. Mouth-watering and refreshing now but will easily sail into the next decade. Screw cap. 12% alc. **RATING** 95 **DRINK** 2022-2032 $35 JF ✪

Viognier 2022, Canberra District What's lovely about this, is that it's quintessentially Clonakilla. It comes finely tuned, with a mix of white stone fruit, apricot kernel, lemon balm and citrusy acidity. The palate extends out evenly and beautifully and there's a lusciousness, but it's not at all weighty. Compelling and delicious. Screw cap. 13.5% alc. **RATING** 95 **DRINK** 2023-2030 $50 JF ✪

Shiraz Viognier 2021, Canberra District Somewhat atypical with lots of upfront acidity and pomegranate tang throughout. There are red and blue fruits in the mix and wafts of warm earth and oak spice. Plus, plenty of fresh herbs and menthol, the latter imparting a cooling sensation. It's tightly coiled, stony and firm, yet the palate is more medium bodied with supple, fine tannins. An intriguing rendition that's enjoyable, nonetheless. Screw cap. 13.5% alc. **RATING** 95 **DRINK** 2022-2035 $130 JF

ŶŶŶŶỸ Chardonnay 2022, Tumbarumba RATING 93 DRINK 2023-2032 $50 JF
O'Riada Shiraz 2021, Canberra District RATING 93 DRINK 2023-2033
$45 JF
Murrumbateman Pinot Noir 2022, Canberra District RATING 92
DRINK 2023-2031 $65 JF
Ceoltoiri 2022, Canberra District RATING 92 DRINK 2024-2032 $50 JF

Clos Clare ★★★★

45 Old Road, Watervale, SA 5452 **Region** Clare Valley
T (08) 8843 0161 **www.closclare.com.au Open** W'ends 11–5 **Winemaker** Sam and
Tom Barry **Est.** 1993 **Dozens** 1600 **Vyds** 2ha
Clos Clare was acquired by the Barry family in '07. Riesling continues to be made from the
2ha unirrigated section of the original Florita vineyard (the major part of that vineyard was
already in Barry ownership). Its red wines come from a vineyard beside the Armagh site.

ŶŶŶŶŶ **Watervale Riesling 2022, Clare Valley** Huge energy and velocity, it's tightly
wound and racy with a filigree of lime, green apple, grapefruit, ginger, talc and
green herbs oscillating between the bouquet and palate. Texture is gently chalky
and mouth-watering, extending exceptionally long while keeping all that fruit,
herbal detail and minerality in a very compact frame. Incredibly refreshing and
lively. Yes, thanks. Screw cap. 12% alc. RATING 95 DRINK 2022-2040 $30 MB ✪

Clovely Estate ★★★★

Steinhardts Road, Moffatdale via Murgon, Qld 4605 **Region** South Burnett
T (07) 3876 3100 **www.clovely.com.au Open** W'ends & public hols 10–5
Winemaker Nick Pesudovs **Est.** 1997 **Dozens** 25 000 **Vyds** 173.76ha
Clovely Estate has the largest vineyards in Qld, with immaculately maintained vines at
2 locations in the Burnett Valley. There are 140ha of red grapes (including 60ha of shiraz)
and 34ha of white grapes. The attractively packaged wines are sold in various styles at
various pricepoints.

ŶŶŶŶỸ **Saperavi 2021, South Burnett** Thick-set, slurpy red of concentrated dark
berries to taste with woody spice, rhubarb and root vegetable savouriness in tow.
It's all happening here. In all that density and richness, good balance and a sense of
freshness. Earthiness, undergrowth characters and meatiness also find a place in the
wine. This is a bold red with a huge volume of perfume and flavour. Screw cap.
14.5% alc. RATING 93 DRINK 2022-2030 $35 MB
Shiraz Saperavi 2019, South Burnett A medium- to full-bodied red wine on
hand. Ripe plum, black olive, salted licorice and clove scents and flavours. Firm
in the palate, rippling with grainy, sinewy tannins that contain a potent array of
concentrated dark fruits and woody spices. It's a powerful red blend: muscular,
robust and a touch rustic, but all well balanced and with charm. Screw cap.
13.8% alc. RATING 93 DRINK 2022-2035 $30 MB ✪
Semillon 2021, South Burnett Tightly wound texture, light, delicate flavours,
citrus-leaning perfume and lick of grassy, green herb detail. Nicely done. Acid
drives the wine while a bit of chalkiness to texture helps things along nicely.
Very refreshing, lively and fresh in this incarnation, it feels like the wine will
gravitate to honeyed and toasty characters with short- to medium-term cellaring.
A bit of a gem. Screw cap. 10.6% alc. RATING 92 DRINK 2022-2030 $35 MB

Clover Hill ★★★★☆

60 Clover Hill Road, Lebrina, Tas 7254 **Region** Northern Tasmania
T (03) 5459 7900 **www.cloverhillwines.com.au Open** Wed–Sun 11–4.30
Winemaker Robert Heywood, Ben Howell **Est.** 1986 **Dozens** 12 000 **Vyds** 23.9ha
Clover Hill was established by Taltarni with the sole purpose of making a premium
sparkling wine. It has 23.9ha of vineyards (chardonnay, pinot noir and pinot meunier) and
its sparkling wine is excellent, combining finesse with power and length. The American

owner and founder of Clos du Val (Napa Valley), Taltarni and Clover Hill has brought these businesses and Domaine de Nizas (Languedoc) under the one management roof, the group known as Goelet Wine Estates.

πππππ **Cuvée Prestige Blanc de Blancs 2010, Tasmania** 10 years on lees; disgorged Nov '21. Straw in hue with a fine, persistent bead. There's a rich, aromatic profile of baked apple, fresh brioche and pastry notes, soft spice, lemon curd and roasting nuts. Biscuity and expansive on the palate with fine, lacy acidity and a distinct sense of elegance and complexity. Lovely drinking. Diam. 12.5% alc. **RATING** 95 **DRINK** 2023-2030 $160 DB
Noir En Bois NV, Tasmania 60/22/18% pinot noir/chardonnay/pinot meunier. The palest of pink blushes in the glass with an energetic bead and mousse. Characters of redcurrant, white peach and strawberry with hints of soft spice, brioche, berry cream and a whiff of vanilla. Expressive and pure with a lovely red berry and cream palate flow, bright sapid acidity and an impressively long finish. Diam. 12.5% alc. **RATING** 94 $55 DB

πππππ **Vintage Riché 2017, Tasmania RATING** 93 **DRINK** 2023-2030 $55 DB
Tasmanian Cuvée Rosé NV, Tasmania RATING 93 $37 DB
Cuvée Foudre NV, Tasmania RATING 93 $55 DB
Cuvee Exceptionnelle Brut Rosé 2017, Tasmania RATING 91
DRINK 2023-2028 $75 DB
Tasmanian Cuvée NV, Tasmania RATING 91 $37 DB

Clyde Park Vineyard ★★★★★

2490 Midland Highway, Bannockburn, Vic 3331 **Region** Geelong
T (03) 5281 7274 **www**.clydepark.com.au **Open** 7 days 11–5 **Winemaker** Terry Jongebloed **Est.** 1979 **Dozens** 6000 **Vyds** 10.1ha
Clyde Park Vineyard, established by Gary Farr but sold many years ago, has passed through several ownership changes. Now owned by Terry Jongebloed and Sue Jongebloed-Dixon, it has significant mature plantings of pinot noir (3.4ha), chardonnay (3.1ha), sauvignon blanc (1.5ha), shiraz (1.2ha) and pinot gris (0.9ha), and the quality of its wines is consistently exemplary.

πππππ **Single Block E Shiraz 2022, Geelong** A saturated crimson purple. A gorgeous wine from the get-go with its lifted aromas of dark cherries, ripe raspberries, florals and spice rack spices. Tightly wound, focused and concentrated, this has all the components to age magnificently over the next 10+ years. In the meantime, give this some air and pair it with aged porterhouse. 140 dozen made. Screw cap. 13.5% alc. **RATING** 96 **DRINK** 2022-2035 $95 PR
Sauvignon Blanc 2022, Geelong Bright straw with green tinges. Gently saline and pristine, this seriously good sauvignon blanc exhibits aromas of fresh gooseberries, white flowers and a touch of freshly cut grass, while the chalky textured palate has lovely line and persistence. Screw cap. 12.5% alc. **RATING** 95 **DRINK** 2022-2026 $35 PR ✪
Pinot Gris 2022, Geelong A bright yellow gold with green tinges. A melange of orchard fruits, pears, honeysuckle and spice announces this very convincing gris. Gently textured, the medium-bodied and beautifully balanced palate has a fine bead of acidity giving the wine structure and length. Good stuff. Screw cap. 12.5% alc. **RATING** 95 **DRINK** 2022-2026 $40 PR ✪
Single Block D Bannockburn Pinot Noir 2022, Geelong Aromas of satsuma plums, dark cherries, rose petals, incense and some potpouri notes. Sweetly fruited and finely tuned on the palate, there's a delicacy that's appealing. The tannins are silky and long and while this can be enjoyed in its youth, this has the potential to improve over time. Screw cap. 13.3% alc. **RATING** 95 **DRINK** 2023-2030 $95 PR

πππππ **Fumé Blanc 2022, Geelong RATING** 93 **DRINK** 2022-2026 $40 PR
Single Block B2 Pinot Noir 2022, Geelong RATING 93 **DRINK** 2023-2023 $95 PR
Shiraz 2022, Geelong RATING 92 **DRINK** 2022-2028 $52 PR

Pinot Noir 2022, Geelong RATING 92 DRINK 2023-2023 $52 PR
Single Block F College Bannockburn Pinot Noir 2022, Geelong
RATING 91 DRINK 2023-2031 $95 PR
Locale Pinot Noir 2022, Geelong RATING 90 DRINK 2022-2026 $32 PR

Coates Wines

185 Tynan Road, Kuitpo, SA 5172 **Region** Adelaide Hills
T 0417 882 557 **www**.coates-wines.com **Open** Sun 11–5 **Winemaker** Duane Coates MW
Est. 2003 **Dozens** 3500

Put simply, Duane Coates MW is a maverick. Fearful of the waft of lime that is the trademark
of many an Australian riesling, for example, he attempts to shift the paradigm to one of
textural intrigue founded on oak, lees and a laissez-faire approach. He is knowledgeable (with
a science degree and a master of oenology, among other accolades), likes nice things and has
tasted widely. He applies a similar aesthetic and empirical algorithm to all his wines, largely
brilliant and inevitably, each of stunning value.

The Riesling 2022, Adelaide Hills A wine of succulence, precision and
breadth requiring patience for the oak to resolve. Yet for those so inclined,
immense rewards await. This reminds me of a contemporary expression from
Pfalz, such extract and power lying reticent. Lemon drop, lime, tamarind,
ginger candy, curry leaf and orchard fruits. Screw cap. 12% alc. RATING 96
DRINK 2022-2035 $35 NG ✪ ♥

The Reserve Chardonnay 2021, Adelaide Hills There are wines twice this
price that barely nudge the quality here. Lees-derived aromas of roasted hazelnut,
curry powder and dried straw. Creamed cashew, sexy oak vanillins, nougatine
and stone fruit allusions aplenty. The oak, a perceivable framework, albeit, nicely
judged in lieu of a mid-term ageing window. This will unravel into a masterpiece.
Screw cap. 13% alc. RATING 96 DRINK 2022-2030 $50 NG ✪

Vin d'Or Semillon 2021, Adelaide Hills A single-vineyard expression, barrel
fermented and left under flor. This is excellent; reeling off scents of parmesan,
raw almond, chamomile, orange blossom, apricot pith and quince paste, ladled
with dried porcini umami with a waft of tatami straw across the ceaseless finish.
A superb wine. Screw cap. 13% alc. RATING 96 DRINK 2022-2035 $125 NG ♥

The Syrah 2021, McLaren Vale This is fine, the clutch of reduction pressed
gently against a framework of oak to infuse a sense of tension as much as a lattice
of structure. Cooler-climatic allusions of iodine, blue fruits, tapenade, salumi and
violet. The drive, long and fresh, belying any sense of warm-climate origins. Little
wonder given the top cru portions of Clarendon and Blewitt Springs fruit in the
mix. Screw cap. 14% alc. RATING 95 DRINK 2022-2030 $30 NG ✪

The Pinot Noir 2021, Adelaide Hills Wild fermented with 15% whole
bunches. Natural mlf and 12 months in French oak (33% new). This is the way
to make pinot from a region challenged by climate. Ample vanillin-cedar oak, a
lithe streamline of grape tannic fibre and riffs on rhubarb, sassafras, dark cherry
and porcini. Requires mid-term ageing, given the tannic mettle. A delicious
expression from a region with very few. Screw cap. 13.5% alc. RATING 94
DRINK 2022-2032 $35 NG ✪

The Gimp Shiraz 2020, McLaren Vale A quasi-homage to warm-climate
Australian expressions of the past, albeit with a far finer weave of tannins and
maritime freshness, all-natural of feel. Llicorella mineral pungency, blue fruits,
charcoal and kirsch rubbing across the gently gritty finish. This is a warm-climate
wine crafted with an artisanal sense of poise and restraint. Screw cap. 14% alc.
RATING 94 DRINK 2022-2032 $35 NG ✪

The Nebbiolo 2020, Adelaide Hills RATING 93 DRINK 2023-2029 $50 NG
The Grenache 2021, McLaren Vale RATING 92 DRINK 2022-2027 $50 NG
The Iberian 2021, Adelaide Hills McLaren Vale RATING 92
DRINK 2022-2028 $35 NG
The Touriga Nacional 2021, McLaren Vale RATING 92 DRINK 2022-2028
$35 NG

Cobaw Ridge

31 Perc Boyers Lane, Pastoria, Vic 3444 **Region** Macedon Ranges
T (03) 5423 5227 **www.**cobawridge.com.au **Open** W'ends 12–5 **Winemaker** Nelly
Cooper, Alan Cooper **Viticulturist** Alan Cooper **Est.** 1985 **Dozens** 1000 **Vyds** 5ha
When the Coopers started planting in the early '80s there was scant knowledge of the
best varieties for the region, let alone the Cobaw Ridge site. They have now settled on
chardonnay and syrah; lagrein and close-planted, multi-clonal pinot noir are more recent
arrivals to thrive. Cobaw Ridge is fully certified biodynamic, and all winery operations are
carried out according to the biodynamic calendar.

Chardonnay 2021, Macedon Ranges Memorably long. It's pure, flinty and
moreish, with sulphides coating lemon-lime and white stone fruit and the ultrafine
acidity, a signature of this vintage, taking charge, but not at the expense of flavour.
Some creamy, miso/cashew-like lees bolster the palate, ensuring this is complex and
detailed. What a wine. Diam. 13.8% alc. **RATING** 97 **DRINK** 2022–2033 $88 JF ✪

il pinko Rosé 2021, Macedon Ranges il pinko is more 'il bronzo' in colour
and as usual, this is stonkingly good. Utterly delicious with rosehip, tamarind,
Angostura bitters, watermelon and rind with flecks of pepper and sumac. There's
a succulence, a juiciness with refreshing acidity yet the palate steals the limelight:
textural, flavoursome, long and pure with some phenolic pull expanding outwards.
Diam. 13% alc. **RATING** 96 **DRINK** 2022–2026 $52 JF ✪ ♥

Lagrein 2021, Macedon Ranges Cobaw Ridge is the champion of lagrein in
Australia, and it's a variety in need of a cool climate. Macedon Ranges fits the bill.
This feels cool and cooling with fine acidity throughout teasing the dark plummy
fruit into submission. Spiced with cinnamon and pepper, this has depth as much
as charm. Diam. 13% alc. **RATING** 96 **DRINK** 2023–2031 $95 JF

l'altra Syrah 2021, Macedon Ranges l'altra is halfway between a rosé and a
red wine and it has a 15% glug of pinot noir in it, too. It's all juicy and tangy and
full of flavour with rosehip and petals, wild strawberries, chinotto and spices with
some basil and menthol. Lovely acidity, refreshing and lively with just enough
tannin to deepen the palate. A red for summer. Diam. 13.4% alc. **RATING** 95
DRINK 2022–2027 $52 JF

Pinot Noir 2021, Macedon Ranges RATING 93 **DRINK** 2023–2033 $88 JF

Cobb's Hill Estate

Oakwood Road, Oakbank, SA 5243 **Region** Adelaide Hills
T (08) 8388 4054 **www.**cobbshillestate.com.au **Open** 7 days 11–5 **Winemaker** Peter
Leske **Viticulturist** Joshua Hicks **Est.** 1997 **Dozens** 4500 **Vyds** 30ha
This Adelaide Hills property (established by Sally and Roger Cook) takes its name from Cobb
& Co, which used it as a staging post in the 1800s. The Cooks raised Angus cattle and grew
cherries on the property before adding vines. Three original vineyards (totalling 10ha) were
planted to sauvignon blanc, chardonnay and riesling. The property was acquired by Nigel
Vinecombe in '16, who also purchased the neighbouring Greenleaf vineyard, thereby adding
6ha of pinot noir, chardonnay and pinot gris. Since the purchase, another 15ha of vines
on the original property have been planted to shiraz, pinot noir, pinot gris, pinot meunier,
chardonnay and riesling.

Stagecoach Shiraz 2021, Adelaide Hills This is good. The cooler,
attenuated '21 vintage providing a helping hand. Hand picked, but a fairly
conventional approach. All the same, the French oak is impeccably nestled.
Aromas of Bing cherry, iodine, white pepper, corn and salumi are spot on. The
mid-weighted, savoury feel is attractive and the finish long. A neat, purposeful
wine. Screw cap. 13.5% alc. **RATING** 91 **DRINK** 2022–2028 $42 NG

Cellar Reserve Chardonnay 2020, Adelaide Hills A solid wine with plenty
to like, but plenty more that could come. Scents of orange blossom, cornmeal,
marzipan and ripe nectarine. This was a hot year, to be sure, but the wine lacks
some drive. Screw cap. 13% alc. **RATING** 90 **DRINK** 2022–2025 $62 NG

Cofield Wines

Distillery Road, Wahgunyah, Vic 3687 **Region** Rutherglen
T (02) 6033 3798 **www**.cofieldwines.com.au **Open** Mon–Sat 9–5, Sun 10–5
Winemaker Damien Cofield, Peter Berks **Viticulturist** Andrew Cofield **Est.** 1990
Dozens 13 000 **Vyds** 15.4ha

Two generations of the Cofield family have developed an impressively broad-based product range with a strong cellar-door sales base. A 20ha property at Rutherglen is planted to shiraz, durif, sangiovese and malbec. Peter Berks joined the winemaker team in '20.

🍷🍷🍷🍷🍷 **Provincial Netherby Shiraz 2021, Rutherglen** Robust and ripe, but there's also a degree of genuine sophistication to this most attractive wine. Fine, fragrant aromas in blueberry, plum, black fruits, earth, woodsy spices with a lively amaro edge. There's an inherent energy across the palate, buoyed by bright red fruits, lively spices, discreet oak and ripe, cherry pip tannins. Everything is in its place. Screw cap. 14.5% alc. **RATING** 95 **DRINK** 2023-2034 $48 JP ✪

🍷🍷🍷🍷 **Provincial Reserve Pinot Noir Chardonnay 2012, King Valley RATING** 92 **DRINK** 2023-2026 $54 JP
Provincial Quartz Vein Durif 2019, Rutherglen RATING 92 **DRINK** 2023-2035 $45 JP
Tempranillo 2021, King Valley RATING 91 **DRINK** 2023-2025 $25 JP ✪
Sauvignon Blanc 2022, King Valley RATING 90 **DRINK** 2023-2027 $24 JP ✪
Durif 2021, Rutherglen RATING 90 **DRINK** 2023-2032 $30 JP

Colab and Bloom

1436 Brookman Road, Willunga, SA 5172 (postal) **Region** South Australia
www.fielddaywineco.com **Open** Not **Winemaker** Daniel Zuzolo **Est.** 2017

Colab and Bloom is a collaboration between wine marketer Nick Whiteway and winemakers and winegrowers throughout South Australia. The emphasis is on fun and fresh wines from emerging varieties. Grapes are sourced from the Adelaide Hills, Southern Fleurieu and Riverland; nero d'Avola is grown at Vasarelli's in Currency Creek, the tempranillo by David Blows in Macclesfield. Grapes are processed across a number of winery locations, including Project Wines in Langhorne Creek, DiFabio in McLaren Flat and Haselgrove in McLaren Vale. The company sits under the umbrella of Field Day Wine Co.

🍷🍷🍷🍷 **Cabernet Sauvignon 2021, Fleurieu** This is in a good drinking place. It offers clear varietal characters of blackcurrant, mint and assorted dry herbs but it's the gloss, or the silk, of it that really makes for enjoyable drinking. It's not earth-shattering, but it's very nicely done. Screw cap. 14% alc. **RATING** 92 **DRINK** 2023-2029 $25 CM ✪
Nero d'Avola 2021, Fleurieu This is jumpy with ripe and sweet raspberry fruits, but it's the layers of musk and associated dry spices that really ramp up the moreishness. You just keep wanting to drink more. It's not complex and it doesn't pretend to be. An overt freshness, not to mention crunchiness, doesn't hurt either. Screw cap. 14% alc. **RATING** 91 **DRINK** 2022-2026 $25 CM ✪
Montepulciano 2021, Fleurieu It's a rustic red, in a good way, with a ruggedness to it. Tar and blueberry flavours mix with bay leaf, meat and toast. Its flavour and mouthfeel make it tailor-made for drinking at a barbecue, though in truth it is worthy of your better glassware. Screw cap. 14.5% alc. **RATING** 91 **DRINK** 2023-2028 $25 CM ✪

Coldstream Hills

29-31 Maddens Lane, Coldstream, Vic 3770 **Region** Yarra Valley
T (03) 5960 7000 **www**.coldstreamhills.com.au **Open** Thurs–Mon 10–5
Winemaker Andrew Fleming, Greg Jarratt, James Halliday AM (Consultant) **Est.** 1985
Vyds 100ha

Founded by James Halliday AM, Coldstream Hills has 100ha of estate vineyards as its base, 3 in the Lower Yarra Valley and 2 in the Upper Yarra Valley. Chardonnay and pinot noir continue to be the principal focus; merlot and cabernet sauvignon came on stream in '97, sauvignon blanc around the same time, Reserve Shiraz later still. A winery was erected in '10 with a capacity of 1500t. There is a plaque in the fermentation area commemorating the official opening on 12 Oct '10 and naming the facility the 'James Halliday Cellar'.

ΨΨΨΨΨ **Deer Farm Vineyard Block E Pinot Noir 2021, Yarra Valley** A light, bright crimson. Boy, this smells good with its aromas of pure raspberry, wild strawberries, pomegranate and crushed violets. Supremely elegant and structured with discreet yet very persistent tannins. Finishes with a lick of amaro bitterness. Impressive. Screw cap. 13% alc. **RATING** 98 **DRINK** 2023-2033 $85 PR ✪ ♥

Deer Farm Vineyard Block D Pinot Noir 2021, Yarra Valley A gorgeous bright crimson. Aromas of dark cherry, ripe raspberries, a hint of pomegranate and Asian spices. There's a gentle creaminess that's perfectly counterbalanced by the wine's firm, yet supple tannins. More immediate than the Block E, it will be a fascinating exercise to see where they both end up 10 years from now. Screw cap. 13% alc. **RATING** 97 **DRINK** 2023-2031 $85 PR ✪

Reserve Chardonnay 2021, Yarra Valley Bright green gold. Pure and expressive with subtle scents of stone fruits, white pears, pink grapefruit and flowers. Similarly restrained and finely tuned on the palate, I really like the overall harmony and balance. Finishes saline and long. A superb wine. Screw cap. 13% alc. **RATING** 97 **DRINK** 2022-2030 $60 PR ✪

ΨΨΨΨΨ **Blanc de Blancs 2017, Yarra Valley** Coldstream Hills sparkling wines are consistently very good and well priced. This is a lovely wine just at the beginning of its evolution. Marine scents sit alongside aromas of lemons, baking spices and ginger. The palate is dry, chalky, structured and impressively long. Diam. 11.5% alc. **RATING** 96 **DRINK** 2022-2028 $45 PR ✪

Deer Farm Vineyard Chardonnay 2021, Yarra Valley Classic, Upper Yarra chardonnay from a great year with a beautifully defined bouquet of just-picked orchard fruits, nashi, some spice and a little saline minerality. Tightly wound, there's excellent drive through the mid-palate as this energetic wine finishes brisk and very long. This will benefit from age, but if you're going to drink it now, please, don't drink it too cold. Screw cap. 13% alc. **RATING** 96 **DRINK** 2022-2029 $45 PR ✪

Reserve Pinot Noir 2021, Yarra Valley Deep crimson red. Concentrated and intense with aromas of black cherry, blueberries, Vietnamese mint, dark chocolate, violets and some oak-derived spice. Densely packed, this muscular wine has ripe, powerful and chewy tannins and, as past Coldstream pinots have shown, this will still look good 20 years from now. Screw cap. 14% alc. **RATING** 96 **DRINK** 2023-2034 $85 PR

The Esplanade Pinot Noir 2021, Yarra Valley A medium bright crimson ruby. Impressive from the get-go. Aromas of ripe raspberries, damson plums, subtle incense and sweet spice from impeccably handled oak. Medium bodied, this perfectly weighted wine is textured, structured, layered and long. The tannins are discreet yet firm, and I'd love to see this in 10 years. Right now, I'd settle for a glass of this and some Peking duck. Screw cap. 13.5% alc. **RATING** 96 **DRINK** 2023-2033 $50 PR ✪

Deer Farm Vineyard Pinot Noir 2021, Yarra Valley A deep-ish bright crimson. Smells a little Gevrey-like, with its dark fruit aromas and ferrous notes together with florals and a subtle hint of licorice root. On the palate, it's perfectly proportioned, concentrated and lithe, too. Sinewy and fine tannins round out a delicious wine that will continue to blossom for at least a decade. Screw cap. 13.5% alc. **RATING** 96 **DRINK** 2022-2032 $50 PR ✪

Pinot Noir Chardonnay 2017, Yarra Valley A bright straw green. This is very fine on the nose with delicate aromas of apples, white peaches, freshly poached red fruits, brioche and a little hazelnut. The palate is equally refined, and this builds nicely with its gentle creaminess and fine bead before finishing taut and long. A refined Aussie sparkling. Diam. 12% alc. **RATING** 95 **DRINK** 2022–2028 $35 PR ✪

The Dr's Block Pinot Noir 2021, Yarra Valley A medium bright garnet. Gently perfumed with aromas of cherries, redcurrants and pomegranate with a little white pepper and spice. Equally gentle on the light- to medium-bodied and silky palate. Screw cap. 14% alc. **RATING** 94 **DRINK** 2023–2028 $50 PR

♟♟♟♟♟ **Pinot Noir 2021, Yarra Valley** **RATING** 93 **DRINK** 2022–2028 $35 PR ✪

Collector Wines

7 Murray Street, Collector, NSW 2581 **Region** Canberra District
T (02) 6116 8722 **www.collectorwines.com.au** **Open** Thurs–Mon 10–4
Winemaker Alex McKay **Est.** 2007 **Dozens** 6000 **Vyds** 6ha
Alex McKay makes exquisitely detailed wines, bending to the dictates of inclement weather on his doorstep, heading elsewhere if need be. Alex was part of a talented team at Hardys' Kamberra Winery and, when it was closed down by Hardys' then new owner CHAMP, he decided to stay in the district. His wines are consistently excellent, their elegance appropriate for their maker. A cellar door renovation, which will increase capacity from 8 to 80, should be complete late '23.

♟♟♟♟♟ **Tiger Tiger Chardonnay 2021, Tumbarumba** If you remember the '80s Steven Greenberg song 'Funkytown', that's cool, although I'm singing Pseudo Echo's rendition while tasting this funky, flinty and fabulous wine. Full of citrus, packed with regional flavour, a zip of texture, oak spice and creamy lees. This is moreish and complex. 'Won't you take me to, Funkytown.' Well, I'm already there with this chardonnay. Screw cap. 12.9% alc. **RATING** 96 **DRINK** 2022–2031 $45 JF ✪

Reserve Shiraz 2019, Canberra District There's a lot in this wine but it starts gently with heady aromas all floral and spicy, the dark fruit comes in next, the spice notes and cedary oak. Fuller bodied with plush tannins and ribbons of acidity moving through the palate. It's gorgeous now but will reward even more in time. Screw cap. 13% alc. **RATING** 96 **DRINK** 2023–2039 $96 JF

Summer Swarm Fiano 2022, Hilltops This has complexity and depth of flavour yet is fresh and so damn drinkable. Honeysuckle, lemon balm, a lemon-saline character, too, with creamed honey and ginger spice. The palate is full of refreshing acidity yet is textural, savoury and moreish. Screw cap. 13.1% alc. **RATING** 95 **DRINK** 2022–2027 $28 JF ✪

Shoreline Sangiovese Rosé 2022, Gundagai Canberra District A pale copper colour and heady aromas, yet the palate steals the show. It's supple, textural, zingy with acidity, savoury and spicy. There's a slip of sweetness on the finish, but it is essentially a dry wine and spot-on. Screw cap. 12.2% alc. **RATING** 95 **DRINK** 2022–2024 $26 JF ✪

Ledger Grüner Veltliner 2022, Tumbarumba White pepper and daikon abound, they are merely some of the gorgeous varietal aromas and flavours here. Hints of lemon, cucumber and preserved ginger with such a creamy texture … then the electric acidity shocks everything into submission, racing towards a long finish. Impressive. Screw cap. 12.8% alc. **RATING** 95 **DRINK** 2022–2028 $34 JF ✪

Marked Tree Red Shiraz 2021, Canberra District An immediately fragrant, spicy, whole-bunch character and meaty reduction kick-start a complex profile. Layers of flavour from red fruits, warm earth and smoky, cured meats to pepper and wood char. A very savoury wine yet the fruit is distinct. Medium-bodied with fine tannins and excellent length. So compelling, so delicious. Screw cap. 13% alc. **RATING** 95 **DRINK** 2024–2034 $34 JF ✪

Rose Red City Sangiovese 2019, Canberra District Alex McKay has an affinity with Italian reds and boy, does it show here. At first deceptively light with sour cherry, warm earth and layers of spice. It builds, moves and entices. It's complex with cherry kernels and amaro on the medium-bodied palate, Italianate tannins coat the mouth and the fresh acidity ensures the next sip is as fabulous as the previous one. Screw cap. 13.2% alc. **RATING** 95 **DRINK** 2022–2030 $34 JF ✪

Colmar Estate

790 Pinnacle Road, Orange, NSW 2800 **Region** Orange
T 0419 977 270 **www**.colmarestate.com.au **Open** Mon–Fri 11–4, W'ends & public hols
10–5 **Winemaker** Will Rikard-Bell **Viticulturist** Ian Pearce **Est.** 2013 **Dozens** 2000
Vyds 5.9ha

Owners Bill and Jane Shrapnel have long loved the wines of Alsace: Colmar is the main
town in that region. The Shrapnels realised a long-held ambition when they purchased
an established, high-elevation (980m) vineyard in May '13. Everything they have done has
turned to gold: notably grafting cabernet sauvignon to pinot noir, merlot to chardonnay, and
shiraz to pinot gris. The plantings are now 1.77ha of pinot noir (clones 667, 777, 115 and
MV6), 1.25ha of chardonnay (clones 95, 96 and P58), 1.24ha of riesling and lesser quantities
of pinot gris, gewürztraminer and the Tahbilk clone of shiraz.

Single Vineyard Reserve Chardonnay 2021, Orange Wildly exotic, the
wine showcases perfectly ripe white nectarine, lily of the valley, Meyer lemon
sorbet and Greek yoghurt. Fine sand, triple-cream brie and oyster mushroom,
there are layers upon layers to unpack. Deep-seated natural acidity is delicate,
with the texture of fine lace on the palate. Superb. Screw cap. 13% alc. **RATING** 96
DRINK 2023-2033 $65 SW ✪

Brut 2017, Orange 80/20% pinot noir/chardonnay. A savvy 5 years on lees
for this méthode traditionnelle sparkling. A lovely yellow plum and Rainier
cherry nose with hints of marigold, crème brûlée and shortbread. Juicy ruby red
grapefruit and a long, fine finish. Sophisticated and complex. Cork. 12% alc.
RATING 95 **DRINK** 2023-2030 $50 SW ✪

Chardonnay Pinot Noir 2015, Orange The red fruit character rings true
for this pinot-dominant méthode traditionnelle sparkling, with rhubarb, cherry
and hints of red apple skin moving into hazelnut skin, almond nougat and barley.
Luscious on the palate and densely packed, this is full of flavour. Cleansing
acidity ensures the palate is long and lengthy. Cork. 12% alc. **RATING** 95
DRINK 2023-2028 $65 SW

Block 5 Riesling 2022, Orange Makrut lime leaf, wild ginger and white
nectarine meet chalkboard dust and cracked bluestone. River water freshness with
an innate power to the weight of the wine. Vivid natural acidity ebbs and flows,
carrying those exotic aromas through a long, lingering finish. Will age gracefully
and glacially. Stunning. Screw cap. 12.5% alc. **RATING** 95 **DRINK** 2022-2038
$40 SW ✪

Single Vineyard Riesling 2022, Orange RATING 93 **DRINK** 2022-2035
$35 SW ✪

Single Vineyard Reserve Riesling 2022, Orange RATING 93
DRINK 2022-2038 $60 SW

Block 2 Chardonnay 2021, Orange RATING 93 **DRINK** 2023-2026 $50 SW

Gewürztraminer 2022, Orange RATING 90 **DRINK** 2023-2028 $40 SW

Condie Estate

480 Heathcote-Redesdale Road, Heathcote, Vic 3523 **Region** Heathcote
T 0404 480 422 **www**.condie.com.au **Open** W'ends & public hols 11–5
Winemaker Richie Condie **Viticulturist** Greg Boisgaud **Est.** 2000 **Dozens** 4500
Vyds 17ha

Richie Condie worked as a corporate risk manager for a multinational company off the back
of a bachelor of commerce degree, but after establishing Condie Estate, completed several
viticulture and winemaking courses, including a diploma of winemaking at Dookie. Having
first established 2.4ha of shiraz, Richie and wife Rosanne followed with 2ha of sangiovese and
0.8ha of viognier. In '10 they purchased a '90-planted, 1.6ha vineyard vineyard where they
established a winery and cellar door, and in '19 a 3rd Heathcote vineyard was added to the mix.

The Max Shiraz 2019, Heathcote It's rich in both flavour and texture, its
plum-filled heart coated in nougat, toast and cream. It feels both elemental and

harmonious, both of which suggest that it will live a long life. It's also dry, and while not overly tannic it feels rock solid, structure-wise. Screw cap. 14.7% alc. **RATING** 94 **DRINK** 2024-2034 $50 CM

The Gwen Shiraz 2019, Heathcote Plenty of guts and a good deal of glory. Roasted plums and spices, smoked meats, cedarwood and cloves, a touch of red licorice. It feels solid and substantial but it also has good spread. A little extra through the finish and it could easily have scored higher. Screw cap. 14.7% alc. **RATING** 94 **DRINK** 2024-2032 $35 CM ✪

🍷🍷🍷🍷🍷 **Giarracca Sangiovese 2021, Heathcote RATING** 93 **DRINK** 2023-2027 $35 CM ✪

Schoolhouse Lane GSM 2021, Heathcote RATING 90 **DRINK** 2023-2028 $35 CM

Cooke Brothers Wines

Shed 8, 89-91 Hill Street, Port Elliot, SA 5212 **Region** South Australia **T** 0409 170 684 **www**.cookebrotherswines.com.au **Open** Fri-Sun 12-5 **Winemaker** Ben Cooke **Est.** 2016 **Dozens** 800

The 3 brothers (eldest to youngest) are: Simon, Jason and Ben. Ben is the partner of Charlotte Hardy, winemaker/owner of Charlotte Dalton Wines. While the elder brothers are not actively involved in the business, Ben has had a long career in wine: 7 years' retail for Booze Brothers, 2 vintages at Langhorne Creek '00-01; and full-time cellar hand/assistant winemaker at Shaw + Smith '03-12 while undertaking wine science and viticulture degrees at CSU from '04-11. If this were not enough, he had 3 northern Californian vintages at the iconic Williams Selyem winery in '08, '12 and '13.

🍷🍷🍷🍷🍷 **Shiraz 2021, Barossa Valley** A contemporary rendition of warm-climate shiraz. Tension imparted by a belt of pulpy reduction. Iodine, green olive, blue and purple fruit allusions and a trail of clove and pepper. Fun drinking. Screw cap. 14.5% alc. **RATING** 92 **DRINK** 2022-2030 $35 NG

Savagnin 2022, Langhorne Creek Lanolin, candle wax, preserved lemon and a salty scrape of gin and Mediterranean tonic. There is plenty to love here: the skinsy architecture, the fractured pucker between a parched lip and the line of subtle fruit and the fill of the mid-palate, ineffable of character but present. A wine in the making. Already a lovely thing. Screw cap. 13% alc. **RATING** 91 **DRINK** 2022-2025 $25 NG ✪

Shiraz 2021, Wrattonbully This is solid. A bit fruit sweet, to be pedantic. Yet the raspberry, clove, aniseed and white pepper accents venture long, drifting effortlessly across a full-weighted palate framed by some vanillin oak tannins. Screw cap. 14.5% alc. **RATING** 91 **DRINK** 2022-2028 $45 NG

Cooks Lot

Ferment, 87 Hill Street, Orange, NSW 2800 **Region** Orange **T** (02) 9550 3228 **www**.cookslot.com.au **Open** Tues-Sat 11-5 **Winemaker** Duncan Cook **Est.** 2002 **Dozens** 4000

Duncan Cook began making wines for his eponymous brand in '02, while undertaking his oenology degree at CSU. He completed his degree in '10 and now works with a number of small growers. Fruit is sourced from vineyards at a range of elevations that are best suited for the varietal and wine style.

🍷🍷🍷🍷🍷 **Iconique Barrique R16R17 Unfiltered Pinot Noir 2019, Orange** Shaved jamon, rhubarb stem, freshly picked red cherries and dried autumn leaves. A scattering of wild strawberries and pink peppercorn with dried ceps, wood cuttings and tree sap. A kaleidoscope of aromas and flavours brimming to the surface like a bubbling brook, cherry stem bitterness with taut tannins and rolling acidity. Multi-dimensional and crafted beautifully. Screw cap. 13% alc. **RATING** 96 **DRINK** 2022-2030 $60 SW ✪ ♥

Allotment No. 666 Pinot Gris 2022, Central Ranges You get a lot of pinot gris for your dollars here. Baked pears, candied ginger, quince pie and apple strudel. Alsace inspired, you cannot accuse this wine of insipidness. It's fleshy with apricot kernel, orange blossom and glacé pineapple. A touch of fruit sweetness backed up by nutmeg, cinnamon and Manuka honey and a long, languid flow over the palate. A dazzling wine. Screw cap. 13% alc. **RATING** 95 **DRINK** 2022-2025 $25 SW ✪ ♥

Iconique Barrique R16R17 Pinot Noir 2019, Orange Red cherries overlaid with blackberries, plum skin and dried meats. Crushed pepper and dried thyme. The wine is tightly knit and still coiled, but opens gradually as hints of cassia and nutmeg creep forward with vanilla bean and leather more prominent. Fine tannins and creeping acidity. A wine with time on its side. Screw cap. 13% alc. **RATING** 95 **DRINK** 2022-2032 $60 SW

Coolangatta Estate ★★★★

1335 Bolong Road, Shoalhaven Heads, NSW 2535 **Region** Shoalhaven Coast
T (02) 4448 7131 **www**.coolangattaestate.com.au **Open** 7 days 10–5
Winemaker Tyrrell's **Est.** 1988 **Dozens** 5000 **Vyds** 10.5ha
Coolangatta Estate is part of a 150ha resort. Some of the oldest buildings were convict-built in 1822. The standard of viticulture is exceptionally high and the contract winemaking is wholly professional. Coolangatta has a habit of bobbing up with medals at Sydney and Canberra wine shows, including gold medals for its mature semillons. In its own backyard, Coolangatta won the trophy for Best Wine of Show at the South Coast Wine Show for 19 out of the show's 20 years.

🍷🍷🍷🍷🍷 **Aged Release Individual Vineyard Wollstonecraft Semillon 2014, Shoalhaven Coast** This aged release is hitting its stride with aromas of lime brûlée tart, caramelised quince and preserved lemon. Acidity is sharp and energetic with a yoghurt creaminess in the mid-palate. There is a yin and yang to the flow of this wine, but plenty of tension to see it through another 5–10 years in the cellar. Screw cap. 11.8% alc. **RATING** 93 **DRINK** 2022-2032 $60 SW

Individual Vineyard Wollstonecraft Semillon 2021, Shoalhaven Coast Lemon pulp, lime cordial and apple blossom followed by kiwi fruit and green pear. Honeycomb and bee pollen. The palate is juicy and full of ripe tree fruits. A wine full of flavour and semillon character. Screw cap. 11.5% alc. **RATING** 92 **DRINK** 2022-2035 $60 SW

Aged Release Estate Grown Semillon 2016, Shoalhaven Coast Lemon wedges, orchard apples and fried bread crumbs are complemented by grapefruit juice and passionfruit blossom. Gentle waves of acidity and a créme fraîche creaminess make for an amicable drink with endless food pairing options. Open and harmonious, it's a wine that's hard not to love. Screw cap. 11.6% alc. **RATING** 92 **DRINK** 2022-2030 $60 SW

Estate Grown Semillon 2021, Shoalhaven Coast Lemon verbena, lime oil and wafts of linden flower are met by yellow apple slices and star fruit. Zesty with a paraffin wax note already developing. The palate is full and generous with clover and honey notes, finishing dry and alert. A pliable wine that is drinking well now. Screw cap. 11.5% alc. **RATING** 90 **DRINK** 2022-2032 $40 SW

Coombe Yarra Valley ★★★★★

673-675 Maroondah Highway, Coldstream, Vic 3770 **Region** Yarra Valley
T (03) 9739 0173 **www**.coombeyarravalley.com.au **Open** Wed–Sun 10–5
Winemaker Travis Bush **Viticulturist** Xavier Mende **Est.** 1998 **Dozens** 10000 **Vyds** 60ha
Coombe Yarra Valley is one of the largest and oldest family estates in the region. Once home to world-famous opera singer Dame Nellie Melba, it continues to be owned and operated by her descendants, the Vestey family. Coombe's wines come from 60ha of vineyards planted in '98 on the site of some of the original vineyards planted in the 1850s. The renovated motor house and stable block contain the cellar door, providore, gallery and restaurant.

🍷🍷🍷🍷🍷 **Tribute Series Nellie Melba Blanc de Blancs 2019, Yarra Valley** Aged on lees for 30 months and bottled with 3.5g/L dosage. Bright green gold. Subtle and refined with its aromas of pink grapefruit, baked bread and marine scents. The bead is fine and persistent, gliding effortlessly across the palate. Finishes dry, long and refreshing. An excellent blanc de blancs. Diam. 13% alc. **RATING** 95 **DRINK** 2022-2026 $65 PR
Pinot Gris 2022, Yarra Valley Pale straw with green tinges. Coombe certainly has a knack for pinot gris, and this subtle wine opens with scents of freshly cut pear, jasmine and a little ginger. Dry, chalky textured, balanced and long. Screw cap. 13% alc. **RATING** 95 **DRINK** 2022-2027 $30 PR ✪

🍷🍷🍷🍷🍷 **Rosé NV, Yarra Valley** **RATING** 93 **DRINK** 2022-2025 $30 PR ✪
Lord Sam 2021, Yarra Valley **RATING** 92 **DRINK** 2022-2029 $80 PR

Cooper Burns ★★★★

494 Research Road, Nuriootpa, SA 5355 **Region** Barossa Valley
T 0428 820 928 **www**.cooperburns.com.au **Open** Fri–Mon 11–4
Winemaker Mark Cooper, Russell Burns **Est.** 2004 **Dozens** 3000
Cooper Burns began as a side project of Mark Cooper and Russell Burns as they worked their winemaking day jobs at Treasury Wine Estates and Torbreck respectively. In '17 they established their winery at Nuriootpa and Russell left Torbreck to work full-time at Cooper Burns. The old homestead garage was renovated in '19 and now serves as the cellar door within the grounds of the winery. Wines produced are shiraz, grenache, GSM, cabernet sauvignon, rosé, riesling and chardonnay.

🍷🍷🍷🍷🍷 **Shiraz 2020, Barossa Valley** A deeply coloured and rich shiraz showing notes of ripe blackberry, black cherry and dark plum fruits along with hints of baking spices, brown sugar, licorice, rum and raisin chocolate, earth and clove. Thickly proportioned with tight sandy tannins and plenty of horsepower for those that seek it on the finish. Screw cap. 14.4% alc. **RATING** 90 **DRINK** 2023-2030 $50 DB
The Bloody Valentine Shiraz 2018, Barossa Valley If you are after a big-boned shiraz with a bottle you can bust out some bicep curls with, this should be up your alley. Plum and blackberry jam, prune juice, espresso, dark spice, fig jam, earth and licorice. Full bodied and powerful, there is undoubtedly opulence and heft here but the tannins lack a little resolution and there is a touch of alcohol heat on the finish. Still, it's impressive in its own way. Screw cap. 15% alc. **RATING** 90 **DRINK** 2023-2028 $100 DB

Cooter & Cooter ★★★★☆

82 Almond Grove Road, Whites Valley, SA 5172 (postal) **Region** McLaren Vale
T 0438 766 178 **www**.cooter.com.au **Open** Not **Winemaker** James Cooter, Kimberly Cooter **Est.** 2012 **Dozens** 800 **Vyds** 23ha
James Cooter comes from a family with more than 20 years in the wine industry. Kimberley is also a hands-on winemaker; her father is Walter Clappis, a veteran McLaren Vale winemaker. Their vineyard, on the southern slopes of Whites Valley, has 18ha of shiraz and 3ha of cabernet sauvignon planted in '96, and 2ha of old-vine grenache planted in the '50s. They also buy Clare Valley grapes to make riesling.

🍷🍷🍷🍷🍷 **Watervale Riesling 2022, Clare Valley** By far the best expression of this wine that I can recall. A flutter of poached quince, preserved lemon muddled in tonic, Granny Smith and orange bitters. The finish is energetic enough, but not shrill, brittle or obviously acidified. Joyful, juicy, beautifully weighted and textural. A true pleasure to drink. Screw cap. 12% alc. **RATING** 95 **DRINK** 2022-2032 $25 NG ✪

🍷🍷🍷🍷🍷 **Grenache 2021, McLaren Vale** **RATING** 93 **DRINK** 2022-2028 $35 NG ✪
Shiraz 2021, McLaren Vale **RATING** 93 **DRINK** 2022-2029 $27 NG ✪

Corang Estate

Shop 2, 1-3 Braidwood Road, Tarago, NSW 2580 **Region** Southern New South Wales
T 0400 102 781 **www**.corangestate.com.au **Open** Fri–Mon 10–4 **Winemaker** Michael
Bynon, Alex McKay **Viticulturist** Michael Bynon, Liz Riley **Est.** 2018 **Dozens** 1500
Vyds 1ha

Corang Estate belongs to Michael and Jill Bynon. Michael has been in the wine industry for
30 years, attending Roseworthy Agricultural College and moving from a marketing career to
the senior corporate ranks. He passed the master of wine tasting examination. Jill spent much
time in France before moving to Australia from her native Scotland in '03. It was here that she
met Michael, and having bought a bush block and erected a small house, they planted 0.5ha
each of shiraz and tempranillo in '18. They also purchase grapes from high-altitude vineyards
comparable to that of their own, which is at 600m.

Prosecco 2022, Hilltops Invitingly fresh and lively, especially on a warm day.
There's plenty of fizz matched to flavours of chamomile and lots of citrus with a
lemon saline kick, too, green apple and fresh herbs. Finishes clean and dry. Cork.
12.5% alc. **RATING** 90 **DRINK** 2022-2024 $26 JF

Corduroy

226 Mosquito Hill Road, Mosquito Hill, SA 5214 (postal) **Region** Adelaide Hills
T 0405 123 272 **www**.corduroywines.com.au **Open** Not **Winemaker** Phillip
LeMessurier **Viticulturist** Mark Vella, Ben Lacey **Est.** 2009 **Dozens** 320

Phillip and Eliza LeMessurier continue the model they originally created in the Hunter under
the tutelage of Andrew Thomas at Thomas Wines. In the Hills, they are matching place and
variety to good effect.

Pedro's Pinot Noir 2021, Adelaide Hills Boasts depth and a modicum of
complexity driven by stemmy spice and scents of bracken, dried porcini, campfire
and chinotto, as if the wine were a little older. Rhubarb and fecund strawberry
riffs deliver some sap and fruit sweetness. The acidity, a bit shrill. Solid drinking.
Screw cap. 12.8% alc. **RATING** 92 **DRINK** 2022-2027 $45 NG
Mansfield Chardonnay 2021, Adelaide Hills A mid-weighted wine of white
fig, cantaloupe and stone fruit allusions propelled to modest length by dutiful
freshness and a little jingle jangle. Yet in all, a style that bridles a contemporary
flintiness with creamy lees and oak handling, presumably a nudge of mlf in
keeping. A wine for those seeking energy and tension, as much as the richer
flavours of yore. Screw cap. 12.8% alc. **RATING** 91 **DRINK** 2022-2028 $45 NG

Coriole

Chaffeys Road, McLaren Vale, SA 5171 **Region** McLaren Vale
T (08) 8323 8305 **www**.coriole.com **Open** 7 days 11–5 **Winemaker** Duncan Lloyd
Viticulturist Mark Bates **Est.** 1967 **Dozens** 30 000 **Vyds** 48.5ha

While Coriole was established in '67, the site and gardens date back to 1860, when the
original farm houses that now constitute the cellar door were built. The oldest shiraz forming
part of the estate plantings was planted in 1917, and since '85 Coriole has been an Australian
pioneer of sangiovese and fiano. More recently, it has planted piquepoul, adding to grenache
blanc, negro amaro, sagrantino, montepulciano and prosecco.

Rubato Reserve Fiano 2022, McLaren Vale Among the finest wines of the
Vale. Period. A striking rendition of fiano, a Campanian variety that increasingly
feels at home here. Skin-inflected riffs on ginger, cumquat and barley water,
with fiano's deep dive of pistachio, wild fennel and stone fruits as a backdrop.
A mid-weighted wine of pithy precision, the prodigious intensity of flavour and
compelling saline length. Screw cap. 13% alc. **RATING** 95 **DRINK** 2023-2028
$55 NG
Willunga 1920 Single Vineyard Shiraz 2021, McLaren Vale This is a
beautifully crafted, prodigiously rich iteration of Vale shiraz. Arguably a bit OTT,

yet one cannot deny the treasure trove of kirsch, mint, anise and mocha expanding with old-vine vinous force. The oak, beautifully embedded. The extraction, à point. A sliver of sweetness emerges across the structural barriers, yet the best approach is simply to give in. Screw cap. 14.5% alc. RATING 95 DRINK 2023-2035 $110 NG

Estate Grown Grenache 2021, McLaren Vale Its spicy/savoury aspect has red fruits staring it down, with an honourable peace for each side. It will live for as long as you wish, but will it repay more than a year or two's patience? Screw cap. 14.4% alc. RATING 95 DRINK 2023-2026 $46 JH ✪

Sangiovese 2021, McLaren Vale This is a three-dimensional wine, the bouquet and palate both attesting to its varietal roots, and taking the opportunity offered by the great vintage, the herbal nuances on the finish adding charisma to the equation. Screw cap. 14.3% alc. RATING 95 DRINK 2023-2041 $30 JH ✪

Lloyd Reserve Shiraz 2020, McLaren Vale Unabashedly full bodied. Black fruit allusions, fennel seed, menthol, smoked salumi and astringent oak tannins that feel almost green at this nascent stage. Yet as the wine opens, the fruit reveals itself to the point of a plush, boysenberry pie sweetness. A very good wine for the style. Screw cap. 14.5% alc. RATING 95 DRINK 2023-2035 $120 NG

Sandalwood 2022, McLaren Vale Blend of grenache gris and piquepoul. A full-weighted and textural experience laden with stone-fruit pithiness, crystallised ginger, almond meal and that waxy, warming scent of herb, scrub and green olives. A wonderful first release barely nudging what it can become. Stunning intensity of flavour and driving length. Very impressive. Screw cap. 13% alc. RATING 94 DRINK 2023-2030 $34 NG ✪

Dancing Fig 2021, McLaren Vale An estate-grown blend of mourvèdre, grenache and shiraz. Juicy and joyful with fig, spicy red and purple fruits and blackberry. In this blessed vintage, the fruit arrived when the winemakers wanted it, here it is juicy acidity that carries the flag. Screw cap. 14.4% alc. RATING 94 DRINK 2023-2033 $28 JH ✪

🍷🍷🍷🍷 Piquepoul 2022, McLaren Vale RATING 93 DRINK 2023-2030 $28 JH ✪

Terre de Fer Shiraz Grenache 2021, McLaren Vale RATING 93 DRINK 2023-2032 $60 NG

Montepulciano 2021, McLaren Vale RATING 93 DRINK 2022-2031 $32 NG ✪

The Soloist Single Vineyard Shiraz 2021, McLaren Vale RATING 93 DRINK 2023-2033 $55 NG

Galaxidia Single Vineyard Shiraz 2021, McLaren Vale RATING 93 DRINK 2023-2031 $65 NG

Vita Reserve Sangiovese 2021, McLaren Vale RATING 93 DRINK 2023-2035 $75 NG

Nero 2022, McLaren Vale RATING 92 DRINK 2022-2026 $30 NG ✪

Fiano 2022, McLaren Vale RATING 92 DRINK 2022-2026 $30 NG ✪

Estate Grown Cabernet Sauvignon 2021, McLaren Vale RATING 92 DRINK 2023-2032 $34 NG

Stonewall Grenache 2021, McLaren Vale RATING 92 DRINK 2023-2030 $60 NG

The Riesling Block Single Vineyard Shiraz 2021, McLaren Vale RATING 92 DRINK 2023-2032 $65 NG

The Optimist Single Vineyard Chenin Blanc 2019, McLaren Vale RATING 92 DRINK 2022-2030 $34 NG

Sparta Shiraz 2021, McLaren Vale RATING 91 DRINK 2022-2028 $28 NG ✪

Pettigala Single Vineyard Shiraz 2021, McLaren Vale RATING 91 DRINK 2023-2032 $65 NG

Corryton Burge ★★★★☆

161 Murray Street, Tanunda, SA 5352 **Region** Barossa Valley
T (08) 8563 7575 **www**.corrytonburge.com **Open** Mon–Fri 9–5, Sat 12–5
Winemaker Trent Burge, Andrew Cockram and Matthew Pellew **Est.** 2020 **Dozens** 4000
A new-ish label with a long history. Siblings Trent (winemaker) and Amelia (marketing)
Burge are 6th-generation Barossans. Trent has spent almost 2 decades working in the family
vineyards and winery, creating his Barossa Boy Wines brand; Amelia returned to the business
in '19, also launching her own Amelia Burge Sparkling Wine range. Their shared enterprise
takes its name from the family's grand 1845 Corryton Park Homestead in Eden Valley.
Sourcing is from the Burge family's 300ha of vines in southern and central Barossa and
Adelaide Hills, and a network of 20 growers as far flung as the Coal River Valley in Tasmania.
Their father Grant Burge plays a mentoring role, and the winemaking team at the family's
Illaparra winery is also acknowledged.

🍷🍷🍷🍷 The Brigadier Cabernet Sauvignon 2019, Barossa A bright, cool-
climate cabernet sauvignon with a punchy aromatic profile of sleek blackberry,
blackcurrant and black cherry fruits sheathed with hints of fine spice, tomato
leaf, cedar, mountain herbs, cassis and rose petals. The balance is bang on with
fruit, tannin and acidity all simpatico and heading in the same direction, which is
deliciousness. Bet you it will cellar nicely, too. Screw cap. 13.5% alc. **RATING** 95
DRINK 2023-2035 $45 DB ❂

🍷🍷🍷🍷🍷 Percival Norman Shiraz 2020, Barossa **RATING** 92 **DRINK** 2023-2030 $45 DB
Riesling 2022, Eden Valley **RATING** 91 **DRINK** 2023-2030 $28 DB ❂
Pinot Gris 2022, Adelaide Hills **RATING** 90 **DRINK** 2023-2023 $28 DB

Corymbia ★★★★★

7046 Caves Road, Redgate WA 6286 **Region** Swan Valley
T 0439 973 195 **www**.corymbiawine.com.au **Open** By appt **Winemaker** Robert
Mann, Genevieve Mann **Viticulturist** Robert Mann, Genevieve Mann **Est.** 2013
Dozens 900 **Vyds** 3.5ha
Rob Mann is a 6th-generation winemaker. He was previously chief winemaker at Cape
Mentelle in Margaret River, where he and wife Genevieve lived. Rob's father had established
a family vineyard in the Swan Valley more than 25 years ago, where they both worked
together in Rob's early career. Genevieve worked as a winemaker in her native South Africa,
as well as France, California and South Australia before meeting Rob and moving to Margaret
River in '07 to be winemaker for Howard Park. They now have 3.5ha in Margaret River and
the Swan Valley, planted to 1.6ha chenin blanc, 0.4ha tempranillo, 0.2ha malbec and 1.3ha
cabernet sauvignon.

🍷🍷🍷🍷🍷 Rocket's Vineyard Chenin Blanc 2022, Swan Valley Talk about presence.
This isn't your average white wine, nor indeed your average chenin blanc. Apple,
pear and apricot flavours are at the heart of it but it's the dry, chalky, grippy
feel of it, the out-and-out length, and the firm, uncompromised structure.
It's flavoursome and mouth-watering at once. Terrific. Screw cap. 12.7% alc.
RATING 95 **DRINK** 2024-2032 $35 CM ❂
Cabernet Sauvignon 2021, Margaret River You'd buy this for its oomph
alone but really, it's the structure and the delicious array of complex flavours that
really draws you in. Lashings of tobacco and bacon fat-like characters mingle
with blackcurrant, clove and something sweeter, like pureed strawberries. Dry,
fine-grained tannin cuts a dry swathe through the finish, setting it up for a long
cellaring future. Screw cap. 13.5% alc. **RATING** 95 **DRINK** 2026-2038 $71 CM
Rocket's Vineyard Tempranillo Malbec 2021, Swan Valley You get
upfront fruit, you get structure, you get character. This feels both familiar and
distinctive at once, with iodine, earth and leather flavours flooded through with
juicy red and black berries, florals and sweet spice. It's both firm and flowing, and
puts smoky, reductive notes to positive effect. Screw cap. 13.7% alc. **RATING** 95
DRINK 2024-2034 $42 CM ❂

Cosmo Wines

187 Victoria Road, Chirnside Park, Vic 3116 **Region** Yarra Valley
T 0408 519 461 **www**.cosmowines.com.au **Open** Fri–Sun 11–5, Mon–Thu 11–4
Winemaker Lindsay Corby **Viticulturist** Lindsay Corby **Est.** 2008 **Dozens** 2500
Vyds 2.25ha

Lindsay Corby operates Bianchet Winery, leasing the winery, and vineyard alongside operating the cellar door and producing wines under the Bianchet Vineyard and Cosmo Wines brands. Founder Lou Bianchet passed away without leaving sufficient records, meaning that the planning and liquor licensing approval was required to re-establish the property detail. Three years' work resulted in the creation of a new business structure with all the necessary approvals in place. Lindsay brings an impressive CV, including cellar door sales, laboratory work and vineyard management, leading to teaching 'The art and science of the vine and wine' at La Trobe University and managing the small campus vineyard.

Estate Cabernet Sauvignon Merlot Cabernet Franc 2019, Yarra Valley
A medium, bright ruby red. Dark cherry fruit aromas together with some cedar, tobacco, a little tomato leaf and a hint of balsamic. A medium-bodied wine that builds nicely on the palate. The tannins are ripe and persistent, auguring well for future potential. Screw cap. 12.6% alc. **RATING** 91 **DRINK** 2023-2028 $35 PR
Bianchet Pinot Noir 2020, Yarra Valley A light, bright ruby with an attractive red fruit and spice-accented nose. The palate is sweet-fruited with fine, caressing tannins and decent length. A wine with immediate appeal. 63 dozen made. Screw cap. 12.2% alc. **RATING** 90 **DRINK** 2022-2026 $40 PR

Coughlan Estate

39 Upper Capel Road, Donnybrook, WA 6239 **Region** Geographe
T 0409 831 926 **www**.coughlanestate.com.au **Open** Thurs–Mon 11–4
Winemaker Bruce Dukes, Remi Guise **Viticulturist** Ryan Gibbs **Est.** 1978
Dozens 2000 **Vyds** 3ha

Coughlan Estate (formerly Barton Jones) has 3ha of semillon, chenin blanc, shiraz and cabernet sauvignon from '78 – the vines are some of the oldest in the region. The vineyard and cellar door are on gentle north-facing slopes, with extensive views over the Donnybrook area.

Riesling Chardonnay 2022, Geographe A really easy-drinking white with distinct personality. Some quince and bitter lemon characters, a bit of sea spray and some green apple elements, all harmonious and pleasing. It's got a tight, lightly chalky texture and flavours extend long on briny acidity. All of this adds up to a delicious, refreshing, personality-imbued drink. Screw cap. 12.6% alc.
RATING 92 **DRINK** 2022-2024 $28 MB ✪
Chenin Blanc 2021, Geographe A chenin with loads of personality, tension, balance and finesse. Scents of Parisian almonds, lemon balm, green apple and faint sea spray. Flavours roll around the palate at medium weight with a slick of pleasing almond milk creaminess and ripe apple, lemon curd and tonic water notes. It's a delight to drink, intense but delivering great DNA of the variety. Get stuck in. Screw cap. 13.2% alc. **RATING** 92 **DRINK** 2022-2026 $34 MB
Rosé Shiraz 2022, Geographe An easy-drinking, crisp and clean rosé. It's strawberries and cream but crunchier than that, though there are strong elements of sweet fruit and vanillin character. It has decent length, a sense of purity and energy, evenness, flow and freshness. It feels well made, is the message. Screw cap. 13.4% alc. **RATING** 91 **DRINK** 2022-2024 $28 MB ✪

Coulter Wines

6 Third Avenue, Tanunda, SA 5352 (postal) **Region** Adelaide Hills
T 0448 741 773 **www**.coulterwines.com **Open** By appt **Winemaker** Chris Coulter
Est. 2015 **Dozens** 3000

Chris Coulter fell in love with wine in the early '90s. In '07 he undertook a winemaking degree and secured work with Australian Vintage Limited, gaining large-volume winemaking experience in Mildura and the Barossa Valley, remaining there through '14 under Australian Vintage Limited, and thereafter as part of the 1847 winemaking team after its acquisition of the Yaldara site. Coulter Wines was born in the '15 vintage as a side project, making wines from another universe – nothing other than SO_2 is added, movements are by gravity and the wine is unfiltered where practicable. He purchases and hand picks grapes from vineyards mainly in the Adelaide Hills.

ΨΨΨΨΨ **C5 Barbera 2022, Adelaide Hills** An Australian barbera that actually tastes like barbera, bearing witness to a confluence of site, clone and handling. Bravo! Dark cherry, camphor and clove bristle with an intent and immediacy that only barbera's acidity can convey. A great food wine. This is far from complex, but it is in the right place and in the right hands. Screw cap. 14.5% alc. **RATING** 94 **DRINK** 2022–2026 $34 NG ✪

ΨΨΨΨΨ **C1 Chardonnay 2022, Adelaide Hills RATING** 93 **DRINK** 2022–2030 $34 NG ✪
Small Batch Sangiovese Cabernet 2021, Adelaide Hills RATING 93 **DRINK** 2022–2035 $50 NG
C4 Experimental Tempranillo 2022, Adelaide Hills RATING 92 **DRINK** 2022–2027 $32 NG
C3 Pinot Noir 2022, Adelaide Hills RATING 92 **DRINK** 2022–2030 $35 NG
C4 Single Vineyard Riesling 2022, Eden Valley RATING 90 **DRINK** 2023–2026 $30 DB

Crabtree Watervale Wines ★★★★

North Terrace, Watervale SA 5452 **Region** Clare Valley
T (08) 8843 0069 **www**.crabtreewines.com.au **Open** 7 days 10.30–5 **Winemaker** Kerri Thompson **Est.** 1984 **Dozens** 5500 **Vyds** 12.1ha
Crabtree is situated in the heart of the historic Watervale district, the tasting room and courtyard (set in the produce cellar of the original 1850s homestead) looking out over the estate vineyard. The winery was founded by Robert Crabtree, who built a considerable reputation for medal-winning riesling, shiraz and cabernet sauvignon. In '07 it was purchased by an independent group of wine enthusiasts, and the winery firmly continues in the tradition of estate-grown premium wines.

ΨΨΨΨΨ **Robert Crabtree Riesling 2022, Clare Valley** Quite intense and concentrated in flavour profile. A riesling of power and presence supporting the aspiration of a reserve wine. Scents of lemon curd, lime juice, warm steel and talc. Flavours set to green apple juice, blackcurrant and lime with an undercurrent of pink grapefruit acidity that stretches long. Feels serious in its style, and fancy. Only 210 dozen made. Screw cap. 13.5% alc. **RATING** 94 **DRINK** 2022–2038 $45 MB

ΨΨΨΨΨ **Watervale Cabernet Sauvignon 2019, Clare Valley RATING** 91 **DRINK** 2022–2030 $32 MB

Craiglee ★★★★★

785 Sunbury Road, Sunbury, Vic 3429 **Region** Sunbury
T (03) 9744 4489 **www**.craigleevineyard.com **Open** 1st Sun each month 11–4
Winemaker Patrick Carmody **Est.** 1976 **Dozens** 2000 **Vyds** 9.5ha
What the Carmody family has achieved since it replanted an historic vineyard site in 1976 is as unlikely as it is remarkable. In a largely unheralded region, and surrounded by burgeoning housing estates, it has consistently produced spicy, peppery, medium-weight shiraz of the highest quality and character, in the process establishing itself among the best of the best producers in Australia. Craiglee's reputation is long-held but, if anything, it continues to rise.

ΨΨΨΨΨ **Shiraz 2019, Sunbury** If Pat Carmody can't make great shiraz, then we should all shut up shop. He's only been doing so for, oh, about 40+ years. There's a DNA imprint to this, with a whorl of dark fruit, warm spices shot through, cedary oak and wafts of red roses. Very savoury though, fuller bodied with archetypal Craiglee tannins supple, shapely and ripe. A lovely wine made by a legend. Screw cap. 13.5% alc. RATING 96 DRINK 2023-2035 $65 JF ✪

Chardonnay 2021, Sunbury It has all the trademark rich flavours yet fine acidity throughout. Ripe stone fruit, citrus and lemon curd with cashew lees bolstering the palate. It's flavoursome but not OTT. It's good. It's Craiglee. Screw cap. 13.5% alc. RATING 95 DRINK 2023-2028 $50 JF ✪

Eadie Shiraz 2019, Sunbury Shiraz without viognier, which might explain why it oscillates between ripe dark fruit and savoury tones, including baking spices and cedary oak. It's a little smoky and meaty, too. The palate is shapely with lots of tannins yet finishes long and satisfying. Screw cap. 13.5% alc. RATING 95 DRINK 2023-2033 $45 JF ✪

JADV Shiraz 2019, Sunbury There's such beautiful texture and a feel to Craiglee shiraz, even this with just a dash of viognier (aka JADV). It remains savoury yet plush with juicy fruit, succulence and such plump tannins. The finish lingers as does the desire to pour another glass, quickly. Screw cap. 13.5% alc. RATING 95 DRINK 2023-2033 $45 JF ✪

🍷🍷🍷🍷🍷 Cabernet Sauvignon 2019, Sunbury RATING 92 DRINK 2024-2033 $45 JF

Craigow ★★★★★

528 Richmond Road, Cambridge, Tas 7170 **Region** Southern Tasmania
T 0418 126 027 www.craigow.com.au **Open** By appt **Winemaker** Frogmore Creek (Alain Rousseau), Tasmanian Vintners **Est.** 1989 **Dozens** 800 **Vyds** 8.75ha

Barry and Cathy Edwards moved from being grapegrowers with only one wine to a portfolio of impressive wines – with long-lived riesling of particular quality, closely attended by pinot noir – while continuing to sell most of their grapes. Craigow's wines express the unique character of the Coal River region. Varieties are selected to suit the area's growing conditions – they're the same cool-climate European varieties that thrive in Burgundy, Alsace and the Loire Valley.

🍷🍷🍷🍷🍷 **Riesling 2022, Tasmania** A wonderfully composed Coal River riesling. Aromas of lemon, lime and crunchy green apple are joined by hints of white flowers, crushed slate, white peach and further back, cool tones of cucumber and freshly sliced fennel. Just a suggestion of texture with pure citrus and peach fruits on rails of porcelain acidity. Vivid and mesmerising drinking. Screw cap. 12% alc. RATING 95 DRINK 2023-2035 $33 DB ✪

Pinot Noir 2021, Tasmania The wine presents itself with a complex, distinctly burgundian air. Finely composed with delicate cherry and raspberry tones cut through with spice, floral notes, sous bois and gentle spice from French oak. Spacious and airy with a graceful, elegant line, it makes for wonderful drinking. Screw cap. 13% alc. RATING 95 DRINK 2023-2032 $50 DB ✪

🍷🍷🍷🍷🍷 Chardonnay 2021, Tasmania RATING 93 DRINK 2023-2027 $35 DB ✪
Sauvignon Blanc 2021, Tasmania RATING 93 DRINK 2023-2027 $33 DB ✪
Rosé 2022, Tasmania RATING 92 DRINK 2023-2025 $33 DB

Crawford River Wines ★★★★★

741 Hotspur Upper Road, Condah, Vic 3303 **Region** Henty
T 0407 332 652 www.crawfordriverwines.com **Open** By appt **Winemaker** Belinda Thomson **Viticulturist** Belinda Thomson **Est.** 1975 **Dozens** 3000 **Vyds** 11ha

Once a tiny outpost in a little-known wine region, Crawford River is now a foremost producer of riesling (and other excellent wines), originally thanks to the unremitting attention to detail and skill of its founder and winemaker, John Thomson. Daughter Belinda has been chief winemaker since '12 and has experience in Marlborough, Bordeaux, Tuscany and the Nahe. Between '08 and '16 she was a senior winemaker and technical director of a winery in Rueda, Spain.

♥♥♥♥♥ **Reserve Riesling 2018, Henty** This is a wine of both power and texture, but more importantly, it's a wine of complexity. It engages you. Citrus rind, grapefruit, petroleum, crushed fennel seeds and bright orange blossom characters put on a display that is at once exquisite and kaleidoscopic. Screw cap. 13% alc. **RATING** 96 **DRINK** 2023-2032 $95 CM ♥

Riesling 2022, Henty Crawford River rieslings are absolute pearls. This is yet another. Intense lime and general citrus flavour with cutting acidity and slips of fruit sweetness. Blossom, rind, juice — we get the whole fruit. This isn't just refreshing, it's revitalising and lifts your spirits. Screw cap. 13.5% alc. **RATING** 95 **DRINK** 2023-2036 $54 CM

Strata Riesling 2022, Henty This is the wine formerly known as Young Vines. This release is both textural and intense. The mouthfeel has a squeakiness, the fruit is pure and open, and for all its citrusy, crushed fennel, open-weave flourishes the flavours still manage to extend beautifully through the finish. Screw cap. 13% alc. **RATING** 95 **DRINK** 2023-2032 $38 CM ✿

Cabernet Sauvignon 2018, Henty Such a dry, elongated style. This sits distinctly in the 'more length than breadth' category. Pencils, boysenberry and redcurrant flavours are seamlessly infused with fragrant and woodsy herb notes. Tannin presents as a firm, taut web through the finish, strong and fine at once. It's a mouth-watering rendition of cabernet, and a very good one at that. Screw cap. 14% alc. **RATING** 94 **DRINK** 2025-2034 $68 CM

♥♥♥♥♀ **Cabernet Sauvignon 2016, Henty RATING** 93 **DRINK** 2022-2031 $60 JP
Beta Sauvignon Blanc Semillon 2018, Henty RATING 90 **DRINK** 2022-2025 $32 JP

 ## Cré   ★★★☆

119 Lorimers Lane Dixons Creek, Vic 3775 **Region** Yarra Valley
T 0402 282 449 **www**.crewines.com.au **Open** W'ends 12–4 **Winemaker** JonJo McEvoy, Oliver Johns **Viticulturist** JonJo McEvoy, Oliver Johns **Est.** 2018 **Dozens** 1100 **Vyds** 4ha

Cré was started in '18 by JonJo McEvoy, Oliver Johns and Angus Hean. The name is Gaelic for clay, a reference to the soils beneath their Dixons Creek vineyard. Two-thirds of production is homegrown, the remainder sourced from vineyards in the Dixons Creek valley and Woori Yallock in the Upper Yarra. Varieties employed include chardonnay, riesling, pinot noir, savagnin, sauvignon blanc, cabernet sauvignon, cabernet franc, merlot and petit verdot. All wines are fermented with indigenous yeasts. The cellar door shares a home with the winemakers' second (and also very natural) label, Fin.

♥♥♥♥♀ **Nouveau Syrah 2021, Yarra Valley** This is so fresh it's crisp. You could serve it chilled. It's light, frisky, racy; all those things. It has more than a little animal-like character. Toast notes, tonic and tobacco all mixed in with fresh, red-berried fruit. It carries an ever-so-slight spritz, too, which emphasises its freshness all the more. Diam. 10.9% alc. **RATING** 90 **DRINK** 2022-2024 $32 CM

Credaro Family Estate   ★★★★☆

2175 Caves Road, Yallingup, WA 6282 **Region** Margaret River
T (08) 9756 6520 **www**.credarowines.com.au **Open** 7 days 10.30–5 **Winemaker** Trent Kelly, Paul Callaghan **Viticulturist** Chris Credaro **Est.** 1988 **Dozens** 25 000 **Vyds** 110ha

The Credaro family settled in Margaret River in 1922, migrating from northern Italy. Initially a few small plots of vines were planted to provide the family with wine in the European tradition. The most recent vineyard acquisition was a 40ha property, with 18ha of vines, in Wilyabrup and the winery has been expanded. Credaro now has 7 separate vineyards, spread throughout Margaret River; Credaro either owns or leases each property and grows and manages the vines with its own viticulture team.

ΥΥΥΥΥ **1000 Crowns Shiraz 2021, Margaret River** Deep, vivid purple crimson. The wine has a menagerie of dark berry fruits of every type in its full-bodied palate. What it does not have are threatening tannins – they are velvety and smooth. The inherent balance of the wine will underwrite a 30–40 year life. Screw cap. 14% alc. **RATING** 95 **DRINK** 2023–2042 $80 JH

Kinship Shiraz 2021, Margaret River This is a pretty smart shiraz, a variety now well and truly established in Margaret River, no apologies needed. It's medium bodied, with bright red and black berry fruits, fine tannins and overall balance. You get your money's worth. Screw cap. 14.5% alc. **RATING** 94 **DRINK** 2023–2036 $40 JH ✪

ΥΥΥΥ **1000 Crowns Chardonnay 2021, Margaret River** **RATING** 93 **DRINK** 2023–2029 $75 JH

1000 Crowns Cabernet Sauvignon 2020, Margaret River **RATING** 93 **DRINK** 2023–2040 $100 JH

Kinship Chardonnay 2022, Margaret River **RATING** 92 **DRINK** 2022–2028 $40 JF

Kinship Cabernet Sauvignon 2021, Margaret River **RATING** 92 **DRINK** 2023–2033 $40 JF

Five Tales Chardonnay 2022, Margaret River **RATING** 90 **DRINK** 2022–2026 $24 JF ✪

CRFT Wines   ★★★★★

45 Rangeview Drive, Carey Gully, SA 5144 **Region** Adelaide Hills
T 0413 475 485 **www**.crftwines.com.au **Open** Fri–Sun 11–5 **Winemaker** Candice Helbig, Frewin Ries **Viticulturist** Candice Helbig, Frewin Ries **Est.** 2012 **Dozens** 2000 **Vyds** 3.2ha

NZ-born Frewin Ries and Barossa-born Candice Helbig, life and business partners, crammed multiple wine lives into a relatively short period, before giving up secure jobs to start CRFT in '12. Frewin's CV includes Cloudy Bay and the iconic Sonoma pinot noir producer Williams Selyem, among others. Candice is a 6th-generation Barossan. She trained as a lab technician before moving to winemaking at Hardys, gaining her degree in oenology and viticulture from CSU and on to Boar's Rock and Mollydooker. The core focus is on small-batch, single-vineyard Adelaide Hills pinot noir, chardonnay and grüner veltliner. The Arranmore vineyard was purchased in '16, gaining organic certification in '19, and wines are made with a minimal-intervention approach.

ΥΥΥΥ **K1 Vineyard Kuitpo Grüner Veltliner 2022, Adelaide Hills** The greatest fidelity to variety shown by this swag of grüner: nettle, white pepper, wild pea fronds and citrus balm. Finely hewn, chiselled and almost pixelated of structural detail, from freshness to sandy slake long. A delicious wine that bodes exciting times for the variety in these parts. Screw cap. 13.5% alc. **RATING** 95 **DRINK** 2022–2027 $31 NG ✪

The Blefari Vineyard Chardonnay 2022, Adelaide Hills Very fine, as much by virtue of its relaxed mid-weighted gait, as its tension. Yet this is tension imparted by an intuitive hand. Toasted hazelnuts, apricot pith, curd and truffled cheese, not dissimilar to good meursault. Long, nicely chewy and strident of confidence. Screw cap. 12.5% alc. **RATING** 95 **DRINK** 2022–2030 $55 NG

The Arranmore Vineyard Chardonnay 2022, Adelaide Hills A febrile, tensile expression, yet with no sacrifice of flavour, nor any forage into the wilderness of hard reduction. A chiselled nose of white peach, nougatine, cashew and just the right amount of flint. The finish is long and contagious of intensity. Very good. Linear, taut and an exemplar for those who seek to make tighter styles of chardonnay. Screw cap. 12% alc. **RATING** 95 **DRINK** 2022–2030 $55 NG

The Swaby Vineyard Chardonnay 2022, Adelaide Hills A ripe, rich, full and flavourful expression. This is no misguided wander into excess. Dried mango, nectarine, peach and an evident curb of vanillin oak imparting its own creamy velour to the fray. The finish is mellifluous, long and finely wrought. Screw cap. 13.5% alc. **RATING** 94 **DRINK** 2022–2030 $55 NG

ABCDEY Arranmore Vineyard Grüner Veltliner 2022, Adelaide Hills RATING 93
DRINK 2022–2028 $31 NG ✪
The Landsdowne Vineyard Chardonnay 2022, Adelaide Hills RATING 93
DRINK 2022–2030 $39 NG
The Mt Bera Vineyard Grüner Veltliner 2022, Adelaide Hills RATING 92
DRINK 2022–2026 $31 NG
The Rohrlach Vineyard Mencia 2022, Barossa Valley RATING 92
DRINK 2022–2026 $30 NG ✪

Crittenden Estate   ★★★★★

25 Harrisons Road, Dromana, Vic 3936 **Region** Mornington Peninsula
T (03) 5981 8322 **www**.crittendenwines.com.au **Open** 7 days 10.30–4.30
Winemaker Rollo Crittenden, Matt Campbell **Viticulturist** Rollo Crittenden, Garry
Crittenden **Est.** 1982 **Dozens** 10 000 **Vyds** 4.8ha
Garry Crittenden was a pioneer on the Mornington Peninsula, establishing the family
vineyard over almost 40 years and introducing a number of avant-garde techniques.
Much has changed – and continues to change – in cool-climate vineyard management.
Crittenden has abandoned the use of synthetic fertilisers in the vineyard, instead focusing
on biological soil health using natural tools such as compost and cover crops. Pinot noir and
chardonnay remain the principal focus at the top tier, but they also produce some remarkable
savagnin made under flor in the Jura style. Today, Garry is semi-retired, with son Rollo
overseeing Crittenden's winemaking and daughter Zoe the marketing side.

ABCDE Cri de Coeur Sous Voile Savagnin 2018, Mornington Peninsula
Four years under flor in old barrels with no intervention, this vin jaune style
is very, very difficult to make. To date, this shows amazing poached quinces,
ripe yellow peach with lemon zest and preserved lemons. Nutty aldehydes are
embossed into the wine, the palate is alive with acidity and vitality. It's complex
and delicious and it gives me goosebumps. Yep. Perfect. Diam. 15.5% alc.
RATING 97 DRINK 2023–2035 $95 JF ✪ ♥

ABCDE Pinot Gris 2022, Mornington Peninsula Full of nashi pear and ginger
spice, baked apples and lemon zest with a touch of clotted cream. Not sweet,
this is textural and rich yet the finish lingers, revitalised thanks to tangy acidity.
Screw cap. 13% alc. RATING 95 DRINK 2023–2027 $37 JF ✪
Cri de Coeur Chardonnay 2021, Mornington Peninsula The mistake with
this wine – or any chardonnay, for that matter – is to serve it too cold. That just
muffles the flavours. Guilty. However, this opened up in no time allowing a full
spread of stone fruit, lemon, mandarin, ginger fluff cake and clotted cream. The
oak is neatly embedded into the body, adding some depth and spicy nuances,
and the superfine acidity drives this to a Formula 1 finish. Diam. 12.5% alc.
RATING 95 DRINK 2023–2031 $95 JF
The Zumma Chardonnay 2021, Mornington Peninsula Smoky, flinty and
a little funky with lots of citrus and stone fruit dressed up with spices and cedar
oak. There's an evenness across the palate with plenty of mouth-watering acidity.
Really delicious. Screw cap. 12.5% alc. RATING 95 DRINK 2023–2031 $65 JF
Cri de Coeur Pinot Noir 2021, Mornington Peninsula A vibrant garnet.
Fragrant with florals and autumn leaves after rain with flavours of morello and
sweet red cherries, tamarind and turmeric, pepper and aniseed melding into
the medium-bodied palate. The raw silk tannins have some sway and are just
coming into unison, with the acidity allowing a lingering finish. Diam. 12.5% alc.
RATING 95 DRINK 2024–2034 $95 JF
Macvin #4 Savagnin NV, Mornington Peninsula Lovely golden amber glint
to the colour; full of honeycomb and quince paste, grilled nuts and seaweed with
moreish aldehydes and wafts of antique furniture fragrance. The palate is clean and
lively with the acidity curtailing the sweetness and evening the palate. The golden
fruit flavour is very much at the forefront, making this absurdly fresh. Screw cap.
17% alc. RATING 95 $95 JF

Peninsula Chardonnay 2021, Mornington Peninsula The name reflects the selection of sites across the Mornington Peninsula; 30% mlf gives the wine a creamy cashew nuance to the fig and stone-fruit palate. Overall, has good line, length and balance; grapefruit makes a final curtain call. Screw cap. 12.5% alc. RATING 94 DRINK 2023–2027 $37 JH

ㅜㅜㅜㅜ Kangerong Chardonnay 2021, Mornington Peninsula RATING 93 DRINK 2023–2030 $45 JF
The Zumma Pinot Noir 2021, Mornington Peninsula RATING 92 DRINK 2024–2034 $65 JF
Peninsula Pinot Noir 2021, Mornington Peninsula RATING 90 DRINK 2023–2026 $37 JF
Kangerong Pinot Noir 2021, Mornington Peninsula RATING 90 DRINK 2024–2030 $45 JF

CS Wine Co ★★★★

600 Banks Road, Marcus HIll, Vic 3222 (postal) **Region** Heathcote
T 0419 568 531 **www**.cswineco.com.au **Open** Not **Winemaker** Charlie Swan
Est. 2014 **Dozens** 400
CS Wine Co is the one-man band of Bellarine-based Charlie Swan. There are 3 wines in the range (shiraz, nero d'Avola and rosé), all made with fruit from a range of Heathcote vineyard sources, Chalmers, Wanted Man and Greenstone among them.

ㅜㅜㅜㅜ Shiraz 2020, Heathcote Contained lusciousness. This is all toast and roasted plums, redcurrant and cloves, with woodsmoke notes threaded through, along with chocolate. In others words, it brings flavour to the table, dark-hearted flavour, and a good deal of it. On a cold night, this will do nicely. Screw cap. 13.5% alc. RATING 93 DRINK 2023–2028 $29 CM
Nero d'Avola 2020, Heathcote Overt floral and mint aromas lead to a dry, almost sturdy palate that lays leather flavours into raspberry, and dry spice into rust. It's a neat, mid-weight and contained wine that doesn't lack charisma. Screw cap. 13.2% alc. RATING 90 DRINK 2023–2027 $29 CM

Cullen Wines ★★★★★

4323 Caves Road, Wilyabrup, WA 6280 **Region** Margaret River
T (08) 9755 5277 **www**.cullenwines.com.au **Open** 7 days 10–4.30 **Winemaker** Vanya Cullen, Andy Barrett-Lennard **Viticulturist** Brian Martin **Est.** 1971 **Dozens** 20 000
Vyds 49ha
A pioneer of Margaret River, Cullen Wines has always produced long-lived wines of highly individual style. The vineyard has progressed beyond organic to biodynamic certification and, subsequently, has become the first vineyard and winery in Australia to be certified carbon positive. Winemaking is in the hands of Vanya Cullen, daughter of founders Kevin and Diana Cullen; she is possessed of an extraordinarily good palate and generosity to the cause of fine wine. Vanya was awarded the Companion's inaugural Viticulturist of the Year in 2022, Cullen's 50th anniversary year.

ㅜㅜㅜㅜㅜ Kevin John Wilyabrup 2021, Margaret River The colour pick-up is substantial, but there's nothing in the bouquet that suggests premature ageing or maderisation, et al. It's complex but harmonious, long and balanced. There's more stone fruit, fig and melon than citrus, but that's intentional, and in tune with the Wilyabrup subregion. Screw cap. 13% alc. RATING 97 DRINK 2023–2041 $160 JH
Diana Madeline Wilyabrup 2021, Margaret River This is a wine that can come from nowhere else, so strong is its sense of place. Expect to swoon over aromas of roses, violets and mulberries doused in baking spices, a ferruginous quality as much as detailed if persuasive tannins. It's complex, complete and structured. Gosh, what a wine. What a woman. The perfect combination. Screw cap. 13.5% alc. RATING 97 DRINK 2025–2045 $160 JF

ɣɣɣɣɣ **Kevin John Wilyabrup 2022, Margaret River** Even if this is a rich rendition full of white stone fruit, quince paste with pomelo dusted in ginger powder and daikon, it has the Kevin John thumbprint. And while that's all well and lovely, it's how this feels that makes it special: dense yet succulent, fleshy and full with umami lees, this is pulsing with flavour and energy and the oak gives off a savoury appearance. As always, compelling. Screw cap. 13.5% alc. **RATING** 96 **DRINK** 2023-2035 $160 JF

Vanya Full Moon Fruit Day Cabernet Sauvignon 2019, Margaret River A wine shaped by 100% cabernet and complete in every way. It's fragrant with florals, woodsy spices, cassis, mulberries with a dusting of cocoa and warm earth. It's medium-bodied, long and detailed with beautifully shaped tannins – fine, ripe and textural. Approachable now yet time will give this more layers and depth. Screw cap. 13% alc. **RATING** 96 **DRINK** 2022-2039 $650 JF

Mangan Vineyard Sauvignon Blanc Semillon 2022, Margaret River A 60/33/7% blend of sauvignon blanc, semillon and verdelho, hand picked on biodynamic fruit and flower days, naturally fermented with no acid additions. It has that oxymoronic coupling of intense, layered tropical fruit and a herbal undercut of lemony acidity. Screw cap. 13% alc. **RATING** 95 **DRINK** 2023-2027 $29 JH ✪

Amber 2022, Margaret River Another excellent rendition with its blood orange zest, glacé lemon, ginger spice, quinine and pliable phenolics that ebb and flow across the palate. Complex yet refreshing; at this youthful stage, the tannins and acidity are doing the tango and will eventually slow down to a bolero. Screw cap. 13% alc. **RATING** 95 **DRINK** 2023-2030 $39 JF ✪

Mangan East Block Wilyabrup 2022, Margaret River An outrageously dark purple hue – so enticing in the glass. Then violets, plums and mulberries come to the fore with squid ink and charcuterie, nori and savoury nuances following closely. The palate is rich and big, packed with decent tannins and a little drying and refreshing acidity to close. Impressive and will mellow more in time. Screw cap. 13.9% alc. **RATING** 95 **DRINK** 2024-2034 $55 JF

Grace Madeline 2022, Margaret River Nothing tropical here, and it's so racy and tight it leaves a smoke trail in its wake. Very youthful with some citrus and coriander, lemon barley water and a briny character; all appealing and the fruit has soaked up the new oak easily. This will only get better in time. Screw cap. 13% alc. **RATING** 95 **DRINK** 2023-2030 $39 JF ✪

Amber 2021, Margaret River A pale amber hue and enticing wafts of potpourri, dried orange peel and fennel, a bit like the fragrance of a calming herbal tea. The palate revs up the taste buds, with neat phenolics adding a gentle grip and chew to the finish and the acidity driving it long. A delicious rendition, again. Screw cap. 12.5% alc. **RATING** 95 **DRINK** 2022-2026 $39 JF ✪

Grace Madeline 2020, Margaret River A stylish, restrained fumé style with pomelo and lemon-lime saline flavours, a touch of guava, too, woodsy spices and mouth-watering, smoky match-struck sulphides. It has texture with some phenolic grip to the finish. Complex and detailed yet its refreshing acidity makes it tempting to drink now although it will garner more complexity with age. Screw cap. 12.5% alc. **RATING** 95 **DRINK** 2022-2030 $39 JF ✪

ɣɣɣɣɣ **Mangan Vineyard Preservative Free Malbec 2022, Margaret River** **RATING** 92 **DRINK** 2022-2025 $50 JF

Wilyabrup Cabernet Sauvignon Merlot 2022, Margaret River **RATING** 92 **DRINK** 2024-2034 $45 JF

Mangan Vineyard Wilyabrup Red Moon 2022, Margaret River **RATING** 92 **DRINK** 2024-2034 $35 JF

Cupitt's Estate   ★★★★★

58 Washburton Road, Ulladulla, NSW 2539 **Region** Shoalhaven Coast
T (02) 4455 7888 **www.cupittsestate.com.au Open** 7 days 11–5 by appt
Winemaker Wally Cupitt **Est.** 2007 **Dozens** 9000 **Vyds** 3ha

Griff and Rosie Cupitt run a combined winery, restaurant, brewery, fromagerie and farm. Rosie studied oenology at CSU and has more than a decade of vintage experience, taking in France and Italy. The Cupitts have 3ha of vines centred on sauvignon blanc and semillon, and also source fruit from Hilltops, Tumarumba, Orange, the Yarra Valley and Canberra District. Sons Wally and Tom now lead the business, as winemaker and general manager respectively.

Merlot 2021, Hilltops The familiar aromas of plums, black cherry and graphite are immediate in this Hilltops merlot. Cinnamon quill, star anise and black gravel come through with a plushness of acid and skinsy tannin grip. This is a wine for drinking with great chatter and plenty of smiles. Screw cap. 14% alc. **RATING** 95 **DRINK** 2022–2030 $38 SW ☻

Fiano 2021, Hilltops Pushed to the limit of extraction here with golden baked pears, Manuka honey and apple strudel. Hay bales, candle wax and enoki mushrooms. A distinct wine that speaks of texture and nutty nuances. A modern style in today's Australian fiano realm. Bold. Screw cap. 12.7% alc. **RATING** 95 **DRINK** 2022–2028 $34 SW ☻

Viognier 2022, Hilltops RATING 93 **DRINK** 2022–2026 $32 SW ☻
Barbera 2021, Hilltops RATING 93 **DRINK** 2022–2032 $38 SW
Sommet Des Colline Cabernet Sauvignon Merlot 2019, Hilltops RATING 93 **DRINK** 2022–2028 $62 SW
Arneis 2022, Canberra District RATING 92 **DRINK** 2022–2025 $32 SW
Dusty Dog Shiraz 2021, Hilltops RATING 92 **DRINK** 2022–2030 $52 SW
Nebbiolo 2021, Hilltops RATING 92 **DRINK** 2022–2030 $36 SW
Dusty Dog Shiraz 2019, Hilltops RATING 91 **DRINK** 2023–2025 $52 SW
Riesling 2022, Hilltops RATING 90 **DRINK** 2022–2030 $32 SW
The Pointer Pinot Noir 2021, Tumbarumba RATING 90 **DRINK** 2022–2025 $42 SW
The Pointer Chardonnay 2021, Tumbarumba RATING 90 **DRINK** 2022–2026 $38 SW
Malbec 2021, Hilltops RATING 90 **DRINK** 2022–2030 $38 SW

Curator Wine Company ★★★★★

28 Jenke Road, Marananga, SA 5355 **Region** Barossa Valley
T 0411 861 604 **www**.curatorwineco.com.au **Open** By appt **Winemaker** Tom White, Daniel Zolotarev **Viticulturist** Sam Dahlitz **Est.** 2012 **Dozens** 5000 **Vyds** 8ha
This business is owned by Tom and Bridget White, who decided to focus on shiraz and cabernet sauvignon from the Barossa Valley, a decision that has been rewarded. The vineyard at Marananga is planted on ancient red soils rich in ironstone and quartzite, and the wines are naturally fermented.

White Label Greenock Vineyard Shiraz 2021, Barossa Valley Inviting aromas of satsuma plum and liqueur cherry fruits cut with hints of baking spices, amaro herbs, violets, olive tapenade, dark chocolate, pastis and roasting meats. Full bodied with a gorgeous fruit density and flow, tightly packed powdery tannin etched with ironstone and graphite and a long, sustained finish. Diam. 14.5% alc. **RATING** 95 **DRINK** 2023–2035 $58 DB

Stonehouse Neldner Vineyard Shiraz 2020, Barossa Valley Bright crimson with lifted aromas of blackberry, black cherry and dark plum fruits. Dark and clove-like with a pinch of volatile acidity sending the blackcurrant notes into the pastille territory. There is a dark, broody presence on the palate with blackstrap licorice and dark chocolate tones coming through with plenty of ripe tannin and drive along its length. It's got some power. Diam. 14.5% alc. **RATING** 95 **DRINK** 2023–2033 $150 DB

Grenache 2021, Barossa Valley Lifted and perfumed with pure, juicy plummy fruits taking centre stage along with hints of dried cranberries, charcuterie, exotic spices, ginger cake, cola, earth and lighter wafts of hoisin, rose petals and jasmine. Those aromas transpose neatly over to a palate that shows great fruit purity, flow and inherent drinkability. Screw cap. 14.5% alc. **RATING** 94 **DRINK** 2023–2027 $35 DB ☻

ＹＹＹＹ **Greenock Vineyard Shiraz 2021, Barossa Valley** RATING 93
DRINK 2023–2033 $58 DB
Cabernet Sauvignon 2020, Barossa Valley RATING 93 **DRINK** 2023–2030
$35 DB ✪
Hamlets Rosé Montepulciano 2022, Barossa Valley RATING 92
DRINK 2023–2025 $25 DB ✪
Shiraz 2021, Barossa Valley RATING 92 **DRINK** 2023–2030 $35 DB
Hamlets Shiraz 2021, Barossa Valley RATING 92 **DRINK** 2023–2028 $30 DB ✪

Curly Flat ★★★★★

263 Collivers Road, Lancefield, Vic 3435 **Region** Macedon Ranges
T (03) 5429 1956 **www**.curlyflat.com **Open** Fri–Mon 12–5 **Winemaker** Matt Harrop,
Ben Kimmorley **Viticulturist** Damien Hall **Est.** 1992 **Dozens** 6000 **Vyds** 14.6ha
Pinot noir of power, chardonnay of both precision and weight, pinot gris of texture and
interest. Curly Flat was founded by Philip Moraghan and Jenni Kolkka in '91, although Jenni
has been the sole owner since '17. It is long-established as an elite producer, a reputation
that has been upheld and extended under the watch of current winemaker Matt Harrop.
Indeed Matt's separation of individual parts of the vineyard, for release as stand-alone wines,
has proven to be both an inspired and a fascinating development.

ＹＹＹＹＹ **Central Pinot Noir 2021, Macedon Ranges** Central is usually my top Curly
Flat pinot thanks to its core of fantastic, concentrated fruit. All ripe and plump yet
neatly contained with juicy pomegranate acidity and lots of twiggy, sappy whole-
bunch flavours, which are not overt just part of this complex wine. Vibrant,
electrifying even. Screw cap. 13.6% alc. RATING 96 **DRINK** 2023–2035 $61 JF ✪
White Pinot 2022, Macedon Ranges From the moment this is poured, its
pale bronze hue enticing, everything falls into place. This has heaps of texture,
vibrancy, zesty acidity and tangy red fruits with a hint of cardamom and terrific
length. Savoury, scintillating and slurpable from go to whoa. Screw cap. 12.5% alc.
RATING 95 **DRINK** 2022–2026 $30 JF ✪
Pinot Noir 2021, Macedon Ranges Plenty of cherry in this, red and morello
in particular. It has some whole-bunch punch both aromatically and on the palate,
zesty and tangy with perky acidity a feature this vintage. Plenty of tannins work
across the medium-bodied palate, too, and there's a lipsmacking, moreish finish.
Screw cap. 13.7% alc. RATING 95 **DRINK** 2023–2035 $61 JF
Chardonnay 2021, Macedon Ranges Ah Curly Flat chardonnay, you good
thing. You tease with tangy fruit all citrusy and white nectarines all spiced up then
the palate tantalises with scrumptious leesy flavours and sweet cedary oak. The
final flirt is a line of fine, pure acidity holding everything neatly in place. Pretty
classy seduction. Screw cap. 13.2% alc. RATING 95 **DRINK** 2022–2033 $50 JF ✪
Pinot Gris 2022, Macedon Ranges This is about as racy as pinot gris can
get. Hence, a bit more citrus to the fresh pear flavours, tangy and juicy with
succulence throughout. Really fine creamy lees, some lemony flavour, too, and
the palate just sings. It's a refreshing style and very pleasing. Screw cap. 12.5% alc.
RATING 94 **DRINK** 2022–2026 $30 JF ✪

ＹＹＹＹＹ **Western Pinot Noir 2021, Macedon Ranges** RATING 93 **DRINK** 2024–2034
$61 JF

Curtis Family Vineyards ★★★★

514 Victor Harbor Road, McLaren Vale, SA 5171 (postal) **Region** McLaren Vale
T 0439 800 484 **www**.curtisfamilyvineyards.com **Open** By appt **Winemaker** Mark
Curtis **Est.** 1973 **Dozens** 10 000 **Vyds** 50ha
The Curtis family traces its history back to 1499 when Paolo Curtis was appointed by
Cardinal de Medici to administer Papal lands in the area around Cervaro. (The name Curtis
is believed to derive from Curtius, a noble and wealthy Roman Empire family.) The family
has been growing grapes and making wine in McLaren Vale since '73, having come to
Australia in '53.

ŦŦŦŦ♀ **Ancestor Shiraz 2020, McLaren Vale** This will placate drinkers of large-framed Aussie reds while piquing the curiosity of those interested in how richness of flavour, structural mettle, oak and sheer tenacity can find harmony. Stewed plum, dried nori, cardamom and menthol lozenge drive long. Some malty oak, a welcome signpost. Already approachable, but this will cellar well all the same. Cork. 14% alc. RATING 92 DRINK 2022–2033 $180 NG

Cavaliere Shiraz 2020, McLaren Vale Another traditional stalwart. This boasts a slightly more contemporary framework than others in the suite. Damson plum, Bing cherry, vanilla pod oak, bitter chocolate and a vivacious floral lift. The tannins, considerably more refined. The finish, relatively effortless and pointed long. Not without charm. Screw cap. 14% alc. RATING 91 DRINK 2022–2030 $70 NG

Martins Vineyard Shiraz 2020, McLaren Vale Old-school and avuncular, reminiscent of the full-bodied, medicinal expressions of shiraz that I drank as a university student. Menthol liniment, spiced cherry, clove, cardamom, licorice strap and vanilla. Warm and expansive, while boasting considerable charm if not a great deal of finesse. Screw cap. 14% alc. RATING 90 DRINK 2022–2030 $50 NG

d'Arenberg   ★★★★

58 Osborn Road, McLaren Vale, SA 5171 **Region** McLaren Vale
T (08) 8329 4888 **www.**darenberg.com.au **Open** 7 days 10.30–4.30
Winemaker Chester Osborn, Jack Walton **Viticulturist** Giulio Dimasi **Est.** 1912
Dozens 220 000 **Vyds** 197.2ha

Nothing, they say, succeeds like success. d'Arenberg kept its 100+yo heritage while moving into the 21st century with flair. At last count, the d'Arenberg vineyards have 40 varieties planted, as well as more than 50 growers in McLaren Vale. Its considerable portfolio of richly robed red wines, shiraz, cabernet sauvignon and grenache are the cornerstones. The iconic 5-level Cube cellar door offers a range of wine experiences including restaurant and a wine sensory room. A founding member of Australia's First Families of Wine.

ŦŦŦŦ♀ **The Hunjee Heartstring Montepulciano 2021, McLaren Vale** A variety with a fine future in these parts, serving up a palette of bright natural acidity and gnarled tannins. Floral, full weighted and complex as a salve of smoked meat, dried tobacco, olive, iodine, clove and thyme, all fired up by a parapet of ferruginous tannin and integrated acidity. The finish, long and effusive. A beacon of light. Screw cap. 15% alc. RATING 93 DRINK 2022–2028 $32 NG ✪

The Biophilic Silurian Cinsault 2021, McLaren Vale A fine opening stanza of purple florals, damson plum, dried herb, mace and a bony thread of saltiness running long. There is a fair whack of heat on this and a firm curb of oak that frankly, could be more judiciously handled. Yet, in all, a very solid wine with plenty to like. Screw cap. 15% alc. RATING 92 DRINK 2022–2028 $32 NG

The Lucky Lizard Chardonnay 2021, Adelaide Hills A mid-weighted and flavourful chardonnay of considerable pedigree, reeling off stone fruit allusions, creamed cashew, dutiful oak accents and white fig. The finish, a plume of canned peach and nougat. Screw cap. 13% alc. RATING 90 DRINK 2022–2026 $34 NG

The Feral Fox Pinot Noir 2021, Adelaide Hills A medicinal, mid-weighted pinot. Despite the core of sweet cherry fruit, rhubarb and herbal complexities of bracken and dried porcini, all laden with personality and umami, the finish is a bit stiff and dry. This is a short-term drinker with loads of flavour. Screw cap. 14% alc. RATING 90 DRINK 2022–2026 $34 NG

The Anthropocene Epoch Mencia 2021, McLaren Vale Purple, glossy and opaque at the core. Pointed aromas of dried nori, lilac, white pepper and blue fruits. The mid-palate, pulpy and expansive, with a skein of peppery tannins meandering a nice course while imbuing a meaty savouriness. The acidity, as is the wont here, is shrill. Yet in this instance, the wine's body can just about handle it. Screw cap. 14.5% alc. RATING 90 DRINK 2022–2025 $32 NG

Dal Zotto Wines

★★★★★

Main Road, Whitfield, Vic 3733 **Region** King Valley
T (03) 5729 8321 **www**.dalzotto.com.au **Open** 7 days 10–5 **Winemaker** Michael
Dal Zotto, Prasad Patil **Est.** 1987 **Dozens** 60 000 **Vyds** 46ha

The Dal Zotto family is a King Valley institution; ex-tobacco growers, then contract
grapegrowers, they are now 100% focused on their Dal Zotto wine range. Founded by
Otto and Elena, ownership has now passed to sons Michael and Christian and their partners
Lynne and Simone, who handle winemaking, sales and marketing respectively. Dal Zotto
is producing increasing amounts of Italian varieties of consistent quality from its substantial
estate vineyard.

🍷🍷🍷🍷 **Pucino VP Prosecco 2022, King Valley** Non-vintage prosecco promotes
the house style. Vintage prosecco, well, now you're talking about a little more
individuality, a little more concentration, with just a touch of gentle savouriness.
The usual energy and exuberance remain but the flavour profile expands and
deepens in honeysuckle, orange peel, quince paste, citrus and pear. There's a
warmth to the texture and overall, that touch of elegance. Crown. 10.9% alc.
RATING 95 **DRINK** 2023-2026 $27 JP ✪
L'Immigrante Prosecco 2021, King Valley A bottle-fermented prosecco
that shows the ever-changing nature and versatility of the grape. Delivers a
sophisticated edge, one enlivened and enhanced by a bready/biscuity perfume
mingling with attractive spring blossoms, honeysuckle, citrus and poached
pear. Expect a supple texture, flavours running deeper with nougat and a light
nuttiness. Hits the prosecco spot. Crown. 11.4% alc. **RATING** 95 **DRINK** 2023-2029
$37 JP ✪
Pucino Col Fondo Prosecco 2021, King Valley A light cloudy lemon colour
introduces the scent of spring – jasmine, citrus blossom, apple with baked pear
and preserved lemon. The palate broadens and runs deep in complex flavours
with additional savouriness through almond skin, grapefruit and poached quince
assisted by a brisk, pulsing bubble. That's a wow! Crown. 10.5% alc. **RATING** 95
DRINK 2023-2026 $31 JP ✪
Pucino Prosecco NV, King Valley The sparkling that started the Australian
prosecco movement, Pucino NV keeps showing the way with both its zest for life
and depth of flavour concentration. Citrus blossom perfume is accompanied by
lemon zest, quince, apple and grapefruit. Akin to a mouthful of lemon sorbet, the
flavours pop with energy and brightness while running deep and long across the
palate. Crown. 10.9% alc. **RATING** 94 $21 JP ✪
Barbera 2021, King Valley The aromas beckon tantalisingly – sour cherry,
mulberry, red licorice, fennel seed, dried herbs, tilled earth. This barbera is such
a delight, so open and inviting and lifted, with fruit to the fore while delivering
plenty of juicy crunch. The tannin presence is fine and ripe. Love the red licorice
spiciness to close. Screw cap. 13.4% alc. **RATING** 94 **DRINK** 2023-2027 $27 JP ✪

🍷🍷🍷🍷 **Pinot Grigio 2022, King Valley RATING** 93 **DRINK** 2023-2026 $22 JP ✪
Arneis 2022, King Valley RATING 93 **DRINK** 2023-2026 $27 JP ✪
Fiano 2022, King Valley RATING 92 **DRINK** 2023-2027 $27 JP ✪
Pinot Bianco 2022, King Valley RATING 92 **DRINK** 2023-2026 $27 JP ✪
Garganega 2022, King Valley RATING 90 **DRINK** 2023-2027 $31 JP

Dalrymple Vineyards

★★★★★

1337 Pipers Brook Road, Pipers Brook, Tas 7254 **Region** Northern Tasmania
T (03) 6382 7229 **www**.dalrymplevineyards.com.au **Open** By appt
Winemaker Peter Caldwell **Est.** 1987 **Dozens** 4000 **Vyds** 17ha

Dalrymple was established by the Mitchell and Sundstrup families; the vineyard and brand
were acquired by Hill-Smith Family Vineyards in late '07. Peter Caldwell has been responsible
for the vineyard, viticulture and winemaking since '10. He brought with him 10 years'
experience at Te Kairanga Wines (NZ) and 2 years with Josef Chromy Wines. His knowledge
of pinot noir and chardonnay is comprehensive. In Dec '12 Hill-Smith Family vineyards

acquired the 120ha property on which the original Frogmore Creek vineyard was established; 10ha of that property is pinot noir specifically for Dalrymple.

ΨΨΨΨΨ **Single Site Cottage Block Pinot Noir 2021, Tasmania** Aromas of ripe plum, red cherry and dried cranberries underscored by hints of fine spice, red licorice, purple floral tones, leaf litter, mushroom broth and game meats. There is an expansive, detailed shape to the wine as it swells with dark and red fruits before a seam of sapid acidity drives the wine to a sustained finish of spicy red fruits and gamey notes. Screw cap. 13.5% alc. **RATING** 95 **DRINK** 2023–2029 $65 DB

Single Site Coal River Valley Pinot Noir 2021, Tasmania A bright mid-ruby hue with red plum, red apple and raspberry fruits leaping from the glass. Hints of exotic spices, pressed flowers, Chinese barbecue, leaf litter, mushroom, amaro herbs and game meats. Bright and focused with a lovely fruit and acid tension, fine, chalky tannins and a mineral-laden acid drive. There is a vitality and shape to this wine that impresses greatly. Screw cap. 14% alc. **RATING** 95 **DRINK** 2023–2033 $65 DB

Single Site Swansea Pinot Noir 2021, Tasmania Pristine red cherry and redcurrant fruits, hints of fine spice, Chinese roast duck, shiitake broth, a light wash of amaro herbs and purple floral notes. Very pretty on the nose, perhaps blossom mixed with some iodine-like coastal influence, finishing complex, gamey and long. Screw cap. 14.5% alc. **RATING** 94 **DRINK** 2023–2028 $65 DB

Single Site Ouse Pinot Noir 2021, Tasmania Mid-ruby with aromas of exotically spiced satsuma plum, red cherry and a mashup of strawberry and raspberry. Hints of mushroom broth, stewed rhubarb, amaro herbs, tobacco pouch, leaf litter, game meats, hoisin and earth. Compact and fine granitic tannins and a brisk minerally cadence with gamey dark and red fruit and plentiful spice on the finish. Screw cap. 13.5% alc. **RATING** 94 **DRINK** 2023–2030 $60 DB

ΨΨΨΨΨ **Pipers River Pinot Noir 2021, Tasmania RATING** 93 **DRINK** 2023–2028 $40 DB

Single Site Estate Cave Block Chardonnay 2021, Tasmania RATING 93 **DRINK** 2023–2029 $50 DB

Single Site Estate Cave Block Chardonnay 2020, Tasmania RATING 92 **DRINK** 2023–2026 $48 DB

Dalwhinnie ★★★★★

448 Taltarni Road, Moonambel, Vic 3478 **Region** Pyrenees
T (03) 5467 2388 **www.**dalwhinnie.wine **Open** 7 days 10–4.30 **Winemaker** Julian Langworthy **Viticulturist** John Fogarty, Sam Bartlett **Est.** 1976 **Dozens** 3500 **Vyds** 23ha
Dalwhinnie was established by Ewan Jones in '73, near Moonabel in Victoria's Pyrenees. At 595m elevation, it is the highest vineyard in the region. The wines have tremendous depth of flavour, reflecting the relatively low yielding but well-maintained vineyards. The vineyards are dry-grown and managed organically, but the quality more than compensates. Fogarty Wine Group acquired the property from the Jones family in '20.

ΨΨΨΨΨ **The Pinnacle Shiraz 2020, Pyrenees** Fabulous wine. Powerful, complex and long. Pure plum into meaty spice into forest berries into fragrant herbs. You can taste the fruit, the soil and the wood, but it all presents as one. And then there's the finish. What a finish. Structured, textural, flavoursome and long. This wine is the complete package. Screw cap. 14% alc. **RATING** 97 **DRINK** 2026–2040 $95 CM ✪

ΨΨΨΨΨ **Moonambel Cabernet 2020, Pyrenees** It's easy enough to list the flavours: spearmint, boysenberry, dark chocolate and pure blackcurrant, but it's the arrangement and more so the flamboyant flourish of them that really impresses. This is Dalwhinnie in dynamic good form. Integrated tannin ripples through the back half of the wine, as do sweet woodsmoke characters, and the finish is full of running and then some. Screw cap. 14.5% alc. **RATING** 96 **DRINK** 2026–2038 $70 CM ✪

Moonambel Shiraz 2020, Pyrenees Pyrenees shiraz matured in all-French oak. It's by no means a massive wine but it feels voluminous thanks to the spread of flavour and expansion through the palate. This is a very good wine. Satsuma plum, soy, sweet spice and jellied cherry notes blend with star anise, cedar and woodsmoke. It's lively, exotic, generous and sophisticated. Screw cap. 14% alc. RATING 95 DRINK 2025–2036 $70 CM

Moonambel Chardonnay 2021, Pyrenees Raciness and flavour, combined with aplomb. Citrus, pear, slate and flint characters launch from the outset, candied fruit and cedar notes emerging as it travels through the mouth. There's nothing lacking about this wine; it seems zippy and refreshing, and will build flesh as it matures, and be better again for it. Screw cap. 13% alc. RATING 94 DRINK 2024–2032 $65 CM

Three Valleys Pinot Noir 2021, Tasmania This sports a bright aromatic profile of red cherry, redcurrant jelly and raspberry coulis with hints of blood orange, exotic spice, shiitake broth, rhubarb, sous bois, dried cranberries and smoked meats. Spiced sour morello cherries and fine tannins feature as the wine departs with a graceful air. Screw cap. 14% alc. RATING 94 DRINK 2023–2030 $55 DB

Dandelion Vineyards ★★★★★

191 Chaffeys Rd, McLaren Vale SA 5171 **Region** South Australia
T (08) 8323 8979 **www.**dandelionvineyards.com.au **Open** 7 days 10–5
Winemaker Elena Brooks **Est.** 2007 **Vyds** 124.2ha
Elena Brooks crafts full-bodied wines across South Australia's premium regions: Adelaide Hills, Eden Valley, Langhorne Creek, McLaren Vale, Barossa Valley and Fleurieu Peninsula. She endeavours to draw upon vineyards untempered by over-management, as much as she strives for a softer impact in the winery. As a result, Dandelion wines are increasingly bright, transparent and stamped by a more sensitive oak regime than in the past. Grenache, a strong suit. At the time of writing, the Wonder Room, a wine bar, cellar door and restaurant, was scheduled to open June '23.

Wonderland of the Eden Valley Riesling 2022 Freshly squeezed lime and grapefruit notes leap out of the glass with hints of bath salts, soft spice, crushed quartz and Christmas lily. Clarity and focus writ large with pure lime fruits on the palate plus lemongrass, dried mandarin rind, finger lime and crushed stone. Coiled and crystalline with a vivid acid line that quivers with minerality and a cadence that takes the breath away. Great stuff. Screw cap. 11.5% alc. RATING 96 DRINK 2023–2033 $60 DB ✪

Red Queen of the Eden Valley Shiraz 2020 Despite the plushness and fruit density on display, there is a wonderful sense of tension in this wine, coiled kinetic energy that resolves on the mid-palate with a finish of great velocity and length. Superb fruit purity and tannin architecture and a sense that cellaring for an extended period will not be a problem. Screw cap. 14.7% alc. RATING 96 DRINK 2023–2037 $300 DB

Enchanted Garden of the Eden Valley Riesling 2022 A steely and wonderfully fragrant riesling showing juicy lime, citrus and grapefruit twang with hints of lemongrass, orange blossom, honeysuckle, rose petal and crushed quartz. It sports a ripping tubular palate shape, playing on the tension between fruit and acidity before snapping across the palate with velocity and precision, a rooster tail of lime and blossom in its wake and a savoury sigh at the end. Yes. Screw cap. 11.8% alc. RATING 95 DRINK 2023–2033 $28 DB ✪

Moonrise Kingdom of McLaren Vale Shiraz Grenache Petite Sirah 2021 60/20/20% shiraz/grenache/petite syrah. A fine blend, conferring a density of fruit, carnal complexities and gritty tannins prowling across a finish marked by a Mediterranean burr of green olive, smoked meats, salt and sapidity. Sure, there is an intensity of fruit sweetness here, but the delivery is one of pixelated grape tannins and a phalanx of structural authority beyond. Screw cap. 14.5% alc. RATING 95 DRINK 2022–2035 $120 NG

Menagerie of the Barossa Grenache Shiraz Mataro 2021 A bunchy 73/19/8% grenache/shiraz/mataro. Slurpalicious red and blue fruits, exotic spice, amaro, roasting meats, purple floral notes, gingerbread, cola and a whole lot of yum. Just deliciously fun, savoury drinking, and that is a beautiful thing. Screw cap. 14% alc. RATING 94 DRINK 2023-2028 $30 DB ✪

Lion's Tooth of McLaren Vale Shiraz Riesling 2021 Distinctive aromas of iodine, blood, smoked charcuterie and tapenade, along with grapey spice. Gritty, pointed and fine. So much more interesting than the simple, pulpy iterations that pervade the landscape. The finish, a perforated chisel's edge of tannins tight enough to evince authority without quelling the joyous fruit. Screw cap. 13.8% alc. RATING 94 DRINK 2022-2028 $40 NG ✪

Faraway Tree of McLaren Vale Grenache 2021 A slake of sandy tannins compresses fecund strawberry, bergamot, pomegranate and hibiscus. A whiff of whole bunches, too, for intrigue. More in common with the contemporary glimpse toward pinot noir than anything heavy. Juicy acidity, beguiling length and dappled sweetness, nothing more. A diaphanous finish of sap and verve. Screw cap. 14.3% alc. RATING 94 DRINK 2022-2028 $120 NG

Midnight Rainbow of McLaren Vale Petite Sirah 2020 Petite sirah (aka durif) is one of those obdurate grape varieties, delivering a morass of dark fruits, spice and almost implacable tannins. The secret is a deft hand when it comes to extraction. A variety of little inherent complexity, but one that delivers force, a menthol savouriness and personality. Sometimes I simply prefer that. A tour de force. Screw cap. 14.5% alc. RATING 94 DRINK 2022-2035 $120 NG

Firehawk of McLaren Vale Shiraz 2020 A rich, thickly layered shiraz with ample freshness underlying, as is the wont here. The craftsmanship, exceptional, manifests as boysenberry, aniseed, clove, lilac, salumi and a llicorella-like burst of sooty tannin and mineral pungency across a luscious finish. Screw cap. 14.5% alc. RATING 94 DRINK 2022-2032 $60 NG

ꚎꚎꚎꚎꚎ **Lionheart of the Barossa Shiraz 2021** RATING 93 DRINK 2023-2029 $30 DB ✪

Pride of the Fleurieu Peninsula Cabernet Sauvignon 2021 RATING 93 DRINK 2025-2035 $40 CM

Treasure Trove of McLaren Vale Grenache 2021 RATING 93 DRINK 2022-2027 $40 NG

Lion's Roar of the Barossa Cabernet Sauvignon 2021 RATING 93 DRINK 2023-2030 $40 DB

March Hare of the Barossa Mataro 2021 RATING 93 DRINK 2023-2030 $60 DB

Lioness of McLaren Vale Shiraz 2021 RATING 92 DRINK 2022-2027 $30 NG ✪

Lion's Roar of the Barossa Cabernet Sauvignon 2020, Barossa Valley RATING 92 DRINK 2023-2033 $40 DB

Lonely Wild of McLaren Vale Grenache 2022 RATING 91 DRINK 2022-2026 $40 NG

Twilight of the Adelaide Hills Chardonnay 2022 RATING 91 DRINK 2023-2027 $28 NG ✪

Honeypot of the Barossa Roussanne 2022 RATING 90 DRINK 2023-2026 $28 DB

Dappled Wines

★★★★★

1 Sewell Road, Steels Creek, Vic 3775 **Region** Yarra Valley
T 0407 675 994 **www**.dappledwines.com.au **Open** By appt **Winemaker** Shaun Crinion
Est. 2009 **Dozens** 800

Owner and winemaker Shaun Crinion was introduced to wine in '99, working for his winemaker uncle at Laetitia Vineyard & Winery on the central coast of California. His career since then has been so impressive I (James) can't cut it short: '00 Devil's Lair, Margaret River and Corbett Canyon Vineyard, California; '02 Houghton, Middle Swan; '03 De Bortoli, Hunter Valley; '04–06 Pipers Brook, Tasmania; '06 Bay of Fires, Tasmania; '06–07 Williams Selyem, California; '08 Domaine Chandon, Yarra Valley; '10 Domaine de Montille, Burgundy; '09– present Dappled Wines (plus part-time for Rob Dolan). His longer-term ambition is to buy or establish his own vineyard.

ŸŸŸŸŸ **Les Vergers Single Vineyard Chardonnay 2021, Yarra Valley** The fireworks come with the finish and aftertaste of this wild-yeast fermented, grapefruit-accented wine. It has exceptional texture, structure and depth. Screw cap. 13% alc. RATING 96 DRINK 2023-2036 $50 JH ✪

Fin de la Terre Single Vineyard Syrah 2021, Yarra Valley Wild-yeast fermented with 100% whole bunches. The colour is deep right to the rim, and it's amazing that the full-bodied palate has so much body and fruit depth given its fermentation. The flavours are all dark and savoury. Striking. Screw cap. 13% alc. RATING 96 DRINK 2023-2046 $45 JH ✪

Champs de Cerises Single Vineyard Pinot Noir 2021, Upper Yarra Valley A voluminous bouquet full of berries and spices leads into a palate that adds fine-spun tannins and forest notes imparted by a whole-bunch component. The texture and structure bode well for the future. Screw cap. 13% alc. RATING 96 DRINK 2023-2031 $50 JH ✪

Appellation Chardonnay 2021, Yarra Valley Apart from Dappled's usual minimal SO_2 (nothing else added) declaration, this is an impeccably balanced and pure chardonnay. White peach, pink grapefruit and cashew provide the flavour. Screw cap. 13% alc. RATING 96 DRINK 2023-2030 $37 JH ✪

Limited Release Tradition Cabernets 2020, Yarra Valley An unusual wine with good hue and depth. Not only are the '81-planted vines very old by Yarra Valley standards, the use of whole bunches (20%) with cabernet is rare. It has seductive flavours and mouthfeel, with a juicy fruit sweetness (not sugar) that flows across the mouth without interruption by tannins or oak. Diam. 13% alc. RATING 95 DRINK 2023-2030 $37 JH ✪

Appellation Pinot Noir 2021, Upper Yarra Valley The colour is light, but the perfumed bouquet is anything but. Rose petals, violets, spices and forest-like aromas fill the bouquet, which is the foundation of the long, poised, savoury palate and its lingering aftertaste. Screw cap. 13% alc. RATING 94 DRINK 2023-2030 $37 JH ✪

David Hook Wines ★★★★★

Pothana Winery, 62 Pothana Lane, Belford, NSW 2335 **Region** Hunter Valley **T** (02) 6574 7164 **www.davidhookwines.com.au Open** Sat 10.30–3.30 by appt **Winemaker** David Hook **Est.** 1984 **Dozens** 10 000 **Vyds** 8ha
David Hook planted the Pothana vineyard in the mid-'80s, and the wines made from it are given the 'Old Vines' banner. This vineyard is planted on the Belford Dome, an ancient geological formation that provides red clay soils over limestone on the slopes and sandy loams along the creek flats; the former for red wines, the latter for white, which has proved an ideal site for the addition and development of Italian varieties pinot grigio, vermentino and pecorino.

ŸŸŸŸŸ **Old Vines Pothana Vineyard Belford Shiraz 2021, Hunter Valley** Bright crimson. Despite (or thanks to) its alcohol of only 13%, the wine is tending to full-bodied territory, with a mix of black fruits and ripe tannins. Its saviour now, or in 30 years, is its balance and typicity. Screw cap. 13% alc. RATING 96 DRINK 2035-2045 $50 JH ✪

Old Vines Pothana Vineyard Belford Semillon 2022, Hunter Valley This wine has an expressive floral bouquet immediately on opening, with citrus blossom to the fore. The palate is utterly delicious, with Tinker Bell acidity threaded through the fabric, blood orange, lime and lemon surging to another level on the finish. Screw cap. 10.5% alc. RATING 95 DRINK 2023-2033 $28 JH ✪

Aged Release Old Vines Pothana Vineyard Belford Shiraz 2018, Hunter Valley Bright crimson through to the rim. A powerful, savoury wine with a full array of spice, leather, blackberry and tannins. Still more to come. Screw cap. 13.5% alc. RATING 95 DRINK 2030–2040 $65 JH

 Nebbiolo 2019, Hilltops RATING 92 DRINK 2022–2030 $42 SW
Pecorino 2022, Hunter Valley RATING 90 DRINK 2022–2025 $35 SW
Sangiovese 2021, Central Ranges RATING 90 DRINK 2023–2026 $35 SW
Aged Release Old Vines Pothana Vineyard Belford Semillon 2014, Hunter Valley RATING 90 DRINK 2023–2029 $50 JH

Dawson James ★★★★

1240B Brookman Road, Dingabledinga, SA 5172 (postal) **Region** Southern Tasmania **T** 0419 816 335 www.dawsonjames.com.au **Open** Not **Winemaker** Peter Dawson, Tim James **Est.** 2010 **Dozens** 1200 **Vyds** 3.3ha
Peter Dawson and Tim James had long and highly successful careers as senior winemakers for Hardys and Accolade Wines. Tim jumped ship first, becoming managing director of Wirra Wirra for 7 years until '07. Now both have multiple consulting roles. They have long had a desire to grow and make wine in Tasmania together, which came to fruition in '10. Dawson James makes single-site chardonnay and pinot noir from 30yo vines on the Meadowbank vineyard in the Derwent Valley.

 Pinot Noir 2020, Tasmania Mid-cherry red in hue with inviting notes of macerated wild strawberries and red and dark cherries. A bed of fine spice with hints of forest floor, rose petal, earth, amaro herbs and a waft of Campari-esque stalky complexity. Fine tannins create shape while fine, lacy acidity lends vitality and drive, finishing long and pure of fruit. Screw cap. 12.6% alc. RATING 94 DRINK 2023–2028 $84 DB
Chardonnay 2019, Tasmania Pale straw with pure aromas of juicy white peach and citrus fruits. Hints of soft spice and nougat, light wafts of struck match, marzipan and white flowers, too. Tightly coiled with scintillating acidity and a wash of citrus fruits and oatmeal on the long, persistent finish. Screw cap. 13% alc. RATING 94 DRINK 2023–2028 $68 DB

De Beaurepaire Wines ★★★★★

182 Cudgegong Road, Rylstone, NSW 2849 **Region** Central Ranges **T** 0429 787 705 www.debeaurepairewines.com **Open** Wed–Sun 11–5 **Winemaker** Richard de Beaurepaire, Will de Beaurepaire, with Lisa Bray, Alex Cassegrain & Jacob Stein (all contract) **Viticulturist** Ray Stewart **Est.** 1998 **Dozens** 12 000 **Vyds** 55ha
The large De Beaurepaire vineyard was planted by Janet and Richard de Beaurepaire in '98 and is situated on one of the oldest properties west of the Blue Mountains, in Rylstone. An elevation of 600m, coupled with limestone soils and frontage to the Cudgegong River, provides grapes very different from the Mudgee norm (hence they prefer to use the broader Central Ranges GI). The regeneratively farmed vineyard is planted to merlot, shiraz, cabernet sauvignon, pinot noir, petit verdot, viognier, chardonnay, semillon and pinot gris.

Jeannette Reserve Rylstone Chardonnay 2019, Central Ranges Grapefruit segments, white peach, honeydew melon and honeysuckle. Filaments of texture splay over the palate with a labne-like creaminess. A marriage of acidity and mlf (15–20%) has you reaching for the next sip. Hazelnut skin bitterness and shards of praline are left lingering. Screw cap. 13% alc. RATING 95 DRINK 2022–2030 $60 SW
Coeur d'Or Rylstone Botrytis Semillon 2021, Central Ranges An electric 'pot of gold' yellow in the glass. Manuka honey, lime marmalade and dried apricots. Needs a decant to blow off some of the bottling aromatics, which allows the treacle caramel, fruit flan and glacé pineapple to unfurl. The wine is lively and dances with acidity and joyous energy. Mace, cinnamon and a dried apricot

skin chew on the finish, adding additional layers of detail. 130g/L RS. Screw cap. 11% alc. **RATING** 95 **DRINK** 2022–2030 $55 SW

🍷🍷🍷🍷⚲ **La Comtesse Rylstone Chardonnay 2021, Central Ranges** **RATING** 93 **DRINK** 2022–2030 $35 SW ✪
Le Chevalier Rylstone Merlot Cabernet Petit Verdot 2019, Central Ranges **RATING** 93 **DRINK** 2022–2030 $35 SW ✪
Bluebird Rylstone Botrytis Viognier 2020, Central Ranges **RATING** 93 **DRINK** 2022–2028 $45 SW
Leopold Rylstone Shiraz Viognier 2018, Central Ranges **RATING** 92 **DRINK** 2022–2026 $65 SW
Blanchefleur Blanc de Blancs 2021, Central Ranges **RATING** 90 **DRINK** 2022–2026 $50 SW
Rylstone Estate Aviatrix Cabernet Sauvignon Shiraz 2021, Central Ranges **RATING** 90 **DRINK** 2022–2028 $45 SW
Billet Doux Rylstone Semillon Sauvignon Blanc 2019, Central Ranges **RATING** 90 **DRINK** 2022–2030 $30 SW

De Bortoli

Pinnacle Lane, Dixons Creek, Vic 3775 **Region** Yarra Valley
T (03) 5965 2271 **www**.debortoli.com.au **Open** 7 days 10–5 **Winemaker** Stephen Webber, Sarah Fagan, Andrew Bretherton **Viticulturist** Rob Sutherland, Andrew Ray, Brian Dwyer **Est.** 1987 **Dozens** 350 000 **Vyds** 520ha

Arguably the most successful of all Yarra Valley wineries, not only in terms of volume of production but also quality. It is run by the wife-and-husband team of Leanne De Bortoli and Steve Webber, but owned by the De Bortoli family. The wines are released in 3 quality (and price) groups: at the top Single Vineyard, then Estate Grown and in 3rd place, Villages. Small-volume labels increase the offer with Melba, La Boheme, an aromatic range of Yarra Valley wines and Vinoque, enabling commercial trials of new varieties and interesting blends. The PHI wines are made from the 7.5ha Lusatia Park vineyard established by the Shelmerdine family in Woori Yallock in '85, purchased in November '15, and from Heathcote. Rutherglen Estate was added to the De Bortoli portfolio in '19.

🍷🍷🍷🍷🍷 **Lusatia Pinot Noir 2021, Yarra Valley** A very bright crimson red. There's a lot going on with scents of perfectly ripened red cherries, delicate spices and rose petals. The palate is perfectly weighted with great depth of fruit but it's oh-so light on its feet. The tannins are ultrafine and persistent. Screw cap. 13.5% alc. **RATING** 97 **DRINK** 2022–2027 $80 PR ✪

🍷🍷🍷🍷🍷 **Melba Amphora Cabernet Sauvignon 2022, Yarra Valley** A gorgeous, bright ruby red. Scents of black cherries, satsuma plums, crushed violets and briary notes. An elegant and complex medium-bodied wine that flows evenly across the palate and, while the wine's suave tannin structure means it can be approached now, I'd love to see how it evolves. Diam. 14% alc. **RATING** 96 **DRINK** 2022–2032 $80 PR
Section A7 Chardonnay 2021, Yarra Valley Bright green gold. A very polished wine offering aromas of white peach and nectarine, tangerine and white flowers. Really light on its feet, this flows effortlessly across the palate before finishing chalky and long. Screw cap. 12.5% alc. **RATING** 96 **DRINK** 2022–2028 $55 PR ✪
Riorret Lusatia Park Pinot Noir 2021, Yarra Valley A very bright ruby crimson. A touch closed; this needs a few good swirls to reveal itself. Savoury with dark plums, black cherry and a little potpourri. On the palate, concentrated yet well balanced with crunchy tannins and bright acidity. Diam. 13.5% alc. **RATING** 96 **DRINK** 2023–2027 $45 PR ✪
Section A8 Syrah 2021, Yarra Valley A medium ruby red. There's a lot of whole-bunch goodness on the bouquet with aromas of dark cherries, blackberries, olive tapenade, potpourri and cracked black pepper. I like how the spicy/meaty palate has good concentration while remaining light on its feet. Has a long, gently tannic finish. Screw cap. 14% alc. **RATING** 96 **DRINK** 2022–2030 $55 PR ✪

Section A5 Chardonnay 2021, Yarra Valley A medium deep and bright green gold. Stone and orchard fruits, marine scents and a little matchstick on the nose, while the palate is simultaneously textured, layered and structured. Screw cap. 12.7% alc. RATING 96 DRINK 2022–2030 $55 PR ✪

PHI Single Vineyard Chardonnay 2022, Yarra Valley A very bright green gold. Exhibiting the Lusatia Park vineyard's trademark purity of fruit, this has aromas of stone and citrus fruits, orange blossom and a little grapefruit pith. Gently textured, chalky, balanced, long and refreshing. That it's so well priced is a bonus! Screw cap. 13.2% alc. RATING 95 DRINK 2023–2027 $32 PR ✪

PHI Lusatia Park Pinot Noir 2022, Yarra Valley Bright cherry red. An immediately appealing wine with its dark cherry fruit, lavender and incense. This has good weight and depth without being heavy. A touch savoury, too, and the tannins are silky and long. Already a joy to drink. Screw cap. 12.7% alc. RATING 95 DRINK 2022–2028 $42 PR ✪

La Boheme Act Four Syrah Gamay 2022, Yarra Valley De Bortoli nails these well-priced, great-drinking red blends. A gorgeous, bright crimson purple and bursting with red cherries, blackberries and spice. Juicy and loaded with flavour, it's got soft tannins and bright acidity to balance. At this price, it might just be the pizza/pasta wine bargain of the year. Screw cap. 13.5% alc. RATING 95 DRINK 2022–2026 $22 PR ✪

PHI Grenache Amphora 2022, Heathcote Clove and general woodsy spice notes float seamlessly through smoked meat, black cherry, roasted plum and redcurrant flavours. It's medium in weight, has a frisky acidic glint in its eye, and finishes with complex, slightly rugged tannin. It's intriguing and more. Screw cap. 14.5% alc. RATING 94 DRINK 2023–2030 $42 CM

PHI Gamay Noir 2022, Yarra Valley A vivid crimson purple. Primary red cherry and strawberry scents with some attractive whole-bunch derived mountain herbs. Mid-weight and gently juicy, finishing with balanced, silky tannins and bright acidity. Screw cap. 14% alc. RATING 94 DRINK 2022–2026 $32 PR ✪

♀♀♀♀♀ **Sparkling Shiraz Durif 2019**, Rutherglen RATING 93 $28 JP ✪

PHI Syrah Grenache 2022, Heathcote RATING 93 DRINK 2023–2028 $32 CM ✪

The Estate Vineyard Pinot Noir 2021, Yarra Valley RATING 93 DRINK 2022–2028 $24 PR ✪

The Estate Vineyard Gamay Noir 2021, Yarra Valley RATING 93 DRINK 2022–2026 $24 PR ✪

The Estate Vineyard Dixons Creek Shiraz 2021, Yarra Valley RATING 93 DRINK 2022–2023 $24 PR ✪

The Estate Vineyard Dixons Creek Chardonnay 2021, Yarra Valley RATING 93 DRINK 2022–2027 $24 PR ✪

Riorret The Abbey Pinot Noir 2021, Yarra Valley RATING 93 DRINK 2022–2027 $45 PR

Vinoque Blanc de Terre 2022, Heathcote RATING 92 DRINK 2023–2026 $25 CM ✪

Rutherglen Estate Renaissance Viognier Roussanne Marsanne 2021, Rutherglen RATING 92 DRINK 2022–2026 $35 JP

Estate Grown Cabernet Sauvignon 2021, Yarra Valley RATING 92 DRINK 2023–2029 $24 PR ✪

Rutherglen Estate Shiraz 2021, Rutherglen RATING 91 DRINK 2022–2027 $24 JP ✪

Rutherglen Petit Moscato Frizzante NV, Rutherglen RATING 90 $22 JP ✪

Grenache Wizardry Rosé 2022, Heathcote RATING 90 DRINK 2023–2025 $24 CM ✪

BellaRiva Sangiovese 2022, Heathcote RATING 90 DRINK 2023–2025 $18 CM ✪

Estate Shelley's Block Marsanne Viognier Roussanne 2021, Rutherglen RATING 90 DRINK 2022–2025 $18 JP ✪

De Bortoli (Riverina)   ★★★★★

De Bortoli Road, Bilbul, NSW 2680 **Region** Riverina
T (02) 6966 0100 **www**.debortoli.com.au **Open** Mon–Sat 9–5, Sun 9–4
Winemaker Julie Mortlock, John Coughlan, Roberto Delgado, Joel Veenhuizen, Jacob
Zanatta **Viticulturist** Kevin De Bortoli **Est.** 1928 **Dozens** 3 500 000 **Vyds** 250ha
Famous for its superb fortified wines and Noble One, which in fact accounts for only a tiny
part of production, this winery also turns out low-priced, competently made varietal wines.
They come from estate vineyards, but also from contract-grown grapes.

ΨΨΨΨΨ **10 Years Old Black Noble Semillon NV, Riverina** Date, fig and almond
log, roasted chestnuts, pecan and soft prunes. Wafts of integrated spirit lead to
barrel notes of vanilla paste, coffee, salted caramel and wood varnish. Baked soda
bread and rye. Takes on new life on the palate with gritty tannins and surging
acidity. Caramelised apples and dried apricots get a new lease on life. This is well
designed, well executed and continues on and on. Stunning. Screw cap. 17.5% alc.
RATING 97 $50 SW ❂

ΨΨΨΨΨ **Old Boys 21 Years Old Tawny NV, Riverina** Figs in syrup, dates and prune
paste. Cumin, cinnamon and garam marsala with wafts of pudding, bitter
chocolate and hard-boiled caramels. An elegance to the rancio with hazelnut
skin, wafer and ground ginger. There is also a bit of quince and apricot paste
with a sour tamarind element that peeks up through the mid-palate. Detailed
and moreish. Screw cap. 19% alc. **RATING** 95 $50 SW
Noble One Botrytis Semillon 2020, Riverina Sweet Wine of the Year. Score
awarded by the Halliday tasting panel at the annual Awards judging. SW writes:
Peach flesh, perfectly ripe mangoes, tangerine and persimmon. Orange blossom,
lemon oil and brandy snaps. Exuberant in fresh fruit and, despite its utter luscious
sweetness, still maintains very persistent acidity to carry the flavours long. A
grip of ruby grapefruit pith, vanilla bean oak and sugared almonds on the
finish. Beautiful now, sensational with decades in the cellar. Screw cap. 9% alc.
RATING 96 **DRINK** 2022–2045 $75 PD ♥

ΨΨΨΨΨ **8 Years Old Fine Tawny NV, Riverina RATING** 92 $30 SW ❂
17 Trees Shiraz 2021, Heathcote RATING 91 **DRINK** 2023–2027 $18 CM ❂
Show Liqueur 8 Years Old Muscat NV, Riverina RATING 91 $50 SW

de Capel Wines   ★★★☆

101 Majors Lane, Lovedale, NSW 2320 **Region** Hunter Valley
T 0419 994 299 **www**.decapelwines.com.au **Open** Thurs–Sun 10–5 **Winemaker** Daniel
Binet **Viticulturist** Jenny Bright **Est.** 2008 **Dozens** 600 **Vyds** 2.2ha
Owners David and Elisabeth Capel's love of wine and a rural life led them to the purchase
of their 11ha property in '01. It wasn't until '08 that they installed all of the vineyard
infrastructure and personally planted 2.2ha of vines under the direction of viticulturist Jenny
Bright. They say, 'We are very fortunate to have the support (and muscle) of our close friends
and family who put in an amazing effort every vintage and help us to hand-pick every single
grape that we grow.'

ΨΨΨΨΨ **Henry Chardonnay 2022, Hunter Valley** Making small quantities of high-
quality red wine is relatively easy if the grapes are of high quality – but white
wines are a different proposition. de Capel's answer comes from contract
winemaker Daniel Binet, with a 10+ years of experience. This is a powerful,
balanced fruit-first chardonnay with a long finish. Screw cap. 12.5% alc.
RATING 93 **DRINK** 2023–2027 $25 JH ❂

De Iuliis   ★★★★★

1616 Broke Road, Pokolbin, NSW 2320 **Region** Hunter Valley
T (02) 4993 8000 **www**.dewine.com.au **Open** 7 days 10–5 **Winemaker** Mike De Iuliis
Viticulturist Mike De Iuliis **Est.** 1990 **Dozens** 15 000 **Vyds** 45ha

The De Iuliis family acquired a property at Lovedale in '86 and planted 18ha of vines in '90, selling the grapes from the first few vintages to Tyrrell's but retaining increasing amounts for release under the De Iuliis label. In '99 the land on Broke Road was purchased and a winery and cellar door were built prior to the '00 vintage. In '11 De Iuliis purchased 12ha of the long-established Steven vineyard in Pokolbin. Winemaker Michael De Iuliis completed postgraduate studies in oenology at Roseworthy; he was a Len Evans Tutorial scholar in '04. He has lifted the quality of the wines into the highest echelon.

Cabernet Sauvignon 2021, Hilltops Mike De Iuliis is understandably enraptured by the 'pristine' fruit of a wine that's a 'fantastic expression of cabernet' with an 'exceptionally fine tannin structure.' It's one of those all-too-rare cabernets to be drinking well now, but with an outlook as long as you wish. Gorgeous bargain. Screw cap. 14% alc. RATING 97 DRINK 2023–2043 $30 JH ✪

Aged Release Single Vineyard 2017, Hunter Valley Aged? Prime of its life, with yet more to come. It was an excellent vintage, and the wine is perfectly poised with its elegance and balance. The first signs of honey are on display in its mouth-watering, citrus-infused, lingering finish. Screw cap. 11% alc. RATING 97 DRINK 2023–2032 $50 JH ✪

Single Vineyard Semillon 2022, Hunter Valley Always comes up trumps, with the full range of lemon citrus, lanolin and acidity just so. It's not sacrilegious to drink it now, but do keep a few bottles for 5 or so years. Screw cap. 11% alc. RATING 95 DRINK 2023–2032 $45 JH ✪

LDR Vineyard Semillon 2022, Hunter Valley This wine came through the heaviest rain encountered for years, the 32yo vines providing a Catherine wheel of alternating lime and lemon fruit flavours, with acidity the staff of life. Screw cap. 11.2% alc. RATING 95 DRINK 2023–2033 $45 JH ✪

Limited Release Chardonnay 2021, Hunter Valley This is a best barrel selection. Much lighter on its feet than the '22 standard release: lovely juicy mid-palate; good line, length and balance, as the late Len Evans might have said. 250 dozen made. Screw cap. 12.2% alc. RATING 95 DRINK 2023–2029 $50 JH ✪

Aged Release LDR Vineyard Shiraz 2017, Hunter Valley This wine's colour, bouquet and palate all say the same thing: it is full-bodied, rich, complex and moderately tannic. The balance, line and length are exemplary, but it demands no fewer than 5 more years, and will still be on an upwards trajectory in 25 years to come. Screw cap. 14.5% alc. RATING 95 DRINK 2030–2040 $90 JH

Special Release Montepulciano 2022, Hunter Valley I was alarmed by the label's promise of a finish of 'gripping tannins and bright acidity'. It hasn't even got a tannic edge, which isn't to say it's lacking structure. It's not. It's lively, with satsuma plum fruit on the come-hither palate, and it has length. Screw cap. 13% alc. RATING 94 DRINK 2023–2036 $40 JH ✪

Special Release Shiraz Pinot Noir 2022, Hunter Valley Tumbarumba Its light colour is clear and star-bright, so don't think the wine lacks flavour or aroma, seemingly emanating from the pinot noir, cherry ex the shiraz. Screw cap. 14% alc. RATING 94 DRINK 2023–2038 $35 JH ✪

Semillon 2022, Hunter Valley RATING 93 DRINK 2023–2024 $25 JH ✪
Special Release Tempranillo 2022, Hunter Valley RATING 92 DRINK 2023–2024 $35 JH
Special Release Pecorino 2022, Hunter Valley RATING 92 DRINK 2023–2027 $30 JH ✪
Shiraz 2021, Hunter Valley RATING 92 DRINK 2023–2027 $25 JH ✪
Chardonnay 2022, Hunter Valley RATING 91 DRINK 2023–2027 $25 JH ✪

Dee Vine Estate

★★★★

Farm, 576 Rossetto Rd, Beelbangera, NSW 2680 (postal) **Region** Riverina
T (02) 6963 5555 **www.deevineestate.com Open** Not **Winemaker** Danny Toaldo, Moreno Chiappin and Danisa Olivera **Est.** 2009

Dee Vine Estate is founded on 2 vineyards established by siblings Michele and Domenico Scarfone soon after they emigrated from southern Italy in 1956. Three generations later, Adrian Bianchini and Fernando Rombola have significantly expanded on the original Nericon holdings, yet the premise remains: to craft affordable Riverina table wines.

Nericon Vineyard Reserve Durif 2019, Riverina Bright and inky purple. The promise of lingonberries, blackberries and mulberry. Nutmeg and licorice root come through in waves, while savoury Kalamata olive and dried rosemary pique interest. Blackcurrant jam and dehydrated berry notes are backed up by dusty tannins and a firm drive of zesty acidity. A satisfying wine that will continue to age well for a decade. Screw cap. 14% alc. **RATING** 90 **DRINK** 2022–2032 $20 SW ✪

D Reserve Shiraz 2018, Adelaide Hills Concentrated black cherry and blackcurrant, traces of blackcurrant leaf and fresh-picked sage open to cardamom, vanilla and cola notes. A lengthy acidity and well-placed dusty tannins carry a pure black cherry flavour. This is straightforward cabernet sauvignon fruit in a bottle. Drinking well now and has years left to mature. Screw cap. 14% alc. **RATING** 90 **DRINK** 2022–2035 $20 SW ✪

Deep Woods Estate ★★★★★

889 Commonage Road, Yallingup, WA 6282 **Region** Margaret River
T (08) 9756 6066 **www.**deepwoods.wine **Open** Mon, Wed–Sun 10–5
Winemaker Julian Langworthy, Andrew Bretherton, Emma Gillespie **Viticulturist** John Fogarty **Est.** 1987 **Dozens** 50 000 **Vyds** 14ha

Deep Woods is a jewel in the crown of the Fogarty Wine Group and produces some of the country's finest wines. The original 14ha vineyard on the Yallingup property is planted mostly to red varieties and chief winemaker Julian Langworthy says it's where the best fruit comes from, especially cabernet sauvignon, destined for the top-tier wines. A Jimmy Watson Trophy winner and *Halliday Wine Companion* Winemaker of the Year in 2019, it's no surprise that Julian also crafts outstanding chardonnay, thanks to thoughtful winemaking and excellent fruit sourced from local growers, ditto rosé and more besides. He says Deep Wood's goal is to make contemporary, compelling, yet distinctly Margaret River wines with an international proposition. The aspiration has been realised.

Reserve Chardonnay 2021, Margaret River A powerful wine that has excellent fruit as its core but morphs quickly towards a savoury spectrum: flinty, funky and wild. The palate gives way to an exhilarating ride full of flavour, with fine acidity extending the length. It's moreish, detailed and very impressive. Screw cap. 13% alc. **RATING** 97 **DRINK** 2022–2033 $65 JF ✪

Reserve Cabernet Sauvignon 2020, Margaret River Structured and compelling with a core of mint choc-coated fruit, baking spices and licorice. So much going on in this powerful wine, yet it is beautiful with fine-grained and plentiful tannins and a finish lingering oh-so-long. Screw cap. 14% alc. **RATING** 97 **DRINK** 2023–2043 $90 JF ✪

Single Vineyard G2 Cabernet Sauvignon 2020, Margaret River This is stupendous. Powerful, rich and detailed. Nothing is out of place. Pristine fruit all mulberries and blueberries dusted in baking spices and yes, ironstone. The tannins are something else – shapely, long and the mouth-watering acidity pulls everything into one long thread of joy. Screw cap. 14% alc. **RATING** 97 **DRINK** 2023–2044 $60 JF ✪

Single Vineyard Cabernet Malbec 2021, Margaret River At once powerful yet contained with the varieties (split unknown) beautifully matched. While the classy cabernet aromas and flavours come through, they are rendered more savoury by the malbec and oak. The fuller-bodied palate is alive and vibrant, flavours build and the tannins have presence, all textural and ripe. The finish lingers long. Screw cap. 14% alc. **RATING** 96 **DRINK** 2023–2043 $50 JF ✪

Single Vineyard Chardonnay 2022, Margaret River Flinty and a little funky with fennel and radish, and yes, stone fruit and citrus in the mix. It is chardonnay, after all. A neat layer of nutty lees, creamy, too, spicy, cedary oak neatly tucked in and the fine acid line that ties everything up ever so neatly. Screw cap. 13% alc. RATING 95 DRINK 2023–2032 $50 JF ✪

Sauvignon Blanc 2022, Margaret River Partial barrel fermentation adds another dimension to the citrus, snow pea and passionfruit of the wine, the rich, varietally precise bouquet marking a multi-layered palate that takes barely a split second to fill every part of the long, lingering palate with its grapefruit and nectarine flavours. As usual, exceptional value. Screw cap. 13% alc. RATING 95 DRINK 2023–2025 $20 JH ✪

Rosé 2022, Margaret River A copper blush followed by a bouquet of red roses, herbs and summer berries. Tastes of those fruits plus toffee apple with some charry radicchio. It has texture, depth and pizzazz, slipping down easily with a lively fresh finish. Screw cap. 13% alc. RATING 95 DRINK 2022–2025 $35 JF ✪

Cabernet Sauvignon Merlot 2021, Margaret River This reveals itself gently as it's not a showy wine but it is elegant and lovely. Delicate aromas, a core of sweet fruit tempered by savoury inputs of woodsy spices, menthol and powdery yet fine tannins with bright acidity driving the long finish. Screw cap. 14% alc. RATING 95 DRINK 2022–2036 $40 JF ✪

🍷🍷🍷🍷 **Shiraz et al 2022, Margaret River** RATING 92 DRINK 2022–2032 $25 JF ✪
Ivory Semillon Sauvignon Blanc 2022, Margaret River RATING 91 DRINK 2023–2032 $17 JH ✪
Hillside Cabernet Sauvignon 2021, Margaret River RATING 90 DRINK 2022–2028 $25 JF ✪

Delamere Vineyards   ★★★★★

Bridport Road, Pipers Brook, Tas 7254 **Region** Northern Tasmania
T (03) 6382 7190 **www.delamerevineyards.com.au Open** Fri–Mon 10.30–4.30, or by appt **Winemaker** Shane Holloway, Fran Austin **Viticulturist** Shane Holloway **Est.** 1982 **Dozens** 5000 **Vyds** 11ha

Planted in '81, Delamere was one of the pioneering estates in the Pipers Brook region in Northern Tasmania. The estate was purchased by Shane Holloway and Fran Austin and their families, Fran joined her husband in '11 after 9 years at Bay of Fires. Today, the Delamere quiver of wines spans fine sparkling wines, several impressive rosé wines and detailed chardonnay and pinot noir from the meticulously tended, close-planted vineyard. All wines speak clearly of the Pipers Brook region and the commitment and experience of the current custodians.

🍷🍷🍷🍷🍷 **Pinot Noir 2021, Tasmania** Typically Tasmanian, this deep-though-brightly coloured wine leans magenta on the rim. A convocation of red, blue, purple and black cherries illuminates the bouquet, but doesn't warn you of the sheer intensity of a spectacular palate. There's both textural and spicy/savoury pinot essence at work. Screw cap. 13.4% alc. RATING 98 DRINK 2023–2037 $65 JH ✪ ♥

Block 3 Chardonnay 2021, Tasmania This is Apple Isle meets Premier Cru Chassagne-Montrachet. A stunning, harmonious wine with wonderfully pure white stone and citrus fruits, hints of soft spice, a light waft of struck-match complexity, oatmeal, white flowers and stone. Crystalline in its clarity and detail with an impressive porcelain acid cadence and a finish that trails off for minutes. Wonderful. Diam. 13.2% alc. RATING 97 DRINK 2023–2032 $120 DB

🍷🍷🍷🍷🍷 **Blanc de Blancs 2016, Tasmania** Pale straw with a fine, persistent bead and notes of baked apple, white peach, apple turnover, soft spice and stone. Biscuity tones wash in on a palate that shows a crystalline-acid focus, invigorating cadence and autolytic complexity. Fading out slowly with pure apple fruit, pastry notes and a wonderful singular acid line. Diam. 12.5% alc. RATING 96 DRINK 2023–2032 $70 DB ✪

Blanc de Blancs 2015, Tasmania Made in the traditional method. A piercing pale-green hue and a burst of lemon citrus on the first taste catch immediate attention. Tasmanian acidity has played a velvet glove game, thus a modest dosage allows the white peach and spice to drive the long, elegant palate. 165 dozen made. Diam. 13% alc. **RATING** 96 **DRINK** 2023–2035 $70 JH ✪ ♥

Non Vintage Rosé NV, Tasmania A wine stacked with spiced strawberries and pomegranate aromas that continue without hesitation on an emphatic high-quality palate. Pale salmon hue and a fine, persistent mousse. The result is a wine of great complexity. Diam. 13.1% alc. **RATING** 96 $42 JH ✪

Chardonnay 2021, Tasmania Hand picked, pressed direct to French barriques and foudres; fermentation and 100% mlf both completed naturally. Ten months' maturation with lees stirring. The spine of tungsten acidity is a unique Tasmanian signature, and not to be undertaken lightly. Screw cap. 13.3% alc. **RATING** 95 **DRINK** 2026–2036 $65 JH

Block 8 Pinot Noir 2021, Tasmania Wonderful clarity and detail on display, with bright red cherry and red-plum tones underlined with fine spice, alpine herbs, macerated berry fruits and French-oak spice. The oak flows in a little more on the palate, which finishes long and pure with fine tannins and bright acidity providing a lovely pulse. Lovely stuff. Diam. 13.5% alc. **RATING** 95 **DRINK** 2026–2032 $135 DB

Vintage Cuvée 2017, Tasmania Characters of baked apple, soft spice, light brioche notes, crushed stone and red apple crunch. Hints of light biscuit and autolysis flow in on the palate, along with hints of white flowers, stone, lemon curd and almond paste. The acidity is fine, lacy and of swift cadence, the dosage modest and the finish clean, crisp and appley. Diam. 12.5% alc. **RATING** 94 **DRINK** 2023–2028 $55 DB

Non Vintage Cuvée NV, Tasmania Pinot noir chardonnay with a '20 base; reserve principally ex '19 and '18. It's the length of the palate that stands out. Pear, blanched almonds, and low-key citrus provide the flavours of a wine with perfect balance. 2500 dozen made. Diam. 12.8% alc. **RATING** 94 $42 JH

Hurlo's Rosé 2022, Tasmania A beautiful salmon pink hue with aromas of redcurrants, raspberry, white peach and ruby grapefruit with hints of soft spice, a wisp of watermelon, wildflowers, crushed river stone and a glimpse of cedar. Some lovely textural elements with crème fraîche and lemon curd on the palate, redcurrant jelly, lemon zest and apple turnover with a mineral-laden pulse and a dry, savoury finish. Impressive. Screw cap. 12.9% alc. **RATING** 94 **DRINK** 2023–2027 $80 DB

🍷🍷🍷🍷♀ **Flyleaf Pinot Noir 2019, Tasmania RATING** 92 **DRINK** 2023–2026 $40 DB

Delatite ★★★★★

390 Pollards Road, Mansfield, Vic 3722 **Region** Upper Goulburn
T (03) 5775 2922 **www**.delatitewinery.com.au **Open** 7 days 11–5 **Winemaker** Andy Browning **Viticulturist** David Ritchie **Est.** 1982 **Dozens** 14 000 **Vyds** 28ha

With its sweeping views across to the snow-clad alps, this is uncompromising cool-climate viticulture. Increasing vine age (first plantings in '68, others between '84–2011) and the adoption of organic (and partial biodynamic) viticulture, have also played a role in providing the red wines with more depth and texture. The white wines are all wild-yeast fermented and are as good as ever.

🍷🍷🍷🍷🍷 **Pinot Gris 2022, Upper Goulburn** Lifted aromas of apple blossom, intense honeysuckle, lime cordial, apple and honeyed spice. Clean acidity aids the delivery of concentrated fruit, spiced apple, lemon drop and nougat flavours. A pastille-like brightness lasts on the finish. Screw cap. 14% alc. **RATING** 95 **DRINK** 2023–2029 $30 JP ✪

Vivienne's Block Reserve Riesling 2021, Upper Goulburn This delicate style of riesling seems so fragile, so finely nuanced in flavour and acidity, but don't be deceived. It's made of more concentrated stuff. Lime cordial, spring blossom, quince, grapefruit pith and white peach arrive bright and intense. Layers of flavour run deep, highlighted by a citrusy acid drive. And so, so tight in its youth. Give it time to spread its wings. Screw cap. 13.5% alc. **RATING** 95 **DRINK** 2022–2030 $60 JP

Late Harvest Riesling 2022, Upper Goulburn Complex, compelling and giving sweet whites a good name. Quince, spiced apple, lime and grapefruit are concentrated in both perfume and flavour. Acidity is an unassuming star, bringing an electric tension to the wine, so much so, the drinker's recognition of sweetness is almost an afterthought. Impressive balance all around. Screw cap. 11.5% alc. **RATING** 95 **DRINK** 2022–2032 $30 JP ✪

🍷🍷🍷🍷🍷 **Pet Nat Riesling Gewürz 2022, Upper Goulburn RATING** 93 **DRINK** 2023–2023 $40 JP
Riesling 2021, Upper Goulburn RATING 92 **DRINK** 2023–2026 $30 JP ✪
Tempranillo 2021, Upper Goulburn RATING 91 **DRINK** 2022–2026 $48 JP
Mansfield Red 2020, Upper Goulburn RATING 91 **DRINK** 2022–2030 $40 JP

Della Fay Wines ★★★★

3276 Caves Road, Yallingup, WA 6284 **Region** Margaret River
T (08) 9755 2747 **www**.dellafay.com **Open** By appt **Winemaker** Michael Kelly
Viticulturist Michael Kelly **Est.** 1999 **Dozens** 3000 **Vyds** 6.4ha
This is the venture of the Kelly family, headed by district veteran Michael Kelly. He gained his degree in wine science from CSU before working at Seville Estate and Mount Mary in the Yarra Valley and Domaine Louis Chapuis in Burgundy, then returning to WA and working for Leeuwin Estate. Michael became the long-term winemaker at Fermoy Estate, while he and his family laid the groundwork for their own brand, buying prime viticultural land in Caves Road, Yallingup, in '99. The focus is on estate-grown cabernet sauvignon, merlot and chardonnay, as well as nebbiolo and vermentino. They also make shiraz from Geographe.

🍷🍷🍷🍷🍷 **Cabernet Sauvignon 2019, Margaret River** Classic regional characters come charging in from mulberries, blackberries and bay leaves to warm earth and nori. It's full bodied, a riper style but still with lots of restraining acidity and no shortage of tannins. Screw cap. 14.5% alc. **RATING** 91 **DRINK** 2024–2034 $38 JF
Shiraz 2019, Geographe A rich, dense and robust style hitting some alcohol warmth on the finish. Still, decent fruit in the mix all dark plums, currants, licorice, cloves and cedary oak. An earthy fragrance, too, which is a Geographe character. Full bodied, lots of tannins and at this price, good value. Screw cap. 15% alc. **RATING** 90 **DRINK** 2023–2028 $25 JF ✪

Denton ★★★★★

160 Old Healesville Road, Yarra Glen, Vic 3775 **Region** Yarra Valley
T 0402 346 686 **www**.dentonwine.com **Open** By appt **Winemaker** Luke Lambert
Viticulturist Julian Parrott **Est.** 1997 **Dozens** 2500 **Vyds** 31.3ha
Leading Melbourne architect John Denton and son Simon established their View Hill vineyard between '97–04. The name View Hill derives from the fact that a granite plug 'was created 370 million years ago, sitting above the surrounding softer sandstones and silt of the valley'. This granite base is most unusual in the Yarra Valley, and, together with the natural amphitheatre that the plug created, has consistently produced exceptional grapes. The principal varieties planted are pinot noir, chardonnay and nebbiolo, plus make an orange wine from ribolla gialla.

🍷🍷🍷🍷🍷 **Chardonnay 2021, Yarra Valley** A very bright green gold. Complex and intriguing with aromas of pear, green apples, a little white nectarine, jasmine and roasted nuts. On the palate, I love the way this manages to be both elegant and intense. The structure and length are spot-on. One of the best Denton wines I've ever tasted. Screw cap. 12.5% alc. **RATING** 97 **DRINK** 2022–2027 $50 PR ✪

🍷🍷🍷🍷🍷 **Shed Rosé 2022, Yarra Valley** A blend of cabernet sauvignon, shiraz and nebbiolo. A pale onion skin hue, this vibrant and subtle wine has aromas of red fruits, blood oranges and lavender. I really like the palate, which is taut, mouth-filling and very refreshing on the chalky, saline and dry finish. A well-priced premium rosé. Screw cap. 11.9% alc. **RATING** 95 **DRINK** 2022-2025 $28 PR ✪
Pinot Noir 2021, Yarra Valley A medium, bright garnet. Expressive on the nose with its bouquet of wild strawberries and a little blood orange together with florals and some secondary forest floor scents. The medium-bodied palate is both silky smooth and structured, relying as much on the wine's bright acidity for its backbone as it does on the fine, gently grippy tannins. Diam. 13.5% alc. **RATING** 95 **DRINK** 2022-2029 $50 PR ✪

🍷🍷🍷🍷🍷 **Shed Pinot Noir 2022, Yarra Valley RATING** 92 **DRINK** 2022-2027 $35 PR
Cabernet Sauvignon 2021, Yarra Valley RATING 92 **DRINK** 2022-2028 $50 PR

Deviation Road

207 Scott Creek Road, Longwood, SA 5153 **Region** Adelaide Hills
T (08) 8339 2633 **www.**deviationroad.com **Open** 7 days 10–5 **Winemaker** Kate Laurie
Est. 1999 **Dozens** 8000 **Vyds** 11.05ha
Continuing a 5-generation family winemaking tradition, Hamish and Kate Laurie created their first wine from the 30yo Laurie family-owned vineyard on Deviation Road in '02. In '04 Hamish and Kate purchased their property at Longwood, which is the current home to 4ha of shiraz and pinot noir, the winery and tasting room.

🍷🍷🍷🍷🍷 **Beltana Blanc de Blancs 2016, Adelaide Hills** An exceptional fizz driven by a whopping 6 years on lees. Sweet lemon tart, candied pear and tarte Tatin. A sumptuous finish of drive, breadth and depth, the freshness swivelling amid the crèmeur while the sweetness meanders alongside. Cork. 12.5% alc. **RATING** 95 **DRINK** 2022-2028 $105 NG ♥
Chardonnay 2022, Adelaide Hills This is very good. The legacy of barrel fermentation and extended lees handling consummated as smoky, flinty riffs of mineral pungency. Baked apple, cantaloupe, cinnamon and creamed cashew. Expansive sweetness, dragged long by juicy, palpably natural acidity. Screw cap. 12.5% alc. **RATING** 95 **DRINK** 2023-2030 $55 NG
Pinot Gris 2022, Adelaide Hills It is a skilled hand that crafts mid-weighted gris as deftly textured, fresh and intense of flavour as this. A wonderful interplay between the thrust of fruit, orchard and autumnal, alongside the parry of structural attributes, both pucker and freshness beautifully measured. Screw cap. 12.5% alc. **RATING** 94 **DRINK** 2022-2026 $30 NG ✪

🍷🍷🍷🍷🍷 **Loftia Vintage Brut 2019, Adelaide Hills RATING** 93 **DRINK** 2022-2028 $48 NG
Altair Brut Rosé NV, Adelaide Hills RATING 93 $42 NG
Pinot Noir 2022, Adelaide Hills RATING 92 **DRINK** 2023-2028 $55 NG
Sauvignon Blanc 2022, Adelaide Hills RATING 91 **DRINK** 2022-2024 $30 NG

Devil's Corner

1 Sherbourne Road, Apslawn, Tas 7190 **Region** East Coast Tasmania
T 0448 521 412 **www.**devilscorner.com.au **Open** 7 days 10–5 **Winemaker** Tom Wallace, Anthony de Amicis **Est.** 1999 **Dozens** 70 000 **Vyds** 175ha
Long the affordable sibling of Tamar Ridge and Pirie within the Brown Family Wine Group, Devil's Corner has grown into a premium wine identity in its own right. Its home is the spectacular and picturesque Hazards vineyard on Tasmania's East Coast, still the largest vineyard in the state, though the company's Kayena vineyard (see Tamar Ridge) is also a substantial source for many of its blends. The cellar door offers sensational views to the Freycinet Peninsula and The Hazards range itself.

ᵠᵠᵠᵠᵠ **Mt Dove Pinot Syrah 2021, Tasmania** Expressive dark cherry and blueberry fruit tones are dotted with fine spice, white pepper, Kalamata olives, dried citrus rind, citrus blossom, sous bois and light game and amaro notes. Superfine, billowing powdery tannins and a nice briny acid drive as the wine fades away slowly, showing excellent balance and an edge of morello cherry sapidity on the exit. Screw cap. 12.5% alc. **RATING** 93 **DRINK** 2023-2029 $70 DB

Resolution Riesling 2022, Tasmania Pale straw in the glass with aromas of freshly squeezed lime, green apple and grapefruit with hints of citrus blossom, crushed slate and oyster shell, almond paste and a whiff of freshly sliced fennel. There's a suggestion of lemon curd on the tight, focused palate that shows serious velocity with a crystalline acid line pushing the wine forward, finishing dry and precise with a briny, limey blast on the exit. Screw cap. 13% alc. **RATING** 92 **DRINK** 2023-2030 $40 DB

Mt Amos Pinot Noir 2018, Tasmania With its velvety dark cherry and berry fruits, exotic spice, gentle amaro tones, dried citrus rind notes and a whiff of orange bitters and game, Mt Amos represents a step up in fruit density and seamless palate flow. Good cellaring potential here, too, with fine-grained tannin architecture and bright acidity providing ample drive and tension. Screw cap. 14% alc. **RATING** 92 **DRINK** 2023-2033 $70 DB

Pinot Grigio 2022, Tasmania King Valley Pale in the glass and serving up characters of crunchy nashi pear, pawpaw and citrus fruits with hints of white flowers, stone and gentle herbal tones. Crisp and inviting with bright acidity and just the merest squeak of texture on the palate, finishing with a pure wave of apple and pear fruits. Screw cap. 12.5% alc. **RATING** 90 **DRINK** 2023-2025 $25 DB ✪

Riesling 2022, Tasmania A vibrant pale straw with green flashes and characters of freshly squeezed lime, green apple and grapefruit with hints of citrus blossom, crushed stone and a whiff of cut fennel. Crisp and refreshing with great precision thanks to a sizzling Tassie acid line, finishing with a blast of apple and lime, crisp and true. Screw cap. 13% alc. **RATING** 90 **DRINK** 2023-2030 $27 DB

Devil's Lair   ★★★★☆

Rocky Road, Forest Grove via Margaret River, WA 6286 (postal) **Region** Margaret River **T** (08) 9759 2000 **www**.devils-lair.com **Open** Not **Winemaker** Travis Clydesdale **Est.** 1990

Devil's Lair has carved out a reputation through a combination of clever packaging and impressive wine quality. The estate vineyards are substantial and are supplemented by contract-grown fruit. High quality Margaret River chardonnay and cabernet remain the focus of the wines produced each vintage; the top-tier 9th Chamber wines only made in exceptional vintages.

ᵠᵠᵠᵠᵠ **Chardonnay 2022, Margaret River** This does not disappoint with its array of grapefruit pith and lemon zest loaded with powdered ginger and galangal plus snips of fresh herbs. Ah, the palate. Long, pure and racy acidity corrals the texture full of creamy, cashew lees into place. Excellent stuff. Screw cap. 13% alc. **RATING** 95 **DRINK** 2023-2032 $50 JF ✪

ᵠᵠᵠᵠᵠ **Dance with the Devil Chardonnay 2022, Margaret River** **RATING** 93 **DRINK** 2023-2028 $25 JF ✪

Cabernet Sauvignon 2021, Margaret River **RATING** 93 **DRINK** 2025-2038 $50 JF

The Hidden Cave Chardonnay 2022, Margaret River **RATING** 91 **DRINK** 2023-2027 $25 JF ✪

Dexter Wines   ★★★★★

210 Foxeys Road, Tuerong, Vic 3915 (postal) **Region** Mornington Peninsula **T** (03) 5989 7007 **www**.dexterwines.com.au **Open** Not **Winemaker** Tod Dexter **Viticulturist** Tod Dexter **Est.** 1987 **Dozens** 2000 **Vyds** 7.1ha

In the mid-1970s, Tod Dexter travelled to the US for a ski season, afterward becoming an apprentice winemaker at Cakebread Cellars, a well-known Napa Valley establishment. After 7 years he returned to the Mornington Peninsula, planting pinot noir (4ha) and chardonnay (3.1ha) in '87. To keep the wolves from the door he became winemaker at Stonier and leased his vineyard to them. Having left Stonier to become the Yabby Lake winemaker, and spurred on by turning 50 in '06, he and wife Debbie established the Dexter label. The quality of his wines has been impeccable, the pinot noir especially so.

Chardonnay 2022, Mornington Peninsula Walks a tightrope with acidity yet layers of flavour on either side stretch out accentuated and long. Expect citrus and a snip of fresh herbs with lots of savoury inputs from the toasty oak but also crushed rocks and smoky sulphides. It has power yet a certain elegance, too. Screw cap. 13% alc. RATING 96 DRINK 2023–2032 $50 JF ✪

Pinot Noir 2022, Mornington Peninsula This is the prettiest, most approachable pinot I can remember from Tod Dexter. It has a lovely mix of cherries and strawberries all delicately spiced with some blood orange and zest keeping it tangy and juicy. Barely medium bodied with supple tannins and finishing gently yet resolutely. Screw cap. 13.5% alc. RATING 95 DRINK 2023–2030 $60 JF

DiGiorgio Family Wines ★★★★

14918 Riddoch Highway, Coonawarra, SA 5263 **Region** Coonawarra
T (08) 8736 3222 **www**.digiorgio.com.au **Open** 7 days 10–5 **Winemaker** Willy Lunn, Bryan Tonkin **Viticulturist** Frank DiGiorgio **Est.** 1998 **Dozens** 25 000 **Vyds** 353.53ha
Stefano DiGiorgio emigrated from Abruzzo, Italy, in 1952. Over the years, he and his family gradually expanded their holdings at Lucindale to 126ha. In '89 he began planting cabernet sauvignon, chardonnay, merlot, shiraz and pinot noir. In '02 the family purchased the historic Rouge Homme winery and its surrounding 13.5ha of vines from Southcorp. The plantings have since been increased to over 350ha, the lion's share to cabernet sauvignon.

Cabernet Sauvignon 2021, Coonawarra This is a firm, well-structured cabernet with black olive, mint, peppercorn and blackcurrant flavours pushing throughout. It sits on the bold side of medium weight, though the meaty dryness of the tannin helps with the impression of size. This will benefit from a few years rest in a cool, dark place. Screw cap. 13.5% alc. RATING 92 DRINK 2025–2033 $35 CM

Kongorong Riesling 2022, Mount Gambier Steely riesling with lime, mineral and bath salt characters shooting straight and direct through the palate. Line and length personified, if perhaps at the expense of flesh. Screw cap. 11.6% alc. RATING 90 DRINK 2025–2035 $25 CM ✪

Emporio Merlot Cabernet Sauvignon Cabernet Franc 2021, Coonawarra Mulberry and briar flavours merge into blackcurrant and milk chocolate. It's both herbal and sweet-fruited at once, the aftertaste showing stringy, slightly bitter herb notes, though it remains pleasant to drink. Some time in the cellar will soften the edges. Screw cap. 13.5% alc. RATING 90 DRINK 2024–2032 $35 CM

 Diletto ★★★★★

131 Lumb Road, Sutherlands Creek, Vic 3331 (postal) **Region** Victoria
T 0402 409 292 **www**.dilettowines.com **Open** Not **Winemaker** Melanie Chester, Ben Mullen **Est.** 2021 **Dozens** 150
Diletto, an Italian word meaning 'to take pleasure', is a new label from Giant Step's winemaker Melanie Chester and Mulline's Ben Mullen (and respective partners). Born out of a love of syrah, their first wine was from the 1969-planted Westgate vineyard just outside of Great Western. There are plans to expand the range to single-vineyard shiraz wines from other great sites in Australia, too.

ΨΨΨΨΨ **Westgate Syrah 2021, Grampians** An auspicious debut. A brilliant crimson purple. Geez, this smells good. Aromas of dark fruits, lavender, graphite, a little olive tapenade and garrigues. Textured with velvety, persistent tannins and bright acidity. A delicious wine, that while hard to keep your hands off even now, will reward at least a decade in the cellar. Screw cap. 13.5% alc. **RATING** 96 **DRINK** 2023-2032 $80 PR

Dinny Goonan   ★★★★☆

880 Winchelsea-Deans Marsh Road, Bambra, Vic 3241 (postal) **Region** Port Phillip **T** 0438 408 420 **www**.dinnygoonan.com.au **Open** Not **Winemaker** Dinny Goonan, Angus Goonan **Est.** 1989 **Dozens** 1500 **Vyds** 5.5ha

The genesis of Dinny Goonan dates back to '88, when Dinny bought a 20ha property near Bambra, in the hinterland of the Otway Coast. Dinny had recently completed a viticulture diploma at CSU and initially a wide range of varieties was planted in what is now known as the Nursery Block. As these came into production Dinny headed back to CSU, where he completed a wine science degree. Production is focused on shiraz and riesling, followed by chardonnay and pinot noir.

ΨΨΨΨΨ **Single Vineyard Riesling 2022, Geelong** A light, bright gold with green tinges. Fragrant and subtle with its melange of freshly squeezed lime, orange blossom, elderflower and just a hint of mint. Dry with citrus pith and bright acidity and finishing long yet tightly wound. Screw cap. 12.5% alc. **RATING** 95 **DRINK** 2023-2032 $32 PR ✪

ΨΨΨΨΨ **Chardonnay 2022, Geelong RATING** 93 **DRINK** 2023-2029 $35 PR ✪
Pinot Noir 2022, Geelong RATING 92 **DRINK** 2023-2027 $35 PR
The Bambra Pinot Noir Chardonnay 2017, Geelong RATING 91 **DRINK** 2022-2025 $45 PR
Single Vineyard Shiraz 2021, Geelong RATING 90 **DRINK** 2022-2026 $34 PR

Dionysus Winery   ★★★★

1 Patemans Lane, Murrumbateman, NSW 2582 **Region** Canberra District **T** 0411 730 724 **www**.dionysus-winery.com.au **Open** W'ends & public hols 10–5 **Winemaker** Michael O'Dea **Est.** 1998 **Dozens** 1000 **Vyds** 4ha

Michael and Wendy O'Dea founded the winery while they had parallel lives as public servants in Canberra. They have now retired, and devote themselves full-time to Dionysus. They purchased their property in '96 and planted chardonnay, sauvignon blanc, riesling, viognier, merlot, pinot noir, cabernet sauvignon and shiraz. Michael has an associate degree in winemaking from CSU and is responsible for viticulture and winemaking; Wendy is responsible for wine marketing.

ΨΨΨΨΨ **Marsanne Roussanne 2022, Hilltops** It's textural and somewhat creamy with a pleasant softness to the acidity and feel across the palate. There's white stone fruit, tangy Meyer lemon and a fleck of spice adding to the flavour profile with neat phenolics on the finish. Screw cap. 13.8% alc. **RATING** 92 **DRINK** 2023-2027 $33 JF

Reserve Riesling 2022, Canberra District It has all the refreshment and drive you could wish for, given the variety. Also, spiced lemon, lime cordial, some bath salts and chalky acidity. It feels soft and easy yet lingers long. Great now and will go some distance. Screw cap. 12% alc. **RATING** 92 **DRINK** 2022-2032 $35 JF

May Riesling 2021, Canberra District A slab of Ossau-Iraty cheese and a glass of chilled May Riesling would be a very fine combo. This is sweet, yet tangy acidity goes in some way to temper that and it's full of saffron, lemon drops, lime cordial and a touch of brittle toffee. 375ml. Screw cap. 10% alc. **RATING** 90 **DRINK** 2022-2026 $35 JF

Dirty Three Wines

★★★★★

64 Cashin Street, Inverloch, Vic 3996 **Region** Gippsland
T 0413 547 932 **www**.dirtythreewines.com.au **Open** Thu–Sun 12–5.30
Winemaker Marcus Satchell **Viticulturist** Marcus Satchell **Est.** 2012 **Dozens** 2500
Vyds 4ha

These days, Marcus Satchell goes by the moniker Mr Gippsland. He's in demand as a contract winemaker, but his own label, run with wife Lisa Sartori, is the real star. The winery is at the back of their cellar door in a cool, industrial site in Leongatha. Sourcing fruit off the Tilson and Berrys Creek vineyards has been key to their vinous success. While Marcus will continue to work with those sites, he and a long-term friend with links to the local dairy industry have decided to collaborate, too. To that end, Marcus has planted his first vineyard, in Leongatha South, with nearly 5ha of chardonnay, pinot noir and riesling with small parcels of mencia, teroldego and refosco. Here's hoping they turn out to be regional heroes one day.

🍷🍷🍷🍷🍷 **All The Dirts Chardonnay 2022, South Gippsland** Exhilarating and incomparable. The power of South Gippsland fruit is on show yet pared back to reveal a beating heart of pink grapefruit, lemon splice and tangy mouth-watering acidity leading off the finely tuned palate. Layers of texture with lees and oak add more to leave an impression of a mighty fine riff. Screw cap. 12.8% alc. **RATING** 97 **DRINK** 2023–2032 $55 JF ✪

🍷🍷🍷🍷🍷 **All the Dirts Pinot Noir 2022, South Gippsland** This is an excellent wine. Quality is not down, no way. This has set its own tune with florals, spice, a riff of red fruits, cherries, raspberries and more. But as always, the palate sings. Oh-so fine tannins glide across the palate and with the equally fine acidity, the finish is long and pure. Screw cap. 13.5% alc. **RATING** 96 **DRINK** 2023–2035 $55 JF ✪

Magic Dirt Pinot Noir 2022, South Gippsland Made with 100% whole bunches it's a big departure in style, says Marcus Satchell. 'It's a polariser,' he reckons. Maybe, maybe not. Yes, there's a fragrant lift, a refreshing stemmy character but the quality fruit, its richness has taken it all in its stride. Complex, savoury, alive and energetic. Persuasive tannins, shapely and textural, work across the full-bodied palate with electrifying acidity. Rock on. Screw cap. 13.2% alc. **RATING** 96 **DRINK** 2023–2035 $120 JF

Dirt Two Pinot Noir 2021, Gippsland Composed and almost gentle with its sway of sweet fruit mingling with some tangy, slightly tart cherries and pomegranate, all lightly spiced and earthy. Mid-weighted and so vibrant, led by its crunchy acidity with raw silk tannins in tow. Screw cap. 13% alc. **RATING** 95 **DRINK** 2023–2035 $65 JF

All The Dirts Chardonnay 2021, South Gippsland Previously known as The Dirty Chardy. A joy to drink with pristine citrus and saline flavours, thirst-quenching acidity and judicious handling of oak that imparts a layer of spice and zip. Finely tuned, savoury, moreish and complex, but most importantly, delicious. Screw cap 12.8% alc. **RATING** 95 **DRINK** 2022–2033 $50 JF ✪

All the Dirts Pinot Noir 2021, South Gippsland Fruit from 5 sites (or dirts) goes towards creating this wine. Heady aromas of red flowers, warm earth and spicy dark fruits. The fuller-bodied palate is flush with sweet cherries yet puts on a savoury show. Finely shaped tannins, super-bright acidity and a slight bitter radicchio/Campari finish, which is appealing, add up to a very good pinot indeed. Screw cap. 13.2% alc. **RATING** 95 **DRINK** 2023–2033 $48 JF ✪

The Dirty Rizza Riesling 2022, Gippsland Firstly, this isn't dirty at all. Hard-pressed whole bunches for flavour and body. The juice is unclarified (or 'dirty') allowing for texture, too. It's a ripper rizza. It's off-dry, allowing the gentle sweetness to temper the lively acidity. It's refreshing and tangy, full of lemon and lime juice/zest with a smidge of creamy curd. I could drink this all day. Lovely wine. Screw cap. 11.5% alc. **RATING** 94 **DRINK** 2022–2032 $38 JF ✪

Dirt Three Pinot Noir 2021, Gippsland Made differently from the Dirt Two Pinot Noir – here it's 100% whole berries and aged in older oak. It's also darker and richer than its sibling and not quite ready to reveal its attributes. Although plenty on offer with wafts of lavender, dark cherries and baking spices. Full bodied with ripe, sweet tannins and a brace of acidity. Feels very tightly wound and nervy. Give it time. Screw cap. 13.5% alc. **RATING** 94 **DRINK** 2024-2034 $65 JF

DogRidge Wine Company ★★★★☆

129 Bagshaws Road, McLaren Flat, SA 5171 **Region** McLaren Vale
T (08) 8383 0140 **www**.dogridge.com.au **Open** Mon–Fri 11–5, w'ends 12–4
Winemaker Fred Howard **Viticulturist** Dave Wright **Est.** 1991 **Dozens** 18000
Vyds 56ha
Dave and Jen Wright (co-owners with Fred and Sarah Howard) had a combined background of dentistry, art and a CSU viticultural degree when they moved from Adelaide to McLaren Flat to become vignerons. They inherited shiraz and grenache vines planted in the early '40s as a source for Château Reynella fortified wines, and their vineyards now include some of the oldest vines in the immediate district. Quality at one end, value-packed at the other.

Fortified Viognier NV This is a superb fortified. Perhaps it is the superlative quality of the spirit that gels varietal spice, apricot pith and ginger to an intoxicating undercurrent of glazed walnuts, orange verbena, tamarind, turmeric and other scents from the floor of the souk, mashed and muddled with pickled cumquat, that makes it all so integrated and mellifluous and delicious. Despite the decadence, the overall impression is miraculously savoury, like all great fortifieds. Ridiculous price! Screw cap. 19% alc. **RATING** 96 $25 NG ❂

Grand Old Brand New Cabernet Sauvignon Shiraz Petit Verdot 2014, McLaren Vale RATING 91 **DRINK** 2022-2025 $40 NG
Butterfingers Barrel Aged Bâtonnage Chardonnay 2021, McLaren Vale
RATING 90 **DRINK** 2022-2026 $30 NG

DogRock Winery ★★★★★

114 Degraves Road, Crowlands, Vic 3377 **Region** Pyrenees
T 0409 280 317 **www**.dogrock.com.au **Open** By appt **Winemaker** Allen Hart
Viticulturist Andrea Hart **Est.** 1998 **Dozens** 1000 **Vyds** 6.2ha
This is the venture of Allen (now full-time winemaker) and Andrea (viticulturist) Hart. Having purchased the property in '98, the planting of shiraz, riesling, tempranillo, grenache, chardonnay and marsanne began in '00 (0.2ha of touriga nacional added in '16 and arinto and azal in '20). Given Allen's former post as research scientist and winemaker with Foster's, the attitude taken to winemaking is unexpected. The estate-grown wines are made in a low-tech fashion, without gas cover or filtration.

Degraves Road Single Vineyard Reserve Shiraz 2021, Pyrenees Ripe cherry plum flavours come adorned in twiggy spice and florals, a swoosh of smoked cedar wrapping it all up beautifully. There's a lot going on here, but it's not a fruit-and-oak bomb. There's savouriness, smokiness, sweetness and more. It's a ripper. Screw cap. 14% alc. **RATING** 96 **DRINK** 2025-2040 $38 CM ❂
Degraves Road Single Vineyard Arinto 2022, Pyrenees Salt on citrus, apples in bloom, herbs with a light smoking. This is both a textural white wine and a highly engaging one, the combination of brine and fruit just begging to be accompanied by food. There's a great deal to like about this. Screw cap. 11.5% alc. **RATING** 94 **DRINK** 2024-2030 $30 CM ❂
Shiraz 2021, Pyrenees Tasty and more. Plum, cedar, mint, musk and smoked meat flavours put on a wildly entertaining, and enjoyable, show. Fresh acidity keeps things lively, but this is a wine built fundamentally on flavour, tannin and length. A creaminess to the texture doesn't hurt either. Screw cap. 13.5% alc. **RATING** 94 **DRINK** 2024-2035 $30 CM ❂
Graciano 2021, Pyrenees The expressive bouquet offers spices and rose petals, the ultrafine palate ups the ante with its length. Tremulous fruits take hold in the

mouth to an unexpected degree, but without significant tannin or oak support. The key is its balance. Screw cap. 12.5% alc. **RATING** 94 **DRINK** 2023–2033 $30 JH ✪

ŸŸŸŸŸ Grenache 2021, Pyrenees **RATING** 93 **DRINK** 2023–2028 $30 CM ✪
Degraves Road Reserve Single Vineyard Chardonnay 2021, Pyrenees **RATING** 93 **DRINK** 2024–2030 $65 CM
El Rojo 2019, Pyrenees **RATING** 93 **DRINK** 2024–2032 $65 CM
Cabernet Sauvignon Shiraz 2021, Pyrenees **RATING** 90 **DRINK** 2023–2030 $30 JH
Cabernet Sauvignon 2021, Pyrenees **RATING** 90 **DRINK** 2024–2031 $30 CM

Domaine A ★★★★★

105 Tea Tree Road, Campania, Tas 7026 **Region** Southern Tasmania
T 0484 001 944 www.domaine-a.com.au **Open** Thurs–Sun 11–5 **Winemaker** Conor van der Reest **Viticulturist** Peter Mueller **Est.** 1973 **Dozens** 5000 **Vyds** 14ha
In '18, ownership of Domaine A passed from Peter Althaus, its long-term custodian, to Moorilla Estate. There were no changes to existing employees, with Conor van der Reest continuing as winemaker, albeit flying solo from the '18 vintage after working closely with Peter for many years prior. Both brands are now owned by philanthropist and collector David Walsh of Mona, Australia's largest private museum. A newly refurbished cellar door/tasting room opened in '22.

ŸŸŸŸŸ Lady A Sauvignon Blanc 2019, Tasmania Complex and captivating with ripe citrus, guava, feijoa and light tropical fruits with underlying hints of wildflowers, crushed river stone, struck flint, honeysuckle, softly spiced baked apples and dried herbs. Great length with a complex wave of fruit, spice and earth, so filigreed with pristine mineral drive and a super-savoury sustained finish. Cork. 13.5% alc. **RATING** 96 **DRINK** 2023–2035 $75 DB ✪ ♥
Pinot Noir 2017, Tasmania A concentrated style, deep in colour with rich blackberry and maraschino cherry with hints of fruitcake spices, cedar, tobacco, fennel gratin, beef jus, licorice and lighter tones of sous bois and dried herbs. Mouth-filling and powerful with tight-grained tannin, layers of spice and herbs and a flexing, black-fruited finish. Impressive and stylistically, one for those seeking power over grace. Cork. 14.9% alc. **RATING** 95 **DRINK** 2023–2033 $85 DB

ŸŸŸŸŸ Merlot 2018, Tasmania **RATING** 93 **DRINK** 2023–2033 $85 DB
Petit a 2016, Tasmania **RATING** 92 **DRINK** 2023–2030 $52 DB

Domaine Asmara ★★★★

Gibb Road, Toolleen, Vic 3551 **Region** Heathcote
T (03) 5433 6133 www.domaineasmara.com **Open** 7 days 9–6.30
Winemaker Sanguine Estate **Est.** 2008 **Dozens** 3000 **Vyds** 12ha
Chemical engineer Andreas Greiving had a lifelong dream to own and operate a vineyard, and the opportunity came along with the global financial crisis. He was able to purchase a vineyard planted to shiraz, cabernet sauvignon, cabernet franc, durif and viognier, and have the wines contract-made. The venture is co-managed by his partner Hennijati who works as a dentist.

ŸŸŸŸŸ Infinity Shiraz 2021, Heathcote Warm, bold and black-fruited. This is an intensely concentrated bottle of red wine. Blackberry, tar, molasses and dried herb notes blend into coffee-cream and orange oil. Spice notes are studded straight into the tannin and while there's obvious alcohol warmth the sheer volume of flavour pushes straight through it. If you like 'em big, you'll love this. Diam. 15% alc. **RATING** 94 **DRINK** 2024–2036 $79 CM

ŸŸŸŸŸ Private Reserve Durif 2021, Heathcote **RATING** 93 **DRINK** 2024–2034 $45 CM
Reserve Shiraz 2021, Heathcote **RATING** 92 **DRINK** 2023–2031 $45 CM

Reserve Cabernet Sauvignon 2021, Heathcote RATING 91
DRINK 2024–2033 $35 CM
Private Collection Shiraz 2021, Heathcote RATING 90 DRINK 2023–2030
$35 CM

Domaine Naturaliste ★★★★★

160 Johnson Road, Wilyabrup, WA 6280 **Region** Margaret River
T (08) 9755 6776 **www.domainenaturaliste.com.au Open** 7 days 10–5
Winemaker Bruce Dukes **Est.** 2012 **Dozens** 12 000 **Vyds** 21ha
Bruce Dukes is wholly talented, and while he makes high-quality acclaimed wines for his own estate – Domaine Naturaliste – he also does this for a raft of other, smaller producers in Margaret River and Geographe. His winemaking style is one of fresh, pure fruit over obvious or intrusive winemaking artifact, and the wines routinely possess a polish and eminent drinkability. Bruce holds both a degree in agronomy from the University of WA and a master's degree in viticulture and agronomy from the University of California (Davis) and has been in Margaret River since '00.

ŶŶŶŶŶ **Purus Chardonnay 2021, Margaret River** The glittering green hue is a pointer to what is to come. Complex barrel ferment aromas bring crushed cashew and a funky wreath of blanched almonds into play. It is the brightest and lightest on its feet of the 3 chardonnay siblings, with fantastic length and perfect balance. Screw cap. 12.5% alc. RATING 97 DRINK 2023–2036 $56 JH ✿

ŶŶŶŶŶ **Floris Chardonnay 2021, Margaret River** The same white grapefruit and nectarine as its Artus Chardonnay sibling, but that's where the similarity ends. This is all about purity and finesse, the fruit flavours strung on a necklace of diamonds, oak incidental. Screw cap. 13.5% alc. RATING 96 DRINK 2023–2035 $35 JH ✿
Artus Chardonnay 2021, Margaret River A wine from the big end of town, built on a scaffold of French oak barrel fermentation and stiletto acidity. Grapefruit and nectarine fill in the masonry. It is layered and balanced. Screw cap. 13% alc. RATING 96 DRINK 2023–2031 $56 JH ✿
Sauvage Sauvignon Blanc 2021, Margaret River Sauvignon Blanc of the Year. It's savoury and dry, but the lemon zest and fruit flavours are the prime movers in showing what can be done even in a vintage that wasn't easy. Screw cap. 13% alc. RATING 96 DRINK 2023–2029 $35 JH ✿ ♥
Le Naturaliste Cabernet Franc 2020, Margaret River While it's a variety that can be so elegant, this is a bigger, richer style yet done well and doesn't go OTT. It's brimming with blueberries, currants and red cherries, spiced to the max with cinnamon and cloves plus a liberal spread of dried herbs. Full bodied, plush with expansive tannins and a lingering finish. Screw cap. 14% alc. RATING 95 DRINK 2023–2033 $89 JF
Morus Cabernet Sauvignon 2019, Margaret River Morus as in mulberries, so expect plenty to feature here. The wine is stately, full of dark ripe fruit, bitter chocolate studded with raisins and nuts, woodsy spices and savoury meaty notes. It's full bodied and dense with expansive tannins and fans of such styles will be pleased. Screw cap. 14% alc. RATING 95 DRINK 2023–2035 $89 JF
Rebus Cabernet Sauvignon 2019, Margaret River The aromas hit at the first twitch of the glass: cassis, olive and tapenade, the medium-bodied palate drawing them into a tightly spun net of tannins. Its best years are in front of it but are well worth waiting for. Screw cap. 14% alc. RATING 95 DRINK 2023–2044 $37 JH ✿
Discovery Syrah 2021, Margaret River Flavours are bright, spicy and unfettered by cedary, charry oak. An array of dark plums, pepper and sumac with supple ripe tannins sashay across the mid-weighted palate with everything refreshed by the tingly acidity. A very good 'drink now' option. Screw cap. 13.5% alc. RATING 94 DRINK 2023–2030 $26 JF ✿

🍷🍷🍷🍷 Rachis Syrah 2021, Margaret River RATING 93 DRINK 2024–2034 $39 JF
Discovery Chardonnay 2021, Margaret River RATING 90 DRINK 2022–2028 $26 JF
Discovery Cabernet Sauvignon 2020, Margaret River RATING 90 DRINK 2023–2029 $26 JF

Domenica Wines ★★★★★

651 Wangaratta-Beechworth Road, Beechworth, Vic 3747 **Region** Beechworth
T (03) 5728 1612 **www.domenicawines.com.au Open** By appt **Winemaker** Peter Graham **Est.** 2012 **Dozens** 1500 **Vyds** 5ha
Domenica Wines is the reincarnation of the previous Ergo Sum joint venture between Rick Kinzbrunner, Michel Chapoutier and Peter Graham. Domenica was established in '12 when Peter bought out Rick and Michel, and he is now the sole owner and winemaker of the business. Shiraz, roussanne and marsanne have a natural affinity with Beechworth's warm, dry summers, granitic soils, slopes and elevation. The region's 2 major varieties are shiraz and chardonnay, and these are cornerstones for Domenica Wines.

🍷🍷🍷🍷🍷 Nebbiolo 2019, Beechworth This showcases amazing, lifted florals and herbals in rosehip and anise with black tea enhancing a core of dark cherry and cranberry. Smooth and supple, the flavour flows and runs deep on a fully integrated palate. No sharp tannic edges here, just a solid base for a long finish and an equally long future. Screw cap. 14% alc. RATING 97 DRINK 2023–2032 $60 JP ✪ ♥

🍷🍷🍷🍷🍷 Chardonnay 2022, Beechworth Subtle and delicate with inner strength, the '22 is but a pup, but so impressive. Brings sunny stone fruits, citrus, mango skin, toasted almond and nougat together under a seamless umbrella of discreet oak and filigree-fine acidity. Flows effortlessly, smoothly, across the tongue. Screw cap. 13% alc. RATING 95 DRINK 2023–2030 $58 JP
Chardonnay 2021, Beechworth Impressive clarity and focus on display. There's an understatement, too – nothing shouts. White nectarine, grapefruit, lemon peel and almond aromas. Supple and smooth with gently creamy flavours running through from stone fruit to pithy grapefruit. Oak is neat and integrated. Draws to a clean, lasting finish. Screw cap. 13.1% alc. RATING 95 DRINK 2023–2030 $55 JP
Gamay 2022, Beechworth From the deep crimson-red colour to the enticing perfume and surprisingly intense flavour profile, this is one serious gamay. Deep earthy notes dressed in black cherry, thyme, oregano and green peppercorn. The acidity remains firm and texture is a feature, both providing a base for the wine's attractive herbals and pepperiness to shine clean and bright. Impressive. Screw cap. 13.2% alc. RATING 94 DRINK 2023–2029 $42 JP

🍷🍷🍷🍷🍷 Estate Shiraz 2021, Beechworth RATING 92 DRINK 2023–2031 $50 JP

Dominique Portet ★★★★★

870 Maroondah Highway, Coldstream, Vic 3770 **Region** Yarra Valley
T (03) 5962 5760 **www.dominiqueportet.com Open** 7 days 10.30–5 **Winemaker** Ben Portet, Tim Dexter **Est.** 2000 **Dozens** 15 000 **Vyds** 9ha
Dominique Portet was one of the first Flying Winemakers, commuting to Clos du Val in the Napa Valley. He then spent over 20 years as managing director of Taltarni and Clover Hill. He then moved to the Yarra Valley, planting cabernet sauvignon, sauvignon blanc, merlot, malbec, cabernet franc and petit verdot. Son Ben is now executive winemaker, Dominique consultant and brand marketer. Ben himself has a winemaking CV of awesome scope, covering all parts of France, South Africa, California and 4 vintages at Petaluma.

🍷🍷🍷🍷🍷 Single Vineyard Chardonnay 2021, Yarra Valley From a high-elevation, steeply sloping Upper Yarra vineyard of red, volcanic soils planted to Bernard/Dijon clones. A chardonnay of elegance and finesse, with all the focus on the fruit (balance the key) and the length that is the Yarra Valley birthmark. Screw cap. 13% alc. RATING 97 DRINK 2023–2041 $42 JH ✪

ΨΨΨΨΨ **Single Vineyard Rosé 2022, Yarra Valley** 75/20/5% cabernet sauvignon/
merlot/malbec. A pale, bright salmon pink. As fresh as a cool mountain stream
with its aromas of just-picked strawberries and raspberries, florals and a hint of
orange zest. Perfectly pitched on the dry, refreshing and long palate. Screw cap.
13% alc. RATING 96 DRINK 2022–2028 $42 PR ✪

Single Vineyard Cabernet Sauvignon Malbec 2021, Yarra Valley Its
bright, deep crimson hue sets the ball rolling, the medium-bodied palate with
raspberries and blackcurrants, the line unwavering, the balance likewise. A wine
of finesse. Screw cap. 13.5% alc. RATING 96 DRINK 2023–2036 $42 JH ✪

Single Vineyard Shiraz 2022, Yarra Valley A bright, medium crimson-ruby
red. Discreet and focused with its aromas of dark cherries, ripe raspberries, spices
and floral scents. The palate is similarly focused with good depth and very fine,
persistent tannins in support. There's a lot to like here. Screw cap. 13.5% alc.
RATING 95 DRINK 2022–2030 $42 PR ✪

Pinot Noir 2021, Yarra Valley A very bright, light crimson. Pretty and
perfumed. Crammed with small red fruits, spices and rose petals. Equally at ease
on the fine-boned and impeccably balanced palate. A wine I'll be following with
interest from now on. Screw cap. 13% alc. RATING 95 DRINK 2023–2028 $60 PR

Fontaine Rosé 2022, Yarra Valley A hand-picked and fragrant blend of
50/35/15% merlot/cabernet sauvignon/shiraz with aromas of wild spring flowers
and spices. The palate is positively fruity (but not sweet). Screw cap. 13% alc.
RATING 94 DRINK 2023–2023 $26 JH ✪

Fontaine Chardonnay 2021, Yarra Valley Sells itself short by emphasising
its drinkability here and now; while the emphasis is on the fruit, there's
complexity and a minimum 5-year life span. Screw cap. 13% alc. RATING 94
DRINK 2023–2027 $26 JH ✪

ΨΨΨΨΨ **Fontaine Cabernets 2021, Yarra Valley** RATING 92 DRINK 2022–2027
$26 PR ✪

Dr Edge   ★★★★★

5 Cato Avenue, West Hobart, Tas 7000 (postal) **Region** Southern Tasmania
T 0439 448 151 **www**.dr-edge.com **Open** Not **Winemaker** Peter Dredge
Viticulturist Peter Dredge **Est.** 2015 **Dozens** 800 **Vyds** 1.5ha
After working as a winemaker for Petaluma, Peter Dredge moved to Tasmania in '09,
spending 7 years within the Accolade group, becoming chief winemaker at Bay of Fires. In
'15 he sourced a small amount of pinot noir from Joe Holyman of Stoney Rise and Gerald
Ellis of Meadowbank to start his own label. He made the wine at Moorilla as a contract
client with sole control of the winemaking process. In '15, during vintage, the Ellis family,
owners of Meadowbank, approached Pete to form a partnership to relaunch Meadowbank.
As part of the deal, Meadowbank has given Pete a sole lease arrangement to 1.5ha, planted
evenly between pinot noir, chardonnay and riesling.

ΨΨΨΨΨ **Chardonnay 2022, Tasmania** Pale straw. Taut yet textured with a slinky array
of white peach, lemon and grapefruit tones underlined with soft spice, roasting
nuts, lemon curd, white flowers, stone and almond paste. Stony and composed
with an umami-rich line of acidity and a real sense of harmony and composition
as it slowly retreats with citrus and a wisp of oatmeal. Screw cap. 12% alc.
RATING 96 DRINK 2023–2029 $60 DB ✪

Chardonnay 2021, Tasmania Taut and terrific with impressive clarity and
detail showing pristine stone and citrus fruit notes along with crunchy green
apple, white flowers, crushed stone, almond paste and a waft of preserved lemon.
There's a chablis-esque nod from sapid, briny acidity that provides velocity and
verve, propelling the wine to a crisp, lingering finish that shows pristine fruit,
excellent composition and an aching sense of umami as it fades. Screw cap.
12% alc. RATING 96 DRINK 2023–2029 $55 DB ✪

North Pinot Noir 2022, Tasmania There is a really cool reductive, struck flint
character on the nose that hovers above the dark cherry and wild strawberry fruits

here. Still airy and filigreed but with a serious stare and a touch of darker spice, amaro herbs, red flowers, dried citrus rind, shiitake broth and light game. The tannins are like powdered granite and there is oodles of mineral energy on the finish. Screw cap. 12.5% alc. **RATING** 95 **DRINK** 2023–2030 $65 DB

South Pinot Noir 2022, Tasmania Bright, light ruby with notes of red cherries, mulberry and raspberry fruits cut with exotic spice, hanging game, amaro herbs, red licorice and citrus blossom. Chalky and airy with a nice blast of raspberry on the palate, a seam of mineral-laden saline acidity and a real lipsmacking finish. A lighter, funkier and filigreed style. Screw cap. 12.5% alc. **RATING** 95 **DRINK** 2023–2030 $65 DB

Pinot Noir 2022, Tasmania Light ruby in colour with notes of red plum, red cherry, wild strawberry and redcurrant with plenty of wild-eyed whole-bunch spice, gamey notes and a lovely chalky tannin vibe, finishing minerally and spacious with amaro-flecked cherry and raspberry fruits. Screw cap. 12.5% alc. **RATING** 94 **DRINK** 2023–2029 $55 DB

South Riesling 2021, Tasmania A light straw hue and aromas of pithy lemon, green apple and peach skin with hints of soft spice, lemon pith, white flowers, grapefruit and crushed stone. There is a textural aspect, a fine swell of lemon pith before the wine swoops across the mid-palate with a tangy, expressive stride finishing with a briny acid cadence and yellow plum and citrus fruits. Lovely. Screw cap. 11.5% alc. **RATING** 94 **DRINK** 2023–2028 $40 DB ✪

🍷🍷🍷🍷 **Pinot Noir 2021, Tasmania** **RATING** 93 **DRINK** 2022–2032 $60 DB
Dr Ongo Pet-Nat 2022, Tasmania **RATING** 91 **DRINK** 2023–2024 $40 DB

Dr. Plonk ★★★★

PO Box 772, McLaren Vale 5172, SA **Region** McLaren Vale
T 0409 533 332 **www**.drplonk.wine **Open** Not **Winemaker** Matt Brown
Viticulturist Richard Leask **Est.** 2004 **Dozens** 800 **Vyds** 12.5ha

Dr. Plonk was borne of maker Matt Brown's experience at Alpha Box & Dice. This experience led to the inaugural bottling of Good Doctor's Tonic in '04. Subsequently, foresight deemed tannat and the late-ripening mourvèdre to be righteous replacements for sauvignon blanc, ripped out in '09 when the 16ha site in the Willunga Foothills became Brown's home base. Later, under the guidance of viticulturalist Richard Leask, montepulciano and carignan were also planted.

🍷🍷🍷🍷 **Fu Rosato Mourvèdre 2022, McLaren Vale** A resinous mid-ruby to chinato/orange peel hue, suggesting longer maceration on skins. Rich and exotic with cinnamon, poached apricot, scented tobacco and volatile riffs on a Turkish bathhouse. Compelling for the adventurous; anathema for the risk-averse. Screw cap. 12.5% alc. **RATING** 90 **DRINK** 2023–2024 $28 NG

The Good Doctor's Antidote Montepulciano 2021, McLaren Vale Wild and weighted. Bristles with intent. A linger of barbecue and well-spiced charcuterie. Vivid aromas of pine needle and mint and sapid dark cherry. Ferrous across the finish, with a rustic whiff of rust, polished leather and a zing of volatility for buzz. Screw cap. 14% alc. **RATING** 90 **DRINK** 2023–2030 $32 NG

The Good Doctor's Tonic Tannat Cabernet Shiraz 2014, McLaren Vale Adelaide Hills An aged release, time bequeathing scents of soy, beef bouillon, polished leather and ferrous sweet earth. The oak, a bit raw. Green. The tannins, obtuse and serving to dry out an otherwise intriguing finale of bombast clad with mint, medicinal herbs and dried black fruits. This is best drunk soon, preferably with richer dishes. Cork. 15.5% alc. **RATING** 90 **DRINK** 2023–2027 $45 NG

Drayton's Family Wines ★★★★

555 Oakey Creek Road, Pokolbin, NSW 2321 **Region** Hunter Valley
T (02) 4998 7513 **www**.draytonswines.com.au **Open** 7 days 10–5 **Winemaker** Mark Smith **Viticulturist** Mick Burgoyne **Est.** 1853 **Dozens** 40 000 **Vyds** 15ha

Six generations of the Drayton family have run the family business; it is now in the hands of Max Drayton, and sons John and Greg. The wines come in part from blocks on the estate vineyards that are over 120 years old and in prime Hunter Valley locations. Mark Smith took over as winemaker from Edgar Vales in time for the '21 vintage.

🍷🍷🍷🍷🍷 **Susanne Semillon 2022, Hunter Valley** Has the concentration achieved by 100yo vines. Won't be released until 2027, and by that time will have grown exponentially on the palate. Free-run juice and balanced acidity give the wine a gold-plated future. Screw cap. 10.5% alc. **RATING** 95 **DRINK** 2027–2037 $60 JH

🍷🍷🍷🍷🍷 **Reserve Semillon 2022,** Hunter Valley **RATING** 93 **DRINK** 2023–2033 $35 JH ✪

Driftwood Estate   ★★★★★

3314 Caves Road, Wilyabrup, WA 6282 **Region** Margaret River
T (08) 9755 6323 **www.**driftwoodwines.com.au **Open** 7 days 11–4 **Winemaker** Kane Grove **Viticulturist** Ryan Gibbs **Est.** 1989 **Dozens** 18 000 **Vyds** 22ha
Driftwood Estate is a well established landmark on the Margaret River scene. Quite apart from offering a casual dining restaurant seating 200 people and a mock Greek open-air theatre, its wines feature striking and stylish packaging and opulent flavours. Its wines are released in 4 ranges: Single Site, Artifacts, The Collection and Oceania.

🍷🍷🍷🍷🍷 **Single Site Chardonnay 2021, Margaret River** At first, oak flavours come to the fore – no surprise as this is a barrel selection. But don't be too hasty. Give this some room to breathe, unfurl and shine. Grapefruit, white nectarines, creamy lemon curd and roasted cashew flavours take over and the palate is held in place by a skein of fine acidity, tight and moreish. Screw cap. 13% alc. **RATING** 96 **DRINK** 2023–2031 $70 JF ✪
Artifacts Fumé Blanc 2022, Margaret River Altogether pleasing and refreshing style with its light spray of tropical fruits, white nectarines and juicy limes plus a strong nettle character. Lively acidity keeps the palate both fresh and refreshed with just enough texture and creaminess to make this something special. Screw cap. 13% alc. **RATING** 95 **DRINK** 2022–2026 $35 JF ✪
Artifacts Petit Verdot 2020, Margaret River Violets, dark fruits, cranberries, cedar and lots of woodsy flavouring, plus tannins from oak and fruit. It's plush and ripe – fans of full-bodied savoury reds should opt for this because it also rewards with freshness. A slightly bitter green walnut finish but a very good drink nonetheless. Screw cap. 14% alc. **RATING** 95 **DRINK** 2022–2033 $35 JF ✪
Single Site Cabernet Sauvignon 2020, Margaret River It's a refined, elegant style and nothing is out of place. Floral and spicy with subtle fruit flavours and savoury attributes. Medium bodied, as that's what Margaret River cabernet is all about, with superfine tannins and great persistence. A lovely wine. Screw cap. 14% alc. **RATING** 95 **DRINK** 2022–2035 $70 JF

🍷🍷🍷🍷🍷 **Artifacts Chardonnay 2022,** Margaret River **RATING** 91 **DRINK** 2023–2029 $35 JF
Artifacts Cabernet Sauvignon 2020, Margaret River **RATING** 91 **DRINK** 2024–2035 $35 JF

🌺 Drury Lane Estate   ★★★★

492 Hermitage Road, Pokolbin, NSW 2320 (postal) **Region** Hunter Valley
T 0423 798 999 **www.**drurylane.com.au **Open** Not **Winemaker** Richard Done **Viticulturist** Liz Riley **Est.** 2021 **Dozens** 833 **Vyds** 8.1ha
Angus Scott was a 4th-generation cattle farmer and cropper who secured an advanced diploma in farm management from the University of Sydney and played professional rugby for over a decade. He wished he could return to the land and build his own farming legacy. Alexandra Scott (née Drury) had a 20-year track record of success working with some of the largest enterprise IT brands in the world. As life partners with young children, they

had dreamt of building a sustainable farming enterprise. When – out of the blue – a 8.5ha vineyard planted in '96 to the 3 most successful varieties (shiraz, chardonnay and semillon) came onto the market they didn't hesitate.

🍷🍷🍷🍷🍷 **Semillon 2022, Hunter Valley** Fragrant, crisp and a long, positive bouquet with lime and lemon in abundance on a long finish. The ever-present crisp and crunchy acidity drives the length and bright aftertaste. Both place of origin and varietal expression from recurrent lime/lemon and Granny Smith apple. Screw cap. 11.6% alc. **RATING** 95 **DRINK** 2023–2032 $30 JH ✪

Duke's Vineyard ★★★★★

1328 Porongurup Road, Porongurup, WA 6324 **Region** Porongurup
T (08) 9853 1107 **www**.dukesvineyard.com **Open** 7 days 11–4.30 **Winemaker** Ben Cane, Rob Diletti **Est.** 1998 **Dozens** 4500 **Vyds** 10ha

Duke's Vineyard was established by renowned West Australian vigneron Ian (Duke) Ranson. Shiraz and cabernet sauvignon have been mainstays for the producer, but it is the rieslings from this estate that have soared over the years, with scintillating and long-lived expressions emerging. The baton was passed with Duke's retirement, seeing winemaker Ben Cane and wife Sarah Date buy the property and brand in April '22. Cane has been concerted in his approach to honouring Duke's legacy, with no clear intent to change anything in the custodianship of the property and wines. Alongside the regional staples, pinot noir, chardonnay, gewürztraminer and sauvignon blanc have been planted to bring additional value to Duke's Vineyard's premier intent.

🍷🍷🍷🍷🍷 **Riesling 2022, Frankland River** A pure and potent riesling loaded with briny minerality and wound tightly with green apple and grapefruit zestiness. Opens with fruit characters married to wet fern, ozone and sea spray notes, the palate likewise apple-meets-grapefruit with flinty mineral elements. Flavours extend long and tightly packed with great concentration of fruit, spice and mineral elements. A winner. Screw cap. 11.2% alc. **RATING** 94 **DRINK** 2022–2035 $38 MB ✪
Magpie Hill Reserve Cabernet Sauvignon 2021, Porongurup This has concentration, palate-staining resonance and a general sense of high drinkability. Scents of clove and pipe tobacco over cassis and lavender, the palate more fruit driven, plummy, but with brined black olive and more clove spice in play. Sits at medium weight, cruises along gently and feels almost refreshing in a way. Elegant, understated and very good. Screw cap. 14% alc. **RATING** 94 **DRINK** 2022–2036 $46 MB

🍷🍷🍷🍷🍷 **The Whole Bunch Shiraz 2021, Porongurup** **RATING** 93 **DRINK** 2022–2030 $66 MB
Single Vineyard Cabernet Sauvignon 2021, Porongurup **RATING** 93 **DRINK** 2022–2030 $29 MB ✪
Protea Sauvignon Blanc 2022, Margaret River **RATING** 92 **DRINK** 2023–2027 $34 MB
Single Vineyard Riesling 2022, Porongurup **RATING** 92 **DRINK** 2022–2030 $29 MB ✪
The First Cab 2021, Porongurup **RATING** 91 **DRINK** 2022–2030 $66 MB

Dune Wine ★★★★★

PO Box 9, McLaren Vale, SA 5171 **Region** McLaren Vale
T 0403 584 845 **www**.dunewine.com **Open** Not **Winemaker** Duncan and Peter Lloyd **Est.** 2016 **Dozens** 1700 **Vyds** 8ha

This is the project of Duncan and Peter Lloyd (of Coriole fame) using fruit sourced from a single vineyard in Blewitt Springs. The brothers grew up immersed in a world of wine, olive oil, illegal goat's cheese and great food. Duncan studied winemaking before leaving McLaren Vale to work in Tasmania and Margaret River, and then in Chianti and the Rhône Valley. He returned to McLaren Vale as he couldn't understand why you would want to live anywhere else.

🍷🍷🍷🍷🍷 **Blewitt Springs Shiraz 2021, McLaren Vale** Dense, deep purple-crimson hue. Black peppercorns, black licorice, dark chocolate, plum, cherry allsorts and leather old and new … yet it doesn't taste full bodied, just complex and shapeshifting. Screw cap. 14% alc. **RATING** 96 **DRINK** 2023–2037 $28 JH ✪
The Empty Quarter 2021, McLaren Vale Predominantly shiraz, grenache and mataro, with a small percentage of touriga nacional. The complex bouquet offers dark fruits and earthy, spicy notes of forest floor taken onboard with enthusiasm by the savoury tannins on the palate and finish. Screw cap. 14.1% alc. **RATING** 95 **DRINK** 2023–2033 $28 JH ✪
Tirari 2021, McLaren Vale A blend of negroamaro, touriga nacional and mataro. A snowstorm of exotic spices and flower petals opens the curtains for a light-bodied wine that is happy in itself and doesn't need any body-building courtesy of tannins or other extract. Screw cap. 13.9% alc. **RATING** 94 **DRINK** 2023–2028 $26 JH ✪

🍷🍷🍷🍷🍸 **Bonaire Rosé 2022, McLaren Vale RATING** 91 **DRINK** 2022–2024 $26 NG ✪
Blewitt Springs Shiraz 2022, McLaren Vale RATING 91 **DRINK** 2022–2027 $28 NG ✪

Eastern Peake
★★★★★

67 Pickfords Road, Coghills Creek, Vic 3364 **Region** Ballarat
T (03) 5343 4245 **www.easternpeake.com.au Open** Tues–Sat 11–3 by appt
Winemaker Owen Latta, Dave Morgan, Charles Mann **Viticulturist** Polly Bowles
Est. 1983 **Dozens** 6000 **Vyds** 5.6ha
Norm Latta and Di Pym established Eastern Peake, 25km northeast of Ballarat on a high plateau overlooking the Creswick Valley, over 40 years ago. In the early years the grapes were sold, but the 5.6ha of vines are now dedicated to the production of Eastern Peake wines. Son Owen Latta has been responsible for the seismic increase in the quality of the wines.

🍷🍷🍷🍷🍷 **Taché 2021, Ballarat** Made from pinot noir. No tinkering, according to Owen Latta. Very classy, delicious and enjoyable from start to finish. Aromas are floral and spicy, savoury and citrusy, same with the palate. Finely tuned with soft raspberry acidity, fine creaminess from the lees and so moreish. Dry but not austere, just an adorable style of rosé. Diam. 12% alc. **RATING** 96 **DRINK** 2022–2027 $38 JF ✪
Intrinsic Chardonnay 2020, Ballarat A richer style yet made in such a way as to express the fruit as much as the place. Poached stone fruit and lemon balm, preserved ginger and lemon accents, buttery, creamy and full bodied. Spicy oak in the background and the acidity a mere part of the equation. Diam. 13% alc. **RATING** 95 **DRINK** 2022–2029 $65 JF
Intrinsic Pinot Noir 2020, Ballarat Intrinsic or otherwise, this is very good, balancing acidity and tannins to a savoury fruit profile. Woodsmoke and chinotto infuse dark cherries and loads of spices with wafts of river mint and forest floor aromas. Complex and fuller bodied with decisive tannins, but not unwieldy as superfine acidity draws it all to a neat end. Diam. 13% alc. **RATING** 95 **DRINK** 2022–2032 $60 JF
Pinot Noir 2021, Western Victoria Juicy, supple, tangy and laden with sweet cherries, kirsch, warming spices and wafts of autumn leaves. The palate has weight extended by pliable, textural tannins, refreshing acidity and really, just a lot to like here. Diam. 13% alc. **RATING** 94 **DRINK** 2022–2031 $48 JF

🍷🍷🍷🍷🍸 **Chardonnay 2021, Western Victoria RATING** 93 **DRINK** 2022–2028 $48 JF

ECK Wines
★★★★

366 Moorabbee Road, Knowsley, Vic 3523 **Region** Heathcote
T (03) 5439 1363 **www.eckwines.com.au Open** By appt **Winemaker** Emily Kinsman
Est. 2019 **Dozens** 1800 **Vyds** 1ha
ECK (pronounced ee-cee-kay) vineyard is centrally located within the Heathcote region on the banks of Lake Eppalock. It was formerly Armstead Estate, whose founder Peter Armstead

planted the first shiraz vines in '03 on an east-facing slope just metres from the lake. Tom and Emily Kinsman purchased the estate in July '17. They grow and source fruit from a number of well-known vineyards across the Heathcote region. Wines have been produced under the ECK label from the '19 vintage.

ŸŸŸŸŸ **Rosé No. 2 2022, Heathcote** Made from cabernet sauvignon and fermented in aged barriques. This is lovely. Bright, perfumed, textured and just plain delicious. Orange oil and cranberry, strawberry and sweet spices, a subtle earthiness. Light but insistent. Moreish but with presence. Screw cap. 11.2% alc. RATING 94 DRINK 2023–2025 $26 CM ✪

Marsanne 2021, Heathcote It's a serious wine without being too earnest or overwrought. Stone fruit and toast flavours swing through a palate whispered with pine, candied citrus and roasted spice. It's dry through the finish to the point of feeling quartz-like. A fair amount of gorgeousness here. Screw cap. 13% alc. RATING 94 DRINK 2024–2028 $30 CM ✪

Shiraz 2020, Heathcote Bold and complex. Sweet plum into blackberry with clove, sweet toast, coffee cream and cedar characters charging through. Both soft and robust. Fruity and smoky and savoury. There's a lot to love here. Screw cap. 14.2% alc. RATING 94 DRINK 2024–2035 $35 CM ✪

ŸŸŸŸŸ **Cabernet Sauvignon 2020, Heathcote** RATING 92 DRINK 2023–2031 $35 CM

Sparkling Shiraz 2019, Heathcote RATING 91 DRINK 2023–2029 $45 CM

Eden Hall   ★★★★

Cnr Boehms Springs Road and E Lorkes Road, Springton, SA 5235 (postal)
Region Eden Valley
T 0400 991 968 **www**.edenhall.com.au **Open** Not **Winemaker** Phil Lehmann
Viticulturist Dan Falkenberg **Est.** 1997 **Dozens** 4000 **Vyds** 33.5ha

David and Mardi Hall purchased the historic Avon Brae Estate in '96. The 120ha property has been planted to cabernet sauvignon (the lion's share, with 11.5ha), riesling (9.3ha), shiraz (8.3ha) and smaller amounts of grüner veltliner and viognier. Around half of the fruit from the estate is made into wine under the Eden Hall label with the remaining fruit sold to 3rd parties such as Yalumba, Rieslingfreak, Soul Growers and Hentley Farm.

ŸŸŸŸŸ **Springton Riesling 2022, Eden Valley** Pale straw with green flashes and aromas of fresh lime and lemon juice, Bickford's lime cordial, orange blossom, lemon zest, crushed stone and a light waft of mandarin. Clean, crisp and dry with just a hint of bath salts appearing on the palate, which powers along nicely thanks to a seam of sizzling acidity. Screw cap. 12.8% alc. RATING 94 DRINK 2023–2028 $25 DB ✪

Springton Riesling 2021, Eden Valley Pale in the glass with aromas of freshly squeezed limes and lemons with hints of orange blossom, crushed quartz, rosehip, makrut lime and citrus zest. Crystalline acidity provides a brisk cadence and the wine displays an impressive amount of clarity and drive, finishing dry and thirst quenching. A great drink from the stellar 2021 vintage. Screw cap. 12.8% alc. RATING 94 DRINK 2023–2028 $25 DB ✪

ŸŸŸŸŸ **Reserve Riesling 2021, Eden Valley** RATING 93 DRINK 2023–2029 $35 DB ✪
Grüner Veltliner 2022, Eden Valley RATING 92 DRINK 2023–2025 $30 DB ✪
Chardonnay 2021, Eden Valley RATING 92 DRINK 2023–2025 $30 DB ✪
Grüner Veltliner 2021, Eden Valley RATING 92 DRINK 2023–2025 $35 DB
Opulence Semi-Sweet Riesling 2022, Eden Valley RATING 92 DRINK 2023–2025 $25 DB ✪
Block 3 Cabernet Sauvignon 2020, Eden Valley RATING 91 DRINK 2023–2030 $40 DB
Reserve Riesling 2022, Eden Valley RATING 90 DRINK 2023–2027 $35 DB
Springton Shiraz 2021, Eden Valley RATING 90 DRINK 2023–2027 $25 DB ✪

Eden Road Wines

3182 Barton Highway, Murrumbateman, NSW 2582 **Region** Canberra District
T 0466 226 808 **www.edenroadwines.com.au Open** Wed–Sun 10–4.30
Winemaker Celine Rousseau **Est.** 2006 **Dozens** 14 000 **Vyds** 5.34ha

The name of this business reflects an earlier time when it also had a property in the Eden Valley. Now based in the Canberra District, having purchased one of the region's oldest vineyards (est. 1972) and wineries at Dookuna. Syrah, sauvignon blanc and riesling are sourced from the estate vineyards, with chardonnay and pinot noir coming from Tumbarumba. Fruit for the Cullarin Block 71 wines comes from a single vineyard at Lake George.

ΨΨΨΨΨ **The Long Road Pinot Gris 2022, Southern New South Wales** An attractive copper blush from some skin contact. Spiced baked apples, nashi pears, cinnamon and musk; delightfully refreshing with some light phenolics adding to the palate weight. Screw cap. 12.5% alc. **RATING** 95 **DRINK** 2023–2026 $30 JF ✪
Sangiovese 2021, Gundagai Seriously good sangiovese with hints of pepper and prosciutto reduction, which adds a meaty, savoury character to juicy and bright cherry flavours. Of course, it's the crunchy acidity and raspy tannins that are key – they're playing their savoury part and giving off an Italian-esque impression. Screw cap. 14.5% alc. **RATING** 95 **DRINK** 2023–2030 $40 JF ✪
Cullarin Block 71 Chardonnay 2022, Canberra District Racy, bright and tight all up, with pure citrus flavours from start to finish, think grapefruit, lemon and finger lime acidity. There's a light layer of creamy, nutty lees just to put a small dint into the acid line. Refreshing and compelling. Screw cap. 11.5% alc. **RATING** 95 **DRINK** 2023–2032 $50 JF ✪

ΨΨΨΨΩ **Chardonnay 2022, Tumbarumba RATING** 93 **DRINK** 2023–2032 $50 JF
Pinot Noir 2022, Tumbarumba RATING 92 **DRINK** 2023–2028 $50 JF

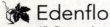 Edenflo

45 Gramp Ave, Angaston, SA 5353 **Region** Eden Valley
T 0420 893 921 **www.edenflowines.com.au Open** By appt **Winemaker** Andrew Wardlaw **Viticulturist** Andrew Wardlaw **Est.** 2016 **Dozens** 1500

Edenflo is an idiosyncratic producer of the best kind. You name it, winemaker Andrew Wardlaw has experimented with it, such are his ever-curious ways. All the wines here are low in sulphur and winemaking intervention, though Andrew's long industry history – he grew up in wine and has extensive experience both locally and internationally – keeps the wines fresh. The 'flo' in the name arguably sums this producer up best: the wines aim to go with the flow of the land and they are grown on.

ΨΨΨΨΩ **Twin Peaks Grenache 2021, Eden Valley Clare Valley** Full-ish in grenache terms, but as complex as all get-out. Orange peel, earth, roasted nut and Dutch chocolate notes sweeping confidently through ripe, sweet cherry flavours. This wine is so juicy it feels joyous; it's deliciously drinkable in a free-flowing way. Cork. 14.8% alc. **RATING** 93 **DRINK** 2022–2027 $45 CM
Syrah 2021, Eden Valley Vibrant purpley red in the glass with notes of slurpy blueberry, juicy plum, boysenberry and mulberry. Hints of orange peel, wild herbs, souk-like spice and warm earth. Fragrant in the mouth with a jasmine-tinged, super-juicy fruit profile. It comes across as a bit natty and there is an undeniable air of joyous drinkability here. Cork. 14.5% alc. **RATING** 92 **DRINK** 2023–2026 $50 DB
Riesling 2022, Clare Valley Light straw with notes of crunchy green apple, freshly squeezed lime juice, lemon curd, clotted cream, wildflowers, soft spice and drying hay. Lemon and apple juice on the palate with tones of soft spice and whey with a precise, focused line and a lovely swoosh of lemon curd on the exit. Screw cap. 11.1% alc. **RATING** 91 **DRINK** 2023–2028 $38 DB
Mezzanine 2022, South Australia Grenache/pinot/syrah. A bruised, purple hue in the glass: super-juicy plum, mulberry and cherry, exotic spices and whiffs

of amaro, a riot of floral tones and something vaguely cidery. Bouncy, light and huge on the drinkability stakes it throws light, chalky tannin shapes and makes for a great little slurper. Screw cap. 13.8% alc. RATING 91 DRINK 2023–2025 $30 DB

Eight at the Gate

15006 Riddoch Highway, Coonawarra SA 5263 **Region** Wrattonbully
T 0400 843 126 **www**.eightatthegate.com.au **Open** Fri–Wed, 10.30–2.30
Winemaker Peter Douglas, Peta Baverstock (sparkling) **Viticulturist** Claire Davies
Est. 2002 **Dozens** 5000 **Vyds** 60ha

Sisters Jane Richards and Claire Davies are part of a SA farming family. They came to it by diverse pathways: Jane left the land, successfully weaving her way up the corporate ladder in the technology world, on a journey that took her to New York and San Francisco. Claire set down her roots in the land, graduating from Roseworthy, working as an assistant winemaker, thereafter as a viticultural consultant in the Di Davidson Consulting group, one of Australia's best. The sisters came together in '02, buying Lanacoona Estate, with an established vineyard planted in '95, now significantly expanded to the present 60ha under the expert eagle eye of Claire.

Family Selection Single Vineyard Chardonnay 2021, Wrattonbully This feels serious from the outset but not at the expense of out-and-out drinkability. Grilled peach, toast, cashew and lime flavours roll powerfully through the palate before bran and quartz-like notes impact the finish. Very good. Screw cap. 13.2% alc. RATING 93 DRINK 2023–2028 $38 CM

Single Vineyard Cabernet Sauvignon 2019, Wrattonbully This is a smooth, well-flavoured wine with just enough of everything that counts. Pure blackcurrant and bay leaf flavours flow through the palate, creamy vanillin oak draped over the top. It's not full on but there's enough richness here to satisfy. The tannin profile, slightly grainy, suggests that it should mature well, too. Screw cap. 14.5% alc. RATING 92 DRINK 2023–2030 $28 CM ✪

Family Selection Single Vineyard Shiraz 2019, Wrattonbully Solid rounds of plum essence and orange oil flavour come dressed in classy cedar and vanilla oak. The extra sauce here is attractive woodsmoke-like characters, likely from that same oak. It's fruity and flowing but has some extra grunt. Screw cap. 14.5% alc. RATING 92 DRINK 2023–2029 $48 CM

Single Vineyard Cabernet Shiraz 2019, Wrattonbully It's simple but not unsatisfying. Raspberry and redcurrant flavours meet vanilla and cream, a flash of mint tossed through for good measure. Improves with air. Screw cap. 14.5% alc. RATING 90 DRINK 2022–2027 $28 CM

1837 Barossa

119–131 Yaldara Drive, Lyndoch, SA 5351 **Region** Barossa Valley
T (08) 7200 1070 **www**.1837barossa.com.au **Open** Wed–Sat 11–9, Sun 11–4
Winemaker Guido Auchli, Peter Gajewski **Viticulturist** Michael Heinrich **Est.** 1837
Vyds 9ha

1837 Barossa commemorates the date on which Colonel William Light named the Barossa. Red wines hail exclusively from the estate near Lyndoch, while whites are sourced from Eden Valley growers. Viticulture is overseen by 5th-generation grower Michael Heinrich, with a philosophy of minimal chemical input. The spectacular estate offers accommodation in its recently refurbished Barossa Manor, including a restaurant and cellar door.

Rapid Crossings Zinfandel 2021, Barossa Bright crimson in the glass with aromas of juicy blueberry, boysenberry and dried cranberry notes with a varietally characteristic blast of spice. There is plenty of fruit heft, fragrant spice and purple floral notes on the palate with dense, fine tannins, bright acidity and, despite the wines alcoholic horsepower, it all comes across as a balanced, meaty and juicy example. Screw cap. 16% alc. RATING 92 DRINK 2023–2028 $26 DB ✪

Barossa Legend Rare Single Block Shiraz 2020 Deep crimson in the glass with characters of ripe satsuma plums, blackberry and macerated berry fruits

undercut with fruitcake spices, licorice, earth, dark chocolate, cedar and some smoky oak-derived barbecue notes in the distance. Fine, grippy tannins and a spice-laden finish. Cork. 14.5% alc. **RATING** 91 **DRINK** 2023–2029 $85 DB
William Jacob Cabernet Sauvignon 2020, Barossa Deep blackberry, blackcurrant and red cherry notes at its core with hints of spice, scattered herbs, cedar, licorice and earth. At the lighter end of full bodied with plenty of fine, powdery tannins, bright acidity and herb-flecked dark and black fruits on the finish. Cork. 14.5% alc. **RATING** 91 **DRINK** 2023–2029 $42 DB

1847 Wines

35 Church Road, Rowland Flat, Barossa Valley, SA 5352 **Region** Barossa Valley
T 0437 804 501 www.1847wines.com **Open** Thurs–Mon 9–4.30 **Winemaker** Sam Kurtz **Viticulturist** Darren Lovell **Est.** 2004 **Dozens** 50 000 **Vyds** 100ha
1847 Winery Group purchased the historic Chateau Yaldara in Lyndoch in '14, deciding to separate the 2 brands and run 1847 on its own merits, based out of Rowland Flat. The flagship wines are the First Pick and Grand Pappy's range. They fit into the traditional, classic Barossa style, full flavoured and structured with bold, balanced lines.

🍷🍷🍷🍷🍷 **Grand Pappy's Shiraz 2019, Barossa Valley** Deep crimson with magenta splashes. Aromas of ripe plum, blackberry jam and black cherry clafoutis along with baking spices, licorice, dark chocolate, crème de cassis and earth. Unctuous and full bodied with an array of ripe black fruits, plenty of spice, tight sandy tannins and an opulent, spicy cassis sheen to the lingering finish. Big and bold. Diam. 14.5% alc. **RATING** 95 **DRINK** 2023–2035 $320 DB

Icon Shiraz 2019, Barossa Valley Deep crimson in the glass with enticing aromas of ripe plum, blackberry and black cherry fruits. A sheath of fine spice and cedar surrounds the fruit along with hints of dark chocolate, cherry clafoutis, licorice, leather, vanilla, tobacco leaf and earth. Impressive fruit density, cascading granitic tannins and a bright acid line, despite its concentration and latent power. One for the cellar. Diam. 14.5% alc. **RATING** 94 **DRINK** 2023–2038 $400 DB
First Pick Shiraz 2019, Barossa Valley Deep crimson and a rich, full-bodied offering with plenty of ripe dark plum, blackberry and cherry notes underscored with hints of baking spices, licorice, dark chocolate, earth, ironstone and espresso. Rich and teetering on the edge of broody, it lies on a raft of tight, grainy tannin and there is no shortage of deep black fruit and spice on the finish. Cork. 14.5% alc. **RATING** 94 **DRINK** 2023–2035 $480 DB
Icon Cabernet Sauvignon 2019, Barossa Valley A seriously good wine at an equally serious pricepoint. There is plenty of structure for an extended life in the cellar, with firm, sandy tannins plunging through red and dark berry fruits layered with hints of spice, roasting meats, cedar, leather, red flowers, red licorice and earth. There is a slightly open, oxidative feel to the palate and I'd think those leathery, mahogany characters would swell with age. Diam. 14.5% alc. **RATING** 94 **DRINK** 2023–2035 $400 DB

🍷🍷🍷🍷🍷 **The Pinnacle Grenache 2017, Barossa Valley RATING** 93 **DRINK** 2023–2030 $160 DB
The Pinnacle Cabernet Shiraz 2016, Barossa Valley RATING 93 **DRINK** 2023–2030 $160 DB
Sparkling Chardonnay Pinot Noir 2016, Adelaide Hills RATING 92 **DRINK** 2023–2028 $50 DB

Elderslie

PO Box 93, Charleston, SA 5244 **Region** Adelaide Hills
T 0404 943 743 www.eldersliewines.com.au **Open** Not **Winemaker** Adam Wadewitz
Est. 2015 **Dozens** 600 **Vyds** 8ha
Winemaker Adam Wadewitz and wine marketer Nicole Roberts bring a wealth of experience gained in many parts of the wine world. They each have their partners (Nikki Wadewitz and Mark Roberts) onboard and also have real-life jobs. In '16 Nicole accepted the position of

executive officer of the Adelaide Hills Wine Region, having had brand development roles with 3 of the Hills' leading winemakers, she now heads up marketing and sales at Bird In Hand. Adam carved out a career at the highest imaginable level, aided by becoming joint dux of the Len Evans Tutorial in '09. He was senior winemaker at Best's, where he made the '12 Jimmy Watson winner; and is now senior winemaker for Shaw + Smith and their associated Tolpuddle Vineyard in Tasmania.

ŸŸŸŸ **Hills Blend #1 2021, Adelaide Hills** Pinot blanc. A highly textural experience that's reliant on a chord of cedar oak as much as a patina of lees-derived miso at its core to define the cadence. Plump, flavourful and gentle of acid. Yet, fresh enough. Baked golden apple, dried hay in the sunshine dictating depth and drive. I'd like less lees work and more simple fruit snap. Yet there is plenty to like here. Screw cap. 13.5% alc. **RATING** 93 **DRINK** 2022-2026 $46 NG

Single Site Nebbiolo 2020, Adelaide Hills At once embracing oak tannins and a slightly darker fruited spectrum (that may be due to a warmer vintage) alongside similar whole-berry musk and rosewater accents. I'd like this a bit denser, carnal and sandalwood-serious. A delicious, albeit prosaic, wine glimpsing a promising future. Screw cap. 14.5% alc. **RATING** 92 **DRINK** 2022-2028 $56 NG

Nebbiolo 2021, Adelaide Hills A pretty, extremely floral nebbiolo that should gain stature and depth with a little age. For now, it's all lilac, red fruits, lavender and a carapace of sandy, pin-bone tannins of impeccable exactitude. There is something resembling contemporary Vale grenache about this, albeit with an edgier tannic slake. Mid-weighted, energetic and approachable. Screw cap. 14% alc. **RATING** 91 **DRINK** 2022-2027 $56 NG

Elderton   ★★★★★

3-5 Tanunda Road, Nuriootpa, SA 5355 **Region** Barossa Valley
T (08) 8568 7878 www.eldertonwines.com.au **Open** Mon–Fri 10–5, w'ends, hols 11–4
Winemaker Julie Ashmead, Brock Harrison **Viticulturist** Peter Wild, Conrad Pohlinger
Est. 1982 **Dozens** 45 000 **Vyds** 65ha

The founding Ashmead family continues to impress. Julie Ashmead (the 5th-generation winemaker at Campbells in Rutherglen) is head of production, overseeing viticulture and winemaking. Elderton has 4 vineyards across the Barossa and Eden valleys. The latter is home to the Craneford vineyard (planted to shiraz, cabernet sauvignon, riesling and chardonnay) and the Mengler Hill vineyard (purchased in '22 from the Mattschoss family and planted to old-vine shiraz, cabernet, riesling and grenache). Elderton's original estate vineyard in the Barossa Valley, Nuriootpa, is planted to shiraz, cabernet sauvignon and merlot dating back to 1894. The Greenock site, planted by the Helbig family in 1915 and purchased in '10, consists of shiraz, grenache, carignan, mourvèdre, cabernet sauvignon, chardonnay and semillon.

ŸŸŸŸŸ **Neil Ashmead Grand Tourer Shiraz 2021, Barossa Valley** Full bodied and full blooded, this wine reflects a great red vintage for the Barossa Valley. Questions of style go out the window with Barossa shiraz, particularly where the US market is concerned. Just give it 20 years. Screw cap. 14.9% alc. **RATING** 95 **DRINK** 2023-2046 $65 JH

Ashmead Family Reserve #2 Shiraz 2021, Barossa Valley A deep, impenetrable crimson with powerful aromas of cassis, macerated plums and black cherry with layers of baking spices, Cherry Ripe, clove, vanilla bean, dark chocolate, salted licorice, violets and a whiff of coconut. Concentrated, inky and sporting plenty of flexing black fruits and spice with super-compact, fine tannins. Screw cap. 14.9% alc. **RATING** 95 **DRINK** 2023-2038 $90 DB

Shiraz 2020, Barossa Big, bold and beautiful. And for good measure, tension between the cooler Eden Valley component (Craneford) and the richer flavours of the Barossa floor. Screw cap. 14.8% alc. **RATING** 94 **DRINK** 2023-2035 $38 JH ✪

ŸŸŸŸŸ **GSM 2022, Barossa RATING** 93 **DRINK** 2023-2028 $38 DB

Ode to Lorraine Cabernet Shiraz Merlot 2020, Barossa Valley RATING 93 **DRINK** 2023-2033 $65 DB

Cabernet Sauvignon 2021, Barossa RATING 92 DRINK 2023–2030 $38 DB
Chardonnay 2022, Eden Valley RATING 91 DRINK 2023–2026 $38 DB
Merlot 2021, Barossa RATING 91 DRINK 2023–2028 $38 DB
Riesling 2022, Eden Valley RATING 90 DRINK 2023–2025 $30 DB

Eldorado Road

Cantina, 46–48 Ford Street, Beechworth, Vic 3747 **Region** Beechworth
T (03) 5725 1698 **www.eldoradoroad.com.au Open** Fri–Sat 11–6, Sun–Mon 11–4
Winemaker Paul Dahlenburg, Ben Dahlenburg, Laurie Schulz **Est.** 2010 **Dozens** 1500
Vyds 4ha

Paul Dahlenburg (nicknamed Bear), Lauretta Schulz (Laurie) and their children leased a
2ha block of shiraz planted in the 1890s. Bear and Laurie knew about the origins of the
vineyard, which was in a state of serious decline after years of neglect. Son Ben returned to
the winery in '16 to assist the family business after several vintages abroad. Years of tireless
work reconstructing the old vines has resulted in tiny amounts of exceptionally good shiraz;
there are also plantings of nero d'Avola, durif, fiano and aucerot.

Perseverance Old Vine Shiraz 2021, Glenrowan Extremely low yields have
produced a highly concentrated fruit intensity with so much life and freshness.
Deep and dense in crimson shades with aromas of dark violet, black fruits,
bramble, thyme, sage and earth. Seamless as it rolls gently, smoothly and long-
lasting to the finish. Something special in so many ways. Screw cap. 14.1% alc.
RATING 97 DRINK 2023–2034 $85 JP ✪ ♥

Dreamfields Fiano 2022, Alpine Valleys Stunning flavour intensity and
textural composition. In possession of both strength and poise, it launches into an
arresting scent of pear, baked apple, peach, melon and almond meal. Runs long,
smooth and concentrated against a mealy, lightly savoury background. That's a
wow! Screw cap. 13% alc. RATING 96 DRINK 2023–2027 $35 JP ✪ ♥
Riserva Nero d'Avola 2021, Beechworth This establishes nero d'Avola as a
serious contender in the Australian red wine arena. Gloriously fragrant in black
cherry, dried herbs, anise and dusty cocoa with savoury, smoky charcuterie notes.
The palate dark fruited and brooding, with supple yet dense tannins. Impressive
on a number of levels, not least that long, lasting finish. Screw cap. 13.7% alc.
RATING 96 DRINK 2023–2030 $65 JP ✪ ♥
Wallflower Viognier Marsanne 2022, Beechworth A field blend that
beautifully reveals why these Rhône Valley varieties make a great couple. Viognier
is full of grace, marsanne rising to the occasion with a delicate floral intensity.
Lifted aromas of honeysuckle, hay and straw, pear and peach. The palate is built
around a core of concentrated fruit with a light beeswax textural element. All
class. Screw cap. 13.3% alc. RATING 95 DRINK 2023–2030 $35 JP ✪
Quasimodo Nero d'Avola Shiraz Durif 2021, North East Victoria A
juicy, medium-bodied wine that is as fresh as a just-picked bunch of spring
daisies. The strands of cherry and blood plum are woven into the wine's
tapestry. It's an exercise in balance and length. Screw cap. 13.7% alc. RATING 95
DRINK 2023–2036 $29 JH ✪

Syrah 2021, Beechworth RATING 92 DRINK 2023–2030 $39 JP

Eldredge

Spring Gully Road, Clare, SA 5453 **Region** Clare Valley
T (08) 8842 3086 **www.eldredge.com.au Open** 7 days 11–5 **Winemaker** Leigh Eldredge
Est. 1993 **Dozens** 7000 **Vyds** 22.97ha

Leigh and Karen Eldredge established their winery and cellar door in the Sevenhill Ranges
at an elevation of 500m above Watervale. The mature estate vineyard is planted to shiraz,
cabernet sauvignon, merlot, sangiovese, riesling and malbec.

ŢŢŢŢ♀ **Spring Gully Riesling 2022, Clare Valley** Spritely, zingy and very tart, this
is a very lean and racy style with lemon juice in mineral water the motif with
briny acidity the other significant player here. It's very brisk and ultra-refreshing
albeit at one speed and razor-sharp in its bite and crispness. It delivers a very
skeletal impression of riesling with aplomb. Screw cap. 11% alc. **RATING** 93
DRINK 2022–2035 $22 MB ✪

Blue Chip Riesling 2022, Clare Valley Lime juice, green apple and some
yeasty, nutty savouriness in the perfume and palate. A faint fruitiness/sweetness
also appears. It's a broadly appealing kind of style, medium bodied and loaded
with flavour. It nails its brief of being distinct. Screw cap. 11.2% alc. **RATING** 92
DRINK 2022–2030 $30 MB ✪

Blue Chip Shiraz 2020, Clare Valley Lush, supple and slurpy shiraz. It's very
dark fruited and sweet, highlighted by booze-soaked berries, vanilla and cola
characters set among ripe plum and kirsch fruit notes. Scents and flavours match
here, the oak a sweet element throughout, but playing quite nicely. Lavish,
opulent, bold. Screw cap. 14.5% alc. **RATING** 92 **DRINK** 2022–2028 $30 MB ✪

Reserve Malbec 2018, Clare Valley Old tobacco pouch scents, whiffs of
ripe plum, some cedar and toast. The palate is juicy, fleshy, deep and round. A
soft and mellow flow of ripe plummy fruit in a sheath of clove and cinnamon
spice, finishing long with fresh, crisp acidity chiming in. It needs more time, but
for now, there's enjoyment in the big seasoning, bold flavours and sweet fruit.
Screw cap. 14.5% alc. **RATING** 91 **DRINK** 2026–2035 $35 MB

Eldridge Estate of Red Hill ★★★★★

120 Arthurs Seat Road, Red Hill, Vic 3937 **Region** Mornington Peninsula
T 0414 758 960 **www**.eldridge-estate.com.au **Open** Fri–Mon 11–5
Winemaker Steve Flamsteed **Est.** 1985 **Dozens** 1000 **Vyds** 3ha
Eldridge Estate has long been considered a totemic producer thanks to the tireless work of
its founders David Lloyd and his late wife, Wendy. The commitment to both quality and
experimentation here was matched only by a commitment to both their local winemaking
community and to Australian wine itself. The estate was sold in '22, the '21 vintage releases
being David's last. The fact that Steve Flamsteed (of Giant Steps fame) has been engaged as
consultant winemaker can be taken as a sign that the new owners are astute, and that ultimate
quality remains the focus.

ŢŢŢŢŢ **Clonal Blend Pinot Noir 2021, Mornington Peninsula** An excellent pinot
noir offering all the perfume the variety can muster, evenly matched to textural
tannins and layers of flavour. Wafts of red roses, spiced cherries, raspberries,
pomegranate and fresh herbs, for starters. The oak is well integrated and blends
with the enticing forest-floor fragrance. While the palate is more medium bodied,
it has terrific structure and length thanks to its raw, silky tannins and fresh acidity.
Screw cap. 13.5% alc. **RATING** 96 **DRINK** 2022–2036 $85 JF

Wendy Chardonnay 2021, Mornington Peninsula This is the most
restrained Wendy to date. In the mix, stone fruit meets Meyer lemon, there's
ginger with a sprinkle of oak spice and remains lithe and juicy as bright acidity
keeps it on a linear thread. A fitting tribute (named in memory of David
Lloyd's late wife) and an excellent wine to finish on a high. Screw cap. 13% alc.
RATING 96 **DRINK** 2022–2031 $75 JF ✪

Single Vineyard Gamay 2021, Mornington Peninsula David Lloyd was
single-minded about pursuing this excellent varietal and to great effect. Arguably,
the 2021 is the finest vintage to date. Brightness, juiciness and layers of woodsy
and warm spices with a flutter of garrigue/fresh herbs plus pepper. Lighter-
framed, with tangy acidity, neat tannins and ready to crack open now. Screw cap.
13% alc. **RATING** 95 **DRINK** 2022–2026 $60 JF

Ellis Wines

52 Garsed Street, Bendigo Victoria 3550 **Region** Bendigo
T 0401 290 315 **www**.elliswines.com.au **Open** Mon–Fri 11–4 **Winemaker** Guy
Rathjen, Nina Stocker **Viticulturist** Bryan Ellis **Est.** 1999 **Dozens** 3000 **Vyds** 54.18ha
Bryan and Joy Ellis own this family business, daughter Raylene Flanagan is the sales manager,
and all 7 of its vineyard blocks are named after family members. For the first 10 years the
Ellises were content to sell the grapes to a range of distinguished producers. However, since
then a growing portion of the crop has been vinified.

ŶŶŶŶŶ **Signature Cabernet Sauvignon 2021, Heathcote** Inviting scents of dark
violet, bramble, cassis and roasting herbs with a cherry-fruit brightness. The palate
is built around impressive structure, carrying good concentrated flavours through
to the finish. Smooth all the way with a rousing woodsy oak presence that
grounds the wine. Screw cap. 14.5% alc. **RATING** 95 **DRINK** 2023–2030 $40 JP ✪
Premium Shiraz 2019, Heathcote A fine follow-up to the excellent '18 with
a similar degree of tightly focused toasty, vanillin French oak and sturdy tannins
lending firm support. Cassis and ripe black plums go hand in hand with licorice,
dark chocolate, black olive and smoky charcuterie notes. Screw cap. 14.9% alc.
RATING 95 **DRINK** 2023–2031 $70 JP
Signature Shiraz 2020, Heathcote Displaying classic Heathcote plushness of
dark fruit and lively spice with plenty of alcohol warmth and oomph. Oak plays
a major role here, too, with French and American oak displaying their presence
throughout the cedary, toasty depth of flavour and woody tannin. The intention
is clear: this is a wine not ready to be opened, just yet. As always, it's your call.
Screw cap. 14.8% alc. **RATING** 94 **DRINK** 2023–2031 $40 JP ✪

ŶŶŶŶŶ **Signature Moscato 2022, Heathcote** **RATING** 91 **DRINK** 2023–2028 $22 JP ✪

Emilian

PO Box 20 Kalorama, Vic 3766 **Region** Yarra Valley
T 0421 100 648 **www**.emilian.com.au **Open** Not **Winemaker** Robin Querre
Est. 2015 **Dozens** 300
Robin Querre is the 4th generation of a family involved in winemaking since 1897,
variously in Saint-Émilion and Pomerol, France. Robin commenced studies in medicine
at the University of Bordeaux, but changed to oenology in 1990. He studied under some
of the Bordeaux greats (such as Yves Glories, Denis Dubourdieu and Aline Lonvaud), and
worked vintages at Château Canon and Moueix, as well as at Rudd Estate in the Napa Valley.
He currently works for Laffort Oenology, a private research company based in Bordeaux,
developing, producing and selling oenological products to winemakers. He and wife Prue
also make small quantities of very good wine in the Yarra Valley.

ŶŶŶŶŶ **L'assemblage Rouge 2022, Yarra Valley** Aromas of boysenberries, spiced
raspberries and violets, which lead onto the light- to medium-bodied, finely
tuned and persistent palate. The tannins are silky and harmonious, and my
feeling is that as good as this is to drink now, it will become even more complex.
Screw cap. 13% alc. **RATING** 96 **DRINK** 2022–2028 $37 PR ✪
Single Vineyard Nebbiolo Rosé 2022, Yarra Valley A pale salmon pink.
Floral accented with aromas of red berries, pomegranate and watermelon. The
palate is as bright as a button. Juicy yet dry, this refreshing and energetic wine
finishes spicy and long. Winemaker Robin Querre has nailed this. Screw cap.
12.5% alc. **RATING** 95 **DRINK** 2022–2025 $25 PR ✪
Single Parcel Chardonnay 2022, Yarra Valley Bright green gold. Aromas
of stone fruits, orange blossom, honeysuckle and a little candied ginger pervade
this quiet and complex wine. Equally restrained on the gently textured and even
palate, there's a nice touch of grip on the finish, too. 125 dozen made. Screw cap.
13% alc. **RATING** 94 **DRINK** 2022–2027 $45 PR

♟♟♟♟♗ Single Parcel Semillon 2022, Yarra Valley RATING 93 DRINK 2022-2029 $37 PR
Single Vineyard Dixons Creek Pinot Noir 2022, Yarra Valley RATING 92 DRINK 2022-2027 $30 PR ✪

Entropy Wines   ★★★★★

254 Trafalgar South Rd Trafalgar South, Vic 3824 (postal) **Region** Gippsland
T 0405 464 988 **www.**entropywines.com **Open** Not **Winemaker** Ryan Ponsford
Viticulturist Ryan Ponsford **Est.** 2015 **Dozens** 1200 **Vyds** 4.7ha

Ryan Ponsford might be new to wine but this young man is smart, loaded with talent, commitment and a penchant for hard work. Formerly an artist working with wet plate photography, his path changed after tasting a pinot noir made by William Downie, and then meeting him in '16. Two years later, William, now a mentor, gifted Ryan some grapes and Entropy began. He's established a nursery block and is gearing up to plant a high-density vineyard at his Traralgon property. He's also reinvigorated 2 neglected vineyards where he sources fruit today, 1 in Warragul and the other Willow Grove. His wines are compelling and the Entropy story is exceptional. A star in the making.

♟♟♟♟♟ **Warragul Vineyard Sauvignon Blanc Semillon 2022, Gippsland** The texture is paramount: flinty, neat phenolics, super-juicy and long to the finish. Oyster shell, briny with slivers of preserved lemon, fresh citrus, wafts of lavender and thyme in between. Take this to lunch and cancel the rest of the day. Diam. 12.5% alc. RATING 96 DRINK 2023-2032 $55 JF ✪
Warragul Vineyard Syrah 2022, Gippsland A spicy, peppery and lively wine, nothing stemmy or bitter. Dark fruit, kirsch and earthy with tar and licorice plus supple, plump, squishy tannins. No new oak influencing the outcome, just beautiful fruit and a savoury perspective. Diam. 13% alc. RATING 95 DRINK 2023-2033 $55 JF
Willow Grove Vineyard Pinot Noir 2022, Gippsland Am I in the presence of greatness? This is captivating and gentle, incorporating supple tannins with a light tug on the finish – lithe, refreshing and purity within. Floral, perfumed, a little spicy, a little slinky and a little bit special. Screw cap. 13.5% alc. RATING 95 DRINK 2023-2031 $78 JF
Willow Grove Vineyard Savagnin 2022, Gippsland This ambrosia is complex and lovely with savoury inflections throughout. Think chamomile, honeycomb and quince, fluffy, creamy lees and fine phenolics. Savagnin, this good, is sexy. Diam. 13.5% alc. RATING 95 DRINK 2023-2030 $55 JF
Warragul Vineyard Riesling 2021, Gippsland This is something else. A powder puff of aromatics all lemon blossom and beeswax with the palate superfine and long; creamy in texture but not too much, citrusy, tangy acidity and yet there's a savoury overlay. Delicious and compelling in equal measure. Diam. 13.5% alc. RATING 95 DRINK 2022-2027 $50 JF ✪
Warragul Vineyard Sauvignon Blanc Semillon 2021, Gippsland This is full of overt tropical fruit and … just kidding. This is so complex and detailed it moves beyond the varieties to more shape and texture. There's a salivating quality, no doubt due to the acidity, yet lees work adds layers of detail and flavour. There's citrus and candied peel with ginger-flecked clotted cream and a hint of linseed. Classy stuff. Diam. 13.5% alc. RATING 95 DRINK 2022-2027 $44 JF ✪
Willow Grove Vineyard Savagnin 2021, Gippsland This wine is rock 'n' roll: electrifying acidity taking centre stage with backup from fine phenolics, creamy lees and complex flavours of camomile, preserved lemon and Japanese pickled ginger, plus hints of creamed honey. It is savoury not fruit-driven wine. There's succulence and texture. I could drink this all day. Diam. 14% alc. RATING 95 DRINK 2022-2028 $44 JF ✪

♟♟♟♟♗ **Willow Grove Vineyard Pinot Noir 2021, Gippsland** RATING 93 DRINK 2022-2028 $60 JF
Warragul Vineyard Syrah 2021, Gippsland RATING 90 DRINK 2024-2031 $49 JF ✪

Eperosa ★★★★★

Lot 552 Krondorf Road, Tanunda, SA 5352 **Region** Barossa Valley
T 0428 111 121 **www**.eperosa.com.au **Open** Fri–Sat 11–5 **Winemaker** Brett Grocke
Est. 2005 **Dozens** 1200 **Vyds** 8.75ha
Eperosa owner and Wine Companion 2021 Winemaker of the Year Brett Grocke qualified as a viticulturist in '01 and, through Grocke Viticulture, consults and provides technical services to over 200ha of vineyards spread across the Barossa Valley, Eden Valley, Adelaide Hills, Riverland, Langhorne Creek and Hindmarsh Valley. He is ideally placed to secure small parcels of organically managed grapes, hand-picked, whole-bunch fermented and foot-stomped, and neither filtered nor fined. The wines are of impeccable quality.

🍷🍷🍷🍷🍷 **Magnolia 1965 Shiraz 2021, Barossa Valley** Vibrant magenta in the glass with plum, blue and dark berry fruits with an array of exotic spices, citrus blossom, bunchy amaro notes, blueberry pie, licorice, liminal garrigue notes, graphite and dark cherries, glossy and pure fruit and a filigreed palate with tight, fine sandy tannin and plenty of mineral energy finishing firmly structured. Cork. 14.8% alc. **RATING** 95 **DRINK** 2023-2033 $60 DB
L.R.C. Shiraz 2021, Barossa Valley A plushly fruited little beauty. Macerated damson plum, black cherry compote, ground spice, a whiff of amaro, leather and dried citrus rind and some graphite/moody notes with a distinctly meaty edge. It's a pretty appealing package with great fruit depth and heft. Cork. 15.1% alc. **RATING** 95 **DRINK** 2023-2038 $55 DB
Magnolia 1896 Shiraz 2021, Barossa Valley Deep magenta crimson with characters of macerated blood plum, blackberry and black cherry fruits with underlying hints of exotic spice, amaro herbs, licorice, dried citrus, brandied fruits, dark chocolate and earth. Less of a floral overtone here and an increased graphite-like depth to the proceedings with compact sandy tannins and a black wave of intense fruit on the finish. Cork. 14.8% alc. **RATING** 95 **DRINK** 2023-2040 $80 DB
SGG 1858 2021, Eden Valley 95/3/2% grenache/mataro/shiraz. Plenty of latent power and tight granitic tannin heft. The fruit is pure and true – all macerated satsuma plum and mulberry tones cut with exotic spice, dried citrus rind, scattered amaro herbs, pressed flowers, ginger cake, black tea, light sarsaparilla and Chinese roast meats. Plenty of muscle and sinew on display here. Cork. 14.9% alc. **RATING** 94 **DRINK** 2023-2033 $60 DB

🍷🍷🍷🍷🍷 **Krondorf 2021, Barossa Valley RATING** 92 **DRINK** 2023-2033 $30 DB ✪

Epsilon ★★★★

43 Hempel Road, Daveyston, SA 5355 **Region** Barossa Valley
T 0417 871 951 **www**.epsilonwines.com.au **Open** By appt **Winemaker** Aaron Southern **Est.** 2004 **Dozens** 3000 **Vyds** 7ha
Taking ownership of the vineyard in '94 when in their 20s, 5th generation grapegrowers Aaron and Julie (nee Kalleske) Southern were content to follow in the footsteps of their ancestors. Friends Jaysen Collins and Dan Standish (Massena Vineyards) helped them realise their dream of producing their own wine in '04.

🍷🍷🍷🍷🍷 **Shiraz 2021, Barossa Valley** Deep crimson with purple flashes in the glass. Jam-packed with juicy blood plum and macerated summer berry fruits with hints of licorice, dark chocolate, fruitcake spices, earth, purple florals, iodine and vanillin oak. There's plenty of depth to the fruit, the tannins are fine and sandy and the finish is awash with spicy, plummy vitality. Screw cap. 14.5% alc. **RATING** 93 **DRINK** 2023-2029 $22 DB ✪
Nineteen Ninety Four Shiraz 2019, Barossa Valley Deep crimson in the glass with notes of blackberry, blood plum and black cherry with hints of fruitcake spices, blackstrap licorice, rum and raisin dark chocolate, crème de cassis, ironstone and earth. Full bodied and mouth-filling with a fine, tannin frame and plush, opulent flow of fruit on the finish. Screw cap. 15% alc. **RATING** 93 **DRINK** 2023-2030 $50 DB

Shiraz 2020, Barossa Valley Deep crimson in colour with inviting notes of juicy plum and blackcurrant dredged in fruitcake spices along with hints of licorice and rum and raisin dark chocolate. Warm earth, ironstone, barbecued meats, graphite and softly spoken cedar. Mouth-filling and flush with fruit, fine tannin and spice, there is a lot to like at this pricepoint. Screw cap. 14.5% alc. RATING 92 DRINK 2023–2028 $22 DB ✪

Ernest Hill Wines ★★★★

307 Wine Country Drive, Nulkaba, NSW 2325 **Region** Hunter Valley
T (02) 4991 4418 **www**.ernesthillwines.com.au **Open** 7 days 10–5 **Winemaker** Mark Woods **Est.** 1999 **Dozens** 6000 **Vyds** 9.2ha
This is part of a vineyard originally planted in the early '70s by Harry Tulloch for Seppelt Wines; it was later renamed Pokolbin Creek vineyard, and later still (in '99) the Wilson family purchased the upper (hill) part of the vineyard, and renamed it Ernest Hill. It is now planted to semillon, shiraz, chardonnay, verdelho, traminer, merlot and tempranillo.

🍷🍷🍷🍷🍷 **Alexander Reserve Premium Hunter Chardonnay 2022** From the Alexander block on the estate vineyard. Nice wine: good line, length and overall balance. Screw cap. 13% alc. RATING 94 DRINK 2023–2028 $45 JH
Shareholders Shiraz 2021, Hunter Valley An attractive phoenix rising from the ashes: its palate is smooth and supple in a medium–bodied, juicy frame. Makes light of the challenges of the vintage. Screw cap. 13.8% alc. RATING 94 DRINK 2023–2033 $32 JH ✪

🍷🍷🍷🍷🍷 **Chicken Shed Chardonnay 2022, Hunter Valley** RATING 91 DRINK 2023–2027 $28 JH ✪
Cyril Premium Hunter Semillon 2022 RATING 90 DRINK 2027–2032 $28 JH
Andrew Watson Reserve Premium Tempranillo 2021, Hunter Valley RATING 90 DRINK 2023–2029 $35 JH

Evans & Tate ★★★★★

Cnr Metricup Road/Caves Road, Wilyabrup, WA 6280 **Region** Margaret River
T (08) 9755 6244 **www**.evansandtate.wine **Open** 7 days 10.30–5 **Winemaker** Matthew Byrne, Feleasha Prendergast **Viticulturist** John Fogarty **Est.** 1970 **Vyds** 12.3ha
Evans & Tate was founded in the early 1970s when its prized Redbrook vineyard was established at Wilyabrup. In 1987 they released the Margaret River Classic Semillon Sauvignon blend, which morphed into the number–one–selling wine from the region. The brand's success as a producer of note has ebbed and flowed over the years, but there is stability now thanks to Fogarty Wine Group taking full ownership; they've injected much–needed funds into vineyards rejuvenation and new plantings. There's a renewed sense of enthusiasm and optimism, and while senior winemaker Matt Byrne has been a steady influence, winemaker Feleasha Prendergast is bringing a fresh perspective, too. Volumes have increased to feed an array of labels but its premium wines under the Redbrook range have never been better. It bodes well.

🍷🍷🍷🍷🍷 **Redbrook Reserve Chardonnay 2020, Margaret River** Tightly wound and structured with grapefruit and lemon and zest, funk and smoky sulphides. Oak is neatly integrated, adding a layer of spice and texture. In one way, this is steely with fine acidity, yet not lacking in flavour. Screw cap. 13.5% alc. RATING 96 DRINK 2022–2032 $65 JF ✪
Redbrook Estate Cabernet Merlot 2020, Margaret River A dark red/inky hue laden with mulberries, plums, cassis and baking spices with wafts of tobacco, menthol/eucalyptus. Full bodied and densely packed with flavour and no shortage of structure or tannins. If you imagine being at a rave, this wine is the DJ mixing it right up. Screw cap. 14.5% alc. RATING 95 DRINK 2024–2040 $40 JF ✪
Redbrook Reserve Cabernet Sauvignon 2019, Margaret River Wonderful fragrance and flavours of mulberries, cranberries, cinnamon and plenty of cedary/ woodsy spices from the oak. It's full bodied, densely packed with flavour and

has no shortage of tannins, albeit ripe and grainy tannins in a youthful context. Decant this then prepare a rack of lamb or roast beef, gather friends for a feast and pour. Screw cap. 14.3% alc. RATING 95 DRINK 2023-2043 $65 JF

🍷🍷🍷🍷🍷 **Redbrook Estate Chardonnay 2020, Margaret River** RATING 93 DRINK 2023-2030 $40 JF
Wild Cape Chardonnay 2021, Margaret River RATING 90 DRINK 2022-2026 $25 JF ✪

Evoi Wines

529 Osmington Road, Bramley, WA 6285 **Region** Margaret River
T 0437 905 100 **www**.evoiwines.com **Open** 7 days 10–5 **Winemaker** Nigel Ludlow **Est.** 2006 **Dozens** 10 000
NZ-born Nigel Ludlow has a graduate diploma in oenology and viticulture from Lincoln University, NZ. Time at Selaks was a stepping stone to Flying Winemaking stints in Hungary, Spain and South Africa, before a return as senior winemaker at Nobilo. He thereafter moved to Victoria, and finally to Margaret River. It took time for Evoi to take shape, the first vintage of chardonnay being made in the lounge room of Nigel's house. After a transition period in a leased space at a commercial winery, '17 saw Evoi open its own winery and cellar door. The quality has been exceptional.

🍷🍷🍷🍷🍷 **Cabernet Sauvignon 2020, Margaret River** Complex and deep from start to finish. A whorl of mulberries and blueberries, baking spices, mocha and oak spice yet it's very savoury. Full bodied, dense and rich; the palate is appealing and smooth with beautiful tannin structure. It'll go some distance. Screw cap. 14% alc. RATING 95 DRINK 2023-2033 $42 JF ✪
The Satyr Reserve 2019, Margaret River 70/20/10% cabernet sauvignon/ petit verdot/malbec. It's a big wine and the oak makes its presence felt, yet good fruit keeps it all under control. Dark berries, chocolate, inky with crushed nori, tobacco verging on freshly rolled pot (just saying) cedary, spicy oak and baking spices come flooding through. Full bodied, rich and ripe with supple tannins. Screw cap. 14% alc. RATING 95 DRINK 2023-2034 $80 JF

🍷🍷🍷🍷🍷 **Malbec 2020, Margaret River** RATING 92 DRINK 2023-2030 $42 JF
Sauvignon Blanc Semillon 2022, Margaret River RATING 90 DRINK 2022-2026 $28 JF
Chardonnay 2021, Margaret River RATING 90 DRINK 2022-2028 $35 JF

Faber Vineyard

233 Haddrill Road, Baskerville, WA 6056 **Region** Swan Valley
T (08) 9296 0209 **www**.fabervineyard.com.au **Open** Fri–Sun 11–4 **Winemaker** John Griffiths **Est.** 1997 **Dozens** 4000 **Vyds** 4.5ha
John Griffiths, former Houghton winemaker, teamed with wife Jane Micallef to found Faber Vineyard. They have established shiraz, verdelho (1.5ha each), brown muscat, chardonnay and petit verdot (0.5ha each). John says, 'It may be somewhat quixotic, but I'm a great fan of traditional warm-area Australian wine styles, wines made in a relatively simple manner that reflect the concentrated ripe flavours one expects in these regions. And when one searches, some of these gems can be found from the Swan Valley.'

🍷🍷🍷🍷🍷 **Donnybrook Durif 2021, Geographe** A bold, big red with sweet fruit, a sheath of firm, granitic tannin, bold flavours and layers and layers of sweet spice. Molten Christmas pudding, ripe plum, kirsch and cola writ large here – huge perfume and flavour profile, indeed. All of this well balanced, an unctuous, lavish red of impeccable credentials and verity to this hearty variety. Screw cap. 14% alc. RATING 94 DRINK 2022-2035 $48 MB
Reserve Shiraz 2020, Swan Valley Dark and dense expression of shiraz with a sumptuous, indulgent feel. Ripe plum, blackcurrants, licorice, turned earth and sweet cola characters on the bouquet – a highly perfumed and intense whiff. The

palate offers more of the sweet/ripe plummy fruit, cherry cola, clove/cinnamon spice and a lick of anise to finish. Very well balanced, too. A prodigious red, done well. Screw cap. 13.5% alc. **RATING** 94 **DRINK** 2022–2035 $93 MB

Cabernet Sauvignon 2020, Frankland River Rich aromas of sweet cassis, sage leaf, clove and tobacco, lush in the palate with similar characters albeit a cool, gently minty lift freshens things. Quite sleek and trim in the mouth; tannins refreshing and gently puckering while faint minerally elements feel woven through. Elegance personified. Screw cap. 14% alc. **RATING** 94 **DRINK** 2022–2032 $65 MB

Grenache 2022, Swan Valley **RATING** 93 **DRINK** 2022–2028 $36 MB
CBP Chenin Blanc 2022, Swan Valley **RATING** 93 **DRINK** 2022–2030 $36 MB
Verdelho 2022, Swan Valley **RATING** 93 **DRINK** 2022–2030 $28 MB ✪
CSM Cabernet Malbec 2021, Frankland River **RATING** 93
DRINK 2022–2030 $48 MB
Petit Verdot 2021, Swan Valley **RATING** 93 **DRINK** 2022–2030 $48 MB
CSS Cabernet Shiraz 2020, Western Australia **RATING** 93
DRINK 2022–2032 $65 MB
Riche Shiraz 2021, Swan Valley **RATING** 92 **DRINK** 2022–2032 $31 MB
Malbec 2021, Western Australia **RATING** 92 **DRINK** 2022–2027 $36 MB
Chenin Blanc 2022, Swan Valley **RATING** 91 **DRINK** 2022–2028 $28 MB ✪

Fallen Giants ★★★★★

4113 Ararat–Halls Gap Road, Halls Gap, Vic 3381 **Region** Grampians
T (03) 5356 4252 www.fallengiants.com.au **Open** By appt **Winemaker** Justin Purser
Viticulturist Rebecca Drummond **Est.** 1969 **Dozens** 3000 **Vyds** 10.5ha
Originally planted in 1969, the (now) Fallen Giants vineyard had once been part of Mount Langi Ghiran, before being bought by the late Trevor Mast. Following his death, it was purchased by siblings Aaron and Rebecca Drummond and renamed Fallen Giants in '13. The name takes its meaning from the local Djab Wurrung and Jardiwadjali peoples and references the creation of Halls Gap. The Drummonds grew up on the Mornington Peninsula; Aaron went on to work for the Rathbone Wine Group, while Rebecca headed into the global financial market trade. Together, they work at making some of the better wines of the Grampians wine region.

Riesling 2022, Grampians The way the acidity comes drenched in flavour here is a joy to behold. Granny Smith apple and lime flavours speak in clear, crisp, bright tones, the effect delicious, the quality obvious. Screw cap. 12.5% alc. **RATING** 95 **DRINK** 2023–2033 $35 CM ✪

Shiraz 2021, Grampians Sweet fruit runs through the wine's generous core, with fistfuls of spice around the edges. This is an easy wine to love. Black cherry and plum, woodsy spice, orange jelly and a mix of black pepper and cloves. It's not a big wine but it's itching to impress, in the most pleasing of ways. Screw cap. 14.5% alc. **RATING** 95 **DRINK** 2024–2036 $45 CM ✪

Cabernet Sauvignon 2021, Grampians Grampians cabernet is hardly flavour of the month, but Fallen Giants is doing its best to change that. This is another excellent release. There's as much pepper as leaf, as much plum as blackcurrant, but there's a sinewy aspect to the tannin that is very cabernet and, as this variety often does, it uses mint/eucalyptus characters to very good effect; adding lift and life to the darkness beneath. Add a briar note to the aftertaste and you're in excellent territory. Screw cap. 14.5% alc. **RATING** 95 **DRINK** 2026–2036 $45 CM ✪

False Cape Wines ★★★★

1054 Willson River Road, Dudley East, SA 5222 **Region** Kangaroo Island
T 0447 808 838 www.falsecapewines.com.au **Open** 7 days 11–5 **Winemaker** Greg Follett, Nick Walker **Viticulturist** Jamie Helyar **Est.** 1999 **Dozens** 6000 **Vyds** 25ha

Julie and Jamie Helyar's False Cape label links 3rd-generation Kangaroo Island farming with 3rd-generation Langhorne Creek grapegrowers. It is the largest vineyard on Kangaroo Island with 25ha of vines (shiraz, sauvignon blanc and cabernet sauvignon and lesser amounts of chardonnay, riesling, pinot gris, merlot and pinot noir). Wines are made by Julie's brother, Greg Follett of Lake Breeze in Langhorne Creek. False Cape is entirely off-grid, completely relying on solar power; the red grape varieties are dry-grown, free-range turkeys providing pest control management and sheep are used for weed management during winter. The wines are consistently well made and low priced.

ΨΨΨΨΨ **The Captain Cabernet Sauvignon 2020, Kangaroo Island** Boysenberry, blackcurrant, choc-mint and peppercorn flavours put on a thoroughly convincing display, but it's the all-round freshness, in the context of fruit intensity, and the length of the well-structured finish that really impress. It's a lovely cabernet, and because it's so inherently balanced it can be enjoyed either in its youth or with age. Screw cap. 14% alc. RATING 94 DRINK 2024-2034 $39 CM ✪

ΨΨΨΨΨ **Lady Ann Rosé 2022, Kangaroo Island** RATING 92 DRINK 2023-2026 $22 CM ✪
Montebello Pinot Gris 2022, Kangaroo Island RATING 92 DRINK 2023-2025 $22 CM ✪
Silver Mermaid Sauvignon Blanc 2022, Kangaroo Island RATING 92 DRINK 2023-2026 $22 CM ✪
Willson River Riesling 2022, Kangaroo Island RATING 92 DRINK 2023-2031 $22 CM ✪
Unknown Sailor Cabernet Merlot 2020, Kangaroo Island RATING 92 DRINK 2023-2030 $27 CM ✪

Farmer's Leap Wines

41 Hodgson Road, Padthaway, SA 5271 **Region** Padthaway
T (08) 8765 5155 **www.**farmersleap.com **Open** 7 days 10–4 **Winemaker** Renae Hirsch
Est. 2004 **Dozens** 15 000 **Vyds** 485ha
Scott Longbottom and Cheryl Merrett are 3rd-generation farmers in Padthaway. They commenced planting the vineyard in '93 on the family property and now have shiraz, cabernet sauvignon, merlot, chardonnay and sauvignon blanc planted. Initially the majority of the grapes were sold, but increasing quantities held for the Farmer's Leap label have seen production rise.

ΨΨΨΨΨ **Shiraz 2021, Padthaway** Some wines just flow effortlessly along, and this is one on them. Plum and redcurrant fruit flavours spread right through the palate, kissed along the way – but only lightly – by creamy oak. No bumps, no surprises, just pure shiraz flavour. Screw cap. 14.5% alc. RATING 90 DRINK 2023-2027 $28 CM
Cabernet Sauvignon 2021, Padthaway This is a faithful rendition of the cabernet sauvignon grape. It offers blackcurrant, boysenberry and subtle bay leaf characters in a juicy, free-flowing way. Middle-of-the-road cabernet, you could call it, in a positive sense. Screw cap. 14% alc. RATING 90 DRINK 2023-2028 $28 CM

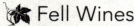 Fell Wines ★★★★

PO Box 210 Goodwood, SA 5034 **Region** McLaren Vale
T 0412 035 765 **www.**fellwines.com.au **Open** Not **Winemaker** Tom Hicks **Est.** 2017
Dozens 400
Fell Wines is the baby of Tom Hicks, of the eponymous Hicks Wines. The name is inspired by the fells (mountains) of northern England and the shepherds, their sheep and their binds to the land. It is the oft-heard story of the wanderer, eager to explore small-batch vinification under the aegis of wild yeast and gentle extraction techniques. The bright labelling of each cuvée confers a certain insouciance, belying the textural precision, intrigue and prodigious drinkability manifest in each bottle. If you are expecting pulpy hipster juice with little

structure, think again! Freshness, fruit and apposite structural latticework are the signatures, as is exceptional value.

🍷🍷🍷🍷🍷 **Fiano 2021, McLaren Vale** I love this rendition of fiano, reliant on a salty wisp of skin contact as much as the pungent maritime ester of freshness that tows it long. Beautifully measured in every facet. Sea spray, tatami straw, white miso, mandarin, tamarind and cumquat. If this was my everyday white I'd be extremely happy. Screw cap. 13.5% alc. **RATING** 94 **DRINK** 2022–2025 $26 NG ✪

🍷🍷🍷🍷🍷 **Sangiovese Rosé 2021, McLaren Vale RATING** 93 **DRINK** 2022–2023 $26 NG ✪
Sangiovese 2021, McLaren Vale RATING 92 **DRINK** 2022–2026 $30 NG ✪
Touriga 2021, McLaren Vale RATING 92 **DRINK** 2022–2024 $30 NG ✪
Grenache 2021, McLaren Vale RATING 92 **DRINK** 2022–2027 $35 NG
Shiraz 2017, McLaren Vale RATING 91 **DRINK** 2022–2025 $30 NG

Fermoy Estate

838 Metricup Road, Wilyabrup, WA 6280 **Region** Margaret River
T (08) 9755 6285 **www.**fermoy.com.au **Open** 7 days 11–5 **Winemaker** Jeremy Hodgson **Viticulturist** Andrew Keig **Est.** 1985 **Dozens** 20 000 **Vyds** 27.28ha
A long-established winery with plantings of semillon, sauvignon blanc, chardonnay, cabernet sauvignon, merlot and shiraz. They are happy to keep a relatively low profile, however difficult that may be given the quality of the wines. Jeremy Hodgson has a first-class honours degree in oenology and viticulture, and a CV encompassing winemaking roles with Wise Wines, Cherubino Consultancy and, earlier, Plantagenet, Houghton and Goundrey Wines.

🍷🍷🍷🍷🍷 **Coldfire Fumé Blanc 2022, Margaret River** A convincing argument for texture with layers of flavour and detail. It's smoky and funky, full of fresh Seville oranges and glacé ones. The phenolics are well handled, there's a moreish, savoury character throughout and some power, too. It feels like a grown-up wine and gee, it's good. Screw cap. 13% alc. **RATING** 95 **DRINK** 2022–2029 $35 JF ✪
Reserve Chardonnay 2021, Margaret River A rich, voluptuous style with the quality fruit masked by decisive winemaking … or perhaps helping it? Flinty, bolshie, plenty of malty oak, layers of creamy lees, lemon curd and a toastiness with streaky bacon. Imagine an extrovert at a party full of introverts, this is such a wine. Screw cap. 13.5% alc. **RATING** 95 **DRINK** 2022–2030 $70 JF
Wilyabrup Reserve Cabernet Sauvignon 2020, Margaret River This is gorgeous. Superfine and long with powdery tannins; there's latent power within yet it hovers around medium bodied. It's structured and detailed, laden with flavour and the oak adds cedar and antique wood aromas plus another layer of tannins. There are also mulberries and blueberries and a kitchen cupboard full of spices. Screw cap. 14% alc. **RATING** 95 **DRINK** 2024–2040 $99 JF
Wilyabrup Cabernet Sauvignon 2020, Margaret River Expect lots of flavour from licorice, cedar, menthol, and brambleberries to cassis. There's some density as much as intensity with lightly drying tannins and cedary oak adding to them, too. Thankfully there's an attractive sweet spot midway, the fruit tempers that and it keeps unfurling. It's wrangling its way out of youth and will be an upstanding fine mature wine one day. Screw cap. 14% alc. **RATING** 94 **DRINK** 2024–2035 $50 JF

🍷🍷🍷🍷🍷 **Blackwater Shiraz Cabernet Malbec 2021, Margaret River RATING** 93 **DRINK** 2023–2034 $40 JF
Merlot 2020, Margaret River RATING 93 **DRINK** 2022–2030 $35 JF ✪
Cabernet Merlot 2020, Margaret River RATING 92 **DRINK** 2023–2035 $30 JF ✪
Rosé 2022, Margaret River RATING 91 **DRINK** 2022–2024 $27 JF ✪
Vintage Brut Rosé 2018, Pemberton RATING 90 **DRINK** 2022–2024 $45 JF
Chardonnay 2021, Margaret River RATING 90 **DRINK** 2022–2027 $35 JF

Ferngrove

276 Ferngrove Road, Frankland River, WA 6396 (postal) **Region** Frankland River
T (08) 9363 1300 **www.ferngrove.com.au Open** Not **Winemaker** Craig Grafton,
Adrian Foot **Viticulturist** Chris Zur **Est.** 1998 **Vyds** 220ha

For over 20 years, Ferngrove has been producing consistent examples of cool-climate wines
across multiple price brackets. The Ferngrove stable includes the flagship Orchid wines, Black
Label, White Label and Independence ranges.

ȲȲȲȲȲ **The Stirlings Mount Hassell Riesling 2022, Great Southern** It's steely and
very racy, brisk and bright with lemon juice, tart green apple juice and crushed
granite minerally notes with briny acidity in tow. Indeed, very minerally as an
expression, compact, lean and refreshing. A pristine, acid-driven style. Screw cap.
12% alc. **RATING** 93 **DRINK** 2023-2035 $35 MB ✪

Majestic Cabernet Sauvignon 2021, Great Southern A leafy expression of
cabernet set to cool, blue fruits with graphite tannins and medium body. Nicely
done in that regard. It feels comfortable and understated, shows detail of spice,
earthy elements and that mineral drawl. Dark cherry, faint mocha, ripe plum
around all that. Attractive scents, fine flavours, good length and a compact, tightly
wound feel. Classy. Screw cap. 14% alc. **RATING** 93 **DRINK** 2022-2035 $40 MB

Orchid Range Cossack Riesling 2022, Great Southern Ultra bright and
vibrant in style with lemon and green apple crispness and crunch, steely mineral
qualities and touches of jasmine tea and floral nuances. Lean or understated, you
choose. It's lively, strongly acid-driven and skeletal but packs in plenty of character.
Screw cap. 11.5% alc. **RATING** 92 **DRINK** 2023-2035 $30 MB ✪

Dragon 2021, Great Southern Pitch-perfect Great Southern shiraz. It's very
pretty in perfume, spicy, red fruited, silky textured, medium weight and offers
excellent drinking in youth. Ticking those boxes! Characters of ripe cherry,
pomegranate juice, cinnamon, pepper, sage leaf and faint briny minerality.
Screw cap. 14% alc. **RATING** 92 **DRINK** 2022-2032 $40 MB

**Orchid Range Queen Of Sheba Cabernet Sauvignon Shiraz 2019,
Great Southern** Brooding, dark fruited, ripe and tinged with mint and
eucalyptus. It flows beautifully, sits at medium weight, finds a gentle pull of
puckering tannin and finishes with light, palate-staining sweet spice and herbs.
A chocolatey note? Sure. It's generous without overdoing it, layers in detail,
too. Well put together and great drinking. Screw cap. 13.5% alc. **RATING** 92
DRINK 2023-2030 $40 MB

Orchid Range Red Spider Nebbiolo 2021, Great Southern Fine and tense
in texture, medium weight, rippling with crushed granite tannins, laced with
dried herbal detail and strongly set to the red cherry zone. It's firm and chewy
yet fresh feeling, too. A strong sense of restraint, complexity and varietal box-
checking. It's a wine that delivers right now but feels best settled into a cellar to
loosen it up a bit. Screw cap. 13.5% alc. **RATING** 91 **DRINK** 2025-2035 $40 MB

Fetherston Vintners

1/99a Maroondah Highway, Healesville, Vic 3777 (postal) **Region** Yarra Valley
T 0417 431 700 **www.fetherstonwine.com.au Open** Not **Winemaker** Chris Lawrence
Viticulturist Chris Lawrence **Est.** 2015 **Dozens** 3500 **Vyds** 22ha

Chris Lawrence and Camille Koll established Fetherston Vintners in '15, a year after Chris
finished an oenology degree with the University of Southern Queensland. Previously at
Yering Station ('10–14) he worked his way up from junior cellar hand to assistant winemaker
before taking on the winemaker role at Sunshine Creek in the Yarra Valley. Camille grew
up in the Yarra. After finishing school, she began a 7-year stint at in marketing at Domaine
Chandon. Chris' late grandfather was Tony Fetherston.

ȲȲȲȲȲ **Chardonnay 2021, Yarra Valley** This has immediate appeal with its white
peach, nectarine and grilled cashew notes. Energetic, with those aforementioned

stone fruits, grapefruit and a hint of fresh vanilla bean, this finishes pithy and long. Impeccably balanced. A lovely wine. Screw cap. 13.1% alc. **RATING** 95 **DRINK** 2022-2025 $42 PR ✪

Single Vineyard Pinot Noir 2021, Yarra Valley A light–medium ruby red. A gorgeous wine from the outset, this opens with aromas of spiced raspberries, a hint of cinnamon, lavender and violets. Equally impressive on the palate. Simultaneously creamy and with silky tannins, this tapers into a long, satisfying finish. Screw cap. 13.2% alc. **RATING** 95 **DRINK** 2022-2025 $42 PR ✪

ΨΨΨΨΨ **Peony Nebbiolo Rosé 2022, Pyrenees RATING** 93 **DRINK** 2022-2024 $28 PR ✪

Camellia Cabernet Malbec 2022, Yarra Valley RATING 93 **DRINK** 2022-2026 $28 PR ✪

Fungi Pinot Noir 2022, Yarra Valley RATING 92 **DRINK** 2023-2027 $32 PR

Magnolia Single Vineyard Albariño 2022, King Valley RATING 90 **DRINK** 2022-2024 $25 PR ✪

Fighting Gully Road ★★★★★

Kurrajong Way, Mayday Hill, Beechworth, Vic 3747 **Region** Beechworth
T 0407 261 373 **www**.fightinggullyroadwines.com.au **Open** By appt **Winemaker** Mark Walpole **Viticulturist** Mark Walpole **Est.** 1997 **Dozens** 3500 **Vyds** 10.5ha
Mark Walpole and his partner Carolyn De Poi found their elevated north-facing site south of Beechworth in '95. They commenced planting the Aquila Audax vineyard in '97 with cabernet sauvignon and pinot noir, expanding with sangiovese, tempranillo, shiraz, petit manseng and chardonnay. In '09 they were fortunate to lease the oldest vineyard in the region, planted by the Smith family in '78 to chardonnay and cabernet sauvignon – in fact, Mark shares the lease with long-time friend Adrian Rodda (see A. Rodda Wines). Mark Walpole is the *Halliday Wine Companion 2024* Viticulturist of the Year.

ΨΨΨΨΨ **Chardonnay 2021, Beechworth** White label. So sunny and upfront delicious, but take your time with this treasure. There is some seriously good viticulture and winemaking behind it, plus it's a top vintage. Summer-fresh scents of nectarine, white peach and citrus, while quality oak brings a warm textural background to layers of fruit, gentle spice, nougat and almond meal. This is archetypal Beechworth chardonnay full of drinking pleasure. Screw cap. 13% alc. **RATING** 95 **DRINK** 2022-2028 $45 JP ✪ ♥

Smith's Vineyard Chardonnay 2021, Beechworth Black label. A complex and compelling chardonnay. At its heart is a mineral, beeswax and slatey core contributing an effortless, natural balance. To that, the winemaker has brought ripe, citrus and stone fruits, introduced some spicy oak and a nougat-like texture. Brings both power and delicacy to the glass. Screw cap. 13.5% alc. **RATING** 95 **DRINK** 2022-2028 $85 JP

Pinot Noir 2021, Beechworth A beautifully fragrant, filigree-fine young pinot noir. Beechworth soil delivers time and time again an effortless, natural balance, which is on display here. Pretty red cherry and strawberry fruit with pepper, spice and floral aromatics, earth and savoury game. Oak is well integrated, tannins are fine and cherry-pip dry. Impressive. Screw cap. 13.5% alc. **RATING** 95 **DRINK** 2023-2028 $45 JP ✪

Syrah 2019, Beechworth With a lightness of touch, shiraz (aka syrah) gives up an arresting array of spices, here led by a light sprinkling of black pepper to elevate some enticing quality black and red fruits. Medium in weight and elegant by design. Screw cap. 14% alc. **RATING** 95 **DRINK** 2022-2030 $65 JP

Sangiovese 2021, Beechworth Classic spiced cherries, wild herbs, cassis and red licorice notes with bright acidity. Ripe and well composed on the palate, it offers fine sinewy tannins and lingering, juicy dark fruits with a lick of pepperiness to close. Screw cap. 14% alc. **RATING** 94 **DRINK** 2021-2026 $35 JP ✪

ŸŸŸŸŸ Verdicchio 2021, Beechworth RATING 93 DRINK 2022–2025 $35 JP ✪
Gros Manseng Moelleux 2021, Beechworth RATING 92 DRINK 2023–2027 $32 JP
Tempranillo 2019, Beechworth RATING 90 DRINK 2023–2026 $45 JP

Fire Gully ★★★★

4051 Caves Road, Wilyabrup, WA 6280 **Region** Margaret River
T (08) 9755 6220 **www.firegully.com.au Open** 7 days 10–5 **Winemaker** Dr Michael Peterkin **Est.** 1988 **Dozens** 5000 **Vyds** 13.4ha
A 6ha lake in a gully ravaged by bushfires gave the name. In '98, Mike Peterkin of nearby Pierro purchased the vineyard. The vineyard, adjacent to Moss Wood, is planted to cabernet sauvignon, merlot, shiraz, semillon, sauvignon blanc and chardonnay. Wines are available for tasting at the Pierro cellar door.

ŸŸŸŸŸ Reserve Shiraz 2020, Margaret River Low yields have had an impact this vintage. Intense flavours of ripe dark plums, warm earth, sumac and tiny red berries, a bit like wild strawberries, yet this still retains its savoury heart. Lots of fruit sweetness across the fuller-bodied palate with supple tannins and good length. Screw cap. 14% alc. RATING 94 DRINK 2022–2030 $60 JF

ŸŸŸŸŸ Reserve Cabernet Sauvignon 2020, Margaret River RATING 93 DRINK 2022–2030 $60 JF
Chardonnay 2021, Margaret River RATING 91 DRINK 2022–2028 $40 JF

First Creek Wines ★★★★★

600 McDonalds Road, Pokolbin, NSW 2320 **Region** Hunter Valley
T (02) 4998 7293 **www.firstcreekwines.com.au Open** 7 days 10–5 **Winemaker** Liz Silkman, Shaun Silkman, Greg Silkman **Est.** 1984 **Dozens** 60 000
First Creek Wines is the family business of Greg Silkman (managing director and winemaker), son Shaun Silkman (chief operating officer and winemaker) and Shaun's wife Liz (chief winemaker). The quality of the wines has been consistently exemplary and there is every reason to believe this will continue in the years to come. Associated business First Creek Winemaking Services is the main contract winemaker operating in the Hunter Valley.

ŸŸŸŸŸ Limited Release Small Batch Vermentino 2022, Hunter Valley This variety is grown all over Corisca, and I've spent days tasting it there. First Creek's effort is extraordinary. It has a perfumed bouquet and a rich palate with a blend of tropical and citrus fruits comforting every part of the mouth and then allowing the inclusion of lime-infused acidity on the finish. Wow. Screw cap. 12.5% alc. RATING 97 DRINK 2023–2035 $35 JH ✪ ♥
Winemaker's Reserve Semillon 2022, Hunter Valley Yet another wine giving the impression it came from a great vintage, with layers of silk and aromas of honeysuckle, stone fruit and pink grapefruit. Great power and life to the finish, the lingering aftertaste is mouth-watering. Screw cap. 11% alc. RATING 97 DRINK 2023–2039 $80 JH ✪
Museum Release Winemaker's Reserve Semillon 2013, Hunter Valley Superb gleaming green colour. The wine obviously had great balance in its youth, and is now reaping the benefit of that start in life. Acidity, as is often the case, provides the structure that the mineral/citrus duo gratefully accept. Screw cap. 10.8% alc. RATING 97 DRINK 2023–2035 $80 JH ✪

ŸŸŸŸŸ Single Vineyard Murphy Vineyard Semillon 2022, Hunter Valley The vibrant pale green colour signals a wine of ultimate finesse; mineral and grapefruit acidity signal the structure and texture. The poise and balance of the wine means a 20-year life span is more likely to be 30 or 40 years given the protection of the screw cap. Screw cap. 11% alc. RATING 96 DRINK 2023–2043 $65 JH ✪
Oakey Creek Vineyard Semillon 2022, Hunter Valley This wine opens with a burst of glorious tropical fruits that also seem to usher finely strung white peach

and pink grapefruit into their mouthfeel. This is such a beautiful semillon. Screw cap. 10.8% alc. **RATING** 96 **DRINK** 2023-2033 $65 JH ✪

Winemaker's Reserve Chardonnay 2021, Hunter Valley Barrel fermentation in French oak enlivens the wine, the full swag of complexity building quickly as it crosses the palate which bursts into song. It has the length one might expect from cool regions such as the Yarra Valley, and leaves the mouth thirsting for more. Lovely stuff. Screw cap. 12.5% alc. **RATING** 96 **DRINK** 2023-2031 $80 JH

Museum Release Murphy Vineyard Semillon 2017, Hunter Valley Pale quartz-green colour; the wine is brilliantly fresh, with crystalline grapefruit acidity that has the most gentle bite. Screw cap. 11.5% alc. **RATING** 96 **DRINK** 2023-2038 $65 JH ✪

Museum Release Winemaker's Reserve Semillon 2017, Hunter Valley This marches to a different tune than to the Murphy Vineyard Semillon; all aspects of the bouquet and palate are more forthcoming, albeit still anchored on yellow grapefruit and its acidity. The colour, too, has a little more colour, though still in a green spectrum. Screw cap. 10.8% alc. **RATING** 96 **DRINK** 2023-2038 $80 JH

Limited Release Small Batch Fiano 2022, Hunter Valley While the wrap-around label professes 'minimal handling' and 'thoughtful winemaking', better would be a 10-second burst as to what the reader should look for. Thus, fiano: 'An Italian variety suited to hot dry conditions that makes scented wines which will repay 3–5 years cellaring. Has a savoury/citrus grip that has you reaching for the second glass.' Screw cap. 12.5% alc. **RATING** 95 **DRINK** 2023-2028 $35 JH ✪

Merton Vineyard Chardonnay 2021, Hunter Valley The vineyard is planted to Dijon/Bernard clones 95 and 96. This vintage clone 95 was the standout; the wine barrel fermented in French puncheons (30% new) which allowed a best-barrel selection. Everything worked as planned in this tangy chardonnay that has excellent intensity and length. Screw cap. 12.5% alc. **RATING** 95 **DRINK** 2023-2029 $65 JH

Marrowbone Vineyard Shiraz 2021, Hunter Valley Good colour. The plum/blackberry swell of fruit is punctuated by spice and licorice on the bouquet. The lively and fresh flavours are in a red/black cherry spectrum and supported by finely milled tannins; made to measure for a 10-year span in the cellar. Its balance is the key now, time will see more savoury nuances developing and a softer tannin profile. Screw cap. 13% alc. **RATING** 95 **DRINK** 2025-2035 $65 JH

Limited Release Small Batch Sangiovese 2021, Hilltops Bright clear crimson. The prettiest sangiovese you'll meet in many a long day. I'm taking mine tonight. Fresh red cherries, some blueberries, and a fresh finish. Screw cap. 12.9% alc. **RATING** 94 **DRINK** 2023-2029 $35 JH ✪

Limited Release Small Batch Malbec 2021, Central Ranges This is a very smart malbec at a price that won't frighten the bank manager. It's full of plum and blackberry fruits, a dab of dark chocolate, and eiderdown soft tannins. Screw cap. 13.5% alc. **RATING** 94 **DRINK** 2023-2031 $35 JH ✪

Limited Release Small Batch Tannat 2021, Hunter Valley Deep purple colour right through to the rim. In its original home, tannat was over-endowed with tannins. This wine certainly has abundant extract (which will please some, though not all). Screw cap. 13% alc. **RATING** 94 **DRINK** 2030-2040 $35 JH ✪

Winemaker's Reserve Shiraz 2021, Hunter Valley The perfumed aromas on the bouquet are full of cherry blossom and spice. I've enjoyed many bottles of 50yo Hunter shiraz without the benefit of screw caps, and am certain that the time for well-made Hunter shiraz is nigh. And this wine does have complexity on a grand scale. Screw cap. 13.5% alc. **RATING** 94 **DRINK** 2023-2031 $80 JH

🍷🍷🍷🍷🍷 **Chardonnay 2021, Hunter Valley RATING** 91 **DRINK** 2023-2030 $25 JH ✪

First Drop Wines   ★★★★

30–38 Barossa Valley Way, Nuriootpa, SA 5355 **Region** Barossa Valley
T 0488 299 233 **www.firstdropwines.com Open** Mon–Sat 10–4 **Winemaker** John
Retsas, Kurt Northam **Est.** 2004 **Dozens** 30 000

First Drop Wines HQ is in the striking 'Home of the Brave' building on the southern edge
of Nuriootpa in the Provenance Barossa precinct. John Retsas is the man behind the dynamic
brand, with delicious wines sourced from vineyards across the Barossa, Adelaide Hills and
McLaren Vale. There is a heavy emphasis on the 'alternative' (appropriate) varieties with
Italian and Portuguese grapes making their presence felt; of course, shiraz, grenache, cabernet
sauvignon and mataro also play a role, with a contemporary slant.

♥♥♥♥♥ **Mother's Milk Shiraz 2021, Barossa** There is no doubt that this wine will
improve but damn it's delicious now. Deep plum and cherry fruits, plenty of spicy
depth with hints of licorice, dark chocolate and earth. It's plush yet has crunch
and cadence as it races off with memories of maraschino cherries, spice and
roasting meats. Screw cap. 14.5% alc. RATING 94 DRINK 2023-2028 $28 DB ✪
Two Percent Shiraz 2020, Barossa A splash (hence the 'two percent') of
muscadelle backs its way into this shiraz. It's not a unique concept but it lends
an exotic, floral edge to the proceedings. There is a deep, spicy resonance that
acts as a base for the rich, ripe plum and blackberry fruits. Licorice-like and
earthy, rich and opulent, there is plenty of concentration on display with compact
sandy tannins and a spicy cassis tide of the finish. Screw cap. 15% alc. RATING 94
DRINK 2023-2033 $50 DB

♥♥♥♥♀ **Following The Sun Prosecco 2022, Riverland** RATING 92 DRINK 2023-2025
$25 DB ✪
Touriga Nacional 2022, McLaren Vale RATING 92 DRINK 2023-2027 $28
DB ✪
Mere et Fils Chardonnay 2021, Adelaide Hills RATING 92
DRINK 2023-2026 $35 DB
Mother's Ruin Cabernet Sauvignon 2019, McLaren Vale RATING 92
DRINK 2023-2033 $28 DB ✪
Forza Nebbiolo 2018, Adelaide Hills RATING 92 DRINK 2023-2028 $60 DB
Endless Summer Pinot Grigio 2022, Adelaide Hills RATING 91
DRINK 2023-2024 $25 DB ✪
Minchia Montepulciano 2019, Adelaide Hills RATING 91 DRINK 2023-2027
$45 DB

Fishbone Wines   ★★★★

422 Harmans Mill Road, Wilyabrup, WA 6285 **Region** Margaret River
T (08) 9755 6726 **www.fishbonewines.com.au Open** Thu–Tue 10–4.30
Winemaker Stuart Pierce **Est.** 2009 **Dozens** 15 000 **Vyds** 9.1ha

Fishbone Wines' 9.1ha vineyard includes chardonnay, tempranillo and cabernet sauvignon;
and newer plantings of malbec, vermentino and pinot noir. The Fishbone wines are created
with minimal intervention. The range includes the 'accessible' Blue Label range, single
vineyard Black Label range and the 'icon' Joseph River wines.

♥♥♥♥♀ **Joseph River Estate Reserve Chardonnay 2021, Margaret River** Flesh
and toastiness, rich stone fruit and grapefruit fruitiness among creamy vanilla
highlights and licks of cinnamon, spice and faint honeyed nuts. Oak has its say
here, but in that it finds good balance and freshness of cool, briny acidity. It feels
pretty classy and yet bombastic at the same time. Should mellow and honey with
time in the cellar. Screw cap. 12.4% alc. RATING 93 DRINK 2023-2035 $65 MB
Black Label Sauvignon Blanc 2022, Margaret River Piercingly fresh with
hints of lime, lemon juice, sugar snap and fresh herbs, all of which rend this
ultra-refreshing. Talc-like acidity gives a layer to the palate and some depth to an
otherwise vibrant, juicy and fruit-driven wine. Screw cap. 12.6% alc. RATING 90
DRINK 2022-2026 $38 JF

Flametree

Cnr Caves Road/Chain Avenue, Dunsborough, WA 6281 **Region** Margaret River
T (08) 9756 8577 **www.flametreewines.com Open** 7 days 10–5 **Winemaker** Cliff Royle
Est. 2007 **Dozens** 20 000

Flametree is one of Margaret River's most successful wineries and yet it owns no vineyards.
It's all about sourcing quality fruit, whether for the entry-level Embers or top-tier, S.R.S.
(Sub Regional Series). Cliff Royle, who joined in '09 as chief winemaker, is savvy when it
comes to fruit choice. He started the S.R.S. range – chardonnay from Wallcliffe and cabernet
sauvignon from Wilyabrup in '10. There's also a Karridale sauvignon blanc. How did he get
there? 'Years of playing around with different parcels of fruit, grading them and being brutal.'
Along the way, Flametree has picked up a raft of awards and accolades.

S.R.S. Wilyabrup Cabernet Sauvignon 2019, Margaret River Fruit
from a small parcel of a single vineyard on an east/northeast facing block in the
Wilyabrup district. Gently held for 30 days on skins after primary fermentation.
Pressed to French oak (50% new) for 12 months' maturation. A beautifully
modulated wine, with silky tannins sliding through the cassis-accented fruit.
Lovely pristine cabernet. Screw cap. 14% alc. **RATING** 97 **DRINK** 2024–2039
$85 JH ✪

S.R.S. Wallcliffe Chardonnay 2022, Margaret River Powerful yet superfine,
long, detailed and rich, although there's a tension throughout with penetrating
acidity. Complexity aplenty. It's also moreish thanks to the sulphides, the excellent
citrus-toned fruit, wave of oak spice adding to what is a superbly balanced wine.
Screw cap. 13% alc. **RATING** 96 **DRINK** 2023–2035 $75 JF ✪
S.R.S. Karridale Sauvignon Blanc 2021, Margaret River It's all about texture
which relentlessly imposes its thumbprint and fruit fragments – pink grapefruit and
apple skin – flying in all directions allied with acidity. Is the price justified? Yes, and
then some. Screw cap. 12% alc. **RATING** 96 **DRINK** 2023–2028 $40 JH ✪
S.R.S. Wilyabrup Cabernet Sauvignon 2020, Margaret River Beauty in
a bottle? Right here, folks. So youthful, divine and on song. Pristine mulberry
and blackberry flavours mingle with cedary oak spice and dark chocolate as wafts
of violets and charcuterie flutter in and out, so too menthol and a hint of green
walnut. The fuller-bodied palate is shored up with firmish tannins but given its
structure, this is a few years away from looking its finest. Screw cap. 14% alc.
RATING 96 **DRINK** 2024–2038 $95 JF
Chardonnay 2022, Margaret River There are some flinty, funky sulphides,
grapefruit, creamy nutty lees, a hint of melon, powdered ginger and honeycomb.
And just when you think, 'Is this all too much of a good thing?' the acidity
comes flowing through, providing energy, zesty appeal, length and refreshment.
A cracking wine for the price. Screw cap. 13% alc. **RATING** 95 **DRINK** 2023–2032
$35 JF ✪
S.R.S. Karridale Sauvignon Blanc 2022, Margaret River A textural,
delicious wine with an abundance of flavour and freshness, too. Feijoa and
pomelo, that's the extent of the tropical fruit spectrum as it builds on the palate
with vanilla slice lees, lime zest and juice. It's thrilling and classy but oh-so-easy to
drink. Screw cap. 13% alc. **RATING** 95 **DRINK** 2023–2030 $40 JF ✪
Chardonnay 2021, Margaret River The bouquet is very complex, with some
funky, struck-match notes immediately obvious, the dominant grapefruit flavours
at ease and a structured mouthfeel. A very impressive wine at this price. Screw
cap. 13% alc. **RATING** 95 **DRINK** 2023–2031 $30 JH ✪
Cabernet Sauvignon 2020, Margaret River Nothing out of place, nothing
overt with the oak or tannins, either, instead the latter are fine and ripe, the
former melded into the body of the wine. Medium weighted with mulberries
and blackberries doused in mocha, herbs and fresh mint. A long carry and a lovely
wine. Screw cap. 14% alc. **RATING** 95 **DRINK** 2023–2035 $45 JF ✪
Cabernet Sauvignon Merlot 2019, Margaret River Rather pitch perfect.
Hitting high notes with mulberries, currants and spicy cedary oak, while the

palate is superfine and long. The tannins are ripe and textural, the acidity refreshing and it is delicious. Today. Now. Screw cap. 14% alc. **RATING** 95 **DRINK** 2023–2033 $35 JF ✪

Sauvignon Blanc Semillon 2022, Margaret River **RATING** 92 **DRINK** 2023–2036 $28 JF ✪
Rosé 2022, Margaret River **RATING** 92 **DRINK** 2023–2025 $30 JF ✪
Embers Chardonnay 2022, Margaret River **RATING** 91 **DRINK** 2023–2026 $25 JF ✪

Flaxman Wines

662 Flaxmans Valley Road, Flaxmans Valley, SA 5253 **Region** Eden Valley
T 0411 668 949 **www**.flaxmanwines.com.au **Open** Thu–Fri, Sun 11–4, Sat 11–5
Winemaker Colin Sheppard **Est.** 2005 **Vyds** 2ha
After visiting the Barossa Valley for over a decade, Melbourne residents Colin and Fi Sheppard decided on a tree change and in '04 found a small, old vineyard overlooking Flaxmans Valley, consisting 1929-planted riesling, shiraz and semillon. The vines are dry grown, hand pruned, hand picked and treated – say the Sheppards – as their garden. Yields are restricted to under 4t/ha and exceptional parcels of locally grown grapes are also purchased. Colin has worked at various Barossa wineries and his attention to detail (and understanding of the process) is reflected in the consistent high quality of the wines.

Riesling 2022, Eden Valley Made with the same unhurried 'don't worry' approach that marks all the Flaxman wines, the aromas and flavours in a lime, lemon and green apple trifecta. Line and length are carried by crisp acidity. 100 dozen made. Screw cap. 12.5% alc. **RATING** 95 **DRINK** 2023–2032 $30 JH ✪
The Stranger 2019, Barossa Contract-grown Barossa shiraz and Eden Valley cabernet sauvignon, skilfully made. Blackberry, black cherry and blackcurrant fruit picked to retain freshness, balance and fine tannins. 50 dozen made. Screw cap. 14% alc. **RATING** 95 **DRINK** 2023–2034 $45 JH ✪
Estate Shiraz 2019, Eden Valley This is superb fruit handled with appropriate respect and care. The vintage was very good, fruit ripeness where you would wish it to be. The only problem is that demand has far outpaced supply. 50 dozen made. Screw cap. 13.5% alc. **RATING** 95 **DRINK** 2023–2040 $120 JH

Semillon 2021, Eden Valley **RATING** 92 **DRINK** 2023–2031 $30 JH ✪
Paladin Shiraz 2019, Barossa Valley **RATING** 92 **DRINK** 2023–2034 $30 JH ✪

Fleet Wines

150 Old Korumburra Rd, Leongatha, Vic 3953 **Region** Gippsland
T 0419 882 838 **www**.fleetwines.com.au **Open** By appt **Winemaker** Lisa Jenkins, Justin Jenkins **Viticulturist** Lisa Jenkins, Justin Jenkins **Est.** 2016 **Dozens** 3000 **Vyds** 7.5ha
One of the most exciting new names on the wine front is Fleet, the brainchild of Lisa and Justin Jenkins. Fruit comes from established sites in Gippsland, Yarra Valley and Mornington Peninsula but their dream has been to establish their own estate, which started in '17 when they bought 21ha at Leongatha. They built a winery in time for the '23 vintage and have planted 2 plots, Block One to pinot noir and chardonnay and Block Two, an east-westerly aspect, to pinot gris and riesling. Lisa is also finishing a bachelor of viticulture at Charles Sturt while both raise their children and vineyard. Eventually, they hope to plant 10ha all up and when the vines are mature enough, Fleet will be all estate made. Until then, Lisa and Justin say they are having fun with the transitional stuff. New cellar door opens spring '23.

Seville Syrah 2022, Yarra Valley Beautifully modulated flavours with such vibrant fruit: all plums, black pepper, dried herbs and pliable tannins that stretch out across the medium-bodied palate. And it's fragrant with florals and spice and all things nice. Diam. 13.2% alc. **RATING** 95 **DRINK** 2023–2032 $45 JF ✪
Nostalgia Leongatha Pinot Noir 2022, Gippsland A bit of a chameleon here as it starts out deceptively light and fine. There are flutters of cherries and

warm spices tempered by tangy cranberry juice–like acidity and fine sandy tannins, then the flavours build and its shape changes. It leaves a lasting impression. Compelling. Diam. 12.2% alc. RATING 95 DRINK 2023–2030 $60 JF

Lichen Pinot Gris 2022, Mornington Peninsula A lovely textural, skinsy gris. Copper pink and cloudy with oodles of personality. Delicate flavours of watermelon and pomegranate juice, pomelo and rosewater. Chalky tannins coat the palate, adding shape and another layer of texture alongside some fluffy, light creamy lees. This is good. Very good and more importantly, delicious. Screw cap. 11.9% alc. RATING 95 DRINK 2022–2025 $32 JF ✪

Lichen Syrah 2022, Yarra Valley A very seductive syrah and incredibly spicy mix of black pepper and baking spices all lifted by florals. Lots going on here. It feels light and easy yet works off a medium-bodied palate with a heart of dark fruit buoyed by Mediterranean herbs. Textural, light tannins and fine acidity in the mix. Screw cap. 12.5% alc. RATING 94 DRINK 2022–2030 $35 JF ✪

ŸŸŸŸŸ **Chorus Pinot Noir et al 2022, Gippsland** RATING 93 DRINK 2023–2027 $50 JF
Noir Gris Red Hill 2022, Mornington Peninsula RATING 93 DRINK 2023–2028 $50 JF
Red Hill Pinot Noir 2022, Mornington Peninsula RATING 92 DRINK 2023–2029 $45 JF
Lichen Pinot Noir 2022, South Gippsland RATING 92 DRINK 2022–2028 $35 JF
Leongatha Pinot Noir 2022, Gippsland RATING 92 DRINK 2023–2028 $45 JF
Rosé 2022, Yarra Valley RATING 91 DRINK 2022–2024 $32 JF
Dixon's Creek Chardonnay 2022, Yarra Valley RATING 90 DRINK 2023–2030 $45 JF
Glen Forbes Chardonnay 2022, South Gippsland RATING 90 DRINK 2023–2030 $45 JF

Flowstone Wines ★★★★★

11298 Bussell Highway, Forest Grove, WA 6286 **Region** Margaret River **T** 0487 010 275 **www.**flowstonewines.com **Open** By appt **Winemaker** Stuart Pym, Janice McDonald **Viticulturist** Stuart Pym **Est.** 2013 **Dozens** 1500 **Vyds** 3ha
Veteran Margaret River winemaker Stuart Pym's career constituted long-term successive roles: beginning with Voyager Estate in '91, thereafter with Devil's Lair, and finishing with Stella Bella in '13, the year he and Perth-based wine tragic Phil Giglia established Flowstone Wines. In '03 Stuart purchased a small property on the edge of the Margaret River Plateau in the beautiful Forest Grove area, progressively planting chardonnay, cabernet sauvignon, gewürztraminer and touriga. From '17, Flowstone leased a vineyard at Karridale, planted to long-established sauvignon blanc and chardonnay.

ŸŸŸŸŸ **Gewürztraminer 2021, Margaret River** Wafts of honeysuckle, roses, Turkish delight and spiced flambé bananas delight. It is wonderfully textural without being heavy. Flavours of lemon rind and glacé lime slip across the fuller-bodied palate with phenolics deftly handled. Screw cap. 13.5% alc. RATING 96 DRINK 2022–2029 $32 JF ✪

Sauvignon Blanc 2021, Margaret River This is stylish, smooth and oh-so slurpable. The palate is long and pure with fine acidity well meshed into the citrus and stone fruit flavours. Plus, there's texture with dabs of lemon and lime curd, some smoky flintiness and the finish lingering long. It's a stunner. Screw cap. 12% alc. RATING 95 DRINK 2022–2028 $36 JF ✪

Queen of the Earth Chardonnay 2020, Margaret River It's a little bit flinty and a little bit funky thanks to moreish sulphides, and it's more than a little bit delicious. Fragrant with florals, grapefruit and lemon, there's a dusting of ginger powder and some sweet-ish woodsy flavours via oak and layers of creamy lees. It's a satisfying drink, too, and feels light to finish thanks to its refreshing acidity. Screw cap. 13% alc. RATING 95 DRINK 2023–2030 $55 JF

ㅜㅜㅜㅜ㇒ Queen of the Earth Sauvignon Blanc 2021, Margaret River RATING 93
DRINK 2023-2028 $55 JF
Chardonnay 2020, Margaret River RATING 93 DRINK 2022-2028 $40 JF
Cabernet Sauvignon 2018, Margaret River RATING 93 DRINK 2023-2033
$40 JF
Moonmilk Shiraz Grenache 2021, Margaret River RATING 92
DRINK 2023-2027 $29 JF ✪

Flying Fish Cove ★★★★

3763 Caves Road, Wilyabrup, WA 6280 **Region** Margaret River
T (08) 9755 6600 **www.flyingfishcove.com Open** By appt **Winemaker** Simon Ding,
Damon Easthaugh **Est.** 2000 **Vyds** 25ha
Flying Fish Cove produces wines under contract for other brands, as well as making its own
wines. Long-serving winemaker Simon Ding had a circuitous journey before falling prey
to the lure of wine, finishing an apprenticeship in metalwork before obtaining a bachelor
of wine science. He joined the Flying Fish Cove team in 2000. Most fruit for Flying Fish
Cove wines is sourced from the Wildberry Farm vineyard in Wilyabrup, planted in '97. The
winery itself is certified organic.

ㅜㅜㅜㅜ㇒ The Wildberry Reserve Cabernet Sauvignon 2021, Margaret River
An elegant style in a way, as it's medium bodied, lightly spiced and very savoury.
Of course, there's the classic regional fruit power of mulberries, blackberries
and some cassis in the mix, with unobtrusive cedar oak adding another layer
of flavour. Partner with hearty fare to mitigate the drying tannins. Screw cap.
14% alc. **RATING** 91 **DRINK** 2023-2033 $49 JF

Forest Hill Vineyard ★★★★★

Cnr South Coast Highway/Myers Road, Denmark, WA 6333 **Region** Great Southern
T (08) 9848 2399 **www.foresthillwines.com.au Open** 7 days 10.30–5 **Winemaker** Liam
Carmody, Guy Lyons **Viticulturist** Ross Pike **Est.** 1965 **Dozens** 12 000 **Vyds** 36ha
This family-owned business is one of the oldest 'new' winemaking operations in WA and was
the site of the first grape plantings in Great Southern in 1965. The quality of the wines made
from the oldest vines (dry-grown) on the property is awesome (released under the numbered
vineyard block labels).

ㅜㅜㅜㅜㅜ Block 9 Shiraz 2021, Mount Barker Single site, dry grown, planted '85 –
a precious vineyard with a rich history. It's all about black fruits laden with
spices, licorice and tannins engraved into the flesh of the fruit. A savoury/
cedary backdrop anchors on those tannins. Screw cap. 14% alc. **RATING** 97
DRINK 2023-2046 $60 JH ✪

ㅜㅜㅜㅜㅜ Riesling 2022, Mount Barker From Block 2, planted in '75. The old vines
provide the seemingly limitless depth to its length, texture and structure, the younger
planting providing the lime blossom bouquet. Lovely cool-grown wine from a very
good region. Screw cap. 12% alc. **RATING** 96 **DRINK** 2023-2037 $29 JH ✪
Block 1 Riesling 2022, Mount Barker Wow, the intensity and drive, the
citrusy impact and mineral detail in acidity. A scintillating riesling of concentration
and power, yet compact in nature. It's heady in perfume: frangipani, green apple,
lime, rose petal and pink grapefruit. The palate a symphony of tart, fresh, juicy,
fruity and spicy all woven beautifully and so exceptionally long. Lingering spice,
gingery and piquant, is lovely. High-pedigree wine here. Screw cap. 12.5% alc.
RATING 96 **DRINK** 2023-2040 $55 MB ✪ ♥
Block 2 Riesling 2022, Mount Barker A very intense and energetic
expression, concentrated, taut and distinguished. Aromas lean into ozone, flint,
green apple, jasmine and blackcurrant with flickers of lime. The palate, more
lime and pink grapefruit orientated, is met with talc, slate-like mineral elements
and gingery spice. It's compact and tense, superbly refreshing and brilliant in its

understatement yet full delivery of character. Wonderful. Screw cap. 12.5% alc. RATING 95 DRINK 2023-2040 $38 MB ✪

Block 5 Cabernet Sauvignon 2021, Mount Barker Cassis, blackcurrant, woody spices, black olive and licorice characters in spades. Evocative perfume delivers dark fruit, toasty, clove spice, leafy herb and anise personality, a roll of fine, lacy, tannins, brambly herb and spice lingering on. Very even, graceful flow, reserved and elegant with excellent persistence of flavour and finesse. An almost refreshing feel overall, too. Very classy. Screw cap. 14% alc. RATING 95 DRINK 2023-2035 $65 MB ♥

Shiraz 2021, Mount Barker A fragrant and elegant bouquet of black cherry, crushed peppercorns and a gently spiced, medium-bodied palate. The long finish is the icing on the cake. Screw cap. 14% alc. RATING 95 DRINK 2023-2041 $34 JH ✪

Block 8 Chardonnay 2022, Mount Barker Lots going on here: flinty mineral notes, soft, just-ripe stone fruits, green apple acidity, a touch of sake-like umami, great intensity and supple texture with some chalky pucker. Delicious drinking, effortless, too, a kind of understatement despite the detail. It feels fancy in its relaxed way. Screw cap. 13% alc. RATING 94 DRINK 2023-2033 $50 MB ♥

🍷🍷🍷🍷🍷 **Malbec 2021, Mount Barker** RATING 93 DRINK 2023-2028 $34 MB ✪
Highbury Fields Chardonnay 2022, Mount Barker RATING 92 DRINK 2023-2032 $25 MB ✪
Highbury Fields Cabernet Sauvignon 2021, Great Southern RATING 92 DRINK 2023-2032 $25 MB ✪
Cabernet Sauvignon 2021, Mount Barker RATING 92 DRINK 2023-2035 $35 MB
Chardonnay 2022, Mount Barker RATING 91 DRINK 2025-2033 $34 MB

Forester Estate

1064 Wildwood Road, Yallingup, WA 6282 (postal) **Region** Margaret River
T (08) 9755 2000 **www.foresterestate.com.au Open** Not **Winemaker** Todd Payne, Kevin McKay **Viticulturist** Kevin McKay **Est.** 2001 **Dozens** 52 000 **Vyds** 33.5ha
Forester Estate is owned by Kevin and Jenny McKay. The name is a nod to the forestry industry that thrived here in the 1850s. Winemaker Todd Payne has had a distinguished career, working in Great Southern, the Napa Valley, Hawke's Bay and the northern Rhône, including a vintage with esteemed producer Yves Cuilleron, before moving back to WA to complete the circle. The estate vineyards were planted in '95 and fruit from older vines is sourced from other growers in the region. The tasting room is housed in a French Renaissance-style castle, built in '07.

🍷🍷🍷🍷🍷 **Sauvignon Blanc 2022, Margaret River** This wine's texture, juicy, tangy fruit and a certain depth of flavour make it immediately enjoyable. Guava, lemon oil and lime juice are the building blocks, racy and clean as it glides across the palate. Here some sweetness kicks in, thwarting a slightly bitter finish. Screw cap. 13.2% alc. RATING 92 DRINK 2022-2028 $30 JF ✪

Forty Paces

428 Pipers Creek Road, Pipers Creek, Vic 3444 (postal) **Region** Macedon Ranges
T 0418 424 785 **www.fortypaceswines.com Open** Not **Winemaker** Jason Peasley
Est. 2001 **Dozens** 100 **Vyds** 0.5ha
Forty Paces has a tiny 0.5ha pinot noir vineyard with MV6, 114, 115 and 777 clones, planted by owner and winemaker Jason Peasley in '01. Jason has no formal training, but was tutored on the job by Stuart Anderson at Epis in the Macedon Ranges. He follows some organic and biodynamic practices in both the vineyard and the winery.

🍷🍷🍷🍷🍷 **Pinot Noir 2021, Macedon Ranges** Dark cherries, all spiced up, wild strawberries, some kirsch, sumac and tamarind with oak spice, too. As usual, mid weighted with supple tannins and the light acidity keeps it buoyant. It's a gentle

wine. One of the most unique pinots thanks to its flavour profile. Screw cap.
13.5% alc. RATING 95 DRINK 2023–2033 $49 JF

ₚₚₚₚₚ **Rosé de Saignée 2022, Macedon Ranges** RATING 92 DRINK 2023–2025
$25 JF

4382 Terroir   ★★★★

28200 New England Hwy, Ballandean, Qld 4382 **Region** Granite Belt
T (07) 4684 1000 **www.**4382terroir.com.au **Open** Wed–Sun 8–4 **Winemaker** Rob
Davidson **Viticulturist** Peter Watters **Est.** 2018 **Dozens**
Rob Davidson and his family are the driving force behind the 4382 Terroir label. They
established their vineyard in '18, only to lose half of it in the '19 bushfire season. The vineyard
was subsequently replanted, and Rob and his partner Judy continue on their vigneron
journey. The 4382 in the winery name is the postcode of Ballandean. Originally, the project
focused only on wines from that postcode, but recent fruit shortfalls have seen 4382 Terroir
sourcing fruit from Riverland to supplement the existing Granite Belt range. Lesser-sung
varieties underpin 4382 Terroir, including saperavi, arinto, sagrantino, durif, lagrein and
fernão pires, among more common semillon and mourvèdre. The diversity is writ large for
this ambitious and dynamic project.

ₚₚₚₚₚ **Viognier 2021, Granite Belt** Scents of fragrant tropical fruits, ginger and green
mango. The palate is lightly chewy, gently puckering and finishes exceptionally
long and fine. Succulent flavours of lime juice drizzled on passionfruit, green apple
and nectarine, with a lick of cashew savouriness in the mix. Good concentration,
too. Screw cap. 13% alc. RATING 94 DRINK 2022–2028 $40 MB

ₚₚₚₚₚ **Arinto 2021, Riverland** RATING 93 DRINK 2022–2025 $35 MB
Fernão Pires 2021, Riverland RATING 92 DRINK 2022–2024 $35 MB
Aglianico 2020, Riverland RATING 92 DRINK 2022–2026 $60 MB
Lagrein 2020, Riverland RATING 92 DRINK 2022–2028 $45 MB
Lagrein 2021, Riverland RATING 90 DRINK 2022–2027 $45 MB

Fourth Wave Wine   ★★★★

Suite 1, Level 3, The Forum, 240-244 Pacific Highway, Charlestown NSW 2290 (postal)
Region Various
T 1300 778 047 **www.**fourthwavewine.com.au **Open** Not **Winemaker** Various
Est. 2009 **Dozens** 300 000
Based in the suburbs of Newcastle, Fourth Wave Wine was founded in '09 by Nicholas and
Frances Crampton, boasting wine industry nous; finance and IT skills respectively. Assisted
by winemaker and consultant Corey Ryan, Fourth Wave makes wine in 6 countries with
the wines packaged under a panoply of brands. A modern-day global negoçiant, if you will.
While savvy marketing is key to their success, the intrinsic qualities of many of the wines
cannot be denied.

ₚₚₚₚₚ **Wild Folk Natural Shiraz 2022, Barossa** This is deep in colour with a
purple flare and resonant notes of pure ripe plum and blackberry dredged with
exotic spice and hints of warm earth, black licorice, pressed purple flowers and
blueberry flan. Pure in the mouth with powdery tannin support and a lot of
drinking enjoyment. Muy bueno! Diam. 14.5% alc. RATING 93 DRINK 2023–2027
$28 DB ✪
Cowpunk Amphora Chardonnay 2022, Tumbarumba This is super-fresh,
and I wouldn't be cellaring it for any great length of time. It's a really good drink:
racy, vibrant with lemon barley water and grapefruit to the fore yet made more
complex by creamy, nutty lees work. It's super-tight across the palate, all moreish
and savoury. Swing top. 12.2% alc. RATING 93 DRINK 2022–2026 $30 JF ✪
Little Giant Cabernet 2021, Coonawarra Great value here. This is a wine of
flavour, structure and length. You don't often get that trio in a wine at this price.
Blackcurrant, bay leaf, cedar and mint notes get the job done, firm tannins pulling
through the finish. It's not a big wine, and you need to enjoy tannin to really see

the beauty of it, but in that context it's a ripper release. Screw cap. 14.5% alc.
RATING 93 DRINK 2023-2032 $22 CM ✪

Take it to the Grave Shiraz 2022, Barossa Terrific value here with a bouncy,
slurpy edge and a wine literally bursting with slurpy, pure plum, blueberry and
boysenberry fruits. Flush with exotic spice and blossomy high tones, fine, sandy
tannins swoop in to support to ripe berry and plum fruits and there is a nice seam
of acidity providing the pulse. Lots of inherent drinkability and enjoyment here.
Screw cap. 14.5% alc. RATING 92 DRINK 2023-2028 $19 DB ✪

Little Giant Single Vineyard Cabernet 2021, Coonawarra Takes the
archetypal flavour of Coonawarra cabernet and adds both elegance and finesse.
Blackcurrant, tobacco, bay leaf and mint flavours come infused with cedar
wood, but what really distinguishes it is the spread of fine-grained tannin and
the evenness of the finish. It's not creamy, per se, but it feels smooth thanks to its
balance and flow. Screw cap. 14.5% alc. RATING 92 DRINK 2024-2031 $32 CM

Little Giant Little Batch Montepulciano 2021, Barossa Valley Purple hued
with vibrant red and dark plum and berry fruits lying on a bed of spice and earth
with liminal floral facets in the distance. Spacious, detailed and swift of pulse, this
makes for easy drinking. Screw cap. 13.5% alc. RATING 92 DRINK 2023-2027
$27 DB ✪

Mania Chardonnay 2021, Tasmania Tamar Valley-sourced chardonnay made
by Jim Chatto. Pale straw with juicy white peach and nectarine notes with citrus,
soft spice, white flowers, nougat, vanilla and crushed stone. Lemon curd and
clotted cream flow in on the palate and the wine trails off with a wake of vanillin
oak, nectarine and citrus. Screw cap. 13% alc. RATING 92 DRINK 2023-2026
$35 DB

Little Giant Single Vineyard Shiraz 2021, Barossa Valley Deep crimson in
the glass with plenty of crunchy plum and summer berry fruits, cut with hints of
spice, earth, licorice, dark chocolate and violets. Bright and swift of line with the
tug of gentle tannins and a bright plummy exit. Screw cap. 14.5% alc. RATING 91
DRINK 2023-2028 $29 DB

Little Giant Single Vineyard Cabernet 2021, Coonawarra Deep crimson
with characters of blackberry, black cherry and blackcurrant fruits with underlying
hints of ground spice, olive tapenade, violets, licorice, cedar, light undergrowth
tones and earth. Some nice deep blackberry pastille fruit on the palate with
pleasant crunch and detail, tight-grained tannin and a deep, macerated black
fruit vibe on the finish. Screw cap. 14.5% alc. RATING 91 DRINK 2023-2028
$15 DB ✪

Cowpunk Organic Chardonnay NV, New South Wales Yellow plum, star
fruit and peach cheeks. Followed by apple crumble and vanilla bean custard. Juicy
but with a softness to the naturally high acidity, which makes for a real drinkability
factor. Well balanced and hits the target for its price. Swing top. 11.7% alc.
RATING 90 $30 SW

Wild Folk GSM 2022, McLaren Vale Unfiltered, unfined and unsulphured.
The result, muted aromas as expected, but a round, full and flavourful mid-palate
jiving with anise, Seville orange, clove, cardamom and jubey dark fruit moves.
The finish, a raft of impressionable fruit sweetness and gentle sooty tannins. Screw
cap. 13.5% alc. RATING 90 DRINK 2022-2024 $28 NG

Wild Folk Nero d'Avola 2022, McLaren Vale Bottled sans fining, filtration,
SO_2 or any other adds. Decent drinking, too. Italianate suggestions of pithy bitter
cherry, herbal bitters, bergamot and something stony and gritty splayed across
the easy, effusive finish. This is fun and well worth a solid chill and a big guzzle.
Diam. 13.5% alc. RATING 90 DRINK 2023-2025 $28 NG

Kindred Spirits Pinot Noir Shiraz 2022, Australia Berried fruit flavour
comes attractively spiced, all peppercorn and anise and purple flowers. It's lively,
frisky even, but there's enough flavour to satisfy and it's far more complex than is
customarily seen at this price. The length of the palate is noteworthy, too. Expect
a light wine but, also, expect a good one. Screw cap. 13.5% alc. RATING 90
DRINK 2023-2026 $12 CM ✪

Little Giant Shiraz 2021, Barossa Deep crimson in the glass with aromas of juicy red and dark plums, mulberry, raspberry coulis and a touch of boysenberry. Deep exotic spice notes and hints of purple flowers, licorice and turned earth. Sweetly fruited with a nice depth of flavour, tight sandy tannins and a bright seam of acidity lending freshness to the proceedings. Screw cap. 14.5% alc. RATING 90 DRINK 2023–2027 $22 DB ✪

Mania Pinot Noir 2021, Tasmania The aromatics are initially a little closed, but with some coaxing show notes of red cherry, mulberry and redcurrant supported by hints of fine spice, rose petals and earth. Supple and brisk on the palate with some sarsaparilla notes and forest floor before tailing off with a touch of sour cherry acidity. Screw cap. 13% alc. RATING 90 DRINK 2023–2027 $37 DB

Little Giant Little Batch Grenache Tempranillo 2021, Barossa Valley Earthy plum and cherry fruits are underscored with hints of spice, cola, pressed flowers, mocha and licorice. Airy and nervy on the palate with a brisk acid cadence, notes of satsuma plum and sour cherry and a lively, easy-drinking feel. Screw cap. 14.5% alc. RATING 90 DRINK 2023–2026 $27 DB

Cabernet 2021, Coonawarra Bright crimson in the glass with notes of blackberry, mulberry and dark plum underlined by spice, earth, violets and cherries with wafts of mint, chocolate and olive tapenade. Light, fine tannins and a savoury palate. There is a lot to like here for the price. Screw cap. 14.5% alc. RATING 90 DRINK 2023–2026 $22 DB ✪

The Hare & The Tortoise Shiraz 2021, Heathcote Intense dark purple in colour – so Heathcote. A super-smart wine for the price, boasting regional trademark black-hearted fruits and plenty of spice. The palate is sturdy, supple and full of ripe flavour and tannins. Screw cap. 14.5% alc. RATING 90 DRINK 2023–2027 $22 JP ✪

Fowles Wine

★★★★☆

1175 Lambing Gully Road, Avenel, VIC 3664 **Region** Strathbogie Ranges **T** (03) 5796 2150 **www.fowleswine.com Open** 7 days, 9–5 **Winemaker** Lindsay Brown, Sam Atherton **Viticulturist** Glenn Chisholm **Est.** 1968 **Dozens** 80 000 **Vyds** 145ha
Fowles Wine is the chief flagbearer of the Strathbogie Ranges region. It's a family-owned winery led by Matt Fowles, its vineyards centred around riesling, chardonnay, shiraz and cabernet sauvignon but with a growing emphasis on pinot noir, sangiovese, arneis, vermentino, sauvignon blanc, mourvèdre, merlot and pinot gris. A great deal of investment has gone into the entire operation over the past decade or more, including the construction of a beautiful new cellar door and restaurant. But at heart, this remains a ground-up operation, soil to table, farm to bottle.

Ladies who Shoot their Lunch Wild Ferment Shiraz 2020, Victoria Black pepper, five-spice, woody spices, aniseed, blackberry, black cherry and earth. The palate is the thing, velvet-like in density, layered in concentrated Rhône-like, spice-filled flavour, and finishing with its now signature long, pepper-dusted finish. Screw cap. 14.4% alc. RATING 95 DRINK 2023–2031 $40 JP ✪

Stone Dwellers Single Vineyard Riesling 2022, Strathbogie Ranges So much life and energy on display here, this riesling consistently brings a lively citrus tang to the glass together with gentle florals, lime zest and quince. Super-dry, super-keen acidity and absolutely refreshing. Could age a treat, too. Screw cap. 12.4% alc. RATING 94 DRINK 2023–2033 $35 JP ✪

Omi's Riesling 2022, Strathbogie Ranges Lime zest, green apple and citrus blossom aromatics to the fore on the bouquet. Beautifully composed in a wine of just 11% alc., the palate is led by honeysuckle with lime, lemon sorbet, fruit tingle touch of sweetness and gentle spice notes that linger. Acidity is filigree fine. 1.5L bottle. Cork. RATING 94 DRINK 2023–2034 $100 JP

Ladies who Shoot their Lunch Wild Ferment Chardonnay 2021, Victoria RATING 92 DRINK 2023–2028 $40 JP

Ladies who Shoot their Lunch Wild Ferment Pinot Noir 2021, Victoria
RATING 92 DRINK 2023-2027 $40 JP
**Stone Dwellers Riesling Museum Release Riesling 2011, Strathbogie
Ranges** RATING 92 DRINK 2023-2028 $85 JP
Ladies who Shoot their Lunch Riesling 2021, Victoria RATING 90
DRINK 2023-2028 $40 JP
Stone Dwellers Single Vineyard Shiraz 2020, Strathbogie Ranges
RATING 90 DRINK 2023-2027 $35 JP

Fox Creek Wines

140 Malpas Road, McLaren Vale, SA 5171 **Region** McLaren Vale
T (08) 8557 0000 **www.foxcreekwines.com Open** 7 days 10–5 **Winemaker** Ben
Tanzer, Steven Soper **Est.** 1995 **Dozens** 35 000 **Vyds** 21ha
Fox Creek has a winemaking history that dates back to '84 when Helen and Dr Jim Watts
purchased a 32ha property in McLaren Vale. The winery has been upgraded to handle the
expanded production of Fox Creek, the increase a function of demand for the full-flavoured,
robust red wines that make up the portfolio. Part of the estate vineyard dates back to the early
1900s, providing the Old Vine Shiraz that carries the Fox Creek banner.

Old Vine Shiraz 2020, McLaren Vale A throaty, old-school shiraz that
performs its dark arts with grace. Camphor, mocha, sooty armchair, Chinese
medicine cabinet, star anise, licorice and shoe polish. The oak, presumably a
good portion American, slathers the forcefield with chocolate brittle, vanilla
and bourbon. The finish, powerful yet warm and, despite the heft, graceful and
rewarding. Screw cap. 14.5% alc. RATING 93 DRINK 2022-2035 $68 NG
Reserve Shiraz 2018, McLaren Vale There is plenty to love here, from the
saturated dark fruits, the underbelly of clove, star anise, cardamom and oak-
derived cinnamon to the swathe of Peking duck lacquer. Yet despite the morass
of fruit and warm, thick mouthfeel, the oak is average and the finish harder than
it needs to be, stunting what should be a long, viscous flow of fruit and medicinal
scrub. A good wine. It should be very good. Screw cap. 14.5% alc. RATING 93
DRINK 2023-2032 $90 NG

Foxeys Hangout

795 White Hill Road, Red Hill, Vic 3937 **Region** Mornington Peninsula
T (03) 5989 2022 **www.foxeys-hangout.com.au Open** 7 days 11–5 **Winemaker** Chris
Strickland **Viticulturist** Chris Strickland, Tony Lee **Est.** 1997 **Dozens** 10 000
Vyds 15ha
After 20 successful years in hospitality operating several cafes and restaurants (including one
of Melbourne's first gastropubs in the early 1990s), brothers Michael and Tony Lee planted
their first vineyard in '97 at Merricks North. The venture takes its name from the tale of
2 fox hunters in the '30s hanging the results of their day's shooting in opposite branches of an
ancient eucalyptus, using the tree as their scorecard. Three of Foxey's vineyards are certified
organic, as is the winery. There is a second cellar door at the Morning Sun vineyard in Main
Ridge, open Thurs–Sun 11–5.

White Gates Chardonnay 2022, Mornington Peninsula Poised and refined
with no shortage of spices and fruit flavour but the texture is key: creamy, cashew-
like lees, the gossamer thread of acidity teasing the palate into submission. Savoury
and mouth-watering, what are you waiting for? Screw cap. 13.5% alc. RATING 96
DRINK 2023-2032 $55 JF ✪
**Kentucky Road 777 Single Vineyard Pinot Noir 2022, Mornington
Peninsula** There's an energy to Kentucky Road, it could be the electrifying
acidity, the way the whole bunches (⅓ all up) have made a positive impact or
maybe it's just magic. Love the tannins here, textural and ever-so-slightly sandy yet
sweet, too, as is the core of fruit of this largely savoury wine. Screw cap. 13% alc.
RATING 96 DRINK 2024-2032 $75 JF ✪

Morning Sun Vineyard Pinot Noir 2022, Mornington Peninsula All I wanted to do was to sit in a comfy chair and drink this wine. So I did. Just a glass, as I'm a professional. It was the gentle sway of tannins, the long thread of refreshing acidity and the neatly packaged box of flavours that made me do it. There's succulence throughout and it's a lovely wine. Screw cap. 13% alc. RATING 96 DRINK 2023–2032 $50 JF ✪

Scotsworth Farm Single Vineyard Pinot Noir 2022, Mornington Peninsula Rich yet finely honed citrusy and stone fruit flavours, the length, the fine acidity and the well-apportioned oak all slip neatly into this wine. While it has substance, depth and complexity, equally important is how good this is to drink. Screw cap. 13.5% alc. RATING 96 DRINK 2023–2032 $55 JF ✪

Pinot Noir 2022, Mornington Peninsula Plenty of tannins and raspberry-like acidity but it's gentle, pretty and supple with watermelon and cherries plus lots of warming spices alongside cardamom and turmeric. It barely gets to medium bodied and with all that juiciness and tang, it's hard to put down. Screw cap. 13% alc. RATING 95 DRINK 2023–2030 $45 JF ✪

Chardonnay 2022, Mornington Peninsula No slouch. It's delicious. Stone fruit and citrus, ginger flower and wood spices, white miso lees and it's creamy with a slight phenolic pull to the finish but the clincher – the lovely acidity all talc-like and refreshing. Screw cap. 13% alc. RATING 95 DRINK 2023–2032 $45 JF ✪

Scotsworth Farm Pinot Noir 2022, Mornington Peninsula Tony Lee says there's a savoury, earthiness to the fruit off this vineyard, and yep, very much so. It adds a layer of complexity to the dark cherry, forest floor, blood orange and chinotto accents. Fuller bodied, with savoury tannins that expand the palate. Screw cap. 13% alc. RATING 95 DRINK 2024–2034 $75 JF

Rosé 2022, Mornington Peninsula A slightly pale cherry red-orange hue. Very spicy with turmeric and cardamom infusing the watermelon and rind flavours. Mouth-watering freshness to this with texture and some neat phenolics following through and adding depth, yet it is delightfully fresh and dry. Screw cap. 13% alc. RATING 95 DRINK 2022–2025 $28 JF ✪

Pinot Meunier Single Vineyard 2021, Mornington Peninsula A variety normally destined for Foxeys' sparkling white, half of the fruit was allowed to fully ripen, which equals a charming red instead. It has plenty of appeal for its red cherries and almost a cherry juice quenching character with cinnamon, pepper and curry leaves adding intrigue. Supple tannins and refreshing acidity lead to a satisfying finish. Such a good drink. Screw cap. 13.5% alc. RATING 95 DRINK 2023–2028 $45 JF ✪

Morning Sun Vineyard Chardonnay 2022, Mornington Peninsula A lovely wine with scents of spring flowers and ginger powder before it moves into more savoury territory with the palate. A saline freshness, root vegetables, especially daikon/radishes, and while there's a layer of creamy lees adding to the texture, it's super-tight and linear. There's an intensity here. It's worth listening to. Screw cap. 13.5% alc. RATING 94 DRINK 2023–2032 $50 JF

♥♥♥♥♡ **White Gates Single Vineyard Pinot Noir 2022, Mornington Peninsula** RATING 92 DRINK 2023–2031 $75 JF

Morning Sun Vineyard Ramato 2022, Mornington Peninsula RATING 92 DRINK 2023–2026 $40 JF

Morning Sun Vineyard Pinot Grigio 2022, Mornington Peninsula RATING 90 DRINK 2022–2025 $40 JF

Frankland Estate   ★★★★★

Frankland Road, Frankland, WA 6396 **Region** Frankland River
T (08) 9855 1544 **www**.franklandestate.com.au **Open** By appt **Winemaker** Brian Kent, Elizabeth Smith, Hunter Smith **Viticulturist** Hunter Smith, Elizabeth Smith **Est.** 1988 **Dozens** 17 000 **Vyds** 32ha

This significant operation is situated on a large sheep property established by Barrie Smith and Judi Cullam. The vineyard has seen progressive growth since '88. The introduction of an array of single-vineyard rieslings has been a highlight, the Isolation Ridge vineyard is organically grown. Frankland Estate is now in the capable hands of 2nd-generation siblings Hunter and Elizabeth Smith. Elizabeth's husband Brian Kent has been at the helm of winemaking for over a decade.

ŸŸŸŸŸ **Isolation Ridge Riesling 2022, Frankland River** Lemon blossom, honeysuckle, lime zest and finger lime acidity, yet softish and almost plush. The palate builds, adding a slip of sexy phenolics, the merest smidge of sweetness and everything in harmony to extend out and excite to the very end. As usual, an elegant, distinct riesling. Screw cap. 12.5% alc. RATING 96 DRINK 2023-2036 $55 JF ✪ ♥

Isolation Ridge Mourvèdre 2021, Frankland River Quite possibly the finest Australian mourvèdre I've tasted. This is something else. Beautifully refined yet has all the fantastic savouriness and meatiness of the variety with ironstone, dried herbs, black plums and sandy, fine tannins. This proves just how magnificent the site is. Screw cap. 14.5% alc. RATING 96 DRINK 2023-2030 $55 JF ✪

Isolation Ridge Syrah 2021, Frankland River Frankland Estate enjoys its prestige as head of the riesling kingdom, but the reds are on a revolutionary path. Will they take the crown? A sneaky 4/2% viognier/mourvèdre added to this excellent, spicy, smoky, juicy, peppery wine. Plush fruit with all the best syrah attributes rising up, including beautiful, savoury and silky tannins. Screw cap. 14.5% alc. RATING 96 DRINK 2023-2035 $55 JF ✪

Olmo's Reward 2020, Frankland River Cabernet franc with glugs of cabernet sauvignon, mourvèdre and a splash of malbec. This is up there as one of the finest. A seamless combination of the varieties morphs into a unified, harmonious red. Supple, fine tannins yet intrinsically powerful in a way, as they coat the fuller-bodied palate, but this never feels big or weighty. The finish is as long as it is beautiful. Screw cap. 14.5% alc. RATING 96 DRINK 2023-2035 $85 JF

Alter Weg Riesling 2022, Frankland River Fine acidity, luscious fruit (in a riesling context), texture and length. What more do you desire? There is more: a little tug of phenolics, the openness on the palate yet slatey and reined in by lemon-sorbet acidity. Moreish, a touch savoury and an excellent drink. Screw cap. 13% alc. RATING 95 DRINK 2023-2035 $39 JF ✪

Franc Organic Cabernet Franc 2022, Frankland River Franc, it's love at first sight (or taste). You're fun, vibrant, juicy and tangy, a little ethereal, too. Awash with spiced red plums, fennel, dried herbs and aromas of freshly tilled earth and florals. Beautiful tannins and refreshing acidity add to the immense pleasure of this exceptional drink. Screw cap. 13.5% alc. RATING 95 DRINK 2023-2028 $39 JF ✪

Grüner Organic 2022, Frankland River Evenly balanced between texture, fruit weight and acidity. And you know what that means? Delicious drinking here, folks. Varietally spot on with hints of stone fruit, just-ripe pears and slatey with a hint of petrichor. Soft dabs of acidity across the palate and creamy lees, too, ensuring this goes down a more savoury, textural route. Screw cap. 13% alc. RATING 95 DRINK 2023-2028 $39 JF ✪

Cabernet Sauvignon 2021, Frankland River Cassis and mulberries, squid ink and bay leaves, astonishing tannins – superfine yet with tensile strength and vibrancy throughout. Gorgeous now and will unfurl gracefully in time. Screw cap. 14% alc. RATING 95 DRINK 2023-2033 $35 JF ✪

ŸŸŸŸŸ **Riesling 2022, Frankland River** RATING 93 DRINK 2023-2030 $32 JH ✪
Chardonnay 2022, Frankland River RATING 91 DRINK 2023-2028 $35 JF
Rocky Gully Shiraz 2021, Frankland River RATING 91 DRINK 2023-2030 $25 JF ✪
Rocky Gully Cabernets 2019, Frankland River RATING 90 DRINK 2023-2028 $25 JF ✪

Fraser Gallop Estate

493 Metricup Road, Wilyabrup, WA 6280 **Region** Margaret River
T (08) 9755 7553 **www.**frasergallopestate.com.au **Open** 7 days 11–4 **Winemaker** Clive
Otto, Ellin Tritt **Viticulturist** Mike Bolas **Est.** 1999 **Dozens** 10000 **Vyds** 21ha
In '99, Nigel Gallop began planting what is now just over 20ha of cabernet sauvignon and
chardonnay (6.8ha each) as well as semillon, petit verdot, cabernet franc, malbec, merlot
and sauvignon blanc. The wines have been made by Clive Otto since '07, and in that time
have amassed an impressive array of domestic and international acclaim. The house style is
very much on the precise, pure end of the spectrum, with the flagship white (the Palladian
Chardonnay) routinely coming in at lower alcohol than many. The Parterre range offers
consistent, indelible, compelling value for money.

ΨΨΨΨΨ **Palladian Chardonnay 2021, Margaret River** A wine that commands
respect, yet it is a wonderful drink. It's complex and detailed with excellent fruit
at its heart, a pulse of refreshing acidity, fabulous smoky oak and hints of funky
sulphides rendering this savoury. It lingers long. It's persuasive. Classy with a
capital C. Screw cap. 12.5% alc. RATING 96 DRINK 2022–2031 $140 JF
Parterre Chardonnay 2021, Margaret River One taste and a laser lightshow
starts up. This is so racy, juicy and succulent it speeds across the palate. Stop.
Reflect. Grapefruit and Meyer lemon, a smidge of creamy lees and lemon curd
texture, plus wood spices with the oak seamless. Mostly, it's mouth-watering,
flinty, fine and exceptionally long. Wonderful wine. Screw cap. 12.5% alc.
RATING 95 DRINK 2022–2031 $60 JF
Parterre Cabernet Sauvignon 2020, Margaret River As usual, a tiptop
Parterre with enticing florals giving way to mulberries and boysenberries, dried
herbs, choc-mint and more besides. It's medium bodied and wonderfully savoury
with powdery tannins and great length. And it will age gracefully. Screw cap.
14% alc. RATING 95 DRINK 2023–2040 $60 JF
Parterre Semillon Sauvignon Blanc 2020, Margaret River Even if appealing
in youth, such an oak-aged style generally needs time to settle and chill out. And
this will follow such a route. In the meantime, it's fragrant with finger lime and
snow peas with a snip of fresh herbs and lots of nutty, toasty oak. There's also a
waxy/lanolin character and no shortage of acidity to keep this alive for another
10 years. Screw cap. 12.5% alc. RATING 95 DRINK 2022–2032 $35 JF ❂
Palladian Cabernet Sauvignon 2019, Margaret River There's plenty of
flavour packed into this from ripe fruit and cedary oak, yet it remains just shy
of full bodied and the palate is far from unwieldy. Blackberries, dark cherries
coated in all manner of spices with wafts of tobacco and choc-mint. It seems a
tad forward but there's depth and structure, too, with hazelnut skin tannins adding
more shape. Screw cap. 14% alc. RATING 95 DRINK 2023–2035 $140 JF

ΨΨΨΨΨ **Wilyabrup Ice Pressed Chardonnay 2022, Margaret River** RATING 93
DRINK 2022–2030 $36 JF
Chardonnay 2022, Margaret River RATING 92 DRINK 2022–2028 $30 JF ❂
Wilyabrup Cabernet Sauvignon 2021, Margaret River RATING 92
DRINK 2022–2035 $35 JF
Wilyabrup Cabernet Merlot 2020, Margaret River RATING 90
DRINK 2023–2035 $30 JF

Fratin Brothers Vineyard

Byron Road, Ararat, Vic 3377 **Region** Grampians
T (03) 5352 3322 **www.**fratinbrothers.com.au **Open** By appt **Winemaker** Michael
Fratin **Viticulturist** Michael Fratin **Est.** 1998 **Dozens** 1200 **Vyds** 3.8ha
The Fratin Brothers vineyard was planted by Dino and Michael Fratin in '98, 30 years after
their father Serge and uncles Dom and Lino established Mount Langi Ghiran Vineyards
(Serge still oversees the vineyard operations). Shiraz cuttings were supplied by Mount Langi
Ghiran, and 2ha of shiraz plus 0.5ha each of sangiovese, chardonnay and tempranillo have
been planted.

ŦŦŦŦŸ **GST 2021, Grampians** 50/35/15% grenache/shiraz/tempranillo. It's sweet-fruited at heart, not to mention creamily textured, but wild/aromatic herb and floral notes bring much-needed complexity to the table and give the wine a sense of completeness. There's some warmth on the finish but this is a good drink. Screw cap. 14.5% alc. **RATING** 92 **DRINK** 2023–2030 $24 CM ✪

Pinot Grigio 2022, Grampians Pear, red apple and citrus flavours meet sherbet bomb candy. It's straight, direct and refreshing but it offers plenty along the way. Good drinking option. Screw cap. 13% alc. **RATING** 91 **DRINK** 2023–2025 $22 CM ✪

Shiraz 2021, Grampians Straightforward in a good way. Plum and currant flavours with an overlay of creamy vanilla. It sits on the bold side of medium weight and feels satisfying from start to finish. Screw cap. 13% alc. **RATING** 91 **DRINK** 2023–2031 $22 CM ✪

Frazer Woods Wines   ★★★★

3856 Caves Road, Wilyabrup, WA 6280 (postal) **Region** Margaret River
T (08) 9755 6274 **www.**frazerwoods.com.au **Open** Not **Winemaker** John Frazer
Est. 1996 **Dozens** 2000 **Vyds** 2ha
Based in Wilyabrup, Frazer Woods is a producer of sparkling wines; white, rosé and red, released under the La Cache and Frazer Woods labels. Jon Frazer and Jan Woods purchased an undeveloped plot of bushland and a paddock in 1985 and set about the long game of transforming it; vines were planted in '96. Irrigation is rare, ferments are natural and the La Cache wines spend a minimum of 5 years on lees. John also runs a contract sparkling wine business, called the Champagne Shed.

ŦŦŦŦŸ **La Cache Chardonnay Pinot Noir 2012, Margaret River** Split between 79/21% chardonnay/pinot noir; disgorged Oct '22. A mid-gold hue, savoury and fine with plenty of acidity and drive. The lees ageing has given this depth yet it's perky, zesty and dry. Diam. 12% alc. **RATING** 91 **DRINK** 2022–2024 $63 JF

Sparkling Shiraz 2008, Margaret River Don't hold onto this any longer – it's dipped well into tertiary territory. Mid-brick yet with a red hue; earthy with lots of baked mushrooms and roast meat flavours. It's full bodied, rich and ripe with decent tannins and a dry finish even if the dosage ensures the finish isn't hard. Good sparkling shiraz in anyone's book. Diam. 14.3% alc. **RATING** 91 **DRINK** 2022–2023 $39 JF

FREEMAN Vineyards   ★★★★

101 Prunevale Road, Prunevale, NSW 2587 **Region** Hilltops
T 0429 310 309 **www.**freemanvineyards.com.au **Open** By appt **Winemaker** Brian Freeman **Viticulturist** Brian Freeman **Est.** 1999 **Dozens** 5000 **Vyds** 200ha
Dr Brian Freeman spent much of his life in research and education, in the latter with a role as head of CSU's viticulture and oenology campus. In '04 he purchased the 30yo Demondrille vineyard and the neighbouring vineyard. A decade later he acquired a number of other vineyards within a 10km radius. In all he has 22 varieties that range from staples such as shiraz, cabernet sauvignon, semillon and riesling through to more exotic varieties such as hárslevelü and Italian varieties prosecco, sangiovese, nebbiolo, rondinella and corvina.

ŦŦŦŦŸ **Fiano Altura Vineyard 2022, Hilltops** It smells of spring with honeysuckle, lemon blossom and ginger flower. Lovely. So too the palate that's stacked with stone fruit and honeycomb, a slip of texture plus bright acidity ensures this is delicious. Screw cap. 13.5% alc. **RATING** 92 **DRINK** 2023–2025 $25 JF ✪

Rondo Rondinella Rosé 2022, Hilltops A dusty bronze-orange hue; lightly spiced with a touch of Campari, Angostura bitters and tangy cherries. Refreshing, lively and has a bit more substance and savouriness than so many rosés on the market. Screw cap. 13% alc. **RATING** 92 **DRINK** 2023–2025 $20 JF ✪

Prosecco 2022, Hilltops A go-to fizz thanks to its vivacity, lemon-lime flavours, baked apple and flutter of fresh herbs. A bit more texture than usual, with creaminess yet lively acidity never far behind. Crown. 11.5% alc. **RATING** 91 **DRINK** 2023–2024 $25 JF ✪

Altura Vineyard Shiraz 2022, Hilltops Flecks of pepper and cardamom infuse the fruit flavours of plums and cherries. It's tangy and juicy, soft and fleshy with grainy tannins and a 'drink me now' attitude. Don't wait. Screw cap. 13.5% alc. **RATING** 91 **DRINK** 2023–2027 $25 JF ✪

Robusta Corvina 2016, Hilltops Is Robusta the love child of Jägermeister and chinotto? Mmm, the mind boggles. This has a bitter herb and spirity, kirsch-like essence; it's rich and powerful and flexes its muscles as those grainy tannins hold sway. This wine is never shy so perhaps approach it without that trait, too. Screw cap. 16.8% alc. **RATING** 91 **DRINK** 2023–2028 $80 JF

Rosso Corvina Rondinella 2022, Hilltops Waves of black and red fruit, chocolate, Italian bitter greens and fennel. The palate is medium bodied and plumped up with raspy, sandy tannins. Good drinking to be had and the perfect pizza wine. Screw cap. 13% alc. **RATING** 90 **DRINK** 2022–2024 $20 JF ✪

Altura Vineyard Cabernet Sauvignon 2022, Hilltops Cassis and currants, wintergreen and charred radicchio with some bitter herbs, too, working with the textural tannins. A little pinched on the finish but food will sort that effect out. Screw cap. 13.4% alc. **RATING** 90 **DRINK** 2023–2028 $25 JF ✪

Robusta Corvina 2015, Hilltops An Aussie take on Italy's amarone – not an easy wine to make in either country. While never shy of alcohol, 17% perhaps pushes the style too far. Some good Italian flavours: charred radicchio and Mediterranean herbs plus rum and raisin chocolate, prunes and dark plums. Full bodied with pomace-like tannins, acidity keeping it on track. Screw cap. **RATING** 90 **DRINK** 2022–2026 $80 JF

Freycinet Vineyard ★★★★★

15919 Tasman Highway via Bicheno, Tas 7215 **Region** East Coast Tasmania **T** (03) 6257 8574 **www**.freycinetvineyard.com.au **Open** 7 days 10–5 **Winemaker** Claudio Radenti, Keira O'Brien **Viticulturist** Claudio Radenti, Keira O'Brien **Est.** 1978 **Dozens** 9500 **Vyds** 16ha

Freycinet's vineyards are situated on the sloping hillsides of a small valley, and the combination of aspect, slope, soil and temperature produces red grapes with unusual depth of colour and ripe flavours. One of the foremost producers of pinot noir, with an enviable track record of consistency; sparkling, riesling and chardonnay are also of the highest quality. In '12 Freycinet acquired part of the neighbouring Coombend property from Brown Brothers, a 42ha property including 5.75ha of vines.

🍷🍷🍷🍷🍷 **R3 Radenti Chardonnay Pinot Noir NV, Tasmania** A multi-vintage approach provides an expansive aromatic profile of apple, oatmeal, soft spice and expressive autolysis notes. Fine, consistent bubbles and impressive fruit stretch taut over a canvas of abundant acid drive and a long, mealy finish. Very impressive. Diam. 13% alc. **RATING** 95 **DRINK** 2022–2030 $65 DB

Riesling 2022, Tasmania A truly lovely East Coast riesling with a long history of success. This has an abundant and fragrant lime/lemon bouquet which is front and centre in the mouth. Tasmanian acidity is there, but it's folded into the bosom of the fruit. Screw cap. 13% alc. **RATING** 95 **DRINK** 2023–2037 $35 JH ✪

Cabernet Merlot 2017, Tasmania Light on the herbaceous notes and packed with bright black fruits on a bed of fine spice, licorice, olive tapenade, cedar, light tobacco and violet tones. Just a hint of cabernet franc lift with a tug of fine, gravelly tannins lending ample support, the line bright and true. Wonderful, graceful drinking now that will improve over time. Screw cap. 13.5% alc. **RATING** 95 **DRINK** 2023–2030 $45 DB ✪ ♥

Pinot Noir 2020, Tasmania A delightful-smelling melange of wild strawberry, red plum, raspberry and red cherry. Notes of five-spice, forest floor, game meats, purple flowers, French oak nuance and red licorice. A picture of grace and elegance on the palate with a smooth, pure-fruit flow, judicious French oak,

bright acidity and a finish that lingers nicely. Screw cap. 14% alc. **RATING** 94
DRINK 2023–2030 $69 DB

ҰҰҰҰ♀ **Wineglass Bay Sauvignon Blanc 2022, Tasmania RATING** 92
DRINK 2023–2023 $30 JH
Louis Pinot Noir 2021, Tasmania RATING 91 **DRINK** 2023–2028 $42 DB
Botrytis 2021, Tasmania RATING 91 **DRINK** 2023–2028 $40 DB
Louis Riesling Schönburger 2022, Tasmania RATING 90 **DRINK** 2023–2026
$28 DB

Frog Choir Wines ★★★☆

At Redgate Winery, Boodjidup Road, Margaret River, WA 6285 **Region** Margaret River
T 0427 777 787 www.frogchoir.com **Open** 7 days 10–4.30 **Winemaker** Bruce Dukes
Viticulturist Bruce Dukes, Naturaliste Vintners **Est.** 1997 **Dozens** 250 **Vyds** 1.2ha
Kate and Nigel Hunt have a micro-vineyard equally split between shiraz and cabernet
sauvignon. It has immaculate address credentials: adjacent to Leeuwin Estate and Voyager
Estate; 6km from the Margaret River township. The hand-tended vines are grown without
the use of insecticides.

ҰҰҰҰ♀ **Cabernet Sauvignon Shiraz 2017, Margaret River** It's full of cassis,
blackberries, mint and oak spices yet plenty of savoury inputs and almost a nori/
Vegemite flavour, which is appealing. Fuller bodied, with ripe tannins and sweet
oak and fruit across the palate. Screw cap. 14% alc. **RATING** 90 **DRINK** 2022–2027
$30 JF

Frogmore Creek ★★★★

699 Richmond Road, Cambridge, Tas 7170 **Region** Southern Tasmania
T (03) 6274 5844 www.frogmorecreek.com.au **Open** Thu–Mon 10–5
Winemaker Alain Rousseau, John Bown **Viticulturist** Danny Belbin **Est.** 1997
Dozens 40 000 **Vyds** 75ha
Frogmore Creek has grown substantially over time, first establishing its own organically
managed vineyard (later sold to Hill-Smith Family Vineyards), and thereafter by a series of
acquisitions. First was the purchase of the Hood/Wellington Wines business; next was the
purchase of the large Roslyn vineyard near Campania; and then (in Oct '10) the acquisition of
Meadowbank Estate – not to be confused with Meadowbank Wines, Derwent Valley – where
the cellar door is now located. In '18, Frogmore Creek opened The Lounge at MAC01, an
urban cellar door/restaurant on Hobart's waterfront, catering to those without the means or
motivation to trek out to Cambridge. Chief winemaker Alain Rousseau has clocked up 20
years with the brand, while vineyard manager Danny Belbin is a 5th generation farmer from
the Coal River Valley.

ҰҰҰҰ♀ **Pinot Noir 2021, Tasmania** Bright cherry red hue. Lifted notes of spiced
cherry, wild strawberry and red plum cut with hints of exotic spice, forest floor,
roast duck, shiitake mushroom and light French-oak spice. Sprightly and pure
with a swift acid cadence and an earthy tone among forest floor, spice and
juicy cherry notes on the palate. Light tannins gently make their presence felt.
Screw cap. 13.6% alc. **RATING** 93 **DRINK** 2023–2029 $48 DB
42°S Pinot Noir 2021, Tasmania Bright cherry hue with lifted notes of spiced
red cherry, wild strawberry and red plum cut through with hints of gentle spice,
ginger cake, purple flowers and gentle oak spice. Light, airy drinking with pure-
spiced cherry fruits and a nice sense of vitality. Screw cap. 13% alc. **RATING** 91
DRINK 2023–2028 $32 DB

Gaelic Cemetery Vineyard ★★★★★

Gaelic Cemetery Road, Stanley Flat, SA 5453 **Region** Clare Valley
www.gaeliccemeteryvineyard.com **Open** By appt **Winemaker** Julian Bermingham
Viticulturist Paul Aworth **Est.** 2005 **Dozens** 2000 **Vyds** 16.8ha

Gaelic Cemetery Vineyard was planted in '96, adjacent to the historic cemetery of the region's Scottish pioneers. Situated in a secluded valley of the Clare hills, the low-cropping vineyard, said the founders, 'is always one of the earliest ripening shiraz vineyards in the region'. The result is hands-off winemaking. Previously owned by the Pike family, Gaelic Cemetery was purchased by Pirathon in '19.

🍷🍷🍷🍷 **McAskill Riesling 2022, Clare Valley** Lime, lemon, green apple and perhaps a yellow fruit note, maybe plum, to my nose. There is a real pithy intensity on the palate with a hint of slinky, chalky texture, some citrus blossom top notes and the distinct feeling that there is some serious latent power simmering away under the pretty exterior. Screw cap. 11% alc. **RATING** 95 **DRINK** 2023–2038 $55 DB

🍷🍷🍷🍷 **Celtic Farm Riesling 2022, Clare Valley** **RATING** 92 **DRINK** 2023–2030 $28 DB ✪

🍇 Gaffy & Neal   ★★★★★

139 Main Creek Road, Red Hill, Vic 3937 **Region** Mornington Peninsula
T 0421 416 239 **www.gaffyandneal.com.au** **Open** By appt **Winemaker** Darrin Gaffy, Douglas Neal **Est.** 2021 **Dozens** 300
Darrin Gaffy is the name behind the excellent Principia Wines; Doug Neal has had a varied career in wine, including a side gig selling Sirugue barrels. Gaffy has been buying them for 20 years and, in between oak conversations, Neal would say 'we should make a chardonnay'. Gaffy & Neal. There's a ring to it. The project began with the '21 vintage when they sourced fruit from around Merricks. Only 2 chardonnays will be made, not exceeding 300 dozen, as Gaffy has no more room at his winery. Both have strong personalities – Gaffy prefers a richer, riper style, Neal a flavoursome yet acid-driven chardonnay. The end result is totally complementary.

🍷🍷🍷🍷 **Merricks North Chardonnay 2021, Mornington Peninsula** There's plenty of flavour via winemaking inputs, but everything's reined in, resulting in a lipsmacking chardy. White peach, citrus, creamy lees and spicy oak flesh out the palate. There's a core of sweet fruit yet it stays in the savoury spectrum overall and fine acidity leads this to a long finish. Very, very satisfying. Screw cap. 13.7% alc. **RATING** 96 **DRINK** 2022–2031 $70 JF ✪
Chardonnay 2021, Mornington Peninsula There's a lot to enjoy with this finely tuned, moreish drink – the citrus, the ginger spice, the light layering of flavour with cashew lees and creaminess. It's a refined style and very good. Simple and stylish labels, too. Screw cap. 13.5% alc. **RATING** 95 **DRINK** 2022–2030 $50 JF ✪

Gala Estate   ★★★★

14891 Tasman Highway, Cranbrook, Tas 7190 **Region** East Coast Tasmania
T 0408 681 014 **www.galaestate.com.au** **Open** 7 days 10–4 by appt **Winemaker** Pat Colombo, Keira O'Brien **Est.** 2009 **Dozens** 5000 **Vyds** 11ha
This vineyard is situated on a 4000ha sheep station, with the 6th, 7th and 8th generations – headed by Robert and Patricia Greenhill. The 11ha vineyard is heavily skewed to pinot noir (7ha), the remainder planted (in descending order of area) to chardonnay, pinot gris, riesling, shiraz and sauvignon blanc. The main risk is spring frost, and overhead spray irrigation serves 2 purposes: it provides adequate moisture for early season growth and frost protection at the end of the growing season.

🍷🍷🍷🍷 **Black Label Pinot Gris 2021, Tasmania** Light straw with an inviting nose of poached pear, citrus and apple with hints of soft spice, clotted cream, lemon curd, dried honey, crushed stone, honeysuckle and lightly roasted cashew notes in the distance. Fine, mineral-laden acidity frames the wine nicely, providing plenty of velocity for the pure pear, citrus and spice core, finishing long and balanced. A lovely example. Screw cap. 13.5% alc. **RATING** 94 **DRINK** 2023–2027 $65 DB

Black Label Emerald Syrah 2021, Tasmania There is a real sense of detail and clarity on display here with pure red and dark berry fruit dotted with spice and hints of dried citrus rind, almond blossom, charcuterie, pepper, red licorice and earth. Spacious and elegant with a bright mineral cadence and an impressive tension between fruit and acidity. Lovely drinking. Screw cap. 14% alc. RATING 94 DRINK 2023–2029 $65 DB

Estate Riesling 2012, Tasmania A deep-straw-coloured museum release that shows complex aromas and flavours. Notes of lime, lemon butter and baked apples with hints of dried hay, marzipan, pressed citrus blossom, buttered cinnamon scroll and fresh apple danish. Long and complex with a lemon curd wake and a lovely minerally energy as it gently fades away. Great drinking now. Screw cap. 11.8% alc. RATING 94 DRINK 2023–2026 $80 DB

ŸŸŸŸŸ **White Label Pinot Gris 2022, Tasmania** RATING 93 DRINK 2023–2026 $37 DB

White Label Pinot Rosé 2022, Tasmania RATING 93 DRINK 2023–2026 $37 DB

1821 Pinot Noir 2021, Tasmania RATING 93 DRINK 2023–2028 $65 DB

Constable Amos Pinot Noir 2019, Tasmania RATING 92 DRINK 2023–2028 $125 DB

Black Label Sparkling Vintage Rosé 2017, Tasmania RATING 91 DRINK 2023–2028 $65 DB

White Label Riesling 2022, Tasmania RATING 91 DRINK 2023–2028 $37 DB

White Label Pinot Noir 2022, Tasmania RATING 91 DRINK 2023–2027 $37 DB

White Label Riesling 2021, Tasmania RATING 91 DRINK 2023–2027 $32 DB

Estate Pinot Noir 2011, Tasmania RATING 90 DRINK 2023–2025 $95 DB

Galafrey   ★★★★☆

Quangellup Road, Mount Barker, WA 6324 **Region** Mount Barker
T (08) 9851 2022 **www**.galafreywines.com.au **Open** 7 days 10–5 **Winemaker** Kim Tyrer **Viticulturist** Nigel Rowe **Est.** 1977 **Dozens** 3000 **Vyds** 12ha
The Galafrey story began when Ian and Linda Tyrer gave up high-profile jobs and moved to Mount Barker to grow grapes and make wine. The dry-grown vineyard they planted continues to be the turning point, the first winery established in an ex-whaling building (long since replaced by a purpose-built winery). The premature death of Ian increased the already considerable difficulties the family had to deal with, but deal with it they did. Daughter Kim Tyrer is now CEO of the business, with Linda in charge of the day-to-day management of Galafrey.

ŸŸŸŸŸ **Dry Grown Reserve Riesling 2022, Mount Barker** Breathtaking with tart lime juice characters, blackcurrant, crunchy green apple tang and a ticklish splash of talc-like minerality. Pure and fruit-driven, albeit at the leaner, more tightly wound end of the spectrum. This is a super-racy expression with impressive drinkability in youth, but a very long future in the cellar. Screw cap. 12% alc. RATING 95 DRINK 2022–2035 $28 MB ✪

ŸŸŸŸŸ **Dry Grown Müller-Thurgau 2022, Mount Barker** RATING 93 DRINK 2022–2025 $28 MB ✪

Dry Grown Cabernet Franc 2021, Mount Barker RATING 93 DRINK 2022–2030 $28 MB ✪

Gapsted Estate   ★★★★

3897 Great Alpine Road, Gapsted, Vic 3737 **Region** Alpine Valleys
T (03) 5751 9100 **www**.gapstedwines.com.au **Open** Thurs–Mon 10–5
Winemaker Andrew Santarossa, Toni Pla Bou, Greg Bennet **Est.** 1997 **Dozens** 250 000
Vyds 256.1ha

Gapsted Estate started life as Gapsted Wines, the major brand of the Victorian Alps Winery. The quality of the wines has led to the expansion of the portfolio, with a focus on alternative varieties. As well as the substantial estate plantings, Gapsted sources fruit from the King and Alpine valleys.

𐂂𐂂𐂂𐂂𐂂 **Valley Selection Fiano 2022, King Valley** Sensitive winemaking here, enhancing both flavour and texture with just a splash of smooth, gentle, vanillin oak input. Expect melon, stone fruits, pear, citrus and apple aromas. Spice and a light herbal interplay bring an added dimension to the palate, and what texture! Fiano has a big future in the King Valley. More, please! Screw cap. 13.5% alc. **RATING** 93 **DRINK** 2023–2026 $30 JP ✪

Ballerina Canopy Sparkling Saperavi NV, King Valley With its notable dark-hearted fruits and lively spice shining, saperavi works well as both a still or sparkling wine. Blackberry, bramble, earth, aniseed and clove exude a warm, wintery feel enlivened by brisk acidity. The palate's texture is supple and even with a savoury vein of chocolate and cherry liqueur running long. Nicely composed. Cork. 14% alc. **RATING** 92 $40 JP

Ballerina Canopy Saperavi 2021, Alpine Valleys A strong band of black fruit and damson plum underscores this intense wine. A vein of florals brings a touch of softness and aromatic lift. The grape's challenging high acidity is brought to heel, not an easy job, to a firm, dry finish. Big, tasty and well built. Screw cap. 15% alc. **RATING** 92 **DRINK** 2022–2032 $35 JP

Secret Harvest Prosecco NV, Alpine Valleys Joins the growing crowd of col fondo-style (with lees) proseccos. Combines both savouriness, citrus brightness and texture, making it a particularly good match with a range of savoury-inspired dishes, especially chicken. Cloudy in colour, brisk in bubble with nutty, yeasty bread dough, preserved lemon and apple aromas. Races across the palate in citrus, green apple, oatmeal, chalky lemon flavours. Crown. 12% alc. **RATING** 90 $30 JP

Secret Harvest Grand Manseng 2022, Alpine Valleys Grand (or gros) manseng is one of the Alpine Valleys' more engaging alternative varieties. Here, it delivers delightful aromatics, spicy notes and smooth textural appeal. Spring blossom, honeysuckle, yellow peach and nectarine aromas. Takes a serious turn on the palate with stewed apple, pear, lively spice and more. Runs long, smooth and deep, finishing clean. Plenty to like here. Screw cap. 13.8% alc. **RATING** 90 **DRINK** 2022–2026 $30 JP

Ballerina Canopy Durif 2021, Alpine Valleys A dark and brooding style that also gives life to durif's beautiful aromatics. Deep red-purple hues. The bouquet brings forth briar, rosemary, earth and berries. Warm and textural across the tongue with generous tannins keeping everything in line. Not so much big as cuddly and, for the durif-phobes, not scary in the least. Screw cap. 15% alc. **RATING** 90 **DRINK** 2022–2034 $35 JP

Valley Selection Montepulciano 2021, King Valley This boasts immediate charm in bright purple-cerise hues and a perfume that sings in cherry, red plum and cranberry fruit with a lift of fresh violets. Plenty of fruit, spice and olive tapenade savouriness, keen acidity keeps the palate linear and super-fresh right to the end. Love to see how it ages, but I don't think I can wait that long. Screw cap. 14.5% alc. **RATING** 90 **DRINK** 2022–2026 $30 JP

Garagiste

★★★★★

72 Blaxland Ave, Frankston South, Vic 3199 (postal) **Region** Mornington Peninsula **T** 0439 370 530 **www**.garagiste.com.au **Open** Not **Winemaker** Barnaby Flanders **Viticulturist** Barnaby Flanders **Est.** 2006 **Dozens** 2200 **Vyds** 6ha

Barnaby Flanders co-founded Allies Wines in '03 with some of the wines made under the Garagiste label. Allies has now gone its own way and Barnaby has a controlling interest in the Garagiste brand. The focus is on the Mornington Peninsula. The grapes are hand-sorted in the vineyard and again in the winery. Chardonnay is whole-bunch pressed, barrel-fermented with wild yeast in new and used French oak, mlf variably used, 8–9 months on lees. Seldom fined or filtered.

ŶŶŶŶŶ **Terre Maritime Chardonnay 2022, Mornington Peninsula** First day open, very good. The next day, even better. So decant, please. It's funky with fine flinty sulphides and a crunchy, minerally sensation across the palate. Citrus and white stone fruit, lightly spiced, creamy lees moreish and savoury. Compelling and stylish. Screw cap. 13% alc. RATING 96 DRINK 2023–2033 $75 JF ✪

Merricks Chardonnay 2022, Mornington Peninsula This wine is made for drinking right now. As in, I need to drink it right now. Lovely to do so. This is pristine, refined and long. Citrus, radish and just-ripe white stone fruit with succulence throughout. White miso and creamy lees, textural and acidity leading all the way. Screw cap. 13% alc. RATING 96 DRINK 2023–2032 $50 JF ✪

Le Stagiaire Chardonnay 2022, Mornington Peninsula This is the best value chardy from the Peninsula because of the quality, not simply the price. Refreshing citrus and white stone fruit, lovely palate weight, textural and even. The acidity leads everything to finish long. Nice one. Again. Screw cap. 13% alc. RATING 95 DRINK 2023–2027 $35 JF ✪

Tuerong Chardonnay 2022, Mornington Peninsula The bright, pale gold-glinting green hue is like a siren saying, 'Drink me, drink me'. Oh, alright then. A supple and juicy, tangy and vibrant offering with fine layers of texture from cashew lees and subtle spicy oak with fine acidity leading the wine into a linear path. Screw cap. 13% alc. RATING 95 DRINK 2023–2032 $50 JF ✪

Tuerong Aligoté 2022, Mornington Peninsula Sadly, I can count on one hand how much Australian aligoté comes my way. Barnaby Flanders makes a damn fine drink out of it. Fennel and lemon are dressed with finger lime and juicy tangy acidity, but it's savoury, too, a little nutty with texture and lovely florals. It has the right amount of complexity without forfeiting deliciousness. Screw cap. 13% alc. RATING 95 DRINK 2023–2027 $38 JF ✪

Merricks Rosé 2022, Mornington Peninsula Grab a bottle and head to the beach with friends armed with paper-wrapped fish and chips. Its pale bronze hue is alive with red fruits and spice but the palate is the clincher: textural, creamy, zesty with superfine acidity to close and hence, dry. A proper pinot noir rosé, and charming at that. Screw cap. 13% alc. RATING 95 DRINK 2023–2026 $38 JF ✪

Merricks Pinot Gris 2022, Mornington Peninsula Barnaby has put his disco pants on with this: flinty sulphides, smoky and very savoury. It's so good. In a way, a pared-back style but still plenty of flavour with crunchy pear, quince doused in spices and a millefeuille of creamy lees. Screw cap. 13% alc. RATING 95 DRINK 2023–2030 $38 JF ✪

Terre de Feu Pinot Noir 2021, Mornington Peninsula Maybe it's the expressive chinotto, amaro and Italian bitter herb characters from 100% whole-bunch fermentation that makes it very appealing and alive. It's by no means overt, overly stemmy or distracting. It adds to the perfume and body of this excellent drink, working with the fruit. Raw silk tannins, fine acidity and a lingering finish all add up to a top-notch pinot. Screw cap. 13.5% alc. RATING 95 DRINK 2023–2031 $75 JF

Merricks Pinot Noir 2022, Mornington Peninsula A bit of a zen wine as it feels calm and soothing – maybe it's the pulpy fruit, the gentle sway of soft tannins, the evenness across the lighter-framed palate or the way it has come together completely. Screw cap. 13.5% alc. RATING 94 DRINK 2023–2029 $50 JF

ŶŶŶŶŶ **Le Stagiaire Pinot Noir 2022, Mornington Peninsula** RATING 93 DRINK 2023–2027 $35 JF ✪

Garden & Field   ★★★★

33 Gnadenberg Road, Moculta SA, 5353 **Region** Barossa Valley
T 0407 684 260 **www.**gardenandfield.com.au **Open** By appt **Winemaker** Peter Raymond
Viticulturist Peter Raymond **Est.** 2009 **Dozens** 100 **Vyds** 5.6ha
It is over 100 years since the Schilling family planted a vineyard. In the late '70s the property was sold and the new owners removed the vines. Another decade passed and the property was again on the market. Viticulturist Peter Raymond and wife Melissa

purchased it and set about preparing 3.6ha for planting. One fine Saturday, a group of octogenarian men armed with picks and shovels came to help plant 3500 vines. Some fruit is sold to other premium producers, but the Raymonds retain enough fruit to make a small amount of their own single-vineyard red wines each year.

🍷🍷🍷🍷🍷 **Gnadenberg Road Shiraz 2019, Barossa** Inky red and serious looking, the wine displays intense aromas of black plum, blackberry and black cherry cut with baking spices, black strap licorice, earth and a fair lick of cedary oak. Great fruit intensity with lots of kirsch and crème de cassis tones and plentiful cedar and spice. It's an opulent, oaky style that will have its fans. Screw cap. 14.8% alc. **RATING** 91 **DRINK** 2023-2030 $145 DB

Gnadenberg Road Cabernet Sauvignon Refosco 2019, Eden Valley Again, a big, bold style with lashings of ripe blackberry and black cherry fruits, layers of dark spice, licorice and earth and a fair lick of cedary oak. The tannins are firm and assertive and it's a wine for those that seek raw horsepower over grace. Impressive nonetheless. Screw cap. 14.5% alc. **RATING** 90 **DRINK** 2023-2029 $75 DB

Gartelmann Wines ★★★★

701 Lovedale Road, Lovedale, NSW 2321 **Region** Hunter Valley
T (02) 4930 7113 **www**.gartelmann.com.au **Open** Mon–Sat 9–5, Sun 10–4
Winemaker Liz Silkman, Annabel Holland **Est.** 1996 **Dozens** 10 000
In '96 Jan and Jorg Gartelmann purchased what was previously the George Hunter Estate – 16ha of mature vineyards, most established by Oliver Shaul in '70. In a change of emphasis, the vineyard was sold and Gartelmann now sources its grapes from the Hunter Valley and other NSW regions, including the cool Rylstone area in Mudgee. Almost 25 years later, in Dec '20, the business was purchased by local chef Matt Dillow who was already running The Deck Café based at Gartelmann.

🍷🍷🍷🍷🍷 **Benjamin Semillon 2022, Hunter Valley** Typical quartz hue, the bouquet with savoury reductive aromas, the palate tightly held to Gartelmann's chest, but should translate with time to a savoury/minerally citrus finish. Will repay cellaring up to 5 years at a minimum. Screw cap. 10.5% alc. **RATING** 92 **DRINK** 2023-2028 $27 JH

Tammy's Riesling 2021, Clare Valley This has been competently made, although there's no statement of future intentions. There's a power of juicy/citrusy fruit, and the length is good. Screw cap. 12.2% alc. **RATING** 90 **DRINK** 2023-2027 $35 JH

Gembrook Hill ★★★★★

Launching Place Road, Gembrook, Vic 3783 **Region** Yarra Valley
T (03) 5968 1622 **www**.gembrookhill.com.au **Open** By appt **Winemaker** Andrew Marks
Est. 1983 **Dozens** 1500 **Vyds** 5ha
Gembrook Hill was established by Ian and June Marks in one of the coolest and most southernmost Upper Yarra Valley sites in 1983. The northeast-facing vineyard is in a natural amphitheatre and the low-yielding vines are unirrigated. Timo Mayer looked after the viticulture and winemaking from 2000–05 when Ian and June's son, Andrew, joined the family farm. Timo and Andrew worked together until '17, also making their own wines at Gembrook Hill. Since then, it's been an all-family affair with June and Andrew Marks, who is in charge of winemaking and viticulture, co-managing Gembrook Hill. Indeed, the only contract labour they use is for picking. As to the wines, Gembrook Hill has produced a superb set; all with their trademark finesse and elegance.

🍷🍷🍷🍷🍷 **Blanc de Blancs 2017, Yarra Valley** Bright gold with green tinges. Lively, complex and understated. Aromas of poached pear, white peach, orange zest, lightly toasted nuts and a little candied ginger. As always with this cuvée, there's rapier-like acidity, but this is more than matched by the wine's intensity and

chalky texture. The 6.15g/L dosage has been perfectly judged. Diam. 11.5% alc.
RATING 97 DRINK 2022-2033 $65 PR ✪ ♥
I.J.M. Pinot Noir 2021, Yarra Valley First produced in '17 as an homage to
Andrew Marks' dad, Ian, this is only the 3rd I.J.M made. A light, bright crimson
purple. Pure fruited and poised, this sublime wine opens with aromas of wild
strawberries, fennel pollen, lavender and violets. Medium bodied, this perfectly
weighted and balanced wine is a total joy to drink now, those who put some
away will be well rewarded. Screw cap. 13% alc. RATING 97 DRINK 2022-2032
$90 PR ✪

🍷🍷🍷🍷🍷 **Sauvignon Blanc 2021, Yarra Valley** A light, bright green gold. A touch
richer and more powerful than '20, there are scents of gooseberries, citrus fruit,
nettles and tangy green herbs. The mid-weight palate has plenty of substance
before finishing chalky textured, refreshing and long. A very nicely balanced wine.
Screw cap. 12.5% alc. RATING 95 DRINK 2023-2026 $33 PR ✪
J.K.M Pinot Noir 2021, Yarra Valley Made in honour of Andrew Marks'
mum, June. A light, bright garnet. Red fruits and whole-bunch derived potpourri
scents come together in this aromatic and finely crafted wine. Sweetly fruited
yet with a savoury edge and fine, gently chewy tannins. Fewer than 100 dozen
produced. Diam. 13% alc. RATING 95 DRINK 2022-2030 $90 PR

🍷🍷🍷🍷♀ **Pinot Noir 2021, Yarra Valley** RATING 93 DRINK 2022-2028 $58 PR

Gemtree Wines   ★★★★★

167 Elliot Road, McLaren Flat, SA 5171 **Region** McLaren Vale
T (08) 8323 0802 **www.**gemtreewines.com **Open** 7 days 11–5 **Winemaker** Mike Brown,
Joshua Waechter **Viticulturist** Melissa Brown **Est.** 1998 **Dozens** 90 000
Gemtree Wines is owned and operated by husband-and-wife team Melissa and Mike
Brown. The vineyards have been certified organic since '11 and are farmed biodynamically,
too. Wines are vegan and made with minimal intervention. The solar-powered cellar door
also provides access to a 1km eco trail, weaving through 10ha of once-barren land that was
transformed into a wetland by the local community.

🍷🍷🍷🍷🍷 **Small Batch Fiano 2022, McLaren Vale** This takes fiano to another level,
defined by a musky, skin-inflected frame of phenolics, chewy and salty, within
which spiced quince, pistachio, fennel oil, almond and preserved lemon riffs play.
Finely tuned phenolics binding flair, flavour and moxie. Superb wine. Cork.
13% alc. RATING 95 DRINK 2022-2027 $35 NG ✪
Subterra Shiraz 2021, McLaren Vale Reductive aromas of neoprene give
way to blueberry, tapenade and iodine. The tannins are salty and nicely gritty,
like coffee grinds between the teeth. There is polish, savouriness and fortitude.
It will age very well indeed. Screw cap. 14% alc. RATING 95 DRINK 2023-2035
$260 NG

🍷🍷🍷🍷♀ **Luna Crescente Fiano 2022, McLaren Vale** RATING 93 DRINK 2022-2027
$26 NG ✪
Small Batch Albariño 2022, McLaren Vale RATING 93 DRINK 2022-2025
$35 NG ✪
Luna de Fresa Rosé 2022, McLaren Vale RATING 93 DRINK 2022-2023
$26 NG ✪
Luna Temprana Tempranillo 2022, McLaren Vale RATING 92
DRINK 2022-2025 $26 NG ✪
Obsidian Shiraz 2021, McLaren Vale RATING 92 DRINK 2023-2035
$100 NG
Ernest Allan Shiraz 2021, McLaren Vale RATING 92 DRINK 2023-2033
$60 NG
Small Batch SBE Grenache 2022, McLaren Vale RATING 90
DRINK 2023-2027 $50 NG

Genista Wines

PO Box 969, Williamstown, SA 5351 **Region** Barossa Valley
www.genistawines.com **Open** Not **Winemaker** Lloyd Broom **Viticulturist** Lloyd Broom
Est. 2017 **Dozens** 100 **Vyds** 3.2ha

Lloyd Broom and Sarah Gregory made the move from Melbourne to the Barossa Valley after purchasing their vineyard in Cockatoo Valley, between the villages of Lyndoch and Williamstown. The vineyards are split into 2 blocks: Home block with 1.6ha of shiraz and Gipson block with 1.2ha of shiraz and 0.4ha of grenache. The wines from this young estate reflect their plantings and ring true to their southern Barossan roots, with rich dark fruits and bright earthy lines.

SG Shiraz Grenache 2021, Barossa Valley Deep red with purple flashes in the glass. Notes of super-juicy plums along with lifted mulberry and boysenberry notes. Abundant spice with hints of orange blossom, rose petals, chocolate, licorice and crème de cassis. The fruit weight and detail are bang on, with fine, gravelly tannin support and a chocolate-dipped, plummy finish that is supple, slinky and very moreish. Screw cap. 14.5% alc. **RATING** 93 **DRINK** 2023–2028 $35 DB ✪ ❂

Duck, Duck, Cat Grenache 2021, Barossa Valley Plenty of ripe plummy fruit and ginger-tinged spice with purple floral notes, cola and earth. Light sandy tannin grip and an inviting, medium-bodied savoury shape across the palate. Screw cap. 14.5% alc. **RATING** 91 **DRINK** 2023–2028 $35 DB

Gentle Folk

PO Box 243 Basket Range, SA 5138 **Region** Adelaide Hills
T 0439 385 567 **www**.gentlefolk.com.au **Open** Not **Winemaker** Gareth Belton
Viticulturist Dylan Grigg **Est.** 2013 **Dozens** 9000 **Vyds** 10ha

Gareth and Rainbo Belton have grown the reputation of Gentle Folk to the point where their wines are now among the most in-demand in all of Australian wine. This is a case of gentle folk making gentle wines, but there's more to it than that: both Gareth and Rainbo are also marine scientists, their (PhD) specialty being marine plants (seaweeds), and there's a sense to everything that they do that the natural order and way of things is their chief informant. The Adelaide Hills region has been crucial – indeed, the driver – of the Australian 'natural wine' movement, and Gentle Folk has been a quiet but inspiring ingredient thereof.

Village Syrah 2022, Adelaide Hills The quality here is glorious. It's so perfumed, so nutty, so fresh with cherry-berried fruit and also so lengthy. It's an intensely peppery wine with gentle chocolate notes drifting through, and it boasts the most insistent-but-integrated tannin. In short, it's a pearler. Diam. 13% alc. **RATING** 97 **DRINK** 2024–2037 $45 CM ✪ ♥

Blanc 2022, Adelaide Hills Barrel-fermented sauvignon blanc. A wine of presence, softness and flow. It boasts quite wonderful fruit concentration and yet it's not heavy; indeed it's tempting to call it pillowy, but then it also has real bite. In flavours terms it offers a mix of gravel, nettle, stone fruit and green pineapple characters, all of which come wafted with curry leaf. It's exquisitely well done. Diam. 13.5% alc. **RATING** 95 **DRINK** 2023–2028 $35 CM ✪

Village Grenache 2022, McLaren Vale Reserved on the nose but the palate is a powerhouse. This is the bright, beautiful face of modern Australian grenache. Red-cherried fruit, tips of red licorice, fragrant herbs and a combination of saltbush, sandalwood and purple flowers. The tannin goes on and on, and the fruit rides with it. Diam. 14% alc. **RATING** 95 **DRINK** 2024–2032 $45 CM ✪

Pinot Noir 2022, Adelaide Hills You'd be hard pressed to find a more energetic pinot noir yet it's also a wine of depth. Juicy, fresh, smoked cherry and plum flavours come infused with bunches of green, fragrant garden herbs. Fine-grained tannin, afterthoughts of orange blossom and a velvety element to the texture; everything is positive here. Diam. 13% alc. **RATING** 94 **DRINK** 2024–2032 $45 CM

Village Sangiovese 2022, Adelaide Hills The amount of flavour here and the length of the finish pushes this wine's quality to clearly above average. Cherry, earth, iodine and roasted spice flavours do all the running here, and impressively so. It's a mid-weight and free-flowing wine, with a bit of X-factor. Diam. 14.5% alc. RATING 94 DRINK 2023–2028 $45 CM

Village Chardonnay 2022, Adelaide Hills This is a convincing chardonnay, full of stone fruit, hay, bacon and smoky oak flavour. The texture is silken without being syrupy, the finish pulsed with acidity but not tart. Give this another 12 months in bottle and it will really sing. Diam. 13% alc. RATING 94 DRINK 2024–2029 $45 CM

ŸŸŸŸŸ **Village Riesling 2022, Adelaide Hills** RATING 93 DRINK 2023–2030 $45 CM
Vin de Sofa 2022, Adelaide Hills RATING 91 DRINK 2023–2025 $32 CM

Geoff Merrill Wines   ★★★★

291 Pimpala Road, Woodcroft, SA 5162 **Region** McLaren Vale
T (08) 8381 6877 **www**.geoffmerrillwines.com.au **Open** Mon–Fri 10–4.30, Sat 12–4.30
Winemaker Geoff Merrill, Scott Heidrich **Est.** 1980 **Dozens** 55 000 **Vyds** 45ha
If Geoff Merrill ever loses his impish sense of humour or his zest for life, high and not-so-high, we shall all be the poorer. The product range consists of 3 tiers: premium (varietal); Reserve, being the older wines, reflecting the desire for elegance and subtlety of this otherwise exuberant winemaker; and, at the top, Henley Shiraz.

ŸŸŸŸŸ **Parham Cabernet Sauvignon 2017, McLaren Vale Coonawarra** I simply can't fail to say it is a massive bottle that must have cost a fortune. Matured in new hogsheads for 26 months. The result is an impressive wine from a cool vintage that favoured the McLaren Vale. Cork. 14.5% alc. RATING 94 DRINK 2024–2030 $95 JH

Reserve Cabernet Sauvignon 2016, Coonawarra McLaren Vale A multi regional blend from a selection of wines that justify further cellaring. The American oak (80% new) is of high quality, and takes command. Merrill says 'The wine represents the best cabernet we have in our cellar,' and there's no doubt that a la Penfolds Bin 707, it's a compelling wine. Screw cap. 14.5% alc. RATING 94 DRINK 2023–2036 $50 JH

Henley Shiraz 2014, McLaren Vale Henley is as Henley does – it polarises opinions. Matured in 100% new hogsheads for 32 months. The texture and length of the palate are its strong points – it's supple and feline. Cork. 14.5% alc. RATING 94 DRINK 2023–2043 $170 JH

ŸŸŸŸŸ **Reserve Shiraz 2016, McLaren Vale** RATING 92 DRINK 2023–2043 $65 JH
Jacko's Shiraz 2016, McLaren Vale RATING 91 DRINK 2023–2030 $30 JH
Reserve Chardonnay 2020, Coonawarra McLaren Vale RATING 90 DRINK 2023–2028 $40 JH

Geoff Weaver   ★★★★★

2 Gilpin Lane, Mitcham, SA 5062 (postal) **Region** Adelaide Hills
T (08) 8272 2105 **www**.geoffweaver.com.au **Open** Not **Winemaker** Geoff Weaver
Est. 1982 **Dozens** 3000 **Vyds** 12.3ha
This is the business of one-time Hardys chief winemaker Geoff Weaver. The Lenswood vineyard was established between '82–88, and invariably produces immaculate riesling and sauvignon blanc and long-lived chardonnays. The beauty of the labels ranks supreme.

ŸŸŸŸŸ **Aged Release Chardonnay 2013, Lenswood** Gleaming yellow-green hue; grapefruit, apple and white peach drive the very expressive and complex palate. A rare chance to see a 9yo chardonnay. Screw cap. 13% alc. RATING 97 DRINK 2023–2027 $70 JH ✪

ŸŸŸŸŸ **Single Vineyard Sauvignon Blanc 2022, Adelaide Hills** A mid-weighted, palpably dry expression that is searingly regional: pithy of texture with riffs on

Meyer lemon, pink grapefruit, spa salts and a splay of talcy freshness mingled with yuzu and makrut lime. Prodigiously long and saliva-sapping juicy. Time on lees has imparted breadth, a dollop of imperceivable sweetness and poise. Very good. Screw cap. 12% alc. **RATING** 94 **DRINK** 2022-2032 $30 NG ✪

Single Vineyard Chardonnay 2021, Adelaide Hills An expressive bouquet of apple, pear and almond leads into a crisp, fresh palate that brings grapefruit into the front row, but with yet more to come. Screw cap. 13.5% alc. **RATING** 94 **DRINK** 2023-2031 $50 JH

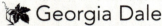# Georgia Dale ★★★★

12 Crowley Road, Healesville, Vic 3777 (postal) **Region** Yarra Valley
T 0416 718 461 **www**.georgiadalewines.com.au **Open** Not **Winemaker** Georgia Dale, Scott Symons **Viticulturist** Gerard Kennedy **Est.** 2019 **Dozens** 250 **Vyds** 10ha
Georgia Dale has made wine at a number of noted wineries across a range of regions, both domestic and international. She has a passion for sparkling wine, thanks in part to stints at Domaine Chandon, Schramsberg Vineyards (US) and Deviation Road, though she also produces viognier, pinot noir and cabernet sauvignon from her Yarra Valley base, as well as sourcing shiraz from the Kennedy vineyard in Heathcote. Her brand XI.XI (Eleven.Eleven) refers to a long string of coincidences across her winemaking career where this number (on batches, barrels etc) was important.

🍷🍷🍷🍷🍷 **XI.XI Barrel Selection Syrah 2021, Heathcote** Aged in 100% new oak for 12 months. That oak is a little too keen, but the fruit beneath is lovely and anyway, it's pretty attractive oak. Smoked cedar and malt flavours flow through plum-shot fruit, the finish then dry and well structured. This wine sits on the bold side of mid-weight and is itching to impress; give it a few extra years in bottle and it will be a delicious dinner partner. Screw cap. 13.5% alc. **RATING** 94 **DRINK** 2025-2035 $50 CM

🍷🍷🍷🍷🍷 **XI.XI Syrah 2021, Heathcote RATING** 93 **DRINK** 2023-2032 $35 CM ✪

Ghost Rock Vineyard ★★★★

1055 Port Sorrell Road, Northdown, Tas 7307 **Region** Northern Tasmania
T (03) 6428 4005 **www**.ghostrock.com.au **Open** 7 days 11–5 **Winemaker** Justin Arnold, Sierra Blair **Viticulturist** Izaak Perkins, Marty Smith **Est.** 2001 **Dozens** 20 000 **Vyds** 30ha
In '01, Cate and Colin Arnold purchased the former Patrick Creek vineyard. The vineyards now total 30ha: pinot noir (14 clones) remains the bedrock of the plantings, with other varieties including chardonnay, pinot gris, riesling and sauvignon blanc. Ownership has passed to son Justin and his wife Alicia (who runs the cellar door). Justin's experience in the Yarra Valley (Coldstream Hills), Margaret River (Devil's Lair) and Napa Valley (Etude) has paid dividends.

🍷🍷🍷🍷🍷 **Bonadale Pinot Noir 2021, Tasmania** Mid-crimson with aromas of red cherry, mulberry and red plum with hits of Chinese barbecue, shiitake broth, spice rack, leaf litter, wild strawberries and earth. Complex, gamey and long with a calm, composed feel and a spread of mountain herbs on the finish. Diam. 13.2% alc. **RATING** 94 **DRINK** 2023-2029 $60 DB

🍷🍷🍷🍷🍷 **Supernatural Cellar Rat 2022, Tasmania RATING** 93 **DRINK** 2023-2027 $30 DB ✪
Sauvignon Blanc 2022, Tasmania RATING 93 **DRINK** 2023-2026 $34 DB ✪
La Filles Pinot Noir 2021, Tasmania RATING 93 **DRINK** 2023-2029 $52 DB
Estate Pinot Noir 2021, Tasmania RATING 93 **DRINK** 2023-2029 $45 DB
Oulton Estate Chardonnay 2021, Tasmania RATING 93 **DRINK** 2023-2027 $52 DB
P3 Rosé 2022, Tasmania RATING 92 **DRINK** 2023-2024 $34 DB
Pinot Gris 2022, Tasmania RATING 91 **DRINK** 2023-2025 $34 DB

Chardonnay 2021, Tasmania RATING 91 DRINK 2023–2027 $45 DB
Catherine Cuvée Exceptionelle 2018, Tasmania RATING 90
DRINK 2023–2027 $49 DB
Riesling 2022, Tasmania RATING 90 DRINK 2023–2029 $34 DB

Giaconda ★★★★★

30 McClay Road, Beechworth, Vic 3747 **Region** Beechworth
T (03) 5727 0246 **www**.giaconda.com.au **Open** By appt **Winemaker** Rick Kinzbrunner,
Nathan Kinzbrunner **Viticulturist** Casey White **Est.** 1982 **Dozens** 3500 **Vyds** 4ha
Giaconda is one of the country's great wine producers, producing one of Australia's greatest
chardonnays. It was founded by mechanical engineer Rick Kinzbrunner in '82 and is devoted
to organic viticulture and traditional winemaking such as gravity flow, wild fermentations and
no filtration. Central to this philosophy is an underground cellar, dug out of solid granite,
creating steady year-round temperatures that lead to prolonged and gentle fermentation.
Slowly, since the '07 vintage, Rick's son, Nathan, has been stepping up. Nathan and Rick
make all the big decisions together, like planting nebbiolo; they sat atop the La Mora hillside in
Barolo in '08 and decided there and then, planting it 2 years later. More recently they decided
to reconnect with roussanne, planting it on the warmer aspects of the Giaconda vineyard.

ŸŸŸŸŸ **Estate Vineyard Chardonnay 2021, Beechworth** The wonder that is
chardonnay is laid out beautifully, masterfully, intelligently and artfully here.
Lifted aromas of orange blossom, peach, nectarine, grapefruit flesh, oatmeal and
grilled nuts with a hint of matchstick. It's plush, luxuriant and textural to taste,
brightened by juicy, filigree-fine, insistent acidity. Both vibrantly youthful and
complex. The vinous adjectives flow. Beautiful. Screw cap. 13.5% alc. RATING 98
DRINK 2023–2037 $140 JP ✿ ♥
Estate Vineyard Pinot Noir 2021, Beechworth What an entrancing wine,
a marriage of power and finesse, not to mention beauty. Deep, bright crimson.
Elevated rose petals, rosehip, plum, maraschino cherry, cranberry, tomato leaf
and thyme perfume. The melding of concentrated fruit, gently spiced oak, lacy,
fine tannins and lifted herbals with the kind of natural balance that stems from
the vineyard's gravel soils offers a truly memorable wine experience. Astonishing.
Cork. 13.8% alc. RATING 98 DRINK 2023–2036 $100 JP ✿ ♥

ŸŸŸŸŸ **Nebbiolo 2019, Beechworth** Power and finesse, aromatic fineness and savoury
overtones. Noted tannin presence, but it's perfectly tailored to the needs of the
fruit. Brings fragrant rose, rosehip, red licorice, anise and pepper together with
cherry, cranberry and earth. A complex grouping of flavours gather on the palate,
formed tight in dry, savoury tannins, running long. And the best part? It's just
beginning its journey. Cork. 14% alc. RATING 96 DRINK 2023–2036 $115 JP

Giant Steps ★★★★★

314 Maroondah Highway, Healesville, Vic 3777 **Region** Yarra Valley
T (03) 5962 6111 **www**.giantstepswine.com.au **Open** 7 days 11–4 **Winemaker** Melanie
Chester, Steve Flamsteed, Jess Clark **Viticulturist** Ashley Wood **Est.** 1997
Dozens 30 000 **Vyds** 60ha
Giant Steps is firmly established among the Australian wine elite. It's long been a quality-
obsessed outfit, but if anything, its sale to Jackson Family Wines in '20 only sharpened the
emphasis on quality. Single-vineyard chardonnay and pinot noir from across the upper and
lower Yarra Valley are the foundation for the winery's reputation, but really every winemaking
excursion this winery takes has a habit of turning to gold. Long-term winemaker Steve
Flamsteed, who is still involved, left the main winemaking post with the wines in impeccable
shape; current head winemaker Melanie Chester has ensured that the changeover has been
both seamless and positive.

ŸŸŸŸŸ **Applejack Vineyard Pinot Noir 2022, Yarra Valley** Pinot Noir of the Year.
Aromas of crushed rose petals, red and black cherries, satsuma plums and subtle
hints of sandalwood and fennel fronds. There's a little charcuterie and a discreet

touch of wet stone. On the palate, this is concentrated, structured and saline, yet you barely notice the tannins due to the core of pure raspberry and cherry fruit. There's a gentle sappiness on the long, lingering finish. Simply irresistible. Screw cap. 13% alc. **RATING** 98 **DRINK** 2022–2032 $90 PR ✪ ♥

Applejack Vineyard Chardonnay 2022, Yarra Valley This is a magnificent wine and the best Giant Steps chardonnay I've tasted. Bright green gold. A stunning bouquet of orchard and stone fruits, grilled nuts, white jasmine and marine scents. Just as complex on the intense yet perfectly balanced palate before finishing spicy, chalky and very long. Screw cap. 12.5% alc. **RATING** 98 **DRINK** 2022–2027 $80 PR ✪

Primavera Vineyard Pinot Noir 2022, Yarra Valley Wonderfully perfumed and vibrant with its aromas of cranberries, wild strawberries, a little Sichuan pepper, fresh citrus oil and musk roses at dusk. A wine of exquisite finesse and excellent depth, the tannins are very fine and long, as is the finish. Screw cap. 13.5% alc. **RATING** 97 **DRINK** 2022–2032 $90 PR ✪

Tarraford Vineyard Chardonnay 2022, Yarra Valley An engaging and lovely wine. Opens with subtle scents of pink grapefruit, orange blossom and coriander seeds. Builds nicely on the gently textured, saline and structured palate before finishing zesty and long. The sort of wine that begs you to take another sip. Screw cap. 13% alc. **RATING** 97 **DRINK** 2022–2027 $80 PR ✪

♟♟♟♟♟ **Pinot Noir 2022, Yarra Valley** A bright ruby crimson. Expressive with aromas of satsuma plums, strawberry coulis, fennel seeds and a hint of star anise. With its core of ripe yet well-delineated fruit and firm-ish, balanced tannins, this is more concentrated and muscular than the '21. It will age well, too. Screw cap. 13% alc. **RATING** 96 **DRINK** 2022–2030 $48 PR ✪

Rosé 2022, Yarra Valley Follows in the footsteps of the exceptional '21. Giant Steps has its fruit sourcing, and minimalist winemaking, down to a fine art. It has an exotic, warm, spice-filled bouquet with musk and strawberry cream flavours. Makes it seem easy. It's not. Screw cap. 12% alc. **RATING** 96 **DRINK** 2023–2023 $30 JH ✪

Sexton Vineyard Pinot Noir 2022, Yarra Valley A deep ruby crimson. The densest and most brooding of the Giant Steps Yarra Valley single-vineyard pinots from '22. You'll find bramble berries, freshly ploughed earth and a little black pepper. Savoury and concentrated on the palate, there is plenty of meat on the bones with substantial and persistent tannins masked by the sheer weight of plush fruit at this stage. Screw cap. 13% alc. **RATING** 96 **DRINK** 2022–2030 $90 PR

Sexton Vineyard Chardonnay 2022, Yarra Valley A bright green gold. The most immediate of the 4 single-vineyard chardonnays from Giant Steps in '22. Perfectly ripened white peach and apricot aromas with scents of German spiced biscuits and a little flint. Textured with good intensity, this silky wine flows effortlessly across the palate. Screw cap. 13% alc. **RATING** 96 **DRINK** 2022–2027 $80 PR

Wombat Creek Vineyard Pinot Noir 2022, Yarra Valley Redcurrants, early season raspberries, pomegranate, coriander seeds and tea rose scents. Vibrant and silky in the mouth, this is both elegant and structured. Finishes even and long with pliant, persistent tannins and juicy acidity. Screw cap. 13% alc. **RATING** 96 **DRINK** 2022–2028 $90 PR

Chardonnay 2022, Yarra Valley A light, bright green gold. Pure fruited with an attractive nose of just ripened orchard and stone fruits, pink grapefruit and orange blossom. A hint of matchstick and just-baked ginger snaps. Concentrated and lithe at the same time, Giant Step's calling card is just as good this vintage, if not better than the super '21 release. Screw cap. 12.5% alc. **RATING** 95 **DRINK** 2022–2027 $48 PR ✪

LDR Pinot Noir Syrah 2022, Yarra Valley A very bright crimson purple. Springs from the glass with violets, cherries, raspberries and a touch of Sichuan pepper. A juicy yet focused and delicious mouthful with satiny tannins. The bargain red wine in the portfolio. Screw cap. 13% alc. **RATING** 95 **DRINK** 2022–2025 $30 PR ✪

Fatal Shore Pinot Noir 2022, Tasmania A bright crimson red, this leaps from the glass with its heady aromas of red raspberries, wild strawberries and redcurrant, a little potpourri and spices such as mace and pink peppercorns. Brightly fruited yet nicely balanced with gently persistent tannins and refreshing acidity, it's so delicious from the get-go, you really can enjoy this now but know that it will still be looking good 5-7 years from now. Screw cap. 13.5% alc. **RATING** 95 **DRINK** 2022-2030 $90 PR

Wombat Creek Vineyard Chardonnay 2022, Yarra Valley From the marginal Wombat Creek vineyard planted at around 400m elevation in the early 1980s. Aromas of yellow grapefruit, gently poached apples, white peach and a little yuzu. With its mouth-watering acidity, this is the most tightly wound of the four Giant Steps chardonnays in '22. Finishes chalky and long. Screw cap. 13.5% alc. **RATING** 94 **DRINK** 2022-2027 $80 PR

Gibson

190 Willows Road, Light Pass, SA 5355 **Region** Barossa Valley
T (08) 8562 4224 **www.**gibsonwines.com.au **Open** 7 days 11–5 **Winemaker** Rob Gibson **Est.** 1996 **Dozens** 11 000 **Vyds** 12.4ha
Rob Gibson spent much of his working life as a senior viticulturist for Penfolds, involved in research tracing the characters that particular parcels of grapes give to a wine, which left him with a passion for identifying and protecting what is left of the original vineyard plantings in Australia. He has a vineyard (merlot) in the Barossa Valley at Light Pass, and one in the Eden Valley (shiraz and riesling) and also purchases grapes from McLaren Vale and the Adelaide Hills.

🍷🍷🍷🍷🍷 **Bin 70 Shiraz 2018, Barossa** Deep crimson in the glass with a classic Barossa nose of plum and black fruits with underlying notes of baking spices, earth, dark chocolate, cedar, vanilla and panforte. Full bodied but shows finesse and grace with excellent fine-grained tannins and a powerful yet composed flow across the palate finishing very long indeed. The oak is present but slides into the fruit beautifully. Cork. 14.9% alc. **RATING** 96 **DRINK** 2023-2043 $345 DB

Australian Old Vine Collection Shiraz 2019, Eden Valley Deep crimson with aromas of rich blackberry, black cherry and dark plum fruits with hints of cedar, brown spices, mace, sage, dark chocolate, pastis and earth. The fruit density and flow are velvety smooth and show great finesse, oak apparent but simpatico with the fruit, tannins firm yet supple and a finish that rides on nicely. A graceful, fruit-rich and balanced Eden Valley shiraz. Cork. 14.5% alc. **RATING** 95 **DRINK** 2023-2040 $110 DB

Australian Old Vine Collection Shiraz 2018, Barossa Deep crimson with aromas of ripe plum, black cherry and blackcurrant fruits, hints of baking spices, dark chocolate, violets, vanilla, cedar, licorice and earth. The initial swell of fruit is luscious and pure, followed by some pretty percussive oak. Tannins are ripe, fine and sandy and there's good mineral energy for such a powerful wine. Traditional Barossa, done really well. Cork. 14.9% alc. **RATING** 95 **DRINK** 2023-2037 $135 DB

🍷🍷🍷🍷🍷 **The Smithy Shiraz Cabernet 2021, Barossa** **RATING** 93 **DRINK** 2023-2033 $39 DB

Bin 60 Museum Release Cabernet Sauvignon Shiraz 2008, Barossa **RATING** 93 **DRINK** 2023-2033 $385 DB

Burkes Hill Riesling 2022, Eden Valley **RATING** 92 **DRINK** 2023-2028 $35 DB

Duke Grenache 2021, Barossa **RATING** 92 **DRINK** 2023-2028 $30 DB ✪

Reserve Shiraz 2020, Barossa **RATING** 92 **DRINK** 2023-2030 $55 DB

The Dirtman Shiraz 2021, Barossa Valley **RATING** 91 **DRINK** 2023-2029 $39 DB

Gilbert Family Wines   ★★★★★

137 Ulan Road, Mudgee, NSW 2850 **Region** Central Ranges
T (02) 6373 1371 **www**.gilbertfamilywines.com.au **Open** Mon 10–2, Thurs
10–4, Fri–Sat 10–5, Sun 10–4 **Winemaker** Simon Gilbert, Will Gilbert **Est.** 2004
Dozens 22 000 **Vyds** 31.5ha

The Gilbert family history is steeped in South Australian agriculture. Joseph Gilbert was
responsible for the movement to viticulture, planting the first vines at Pewsey Vale in the Eden
Valley in 1847. His great-great-grandson Simon Gilbert is now a 5th-generation winemaker
and it was in 2004 that Gilbert Family Wines began to tell its story. Today Simon is joined
by his son and 6th-generation winemaker Will Gilbert. Crafting wines from Mudgee,
Orange and the Eden Valley, with developments also in the Hilltops, the pair produce both
traditional and progressive wines with a regional focus.

🍷🍷🍷🍷🍷 **Blancs de Blancs #2 Chardonnay 2016, Orange** Second disgorgement of
the '16 vintage. Marine fossils, oyster shell, white pomelo pith and sweet alyssum.
Candlenut, young almonds and ricotta. The extended lees ageing (68 months)
adds facets of bread dough, shortbread and white pepper. Rife with energy,
tension and vigour. A sparkling wine that leads the way for its style and substance.
Cork. 12.2% alc. **RATING** 97 **DRINK** 2022-2032 $78 SW ✿ ♥

gilbert Museum Release Chardonnay 2016, Orange Baked apples, peach
cobbler and upside-down pineapple cake. Warmed Anzac biscuits, candied
ginger and grated nutmeg, walnut paste and curry leaf. Driving acidity, but it's
the latticework of texture and flavour depth that you'll be swooning over. Power
and sophistication, it's all here. Screw cap. 13% alc. **RATING** 97 **DRINK** 2022-2028
$60 SW ✿ ♥

🍷🍷🍷🍷🍷 **gilbert Museum Release Riesling 2016, Orange** Makrut lime leaves,
lemon-lime cordial, candied green apple and dried hay. Succulent acidity followed
by sunflower kernel, silver needle tea and a woven fabric of texture. This is
only beginning to hit its stride with baked clay minerality, a dense chew to the
fruit and a flavour length for days. Intricate. Screw cap. 12% alc. **RATING** 96
DRINK 2022-2035 $60 SW ✿ ♥

Méthode Traditionelle #2 2016, Orange Second disgorgement of the '16
vintage. Chardonnay, pinot noir, meunier. Traditional method, 68 months on lees.
Zero dosage. Musk and alpine strawberry, crab apples and lilly pilly fruit. Orange
blossom honey, buttered toast and cashew butter. Pink salt flakes and quince. The
choice to omit dosage allows the intensity of red-berried fruit to shine while
maintaining lees complexity and fragility. A class act. Cork. 12.6% alc. **RATING** 95
DRINK 2022-2028 $78 SW

gilbert Pinot Noir 2022, Orange Alpine strawberry, rhubarb and cranberry.
Brazilian chilli kiss peppers, goji and rosehip. The carbonic component (30%)
has elevated the already fragrant perfume. Lithe, slinky and deft on her feet, with
swift acidity, exotic florals and elegance of movement across the palate. Structurally
sound tannins and a kinesthetic awareness of form. An assured wine and hard to
beat at the price. Screw cap. 13.5% alc. **RATING** 95 **DRINK** 2022-2028 $36 SW ✿

gilbert Sauvignon Blanc 2022, Orange Year in, year out this wine manages
to achieve a balance between textural architecture and the bright, lively and telltale
signs of the variety. Pineapple core, passionfruit curd, edamame and honeydew.
On the palate, the wine continues to evolve with a pulpiness of ripe fruit and
fullness of mouthfeel. Oak supports the array of fresh produce. Screw cap.
12% alc. **RATING** 95 **DRINK** 2022-2028 $30 SW ✿ ♥

gilbert Chardonnay 2021, Orange The wine opens with crushed chalk,
pomelo, lemon pith and churned ricotta. Water crackers, silver needle tea and
lemongrass follow. There is a mealiness on the palate, oatmeal and crushed
almond. A fine line of blue rock and seashell. Acidity reigns supreme, forceful but
coaxing. The palate slips and slides along. A slinky little number and built for the
long haul. Screw cap. 12.5% alc. **RATING** 95 **DRINK** 2022-2030 $56 SW

**Gilbert + Gilbert Single Vineyard Museum Release Riesling 2017,
Eden Valley** Makrut lime leaf, bush lemon and sour green apple. Summer rain,

hot wet concrete and struck stone. Undulating acidity and flavours of golden kiwi, lemongrass and greengage plums. A gentle almond milk nuttiness and flaky pastry. Alive with fruit, zesty drive and long length. Screw cap. 12.4% alc. **RATING** 95 **DRINK** 2022–2028 $36 SW ✪

gilbert Museum Release Shiraz 2017, Orange Raspberry coulis, blackberries and pomegranate molasses. Baked red clay, dried tea leaves, tonka bean and carob. The fruit weight is explosive upfront then melts away into savoury dried herbs and cooking spices. Cardamom, clove and coffee pod. The aqueous way it flows across the palate is a highlight. Superb. Screw cap. 14% alc. **RATING** 95 **DRINK** 2022–2028 $42 SW ✪ ❤

🍷🍷🍷🍷🍸 **gilbert Chardonnay 2022, Orange RATING** 93 **DRINK** 2022–2032 $36 SW
gilbert Rosé 2022, Mudgee RATING 92 **DRINK** 2022–2025 $26 SW ✪
gilbert Nashdale Pinot Noir 2021, Orange RATING 92 **DRINK** 2022–2030 $56 SW
gilbert Nashdale Chardonnay 2019, Orange RATING 92 **DRINK** 2022–2028 $56 SW
gilbert Pétillant Naturel Riesling 2022, Central Ranges RATING 91 **DRINK** 2022–2024 $28 SW ✪
gilbert Pétillant Naturel Rosé Sangiovese 2022, Mudgee RATING 90 **DRINK** 2022–2024 $28 SW
gilbert Blanc 2022, Hilltops Orange RATING 90 **DRINK** 2022–2026 $26 SW

Gilberts   ★★★★

30138 Albany Highway, Kendenup via Mount Barker, WA 6323 **Region** Mount Barker **T** 1800 708 110 www.gilbertwines.com.au **Open** Thu–Mon 10–5 **Winemaker** West Cape Howe **Est.** 1985 **Dozens** 3000 **Vyds** 9ha

Once a part-time occupation for 3rd-generation sheep and beef farmers Jim and Beverly Gilbert, but now a full-time job and a very successful one. In '14 the 4th generation, sons Clinton and Matthew, joined the management of the business. The mature vineyard (shiraz, chardonnay, riesling and cabernet sauvignon) coupled with contract winemaking at West Cape Howe, has long produced high-class wines.

🍷🍷🍷🍷🍸 **Riesling 2022, Mount Barker** A strong perfume of lemon verbena, lime oil, fig leaf, blackcurrant and green apple, with whiffs of frangipani in the mix. The palate is concentrated and strongly set to sweet lime and green apple characters with a rod of steely, flinty minerality shot through. A bolder expression of riesling, done with distinction. Screw cap. 11% alc. **RATING** 92 **DRINK** 2022–2033 $32 MB
Estate Hand Picked Chardonnay 2021, Mount Barker A soft and supple chardonnay of green melon, sweet nectarine, cool, limey acidity and creamy vanilla sweetness. A bit of flinty, smoky minerality also plays a hand. As chardonnay goes, there's a good sense of complexity with full perfume and layers of fruit, spice and winemaking influence all pitching in. Screw cap. 12.5% alc. **RATING** 92 **DRINK** 2022–2027 $35 MB
Reserve Shiraz 2020, Mount Barker Redolent of ripe raspberries, blackcurrant jam, strong cedar, twiggy herbs and white pepper. Flavours roll thick and dry with potent red berry fruit, woody spices and pepper. A touch of saltiness is apparent through the chewy, chalky (and lingering) finish. It's a red wine of power and presence that finds reasonable balance, delivering a full-flavoured expression. Screw cap. 14.5% alc. **RATING** 91 **DRINK** 2022–2035 $45 MB

Gipsie Jack Wine Co   ★★★★

The Winehouse, 1509 Langhorne Creek Road, Langhorne Creek, SA 5255 **Region** Langhorne Creek **T** (08) 8537 3029 www.thewinehouse.com.au **Open** 7 days 10–4 **Winemaker** John Glaetzer, Ben Potts **Est.** 2004

The partners of Gipsie Jack are John Glaetzer and Ben Potts, named after John Glaetzer's Jack Russell dog Gipsie. Glaetzer and Potts say, 'We want to make this label fun, like in the 'old days'. No pretentiousness, no arrogance, not even a back label. A great wine at a great price, with no discounting.'

ΨΨΨΨΨ **The Terrier Shiraz Cabernet Sauvignon 2021, Langhorne Creek** The usual skills of John Glaetzer and Ben Potts launch the wine with a most expressive bouquet and well-balanced palate. A bit edgy at the time of tasting, but still the usual over-delivery. Screw cap. 14.4% alc. **RATING** 90 **DRINK** 2023–2029 $19 JH ✪

Glaetzer Wines

PO Box 824 Tanunda, SA 5352 **Region** Barossa Valley
T (08) 8563 0947 **www.glaetzer.com Open** Not **Winemaker** Ben Glaetzer **Est.** 1996
Dozens 15 000 **Vyds** 20ha

With a family history in the Barossa Valley dating back to 1888, Glaetzer Wines was established by Colin Glaetzer after 30 years of winemaking experience. Son Ben worked in the Hunter Valley and as a Flying Winemaker in many of the world's wine regions before returning to Glaetzer Wines and assuming the winemaking role. The wines are made with great skill and abundant personality.

ΨΨΨΨΨ **Amon-Ra Unfiltered Shiraz 2021, Barossa Valley** A wine of impact and purity. Beautiful ripe black plum, cassis and black cherry fruits with hints of cedar, baking spices, dark chocolate, licorice, nutmeg, espresso, earth and graphite. Power and harmony writ large with cascading tannin, lacy acidity and great depth and concentration. It's a cracker. Cork. 15% alc. **RATING** 96 **DRINK** 2023–2043 $100 DB

Anaperenna 2021, Barossa Valley It's a deeply fruited affair, all cassis, blackberry and black cherry tones with impressive weight, depth and purity. It's not a wine for the oak-shy, as the cedar and vanilla tones make their presence felt, but all that fruit just sucks it up like a greedy Labrador. Finishing bold with tight, compact powdery tannin and cassis leaving the impression that this will cellar like a champion. Cork. 15% alc. **RATING** 95 **DRINK** 2023–2040 $52 DB

ΨΨΨΨΨ **Bishop Shiraz 2020, Barossa Valley RATING** 93 **DRINK** 2023–2030 $30 DB ✪
Wallace Shiraz Grenache 2021, Barossa Valley RATING 92
DRINK 2023–2032 $23 DB ✪
Wallace Shiraz Grenache 2020, Barossa Valley RATING 91
DRINK 2023–2028 $23 DB ✪

Glandore Estate

1595 Broke Road, Pokolbin, NSW 2320 **Region** Hunter Valley
T (02) 4998 7140 **www.glandorewines.com Open** 7 days 10–5 **Winemaker** Duane Roy,
Nick Flanagan **Est.** 2004 **Dozens** 9000 **Vyds** 8ha

Glandore Estate is the reincarnation of the Brokenback vineyard established as part of Rothbury Estate in the early '70s, but it had an even longer history. It was purchased by legendary grapegrowers Mick and Jack Phillips in the '30s, and given the Glandore name. Owners David Madson, John Cambridge and Peter McBeath, who acquired the property in '04 (with existing chardonnay vines), extended the plantings with savagnin, semillon and viognier. Tempranillo, sangiovese, nebbiolo and pinot grigio have been added. Fruit is also sourced from across NSW.

ΨΨΨΨΨ **Cellarhands Oakey Creek Vineyard Semillon 2022, Hunter Valley** Very expensive packaging will be the end of the wine when the one-piece natural cork allows the transfer of oxygen as the wine ages. There's some very good semillon in the bottle, and no sign yet of madeirisation or outright oxidation. The score is for today, not tomorrow. Cork. 11% alc. **RATING** 94 **DRINK** 2023–2025 $80 JH

ΨΨΨΨΨ **Sangiovese 2021, Hilltops RATING** 91 **DRINK** 2023–2028 $38 JH
Cellarhands Lauriston Vineyard Shiraz Malbec 2021, Macedon Ranges
RATING 90 **DRINK** 2023–2025 $120 JH

Glenguin Estate ★★★★★

Milbrodale Road, Broke, NSW 2330 (postal) **Region** Hunter Valley
T 0417 685 304 **www.**glenguinestate.com.au **Open** Not **Winemaker** Robin Tedder
MW, Rhys Eather **Viticulturist** Dave Grosser, Andrew Tedder **Est.** 1993 **Dozens** 2000
Vyds 4.2ha

Glenguin Estate was established by the Tedder family, headed by Robin Tedder MW. It is close to Broke and adjacent to Wollombi Brook. The backbone of the production comes from plantings of Busby clone semillon and shiraz with an average vine age of 30 years. Vineyard manager Andrew Tedder, who has considerable experience with organics and biodynamics, is overseeing the ongoing development of Glenguin's organic program.

♟♟♟♟♟ **Aged Release Glenguin Vineyard Semillon 2017, Hunter Valley** Gleaming green gold. From the stellar '17 vintage, the bouquet and palate both speak with clarion quality of lime, lemon, toast and cashew, the back palate and finish with the high-tensile acidity of Hunter semillon. Screw cap. 11% alc. **RATING** 96 **DRINK** 2026–2032 $30 JH ✪

Glenlofty Estate ★★★★★

123 Glenlofty-Warrenmang Road, Glenlofty, Vic 3469 **Region** Pyrenees
T (03) 5354 8228 **www.**glenloftywines.com.au **Open** By appt **Winemaker** Carmel
Keenan, Scott Gerrard **Viticulturist** Scott Gerrard **Est.** 1995 **Dozens** 40000 **Vyds** 136ha

The vineyard was established by Southcorp after exhaustive soil and climate research to supply grapes for Seppelt and Penfolds wines. In Aug '10 Treasury Wine Estates sold the vineyard to Canadian-based Roger Richmond-Smith and winemaking moved to Blue Pyrenees Estate. Glenlofty Wines subsequently purchased the nearby 30ha Decameron Station, bringing the total vineyard holdings to over 130ha. In April '19 Glenlofty Wines also purchased Blue Pyrenees Estate, making it the largest producer in the Pyrenees.

♟♟♟♟♟ **Estate Syrah 2021, Pyrenees** Alive with spice, flooded with fruit, curled with tannin and awash with all manner of complexities through the finish. This is what it's all about. Plums, woodsy spice notes, florals and jellies and mints. This is savoury, warm, fruit driven and deep all at once, and boasts a deliciously smoky/graphite-like aftertaste. It's a wonderful drink. Screw cap. 14.5% alc. **RATING** 96 **DRINK** 2024–2035 $35 CM ✪

The Ridge Block Shiraz 2020, Pyrenees There's a substantial volume of fruit here matched to a significant amount of saucy, smoky oak. While 'more of everything' isn't always a great tactic, it works well here. This is a drastically seductive red wine. Plum, cedar, clove and choc-mint characters pour on the flavour, but the wine somehow remains fresh and frisky throughout. Excellent. Screw cap. 13.5% alc. **RATING** 95 **DRINK** 2023–2032 $50 CM ✪

Estate Cabernet Sauvignon 2020, Pyrenees This is a wine of structure and length but it's the juiciness of the fruit that really elevates it. Indeed while it has the scaffolding to age it's so fresh and lively that you could drink it pretty much any time. Boysenberry, blackcurrant, mint and cedar-sawdust characters present deliciously here. Wine quality at this estate has really stepped up a gear of late. Screw cap. 13.5% alc. **RATING** 94 **DRINK** 2024–2034 $35 CM ✪

The Decameron Block Cabernet Sauvignon 2020, Pyrenees Strong flavours of blackcurrant, cedar, bay leaf and mint put on a velvety, fresh, mouth-filling display. It's not in any way overcooked, and yet it really serves up the flavour. Tannin is a little over-exuberant, as is oak, but both will settle. The mint notes here are overt too, but the quality is serious. Screw cap. 13% alc. **RATING** 94 **DRINK** 2025–2035 $50 CM

♟♟♟♟♟ **Estate Chardonnay 2021, Pyrenees RATING** 93 **DRINK** 2024–2030 $35 CM ✪
GO Shiraz 2019, Pyrenees RATING 93 **DRINK** 2023–2030 $25 CM ✪
Estate Shiraz 2020, Pyrenees RATING 91 **DRINK** 2024–2031 $35 CM

Glenwillow Wines

Bendigo Pottery, 146 Midland Highway, Epsom, Vic 3551 **Region** Bendigo
T 0428 461 076 **www.**glenwillow.com.au **Open** Thurs–Mon & public hols 10.30–5
Winemaker Adam Marks, Brendan Lane **Viticulturist** Peter Fyffe **Est.** 1999
Dozens 750 **Vyds** 3ha

Peter and Cherryl Fyffe began their vineyard at Yandoit Creek, 10km south of Newstead, in '99. They planted 1.8ha of shiraz and 0.3ha of cabernet sauvignon, later branching out with 0.6ha of nebbiolo and 0.1ha of barbera. Planted on a mixture of rich volcanic and clay loam interspersed with quartz and buckshot gravel, the vineyard has an elevated north-facing aspect, which minimises the risk of frost. The cellar door operates from Bendigo Pottery.

Reserve Shiraz 2017, Bendigo A complex and age-worthy reserve red. Released as a 6yo wine, it is moving into some attractive secondary development of game, earthy mushroom and chocolate set against a background of blackberry and spice. It is clearly enjoying the onset of middle age. Velvety tannins smooth the journey. Screw cap. 14.2% alc. **RATING** 92 **DRINK** 2022–2030 $60 JP

Golden Grove Estate

Sundown Road, Ballandean, Qld 4382 **Region** Granite Belt
T (07) 4684 1291 **www.**goldengroveestate.com.au **Open** Mon–Tue, Thu–Sun 9–4
Winemaker Ray Costanzo **Viticulturist** Sam Costanzo, Jason Costanzo **Est.** 1993
Dozens 4000 **Vyds** 15ha

Golden Grove Estate was established by Mario and Sebastian Costanzo in '46, producing stone fruits and table grapes. The first wine grapes (shiraz) were planted in '72 but it was not until '85, when ownership passed to son Sam and his wife Grace, that the use of the property began to change. In '93 chardonnay and merlot joined the shiraz, followed by cabernet sauvignon, sauvignon blanc and semillon. The baton has been passed down another generation Ray Costanzo, who has lifted the quality of the wines remarkably and has also planted tempranillo, durif, barbera, malbec, mourvèdre, vermentino and nero d'Avola. Its consistent wine show success over recent years with alternative varieties is impressive.

Rare Tawny Small Batch Release 15 Years Aged NV, Granite Belt Excellent fortified wine with strong rancio, woody spice, dried fruit-and-nut characters and clean, refreshing spirit integrated beautifully. Strong scents of fruit and nut dark chocolate, mustard powder, cocoa powder, licorice, cinnamon and toffee. Similar flavours with a little tannin grip and that cool spirit character keeping things fresh and perky. Really well done. 500ml. Screw cap. 21.5% alc. **RATING** 94 $65 MB

Joven Tempranillo 2022, Granite Belt RATING 92 **DRINK** 2022–2024 $35 MB
Rosé Brosé 2022, Granite Belt RATING 92 **DRINK** 2022–2024 $26 MB ✪
Vermentino 2022, Granite Belt RATING 92 **DRINK** 2022–2024 $35 MB
Nero d'Avola 2021, Granite Belt Murray Darling RATING 91 **DRINK** 2022–2024 $35 MB

Golding Wines

52 Western Branch Road, Lobethal, SA 5241 **Region** Adelaide Hills
T (08) 8189 4500 **www.**goldingwines.com.au **Open** by appt **Winemaker** Natasha Mooney **Viticulturist** Darren Golding **Est.** 2002 **Dozens** 11 000 **Vyds** 27ha

The Golding family story began in the Adelaide Hills 3 generations ago through market gardening and horticulture. Viticulture became part of the picture in '95 when their Western Branch Road vineyard was planted. Darren and Lucy Golding took the helm in '02, launching the Golding Wines brand. Viticultural holdings have increased recently with the purchase of more vineyards and new plantings of gamay added to the existing pinot noir, shiraz, chardonnay, savagnin, pinot gris and sauvignon blanc. The cellar door and restaurant are in their rustic sandstone barn.

ȲȲȲȲȲ **Marjorie Blanc de Blancs 2016, Adelaide Hills** A toasty, aspirational style of fizz with iodine, creamy breadth, brioche and truffle suggestive of long lees ageing. Granny Smith apple, pistachio, quince and apricot pithiness are driven long and broad by a skein of saline freshness and a perky bead. Impressive. Cork. 12.5% alc. **RATING** 93 **DRINK** 2022-2030 $65 NG

Ombre Gamay 2022, Adelaide Hills Very good gamay. Drinks akin to a warm-vintage beaujolais, auguring well for the variety in these parts. Chinotto and strewn herbs. Mid-weighted of frame. The finish, ostensibly dry and gristly before a burst of sweet cherry fruit, uncluttered and pure and liberating, makes for a delicious wine. Screw cap. 13% alc. **RATING** 93 **DRINK** 2022-2026 $32 NG ✪

Gomersal Wines   ★★★★

203 Lyndoch Road, Gomersal, SA 5352 **Region** Barossa Valley
T (08) 8563 3611 **www.gomersalwines.com.au Open** Thurs–Sun 10–4
Winemaker Barry White **Viticulturist** Barry White **Est.** 1887 **Dozens** 10200
Vyds 20.2ha
The 1887 establishment date has a degree of poetic licence. In 1887 Friedrich W Fromm planted the Wonganella vineyards, following that with a winery on the edge of the Gomersal Creek in '91; it remained in operation for 90 years, finally closing in '83. In '00 a group of friends bought the winery and re-established the vineyard, planting 17ha of shiraz, 2.2ha of mourvèdre and 1ha of grenache.

ȲȲȲȲȲ **Shiraz 2019, Barossa Valley** Deep crimson in the glass, there is plenty of inky fruit depth and flex here thanks to the black, cracking soils out on the Gomersal plains. Rich dark plum and blackberry fruits, abundant spice and meaty nuance, rum and raisin chocolate, clove and vanillin with a compact, dense flow of fruit, gingery spice and a muscular, sandy tannin framework. Screw cap. 14.5% alc. **RATING** 91 **DRINK** 2023-2029 $25 DB ✪

Cabernet Sauvignon 2019, Barossa Valley Crimson in the glass and bursting with macerated plums, blackberry, fig and lighter mulberry tones. Hints of baking spices, roasting meats, turned earth, pressed flowers and choc-mint. Muscular with a swoop of sour cherry and cassis on the palate, which shows rich black fruit, fine sandy tannins and not a peep from any herbaceous notes. Screw cap. 14.5% alc. **RATING** 90 **DRINK** 2023-2029 $25 DB ✪

Goona Warra Vineyard   ★★★☆

790 Sunbury Road, Sunbury, Vic 3429 (postal) **Region** Sunbury
T (03) 9740 7766 **www.goonawarra.com.au Open** Not **Winemaker** Richard Buller, Kirilly Gordon **Est.** 1863 **Dozens** 2500 **Vyds** 5.27ha
A historic stone winery, originally established under this name by a 19th-century Victorian premier. Excellent tasting facilities, an outstanding venue for weddings and receptions. The public-facing side of the winery is closed until late '23 (or early '24) while significant renovations take place, including a new cellar door. The winery is still operating in the meantime.

ȲȲȲȲȲ **Chairmans Reserve Shiraz 2019, Sunbury** A richly flavoured, solid offering and seems a bit old-school in a way yet in a good way, too. It's voluptuous with black, ripe fruit blanketed in baking spices and bourbon-flavoured oak. Full bodied, with shapely tannins and a freshness throughout. It has plenty to offer. To get the best out of it, match with hearty food. Screw cap. 14% alc. **RATING** 93 **DRINK** 2023-2033 $40 JF

Grampians Estate   ★★★★☆

1477 Western Highway, Great Western, Vic 3377 **Region** Grampians
T (03) 5354 6245 **www.grampiansestate.com.au Open** 7 days 10–5
Winemaker Andrew Davey, Tom Guthrie **Est.** 1989 **Dozens** 2000 **Vyds** 8ha

Graziers Sarah and Tom Guthrie began their diversification into wine in '89, but their core business continues to be fat lamb and wool production. They have acquired the Garden Gully winery at Great Western, giving them a cellar door and a vineyard with 140+yo shiraz and 100+yo riesling. Grampians Estate followed its success of being Champion Small Winery of Show at the Australian Small Winemakers Show for the 2nd year running in '18 by winning the Premier's Trophy for Champion Wine of Victoria in '19. These successes led to a major expansion of the cellar door, with a new cafe and outdoor area.

ΨΨΨΨΨ **Rutherford Sparkling Shiraz 2020, Grampians** Complex in style with mushroom, game, ripe plum and blueberry flavours shooting through a creamy yet dry palate. There are subtle chocolate characters here, too, and good overall intensity, though it dries and flattens significantly through the finish. Cork. 14% alc. **RATING** 93 **DRINK** 2024-2032 $40 CM

Streeton Reserve Shiraz 2020, Grampians Choc-mint oak sits hand-in-glove with plum-shot fruit. There are clove and assorted roasted/sweet spice notes here, but it's essentially a wine of fruit and oak with a little regional pepper on show. Red/black licorice flavours boost the wine as it breathes, bringing game and dried herbs notes with them. It's an enjoyable wine to drink. Screw cap. 14% alc. **RATING** 93 **DRINK** 2024-2033 $80 CM

Field's Crossing Grenache 2021, Grampians There's some alcohol warmth to this wine but it remains elegant and light, in a good way, with raspberry, earth and dried herb characters signing brightly through the palate. A light sheet of dry, spicy tannin plays a key role; it helps both set and maintain the savoury, dry and elegant tone. It's clear that there's quality to be had here. Screw cap. 14.5% alc. **RATING** 92 **DRINK** 2023-2028 $28 CM ✪

Mafeking Shiraz 2021, Grampians One sip and you're into a pool of plums, a few more and the spice notes begin to appear. This is one of those mid-weight wines that evolves in the glass, pepper and spice taking time to be coaxed forward while the fruit has the door open before you'd even had a chance to knock. Vanillin oak, served in moderate volume, helps keep it all tied nicely together. Screw cap. 14.3% alc. **RATING** 91 **DRINK** 2023-2030 $25 CM ✪

Corriedale Cabernet Sauvignon 2021, Grampians It tastes of chocolate powder and boysenberry, blackcurrant and bay leaves. Technically it's medium in weight, but it sits on the lighter side of that marker. This wine's real appeal lies in its succulent, even-tempered flow. Screw cap. 14.5% alc. **RATING** 90 **DRINK** 2023-2028 $30 CM

Granite Hills ★★★★★

1481 Burke and Wills Track, Baynton, Vic 3444 **Region** Macedon Ranges **T** (03) 5423 7273 **www**.granitehills.com.au **Open** by appt **Winemaker** Llew Knight, Rowen Anstis **Viticulturist** Andrew Conforti **Est.** 1970 **Dozens** 5000 **Vyds** 11.5ha

Granite Hills is one of the enduring classics, having pioneered the successful growing of riesling and shiraz in an uncompromisingly cool climate. The vineyard includes riesling, chardonnay, shiraz, cabernet sauvignon, cabernet franc, merlot and pinot noir (the last also used in its sparkling wine). The rieslings age superbly, and the shiraz was the forerunner of the cool-climate school in Australia.

ΨΨΨΨΨ **Knight Riesling 2022, Macedon Ranges** Year in, year out, a cracking rizza. This is liquid synchronicity: wafts of citrus, juicy and tangy across the palate yet so even and pure, too. Wonderful texture and length. A wine to celebrate the end of a day no matter how it panned out because this will bring a smile and much joy. Screw cap. 13.5% alc. **RATING** 96 **DRINK** 2022-2032 $30 JF ✪

Knight Grüner Veltliner 2022, Macedon Ranges Spot-on aromas and flavours of honeysuckle, lemon blossom, camomile and beeswax. The palate fleshes out with some creaminess, neat phenolics and juicy acidity. Textural and delicious. Screw cap. 13.5% alc. **RATING** 95 **DRINK** 2022-2028 $30 JF ✪

Knight Chardonnay 2021, Macedon Ranges Whoosh! This takes off at breakneck speed thanks to a g-force of acidity that eventually slows down, allowing all the flavours to catch up. A lemon, lime and bitters tang, really citrusy and ultra-refreshing yet just a slip of texture. This will flesh out in time. Screw cap. 13% alc. **RATING** 95 **DRINK** 2023–2031 $40 JF ✪

The Gordon 2017, Macedon Ranges 80/10/10% cabernet sauvignon/ cabernet franc/merlot. Drinking perfectly with its cassis and currants, a hint of fruitcake mix, cigar box and cedary oak. The palate is beautifully modulated with ripe, pomace-like tannins and length. Screw cap. 14% alc. **RATING** 95 **DRINK** 2023–2030 $35 JF ✪

🍷🍷🍷🍷🍷 **Knight Gamay Noir 2021, Macedon Ranges** **RATING** 92 **DRINK** 2023–2030 $40 JF

Green Door Wines

1112 Henty Road, Henty, WA 6236 **Region** Geographe
T 0439 511 652 **www.greendoorwines.com.au** **Open** Thurs–Sun 11–4.30
Winemaker Ashley Keeffe, Vanessa Carson **Est.** 2007 **Dozens** 1200 **Vyds** 4ha
Ashley and Kathryn Keeffe purchased what was then a rundown vineyard in '06. With a combination of new and pre-existing vines, the vineyard includes fiano, mourvèdre, grenache, verdelho, tempranillo and shiraz. The wines are made in a small onsite winery using a range of winemaking methods, including the use of amphora pots.

🍷🍷🍷🍷🍷 **Amphora Monastrell 2021, Geographe** This wine somehow manages to combine presence with a lightness of touch. It's not thick or dense but its personality has a force to it. It's driven by red cherry, plum, strawberry and leather flavours – with clove, woodsmoke and cedar as highlights – but it has its own, dry, long-lasting magic. Screw cap. 14% alc. **RATING** 95 **DRINK** 2024–2030 $40 CM ✪

Fiano 2022, Geographe Beautiful, lively, bright-fruited flavour here. It has a pulpy aspect, almost always a good thing. Grapefruit and lemons, limes and florals. Intensity is of note, as is texture, without either being over the top. This is a fundamentally delicious wine to drink. Screw cap. 13.5% alc. **RATING** 94 **DRINK** 2023–2027 $28 CM ✪

🍷🍷🍷🍷🍷 **Amphora Tempranillo 2021, Geographe** **RATING** 93 **DRINK** 2023–2028 $40 CM

Greenock Creek Wines

450 Seppeltsfield Road, Marananga SA 5355 **Region** Barossa Valley
T (08) 8563 2898 **www.greenockcreekwines.com.au** **Open** 7 days 11–5
Winemaker Alex Peel, Peter Atyeo **Viticulturist** Peter Atyeo **Est.** 1984 **Dozens** 7000 **Vyds** 26ha
Founders Michael and Annabelle Waugh deliberately accumulated a series of old dryland, low-yielding Barossa vineyards back in the '70s, aiming to produce wines of unusual depth of flavour and character. They succeeded handsomely in this aim, achieving icon status and stratospheric prices in the US, making the opinions of Australian scribes irrelevant. The Waughs retired in '18 and the business was sold to a group headed by Sydney-based Jimmy Chen. Peter Atyeo stayed on as vineyard manager and winemaker, with Alex Peel (formerly Ross Estate and Yaldara) stepping in as senior winemaker. Older vineyards were remediated, new sites brought into the fold, and winemaking facilities updated.

🍷🍷🍷🍷🍷 **Roennfeldt Road Shiraz 2018, Barossa Valley** Shiraz sourced from 120yo vines. Concentration is always a leitmotif for this estate, but there is freshness and vitality, too, and that is what I dig. Super-ripe blackberry and black cherry fruits, fruitcake, espresso, prune juice, rum and raisin chocolate, roasting meats and licorice. Textured and velvety with compact chocolatey tannins. An altogether impressive wine. Cork. 14.5% alc. **RATING** 97 **DRINK** 2023–2040 $300 DB

🍷🍷🍷🍷🍷 **Fifteen Claims Shiraz 2020, Barossa Valley** Head-spinning concentration and latent power. It's like everything has been distilled down to its essence and squeezed into the bottle, such is the fruit purity and tannin architecture. Black fruits, layered spice, licorice and olive tapenade sheathed in dark chocolate and earth, finishing long and powerful with a spicy, cedary plume. Cork. 16% alc. RATING 96 DRINK 2023–2035 $120 DB

Creek Block Limited Release Shiraz 2020, Barossa Valley Some serious flexing of the shiraz muscles here with superb fruit intensity and density. Pure and opulent yet showing clarity and a vivid line despite its proportions. Cassis and macerated plums, layered spice, licorice, dark chocolate and earth. Tight, kinetic tannins and a toothsome finish that shows surprising balance for the level of horsepower within. Impressive stuff. Cork. 16% alc. RATING 96 DRINK 2023–2038 $200 DB

Roennfeldt Road Cabernet Sauvignon 2018, Barossa Valley An impressive beast showing remarkable freshness for the levels of concentration and fruit weight. Insanely opulent blackberry, blackcurrant and black cherry fruits, deeply layered spice, cedar, tobacco leaf, licorice, herbs, fruitcake and cassis. Everything is framed by ferrous tannins and bright acidity, and the finish shows great sustain, latent power and balance. Cork. 14.5% alc. RATING 96 DRINK 2023–2040 $300 DB ♥

Apricot Block Shiraz 2021, Barossa Valley The Apricot Block presents as one of the broodier offerings in the Greenock Creek quiver. Characters of blackberry and cherry, prune, brandied fruits and macerated plums cut with spice, dried citrus rind and earth with a fine, chocolatey tannin bite and a crème de cassis-like intensity to the fruit on the finish. Cork. 15% alc. RATING 95 DRINK 2023–2038 $60 DB ✪

Alices Shiraz 2021, Barossa Valley A quick blast of blackberry pastille gives way to opulent blackberry and cherry fruits with hints of baking spices, dark chocolate-dipped raspberries and pressed purple flowers. If you peer deep into the distance, there are some liminal leathery/mahogany notes, too, wrapping the ripe, long tannins in a warm embrace. As always, mighty impressive stuff. Cork. 15.5% alc. RATING 95 DRINK 2023–2038 $50 DB ✪

Cabernet Sauvignon 2021, Barossa Valley Nary a herbaceous note in sight, the wine presents a rolling swell of red and blackberry and cherry fruits, cut with spice and cedar along with hints of crème de cassis, roasting game and turned earth. Fine, toothsome tannins and a bright sapid line of acidity provide ample cadence and support, finishing long, spicy and awash in pure fruit. Cork. 14.5% alc. RATING 95 DRINK 2023–2025 $55 DB

Jaensch Block Shiraz 2020, Barossa Valley There's a little more compression in this wine, a little more width to the shoulders and less of a sleek cadence … more of a tubular swell of pure fruit. The fruity purity and opulence are classic Greenock Creek — all rich plum and berry fruits, cassis and kirsch, dredged with spice, cedary oak and earth. The tannins are different, too, fine, compact and clay-like. It's an impressive beast. Cork. 16% alc. RATING 95 DRINK 2023–2035 $60 DB

Seven Acre Shiraz 2020, Barossa Valley Deeply coloured with broody-edged characters of blackberry, black cherry and dark plum with hints of roasting meats, olive tapenade, cedar, vanilla, blueberry pie, fruitcake, ironstone, dark chocolate, licorice and violets. Toothsome and textured, compact in tannin with surprising vivacity and acid cadence, focusing and accelerating on the back palate before exiting with a rich, black-fruited roostertail. Woah! Cork. 15.5% alc. RATING 95 DRINK 2023–2035 $70 DB

Block 3 Shiraz 2021, Barossa Valley Deep magenta, the aromatic profile swells with ripe blackberry, mulberry and boysenberry fruits cut through with hints of baking spices, chocolate bullets, purple floral top notes, earth, mocha and licorice. The fruit on the palate is opulent and shows a dusting of frangipani before it rises with thick, powdery tannin heft and an impressively concentrated finish. Cork. 15.5% alc. RATING 94 DRINK 2023–2033 $50 DB

ⵛⵛⵛⵛⵛ **High Ridge Cabernet Sauvignon 2021**, Barossa Valley RATING 93 DRINK 2023–2033 $45 DB

Durif 2021, Barossa Valley RATING 93 DRINK 2023–2030 $30 DB ✪

Mataro 2021, Barossa Valley RATING 93 DRINK 2023–2027 $40 DB
Poplar Holme Shiraz 2020, Barossa Valley RATING 93 DRINK 2023–2030
$45 DB
Cornerstone Grenache 2022, Barossa Valley RATING 92 DRINK 2023–2030
$40 DB
Grenache 2022, Barossa Valley RATING 92 DRINK 2023–2028 $30 DB ✪
Casey's Block Shiraz 2021, Barossa Valley RATING 92 DRINK 2023–2033
$38 DB
Four Cuttings Cabernet Sauvignon 2020, Barossa Valley RATING 92
DRINK 2023–2029 $45 DB
Stone Block Shiraz 2020, Barossa Valley RATING 92 DRINK 2023–2030
$45 DB
Shiraz 2020, Barossa Valley RATING 91 DRINK 2023–2027 $35 DB

GREENWAY Wines

350 Wollombi Road, Broke, NSW 2330 **Region** Hunter Valley
T 0418 164 382 www.greenwaywines.com.au **Open** Fri 11–3, Sat 11–4, Sun 11–3 or
by appt **Winemaker** Daniel Binet **Viticulturist** Neil Grosser **Est.** 2009 **Dozens** 650
Vyds 6.5ha
GREENWAY Wines is a small family-run business and the passion project of architect Anne
Greenway. The sustainably managed vineyard is nestled against Wollombi Brook near Broke.
Small quantities of single-vineyard estate wines are produced only in the best vintages.

🍷🍷🍷🍷 Arté Grigio 2022, Hunter Valley Complexity was achieved via extended skin
contact and 10% barrel fermentation, announced by its russet salmon pink hue.
Love it or hate it, food for lengthy discussion. Screw cap. 12% alc. RATING 90
DRINK 2023–2026 $30 JH

Grey-Smith Wines

8 Helen Street, Coonawarra, SA 5263 **Region** Coonawarra
T 0429 499 355 www.grey-smith.com.au **Open** By appt **Winemaker** Ulrich Grey-
Smith **Viticulturist** Paul Chiesa **Est.** 2012 **Dozens** 250
Ulrich Grey-Smith travelled wine roads near and far before establishing his eponymous
business. The original foundation for this career was the completion of the bachelor's degree
in oenology at Roseworthy Agricultural College ('87–90). His business goes well beyond
the small amount of sparkling wine he makes, to all sides of making and selling wine. Ulrich
works as a consultant, as a freelance winemaker, and for many years was executive officer and
secretary of the Limestone Coast Grape & Wine Council Inc.

🍷🍷🍷🍷 Chardonnay 2018, Mount Gambier It tastes of peaches and cedar, and it
tastes good. It's a full-bodied style with steel and citrus flavours driving through
a world of sunny, ripe stone fruit. Indeed it's remarkable, given the low alcohol
reading, just how much flavour there is here, though the cut of citrus helps keep it
running appreciably out through the finish, too. Screw cap. 12.1% alc. RATING 92
DRINK 2023–2028 $30 CM ✪
Blanc de Blancs NV, Mount Gambier From the 2016 vintage, but no vintage
on the label. Five years on lees and zero dosage. Flamboyant on the nose and then
steely and dry on the palate. All manner of lees, apple, grapefruit and stone fruit
aromas mixed in with stone and wood, though the palate is then severe in its dry,
unyielding presentation. It's easy to suspect that the best years of this wine are
many years hence. Crown. 12% alc. RATING 90 $50 CM

Groom

28 Langmeil Road, Tanunda, SA 5352 (postal) **Region** Barossa Valley
T (08) 8563 1101 www.groomwines.com **Open** Not **Winemaker** Daryl Groom, Lisa
Groom, Jeanette Marschall **Est.** 1997 **Dozens** 2000 **Vyds** 27.8ha

The full name of the business is Marschall Groom Cellars, a venture established by David and Jeanette Marschall and Daryl and Lisa Groom. Daryl was a highly regarded winemaker at Penfolds before he moved to Geyser Peak in California. Years of discussion between the families resulted in the purchase of a 35ha block of bare land adjacent to Penfolds' 130yo Kalimna vineyard. Shiraz was planted in '97, followed by the purchase of an 8ha sauvignon blanc vineyard in the Adelaide Hills. In '00, 3.2ha of zinfandel was planted on the Kalimna Bush Block.

ŸŸŸŸŸ **Shiraz 2021, Barossa Valley** Deep crimson with notes of blackberry jam, plums and boysenberry with hints of licorice, rum and raisin chocolate, clove, cedar, vanilla and punchy oak. The rich fruit shines through with increased volume on the palate, still with a sheen of cedar and pipe tobacco, before slowly fading with tones of spice, crème de cassis and chocolate, tight compact tannins giving shape. Cork. 14.5% alc. **RATING** 95 **DRINK** 2023-2033 $50 DB ✿

Bush Block Zinfandel 2021, Barossa Valley Deep, saturated crimson in the glass with aromas of deep, dark baking spices, blackberry jam, macerated black cherries, rum and raisin chocolate, sarsaparilla, brandied fruit and mince pies. Big, mouth-filling and bold but wonderfully balanced with chocolatey tannins, no shortage of spice and a swell of deep, black-fruited texture as it trails off leaving a wake of spice. Cork. 14.5% alc. **RATING** 95 **DRINK** 2023-2029 $30 DB ✿

ŸŸŸŸŸ **Sauvignon Blanc 2022, Adelaide Hills** **RATING** 90 **DRINK** 2023-2025 $24 DB ✿

Grosset ★★★★★

King Street, Auburn, SA 5451 **Region** Clare Valley
T 1800 088 223 **www**.grosset.com.au **Open** 10–5 Wed–Sun (Spring)
Winemaker Jeffrey Grosset, Brent Treloar **Est.** 1981 **Dozens** 9500 **Vyds** 21ha
Jeffrey Grosset wears the unchallenged mantle of Australia's foremost riesling maker. Grosset's pre-eminence is recognised both domestically and internationally; however, he merits equal recognition for the other wines in his portfolio: chardonnay and pinot noir from the Adelaide Hills and Gaia, a bordeaux blend from the Clare Valley; Apiana Fiano and Nereus, a shiraz-based wine wih a touch of nero d'Avola. Jeffrey's quietly spoken manner conceals a steely will. Four estate-owned vineyards in the Clare Valley are certified organic and biodynamic.

ŸŸŸŸŸ **Piccadilly Chardonnay 2021, Adelaide Hills** Pale quartz-green. Grosset's oenological mastery comes down to 3 words: purity, balance and length. The late wine writer Tony Keys' approach was, 'When I taste a wine from a well-regarded winery I start with the maximum score (of 10) and deduct 0.1 for each fault.' He would have given this wine the maximum. I'm almost there. Screw cap. 13.5% alc. **RATING** 97 **DRINK** 2023-2040 $75 JH ✿

ŸŸŸŸŸ **G110 2022, Clare Valley** Great energy, chalky pucker and a strong sense of minerality. Tightly wound, strong with lime juice, green apple tang and pink grapefruit zestiness all bound with saline and talc-like crunch and chew. Aromatics are a little scarce at present, but it will open up gloriously. It leaves a little residual nuttiness/yeastiness with each sip and is pleasing in its faint savouriness. Screw cap. 12.9% alc. **RATING** 96 **DRINK** 2023-2040 $135 MB

Springvale Riesling 2022, Clare Valley A high-tension, fragrant Springvale release. Bright, floral perfume of lime blossom, ozone, blackcurrant and green apple. A strong spectrum of citrus flavours are the currency here: lemon, lime and a squirt of pulpy grapefruit zing with a faintly yeasty, almond-like character to finish. Quiet complexity and vitality are writ large here. Excellent. Screw cap. 12.9% alc. **RATING** 95 **DRINK** 2022-2040 $51 MB

Polish Hill Riesling 2022, Clare Valley As always, an intense and concentrated expression of Clare Valley riesling. Powerful scents of mixed citrus peel, lime essence, lemongrass and ozone with faint, exotic spice and blackberry characters in the mix. The palate delivers a juiciness, brightness of flavour and a little powdery grip to finish. A couple of years' grace would yield additional enjoyment. Screw cap. 12.9% alc. **RATING** 95 **DRINK** 2024-2040 $75 MB

Alea Riesling 2022, Clare Valley A moreish, off-dry riesling with pitch-perfect sweetness and acidity, mouth-watering and fresh in its feel. Scents of green apple, makrut lime leaf and lemon lozenges. Flavours combine with the crunch and sweetness of green apple with a good squeeze of tangy lime juice. Gentle fruit sweetness is abetted by cool, briny, lemony acidity. Ultra appealing and yet with a sense of detail and minerally complexity. An outstanding release. Screw cap. 12.5% alc. **RATING** 95 **DRINK** 2022-2035 $45 MB

Gaia 2020, Clare Valley A wine of great density and energy with requisite tannin, acidity, lavish fruit and spice detail. Aromas of dark plum, mahogany, exotic spice, dried herbs and anise. Flavours set between that dark fruit character and woody elements, more dried herbs and a gravelly minerality. It extends beautifully and long, rippling with fine tannin and tightening in a satisfying way. A wine that unfurls well now, with time, but cellaring will reward likewise. Screw cap. 14% alc. **RATING** 95 **DRINK** 2023-2040 $100 MB ❤

ⵉⵉⵉⵉⵉ **Apiana 2022, Clare Valley RATING** 93 **DRINK** 2022-2029 $51 MB
Nereus 2021, Clare Valley RATING 93 **DRINK** 2023-2027 $52 MB

Grounded Cru ★★★★★

49 Ingoldby Road, McLaren Flat, SA 5052 **Region** McLaren Vale
T 0438 897 738 **www**.groundedcru.com.au **Open** By appt **Winemaker** Geoff Thompson, Matt Jackman **Viticulturist** Geoff Thompson, Matt Jackman **Est.** 2015 **Dozens** 18 000

Grounded Cru draws fruit from high-quality vineyards in McLaren Vale, Langhorne Creek and the Adelaide Hills, regions that maker Geoff Thompson believes 'talk to each other' due to a complementary patina of mesoclimates, soil types, rainfall, altitude and varying degrees of maritime influence. Thompson was formerly chief winemaker at McPherson Wines in Nagambie. Conversely, his approach at Grounded Cru is one that seeks textural intrigue over obvious fruit, with European styling melded to Australian generosity.

ⵉⵉⵉⵉⵉ **Cru Grenache 2021, McLaren Vale** This is deft winemaking under a banner of regional fealty, natural freshness and high-quality fruit. Scented gloriously with persimmon, red cherry, kirsch and exuberant florals, this is a stunning grenache, transparent, succulent and mid-weighted of feel, auguring so well for future cuvées as the shapeshifting of a relatively new address takes place. Screw cap. 14.2% alc. **RATING** 95 **DRINK** 2022-2027 $30 NG ✪

Cru Shiraz 2021, McLaren Vale Violets, smoked meats, dried nori and pepper grind, all neatly compressed into a vortex of tension and freshness by well-placed oak and deft reductive handling. A lovely wine, finishing as plush as it is vibrant. Screw cap. 14.9% alc. **RATING** 95 **DRINK** 2022-2032 $30 NG ✪

Inc Cabernet Sauvignon 2020, McLaren Vale There is something about McLaren Vale cabernet that transcends typecasts, delivering wines of considerable force, albeit with tannic fortitude and sea-salty restraint. Miraculously, these confluences serve a sense of savouriness and moreish delivery: sage, bay leaf, anise, tea tree, blackcurrant and a long smear of tapenade across the impressive finish. Screw cap. 14.5% alc. **RATING** 95 **DRINK** 2022-2035 $55 NG

Cru GSM 2021, McLaren Vale A fine Rhône-inspired blend. The result is a potpourri of red and darker fruit allusions and a mandala of textural weaves. Spiced berries, pepper-crusted charcuterie, iodine and a ferrous girth of finely wrought tannins, assertive but nothing to stultify the density and pulse of this lovely wine. Richness and tension, all at once. Great GSM. Screw cap. 14.7% alc. **RATING** 94 **DRINK** 2022-2030 $30 NG ✪

Inc Shiraz 2020, McLaren Vale This is a traditional Australian idiom rendered with an incantation of class and tension. Saturated blue and black fruits, a good smear of anise, a waft of menthol, an asado of assorted meats and a thick fibre

of dutiful freshness and gritty tannin running long across a full-chested girth.
Screw cap. 14.9% alc. RATING 94 DRINK 2022-2035 $55 NG

♈♈♈♈♈ Cru Pinot Gris 2022, Adelaide Hills RATING 93 DRINK 2022-2025
$26 NG ✪
Cru Sauvignon Blanc 2022, Adelaide Hills RATING 92 DRINK 2022-2025
$26 NG ✪
Cru Grenache Rosé 2022, McLaren Vale RATING 91 DRINK 2022-2023
$26 NG ✪

Grove Estate Wines   ★★★★

4100 Murringo Road, Young, NSW 2594 **Region** Hilltops
T (02) 6382 6999 **www.groveestate.com.au Open** 7 days 9–4.30 **Winemaker** Brian
Mullany, Tim Kirk, Bryan Martin **Est.** 1989 **Dozens** 4000 **Vyds** 100ha
Grove Estate vineyard was re-established in '89 by Brian and Suellen Mullany on the site
where grapes were first planted in Lambing Flat in 1861 by Croatian settlers who brought
vine cuttings with them from Dalmatia. Further plantings in '98 were made on their Bit
O' Heaven vineyard, the 2 sites with vastly different soils. One of the original pickers' huts
has been refurbished as the cellar door. The wines are made at Clonakilla by Tim Kirk and
Bryan Martin.

♈♈♈♈♈ The Italian Sangiovese Barbera Sagrantino Nebbiolo 2022, Hilltops
It does work. Intense sweet fruit and woodsy spices, cherry pips and cardamom.
A drink-now style and you'd be happy you did. Screw cap. 13.5% alc. RATING 91
DRINK 2022-2025 $28 JF ✪
Tempranillo 2021, Hilltops While this has lovely cherry and redcurrant
flavours, it's savoury, tangy and tart. Mouth-watering, even. There are some meaty
reduction adds and those distinct temp tannins appear out of nowhere all stealth-
like. Yet definitely a joven style. Screw cap. 13% alc. RATING 91 DRINK 2022-2028
$28 JF ✪
Think Outside The Circle Fiano 2022, Hilltops Don't chill this down too
much because it's a textural style and it needs to unfurl in the glass. While acidity
weaves in and out, this is full of creamed honey, poached pears and honeysuckle.
Screw cap. 12.5% alc. RATING 90 DRINK 2022-2025 $25 JF ✪
Think Outside The Circle Innocence Viognier 2022, Hilltops For a
viognier, this is restrained and almost tight – unheard of! Still, there's a bit of
gold colour and texture with some phenolic pull to the finish. In between,
some apricot kernels, dried pears and spiced preserved lemon; overall rather
savoury. It's an unusual style and appealing. Screw cap. 12.5% alc. RATING 90
DRINK 2022-2025 $22 JF ✪
Al Dente Rosé Nebbiolo Cabernet Sauvignon 2022, Hilltops An attractive
pastel cherry hue and fragrant with flavours of rosehip, hibiscus infusion and cassis
plus strawberries and cream. The palate is refreshing thanks to the acidity and
there's a slip of texture, too. Screw cap. 12.5% alc. RATING 90 DRINK 2022-2024
$25 JF ✪
The Cellar Block Shiraz 2021, Hilltops Packed with juicy and sweet fruit
doused in pepper and cedary oak. It's a bit intense at first with plenty of tannins,
all ripe and shapely working off a full-bodied palate. Some grip on the finish
yet bright, so bright I almost need sunglasses to taste this. Screw cap. 14.5% alc.
RATING 90 DRINK 2024-2034 $40 JF

Gundog Estate   ★★★★★

101 McDonalds Road, Pokolbin, NSW 2320 **Region** Hunter Valley
T (02) 4998 6873 **www.gundogestate.com.au Open** 7 days 10–5 **Winemaker** Matt
Burton **Est.** 2010 **Dozens** 7000 **Vyds** 5ha
Matt Burton makes 4 different Hunter semillons and shiraz from the Hunter Valley,
Murrumbateman and Hilltops, primarily purchased from other growers. The cellar door is

located in the historic Pokolbin schoolhouse. Matt also collaborates with Dylan McMahon of Seville Estate on a Yarra Valley range, Burton McMahon (see separate entry). A second Gundog cellar door can be found at 42 Cork Street, Gundaroo.

ŸŸŸŸŸ The Chase Semillon 2022, Hunter Valley The length and juicy persistence of this wine are very impressive. It glides across the mouth, the finish brooking no downside, the finesse and balance both remarkable. Screw cap. 11% alc. RATING 95 DRINK 2023-2032 $40 JH ✪

Rare Game Shiraz 2021, Hunter Valley Don't be deceived by the relatively light, clear colour. The bouquet is expressive and complex, the palate vibrant and clearly delineated. The juicy red fruits are set against perfectly weighted tannins, all framed by gently savoury tannins. The sheer balance makes it easy to drink without any introspection and overlooks the quality – and longevity. Screw cap. 13% alc. RATING 95 DRINK 2023-2043 $80 JH

Wild Semillon 2022, Hunter Valley An off-dry finish, the low-level sweetness reflects the stopping of the ferment, the phenolics derived from skins. Defies its elegance and freshness, yet Matt Burton came up with the answers. Screw cap. 11.5% alc. RATING 94 DRINK 2023-2027 $40 JH ✪

Smoking Barrel Red 2021, Hilltops Hunter Valley 'This is one of our most popular wines,' says Gundog Estate, and it's not hard to see why, with both quality and price on the money. The colour, presumably thanks to the Hilltops contribution, is bright and deep, the palate rich and layered with ripe plum and cherry fruit. Screw cap. 13.5% alc. RATING 94 DRINK 2023-2028 $35 JH ✪

ŸŸŸŸ♀ Hunter's Semillon 2022, Hunter Valley RATING 93 DRINK 2023-2029 $30 JH ✪

Hunter's Shiraz 2021, Hunter Valley RATING 92 DRINK 2025-2036 $45 JH

Haan Estate ★★★★

148 Siegersdorf Road, Tanunda, SA 5352 (postal) **Region** Barossa Valley
T 0412 804 824 **www.**haanestate.com.au **Open** Not **Winemaker** Jo Irvine **Est.** 1993
Dozens 5000 **Vyds** 16.3ha
Established in 1993 by the Haan Family, Haan Estate is enjoying a revival under the direction of George Zaal and associate Mingrong Meng of Shanghai. The estate vineyard is planted to shiraz (5.3ha), merlot (3.4ha), cabernet sauvignon (3ha), viognier (2.4ha), cabernet franc (1ha) and malbec, petit verdot and semillon (0.4ha each). Oak use is determined by the vintage and the wines are matured for up to 24 months in new and used barrels and puncheons. The oak undoubtedly plays a role in the shaping of the style of the Haan wines, but it is perfectly integrated and the wines have the fruit weight to carry the oak.

ŸŸŸŸ♀ Wilhelmus 2020, Barossa Valley Cabernet sauvignon/merlot/cabernet franc/malbec/petit verdot. Deep crimson with rich blackberry, blackcurrant and red cherry fruits sheathed in baking spices, violets, cedar, tobacco leaf, polished leather, cassis, sage and licorice. Plenty of fruit weight with red-fruit high tones on the palate, spicy oak and grainy tannin grip. A little bit of heat shows through on the long, powerful finish. Cork. 15% alc. RATING 93 DRINK 2023-2033 $65 DB

Merlot Cabernet Franc 2018, Barossa Valley Cabernet franc plays its part here, opening up the aromatic profile and providing some light, leafy high tones to the deep, plummy fruit of the merlot. There is a thick bed of oak spice and hints of red cherry, polished leather, citrus blossom, licorice and mocha, too, framed by chalky tannins and just a scattering of herbs on the exit. Screw cap. 15% alc. RATING 93 DRINK 2023-2028 $25 DB ✪

Estate Shiraz Viognier 2018, Barossa Valley Deep crimson with vibrant aromas of satsuma plum, blueberry and boysenberry along with hints of baking spices, licorice, purple flowers and spicy oak. The fruit on the palate is pure and true with powdery tannins in support and a deep fan of ripe fruit and spice on the finish. Screw cap. 15% alc. RATING 92 DRINK 2023-2028 $25 DB ✪

Shiraz Cabernet Sauvignon 2018, Barossa Valley Deep, bright crimson with vibrant blackberry, black cherry and blackcurrant fruits studded with baking spices, licorice, dark chocolate, cherry clafoutis and earth. Well weighted with a light wash of scattered herbs, oak spice and a hint of pressed flowers on the finish, which shows dense, chalky tannin grip and a medium length. Screw cap. 15.5% alc. **RATING** 91 **DRINK** 2023–2028 $25 DB ✪

Haddow + Dineen ★★★★☆

c/- Bruny Island Cheese Co, 1807 Bruny Island Main Road, Great Bay, Tas 7150 (postal)
Region Tasmania
T 0412 478 841 **www**.haddowanddineen.com.au **Open** Not **Winemaker** Jeremy Dineen and Nick Haddow **Est.** 2017 **Dozens** 800 **Vyds** 2.6ha
This is a collaborative winemaking project involving winemaker Jeremy Dineen and cheesemaker Nick Haddow. Jeremy was chief winemaker at Josef Chromy from '05 to '20, his knowledge and skill self-evident. Nick Haddow is a cheesemaker and author with a string of awards to his name, but is perhaps best known now for his culinary crusading on SBS' *Gourmet Farmer*. Haddow + Dineen sources from a single vineyard at the mouth of the Tamar River on white quartz gravel. Their wines have no additions other than a small amount of SO₂, and are not fined or filtered.

🍷🍷🍷🍷🍷 **Private Universe Pinot Noir 2021, Tasmania** A superb pinot noir awash with dark cherry and macerated wild-strawberry fruit notes undercut with hints of amaro herbs, fine spice, game meats, chinotto, shiitake broth and earth. The aromas transpose neatly onto the palate, which is harmonious and detailed with wonderful fruit purity, deep spice and a bright acid pulse finishing long and decidedly moreish. Lovely stuff. Screw cap. 13.2% alc. **RATING** 95 **DRINK** 2023–2028 $55 DB

Crows Descended 2021, Tasmania Tasmanian shiraz is a rare beast. Blow me down if it isn't lovely. Awash with red and dark plummy fruits on a bed of spice, dots of cream and roasting meats, purple floral notes and just a sprinkle of pepper. Tight, fine tannins and racy acidity wrap up a lovely inaugural release. Screw cap. 13.5% alc. **RATING** 94 **DRINK** 2023–2030 $55 DB

Hahndorf Hill Winery ★★★★★

38 Pain Road, Hahndorf, SA 5245 **Region** Adelaide Hills
T (08) 8388 7512 **www**.hahndorfhillwinery.com.au **Open** Mon–Sat 10–5
Winemaker Larry Jacobs **Viticulturist** Larry Jacobs **Est.** 2002 **Dozens** 8000 **Vyds** 6.5ha
Larry Jacobs and Marc Dobson purchased Hahndorf Hill Winery in '02. Larry and Marc established the near-iconic Mulderbosch Wines in '88. It was purchased at the end of '96 and the pair eventually found their way to Australia and Hahndorf Hill. Now a specialist in Austrian varieties, they have imported 6 clones of grüner veltliner and 2 clones of st laurent into Australia and also produce blaufränkisch and zweigelt.

🍷🍷🍷🍷🍷 **GRU Grüner Veltliner 2022, Adelaide Hills** A very complex wine with 3 very different vinification pathways. Some crushed with skin contact and cultured yeast; some crushed and full solids, juice wild fermented in old barriques; and a 3rd parcel cool-fermented in stainless steel with cultured yeast, then matured in oak large and small. The final blended wine has a distinct swish of perfume and cinnamon spice on the bouquet; the palate is mouth-filling to begin, but then swells aromatically to the finish and lingering aftertaste. Screw cap. 13% alc. **RATING** 96 **DRINK** 2023–2033 $32 JH ✪

Green Angel Late Harvest Grüner Veltliner 2021, Adelaide Hills This has 131g/L of RS. Its green-gold colour is the starting point, blanched almond and stone fruit take the stage next, with incipient honey close by and Meyer lemon-tinged acidity to close. Will be very long-lived. Screw cap. 10.5% alc. **RATING** 95 **DRINK** 2023–2036 $35 JH ✪ ♥

White Mischief Grüner Veltliner 2022, Adelaide Hills Tropical fruits play a role in the complex, gently honeyed flavours, with juicy acidity just when and where it's needed. Screw cap. 13.5% alc. **RATING** 94 **DRINK** 2023–2032 $25 JH
Brother Nature Field Blend 2022, Adelaide Hills Hahndorf Hill's first field blend was 7 years in the making. In descending order: hárslevelü/pinot blanc/welschriesling/riesling/savagnin/grüner veltliner/chenin blanc/chardonnay/sauvignon blanc/muscat blanc/gewürztraminer/muscadelle. The bouquet's perfume floats airily out of the glass, spice to the fore, and the palate does indeed have cleansing acidity. Screw cap. 12% alc. **RATING** 94 **DRINK** 2023–2032 $39 JH ✪

🍷🍷🍷🍷 **The Foundling Saint Laurent 2020, Adelaide Hills RATING** 93 **DRINK** 2023–2040 $65 JH

Hamelin Bay Wines   ★★★☆
McDonald Road, Karridale, WA 6288 **Region** Margaret River
T 0417 954 168 **www.**hbwines.com.au **Open** 7 days 10.30–4.30 **Winemaker** Andrew Pruyn **Viticulturist** Dean Fairey **Est.** 1992 **Dozens** 5000 **Vyds** 23.5ha
The Hamelin Bay vineyard was established by the Drake-Brockman family, pioneers of the region. Richard Drake-Brockman's great-grandmother, Grace Bussell, was famous for her courage when, in 1876, aged 16, she rescued survivors of a shipwreck not far from the mouth of the Margaret River. Richard's great-grandfather Frederick, known for his exploration of the Kimberley, read about the feat in Perth's press and rode 300km on horseback to meet her – they married in 1882. Hamelin Bay's vineyard and winery is located within a few kms of Karridale, which were named in honour of these pioneering families.

🍷🍷🍷🍷 **Five Ashes Vineyard Sauvignon Blanc 2022, Margaret River**
Quintessential stuff here. Big perfume of green herbs, cut grass and passionfruit. Grass and passionfruit on the palate too, but with lemony acidity and a talc-like minerally vein. Well balanced. It's fresh as, bright as, a vibrant expression of the variety. Tight and racy. Drink in its summery youth. Screw cap. 13.5% alc. **RATING** 90 **DRINK** 2022–2024 $26 MB

Handpicked Wines   ★★★★★
50 Kensington Street, Chippendale, NSW 2008 **Region** Various
T (03) 5983 0039 **www.**handpickedwines.com.au **Open** Mon–Fri 11–10, w'ends 10–10
Winemaker Peter Dillon, Rohan Smith **Est.** 2001 **Dozens** 100 000 **Vyds** 83ha
Handpicked Wines is a multi-regional business with a flagship vineyard and winery on the Mornington Peninsula and vineyards in the Yarra Valley, Barossa Valley and Tasmania. They also make wines from many of Australia's leading fine wine regions. Five of Handpicked's vineyards focus on high-quality pinot noir and chardonnay – 2 in Tasmania's Tamar Valley, Capella vineyard in the Mornington Peninsula and 2 in the Yarra Valley, including Wombat Creek in the Upper Yarra, the highest elevation vineyard in the valley. Director of winemaking Peter Dillon travels extensively to oversee quality throughout the regions; he and assistant winemaker Rohan Smith work closely with a team of viticulturists who manage the vineyards. There is a second cellar door at 80 Collins Street, Melbourne.

🍷🍷🍷🍷🍷 **Capella Vineyard Pinot Noir 2021, Mornington Peninsula** Plenty of juicy fruit leading the way. Very tangy and succulent thanks to refreshing acidity yet you'll find fine tannins and the savoury/smoky tones of the oak adding to the depth and texture across the lighter-framed palate. The finish is long and pure. Captivating. Screw cap. 12% alc. **RATING** 95 **DRINK** 2023–2031 $95 JF
Highbow Hill Vineyard Chardonnay 2021, Yarra Valley Well hello, Highbrow Hill. You're putting on the charm with this complete wine. Lemon zest and juice, white stone fruit, cedary, spicy oak, a little smoky, a little flinty and those moreish sulphides add to the savoury profile. Brimming with energising acidity ensuring a lingering and long finish. Terrific. Screw cap. 12.4% alc. **RATING** 95 **DRINK** 2022–2031 $70 JF

Collection Chardonnay 2021, Tasmania Supercharged flavours of grapefruit, lemon and white stone fruit yet very much in the savoury spectrum and held together by gossamer-like acidity. There's succulence and restraint on the palate with some funky, flinty flavour, fine creamy lees and woodsy spices adding more detail. Screw cap. 12.2% alc. RATING 95 DRINK 2023–2031 $50 JF ✪

Auburn Road Vineyard Pinot Noir 2021, Tasmania A lovely garnet hue to start, heady aromas of florals and spice then an explosion of flavour on the full-bodied palate. Dark cherries, squishy raspberries, fine oak spice, orange peel and rhubarb combine as one complex flavour profile. Tannins are firm and acidity refreshing. Screw cap. 12.8% alc. RATING 95 DRINK 2023–2034 $90 JF

Highbow Hill Vineyard Pinot Noir 2021, Yarra Valley While it doesn't have its usual power, this remains finely tuned, expressive and lovely. Cherries and rhubarb, mint and Asian five-spice, cedary oak and savoury inflections. Screw cap. 13.3% alc. RATING 95 DRINK 2023–2033 $90 JF

Collection Pinot Noir 2021, Yarra Valley A bit more complexity and this would be something else. It's still lovely, gently fruited, lightly spiced, with fine tannins and refreshing acidity that ensures the finish lingers. Screw cap. 12.8% alc. RATING 94 DRINK 2023–2031 $60 JF

🍷🍷🍷🍷🍷 **Wombat Creek Vineyard Chardonnay 2021, Yarra Valley** RATING 93 DRINK 2023–2030 $70 JF

Wombat Creek Vineyard Pinot Noir 2021, Yarra Valley RATING 93 DRINK 2023–2031 $90 JF

Collection Chardonnay 2021, Yarra Valley RATING 93 DRINK 2022–2031 $50 JF

Collection Chardonnay 2021, Mornington Peninsula RATING 92 DRINK 2022–2030 $50 JF

Collection Pinot Noir 2021, Mornington Peninsula RATING 91 DRINK 2023–2031 $60 JF

Collection Pinot Noir 2021, Tasmania RATING 91 DRINK 2024–2034 $60 JF

Capella Vineyard Chardonnay 2021, Mornington Peninsula RATING 91 DRINK 2023–2031 $70 JF

Regional Selections Shiraz 2021, McLaren Vale RATING 90 DRINK 2023–2029 $29 JF

Hanging Rock Winery   ★★★★☆

88 Jim Road, Newham, Vic 3442 **Region** Macedon Ranges
T (03) 5427 0542 **www.**hangingrock.com.au **Open** 7 days 10–5 **Winemaker** Robert Ellis **Est.** 1983 **Dozens** 20 000 **Vyds** 14.5ha
The Macedon area has proved marginal in spots and the Hanging Rock vineyards, with their lovely vista towards the rock, are no exception. Founder John Ellis thus elected to source additional grapes from various parts of Victoria to produce an interesting and diverse range of varietals at different pricepoints. John's children Ruth and Robert are integral to the business today; Robert has an oenology degree from the University of Adelaide, after that working as a Flying Winemaker in Champagne, Burgundy, Oregon and Stellenbosch and Ruth has a degree in wine marketing from the University of Adelaide.

🍷🍷🍷🍷🍷 **Jim Jim Pinot Noir 2020, Macedon Ranges** It's not a big wine but there's plenty of flavour punch. Poached rhubarb with black pepper and turmeric, macerated sweet cherries doused in baking spices with slips of cedary oak and tangy acidity. It highlights the cool-climate credentials of the high vineyard with some alpine herbs and a fineness throughout. Lovely drink. Screw cap. 13% alc. RATING 94 DRINK 2022–2033 $60 JF

🍷🍷🍷🍷🍷 **Kindred Riesling 2022, Strathbogie Ranges** RATING 93 DRINK 2023–2030 $28 JP ✪

Jim Jim Sauvignon Blanc 2022, Macedon Ranges RATING 93 DRINK 2022–2028 $35 JF ✪

The Jim Jim Three 2022, Macedon Ranges RATING 93 DRINK 2022-2028 $35 JF ✪
JSE Members Reserve Shiraz 2020, Heathcote RATING 93 DRINK 2023-2032 $50 JP
Pinot Noir 2021, Macedon Ranges RATING 91 DRINK 2022-2026 $35 JF
Brut Cuvée XVIII NV, Macedon Ranges RATING 90 $50 JF
Jim Jim Chardonnay 2021, Macedon Ranges RATING 90 DRINK 2023-2030 $50 JF

Harcourt Valley Vineyards ★★★☆

3339 Calder Highway, Harcourt, Vic 3453 **Region** Bendigo
T (03) 5474 2223 **www**.harcourtvalley.com.au **Open** Sun 12–4 **Winemaker** Quinn Livingstone **Viticulturist** Quinn Livingstone **Est.** 1976 **Dozens** 2000 **Vyds** 4ha
Harcourt Valley Vineyards was planted in 1976. It has the oldest planting of vines in the Harcourt Valley. Quinn Livingstone (2nd-generation winemaker) is making a number of small-batch wines. Minimal fruit handling is used in the winemaking process. The tasting area overlooks the vines, with a large window that allows visitors to see the activity in the winery.

ⵧⵧⵧⵧⵧ **Rosé 2022, Heathcote** This malbec/cab franc blend brings gentle musk confection notes and ginger spice together with summery berry and cherry fruits, to produce one delicious, lively rosé. Acidity keeps the right side of approachable. Drink young to enjoy the vibrancy and life. Screw cap. 11.6% alc. **RATING** 91 **DRINK** 2022-2025 $20 JP ✪

Hardys ★★★★★

202 Main Road, McLaren Vale, SA 5171 **Region** McLaren Vale
T (08) 8329 4124 **www**.hardyswines.com **Open** Sun–Fri 11–4, Sat 10–4
Winemaker Helen McCarthy **Viticulturist** Adam Steer **Est.** 1853
This 170+yo brand is part of the Accolade Wines group. The eponymous Eileen Hardy label is named for matriarch Eileen Hardy OBE; the inaugural Eileen Hardy Shiraz was released in '73 in honour of her 80th birthday. In line with the enormous scale of production, grapes are sourced from around Australia. The cellar door houses a museum that traces the history of the brand through stories and old winemaking equipment.

ⵧⵧⵧⵧⵧ **The Eight (VIII) Cabernet Shiraz 2016, Frankland River McLaren Vale Coonawarra** An elegant wine with pure, detailed blackberry and plum notes supported by layered spice, dark chocolate, black pepper, earth and softly spoken cedar tones. There's an air of grace across the palate with balanced, cascading ripe tannins and supple-yet-savoury form from ripe fruit and a finish that lingers wonderfully. Screw cap. 14.4% alc. **RATING** 96 **DRINK** 2021-2045 $250 DB
Eileen Hardy Chardonnay 2021, Tasmania Pale straw in the glass with pristine aromas of white peach, nectarine, lemon and grapefruit with hints of cashew-like oak, almond, white flowers, roasting nuts and gentle, spicy oak. Showing excellent tension, texture and drive, the aromas transpose neatly onto the palate, which lingers persistently with pristine stone and citrus fruits framed by tight acidity and nicely judged French-oak nuance. Screw cap. 13.5% alc. **RATING** 95 **DRINK** 2023-2030 $130 DB
Eileen Hardy Pinot Noir 2021, Tasmania Dreamy, creamy oak flits above bright red cherry fruits with underlying notes of fine spice, forest floor and mushroom broth. Very much an acid-driven wine with a fine structure and sapid exit that tends to savoury with time in the mouth. Diam. 13% alc. **RATING** 94 **DRINK** 2022-2028 $135 DB

ⵧⵧⵧⵧⵧ **Eileen Hardy Shiraz 2020, McLaren Vale** RATING 93 DRINK 2025-2040 $153 NG
HRB Chardonnay 2021, Yarra Valley Margaret River Pemberton RATING 92 DRINK 2023-2025 $35 PR

Hare's Chase

56 Neldner Road, Marananga, SA 5355 **Region** Barossa Valley
T 0434 160 148 **www**.hareschase.com **Open** By appt **Winemaker** Matt Reynolds
Est. 1998 **Dozens** 5000 **Vyds** 16.8ha

Hare's Chase was created by 2 families, headed respectively by (ex Penfolds) Peter Taylor as then winemaker, with over 30 vintages' experience, and Mike de la Haye as general manager. Together they purchased a 100+yo vineyard in the Marananga Valley area of the Barossa Valley in '97, though the brand has changed hands multiple times since. The vineyard has some of the best red soil available for dry-grown viticulture. Extensive replanting means that three-quarters of the vineyard is planted to now 20+yo shiraz vines, with some mataro, cabernet sauvignon and tempranillo.

🍷🍷🍷🍷🍷 **Lepus 2020, Barossa Valley** This shiraz is a deep, impenetrable crimson in the glass with aromas of pure cassis, kirsch and dark plum fruits underscored by hints of baking spices, licorice, espresso, dark chocolate and earth. Thick and powerful with a deep black fruit presence, a sense of broodiness and chocolate bullet/spicy depth. Cork. 14.8% alc. **RATING** 94 **DRINK** 2023-2033 $178 DB

🍷🍷🍷🍷🍷 **Vigilance Marananga Shiraz 2020, Barossa Valley RATING** 93
DRINK 2023-2030 $50 DB
Ironscraper Shiraz 2020, Barossa Valley RATING 91 **DRINK** 2023-2029 $35 DB
The Springer Shiraz 2020, Barossa Valley RATING 90 **DRINK** 2023-2027 $35 DB

Harewood Estate

1570 Scotsdale Road, Denmark, WA 6333 **Region** Great Southern
T (08) 9840 9078 **www**.harewood.com.au **Open** Fri–Mon 10–4 (school hols 7 days)
Winemaker James Kellie **Est.** 1986 **Dozens** 15000 **Vyds** 20ha

In '03, James and Careena Kellie, responsible for the contract making of Harewood's wines since '98, purchased the Harewood Estate. They constructed a 300t winery, offering both contract winemaking services and the ability to expand the Harewood range to include subregional wines from across the Great Southern region.

🍷🍷🍷🍷🍷 **Flux-VII White Blend 2022, Denmark** A blend of sauvignon blanc/semillon/riesling. Scents of lemon curd and quince, nashi pear and almonds. The palate is much more keen and quick, a zesty shiver of lemon-lime with pink grapefruit and faint almond/nougat notes. A vibrant, tightly wound and thirst-quenching expression on hand. Very pleasing. Screw cap. 12.5% alc. **RATING** 92 **DRINK** 2023-2026 $30 MB ✪
Museum Release Riesling 2013, Porongurup A rich and full expression of riesling bolstered with briny acidity – the mature release sees the wine in good stead, perhaps a little pudgy and soft, but with energy underlying. Scents of ripe apple, toast, honey and flint. Flavours of honey-dipped apples, light caramel and peach with lime juice squeezed over the lot. It's ready to roll now. Screw cap. 12% alc. **RATING** 92 **DRINK** 2023-2025 $45 MB

Hart of the Barossa

Cnr Vine Vale Road/Light Pass Road, Tanunda, SA 5352 **Region** Barossa Valley
T 0412 586 006 **www**.hartofthebarossa.com.au **Open** Fri–Sat 11–4 or by appt
Winemaker Michael Hart, Alisa Hart, Rebekah Richardson **Est.** 2007 **Dozens** 2000 **Vyds** 6.5ha

The ancestors of Michael and Alisa Hart arrived in SA in 1845, their first address (with 7 children) a hollow tree on the banks of the North Para River. Michael and Alisa personally tend the vineyard, which is the oldest certified organic vineyard in the Barossa Valley and includes a patch of 120yo shiraz. The quality of the wines coming from these vines is exceptional; unfortunately, there is only enough to make very small quantities each year. The other wines made are also impressive, particularly given their prices.

ŸŸŸŸŸ **Ye Faithful Limited Release Old Vine Shiraz 2018, Barossa Valley**
Impenetrable red purple in the glass with opulent characters of crème de cassis, blackberry, black plum and kirsch on a canvas of deep baking spices, black licorice, Barossa earth, cedar, vanilla, tobacco leaf and oak spice. Pure and powerful with considerable fruit weight, ample, fine granitic tannin, bright acidity and a lengthy vapour trail of cassis, cedar and spice on the finish. Impressive. Screw cap. 14.5% alc. **RATING** 95 **DRINK** 2023–2033 $115 DB

ŸŸŸŸŸ **Vine Vale Mataro 2021, Barossa Valley** RATING 92 DRINK 2023–2028 $30 DB ✪
The Höhepunkt Grenache 2021, Barossa Valley RATING 92 DRINK 2023–2028 $35 DB
Ye Brave Limited Release Shiraz 2020, Barossa Valley RATING 92 DRINK 2023–2028 $35 DB
Two Barrels Cabernet Sauvignon Shiraz 2020, Barossa RATING 90 DRINK 2023–2030 $45 DB

Harvey River Estate   ★★★☆

Third Street, Harvey, WA 6220 **Region** Geographe
T (08) 9729 2085 **www.**harveyriverestate.com.au **Open** Wed–Sat 10–4, Sun 10–2
Winemaker Stuart Pierce **Est.** 1999 **Dozens** 20 000 **Vyds** 18.5ha
Harvey River Estate has a long and significant tradition of winemaking in WA's southwest. The Sorgiovanni family have been farming and making wine on the original property since Guiseppe (Joe) arrived from Italy in 1928. The Harvey River Estate label was established in '99, the fruit for these wines is predominantly from the family-owned vineyards in Geographe.

ŸŸŸŸŸ **Magellan Muscat NV, Geographe** Bright and fresh with clean spirit, gentle woody spice accents, floral lift and layers of salted caramel, toast, honeycomb, sugared almonds and sweet spices. Lush and shapely on the palate, edged with fine, silty tannins and finishing with lingering honey and toast characters. A vibrant expression, readily drinkable and enjoyable in this more energetic iteration. Screw cap. 19% alc. **RATING** 92 $40 MB

Haselgrove Wines   ★★★★★

187 Sand Road, McLaren Vale, SA 5171 **Region** McLaren Vale
T (08) 8323 8706 **www.**haselgrove.com.au **Open** 7 days 11–5 **Winemaker** Andrew Locke **Est.** 1981 **Dozens** 45 000 **Vyds** 9.7ha
Italian-Australian industry veterans Don Totino, Don Luca, Tony Carrocci and Steve Maglieri decided to purchase Haselgrove 'over a game of cards and couple of hearty reds' in '08. The modern small-batch winery is known for its reds, producing shiraz, cabernet sauvignon and GSM blends as well as chardonnay and fiano, among others.

ŸŸŸŸŸ **Il Padrone Shiraz 2020, McLaren Vale** An example of true expertise. Violet, llicorella, a sachet of clove, pepper and alternate Indian spice as blueberry, mulberry and every other berry expand across a cuddle of salubrious oak. The finish, a smooth operator, yet one of savouriness, impeccably managed tannins, impressive length and a calling card of class. Screw cap. 14.5% alc. **RATING** 95 **DRINK** 2022–2032 $55 NG

ŸŸŸŸŸ **Protector Cabernet Sauvignon 2020, McLaren Vale** RATING 93 DRINK 2022–2030 $40 NG
Catkin Shiraz 2020, McLaren Vale RATING 93 DRINK 2022–2032 $40 NG
The Lear Shiraz 2021, McLaren Vale RATING 92 DRINK 2023–2035 $90 NG
First Cut Shiraz 2020, McLaren Vale RATING 92 DRINK 2022–2028 $26 NG ✪
Staff Chardonnay 2021, Adelaide Hills RATING 91 DRINK 2022–2026 $35 NG
The Cruth Shiraz 2021, McLaren Vale RATING 90 DRINK 2023–2035 $150 NG
First Cut Cabernet Sauvignon 2020, McLaren Vale RATING 90 DRINK 2022–2027 $26 NG

Hatherleigh Vineyard   ★★★★☆

35 Redground Heights Road, Laggan, NSW 2583 **Region** Various
T 0418 688 794 **www**.nickbulleid.com/hatherleigh **Open** By appt **Winemaker** Stuart
Hordern, Nick Bulleid MW **Viticulturist** Nick Bulleid MW **Est.** 1996 **Dozens** 240
Vyds 1ha
This is the venture of long-term Brokenwood partner and peripatetic wine consultant Nick
Bulleid MW. The vineyard in the Southern Tablelands was planted exclusively to pinot noir
between 1996 and '99, but part thereafter grafted to a clonal mix of MV6 (predominant),
and chardonnay clone 95. The wines are made at Brokenwood under the joint direction of
Stuart Hordern and Kate Sturgess.

🍷🍷🍷🍷🍷 Chardonnay 2021, Southern New South Wales Now, this is impressive,
basking in cool-climate flavours from grapefruit, lemon zest and lime sorbet-like
acidity. Lovely tension across the palate, which is steely and tight, yet with light
layers of creamy lees, grilled nuts and lacy phenolics that add some weight. Classy
chardy. Screw cap. 12.8% alc. RATING 95 DRINK 2023–2031 $40 JF ✪

🍷🍷🍷🍷🍷 Pinot Noir 2019, Southern New South Wales RATING 90 DRINK 2023–2025
$40 JF

Hay Shed Hill Wines   ★★★★★

511 Harmans Mill Road, Wilyabrup, WA 6280 **Region** Margaret River
T (08) 9755 6046 **www**.hayshedhill.com.au **Open** 7 days 10–5 **Winemaker** Michael
Kerrigan **Est.** 1973 **Dozens** 24 000 **Vyds** 18.55ha
Mike Kerrigan, former winemaker at Howard Park, acquired Hay Shed Hill in late '06 (with
co-ownership by the West Cape Howe syndicate). The estate-grown wines are made under
the Vineyard and Block series, the latter made from separate blocks within the vineyard. The
Pitchfork wines are made from contract-grown grapes in the region and the KP Wines label
is a collaboration between Michael and his daughter Katie Priscilla Kerrigan.

🍷🍷🍷🍷🍷 Cabernet Sauvignon 2020, Margaret River A classic high-quality Margaret
River cabernet with more depth to rounded, fleshy fruit and quality oak than is
usual with this wine. It exudes cassis and has an excellent ripe tannin structure.
Screw cap. 14% alc. RATING 96 DRINK 2023–2035 $26 JH ✪
KP Naturally Rosé 2022, Geographe What a gorgeous drink. The palest
copper blush, mildly cloudy with heady aromas and flavours of raspberries and
spice, but it's the texture that tantalises. Creamy and smooth, savoury and light
to the very end, finishing with a zap of acidity. Screw cap. 12.5% alc. RATING 95
DRINK 2022–2025 $28 JF ✪
Block 1 Semillon Sauvignon Blanc 2021, Margaret River This is a
particularly attractive example of semillon/sauvignon blanc, with a layer of white
peach and passionfruit joining the more usual lemon and snow pea. Subtle creamy
oak nuances add to the length of the finish. Screw cap. 12% alc. RATING 95
DRINK 2023–2025 $29 JH ✪
Morrison's Gift 2020, Margaret River A blend of Bordeaux's 5 varieties that
offers a rare mix of juicy and dusty aromas and flavours. The palate and finish
are very long, the aftertaste (and the price) mouth-watering, the tannins spicy.
Screw cap. 14% alc. RATING 95 DRINK 2023–2030 $24 JH ✪
Block 2 Cabernet Sauvignon 2020, Margaret River If the fabulous dark
red hue or heady aromas don't make your heart flutter, check your pulse. Full of
violets, blackcurrant pastilles, mulberries and nori with the cedary/menthol oak
adding fragrance and more shape to the full-bodied palate. While the flavours
are rich and intense, this is smooth and plush with finely apportioned tannins.
Screw cap. 14% alc. RATING 95 DRINK 2024–2040 $60 JF

🍷🍷🍷🍷🍷 KP Naturally Riesling Pet Nat 2022, Mount Barker RATING 93
DRINK 2022–2024 $35 JF ✪
Shiraz Tempranillo 2020, Margaret River RATING 92 DRINK 2022–2028
$22 JF ✪

Pitchfork Cabernet Merlot 2020, Margaret River RATING 91
DRINK 2023-2027 $15 JH ✪
Semillon Sauvignon Blanc 2022, Margaret River RATING 90
DRINK 2022-2024 $22 JF ✪
Pitchfork Pink 2022, Margaret River RATING 90 DRINK 2022-2023 $17 JF ✪
Cabernet Merlot 2020, Margaret River RATING 90 DRINK 2022-2028
$22 JF ✪

Hayes Family Wines

102 Mattiske Road, Stone Well, SA 5352 **Region** Barossa Valley
T 0499 096 812 **www**.hayesfamilywines.com **Open** Fri–Sat 10.30–4.30 or by appt
Winemaker Andrew Seppelt **Viticulturist** Amanda Mader **Est.** 2014 **Dozens** 5000
Vyds 20ha
Hayes Family Wines is a family-owned producer nestled among organically farmed vineyards
in Stone Well on the western ridge of the Barossa Valley. Shiraz, grenache, mataro and
semillon are produced from estate vines in Stone Well dating back to 1870, as well as small-
batch, single-vineyard wines from Ebenezer, Koonunga, Williamstown and the Eden Valley.

🍷🍷🍷🍷🍷 Three Kings 2021, Barossa Valley 45/35/20% grenache/shiraz/mataro
ex three leading growers, each to one variety. An utterly exceptional colour,
soft as silk mouthfeel and a seamless fusion of flavours. Equally enjoyable is the
alcohol, which tastes closer to 13.5% than 14.5%. Cork. 14.5% alc. RATING 96
DRINK 2023-2041 $80 JH
Estate Stone Well Block 1 Shiraz 2021, Barossa Valley Glossy blackberry
and plum fruits with hints of warm earth, baking spices, ironstone, blueberry pie,
barbecued meats, cedar, chocolate bullets and violets. Unctuous fruit density with
tightly packed, powdery tannins and a slew of glistening blackberry fruits on the
long finish. Just the merest hint of heat, but blimey it's good drinking. Screw cap.
14.5% alc. RATING 95 DRINK 2023-2032 $70 DB
Estate Stone Well Block 9 Shiraz 2021, Barossa Valley Deep, purple-edged
crimson in the glass with aromas of ironstone-flecked blackberry, black cherry
and blood plum supported by baking spices, shoyu, licorice, dark chocolate, earth,
iodine and roasting meats. There's a deep fruit presence here, powdery tannins and
super-rich black fruits, spice and veal jus notes on the long finish. Impressive stuff.
Screw cap. 14.5% alc. RATING 95 DRINK 2023-2033 $70 DB
Primrose Vineyard Mataro 2021, Barossa Valley A very attractive wine,
supple and long, plum and blackberry fruit the drivers within a perfectly balanced
palate. With only 55 dozen made, there's no showboating here. Screw cap.
14.1% alc. RATING 94 DRINK 2023-2033 $40 JH ✪
Koonunga Shiraz 2021, Barossa Valley Deep, purple-flecked crimson with
bright blueberry, satsuma plum and cassis notes along with hints of baking spices,
jasmine, licorice, dark chocolate, cherry clafoutis and warm earth. There is a glorious
plume of opulent black fruits that leaves a spice trail across the palate, while tight, fine
sandy tannins and bright acidity provide the pulse for what is a very enjoyable drink
indeed. Screw cap. 14.8% alc. RATING 94 DRINK 2023-2030 $55 DB

🍷🍷🍷🍷♀ Stone Well Vineyard Shiraz 2021, Barossa Valley RATING 93
DRINK 2023-2030 $45 DB
Estate Block 3 Mataro 2021, Barossa Valley RATING 93 DRINK 2023-2031
$40 JH
Shiraz 2021, Barossa Valley RATING 93 DRINK 2023-2030 $38 DB
Cabernet Sauvignon 2021, Barossa Valley RATING 93 DRINK 2023-2030
$38 DB
Fromm Vineyard Shiraz 2021, Barossa Valley RATING 93 DRINK 2023-2030
$70 DB
Hoffmann DV Shiraz 2021, Barossa Valley RATING 93 DRINK 2023-2033
$70 DB

HEAD Wines

PO Box 58, Tanunda, SA 5352 **Region** Barossa Valley
T 0413 114 233 **www**.headwines.com.au **Open** By appt Feb–Apr **Winemaker** Alex
Head **Est.** 2006 **Dozens** 9000

In '97, Alex Head finished a degree in biochemistry from Sydney University. Experience in
fine wine stores, importers and an auction house was followed by vintage work at Tyrrell's,
Torbreck, Laughing Jack and Cirillo Estate. The names of his flagship reds reflect his
fascination with Côte Rôtie in the northern Rhône – the 2 aspects in this famous appellation
are known as Côte Blonde and Côte Brune. Head's Blonde comes from an east-facing slope
in the Stone Well area, while The Brunette comes from a very low-yielding vineyard in the
Moppa area.

ΨΨΨΨΨ Wilton Hill Barossa Ranges Shiraz 2020, Eden Valley Deep, saturated
crimson with an impressive array of ripe dark and black fruits set on a bed of
fine spice. Hints of pressed flowers, crushed stone, tobacco leaf, sage, graphite,
black pepper and roasting meats. Very nicely composed indeed with a restrained,
elegant line, fine granitic tannins and a distinctly savoury, European-style shape
to the sustained finish. Pitch-perfect balance. Tremendous stuff. Diam. 14.5% alc.
RATING 97 **DRINK** 2023-2035 $149 DB

ΨΨΨΨΨ Ancestor Vine Central Grounds Shiraz 2021, Barossa Valley Brilliant,
vivid crimson in the glass with inviting aromas of satsuma plum and dark cherry
dusted with exotic spices and jasmine with hints of cocoa powder, graphite,
crushed stone and roasting meats. Fruit purity is on point with impressive flow
and structure thanks to bright acidity and compact, fine tannins. Beautifully
balanced yet concentrated, detailed and just great drinking. Diam. 15% alc.
RATING 96 **DRINK** 2023-2038 $109 DB

Old Vine Grenache 2021, Barossa Its deep crimson-purple hue rings the bell
to approach with care. There's so much happening in the bouquet it's mesmeric,
like a great burgundy that you hesitate to taste for fear of losing the magic of the
aromas. The power of the drive here takes you deep into a shaded forest with its
violets and wild orchids. It's a wine needing 20-30 years to reveal all. Screw cap.
14.5% alc. **RATING** 96 **DRINK** 2023-2046 $40 JH ✪

The Brunette Shiraz 2021, Barossa 90/10% shiraz/cabernet sauvignon. Deep
magenta with aromas of bright, ripe plum and blackberry fruits cut with exotic
spices, purple flowers, ironstone, licorice, graphite and earth. Textural and resonant
with a dark fruit flow, the gentle tug of granitic tannins framed by bright acidity
and a long, supple finish. Screw cap. 14.5% alc. **RATING** 95 **DRINK** 2023-2035
$73 DB

Head Red GSM 2021, Barossa Blimey. This is a hell of a wine at $28, and
follows its own path, picking the best bits of the Old Vine and the humble Head
Red grenaches. Thus it borrows structure from the Old Vine, and vibrancy
from Head Red. Overall, the balance and harmony brook no dissent. Screw cap.
14% alc. **RATING** 95 **DRINK** 2023-2033 $28 JH ✪

Head Red Cabernet Sauvignon 2021, Barossa Elegance is the feature of all
the Head Red wines. Balance is a *sine qua non* traveller of elegance; drilling down
further, Alex Head's handling of tannin is masterful – as here, at 13.5% alcohol!
That's meant to be impossible, but clearly it's not. Blackcurrant/cassis floods the
mouth, and other fruits (plum the most obvious) join in. Screw cap. **RATING** 95
DRINK 2023-2036 $28 JH ✪

The Contrarian Shiraz 2021, Barossa Uncommonly deep in colour given
the whole bunches, likewise the density of the savoury black fruits. It's hard to
reconcile this wine and its '20 sibling (red cherry fruits), but so be it. While rich
and medium- to full-bodied, the black fruits and spice (rather than tannins) carry
the day. Screw cap. 14.2% alc. **RATING** 95 **DRINK** 2023-2041 $40 JH ✪

Grenache Rosé 2022, Barossa Pale salmon pink. It has a floral/musk/spice
bouquet and a textural palate, neither sweet nor dry. I totally agree with Alex

Head's suggestion that it be served as an aperitif or with spicy food. Screw cap. 13% alc. **RATING** 94 **DRINK** 2023–2024 $28 JH ✪

The Blonde Shiraz 2021, Barossa Deep magenta, plush and perfumed with ripe plum, black cherry and blackberry fruits, dark spice, orange blossom, licorice, dark chocolate, sage and earth. Voluminous with a sense of latent power, tightly packed granitic tannin and a long, darkly spiced finish. Screw cap. 14.5% alc. **RATING** 94 **DRINK** 2023–2025 $57 DB

Head Red Shiraz 2021, Barossa The sage-flecked elegance of Eden Valley fruit comes through in this wine, while retaining fruit purity and impeccable balance and flow. Layered with spice, hints of violets, and fine powdery tannin, finishing long for a wine at this price. Screw cap. 14.5% alc. **RATING** 94 **DRINK** 2023–2029 $28 DB ✪

The Contrarian Viognier 2021, Eden Valley Alex Head is a fan of the wines of Château-Grillet in the northern Rhône, and I can totally see where he is going with this baby. It's flighty and filigreed with lovely sapid citrus fruits dusted with apricot nuance, soft spice, clotted cream, white flowers, a whiff of struck match and crushed stone. Textured yet taut and driven with plenty of clarity, detail and minerally persistence on the finish. Screw cap. 11.5% alc. **RATING** 94 **DRINK** 2023–2028 $40 DB ✪

🍷🍷🍷🍷🍷 Riesling 2021, Eden Valley **RATING** 93 **DRINK** 2023–2029 $28 DB ✪
Old Vine Shiraz 2021, Barossa **RATING** 92 **DRINK** 2023–2028 $40 DB

Heathcote Estate ★★★★☆

Drummonds Lane, Heathcote, Vic 3523 (postal) **Region** Heathcote
T (03) 5974 3729 **www**.yabbylake.com **Open** at Yabby Lake 7 days 10–4
Winemaker Tom Carson, Chris Forge, Luke Lomax **Viticulturist** Paul Viggers **Est.** 1998
Dozens 5000 **Vyds** 35ha
Heathcote Estate and Yabby Lake Vineyard (see separate entry) are owned by the Kirby family of Village Roadshow Ltd. They purchased a prime piece of Heathcote red Cambrian soil in '99, planting shiraz and a little grenache; they have since added nebbiolo. The hugely talented Tom Carson has been group winemaker since '08, adding lustre to the winery and its wines. The estate vineyard was certified organic in '21.

🍷🍷🍷🍷🍷 **Single Vineyard Shiraz 2021, Heathcote** Complex shiraz with herb, meat, woodsmoke and mint characters rippling through cherry-plum fruit flavour. It's cool and composed but flavoursome too, with clove notes running out ahead of it all and excellent length to the finish. It's not the heaviest of Heathcote red wines and it doesn't need to be; it has a whole lot else going on besides. Screw cap. 13.5% alc. **RATING** 95 **DRINK** 2024–2036 $50 CM ✪

Single Vineyard Nebbiolo 2021, Heathcote Has the typical light colour of nebbiolo that bears no relation to the savoury tannins of the variety, here running through start to finish and positively demanding food, preferably an Italian ragout. An inaugural release, with classic pomegranate and rose petal aromas. Screw cap. 14% alc. **RATING** 94 **DRINK** 2023–2039 $50 JH

🍷🍷🍷🍷🍷 Primal Organic Preservative Free Shiraz 2022, Heathcote **RATING** 90 **DRINK** 2023–2023 $30 JH

Heathcote Winery ★★★★

185 High Street, Heathcote, Vic 3523 **Region** Heathcote
T (03) 5433 2595 **www**.heathcotewinery.com.au **Open** 7 days 11–5
Winemaker Rachel Gore **Est.** 1978 **Dozens** 8000 **Vyds** 11ha
Heathcote Winery's cellar door is situated in the main street of Heathcote, housed in a restored miner's cottage built 1854 to cater for the huge influx of gold miners. The first vintage was processed in 1983, following the planting of the vineyards in '78. Shiraz and shiraz viognier account for most of the production.

ΤΤΤΤΤ **Slaughterhouse Paddock Single Vineyard Shiraz 2020, Heathcote**
Eucalyptus notes are strong here, but so too is the power of fruit. Saturated
plum, cloves, vanilla cream and caramel notes are lifted by the mint and gum leaf
characters. It's velvety, plush, all those things. Talk about seductive. Screw cap.
14.5% alc. RATING 94 DRINK 2024-2034 $60 CM
The Origin Single Vineyard Shiraz 2020, Heathcote A dense, ripe,
commanding wine. It's bold with plum, mint, clove and black cherry flavours
and is riddled with smoky, cedary oak, but it still manages to feel both
harmonious and balanced. There's more oak and more fruit on the finish,
along with tannin, and it keeps pulsing there for a good while. Screw cap.
14.5% alc. RATING 94 DRINK 2025-2035 $60 CM
The Wilkins Shiraz 2019, Heathcote Mint, cream, cedar wood and saturated
plums. It's thick with oak and thick with flavour. This is one of those wines
that coats the mouth, its charms on full display from the very first sip. It remains
satisfying all the way, though it takes air (preferably in a decanter) for the finish to
really extend. Screw cap. 14.5% alc. RATING 94 DRINK 2024-2036 $120 CM

ΤΤΤΤΤ **Mail Coach Shiraz 2021, Heathcote** RATING 93 DRINK 2024-2032 $35 CM ✪
Mail Coach Viognier 2022, Heathcote RATING 91 DRINK 2024-2028
$35 CM
Vermentino 2022, Heathcote RATING 91 DRINK 2023-2026 $30 CM
Grenache Rosé 2022, Heathcote RATING 90 DRINK 2023-2026 $30 CM

Heathvale   ★★★★★

300 Saw Pit Gully Road, via Keyneton, SA 5353 **Region** Eden Valley
T 0407 600 487 **www**.heathvale.com **Open** By appt **Winemaker** Trevor March, Tony
Carapetis (Consultant) **Est.** 1987 **Dozens** 1200 **Vyds** 9ha
The origins of Heathvale go back to 1865, when William Heath purchased the property,
building the homestead and establishing the vineyard. Today it's owned by Trevor March, who
re-established the vineyards in 1987, planting shiraz, cabernet sauvignon, riesling, sagrantino
and tempranillo. The winemaking is now under the control of consultant Tony Carapetis
(Quattro Mano).

ΤΤΤΤΤ **The Reward Shiraz 2020, Eden Valley** An impressive shiraz that shows a
deep crimson colour and characters of damson plum, boysenberry and mulberry
undercut with layers of fine spice, licorice, purple flowers, choc-berry fruits
and lighter wafts of mint and blackberry pastille. Tight, granitic tannins provide
support while quartz-like acidity cuts through as it powers to a lingering finish.
Very nice. Diam. 15% alc. RATING 95 DRINK 2023-2030 $69 DB

Hedonist Wines   ★★★★

Rifle Range Road, McLaren Vale, SA 5171 (postal) **Region** McLaren Vale
T (08) 8323 8818 **www**.hedonistwines.com.au **Open** Not **Winemaker** Walter Clappis,
Kimberly Cooter, James Cooter **Est.** 1982 **Dozens** 18 000 **Vyds** 35ha
Walter Clappis has been making wine in McLaren Vale for near on 40 years and has won
innumerable trophies and gold medals, including the prestigious George Mackey Memorial
Trophy with his '09 The Hedonist Shiraz, chosen as the best wine exported from Australia
that year. Daughter Kimberly and son-in-law James Cooter support him on the winery
floor. The certified organic and biodynamic estate plantings of shiraz, cabernet sauvignon,
tempranillo and grenache are the cornerstones of the business.

ΤΤΤΤΤ **Ecology Shiraz 2021, McLaren Vale** Blueberry coulis, lilac and aniseed.
Lifted aromas, enticing and auguring well for the energy to come. Some
reductive tension, nicely handled. Plush and pulpy, yet far from any throwaway
semi-carbonic style. A rim of tannin and a tranche of salty freshness soused with
some whole-bunch spice makes sure of that. Good drinking. Screw cap. 14% alc.
RATING 93 DRINK 2022-2030 $35 NG ✪

Ecology Grenache 2021, McLaren Vale Transparency, freshness and a pinot-esque fidelity. Ume, violet, bergamot, red licorice and dried raspberries doused in brine. Saline freshness and spindly tannin corral the fray and compress any excess. Good use of the right oak. Lacking in mid-palate intensity, but nicely done. Screw cap. 14% alc. **RATING** 93 **DRINK** 2022-2027 $35 NG ✪

GSM 2021, McLaren Vale Plenty of pleasure on offer here. Charcoal-grilled meat, worn leather, aniseed and a potpourri of garrigue-like spices dousing a core of kirsch and stewed damson plum. The tannins, spindly and shapely, compress the fruit into a vortex of just enough tension. The acidity, a little shrill. Screw cap. 14% alc. **RATING** 91 **DRINK** 2022-2025 $28 NG ✪

Cabernet Sauvignon 2021, McLaren Vale A lovely scent of mulch, bark, currant of both hues and black olive tapenade. Sage and bay leaf imbue a savouriness to the tannins, rolled just tight enough for tension, but loose enough for imminent pleasure. Excellent drinking for the money. Screw cap. 14% alc. **RATING** 91 **DRINK** 2022-2027 $26 NG ✪

The Hedonist Sangiovese 2022, McLaren Vale A versatile, mid-weighted wine for the everyday table. Chinotto, tapenade, anise and a dried herbal twine finding confluence with a frisk of acidity and flirt of tannin, nicely edgy, to keep things on a savoury rail. Screw cap. 13.5% alc. **RATING** 90 **DRINK** 2022-2026 $28 NG

The Hedonist Shiraz 2021, McLaren Vale Hitting all the right notes: floral, meaty, gently ferrous and brimming with dark-fruit allusions underlain by charcuterie, briar, clove and peppery freshness. Solid. The sturdy, yet lithe tannic mould is particularly impressive. Screw cap. 14% alc. **RATING** 90 **DRINK** 2023-2027 $26 NG

Heggies Vineyard ★★★★

Heggies Range Road, Eden Valley, SA 5235 **Region** Eden Valley
T (08) 8561 3200 **www**.heggiesvineyard.com **Open** By appt **Winemaker** Marc van Halderen **Est.** 1972 **Dozens** 15 000 **Vyds** 62ha

Heggies was the 2nd of the high-elevation (570m) vineyards established by the Hill-Smith family, following the revival of Pewsey Vale vineyard in 1961. Plantings on the 120ha former grazing property began in '73; the principal varieties are riesling and chardonnay.

🍷🍷🍷🍷 **Estate Riesling 2022, Eden Valley** Firing on all cylinders with classic Eden Valley characters of freshly squeezed limes, Bickford's lime cordial and Christmas lily. There are some lemon curd aspects on the palate and a lovely quartz-like acidity providing ample velocity and crispness. Screw cap. 11.5% alc. **RATING** 93 **DRINK** 2023-2030 $26 DB ✪

Reserve Chardonnay 2021, Eden Valley Pale straw with the merest flash of green in the glass. Notes of juicy white peach and nectarine with a splash of grapefruit lift. Hints of cinnamon, nougat, white flowers, stone, struck flint, apple pastries and nicely judged French oak. Detailed and long with excellent clarity, sapid, lipsmacking acidity and pure, lightly oak-spiced stone and citrus fruits on the long, crystalline finish. Screw cap. 12% alc. **RATING** 93 **DRINK** 2023-2026 $50 DB

Estate Chardonnay 2021, Eden Valley Pale straw in the glass with aromas of bright nectarine and white peach with hints of grapefruit, white flowers, crushed quartz and lighter wafts of vanillin oak and marzipan. Plenty of flesh and textural verve with clotted cream and citrus rind notes joining in on the palate as it builds for a long, sustained finish. Screw cap. 13% alc. **RATING** 93 **DRINK** 2023-2027 $35 DB ✪

Cloudline Chardonnay 2022, Eden Valley Pale straw in the glass with aromas of bright white peach, nectarine and citrus with hints of soft spice, nougat, almond blossom, crème fraîche and stone. Finely honed and precise on the palate with tight grapefruit-like acidity driving the ripe stone fruits forward to a crisp, dry and utterly moreish finish. Great value. Screw cap. 13% alc. **RATING** 92 **DRINK** 2023-2027 $22 DB ✪

Heirloom Vineyards

PO Box 39, McLaren Vale, SA 5171 **Region** South Australia
T (08) 8323 8979 **www**.heirloomvineyards.com.au **Open** Not **Winemaker** Elena
Brooks **Est.** 2004

Another venture for winemaker Elena Brooks and her husband Zar. Dandelion Vineyards
and Zonte's Footstep came along first, and continue, but other partners are involved in
those ventures. The lofty aims of Heirloom are 'to preserve the best of tradition, the unique
old vineyards of SA, and to champion the best clones of each variety, embracing organic
and biodynamic farming'. Fruit is sourced from across SA and the quality of the wines has
been consistently very good.

Anevo Fortress Grenache Touriga Tempranillo 2021, McLaren Vale The
super-heavyweight bottle is a model of everything you might seek in McLaren
Vale grenache and friends. It soars with red fruits that make applause mandatory,
then dips into more sombre fruits bordering jam or liqueur. Screw cap. 14.2% alc.
RATING 95 **DRINK** 2023–2040 $80 JH
A'Lambra Shiraz 2021, Barossa Valley Dense, opaque, old-blood liquid
that stains the glass as it is swirled. There are untold layers of very black fruits
here, plus a dab of chocolate borrowed from McLaren Vale. I'm not in 2 minds
about this, it's more like 20. So precocious. Screw cap. 14.5% alc. **RATING** 95
DRINK 2023–2071 $120 JH

Alcala Grenache 2022, McLaren Vale **RATING** 93 **DRINK** 2023–2030 $80 NG
Alcazar Castle Pinot Noir 2022, Adelaide Hills **RATING** 93
DRINK 2023–2030 $80 NG
Assen's Fortalice Chardonnay 2022, Adelaide Hills **RATING** 93
DRINK 2023–2032 $60 NG
Touriga 2022, McLaren Vale **RATING** 92 **DRINK** 2022–2027 $40 NG
Anevo Fortress Grenache Touriga Tempranillo 2022, McLaren Vale
RATING 92 **DRINK** 2023–2030 $70 NG
Shiraz 2021, McLaren Vale **RATING** 92 **DRINK** 2022–2028 $40 NG
The Velvet Fog Pinot Noir 2022, Adelaide Hills **RATING** 91
DRINK 2023–2028 $40 NG
Shiraz 2021, Barossa Valley **RATING** 91 **DRINK** 2023–2028 $40 DB

Helen's Hill Estate

16 Ingram Road, Lilydale, Vic 3140 **Region** Yarra Valley
T (03) 9739 1573 **www**.helenshill.com.au **Open** Thurs–Mon 10–5 **Winemaker** Scott
McCarthy **Viticulturist** Robyn and Andrew McIntosh **Est.** 1997 **Dozens** 12 000
Vyds 30ha

Helen's Hill Estate is named after the previous owner of the property, Helen Fraser. Venture
partners Andrew and Robyn McIntosh and Roma and Allan Nalder combined childhood
farming experience with more recent careers in medicine and finance to establish the estate.
It produces 2 labels: Helen's Hill Estate and Ingram Road, both made onsite. Scott McCarthy
has worked in the Barossa and Yarra valleys, Napa Valley, Languedoc, the Loire Valley and
Marlborough. The winery, cellar door complex and elegant 140-seat restaurant command
some of the best views in the valley.

Breachley Block Single Vineyard Chardonnay 2021, Yarra Valley A wine
of elegance and purity, reflecting the perfect vintage conditions. It has white
stone fruit, green apple, a gentle thrust of pink grapefruit, and creamy cashew,
all coalescing on the long, lingering finish. Screw cap. 12.6% alc. **RATING** 97
DRINK 2023–2032 $37 JH ✪

First Light Single Clone Reserve Pinot Noir 2021, Yarra Valley The scent-
filled bouquet wastes no time in imposing itself on the senses, the palate following
suit, with red berries and cherries to the fore. Diam. 12.8% alc. **RATING** 96
DRINK 2023–2036 $65 JH ✪

Zenith Reserve Single Vineyard Shiraz 2020, Yarra Valley Sourced from the top 4 rows of shiraz. A complex medium- to full-bodied shiraz, with blackberry and plum fruit backed by positive tannins. It has a 30+ year outlook for cellaring. Diam. 14.5% alc. **RATING** 95 **DRINK** 2025–2050 $65 JH

Lana's Single Vineyard Rosé 2022, Yarra Valley 100% cabernet sauvignon. This is a powerhouse rosé to drink with food. No panic about consumption because there's a 5+ year window of opportunity. Screw cap. 12.6% alc. **RATING** 94 **DRINK** 2023–2029 $30 JH ✪

Long Walk Single Vineyard Pinot Noir 2021, Yarra Valley The immediately expressive and complex bouquet sets the scene for a delicious pinot in a drink now or later framework. Cherry and rhubarb sit within a spicy, savoury support role. Its balance and length are right on the money. Screw cap. 13% alc. **RATING** 94 **DRINK** 2023–2037 $37 JH ✪

🍷🍷🍷🍷♀ **Roma's Grace Blanc de Noir 2021, Yarra Valley RATING** 93 **DRINK** 2023–2026 $60 JH

Empress Reserve Single Vineyard Chardonnay 2021, Yarra Valley RATING 92 **DRINK** 2023–2025 $65 JH

Ingram Road Pinot Noir 2021, Yarra Valley RATING 91 **DRINK** 2023–2026 $24 JH ✪

Helm ★★★★★

19 Butts Road, Murrumbateman, NSW 2582 **Region** Canberra District **T** (02) 6227 5953 **www.**helmwines.com.au **Open** Fri–Mon 10–4 **Winemaker** Ken Helm, Rory Shingles **Viticulturist** Thomas Lefebvre **Est.** 1973 **Dozens** 5000 **Vyds** 10ha

In '23, Helm Wines celebrated its 50-year anniversary and Ken Helm AM's 47th riesling vintage. Riesling has been an all-consuming interest, ultimately rewarded with rieslings of consistently high quality. In 2000, he established the Canberra International Riesling Challenge, putting the region on the world stage. Ten years later, Ken was awarded a Member of the Order of Australia (AM) for his contribution to the Australian wine industry. In '17 Helm completed construction of a separate 40 000L winery purely for riesling, the old winery is now dedicated to producing cabernet sauvignon.

🍷🍷🍷🍷🍷 **Premium Riesling 2022, Canberra District** A more textural offering this vintage giving it a fuller feel across the palate. In-between, plenty of citrus tones, lemon sherbet with juicy lemon-lime punctuated by a sliver of stone fruit. Composed and fine, long and pure. A slight furry grip on the finish but in a good way. Screw cap. 11% alc. **RATING** 95 **DRINK** 2022–2035 $60 JF

🍷🍷🍷🍷♀ **Classic Dry Riesling 2022, Canberra District RATING** 93 **DRINK** 2022–2032 $45 JF

Riesling Rosé 2022, Canberra District RATING 92 **DRINK** 2022–2024 $35 JF

Half Dry Riesling 2022, Canberra District RATING 92 **DRINK** 2022–2030 $35 JF

Henley Park Wines ★★★★

6 Swan Street, Henley Brook, WA 6055 **Region** Swan Valley **T** (08) 9296 4328 **www.**henleywine.com **Open** W'ends & public hols 10–5 **Winemaker** Claus Petersen, Lisbet Petersen **Est.** 1935 **Dozens** 5000 **Vyds** 4.5ha

In late 2021, Henley Park winery was taken over by winemaker Lance Parkin (ex-Houghton, currently Battles Wine, his family winemaking project). Lance and colleague Troy Overstone (also ex-Houghton) both run the operations of winery and vineyard for Henley Park. The farming is shifting to organic practices and the winemaking is labelled as 'minimalist approach'.

🍷🍷🍷🍷♀ **Chardonnay 2022, Swan Valley** A flavoursome chardonnay, away from the vogue of more skeletal, racy styles, with requisite stone fruit, ripe apple and toasty nuances, cinnamon spice and some creamy vanillin characters. Balanced, too, despite the heft and fleshiness, with a cool, refreshing finish. Delightful expression. Screw cap. 13% alc. **RATING** 93 **DRINK** 2023–2030 $35 MB ✪

Chenin Blanc 2022, Swan Valley This is the first release by winemaker Lance Parkin. It's a textural white set just below medium weight. It's bright, vibrant and crisp, showcasing typical tonic water, cucumber and preserved lemon qualities of Swan Valley chenin blanc with gentle savouriness and a light, briny minerality in tow. Quietly complex, delicious, refreshing and a wonderful thing to drink. Screw cap. 12.5% alc. **RATING** 93 **DRINK** 2022–2025 $25 MB ✪

Henschke

1428 Keyneton Road, Keyneton, SA 5353 **Region** Eden Valley
T (08) 8564 8223 **www**.henschke.com.au **Open** Mon–Sat 9–4.30 & public hols 10–3
Winemaker Stephen Henschke **Viticulturist** Prue Henschke **Est.** 1868 **Dozens** 30 000
Vyds 100ha

Henschke is the foremost medium-sized wine producer in Australia. Stephen and Prue Henschke have taken a crown jewel and polished it to an even greater brilliance. Year on year they have quietly added labels for single vineyards, single varieties or blends. The wines hail from the Eden Valley (the majority), the Barossa Valley or the Adelaide Hills. There's a compelling logic and focus – no excursions to McLaren Vale, Coonawarra, etc. Recognition as Winery of the Year in the '21 Companion was arguably long overdue. A founding member of Australia's First Families of Wine. Prue Henschke is the inaugural inductee to the James Halliday Hall of Fame (see page 33).

🍷🍷🍷🍷🍷 **Hill of Grace 2018, Eden Valley** The 60th anniversary of what is widely considered Australia's finest single-vineyard wine. It is an elegant, beautiful shiraz, with tannin–acid architecture on point, the fruit depth just stunning and dotted with five-spice, sage, pepper, charcuterie, crushed quartz and the most lovely, kinetic tannin structure. Harmony and grace on the sustained finish. Voluminous and complex, with amazing fruit density and just a complete wine. A classic! Screw cap. 14.5% alc. **RATING** 99 **DRINK** 2023–2070 $950 DB ♥

Mount Edelstone 2018, Eden Valley Picture perfect blackberry and blackcurrant fruits, shades of mixed spice, purple floral tones, earth, licorice, rosehip and crushed quartz. This shiraz is a gorgeous expression of site, pure with long, ripe tannins, lacy mineral-laden acidity providing clarity and drive and a finish that sails on for some time before finishing chalky and sustained. Screw cap. 14.5% alc. **RATING** 98 **DRINK** 2023–2045 $245 DB

Julius Riesling 2022, Eden Valley A reserve selection honouring ancestor Julius Henschke, always a wine of utmost quality. Its flowery, fragrant lime and lemon aromas soar from the glass, the palate with its spear of unsweetened lime and lemon finish and aftertaste underlining its intensity and quality. Screw cap. 12.5% alc. **RATING** 97 **DRINK** 2023–2037 $49 JH ✪

Hill of Roses 2018, Eden Valley A core of pure blackberry and dark plum characters leap from the glass with hints of blackcurrant pastille, sage, bay leaf, dried meats, earth and a gentle violet note. A wonderfully balanced shiraz with a pure, savoury fruit flow flecked with spice and gentle herbs on the finish. Powdered, granitic tannins frame the wine beautifully, finishing mineral-laden with crystal clear definition and impressive persistence. Vinolok. 14.5% alc. **RATING** 97 **DRINK** 2023–2045 $455 DB

🍷🍷🍷🍷🍷 **Johann's Garden 2021, Barossa Valley** 92/8% grenache/mataro. Magenta-splashed crimson in the glass with super-pure fruit tones on display: red and dark plum, blueberry and boysenberry with underlying hints of exotic spice, gingerbread, purple floral tones, teacake, rhubarb, cherry clafoutis and mountain herbs. Succulent yet tending savoury on the finish with a real sense of purity and grace; superfine powdery tannin lending gentle support and a bright, mineral line. Screw cap. 14.5% alc. **RATING** 96 **DRINK** 2023–2035 $64 DB ✪

Cyril Henschke 2018, Eden Valley Bright blackberry and blackcurrant fruits with top notes of redcurrant and red cherry. Olive tapenade, cedar, light briar notes and mountain herbs. Fine lacy acidity and tight, powdery tannin provide the frame, and there is no doubt that this cabernet will age magnificently. Screw cap. 14.5% alc. **RATING** 96 **DRINK** 2023–2043 $175 DB ♥

The Wheelwright Vineyard 2018, Eden Valley 100% shiraz. Pure mulberry, blueberry and blackberry fruits with hints of fine spice, sage, bay leaf, licorice, dark chocolate and crushed stone. Firm granitic tannins melt into the wine, pure and true with a fine, lively cadence and superb fruit density and detail on display. Drink or hold. Screw cap. 14.5% alc. **RATING** 96 **DRINK** 2023–2040 $150 DB

Apple Tree Bench 2019, Barossa Valley A shiraz/cabernet blend. Deep magenta crimson and packed with blackberry and plum fruits with hints of spice, clove, mace, orange blossom and blackberry pastille. Long of finish with a lovely mineral line and finely honed tannins, pure and true on the exit. Screw cap. 14.5% alc. **RATING** 95 **DRINK** 2023–2040 $70 DB

Hill of Peace 2018, Eden Valley Semillon from vines planted in 1952 on the Henschke Hill of Grace vineyard. Pure curd-like lemon fruit notes with hints of white flowers, lanolin, crushed quartz, lemon zest and river stone. Textural and flowy with great tension and detail, a pure lemony core, crystalline acid line and a sustained finish. Screw cap. 11.4% alc. **RATING** 95 **DRINK** 2023–2025 $70 DB

Louis Semillon 2021, Eden Valley A succulent release with an expansive mid-palate showing pristine characters of lemon, grapefruit, lemon curd, clover blossom, crushed stone, lanolin, cut grass and white flowers. There's a lovely waxy, textural element and a sapid acid line that drives the wine forward, finishing long and lemony with light mountain herbs on the exit. Screw cap. 12% alc. **RATING** 94 **DRINK** 2023–2033 $35 DB ✪

Tappa Pass Vineyard Selection Shiraz 2020, Barossa Deeply coloured, bright and fragrant with a generous fruit profile of black and blue fruits with layers of spice, dried herbs, licorice, dark chocolate and purple floral and orange blossom tones. Excellent fruit purity and the fine tannins resolve nicely, the wine finishing long, concentrated with great focus and detail. Screw cap. 14.5% alc. **RATING** 94 **DRINK** 2023–2040 $123 DB

Keyneton Euphonium 2019, Barossa 52/25/12/11% shiraz/cabernet sauvignon/cabernet franc/merlot. Deep crimson. Blackcurrant, blood plum and blackberry fruits with hints of baking spices, vanillin, tobacco leaf, cedar, licorice and stone. Fine tannin grip with lots of detail and a sense of suppleness to its form, concentrated yet showing restraint and elegance as the wine slowly fades. Screw cap. 14.5% alc. **RATING** 94 **DRINK** 2023–2035 $66 DB

♟♟♟♟♟ **Stone Jar Tempranillo 2021, Eden Valley** **RATING** 93 **DRINK** 2023–2030 $50 DB

Marble Angel Vineyard Cabernet Sauvignon 2020, Barossa Valley **RATING** 93 **DRINK** 2023–2035 $78 DB

Roeslein Barbera 2021, Eden Valley **RATING** 92 **DRINK** 2023–2026 $37 DB

Henry's Seven 2021, Barossa **RATING** 92 **DRINK** 2023–2030 $38 DB

Five Shillings 2021, Barossa **RATING** 92 **DRINK** 2023–2030 $35 DB

The Rose Grower Nebbiolo 2020, Eden Valley **RATING** 92 **DRINK** 2023–2035 $50 DB

Peggy's Hill Riesling 2022, Eden Valley **RATING** 91 **DRINK** 2023–2032 $26 JH ✪

Innes Vineyard Littlehampton Pinot Gris 2022, Adelaide Hills **RATING** 90 **DRINK** 2022–2028 $37 NG

Hentley Farm Wines ★★★★★

Cnr Jenke Road/Gerald Roberts Road, Seppeltsfield, SA 5355 **Region** Barossa Valley **T** (08) 8562 8427 **www**.hentleyfarm.com.au **Open** 7 days 10–4 **Winemaker** Andrew Quin **Est.** 1997 **Dozens** 20 000 **Vyds** 44.7ha

Keith and Alison Hentschke purchased Hentley Farm in '97, as a mixed farming property with an old vineyard. Keith studied agricultural science at Roseworthy, later adding an MBA. During the '90s he had a senior production role with Orlando, before moving on to manage Fabal, one of Australia's largest vineyard management companies. Establishing a great vineyard like Hentley Farm required all of his knowledge. A total of 38.2ha were planted between '99 and '05. In '04 an adjoining 6.5ha vineyard, christened Clos Otto, was acquired. Shiraz dominates the plantings, with 32.5ha.

ΤΤΤΤΤ **Clos Otto Shiraz 2020, Barossa Valley** Deep, inky crimson in the glass. Opulent aromas of ripe satsuma plum, black cherry and blueberry fruits layered with dark spice, ironstone, tapenade, violets, kirsch, cocoa and soft vanillin oak. Like slipping into a velvet armchair, all-enveloping fruit and spice with a stunning chocolatey tannin profile and a finish that shows excellent sustain. Balanced, graceful and plush, geez it's good. Cork. 14.8% alc. **RATING** 97 **DRINK** 2023-2040 $270 DB

ΤΤΤΤΤ **The Old Legend Grenache 2021, Barossa Valley** Aromas of gingerbread and an array of blossom notes flutter above the pure dark plum, cranberry and mulberry fruits. Hints of raspberry coulis, matcha, cola, turned earth and berry flan. Perfectly weighted. A plush, ripe and savoury-shaped beauty with tight, powdery tannins and ever-present spiced plum and raspberry on the exit. Tremendous stuff. Screw cap. 14.5% alc. **RATING** 96 **DRINK** 2023-2033 $70 DB ✪

The Beauty Shiraz 2020, Barossa Valley Co-fermented with a small portion of viognier which has had the desired elevation of colour (vivid crimson) and added vinous speed to a yearling racehorse. It is light, lively and refreshing with its red fruits standing up to the black. Its tannins are also remarkable in their taste as well as structure. Screw cap. 14.5% alc. **RATING** 96 **DRINK** 2023-2040 $70 JH ✪

The Beast Shiraz 2020, Barossa Valley A purple-splashed beast of a wine with the estate's characteristic plush black and dark berry fruits. Abundant spice and hints of cedar, vanilla bean, licorice, dark chocolate, tobacco pouch, pressed flowers and roasting meats. Plush and opulent with super-compact sandy tannins and all the structure to age well, should you be able to keep your mitts off it. Screw cap. 15% alc. **RATING** 96 **DRINK** 2023-2043 $95 DB

The Beast Shiraz 2021, Barossa Valley Plush macerated plum, blueberry and boysenberry fruits cut deep with spice, vanilla bean, dark chocolate, tobacco, roasting meats and some pretty punchy cedar oak tones at this stage of its evolution. Opulent and pure with stunning fruit weight and flow, tight, chalky tannin and a wall of spiced dark and black fruit on the lingering finish. Screw cap. 15% alc. **RATING** 95 **DRINK** 2023-2043 $95 DB

The Beauty Shiraz 2021, Barossa Valley A glass-staining purple-crimson hue. Pure macerated plum and black fruits with underlying hints of dark spice, earth, purple flowers, dark chocolate bullets and graphite. Sports a very stony, savoury disposition with tightly packed tannin grunt and a super-long finish featuring concentrated plum, blackberry, spice and earth. Screw cap. 14.5% alc. **RATING** 95 **DRINK** 2023-2043 $70 DB

The Old Legend Grenache 2022, Barossa Valley Top notes of dried citrus rind, exotic spice, citrus blossom, gingerbread and sage flit above the pure plum, raspberry and red berry fruits. Perhaps a little touch of Turkish delight and cola in there, too, along with fine sandy tannin and a nervy fresh acid line with just a wisp of heat apparent on the finish. Super. Screw cap. 14.8% alc. **RATING** 94 **DRINK** 2023-2033 $70 DB

The Stray Grenache Shiraz 2022, Barossa Valley Deep magenta-splashed crimson with a landslide of juicy ripe plum, boysenberry and blueberry fruits sheathed in hints of ground spice, ginger cake, citrus blossom, cola, dark chocolate, vanilla bean, raspberry coulis and earth. A nice calm, composed feel to this one, bright acidity shining some light and super-compact sandy tannin for gentle support. Screw cap. 14.8% alc. **RATING** 94 **DRINK** 2023-2030 $35 DB ✪

Shiraz 2021, Barossa Valley Deep purple-edged crimson in the glass, it's packed with super-ripe blood plum, blueberry and black cherry fruits underscored with dark spices, crème de cassis, licorice, dark chocolate, dried herbs and liminal wafts of truffle, pepper and orange blossom. Unctuous with velvety black and blue fruits and a trail of spice on the exit. Screw cap. 14.8% alc. **RATING** 94 **DRINK** 2023-2033 $36 DB ✪

The Stray Grenache Shiraz 2021, Barossa Valley Deep, purpley-edged crimson with an avalanche of plush, velvety plum and black berry fruits, undercut with spice, licorice, dark chocolate, ginger cake, violets, raspberry jam, berry cream, vanilla bean and earth. There is a really impressive fruit purity on display here, tannins ripe and gently gripping the roof of the palate, plush and long and a perfect example of contemporary Barossan wine. Great value. Screw cap. 14.5% alc. **RATING** 94 **DRINK** 2023-2024 $35 DB ✪

♀♀♀♀♀ **Riesling 2022, Eden Valley** **RATING** 93 **DRINK** 2023-2028 $28 DB ✪
Cabernet Sauvignon 2021, Barossa Valley **RATING** 92 **DRINK** 2023-2033 $35 DB
The Quintessential Shiraz Cabernet 2021, Barossa Valley **RATING** 92 **DRINK** 2023-2030 $70 DB

Herbert Vineyard ★★★★

Bishop Road, Mount Gambier, SA 5290 **Region** Mount Gambier
T 0408 849 080 **www.**herbertvineyard.com.au **Open** By appt **Winemaker** David Herbert **Est.** 1996 **Dozens** 550 **Vyds** 1.77ha
David and Trudy Herbert have 1.77ha planted to pinot noir (1.32ha), with smaller amounts of cabernet sauvignon, cabernet franc, shiraz, pinot gris and merlot. They have built a 2-level (mini) winery overlooking a 1300 square-metre maze, which is reflected in the label logo.

♀♀♀♀♀ **Cabernet + 2021, Mount Gambier** It's a lighter style of cabernet but it's still a worthy one. It tastes of boysenberry more than it does of blackcurrant; it's a painting in watercolours rather than oil. It flows juicily along, trailing fresh, aromatic herb notes. There's a grapey dryness to the finish, which works well. Screw cap. 13.4% alc. **RATING** 90 **DRINK** 2023-2030 $27 CM

Pinot Noir 2021, Mount Gambier Bright in colour, flavour and personality. Red cherry, strawberry and smoked meat characters are cut through with a combination of apple juice acidity and sweet spice. It's juicy in general but firm through the finish, with twiggy, smoked herb notes whispering through the aftertaste. Screw cap. 13.1% alc. **RATING** 90 **DRINK** 2023-2028 $26 CM

Heritage Estate ★★★★

747 Granite Belt Drive, Cottonvale, Qld 4375 **Region** Granite Belt
T (07) 4685 2197 **www.**heritageestate.wine **Open** 7 days 10–4 **Winemaker** Stephen Oliver **Viticulturist** Stephen Oliver, Robert Fenwick **Est.** 1990 **Dozens** 4000 **Vyds** 20ha
Heritage Estate is owned by Robert and Therese Fenwick. There are 2 estate vineyards in the Granite Belt: one at Cottonvale (north) which grows white varieties; and the other at Ballandean (south), a slightly warmer site planted to red varieties and marsanne.

♀♀♀♀♀ **Sagrantino 2021, Granite Belt** Broad-shouldered, dark fruited, and lashed with spice, florals and nutty savouriness. A strong fragrance of ripe plum, nutmeg, clove, hazelnuts and lavender with a whiff of white pepper. The palate is lush, supple and yet tightens on emery board tannins, finishing long and fresh with blood orange acidity and a lick of pleasing bitterness. Lots of dark, ripe fruit flavours, some cola and more savoury nuttiness with lashings of nutmeg and clove spice. A stellar rendition. Screw cap. 14.3% alc. **RATING** 94 **DRINK** 2022-2030 $40 MB ✪

♀♀♀♀♀ **Somme Riesling 2022, Granite Belt** **RATING** 92 **DRINK** 2023-2030 $28 MB ✪
Single Vineyard Syrah 2021, Granite Belt **RATING** 92 **DRINK** 2022-2030 $35 MB
Marsanne 2021, Granite Belt **RATING** 92 **DRINK** 2022-2027 $32 MB
Savagnin 2022, Granite Belt **RATING** 91 **DRINK** 2022-2027 $33 MB
Pinot Gris 2022, Granite Belt **RATING** 91 **DRINK** 2023-2028 $29 MB

Hesketh Wine Company ★★★★

827 Mt Barker Road, Verdun, SA 5245 **Region** South Australia
T (08) 8362 8622 **www.**heskethwinecompany.com.au **Open** Mon–Thurs 10–5, Fri–Sat
10–10, Sun 10–6 **Winemaker** Keeda Zilm, Andrew Hardy, Luke Broadbent **Est.** 2006
Dozens 40 000

Established by Jonathon Hesketh in '06, this label is now part of The Usual Suspects
Collective, which also has Ox Hardy Wines and Parker Coonawarra Estate under its wing,
among others. Jonathon, who still oversees the winery's operations, spent 7 years as the
global sales and marketing manager of Wirra Wirra, and 2.5 years as general manager of
Distinguished Vineyards in NZ. He is also the son of Robert Hesketh, one of the key players
in the development of many facets of the SA wine industry. A new cellar door/tasting room/
pizza kitchen opened in '22 at Grünthal in the Adelaide Hills.

♀♀♀♀♀ G.A.R. Great Australian Red 2021, Coonawarra McLaren Vale
Coonawarra cabernet and McLaren Vale shiraz. Plush aromas of cedar-framed
blackberry and satsuma plum fruits with plenty of fine spice and notes of tobacco,
licorice, dark chocolate and earth. Ripe and full bodied with chocolatey tannin
grip and a finish stacked with dark and black fruits and oak spice that lingers
nicely. Screw cap. 13.5% alc. **RATING** 93 **DRINK** 2023-2033 $60 DB

Regional Selections Riesling 2022, Eden Valley Sporting classic Eden
Valley aromas of freshly squeezed lime juice and Christmas lily with underlying
hints of crushed quartz, jasmine, light pastis tones and almond blossom. A light
phenolic textural component comes into play on the palate, which shows sapid
acidity and excellent fruit purity and drive. Value. Screw cap. 12% alc. **RATING** 92
DRINK 2023-2033 $24 DB ✪

Penola Cabernet Sauvignon 2021, Coonawarra Crimson in the glass
with a bright, red-fruited edge to the blackberry and blackcurrant core. Hints
of fine spice, cedar, licorice, dried herbs, pressed flowers, tobacco and gentle
undergrowth. Red plum and blackberry fruits on the palate cut with spice and
herbs with lovely lacy acidity driving things along and ripe tannin architecture.
Screw cap. 14.5% alc. **RATING** 92 **DRINK** 2023-2030 $34 DB

Regional Selections Fiano 2022, Clare Valley Pale in the glass with green
flashes and characters of green apple, grapefruit, nashi pear and custard apple.
Hints of white flowers, pine nuts, crushed stone and marzipan with some light
creamy notes joining in on the palate, which is sizzlingly crisp and dry with a real
mineral salt vibe to the acid profile. Nervy, focused and great refreshing drinking.
Screw cap. 12% alc. **RATING** 91 **DRINK** 2023-2026 $24 DB ✪

Regional Selections Cabernet Sauvignon 2021, Coonawarra No shortage
of lush blackberry and blackcurrant fruits on display backed up by spice, violets,
licorice, crème de cassis, tobacco and lighter undergrowth tones. Sweetly fruited
with clove and cinnamon spices, characteristic focused acidity and some fine,
powdery tannin support. Screw cap. 14.5% alc. **RATING** 91 **DRINK** 2023-2030
$24 DB ✪

Ebenezer Shiraz 2021, Barossa Valley Light on its feet for Barossa shiraz.
Fruit notes of satsuma plum and blackberry dotted with hints of fruitcake spices,
dark chocolate, licorice, violets, olive tapenade and pan juices. Medium-bodied
with a savoury palate shape, fine sandy tannin grip and some morello cherry
twang to the acidity. Screw cap. 14.5% alc. **RATING** 91 **DRINK** 2023-2029 $34 DB

Negroamaro 2021, Barossa Valley Bright cherry red in the glass with
bouncy aromas of red cherry, cranberry and red plummy fruit underlined with
fine spice, hints of orange blossom, red licorice and a touch of almond paste.
Light and spacious in the mouth with juicy fruit, fine tannins and a racy line.
Great, refreshing drinking. Screw cap. 13% alc. **RATING** 91 **DRINK** 2023-2026
$24 DB ✪

Hewitson

66 Seppeltsfield Road, Nuriootpa, SA 5355 **Region** Adelaide
T (08) 8212 6233 **www.**hewitson.com.au **Open** Mon–Sat 11–5 **Winemaker** Dean
Hewitson **Viticulturist** Dean Hewitson **Est.** 1998 **Dozens** 25 000 **Vyds** 12ha

Dean Hewitson was a winemaker at Petaluma for 10 years, during which time he managed
to do 3 vintages in France and one in Oregon, as well as undertaking his master's at
the University of California, Davis. The wines are immaculately made from a technical
viewpoint. Dean sources old vine mourvèdre from Friedrich Koch's Old Garden vineyard,
planted in 1853 at Rowland Flat, as well as shiraz and grenache from (up to) 110yo vines
in Tanunda and riesling from 30+yo vines in the Eden Valley. Cabernet sauvignon, shiraz,
mourvèdre and muscat blanc are estate grown.

ＹＹＹＹＹ **Barrel 1853 Shiraz Mourvèdre 2020, Barossa Valley** Rich and meaty
with exotically spiced dark plum, blackberry and cherry fruits, smoked meats,
charcuterie, purple flowers and earth. Ferruginous and mineral-driven with a real
sense of grace and shimmering clarity to its form, the finish sails persistently with
a chalky, savoury tannin grip, gamey complexity and a real sense of purpose and
place. Diam. 14% alc. **RATING** 97 **DRINK** 2023–2043 $450 DB ♥

ＹＹＹＹＹ **Old Garden Vineyard Mourvèdre 2020, Barossa Valley** The 1853-planted
Old Garden vineyard is thought to be the oldest mourvèdre vineyard in the
world. This shows such amazing balance, tension and detail … all meaty dark
and black fruits, exotic spice, biscuity oak and amaro herbs. Savoury and wild,
it is the benchmark for the variety in Australia for good reason. Diam. 14% alc.
RATING 96 **DRINK** 2023–2035 $88 DB

Barrel 1853 Shiraz Mourvèdre 2019, Barossa Valley Rich and pure
with deep plum and macerated black fruits with exotically spiced nuance. It's
earthy and multi-layered with a gorgeous fruit flow and presence and trademark
savouriness. Tannins, fine and powdery, resolve nicely into the wine as the fruit
slowly sails off into the distance. Diam. 14% alc. **RATING** 96 **DRINK** 2023–2033
$450 DB

Gun Metal Riesling 2022, Eden Valley Devastating October hail destroyed
some Eden Valley vineyards, but those that escaped were blessed with a superb
late/prolonged summer. Wines such as this are full to the brim with juicy lime
and lemon fruit balanced by crisp acidity. Lovely vintage, saved from the jaws of
hell. Screw cap. 12.5% alc. **RATING** 95 **DRINK** 2023–2032 $28 JH ✪

Miss Harry Grenache Shiraz Mourvèdre 2022, Barossa Valley Oodles
of bright red cherry, wild strawberry and cranberry fruit tones on a bed of exotic
spice with hints of citrus blossom, dried herbs, red licorice, gingerbread and
roasting meats. Calm, savoury and pure, sporting a wicked red and dark fruit flow,
gentle tannins and, the bottom line is, it's a real joy to drink. Screw cap. 13.5% alc.
RATING 95 **DRINK** 2023–2029 $30 DB ✪

Miss Harry Grenache Shiraz Mourvèdre 2021, Barossa Valley This is a
very attractive GSM, a blend which doesn't always live up to expectations. Here
the fruits are vibrant and supported by some delicious strands of high-toned
spice you might find in a classy pinot noir. Screw cap. 14% alc. **RATING** 95
DRINK 2023–2031 $28 JH ✪

Monopole Mother Vine Shiraz 2020, Barossa Valley Deep plum and black
fruits cut with baking spices, roasting meats, tobacco pouch, vanilla bean, cedar,
pan juices, dark chocolate and earth. Savoury, meaty and intense with chocolatey
tannins and a rich rum and raisin chocolate vibe on the opulent finish. Diam.
14% alc. **RATING** 95 **DRINK** 2023–2040 $150 DB

The Ancients Shiraz 2020, Barossa Valley Super-ripe satsuma plum, black
cherries and macerated summer berry fruits. There are layers of deep spice,
licorice, earth, violets and cassis and a lovely supple, savoury shape across the
palate, fine sandy tannin adding support. The finish trails off persistently with
a very composed, calm and pure-fruited air. Screw cap. 14% alc. **RATING** 95
DRINK 2023–2033 $50 DB ✪

Monopole Mother Vine Shiraz 2019, Barossa Valley The 'mother vine' (a survivor of an 1853 planting) provided the cuttings which Dean Hewitson patiently built up. The wine is medium-bodied, with blackberry and plum to the fore and oak unimportant. You are drinking clonal history. Diam. 14% alc. RATING 95 DRINK 2023–2029 $150 JH

Old Garden Vineyard Mourvèdre 2019, Barossa Valley The fruit is plush and deep, studded with exotic spice, pressed flowers, earth, biscuity oak and whole-bunchy lift. The tannins are fine and the oak notes swell on the palate, but the fruit is up for it, lingering persistently on the finish with trademark savouriness. Diam. 14% alc. RATING 95 DRINK 2023–2033 $88 DB

The Mad Hatter Shiraz 2021, Barossa Valley Classic aromas of satsuma plum and summer berry fruits layered with baking spices, licorice and dark chocolate. Nary a hair out of place on the palate with impressive fruit purity and a harmonious, dark savoury flow to the wines' form; powdery tannin in support with a minerally driveline. Cork. 14% alc. RATING 94 DRINK 2023–2030 $50 DB

The Mad Hatter Shiraz 2020, Barossa Valley Consistently an impressive offering with its slinky, textural and wonderfully pure fruit profile displaying juicy plummy fruits layered with spice, earth, violets and well-judged French oak nuance. The tannins superfine and powdery, the line bright and vivid, it's just a lovely wine to drink. Cork. 14% alc. RATING 94 DRINK 2023–2030 $50 DB

♟♟♟♟♟ **Baby Bush Mourvèdre 2021, Barossa Valley** RATING 93 DRINK 2023–2030 $30 DB ✪

Ned & Henry's Shiraz 2021, Barossa Valley RATING 93 DRINK 2023–2029 $30 DB ✪

LuLu Shiraz 2020, Barossa Valley RATING 93 DRINK 2023–2029 $26 DB ✪

Belle Ville Rosé 2022, Barossa Valley RATING 92 DRINK 2023–2026 $30 DB ✪

Truffle Row Carignan Syrah 2021, Barossa Valley RATING 92 DRINK 2023–2029 $35 JH

Hickinbotham Clarendon Vineyard ★★★★★

92 Brooks Road, Clarendon, SA 5157 **Region** McLaren Vale
T (08) 8383 7504 **www**.hickinbothamwines.com.au **Open** By appt **Winemaker** Chris Carpenter, Peter Fraser **Viticulturist** Michael Lane **Est.** 2012 **Dozens** 4800 **Vyds** 87ha
Alan Hickinbotham planted his namesake vineyard to dry-grown cabernet sauvignon and shiraz in '71. His father, Alan Robb Hickinbotham, co-founded the oenology diploma at Roseworthy in 1936. Jackson Family Wines bought the estate in '12; it is run as a separate business to its Yangarra Estate Vineyard. The vineyard has been farmed according to organic and biodynamic practices since '19.

♟♟♟♟♟ **Trueman Cabernet Sauvignon 2021, McLaren Vale** A large-framed wine defined by a serendipitous ripening season and skilled craftsmanship. The tannins, impeccably managed and refined. The oak, all sex appeal. The sheer density of currant, sage, black olive, rosemary and thyme, an immaculate forcefield. This is built for the cellar. Screw cap. 14% alc. RATING 95 DRINK 2023–2035 $90 NG ♥

The Peake Cabernet Shiraz 2021, McLaren Vale Majority cabernet (60%) riding riffs of cassis, mint, sage, tapenade and bay leaf over shiraz's warmer chord. A rich wine of immaculate tannic cladding. The mocha-cedar of the oak is salubrious of feel rather than obtuse or excessive. Maritime freshness, a stylish undercarriage infusing energy while towing impressive length. This is an immensely classy wine that sets the bar high. Screw cap. 14.5% alc. RATING 95 DRINK 2024–2040 $225 NG

Brooks Road Shiraz 2021, McLaren Vale Full-weighted and plush, yet managing to come across as fresh, poised and eminently drinkable all at once. Not an easy feat. Raspberry coulis, clove, star anise and black plum. The tannins, impeccably managed, as is the wont here, with a fine line of savoury chew. The freshness, bright and salty. Excellent wine. Screw cap. 14% alc. RATING 95 DRINK 2023–2032 $90 NG

The Nest Cabernet Franc 2021, McLaren Vale 15 months in French barriques (60% new), an approach dictating a certain classicism of feel to this savoury, full-weighted and immensely expressive wine. Aromas of pencil lead, graphite, redcurrant, chilli and pimento. Lithe of tannic persuasion and long of finish. This is delicious. Screw cap. 14% alc. RATING 94 DRINK 2023–2032 $90 NG ♥

 Mr. Grant Malbec 2021, McLaren Vale RATING 93 DRINK 2023–2030 $90 NG
The Revivalist Merlot 2021, McLaren Vale RATING 92 DRINK 2023–2030 $90 NG

Hidden Creek ★★★★

Eukey Road, Ballandean, Qld 4382 **Region** Granite Belt
T (07) 4684 1383 **www**.hiddencreek.com.au **Open** W'ends 10–4 **Winemaker** Andy Williams **Viticulturist** Dan Folkers **Est.** 1995 **Dozens** 600 **Vyds** 2.5ha
Located at 1000m on a ridge overlooking the Severn River Valley. The granite boulder–strewn hills mean that the 70ha property only provides 2.5ha of vineyard, in turn divided into 3 different blocks planted to shiraz, viognier, tempranillo and more recently marsanne. Other varieties are sourced from local growers.

 Verdelho 2022, Granite Belt Easy-drinking style with plenty of depth and charisma. Scents of tinned tropical fruits, quince, ginger and clove. The palate delivers more tropical fruits but they're a bit more subdued, ably balanced by more spicy ginger, touches of sweet spice and some lime pickle to finish. Quite plush on the palate, but finishes fresh and trails long after each spice with limey acidity and spice. Very good. Screw cap. 13.5% alc. RATING 93 DRINK 2023–2026 $36 MB
Viognier 2022, Granite Belt Juicy, with plenty of hallmark apricot, dried coconut, sugared almond and floral characters going on. Pretty in perfume of all those notes, delightful in the mesh of those flavours likewise. While relatively overt, it holds an easy charm and freshness on its side. Well judged in its style. Screw cap. 12.5% alc. RATING 91 DRINK 2023–2025 $36 MB
Syrah 2021, Granite Belt A soft and supple red wine set to medium weight. Ripe red berry fruits to sniff on, some sweet spice, scents of minty herbs and white pepper, too. The palate feels silky, extends well of velvety tannins and has appealing, green herb and white pepper seasoning. Screw cap. 13% alc. RATING 91 DRINK 2022–2028 $35 MB
Joven Tempranillo 2022, Granite Belt A nouveau style. It's bright, fresh, a little crunchy in texture, vibrant in its personality, low in oak seasoning and generally appealing for early (chilled?) drinking. Scents and flavours of cherry cola, sarsaparilla, cinnamon and aniseed. Pretty as. A little rough around the edges tannins aren't too bad in the scheme of things. Go forth! Screw cap. 13% alc. RATING 90 DRINK 2023–2026 $38 MB

Higher Plane ★★★★★

98 Tom Cullity Drive, Cowaramup, WA 6284 **Region** Margaret River
T (08) 9755 9000 **www**.higherplanewines.com.au **Open** At Juniper Estate, 7 days 10–5 **Winemaker** Luc Fitzgerald **Viticulturist** Ianto Ward **Est.** 1997 **Dozens** 2000 **Vyds** 15.9ha
Higher Plane was purchased by Roger Hill and Gillian Anderson, owners of Juniper, in '06. The brand was retained with the intention of maintaining the unique aspects of the site in the south of Margaret River, distinct from those of Wilyabrup in the north. The close-planted vineyard is sustainably farmed using organic principles. Following the passing of Roger, son Tom now runs the business. Chardonnay, sauvignon blanc, and cabernet sauvignon are the major plantings, with smaller amounts of shiraz, malbec, fiano and verdejo. The aim is to craft wines of varieties and techniques not traditionally associated with the region.

▼▼▼▼▼ **Sun Dips Low Fiano 2022, Margaret River** This is excellent. Dried and fresh pears, peach and honeycomb, flinty, smoky with a light touch of savouriness. Beautifully handled phenolics add texture and shape across the palate and the ever-important acidity ties it all up neatly. Screw cap. 13% alc. **RATING** 95 **DRINK** 2023-2026 $29 JF ✪

Led Astray Fumé Blanc 2022, Margaret River Fruit off a single vineyard in Karridale, whole-bunch pressed to tank, settled then popped into used French barriques for a wild ferment, 7 months on lees. No wonder this is good. It has texture matched to flavour and complexity throughout. Flutters of lavender, stone fruit, lemongrass, guava and tangy citrus with the palate augmented by creamy lees and tangy acidity. It's classy but so easy to drink. Screw cap. 13% alc. **RATING** 95 **DRINK** 2023-2027 $29 JF ✪

Vanishing Point Syrah 2022, Margaret River Not sure why it's called Vanishing Point, but this is guaranteed to lift one's spirit. It's so delicious with dark plums, tangy raspberries and black cherries all lightly spiced with fine tannins and thirst-quenching acidity. Gosh, this is good. Screw cap. 13.5% alc. **RATING** 95 **DRINK** 2023-2028 $29 JF ✪

Time For Heroes Malbec 2022, Margaret River This is bloody delicious. I don't think I've had a more enjoyable 'drink now' malbec. Trademark deep purple boysenberries and blueberries, sweet fruit across the mid-weighted palate and so much energy with lovely tannins all grainy and ripe, vibrant acidity zipping in and out. A cracking wine. Screw cap. 13% alc. **RATING** 94 **DRINK** 2022-2028 $29 JF ✪

▼▼▼▼▽ **Three's Company Field Blend 2022, Margaret River** **RATING** 93 **DRINK** 2023-2026 $29 JF ✪

Forest Grove Chardonnay 2021, Margaret River **RATING** 93 **DRINK** 2023-2029 $28 JH ✪

Two to Tango Cabernet Malbec 2021, Margaret River **RATING** 93 **DRINK** 2023-2030 $29 JF ✪

Jewels of Karridale Chardonnay 2022, Margaret River **RATING** 92 **DRINK** 2024-2031 $29 JF ✪

Syrah 2021, Margaret River **RATING** 92 **DRINK** 2023-2031 $29 JF ✪

Hill-Smith Estate ★★★★☆

40 Eden Valley Road, Angaston, SA 5353 (postal) **Region** Eden Valley
T (08) 8561 3200 **www**.hillsmithestate.com **Open** Not **Winemaker** Louisa Rose
Est. 1979 **Dozens** 5000 **Vyds** 12ha
Hill-Smith Estate is owned by the Hill-Smith Family of Pewsey Vale and Heggies Vineyard fame. The primary Eden Valley vineyard is planted to chardonnay. The Parish vineyard in Tasmania's Coal River Valley was purchased from Frogmore Creek in '12.

▼▼▼▼▼ **Parish Vineyard Single Estate Coal River Valley Riesling 2022, Tasmania** Pale straw with aromas of lime, grapefruit, green apple and light peach tones. Hints of white flowers, almond paste, crushed stone, lemon curd and grapefruit pith. Some lovely slinky texture on the palate with pristine citrus and apple fruits, a mineral-laden seam of acidity that drives the wine forward and a dry, sizzling and focused finish. Screw cap. 12% alc. **RATING** 94 **DRINK** 2023-2029 $35 ✪

Hither & Yon ★★★★

17 High Street, Willunga, SA 5172 **Region** McLaren Vale
T (08) 8556 2082 **www**.hitherandyon.com.au **Open** 7 days 11–4 **Winemaker** Richard Leask **Viticulturist** Richard Leask **Est.** 2012 **Dozens** 10 000 **Vyds** 78ha
Brothers Richard and Malcolm Leask started Hither & Yon in '12, the Old Jarvie label added in '16. The grapes are sourced from 78ha of family vineyards at 7 sites scattered around McLaren Vale. Richard manages the vineyards while Malcolm runs the business. The historic, tiny cellar door was originally the Willunga butcher's shop built in the 1860s. The Hither & Yon labels feature the brand's ampersand, with a different artist creating the artwork for each wine.

Carignan 2022, McLaren Vale This is good. A variety endowed with astringent mettle and inherently high acidity. Placated, toned and let loose with what feels like gentle extraction and the right sort of oak treatment. Red pastille, kirsch, bergamot and a herbal tannic twine directing the fray. Mid-weighted, fresh, intense of flavour and yet light on its feet. Immensely versatile at the table. Good drinking. Diam. 14% alc. **RATING** 91 **DRINK** 2023-2028 $33 NG

Shiraz 2021, McLaren Vale Scents of dark cherry, tea tree, mint and green peppercorn. Iodine and a swab of tapenade, too. This is good drinking for the money. Flavour, poise and refreshment in spades, with a lithe tannin profile tucking in the seams for savouriness over overt fruit. Screw cap. 14.5% alc. **RATING** 91 **DRINK** 2022-2026 $29 NG

Pinot Noir 2022, Adelaide Hills This is a delicious, fuller-weighted pinot noir of ample fruit, optimal ripeness and giddy drinkability. Crushed strawberries, clove, root spice and Seville orange notes meander about a svelte tannic twine. Nothing particularly complex here, but loads to love for those seeking an immediate flavour fix. Diam. 14% alc. **RATING** 90 **DRINK** 2023-2026 $36 NG

Grenache Mataro 2021, McLaren Vale Partial carbonic riffs on blue and red pastille notes. A core of sweeter kirsch, with a firm curb of ferrous, herb-clad tannins to corral any excess. Good drinking, but needs more succulence and intensity. Diam. 14.5% alc. **RATING** 90 **DRINK** 2022-2026 $29 NG

Hobbs Barossa Ranges ★★★★★

Artisans of the Barossa, 24 Vine Vale Road, Tanunda, SA 5352 **Region** Barossa Valley **T** (08) 8563 3935 **www**.hobbsvintners.com.au **Open** 7 days 11–5 **Winemaker** Pete Schell, Chris Ringland (Consultant), Allison and Greg Hobbs **Est.** 1998 **Dozens** 1500 **Vyds** 6.2ha

Hobbs Barossa Ranges is the venture of Greg and Allison Hobbs. The estate vineyards revolve around 1ha of shiraz planted in 1905, 1ha planted in '88, 1ha planted in '97 and 1.82ha planted in '04; just two rows are planted to viognier. Gregor Shiraz, an Amarone-style shiraz in full-blooded table-wine mode is produced by cane cutting, followed by further desiccation on racks.

Gregor Shiraz 2020, Barossa Deep, intense and resonant with gorgeous black fruits, clove, cinnamon, milk chocolate, Dutch salted licorice, espresso, brandied fruit, ironstone, roasting meats and earth. There is a head-spinning texture and intensity to the fruit, with serious impact and latent horsepower, yet showing impeccable balance and verve. One of the best Gregors I've seen. Screw cap. 15.7% alc. **RATING** 96 **DRINK** 2023-2038 $150 DB

1905 Shiraz 2020, Eden Valley I like Greg Hobbs. There is no B.S. Very much like his wines, which are built in a muscular, opulent style, and there ain't nothing wrong with that. Full-bodied with deep, rich plum and macerated black fruit notes with hints of cedar, vanilla, baking spices, licorice and dark chocolate. Powerful and intense with plenty of fruit depth, oak and concentration. Strap in. Agglomerate. 15.6% alc. **RATING** 95 **DRINK** 2023-2035 $170 DB

Hochkirch Wines ★★★★★

7389 Hamilton Highway, Tarrington, Vic 3301 **Region** Henty **T** (03) 5573 5200 **www**.hochkirchwines.com.au **Open** By appt **Winemaker** John Nagorcka **Est.** 1990 **Dozens** 4000 **Vyds** 10ha

Jennifer and John Nagorcka developed Hochkirch in response to the very cool climate: growing season temperatures are similar to those in Burgundy. A high-density planting pattern was implemented, with a low fruiting wire taking advantage of soil warmth in the growing season, and the focus was placed on pinot noir (5ha), with lesser quantities of riesling, chardonnay, semillon and shiraz. The Nagorckas have moved to Demeter certified biodynamic viticulture and the vines are not irrigated.

Maximus Pinot Noir 2021, Henty It's not upfront and that's a good thing. Deep-seated but varietal characters of black cherry, animale, twiggy herbs and root vegetables. It's firm with fine-grained tannin and feels confident through the finish. All it needs is time; a few years at least. Cork. 13% alc. **RATING** 95 **DRINK** 2026–2033 $60 CM

Syrah 2021, Henty Wonderfully complex and engaging. It's awash with bunches of herbs, game, black cherry, violet and cedar characters, with a textural nuttiness as a final coat. It somehow – it's difficult to tell how – feels both plush and sinewy at once, thanks to the stringiness of its tannin perhaps, and the peppery, bunchy, leafy aspect of its aftertaste. In any case it's a wine that tastes wild, in a positive way. Cork. 13% alc. **RATING** 95 **DRINK** 2025–2033 $50 CM ✪

Tarrington Vineyards Pinot Noir 2021, Henty Light and sinewy with textbook structure and, more to the point, length. The flavour itself is sweet-sour, the spice notes liberal, the inflections myriad. It flirts with being too lean or rather too sour but the compensations are significant. It will be beautiful in time. Cork. 12.5% alc. **RATING** 94 **DRINK** 2026–2033 $60 CM

♟♟♟♟ **Village Pinot Noir 2021, Henty** **RATING** 93 **DRINK** 2024–2032 $50 CM

Hoddles Creek Estate

★★★★★

505 Gembrook Road, Hoddles Creek, Vic 3139 **Region** Yarra Valley
T (03) 5967 4692 **www**.hoddlescreekestate.com.au **Open** By appt **Winemaker** Franco D'Anna, Chris Bendle **Viticulturist** Franco D'Anna **Est.** 1997 **Dozens** 30 000 **Vyds** 33.3ha
The D'Anna family established their vineyard on a property that had been in the family since in 1960. Son Franco is the viticulturist and inspired winemaker; he graduated to chief wine buyer by the time he was 21. He completed a bachelor of commerce before studying viticulture at CSU. A vintage at Coldstream Hills, then 2 years' vintage experience with Peter Dredge at Witchmount and, with Mario Marson (ex-Mount Mary) as mentor in '03, put an old head on young shoulders.

♟♟♟♟♟ **1er Chardonnay 2021, Yarra Valley** The bouquet is ethereal yet arrests attention, but it's the amazing intensity of the wine on the palate that's breathtaking. The grapefruit/white peach duo meet their match with the electrifying acidity, creating layers of flavour that are welded together, yet never say too much. Screw cap. 13.2% alc. **RATING** 98 **DRINK** 2023–2041 $65 JH ✪ ♥

1er Pinot Noir 2021, Yarra Valley The scented bouquet has all the marks of the vintage: warm spices, red flowers, plum and forest floor. The silky, supple palate sweeps all that has gone before into an intense, pulsating blaze of dark cherry, savoury spices and fine-strung tannins. Screw cap. 13.2% alc. **RATING** 97 **DRINK** 2023–2041 $65 JH ✪

PSB Pinot Noir 2021, Yarra Valley A wine laden with red cherry, plum, rhubarb and pomegranate. It caresses the mouth through its journey; its generosity is remarkable, but so is its finesse. This is utterly different from the other top wines of the Yarra Valley. Its future will be measured in decades. Screw cap. 13.2% alc. **RATING** 97 **DRINK** 2023–2045 $70 JH ✪

♟♟♟♟♟ **Chardonnay 2021, Yarra Valley** You would be hard-pressed to find a better-value Australian chardonnay. Indeed, this may just be the best value chardonnay in the world! There's a hint of matchstick to go with the yellow nectarine fruit and grilled cashew, while the medium-bodied palate is delicious, flavour filled, refreshing and long. Screw cap. 13.2% alc. **RATING** 96 **DRINK** 2022–2026 $25 PR ✪

Pinot Noir 2021, Yarra Valley Vivid deep crimson hue. Cherry, raspberry, strawberry all populate the intense but perfectly created pinot, each reflected in a Catherine wheel of pinot noir essence. Hoddles Creek does it again and again. Australia's best value pinot? Screw cap. 13.2% alc. **RATING** 96 **DRINK** 2023–2031 $25 JH ✪

Syberia Chardonnay 2020, Yarra Valley Just starting on a long road to a destination utterly different to that suggested by the name. This is a beautiful Yarra Valley chardonnay, a class of intense competition, yet it's right up there. It's a quiet beauty, happy and secure thanks to the balance and harmony of its fruit, acidity and oak. Screw cap. 12.8% alc. **RATING** 96 **DRINK** 2023–2032 $70 JH ✪

Hollick Estates

11 Racecourse Road, Penola, SA 5277 **Region** Coonawarra
T (08) 8737 2318 **www**.hollick.com **Open** Mon–Fri 9–5, Sat–Sun 11–5
Winemaker Jordan Cory **Est.** 1983 **Dozens** 40000 **Vyds** 88ha
Established in 1983 by the Hollick family, Hollick Estates' vineyard, winery, restaurant and
cellar door overlooks Coonawarra. The estate-grown wines come from 3 vineyards, 2 in
Coonawarra and 1 in nearby Wrattonbully, reflecting the characteristics of each site. The
classic Coonawarra varieties of cabernet sauvignon, shiraz and chardonnay are made, along
with The Nectar (botrytis riesling), barbera and tempranillo.

Ravenswood Cabernet Sauvignon 2020, Coonawarra Powerhouse
cabernet. Coffee grounds and blackberry, strings of herbs, woodsmoke and cedar
wood. Warm-hearted, sexy, brooding … all those things. For all these rumblings
though it remains cabernet sauvignon to its back teeth, offering both cool and
warm notes that make gravity look easy, pumping tannin into fruit and keeping it
all seamless. Screw cap. 14.9% alc. **RATING** 95 **DRINK** 2027-2042 $89 CM
Wilgha Shiraz 2020, Coonawarra This is awash with plum, musk and red
licorice flavours, and yet there are herb, tobacco, meat and wood spice characters
here in good measure, which gives it something of a cabernet-like edge. A full-
throttle-but-complex wine that aims to impress, and does exactly that. Screw cap.
14.9% alc. **RATING** 94 **DRINK** 2026-2036 $69 CM

Old Vines Cabernet Sauvignon 2021, Coonawarra RATING 93
DRINK 2024-2035 $36 CM
The Nectar Botrytis 2022, Coonawarra RATING 91 **DRINK** 2023-2028
$27 CM ✪
The Gondolier Barbera 2022, Wrattonbully RATING 90 **DRINK** 2023-2026
$23 CM ✪

Hollydene Estate ★★★★

3483 Golden Highway, Jerrys Plains, NSW 2330 **Region** Hunter Valley
T (02) 6576 4110 **www**.hollydeneestate.com **Open** Sat–Thurs 8.30–4, Fri 8.30–6
Winemaker Matt Burton **Est.** 1965 **Dozens** 7000 **Vyds** 40ha
Karen Williams has 3 vineyards and associated properties, all established in the '60s. They
are Hollydene Estate, Wybong Estate and Arrowfield; the latter one of the original vinous
landmarks in the Upper Hunter. The 3 vineyards produce grapes for the Hollydene Estate and
Juul labels. Hollydene also makes sparkling wines from the Mornington Peninsula.

Museum Release Estate Semillon 2017, Upper Hunter Valley The
gold-green hue would be expected of a 10yo semillon, not a 5yo. Rich, layered,
some honey in the mix. Slightly phenolic, although it was fined. Good value for
immediate drinking. Screw cap. 11% alc. **RATING** 93 **DRINK** 2023-2025 $29 JH ✪
Juul Blanc de Blancs 2008, Mornington Peninsula Traditional method,
disgorged May '22. The previous disgorgement was tasted by another member
of the panel in Dec '16 when it had 6 years on lees, and 1 year on cork. This
iteration has full yellow colour, and one guesses must have had a higher dosage.
Diam. 12.5% alc. **RATING** 91 **DRINK** 2023-2023 $85 JH
Blanc de Noirs 2008, Mornington Peninsula Traditional method, a blend of
pinot noir and pinot meunier, disgorged May '22. The previous disgorgement was
highly rated by another member of the panel in January '17, but seems to have
lost weight rather than gained it; ditto complexity. Diam. 12.5% alc. **RATING** 90
DRINK 2023-2023 $50 JH
Reserve Chardonnay 2021, Upper Hunter Valley French oak is mentioned
several times on the back label, and the wine does indeed have plenty of cashew/
toast on both the bouquet and palate. Good drinking now. Screw cap. 13.5% alc.
RATING 90 **DRINK** 2023-2024 $36 JH

Holm Oak

11 West Bay Road, Rowella, Tas 7270 **Region** Northern Tasmania
T (03) 6394 7577 **www.holmoakvineyards.com.au Open** Mon–Fri 10–3
Winemaker Rebecca Duffy **Viticulturist** Tim Duffy **Est.** 1983 **Dozens** 15000
Vyds 15ha

Holm Oak takes its name from its grove of oak trees, planted around the beginning of the 20th century. A boutique family affair, winemaker Rebecca Duffy has extensive winemaking experience in Australia and California; and husband Tim, a viticultural agronomist, manages the vineyard (pinot noir, pinot gris, cabernet sauvignon, chardonnay, riesling and small amounts of merlot, arneis, shiraz and cabernet franc). Cellar door, winery, family home (and a pet pig named Pinot) all co-exist on the vineyard site.

Riesling 2022, Tasmania A flawless riesling at every point, the bouquet highly floral with white flower and powdery apple blossom before the sheer power of the mouth-watering lime juice and Meyer lemon take control. The length is prodigious, with the flavours lingering in the mouth for a seeming eternity. Screw cap. 11.8% alc. **RATING** 97 **DRINK** 2023–2042 $30 JH ✪

The Wizard Pinot Noir 2020, Tasmania The colour is deep and the bouquet profound, with warm earth, talc, forest leaf, herb litter and a tendril of meat glaze all coming into play on the long, complex, medium-bodied palate. A peacock's tail fans in full display on the finish and aftertaste. Screw cap. 13.5% alc. **RATING** 97 **DRINK** 2023–2035 $65 JH ✪

Pinot Noir 2021, Tasmania The colour is deep in pinot terms, and the palate duly delivers. Its texture and structure are spot on, with spicy tannins running through black cherry and plum fruit in an even, lingering stream. Screw cap. 13.5% alc. **RATING** 96 **DRINK** 2023–2036 $38 JH ✪

The Protégé Pinot Noir 2022, Tasmania The extraordinarily bright colour sets the antennae waving, and the palate is equally good. It's an exercise in purity, all red fruits (cherry, strawberry et al.) with spices waiting to add their impact a few years down the track. And by the way, it wasn't besmirched by oak. Screw cap. 13% alc. **RATING** 95 **DRINK** 2023–2028 $28 JH ✪

The Wizard Chardonnay 2021, Tasmania Pale straw in the glass with inviting characters of grapefruit, green apple, lemon and stone fruit. There is a layer of fine spice along with hints of white flowers, lemon curd, nougat and dreamy oak flitting around. Drive is plentiful on the palate with a porcelain acidity setting a brisk cadence. Screw cap. 13% alc. **RATING** 95 **DRINK** 2023–2027 $65 DB

Shiraz 2021, Tasmania Tasmanian shiraz has well and truly arrived, needing no excuses. The crimson-purple hue carries through to the rim, the bouquet and palate offering reprises each time you go back for another sip, with pepper, fresh earth, dark fruits, tannins and oak all contributing. Screw cap. 13.2% alc. **RATING** 95 **DRINK** 2023–2046 $50 JH ✪

Chardonnay 2021, Tasmania There is something special about the '21 vintage, which blessed all cool-climate wines and invested them with purity and finesse. Balance is achieved with 30% new French oak and mlf, extended lees contact will take the wine through to maturity 5 years hence, and won't stumble at any point into the far future. Screw cap. 12.5% alc. **RATING** 95 **DRINK** 2023–2031 $38 JH ✪

Pinot Gris 2022, Tasmania This wine has been beautifully made, with the lightest of touches from Rebecca Duffy: 10% wild fermented in used oak and 10% in tank, with 3 months on lees. 7g/L acidity and 4g/L RS complete the deal. Screw cap. 12.8% alc. **RATING** 94 **DRINK** 2023–2027 $30 JH ✪

Pinot Noir Chardonnay NV, Tasmania RATING 92 $45 DB
Sparkling Rosé NV, Tasmania RATING 91 $45 DB

Home Hill

38 Nairn Road, Ranelagh, Tas 7109 **Region** Southern Tasmania
T (03) 6264 1200 **www**.homehillwines.com.au **Open** 7 days 10–5 **Winemaker** Catalina
Collado **Viticulturist** Sean Bennett **Est.** 1993 **Dozens** 3500 **Vyds** 10.2ha

Terry and Rosemary Bennett planted their first 0.5ha of vines in '94 on gentle slopes in the beautiful Huon Valley. The plantings have gradually been increased to 10.2ha, including pinot noir, chardonnay, pinot gris and sylvaner. Home Hill has had great success with its exemplary pinot noirs, consistent multi-trophy and gold medal winners in the ultra-competitive Tasmanian Wine Show. Impressive enough but pales into insignificance in the wake of winning the Jimmy Watson Trophy at the Melbourne Wine Awards '15.

Kelly's Reserve Chardonnay 2021, Tasmania Pale straw in the glass with detailed white peach and citrus characters sheathed by gentle-oak spice and hints of white flowers, marzipan, French-oak nuance and stone. Impressive clarity and porcelain acidity on a palate that presents tight and focused. Finishes with a hint of nutty, vanillin oak, pristine citrus fruits and a clean, sapid flick of its tail. Lovely. Screw cap. 13.8% alc. **RATING** 95 **DRINK** 2024–2028 $40 DB ✪

Kelly's Reserve Pinot Noir 2021, Tasmania Bouncy, vibrant cherry red in the glass with notes of wild strawberry, red and dark cherry and red plum undercut with fine spice, forest floor, red licorice and dreamy French oak wafts. A display of pure cherry and berry fruits fan out on the palate. Superfine tannins, bright acidity and a persistent finish that fades with memories of cherry pastry and exotic spice. Screw cap. 14.1% alc. **RATING** 95 **DRINK** 2023–2032 $110 DB

Ms Daisy Cuvée 2018, Tasmania RATING 93 **DRINK** 2023–2026 $50 DB
Estate Pinot Noir 2021, Tasmania RATING 93 **DRINK** 2023–2028 $60 DB
Kelly's Cuvée 2018, Tasmania RATING 92 **DRINK** 2023–2026 $50 DB

HOOSEGG

45 Caldwell Lane, Orange NSW 2800 **Region** Orange
T 0448 983 033 **www**.hoosegg.com **Open** By appt **Winemaker** Philip Shaw
Viticulturist Philip Shaw **Est.** 1984

This seems certain to be the last oenological resting place of Philip Shaw, the genius who made the Rosemount Estate empire possible. After its merger to Southcorp in '01, he saw the writing on the wall and jumped ship, soon after excising 47ha from his '89-planted Koomooloo vineyard for Philip Shaw Wines. In '15 he passed ownership of Philip Shaw Wines to his sons, Damian and Daniel, and built a 50t winery for his business HOOSEGG. In a complete turnaround from 30+ years at the helm on one of Australia's largest wine producers, here Philip's exceptional wines are small batch and hand made.

Double Happy Cabernet Sauvignon 2019, Orange Superlative in precisely picked blackberries, mulberry and plum skin. Black raspberry and tulip with a medley of peppercorn, Kalamata olive, bay leaf and thyme. Cigar box and sweet chewing tobacco, mocha and potting soil. The wine flows seamlessly with sandy tannins, propulsive acidity and unification of oak. There is flavour for days here. Beautiful to behold. Cork. 13.5% alc. **RATING** 97 **DRINK** 2022–2035 $140 SW ♥

Jade Moon Cabernet Franc 2019, Orange Violets, cherries and a briar of thistle and shrub. A wine whose intoxicating perfume is overwhelming and often undersold. Cassis, blueberries and volcanic black rock. Tannins are sinewy and finely woven together to create a lacework of exalted texture. Salted licorice, cardamom and cocoa beans. A magnificent celebration of the variety, this wine sings a song of thriving vines, place and artistry. Cork. 13.4% alc. **RATING** 96 **DRINK** 2022–2032 $140 SW ♥

Mountain Dragon Merlot 2019, Orange Few take the time to grow, care and craft merlot in such a way. Damson plum, fresh prune and blackberry leaf. Juniper, allspice and black peppercorns are threaded throughout. Tiny additions of cabernet sauvignon and shiraz frame that plummy fruit like a gilded picture, ensuring the wine will age gracefully and glacially. Sits comfortably in the mid palate and acidity carries the flavours of granite, turned earth and vanilla bean on and on. Cork. 13.4% alc. **RATING** 95 **DRINK** 2022–2030 $118 SW

Self Made-Up Man 2019, Orange 35/32/21/12% shiraz/cabernet sauvignon/ merlot/cabernet franc. Raspberry, pomegranate, cherry and blackcurrants. Allspice, cardamom, cedar and boot polish follow. Grainy tannins sit upfront and acidity rolls on. Oak stands in support like the hooves of a Clydesdale. Finishes savoury and dry with finely sprinkled white pepper. Screw cap. 13.4% alc. **RATING** 95 **DRINK** 2022–2032 $58 SW

Everything is Going According to Plan Chardonnay 2019, Orange Struck match and cracked bluestones. Wild jasmine, lemonade fruit, white peach and sunflower seed. Coconut nougat, ginger snaps and creamed butter. Oak is plentiful and glossy, nicely weighted mlf and migration across the palate. Quite seamless in nature. Screw cap. 13.1% alc. **RATING** 95 **DRINK** 2022–2028 $58 SW

Magic Monkey Shiraz 2019, Orange This has black fruit at its core with slivers of raspberry coulis and pomegranate. White pepper, allspice and clove studs, a hint of bay leaf and rosemary stem. The wine is lithe and slinky on the palate with classy oak behind it all. The layers of spice come alive with nutmeg, tonka bean and caraway. A beautifully poised wine with plenty of production but full of class. Cork. 13.5% alc. **RATING** 94 **DRINK** 2022–2028 $118 SW

Houghton   ★★★★★

4070 Caves Road, Wilyabrup, WA 6280 **Region** Swan Valley
T (08) 9755 6042 **www**.houghton-wines.com.au **Open** 7 days 11–5
Winemaker Courtney Treacher **Viticulturist** Stephen Kirby **Est.** 1836 **Dozens** 43 000
Houghton's reputation was once largely dependent on its (then) White Burgundy. Its portfolio now changed to a kaleidoscopic range of high-quality wines from the Margaret River, Frankland River, Great Southern and Pemberton regions to the fore. In Nov '19 the Houghton property was sold to the Yukich family, who had acquired part of the property in '90 and established Oakover Wines. The reunited vineyard relaunched as Nikola Estate (see separate entry), in honour of Nikola Yukich, who emigrated from Croatia and planted vines in the Swan Valley over 90 years ago. The Houghton brand was retained by Accolade.

ΨΨΨΨΨ C.W. Ferguson Cabernet Malbec 2020, Frankland River Cabernet & Family of the Year. Score awarded by the Halliday tasting panel at the annual Awards judging. MB writes: A mellow, medium- to fuller-weight expression rippling with choc-raspberry, forest berry coulis, clove, dark chocolate, mint and eucalyptus. All nicely played, balanced and even. A potent flow on the palate, so inky and rich, and a chewy corset of silty, crushed rock tannins. It's a bold strike of cab malbec but finds judicious balance and a sense of vibrancy. It speaks fluently of quality fruit and the finesse of winemaking. Screw cap. 14% alc. **RATING** 98 **DRINK** 2026–2040 $78 PD ♥

Gladstones Cabernet Sauvignon 2020, Margaret River There's no denying the presence of the variety and its region. It's intensely flavoured: full of mulberries and cassis, five-spice and cedary oak with wafts of violets and cooling menthol. It's fuller bodied and structured but not weighty, it seems to effortlessly work across the palate with shapely tannins and refreshing acidity. Screw cap. 13.5% alc. **RATING** 95 **DRINK** 2023–2038 $100 JF

Jack Mann Single Vineyard Cabernet Sauvignon 2020, Frankland River A blockbuster wine. Deeply scented, loaded with blackforest cake, rum and raisin chocolate, ripe plum and cassis notes with whiffs of violets and vanilla cream. The palate is intense, so concentrated and thick, more of the blackforest cake, panforte, rum and raisin with firm tannins rippling around, dry, woody spices woven through and a good extension of flavour. Hold onto your hat. Screw cap. 14% alc. **RATING** 94 **DRINK** 2026–2040 $175 MB

House of Arras

Bay of Fires, 40 Baxters Road, Pipers River, Tas 7252 **Region** Northern Tasmania
T (03) 6362 7622 **www.**houseofarras.com.au **Open** Thurs–Mon 10–5 by appt
Winemaker Ed Carr **Est.** 1995

House of Arras is considered the benchmark at the pointy end of our country's outstanding sparkling wine producers. Pristine fruit from some of Tasmania's top vineyard sites and having Australia's most awarded sparkling winemaker, Ed Carr, at the helm is a combination that is hard to beat. The composition, complexity and structure of the estate sparkling wines and their track record on the wine show circuit are a testament to Ed's exceptional skill as a sparkling winemaker and the commitment of House of Arras to produce the finest sparkling wines in the land. World-class wines that proudly express their origin.

ᵀᵀᵀᵀᵀ **Rosé 2014, Tasmania** Expansive and inviting aromas of bright red fruits and citrus underlined with soft spice, fresh brioche and light sea-spray notes. Immaculate tension on the palate, with autolysis notes wrapping their arms around pure red fruits while walking the ridgeline of grace and latent power with aplomb. A stunning wine. Diam. 13.5% alc. **RATING** 97 **DRINK** 2023–2032 $130 DB
EJ Carr Late Disgorged 2007, Tasmania Disgorged Feb '22. Deep straw with an ultrafine bead. Characters of redcurrant, red apple, shiitake, crushed oyster shell, fresh brioche and soft spice. Beautifully expansive, yet taut on the palate with toasty pastry and almond meal notes with pitch-perfect tension and an impressive sense of grace and elegance. Diam. 12.5% alc. **RATING** 97 **DRINK** 2023–2032 $266 DB ♥

ᵀᵀᵀᵀᵀ **Grand Vintage 2014, Tasmania** Pale straw with an ultrafine, energetic bead and mousse. Notes of green apple, redcurrant, fresh brioche, white flowers, oyster shell and soft spice. Expansive and pure, with toasty elements floating in on the palate. They're joined by notes of nougat, vanilla bean, roasted nuts and liminal hints of white truffle and stone. Achingly pure, with a taut sense of grace. Beautiful. Diam. 13.3% alc. **RATING** 96 **DRINK** 2023–2030 $119 DB
Blanc de Blancs 2014, Tasmania Abundant leesy complexity on display here with notes of green apple, fresh-baked apple pastries, complex autolysis hints, juicy white peach, dried honey, clotted cream, nougat and jasmine. Persistent and long with scintillating acid drive and toasty roasted nut and brioche notes entering on the finish. A picture of latent power and grace. Diam. 13.2% alc. **RATING** 95 **DRINK** 2023–2026 $130 DB

ᵀᵀᵀᵀᵀ **Brut Elite NV, Tasmania RATING** 93 $65 DB
Origin South Brut Cuvée NV, Tasmania RATING 92 $35 DB
A by Arras Premium Cuvée Rosé NV, Tasmania RATING 92 $35 DB
A by Arras Premium Cuvée NV, Tasmania RATING 91 $35 DB

Howard Park

Miamup Road, Cowaramup, WA 6284 **Region** Margaret River
T (08) 9756 5200 **www.**burchfamilywines.com.au **Open** 7 days 10–5 **Winemaker** Nic Bowen, Mark Bailey **Viticulturist** David Botting, Steve Kirby **Est.** 1986 **Vyds** 183ha

Over the last 30 years, the Burch family has slowly acquired vineyards in Margaret River and Great Southern. The Margaret River vineyards range from Leston in Wilyabrup to Allingham in southern Karridale; Great Southern includes Mount Barrow and Abercrombie, with Houghton cabernet clones, planted in '75, all in Mount Barker. The feng shui–designed cellar door is a must-see. A founding member of Australia's First Families of Wine.

ᵀᵀᵀᵀᵀ **Chardonnay 2021, Margaret River** This classy wine has the freshness and bite of melon, white peach and grapefruit of Karridale. There is a light touch of funk on the bouquet that brings complexity forward, highlighting the grapefruit contribution. Screw cap. 13% alc. **RATING** 96 **DRINK** 2023–2030 $60 JH ✪
ASW Cabernet Sauvignon Shiraz 2020, Margaret River Cabernet sauvignon from Block 29 with shiraz from Block 4, though no percentage is

given for either varietal. Well, for my money the cabernet's contribution has been of critical importance, providing the tannin structure, the cool and controlled fruit, and the cedary nuances that create the wine's length. And that fresh acidity. Screw cap. 14.5% alc. RATING 96 DRINK 2023-2040 $75 JH ✪

Miamup Rosé 2022, Margaret River Now, isn't this a glass of good cheer with its assortment of red fruits, white peach dazzled in spice and lemon-saline flavours. There's more, with texture, refreshing acidity and an overall succulence meaning another glass is guaranteed to be enjoyed. Screw cap. 12.5% alc. RATING 95 DRINK 2022-2024 $29 JF ✪

Arbor Novae Chenin Blanc 2022, Margaret River This is particularly smart. Dried wildflowers, quince and barely ripe pears, Japanese pickled ginger and whiffs of red shiso. Ah, but the palate. Racy, tangy and juicy yet with plenty of texture. The finish tears away and all that's left is an empty glass. Screw cap. 12.5% alc. RATING 95 DRINK 2022-2030 $35 JF ✪

Chardonnay 2022, Margaret River Here's the list: citrusy flavours, pristine stone fruit, ginger spice, creamy lees and lightly toasty, attractive cedary oak offering savoury inputs. And the length, very good length thanks to the acidity. All the boxes have been ticked for a most excellent chardonnay. Screw cap. 12.5% alc. RATING 95 DRINK 2023-2033 $60 JF

🍷🍷🍷🍷 **Petit Jeté Brut NV, South West Australia** RATING 93 $32 JF ✪
Grenache 2022, Swan Valley RATING 93 DRINK 2022-2027 $29 JF ✪
Miamup Sauvignon Blanc Semillon 2022, Margaret River RATING 93 DRINK 2022-2025 $29 JF ✪
Miamup Chardonnay 2022, Margaret River RATING 93 DRINK 2022-2030 $29 JF ✪
Riesling 2022, Great Southern RATING 93 DRINK 2022-2033 $35 JF ✪
Flint Rock Shiraz 2020, Great Southern RATING 93 DRINK 2022-2030 $25 JF ✪
Sauvignon Blanc 2022, Western Australia RATING 92 DRINK 2022-2026 $32 JF
Flint Rock Riesling 2022, Great Southern RATING 92 DRINK 2022-2032 $29 JF ✪
Flint Rock Chardonnay 2022, Great Southern RATING 92 DRINK 2022-2028 $29 JF ✪
Jete Rosé NV, Great Southern RATING 91 $46 JF
Flint Rock Pinot Noir 2022, Great Southern RATING 90 DRINK 2022-2027 $29 JF

Howard Vineyard   ★★★★★

53 Bald Hills Road, Nairne, SA 5252 **Region** Adelaide Hills
T (08) 8188 0203 **www.**howardvineyard.com **Open** 7 days by appt **Winemaker** Tom Northcott **Viticulturist** Nathan Foreman **Est.** 1997 **Dozens** 25 000 **Vyds** 60ha
Howard Vineyard is a family-owned Adelaide Hills winery set among towering gum trees, and terraced lawns. All the wines are estate-grown. Winemaker Tom Northcott has a bachelor degree in viticulture and oenology from Adelaide University, and has worked vintages in the South of France, Barossa Valley, Western Australia and Tasmania.

🍷🍷🍷🍷🍷 **Amos Chardonnay 2021, Adelaide Hills** A fine beam of nougatine and toasted hazelnut reminds me of quality burgundy. Glazed quince, apricot kernel, raw almond and praline, too. I do wish there was a little more chewy texture and less acidity. An expansive and lovely wine. Diam. 13% alc. RATING 95 DRINK 2022-2032 $60 NG

Amos Cabernet Sauvignon 2021, Adelaide Hills Refined aromas of mulberry, crème de cassis, tomato bush and mint. Long, lithe, mid-weighted, savoury and refined, with an immaculate patina of tannins. Very good wine. Screw cap. 14.5% alc. RATING 95 DRINK 2022-2030 $60 NG

ㅊㅊㅊㅊㅊ Amos Shiraz 2021, Adelaide Hills RATING 93 DRINK 2023-2033 $60 NG
Amos Pinot Noir 2021, Adelaide Hills RATING 93 DRINK 2022-2031
$60 NG
Amos Blanc de Noirs 2014, Adelaide Hills RATING 92 DRINK 2022-2028
$80 NG
Shiraz 2021, Adelaide Hills RATING 92 DRINK 2022-2027 $35 NG
Block Q Sauvignon Blanc 2022, Adelaide Hills RATING 91
DRINK 2022-2024 $25 NG ✪
Sangiovese 2022, Adelaide Hills RATING 91 DRINK 2022-2027 $40 NG
Rosé 2022, Adelaide Hills RATING 91 DRINK 2022-2023 $35 NG

Hugh Hamilton Wines ★★★★★

94 McMurtrie Road, McLaren Vale, SA 5171 **Region** McLaren Vale
T (08) 8323 8689 **www**.hughhamiltonwines.com.au **Open** 7 days 11–5
Winemaker Nic Bourke **Est.** 1991 **Dozens** 18 500 **Vyds** 21.4ha

In '14, 5th-generation family member Hugh Hamilton handed over the reins to daughter
Mary. The business embraces both mainstream and alternative varieties, its 85+yo shiraz and
65+yo cabernet sauvignon at its Blewitt Springs vineyard providing the ability to develop
the Black Blood range. There have been changes: in the way the vines are trellised, picking
and fermenting in small open fermenters, using gravity for wine movements and maturation
in high-quality French oak. The Tonnellerie trio of wines, made from the same shiraz fruit,
are raised in oak from different French cooperages: Ermitage, Vicard and François Frères.
The cellar door is lined with the original jarrah from Vat 15 of the historic Hamilton's Ewell
winery, the largest wooden vat ever built in the Southern Hemisphere.

ㅊㅊㅊㅊㅊ Black Blood II Shiraz 2021, McLaren Vale Red licorice, purple pastille,
blueberry and a potpourri of clove, cardamom and pepper. A powerful wine, to
be sure. But there is a levity, poise and welcome drinkability. Fine length, to boot.
Screw cap. 14.8% alc. RATING 95 DRINK 2022-2032 $84 NG
Tonnellerie Unoaked Shiraz 2020, McLaren Vale Matured in older barrels
and thus, the rather misleading moniker, 'unoaked'. If it weren't for that subtle
oak the tannins would be nowhere near as good as they are. And they are very
good. Scents of blue fruits, clove, aniseed and raspberry bonbon. The classy floral
nose suggestive of the lithe, yet firm; forceful, yet elegant; rich and yet subtle wine
to come. Screw cap. 14.8% alc. RATING 95 DRINK 2022-2032 $55 NG
The Oddball Saperavi 2020, McLaren Vale This is very good. An ancient
variety of a dense tannins and colour. Yet the extraction is deft, comprehending
the need for some structure without risking excessive dryness. Especially with
a variety as endowed as this. Opaque. Riffs on kirsch, bracken and lilac. The
tannins, alloyed enough, yet sufficiently gritty to guide length and dictate a
welcome savouriness. Cork. 14.9% alc. RATING 95 DRINK 2022-2030 $74 NG
Black Blood III Shiraz 2021, McLaren Vale Sourced from the elevated stands
of Blewitt Springs. By far the freshest and more lifted of the troika of Black
Blood cuvées. Aniseed, a smear of black olive and the iodine florals of a reductive
approach in the cellar. Some menthol dryness across the finish. A very good wine.
Screw cap. 14.5% alc. RATING 94 DRINK 2022-2030 $84 NG

ㅊㅊㅊㅊㅊ The Nimble King Cabernet Sauvignon 2021, McLaren Vale RATING 93
DRINK 2022-2030 $55 NG
Black Ops Shiraz Saperavi 2021, McLaren Vale RATING 93
DRINK 2022-2028 $39 NG
Black Blood I Shiraz 2021, McLaren Vale RATING 93 DRINK 2022-2030
$84 NG
Jekyll & Hyde Shiraz Viognier 2020, McLaren Vale RATING 93
DRINK 2022-2032 $55 NG
Tonnellerie Francois Frères Shiraz 2020, McLaren Vale RATING 93
DRINK 2024-2032 $55 NG
The Ruffian Liqueur Muscat NV, Rutherglen RATING 93 $35 NG ✪

The Mongrel Sangiovese 2022, McLaren Vale RATING 92 DRINK 2023-2027 $33 NG

The Rascal Shiraz 2021, McLaren Vale RATING 92 DRINK 2022-2030 $35 NG

Oddball the Great Saperavi 2019, McLaren Vale RATING 92 DRINK 2022-2035 $154 NG

The Moocher Mourvèdre 2021, McLaren Vale RATING 91 DRINK 2023-2031 $35 NG

Loose Lips NV, McLaren Vale Adelaide Hills RATING 90 DRINK 2023-2028 $38 NG

Humis Vineyard ★★★★

3730 Heathcote-Rochester Road, Corop, Vic 3559 **Region** Heathcote
T 0419 588 044 **www.**humisvineyard.com **Open** By appt **Winemaker** Missy Jones
Viticulturist Hugh Jones **Est.** 2010 **Dozens** 1000 **Vyds** 22.5ha
In '10, with the wine industry on its knees and a drought in full swing in Heathcote, Hugh and Michelle (Missy) Jones saw a dusty paddock running down to a dry Lake Cooper with a 'for sale' sign. The decision was obvious: buy. The ace in the hole was the irrigation water available to the property. New plantings of Rhône varietals such as grenache, grenache blanc, picpoul and marsanne were chosen for their heat and drought resistance.

Grenache 2022, Heathcote Pitch-perfect scents of sweet spice and blueberry lead to a super-delicious palate laden with bright red berried fruit, violets, crushed fennel and musk. The appeal of this wine is obvious, in the best of ways. It's bright, perfumed, strung with fine-grained, flavoursome tannin and while complex, it's juicy and energetic throughout. It's a light and lovely wine. Screw cap. 14.5% alc. **RATING** 94 **DRINK** 2023-2029 $29 CM

Grenache Rosé 2022, Heathcote RATING 90 **DRINK** 2023-2025 $23 CM

Hungerford Hill ★★★★☆

2450 Broke Road, Pokolbin, NSW 2320 **Region** Hunter Valley
T (02) 4998 7666 **www.**hungerfordhill.com.au **Open** 7 days 10-5 **Winemaker** Bryan Currie **Est.** 1967 **Dozens** 22 000 **Vyds** 5ha
Sam and Christie Arnaout purchased Hungerford Hill in Dec '16, planning to refocus the 50yo label on its Hunter Valley origin, also adding significant new Lower Hunter vineyards at Sweetwater and Dalwood – the oldest continuously operating vineyard in Australia. Hungerford Hill uses these vineyards to bolster its Hunter Valley wines while continuing its 20+-year association with the cool-climate Tumbarumba and Hilltops regions.

Pinot Meunier 2022, Tumbarumba It's a sunny day, lunch is ready and you're hankering for a juicy red. One with plenty of flavour and punch. Well, here it is: a heady, spicy and lively offering with fine silk tannins, plenty of refreshing acidity and so good that everyone will be raising their hand when asked, who wants a glass of pinot meunier? Screw cap. 13.5% alc. **RATING** 95 **DRINK** 2023-2028 $45 JF

Tempranillo 2022, Hilltops RATING 93 **DRINK** 2024-2029 $45 JF
Sauvignon Blanc 2022, Tumbarumba RATING 90 **DRINK** 2022-2025 $27 JF
Pinot Gris 2022, Tumbarumba RATING 90 **DRINK** 2022-2025 $27 JF

Hurley Vineyard ★★★★★

101 Balnarring Road, Balnarring, Vic 3926 (postal) **Region** Mornington Peninsula
T (03) 5931 3000 **www.**hurleyvineyard.com.au **Open** Not **Winemaker** Kevin Bell
Est. 1998 **Dozens** 1100 **Vyds** 3.5ha
It's never as easy as it seems. Despite leading busy city lives, Kevin Bell and wife Tricia Byrnes have done most of the hard work in establishing Hurley Vineyard themselves, with some help from family and friends. Kevin completed the applied science (wine science) degree at CSU,

drawing on a wide circle of fellow pinot noir makers in Australia and Burgundy. He has not allowed a significant heart issue to prevent him continuing with his first love.

ŢŢŢŢŢ **Garamond Balnarring Pinot Noir 2021, Mornington Peninsula** The most balanced and complete of Hurley's pinots this vintage, with more flesh to the bones. Dark fruit, ripe, tangy and sometimes sweet, punchy acidity yet firm tannins and smoky, charry oak acting as a backdrop to the full-bodied palate. Diam. 13.3% alc. **RATING** 95 **DRINK** 2024–2034 $110 JF

ŢŢŢŢŢ **Hommage Balnarring Pinot Noir 2021, Mornington Peninsula** **RATING** 93 **DRINK** 2024–2034 $90 JF
Lodestone Balnarring Pinot Noir 2021, Mornington Peninsula **RATING** 92 **DRINK** 2024–2031 $90 JF

Hutton Vale Farm ★★★★

65 Stone Jar Road, Angaston, SA 5353 **Region** Eden Valley
T (08) 8564 8270 **www**.huttonvale.com **Open** By appt **Winemaker** Kym Teusner
Est. 1960 **Dozens** 1500 **Vyds** 27.1ha
John Howard Angas arrived in SA in 1843 and gave his name to Angaston, purchasing and developing significant farming property. He named part of this Hutton Vale, a property that is now owned by his great-great-grandson John and wife Jan Angas. The Angases grow the grapes and Kym Teusner is responsible for the winemaking, sales and marketing of Hutton Vale wines.

ŢŢŢŢŢ **Riesling 2022, Eden Valley** Succulent and scintillating rizza with bright fruit flavour, tension and energy to burn. Loaded with lime and frangipani on the bouquet with whiffs of ginger and blackcurrant. The palate is lightly juicy but clipped with fine, powdery pucker and bolstered with briny, mineral tang. More lime, floral palate elements, candied orange peel and gingery notes to taste too. Lots of flavour, but freshness on song. A delight. Screw cap. 12.2% alc. **RATING** 94 **DRINK** 2022–2035 $35 MB ✪
Cabernet Sauvignon 2019, Eden Valley Dark and brooding cabernet with inky, ripe plummy fruit characters, touches of Christmas pudding, raisin and nuts with a lick of choc-mint in the mix. Scents and flavours echo each other well, the palate dense, saturated in flavour yet finds a trim of light, gummy tannin to tighten and freshen things. A bold red, done impeccably. Screw cap. 14.5% alc. **RATING** 94 **DRINK** 2022–2035 $70 MB

ŢŢŢŢŢ **Off Dry Riesling 2022, Eden Valley** **RATING** 93 **DRINK** 2022–2028 $35 MB ✪
Shiraz 2019, Eden Valley **RATING** 93 **DRINK** 2022–2035 $75 MB

Il Cattivo ★★★★

65 Bay View Road, Port Elliot, SA, 5212 (postal) **Region** Currency Creek
T (08) 7079 1033 **www**.ilcattivo.com.au **Open** Not **Winemaker** Anthony Catinari, Richard Bate **Viticulturist** Anthony Catinari **Est.** 2017 **Dozens** 1550 **Vyds** 1ha
Il Cattivo is owned by property developer Anthony Catinari, whose 2017-planted estate vineyard overlooks Fisherman's Bay on the south coast of the Fleurieu Peninsula. The 1ha vineyard is planted to fiano and montepulciano, channeling Anthony's family roots in Italy's Abruzzo. Additional fruit is sourced from McLaren Vale and the Adelaide Hills, and more plantings of Italian and Spanish varieties, as well as Georgian variety saperavi, are planned.

ŢŢŢŢŢ **Fiano 2022, Langhorne Creek** This presents as both fresh and complex. Pulpy fruit, custard powder notes, a sweet hay aspect and a mix of crushed fennel and peach through the finish. It's not your standard fare – those custard powder notes won't be for everyone – but it's quite a ride. Screw cap. 12% alc. **RATING** 91 **DRINK** 2023–2026 $24 CM ✪
Nebbiolo 2021, Southern Fleurieu This is a decent rendition of the variety. Red licorice, tar, rust and orange-blossom characters come infused

with woodsmoke and sweet spice. It finishes appropriately dry though even as it does, the fruit and spice notes keep rolling on through. Screw cap. 13.5% alc. **RATING** 91 **DRINK** 2023-2028 $35 CM

Tempranillo 2022, Adelaide Hills This is a bright, energetic tempranillo, released young, with cherry-berry flavours tumbling throughout, along with dry spice and eucalyptus notes. It's a bit drier and more tannic than is custom with the 'joven' style but that's not in any way a bad thing. Screw cap. 13% alc. **RATING** 90 **DRINK** 2023-2026 $28 CM

Ilya Vineyards   ★★★★

343 Toops Hills Rd, Kuitpo, SA 5201 **Region** Adelaide Hills
T 0419 801 796 www.ilyavineyards.com **Open** By appt **Winemaker Est.** 1997
Dozens 200 **Vyds** 66ha

Ilya Vineyards is located in Kuitpo, an unofficial subregion of the Hills marked by ironstone soils. The site was purchased in '97 by Paul and Sharon Bushell with the aim of making cool-climate wines from estate-grown fruit. The culture here is one of an understated restraint. A calm composure. The comprehension that while nature's whimsies can be honed to an extent, they will ultimately usurp excessive winemaking or vineyard (mis)management. Subsequently, the wines are mid-weighted, judiciously oaked, impeccably balanced and delicious to drink. These are the sort of wines that reflect a steady hand and a good place to grow grapes, stimulating the intellect without getting in the way of conversation.

Trial Blend No.1 Shiraz Pinot Noir 2021, Adelaide Hills Perhaps the best shiraz/pinot noir blend in these parts. Infuses the raspberry waft of fruit and cushy mid-palate with just enough herbs, spice and astringency to prevent banality, confer intrigue and evince just enough structural authority to keep the drinker interested. Pepper, clove, red fruit accents, orange zest and a slick of red licorice. Delicious! Screw cap. 14% alc. **RATING** 93 **DRINK** 2022-2025 $28 NG

Shiraz 2021, Adelaide Hills Mid-weighted of feel, with a ferrous curb of tannins directing iodine, pâté en croute, sapid red and blue fruit accents and a whole-bunch volley of clove, peppercorn and mezcal. The acidity is crystalline and natural of feel, whetting my palate. The finish of flow and impressive linger. Screw cap. 14% alc. **RATING** 92 **DRINK** 2022-2027 $28 NG ✪

Single Vineyard Pinot Noir 2021, Adelaide Hills A judicious confluence of bunchy clove, sarsaparilla and dill accents with a core of red cherry sappiness, briary tannins stemming any excess. A free flow of herbs, spices and fruit from attack to finish. A beautifully composed wine and at the price, stellar value. Screw cap. 13.5% alc. **RATING** 92 **DRINK** 2022-2027 $28 NG ✪

Single Vineyard Cabernet Sauvignon 2019, Adelaide Hills A beautifully proportioned wine for the price, and stylised to perfection. Currant, anise, mint and sage flecking the sort of long-limbed tannins that impart savouriness as much as a gentle authority. Just the ticket for everyday drinking. Screw cap. 14% alc. **RATING** 91 **DRINK** 2022-2030 $28 NG ✪

In Praise of Shadows   ★★★★

212 Seaview Road, McLaren Vale, SA 5171 **Region** McLaren Vale
T 0411 518 037 www.inpraiseofshadows.com.au **Open** By appt **Winemaker** Rob Mack, Brett Trewartha **Est.** 2017 **Dozens** 3000

Inspired by the eponymous essay on Japanese aesthetics by Jun'ichirō Tanizaki, In Praise of Shadows wines are about an immediacy, pleasure and the embrace of what lies in front of our eyes, rather than that which has fallen to the wayside of the past. In essence, Ikigai, or our reason for being. The wines, fine-boned, energetic and floral, are Mediterranean-accented, befitting McLaren Vale and the elevated reaches of Blewitt Springs and Clarendon, from whence much of the fruit is sourced. An emphasis is placed on organic material and a less-is-more approach, without it being a mantra.

Akira Grenache 2021, McLaren Vale This is better the second day, than the first. Musk, rosewater, a scent of Indian spice and a whiff of the clove, star anise and cinnamon of the souk. Cocoa oak, too, upon opening. Quite the magic carpet ride, with a bark-like ripple of tannin to conclude. The motivation here is admirable. Delicious. Screw cap. 13.2% alc. **RATING** 93 **DRINK** 2022–2026 $60 NG

Shiraz 2022, McLaren Vale This is a smoky, delicious and unashamedly hedonistic sort of shiraz that's skilfully pared back into a mould of spicy, lifted freshness. Riffs on barbecued baby back ribs, charcuterie and porcini dashi muddled with lilac, dried lavender, nori, clove, pepper grind and purple pastille. Loosely knit yet refined, with just enough tension for poise and accessible delivery. Screw cap. 14.2% alc. **RATING** 92 **DRINK** 2023–2026 $30 NG ✪

Komorebi Grenache 2021, McLaren Vale Pretty aromas of ume, cranberry, mashed strawberry, Seville orange and rosehip tea. While the acidity is crunchy, the tannins are wiry and astringent, backed by an underlying greenness. Prosaic. Screw cap. 13.2% alc. **RATING** 92 **DRINK** 2022–2026 $60 NG

Mankai 2022, McLaren Vale Grenache/touriga/monastrell/graciano. An exciting blend that augurs as well for the present as the future. Touriga's florals, purple fruits and iodine-freshness at the fore. Sangria, white pepper and a smattering of thyme and dill across the finish. Contagious of energy. Fun to drink. Screw cap. 13% alc. **RATING** 91 **DRINK** 2022–2024 $28 NG ✪

Sakura Rosé 2022, McLaren Vale Majority sangiovese, with a burst of grenache at its core. A mid-weighted and highly textural rosé. Dried thyme, pomegranate, red cherry and musk with a curl of fibrous tannins imparting chew and a gentle authority to the finish. Screw cap. 13% alc. **RATING** 91 **DRINK** 2022–2023 $28 NG ✪

Shiraz 2021, McLaren Vale A ferrous, savoury, mid-weighted and immensely rewarding warm-climate shiraz. Dried salumi, iodine and a yeasty beef stock–marmite equation, ladling oodles of umami across the mid-palate. Plenty of Indian spice, ground pepper and bunchy complexity layering the pushy, vibrant finish. Delicious drinking. Screw cap. 13.4% alc. **RATING** 91 **DRINK** 2022–2027 $30 NG

Lusko Fusco 2022, McLaren Vale Adelaide Hills Tempranillo/touriga/graciano. While there is an element of monotony to these ersatz field blends, this strikes a pose. At least by virtue of its formed tannic kit, meandering beneath root spice, tamarind and Cherry Ripe notes. Good, savoury drinking. Screw cap. 12.5% alc. **RATING** 90 **DRINK** 2022–2025 $30 NG

Cabernet Franc 2022, McLaren Vale An exuberantly aromatic, pulpy, mid-weighted style. Semi-carbonic fermentation has been used to good effect. Lilac, rosewater and bergamot. Redcurrant and campfire, beyond. The finish is effortless and lithe, with just enough grippy tannin to evince poise and authority. Screw cap. 13% alc. **RATING** 90 **DRINK** 2022–2026 $30 NG

Mankai 2021, McLaren Vale Garnacha/monastrell/touriga/graciano. A slurpy wine with a bristle of tannin and squeegee of maritime salinity, for freshness. Lilac, crisp nori, blue-to-purple fruit allusions and some dried thyme scattered across the slightly edgy finish. I'd be drinking this with a good chill and a giddy smile. Screw cap. 13.3% alc. **RATING** 90 **DRINK** 2022–2025 $28 NG

Indigo Vineyard ★★★★

1221 Beechworth-Wangaratta Road, Everton Upper, Vic 3678 **Region** Beechworth **T** (03) 5727 0233 **www**.indigovineyard.com.au **Open** 7 days 11–4 **Winemaker** Lilian Carter **Viticulturist** Daniel Abotomey **Est.** 1999 **Dozens** 6000 **Vyds** 46ha
Indigo Vineyard has a little under 50ha of vineyards planted to 12 varieties, including the top French and Italian grapes. The business sells about half of its fruit to Brokenwood, where Indigo wines are made by Kate Sturgess and Stuart Hordern.

🍷🍷🍷🍷🍷 **Pinot Grigio 2021, Beechworth** Plenty of zing from appley fresh, bright acidity. The mid-palate texture brings all manner of food possibilities with it. And in between, there is the most delightful array of floral aromatics, nashi pear, a hint of spice and a range of delicious apple – fresh and cooked – finishing with just a touch of sweet biscuit. Screw cap. 12.9% alc. **RATING** 95 **DRINK** 2022–2026 $25 JP ✪ ♥

Inkwell ★★★★★

377 California Road, Tatachilla, SA 5171 **Region** McLaren Vale
T 0468 883 776 www.inkwellwines.com **Open** Wed–Sun 11–5 **Winemaker** Dr. Irina Santiago-Brown **Viticulturist** Dr. Irina Santiago-Brown **Est.** 2003 **Dozens** 4000 **Vyds** 12ha
Inkwell was born in '03 when Dudley Brown moved to Australia from California and bought a rundown vineyard on the serendipitously named California Road. He inherited 5ha of neglected shiraz, and planted an additional 7ha to viognier (2.5ha), primitivo (2.5ha) and heritage shiraz clones (2ha). The 5-year restoration of the old vines and establishment of the new reads like the ultimate handbook for aspiring vignerons. Dr. Irina Santiago-Brown has since joined Dudley at Inkwell as chief winemaker, viticulturist and life partner; she is an advocate for sustainable viticulture, with the world's first PhD in the subject.

ΨΨΨΨΨ **Sweet Jane Viognier 2021, McLaren Vale** An insanely good fortified that melds viognier's aromatic virtuosity of peach and crystalline ginger spice with a dab of spirit impeccably embedded into the fray. Some aldehydes lift, while a jolt of volatility energises. Jura-esque. This is lo-fi fortification as an art form. Of the highest order. Screw cap. 16.4% alc. **RATING** 97 **DRINK** 2022–2040 $50 NG ✪ ♥

ΨΨΨΨΨ **Deeper Well Shiraz 2016, McLaren Vale** This is very good indeed. Refines and tames the excess of sweet fruit inherent to the region with an intuitive approach to minimalism. A dusty swathe of tannins, deeply Mediterranean of shape, placates tamarind, clove, fenugreek, beef bouillon, sour pickled cherry and rust, a ferrous bone of tannins joining attack to the immaculate spread of a finish. Screw cap. 13.7% alc. **RATING** 95 **DRINK** 2023–3032 $100 NG

ΨΨΨΨΨ **Road to Joy Shiraz Primitivo 2020, McLaren Vale RATING** 93 **DRINK** 2022–2028 $26 NG ✪
Deeper Well Shiraz 2018, McLaren Vale RATING 93 **DRINK** 2023–2032 $80 NG
One Love Cabernet Shiraz 2017, McLaren Vale RATING 93 **DRINK** 2022–2026 $80 NG
Deeper Well Shiraz 2015, McLaren Vale RATING 93 **DRINK** 2023–2027 $100 NG
Pressure Drop Cabernet Sauvignon 2020, McLaren Vale RATING 92 **DRINK** 2023–2030 $40 NG
One Love Cabernet Shiraz 2018, McLaren Vale RATING 92 **DRINK** 2023–2032 $80 NG
Dub Style Touriga 2022, South Australia RATING 90 **DRINK** 2022–2024 $30 NG

Innocent Bystander ★★★★

316 Maroondah Highway, Healesville, Vic 3777 **Region** Yarra Valley
T (03) 5999 9222 www.innocentbystander.com.au **Open** Mon–Tue 12–5, Thurs 12–5, Fri–Sun 12–10 **Winemaker** Joel Tilbrook, Cate Looney, Geoff Alexander, Katherine Brown, Tom Canning **Est.** 1997 **Dozens** 49 000 **Vyds** 45ha
Brown Brothers bought the Innocent Bystander brand (including Mea Culpa) from Giant Steps in '16, relocating the cellar door next door in the old White Rabbit Brewery site. Its business is in 2 completely different wine categories, both fitting neatly together. On one hand is the big volume of vintage moscato, the grapes coming from the King Valley; and non vintage prosecco, similarly sourced. The other side of the business is the premium, high-quality Yarra Valley single varietal wines with substantial brand value.

ΨΨΨΨΨ **Mea Culpa Pinot Noir 2021, Yarra Valley** A light, bright cherry red. This needs a good swirl before revealing sweet, brambly red fruits and a little spice. The palate is generously flavoured with those aforementioned red fruits and quite firm tannins that just need another 6 months or so to settle down. Screw cap. 12.1% alc. **RATING** 92 **DRINK** 2023–2027 $49 PR

Iron Gate Estate

178 Oakey Creek Road, Pokolbin, NSW 2320 **Region** Hunter Valley
T (02) 4998 6570 **www**.irongateestate.com **Open** 7 days 10–4, by appt
Winemaker Geoff Broadfield, Jade Hafey **Est.** 1996 **Dozens** 4500 **Vyds** 8.8ha
Iron Gate Estate would not be out of place in the Napa Valley, which favours bold
architectural statements made without regard to cost; no expense was spared in equipping
the winery or on the lavish cellar door facilities. The winery and its equipment have been
upgraded since the arrival in '18 of veteran winemaker Geoff Broadfield, who has reshaped
the business plan. The Primera range includes wines that are the best expression of a given
variety from the estate and NSW regions.

99999 **Primera Chardonnay 2022, Hunter Valley** Two-thirds fermented in
predominantly new French oak, the remainder in stainless steel tank; matured
on lees for 6 months. The vinification worked well, the new oak absorbed
by the white peach and citrus flavours. Screw cap. 12.7% alc. **RATING** 92
DRINK 2023–2027 $40 JH
Portero 2022, Hunter Valley Hilltops An interesting 65/35% blend of
Hunter Valley chardonnay and Hilltops semillon, which poses the question
whether reversing the varietal regional blend (ie Hunter Valley semillon and
Hilltops chardonnay) would make an even better wine – theoretical, of course.
This is a bright, fresh and breezy wine, citrus in the driver's seat, and would easily
gain in complexity/mouthfeel with a few years in bottle. Screw cap. 12.2% alc.
RATING 91 **DRINK** 2023–2028 $35 JH

Ironcloud Wines

Suite 16, 18 Stirling Highway, Nedlands, WA 6009 (postal) **Region** Geographe
T 0401 860 891 **www**.ironcloudwines.com.au **Open** Not **Winemaker** Michael Ng
Est. 1999 **Dozens** 2500 **Vyds** 11ha
In '03 owners Warwick Lavis and Geoff and Karyn Cross purchased the then-named Pepperilly
Estate, which had been planted in 1999 on red gravelly loam soils. Peppermint trees line the
Henty Brook, the natural water source for the vineyard. Winemaker Michael Ng, who joined
the team in '17, is ex chief winemaker for Rockliffe.

99999 **Rock of Solitude Ferguson Valley Touriga 2021, Geographe** Wonderful
perfume of sour cherry, paprika, mint and black jelly beans. Similar in flavour
with that black jelly bean and/or licorice character more prominent and
splashed with cherry cola notes. Vibrant expression, generous and yet brisk with
cranberry-like acidity, edged with fine, lacy tannin and mouth-puckering, tart
red berry fruit lingers. Great energy and personality here; a charming drink.
Screw cap. 14.5% alc. **RATING** 91 **DRINK** 2023–2028 $35 MB

Irvine ★★★★

63 Valley Road, Angaston, SA 5353 **Region** Eden Valley
T (08) 8564 1110 **www**.irvinewines.com.au **Open** By appt **Winemaker** Lachlan
Duncan **Viticulturist** Peter Miles **Est.** 1983 **Dozens** 20 000 **Vyds** 140ha
When James (Jim) Irvine established his eponymous winery in '83, he chose to produce
merlot from the Eden Valley. He was a much-in-demand consultant, bobbing up in all sorts of
places. Yet when he decided to sell the business in '14, its potential was greatly increased with
the investment of the purchasing Wade and Miles families. Henry Winter Miles had planted
0.8ha of shiraz in 1867 and successive generations had added to the vineyard portfolio from
1967, both acquiring existing vineyards and planting others. Henry's great-grandson Peter
Miles and partner John Wade collectively own 160ha spread through the Barossa and Eden
valleys, although only 140ha fall within the Irvine partnership.

99999 **The Estate Cabernet Sauvignon 2020, Barossa** Medium crimson in the
glass. Here is a vibrant expression of cabernet sauvignon showing bright characters
of blackberry, dark cherry and macerated berry fruits on a base of fine spice,

scattered herbs, licorice, cedar and pressed flowers. Fine acidity and chalky tannin wrap things up as the wine fades in a swell of herb and spice-flecked black fruits. Screw cap. 14.6% alc. **RATING** 91 **DRINK** 2023–2028 $35 DB

Altitude Primitivo 2020, Eden Valley Red cherry and redcurrant notes flit above darker fruit, plum and summer berries. Hints of all sorts of spices: cinnamon, mace, bay leaf and star anise along with pressed purple and red flowers, morello cherries and berry pastries. Some nice airy space on the palate with a twang of sour morello cherry, mixed spice and powdery tannin scaffolding with a sapid mineral line. Screw cap. 14.7% alc. **RATING** 91 **DRINK** 2023–2027 $35 DB

The Estate Shiraz 2020, Barossa Valley Deep crimson with characters of blackberry, black cherry and macerated plums with hints of baking spices, dark chocolate, earth, licorice and vanillin oak. Bright acidity and powdery tannin frame the fruit, which shows a redder aspect on the palate, perhaps with a swish of morello cherry on the medium-length finish. Screw cap. 14.8% alc. **RATING** 91 **DRINK** 2023–2030 $35 DB

Spring Hill Riesling 2022, Eden Valley Pale straw in the glass with notes of freshly squeezed lime, green apple and citrus along with hints of crushed stone, orange blossom, lemon curd and a whiff of marzipan in the back. Expansive and sapid with some clotted cream showing itself before the wine focuses with a sizzling acid step and pure citrus-laden exit. Screw cap. 12.8% alc. **RATING** 90 **DRINK** 2023–2028 $25 DB ✪

Spring Hill Shiraz 2021, Barossa Deeply coloured, perfumed and packed with juicy blackberry, mulberry and dark plum fruits. Sports an abundance of spice, licorice, dark chocolate and purple floral high tones. Medium bodied with a juicy fruit flow, fine, sandy tannins and a bright acid line, it makes for good drinking and excellent value for money. Screw cap. 14.6% alc. **RATING** 90 **DRINK** 2023–2027 $25 DB ✪

The Estate Shiraz 2021, Eden Valley A plush shiraz sporting a deep hue and notes of blackberry and dark cherry fruit with hints of fine spice, tobacco, sage, bay leaf, briar, licorice, macerated summer berry fruits and some vaguely musky spice tones. There is some nice texture and depth to the fruit, the tannins fine, sandy and supple, and there's a sweep of sour cherry and earth on the medium-length finish. Screw cap. 14.7% alc. **RATING** 90 **DRINK** 2023–2030 $35 DB

J.M. Lentini

23 Gawley Street, Nuriootpa, SA 5355 (postal) **Region** Barossa Valley
T 0412 537 490 **www.**jmlentini.com.au **Open** Not **Winemaker** John Lentini **Est.** 2016
Dozens 100

Automotive design engineer John Lentini established his eponymous brand in '16 after 14 years making wines for family and friends in his suburban Melbourne garage. Regular visits to the Barossa introduced him to the winemakers and growers of the region, enabling him to realise his vision to 'make single-vineyard wines that naturally convey the characteristics of the site and vintage'. His mandate is pure expressions of shiraz from the cooler sites of the Barossa, in particular the Eden Valley. The range currently comprises just one wine, with the hope of expanding to showcase the diversity of site expressions across the Barossa.

🍷🍷🍷🍷 **Syrah 2021, Eden Valley** Some lovely fruit purity on display here, with juicy satsuma plum and black cherry fruit notes supported with hints of fine spice, violets, licorice, earth and lighter wafts of sage and graphite. Well weighted and pure in the mouth with crushed quartz tannins providing a great frame for the fruit. Bright of acid and displaying a graceful air on the exit. Cork. 14.5% alc. **RATING** 92 **DRINK** 2023–2029 $60 DB

Jack Estate

15025 Riddoch Highway, Coonawarra, SA 5263 **Region** Coonawarra
T (08) 8736 3130 **www.**jackestate.com **Open** By appt **Winemaker** Conrad Slabber
Est. 2011 **Dozens** 10 000 **Vyds** 221ha

Jack Estate was founded in '11 by a group of grapegrowers who acquired the large Mildara Blass winery in Coonawarra. Wines are sourced from the estate vineyards in Coonawarra (1ha of cabernet sauvignon) and the Murray Darling (200ha). Jack Estate also sources grapes from neighbouring grapegrowers in Coonawarra and Wrattonbully to complete their 3-tiered range.

🍷🍷🍷🍷 **Cabernet Sauvignon 2019, Coonawarra** There's some substance to this wine but it's neat with it. Blackcurrant, boysenberry, cedar wood and gum leaf flavours come skilfully churned with tannin. Both texture and length are in a good place but it's the sheer volume of well-managed flavour that will win people over. Screw cap. 14.5% alc. **RATING** 93 **DRINK** 2024–2034 $25 CM ✪
Shiraz 2019, Coonawarra Wrattonbully There's a fair amount of gum leaf flavour here but it's flush with fresh, curranty fruit and the mouthfeel is feathery soft too. This is a wine made for good, pure, straightforward drinking pleasure, and that's exactly what it provides. Screw cap. 14.5% alc. **RATING** 91 **DRINK** 2023–2030 $22 CM ✪

Jack Rabbit Vineyard ★★★★

85 McAdams Lane, Bellarine, Vic 3221 **Region** Geelong
T (03) 5251 2223 **www**.jackrabbitvineyard.com.au **Open** 7 days 10–5 **Winemaker** Nyall Condon **Viticulturist** David Sharp **Est.** 2010 **Dozens** 5000 **Vyds** 20ha
Nestled onsite next to the acclaimed Jack Rabbit Restaurant is 1.5ha of pinot noir. Jack Rabbit Vineyard also owns another 18.5ha of vineyards across The Bellarine, planted on sandy loam, clay and volcanic-influenced soils, all going in to their range of estate-grown wines.

🍷🍷🍷🍷 **The Bellarine Shiraz 2021, Geelong** A bright, medium crimson red. Red berries intermingle with cracked pepper and crushed violets, while the medium-bodied palate is pliant and gently textured with satiny tannins rounding out a nicely put together wine. Screw cap. 14% alc. **RATING** 93 **DRINK** 2022–2027 $48 PR
The Bellarine Pinot Grigio 2022, Geelong A light, bright green gold. Bright and fresh on the nose, too, with scents of freshly sliced pears, yellow apples and some almond kernel. The palate is nicely textured and dry, finishing chalky and long. A very good example. Screw cap. 12.5% alc. **RATING** 92 **DRINK** 2022–2027 $38 PR
The Bellarine Rosé 2022, Geelong A light, bright onion skin colour. Savoury for a pinot noir rosé, which I like, and complemented by strawberry and citrus scents and a touch of springtime herbs. Dry, textural and refreshing. A premium rosé at a premium price! Screw cap. 11.9% alc. **RATING** 92 **DRINK** 2022–2025 $38 PR
The Bellarine Riesling 2022, Geelong A light, bright straw with green tinges. Aromas of citrus fruits and jasmine can be found in this subtle riesling. Tightly wound with lemon pith and honeysuckle flavours on the palate, this finishes with decent length and freshness. Screw cap. 11.5% alc. **RATING** 91 **DRINK** 2022–2028 $38 PR
The Bellarine Pinot Noir 2021, Geelong A bright, medium cherry red. While it's a touch oaky at this stage, there's also an attractive melange of crushed strawberries, cherries and dried roses. Light- to medium-bodied, the palate is silky smooth and elegant. Screw cap. 12.5% alc. **RATING** 91 **DRINK** 2022–2025 $48 PR

Jackson Brooke ★★★★

126 Beaconsfield Parade, Northcote, Vic 3070 (postal) **Region** Henty
T 0466 652 485 **www**.jacksonbrookewine.com.au **Open** Not **Winemaker** Jackson Brooke **Est.** 2013 **Dozens** 1400
Jackson Brooke left the University of Melbourne in '04 with a science degree before studying oenology at Lincoln University in NZ. A vintage at Wedgetail Estate in the Yarra Valley was followed by Japan, Southern California and then 3 years as assistant winemaker to Ben Portet.

He sources shiraz from the Grampians and riesling, pinot noir and pinot meunier from Henty, making boutique wines out of a rented space at Witchmount Estate.

ŸŸŸŸŸ **Westgate Vineyard Shiraz 2021, Grampians** This wine puts savouriness on the front foot, its back end firmly planted in blueberry and plum goodness. There are so many leaf and sweet spice and mezcal and graphite and walnut and pepper characters swirling about here, and it's these aspects that define it. It will be your thing, or it won't be. But within its overt savoury style, it's excellent. Screw cap. 14.5% alc. RATING 94 DRINK 2023–2032 $30 CM ✪

Cobboboonee Vineyard Chardonnay 2020, Henty Yes, there's flavour here, but this is a wine both built on acidity and designed to soar impressively through the finish. Custard apple, lime, nectarine and grapefruit flavours whisper with honeysuckle and flint, but it's the extended finish that really impresses. Stand back. Wait. This will mature well. 180 dozen made. Screw cap. 12.5% alc. RATING 94 DRINK 2024–2032 $30 CM ✪

Jacob's Creek

2129 Barossa Valley Way, Rowland Flat, SA 5352 **Region** Barossa Valley
T 1300 154 474 **www**.jacobscreek.com **Open** 7 days 10–4.30 **Winemaker** Dan Swincer **Est.** 1973 **Dozens** 5700 000 **Vyds** 740ha
Jacob's Creek (owned by Pernod Ricard) is one of the largest-selling brands in the world, and the global success of the base range has had the perverse effect of prejudicing many critics and wine writers who sometimes fail to objectively look behind the label and taste what is in fact in the glass.

ŸŸŸŸŸ **Survivor Vine Riesling 2022, Barossa** Pale in the glass with lifted aromas of freshly squeezed lime, Bickford's lime cordial and grapefruit with hints of orange blossom, crushed river stone, white flowers, almond paste and bath salts. Dry, fruit-pure and displaying a lovely sense of composure with a bright mineral line and an expressive, limey finish. Screw cap. 12% alc. RATING 94 DRINK 2023–2030 $75 DB

Survivor Vine Shiraz 2021, Barossa Super-ripe plum, blueberry and mulberry mesh with hints of baking spices, licorice, dark and milk chocolate and purple floral tones. Oak makes its presence known with cedar and vanilla notes flowing in, tannins ripe and dense and a distinct berry cream aspect to the finish. A very polished wine. Cork. 14% alc. RATING 94 DRINK 2023–2035 $90 DB

Organic Shiraz 2019, McLaren Vale Excellent aromatic intensity in pure blood plum and black cherry fruits sheathed with hints of fine spice, graphite, turned earth and purple floral tones. The fruit flow is true and balanced with compact, gypsum-like tannins and the oak presence is fairly softly spoken, with cedar making its presence felt only on the persistent finish. Cork. 14% alc. RATING 94 DRINK 2023–2030 $60 DB

ŸŸŸŸŸ **Biodynamic Shiraz 2017, McLaren Vale** RATING 93 DRINK 2023–2028 $60 DB

Our Limited Release Pinot Noir Chardonnay Pinot Meunier NV, Adelaide Hills RATING 92 $30 DB ✪

Jansz Tasmania

1216b Pipers Brook Road, Pipers Brook, Tas 7254 **Region** Northern Tasmania
T (03) 6382 7066 **www**.jansz.com.au **Open** 7 days 11–4 **Winemaker** Jennifer Doyle
Viticulturist Jennifer Doyle **Est.** 1985 **Dozens** 38 000 **Vyds** 30ha
Jansz is part of Hill-Smith Family Vineyards and was one of the early sparkling wine labels in Tasmania, stemming from a short-lived relationship between Heemskerk and Louis Roederer. Its 15ha of chardonnay, 12ha of pinot noir and 3ha of pinot meunier correspond almost exactly to the blend composition of the Jansz wines. Part of the former Frogmore Creek Vineyard, purchased by Hill-Smith Family Vineyards in '12, is dedicated to the needs of Jansz Tasmania.

ΨΨΨΨΨ **Pontos Hills Vintage Cuvée 2018, Tasmania** Pale straw with a fine, lively bead and aromas of preserved lemon, baked apple, fresh biscuits, hazelnuts, poached pears, nougat and white flowers. A tweak of pithy grapefruit phenolics on the finish and a crisp, fine line of natural acidity sets a cracking cadence. Lovely drinking. Diam. 12% alc. RATING 94 DRINK 2023–2030 $50 DB
Premium Vintage Cuvée 2018, Tasmania Light straw in the glass with a fine, energetic bead and mousse. Aromas of green apple, lemon curd, redcurrants, brioche, oyster shell, nougat, hazelnuts and crushed stone. Scintillating clarity and drive from the natural acidity with notes of clotted cream and light biscuit tones and a dry, crisp finish that lingers nicely and shows plenty of detail. Diam. 12.5% alc. RATING 94 DRINK 2023–2030 $50 DB
Late Disgorged Vintage Cuvée 2014, Tasmania Mid-straw in the glass with an enthusiastic fine bead and mousse. Aromas of green apple, lemon curd, poached pears, toasted almonds, white flowers, clotted cream and tones of freshly baked pastries. Creamy yet focused with a crystalline acid drive, lemon and apple fruit flavours, soft spice and a long, dry and refreshing finish. Diam. 12.5% alc. RATING 94 DRINK 2023–2028 $60 DB

ΨΨΨΨΨ **Single Vineyard Vintage Chardonnay 2018, Tasmania** RATING 93 DRINK 2024–2029 $65 DB
Premium Rose NV, Tasmania RATING 92 $30 DB ✪
Premium Cuvée NV, Tasmania RATING 92 $30 DB ✪

Jasper Hill ★★★★★

88 Drummonds Lane, Heathcote, Vic 3523 **Region** Heathcote
T (03) 5433 2528 **www**.jasperhill.com.au **Open** By appt **Winemaker** Ron Laughton, Emily McNally **Est.** 1979 **Dozens** 2000 **Vyds** 26.5ha
The red wines of Jasper Hill, crafted by father-daughter team Ron Laughton and Emily McNally, are highly regarded and much sought after. The low-yielding dry-grown vineyards are managed organically and tended by hand. As long as vintage conditions allow, these are wonderfully rich and full-flavoured wines. Emily also purchases fruit from Heathcote for her 2 side projects, creating Lo Stesso Fiano and Shiraz with friend Georgia Roberts, as well as Occam's Razor Shiraz.

ΨΨΨΨΨ **Georgia & Friends Shiraz 2021, Heathcote** Some wines just have that extra spread, that extra run, and this is one of them. Blackberry, coal, cloves, meaty spice and floral elements combine to dramatic effect here, but it's the persistence of the finish and the integrated grain of the tannin that really brings on the wow. Screw cap. 15% alc. RATING 95 DRINK 2025–2035 $82 CM
Lo Stesso Fiano 2022, Heathcote Sure, there's flavour here but it's the texture that draws you in. We're not talking about softness or smoothness, we're talking about chalk and quartz. It has that wheat-like crackle to it, that dryness in the context of juicy fruit. Citrus, wax and floral notes add life to this wine but there's a lot going on besides. Screw cap. 13.5% alc. RATING 94 DRINK 2023–2026 $30 CM ✪
Occam's Razor Shiraz 2021, Heathcote The alcohol sounds high, but in reality, this wine carries it with ease. Blueberry, aniseed and plum flavours charge seductively from the gate, trailing woodsy spice, dried herb and gum leaf notes in their wake. This is a wine of both substance and polish, and while its aromas have been blown off slightly there's more than enough on the palate to keep you engrossed. Cork. 15% alc. RATING 94 DRINK 2024–2032 $46 CM

ΨΨΨΨΨ **Georgia's Paddock Riesling 2022, Heathcote** RATING 91 DRINK 2022–2028 $41 CM

 JC's Own

26 Sturt Street, Angaston, SA 5353 (postal) **Region** Barossa Valley
T 0408 821 737 **www**.jcsown.com **Open** Not **Winemaker** Jaysen Collins **Est.** 2015
Dozens 139

Many Barossa wine drinkers will know winemaker Jaysen Collins who, along with Dan Standish, established the Massena wine brand. JC's Own is where Jaysen gets to push the boundaries a little while playing with great vineyard sites and growers he has built relationships with over the years. The quiver includes wines from the Adelaide Hills to his Barossa home; from funky, multi-variety, skin-contact whites and carbonic maceration grenache through to sturdy single-vineyard Barossa shiraz. The beautifully packaged and enchanting wines are a prime example of the 'New Barossa' style.

ŶŶŶŶŶ **Ferine Grenache 2021, Barossa** A wild-eyed, super-fragrant grenache. Magenta-splashed crimson with a wild nose of redcurrant jelly, watermelon, raspberry coulis and dried citrus rind with underlying shades of exotic spice, hanging meats, amaro, pressed citrus blossom, game, earth and leaf litter. Spacious and airy with a meaty, funky edge finishing chalky and savoury with some morello cherry and a vivid, sapid cadence. Cork. 14.5% alc. **RATING** 94 **DRINK** 2023-2028 $34 DB ✪

Single Vineyard Greenock Shiraz 2020, Barossa Deep blackberry, black cherry and satsuma plum notes with hints of baking spices, licorice, dark chocolate, ironstone, olive tapenade, tobacco, cedar, roasting meats and earth. Bright acidity drives the deep black fruits along nicely, with fine sandy tannins lending support. Cork. 14% alc. **RATING** 94 **DRINK** 2023-2035 $65 DB

ŶŶŶŶŶ **Bluebird Grenache 2022, Barossa** **RATING** 93 **DRINK** 2023-2030 $34 DB ✪
Stratum Shiraz 2021, Barossa **RATING** 93 **DRINK** 2023-2030 $34 DB ✪
Freestyler 2021, Eden Valley Barossa Valley Adelaide Hills **RATING** 93 **DRINK** 2023-2026 $34 DB ✪

Jeanneret Wines

22 Jeanneret Road, Sevenhill, SA 5453 **Region** Clare Valley
T (08) 8843 4308 **www**.jeanneretwines.com **Open** Mon–Sat 10–5 & public hols,
Sun 12–5 **Winemaker** Ben Jeanneret, Harry Dickinson **Est.** 1992 **Dozens** 18 000
Vyds 36.5ha

Ben Jeanneret has progressively built the range and quantity of wines he makes at the onsite winery. In addition to the estate vineyards, Jeanneret contract buys from an additional 20ha of hand-pruned, hand-picked, dry-grown vines spread throughout the Clare Valley.

ŶŶŶŶŶ **Cabernet Shiraz 2019, Clare Valley** Lush, ripe berry fruit characters, cola and vanilla cream with sweet, cinnamon spice – that's the ticket. Firm on the palate, a little bitey with lemony acidity, but with good tannin working in structure. More is revealed as the wine opens, indeed the tannins are the ace in the hole, proper, tense and palate resetting. Should please those seeking a dark, deep Clare red. Screw cap. 14.5% alc. **RATING** 92 **DRINK** 2022-2030 $30 MB ✪

Jericho Wines

211 Kays Road, McLaren Vale, SA 5171 **Region** Adelaide Hills
T 0410 519 945 **www**.jerichowines.com.au **Open** By appt **Winemaker** Neil and Andrew Jericho **Est.** 2012 **Dozens** 5000

The family winemaking team consists of father and son, Neil and Andrew Jericho. Neil has over 45 years of winemaking experience in Rutherglen, King Valley and the Clare Valley; and Andrew over 15 years in McLaren Vale working as senior winemaker for Maxwell Wines and Mollydooker. Andrew obtained his bachelor of oenology from the University of Adelaide and obtained experience at Grace Vineyard in the Shanxi Province of China. His partner Kaye is an experienced vintage widow, their eldest daughter Sally worked for Wine Australia for a decade and has degrees in marketing and accounting. Youngest son Kim was torn between oenology, hospitality and graphic design; he opted for the latter, hence designing the highly standout label and Jericho branding.

ΨΨΨΨΨ **Kuitpo Lockett Vineyard Fumé Blanc 2021, Adelaide Hills** This is as close as Australia gets to fine Sancerre. Gooseberry, lemon drop, hedgerow, lees-derived pastry notes, ginger, tatami straw and quince. No vapid tropical accents or tangy acidity. Strident, powerful and pungent of mineral force, with a belt of oak (50% new) restraining vivid intensity as much as promoting wonderful complexity. A stellar wine! Screw cap. 13.5% alc. RATING 96 DRINK 2023–2030 $42 NG ✪ ♥
Vintage Fortified Touriga Nacional 2020, McLaren Vale This is a prodigiously complex fortified. Date, clove, cinnamon stick, preserved Seville orange, ginger cake and cumquat barely cover it, such is the kaleidoscope. Like peering into a Vikram Seth novel before being whisked to Marrakech by some magic carpet. Very fine. Note that this was not made oxidatively, meaning that it can't be opened and left indefinitely. Screw cap. 18.3% alc. RATING 96 DRINK 2023–2040 $40 NG ✪
Limited Release Average 24 Years Age Tawny NV, Australia A kaleidoscopic blend with an average age of 24 years (some components exceeding 60), each a rivet in a greater weld of poise, grace and prodigious complexity. Yet this is not the hedonistic sort of fortified that bludgeons with a molasses-sweet oiliness, but one that lilts long, gracing the palate with date, tamarind, clove, orange balm and incense, akin to entering Ali Baba's cave on tiptoes. Cork. 19.8% alc. RATING 96 $80 NG

ΨΨΨΨΨ **Bracken Vineyard Grenache 2021, McLaren Vale** RATING 93 DRINK 2022–2027 $38 NG
Ancient Stones Shiraz 2021, McLaren Vale RATING 93 DRINK 2023–2032 $80 NG
Selected Vineyards GSM 2021, McLaren Vale RATING 93 DRINK 2022–2027 $27 NG ✪
Selected Vineyards S3 Shiraz 2021, McLaren Vale RATING 93 DRINK 2023–2028 $27 NG ✪
Bracken Vineyard Shiraz 2021, McLaren Vale RATING 92 DRINK 2022–2032 $38 NG
Ilya Vineyard Syrah 2021, Adelaide Hills RATING 92 DRINK 2023–2030 $38 NG
Selected Vineyards Rosé 2022, Adelaide Hills RATING 91 DRINK 2023–2024 $27 NG ✪
Selected Vineyards Fiano 2022, Adelaide Hills RATING 90 DRINK 2022–2026 $27 NG

Jester Hill Wines   ★★★★

292 Mount Stirling Road, Glen Aplin, Qld 4381 **Region** Granite Belt
T (07) 4683 4380 **www**.jesterhillwines.com.au **Open** 7 days 10–5 **Winemaker** Stephen Oliver, Michael Bourke **Est.** 1993 **Dozens** 2000 **Vyds** 7.3ha
A family-run vineyard situated in the pretty valley of Glen Aplin in the Granite Belt. Owners Michael and Ann Bourke aim to concentrate on small quantities of premium-quality wines reflecting the full-bodied style of the region. Most recently they have planted sangiovese and roussanne.

ΨΨΨΨΨ **Touchstone Shiraz 2018, Granite Belt** A full-figured red of slick texture, concentrated inky fruit, spice flavours and lavish wood seasoning. Scents of cola, vanilla, coconut and ripe plum with whiffs of clove and cedar. Sweet and ripe fruit to taste with layers of coconut, chocolate and cola on stewed plum and raspberry jelly. There's a lot going on here and it's distinctly a big, bold, old-school style. Screw cap. 14.5% alc. RATING 92 DRINK 2022–2028 $60 MB
Touchstone Petit Verdot 2018, Granite Belt Inky, potent red wine of cuddly texture and supple tannins. Scents of ripe plum, mulberry and blackcurrant jam with savoury elements of salted licorice and sage leaf. Bold and spicy to taste with

dark berry, faint raisin and dark chocolate flavours gently spiked with saltbush and sage. Even and well balanced despite the density. Screw cap. 14.5% alc. **RATING** 92 **DRINK** 2022–2028 $48 MB

Touchstone Roussanne 2019, Granite Belt Scents of nashi pear, cashew, clove and woody spices – very aromatic and immediately appealing. Flavours lean into that nashi pear character with layers of clove spice, a squeeze of lime, some ginger and quinine in the mix, too. Squeaky texture runs long and tight through a persistent finish. An intriguing expression. Screw cap. 13% alc. **RATING** 91 **DRINK** 2022–2028 $36 MB

Touchstone Shiraz 2016, Granite Belt An inky, potent red wine with a full flourish of ripe, stewed berry fruits, salted plum, licorice and black pepper characters. Soft and supple on the palate, with ripe red berry fruit layered with salted licorice and fine, feathery tannins. It feels easy-drinking, albeit in a bolder, richer, sweet-hearted wine style. Harmonious feel too. In a good place. Screw cap. 14% alc. **RATING** 91 **DRINK** 2022–2028 $48 MB

Shiraz Roussanne 2019, Granite Belt Dark cherry, cinnamon spice and kirsch aromas lifted with sweet, floral scents of jasmine and frangipani. The palate has an inherent sweetness, more kirsch and sweet spices, and a lick of stone fruit, too. Tannin feels gravelly and grippy, pulling in the fruitiness of the wine and the finish is cool and reserved. Screw cap. 14.5% alc. **RATING** 90 **DRINK** 2022–2028 $48 MB

Touchstone Cabernet Sauvignon 2010, Granite Belt A mature release at the ultra full flavoured end of the spectrum. Slick texture, plush tannins and a strong sense of very ripe fruit, sweet spice and nutty savouriness. Inky and concentrated, the wine is breathy with booze-soaked plum and berries, ripe, rich currant and raisin characters and licks of malt, bourbon, cola and dark chocolate. Screw cap. 15.5% alc. **RATING** 90 **DRINK** 2022–2027 $60 MB

Jilyara

2 Heath Road, Wilyabrup, WA 6280 **Region** Margaret River
T 0407 552 402 **www**.jilyara.com.au **Open** Thurs 10–6, Fri 10–9, Sat 10–9, Sun 10–6 at Origins Market **Winemaker** Kate Morgan **Viticulturist** Craig Cotterell **Est.** 2018 **Dozens** 3500 **Vyds** 9.7ha

The Cotterell family planted the 9.7ha Jilyara vineyard in '95. Until '17 the crop was sold to other producers in the region. They have 6.4ha of cabernet sauvignon, 0.9ha each of malbec and sauvignon blanc, 0.8ha of chardonnay, 0.4ha of merlot and 0.3ha of petit verdot. There are 3 tiers: at the top The Williams' Block duo of chardonnay and cabernet sauvignon; next comes the Heath Road banner with chardonnay, malbec and cabernet sauvignon; the last group is Honeycomb Corner with a sauvignon blanc and cabernet sauvignon.

The Williams' Block Cabernet Sauvignon 2021, Margaret River A composed, gentle wine in a way, although it has plenty of flavour and a presence. Lovely aromatics: floral, spicy and earthy with requisite leafy freshness. Mulberries, blackberries and plums are spiced up, even with a hint of pepper, as flavours build on the fuller-bodied palate. Textural, grainy tannins and fine acidity lead to a convincing long finish. Screw cap. 14.5% alc. **RATING** 93 **DRINK** 2023–2036 $75 JF

The Williams' Block Chardonnay 2021, Margaret River This comes across as super-tight and restrained, led by acidity, which reins in what fruit flavour there is – a smidge of lemon, grapefruit and barely ripe melon. A light touch of creamy lees and wood spices add some texture to the palate. A good wine in need of more time. Screw cap. 12% alc. **RATING** 91 **DRINK** 2023–2031 $75 JF

Heath Road Chardonnay 2022, Margaret River Very perky acidity greets the palate and puckers the mouth, so with appropriate food, this reveals more. Stone fruit, lemon-lime tart, nutty oak and a little moreish. Screw cap. 12.5% alc. **RATING** 90 **DRINK** 2023–2027 $90 JF

Heath Road Cabernet Sauvignon 2021, Margaret River A neat mix of mulberries and cranberries, leafy freshness and oak spices. Fuller bodied.

Tannins are shapely and distinctive with a slight bitter radicchio finish. All in all a good drink now and for some time yet. Screw cap. 14.5% alc. **RATING** 90 **DRINK** 2023–2033 $90 JF

Heath Road Malbec 2021, Margaret River There's no shortage of colour in this gleaming purple-red wine. It's also full of dark fruit, all plummy and cherry with curry leaves, espresso and dark chocolate. Full bodied and plush with ripe, fleshy tannins and raspberry sorbet acidity. Straightforward in a way but decent drinking to be had. Screw cap. 13.5% alc. **RATING** 90 **DRINK** 2023–2030 $35 JF

Jim Barry Wines ★★★★★

33 Craig Hill Road, Clare, SA 5453 **Region** Clare Valley
T (08) 8842 2261 **www.**jimbarry.com **Open** Mon–Sat 10–4 **Winemaker** Tom Barry, Ben Marx, Topsi Wallace **Viticulturist** Derrick Quinton **Est.** 1959 **Dozens** 80 000 **Vyds** 380ha

Jim Barry's wine business is led by Peter Barry; the 3rd generation represented by Peter and Sue Barry's children, Tom, Sam and Olivia. Tom's wife is also called Olivia, and she (Olivia Hoffmann) has set a whirlwind pace, graduating with a bachelor of commerce from the University of Adelaide, then a master of wine business. Peter purchased the famed Florita Vineyard with his brothers in '86 (one of the oldest vineyards in the Clare Valley, planted in '62). The 2nd generation also purchased Clos Clare in '08 with its high-quality vineyards (see separate entry). A founding member of Australia's First Families of Wine.

ΨΨΨΨΨ **The Florita Riesling 2022, Clare Valley** Understated, yet piles on the detail with minerally inflections, powdery/chalky texture, barely there savoury elements and a cavalcade of citrus, floral and pithy elements. It's decidedly intense, concentrated to the max and has a superb carry of flavour, lingering with palate-staining fruit, spice and minerality in spades. Darn awesome. Screw cap. 12% alc. **RATING** 96 **DRINK** 2022–2040 $60 MB ✪

The Armagh Shiraz 2020, Clare Valley Deeply concentrated, impossibly silky, balanced, long, palate-staining and vibrant. A cavalcade of mixed forest berries, clove, cinnamon, fresh tobacco, dark chocolate and leafy, eucalyptus-like herbal lift. Seamless, yet cinched with fine, silty tannin, all bolstered and lifted with a cool, briny acid profile. Elegant, and yet with power and presence. Screw cap. 13.8% alc. **RATING** 96 **DRINK** 2025–2045 $450 MB ♥

Lodge Hill Riesling 2022, Clare Valley The vineyard has 480m elevation, which is the key to the fine-boned structure of this classic riesling. A mix of crisp acid and lime juice progressively gains intensity on the back palate, finish and aftertaste. Screw cap. 12% alc. **RATING** 95 **DRINK** 2023–2032 $25 JH ✪

Loosen Barry Wolta Wolta Dry Riesling 2020, Clare Valley A collaboration between the Barry family and Dr Loosen in Mosel, Germany. This has energy, beautiful, succulent texture, filigreed acidity and perfume in spades. Good concentration of flavour, freshness and tension. It's all green apple, lime, lemon, grapefruit, thyme and ginger elements with a dash of pepper. There's detail, delicacy and structure here. Screw cap. 12.1% alc. **RATING** 95 **DRINK** 2022–2035 $120 MB

Spring Farm Block 18 Riesling 2013, Clare Valley Magnificent. Complex, supple and loaded with honey toast, truffle and sugared almond. The calling cards of lime, preserved lemon and spicy ginger work their magic in bouquet and palate. Complexity, structure and vitality all here, too. Superb. Screw cap. 12% alc. **RATING** 95 **DRINK** 2022–2030 $100 MB

Spring Farm Block 114 Riesling 2013, Clare Valley Supple, soft, succulent and lively. Zesty acidity set under marzipan, truffle, brown lime and dried apple fruits. The perfume is similarly set – evocative, rich and bright. While the wine feels ostensibly mellow, vigour comes from acidity, all briny and uplifting. The wine delivers great energy despite its mature characters. Good stuff, Barry family. Screw cap. 12% alc. **RATING** 95 **DRINK** 2022–2035 $100 MB

Expression by Tom Barry Riesling 2022, Clare Valley A wine imbued with textural glide and amplitude, taking on complex savoury elements among pristine citrus and green apple fruit characters. Scents of lime pickle, ginger and faint almond. The flavours echo with lime pickle, piquant ginger, and a gentle, halva-like sweet-savoury nuttiness. It's a compelling wine. Bravo. Screw cap. 12% alc. **RATING** 94 **DRINK** 2022–2035 $35 MB ✪

Cellar Release The Florita Riesling 2016, Clare Valley Soft and supple, albeit with a core of very limey acidity enlivening the gentle, attractive decay. Honey toast, lemon butter, brown lime and dried apple scents and flavours aplenty, with a rollicking swish of briny acidity. Indeed, you can see the maturity and revel in the complexity, but also find yourself perked up with each sip. It's in a great place. Best drunk now-ish but can be held longer, too. Screw cap. 11.3% alc. **RATING** 94 **DRINK** 2022–2030 $70 MB

🍷🍷🍷🍷🍷 **Assyrtiko 2022, Clare Valley RATING** 93 **DRINK** 2022–2025 $40 MB
Single Vineyard McKay's Riesling 2022, Clare Valley RATING 93 **DRINK** 2022–2030 $35 MB ✪
Expression by Tom Barry Malbec 2021, Clare Valley RATING 93 **DRINK** 2022–2030 $35 MB ✪
Watervale Riesling 2022, Clare Valley RATING 92 **DRINK** 2023–2032 $22 JH ✪
The Farm Single Vineyard Cabernet Sauvignon 2021, Clare Valley RATING 92 **DRINK** 2022–2030 $35 MB
The Farm Single Vineyard Cabernet Malbec 2021, Clare Valley RATING 92 **DRINK** 2022–2030 $35 MB
The McRae Wood Shiraz 2020, Clare Valley RATING 92 **DRINK** 2022–2036 $60 MB
Lodge Hill Shiraz 2021, Clare Valley RATING 90 **DRINK** 2022–2030 $25 MB ✪

JJ Hahn

Cnr Seppeltsfield and Stelzer Roads, Stonewell, SA 5352 **Region** Barossa Valley
T (08) 8562 3300 **www**.jjhahnwineco.com **Open** Mon–Sat 10–4.30 **Winemaker** Rolf Binder, Tom White and Dan Zolotarev **Viticulturist** Sam Schiller **Est.** 1997 **Dozens** 6000
Established in '97 as a collaboration with James and Jackie Hahn, who retired in '10, this is a brand of sibling winemakers Rolf Binder and Christa Deans, alongside sister labels Magpie Estate and formerly also Rolf Binder Wines. Rolf remains involved in the winemaking; he has also extended distribution internationally. Exclusively devoted to red wines, the range celebrates the traditional varieties of shiraz, cabernet sauvignon and merlot. Tom White of Curator Wine Co has been winemaker at JJ Hahn since '22; he will purchase the brand in '23.

🍷🍷🍷🍷🍷 **Western Ridge 1975 Planting Shiraz 2021, Barossa Valley** A rich, broody rendition of Western Ridge fruit, savoury in stature and flecked with hints of ironstone, spice and earth. There is a lovely texture supported by chocolatey tannins and plenty of latent horsepower beneath the dark-fruited surface. Some excellent cellaring potential here. Screw cap. 14% alc. **RATING** 95 **DRINK** 2023–2035 $40 DB ✪

1890s Vineyard Shiraz 2017, Barossa Valley Red and dark plum fruits, layered baking spices, red licorice, turned earth, roasting meats and dark chocolate. American oak influence shows through, but there is a real sense that this could only be from the Barossa. It's calm and collected with leather and mahogany tones on the finish, fine milk chocolate tannins and regional familiarity. Screw cap. 14.5% alc. **RATING** 95 **DRINK** 2023–2035 $85 DB

Homestead Cabernet Sauvignon 2021, Barossa Valley Deep magenta in the glass with aromas of blackberry, blackcurrant and black cherry. Plenty of spice and earth with hints of scattered herbs, licorice and a light dusting of amaro in the background. Deep, resonant and fruit pure, there is structure here for cellaring and a rising tide of rich, blackberry pastille-like fruit on the long finish. Screw cap. 14% alc. **RATING** 94 **DRINK** 2023–2032 $35 DB ✪

𝓣𝓣𝓣𝓣𝓠 **Hermann's Vineyard Shiraz 2021, Barossa Valley** RATING 90
DRINK 2023–2029 $35 DB

John Duval Wines

Artisans of the Barossa, 24 Vine Vale Road, Tanunda, SA 5352 **Region** Barossa Valley
T (08) 8562 2266 **www**.johnduvalwines.com **Open** 7 days, 11–5 **Winemaker** John
Duval **Est.** 2003 **Dozens** 8000

John Duval is an internationally recognised winemaker, having been the custodian of
Penfolds Grange during his role as chief red winemaker from 1986–2002. He established his
eponymous brand in '03 after almost 30 years with Penfolds and provides consultancy services
to clients all over the world. While his main focus is on old-vine shiraz, he has extended
his portfolio with other Rhône varieties. John was joined in the winery by son Tim in '16.
Wines can be tasted at Artisans of the Barossa.

𝓣𝓣𝓣𝓣𝓣 **Annexus Mataro 2021, Barossa Valley** Dark plum, mulberry and macerated
berry fruit are cut with notes of exotic spice, hanging meats, licorice, earth and
light purple floral tones. There is a lovely fruit density and texture here, pure yet
savoury edged with tight, sandy tannin support and a spicy red and dark-fruited
finish. Screw cap. 14.5% alc. RATING 96 DRINK 2023–2033 $70 DB ✪
Annexus Grenache 2021, Barossa Valley Gingery and red-fruited with top
notes of jasmine and orange blossom with hints of red licorice, pressed flowers,
crushed stone and a light whiff of marzipan. Graceful and pure with lovely
palate weight and brisk cadence, finishing long and spicy. Screw cap. 14.5% alc.
RATING 95 DRINK 2023–2030 $70 DB
Entity Shiraz 2021, Barossa Vibrant and pure at heart with deep black plum,
black cherry and boysenberry fruits, plentiful exotic spice, violets, licorice and
wafts of light cedar and vanillin oak. Impressive fruit depth, sandy tannin support
and long, plush finish of spicy black fruits and earth. Screw cap. 14.5% alc.
RATING 95 DRINK 2023–2033 $55 DB
Concilio Shiraz 2021, Barossa Valley High-quality grapes and flawless
winemaking. Bright and very deeply coloured. While nigh-on full bodied, the
harmony and balance of the black fruits and supple tannins make it oh-so-easy to
drink. Screw cap. 14% alc. RATING 94 DRINK 2023–2031 $30 JH ✪
Plexus Shiraz Grenache Mourvèdre 2021, Barossa Bright aromas of red
and dark plum, mulberry and boysenberry mesh with hints of earth, licorice,
spice, roasting meats and violets. Lovely fruit purity with tight-grained tannin
providing the framework and bright acidity the pulse, finishing plush and pure.
A wonderful red. Screw cap. 14.5% alc. RATING 94 DRINK 2023–2028 $40 DB ✪
Annexus Shiraz 2021, Eden Valley Deep blackberry and black plums with
hints of fine spice, roasting meats, black licorice, cassis, violets and earth. There is
a sense of grace and latent power on the palate, with pure fruit and plenty of detail
across fine, compact tannins and bright acidity that propels the wine forward.
Screw cap. 14.5% alc. RATING 94 DRINK 2023–2030 $70 DB
Concilio Grenache Shiraz 2020, Barossa Valley It's a cracker – weighted
just-so and laden with sour cherry and red plum fruits, exotic spices, gingerbread,
red licorice and earth. Swift of cadence and great savoury drinking. Screw cap.
14.5% alc. RATING 94 DRINK 2023–2029 $40 DB ✪
Plexus Shiraz Grenache Mourvèdre 2020, Barossa Valley Gorgeously
perfumed with red cherry, raspberry and mulberry fruits flecked with violets and
jasmine with hints of ginger cake, red licorice, earth, cola and crushed stone.
There is a lively acid cadence, superfine powdery tannins and an array of gingery
spice and red fruit that fans out nicely on the finish. A bargain. Screw cap.
14.5% alc. RATING 94 DRINK 2023–2029 $40 DB ✪

𝓣𝓣𝓣𝓣𝓠 **Plexus Roussanne Marsanne Viognier 2022, Barossa** RATING 93
DRINK 2023–2026 $30 DB ✪
Concilio Grenache Shiraz 2021, Barossa Valley RATING 92
DRINK 2023–2028 $30 DB ✪

John Kosovich Wines ★★★★☆

180 Memorial Avenue, Baskerville, WA 6056 **Region** Swan Valley
T (08) 9296 4356 **www**.johnkosovichwines.com.au **Open** Wed–Mon 10.30–4.30
Winemaker Anthony Kosovich **Viticulturist** Ray Kosovich **Est.** 1922 **Dozens** 2000
Vyds 10.9ha

Ivan (known as Jack) Kosovich and his brothers immigrated from Croatia shortly before the outbreak of WWI and Jack purchased the property in 1922. A 7m white gum beam cut from a tree felled by Jack in the nearby hills became the supporting structure for the cellar roof. Son, John, took over winemaking aged 15, making fortified wines and rough red wines. In the '60s, John changed the vineyard to produce white wines. Riesling was the first variety planted, chenin blanc, chardonnay and verdelho followed. In '89 John established a 3.5ha vineyard in Pemberton, changing the face of the business forever, albeit continuing with the magnificent Rare Muscat. In '95 John became a member of the Order of Australia for his long contribution to the wine industry. Son Anthony (Arch) came on board in '94, taking over the winemaking a few years later.

♆♆♆♆♆ **Bottle Aged Reserve Chenin Blanc 2018, Swan Valley** Other White/ Blend of the Year. Score awarded by the Halliday tasting panel at the annual Awards judging. MB writes: Released as a 5yo wine. Strong, lemony scents with accents of honeycomb, wet fern, pineapple and tonic water. The palate is squeaky and crisp, showing more lemony characters with dashes of tonic water, bay leaf and briny minerality with some chalkiness in texture, too. Gentle maturation endows savoury elements and some honey-butter notes. It's in a brilliant place, vivid for the variety and maturing graciously. Screw cap. 12.8% alc. **RATING** 98 **DRINK** 2023–2040 $54 PD ♥

♆♆♆♆♀ **100 Year Anniversary Chenin Blanc 2022, Swan Valley RATING** 93 **DRINK** 2023–2035 $40 MB
Autumn Harvest Semillon 2018, Swan Valley RATING 93 **DRINK** 2023–2030 $38 MB
Pinot Noir 2021, Pemberton RATING 92 **DRINK** 2023–2030 $48 MB

John's Blend ★★★★

Bridge Road, Langhorne Creek, SA 5255 **Region** Langhorne Creek
T (08) 8537 3029 **www**.johnsblend.com.au **Open** At The Winehouse, Langhorne Creek
Winemaker John Glaetzer **Est.** 1974 **Dozens** 2000 **Vyds** 23ha

John Glaetzer was Wolf Blass's right-hand man almost from the word go; the power behind the throne of the 3 Jimmy Watson trophies awarded to their wines ('74, '75, '76) and the small matter of 11 Montgomery trophies for Best Red Wine at the Adelaide Wine Show. This has always been a personal venture on the side, as it were, of John and wife Margarete, officially sanctioned, of course, and needing little marketing effort.

♆♆♆♆♀ **Margarete's Shiraz 2020, Langhorne Creek** Packed to the rafters with fruit and oak, in classic 'no wood, no good' style. Needs years to show its best. Screw cap. 14.5% alc. **RATING** 92 **DRINK** 2023–2040 $38 JH
Individual Selection Cabernet Sauvignon 2019, Langhorne Creek There's no shortage of meat (oak) on the bones of this wine, and if you are hooked on the oak, the wine of each vintage will not let you down. Cork. 14.5% alc. **RATING** 90 **DRINK** 2023–2029 $38 JH

Jones Winery & Vineyard ★★★★★

61 Jones Road, Rutherglen, Vic 3685 **Region** Rutherglen
T (02) 6032 8496 **www**.joneswinery.com **Open** By appt **Winemaker** Mandy Jones, Benjamin Jones **Viticulturist** Arthur Jones **Est.** 1860 **Dozens** 3500 **Vyds** 10ha

Jones Winery & Vineyard stands as testament to a rich winemaking tradition. Since 1927, the winery has been owned and operated by the Jones family. Two blocks of old vines have been preserved (including 1.69ha of shiraz), supported by further blocks progressively planted between '75 and the present day. Today, the winery is jointly run by winemaker Mandy Jones, who brings years of experience working in Bordeaux, and her brother Arthur Jones. Together they produce a small range of boutique wines.

LJ 2021, Rutherglen Shiraz/grenache. An expressive, aromatic profile with a seamless beauty defining the palate. Relates to its terroir with earthiness and bold, ripe, dark-berried fruit. But then it lifts, producing supple, fine layers of oak nuance, spicy flavour and fine-grained tannins against a supple, svelte palate. Screw cap. 13.1% alc. **RATING** 95 **DRINK** 2023–2033 $90 JP

Rare Muscat NV, Rutherglen The base wine for this fortified goes back to 1922. It's used sparingly, blended with younger wines ('younger' being a relative term in Rutherglen) and neutral spirit. The result is richly concentrated, complex in prune, raisin, fruitcake, caramel and wood-aged nuttiness with a thread of licorice that brings an extra layer of interest. 500ml. Vinolok. 18.5% alc. **RATING** 95 $160 JP

J6 Six Generations Durif Vin de Liqueur 2021, Rutherglen **RATING** 93 **DRINK** 2023–2027 $40 JP

Shiraz Malbec 2021, Rutherglen **RATING** 91 **DRINK** 2023–2030 $25 JP ✪

Josef Chromy Wines   ★★★★☆

370 Relbia Road, Relbia, Tas 7258 **Region** Northern Tasmania
T (03) 6335 8700 **www.**josefchromy.com.au **Open** 7 days 10–5 **Winemaker** Ockie Myburgh **Viticulturist** Kellie Graham **Est.** 2004 **Dozens** 40 000 **Vyds** 60ha

Josef Chromy escaped from Czechoslovakia in 1950, arriving in Tasmania 'with nothing but hope and ambition'. He went on to own or develop such well-known Tasmanian wine brands as Rochecombe (now Bay of Fires), Jansz, Heemskerk and Tamar Ridge. In '07, aged 76, Josef launched Josef Chromy Wines. The foundation of the business is the Old Stornoway vineyard, with 60ha of mature vines. Talented and hard-working winemaker Jeremy Dineen handed over the reins to his capable offsider Ockie Myburgh in January '21. In April '22, the brand was acquired by Paragon Wine Estates, which is part of the Woolworths-owned Endeavour Group.

Sauvignon Blanc 2022, Tasmania The wine has abundant varietal flavour, with rich tropical notes running from lychee to passionfruit, and a crosshatch of snow pea and minerally acidity. Screw cap. 13.5% alc. **RATING** 95 **DRINK** 2023–2028 $33 JH ✪

Riesling 2022, Tasmania A sea-breeze fresh, crisp and minerally bouquet is joined by lemon zest on the long palate. Screw cap. 12.8% alc. **RATING** 94 **DRINK** 2023–2029 $33 JH ✪

ZDAR Pinot Noir 2021, Tasmania Bright ruby in the glass with a wonderfully pure nose of ripe cherry and plum fruits underscored with hints of fine spice, undergrowth, citrus zest, mushroom broth, beetroot and earth. There is a lovely savoury sense of harmony and composition to this wine. It's pure and spicy with fine powdery tannin and a sweep of morello cherry on the finish. Great drinking. Screw cap. 13.3% alc. **RATING** 94 **DRINK** 2023–2030 $80 DB

Pinot Noir 2021, Tasmania A bright cherry hue with aromas of black cherry, plum, exotic spice, licorice, berry turnover and ample stalky nuance. Textured and mouth-filling with powerful (yet graceful) deep-spiced cherry and plum fruits with hints of earth and game. Almost burgundian in its demeanour, with a gentle tug of fine tannin lending support and structure. Screw cap. 13.4% alc. **RATING** 94 **DRINK** 2023–2028 $43 DB

Chardonnay 2022, Tasmania **RATING** 93 **DRINK** 2023–2028 $43 DB
Chardonnay 2021, Tasmania **RATING** 93 **DRINK** 2023–2027 $43 DB
Finesse Brut 2018, Tasmania **RATING** 92 **DRINK** 2023–2026 $50 DB
Brut Finesse Rosé 2017, Tasmania **RATING** 91 **DRINK** 2023–2025 $50 DB
PEPIK Pinot Noir 2021, Tasmania **RATING** 91 **DRINK** 2023–2026 $27 DB ✪

Joshua Cooper Wines ★★★★★

PO Box 263 Kyneton, Vic 3444 **Region** Victoria
T 0420 689 128 **www.**joshuacooperwines.com.au **Open** Not **Winemaker** Joshua
Cooper **Viticulturist** Joshua Cooper **Est.** 2012 **Dozens** 2000 **Vyds** 8ha
Occasionally, a winemaker comes along who has the gift of presence and crafts compelling
wines. Josh Cooper is one. Astonishing as he's only in his mid-30s. Sure, it's destiny; his
parents are Allan and Nellie Cooper of Cobaw Ridge fame but Josh is forging his unique
path. Aside from gentle, thoughtful winemaking, his love of the Macedon Ranges and his
respect for vinous history (drinking many old vintages of Balgownie Estate and Virgin Hills
with his father) have inspired some of his wines, sourced from old vineyards such as Balgownie
Estate. How serendipitous. In '21, he bought 8ha in the Macedon Ranges, high-density
plantings of chardonnay with some pinot noir will be completed in '24. With the new, he
won't be giving up the old established sites. It's all complementary and full of synergy. Joshua
Cooper is the *Halliday Wine Companion 2024* Best New Winery.

Balgownie Vineyard 1970 Block Cabernet Sauvignon 2021, Bendigo
What a wine. The beauty and quality of fruit shine: inky cassis, violets, nori, some
bresaola-like reduction, Middle Eastern spices, dark chocolate and more. But the
palate – whoa! Slinky, supple, sensual tannins glide across. Fine acidity to close
after a ridiculously long finish. I think I've died and gone to heaven. Agglomerate.
13% alc. **RATING** 97 **DRINK** 2024–2040 $100 JF ✪ ♥

Ray-Monde Vineyard Pinot Noir 2021, Port Phillip The fruit is sweet and
juicy, savoury and ripe laden, with Middle Eastern spices, warm earth, blood
orange and zest with an appealing truffled salami note. The tannins are fine
and stretchy, the acidity invigorating and the finish lingers long. Diam. 13% alc.
RATING 96 **DRINK** 2023–2033 $65 JF ✪

Doug's Vineyard Pinot Noir 2021, Macedon Ranges Somewhat speechless
after tasting this. This is such a beautifully crafted wine from beautifully grown
fruit. My heart fluttered as the fine tannins and energising acidity drew long
and succinctly across the palate. Before that, a wave of dark fruit, all manner of
spices with pepper, chinotto and the scent of autumn leaves after a downpour
lingered. Savoury, a real succulence and such a delicious drink. Diam. 13.5% alc.
RATING 96 **DRINK** 2023–2031 $65 JF ✪

Dash Farms Mount Alexander Chardonnay 2021, Central Victoria
While there are flickers of stone fruit and citrus, this is parked in the savoury
aisle. Briny and stony with clotted cream and white miso lees flavours. The palate
is generous but contained, with that distinct lemon oil character from the new
Stockinger barrel, and then the acidity races along allowing it to finish on a high.
Compelling stuff. Diam. 13.5% alc. **RATING** 95 **DRINK** 2023–2030 $65 JF

**Dash Farms Mount Alexander Cabernet Sauvignon 2021, Central
Victoria** Dark, inky and enticing with lavender and violets, menthol, milk
chocolate, new leather and a waft of a just-whittled pencil while the dark fruit is
all blackberries and cassis. Medium bodied, precision tannins with some texture
and a fine finish. If anyone can make cabernet cool, it's Josh Cooper. Diam.
14% alc. **RATING** 95 **DRINK** 2023–2038 $50 JF ✪

Shay's Flat Landsborough Valley Cabernet Sauvignon 2021, Pyrenees
Always an interesting expression of cabernet from this region – more eucalyptus,
more savoury and tannins slightly more drying, in a good way as there's plenty
of fruit to temper all that. Cassis and blackberries loom large, spicy oak and
potpourri with a fuller-bodied palate and just a slight green edge, a cardamom
character, on the finish. Screw cap. 13% alc. **RATING** 95 **DRINK** 2023–2036 $65 JF

Jumy Estate ★★★★

28 Ellsworth Crescent, Camberwell, Vic 3124 (postal) **Region** Yarra Valley
T 0433 591 617 **Open** Not **Winemaker** Ben Haines **Est.** 2015 **Dozens** 2000

Jumy Estate was founded in '15 by leading architect Linda Wang and structural engineer Roy Zhang. Highly regarded winemaker Ben Haines' brief is to produce wines that are engaging and distinct, and capture the sense of place.

ODE1952 Signature Series Pinot Noir 2021, Yarra Valley A light, bright crimson. Light on its feet, too, with aromas of strawberries and redcurrants, the dried herbs and floral whole-bunch notes already well integrated. Sappy and persistent on the palate, this is a well-put together wine. Diam. 12.8% alc. **RATING** 93 **DRINK** 2023-2028 $33 PR ✿

ODE1952 Signature Series Chardonnay 2022, Yarra Valley Bright green gold. More savoury and complex than the '21 release. Ripe stone fruits and melon intermingle with a little nougat and grilled cashew. Rich through the chalky textured mid-palate before finishing lemony and long. Diam. 12% alc. **RATING** 92 **DRINK** 2023-2026 $31 PR

ODE19 Jumy Signature Series Shiraz 2020, Grampians A medium, bright ruby red. Lifted with aromas of red and black fruits and lots of cracked black pepper and other spice rack spices. Medium bodied, this silky and already delicious wines flows evenly across the palate. Diam. 13.5% alc. **RATING** 91 **DRINK** 2023-2026 $30 PR

ODE1952 Signature Series Pinot Noir 2022, Yarra Valley Bright crimson. While it's a touch closed at present, there's still plenty to like in the form of bright red fruits, pomegranate, a little white pepper and some floral notes. The palate is light yet finely tuned with good acidity and very fine-grained tannins in support. A well-made wine at the more delicate end of the pinot noir spectrum. Screw cap. 11.5% alc. **RATING** 90 **DRINK** 2023-2027 $33 PR

Juniper ★★★★★

98 Tom Cullity Drive, Cowaramup, WA 6284 **Region** Margaret River **T** (08) 9755 9000 **www**.juniperestate.com.au **Open** 7 days 10–5 **Winemaker** Mark Messenger, Luc Fitzgerald **Viticulturist** Ianto Ward **Est.** 1973 **Dozens** 12 000 **Vyds** 34.31ha

Roger Hill and Gillian Anderson purchased the Wrights' Wilyabrup property – one of the founding vineyards in the region – in '98, driven by the 25yo vineyard with dry-grown cabernet as the jewel in the crown. They also purchased complementary vineyards in Forest Grove (Higher Plane) and Wilyabrup; the vineyards are sustainably farmed using organic principles. Following the passing of Roger, son Tom (formerly a winemaker in the Yarra Valley) is now running the business while original winemaker Mark Messenger is still at the helm.

Cornerstone Wilyabrup Chardonnay 2021, Margaret River Scintillating chardonnay. Pure, pristine fruit, superfine and long; the palate an exercise in restraint. There's 45% new French oak involved, which the fruit has completely taken it in its stride. Bravo. Screw cap. 12.5% alc. **RATING** 97 **DRINK** 2023-2033 $60 JF ✿ ♥

Cornerstone Wilyabrup Cabernet Sauvignon 2016, Margaret River Smashing wine. This cabernet has come from the best address in town, but it doesn't make a thing about it. It's elegant, it's long and precisely sculpted, and its varietal expression is one of extreme purity. Screw cap. 14% alc. **RATING** 97 **DRINK** 2023-2040 $90 JH ✿

Heritage Shiraz 2019, Margaret River A lot of depth here, fuller bodied, rich and savoury with plenty of spice (including sumac and pepper), shapely, ripe tannins and an expansive palate. Excellent Margaret River shiraz, and it's here to stay. Screw cap. 14.5% alc. **RATING** 96 **DRINK** 2023-2033 $40 JF ✿ ♥

Cornerstone Wilyabrup Cabernet Sauvignon 2018, Margaret River It wears its (sub)regional stamp brilliantly as it flaunts violets, mulberries, mocha, freshly rolled tobacco and damp earth. It's just wonderful. There's more. The palate is layered with cedary oak and raw silk/slightly powdery tannins. Rather savoury, lightly spiced and finishes with precision and terrific length. Screw cap. 14% alc. **RATING** 96 **DRINK** 2023–2038 $90 JF

Canvas Malbec 2022, Margaret River Could Mark Messenger be Mr Malbec? OK, he's more than that but he handles this variety superbly. Outrageous purple, excellent fruit all tangy, buoyant and vibrant. A touch of meaty reduction adds to the savoury profile with sandy tannins and juiciness throughout. Screw cap. 13.5% alc. **RATING** 95 **DRINK** 2022–2028 $32 JF ❂

Canvas Nouveau 2022, Margaret River Shiraz/cabernet sauvignon/ tempranillo. A poppy, bright and juicy drink. A bright red hue delights, so too the aromas of roses, red licorice, star anise and more. Best of all, the palate is crisp, dry and juicy with a saline-like acidity. Love it. Nouveau-styles are trending in Margaret River, which is great because if you serve the wines chilled in warm weather, enjoyment follows. Screw cap. 13% alc. **RATING** 95 **DRINK** 2022–2024 $29 JF ❂

Estate Aquitaine Rouge 2019, Margaret River A bang-on blend of 57/19/12/8/4% cabernet sauvignon/merlot/malbec/cabernet franc/petit verdot. Talk about harmony. Everything is in place, the heady aromas of violets and yes, it smells of Margaret River. The whorl of dark fruit, the layer of spice, the supple, fine texture and exceptional tannins. Stunning now and will hang around for many years hence. Screw cap. 14% alc. **RATING** 95 **DRINK** 2023–2039 $40 JF ❂

ΨΨΨΨϘ **Crossing Original White 2022, Margaret River RATING** 92 **DRINK** 2022–2024 $18 JF ❂
Crossing Shiraz 2018, Margaret River RATING 92 **DRINK** 2023–2030 $40 JH
Canvas Tempranillo 2021, Margaret River RATING 91 **DRINK** 2022–2029 $29 JF
Three Fields Cabernet Sauvignon 2021, Margaret River RATING 91 **DRINK** 2024–2034 $35 JF

Just Red Wines   ★★★☆

2370 Eukey Road, Ballandean, Qld 4382 **Region** Granite Belt **T** (07) 4684 1322 **www**.justred.com.au **Open** 7 days 10–5 **Winemaker** Tony and Michael Hassall **Est.** 1998 **Dozens** 1500 **Vyds** 2.8ha

Tony, Julia and Michael Hassall have planted shiraz and merlot (plus later additions of cabernet sauvignon, tannat and viognier). Just Red Wines is in a unique climatic region just west of the Great Dividing Range near the New South Wales border. The elevation of almost 900m provides cool nights in the summer and very cool winters. The warm Queensland sunshine is particularly suited to growing red wine and hence they have chosen to specialise.

ΨΨΨΨϘ **Tannat 2021, Granite Belt** Tannat seems to resonate with the Granite Belt. Dark, plummy fruit is coupled to black olive, fennel and clove/cinnamon-spice characters. While there's depth of flavour, the wine lifts on rails of cool acidity and finds good tension from ripples of sandy tannin. Oak seasoning lends a little overtness in malty scents and flavours, but feels mostly meshed in the richness of inherent fruit and spice. Should mature with interest, too. Screw cap. 13.1% alc. **RATING** 90 **DRINK** 2022–2035 $35 MB

Juxtaposed

PO Box 655, McLaren Vale, SA 5171 **Region** McLaren Vale **T** 0450 000 373 **www**.juxtaposed.com.au **Open** By appt **Winemaker** Dr Wes Pearson **Viticulturist** Peter Bolte **Est.** 2010 **Dozens** 2000 **Vyds** 3ha

Justaposed (previously Dodgy Brothers) is a partnership between Canadian-born winemaker Wes Pearson, viticulturist Peter Bolte and grapegrower Peter Sommerville. Wes graduated from the University of British Columbia's biochemistry program in '08, along the way working at wineries including Château Léoville-Las Cases in Bordeaux. Also in '08 he and his family moved to McLaren Vale, and after working at several wineries, he joined the Australian Wine Research Institute as a research scientist. Peter Bolte has almost 40 vintages in McLaren Vale under his belt and was the original Dodgy Brother. Peter Sommerville's vineyard provides cabernet sauvignon, cabernet franc and petit verdot.

🍷🍷🍷🍷🍷 **Wait Vineyard Grenache 2021, McLaren Vale** A levity to the density, a fibrous grittiness to the tannins and wonderful, saliva-pulling freshness, each a weave in a veil of mystique, elegance and beauty. Kirsch, bergamot, thyme, lavender … irrelevant, for this is a textural maze of real intrigue. A veritable bargain, too. Screw cap. 14% alc. RATING 96 DRINK 2022-2032 $49 NG ✪

Minchella Vineyard Shiraz 2021, McLaren Vale A very good shiraz. Clove, mace, allspice, blue fruits, charcuterie, aniseed and beautifully extracted tannins, oak and grape, curtailing the fruit sweetness. Simple mercy! Gritty and llicorella-pungent of feel. The tannins and the oak make this wine. Screw cap. 14.3% alc. RATING 95 DRINK 2022-2032 $37 NG ✪

Smart Vineyard Grenache 2021, McLaren Vale I've been oscillating between this and its Wait vineyard sibling. While this is not the winner, I suggest you buy both. This may well outpace the other in time. There is more intensity, sap and oomph. Ferrous, even. Yet the mocha seams of oak are more obvious. But so much to adore. Raspberry bonbon, candied orange peel, vanilla, cardamom and the tamarind entrée of the Marrakech souk. Screw cap. 14.3% alc. RATING 95 DRINK 2022-2030 $49 NG ✪

Wait Vineyard Old Vine Shiraz 2021, McLaren Vale A fine, hot-climate shiraz. A stark juxtaposition against grenache's innate feel in these parts, this is pulpy and extracted in the vein of freshness with oak compressing the seams as a bane of tension. Iodine, purple fruits, vanilla, cardamom, clove, lots of lavender and a plush finish marked by shiraz's unavoidable burst of hedonistic sweetness. Screw cap. 14.2% alc. RATING 94 DRINK 2022-2032 $37 NG ✪

🍷🍷🍷🍷 **Old Vine Grenache 2021, McLaren Vale** RATING 93 DRINK 2022-2030 $37 NG

Sangiovese 2021, McLaren Vale RATING 93 DRINK 2022-2028 $33 NG ✪

Fiano 2022, McLaren Vale RATING 92 DRINK 2022-2028 $33 NG

Kaesler Wines   ★★★★★

Barossa Valley Way, Nuriootpa, SA 5355 **Region** Barossa Valley
T (08) 8562 4488 **www.**kaesler.com.au **Open** 7 days 11–5 by appt **Winemaker** Tim Dolan, Stephen Dew **Viticulturist** Nigel Van Der Zande **Est.** 1990 **Dozens** 20 000 **Vyds** 38ha
The first members of the Kaesler family were Silesian immigrants who settled in the Barossa Valley in 1845. The vineyards date back to 1893 and some of the old dry-grown shiraz remains today. Kaesler family ownership ended in 1968 and the company was eventually acquired by former flying winemakers Reid and Bindy Bosward, in conjunction with the same investment group who have since purchased Yarra Yering. Together they have set about regenerating the vines and the estate. The old brick horse stable now holds a private tasting room and the original farm cottages offer accommodation.

🍷🍷🍷🍷🍷 **Old Vine Semillon 2022, Barossa Valley** Barossa semillon gets nowhere near the recognition it deserves, and here is a prime example of why we should all be drinking more of it. Water white with a splash of green and notes of crunchy green apple and lemon fruits with hints of marzipan, white flowers, crushed quartz and lemon zest. Dry, vivid and savoury on the palate with pristine fruit, sensational acid drive and all the detail, clarity and enjoyment you could hope for. Screw cap. 11% alc. RATING 95 DRINK 2023-2033 $25 DB ✪

The Fave Grenache 2021, Barossa Valley Almost pinot-esque in hue with pretty aromas of raspberry coulis, red plum and cranberry with hints of exotic spices, jasmine, red licorice, gingerbread, raspberry cola and earth. Detailed with a spacious mouthfeel, fine, sandy tannins and a long, floral-flecked finish. Beautiful drinking. Screw cap. 13.5% alc. RATING 95 DRINK 2023-2028 $45 DB ✪

Old Bastard Shiraz 2020, Barossa Valley Consistently impressive for its fruit density, textural flow and latent horsepower. Opulent blackberry, black cherry and plum fruit cut with hints of baking spices, dark chocolate, licorice, earth and violet top notes. Pure and beautifully weighted with savoury, gypsum-like tannins, bright acidity and impressive balance of the depth of fruit finishing long, true and distinctly Barossan. Cork. 14.5% alc. **RATING** 95 **DRINK** 2023–2033 $90 DB

ＹＹＹＹＹ Stonehorse Riesling 2022, Clare Valley **RATING** 93 **DRINK** 2022–2030 $25 MB✪
Cabernet Sauvignon 2020, Barossa Valley **RATING** 93 **DRINK** 2023–2029 $45 DB
Avignon Grenache Mourvèdre 2020, Barossa Valley **RATING** 93 **DRINK** 2023–2030 $40 DB
Love Child Viognier 2022, Barossa Valley **RATING** 91 **DRINK** 2023–2026 $45 DB

Kalleske ★★★★★

6 Murray Street, Greenock, SA 5360 **Region** Barossa Valley
T (08) 8563 4000 **www.kalleske.com Open** 7 days 10–5 **Winemaker** Troy Kalleske
Viticulturist Kym Kalleske **Est.** 1999 **Dozens** 10000 **Vyds** 50ha
The Kalleske family has been growing and selling grapes on a mixed farming property at Greenock for over 140 years. Sixth-generation Troy Kalleske, with brother Tony, established the winery and created the Kalleske label in '99. The vineyard is planted mainly to shiraz (31ha) and grenache (7ha), with smaller amounts of chenin blanc, semillon, viognier, cabernet sauvignon, mataro, durif, petit verdot, tempranillo and zinfandel. The vines vary in age, with the oldest dating back to 1875. All are grown biodynamically.

ＹＹＹＹＹ Eduard Old Vine Shiraz 2020, Barossa Valley Ripe blackberry, black cherry and macerated plums with baking spices, blackcurrant pastille, panforte, grilled fig, high-cocoa dark chocolate, olive tapenade, chocolate-dipped cherries and earth. Fine, high-resolution pithy tannin support and a long finish featuring a full-bodied swell of cassis, plum, spice and earth with a velvety yet sinewy edge. Screw cap. 15% alc. **RATING** 96 **DRINK** 2023–2040 $90 DB
Greenock Single Vineyard Shiraz 2021, Barossa Valley Kalleske's Greenock shiraz is always rich in subregional DNA. Here, great concentration and density, ferrous-edged tannins and a smooth, velvety palate of deep plum and dark berry fruits with underlying baking spices, licorice, dark chocolate, olive tapenade and earth. Structured yet possessing energy and drive. An excellent release. Screw cap. 14.5% alc. **RATING** 95 **DRINK** 2023–2035 $45 DB ✪
Old Vine Single Vineyard Grenache 2021, Barossa Valley Deep red and dark satsuma plum and dark cherry tones with light cranberry top notes and underlying hints of ground spice, gingerbread, red licorice, pressed citrus blossom, sarsaparilla, vanilla and earth. Calm and composed with detail, density and savoury flow framed by fine billowing tannin and vivid mineral drive. Screw cap. 15% alc. **RATING** 95 **DRINK** 2023–2033 $50 DB ✪

ＹＹＹＹＹ Zeitgeist Shiraz 2022, Barossa Valley **RATING** 93 **DRINK** 2023–2027 $29 DB✪
Parallax Grenache 2022, Barossa Valley **RATING** 93 **DRINK** 2023–2027 $29 DB✪
Moppa Shiraz 2021, Barossa Valley **RATING** 93 **DRINK** 2023–2033 $30 DB✪

Kanta ★★★★☆

22-26 Vardon Lane, Adelaide, SA 5000 (postal) **Region** Adelaide Hills
T (08) 8232 5300 **Open** Not **Winemaker** Egon Muller **Est.** 2005 **Dozens** 1000
This virtual winery is a joint venture between famed Mosel-Saar-Ruwer winemaker (and proprietor) Egon Müller and Michael Andrewartha from Adelaide's East End Cellars. The focus is on riesling, with fruit sourced from a high-altitude site near Echunga in the Adelaide Hills.

ΨΨΨΨΨ **Egon Müller Riesling 2021, Adelaide Hills** Tight, steely, sulphurous and limey upon opening. An aggressive swoosh liberates camphor, orange bitters and cumquat. The fly of chalky salinity, juicy acidity and Meyer lemon pucker, serves as the lattice, the stage, to drive this delicious wine into a long future. Screw cap. 13.5% alc. RATING 94 DRINK 2022–2032 $30 NG ✪

Karrawatta ★★★★★

164 Greenhills Road, Meadows, SA 5201 **Region** Adelaide Hills
T (08) 8537 0511 **www.karrawatta.com.au Open** 7 days 11–4 **Winemaker** Mark Gilbert **Viticulturist** Mark Gilbert **Est.** 2012 **Dozens** 5000 **Vyds** 59.25ha
Mark Gilbert is the great-great-great-grandson of Joseph Gilbert, who established the Pewsey Vale vineyard and winery in 1847. Joseph Gilbert had named the property Karrawatta, but adopted Pewsey Vale after losing the toss of a coin with his neighbour. The Karrawatta of today has 12.43ha of vines in the Adelaide Hills, 38.07ha in Langhorne Creek and 8.75ha in McLaren Vale. The vineyards are all hand pruned, the small-batch wines fashioned with minimum intervention.

ΨΨΨΨΨ **Anth's Garden Grand Vin Chardonnay 2021, Adelaide Hills** Classy chardonnay. More sturm of phenolics and drang of salty freshness than most. Thoroughly intriguing as a result. Very savoury. The waft of apricot kernel, peach and quince is secondary to the texture. A peaty, lees-derived core. The oak nestled beautifully, yet assertive, galvanising the fruit. A plume of acidity tows impressive length. Cork. 12.5% alc. RATING 96 DRINK 2022–2031 $150 NG
Tutelina Shiraz 2020, McLaren Vale Langhorne Creek Adelaide Hills A heady wine that is beautifully crafted. Salubrious oak tannins, mocha, cocoa nib and a luxurious flow of dark fruits and spice. Sometimes less is more, but there are moments to revel in excess. Here it is! Screw cap. 14.9% alc. RATING 95 DRINK 2024–2035 $275 NG
Spartacus Cabernet Sauvignon Malbec Shiraz 2020, Langhorne Creek Like a modern bordeaux, such is the quality of the oak and the precision of the tannins, alloyed ballbearings on the attack, and a rub of chamois at the finish. Dark fruits, chocolate and bouquet garni. Despite the richness and rather obvious power, there is a sophistication, savouriness and lovely glide to this beautiful behemoth. Cork. 14.6% alc. RATING 94 DRINK 2024–2038 $92 NG
Joseph Grand Vin Shiraz 2018, Langhorne Creek A wine of a palate-staining largesse. Yet with sass, uncanny energy and vibrant aromatics all belying the heady alcohol. Miraculously, it works. Not a 3-glass proposition, perhaps, but certainly a wine of flair and intelligent composition. Lilac, blueberry and nori cascade along a trajectory of growing fruit sweetness and intensity, lathering the thick finish with kirsch, rosemary and lavender notes. Screw cap. 15.5% alc. RATING 94 DRINK 2022–2030 $150 NG
Christo's Paddock Grand Vin Cabernet Sauvignon 2018, Langhorne Creek A sumptuous, hot-climate cabernet from a low-yielding vintage. Distinctly maritime, with a plume of briny black olive/sea spray freshness. Dried sage segues to a morass of dark-fruit allusions, corralled by a curb of mocha oak. Cork. 14.9% alc. RATING 94 DRINK 2022–2035 $150 NG

ΨΨΨΨΨ **Popsie Blanc de Blancs Chardonnay 2019, Adelaide Hills** RATING 93 DRINK 2023–2032 $62 NG
Dairy Block Shiraz 2021, Adelaide Hills RATING 93 DRINK 2022–2030 $42 NG
Chapel Hill Road Bush Vine Grenache 2021, McLaren Vale RATING 93 DRINK 2022–2030 $46 NG
Dairy Block Grand Vin Shiraz 2018, Adelaide Hills RATING 93 DRINK 2022–2032 $150 NG
Anna's Sauvignon Blanc 2022, Adelaide Hills RATING 92 DRINK 2022–2024 $34 NG
Ace of Trumps Chapel Hill Road Shiraz 2021, McLaren Vale RATING 92 DRINK 2022–2032 $62 NG

Sophie's Hill Pinot Grigio 2022, Adelaide Hills RATING 91
DRINK 2022–2024 $34 NG
The Meddler Malbec 2020, Langhorne Creek RATING 91 DRINK 2022–2032
$54 NG
Anth's Garden Chardonnay 2021, Adelaide Hills RATING 90
DRINK 2022–2027 $46 NG

Kate Hill Wines

21 Dowlings Road, Huonville, Tas 7109 **Region** Southern Tasmania
T 0448 842 696 **www**.katehillwines.com.au **Open** Wed–Sun 11–4 **Winemaker** Kate
Hill **Est.** 2008 **Dozens** 2000 **Vyds** 4ha
When Kate Hill and her husband Charles came to Tasmania in '06, Kate had worked as a
winemaker in Australia and overseas for 10 years. Having always sourced fruit from vineyards
across Southern Tasmania, '16 saw them also planting 4ha of their own pinot noir, chardonnay
and shiraz. A cellar door followed in '17. The aim is to produce approachable, delicate wines.

ŸŸŸŸŸ **Shiraz 2020, Tasmania** Think red plum and red cherry with a dollop of
raspberry high tones. There are hints of red licorice, roasting game, orange
blossom, dried citrus rind and exotic spice in the mix with a sense of space and
detail that's almost pinot-like in stature. Tight, fine chalky tannin and bright
Tassie acid drive seal the deal as the wine fades with notes of sour cherry and
spice. Screw cap. 12.5% alc. RATING 93 DRINK 2023–2029 $55 DB
Huon Valley Chardonnay 2021, Tasmania Inviting aromas of lemon, green
apple and melon fruits underscored by hints of crushed stone, white flowers,
almond paste, light vanillin oak, nougat and oatmeal. Clean and crisp with some
nice detail and a lovely line of crystalline acidity that propels the wine forward,
finishing in a blast of citrus and soft spice. Screw cap. 12.6% alc. RATING 92
DRINK 2023–2026 $42 DB
Huon Valley Pinot Noir 2020, Tasmania Pale crimson with plenty of forest
floor/mushroom notes that act as a base for the red cherry and raspberry fruit
tones. Hints of spice, redcurrant jelly, master stock and light, gamey notes join
in along with gentle, fine tannin and bright acid drive. Screw cap. 13.2% alc.
RATING 92 DRINK 2023–2028 $60 DB
Pinot Noir 2018, Tasmania Pale crimson with aromas of red cherry, plum and
raspberry on a bed of fine spice with hints of purple flowers, earth, redcurrant
jelly and light game tones. Some nice detail on the palate with a grainy tannin
presence and a wash of sour cherry and spice on the finish. Screw cap. 12.8% alc.
RATING 90 DRINK 2023–2027 $42 DB

Kay Brothers

57 Kays Road, McLaren Vale, SA 5171 **Region** McLaren Vale
T (08) 8323 8211 **www**.kaybrothers.com.au **Open** 7 days 11–5 **Winemaker** Duncan
Kennedy **Viticulturist** Duncan Kennedy **Est.** 1890 **Dozens** 10 000 **Vyds** 22ha
Kay Brothers is a traditional family winery with a rich history dating back to 1890. One of
5 wineries in the Vale with vines planted in the 1880s (the others being Paxton, Ox Hardy,
Richard Hamilton and d'Arenberg), the 20ha estate includes the original 1.5ha of Block 6
shiraz vines planted in 1892. The full-flavoured red and fortified wines can be particularly
good. Both vines and wines are going from strength to strength here.

ŸŸŸŸŸ **Block 6 Shiraz 2020, McLaren Vale** This release represents a profound change
at this address from a culture of rich wines hewn of old vines and traditional
winemaking, to one of earlier harvesting and a grasp for freshness. Sure, the
ancient vines remain. Yet despite the palpable intensity and drive, there is a
twiggy dryness, a paucity of amplitude and a generosity that is synergistic with
an early harvest window. Olive and dark fruits, sure. Time may bestow further
beauty. I score with the benefit of the doubt. Screw cap. 13% alc. RATING 95
DRINK 2022–2030 $125 NG

ΥΥΥΥΥ Grenache Rosé 2022, McLaren Vale RATING 93 DRINK 2022–2023
$25 NG ✪
Basket Pressed Mataro 2021, McLaren Vale RATING 93 DRINK 2022–2030
$33 NG ✪
GSM Grenache Shiraz Mourvèdre 2021, McLaren Vale RATING 93
DRINK 2022–2025 $39 NG
Petit Blanc 2022, McLaren Vale RATING 92 DRINK 2022–2024 $25 NG ✪
Griffon's Key Reserve Grenache 2021, McLaren Vale RATING 92
DRINK 2022–2028 $70 NG
Hillside Shiraz 2020, McLaren Vale RATING 92 DRINK 2023–2035 $49 NG
Basket Pressed Merlot 2021, McLaren Vale RATING 91 DRINK 2022–2030
$33 NG
Basket Pressed Shiraz 2021, McLaren Vale RATING 91 DRINK 2022–2025
$39 NG
Basket Pressed Grenache 2021, McLaren Vale RATING 90
DRINK 2022–2027 $33 NG

Keith Tulloch Wine

989 Hermitage Road, Pokolbin, NSW 2320 **Region** Hunter Valley
T (02) 4998 7500 **www.keithtullochwine.com.au Open** By appt Thurs–Sat 10–4,
Sun 10–3 **Winemaker** Keith Tulloch, Brendan Kaczorowski, Alisdair Tulloch
Viticulturist Brent Hutton **Est.** 1997 **Dozens** 10 000 **Vyds** 15ha
Keith Tulloch is, of course, a member of the Tulloch family, which has played a leading role
in the Hunter Valley for over a century. Formerly a winemaker at Lindemans and Rothbury
Estate, he developed his own label in '97. There is the same almost obsessive attention to
detail, the same almost ascetic intellectual approach, the same refusal to accept anything but
the best as that of Jeffrey Grosset. In Apr '19 the winery became the first Hunter Valley winery
to become certified carbon neutral under the National Carbon Offset Standard (NCOS).

ΥΥΥΥΥ **Latara Vineyard Semillon 2022, Hunter Valley** No mlf, no time on lees.
This is a compelling wine of purity and flawless balance. There's plenty of
lemon, lemongrass and steely freshness leaving no room for argument: this will
be a stunner with a decade or 2 in the cellar. Screw cap. 11% alc. RATING 96
DRINK 2023–2037 $37 JH ✪
Field of Mars Block 4 Chardonnay 2021, Hunter Valley The decision not
to use any new oak was intelligent, serving to focus on the purity of the wine.
The palate is long and harmonious, and while it has the cohesion to lay the way
for current consumption, it will repay a few years of maturation in bottle. Only
50 dozen made. Screw cap. 13% alc. RATING 96 DRINK 2023–2036 $75 JH ✪
Field of Mars Block 1 Shiraz 2021, Hunter Valley 10% whole bunches,
10 days fermentation on skins, pressed off for mlf in a single 1500L French foudre
and aged in the same vessel for 14 months. Highly fragrant and positively juicy,
all the decisions from vine to bottle were perfectly timed and pitched. 165 dozen
made. Screw cap. 13% alc. RATING 96 DRINK 2023–2041 $95 JH
Ewen Vineyard Chardonnay 2022, Hunter Valley Racked to French
barriques (10% new), matured on lees with bâtonnage twice a month. An elegant
chardonnay, fresh and seamless, the accent on white peach and melon fruit
supported by citrusy acidity, the oak no more than a whisper. 280 dozen made.
Screw cap. 12.5% alc. RATING 95 DRINK 2023–2030 $45 JH ✪
McKelvey Vineyard Chardonnay 2022, Hunter Valley Racked cloudy to
225L French barriques (10% new), 7 months on lees. Has the elegance and fluid
mouthfeel of the same ilk as the Ewen vineyard, the finish long and harmonious.
280 dozen made. Screw cap. 12.5% alc. RATING 95 DRINK 2023–2030 $45 JH ✪
Field of Mars Block 2 Semillon 2021, Hunter Valley Clear juice
inoculated with DV10 champagne yeast, cool-fermented. Starts with intensity
and progressively builds onto another plane. Likewise, lemon juice and stiletto
acidity underwrite the purity of the long, finely drawn, palate. 95 dozen made.
Screw cap. 10.5% alc. RATING 95 DRINK 2023–2036 $55 JH

Field of Mars Block 3 Semillon 2021, Hunter Valley Similar vinification to that of Block 2. A bolder style than the Block 2, says Keith Tulloch, and it's certainly true that this is more consumer-friendly, the acidity bordering on succulent. Its flavour drivers are as one, with purity not in doubt. 165 dozen made. Screw cap. 10.5% alc. RATING 95 DRINK 2023–2030 $55 JH

The Kester Shiraz 2021, Hunter Valley Matured in a French foudre and puncheons for 14 months. The vivid hue is a confident start off the back of 13% alc. (a feature of the vintage); a supple medium-bodied wine that shows, but carries, the use of oak. Screw cap. 13% alc. RATING 95 DRINK 2023–2046 $80 JH

Shiraz Viognier 2021, Hunter Valley 95/5% shiraz/viognier blend, co-fermented, destemmed but not crushed to retain whole berries, cultured yeast and 7–10 days on skins; mlf in French oak. A light- to medium-bodied wine, pretty as one can be, patience not needed. Screw cap. 13% alc. RATING 94 DRINK 2023–2036 $38 JH ✪

Tawarri Vineyard Shiraz 2021, Hunter Valley Whole bunches (10%), 3-day cold soak; 10 days on skins; pressed off for mlf in a single 1500L French foudre and aged in the same vessel for 14 months. Was the foudre new, I wonder? Or is it the vineyard site, splendidly aloof at an elevation of 460m? Has a long future, and needs it. 165 dozen made. Screw cap. 13.5% alc. RATING 94 DRINK 2023–2046 $50 JH

𝟵𝟵𝟵𝟵𝟵 Chardonnay 2022, Hunter Valley RATING 92 DRINK 2024–2027 $38 JH
Semillon 2022, Hunter Valley RATING 92 DRINK 2023–2030 $32 JH

Kellybrook   ★★★★☆

Fulford Road, Wonga Park, Vic 3115 **Region** Yarra Valley
T (03) 9722 1304 www.kellybrookwinery.com.au **Open** Fri–Sun 11–5
Winemaker Stuart Dudine **Est.** 1962 **Dozens** 3000 **Vyds** 8.4ha
The vineyard is at Wonga Park, one of the gateways to the Yarra Valley. A very competent producer of cider and apple brandy (in Calvados style) as well as table wine. When it received its winery licence in '70, it became the first winery in the Yarra Valley to open its doors in the 20th century, a distinction often ignored or forgotten.

𝟵𝟵𝟵𝟵𝟵 **Blanc de Blancs 2019, Yarra Valley** Barrel fermentation before 33 months on lees; disgorged with a dosage of 6g/L. Light, bright straw with green tinges. A complex bouquet of citrus fruits, quince, ginger and a little marzipan. Dry, focused and elegant on the palate, this will continue to improve and develop with time. Diam. 12% alc. RATING 95 DRINK 2022–2027 $45 PR ✪

𝟵𝟵𝟵𝟵𝟵 Willowlake Vineyard Pinot Noir 2021, Yarra Valley RATING 93 DRINK 2022–2028 $40 PR
Willowlake Vineyard Chardonnay 2021, Yarra Valley RATING 92 DRINK 2022–2026 $40 PR
Siwa Chardonnay 2021, Yarra Valley RATING 92 DRINK 2022–2026 $40 PR
Estate Shiraz 2020, Geelong RATING 91 DRINK 2022–2026 $40 PR
Edenesque Chardonnay 2022, Yarra Valley RATING 90 DRINK 2022–2025 $30 PR
Edenesque Pinot Noir 2021, Yarra Valley RATING 90 DRINK 2022–2026 $30 PR

Kennedy   ★★★★

Maple Park, 224 Wallenjoe Road, Corop, Vic 3559 (postal) **Region** Heathcote
T (03) 5484 8293 www.kennedyvintners.com.au **Open** Not **Winemaker** Glen Hayley, Gerard Kennedy **Viticulturist** Barney Touhey **Est.** 2002 **Dozens** 3000 **Vyds** 29.2ha
Having been farmers in the Colbinabbin area of Heathcote for 27 years, John and Patricia Kennedy were on the spot when a prime piece of red Cambrian soil on the east-facing slope of Mount Camel Range became available for purchase. They planted 20ha of shiraz in '02, further plantings of shiraz, tempranillo and mourvèdre followed in '07. John and Patricia's

geologist son Gerard returned to the family business in '15 and oversees the winemaking and activities in the vineyard.

ŸŸŸŸŸ **Cambria Shiraz 2020, Heathcote** It sits on the bold side of medium weight and is as seamless as it is seductive. Black cherry, wheat, cedar and ripe plum flavours put on an entirely convincing show, with woodsmoke and mint notes adding to the highlights. It's cohesive, it's impressive and it's moreish. Screw cap. 14% alc. **RATING** 94 **DRINK** 2024–2034 $40 CM ✪

ŸŸŸŸŸ **Pink Hills Rosé 2022, Heathcote** **RATING** 93 **DRINK** 2022–2026 $25 CM ✪
Henrietta Shiraz 2021, Heathcote **RATING** 93 **DRINK** 2023–2031 $30 CM ✪
Henrietta Rosé 2022, Heathcote **RATING** 92 **DRINK** 2023–2025 $24 CM ✪
Henrietta Tempranillo 2022, Heathcote **RATING** 90 **DRINK** 2023–2027 $25 CM ✪

Kerri Greens ★★★★★

38 Paringa Road, Red Hill South, Vic 3937 **Region** Mornington Peninsula
T (03) 5989 2572 www.kerrigreens.com **Open** Sat 11–5, Fri, Sun 12–5
Winemaker Tom McCarthy, Lucas Blanck **Viticulturist** Lucas Blanck, Tom McCarthy
Est. 2015 **Dozens** 1000

Kerri Greens (named after a local surf break) offers excellent and energising wines. Tom McCarthy (son of local Peninsula producers Kathleen Quealy and Kevin McCarthy) is the lead winemaker at Quealy Wines these days and Lucas Blanck (son of winemaker Frederic, from Domaine Paul Blanck in Alsace) is viticulturist. Organics, sustainability and treading gently are important considerations. It's also a family business strengthened by their wives, Alyce Blanck and Sarah Saxton, who are very much at the forefront. This young quartet is respectful of a wine region that nurtures them, yet not afraid to shake things up. In mid '23, Lucas and Alyce took over sole ownership of Kerri Greens.

ŸŸŸŸŸ **Duke Chardonnay 2021, Mornington Peninsula** This is ethereal with fine gossamer-like acidity holding together citrus, lemon cream and white nectarine flavours. There's texture and creaminess across the palate, but it too is restrained and there's a lipsmacking tonic water/saline character, without the sweetness of course. Moreish, savoury and a stunning drink. Bravo. Screw cap. 12.6% alc. **RATING** 96 **DRINK** 2022–2031 $62 JF ✪
Pig Face Chardonnay 2022, Mornington Peninsula Refreshment with a capital R. Deceptive at first as its tightly wound with spider-silk-tight acidity encasing the dabs of grapefruit, lemon salts and seashell. Then enticing wafts of flinty sulphides, spicy oak and nutty lees come to the fore. Not much, flavours are dialled down to subtle. Classy stuff and moreish to the last drop. Screw cap. 12.6% alc. **RATING** 95 **DRINK** 2023–2030 $36 JF ✪
Sage Phoque 2021, Mornington Peninsula A complex, compelling and textural rosé. A copper-Campari hue and tastes a bit like it, too, as this is incredibly savoury, more of an absence of fruit in a way. Amaro, chinotto, saline even, yet it is refreshing and dry with mouth-watering acidity. Serious wine and seriously good, too. Screw cap. 13% alc. **RATING** 95 **DRINK** 2022–2026 $36 JF ✪
Foothills Pinot Noir 2021, Mornington Peninsula Such clarity to this both in colour and flavours, with the latter an amalgam of spiced cherries and plums, licorice and menthol, sumac and cedary oak. It's medium bodied with sweet fruit bombing the palate, acidity lengthening the finish and textural tannins shoring up everything beautifully. Screw cap. 13.2% alc. **RATING** 95 **DRINK** 2023–2033 $45 JF ✪
Citrea Riesling 2021, Mornington Peninsula Riesling with texture, depth and flavour from whole bunches, wild fermentation in seasoned oak, mlf too and around 11 months on solids. Beautiful fruit flavours abound with yellow peach, lemon curd and glacé lime. Spicy, rich and a palate that's plump and yet tempered by fine acidity. Excellent drop. Screw cap. 13.2% alc. **RATING** 95 **DRINK** 2022–2031 $36 JF ✪

Duke Pinot Noir 2021, Mornington Peninsula A very fine drink, pretty and ethereal. Flavours oscillate between tangy-sweet fruit to savoury elements: cherries and pips, poached rhubarb and blood orange with Angostura bitters. The palate squeezes in at medium bodied with fine, sandy tannins and such uplifting acidity to close long and pure. Screw cap. 12.8% alc. RATING 95 DRINK 2024–2032 $65 JF

ɤɤɤɤ **Samphire Sauvignon Blanc 2022, Mornington Peninsula** RATING 93 DRINK 2023–2028 $32 JF ○
Oxydental Chardonnay 2021, Mornington Peninsula RATING 92 DRINK 2023–2026 $36 JF
Pinots de Mornington Rosé 2022, Mornington Peninsula RATING 91 DRINK 2022–2024 $32 JF
Effet-Mer Syrah 2021, Mornington Peninsula RATING 90 DRINK 2024–2031 $40 JF

Kerrigan + Berry   ★★★★★

PO Box 221, Cowaramup, WA 6284 **Region** South West Australia
T (08) 9755 6046 **www**.hayshedhill.com.au **Open** at Hay Shed Hill 7 days 10–5
Winemaker Michael Kerrigan, Gavin Berry **Est.** 2007 **Dozens** 1500
Owners Michael Kerrigan and Gavin Berry have been making wine in WA for a combined period of over 50 years. This is strictly a weekend and after-hours venture, separate from their respective roles as chief winemakers at Hay Shed Hill (Michael) and West Cape Howe (Gavin). They have focused on what is important, and explain, 'We have spent a total of zero hours on marketing research, and no consultants have been injured in the making of these wines'.

ɤɤɤɤɤ **Riesling 2022, Mount Barker** The bouquet is a meadow of spring flowers crushed underfoot, with a sprig of lavender for good measure. The palate takes up the story, with juicy makrut lime, lemon and crisp acidity all on the same page. Screw cap. 11.5% alc. RATING 96 DRINK 2023–2032 $29 JH ○

ɤɤɤɤ **Chardonnay 2021, Margaret River** RATING 93 DRINK 2023–2027 $39 JH

Kersbrook Hill   ★★★★

1498 South Para Road, Kersbrook, SA 5231 **Region** Adelaide Hills
T (08) 8389 3301 **www**.kersbrookhill.com.au **Open** 7 days 10–5.30 **Winemaker** Paul Clark, Nigel Nessi **Viticulturist** Paul Clark **Est.** 1998 **Dozens** 8000 **Vyds** 11ha
Paul and Mary Clark purchased what is now the Kersbrook Hill property, then grazing land, in 1997, planting 0.4ha of shiraz on a reality-check basis. Encouraged by the results, they increased the plantings to 3ha of shiraz and 1ha of riesling 2 years later. Yet further expansion of the vineyards has seen the area under vine increased to 11ha, cabernet sauvignon (with 6ha) the frontrunner.

ɤɤɤɤɤ **Barrel Aged Tawny NV, Adelaide Hills** 15 years on average. Molasses, brûlée, walnut husk and a Moroccan souk sweep across tamarind, raisin and bergamot. Dried date and cardamom pulse across a long, viscous finish. There is a lot to feel out. A very good wine. 350ml. Screw cap. 19.5% alc. RATING 95 $35 NG ○

Kies Family Wines   ★★★★

Lot 2 Barossa Valley Way, Lyndoch, SA 5381 **Region** Barossa Valley
T (08) 8524 4110 **www**.kieswines.com.au **Open** 7 days 9–4 **Winemaker** Joanne Irvine **Est.** 1969 **Dozens** 5000 **Vyds** 30ha
The Kies family has been resident in the Barossa Valley since 1857; the present generation of winemakers is the 5th. Until 1969 the family sold almost all their grapes, but in that year they launched their own brand, Karrawirra. The coexistence of Killawarra forced a name change in '83 to Redgum Vineyard; this business was subsequently sold. Later still, Kies Family Wines

opened for business, drawing upon vineyards (up to 100yo) that had remained in the family throughout the changes, offering a wide range of wines through the 1880 cellar door.

ŶŶŶŶŶ **The Suit Cabernet Sauvignon 2020, Barossa Valley** Deep blackberry and blackcurrant pastille fruit characters with hints of baking spices, tobacco, polished leather, violets, licorice and cedar. A core of cassis-like fruit on the palate, and chocolatey, toothsome ripe tannins as the wine sails off. Would cellar nicely. Cork. 15% alc. **RATING** 94 **DRINK** 2023-2035 $50 DB
Dedication Shiraz 2020, Barossa Valley Deep, tobacco-flecked plum, blackberry and black cherry fruits dredged with baking spices, licorice, dark chocolate, violets, cedar and earth. It sits at the lighter end of full bodied with notes of leather and mahogany before setting off with dark and black berry fruits, spices tending savoury at the end. Cork. 14.5% alc. **RATING** 94 **DRINK** 2023-2033 $55 DB

ŶŶŶŶŶ **Klauber Block Shiraz 2020, Barossa Valley** **RATING** 93 **DRINK** 2023-2030 $35 DB ✪
Chaff Mill Cabernet Sauvignon 2020, Barossa Valley **RATING** 92 **DRINK** 2023-2033 $35 DB

Kilikanoon Wines ★★★★★

30 Penna Lane, Penwortham, SA 5453 **Region** Clare Valley
T (08) 8849 2356 **www**.kilikanoon.com.au **Open** 7 days 11–5 **Winemaker** Peter Warr, Mercedes Paynter **Viticulturist** Troy van Dulken **Est.** 1997 **Dozens** 100 000 **Vyds** 120ha
Kilikanoon has travelled in the fast lane since winemaker Kevin Mitchell established it in 1997 on the foundation of 6ha of vines he owned with father Mort. With the aid of investors, its 100 000 dozen production comes from 120ha of estate-owned vineyards. A major restructure has been completed with the acquisition of the winery that it had hitherto leased, along with the ownership of the 16.35ha Mount Surmon vineyard. This very substantial business in the Clare Valley produces 85% red wines, with a further focus on grenache. Kilikanoon accounts for over 35% of the region's production of this variety.

ŶŶŶŶŶ **Mort's Reserve Watervale Riesling 2022, Clare Valley** Lots of energy here. Lime and lemon to the fore, with just-ripe green apple, fennel and a touch of blackcurrant. Sleek in texture, very long and fine to finish. Maybe missing a little mid-palate stuffing … racy, anyway, with some powdery pucker in tow and great texture. Feels polished, primped and preened. Screw cap. 11% alc. **RATING** 94 **DRINK** 2022-2040 $50 MB
Morrison Shiraz Cabernet 2020, Clare Valley A silky, medium-weight cabernet shiraz. Very perfumed, fine tannins, good length. The fragrant bouquet redolent of blueberry and mulberry with a lift of choc-mint, eucalyptus and white pepper. The palate feels pure in its berry fruit flavours with the faintest suggestion of cedar-clove oak. There's leafy mintiness lending freshness and lift, a dash of white pepper and salted licorice, too. It's in very good shape. Screw cap. 14.5% alc. **RATING** 94 **DRINK** 2022-2032 $55 MB ♥
Walton 1946 Grenache 2020, Clare Valley Slurpy, concentrated, slick and rich. Stewed plum, new leather, Asian five-spice and light minty elements all working together in bouquet and palate. Very intense, concentrated and held together with a ribbons of grippy, grunty tannin, but the overall feel sees balance as a motif even with the potency of the wine. Big, and done well. Screw cap. 14.5% alc. **RATING** 94 **DRINK** 2022-2035 $96 MB
Oracle Shiraz 2019, Clare Valley Mellifluous, rich and sweet-hearted. Ripe cherry compote, black olive and choc-licorice to sniff on. The palate is more sweet and plummy, laced with fine, powdery tannins and a lick of smoky minerality in tow, all dusted with clove-woody spice. There's a lovely flow to this wine, suppleness, too. An impressive expression of a regional staple, boldly done. Screw cap. 14.5% alc. **RATING** 94 **DRINK** 2022-2035 $96 MB

ŸŸŸŸ♀ **Small Batch Kx Cabernet Malbec 2020**, Clare Valley RATING 93
DRINK 2022-2026 $35 MB ✪
Small Batch Kx Rosé 2022, Clare Valley RATING 92 DRINK 2022-2024
$25 MB ✪
Attunga 1865 Shiraz 2020, Clare Valley RATING 92 DRINK 2022-2035
$250 MB
Small Batch Kx Riesling 2022, Clare Valley RATING 91 DRINK 2022-2030
$25 MB ✪
Skilly Valley Pinot Gris 2022, Clare Valley RATING 91 DRINK 2022-2024
$25 MB ✪
Small Batch Kx Grenache 2021, Clare Valley RATING 91 DRINK 2022-2027
$35 MB
Mort's Cut Watervale Riesling 2020, Clare Valley RATING 91
DRINK 2022-2025 $30 MB
Small Batch Kx Montepulciano 2020, Clare Valley RATING 90
DRINK 2022-2026 $35 MB
Blocks Road Cabernet Sauvignon 2019, Clare Valley RATING 90
DRINK 2022-2030 $40 MB

Kimbarra Wines ★★★★

422 Barkly Street, Ararat, Vic 3377 **Region** Grampians
T 0428 519 195 www.kimbarrawines.com.au **Open** By appt **Winemaker** Peter Leeke,
Justin Purser, Adam Richardson **Est.** 1990 **Dozens** 180 **Vyds** 11ha
Peter Leeke has 8.5ha of shiraz, 1.5ha of riesling and 1ha of cabernet sauvignon – varieties that
have proven best suited to the Grampians region. The particularly well-made, estate-grown
wines deserve a wider audience.

ŸŸŸŸ♀ **Riesling 2022, Grampians** The intensity of the lime flavours is really quite
something. It's like squeezing a ripe, juicy lime, warmed from the sun, sweet and
zesty at once. It's relatively simple but it's enormously engaging, simultaneously.
A joy to drink. Screw cap. 12% alc. RATING 93 DRINK 2023-2032 $30 CM ✪
Shiraz 2021, Grampians Black pepper and cloves, sweet plum and cherry,
flashes of woodsy spice and walnut. It's of average intensity and above average
quality. Tannin, lacy, has been finely judged. This is the archetypal now-or-later
wine. Screw cap. 14.5% alc. RATING 93 DRINK 2023-2033 $30 CM ✪

Kimbolton Wines ★★★★★

29 Burleigh Street, Langhorne Creek, SA 5255 **Region** Langhorne Creek
T (08) 8537 3002 www.kimboltonwines.com.au **Open** 7 days 11–4 **Winemaker**
Contract **Est.** 1998 **Dozens** 2500 **Vyds** 55ha
The Kimbolton property originally formed part of the Potts Bleasedale estate. In 1946 it was
aquired by Henry and Thelma Case, grandparents of current owners, brother and sister Nicole
Clark and Brad Case. The grapes from the vineyard plantings (cabernet sauvignon, shiraz,
malbec, fiano, carignan and montepulciano) are sold to leading wineries, with small amounts
retained for the Kimbolton label. The cellar door is made from a 'unique mix of high-gloss
navy industrial shipping containers' and timber, including a rooftop viewing platform.

ŸŸŸŸ **The Rifleman Shiraz 2020, Langhorne Creek** From a 1ha block planted
in 1993. Fermented in small open fermenters, hand-plunged thrice daily;
pressed to small open top fermenters, 7 days on skins; matured in 100% new
French oak. Strict barrel selection resulted in a make of only 100 dozen. Plum,
mulberry and blackberry fruit flavours all help. Screw cap. 14.5% alc. RATING 95
DRINK 2025-2040 $60 JH
The Rifleman Cabernet Sauvignon 2020, Langhorne Creek Pressed to
100% new French barrels for a strict best barrels selection; only 100 dozen made.
Supple, medium- to full-bodied palate; juicy cassis/choc mint flavours upfront,
with tannins and (surprisingly) oak in the back seat. Screw cap. 14.3% alc.
RATING 95 DRINK 2023-2035 $60 JH

The Rifleman Chardonnay 2022, Adelaide Hills Barrel fermented in French oak (20% new) followed by 8 months' maturation. A rich, pleasantly fleshy chardonnay ready to roll right now. Screw cap. 13% alc. **RATING** 94 **DRINK** 2023–2029 $36 JH ✪

🍷🍷🍷🍷♀ **Single Vineyard Brad's Block Montepulciano 2022, Langhorne Creek** **RATING** 92 **DRINK** 2023–2030 $30 JH ✪
Single Vineyard Fig Tree Cabernet Sauvignon 2021, Langhorne Creek **RATING** 92 **DRINK** 2026–2031 $28 JH ✪
Single Vineyard M14 Fiano 2022, Langhorne Creek RATING 90 **DRINK** 2026–2031 $25 JH ✪
Single Vineyard VSP Shiraz 2021, Langhorne Creek RATING 90 **DRINK** 2023–2036 $25 JH ✪

Kingsley Grove Estate

49 Stuart Valley Drive, Goodger, Qld 4610 **Region** South Burnett
T (07) 4162 2229 www.kingsleygrove.com **Open** 7 days 10–5 **Winemaker** Simon Berry **Viticulturist** Peter Stewart **Est.** 1998 **Dozens** 1000 **Vyds** 10ha
Patricia Berry and late husband Michael founded a substantial vineyard near Kingaroy, an area better known for growing peanuts. The VSP-trellised vines are grown in a north–south orientation that best accommodates the hot Queensland summer sun with a computer-controlled irrigation system. The wines are made onsite by son Simon Berry.

🍷🍷🍷🍷♀ **Rum Barrel Fort Semillon NV, South Burnett** This fortified is made from wines blended since '06 and matured for 14 years before finishing in rum barrels. It shows its rum credentials in molasses and treacle elements, but also feels quite fresh despite the cavalcade of woody spices, raisin notes and kirsch elements. It's lighter than you'd think in some respects, albeit flavour-packed and vibrant. Unique, great drinking. Stopper. 17.5% alc. **RATING** 93 $100 MB

Kirrihill Wines

948 Farrell Flat Road, Clare, SA 5453 **Region** Clare Valley
T (08) 8842 1233 www.kirrihill.com.au **Open** By appt **Winemaker** Andrew Locke, Alexandra Wardlaw **Viticulturist** Dick Brysky **Est.** 1998 **Dozens** 45 000 **Vyds** 250ha
The Kirrihill story started in the late '90s. The aim was to build a business producing premium wines from temperate vineyards that represent the unique characters of the Clare Valley. Grapes are sourced from specially selected parcels of Kirrihill's 600ha of vineyards. Andrew Locke, with vintage experience in the Loire Valley, Tuscany, Sonoma Valley and Spain, joined Kirrihill as chief winemaker in '20.

🍷🍷🍷🍷♀ **E.B.'s The Settler Watervale Riesling 2022, Clare Valley** A fuller-flavoured and potent expression of riesling. Deep concentration with chalky, puckering fringes and a good textural experience. Strong scents of lime juice, dried citrus peel and talc. The palate shows more of that lime juice with gingery elements, piquant almost with a zingy tangle of lemony acidity through the mid-palate. A pretty intense wine on hand. Good. Screw cap. 12% alc. **RATING** 91 **DRINK** 2022–2033 $35 MB

Knappstein ★★★★☆

2 Pioneer Avenue, Clare, SA 5453 **Region** Clare Valley
T (08) 8841 2100 www.knappstein.com.au **Open** 7 days 10–4 **Winemaker** Michael Kane, Mike Farmilo (Consultant) **Est.** 1969 **Dozens** 75 000 **Vyds** 114ha
Knappstein's full name is Knappstein Enterprise Winery, reflecting its history before being acquired by Petaluma, then part of Lion Nathan, followed by Accolade. After a period of corporate ownership, Knappstein has now come full circle and is back in private ownership, purchased in '19 by Yinmore Wines. Despite these corporate chessboard moves, wine quality has remained excellent. The wines are produced from the substantial mature estate Enterprise, Ackland, Yertabulti and The Mayor's vineyards.

🍷🍷🍷🍷🍷 **Ackland Single Vineyard Watervale Riesling 2022, Clare Valley** Bright, vibrant, juicy and refreshing. That's a lot of boxes ticked already. It's an intense and inwardly concentrated expression. Zingy, zesty and loaded with tart, lemony citrus characters overlaid with pink grapefruit and licks of stony, minerally notes. The perfume and palate are in sync, the wine incredibly refreshing, almost breathtaking. It's one for the acid hounds, well balanced in its way, and detailed/complex too. Well played. Screw cap. 12% alc. **RATING** 94 **DRINK** 2022–2035 $30 MB ✪

🍷🍷🍷🍷🍷 **Enterprise Vineyard Cabernet Sauvignon 2020, Clare Valley** **RATING** 93 **DRINK** 2022–2035 $53 MB
The Insider 2022, Clare Valley **RATING** 92 **DRINK** 2022–2030 $30 MB ✪
Riesling 2022, Clare Valley **RATING** 92 **DRINK** 2022–2030 $22 MB ✪
Enterprise Vineyard Spring Farm Riesling 2022, Clare Valley **RATING** 92 **DRINK** 2022–2035 $30 MB ✪
Insider Shiraz Malbec 2020, Clare Valley **RATING** 92 **DRINK** 2022–2028 $30 MB ✪
Mayors Vineyard Shiraz 2020, Clare Valley **RATING** 92 **DRINK** 2022–2035 $53 MB

Knee Deep Wines ★★★☆

22 Rathay Street, Victoria Park, WA 6100 (postal) **Region** Margaret River
T (08) 9755 6776 **www.kneedeepwines.com.au** **Open** Not **Winemaker** Kate Morgan
Est. 2000 **Dozens** 5000

Perth surgeon and veteran yachtsman Phil Childs and wife Sue established Knee Deep in 2000. The name was inspired by the passion and commitment needed to produce premium wine and as a tongue- in-cheek acknowledgement of jumping in 'boots and all'. The brand passed to the Holden family in '17, Matt and Clair Holden having worked alongside the Childs family for 5 years.

🍷🍷🍷🍷🍷 **Birdhouse Cabernet Sauvignon 2021, Margaret River** While the tannins are coming across a bit gangly, elbowing their way across the fuller-bodied palate, there's depth and plenty of varietal fruit at play. Lots of cassis and blackberries infused with licorice and oak spice. A bit more time in bottle will help. Screw cap. 14.5% alc. **RATING** 90 **DRINK** 2024–2033 $39 JF

Koerner Wine ★★★★★

935 Mintaro Road, Leasingham, SA 5452 **Region** Clare Valley
T 0408 895 341 **www.koernerwine.com.au** **Open** By appt **Winemaker** Damon Koerner **Est.** 2014 **Dozens** 4000 **Vyds** 60ha

Brothers Damon and Jonathan (Jono) Koerner grew up in the Clare Valley but flew the coop to work and study in other parts of Australia and abroad. Their family vineyard had been owned and managed by their parents, Anthony and Christine Koerner, for 40 years. They have since passed ownership and management of the vineyards on to their sons; the vineyards are now being converted to organics. The pair have made a good dent in modernising the 'classic' Clare Valley style, specialising in early picked, minimal-intervention wines and utilising terracotta and ceramic fermenters. Koerner wines are mostly made from the family vineyard, Gullyview, with some fruit sourced from neighbouring vineyards, Parish and Vivian. A major point of difference from other Clare Valley wineries is the use of synonyms for well-known varieties, as well as adopting Australian name usage, turning the world upside-down with left-field winemaking practices.

🍷🍷🍷🍷🍷 **Parish Riesling 2022, Clare Valley** Grapefruit, lime and bath-salt flavours burst convincingly through the palate before gradually easing out through the finish. There's a gently herbal, tonic-like note, too. Once again we're in terrific territory here. Diam. 11.8% alc. **RATING** 95 **DRINK** 2024–2035 $50 CM ✪
Watervale Riesling 2022, Clare Valley This is a pure, textural riesling that's both true to its origins and variety but also has its own distinctive characters.

Lemon and lime notes come crisp and clear before earth, stone and hay-like notes sweep in. It has both interest and pure pleasure covered. Diam. 12% alc. **RATING** 95 **DRINK** 2023–2035 $38 CM ✪

Gullyview Riesling 2022, Clare Valley This is a dry, pebbly style with citrus juice and floral characters building as the wine breathes. It has cut, thrust and body, but it's the savoury, stony, 'of the earth' aspect that really beguiles. A grippyness to the texture is the icing on the cake. Diam. 12.3% alc. **RATING** 95 **DRINK** 2023–2035 $50 CM ✪

Rolle Vermentino 2022, Clare Valley Citrus and grapefruit pulp flavours meet tonic water and brine. It's textural, flavoursome and charismatic, but mostly it's just a beautiful wine to drink. A gentle grip on the finish works well, too. Diam. 10.8% alc. **RATING** 94 **DRINK** 2023–2026 $45 CM

Gullyview Vineyard Cannonau Grenache 2021, Clare Valley It's not big wine in any sense but there are myriad elements in play and the general effect is transfixing. Bacon, cherries, woodsy spices, decaying roses and a red licorice note. Tannin attempts to be earthen and dry but the juicy, mouth-watering fruit just rushes on through. Lovely. Diam. 13% alc. **RATING** 94 **DRINK** 2023–2030 $45 CM

The Clare 2021, Clare Valley A blend of cabernet sauvignon, cabernet franc, grenache, malbec, carignan and sciacarello. Blackcurrant, choc-mint flavours are the main drivers, but there's attitude here, too, most of it via complex herb and tobacco-like notes, though the wine's 'natural' free-flowing feel is also a key aspect. It's very good. Diam. 13.1% alc. **RATING** 94 **DRINK** 2023–2032 $35 CM ✪

🍷🍷🍷🍷🍷 **La Korse 2022, Clare Valley RATING** 93 **DRINK** 2023–2027 $38 CM
Classico 2021, Clare Valley RATING 93 **DRINK** 2023–2029 $50 CM
Vivian Vineyard Nielluccio Sangiovese 2021, Clare Valley RATING 92 **DRINK** 2022–2026 $45 CM
Pigato Vermentino 2022, Clare Valley RATING 91 **DRINK** 2022–2025 $38 CM
Mammolo 2022, Clare Valley RATING 91 **DRINK** 2024–2028 $45 CM

Koomilya ★★★★★

60 Olivers Rd, McLaren Vale, SA 5171 **Region** McLaren Vale
T (08) 8323 8000 **www**.pannell.com.au **Open** 7 days 11–4 **Winemaker** Stephen Pannell **Viticulturist** Stephen Pannell **Est.** 2015 **Dozens** 2000 **Vyds** 13ha
The Koomilya vineyard is wedged between the original Upper Tintara vineyard planted in 1862, and the Hope Farm or Seaview vineyard established in the early 1850s. More than 15ha of native bush and scrub, with a creek line that flows through the heart of the property, all have a moderating influence on the microclimate of the property. In '12, Stephen Pannell and his wife Fiona embarked on rejuvenating it with organic farming, weeding the native bush and removing olive trees to create biochar to return as charcoal to the soil. Plantings of new varieties have followed, with a small set of wines created to specifically reflect the location, accent and circumstances of the seasons throughout each particular vintage.

🍷🍷🍷🍷🍷 **JC Block Shiraz 2019, McLaren Vale** The tannins, a ferruginous torque and resolutely of place. A good place, with 47yo vines on grey, slaty siltstone. The sense of native scrub is strong. Briny olive pip. Biltong. Kirsch. The tannins scrape the mouth, like grazed knees as a kid, and a smile still beaming. A brilliant wine. Screw cap. 14% alc. **RATING** 97 **DRINK** 2024–2034 $120 NG ♥

🍷🍷🍷🍷🍷 **GT Block Shiraz 2019, McLaren Vale** I can't stop mumbling about the wine's freshness and savour. Blue pastille, redcurrant, clove, lilac and dried salumi blend with a sachet of Indian spice that splits further with each sip. Clove, tamarind and sandalwood, too. The lightest of feel, yet framed by a jittery nerve of filigreed tannins and perky freshness. Delicious already, but you'd be a fool not to give this time. Screw cap. 13.5% alc. **RATING** 96 **DRINK** 2025–2035 $120 NG

DC Block Shiraz 2019, McLaren Vale The most reductive among the Koomilya shiraz trinity. Think mottled raspberry, cocoa, Bing and morello cherries, pomelo and moist leather, all slung over terracotta tiles to dry out. The carapace of tannin is scaly and detailed, yet far from the ferrous girth of the JC, or the nerve and detail of the GT. While this will age well, it is surely the cuvée to breach first. Screw cap. 14% alc. **RATING** 95 **DRINK** 2022-2032 $120 NG

Koonowla Wines   ★★★☆

18 Koonowla Road, Auburn, SA 5451 (postal) **Region** Clare Valley
T (08) 8849 2270 **www.koonowla.com Open** Not **Winemaker** Con Moshos
Viticulturist Damien Harris **Est.** 1997 **Dozens** 5000 **Vyds** 90ha
Koonowla is an historic Clare Valley property situated just east of Auburn. It was first planted with vines in the 1890s. A disastrous fire in 1926 destroyed the winery and wine stocks, and the property converted to grain and wool production. Replanting of vines began in '85 and accelerated in the early '90s. Purchased by the George family in September '19 – led by Nick George and his son Alex – wines are now made at Tapanappa by Con Moshos.

ㆍ**Reverence Pinot Gris 2022, Clare Valley** This has hallmark slickness and vitality in texture, with greasy apple, nashi pear and cashew savouriness, a lift of pleasing white vinegary tang and a dash of sweet, exotic spice. Feels a little loose-knit and edgy in the best sense; a cool, wild streak but retains drinkability. Count me in. Screw cap. 13.5% alc. **RATING** 91 **DRINK** 2022-2024 $28 MB ✪

Kooyong   ★★★★★

263 Red Hill Road, Red Hill **Region** Mornington Peninsula
T (03) 5989 4444 **www.kooyongwines.com.au Open** 7 days 11–5 **Winemaker** Tim Perrin **Viticulturist** Stuart Marshall **Est.** 1996 **Dozens** 13000 **Vyds** 40ha
Kooyong, owned by Giorgio and Dianne Gjergja, released its first wines in '01. The vineyard is primarily planted to pinot noir and chardonnay, with a little (3ha) pinot gris and (0.97ha) shiraz added more recently. The Single Block wines sit at the top of the portfolio and the best of the remaining parcels go into the Estate range. The Massale Pinot Noir and Clonale Chardonnay are multi-vineyard blends.

ㆍ**Faultline Single Block Chardonnay 2021, Mornington Peninsula** There's finesse across the tight palate with fresh lemon and grapefruit and some flinty sulphides. Plus the perfect amount of nutty lees. Moreish, savoury, complex and delicious. Screw cap. 13.5% alc. **RATING** 96 **DRINK** 2022-2031 $60 JF ✪
Ferrous Single Block Pinot Noir 2021, Mornington Peninsula There's a bit more depth and weight to Ferrous this year, making it particularly appealing now even with the perky, crunchy acidity making a mark. Plenty of fleshy tannins, woody spices, chinotto, ironstone, red cherries and pips along for the ride. Screw cap. 13% alc. **RATING** 95 **DRINK** 2022-2033 $75 JF
Estate Chardonnay 2021, Mornington Peninsula With thoughtful winemaking, it's more than a safe bet – it's an excellent option. Stone fruit and peach fuzz, lemon and creamy lees, yet a taut palate from the fine acidity. Everything in place and this is delicious now. Screw cap. 13.5% alc. **RATING** 95 **DRINK** 2022-2030 $44 JF ✪
Farrago Single Block Chardonnay 2021, Mornington Peninsula No shortage of flavour yet tightly composed to show off a more linear thread. Layers of citrus and grapefruit pith, white peach and vanilla pod plus cedary spices from oak. Vanilla custard and nutty lees add texture. Screw cap. 13.5% alc. **RATING** 95 **DRINK** 2022-2030 $60 JF

ㆍ**Massale Pinot Noir 2022, Mornington Peninsula RATING** 93 **DRINK** 2023-2028 $36 JF
Haven Single Block Pinot Noir 2021, Mornington Peninsula RATING 93 **DRINK** 2024-2033 $75 JF
Clonale Chardonnay 2022, Mornington Peninsula RATING 92 **DRINK** 2022-2027 $34 JF

Meres Single Block Pinot Noir 2021, Mornington Peninsula RATING 92
DRINK 2023–2031 $75 JF
Beurrot Pinot Gris 2022, Mornington Peninsula RATING 90
DRINK 2022–2026 $32 JF
Estate Shiraz 2021, Mornington Peninsula RATING 90 DRINK 2023–2030
$44 JF
Estate Pinot Noir 2021, Mornington Peninsula RATING 90
DRINK 2024–2031 $54 JF

Kosciuszko Wines ★★★☆

Capital Wines, 13 Gladstone Street, Hall, ACT 2618 **Region** Tumbarumba
T 0417 036 436 **www.**kosciuszkowines.com.au **Open** Thurs–Sun 10.30–4
Winemaker Robert Bruno, Alex McKay, Greg Gallagher **Viticulturist** Juliet Cullen
Est. 2005 **Dozens** 1500
Kosciuszko Wines is the venture of the energetic Bill and Maria Mason. Bill has been
distributing wine in Canberra since '04, with a small but distinguished list of wineries, which
he represents with considerable marketing flair. In '18 Bill purchased Kosciuszko Wines from
founding winemaker Chris Thomas after working with Chris and Kosciuszko Wines
for a number of years. Bill sources his fruit from pioneering grapegrower Julie Cullen's
Tumbarumba vineyard.

🍷🍷🍷🍷 **Sangiovese Rosé 2022, Tumbarumba** Sangiovese's acidity and gorgeous
flavours make it ideal for rosé. Expect rosehip, watermelon, musk and redberries
to make their flavour presence known. There's some light texture as the acidity
comes to the fore and freshens up the palate in anticipation of the next sip.
Screw cap. 12.5% alc. RATING 91 DRINK 2022–2024 $27 JF ✪

Krinklewood Biodynamic Vineyard ★★★★☆

712 Wollombi Road, Broke, NSW 2330 **Region** Hunter Valley
T (02) 6579 1322 **www.**krinklewood.com **Open** Fri–Sun 10–5 **Winemaker** Valentina
Moresco **Viticulturist** Chris Martin **Est.** 1981 **Dozens** 7500 **Vyds** 14.5ha
Krinklewood is a certified biodynamic organic winery. Every aspect of the property is
managed in a holistic and sustainable way; extensive herb crops, native grasses and farm
animals all help to maintain healthy soil biology. In '20, young entrepreneur Oscar Martin
bought Krinklewood from winemaker Rod Windrim.

🍷🍷🍷🍷 **Semillon 2022, Hunter Valley** Crushed free-run juice retained; impeccably
handled with cool fermentation in tank and clearly with attention to detail.
Layered lime/lemon flavours which aren't threatened by acidity, rather sustained
by it. 'Having your cake and eating it' stuff. Screw cap. 11.5% alc. RATING 95
DRINK 2023–2033 $35 JH ✪
Wild Shiraz 2021, McLaren Vale 'Australia' is as far as it goes in the regional
claim on the label, although McLaren Vale is its origin; and the variety, place and
vintage all come together in a rich palate. By some distance the best Krinklewood
shiraz in this tasting. Screw cap. 14% alc. RATING 94 DRINK 2023–2039 $32 JH ✪

🍷🍷🍷🍷 **Basket Press Shiraz 2021, Hunter Valley** RATING 91 DRINK 2028–2031
$75 JH
Limited Release Terre Rouge 2021, McLaren Vale RATING 90
DRINK 2025–2028 $120 JH

Krondorf ★★★★

32–34 Murray Street, Tanunda, SA 5352 (postal) **Region** Barossa
T (08) 8561 2298 **www.**krondorfwines.com.au **Open** Not **Winemaker** Nick Badrice
Viticulturist Nick Badrice **Est.** 1978 **Dozens** 30 000 **Vyds** 30ha
The small hamlet of Krondorf, German for 'Crown Village,' was established by a handful of
Silesian families in 1847 and has become a name intrinsically linked with the Australian wine

industry. The brand itself came into being during the 1960s and '70s and a group of young winemakers, led initially by Grant Burge, carved a reputation for the wine culminating in taking out the Jimmy Watson Trophy in '80. The label has been through its ups and downs but has been recently revitalised with winemaker Nick Badrice in charge, producing wines that speak strongly of both the region and the brand's historical bloodline.

Single Site Moculta Shiraz 2020, Eden Valley Wines from this little pocket of Moculta, in the northern Eden Valley, are a stepping stone between the thundering depth of valley floor fruit and the finer lines of higher altitudes. Deeply coloured with ripe blackberry and black cherry fruits with hints of baking spices, licorice, sage, violets and earth; a bit tighter in acidity, tannins a little more granitic, finishing long and elegant. Screw cap. 14.5% alc. **RATING** 94 **DRINK** 2023–2033 $40 DB ✪

Stone Altar Old Vine Grenache 2021, Barossa **RATING** 93 **DRINK** 2023–2030 $65 DB
Single Site GSM Grenache Shiraz Mourvèdre 2021, Barossa Valley **RATING** 93 **DRINK** 2023–2029 $40 DB
Founder's View Grenache 2021, Barossa Valley **RATING** 92 **DRINK** 2023–2028 $24 DB ✪
Old Salem Shiraz 2020, Barossa Valley **RATING** 92 **DRINK** 2023–2030 $35 DB

Krystallo Estate

3630 Midland Highway, Lima South, Vic 3673 (postal) **Region** Upper Goulburn
T (03) 5768 2685 **www**.krystalloestate.com.au **Open** Not **Winemaker** Rob Dolan
Est. 1988 **Dozens** 1200 **Vyds** 8ha
Krystallo Estate is a family-run winery in Lima South, a cool, elevated region between Mansfield and Benalla. In '09, Jim and Maria Kakridas purchased Nillahcootie Estate, planted to traditional cabernet, shiraz, merlot and semillon. They later expanded the estate by purchasing the vineyard next door, planted to Mediterranean varieties. Wines sourced from the former are bottled under the Nillahcootie label; the latter under the Belitso label, named after family patriarch, Giorgios Belitso Kakridas. Greek varieties are planned too, as is a cellar door.

Belitso Malvasia 2021, Upper Goulburn This malvasia makes no bones of its fullness in flavour, its touches of nuttiness and gentle aromatics. Honeysuckle, lantana, yellow peach skin and quince paste aromas are generous. They are joined by a complex nutty character to taste, which is greatly enhanced by a warm textural smoothness. The food-matching possibilities are many. Screw cap. 13.2% alc. **RATING** 91 **DRINK** 2022–2026 $23 JP ✪

Kurtz Family Vineyards

731 Light Pass Road, Angaston, SA, 5353 **Region** Barossa Valley
T 0418 810 982 **www**.kurtzfamilyvineyards.com.au **Open** By appt **Winemaker** Steve Kurtz **Viticulturist** Steve Kurtz **Est.** 1996 **Dozens** 3000 **Vyds** 18.1ha
The Kurtz family vineyard is at Light Pass. It has 9ha of shiraz, the remainder planted to cabernet sauvignon, grenache, mataro, malbec and petit verdot. Steve Kurtz has followed in the footsteps of his great-grandfather Ben Kurtz, who first grew grapes at Light Pass in the '30s. During a career working first at Saltram and then at Foster's until '06, Steve gained invaluable experience from Nigel Dolan, Caroline Dunn and John Glaetzer, among others.

Lunar Block Individual Vineyard Shiraz 2019, Barossa Valley Deep-set blackberry, satsuma plum and boysenberry with hints of baking spices, earth, spearmint and black licorice with oak-derived coconut, vanilla and tobacco leaf. Opulent and rich, with spicy, pure black fruits, plenty of oak and a licorice-accented tail with firm, compact tannins and a persistent finish. A robust style. Screw cap. 14.5% alc. **RATING** 92 **DRINK** 2023–2030 $75 DB
Uncle Tony's Mataro 2019, Barossa Valley Deep crimson in the glass with notes of blackberry fruits and black cherry cut through with deep spices, vanillin,

cedar, earth, roasting meats and licorice. The oak turns up a bit on the palate, which is rich and opulent with tight, compact tannin and an earthy, savoury swell of black fruit on the finish. Screw cap. 14.5% alc. **RATING** 92 **DRINK** 2023–2028 $35 DB

Schmick Shiraz 2018, Barossa Valley Deep crimson in the glass with opulent aromas of crème de cassis, plum jam and black cherry along with hints of baking spices, dark chocolate, espresso, cedar and vanillin oak. Full bodied and fruit pure with bright acidity, gravelly tannin heft and a pleasing, persistent finish. One for lovers of muscular Barossan styles. Screw cap. 15% alc. **RATING** 92 **DRINK** 2023–2033 $100 DB

Charlies Grenache 2020, Barossa Valley Crimson in the glass with aromas of satsuma plum, dark cherry and berry fruits. Hints of spice, warm earth, licorice, fig and tea leaves. A traditional loose-knit Barossa style with compact, sandy tannins, bright acidity and a spicy trail of plum and violets on the finish. Screw cap. 14.5% alc. **RATING** 90 **DRINK** 2023–2028 $35 DB

Seven Sleepers Shiraz 2020, Barossa Valley Pretty sharp value here at sub-$20 a bottle. Deep crimson in the glass with loads of ripe plum and blackberry fruits cut with baking spices, dark chocolate, licorice and earth. A pleasing flow of ripe fruit, a dusty tannin architecture and a savoury finish that is flush with fruit and spice. Screw cap. 14.5% alc. **RATING** 90 **DRINK** 2023–2027 $18 DB ✪

Kyneton Ridge ★★★★

517 Blackhill Road, Kyneton, Vic 3444 **Region** Macedon Ranges
T 0408 841 119 **www**.kynetonridge.com.au **Open** Fri–Sun & public hols 11–5
Winemaker Patrick Wood **Viticulturist** Tom Handyside **Est.** 1997 **Dozens** 1200
Vyds 4ha

Kyneton Ridge is the dedicated project of Andrew and Angela Wood, who bought the property in '19. This is their first foray into wine, although their winemaker son, Patrick, is very much hands on. Originally established by John Boucher and partner Pauline Russell in '97, the Woods have subsequently added nebbiolo, riesling, more chardonnay plus cabernet sauvignon, covering about 4.5ha, while still sourcing shiraz from Heathcote. Time, energy and money were spent on renovating the winery and cellar door, with a cafe and arts space opening in '21. The winery has been at full production since the '22 vintage.

ŸŸŸŸŸ **Sparkling Shiraz NV, Heathcote** Ah, sparkling shiraz. As Aussie as, well, sparkling shiraz. You'd be happy with a glass of this on any day, not just Christmas Day, folks. It's fresh and lively with a core of dark plums spiced up with cinnamon and a hint of pepper. It finishes dry and refreshingly so. Diam. 14.5% alc. **RATING** 93 $35 JF ✪

Reserve Pinot Noir 2021, Macedon Ranges You can get stuck on the lovely aromatics for ages before tasting the wine. Full of roses, strawberry compote, warm earth, sumac, cherries and pips. The palate is reined in by plenty of acidity and it remains in the driver's seat with fine tannins in tow. Not a big wine and it appeals for its restraint and perfume. Screw cap. 12.2% alc. **RATING** 93 **DRINK** 2022–2030 $40 JF

Sparkling Reserve Pinot Noir Chardonnay 2015, Macedon Ranges Aromas and flavours range from bruised apple, nougat and buttered toast to preserved lemons and dried pears. The light intro of aldehydes adds another layer of complexity, as do the tannins. Plenty of acidity driving this and refreshing the palate, which is nice and dry. A low-ish dosage. Diam. 12% alc. **RATING** 92 **DRINK** 2022–2025 $40 JF

Cabernet Shiraz 2021, Macedon Ranges A lighter style, yet it's not lacking flavour or fruit weight. The colour is super-bright and enticing, and the leafy freshness of the cabernet, more of a raspberry leaf character, is very appealing. There's also licorice root, cassis and red plums. Fleshy and tangy across the palate, sweet-ish fruit and the tannins have meshed well. It's a real surprise and delight. Screw cap. 13.5% alc. **RATING** 92 **DRINK** 2022–2027 $28 JF ✪

Shiraz 2021, Heathcote Inky purple hue with fruit to match, as in black plums and ripe blueberries. Fuller bodied, the texture is supple and smooth with ripe tannins, some coconut rough chocolate, menthol and woodsy spices in the mix. It's rich and delicious and best enjoyed in its youth. It just feels right to drink now. Screw cap. 14.5% alc. **RATING** 92 **DRINK** 2022-2027 $30 JF

Skipping Rabbit Pinot Noir 2022, Macedon Ranges Bursting with youthful flavours, all juicy fruit with a vibrancy across the palate. Sweet cherries, raspberries, some red lollies and woodsy spices with tangy acidity in tow. Tannins have some grip, but the palate is rather fine and lighter framed. Lovely and easy to like. Screw cap. 13.5% alc. **RATING** 90 **DRINK** 2023-2029 $30 JF

Chardonnay 2022, Bendigo At first a little estery and shy, this opened up nicely in the glass. Spiced stone fruit, grilled pineapple, lemon balm and mandarin followed by a light spread of creamy lees. Acidity tightens the finish. Screw cap. 12% alc. **RATING** 90 **DRINK** 2023-2026 $32 JF

L.A.S. Vino ★★★★★

PO Box 361 Cowaramup, WA 6284 **Region** Margaret River
T www.lasvino.com **Open** Not **Winemaker** Nic Peterkin **Est.** 2013 **Dozens** 800
Owner Nic Peterkin is the grandson of the late Diana and Kevin Cullen (Cullen Wines) and the son of Mike Peterkin (Pierro). After graduating from the University of Adelaide with a master's degree in oenology and travelling the world as a Flying Winemaker, he came back to roost in Margaret River with the ambition of making wines that are a little bit different, but also within the bounds of conventional oenological science. He intends to keep the project small.

ΨΨΨΨΨ **Wildberry Springs Chardonnay 2021, Margaret River** There is just something special about this wine. It has all the power and thrust of Wilyabrup fruit, yet remains tight and linear. The wine is fermented in quartz amphora and aged 10 months, which partly explains the pure chardonnay character shining through. It has depth and refinement with a seemingly everlasting finish. Superb drink. Diam. 13.5% alc. **RATING** 96 **DRINK** 2022-2033 $80 JF

CBDB Chenin Blanc Dynamic Blend 2021, Margaret River Fragrant with white blossom and ginger flower. Quite high-toned in a way, with apple pie, creamed honey, quince paste and lively lemon-lime juice and zest. It's racy thanks to the refreshing, brisk acidity, yet with plenty of slippery texture. It's a gorgeous wine. And seriously, how can you not love a wine called CBDB (chenin blanc dynamic blend)? Diam. 13.5% alc. **RATING** 96 **DRINK** 2022-2032 $60 JF ✪

Albino PNO Rosé 2021, Margaret River Searching for a rosé with texture, flavour and an X-factor? Look no more. Pale copper hue with a savoury twang alongside a whisper of red fruits, baked apple and lemon zest. Tangy and juicy, with plenty of spicy character, but it's the palate that sings. Lively, refreshingly pure and long. Diam. 12.5% alc. **RATING** 95 **DRINK** 2022-2025 $55 JF

Barrels of Metricup Chardonnay 2021, Margaret River Packed with flavour from white peach, citrus and lemon balm to ginger flower, yet it's definitely a savoury drink. Fuller bodied with creamy lees and plenty of mouth-watering acidity. It's buoyant and lively with good tension and great definition. Diam. 13.5% alc. **RATING** 95 **DRINK** 2022-2030 $70 JF

Granite Grenache 2021, Geographe This is heady with wild strawberries, pomegranate and raspberry jubes with a sprinkle of woodsy spices and a hint of fresh herbs. It's vibrant with supple, sweet tannins across the mid-weighted palate and a bright acidity that makes this refreshing and pleasing in equal measure. Diam. 13.5% alc. **RATING** 94 **DRINK** 2022-2028 $60 JF

La Cantina King Valley ★★★☆

54 Honey's Lane, King Valley, Vic 3678 **Region** King Valley
T (03) 5729 3615 **www.**lacantinakingvalley.com.au **Open** 7 days 10–5 (10–6 during daylight savings) **Winemaker** Peter Corsini **Viticulturist** Peter Corsini **Est.** 1996
Dozens 6000 **Vyds** 25ha

Gino and Peter Corsini have 25ha of pinot grigio, chardonnay, dolcetto, sangiovese, nebbiolo, tempranillo, shiraz and, more recently, saperavi. They sell half and retain the rest to produce their estate wines. The wines are made without the use of sulphur dioxide.

🍷🍷🍷🍷🍷 **Saperavi 2021, King Valley** Inky and deepest purple in colour, this saperavi is one big, bold ball of dense colour, aroma and flavour. Dutch licorice, black cherry, prune, earth and clove mix dark brooding intensity with savoury tannin nuance in this rich, hedonistic wine. Fantastic barbecue accompaniment. Screw cap. 14.8% alc. **RATING** 90 **DRINK** 2023–2028 $28 JP

La Kooki Wines
★★★★☆

12 Settlers Retreat, Margaret River, WA 6285 (postal) **Region** Margaret River
T 0447 587 15 **www**.lakookiwines.com.au **Open** Not **Winemaker** Eloise Jarvis, Glenn Goodall **Est.** 2017 **Dozens** 335
Eloise Jarvis and Glen Goodall have 50 years of winemaking experience between them. They met studying eonology in South Australia in the '90s and after vintages abroad they settled in WA, Eloise initially working for Cape Mentelle and Glenn for Xanadu, where he remains today as head winemaker. They wanted to create something different, together, drawing on their relationships with local growers to produce drinkable wines that are 'a little bit kooki'.

🍷🍷🍷🍷🍷 **Rosé Blonde 2022, Margaret River** Fragrant with raspberries and wild strawberries with a dusting of spice. The palate is lively and while a fine thread of acidity teases out the fruit profile, it is savoury. Tangy, juicy, slightly creamy and deliciously dry. Screw cap. 13% alc. **RATING** 95 **DRINK** 2022–2024 $28 JF

🍷🍷🍷🍷🍷 **Las Piedras Tempranillo 2021, Geographe RATING** 90 **DRINK** 2023–2030 $40 JF

La Linea
★★★★☆

36 Shipsters Road, Kensington Park, SA 5068 (postal) **Region** Adelaide Hills
T (08) 8431 3556 **www**.lalinea.com.au **Open** Not **Winemaker** Peter Leske
Viticulturist Peter Leske **Est.** 2007 **Dozens** 3000 **Vyds** 8ha
La Linea is a partnership between experienced wine industry professionals Peter Leske (ex-Nepenthe), Alanna Pepper and David LeMire MW. Peter was among the first to recognise the potential of tempranillo in Australia and his knowledge of it is reflected in the 3 wine styles made from the variety: a dry rosé, a dry red blended from several Adelaide Hills vineyards, and Sureño, made in select vintages from specific sites at the southern end of the Hills. The team pioneered mencia – the red variety from northwest Spain – in the Hills. They also produce off-dry riesling from an elevated single-site vineyard in Lenswood.

🍷🍷🍷🍷🍷 **Vertigo 25GR Riesling 2022, Adelaide Hills** A fine-boned, off-dry expression. Citrus verbena, lime blossom and sherbet accents strewn with fennel seed and curry leaf. Highly strung, with riesling's whirl of acidity sweeping the sugar into a place of palpable dryness. Penetrative and tenacious. As balletic and precise as it is intense and palate staining. Very good drinking. Screw cap. 10.5% alc. **RATING** 93 **DRINK** 2022–2035 $24 NG
Sureño Tempranillo 2021, Adelaide Hills A bony, nicely astringent framework houses darker fruit allusions, a smear of anise and black olive and a trail of dried thyme, lavender and sage. The finish is persistent, if not drying, at this embryonic stage. A lovely wine, likely better in a few years. Screw cap. 13.5% alc. **RATING** 93 **DRINK** 2022–2029 $35 NG
Mencia 2021, Adelaide Hills Like a cool-climate syrah without quite the same degree of acidity and a leafier, more gently astringent tannin profile. Iodine, graphite, lilac, peat and blueberry. Mid-weighted, fresh enough and very digestible. Screw cap. 13% alc. **RATING** 92 **DRINK** 2022–2025 $30 NG
Tempranillo 2021, Adelaide Hills Sappy, pithy, vibrant, mid-weighted and beautifully poised. A lattice of supple astringency, well-nestled vanillin oak and vibrant freshness supporting lilac florals, sweet cherry, raspberry bonbon and a

sachet of dried sage and garden herb. Very good drinking. Screw cap. 13.5% alc.
RATING 92 DRINK 2022-2027 $27 NG ✪

Tempranillo Rosé 2022, Adelaide Hills There is no holding back when
it comes to flavour here, with orange verbena, cumquat, ruby grapefruit and
muddled cherry. A raft of almost sandy salinity and pucker grabbing the finish,
promoting the flavours while placating any sense of excess. I like this. Screw cap.
12.5% alc. RATING 91 DRINK 2022-2024 $24 NG ✪

La Pleiade

M. Chapoutier Australia, 141-143 High Street, Heathcote Vic 3523 **Region** Heathcote
T (03) 9602 1570 **www.mchapoutier.com.au Open** Mon–Wed, Fri 10–2 Sat–Sun 10–5
Winemaker Ron Laughton, Michel Chapoutier **Viticulturist** Emily Laughton **Est.** 1998
Dozens 500 **Vyds** 8ha

A joint venture of Michel and Corinne Chapoutier and Ron and Elva Laughton. In spring
'98 a vineyard of Australian and imported French shiraz clones was planted. The vineyard is
run biodynamically and the winemaking is deliberately designed to place maximum emphasis
on the fruit quality. La Pleiade is available for tasting at M. Chapoutier in Heathcote.

🍷🍷🍷🍷 **Shiraz 2019, Heathcote** This is a big, warm, relatively simple wine with
blackberry and dark chocolate characters. Yes, there are floral notes, but it's the
might and power that defines it. Firm-ish tannin keeps it all in check. Charm and
high alcohol don't usually go hand-in-hand, but this somehow manages it. Cork.
15.5% alc. RATING 93 DRINK 2023-2032 $68 CM

La Prova

102 Main Street, Hahndorf, SA 5245 **Region** Adelaide Hills
T (08) 8388 7330 **www.laprova.com.au Open** 1st w'end of the month 11–5 or by appt
Winemaker Sam Scott **Est.** 2009 **Dozens** 5000

Sam Scott's great-grandfather worked for Max Schubert and passed his knowledge down
to Sam's grandfather. Sam enrolled in business at university, continuing the casual retailing
with Booze Brothers – which he'd started while at school – picking up the trail with Baily
& Baily. Next came wine wholesale experience with David Ridge, selling iconic Australian
and Italian wines to the trade. This led to a job with Michael Fragos at Tatachilla in '00 and
since then he has worked across Australia and in California.

🍷🍷🍷🍷 **Uno Fiano 2021, Adelaide Hills** Made from the first fiano vines planted in the
Adelaide Hills. A lovely wine that swings along with the idea that fiano produces
texture and structure of its own. Could it be a mature chenin blanc, a viognier, a
mature marsanne? All or any, but does it matter? Screw cap. 13.3% alc. RATING 96
DRINK 2023-2028 $35 JH ✪

Fiano 2022, Adelaide Hills Mid-weighted, gently unctuous and expansive.
Riffs on pistachio, marzipan, wild fennel and glazed quince unravel along a
rail of phenolics and saline freshness. Fine length, density and Mediterranean
marrow. Something to chew on, as much as something dangerously easy to drink.
Screw cap. 13.3% alc. RATING 95 DRINK 2022-2027 $28 NG ✪

Pinot Grigio 2022, Adelaide Hills A little slow out of the blocks, but
has cascades of lime, pear and Granny Smith apple on the palate, girdled by
crunchy acidity on the lingering finish. Screw cap. 12.5% alc. RATING 95
DRINK 2023-2026 $27 JH ✪

Aglianico Rosato 2022, Adelaide Hills A mid-coral hue, segueing to an
orb of thyme, mint and small red berries, textural and energetic, as if they are
popping through the mouth with each sip. A refined rosé of sap, succulence and
compelling intensity, as the fruit unwinds into a ferrous sphere and a long linger.
Screw cap. 13% alc. RATING 95 DRINK 2022-2024 $27 NG ✪

Sangiovese 2021, Adelaide Hills Wild-yeast fermented with over a month
on skins to extract the tannins, doing so with skilled restraint. Sure, the wine
has a savoury carapace, but there's its overall impact of cherries of every kind to
provide balance. Screw cap. 14% alc. RATING 95 DRINK 2023-2030 $28 JH ✪

ΨΨΨΨΨ Nebbiolo Rosato 2022, Adelaide Hills RATING 93 DRINK 2023–2023
$28 JH ✪
Pinot Grigio 2022, Adelaide Hills RATING 93 DRINK 2022–2024 $27 NG ✪
Uno Barbera 2021, Adelaide Hills RATING 92 DRINK 2022–2026 $35 NG
Prosecco 2022, King Valley RATING 91 DRINK 2022–2024 $27 NG ✪

Lake Breeze Wines ★★★★★

Step Road, Langhorne Creek, SA 5255 **Region** Langhorne Creek
T (08) 8537 3017 **www.**lakebreeze.com.au **Open** 7 days 10–5 **Winemaker** Greg Follett
Viticulturist Tim Follett **Est.** 1987 **Dozens** 25 000 **Vyds** 95ha
The Folletts have been farmers at Langhorne Creek since 1880, and grapegrowers since
the 1930s. Part of the grape production is sold, but the quality of the Lake Breeze wines is
exemplary, with the red wines particularly appealing.

ΨΨΨΨΨ **Arthur's Reserve Cabernet Sauvignon Malbec Petit Verdot 2020,
Langhorne Creek** A high-quality wine that is supple yet complex, with
blackcurrant fruit riding on the back of ripe tannins and integrated oak. The
blend is made 20 months post-vintage and spends a further 15 months in
barrel thereafter. Lake Breeze's flagship wine. Screw cap. 14% alc. **RATING** 98
DRINK 2023–2043 $48 JH ✪ ♥
The Drake Cabernet Sauvignon Shiraz 2018, Langhorne Creek Still
exceptionally youthful crimson-purple hue. This is a blend of the best 2 barrels
of vintage, its components matured in French barriques (90% new) for 20 months.
The oak is high quality, but the wine needs more time in bottle to integrate. That
integration is simply a matter of time, because the fruit and tannins are already
balanced. Screw cap. 14.2% alc. **RATING** 97 **DRINK** 2028–2043 $80 JH ✪

ΨΨΨΨΨ **Vermentino 2022, Langhorne Creek** This is a super-delicious wine. There's
a Catherine wheel of tropical fruits, guava and passionfruit persistent, then a blaze
of Meyer lemon on the finish and aftertaste. Screw cap. 12% alc. **RATING** 95
DRINK 2023–2030 $20 JH ✪
Winemaker's Selection Shiraz 2021, Langhorne Creek Only made in the
best vintages. Again and again, the quality of the '21 vintage comes through,
hot and strong, here on the rich and juicy plum and blackberry-fruited palate.
Screw cap. 14.5% alc. **RATING** 95 **DRINK** 2026–2036 $48 JH ✪
Section 54 Shiraz 2021, Langhorne Creek Fruit from a mix of 50yo vines.
The '21 vintage has imparted an extra depth to the palate with its plum and
cherry fruit engendering an uncommon elegance and opulence. A lot of wine
for the price. Screw cap. 14.5% alc. **RATING** 95 **DRINK** 2023–2038 $26 JH ✪
Cabernet Sauvignon 2021, Langhorne Creek 6/3% malbec/petit verdot,
blended with the cabernet at 15 months, bottled unfined after 20 months in
French barriques (65/35% second fill/new). Extraordinary price for so much
work and oak. That oak is somewhat obvious, simply needing a year or 2 to pull
in behind the cassis/blackcurrant fruit. Already a high-quality wine with more in
store. Screw cap. 14% alc. **RATING** 95 **DRINK** 2025–2040 $28 JH ✪
Nero d'Avola 2022, Langhorne Creek Whole-berry fermentation, matured
in used French barriques for 7 months. Attractive juicy red berry fruits, fine
tannins provide texture. Delicious wine, but drink soonish. Screw cap. 13.8% alc.
RATING 94 **DRINK** 2023–2025 $24 JH ✪
Bernoota Shiraz Cabernet 2021, Langhorne Creek A lot of effort
went into making this $22 wine. Open-fermented for 8-10 days, finished in
American oak; matured 20 months in a wide variety of American and French
barriques. The wine is a flood of dark fruit. Screw cap. 14.5% alc. **RATING** 94
DRINK 2023–2031 $22 JH ✪
Reserve Chardonnay 2021, Langhorne Creek Machine-harvested, 45% mlf;
barrel fermented and matured in French oak (30% new). Well made, and deserved
its Trophy Best White, Rosé or Sparkling Langhorne Creek Wine Show '22. It
is a mix of grapefruit and green apple; oak integrated and balanced. Screw cap.
14% alc. **RATING** 94 **DRINK** 2024–2027 $26 JH ✪

ŶŶŶŶ♀ **Old Vine Grenache 2022, Langhorne Creek** RATING 93 DRINK 2023–2030 $30 JH ✪
Malbec 2021, Langhorne Creek RATING 93 DRINK 2025–2030 $30 JH ✪
Rosato 2022, Langhorne Creek RATING 91 DRINK 2023–2024 $20 JH ✪
Bull Ant Cabernet Merlot 2021, Langhorne Creek RATING 91 DRINK 2023–2027 $19 JH ✪
Bull Ant Shiraz 2021, Langhorne Creek RATING 90 DRINK 2023–2028 $19 JH ✪

Lake Cooper Estate ★★★★

1608 Midland Highway, Corop, Vic 3559 **Region** Heathcote
T (03) 9387 7657 **www.lakecooper.com.au Open** By appt **Winemaker** Paul Boulden, Richard Taylor **Viticulturist** Rick Milland **Est.** 2014 **Dozens** 71 600 **Vyds** 45ha
Lake Cooper Estate is a substantial venture in the Heathcote region, set on the side of Mount Camel Range with panoramic views of Lake Cooper, Greens Lake and the Corop township. There are plans for the construction of a 300t winery, cellar door, restaurant and accommodation, with a complete overhaul of winemaking practices by the highly experienced Paul Boulden and Richard Taylor.

ŶŶŶŶŶ **Rhapsody Reserve Shiraz 2021, Heathcote** This is a smooth, sweet and generously proportioned red. It's awash with saturated plum, peppercorn, toast and cedar flavours, and it's all delivered with a creamy mouthfeel. It's straightforward, and it's good with just enough tannin to see it mature well into the future. Screw cap. 14.5% alc. RATING 94 DRINK 2024–2036 $60 CM

ŶŶŶŶ♀ **Reserve Cabernet Sauvignon 2021, Heathcote** RATING 93 DRINK 2024–2032 $30 CM ✪
Shiraz 2021, Heathcote RATING 93 DRINK 2024–2032 $30 CM ✪
Marsanne 2019, Nagambie Lakes RATING 91 DRINK 2024–2030 $22 CM ✪

Lake George Winery ★★★★

173 The Vineyards Road, Lake George, NSW 2581 **Region** Canberra District
T 0(2) 4848 0182 **www.lakegeorgewinery.com.au Open** Thurs–Sun 10–4
Winemaker Nick O'Leary, Malcolm Burdett, Carla Rodeghiero **Viticulturist** Thomas Lefebvre **Est.** 1973 **Dozens** 3000 **Vyds** 8ha
Lake George Winery, a dry-grown site on what was once the Westering vineyard, celebrated its 50th vintage in '23. There's a sense of rejuvenation and renewal thanks to the dedication of owner Sarah McDougall. In '18, she and her late husband Anthony took ownership and set about improving the growing practices, eschewing herbicides and embracing sustainability. 'All the magic happens in the vineyard and if you grow really beautiful fruit, then making the wine comes easily,' Sarah says. Better vineyard management has been stepped up thanks to the input of consultant viticulturist Thomas Lefebvre. Anthony died in '22 and Sarah wants to continue his legacy of caring for the land. It bodes well for future generations.

ŶŶŶŶ♀ **Riesling 2022, Canberra District** A glass of this will awaken your senses thanks to its perky acidity. Intense flavours of citrus, green apple and apple skins with a flash of fresh basil. More time to flesh out will be welcome and the wine better as a result. Screw cap. 11.5% alc. RATING 91 DRINK 2023–2032 $29 JF

Landaire at Padthaway Estate ★★★★☆

Riddoch Highway, Padthaway, SA 5271 **Region** Padthaway
T 0417 408 147 **www.landaire.com.au Open** Fri–Sun 11–4 or by appt
Winemaker Contract **Est.** 2012 **Dozens** 2000 **Vyds** 200ha
David and Carolyn Brown have been major grapegrowers in Padthaway for 2 decades, Landaire evolved from a desire, after many years of growing grapes at their Glendon vineyard,

to select small quantities of the best grapes to produce wines under their own label. It has proved a sure-fire recipe for success. The 1850s stables have since been converted into a cellar door, with accommodation available in the original 1901 shearers' quarters and 1947 cottage. In '17 Carolyn and David purchased nearby Padthaway Estate.

🍷🍷🍷🍷🍷 **Chardonnay 2021, Padthaway** Chardonnay and White Wine of the Year. Score awarded by the Halliday tasting panel at the annual Awards judging. CM writes: Wow, this is serious business. Indeed the word glorious immediately springs to mind. Toast, flint, grilled white peach, nougat and lemon curd characters come charging at you, first sip until the last, compellingly, authoritatively. Jumps straight out of the box and once it's out, there's no stopping it. Screw cap. 12.5% alc. RATING 98 DRINK 2023-2030 $37 PD ✪ ♥

Block 22 Shiraz 2018, Padthaway This is a substantial red wine with the structure and length to match. Blackberry and pure plum, cedar wood and mint characters sweep warmly through the palate, asphalt and floral notes coming along for the ride. There's a boozy aspect to this, it sits on the outer edges of ripeness, but the overall balance and the length of the finish make this a successful version of the full-throttle style. Cork. 15% alc. RATING 94 DRINK 2024-2034 $60 CM

🍷🍷🍷🍷🍷 **Cabernet Sauvignon 2021, Padthaway** RATING 93 DRINK 2024-2034 $40 CM

Eliza Blanc de Blancs 2019, Padthaway RATING 91 DRINK 2023-2026 $48 CM

Single Vineyard Shiraz 2021, Padthaway RATING 91 DRINK 2024-2032 $40 CM

Pinot Gris 2022, Padthaway RATING 90 DRINK 2023-2025 $28 CM

Lane's End Vineyard ★★★★

885 Mount William Road, Lancefield, Vic 3435 **Region** Macedon Ranges **T** (03) 5429 1760 **www.**lanesend.com.au **Open** By appt **Winemaker** Howard Matthews **Viticulturist** Nicky Ralph, Howard Matthews **Est.** 1985 **Dozens** 400 **Vyds** 2ha

Howard Matthews and family purchased the former Woodend Winery in '00, with 1.8ha of chardonnay and pinot noir and a small amount of cabernet franc dating back to the mid-'80s. The cabernet franc has been grafted over to pinot noir and the vineyard is now made up of 1ha each of chardonnay and pinot noir (5 clones). Howard has been making the wines for over a decade.

🍷🍷🍷🍷🍷 **Pinot Noir 2020, Macedon Ranges** A distinct eucalyptus fragrance here, verging towards peppermint. Yet, there's also a buffer of flavour from dark fruit, woodsy spices, licorice and charcuterie. Plus, toasty, slinky oak adds tannins, weight and flavour. Medium bodied, supple, vibrant and driven by refreshing acidity. It's better with food. Screw cap. 13% alc. RATING 92 DRINK 2023-2028 $50 JF

L'autre Pinot Noir 2021, Macedon Ranges L'autre's signature is its lightness with pared-back flavours and a certain restraint. An old-wood character infuses the just-ripe red cherries and there's spice, wintergreen and lemony acidity. The tannins are supple and way in the background, so this adds up to a drink-now red. Screw cap. 13% alc. RATING 91 DRINK 2022-2026 $35 JF

Rosé 2022, Macedon Ranges It's juicy and refreshing with watermelon, strawberries and musk lollies. There's a softness across the palate with tangy lemony acidity and while a drier style, there's a lick of sweetness on the finish. Screw cap. 12.9% alc. RATING 90 DRINK 2022-2024 $27 JF

Cottage Chardonnay 2022, Macedon Ranges This is refreshment in a glass. A well-balanced combo of citrus flavours with a hint of creamy lees and florals. There's a succulence, vibrancy and, while uncomplicated, it is convincing. All in all, delicious. Screw cap. 13% alc. RATING 90 DRINK 2022-2026 $30 JF

Lange Estate

663 Frankland-Cranbrook Road, Frankland River, WA 6396 **Region** Frankland River
T 0438 511 828 **www**.langeestate.com.au **Open** By appt **Winemaker** Liam Carmody
and Guy Lyons **Viticulturist** Kim Lange, Lee Haselgrove **Est.** 1997 **Dozens** 7000
Vyds 20ha

The eponymous Lange Estate is owned and run by the family: Kim and Chelsea, their
children Jack, Ella and Dylan, together with parents Don and Maxine. The vineyard is situated
in the picturesque Frankland River, tucked away in the far northwestern corner of the Great
Southern. The vineyard, with an elevation of almost 300m and red jarrah gravel loam soils,
produces wines of great intensity.

Providence Road Riesling 2022, Frankland River Quite an intense,
concentrated expression, but the zesty core of limey acidity is up to the task,
there's a gentle wave of nutty savouriness and the lightly powdery texture is a
treat. An energetic perfume canvasses jasmine, dried citrus peel, green apple
and blackcurrants, with flavours set to ripe green apple and lemon/lime with
a long, steely finish. A strong showing here. Screw cap. 13% alc. **RATING** 93
DRINK 2022–2035 $32 MB ✪

Fifth Generation Cabernet Sauvignon 2021, Frankland River Satiny,
plush and layered with medium-weight dark plum, cassis and white pepper/
herbal elements. Fine, taut ribbons of tannin, cool acidity and a minerally nuance
that lends complexity, too. Above all, really delicious flavours, moreish and fruit
driven but stippled with woody seasoning and herbal fruit character. Very good.
Screw cap. 14% alc. **RATING** 93 **DRINK** 2022–2034 $50 MB

Providence Road Cabernet Sauvignon 2021, Frankland River A
neat and tidy expression. Dark fruited and dusted with clove, some tobacco
characters, black tea tannins, dried rose petals and dark cocoa. It's quite firm but
also succulent and refreshing. Quite concentrated and dense, too. Screw cap.
14% alc. **RATING** 92 **DRINK** 2022–2030 $32 MB

Langmeil Winery

Cnr Langmeil Road/Para Road, Tanunda, SA 5352 **Region** Barossa Valley
T (08) 8563 2595 **www**.langmeilwinery.com.au **Open** 7 days 10–4 **Winemaker** Paul
Lindner **Est.** 1996 **Vyds** 33.12ha

Langmeil Winery, owned and operated by the Lindner family, is home to what may be the
world's oldest surviving shiraz vineyard, The Freedom 1843. The historic, now renovated,
site was once an important trading post and is also the location of the Orphan Bank vineyard.
This plot of shiraz vines, originally planted in the 1860s, was transplanted from Tanunda to
the banks of the North Para River in 2006.

The Freedom 1843 Shiraz 2020, Barossa Valley A thick, rolling swell of
blackberry breaking over the palate dotted with spice, licorice, dark chocolate,
violets, roasting meats and earth. Velvety and showing an incredible concentration
of fruit and superfine, ripe tannin. They've seen a lot have these old vines, but
they still deliver wines of remarkable heft and power. And this is a great example.
Screw cap. 15% alc. **RATING** 96 **DRINK** 2023–2050 $185 DB

Pure Eden Shiraz 2020, Eden Valley There is an impressive depth and
intensity to the red and blue fruits on display here. Plush and opulent with hints
of sage, bay leaf, brown spice, violets, olive tapenade, cedar, vanilla bean, licorice
and earth. A weighty, succulent flow of black fruit on the palate, crushed-quartz
tannins and a finish that is more latent power than grace … and sometimes that is
just fine. Screw cap. 14.5% alc. **RATING** 95 **DRINK** 2023–2040 $170 DB

Kernel Cabernet Sauvignon 2020, Barossa RATING 93 **DRINK** 2023–2033
$55 DB

Jackaman's Cabernet Sauvignon 2020, Barossa Valley RATING 93
DRINK 2023–2035 $15 DB ✪

Orphan Bank Shiraz 2020, Barossa RATING 93 **DRINK** 2023–2033 $75 DB

Lineage Shiraz 2017, Barossa RATING 93 DRINK 2023-2033 $500 DB
Stelle Nere Shiraz NV, Barossa RATING 92 $55 DB
Wattle Brae Riesling 2022, Eden Valley RATING 92 DRINK 2023-2030 $30 DB ✪
Black Beauty Malbec 2021, Barossa RATING 92 DRINK 2023-2027 $30 DB ✪
Hallowed Ground Shiraz 2020, Barossa RATING 92 DRINK 2023-2033 $55 DB
Della Mina Sangiovese Barbera 2021, Barossa RATING 91 DRINK 2023-2027 $30 DB
Prime Cut Shiraz 2021, Barossa RATING 91 DRINK 2023-2028 $25 DB ✪
Valley Floor Shiraz 2020, Barossa RATING 91 DRINK 2023-2028 $35 DB
Rough Diamond Grenache 2021, Barossa RATING 90 DRINK 2023-2026 $25 DB ✪
Wild Child Cabernet Sauvignon 2021, Barossa RATING 90 DRINK 2023-2029 $25 DB ✪
Legendary Cabernet Shiraz 2020, Barossa RATING 90 DRINK 2023-2027 $30 DB

Lark Hill ★★★★★

31 Joe Rocks Road, Bungendore, NSW 2621 **Region** Canberra District **T** (02) 6238 1393 **www**.larkhill.wine **Open** Fri–Sun 11.30–5 **Winemaker** Chris Carpenter **Est.** 1978 **Dozens** 7000 **Vyds** 14ha

The Lark Hill vineyard is situated at an elevation of 860m, offering splendid views of the Lake George escarpment. The Carpenters make wines of real quality, style and elegance, particularly their pinot noirs in favourable vintages. Significant changes came in the wake of son Chris gaining a double degree in wine science and viticulture through CSU and the organic/biodynamic certification of the vineyard and wines in '03. Lark Hill planted the first grüner veltliner in Australia in '05 and in '11 purchased 1 of the 2 Ravensworth vineyards from Michael Kirk, with plantings of sangiovese, shiraz and viognier. This site, now known as the Dark Horse vineyard, was converted to organic and biodynamic farming in '13, with teroldago and gargenega planted in '21 and fahlangina in '22. Fruit for the Regional series is purchased from several sites around Canberra.

🍷🍷🍷🍷🍷 **Roxanne! Petillant Naturel 2021, Canberra District** This is what pét-nat should be all about: vibrant, fresh and flavoursome yet with complexity. Red berries and watermelon, spicy with crunchy acidity and lovely texture – slightly creamy with a light savoury, phenolic pull to the finish and a slip of sweetness to round everything out. Crown. 11.5% alc. RATING 95 DRINK 2022-2026 $30 JF ✪
Lark Hill Vineyard Chardonnay 2019, Canberra District A very fine chardonnay. It has plenty of flavour but is by no means a big wine, acidity takes care of that rendering it fine and long. Savoury with flinty aromas, a touch of cashew butter/leesy flavour and smoky bacon from the oak. A complex, compelling wine. Screw cap. 12.5% alc. RATING 95 DRINK 2022-2030 $55 JF
Lark Hill Vineyard Pinot Noir 2021, Canberra District Such an elegant, fine expression with its nod to the cooler vintage. Florals and spice come first, then red cherries and squishy raspberries, the oak is gentle and adds a sheath of textural tannins plus spice yet the palate is lighter framed. A gorgeous, pretty drink for today. Screw cap. 13.5% alc. RATING 94 DRINK 2022-2030 $55 JF

🍷🍷🍷🍷🍷 **Dark Horse Vineyard Marsanne 2019, Canberra District** RATING 93 DRINK 2024-2034 $45 JF
Lark Hill Vineyard Riesling 2022, Canberra District RATING 92 DRINK 2024-2034 $55 JF
Dark Horse Vineyard Sangiovese 2022, Canberra District RATING 92 DRINK 2022-2027 $30 JF ✪
Lark Hill Vineyard Grüner Veltliner 2021, Canberra District RATING 92 DRINK 2023-2030 $45 JH
Dark Horse Vineyard Marsanne 2021, Canberra District RATING 92 DRINK 2023-2024 $30 JH ✪

Ley-Line Lark Hill Vineyard Riesling 2022, Canberra District RATING 92 DRINK 2023-2028 $55 JH

Regional Grenache 2022, Hilltops RATING 91 DRINK 2022-2025 $30 JF

Regional Riesling 2022, Hilltops RATING 90 DRINK 2022-2028 $25 JF ✪

Hudson Vineyard Mourvèdre 2021, Hilltops RATING 90 DRINK 2023-2027 $30 JH

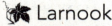 Larnook   ★★★★

7 Settlement Rd, McLaren Flat, SA 5171 (postal) **Region** McLaren Vale
T 0419 811 564 **www**.larnookwines.com.au **Open** Not **Winemaker** Alexia Roberts
Viticulturist Alexia Roberts **Est.** 2021 **Dozens** 650 **Vyds** 1.84ha

Larnook means to build a habitation, camp or nest in the language of the Kulin nation. Winemaker Alexia Roberts and her family recently built their own nest atop a rise in Blewitt Springs in McLaren Vale, planted to old bush-vine grenache dating from 1922, alongside younger shiraz plantings from '99. Wines under the subregional Blewitt Springs Single Site series come from the property, while others are sourced from elsewhere within the Vale. For such a young project, the quality is high. Here, attention is paid to retaining freshness and employing the broader textural girth that comes with that. A name to watch.

🍷🍷🍷🍷 **Blewitt Springs Shiraz 2022, McLaren Vale** A lustrous crimson, mid-weighted of feel and brimming with considerable energy, although it feels an echo of the strong voice it wants to be. Fine aromas: black sooty rock, licorice strap, blueberry, tapenade and nori. The freshness is undeniable, with pithy tannins macerated in dried lavender directing considerable length. Screw cap. 13.8% alc. RATING 92 DRINK 2023-2028 $45 NG

Rosé 2022, McLaren Vale Very good rosé. Cool-fermented to promote fruit and freshness, stirred to imbue breadth. Tangerine, musk, cumquat and raspberry riffs shimmy across a chord of juicy, saline acidity. Suitably moreish, dry and textural to force a second and third glass. Screw cap. 12.6% alc. RATING 92 DRINK 2022-2023 $27 NG ✪

Blewitt Springs Grenache 2022, McLaren Vale Almost nebbiolo-esque aromas of orange peel and sandalwood melding with clove and cardamom. Chinotto, too. A spicy, mid-weighted and immensely savoury grenache. The only caveat is that this lacks depth, sap and pulse, despite the nicely wrought, gritty tannins serving as the conclusion. Screw cap. 14% alc. RATING 90 DRINK 2023-2026 $45 NG

Tempranillo 2022, McLaren Vale Vibrant and mid-weighted, with pithy tannins compressing forestry aromas of boysenberry and bracken alongside anise, violet and sassafras. Fun. The finish, effusive and of perfect, easygoing length for the imminently approachable style. Screw cap. 14% alc. RATING 90 DRINK 2023-2026 $30 NG

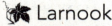 Latitude 32   ★★★★☆

266 Deaseys Road, Pokolbin, NSW 2320 (postal) **Region** Hunter Valley
T 0402 968 688 **www**.latitude32wines.com **Open** Not **Winemaker** Damien Stevens
Viticulturist Ken Bray **Est.** 2019 **Dozens** 1250 **Vyds** 4ha

Emma and David White once described themselves as corporate renegades and were known by their friends as 'wine chasers'. But no more. Emma 'retired' at the age of 40 from her career as CFO and COO of large multinational construction and development businesses and has enrolled in vini/viti courses, making international study trips focusing on new varieties for the Hunter Valley. In '21 they planted (by hand) 1ha of shiraz, and intend to plant a further 5ha (the method of planting not specified). Their wines are made in the old (and large) Lindeman's winery on McDonalds Road, where they work collegially with winemaker Damien Stevens. Their philosophy is to create wines that will truly tell the story of place and time, embracing vintage variation rather than seeking to hide it.

🍷🍷🍷🍷 **Sangiovese 2019, Hilltops** The Hilltops region experienced a warm and dry vintage, here reflected by the depth of the bright colour (in sangiovese parlance).

A pretty snappy example of a variety that can be sulky at best, bitter at worst. So, hats off to the 104 dozen made, and enjoy the lively red cherry fruits. Screw cap. 13.2% alc. **RATING** 95 **DRINK** 2025–2035 $32 JH ✪

Semillon 2022, Hunter Valley The analysis of 9.2g/L of TA and pH of 2.88 tells all for a semillon with a near-endless future and demands a decade at the least, giving it time for flesh to form around the acid framework. Its purity and length are as one. Screw cap. 11.2% alc. **RATING** 94 **DRINK** 2023–2042 $30 JH ✪

The Dux Shiraz 2019, Hunter Valley A very good vintage building on the great '17 and '18 vintages, the only downside the depressed production at 120 dozen bottles. This is a powerful and complex wine, its full colour waving the quality flag. A luscious dark fruit chord runs the length of the palate, tannins a wholly appropriate structure underpinning the fruit. Nothing has been left behind. Screw cap. 14% alc. **RATING** 94 **DRINK** 2026–2049 $45 JH

🍷🍷🍷🍷 **Limited Edition Semillon 2021, Hunter Valley RATING** 93 **DRINK** 2023–2026 $30 JH ✪

Laughing Jack ★★★★★

194 Stonewell Road, Marananga, SA 5355 **Region** Barossa Valley
T (08) 8562 3878 **www.**laughingjackwines.com.au **Open** Fri–Sat 10–4 **Winemaker** Shawn Kalleske **Viticulturist** Kalleske family **Est.** 1999 **Dozens** 6500 **Vyds** 44.2ha
Laughing Jack is owned by Shawn and Briony Kalleske, with brothers Nathan and Damon Kalleske. The 3 estate vineyards in Marananga, Greenock and Moppa are primarily planted to shiraz, with lesser amounts of semillon and grenache. Vine age varies considerably, with old, dry-grown shiraz the jewel in the crown. As any Australian knows, the kookaburra is also called the laughing jack, and there is a resident flock of kookaburras in the stands of blue and red gums surrounding the vineyards.

🍷🍷🍷🍷🍷 **Moppa Hill Block 6 Shiraz 2020, Barossa Valley** Calm and composed, this savoury-leaning shiraz shows deep, ripe blackberry and dark plum fruits on a bed of baking spices, dark chocolate, olive tapenade, licorice and earth. It sports a powdery tannin grip, and an impressively sustained finish. Screw cap. 14.5% alc. **RATING** 95 **DRINK** 2023–2033 $50 DB ✪

Augustus Shiraz 2020, Barossa Valley Deeply coloured with aromas of blackberry, black cherry and cassis with abundant baking spices, olive tapenade, ironstone, cedar, Cherry Ripe, chocolate bullets and earth. Plenty packed into the palate with a cassis-like roll of fruit, spice and cedar. Tight and compact tannins and a classic western Barossan flow on the finish. Screw cap. 14.5% alc. **RATING** 94 **DRINK** 2023–2033 $50 DB

🍷🍷🍷🍷 **Rosé 2022, Barossa Valley RATING** 92 **DRINK** 2023–2026 $28 DB ✪
Jack's Shiraz 2020, Barossa Valley RATING 91 **DRINK** 2023–2028 $28 DB ✪
Jack's Shiraz Cabernet 2020, Barossa Valley RATING 91 **DRINK** 2023–2028 $28 DB ✪

Laurel Bank ★★★★

130 Black Snake Lane, Granton, Tas 7030 **Region** Southern Tasmania
T (03) 6263 5977 **www.**laurelbankwines.com.au **Open** By appt **Winemaker** Greer Carland **Est.** 1986 **Dozens** 1700 **Vyds** 3.5ha
Laurel Bank was established by Kerry Carland in '86 but deliberately kept a low profile by withholding release of most of its early wines. When the time came, Kerry entered the Hobart Wine Show in '95 and won the trophy for Most Successful Tasmanian Exhibitor. These days, Kerry's daughter Greer is the extremely qualified winemaker, with a degree in oenology, vintages in Chile, Oregan and Burgundy under her belt and 12 years as senior winemaker at Winemaking Tasmania (now Tasmanian Vintners). She also produces wines for her own label, Quiet Mutiny, on the side.

ＹＹＹＹＹ **Pinot Noir 2021, Tasmania** Mid-ruby in the glass with aromas of red cherry, raspberry and redcurrant fruits seamlessly meshing with hints of fine spice, sous bois, wildflowers, dried herbs, amaro and a gentle note of game. Harmonious and pure in the mouth with a glide of morello cherries and plenty of spicy, amaro complexity. Screw cap. 13.7% alc. **RATING** 94 **DRINK** 2023–2030 $39 DB ✪

ＹＹＹＹＹ **Sauvignon Blanc 2022, Tasmania** **RATING** 93 **DRINK** 2023–2026 $26 DB ✪
Riesling 2022, Tasmania **RATING** 92 **DRINK** 2023–2030 $26 DB ✪

Leconfield   ★★★★★

15454 Riddoch Highway, Coonawarra, SA 5263 **Region** Coonawarra
T (08) 8323 8830 **www.leconfieldwines.com** **Open** 7 days 11–4 **Winemaker** Paul Gordon, Greg Foster **Viticulturist** Bendt Rasmussen **Est.** 1974 **Dozens** 25000 **Vyds** 43.7ha
Sydney Hamilton purchased the unplanted property that was to become Leconfield in '74, having worked in the family wine business for over 30 years until his retirement in the mid '50s. When he acquired the property, and set about planting it, he was 76 and reluctantly bowed to family pressure to sell Leconfield to nephew Richard in '81. Richard has progressively increased the vineyards to their present level, over 75% dedicated to cabernet sauvignon – for long the winery's specialty.

ＹＹＹＹＹ **Old Vines Riesling 2021, Coonawarra** Excellent intensity of flavour here. Lime and mandarin with citrus leaf notes and assorted florals. One sip and you're hooked. In fact, just the smell is enough to lure you in, its aromas both flamboyant and convincing at once. The fruit! The array! This is already terrifically complex. Screw cap. 12.5% alc. **RATING** 95 **DRINK** 2023–2030 $28 CM ✪
The Sydney Reserve Cabernet Sauvignon 2019, Coonawarra There's a power of fruit here though it's not over the top. Indeed, it's quite measured. The backbone is all blackcurrant and plum, clove, smoked cedar and licorice all playing varying roles. Tobacco and mint work through the finish, adding savouriness and lift. Screw cap. 14.5% alc. **RATING** 94 **DRINK** 2026–2036 $80 CM

ＹＹＹＹＹ **Cabernet Franc 2021, Coonawarra** **RATING** 93 **DRINK** 2023–2031 $32 CM ✪
Cabernets 2021, Coonawarra **RATING** 92 **DRINK** 2024–2032 $32 CM
Merlot 2021, Coonawarra **RATING** 92 **DRINK** 2023–2031 $28 CM ✪
Chardonnay 2021, Coonawarra **RATING** 92 **DRINK** 2023–2028 $28 CM ✪
Shiraz 2021, Coonawarra **RATING** 91 **DRINK** 2023–2030 $28 CM ✪

Leeuwin Estate   ★★★★★

Stevens Road, Margaret River, WA 6285 **Region** Margaret River
T (08) 9759 0000 **www.leeuwinestate.com.au** **Open** 7 days 10–5 **Winemaker** Tim Lovett, Phil Hutchison, Breac Wheatley **Viticulturist** David Winstanley **Est.** 1974 **Dozens** 50000 **Vyds** 160ha
This outstanding winery and vineyard is owned by the Horgan family, founded by Denis and Tricia, who continue their involvement, with son Justin Horgan and daughter Simone Furlong joint chief executives. The Art Series Chardonnay is, in my (James') opinion, Australia's finest example based on the wines of the last 30 vintages. The large estate plantings, coupled with strategic purchases of grapes from other growers, provide the base for high-quality Art Series Cabernet Sauvignon and Shiraz; the hugely successful, quick-selling Art Series Riesling and Sauvignon Blanc; and lower-priced Prelude and Siblings wines.

ＹＹＹＹＹ **Prelude Vineyards Chardonnay 2021, Margaret River** Only Leeuwin Estate could come up with a second label of such extreme quality. The quartz-green colour heralds a laser-cut wine of great purity with a perfumed, grapefruit-accented bouquet underscored by cleansing, refreshing acidity on the palate. Oak was an agent in its structure but plays no part on its palate. Screw cap. 13% alc. **RATING** 97 **DRINK** 2023–2036 $40 JH ✪

Art Series Chardonnay 2020, Margaret River A wine that remains at the top of its game – it's a pure expression of place as much as the producer. It's refreshing, classy and superfine, the acidity reining everything in and towards an outrageously long finish. Mesmerising. Screw cap. 13.5% alc. **RATING** 97 **DRINK** 2022–2032 $125 JF

Art Series Cabernet Sauvignon 2019, Margaret River It's masterful to craft a wine that is this effortlessly structured, detailed, powerful and concentrated. Mulberries, cassis, warm spices, violets and cedary oak come together in harmony while the tannins sashay across the palate. Flavours persist, as does the finish, and it will age beautifully but hard to resist now. Impressive wine. Screw cap. 13.5% alc. **RATING** 97 **DRINK** 2024–2042 $89 JF ✪

🍷🍷🍷🍷🍷 **Art Series Riesling 2022, Margaret River** Margaret River is not renowned for riesling but this producer is, and, as per usual, this is a good one. It's spicy, tangy and full of florals, citrus with lemon bath salts and a sprig of mint. Dry, long and pure. Screw cap. 12% alc. **RATING** 95 **DRINK** 2022–2030 $25 JF ✪

Prelude Vineyards Cabernet Sauvignon 2020, Margaret River There's a fineness to this, subtly from the aromas and flavours to the palate. Medium bodied, supple tannins, a skein of acidity tying everything together and lengthening the palate. It's a little deceptive, too, because there's plenty of detail yet it's lovely to drink now. Screw cap. 13.5% alc. **RATING** 95 **DRINK** 2023–2035 $32 JF ✪

Art Series Shiraz 2020, Margaret River This leaves such an impression on so many fronts: firstly, the fabulous red-purple hue followed by aromas of dark fruits, baking spices and warm earth and finally, its texture. The fuller-bodied palate unfurls eventually to reveal layers of flavour, grainy tannins and acidity ensuring it finishes long. Screw cap. 13.5% alc. **RATING** 95 **DRINK** 2023–2035 $46 JF ✪

🍷🍷🍷🍷🍸 **Rosé 2022, Margaret River RATING** 93 **DRINK** 2022–2024 $27 JF ✪
Art Series Sauvignon Blanc 2022, Margaret River RATING 93 **DRINK** 2022–2026 $31 JF ✪
Siblings Shiraz 2020, Margaret River RATING 92 **DRINK** 2022–2032 $25 JF ✪
Siblings Sauvignon Blanc 2022, Margaret River RATING 90 **DRINK** 2022–2025 $25 JF ✪

Lenton Brae Wines

★★★★☆

3887 Caves Road, Margaret River, WA 6285 **Region** Margaret River
T (08) 9755 6255 **www**.lentonbrae.com **Open** 7 days 10–5 **Winemaker** Vanessa Carson, Russell Cocker **Viticulturist** Russell Cocker **Est.** 1982 **Dozens** 15 000 **Vyds** 8ha

The late Bruce Tomlinson established Lenton Brae in '82 with wife Jeanette. Bruce was an architect and designed the now heritage-listed winery. In time, it became highly regarded as a producer of elegant wines. They sold half of the business in '91 to the Jackson family and the Jacksons took over as sole owners in '21 after the business went into liquidation. In '22, the cellar door was stylishly revamped, along with a sense of renewal perhaps.

🍷🍷🍷🍷🍷 **Cabernet Sauvignon 2021, Margaret River** While this has the exuberance of youth, it also has a firm foundation to age well. It is an elegant style with a core of sweet fruit, upfront acidity but in-check and lovely tannins. There's almost a purity to this. Just as I was thinking I'd like to taste this in a few years time, it unfurls in the glass and delights more. Screw cap. 13.5% alc. **RATING** 95 **DRINK** 2024–2035 $80 JF

🍷🍷🍷🍷🍸 **Karridale Sauvignon Blanc 2022, Margaret River RATING** 91 **DRINK** 2022–2027 $40 JF
In Good Hands Chenin Blanc 2022, Margaret River RATING 90 **DRINK** 2022–2025 $36 JF
Wilyabrup Cabernet Sauvignon 2021, Margaret River RATING 90 **DRINK** 2024–2032 $38 JF

Leo Buring

Sturt Highway, Nuriootpa, SA 5355 (postal) **Region** Eden Valley
T 1300 651 650 **Open** Not **Winemaker** Marie Clay **Est.** 1934

Between 1965 and '00, Leo Buring was Australia's foremost riesling producer, with a rich legacy left by former winemaker John Vickery. The brand began with many varieties and wine styles before honing in on riesling – it's been the only varietal made for the past 25 years or so. Top of the range are the Tasmanian Leopold rieslings, supported by Clare and Eden valley rieslings at significantly lower prices.

DW Z20 Leopold Riesling 2022, Tasmania An impeccable, perfumed riesling of serious clarity and tension. Pale in the glass with notes of lemon, green apple and lime framed by orange blossom and jasmine with hints of crushed slate, marzipan, lemon sorbet, grapefruit pith and a suggestion of preserved lemon. Riding true on rails of crystalline mineral-laden acidity with precision and purity. A beautiful wine. Screw cap. 12% alc. **RATING** 96 **DRINK** 2023–2033 $45 DB ✪

Leopold Riesling 2021, Tasmania Pale straw in the glass with aromas of green apple, lime and grapefruit juice and hints of orange blossom, crushed stone, marzipan, pressed white flowers and almond paste. Tight, shimmering acidity ramps up on the palate where the citrus fruits are joined by a light wash of dried herbs, leaving a wake of green apple, grapefruit and blossom. Screw cap. 11% alc. **RATING** 94 **DRINK** 2023–2028 $45 DB

Dry Riesling 2022, Eden Valley **RATING** 93 **DRINK** 2023–2033 $20 DB ✪

Leogate Estate Wines

1693 Broke Road, Pokolbin, NSW 2320 **Region** Hunter Valley
T (02) 4998 7499 **www**.leogate.com.au **Open** 7 days 10–5 **Winemaker** Mark Woods
Est. 2009 **Dozens** 30 000 **Vyds** 127.5ha

Bill and Vicki Widin purchased the substantial 1960s-planted Brokenback vineyard in '09, the original 50ha comprising semillon, chardonnay and shiraz. By '13, they'd built a winery and cellar door – a suite of 20 luxury villas was built in '22. Over time, they've added verdelho, pinot gris, gewürztraminer and tempranillo to the original vineyard. In '16 Leogate purchased a 61ha certified organic vineyard at Gulgong (Mudgee) planted to shiraz, cabernet sauvignon and merlot. Leogate acquired the Black Cluster vineyard in '20. It's predominantly planted to old-vine shiraz, with some semillon in tow.

Cellar Release The Basin Reserve Shiraz 2018, Hunter Valley A beautiful shiraz from its crimson-purple colour to its fragrant bouquet, precursors to the stunning palate where silk and velvet purple and black fruits join hands with fine-spun tannins, a memory of Hunter earth and dark spices. Screw cap. 14% alc. **RATING** 97 **DRINK** 2025–2050 $115 JH

Museum Release Malabar Reserve Shiraz 2014, Hunter Valley The bouquet is warm and inviting, with Hunter dust on the bouquet, then radically changing the game with an intense and wonderfully fresh palate of exceptional length. This was also tasted on release in '16 and as a Cellar Release in '20 and it just gets better. Screw cap. 14% alc. **RATING** 97 **DRINK** 2023–2033 $80 JH ✪

Museum Release Creek Bed Reserve Chardonnay 2013, Hunter Valley Excellent bright yellow-green. A lovely chardonnay, still full of life and zero phenolics. White stone fruit, melon, Granny Smith apple and citrusy acidity all in harmonic song. Screw cap. 13% alc. **RATING** 97 **DRINK** 2023–2030 $50 JH ✪

Museum Release Reserve Semillon 2010, Hunter Valley The wine is freaky. Fresh and crisp, still with lemon zest and Meyer lemon purity of the highest order, acidity doing its job no more, no less. Screw cap. 11.4% alc. **RATING** 97 **DRINK** 2023–2040 $70 JH ✪

Cellar Release Western Slopes Reserve Shiraz 2018, Hunter Valley It's full of luscious red and black berries and cherries in a medium- to full-bodied frame. These wines are made in very small quantities, with high level of attention to detail. Screw cap. 14% alc. **RATING** 96 **DRINK** 2027–2037 $115 JH

Creek Bed Reserve Semillon 2022, Hunter Valley This offers another level of intensity and racy purity. Lime, lemon and flinty flavours drive the palate to exceptional length, however far it may be from the opening of business now. Screw cap. 10.5% alc. RATING 95 DRINK 2023–2042 $38 JH ✪

Vicki's Choice Reserve Chardonnay 2021, Hunter Valley Two parcels: 90% pressed to new and used French hogsheads; wild-yeast fermentation and partial mlf, the remaining 10% fermented in stainless steel. Blended and bottled after 10 months' maturation. As with all the Leogate chardonnays, there's plenty to chew on, both length and depth, peach the core of the lengthy palate. Screw cap. 13% alc. RATING 95 DRINK 2023–2031 $70 JH

H10 Block Reserve Chardonnay 2021, Hunter Valley 60% wild-yeast fermented in new and 1yo hogsheads, partial mlf; 40% in stainless steel. Radically different from the Creek Bed Reserve; rounder and richer with white and yellow peach, plus melon. Screw cap. 13% alc. RATING 95 DRINK 2023–2034 $42 JH ✪

Cellar Release Malabar Reserve Shiraz 2018, Hunter Valley From an excellent vintage, and this wine shows it, but it has retreated somewhat. It's very complex and structured but retains the points it garnered on first tasting as a new release in February '20. Screw cap. 14.5% alc. RATING 95 DRINK 2024–2044 $70 JH

Museum Release Brokenback Vineyard Shiraz 2014, Hunter Valley An elegant, relaxed wine; secure for another 5 or so years thanks to its impeccable balance and freshness. Screw cap. 14% alc. RATING 95 DRINK 2023–2030 $70 JH

Black Cluster Army Block Semillon 2022, Hunter Valley The name may not suggest it, but this 'Block' is a 15ha planting of semillon that is over 50yo. Its (figuratively) sour lemon flavour, hunting in tandem with firm acidity, makes for a semillon of purity and elegance in the best old-fashioned style. Screw cap. 11.5% alc. RATING 94 DRINK 2023–2032 $22 JH ✪

Brokenback Vineyard Semillon 2022, Hunter Valley This vineyard was created by the one and only Len Evans AO OBE, who would have been proud to taste this wine. The screw cap revolutionised the cellaring of young semillons such as this (and every other semillon in its infancy, as it were). This just happens to be delicious now. Screw cap. 10.5% alc. RATING 94 DRINK 2023–2037 $22 JH ✪

Museum Release Vicki's Choice Reserve Chardonnay 2012, Hunter Valley 90% wild fermented and partial mlf in new and 1-2yo French hogsheads, the balance in stainless steel. Shows its age and simply serves to highlight the class of its '13 Creek Bed Reserve sibling. Screw cap. 13% alc. RATING 94 DRINK 2023–2028 $80 JH

🍷🍷🍷🍷🍷 **Black Cluster Shiraz 2021, Hunter Valley** RATING 93 DRINK 2026–2046 $35 JH ✪

Brokenback Tempranillo 2019, Hunter Valley RATING 93 DRINK 2023–2028 $40 JH

Cellar Release H10 Block Reserve Chardonnay 2018, Hunter Valley RATING 93 DRINK 2023–2024 $42 JH

Malabar Reserve Chardonnay 2021, Hunter Valley RATING 92 DRINK 2023–2028 $38 JH

Creek Bed Reserve Chardonnay 2021, Hunter Valley RATING 92 DRINK 2023–2030 $38 JH

Leura Park Estate ★★★★

1400 Portarlington Road, Curlewis, Vic 3222 **Region** Geelong
T (03) 5253 3180 **www.leuraparkestate.com.au Open** Thurs–Sun 11–4
Winemaker Darren Burke **Viticulturist** David Sharp **Est.** 1995 **Dozens** 3000 **Vyds** 16ha
Leura Park Estate's vineyard is planted to chardonnay (50%), pinot noir, pinot gris, sauvignon blanc, riesling, shiraz and cabernet sauvignon. Owners David and Lyndsay Sharp are committed to minimal interference in the vineyard and have expanded the estate-grown wine range to include Vintage Grande. The erection of a winery for the '10 vintage has contributed to increased production and ongoing wine show success.

🍷🍷🍷🍷♀ **Bellarine Peninsula Sauvignon Blanc 2021, Geelong** Bright straw gold with green tinges. Restrained, with aromas of white nectarines, gooseberries and nettles. On the palate, this attractive and well-put-together wine is light, chalky textured and long. Screw cap. 12.5% alc. RATING 93 DRINK 2022–2025 $38 PR

Limited Release Block 1 Reserve Chardonnay 2021, Geelong
An immediate and attractive nose with aromas of ripe stone fruits, some grapefruit pith and grilled nuts. Generous and full flavoured on the palate, it's finely tuned and well balanced, too. Screw cap. 13% alc. RATING 93 DRINK 2022–2026 $50 PR

Bellarine Peninsula Riesling 2022, Geelong A bright green gold. Lifted florals sit alongside fresh lime and citrus scents in this dry, poised and nicely balanced wine of refreshing acidity. Screw cap. 11.5% alc. RATING 92 DRINK 2022–2029 $38 PR

Bellarine Peninsula Chardonnay 2021, Geelong A deep-ish bright green gold. Ripe stone fruits, honeysuckle, a little oak-derived vanillin and some orange blossom can all be found on the bouquet. Ample, gently creamy and long, there's a fine bead of acidity running through, keeping things fresh. Screw cap. 12.5% alc. RATING 92 DRINK 2022–2026 $38 PR

Bellarine Peninsula Pinot Noir 2021, Geelong A light, bright ruby red. Cool aromas of freshly picked cherries, bracken and spice meld together in this appealing wine. It has good weight and texture and, while it's already drinking well, it should continue to do so for a few years yet. Screw cap. 12.5% alc. RATING 92 DRINK 2022–2028 $48 PR

Yublong Limited Release Cabernet Sauvignon 2021, Geelong A medium deep cherry red. Fragrant with red and black fruits, cedar and some bell pepper. On the palate, this elegant wine is medium bodied, cool fruited and finely detailed. Will be even better as it softens and opens up. Screw cap. 13.5% alc. RATING 92 DRINK 2022–2029 $48 PR

25 d'Gris Bellarine Peninsula Pinot Gris 2022, Geelong A medium gold with green tinges. Definitely gris and not grigio with its aromas of ripe white peaches, waxy apples and spice, while the palate is generous and textured but dry and balanced. It's very tasty right now. Screw cap. 13.5% alc. RATING 91 DRINK 2022–2025 $38 PR

Levrier Wines by Jo Irvine ★★★★☆

928 Research Road, Nuriootpa, SA 5355 **Region** Barossa Valley
T (08) 8562 3888 **www.levrierwines.com.au Open** By appt **Winemaker** Joanne Irvine
Est. 2014 **Dozens** 3000

'Levrier' is French for greyhound, and Jo Irvine has looked after retired racing greyhounds for 20 years. Jo is also enjoying a second lease on life. At 35 she gave up her nursing career, working vintages in the US while earning her viticulture and oenology degree before coming home to start a consulting business and make wines for her father, Jim Irvine, at Irvine Wines. Jim sold that business in '14, after which Jo went out on her own, releasing the first wines under the Levrier label in '16. The wines she makes on her own account are named for famous racing greyhounds: Sorter, Argos, Anubis and Peritas. Levrier's cellar door is also distinctly dog friendly, with a fenced dog park for visiting hounds, and resident wine greyhounds Georgie and Daphne often onsite.

🍷🍷🍷🍷🍷 **Anubis Single Vineyard Cabernet Sauvignon 2016, Eden Valley**
Burnished yet still deep crimson in the glass with notes of satsuma plums and macerated summer berry fruits. Hints of baking spices, violets, roasting meats, licorice, olive tapenade, turned earth, tobacco and cedar. Fine, sandy tannin, lacy acidity and some sour cherry notes joining in on the palate. Finishes long and very moreish. Screw cap. 14.5% alc. RATING 95 DRINK 2023–2028 $70 DB

Meslier Brut Rosé NV, Adelaide Hills Petit meslier is a rare champagne variety. An intriguing wine, as reliant on a rail of chewy phenolics as it is on chalky freshness. Plenty creamy and refined. Musk stick, tiny red berries and a lilt of Turkish delight. The structured finish feels pliant and dry, a welcome

juxtaposition to the intensity of flavour on show. Cork. 11% alc. **RATING** 94
$50 NG

Anubis Single Vineyard Cabernet Sauvignon 2018, Eden Valley Rich
blackberry, black cherry and macerated plums on a bed of deep spice with hints
of tobacco leaf, cedar, pencil lead, dried herbs, licorice, espresso and earth. Some
fig and prune join in on the palate, which shows substantial power and heft, solid
fruit density, chocolatey tannins, espresso and a core of cassis fruit on the exit.
Screw cap. 14.5% alc. **RATING** 94 **DRINK** 2023–2033 $70 DB

♟♟♟♟♀ **Cabernet Franc 2020, Barossa** **RATING** 93 **DRINK** 2023–2028 $35 DB
Peritas Single Vineyard Zinfandel 2018, Barossa Valley **RATING** 92
DRINK 2023–2028 $60 DB
Peritas Single Vineyard Zinfandel 2017, Barossa Valley **RATING** 92
DRINK 2023–2028 $55 DB
Merlot 2018, Barossa **RATING** 90 **DRINK** 2023–2028 $35 DB
Argos Single Vineyard Shiraz 2016, Barossa **RATING** 90 **DRINK** 2023–2028
$45 DB

Lienert Vineyards   ★★★★

Artisans of Barossa, 16 Vine Vale Road, Tanunda, SA 5352 **Region** Barossa Valley
T (08) 8524 9062 **www.**lienert.wine **Open** 7 days 9–5 **Winemaker** James Lienert
Viticulturist John Lienert **Est.** 2001 **Dozens** 5000 **Vyds** 100ha
Lienert Vineyards is a partnership between brothers John and James Lienert, who have
converted the family's farmland on the Barossa Valley's western ridge from cropping to
vineyards, planting the first vines in the distinctive terra rossa soils in '01. John manages the
vineyard, which also supplies fruit to a number of Barossa wineries. James makes wines under
the Lienert Vineyards and Jack West labels from selected blocks.

♟♟♟♟♟ **Leinert Grenache 2021, Barossa Valley** I've got to say, I'm loving what John
and James Lienert are doing. Here it's grenache, bright and airy in the mouth with
beautiful ripe, ginger-spiced plums and red fruits with hints of Asian spices, earth,
purple flowers, cola and licorice. Savoury, composed and just straight-up great
drinking. Screw cap. 14% alc. **RATING** 94 **DRINK** 2023–2027 $45 DB

♟♟♟♟♀ **Tierra del Puerco Field Marshall Shiraz 2020, Barossa Valley** **RATING** 92
DRINK 2023–2026 $25 DB

Lightfoot Wines   ★★★★★

717 Calulu Road, Bairnsdale, Vic 3875 **Region** Gippsland
T (03) 5156 9205 **www.**lightfootwines.com **Open** Fri–Sun 11–5 **Winemaker** Alastair
Butt, Tom Lightfoot **Viticulturist** Tom Lightfoot, Matt Mahlook **Est.** 1995
Dozens 10 000 **Vyds** 29.3ha
Formerly Lightfoot & Sons. Brian and Helen Lightfoot first established a vineyard of
predominantly pinot noir and shiraz, with some cabernet sauvignon and merlot, on their
Myrtle Point farm in the late '90s. In the early days, most of the grapes were sold, but with the
arrival of Alastair Butt (formerly of Brokenwood and Seville Estate) and sons Tom and Rob
Lightfoot taking over the business around '08 (Tom in the vineyard and cellar, Rob overseeing
sales and marketing), the focus has shifted to producing estate wines. Cabernet and merlot
have since been replaced with more chardonnay, some gamay, pinot grigio and pinot noir.

♟♟♟♟♟ **River Block Shiraz 2021, Gippsland** Gippsland shiraz doesn't come any
better than this. The dark garnet hue entices as much as the heady aromatics
of blueberries, plums and earthy red clay – and its delightfully savoury. Medium
bodied, excellent tannins all plush and velvety and the finish so persistent.
Impressive. Screw cap. 13% alc. **RATING** 96 **DRINK** 2023–2035 $60 JF
Myrtle Point Vineyard Pinot Noir 2021, Gippsland So appealing both
aromatically and with its flavour profile. A varietal ride with sweet cherries,
warm spices, orange zest over rhubarb plus some attractive cedary oak nuances.

It's supple and fine on the medium-bodied palate, the tannins particularly lovely and lacy. Screw cap. 13.5% alc. **RATING** 95 **DRINK** 2022–2029 $35 JF ✪

Cliff Block Pinot Noir 2018, Gippsland This has so much pizzazz it could lead a dance party. Upfront, macerated cherries and baking spices, oak spices, too, wafts of autumn leaves, chinotto and menthol. Full bodied, with dense fruit across an expansive palate where tannins have in-built texture and firmness. There's a slightly bitter charred radicchio flavour to the finish, which adds to this complex wine. Screw cap. 13.8% alc. **RATING** 95 **DRINK** 2023–2033 $60 JF

🍷🍷🍷🍷 **Darkfoot Chardonnay NV, Gippsland RATING** 93 $60 JF
Beaujangles Pinot Noir 2022, Gippsland RATING 91 **DRINK** 2022–2025 $40 JF
Rosé Pinot Noir 2022, Pyrenees Gippsland RATING 90 **DRINK** 2023–2023 $25 JF ✪
Myrtle Point Vineyard Shiraz 2021, Gippsland RATING 90 **DRINK** 2023–2033 $35 JF

Lillypilly Estate   ★★★★☆

47 Lillypilly Road, Leeton, NSW 2705 **Region** Riverina
T (02) 6953 4069 **www**.lillypilly.com **Open** Mon–Sat 10–5, Sun by appt
Winemaker Robert Fiumara **Est.** 1972 **Dozens** 10 000 **Vyds** 30ha
Botrytised white wines are by far the best offering from Lillypilly, with the Noble Muscat of Alexandria unique to the winery. These wines have both style and intensity of flavour and can age well. Their table wine quality is always steady – a prime example of not fixing what is not broken.

🍷🍷🍷🍷 **Museum Release Noble Blend 1st Rendition 2008, Riverina** Semillon, muscat and riesling make up this museum release. An intoxicating and heady mix of orange marmalade, candied quince and crème caramel. Sweet paprika, galangal and ground coriander add a savoury quality. Acidity maintains momentum across the palate as dried apricot and sweet fig notes linger on. A wonderful journey. Screw cap. 11% alc. **RATING** 95 **DRINK** 2022–2032 $42 SW ✪

🍷🍷🍷🍷 **Noble Harvest 2021, Riverina RATING** 93 **DRINK** 2022–2035 $30 SW ✪

limefinger   ★★★★★

18 Edwards Rd, Polish Hill River, SA 5453 **Region** Clare Valley
T 0417 803 404 **www**.limefingerwine.com.au **Open** By appt **Winemaker** Neil Pike
Viticulturist Neil Pike **Est.** 2020 **Dozens** 400 **Vyds** 0.5ha
Neil Pike has been part of the Clare Valley wine scene for 40 years and helped create and craft the success of Pikes Wines. In '20, he retired from that juggernaut so the next generation could takeover. It was time, but he wasn't finished with riesling. 'I truly love making wine, riesling in particular, and I certainly love drinking riesling. So limefinger is good fun.' Just 2 rieslings are made, one sourced from a vineyard he's long admired in Watervale, the other from the 500 vines planted at his home property in Polish Hill River.

🍷🍷🍷🍷🍷 **Solace Riesling 2022, Clare Valley** Riesling of the Year. Score awarded by the Halliday tasting panel at the annual Awards judging. MB writes: So scintillating, so pure, so much energy, so minerally. Scents of lime (of course), pink grapefruit and honeysuckle with a whiff of warm slate. The palate is compact, racy and very long. More of those lime characters, tightly bundled with an incredible mineral character that races through the wine, extending it on lacy threads to infinity. Screw cap. 11% alc. **RATING** 98 **DRINK** 2022–2040 $38 PD ✪ ❤

The Learnings Watervale Riesling 2022, Clare Valley Immense charm and detail here. Scents of grapefruit, ginger, makrut lime, lemongrass and a kind of candied citrus peel thing going on. Flavours are concentrated and energised with cool, minerally acidity. Tastes like gin and tonic with a big splash of pink grapefruit juice in it, or something like that. Complex and serious – this is stellar stuff. Screw cap. 12% alc. **RATING** 95 **DRINK** 2022–2037 $38 MB ✪

Lindeman's

Level 8, 161 Collins Street, Melbourne 3000 (postal) **Region** Coonawarra
T 1300 651 650 **www**.lindemans.com **Open** Not **Winemaker** Elizabeth Marwood
Est. 1965

Lindeman's Coonawarra vineyards have assumed a greater importance than ever thanks to the move towards single-region wines. The Coonawarra Trio of Limestone Ridge Vineyard Shiraz Cabernet, St George Vineyard Cabernet Sauvignon and Pyrus Cabernet Sauvignon Merlot Malbec are all of exemplary quality.

Trio St George Vineyard Cabernet Sauvignon 2021, Coonawarra This has fruit and oak and gives a general impression of power, but it's the firmness of the tannin that roots its quality to the spot. This is a seriously good St George. Blackcurrant, mint, florals and cedar with woodsmoke and fragrant herbs as whispers. It's structured, it's powerful and it's persistent. Screw cap. 14% alc. **RATING** 96 **DRINK** 2028-2046 $70 CM ✪

Trio Pyrus Cabernet Sauvignon Merlot Malbec 2021, Coonawarra This has cellar-worthiness written all over it. It's complex, herbal, slipped with silk and well fruited. Graphite, bay leaves, redcurrant and cedar play into twiggy spice and mint notes. It's not a heavy wine but it's fascinating, thanks to the array of flavours. The length of the finish is beyond impressive. Screw cap. 14% alc. **RATING** 96 **DRINK** 2027-2046 $70 CM ✪

Trio Limestone Ridge Vineyard Shiraz Cabernet 2021, Coonawarra Dense plum, blackcurrant and saltbush flavours gradually merge into salted caramel, vanilla and bay leaf. This is a substantial red wine, smooth to the touch, with a salty edge but ample fruit and oak flavour. It feels both seamless and, right now, a bit surly, though time will well and truly sort out the latter. Screw cap. 14% alc. **RATING** 94 **DRINK** 2027-2046 $70 CM

Lindenderry Estate

142 Arthurs Seat Road, Red Hill, Vic 3937 **Region** Mornington Peninsula
T (03) 5989 2933 **www**.lindenderry.com.au **Open** Sat–Sun 12–3 **Winemaker** Barnaby Flanders **Est.** 1999 **Dozens** 1000 **Vyds** 3.35ha

Lindenderry Estate in Red Hill is a sister operation to Lancemore Hill in the Macedon Ranges and Lindenwarrah at Milawa. It has a 5-star country house hotel, conference facilities, a function area, day spa and restaurant on 16ha of gardens. It also has a little over 3ha of vineyards, planted equally to pinot noir and chardonnay. Notwithstanding the reputation of the previous winemakers for Lindenderry, the wines now being made by Barney Flanders are the best yet. He has made the most of the estate-grown grapes, adding cream to the cake by sourcing some excellent Grampians shiraz.

Pinot Noir 2022, Macedon Ranges Whole bunches in the ferment add a lovely smoky, perfumed lift. Savoury with forest floor aromas and macerated cherries with woodsy spices. The palate chimes in at medium bodied with raspberry-like acidity playing tag with the ripe, textural tannins. Nice one. Screw cap. 13.5% alc. **RATING** 95 **DRINK** 2023-2032 $50 JF ✪

Pinot Noir 2022, Mornington Peninsula This is superfine and delicious. Gorgeous fruit and sensitive winemaking have turned this into a savoury drink with cherries and pips, cedary oak spices and Asian five-spice. Sandy tannins sashay across the palate with fine acidity, too. Screw cap. 13% alc. **RATING** 95 **DRINK** 2023-2032 $50 JF ✪

Chardonnay 2022, Mornington Peninsula A charming chardonnay. Fragrant with the palate showing off lemon and mandarin, just enough creamy lees to add a layer of texture, some smokin' sulphides turning this moreish and savoury with powder puff acidity to close. Screw cap. 13% alc. **RATING** 95 **DRINK** 2023-2032 $55 JF

Pinot Gris 2022, Macedon Ranges Textural, rich and fragrant. It starts with florals from lavender to honeysuckle with a palate full of stone fruit, honeydew and ginger spice but more than anything, it's savoury, too. Neat phenolics, luscious but not too heavy with dabs of clotted cream and a powder puff of acidity. Screw cap. 13% alc. **RATING** 94 **DRINK** 2023–2028 $35 JF

Shiraz 2021, Mornington Peninsula Highly aromatic and enticing. Florals, woodsmoke and spice come to the fore and the palate follows with dark cherries and plums, sweet cinnamon and cedar/clove oak yet savoury and complex. It's parked at medium bodied with grainy tannins and a lithe acidity -- gee, this is good. Screw cap. 13.5% alc. **RATING** 94 **DRINK** 2023–2033 $50 JF

♈♈♈♈♈ **Sparkling Rosé Pinot Noir 2019, Macedon Ranges** **RATING** 93 **DRINK** 2023–2025 $60 JF

Rosé 2022, Macedon Ranges **RATING** 92 **DRINK** 2023–2025 $35 JF

Linke Wines ★★★☆

60A Seppeltsfield Rd, Nuriootpa, SA 5355 (postal) **Region** Barossa Valley
T 0407 025 363 **www**.linkewines.com.au **Open** Not **Winemaker** Brock Harrison
Viticulturist Scott Linke **Est.** 2002 **Dozens** 5000 **Vyds** 30ha

Linke Wines is a 5th generation Tanunda-based producer who previously supplied grapes to Barossa Valley wineries such as St Hallett and Langmeil. It has been producing Linke Shiraz and Cabernet Sauvignon since the '02 vintage from their Stone Well and Dorrien blocks, as well as a dry-grown riesling from the cooler climes of the Eden Valley.

♈♈♈♈♈ **Dry Grown Riesling 2022, Eden Valley** Freshly squeezed lime and Bickford's lime cordial with hints of orange blossom, crushed quartz, almond paste and white flowers. There is a steely focus to the wine with a sizzling line of acidity cutting across the palate, focused limey fruit and the gentle wash of blossom on the crisp finish. Screw cap. 12.3% alc. **RATING** 91 **DRINK** 2023–2027 $35 DB

Lino Ramble ★★★★

11 Gawler Street, Port Noarlunga, SA 5167 **Region** McLaren Vale
T 0409 553 448 **www**.linoramble.com.au **Open** By appt **Winemaker** Andy Coppard
Est. 2012 **Dozens** 3500

After 20 years of working for other wine companies, big and small, interstate and international, Andy Coppard and Angela Townsend say, 'We've climbed on top of the dog kennel, tied a cape around our necks, held our breaths, and jumped'. And if you are curious about the name, the story has overtones of James Joyce's stream of consciousness mental rambles.

♈♈♈♈♈ **Gomas Grenache 2021, McLaren Vale** A jubey, full-bodied wine that plays the regional card of translucent freshness, glimpsing a 'je ne sais quoi' pinosity. Yet the candied orange, red cherry and pomegranate are quintessentially of the Vale. The fruit sweetness, too, oozing over the sandy tannins and slightly obvious oak. Some menthol dryness at the finale. Screw cap. 14.6% alc. **RATING** 92 **DRINK** 2022–2026 $50 NG

Dot to Dot Arinto 2022, McLaren Vale This Portuguese indigene feels intuitive here. Chamomile, baked quince, marzipan, mirabelle and freshly lain tatami straw. A mid-weighted wine that is stuffed with intensity and chew as much as saline freshness. A delicious wine that's built for the table. Screw cap. 12.8% alc. **RATING** 91 **DRINK** 2022–2025 $25 NG

Vinyl Pinot Grigio 2022, South Australia Good grigio with sap, verve and drive. Blended Granny Smith, nashi pear and wild fennel. A skein of peppery acidity tows solid length. Screw cap. 12.4% alc. **RATING** 90 **DRINK** 2022–2024 $25 NG

Lithostylis ★★★★☆

17 Church Street, Leongatha, Vic 3953 (postal) **Region** Gippsland
T (03) 5662 2885 **www**.lithostylis.com **Open** Not **Winemaker** Dean Roberts
Viticulturist Dean Roberts **Est.** 2006 **Dozens** 300 **Vyds** 2.25ha

Dean and Dayna Roberts purchased their '97-planted vineyard in '06. They say 'Organic and biodynamic practices are preferred, but not dogmatically pursued. Winemaking is limited to essential interventions.' Dean began his career with a viticulture diploma from Swinburne University, Lilydale, in '02, becoming vineyard manager for Diamond Valley Vineyards, simultaneously undertaking further winemaking studies. He then completed a vintage at Ponzi Wines in Oregon, and on returning to Australia had a short, but intense, period of employment with Bass Phillip. He now works as a vineyard management contractor, and on the winemaking front receives assistance from Dayna, who has a biomedical science degree from Monash University.

ŸŸŸŸŸ **The Obelisk Pinot Noir 2021, Gippsland** Good South Gippsland pinot leaves a lasting and impressive impression. This is a perfect example. It has structure, depth and so much gorgeous fruit, but it's neither fruity nor weighty. Full bodied, ripe velvety tannins, it pulses with energy and drive. Diam. 13.8% alc. **RATING** 95 **DRINK** 2022–2033 $48 JF ✪

Monolith Chardonnay 2021, Gippsland In true regional style, this seems restrained and slow to reveal its true self. But it does. Soon the citrus flavours give way to spiced stone fruit, layers of creamy texture all nutty and flecked with oak flavours. It's fleshy and succulent with a lovely savouriness throughout. And of course, plenty of fine acidity lengthening out the palate. Diam. 12.8% alc. **RATING** 94 **DRINK** 2022–2030 $40 JF ✪

ŸŸŸŸŸ **Cuvée Oberon 2018, Gippsland RATING** 93 **DRINK** 2022–2025 $58 JF
Ironstone Pinot Noir 2019, Gippsland RATING 92 **DRINK** 2022–2025 $30 JF ✪
Chardonnay 2021, South Gippsland RATING 91 **DRINK** 2022–2026 $30 JF

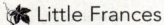

Little Frances

478 Stanley Road, Beechworth, Vic 3747 **Region** Beechworth
T 0476 771 438 **www**.littlefrances.com.au **Open** By appt **Winemaker** Erin Frances Pooley **Est.** 2012 **Dozens** 2000

Little Frances is Erin Frances Pooley, an intrepid winemaker behind ventures in Australia and California. Born in Sydney, she moved to the US to work vintage in '07, founding Little Frances in '12 with 2t of semillon from Lake County, north of Napa Valley. The line expanded to include sauvignon blanc, chenin blanc and merlot. In '20, she returned home looking to make Beechworth her Australian winemaking base. 'The granite, altitude and climate of Beechworth was always my goal,' she says. Erin, no relation to the Pooley winemaking family in Tasmania, relies on growers throughout the Beechworth region and has found a new winemaking home in an old apple processing shed on the Beechworth–Stanley Road. Her goal of expanding Little Frances across 2 hemispheres is now complete.

ŸŸŸŸŸ **Shiraz 2022, Beechworth** Confidently captures the energy, lively spice and red-fruited beauty of Beechworth shiraz. Boasts mid-weight appeal with bright red berries, plums, star anise, sage and green peppercorns with some meaty, toasty oak. Ripe cherry tannins contribute to the energy of the wine. The rich vein of peppery spice lasts and lasts on the finish. Diam. 13.8% alc. **RATING** 92 **DRINK** 2023–2030 $42 JP

Chardonnay 2021, Yarra Valley Aromas of yellow apples, stone fruits, a little lemon curd and some toasted hazelnuts can all be found on this gentle and engaging wine. Equally quiet and refined on the palate, the finish is chalky and long. Pair it with grilled white fish and don't serve it too cold! Diam. 12% alc. **RATING** 92 **DRINK** 2022–2027 $45 PR

Merlot 2022, Beechworth Erin Frances Pooley certainly boasts some excellent contacts for quality fruit. Merlot is a case in point. Erin has highlighted the grape's bevy of floral aromatics – rose, violet, bay leaf, anise – with arresting black cherry and plum. Keeps a trim presence in fine-grained tannins while maintaining a sleek textural flow. Diam. 13.5% alc. **RATING** 91 **DRINK** 2023–2028 $42 JP

Living Roots

159 Tynan Rd, Kuitpo SA 5201 **Region** Adelaide Hills
T www.livingrootswine.com **Open** By appt **Winemaker** Sebastian Hardy, Anthony
Neilson **Est.** 2016 **Dozens** 4400

Living Roots can be found in both the Finger Lakes region of New York and South
Australia's Adelaide Hills. It was founded by husband-and-wife team Sebastian (an Adelaide
native and 6th generation winemaker) and Colleen Hardy (a New York native and marketer).
The intercontinental label pays homage to family heritage while also branching out to new
vineyards, styles and techniques. Grapes are sourced from a number of growers, including
both of the Hardys' families, highlighting the natural strengths of each variety and climate in
vastly different corners of the globe.

ΨΨΨΨ **Pepperberry Shiraz 2019, Adelaide Hills** Takes a whirl to open, yet delivers
intrigue and promise. Liminal of style, glimpsing the meaty wilderness of the
Rhône while allowing a surfeit of typically Australian plum, cherry and blueberry
to flow freely. The ferrous mid-palate, smeared with olive and sarsaparilla, is
untamed in an effortless way, making for inviting drinking. Screw cap. 13.3% alc.
RATING 94 **DRINK** 2022-2028 $34 NG ✪

ΨΨΨΨ **Petite Sirah Syrah 2021, Adelaide Hills RATING** 92 **DRINK** 2022-2028
$34 NG
Pinot Noir 2020, Adelaide Hills RATING 92 **DRINK** 2022-2026 $34 NG
Rizz Fizz Riesling 2021, Adelaide Hills RATING 91 **DRINK** 2022-2024 $30 NG

Liz Heidenreich Wines ★★★★

PO Box 783, Clare, SA 5453 **Region** Clare Valley
T 0407 710 244 **www.**lizheidenreichwines.com **Open** Not **Winemaker** Liz
Heidenreich **Est.** 2018 **Dozens** 2000 **Vyds** 6ha

In 1866, Liz Heidenreich's great-great-grandfather Georg Adam Heidenreich, a Lutheran
minister, was sent from Hamburg to the Barossa Valley to provide religious care. In 1936,
Liz Heidenreich's grandfather planted vines at Vine Vale; those vines still in production, still
owned and managed by the Heidenreich family. Liz decided to follow her family heritage and
enrolled in a post-graduate winemaking degree course at the University of Adelaide. She says
her spiritual wine homes are the Barossa and Clare valleys.

ΨΨΨΨ **Watervale Riesling 2022, Clare Valley** 2g/L RS – not sweet whatsoever,
but there's a little extra pliancy and bounce. Scents of red apple, blackcurrant,
pink grapefruit and flint. Flavours are also red apple oriented, doused in lime
juice, flecked with ginger and finishing steely and flinty. Drinkability is high
here. Refreshment factor, too. Screw cap. 12% alc. **RATING** 93 **DRINK** 2022-2035
$25 MB ✪
Rufus Block 2020, Barossa Valley Lots of sweet, ripe fruit aromas, a warm
compote of forest berries, dark chocolate, vanilla, cinnamon and minty elements.
The flavours similarly concentrated with berry, choc-mint and a light grip of
cinnamon-dusted silty tannins. It's potent, mouth-filling and opulent, warm,
round and finishes dusty. Pleasure zone stuff. Screw cap. 14% alc. **RATING** 92
DRINK 2022-2028 $35 MB

Lloyd Brothers ★★★★

34 Warners Road, McLaren Vale, SA 5171 **Region** McLaren Vale
T (08) 8323 8792 **www.**lloydbrothers.com.au **Open** 7 days 11-5 **Winemaker** Gonzalo
Sanchez **Est.** 2002 **Dozens** 10 000 **Vyds** 42.4ha

Lloyd Brothers is owned and operated by David and Matthew Lloyd, 3rd-generation
McLaren Vale vignerons. Their 25ha estate overlooks the township, and is planted to 20ha
shiraz, 2.5ha bush-vine grenache and 1ha bushvine mataro (plus 18.9ha of sauvignon blanc,
chardonnay, pinot gris and shiraz in the Adelaide Hills). Most recently, David planted what
may be the first picpoul grapes in the Hills.

ΨΨΨΨΨ **Nouveau 2022, McLaren Vale** This is a great deal of fun. Bright and mid-weighted of mouthfeel, yet pulpy, effusive of energy and silken. Tamarind, sour cherry, strawberry and a skein of white pepper-doused acidity towing length. Crafted with consideration for the contemporary table. Interchangeable with top tier rosé, albeit, considerably more versatile. Kapow! Screw cap. 14% alc. RATING 93 DRINK 2022-2024 $28 NG ✪

Estate Blend GSM 2021, McLaren Vale 65/30/5% grenache/shiraz/mourvèdre. I'd like to see more of the latter to confer savouriness, more tannin and less obvious fruit. Plenty rich and lively, though. Delicious, if not a bit sweet, with briar, cardamom and clove restraining kirsch, lilac and spiced plum. Screw cap. 14.5% alc. RATING 93 DRINK 2021-2025 $32 NG ✪

Estate Shiraz 2021, McLaren Vale A smooth operator, exuding a phalanx of dark fruits, a potpourri of spice, anise and mocha- to vanillin-oak overtones. Full bodied, to be sure, but far from heavy. This will appease those seeking weight as much as freshness and a strong regional voice. Screw cap. 14.5% alc. RATING 92 DRINK 2022-2032 $35 NG

Syrah 2021, Adelaide Hills This is exceptional for the price. Mid-weighted of feel and brimming with the cool aura of high-quality syrah. Dried nori, blueberry, lilac and a swab of green olive tapenade. Best is the pepper-doused skein of freshness and furl of tannin at the finish, driving and corralling this immensely savoury and nourishing wine. Delicious. Screw cap. 14% alc. RATING 92 DRINK 2022-2027 $32 NG

Picpoul 2022, Adelaide Hills Picpoul, or 'lip stinger' in French, suits these parts. Lightweight and tensile, the grape's physiognomy, affinity with maritime settings and high-acid kit imparts an aura of confidence and optimism. Real freshness, natural of feel. Pithy and textural, to boot. Preserved lemon rind, nashi pear granita, yuzu, frangipani and spa salts careen long, with a salty linger. Screw cap. 11.5% alc. RATING 91 DRINK 2022-2026 $26 NG ✪

Pinot Noir Syrah 2021, Adelaide Hills A sappy, mid-weighted expression boasting red-fruit allusions, a whiff of hibiscus and some whole-bunch derived clove and white pepper accents. Sits effortlessly in the mouth. Deserved of a wide array of foods to do its versatility justice. A crunchy, imminently digestible simplicity is a virtue rather than a bane. Delicious! Screw cap. 13.5% alc. RATING 91 DRINK 2022-2024 $32 NG

Hills & Coast Shiraz 2021, McLaren Vale This is a pricepoint that hovers between possibility and improbability. Improbable because there is so little wine worth drinking in this zone. Lo and behold, this is good! Sure, the oak tannins are a bit scratchy, but the fruit is luscious. Blue and black fruits, florals, a strap of chewy licorice and a lick of vanilla. What's not to like? Screw cap. 14.5% alc. RATING 90 DRINK 2022-2027 $20 NG ✪

Lobethal Road Wines   ★★★★☆

2254 Onkaparinga Valley Road, Mount Torrens, SA 5244 **Region** Adelaide Hills **T** (08) 8389 4595 **www.**lobethalroad.com **Open** Thurs–Mon 11–5 **Winemaker** Michael Sykes **Viticulturist** David Neyle **Est.** 1998 **Dozens** 7500 **Vyds** 10.5ha
Dave Neyle and Inga Lidums bring diverse, but very relevant, experience to the Lobethal Road vineyard; the lion's share planted to shiraz, with smaller amounts of chardonnay, tempranillo, sauvignon blanc, graciano, pinot gris and roussanne. Dave has been in vineyard development and management in SA and Tasmania since '90. Inga has 25+ years' experience in marketing and graphic design, with a focus on the wine and food industries. The property is managed with minimal chemical input.

ΨΨΨΨΨ **Maja Late Disgorged 2017, Adelaide Hills** A beautifully defined nose of flint, candied citrus peel, chalk and brioche. Expansive girth, tenacious length and a palpable sense of dryness. A compelling marrow of complexity following 5 years on lees. Extremely classy domestic fizz. Diam. 12.3% alc. RATING 95 DRINK 2022-2028 $60 NG

Bacchant Chardonnay 2021, Adelaide Hills The regional pendulum is swinging away from reduction and here is a prime example of allowing the fruit, subtle and orchard of idiom, to flow effortlessly. Some creamy lees work and a dab of oak make for a subtle foundation, promoting transparency of place, culture and cultivar. Diam. 13.4% alc. RATING 94 DRINK 2022–2030 $45 NG

ŶŶŶŶŶ Maja Late Disgorged 2014, Adelaide Hills RATING 93 DRINK 2022–2035 $65 NG
Pinot Gris 2022, Adelaide Hills RATING 92 DRINK 2022–2025 $25 NG ✪
Bacchant Shiraz 2021, Adelaide Hills RATING 92 DRINK 2022–2030 $45 NG
Roussanne 2021, Adelaide Hills RATING 92 DRINK 2022–2026 $25 NG ✪

Logan Wines   ★★★★★

1320 Castlereagh Highway, Apple Tree Flat, Mudgee, NSW 2850 **Region** Mudgee
T (02) 6373 1333 **www**.loganwines.com.au **Open** 7 days 10–5 **Winemaker** Peter Logan, Jake Sheedy **Viticulturist** Graeme Brown **Est.** 1997 **Dozens** 50 000
Logan is a family-owned and -operated business with an emphasis on cool-climate wines from Orange and Mudgee. Owner and head winemaker Peter Logan majored in biology and chemistry at Macquarie University, moving into the pharmaceutical world working as a process chemist. In a reversal of the usual roles, his father encouraged him to change careers and Peter obtained a graduate diploma in oenology from the University of Adelaide in '96. The winery and tasting room are situated on the Mudgee vineyard in Apple Tree Flat.

ŶŶŶŶŶ Ridge of Tears Shiraz 2021, Mudgee Stewed rhubarb, pomegranate juice and juniper berries lead to sappy blackcurrant stems, cardamom pods and fennel seeds. Lifted acidity brings forth baking spices and tightly knit, fine tannins. A wine of grace and poise. Screw cap. 13.5% alc. RATING 95 DRINK 2022–2035 $60 SW
Ridge of Tears Riesling 2021, Orange Green apple, wild sweet alyssum flower, lime sorbet and crushed sandstone. The palate is brimming with mouth-watering acidity and finite fruit sweetness. This is a riesling latent with texture and power wrapped in pretty florals. Screw cap. 12% alc. RATING 95 DRINK 2022–2042 $50 SW ✪

ŶŶŶŶŶ Vintage M Cuvee 2019, Orange RATING 93 DRINK 2022–2027 $45 CM
Pinot Noir 2021, Orange RATING 93 DRINK 2022–2035 $45 SW
Clementine Pinot Gris 2022, Central Ranges RATING 92 DRINK 2022–2028 $25 SW ✪
Weemala Riesling 2022, Clare Valley Orange RATING 92 DRINK 2022–2032 $20 SW ✪
Weemala Pinot Noir 2022, Orange RATING 92 DRINK 2022–2028 $20 SW ✪
Clementine de la mer 2022, Central Ranges RATING 91 DRINK 2022–2028 $25 SW ✪
Shiraz 2021, Orange RATING 91 DRINK 2022–2030 $45 SW
Sauvignon Blanc 2022, Orange RATING 90 DRINK 2022–2030 $25 SW ✪
Weemala Pinot Gris 2022, Orange RATING 90 DRINK 2022–2028 $20 SW ✪

Lone Palm Vineyard   ★★★★

PO Box 288, Tanunda, SA 5352 **Region** Barossa Valley
T 0411 861 604 **www**.lonepalmvineyard.com.au **Open** Not **Winemaker** Thomas White **Est.** 2019 **Dozens** 1500 **Vyds** 7ha
Lone Palm has 7ha of shiraz, planted in '92, at Marananga on the western ridge of the Barossa Valley. The vineyard gets its name from a single old palm tree next to the original cottage, built in the late 1800s. The wines are made in a generous style, open-fermented slowly and gently basket-pressed.

ŶŶŶŶŶ Hillside Shiraz 2021, Barossa Valley Deep blackberry and black cherry fruits with hints of macerated plums, dark chocolate, fruitcake spice, cedar, Cherry Ripe, licorice, olive tapenade and pan juices. Cassis and kirsch on the palate with some broody graphite tones, oak spice, chocolatey tannin and latent power. Screw cap. 14.5% alc. **RATING** 93 **DRINK** 2023-2033 $120 DB

Crossings Shiraz 2022, Barossa Valley Deep magenta with aromas of satsuma plum, blueberry and dark cherry cut with baking spices, earth, violets, licorice and fruitcake. These transpose neatly over to the palate, which shows excellent fruit density, fine tannin and layered spice and dark fruits on the finish. Screw cap. 14.5% alc. **RATING** 92 **DRINK** 2023-2030 $60 DB

Hillside Shiraz 2020, Barossa Valley Deep crimson in colour with a vibrant, plummy nose of macerated plums and mulberry fruits. Plenty of spice layered below along with hints of licorice, violets, cedar, cassis and earth. These aromas transpose neatly over to the palate, which shows fine, chocolatey tannins and good sustain on the exit. Screw cap. 14.5% alc. **RATING** 92 **DRINK** 2023-2033 $120 DB

Crossings Shiraz 2021, Barossa Valley Vibrant crimson with bright-smelling red plum, nectarine and red cherry fruits with hints of spice, red licorice, citrus blossom, dried citrus rind, cedar and earth. Quite sprightly and lively in the mouth with a raft of red berry fruits, fine, sandy tannins and an energetic line of acidity for propulsion. Screw cap. 14.5% alc. **RATING** 91 **DRINK** 2023-2030 $60 DB

Crossings Shiraz 2020, Barossa Valley Deep crimson with plush, plummy fruit on a bed of baking spices, purple flowers, dark chocolate, licorice and earth. Fresh and sprightly on the palate with lovely ripe plummy fruit, gentle sandy tannins and a spicy plume of fruit and earth on the exit. Screw cap. 14.5% alc. **RATING** 91 **DRINK** 2023-2030 $60 DB

Lone Star Creek Vineyard ★★★★

75 Owens Rd, Woori Yallock, Vic 3139 (postal) **Region** Yarra Valley
T 0414 282 629 **www**.lonestarcreekwines.com.au **Open** Not **Winemaker** Franco D'Anna **Viticulturist** Steve Sadlier **Est.** 1997 **Dozens** 800 **Vyds** 22ha
The Lone Star Creek vineyard was established in '97 by Robin Wood and Gillian Bowers, who are primarily contract growers; '17 was the first vintage under their own label. Pinot noir (52%), pinot gris (23%), chardonnay (15%), sauvignon blanc (5%) and syrah (5%) are planted. Situated on the border of Woori Yallock and Hoddles Creek, the cool-climate Upper Yarra fruit was sold to wineries including Hoddles Creek Estate, so when the time came to start producing wine under the Lone Star Creek Vineyard label, enlisting Hoddles Creek's own Franco D'Anna as winemaker was an obvious choice. The vineyard is not subject to strictly organic management, but the philosophy with both the viticulture and winemaking is one of minimal intervention.

ɬɬɬɬ **Pinot Gris 2022, Yarra Valley** A varietal pale salmon hue. I really like the touch of reduction with its delicate pear, strawberry and spice aromas. Has excellent freshness to go with the textural mid-palate before finishing chalky and dry. Screw cap. 12.5% alc. **RATING** 93 **DRINK** 2022-2025 $24 PR ✪

Syrah 2021, Yarra Valley A youthful crimson-purple, this needs a few swirls to open up before revealing some aromas of white plum and dark cherry fruits, freshly cracked green peppercorn and a hint of dark cocoa nibs. The palate is savoury and with its sinewy tannins, this crying out for some food or another year or two in the bottle. Screw cap. 12.5% alc. **RATING** 90 **DRINK** 2022-2027 $33 PR

Lonely Shore ★★★★

18 Bavin Street, Denmark, WA 6333 (postal) **Region** Denmark
T 0418 907 594 **www**.lonelyshore.com.au **Open** Not **Winemaker** Liam Carmody **Est.** 2014 **Dozens** 200 **Vyds** 2ha
Liam Carmody graduated from Curtin University in '03, since working in Sonoma, California, NZ, France, South Africa and the Mornington Peninsula before settling in Denmark and taking up a full-time winemaking role at Forest Hill. Thus Lonely Shore is very much a busman's holiday. The grapes come from the dry-grown DeiTos vineyard near Manjimup.

ɬɬɬɬ **DeiTos Vineyard Pinot Noir 2022, Manjimup** A lovely perfume of sour cherry, smoky spice, truffle, dried herb and eucalyptus. The palate is set similarly with very firm, dry and smoky tannins, dried cherry, licorice and a smoky spice finish. Very savoury, succulent and structured overall. It's a serious feeling wine, but a bit out of the box, and in that, not untoward. Screw cap. 13% alc. **RATING** 93 **DRINK** 2023–2035 $45 MB

Longhouse Wines ★★★★

385 Palmers Lane, Pokolbin, NSW 2320 **Region** Hunter Valley
T 0412 564 777 **www**.longhousewines.com.au **Open** By appt **Winemaker** Greg Schipp, Jo Baker, James Clarke **Est.** 2011
Longhouse Wines began when architecture student Jo Baker decided to teach architecture students to move beyond the classroom and give them practical experience in building. The Palmers Lane property was purchased, and the Longhouse designed. Over the next 2 years, students from across Australia and overseas came to the building site, picked up tools, and put the three-unit building together. There was also a neglected chardonnay vineyard around the Longhouse, and Jo (with a dual architecture and horticultural background), Greg Schipp (a Newcastle lawyer studying wine science at CSU) and James Clarke (a Newcastle doctor) set about the revitalisation of the vineyard.

♟♟♟♟♀ **H Single Vineyard Grenache 2021, McLaren Vale** A good grenache. Sap and sweetness of fruit are placated by salty freshness and some welcome tannic mettle. Gentle, mind you. But beautifully proportioned as riffs of kirsch, pomegranate and Seville orange peel linger long and sweet. Screw cap. 14.5% alc. **RATING** 92 **DRINK** 2022–2025 $35 NG

Longview Vineyard ★★★★★

154 Pound Road, Macclesfield, SA 5153 **Region** Adelaide Hills
T (08) 8388 9694 **www**.longviewvineyard.com.au **Open** Wed–Sun 11–4, Mon–Tues by appt **Winemaker** Peter Saturno, Brian Walsh **Viticulturist** Chris Mein **Est.** 1995 **Dozens** 20 000 **Vyds** 60ha
With a lifelong involvement in wine and hospitality, the Saturno family has been at the helm of Longview since '07. Plantings of barbera, grüner veltliner, riesling, pinot noir and new clones of chardonnay and pinot grigio were added to the existing shiraz, cabernet sauvignon, nebbiolo and sauvignon blanc. A new cellar door and kitchen was unveiled in '17, adding to 16 accommodation suites, a popular function room and unique food and wine events in the vineyard.

♟♟♟♟♟ **The Piece Shiraz 2020, Adelaide Hills** This is exceptional from the perspective of intensity, complexity and polished tannins, the latter a confluence of classy oak and massaged grape skins. A nourishing nose of umami-doused beef broth and spiced salumi. Thereafter, iodine, a sachet of Indian spices, a smear of tapenade, lapsang souchong and star anise. Screw cap. 13.5% alc. **RATING** 96 **DRINK** 2023–2035 $100 NG

Wagtail Pinot Noir Chardonnay Brut 2018, Adelaide Hills The first fermentation in oak, serving to build texture while conferring structural mettle. The second in bottle, with 42 months on lees imparting autolytic detail and further bandwidth of intensity. A seismic shift from the peachy attack to the chalky finish. Lovely domestic fizz. Diam. 12% alc. **RATING** 95 **DRINK** 2022–2030 $50 NG

Macclesfield Chardonnay 2021, Adelaide Hills Very good chardonnay. Taut, pungent and tensile, with relief provided by a creamy core of almond meal, white miso, nougatine and curd. Stone-fruit accents from white peach to nectarine carouse along bright acid lines. An attractive chewiness at the seams and a finish of compressed energy spring to life with a whirl of the glass. Lovely drinking. Screw cap. 12.5% alc. **RATING** 95 **DRINK** 2022–2032 $45 NG ✪

Whippet Sauvignon Blanc 2022, Adelaide Hills A late, cool vintage gave birth to a sauvignon blanc with a full suite of flavours ranging from snow peas to citrus to tropical. Good acid balance, too. Screw cap. 12.5% alc. **RATING** 94 **DRINK** 2023–2025 $25 JH ✪

🍷🍷🍷🍷🍷 Juno Rosato 2022, Adelaide Hills RATING 93 DRINK 2023-2024 $28 JH ✪
Macclesfield Riesling 2022, Adelaide Hills RATING 93 DRINK 2022-2030 $30 NG ✪
Macclesfield Cabernet Sauvignon 2021, Adelaide Hills RATING 93 DRINK 2023-2033 $45 NG
Jupiter Barbera 2021, Adelaide Hills RATING 93 DRINK 2022-2026 $40 NG
Macclesfield Syrah 2021, Adelaide Hills RATING 92 DRINK 2022-2029 $45 NG
Yakka Shiraz 2021, Adelaide Hills RATING 91 DRINK 2022-2027 $30 NG

Lost Buoy Wines

Level 7/431 King William St, Adelaide SA 5000 (postal) **Region** McLaren Vale
T 0438 803 876 **www.**lostbuoywines.com.au **Open** Not **Winemaker** Matt O'Leary
Est. 2010 **Dozens** 8000 **Vyds** 6.5ha
The Lost Buoy vineyard is perched high on the cliffs at Port Willunga in McLaren Vale, overlooking the Gulf of St Vincent. The 6.5ha 'home block' is planted to grenache and shiraz, the region's foundation varieties. The shiraz, grenache and rosé are made from estate-grown grapes, while the sauvignon blanc is sourced from the Adelaide Hills. The brand was purchased by Savitas Wines in '18 and all the wines are now made by Matt O'Leary.

🍷🍷🍷🍷🍷 Grenache 2021, McLaren Vale Yes there's some alcohol warmth but the flavours are excellent. Mineral, sweet raspberry, earth and sweet spice, the finish an attractive amalgam of rust, wood, fruit and flowers. The flavours themselves feel fresh, neat and unfettered. Screw cap. 15.5% alc. RATING 91 DRINK 2023-2027 $25 CM ✪
Shiraz 2021, McLaren Vale Simple but effective. Plum and milk chocolate flavours and fresh with them; there's good energy here. Raspberry and sweet hay/clove notes add extra lift and life. It all works nicely. Drink it young. Screw cap. 14.5% alc. RATING 91 DRINK 2023-2028 $25 CM ✪

Lost Farm Wines ★★★★☆

527 Glynburn Road, Hazelwood Park, SA 5063 (postal) **Region** Tasmania
T (08) 8397 7100 **www.**lostfarmwines.com.au **Open** Not **Winemaker** Richard Angove
Est. 2018 **Dozens** 2000
Fifth-generation South Australian winemaker and grapegrower Richard Angove fell in love with the Tamar Valley while working vintage in '08, but it took him a decade to realise his ambition to work with a small group of growers to produce wines in the region. Sparkling, pinot noir and a stunning chardonnay are made from well-established vineyards in the Tamar Valley.

🍷🍷🍷🍷🍷 Chardonnay 2021, Tasmania Pale straw in the glass with a striking nose of juicy white peach, citrus and nectarine fruits underscored by dreamy, cashew-like French oak, white flowers, oatmeal, almond paste and stone. Tight, scintillating acidity provides a vital pulse and the wine finishes with impressive clarity and detail. Fans out beautifully with a textural, light-phenolic tweak and a lovely white peach, citrus and roasted nut flourish. Screw cap. 13% alc. RATING 96 DRINK 2023-2029 $42 DB ✪
Pinot Noir 2021, Tasmania Bright, vibrant cherry red in the glass. A shy nose of red and dark cherry, raspberry and wild strawberry that opens with time in the glass. Deep spice and purple floral notes are joined by roasting game meats, hints of forest floor and a touch of creamy oak. Bright acidity and gentle tannins, with a medium-length finish that shows a chalky, savoury flourish. Screw cap. 13% alc. RATING 94 DRINK 2023-2028 $42 DB

🍷🍷🍷🍷🍷 Vintage Pinot Noir Chardonnay 2016, Tasmania RATING 91 DRINK 2023-2026 $50 DB

Lost Penny

538 Carrara Hill Road, Ebenezer, SA 5355 **Region** Barossa Valley
T 0418 857 094 **www**.lostpennywines.com **Open** By appt **Winemaker** Carol Riebke
Viticulturist Nick Riebke **Est.** 2017 **Dozens** 1800 **Vyds** 30ha
Sixth-generation Barossan winemaker and grapegrower couple Carol and Nick Riebke bottle shiraz, cabernet sauvignon and grenache primarily from their estate vineyard in Ebenezer, passed down through Nick's family since the late 1800s. Carol learnt her craft under Barossa winemaking legend John Glaetzer before establishing their family brand. 'We're gamblers!' Nick admits. 'It's the risk, the anticipation and the intrigue about what the next season will bring that keep us coming back for more!'

1891 Penny Shiraz 2020, Barossa Valley Deep crimson with aromas of bold black fruits and cassis with hints of blackstrap licorice, dark chocolate, deep spice, earth and violet. Full bodied, more cedary, vanillin oak flows in on the palate with a curtain of tight tannin and a swell of spice, cassis-like fruit on the finish. Diam. 15% alc. **RATING** 91 **DRINK** 2023–2029 $60 DB

Mischief Maker Montepulciano 2021, Barossa Valley Bright, purple-edged crimson in the glass, there is a real stony, savoury sense of composure about this wine. Plenty of red cherry and plummy notes with underlying tones of red licorice, earth, soft spice and purple florals, the tannins are powdery and fine and the acidity cuts a brisk pace, finishing with a flow of sour red cherry and spice. Diam. 13.5% alc. **RATING** 90 **DRINK** 2023–2025 $30 DB

Almond Row Shiraz 2020, Barossa Valley Vibrant crimson in the glass with aromas of blood plum, blackberry and cassis with hints of fruitcake spices, licorice and dark chocolate. Good fruit intensity and depth on the palate with some blue fruit high tones, gypsum-like tannins, bright acidity and a savoury, black-fruited palate shape on the exit. Diam. 14.5% alc. **RATING** 90 **DRINK** 2023–2027 $30 DB

Lou Miranda Estate

1876 Barossa Valley Way, Rowland Flat, SA 5352 **Region** Barossa Valley
T (08) 8524 4537 **www**.loumirandaestate.com.au **Open** Mon–Fri 10.30–4, w'ends 11–4
Winemaker Angela Miranda **Viticulturist** Andrew Nash **Est.** 2005 **Dozens** 20 000
Vyds 23.29ha
Lou Miranda's daughters Lisa, Angela and Victoria are the driving force behind the estate, albeit with continuing hands-on involvement from Lou. The jewels in the crown of the estate plantings are 0.5ha of mourvèdre planted in 1897 and 1.5ha of shiraz (and a tiny 0.14ha grenache) planted in 1907. The remaining vines have been planted gradually since '95, the varietal choice widened by cabernet sauvignon, merlot, chardonnay and pinot grigio.

Fierce III Shiraz Grenache Mataro 2019, Barossa A plummy, spicy SGM. Deep crimson, fragrant and flush with pure black and red fruits cut with baking spices, turned earth, pressed flowers, raspberry coulis, roasting meats and licorice. Tight and sinewy with compact, sandy tannin support and a spicy black-fruited finish. Screw cap. 14.5% alc. **RATING** 91 **DRINK** 2023–2028 $45 DB

Fierce III Shiraz 2019, Barossa Valley Deep crimson in the glass with notes of blackberry jam, crème de cassis and macerated dark plums. It's followed by a purple, floral flourish of licorice, baking spices and earth. Sinewy and black-fruited in the mouth with compact tannins and graphite-esque broodiness to finish. Screw cap. 14.5% alc. **RATING** 90 **DRINK** 2023–2028 $45 DB

Lowestoft

680 Main Road, Berriedale, Tas 7011 **Region** Tasmania
T (08) 9282 5450 **www**.lowestoft.wine **Open** By appt **Winemaker** Liam McElhinney
Viticulturist John Fogarty **Est.** 2019 **Dozens** 1250 **Vyds** 3ha
A premium Tasmanian brand of WA-based Fogarty Wine Group, which purchased the 3ha Lowestoft vineyard and historic house at Berriedale in '19. Substantial plantings on 2 properties at Forcett and Richmond in the Coal River Valley bring the group's holdings to

some 200ha, making it Tasmania's 2nd-largest vineyard owner. Winemaking is conducted at Tasmanian Vintners, the state's biggest contract facility, in which the group purchased a 50% share. Lowestoft joins Fogarty's lauded suite of boutique wineries across Western Australia, Lake's Folly in the Hunter Valley and Dalwhinnie in the Pyrenees.

🍷🍷🍷🍷🍷 **La Meilleure Chardonnay 2021, Tasmania** Pale straw in the glass with aromas of white peach, nectarine and grapefruit with a nice match/sulphide nuance and hints of soft spice, oatmeal, white flowers, nougat, lemon curd and clotted cream. There is impressive detail, clarity and composition here with a long, wonderfully expressive pure flow across the palate on rails of mineral and stone. A picture of tension and release. Beautiful drinking. Screw cap. 13.1% alc. **RATING** 97 **DRINK** 2023–2033 $100 DB ✪

🍷🍷🍷🍷🍷 **La Maison Pinot Noir 2021, Tasmania** Pure red plum and dark cherry fruits strut their stuff here with hints of five-spice, sous bois, dried raspberry, cranberry, black tea and vanilla, with light roast game further in the distance. Savoury and true with excellent fruit depth and purity, chalky tannins providing support. Screw cap. 14% alc. **RATING** 96 **DRINK** 2023–2035 $130 DB
Chardonnay 2021, Tasmania An immediate wash of mealy lemon, grapefruit, white peach and nectarine fruit notes with hints of fine spice, white flowers, flint, crushed river stone, nougat, oyster shell and sexy French oak. There is a swirl of struck-match complexity in the mix, and the wine presents an expansive palate with plenty of clarity, tension and complexity. A long, dreamy finish, too. Screw cap. 13% alc. **RATING** 95 **DRINK** 2023–2030 $75 DB
Pinot Noir 2021, Tasmania A bright, complex pinot noir. Pure red and dark cherry, raspberry and wild strawberry fruits with hints of five-spice, teacake, mushroom, purple floral and subtle leaf litter tones. There is a nice sense of space and clarity, fine acidity providing the pulse and a sustained finish studded with game, amaro and spice. Screw cap. 14% alc. **RATING** 95 **DRINK** 2023–2030 $75 DB
Single Vineyard Pinot Noir 2021, Tasmania Bright cherry fruit studded with spice, pomegranate, pressed flowers, cranberry, mountain herbs and subtle undergrowth at the core. There is a pleasing depth to the dark cherry and wild strawberry fruits with fine powdery tannins, a bright mineral-laden line and a composed, savoury swish of the tail on the exit. Screw cap. 13.5% alc. **RATING** 95 **DRINK** 2023–2030 $100 DB

🍷🍷🍷🍷🍷 **Reserve Brut Méthode Traditionnelle NV, Tasmania RATING** 92 $75 DB

Lyons Will Estate ★★★★★

60 Whalans Track, Lancefield, Vic 3435 **Region** Macedon Ranges
T 0412 681 940 **www.**lyonswillestate.com.au **Open** Sat–Sun 11–5 **Winemaker** Oliver Rapson, Renata Morello **Viticulturist** Oliver Rapson, Renata Morello **Est.** 1996
Dozens 1500 **Vyds** 6.5ha

Oliver Rapson (with a background in digital advertising) and Renata Morello (a physiotherapist with a PhD in public health) believed the Macedon Ranges has the best of both worlds: less than an hour's drive to Melbourne, ideal for pinot and chardonnay and still sparsely settled. The property had 2ha of vines planted in '96: pinot noir and chardonnay. Over time they have extended the pinot noir and chardonnay and also planted riesling and gamay. Oliver makes the pinot noir and chardonnay, Renata the riesling and gamay.

🍷🍷🍷🍷🍷 **Riesling 2022, Macedon Ranges** Spine-tingling freshness from go to whoa thanks to its superfine acidity. There's more, the lime juice and zest, wafts of lemon verbena and the overall talc-like texture ensure this is a lovely drink with or without food. Diam. 11.3% alc. **RATING** 95 **DRINK** 2022–2032 $39 JF ✪
Pinot Noir 2021, Macedon Ranges Gosh, this is packed with flavour, fine tannins and plenty of acidity. Sure, there's the usual eucalyptus/mint character but there's so much else here it's just like seasoning. Spiced red and morello cherries, sumac and pepper with splashes of Averna with cedary oak bolstering the palate. Screw cap. 12.8% alc. **RATING** 95 **DRINK** 2024–2034 $48 JF ✪

ŤŤŤŤŢ Rosé 2022, Macedon Ranges RATING 93 DRINK 2022–2025 $33 JF ✪
Chardonnay 2021, Macedon Ranges RATING 92 DRINK 2023–2031 $42 JF
Pinot Noir 2020, Macedon Ranges RATING 91 DRINK 2023–2029 $45 JF

M. Chapoutier Australia   ★★★★★

141–143 High Street, Heathcote, Vic 3523 **Region** Various
T (03) 5433 2411 **www**.mchapoutieraustralia.com **Open** W'ends 10–5 or by appt
Winemaker Michel Chapoutier **Est.** 1998 **Dozens** 8000 **Vyds** 48ha
M. Chapoutier Australia is the eponymous offshoot of the famous Rhône Valley producer. The
business focuses on vineyards in the Pyrenees, Heathcote and Beechworth with collaboration
from Ron Laughton of Jasper Hill and Rick Kinzbrunner of Giaconda. After first establishing
a vineyard in Heathcote adjacent to Jasper Hill, Chapoutier purchased the Malakoff vineyard
in the Pyrenees to create Domaine Terlato & Chapoutier (the Terlato & Chapoutier joint
venture was established in 2000; Terlato still owns 50% of the Malakoff vineyard). In '09
Michel Chapoutier purchased 2 neighbouring vineyards, Landsborough Valley and Shays Flat;
all these are now fully owned by Tournon. (Tournon consists of Landsborough Valley and
Shays Flat estates in the Pyrenees and Lady's Lane Estate in Heathcote.)

ŤŤŤŤŤ **Domaine Terlato & Chapoutier L-Block Shiraz 2019, Pyrenees** Smoky
oak notes and cherry/plum fruit meet woody spice, game, peanut oil and floral
elements. It's complex, silken, blessed with fine-grained tannin and has good
extension through the finish. There's a lot going on in this wine but it feels
svelte throughout, always a good combination. Cork. 14.5% alc. **RATING** 95
DRINK 2024–2034 $80 CM
...Ergo Sum Shiraz 2018, Beechworth Good Beechworth shiraz always has
an X-factor, and this is good Beechworth shiraz. Blueberry and blackberry jelly
flavours are served with liberal splashes of sweet spice and florals. Anise, violets,
deli meats and toast – all these characters have walk-on roles. It's a delicious
experience. Screw cap. 14.1% alc. **RATING** 95 **DRINK** 2023–2032 $68 CM

ŤŤŤŤŢ **Domaine Terlato & Chapoutier Lieu-Dit Malakoff Shiraz 2019,** Pyrenees
RATING 93 **DRINK** 2023–2030 $40 CM
Tournon Lady's Lane Vineyard Shiraz 2019, Heathcote **RATING** 92
DRINK 2023–2028 $50 CM
Tournon Mathilda Viognier Marsanne 2021, Victoria **RATING** 90
DRINK 2023–2026 $20 CM ✪

Mac Forbes   ★★★★★

770 Healesville – Koo Wee Rup Road, Healesville, Vic 3777 **Region** Yarra Valley
T 0484 091 031 **www**.macforbes.com **Open** 1st Sat of the month 11–4 **Winemaker**
Hannah Hodges **Viticulturist** Owen Littlejohns **Est.** 2004 **Dozens** 8000 **Vyds** 13ha
Mac Forbes cut his teeth at Mount Mary, where he was winemaker for several years before
heading overseas in '02. He spent 2 years in London working for Southcorp in a marketing
role, then travelled to Portugal and Austria to gain further experience. He returned to the
Yarra Valley prior to the '05 vintage, purchasing grapes to make his own wines. Today, Mac
makes a Victorian range and a Yarra Valley range from grower fruit, and a single-vineyard
range from his own sites, which have been increasing and improving through trial and
error since he got his hands on the Woori Yallock vineyard in '11. They have been dry
farmed since '15, with a move towards organics from '17.

ŤŤŤŤŤ **RS15 Riesling 2022, Strathbogie Ranges** A pale, bright green gold. Very
restrained with its delicate bouquet of green apple, nashi pear and pink grapefruit.
Chalky textured, finely detailed and with balanced and perfectly integrated acidity,
you'd struggle to guess that this has 15g/L of R.S. A beautifully put-together wine
that should age effortlessly. Screw cap. 10.5% alc. **RATING** 96 **DRINK** 2022–2032
$45 PR ✪ ♥
Yarra Junction Village Chardonnay 2022, Yarra Valley It's a coin toss
between this and the Woori Yallock as my pick of the Village series wines

in '22. Complex with aromas of tangerines, just-ripened orchard fruits, pink grapefruit and a little oyster shell. Tightly wound with great acidity. Balanced and mouthcoating, finishing pithy and long. Screw cap. 11.5% alc. **RATING** 96 **DRINK** 2022-2028 $55 PR ✪

Woori Yallock Village Chardonnay 2022, Yarra Valley A very bright green gold. Opens with aromas of red apples, white nectarines, lemon-scented verbena and an attractive vanillin spice character. Seamless on the palate but still compact and tightly wound. Finishes long, taut and saline. Excellent now and it will age well. Screw cap. 12% alc. **RATING** 96 **DRINK** 2022-2028 $55 PR ✪

Yarra Junction Village Pinot Noir 2022, Yarra Valley A very bright crimson purple. Opens with scents of spiced raspberries, pomegranate, rose petals and mountain herbs. A lot is going on here! Very bright on the finely tuned, pure fruited, structured and well-balanced palate, too. I like this a lot now, but all the components are here for this to age effortlessly. Screw cap. 11.5% alc. **RATING** 96 **DRINK** 2022-2028 $55 PR ✪

Syrah 2022, Yarra Valley Deep ruby red. Vibrant and focused on the nose with an array of red and blue fruits, violets and mountain herbs. Medium bodied and plush, this delicious and energetic wine is framed by silky, very persistent tannins and juicy acidity. A thoughtful and well-put-together wine. Screw cap. 13.5% alc. **RATING** 96 **DRINK** 2022-2030 $38 PR ✪

Riesling 2022, Strathbogie Ranges A brilliant green gold. Very pure fruited with fresh citrus and jasmine, some lime pith and orange blossom. Gentle and chalky textured, the balance between the fruit, sugar (3g/L RS) and acidity is absolutely spot on. Screw cap. 12.5% alc. **RATING** 95 **DRINK** 2022-2032 $33 PR ✪

Coldstream Village Pinot Noir 2022, Yarra Valley A light ruby red. Aromas of freshly poached strawberries, spices and a hint of rose petals make for the most accessible, at this stage, of the 5 Village pinots in '22. Already delicious with its generous yet gentle palate and supple tannins. Just a lovely drink. Screw cap. 12% alc. **RATING** 95 **DRINK** 2022-2028 $55 PR

Gladysdale Village Pinot Noir 2022, Yarra Valley A light, bright crimson. Cool fruited with aromas of raspberries, redcurrants and a little pomegranate together with some gentle florals and spice. There's good vibrancy on the palate, too, with fine-grained, silky tannins and chalky acidity keeping the wine balanced and structured. Screw cap. 11% alc. **RATING** 94 **DRINK** 2022-2030 $55 PR

Gembrook Village Pinot Noir 2022, Yarra Valley Fragrant and darkly fruited, this offers black cherries and satsuma plums with hints of earth, clove and bay leaf. Firmly structured but well balanced, the medium-bodied palate is sapid, ferrous and long. Built to go with aged rib eye and the like, this will become more complex and softer with time. Screw cap. 12% alc. **RATING** 94 **DRINK** 2022-2032 $55 PR

EB79 Mencia 2021, Yarra Valley Spicy and full of intrigue with its aromas of ripe satsuma plums, dark sour cherry, crushed violets and dark cacao nibs. Medium bodied, this fruit-driven wine saturates the palate with fruit and tannins while remaining fresh and very digestible. It's handling protein and spice in its stride right now. Cork. 12.5% alc. **RATING** 94 **DRINK** 2022-2028 $40 PR ✪

🍷🍷🍷🍷 **Chardonnay 2022, Yarra Valley** **RATING** 93 **DRINK** 2022-2026 $38 PR
RS20 Riesling 2022, Strathbogie Ranges **RATING** 93 **DRINK** 2022-2028 $45 PR
EB80 G-Train Grenache 2021, Yarra Valley **RATING** 93 **DRINK** 2022-2027 $40 PR
Gladysdale Village Chardonnay 2022, Yarra Valley **RATING** 92 **DRINK** 2022-2028 $55 PR
EB81 Suave, Hey Garganega 2022, King Valley **RATING** 92 **DRINK** 2022-2026 $40 PR
Pinot Noir 2022, Yarra Valley **RATING** 92 **DRINK** 2022-2028 $38 PR
By Any Other X01 Rosé 2022, Strathbogie Ranges **RATING** 92 **DRINK** 2022-2024 $28 PR ✪

Woori Yallock Village Pinot Noir 2022, Yarra Valley RATING 90
DRINK 2022-2027 $55 PR
Hugh Cabernets 2021, Yarra Valley RATING 90 DRINK 2023-2029 $85 PR

Macaw Creek Wines

Macaw Creek Road, Riverton, SA 5412 **Region** Mount Lofty Ranges
T (08) 8847 2657 www.macawcreekwines.com.au **Open** By appt **Winemaker** Rodney
Hooper **Est.** 1992 **Dozens** 8000 **Vyds** 10ha
The property on which Macaw Creek Wines is established has been owned by the Hooper
family since the 1850s, but development of the estate vineyards did not begin until 1995.
The Macaw Creek brand was established in '92 with wines made from grapes from other
regions. Rodney Hooper is a highly qualified and skilled winemaker with experience in many
parts of Australia and in Germany, France and the US. The wines are certified organic and
free of preservatives.

🍷🍷🍷🍷 **Reserve Shiraz 2020, Langhorne Creek** The oak handling feels apposite,
buried amid the wine's hot-climate extract and weight. There is plenty there, to
be sure, yet the decorous oak tannins find confluence with the flow of darker
fruits, anise and bitter mint chocolate. The heavy, chocolatey style is defined by
skilfully extracted grape tannins, gritty, chewy and juicy, across the tail. Good
drinking. Screw cap. 14% alc. RATING 91 DRINK 2022-2032 $35 NG

McGlashan's Wallington Estate

225 Swan Bay Road, Wallington, Vic 3221 **Region** Geelong
T (03) 5250 5760 www.mcglashans.com.au **Open** Fri–Sun 11–5 **Winemaker** Robin
Brockett (Contract) **Est.** 1996 **Dozens** 2500 **Vyds** 12ha
Russell and Jan McGlashan began the establishment of their vineyard in 1996. Chardonnay
(6ha) and pinot noir (4ha) make up the bulk of the plantings, the remainder shiraz and pinot
gris (1ha each). The wines are made by Robin Brockett, with his usual skill and attention to
detail. The cellar door is shared with FarmDog brewing.

🍷🍷🍷🍷 **Bellarine Peninsula Shiraz 2021, Geelong** Ripe red and blue fruits sit
alongside aromas of lavender, sage and cracked black pepper. Even though this
had just been bottled when I tasted it, the oak is already well integrated. As for
the palate, it's ripe and sweet fruited but equally it's balanced with good acidity
and silky, plush tannins in support. A very pleasurable mouthful. Screw cap.
14% alc. RATING 92 DRINK 2022-2028 $42 PR
Bellarine Peninsula Rosé 2022, Geelong 60/40% pinot noir/shiraz. A light,
bright salmon colour. This flavourful and fruit-driven rosé has aromas of bright
red fruits and a touch of citrus. Dry, with a refreshing orange pith flourish on the
finish. Screw cap. 12.5% alc. RATING 91 DRINK 2022-2024 $35 PR

McGuigan Wines

447 McDonalds Road, Pokolbin, NSW 2320 **Region** Hunter Valley
T (02) 4998 4111 www.mcguiganwines.com.au **Open** 7 days 10–5
Winemaker Thomas Jung **Est.** 1992 **Dozens** 4.3 million **Vyds** 2000ha
McGuigan Wines is an Australian wine brand operating under parent company Australian
Vintage Ltd. McGuigan represents 4 generations of Australian winemaking and, while its
roots are firmly planted in the Hunter Valley, its vine holdings extend across SA, from the
Barossa Valley to the Adelaide Hills and the Eden and Clare valleys, into Vic and NSW.
McGuigan Wines' processing facilities operate out of 3 core regions: the Hunter Valley,
Murray Darling and the Barossa Valley.

🍷🍷🍷🍷🍷 **Personal Reserve Vanessa Vale Vineyard Shiraz 2019, Hunter Valley** The
deep colour has changed little since bottled, the body with pools of luscious black
fruits, tannins that, given enough time, will make a complete wine. This wine

needs 15+ years to slim down and develop spices and other complexities of age. Cork. 14.5% alc. **RATING** 94 **DRINK** 2025–2035 $60 JH

ŶŶŶŶ **Bin 9000 Semillon 2022, Hunter Valley** **RATING** 92 **DRINK** 2023–2030 $25 JH ✪
Personal Reserve Hunter Ridge Vineyard Chardonnay 2022, Hunter Valley **RATING** 92 **DRINK** 2023–2028 $40 JH

McHenry Hohnen Vintners ★★★★★

10406 Bussell Hwy, Witchcliffe, WA 6285 **Region** Margaret River
T (08) 9757 9600 **www**.mchenryhohnen.com.au **Open** 7 days 10.30–4.30
Winemaker Jacopo Dalli Cani, Henry Wynn **Viticulturist** Simon Keall **Est.** 2004
Dozens 7500 **Vyds** 50ha
The McHenry and Hohnen families have a long history of grapegrowing and winemaking in Margaret River. They joined forces in '04 to create McHenry Hohnen with the aim of producing wines honest to region, site and variety. Vines have been established on the McHenry, Calgardup Brook and Rocky Road properties, all farmed biodynamically.

ŶŶŶŶŶ **Sauvignon Blanc 2022, Margaret River** Texture aplenty. Expect a fragrance of makrut lime and curry leaves, it's smoky and a little flinty, citrusy with finger lime pop and some creaminess. It's a fantastic drink, refreshing and lively yet complex and detailed. Screw cap. 13% alc. **RATING** 96 **DRINK** 2022–2030 $35 JF ✪ ♥
Burnside Vineyard Chardonnay 2021, Margaret River This wine is citrusy, fine and flinty with delicate sulphides. Yum. It builds and unfurls with a subtle line of lees and texture. Ooh. And then explodes with racy acidity and electrifying energy to ensure it finishes long and pure. Woah! Screw cap. 13.3% alc.
RATING 96 **DRINK** 2022–2032 $80 JF
Calgardup Brook Vineyard Chardonnay 2021, Margaret River Precision, definition and length. There's the usual citrus theme going on here, the pink grapefruit and pith, zest and juicy acidity. There's also the flintiness, the seamless integration of oak, the attention to detail throughout and mostly, the energy and drive. Complex and complete. Screw cap. 13% alc. **RATING** 96 **DRINK** 2022–2032 $80 JF
Rolling Stone 2019, Margaret River A harmonious wine, certainly firmly structured with stately tannins but all in sync. Aromas and flavours roll through like waves: fresh tobacco, violets, nori, cassis and mulberries, cedary oak and spices with a whiff of menthol in the background. Full bodied, detailed and complex. Just wow. Screw cap. 14% alc. **RATING** 96 **DRINK** 2024–2040 $135 JF
Chloé 2022, Margaret River Mataro is the stepping stone for this super-dry and refreshing rosé. Aromas merely flutter in – rose petal, a dusting of spice and smoked meats. The palate is where all the action lies. Racy thanks to its acidity, plus there's texture and a light phenolic grip making this pleasing to the last drop. Screw cap. 12.8% alc. **RATING** 95 **DRINK** 2022–2024 $35 JF ✪
Apiary Block Chardonnay 2022, Margaret River Cloudy with a lovely straw hue, mineral character and flavour aplenty ranging from citrus, lime jelly and ginger spice to lemon curd. It's long and pure with texture, depth and fine-acid structure. It's ultra-refreshing and so damn drinkable. Deceptive, because it's not a simple wine. It has detail and layers. I could drink this all day. Or night. Screw cap. 13% alc. **RATING** 95 **DRINK** 2022–2028 $35 JF ✪
Hazel's Vineyard Chardonnay 2021, Margaret River Great wine. Yellow stone fruit, grapefruit and pith plus a range of spices. The flavours build across the generous palate filled out by creamy, nutty lees and some chicken stock flavours, which are lees derived. Yup, moreish and savoury. Screw cap. 13.3% alc.
RATING 95 **DRINK** 2022–2031 $80 JF
Laterite Hills Chardonnay 2021, Margaret River Laterite Hills is about sourcing fruit off several sites and blending it into one harmonious wine. It works a treat. This is composed, delicious and stylish. Expect white peach, grapefruit, tangy zest and finger lime pop. There's texture, a slip of creaminess

and neat acidity to bring it all together. Screw cap. 12.9% alc. **RATING** 95 **DRINK** 2022-2031 $45 JF ✪

Hazel's Vineyard Grenache Shiraz Mataro 2021, Margaret River This is smokin'. Lovely, tangy, juicy fruit all spiced up with pepper and cinnamon, sarsaparilla and turmeric, cured meats making an appearance. Lots on the go with raw silk tannins, plenty of refreshing acidity and evenness across the medium-bodied palate. Screw cap. 14.5% alc. **RATING** 95 **DRINK** 2023-2031 $45 JF ✪ ♥

♟♟♟♟♀ **Marsanne Roussanne 2022, Margaret River RATING** 93 **DRINK** 2022-2028 $35 JF ✪
BDX 2021, Margaret River RATING 93 **DRINK** 2024-2035 $45 JF
Hazel's Vineyard Tempranillo 2021, Margaret River RATING 93 **DRINK** 2023-2030 $45 JF
Hazel's Vineyard Zinfandel 2021, Margaret River RATING 92 **DRINK** 2023-2031 $55 JF

McKellar Ridge Wines   ★★★★

2 Euroka Avenue, Murrumbateman, NSW 2582 **Region** Canberra District
T 0409 780 861 **www**.mckellarridgewines.com.au **Open** Sat 10-4, Sun 12-4 or by appt
Winemaker John Sekoranja, Marina Sekoranja **Viticulturist** John Sekoranja, Marina Sekoranja **Est.** 2005 **Dozens** 800 **Vyds** 5.5ha
Call it serendipity, but the day John Sekoranja retired from a corporate life in '16, he and wife Marina were at a wine dinner and met McKellar Ridge's founders, Brian and Janet Johnston. They struck up a friendship and soon enough the Sekoranjas were doing vintage. As it turned out, the Johnstons were retiring. Enter new owners John and Marina. While Marina gave up a successful nutrition and dietetic business, both are completing degrees in wine science at Charles Sturt University. Riesling, shiraz, shiraz-viognier and Bordeaux varieties form the core range. With close to 5ha to manage, including the cellar door on weekends, they are busy. And Marina says they are loving every minute of it.

♟♟♟♟♀ **Shiraz 2021, Canberra District** This took out Top Gold and Best Red at the 2022 Australian Cool Climate Wine Show, which is terrific. It is oaky, sweet and cedary with plush dark fruit all plums and blueberries laden with spices and tamarind. Fleshy on the palate and fuller bodied with gritty tannins that just catch on the finish. More time in bottle or a chargrilled steak if opening tonight. Screw cap. 13.4% alc. **RATING** 93 **DRINK** 2023-2033 $50 JF

McLeish Estate Wines   ★★★★★

462 De Beyers Road, Pokolbin, NSW 2320 **Region** Hunter Valley
T (02) 4998 7754 **www**.mcleishestatewines.com.au **Open** 7 days 10-5
Winemaker Xanthe Hatcher **Viticulturist** Ted Nicolai **Est.** 1985 **Dozens** 8000 **Vyds** 17ha
Bob and Maryanne McLeish have established a particularly successful business based on estate plantings. The wines are of consistently high quality, and more than a few have accumulated show records leading to gold medal-encrusted labels. Xanthe Hatcher (Pooles Rock) took over the contract winemaking from Andrew Thomas in '20.

♟♟♟♟♟ **Reserve Semillon 2022, Hunter Valley** Hand-picked fruit ex-Block 3 of the estate vineyard. Whole-bunch pressed, fermented with a neutral yeast. When complexity merges with purity you have something special. Very difficult to spit the wine out in the course of tasting numerous young semillons. Screw cap. 11.4% alc. **RATING** 96 **DRINK** 2023-2042 $45 JH ✪
Cellar Reserve Semillon 2016, Hunter Valley Uses the usual McLeish approach of picking at a series of baumés – truly a wine made in the vineyard. Toast has made its appearance on the bouquet; lemon juice/butter/zest on the rewarding palate. Screw cap. 10.5% alc. **RATING** 96 **DRINK** 2023-2036 $80 JH
Cellar Reserve Cabernet Sauvignon 2016, Hunter Valley The back label opines 'Cellaring potential – superb drinking pleasure through to 2022' but the

wine has beaten the odds by a considerable margin. It's earthy/leathery in the best Hunter tradition, and the fruit and tannins are each in lockstep. Screw cap. 14% alc. **RATING** 94 **DRINK** 2023-2030 $50 JH

Cellar Reserve Semillon 2006, Hunter Valley Cork sealed, and the wine's still in good health, specifically not madeirised or oxidised. This does no more than remind me that no 2 bottles sealed with cork will be exactly the same. The only question is how different will they be? PS the cork came out without fracture and had done its job very well. Cork. 10.8% alc. **RATING** 94 **DRINK** 2023-2026 $125 JH

🍷🍷🍷🍷 **Cellar Reserve Tri Moir 2013, Hunter Valley** **RATING** 93 **DRINK** 2023-2026 $50 JH

Dwyer Rosé 2022, Hunter Valley **RATING** 91 **DRINK** 2023-2024 $28 JH ✪

Chelsea 2022, Hunter Valley **RATING** 90 **DRINK** 2023-2026 $32 JH

McPherson Wines

199 O'Dwyer Road, Nagambie, Vic 3608 (postal) **Region** Nagambie Lakes
T (03) 9263 0200 **www.**mcphersonwines.com.au **Open** Not **Winemaker** Jo Nash
Est. 1968 **Dozens** 500 000 **Vyds** 262ha

McPherson Wines is, by any standards, a substantial business. Made at various locations from estate vineyards and contract-grown grapes, they represent very good value across a range of labels. Winemaker Jo Nash has been at the helm for many years and co-owner Alistair Purbrick (Tahbilk) has a lifetime of experience in the industry. Quality is unfailingly good.

🍷🍷🍷🍷 **Bella Luna Fiano 2021, Victoria** Fiano is fast becoming a mainstream wine thanks to its suitability to a range of climates and its light savoury, textural appeal. Bella Luna brings those qualities to light, exploring complex preserved lemon, quince, spiced apple and pear aromas and flavours. Good balance across the palate with fruit playing strong against a smooth and supple background. Top value. Screw cap. 11.5% alc. **RATING** 90 **DRINK** 2022-2025 $19 JP ✪

McWilliam's

Jack McWilliam Road, Hanwood, NSW 2680. **Region** Riverina
T (02) 6963 3400 **www.**mcwilliams.com.au **Open** By appt **Winemaker** Russell Cody, Mel McWilliam, Stephanie Lucas **Est.** 1913 **Vyds** 20ha

The McWilliam's brand and Hanwood vineyard was purchased by Calabria wines in '21 (McWilliam's Mount Pleasant winery and vineyards were bought by Medich Family Office). The exceptional-value offerings of Hanwood Estate in Griffith remain anchors of the brand. Yet McWilliam's viticultural resources have expanded to include Hilltops, Tumbarumba and Canberra whence wines of considerable detail, cool-climate clarity and exceptional value are crafted under the aegis of chief winemaker Russell Cody. While the Single Vineyard suite sets the pace, the 660 range is brilliant, defined by a series of wines that are surely among the country's greatest bargains. A new cellar door opens mid-'23.

🍷🍷🍷🍷🍷 **Hanwood Very Rare Tawny Aged 30 Years NV, Riverina** Red raspberry with a black cherry core. Ristretto espresso, brandy orange, red oak and raw maple. The wine's aromas twist and turn. Red apple skin, sumac and true cinnamon on a taffeta of silk threads interwoven with delicious rancio, mushroom and saffron. Tannins cradle the wine with a warmth that speaks of clean spirit, soulful tenderness and appreciation. Magnificent. Screw cap. 19.5% alc. **RATING** 98 $175 SW ♥

🍷🍷🍷🍷🍷 **Eliza Jane Shiraz 2018, Canberra District** Gosh, this is good with its deep, dark purple hue, concentrated fruit and shapely tannins. Plums, lots of spice and cedary oak nicely placed through, baking spices, pepper and a hint of menthol. The palate fleshes out, fuller-bodied with ripe plush tannins. Alas, only 606 bottles were made. Screw cap. 13.5% alc. **RATING** 96 **DRINK** 2023-2033 $100 JF

Hanwood Rare Tawny Aged 20 years NV, Riverina Fig Newtons, wild rosella, caraway seeds and orange rind. Luxurious on the palate followed by a landslide of spice and rancio. Mace, allspice, Sichuan flowers and liqueur cherries. Roast walnuts and cinnamon. Highly detailed and expressive. Screw cap. 19.5% alc. RATING 96 $80 SW

Single Vineyard Shiraz 2021, Canberra District The Single Vineyard has its own personality and depth. It's very good. Savoury, and while the fruit is excellent, it's all a part of the flavour profile, not dominating in any way. Fine tannins and hints of cardamom and pepper with juicy acidity slipping across the medium-weighted palate. Screw cap. 13.5% alc. RATING 95 DRINK 2023–2033 $40 JF ✪

Single Vineyard Chardonnay 2021, Tumbarumba Tumbarumba certainly knows how to turn on the chardonnay charm. Beautiful citrus flavours and spice all in balance with the more savoury components, some chicken stock and popcorn coming off the creamy lees traits. Linear and pure, the acidity is so refreshing and just extends the palate out for ages. Love it. Screw cap. 12.5% alc. RATING 95 DRINK 2022–2031 $40 JF ✪

Hanwood Rare Muscat Aged 20 Years NV, Riverina This first speaks of red berried fruits, as good Muscats should. Steeped morello cherries, plum and figs meet glazed peaches, orange zest and perfumed bergamot. Red fruit comes through on the mid-palate and the rancio complements the touch of tannin grip. Walnut and crème caramel sauce are the lasting notes. A very elegant muscat with a silky smooth finish. Screw cap. 18.5% alc. RATING 95 $80 SW

McW Reserve 660 Cabernet Sauvignon 2019, Hilltops This is excellent. Plush and giving with deliciously ripe fruit, spicy and fleshy across the palate yet very much a savoury style. The tannins are fine yet shapely and the finish lingers long. For the price, gee, this is stonkingly good. Screw cap. 14% alc. RATING 94 DRINK 2023–2029 $25 JF ✪

Hanwood Rare Topaque Aged 20 years NV, Riverina Chestnut in the glass with aromas of Medjool date, cinnamon, nutmeg and coffee bean. The palate invokes a chocolate/caramel creaminess with sarsaparilla and hazelnut skin bitterness. There is a peak of acidity to balance the lusciousness and a strong almond toffee note on the finish. A good balance of spice and roasted nuts among the sweetness. Screw cap. 18% alc. RATING 94 $80 SW

ŶŶŶŶŶ **McW Reserve 660 Syrah 2021, Canberra District** RATING 90 DRINK 2022–2030 $25 JF ✪
Single Vineyard Pinot Noir 2021, Tumbarumba RATING 90 DRINK 2023–2029 $40 JF

MadFish Wines   ★★★★

137 Fifty One Road, Cowaramup, WA 6284 **Region** Margaret River
T 08 9756 5200 **www.**madfishwines.com.au **Open** 7 days 10–5 **Winemaker** Nic Bowen, Mark Bailey **Viticulturist** Dave Botting **Est.** 1992
Named after a renowned bay in the Great Southern (near Denmark), MadFish was established by Howard Park as a standalone brand with a focus on expressive, affordable, drink-now wines. Sourced from long-term growers in the state's southwest. In its 30+ year history it has grown to become a widely recognised and exported wine brand. Today, as always, the wines are made by Nic Bowen and Mark Bailey, and at the same facility. In '07, Gold Turtle was established, projected as a regional (GI specific) tier of wines exclusively for Endeavour Drinks. In the past few years both Gold Turtle and MadFish have expanded to include sparkling wines. Further regional expansion may be imminent.

ŶŶŶŶŶ **Gold Turtle Grenache 2020, Swan Valley** Always a lovely surprise to find a well-priced grenache that keeps a savoury outlook. This is terrific. Hints of cranberries and raspberries, very spicy with grainy tannins. It's lighter framed and gluggable. Screw cap. 14% alc. RATING 91 DRINK 2022–2026 $23 JF ✪
Gold Turtle Shiraz 2021, Margaret River Terrific colour, a bright dark purple with a shot of red, and full of spiced plums and berries flecked with dried herbs. Soft and supple yet there are some shapely tannins and refreshment throughout.

Neat wine. Neat price. Screw cap. 14% alc. **RATING** 90 **DRINK** 2022-2028 $17 JF

Cabernet Sauvignon Merlot 2021, Western Australia I don't mind this wine – one to enjoy now, at a barbecue, but it'll mellow in a few more years. Cassis and cherries, cedary, woodsy spice, a hint of fresh herbs and some sway with the tannins. It works across a medium-bodied palate and has plenty of refreshing acidity and a touch of detail. Screw cap. 14% alc. **RATING** 90 **DRINK** 2022-2028 $19 JF ✪

Madman's Gully   ★★★★

31 Newbound Lane, Beechworth Vic 3747 (postal) **Region** Beechworth
T 0425 774 660 **www.**madmansgullywines.com.au **Open** Not **Winemaker** Jo Marsh **Viticulturist** Fiona Wigg **Est.** 2009 **Dozens** 180 **Vyds** 0.4ha
The name Madman's Gully is attributed to the antics of a naked Scotsman protecting his claim on the 1850s goldfields, which produced much of the riches on which Beechworth was built. Fiona Wigg has a background in agricultural science, accumulating many years of practical experience as a viticulturist. During Fiona's time as a vineyard manager at Seppelt Great Western she developed an interest in elegant, cool-climate shiraz, which led to the search for a suitable vineyard site of her own. With husband Ross she established a small patch of shiraz vines in '09 on the edge of the old Madman's Gully goldfield above Beechworth.

♟♟♟♟ **Syrah 2021, Beechworth** Beechworth shiraz can be striking in its delicacy and fineness. This is one such example. Light and fragrant in red cherry, blueberry, bush scents and white pepper. The palate's bright and juicy red fruit and herbal flavours are underpinned by discreet oak spice and fine tannins. A lingering layer of pepper and anise brings this little charmer to a long finish. Will age reliably for the medium term. Screw cap. 13.8% alc. **RATING** 92 **DRINK** 2023-2031 $42 JP

Main Ridge Estate   ★★★★★

80 William Road, Red Hill, Vic 3937 **Region** Mornington Peninsula
T (03) 5989 2686 **www.**mre.com.au **Open** W'ends & public hols 11–5 by appt
Winemaker James Sexton **Viticulturist** Linda Hodges **Est.** 1975 **Dozens** 1200 **Vyds** 2.8ha
Credit to young James Sexton and especially his parents Tim and Libby, who bought the renowned estate from luminaries Nat and Rosalie White in '15. Fast forward to today, James has completed his wine science degree from Charles Sturt University and says vineyard management is key. That means reinvigorating the sites, eschewing herbicides and pesticides, all the while working on soil health and changes to canopy management. He's learnt quickly. There's always been little room for expansion, but in '21, neighbours and friends John and Julie Trueman decided to ease into retirement. Now the Trueman Pinot Noir and Chardonnay are part of the Main Ridge Estate family. Distinctly different, as they should be. While respectful of the Main Ridge Estate heritage, the wine labels have undergone a subtle revamp.

♟♟♟♟ **Trueman Vineyard Chardonnay 2021, Mornington Peninsula** Refined and long with splashes of citrus, white nectarine, powdered ginger and lemon cream. Lovely chalky acidity, refreshing, tangy and a little briny. It's on song. Alas, a measly 50 dozen made. Screw cap. 13.2% alc. **RATING** 95 **DRINK** 2022-2031 $50 JF ✪

The Acre Pinot Noir 2021, Mornington Peninsula A refined and composed outcome with such suppleness across the fuller-bodied palate. Dark cherries, blood orange and zest, a whiff of pine needles and woodsy spices. While there's no shortage of acidity, the palate feels almost gentle and soft with stretchy tannins. A lovely drink. Screw cap. 14.1% alc. **RATING** 95 **DRINK** 2022-2025 $85 JF

Half Acre Pinot Noir 2021, Mornington Peninsula There's a bit more intensity, richness and depth to this compared to its Acre sibling. Waves of flavour from dark cherries to rhubarb, blood orange, amaro, bitter herbs and lots of spices. They all layer across the palate, finally meeting up with plush tannins and crunchy acidity. Very refreshing and complex. Screw cap. 14.3% alc. **RATING** 95 **DRINK** 2022–2035 $95 JF

Chardonnay 2021, Mornington Peninsula This wine is stamped strongly with the estate DNA. Ripe stone fruit, lemon and grilled peach, a little flinty, creamy and a touch of oyster shell brininess. The palate fleshes out with lots of texture yet the fine acidity keeps this on an even keel. Lovely. Screw cap. 13.2% alc. **RATING** 95 **DRINK** 2023–2031 $65 JF

ŸŸŸŸŸ **Trueman Vineyard Pinot Noir 2021, Mornington Peninsula RATING** 93 **DRINK** 2023–2034 $50 JF

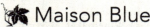 # Maison Blue ★★★☆

139 Little Road, Willunga, SA 5172 (postal) **Region** McLaren Vale **T** (07) 3075 7595 **www.**maisonblue.com.au **Open** Not **Winemaker** Mike Farmilo **Viticulturist** Gregg Ross **Est.** 1995 **Dozens** 50 000 **Vyds** 14.2.ha

A new producer responsible for well-made wines of a traditional bent: forward fruit, tempered oak and bright acidity. Maison Eros is the top tier; an entry-level range is sourced from various regions outside the Vale. There is little to surprise the domestic drinker, but the weighty bottles and cork closures suggest that the wines are primarily destined for export.

ŸŸŸŸŸ **Maison Eros Shiraz 2020, McLaren Vale** Despite the throaty warmth, this is good. Rich, yet efforts at refinement are palpable. A splay of dried nori, Bing cherry, charcuterie and ground pepper all corralled by quality oak and maritime salinity. The finish is just a bit hot. Cork. 15% alc. **RATING** 91 **DRINK** 2022–2030 $45 NG

Majella ★★★★★

Lynn Road, Coonawarra, SA 5263 **Region** Coonawarra **T** (08) 8736 3055 **www.**majellawines.com.au **Open** 7 days 10–4 **Winemaker** Bruce Gregory, Michael Marcus **Viticulturist** Steven Lynn **Est.** 1968 **Dozens** 30 000 **Vyds** 70ha

The Lynn family has been in residence in Coonawarra for over 4 generations, starting as storekeepers, later graduating into grazing. The Majella property was originally owned by Frank Lynn, then purchased in '60 by nephew George. In '68 Anthony and Brian (the Prof) Lynn established the vineyards, since joined by Peter, Stephen, Nerys and Gerard. Bruce Gregory has been at the helm for every wine made at Majella with Michael Marcus joining the winemaking team in '08. The Malleea is one of Coonawarra's classics, The Musician one of Australia's most outstanding red wines selling for less than $20 (having won many trophies and medals). The largely fully mature vineyards are principally shiraz and cabernet sauvignon, with a little riesling and merlot.

ŸŸŸŸŸ **The Malleea 2018, Coonawarra** Blackcurrant fruit comes married to cedar oak, ripe redcurrant is rolled into cream, bay leaf and tobacco notes edge towards choc-mint. This is both a seamless wine and a firm one, the fruit and oak rippled through with fine-grained tannin, the finish full of both running and swagger. Screw cap. 14.5% alc. **RATING** 95 **DRINK** 2025–2045 $80 CM

Cabernet Sauvignon 2020, Coonawarra Tannin spreads from the mid-palate onwards, assertive and dry, fine grained but commanding. It gives a pronounced sense of gravity, but it also calls into question the wine's balance. It otherwise offers trademark blackcurrant, boysenberry, mint and cedar flavours, all of which are delivered in both delicious and substantial volume. Screw cap. 14.5% alc. **RATING** 94 **DRINK** 2026–2038 $35 CM ✪

GPL68 Cabernet Sauvignon 2018, Coonawarra This is an elegant release with mulberry and boysenberry characters flowing through pure blackcurrant and mint. Cedar oak is present but neatly settled into the fruit, while fragrant tobacco notes work beautifully as highlights. This wine was tasted as a 4yo release, appearing fresh to the point of friskiness. Screw cap. 14.5% alc. **RATING** 94 **DRINK** 2024–2034 $130 CM

ȲȲȲȲȲ Shiraz 2020, Coonawarra RATING 93 DRINK 2024–2035 $35 CM ✪
The Musician Cabernet Shiraz 2021, Coonawarra RATING 92
DRINK 2023–2030 $19 CM ✪
Sparkling Shiraz 2021, Coonawarra RATING 91 DRINK 2022–2026 $40 CM
Merlot 2021, Coonawarra RATING 91 DRINK 2023–2030 $30 CM

Malcolm Creek Vineyard   ★★★☆

33 Bonython Road, Kersbrook, SA 5231 **Region** Adelaide Hills
T 0404 677 894 **www**.malcolmcreekwines.com.au **Open** W'ends & publics hols by appt
Winemaker Peter Leske, Michael Sykes **Viticulturist** Infield **Est.** 1982 **Dozens** 800
Vyds 2ha
Malcolm Creek was the retirement venture of Reg Tolley, who decided to upgrade his
retirement by selling the venture to Bitten and Karsten Pedersen in '07. The wines are
invariably well made and develop gracefully; they are worth seeking out, and are usually
available with some extra bottle age at a very modest price.

ȲȲȲȲȲ Chardonnay 2021, Adelaide Hills A mid-weighted chardonnay of flavour,
considerable charm and a welcome exactitude, sans excessive clutter of reduction
or oak. A gracious free flow of tangerine, nectarine and white fig curled around a
hearth of gently creamy oak and leesy almond meal. Good drinking. Screw cap.
13% alc. RATING 92 DRINK 2022–2028 $30 NG ✪

Mandala   ★★★★★

1568 Melba Highway, Dixons Creek, Vic 3775 **Region** Yarra Valley
T (03) 5965 2016 **www**.mandalawines.com.au **Open** Mon–Fri 1–4, w'ends 10–5
Winemaker Charles Smedley, Rachel Gore **Est.** 2007 **Dozens** 10 500 **Vyds** 29ha
Mandala is owned by Charles Smedley, who acquired the established vineyard in '07. The
vineyard has vines up to 25 years old, but the spectacular restaurant and cellar door complex
is a more recent addition. The vineyards are primarily at the home base in Dixons Creek,
with chardonnay (9.1ha), pinot noir (6.1ha), cabernet sauvignon (4.4ha) and shiraz (1.7ha).
There is a separate 4.4ha vineyard at Yarra Junction planted entirely to pinot noir with an
impressive clonal mix.

ȲȲȲȲȲ The Mandala Butterfly Cabernet Sauvignon 2021, Yarra Valley Classic
cool-climate cabernet with aromas of pure blackcurrant fruit, gentle cedar notes,
freshly crushed black pepper and jasmine. Medium bodied and impeccably
balanced, ultrafine and persistent tannins make this approachable now, with the
promise of more to come. Screw cap. 14.4% alc. RATING 96 DRINK 2023–2032
$70 PR ✪
Gathering LD Blanc de Blancs Chardonnay 2015, Yarra Valley Disgorged
July '22 with zero dosage after 72 months on lees. Light bright straw with green
tinges. This is both fresh and complex with its aromas of just–ripened apricots,
preserved lemon and baking spices. Dry, chalky and long, this manages to be quite
rich and full flavoured, yet refined at the same time. Delicious. Diam. 12.5% alc.
RATING 95 DRINK 2022–2026 $70 PR
The Prophet Pinot Noir 2022, Yarra Valley Brambly red fruits, cherry skins,
juniper and warm spices. Quite a bit more depth and concentration than the
estate pinot of the same year, the palate is balanced with vibrant acidity and gently
grippy and persistent tannins. A lovely wine. Screw cap. 13% alc. RATING 95
DRINK 2023–2032 $70 PR
The Mandala Compass Chardonnay 2022, Yarra Valley Immediately
appealing and perfumed with aromas of ripe apricots, honeysuckle and just a
whiff of fresh vanilla bean from the oak, which is already nicely integrated. There's
good volume and vibrancy on the palate, a fine vein of acidity running through
the wine before finishing chalky and long. Screw cap. 13% alc. RATING 95
DRINK 2023–2029 $70 PR

Fumé Blanc 2022, Yarra Valley A bright straw green-gold. Bursting from the glass with its aromas of ripe tropical fruits, greengages and some attractive herbal notes. Dry, chalky and long, this really is a lovely example of the style. Screw cap. 13% alc. RATING 94 DRINK 2023–2025 $35 PR ✪

Chardonnay 2022, Yarra Valley RATING 93 DRINK 2023–2028 $35 PR ✪
Rosé 2022, Yarra Valley RATING 93 DRINK 2023–2024 $25 PR ✪
Pinot Noir 2022, Yarra Valley RATING 93 DRINK 2023–2029 $35 PR ✪
The Rock Shiraz 2021, Yarra Valley RATING 93 DRINK 2022–2028 $70 PR
Pinot Gris 2022, Mornington Peninsula RATING 91 DRINK 2023–2025 $25 PR ✪

Mandoon Estate ★★★★★

10 Harris Road, Caversham, WA 6055 **Region** Swan District
T (08) 6279 0500 **www**.mandoonestate.com.au **Open** 7 days 10–5 by appt
Winemaker Ryan Sudano, Mathieu Enderle **Est.** 2009 **Dozens** 10 000 **Vyds** 50ha
Mandoon Estate, headed by Allan Erceg, made a considerable impression with its wines in a very short time. In '08 the family purchased a site in Caversham in the Swan Valley, with vines planted as early as 1895. Construction of the winery was completed in time for the first vintage in '10. They also purchased a further 20ha in Margaret River. Winemaker Ryan Sudano has metaphorically laid waste to Australian wine shows with the quality of the wines he has made from the Swan Valley, Frankland River and Margaret River.

Discovery Series Bush Vine Grenache 2021, Swan Valley Complex, layered and long; a palate of cherry bolstered with plum and a hint of tobacco. Despite its authority, the palate is fresh and the finish gains another degree as fine tannins come into play, but in no way threaten the compelling length. 65 dozen made. Screw cap. 14.5% alc. RATING 97 DRINK 2023–2030 $70 JH ✪
Reserve Research Station Cabernet Sauvignon 2018, Margaret River This is made from a small trial block planted in 1976. Some years ago, Mandoon Estate acquired the neglected block and rehabilitated it. Given the Margaret River's great 2018 vintage, it is no surprise to find this a magical, succulent, cabernet. Screw cap. 14% alc. RATING 97 DRINK 2023–2048 $84 JH ✪

Block 1895 Verdelho 2022, Swan Valley This triggered memories of Western Australian winemaker Jack Mann, who held that a white wine should be able to be diluted with 50% water to be taken seriously. This wine has both flavour and texture from cool fermentation in tank, and certainly is to be taken seriously. Screw cap. 13.5% alc. RATING 95 DRINK 2023–2029 $30 JH ✪

Sauvignon Blanc 2022, Margaret River RATING 93 DRINK 2023–2025 $23 JH ✪
Discovery Series Chenin Blanc 2022, Swan Valley RATING 90 DRINK 2022–2025 $35 MB

Manser Wines ★★★★

c/- 3 Riviera Court, Pasadena, SA 5042 (postal) **Region** Adelaide Hills
T 0400 251 168 **www**.manserwines.com.au **Open** Not **Winemaker** Phil Christiansen
Est. 2015 **Dozens** 1000 **Vyds** 6ha
Phil Manser has teamed up with brother Kevin and father Bernie to run the family vineyard. It was established by Tim James, a skilled winemaker with senior winemaking and management roles at Hardys and Wirra Wirra. He planted 4 clones of shiraz randomly throughout the vineyard in '97, a common practice in France. The Mansers acquired the property in '15, Tim remaining an enthusiastic spectator during vintage. They also source fruit from a 65yo vineyard in Blewitt Springs and a third vineyard on the McMurtrie Mile.

Block 4 Shiraz 2021, Adelaide Hills A contemporary expression, tautly furled around a bone of reduction splaying dried nori, violet, purple fruits and tapenade across a buoyant mid-palate. A waft of menthol is slightly drying, yet the finish is long, penetrative and quite fine. The flow, effortless, without the jingle jangle of extraneous winemaking. Best, it tastes like the Adelaide Hills. Screw cap. 14.9% alc. **RATING** 93 **DRINK** 2022–2029 $65 NG

100 Year Old Vines Reserve Grenache 2021, McLaren Vale The lifted delicacy of old-vine grenache from Australia's grand cru equivalent on show. Rosewater, lavender, pithy red cherry, cranberry and kirsch. The structural lattice, fine-boned and silty. Yet the mid-palate is hollow and the finish, a bit too tangy. Screw cap. 14.5% alc. **RATING** 91 **DRINK** 2022–2028 $65 NG

Many Hands Winery   ★★★★

2 Maxwells Road, Coldstream, Vic 3770 **Region** Yarra Valley
T 0400 035 105 **www**.manyhandswinery.com.au **Open** Fri–Mon 10–5
Winemaker Tony Indomenico **Viticulturist** Tony Indomenico **Est.** 2010 **Dozens** 1000
Vyds 2.6ha
Owners Jennifer Walsh and Tony Indomenico were looking for a tree change when in '10 they came across a 2.6ha vineyard that had been planted in 1982 to 6 mainstream varieties, but not always looked after. The first task was to rehabilitate the vineyard and thereafter build a restaurant offering Italian food reflecting Tony's Sicilian heritage.

🍷🍷🍷🍷🍷 **Cabernet Sauvignon Cabernet Franc 2020, Yarra Valley** A medium deep, bright crimson. From a cooler year in the Valley for cabernet varieties, this leaps out of the glass with its aromas of dark cherries, lifted violets, a touch of bell pepper and a hint of cedar from the already well-integrated oak. Medium bodied with ultrafine, persistent tannins, this will provide a lot of enjoyment in the ensuing years. Diam. 13.5% alc. **RATING** 94 **DRINK** 2022–2032 $49 PR
Pinot Noir 2018, Yarra Valley A bright crimson cherry-red. Nicely perfumed with sappy red and black fruits, spice rack spices and a little earth. Well weighted, this medium-bodied and densely packed wine is firmly structured yet still retains finesse. Approachable now, I suspect this will continue to improve and unfurl for some time to come. Diam. 13.5% alc. **RATING** 94 **DRINK** 2022–2028 $49 PR

🍷🍷🍷🍷 **Rosé 2019, Yarra Valley** **RATING** 93 **DRINK** 2022–2022 $35 PR ✪
Sangiovese 2020, Yarra Valley **RATING** 90 **DRINK** 2022–2026 $35 PR

Marchand & Burch   ★★★★☆

PO Box 180, North Fremantle, WA 5159 **Region** Great Southern
T (08) 9336 9600 **www**.burchfamilywines.com.au **Open** Not **Winemaker** Janice McDonald, Pascal Marchand **Est.** 2007 **Dozens** 2000 **Vyds** 8.46ha
A joint venture between Canadian-born and Burgundian-trained Pascal Marchand and Burch Family Wines. Grapes are sourced from single vineyards and, in most cases, from single blocks within them (4.51ha of chardonnay and 3.95ha of pinot noir, variously situated in Mount Barker and Porongurup). Biodynamic practices underpin the viticulture in the Australian and French vineyards, and Burgundian viticultural techniques have been adopted here (e.g. narrow rows and high-density plantings, Guyot pruning, VSP and leaf and lateral shoot removal).

🍷🍷🍷🍷🍷 **Rosé 2022, Western Australia** An ultra-refreshing rosé thanks to its mouth-watering acidity. Plenty of flavour, too. Expect a dollop of creamy texture to the riff of red berries, stone fruit and a subtle layering of spice. Good energy and very good drinking. Screw cap. 13% alc. **RATING** 95 **DRINK** 2022–2024 $28 JF ✪
Villages Chardonnay 2022, Great Southern There's the texture, the refreshing acidity and the citrusy flavours that combine to make this a very appealing drink. Lemon and lime with splashes of grapefruit juice, a dusting of ginger spice and vanilla pod oak. A more restrained style this vintage and all the better for it. Screw cap. 12.5% alc. **RATING** 94 **DRINK** 2022–2032 $42 JF
Villages Shiraz 2021, Great Southern The fantastic dark red-black hue, the swaying aromas of woodsmoke, dark fruits, baking spices and florals all point to a very big wine. It isn't so. Yes, there's density, richness, plushness and a full-bodied

palate but everything in its place is contained and smooth. Screw cap. 14.5% alc.
RATING 94 DRINK 2022–2033 $60 JF

ŸŸŸŸ♀ **Mount Barrow Pinot Noir 2022, Mount Barker** RATING 93
DRINK 2023–2033 $62 JF
Villages Pinot Noir 2022, Great Southern RATING 91 DRINK 2023–2030
$42 JF

Marco Lubiana   ★★★★☆

60 Rowbottoms Road, Granton, Tas 7030 **Region** Tasmania
T 0429 637 457 **www.marcolubiana.com.au Open** Wed–Sun 10–4 **Winemaker** Marco
Lubiana **Viticulturist** Marco Lubiana, Steve Lubiana **Est.** 2018 **Dozens** 800 **Vyds** 4ha
Marco Lubiana is inspired by planet Earth, the history of Burgundy and that of his
winegrowing family. He discovered the great wines of France and Italy while working at East
End Cellars. His first vintage at his parents' winery was '18, followed by an internship in the
Cote d'Or during the '19 vintage. He returned home to the Derwent River Valley in '18
to make his first vintage in his parents' winery. His sourcing is from a diverse array of clones
exclusively in his parents' biodynamic vineyards in the Derwent and Huon valleys, and his
focus rests entirely on chardonnay and pinot noir as still wines, with barrel-fermented vintage
sparkling in the pipeline. Sulphur dioxide is used sparingly – in some cases not at all.

ŸŸŸŸŸ **Huon & Derwent Chardonnay 2021, Tasmania** A wonderful wine full of
bright white peach, nectarine and lime characters with wisps of nougat, lemon
curd, oatmeal, soft oak spice, white flowers and stone. Great clarity and detail
throughout with a shimmering acidity and long finish with a touch of meal. Such
an exciting young addition to the Tassie wine scene. Cork. 13% alc. RATING 95
DRINK 2023–2027 $60 DB
Lucille & Ruscello Vineyard Pinot Noir 2021, Tasmania What a pretty
smelling wine, and with pinosity to burn. Amaro and exotic spice-flecked dark
cherry fruits cut with notes of pressed flowers, earth, shiitake broth and light
gamey whiffs. Bright, complex and a joy to drink with oodles of space and
detail, plus a wonderful twangy, sapid acid line. Screw cap. 13.5% alc. RATING 94
DRINK 2023–2028 $57 DB

Marcus Hill Vineyard   ★★★★

560 Banks Road, Marcus Hill, Vic 3222 (postal) **Region** Geelong
T 0421 728 437 **www.marcushillvineyard.com.au Open** By appt **Winemaker** Chip
Harrison **Est.** 2000 **Dozens** 1000 **Vyds** 3ha
In '00, Richard and Margot Harrison, together with 'gang-pressed friends', planted 2ha of
pinot noir overlooking Point Lonsdale, Queenscliff and Ocean Grove, a few kms from Bass
Strait and Port Phillip. Since then chardonnay, shiraz, more pinot noir, and 3 rows of pinot
meunier have been added. The vineyard is run with minimal sprays, and the aim is to produce
elegant wines that truly express the maritime site.

ŸŸŸŸ♀ **Bellarine Peninsula Pinot Noir 2020, Geelong** A light, bright brick colour.
This has immediate appeal with its aromas of red fruits, pomegranate, musk and
some gentle, sweet spice. Fleshes out nicely on the palate and the tannins are fine
and detailed. Screw cap. 13% alc. RATING 92 DRINK 2022–2025 $35 PR
Bellarine Peninsula Chardonnay 2021, Geelong This interesting wine sits
at the richer end of the chardonnay spectrum. Aromas of lime leaf, mango skin
and fresh guava along with just a hint of oak-derived crème brûlée. Mouth-filling
yet balanced by the wine's fresh acidity, this will handle richer seafood dishes with
ease. Screw cap. 12.5% alc. RATING 91 DRINK 2022–2025 $35 PR
Bellarine Peninsula Pinot Meunier 2020, Geelong Aromas of amaretto
cherries and a lick of smoked paprika. This savoury edge follows onto the palate,
which also has a core of sweet cherry fruit. A silky, fruit-forward wine with fine
tannins. Screw cap. 13% alc. RATING 90 DRINK 2022–2024 $35 PR

Margan Wines

1238 Milbrodale Road, Broke, NSW 2330 **Region** Hunter Valley
T (02) 6579 1317 **www.**margan.com.au **Open** 7 days 10–5 **Winemaker** Andrew
Margan, Ollie Margan **Viticulturist** Andrew Margan, Alessa Margan **Est.** 1996
Dozens 25 000 **Vyds** 100ha

Margan Vineyards was established by Andrew and Lisa Margan in '96. Today it incorporates
2 of the 2nd generation, Alessa and Ollie, working in the vineyard and winery respectively.
Andrew continues to oversee the viticultural and winemaking side; Lisa, the tourism and
restaurant. The estate boasts 100ha of vines and the vineyards are largely on the lauded
Fordwich Sill, a geological formation dating back 200 million years. They are a mix of old
vines (50+ years) planted to traditional varieties including semillon, chardonnay and shiraz, as
well as younger plantings of new and exciting varieties albariño and barbera. Field blends of
shiraz/mourvèdre and tempranillo/graciano/shiraz are unique to the region.

**White Label Single Vineyard Timbervines Chardonnay 2022, Hunter
Valley** This wine is sourced from a 1ha block planted on the red volcanic soil of
Margan's 1972-planted Timbervines vineyard. Its fragrant bouquet heralds a palate
of high-quality chardonnay, white peach and grapefruit running throughout a
classy wine. Screw cap. 12.5% alc. **RATING** 96 **DRINK** 2023–2030 $80 JH
Aged Release Francis John Semillon 2018, Hunter Valley Wow. Doesn't
this throw all manner of aromas and flavours (peach and lemon) into the
convincing and still youthful palate. I'm taking this one home with me. Screw cap.
12% alc. **RATING** 96 **DRINK** 2023–2032 $60 JH ✪
White Label Single Vineyard Ceres Hill Barbera 2021, Hunter Valley
From a 3ha block within the Ceres Hill vineyard. Planted in 1998, it has
flourished, so don't pay any attention to the wine's slightly turbid wishy-washy
colour. But do pay attention to the palate and its finish. It's only just in medium-
bodied territory, but it has magical savoury acidity (an oxymoron, I know, but it's
the wine). Screw cap. 13.5% alc. **RATING** 95 **DRINK** 2025–2031 $40 JH ✪
**White Label Single Vineyard Timbervines Tempranillo Graciano Shiraz
2021, Hunter Valley** The juicy red fruits positively leap out of the glass,
although it's not a one-trick pony, the 3 varieties coming together wonderfully
well, synergy at work from start to finish. This is another good wine, value in big
block letters. I see it as a medium-bodied wine, ready and waiting. Screw cap.
13.5% alc. **RATING** 95 **DRINK** 2023–2033 $40 JH ✪
**White Label Single Vineyard Saxonvale Shiraz Mourvèdre 2021, Hunter
Valley** The 50yo vines were interplanted as a field blend, picked at the same time
even though the mourvèdre wasn't fully ripe. It drops the alcohol to 13% and
results in an elegant, medium-bodied palate with red and blue fruits. A lovely
wine. Screw cap. 13% alc. **RATING** 95 **DRINK** 2023–2036 $50 JH ✪
Aged Release Single Vineyard Timbervines Shiraz 2019, Hunter Valley
The fruit came from the red volcanic soil of the Fordwich Sill. The label states
it is 'an ageing style of Hunter Valley shiraz.' The wine is exactly that, composed
of the best 10 barrels from the best blocks, and while full bodied, has a delicious
river of freshness running through the length of the palate. Screw cap. 13.5% alc.
RATING 95 **DRINK** 2029–2039 $100 JH
**White Label Single Vineyard Ceres Hill Chardonnay 2022, Hunter
Valley** An elegant chardonnay, poised and balanced, and with excellent length.
The fruit flavours are focused on grapefruit, perhaps reflecting the low-ish
alcohol. Less intense than its Timbervines sibling. Screw cap. 12% alc. **RATING** 94
DRINK 2023–2029 $50 JH
White Label Single Vineyard Ceres Hill Semillon 2022, Hunter Valley
A juicy palate with Meyer lemon the anchor, the Hunter Valley acidity kicking
in on the finish and mouth-watering aftertaste. Screw cap. 11.5% alc. **RATING** 94
DRINK 2025–2035 $40 JH ✪
**White Label Single Vineyard Fordwich Hill Semillon 2022, Hunter
Valley** From a 1ha block planted '74 on red volcanic soil. Complexity rules from
start to finish, diminishing the focus but adding length as the flavours come and

go, and range from lemongrass to quince et al. Screw cap. 12% alc. **RATING** 94 **DRINK** 2023-2029 $40 JH ✪

🍷🍷🍷🍷🍷 White Label Single Vineyard Fordwich Hill Chardonnay 2022, Hunter Valley **RATING** 93 **DRINK** 2023-2029 $40 JH
Semillon 2022, Hunter Valley **RATING** 92 **DRINK** 2023-2027 $22 JH ✪
White Label Single Vineyard Ceres Hill Albariño 2022, Hunter Valley **RATING** 90 **DRINK** 2023-2025 $35 JH

Marri Wood Park

28 Whittle Road Yallingup WA 6282 **Region** Margaret River
T 0438 525 580 **www**.marriwoodpark.com.au **Open** 7 days 11–4 **Winemaker** Nic Peterkin **Viticulturist** Julian Wright **Est.** 1992 **Dozens** 1500 **Vyds** 6.5ha
Established '92 in Yallingup, Marri Wood Park is a boutique, family-owned producer with an impressive range of wines from a bouncy, natty pét-nat to serious and classic Margaret River varieties. Natalie Wright and her father Julian moved to Yallingup in '04 to take over the vineyard that had been managed for them for 11 years. Today they have 6.5ha of Demeter-certified, biodynamic vineyards planted to cabernet sauvignon, sauvignon blanc, chenin blanc and semillon. The emphasis is on an ecologically beneficial approach to farming that yields top-quality wine grapes, and is sustainable and in tune with the environment.

🍷🍷🍷🍷🍷 Chenin Blanc 2021, Margaret River Heady aromatics and flavours of quince blossom, lemon with a whiff of pepper and woodsy spices, plus lime curd and a delicious, thirst-quenching lemon-saline character. Refreshing acidity, some quince-like tannins are also in the mix. An excellent wine. Screw cap. 13.5% alc. **RATING** 95 **DRINK** 2023-2035 $40 JF ✪

🍷🍷🍷🍷🍷 Sauvignon Blanc Semillon 2022, Margaret River **RATING** 93 **DRINK** 2022-2030 $32 JF ✪
Sauvignon Blanc 2021, Margaret River **RATING** 93 **DRINK** 2022-2028 $38 JF
Bratty Nat Pétillant Naturel 2022, Margaret River **RATING** 92 **DRINK** 2022-2024 $35 JF
Reserve Chenin Blanc 2009, Margaret River **RATING** 90 **DRINK** 2022-2024 $49 JF

Massena Vineyards

26 Sturt Street, Angaston, SA 5353 **Region** Barossa Valley
T 0408 821 737 **www**.massena.com.au **Open** By appt **Winemaker** Jaysen Collins **Est.** 2000 **Dozens** 5000 **Vyds** 4ha
Massena Vineyards draws upon 1ha each of mataro, saperavi, petite sirah and tannat at Nuriootpa, also purchasing grapes from other growers. It is an export-oriented business, although the wines can also be purchased from better wine shops and online, which, given both the quality and innovative nature of the wines, seems more than ordinarily worthwhile.

🍷🍷🍷🍷🍷 Old Vine Semillon 2022, Barossa Valley Light straw in the glass with characters of pithy lemon, grapefruit and peach with hints of lemon curd, mountain herbs, soft spice and yellow flowers. Stony, savoury and long on the finish, with a bright acid drive and a fan of mountain herbs. Screw cap. 14.5% alc. **RATING** 90 **DRINK** 2023-2027 $22 DB ✪

Matriarch & Rogue

279 Main North Road, Clare, SA 5453 **Region** Clare Valley
T 0419 901 892 **www**.matriarchandrogue.com.au **Open** By appt **Winemaker** Marnie Roberts **Est.** 2014 **Dozens** 3000
The catchy name is based on 5 sisters who are the 3rd generation of the Byrne family, with a history going back to the family's home in Ireland. The sisters are known as the Patrick Byrne girls, and the wines are a tribute to the strong women of the family, and the rogues

they married. Winemaker and proprietor Marnie Roberts is, one assumes, one of the strong women.

ΨΨΨΨΨ Jean Malbec 2021, Clare Valley Fleshy, bright, deep and dark but with all the comely softness and suppleness requisite of early drinking. There's also a crispness to the fringes of the plummy, sweet-spicy sluice, and, importantly, a smudge of palate-resetting tannin to finish. Deeply flavoured, a fog of pulsing ripe, plummy fruit and violet floral lift to sniff on. Drink in the flourish of its youth. Screw cap. 14% alc. **RATING** 93 **DRINK** 2022–2026 $30 MB ✪

Rogues Of The Resistance Pecorino 2022, Adelaide Hills One of those straightforward and simple white wines, easy drinking, crisp and bright. Has green pear, bath salts and waxy elements in scents and flavours. Simple, light on, some nice grip, refreshing. It's basic, but delivers good DNA of the variety and finds a strong mineral line all ticklish and mouth-watering to close. Screw cap. 12.7% alc. **RATING** 91 **DRINK** 2022–2024 $40 MB

Rogues Of The Resistance Aglianico 2020, Riverland Scents of pickled cherry, white strawberry, clove, white pepper and thyme. The palate a crackle of energetic cranberry-drink tang and dryness, wispy with sandy tannins. Finishes with pomegranate juice tartness and refreshing character. Not overly complex, but drinkability works a treat. Screw cap. 13.3% alc. **RATING** 91 **DRINK** 2022–2026 $40 MB

Rogues Of The Resistance Cabernet Franc 2021, Clare Valley Very juicy, very bright. A lively mix of green herb, white pepper, jammy mulberry fruitiness and some saline/minerally characters. Bouquet and palate in check on that. It's sloshy and loose-knit but finds crisp edges and a vibrancy that suggests a chill is probably the best idea. A cracker alt-style for the region. Drink young. Screw cap. 12.7% alc. **RATING** 90 **DRINK** 2022–2025 $40 MB

Montepulciano 2020, Adelaide Hills A throaty, hefty montepulciano, inky and thick set, slurpy and soft. Pleasurable texture and a fog of kirsch, ripe cranberry, cherry cola and sweet spice scents. Fruit flavours are sweet and ripe – a slosh of kirsch, plum, black cherries and cinnamon dusted around the lot. Warming, lush and exuberant. Screw cap. 14.5% alc. **RATING** 90 **DRINK** 2022–2027 $25 MB ✪

Rogues Of The Resistance Mencia 2020, Riverland A bright and lively red wine, leaning towards a chilled red in style but for the concentration of flavours and intensity. It's fragrant of red cherry, pomegranate juice, old spices and clove. Flavours are softer – warm, brown spice starts and finishes the wine, in the midst a wash of pleasing sour plum and blackcurrant characters, with a minty, herbal lift. Nice drinking here. Screw cap. 12.6% alc. **RATING** 90 **DRINK** 2022–2025 $40 MB

Maverick Wines

981 Light Pass Road, Vine Vale, Moorooroo, SA 5352 **Region** Barossa Valley
T 0402 186 416 **www.**maverickwines.com.au **Open** Fri–Sun 11–4 **Winemaker** Ronald Brown **Viticulturist** Ronald Brown **Est.** 2004 **Dozens** 6000 **Vyds** 30ha
This is the business established by highly experienced vigneron Ronald Brown. It has evolved, now with 7 vineyards across the Barossa and Eden valleys, all transitioned into biodynamic grape production. The vines range from 40 to almost 150 years old, underpinning the consistency and quality of the wines.

ΨΨΨΨΨ Ahrens' Creek Ancestor Vine Shiraz 2020, Barossa Valley The vines were planted by then newly arrived migrant Mick Ahrens, and, as old vines can do, sailed through the at times challenging vintage. This is a beautiful shiraz, medium bodied with its deep river of dark chocolate, blackberry fruit, filagreed tannins and positive oak. Diam. 14% alc. **RATING** 97 **DRINK** 2023–2050 $320 JH

ΨΨΨΨΨ The Maverick Shiraz Cabernet Sauvignon 2020, Barossa Elegant and fruit-pure with an iodine-like sheen to the deep blackberry and black cherry fruits. Layers of baking spices, roasting meats, blood pudding, dark chocolate and impressively judged oak along with compact granitic tannins and bright

acidity with excellent length on the finish. Diam. 14.5% alc. **RATING** 96
DRINK 2023-2035 $320 DB

Ahrens' Creek Cabernet Sauvignon 2020, Barossa Valley Opulent
blackberry, black cherry and dark plum fruits are cut through with hints of
cedary oak, vanilla bean, clove, baking spice, licorice and dark chocolate. Full
bodied with fine, granitic tannin heft, bright acidity and a wonderful depth and
presence. Diam. 14.5% alc. **RATING** 96 **DRINK** 2023-2035 $180 DB

Ahrens' Creek Mourvèdre 2021, Barossa Valley Notes of dark plum,
mulberry and boysenberry fruits with hints of souk-like spices, redcurrant jelly,
veal jus, iodine, roasting game meats, pressed flowers and earth. There is a sour
cherry aspect on the palate and a wonderful array of Asian spices and gamey
notes with fine, granitic tannins, bright acidity and a sapid, spicy finish. Diam.
14.5% alc. **RATING** 95 **DRINK** 2023-2029 $180 DB

Ahrens' Creek Shiraz 2020, Barossa Valley Very old (ancestor) vines have
produced a savoury, earthy wine that's very different from its Ahrens' Creek
Ancestor Vine Shiraz sibling. There's a hint of bitter chocolate that comes and
goes in a wine full of interest. Diam. 14.5% alc. **RATING** 95 **DRINK** 2023-2035
$180 JH

♥♥♥♥♀ **Ahren's Creek Ancestor Vine Grenache 2021, Barossa Valley** **RATING** 93
DRINK 2023-2028 $180 DB

Twins Barrel Reserve Grenache Mourvèdre Shiraz 2021, Barossa Valley
RATING 93 **DRINK** 2023-2028 $50 DB

Barossa Ridge Cabernets 2020 **RATING** 92 **DRINK** 2023-2028 $180 DB

Barossa GMS Grenache Mourvèdre Shiraz 2021, Barossa Valley
RATING 91 **DRINK** 2023-2026 $50 DB

Max & Me ★★★★★

Eden Valley Hotel, 11 Murray Street, Eden Valley, SA 5235 **Region** Eden Valley
T 0403 250 331 **www**.maxandme.com.au **Open** 7 days 12–5 **Winemaker** Philip
Lehmann **Viticulturist** Philip Lehmann **Est.** 2011 **Dozens** 900 **Vyds** 10.22ha

Max is the name of Phil Lehmann's rescue German shepherd/whippet cross, who introduced
Phil to his (then) wife-to-be Sarah during a visit to the Barossa. A dog lover from way back,
she fell in love with Max and Phil made it clear she wouldn't get Max unless she married him
(Phil). Phil had previously purchased the Boongarrie Estate with 5.25ha of shiraz and 4.97ha
of cabernet sauvignon. They converted the vineyard to (non-certified) organic management,
with no herbicides and only copper/sulphur sprays. The benefits are self-evident, reflected
in the high quality of the wines made since '11. Plantings of gamay, riesling and grenache
came in '21.

♥♥♥♥♥ **Boongarrie Vineyard Shiraz 2021, Eden Valley** Lifted aromas of satsuma
plum, boysenberry and crunchy blueberry fruits cut with hints of spice, citrus
blossom, licorice, chocolate, olive tapenade and earth. It sports excellent fruit
purity and detail, a mineral-laden acid cadence and a powdery tannin architecture
with a real sense of harmony and verve. The best release yet from this vineyard.
Screw cap. 13.2% alc. **RATING** 95 **DRINK** 2023-2033 $60 DB

Boongarrie Vineyard Cabernet Sauvignon 2021, Eden Valley There is a
brightness to the aromatic profile, a high-toned blackberry pastille note that sits
above the black cherry fruits with hints of rose petals, licorice, wild herbs, tobacco
leaf, pressed flowers, marzipan and earth. Impressive granitic tannins appear ripe
and willing to lend support, while Eden Valley acidity provides a vibrant pulse.
Screw cap. 13.8% alc. **RATING** 95 **DRINK** 2023-2033 $50 DB ✪

Springton Vineyard Grenache 2022, Eden Valley Vivid and zesty with
impressively pure plum and red berry fruits, a plume of gingery spice and hints of
cola, citrus blossom and red licorice. Great velocity and chalky tannin grip all add
up to a great little first run for this new wine. Very nice! Screw cap. 13.3% alc.
RATING 94 **DRINK** 2023-2030 $55 DB

Woodcarvers Vineyard Mirooloo Road Riesling 2022, Eden Valley
RATING 93 DRINK 2023–2030 $30 DB ✪
Boongarrie Vineyard Whole Bunch Syrah 2021, Eden Valley RATING 93
DRINK 2023–2030 $50 DB
Boongarrie Vineyard Shiraz 2020, Eden Valley RATING 93
DRINK 2023–2033 $60 DB
The House Blend Shiraz Cabernet Sauvignon 2021, Eden Valley
RATING 92 DRINK 2023–2030 $40 DB
Pinot Noir 2021, High Eden RATING 91 DRINK 2023–2028 $65 DB

Maxwell Wines ★★★★

19 Olivers Road, McLaren Vale, SA 5171 **Region** McLaren Vale
T (08) 8323 8200 **www.**maxwellwines.com.au **Open** 7 days 10–5 **Winemaker** Kate
Petering, Mark Maxwell **Viticulturist** Richard Wellsmore **Est.** 1979 **Dozens** 30 000
Vyds 40ha
Maxwell Wines has carved out a reputation as a premium producer in McLaren Vale, making
some excellent red wines in recent years. The majority of the vines on the estate were planted
in '72, including 19 rows of the highly regarded Reynella clone of cabernet sauvignon. The
Ellen Street shiraz block in front of the winery was planted in '53. Kate Petering, formerly
chief winemaker at Mount Langi Ghiran, was appointed head winemaker in March '19.

 Nero 2021, McLaren Vale Nero d'Avola, a robust variety suited to dry, warm
climates, performs well here. It's responsible for effusively fruity wines swathed in
dusty tannins that generally, at least in its home turf of Sicily, drink well young.
Among the better regional expressions due to the refined belt of tannin. Blood
plum, lilac, a twine of dried marjoram, thyme and some well-appointed oak
framework, all impeccably assembled. Excellent drinking. Screw cap. 14.2% alc.
RATING 93 DRINK 2023–2026 $42 NG
Minotaur Reserve Shiraz 2021, McLaren Vale A powerful mould of dark
fruits, molten licorice and salubrious coffee oak cladding. This is a style for the
hedonist, with an abundance of pretty much everything, like the Spanish quarter
in Naples. And yet, despite it all, there is considerable craftsmanship involved to
promote freshness and restrain the oak from excess. OTT, but in the best way.
Diam. 14% alc. RATING 92 DRINK 2023–2032 $115 NG
Clan Wine Club Grenache Blanc 2022, McLaren Vale The wines here have
grown in stature and with such strident convincing. A defter touch, the right
varieties … and so the story goes. Fine aromas, fidelitous to type: yellow plum,
dried tatami mat and a toasted nutty brûlée verging on marzipan. Picked on the
side of freshness. Screw cap. 12.5% alc. RATING 91 DRINK 2023–2028 $42 NG
Ellen Street Shiraz 2020, McLaren Vale An unabashed, full-throttle shiraz,
drawing on smoky barrel ferment aromas to corral a stream of saturated dark-
and blue-fruit allusions. Plenty floral and lifted. Clove and allspice, too. Firm oak
rims. This ticks the boxes for the traditional drinker of throaty South Australian
wines with an additional notch of flair. Screw cap. 14.5% alc. RATING 90
DRINK 2023–2032 $42 NG

Mayer ★★★★★

66 Miller Road, Healesville, Vic 3777 **Region** Yarra Valley
T (03) 5967 3779 **www.**timomayer.com.au **Open** By appt **Winemaker** Timo Mayer,
Rivar Ferguson-Mayer **Est.** 1999 **Dozens** 2000 **Vyds** 3ha
Timo Mayer teamed with partner Rhonda Ferguson to establish Mayer on the slopes of
Mt Toolebewong, 8km south of Healesville. The steepness of those slopes is presumably
'celebrated' in the name given to the vineyard (Bloody Hill). Pinot noir has the lion's
share of the high-density vineyard, with smaller amounts of shiraz and chardonnay. Mayer's
winemaking credo is 100% whole bunches (with a focus on syrah, cabernet, gamay, merlot,
nebbiolo, sangiovese and tempranillo), minimal interference and handling; all wines are all
unfined and unfiltered.

ŸŸŸŸŸ **Syrah 2022, Yarra Valley** A saturated crimson purple. It's got blackberries, black cherries and satsuma plums. But wait, there's more. It's also got crushed violets, iodine, charcuterie and allspice. Like an exquisitely tailored velvet suit, this is sumptuous but perfectly proportioned with fine-grained and persistent tannins rounding out a wine that will provide considerable pleasure. Diam. 13% alc. RATING 97 DRINK 2022-2036 $65 PR ✪

Chardonnay 2022, Yarra Valley Brightly fruited with white peach, green apple, lemon verbena and very lightly grilled nuts. Pure-fruited and flinty. The acidity is fine-boned and there's a grapefruit pithiness on the finish adding to the wine's complexity and length. Should age very nicely indeed. Diam. 12.5% alc. RATING 97 DRINK 2022-2027 $60 PR ✪

ŸŸŸŸŸ **Bloody Hill Villages Coldstream Shiraz 2022, Yarra Valley** Pink peppercorns and cured meats with ripe raspberry coulis and dark cassis. There's a hint of mint, too. Even better on the palate, which also reveals some black olive tapenade and Asian spices. Fine, almost pinot-like tannins to finish. A steal at this price. Diam. 13% alc. RATING 96 DRINK 2022-2028 $34 PR ✪

Bloody Hill Villages Coldstream Pinot Noir 2022, Yarra Valley Gorgeous from the outset with aromas of violets, red cherries and lavender. Some strawberry sherbet even. Pure-fruited and fine-boned, this elegant and gently sinewy wine is a pleasure to drink now, but has the structure to improve over the next few years. Diam. 12.5% alc. RATING 96 DRINK 2022-2027 $38 PR ✪

Bloody Hill Villages Healesville Pinot Gris 2022, Yarra Valley Pinot Gris of the Year. A fresh and appealing pinot gris. This has some nashi pear and grapefruit pith with a hint of apricot kernel. On the palate, you'll find white nectarine, some pickled ginger and, equally importantly, a touch of grip giving the wine shape and structure. A no-brainer for spicy Thai food and the like. Diam. 12.5% alc. RATING 96 DRINK 2022-2025 $34 PR ✪ ♥

Pinot Noir 2022, Yarra Valley A bright crimson red. Very pure-fruited and perfumed. Perfectly ripened raspberries and strawberries intermingle with scents of sandalwood, allspice and a touch of cardamom. Already delicious, this is also well-structured with fine tannins and bright acidity. Diam. 12.5% alc. RATING 96 DRINK 2022-2033 $65 PR ✪

Nebbiolo 2022, Yarra Valley With aromas of perfectly ripened red raspberries, freshly cut flowers and Mediterranean dried herbs, this is more serious than last year's release. It's amazing, too, just how well the fruit has swallowed up the whole bunches. There's excellent depth of fruit on the palate and with its firm yet supple nebbiolo and whole-bunch tannins, this has all the components to age superbly. Bravo! Diam. 13% alc. RATING 96 DRINK 2022-2032 $65 PR ✪

Volcanic Chardonnay 2022, Yarra Valley White peach and floral notes intermingle with some spice and gentle flint aromas. The palate is energetic and fresh with a hint of lemon oil coming through in the long, crunchy and saline finish. Good stuff. Screw cap. 12.5% alc. RATING 96 DRINK 2023-2023 $60 PR ✪

Cabernet 2022, Yarra Valley Fragrant with cranberries, boysenberries, plum skins, a little olive tapenade and well-judged florals from the whole bunches. Medium bodied, this juicy red is neither forced nor extracted and the sinewy, fine and long tannins are already in perfect harmony with the fruit. A delicious and atypical cabernet. Diam. 13% alc. RATING 95 DRINK 2023-2031 $65 PR

Volcanic Syrah 2022, Yarra Valley A gorgeous bright crimson and an intriguing nose with bright maraschino cherries, red apple skin, satsuma plums and violets. Really bright and crunchy-fruited on the palate and the tannins are fine and sophisticated. The perfect wine for steak frites. Screw cap. 12.5% alc. RATING 95 DRINK 2023-2023 $60 PR

Dr Mayer Pinot Noir 2022, Yarra Valley A cornucopia of whole-bunch spices and fresh herbal notes to go with the wine's briary red fruits. Firmly structured and still quite compact on the palate, this just needs a year or so for the tannins and whole bunches to assimilate into the wine. Diam. 12.5% alc. RATING 94 DRINK 2022-2030 $65 PR

Volcanic Pinot Noir 2022, Yarra Valley Vibrant and pristine with aromas of new season raspberries, pomegranate and subtle incense from the whole bunches, which have already integrated seamlessly into the wine. There's a freshness on the palate, some sweet spice and the tannins are fine. Finishes gently sappy and persistent. Screw cap. 13% alc. **RATING** 94 **DRINK** 2023–2023 $65 PR

Bloody Hill Villages Panton Hill Chardonnay 2022, Yarra Valley **RATING** 93 **DRINK** 2022–2026 $38 PR
Merlot 2022, Yarra Valley **RATING** 93 **DRINK** 2022–2032 $65 PR
Gamay 2022, Yarra Valley **RATING** 93 **DRINK** 2022–2028 $55 PR
Tempranillo 2022, Yarra Valley **RATING** 92 **DRINK** 2022–2029 $60 PR

Mayfield Vineyard   ★★★★☆

954 Icely Road, Orange, NSW 2800 **Region** Orange
T (02) 6365 9292 **www**.mayfieldvineyard.com.au **Open** W'ends 10–4 **Winemaker** Drew Tuckwell **Viticulturist** Charles Simons **Est.** 1998 **Dozens** 12000 **Vyds** 17ha
The history of Mayfield dates back to 1815 when explorer William Charles Wentworth was granted a Mayfield Crown Grant from the governor of NSW. Today the Settlers Cottage is a heritage-listed homestead and popular accommodation. Vines were first planted in '99 and Mayfield vineyard was born. Since ownership changed hands in '21, Mayfield has been given a breath of cool, crisp Orange air from root to bottle under the guidance of co-owner, general manager and viticulturist Charles Simons. Single-vineyard wines, minimal intervention and a focus on elegance, refinement and vivacity are at its core.

Eighteen Fifteen Chardonnay 2022, Orange Latent power from start to finish with the developing Mayfield signature style of finesse and grace. Lemon aspen, lime cordial and white nectarine. Crushed sandstone and struck match. A yoghurt creaminess is followed by darting acidity and a touch of phenolic bitterness on the finish. A steal at the price. Screw cap. 12.5% alc. **RATING** 95 **DRINK** 2022–2032 $37 SW ✪

Backyard Riesling 2022, Orange **RATING** 93 **DRINK** 2022–2032 $34 SW ✪
Single Vineyard Chardonnay 2021, Orange **RATING** 93 **DRINK** 2022–2035 $37 SW
Five Rows Cabernet Franc Merlot Cabernet Sauvignon Petit Verdot 2022, Orange **RATING** 91 **DRINK** 2022–2026 $30 SW
Sophie's Godmother Sauvignon Blanc 2022, Orange **RATING** 90 **DRINK** 2022–2025 $28 SW

Mayford Wines   ★★★★★

6815 Great Alpine Road, Porepunkah, Vic 3740 (postal) **Region** Alpine Valleys
T (03) 5756 2528 **www**.mayfordwines.com **Open** Not **Winemaker** Eleana Anderson
Viticulturist Bryan Nicholson **Est.** 1995 **Dozens** 1000 **Vyds** 3.9ha
In '95, Bryan Nicholson planted a small amount of shiraz, chardonnay and tempranillo. Further plantings of shiraz, tempranillo, cabernet sauvignon and malbec increased the vineyard to 3.9ha, with more plantings planned. Wife and co-owner Eleana Anderson was a Flying Winemaker, working 4 vintages in Germany while completing her wine science degree at CSU. Vintages in Australia included one at Feathertop (also at Porepunkah), where she met Bryan. Eleana practises minimalist winemaking, declining to use enzymes, cultured yeasts, tannins and copper. Wines can be tasted at Billy Button's cellar door in Bright (see separate entry).

Porepunkah Tempranillo 2021, Alpine Valleys What a comeback! Tempranillo shines in the fabulous '21 vintage. Great vibrancy of colour in deep purple hues. Offers up a striking perfume of well-defined dark cherries, plum, earth, dried rosemary, dusty cocoa and red licorice. An effortless beauty unfolds across the palate. Medium bodied, supple and textural. Give it time. Screw cap. 13.9% alc. **RATING** 96 **DRINK** 2022–2033 $42 JP ✪

Porepunkah Shiraz 2019, Alpine Valleys A wine of pure class. Perfectly reflects the Alpine Valleys' ability to compete when it comes to quality shiraz. Arrives integrated and balanced with a budding complexity. Dark plum, black berries, a shopping list of spices including anise and just a touch of intriguing eucalyptus. The ground work for a big future is set against a nuanced display of smoky oak and fine tannins. Screw cap. 13.9% alc. **RATING** 96 **DRINK** 2022–2034 $42 JP ✪

Porepunkah Chardonnay 2021, Alpine Valleys A fine-featured chardonnay with acidity taking charge, slowly revealing a delicacy of citrus fruits (grapefruit, lemon zest) with pear skin, a gentle spiciness and some nutty influences. Coming together beautifully and deliciously now, give it more time and you will be rewarded. Screw cap. 13% alc. **RATING** 95 **DRINK** 2022–2030 $42 JP ✪

Maygars Hill Winery ★★★★★

115 Longwood-Mansfield Road, Longwood, Vic 3665 **Region** Strathbogie Ranges
T 0402 136 448 **www**.maygarshill.com.au **Open** By appt **Winemaker** Contract
Est. 1997 **Dozens** 900 **Vyds** 3.2ha

Jenny Houghton purchased this 8ha property in '94, planting shiraz (1.9ha) and cabernet sauvignon (1.3ha). The name comes from Lieutenant Colonel Maygar, who fought with outstanding bravery in the Boer War in South Africa in 1901 and was awarded the Victoria Cross. The shiraz and cabernet sauvignon, both in Reserve and standard guise, have been consistently excellent for a number of years. In mid-2021, the winery was sold to established vineyard owners from North East Victoria.

🍷🍷🍷🍷🍷 **Cabernet Sauvignon 2021, Strathbogie Ranges** Strathbogie Ranges cabernet is mighty good, often nudging out the region's fave (shiraz) in the quality stakes. This is such a wine, stunningly so. Composed and complex with an enticing aromatic bouquet in cassis, mulberry, black cherry, bush mint and the liveliest of spices. Dark fruits rule the taut, well-structured palate with a juicy swathe of flavour, herbal notes and integrated oak tannins. This will age superbly. Screw cap. 14% alc. **RATING** 95 **DRINK** 2023–2034 $32 JP ✪ ♥

Beersheba Cabernet Sauvignon 2021, Strathbogie Ranges Built for a long journey, Beersheba slowly, slowly, reveals its inner beauty. Consider a decant to do it full justice. Brandishes regional eucalyptus in tandem with cassis, blackberries, bramble, a full array of dried herbs and chocolate and woodsy oak. It's all tightly controlled at the moment and dressed firmly in cherry pip-dry tannins. Give it the time it demands and deserves. Screw cap. 13.1% alc. **RATING** 95 **DRINK** 2023–2038 $45 JP ✪

🍷🍷🍷🍷 **Shiraz 2021, Strathbogie Ranges RATING** 92 **DRINK** 2023–2031 $30 JP ✪

mazi wines ★★★★

5 Wilbala Road, Longwood, SA 5153 (postal) **Region** McLaren Vale
T 0406 615 553 **www**.maziwines.com.au **Open** Not **Winemaker** Alex Katsaros,
Toby Porter **Est.** 2016 **Dozens** 6000

Lifelong friends Toby Porter and Alex Katsaros always talked about making wine together as an adjunct to their day jobs in wine. Toby has been a winemaker at d'Arenberg for 15+ years and Alex had 10 years' experience working with alternative varieties here and abroad. They decided to only make rosé, and more power to them in doing so. McLaren Vale is the sole source for their grapes, focusing on grenache, but they are happy to work with bush-vine mataro. The aim is to produce fresh wines with vibrant fruit. The derivation of the name is as simple as that of their raison d'être – it is Greek for together.

🍷🍷🍷🍷🍷 **Grenache Rosé 2022, McLaren Vale** A mid-coral with onion skin edges. Bright and effusive, with musk stick, loganberry, dried thyme and fecund raspberry scents. The palate is mid-weighted and textural, nicely judged between freshness and flavour. This is a very good rosé, be it in an Australian context alone, or an international one. Screw cap. 13% alc. **RATING** 94 **DRINK** 2022–2023 $26 NG ✪

ＹＹＹＹＹ Limited Release Rosé 2022, McLaren Vale **RATING** 93 **DRINK** 2022-2025
$48 NG

Mataro Cinsault Grenache Rosé 2022, McLaren Vale **RATING** 92
DRINK 2022-2024 $25 NG ✪

Tóra Mataro Cinsault 2022, McLaren Vale **RATING** 91 **DRINK** 2022-2024
$25 NG ✪

Mazza Wines ★★★★

PO Box 480, Donnybrook, WA 6239 **Region** Geographe
T 0417 258 888 **www.mazza.com.au Open** Not **Winemaker** Contract **Est.** 2002
Dozens 1000 **Vyds** 4ha

David and Anne Mazza were inspired by the great wines of Rioja and the Douro Valley, and
continue a long-standing family tradition of making wine. They have planted the key varieties
of those 2 regions: tempranillo, graciano, bastardo, sousão, tinta cão and touriga nacional.
They believe they were the first Australian vineyard to present this collection of varieties on
a single site and I am reasonably certain they are correct.

ＹＹＹＹＹ Planta Fina 2022, Geographe Mazza Wines is the only producer of
planta fina, a rare Spanish variety, in Australia. Sea spray and red apple scents
in abundance with a touch of hazelnut and candle wax. The palate shows
more red apple, licks of briny minerality and a dip of almond finishing
long, fine and refreshing with a pink grapefruit tang. It's an utter delight of
impeccable credentials. Only 45 cases made. Screw cap. 11% alc. **RATING** 93
DRINK 2023-2025 $28 MB ✪

Bastardo Fortified Touriga Nacional 2018, Geographe A bright and
vibrant fortified wine. Scents of candied cherry, toffee apple, dried orange,
kirsch and fernet. The palate is slippery and opulent but clean and fresh-feeling
with more of the kirsch, fernet and orange characters, a lick of sweet spice and
some chocolatey elements. It's well judged in its style, rich and luxurious. Good
drinking. Screw cap. 17% alc. **RATING** 92 **DRINK** 2023-2030 $30 MB ✪

Mazzini ★★★☆

131 Lumb Rd, Sutherlands Creek VIC 3331 (postal) **Region** Geelong
T 0448 045 845 **www.mazziniwines.com.au Open** Not **Winemaker** Ray Nadeson,
Duncan Lowe **Est.** 2016 **Dozens** 400

Mazzini Wines was established in 2016 by Paul and Karen Marinelli after fostering strong
connections with the Geelong wine industry. Mazzini Wines doesn't boast the usual winery,
vineyard and cellar door but rather operates as a form of négociant/wine merchant, sourcing
fruit from some of the region's most promising individual vineyards and utilising the skills of
experienced local winemakers Ray Nadeson and Duncan Lowe. The colourful Mazzini wine
labels are a nod to Paul's Italian heritage and the name of his Nonno's street in Mola di Bari
in Puglia, Italy. The wines are intended to reflect the hands-on and pure approach to produce
he grew up admiring in his family.

ＹＹＹＹＹ Single Vineyard Pinot Noir 2022, Geelong A bright cherry red. Aromas
of sour cherry, blood oranges and spice emanate from this well-made wine. In
the mouth, it's silky with good depth of fruit and fine, supple tannins to close.
Screw cap. 12.5% alc. **RATING** 92 **DRINK** 2022-2027 $35 PR

MBK ★★★★

14 Meredyth Street, Millswood, SA 5034 (postal) **Region** Barossa Valley
T (08) 8344 5691 **Open** Not **Winemaker** Steve Baraglia **Est.** 2014 **Dozens** 400

MBK (and parent company, Mabenki) is derived from the names of the 3 founders: Mario
Barletta, Ben Barletta and Kim Falster. Brothers Ben and Mario came from a retail background
(Walkerville Cellars, Adelaide), Kim Falster is their wine-loving friend. The company started
in '14, but its genesis was back in '93, making 'house wine' to sell in the store. They have

never missed a vintage, but wines were sold exclusively to a private customer base. The '21 vintage represented the first commercial release of the MBK label.

Watervale Riesling 2022, Clare Valley Scents of green apple juice, lime and frangipani. Juicy and bright to taste, more green apple juice here, another squeeze of lime and faint nougat savouriness. It's a bright and lively expression of good poise and length that drinks with charm and shows intensity of fruit character. Nicely done. Screw cap. 12% alc. **RATING** 93 **DRINK** 2022-2030 $25 MB ✪
Greenock Creek Shiraz 2020, Barossa Valley Super-deep magenta with inviting aromas of ripe satsuma plum, blackberry and black cherry fruits with hints of baking spices, Dutch licorice, brandied fruit, dark chocolate and earth. Opulent and rich with a deep, black fruit flow, plenty of spice and ferrous, graphite-like tones and super-compact ripe tannins, finishing long and true. Screw cap. 14.5% alc. **RATING** 92 **DRINK** 2023-2033 $30 DB ✪

Meadowbank Wines ★★★★★

652 Meadowbank Road, Meadowbank, Tas 7140 **Region** Southern Tasmania
T 0439 448 151 **www.**meadowbank.com.au **Open** By appt **Winemaker** Peter Dredge
Viticulturist Gerald Ellis **Est.** 1976 **Dozens** 800 **Vyds** 52ha
In '76 Gerald and Sue Ellis picked the first grapes from their large Glenora property at the top end of the Derwent River. There have been 4 major expansions since, a 10ha planting of pinot noir, chardonnay, syrah and gamay in '16 lifting the total to 52ha, the major part as fully mature vines. Meadowbank supplies grapes to 6 or so small wineries and also leases 32ha to Accolade. Peter Dredge, having been closely associated with the vineyard for 6 years, formed a partnership with the Ellis family (Gerald, Sue, daughter Mardi and her husband, Alex Deane) to relaunch Meadowbank. The wines are made by Peter at his contract winemaking facility from the portion of vineyard set aside for the Meadowbank wines.

Pinot Noir 2022, Tasmania There is an instant appeal here with spiced red cherry, wild strawberry and raspberry coulis notes cut with hints of dried citrus blossom, smoked meats, sous bois, softly spoken cedary tones, struck flint and char siu. Fine, billowing river-silt tannins, a mineral-laden line and a nice umami nudge as the wine slowly retreats with gentle game, spice and savoury red fruits. Screw cap. 12.5% alc. **RATING** 95 **DRINK** 2023-2033 $60 DB
Chardonnay 2022, Tasmania Great length of flavour and drive. White peach, nectarine, green apple and grapefruit tones with underlying hints of nougat, crushed river stone, wildflowers, flint, dried herbs and softly spoken cashew oak. Dots of oatmeal and soft spice throughout with an enticing mineral line, excellent tension and detail finishing long and pure. Screw cap. 12.5% alc. **RATING** 95 **DRINK** 2023-2029 $60 DB
Riesling 2022, Tasmania Purity and drinkability writ large. Light straw in colour with pure aromas of Meyer lemon, lime and peach skin with notes of crushed stone, pressed white flowers, almond paste, dried mandarin rind and hints of poached pear. A wonderfully textural wine, playing on the tension between fruit and acidity, sapid yet expressive, enchanting at the moment with a lot of promise. Screw cap. 12% alc. **RATING** 95 **DRINK** 2023-2033 $39 DB ✪
Chardonnay 2021, Tasmania Notes of juicy white peach, nectarine, apple and grapefruit with hints of white flowers, marzipan, roasted cashews, Meyer lemon and nicely judged French oak. Oatmeal notes swell on the mid-palate before being reined in by tight, mineral-laden acidity. Finishes long and pure with excellent clarity and drive. Screw cap. 12.5% alc. **RATING** 95 **DRINK** 2023-2028 $60 DB
Pinot Noir 2021, Tasmania A funky-edged little beauty with struck flint floating over the bright cherry and macerated strawberry fruits. Exotically spiced with a beautifully pure fruit profile, layered forest floor and Chinese roast duck notes. Fine, gentle tannin architecture and porcelain-fine acid drive. It's lovely. Diam. 12.5% alc. **RATING** 95 **DRINK** 2022-2030 $60 DB

Blanc de Blancs 2017, Tasmania Pale straw with a fine, energetic bead and aromas of grapefruit, green apple, lemon barley, crushed stone and white flowers plus marzipan and brioche notes. Nashi pear and some light, soft spice flow in on the palate, which shows fine, saline acidity and some nice tension and detail before fading off with gently spiced grapefruit and peach. Diam. 11.5% alc. **RATING** 94 **DRINK** 2023–2030 $85 DB

Syrah 2021, Tasmania Purpley-hued with vivid blue fruits, satsuma plums and some crunchy cranberry notes. Hints of exotic spice and amaro herbs, orange blossom, light meaty notes and a rocky minerality. Supple and super-pure with tight, compact granitic tannins and an energetic acid cadence, finishing plummy and very moreish. Screw cap. 12.5% alc. **RATING** 94 **DRINK** 2023–2028 $60 DB

ȲȲȲȲȲ **Gamay 2022, Tasmania RATING** 93 **DRINK** 2023–2026 $50 DB
Pinot Meunier 2022, Tasmania RATING 91 **DRINK** 2023–2025 $39 DB

Medhurst
★★★★★

24–26 Medhurst Road, Gruyere, Vic 3770 **Region** Yarra Valley
T (03) 5964 9022 **www**.medhurstwines.com.au **Open** Thurs–Mon & public hols 11–5
Winemaker Simon Steele **Est.** 2000 **Dozens** 6000 **Vyds** 12ha

The wheel has come full circle for Ross and Robyn Wilson. In the course of a very distinguished corporate career, Ross was CEO of Southcorp when it brought the Penfolds, Lindemans and Wynns businesses under its banner. Robyn spent her childhood in the Yarra Valley, her parents living less than a km away from Medhurst. The vineyard is planted to low-yielding sauvignon blanc, chardonnay, pinot noir, cabernet sauvignon and shiraz vines. The winery focuses on small-batch production and also provides contract winemaking services. The arrival of Simon Steele (his loss much mourned by Brokenwood) has enhanced the already considerable reputation of Medhurst.

ȲȲȲȲȲ **Estate Vineyard Chardonnay 2022, Yarra Valley** Another impeccable Medhurst chardonnay. This is singing with aromas of perfectly ripened white nectarine, peach, pink grapefruit and a little lightly grilled cashew. Equally pure fruited on the gently textured palate, which also has a fine vein of acidity coursing through. A truly lovely wine. Screw cap. 13% alc. **RATING** 97 **DRINK** 2022–2027 $50 PR ✪

Reserve Pinot Noir 2021, Yarra Valley Delicately perfumed with a bouquet of crystalline red fruits, pomegranate and rose petals, this is a wine that reveals itself slowly, and in waves. Fine boned, silky and structured, it's a joy to drink now but will only continue to build and improve. Screw cap. 13% alc. **RATING** 97 **DRINK** 2022–2031 $95 PR ✪

ȲȲȲȲȲ **Reserve Chardonnay 2021, Yarra Valley** Bright green gold. This is an essay in restraint and latent power, with aromas of stone fruits, tangerine oil, lemon curd and marine scents. Concentrated, structured and long, this has been built to last and it would be fascinating to follow this wine's evolution over the next 5–7 years, if not longer. Screw cap. 13% alc. **RATING** 96 **DRINK** 2022–2028 $95 PR

Estate Vineyard Pinot Noir 2022, Yarra Valley A light, very bright crimson red. Red fruits, lavender and spice are all present on the nuanced bouquet. Even better on the palate, which has excellent depths framed by chalky, persistent tannins and bright acidity. Good, but definitely a wine that will continue to improve for at least the next 2–3 years. Screw cap. 13% alc. **RATING** 95 **DRINK** 2022–2028 $55 PR

YRB 2022, Yarra Valley A vivid crimson purple, this leaps out of the glass with its vibrant mix of ripe raspberries, potpourri spices and pink peppercorns. Medium bodied with some concentration and tannin from the syrah while remaining supple and light on its feet. A delicious wine that can be enjoyed now but will still be looking good in 4–5 years. Screw cap. 13% alc. **RATING** 95 **DRINK** 2022–2027 $50 PR ✪

Estate Vineyard Rosé 2022, Yarra Valley An estate blend of cabernet sauvignon and shiraz from '00-planted D and E Blocks. The faint salmon hue reflects the whole-bunch pressing used to make this a purpose-built wine from the ground up. Screw cap. 13% alc. RATING 95 DRINK 2023–2028 $30 JH ✪

Meerea Park

Pavilion B, 2144 Broke Road, Pokolbin, NSW 2320 **Region** Hunter Valley
T (02) 4998 7474 **www**.meereapark.com.au **Open** 7 days 10–5 **Winemaker** Rhys Eather **Viticulturist** Rhys Eather **Est.** 1991 **Dozens** 8000
This is the project of Rhys and Garth Eather, whose great-great-grandfather, Alexander Munro, established a famous vineyard in the 19th century known as Bebeah. While the range of wines chiefly focuses on semillon and shiraz, it extends to other varieties (including chardonnay) and also into other regions. Meerea Park's cellar door is located at the striking Roche Estate, situated on the corner of Broke Road and McDonald Road. The quality of the wines is outstanding.

🍷🍷🍷🍷 **Cellar Release BLACK Shiraz 2018, Hunter Valley** The second in line of the drought-ravaged '17, '18 and '19 vintages. The grapes come from 2 highly praised vineyards, with the best 3 barrels chosen. A superb shiraz that plays a trick of presenting a wine that is so damn good it can be enjoyed tonight or 50 years hence. Sets the price bar for Hunter shiraz. Screw cap. 14% alc. RATING 98 DRINK 2023–2058 $300 JH

🍷🍷🍷🍷 **Alexander Munro Individual Vineyard Chardonnay 2022, Hunter Valley** Fruit was whole-bunch pressed, fermented and then matured for 10 months in French hogsheads (40% new). A full-bodied chardonnay, with concentration and length, the fruit having absorbed the oak. Screw cap. 12.5% alc. RATING 95 DRINK 2023–2031 $55 JH
Terracotta Individual Vineyard Syrah 2021, Hunter Valley 85/15% shiraz/marsanne. Co-fermentation has resulted in a light vivid magenta, the light- to medium-bodied palate also vibrant. Screw cap. 13.5% alc. RATING 95 DRINK 2023–2033 $70 JH
Hell Hole Individual Vineyard Shiraz 2021, Hunter Valley Hand-picked fruit from the 50–60yo vines. Matured in French hogsheads (40% new) for 16 months; minimal filtration and nil fining. Consistently a most attractive medium-bodied shiraz. Screw cap. 13.5% alc. RATING 95 DRINK 2023–2038 $60 JH
Old Vine Semillon 2016, Hunter Valley Sourced from a 50yo vineyard in Pokolbin. An exceptionally light and bright quartz green for a 6yo semillon. A complex bouquet that's faintly reductive, but not at all faulty. On the palate, the lemon citrus flavour is intense and long. Screw cap. 11.5% alc. RATING 95 DRINK 2023–2036 $40 JH ✪
Hell Hole Individual Vineyard Semillon 2022, Hunter Valley The bouquet is closed on release in March '23, but the juicy, sweet fruit on the palate is very attractive (the sweetness is fruit, not sugar, derived). Good length and balance. Screw cap. 11% alc. RATING 94 DRINK 2023–2035 $35 JH ✪
Terracotta Individual Vineyard Semillon 2021, Hunter Valley The grapes come from old vines on the Lochleven vineyard, with excellent juicy Meyer lemon fruit and crunchy acidity, length likewise very good. No-frills vinification. The future is bright. Screw cap. 11% alc. RATING 94 DRINK 2025–2035 $40 JH ✪

🍷🍷🍷🍷 **XYZ Semillon 2022, Hunter Valley** RATING 93 DRINK 2023–2029 $30 JH ✪
The Aunts Individual Vineyard Shiraz 2021, Hunter Valley RATING 93 DRINK 2023–2036 $40 JH
Reserve Pinot Noir 2022, Hunter Valley RATING 90 DRINK 2023–2026 $50 JH
XYZ Shiraz 2021, Hunter Valley RATING 90 DRINK 2023–2026 $30 JH

Mercer Wines   ★★★★★

426 McDonalds Rd, Pokolbin, NSW 2320 **Region** Hunter Valley
T 1300 227 985 **www**.mercerwines.com.au **Open** 7 days 10–5 **Winemaker** Aaron
Mercer, Kiri Irving **Est.** 2019 **Dozens** 4000

After several years at the bastion of organic Hunter Valley viticulture, Tamburlaine, Aaron
Mercer set out under his own banner. Aaron has been exposed to a litany of wine styles
through his experience across the region, with stints at Tyrrell's and Brokenwood, in addition
to work in France, Germany and California, where he sourced fruit along the Central
Coast from Bien Nacido, Paso Robles and Monterey. Yet it is the draw of the Hunter,
where Mercer was born, that defines his current MO: crafting wines in small batches to
showcase the Hunter's best turf, complemented at times with fruit from cooler reaches of
inter-regional NSW.

🍷🍷🍷🍷 **Montepulciano Rosso 2021, Central Ranges** This wine is vibing.
Blackberries, fluorescent dragonfruit and rambutans. Swiss chard leaves, dried
thyme and oregano. Crushed and sparkling volcanic soils. Rhythmic on the
palate, symmetrical and uniquely savoury. Tannins are varietally spot-on and carry
nuanced flavours. Finishes with a puckering slurp of audacity. Get in! Screw cap.
14% alc. **RATING** 95 **DRINK** 2022–2028 $32 SW ✪ ♥
Limited Release Shiraz 2021, Hunter Valley Vivid rim. Attractive medium-
bodied shiraz in archetypal Hunter style. Drink now for the vibrancy of the
blackberry and black cherry fruit, or cellar for decades as the spicy/fresh earth
flavours build, sustained by the ripe but fine tannins already on show. Screw cap.
14% alc. **RATING** 95 **DRINK** 2023–2043 $60 JH

🍷🍷🍷🍷 **Bianco 2022, Hunter Valley RATING** 92 **DRINK** 2023–2027 $28 JH ✪
Rosato Sangiovese 2022, Orange RATING 92 **DRINK** 2022–2025 $28 SW ✪
Organic Chardonnay 2022, Orange RATING 92 **DRINK** 2022–2028 $30 SW ✪
Limited Release Chardonnay 2022, Tumbarumba RATING 92
DRINK 2024–2032 $50 JF
Joven Tempranillo 2022, Hilltops RATING 91 **DRINK** 2022–2025 $30 JF
Barbera Novello 2022, Orange RATING 90 **DRINK** 2022–2027 $32 SW
Limited Release Semillon 2022, Hunter Valley RATING 90
DRINK 2023–2028 $40 JH

Mérite Wines   ★★★★

PO Box 167, Penola, SA 5277 **Region** Wrattonbully
T 0437 190 244 **www**.meritewines.com **Open** Not **Winemaker** Michael Kloak,
Colleen Miller **Viticulturist** Michael Kloak, Colleen Miller **Est.** 2000 **Dozens** 2000
Vyds 45ha

Mérite Wines was the end of Mike Kloak and Colleen Miller's protracted search for high-
quality viticultural land, with a particular focus on the production of merlot. However, it's
not a case of all eggs in the same basket; malbec, cabernet sauvignon and shiraz have also been
planted. It was not until '13 that the first small amount of wine was made (most of the grapes
were, and will continue to be, sold to other winemakers).

🍷🍷🍷🍷 **Single Vineyard Cabernet 2020, Wrattonbully** For the most part, it's a fleshy
cabernet with good/attractive fruit flavour, firming and freshening through the
finish in the process of elevating its quality. Blackcurrant, violet, mint and twiggy-
herb flavours combine successfully throughout, with resiny oak showing through
the aftertaste. A well-made, and well-flavoured, red wine. Screw cap. 14.5% alc.
RATING 94 **DRINK** 2024–2034 $60 CM
Q Single Vineyard Merlot 2020, Wrattonbully This is a merlot worth
hunting down. The flavours shoot through the wine in convincing style, bringing
nuance but also out-and-out fruit flavour, of both the red and black berried kind.
It's neat, firm, polished and generally well finished, with just enough grain to keep
it feeling real. Screw cap. 14% alc. **RATING** 94 **DRINK** 2023–2031 $32 CM ✪

Single Vineyard Merlot 2018, Wrattonbully This is polished and plush with sweet, berried fruit rolling attractively through the palate, complemented by cedar, violet, bay leaf and graphite characters. It feels complex in its own, easygoing way, though as it breathes the intricacy of the tannin is revealed, for the positive. A creaminess to the texture ramps up the pleasure that little bit more. Cork. 14% alc. RATING 94 DRINK 2024-2034 $60 CM

🍷🍷🍷🍷 **Malbec 2021, Wrattonbully** RATING 92 DRINK 2023-2032 $45 CM

Merricks Estate ★★★★☆

97 Thompson Lane, Merricks, Vic 3916 **Region** Mornington Peninsula
T 0419 135 037 **www**.merricksestate.com.au **Open** 1st w'end of each month 12–5
Winemaker Simon Black (Contract) **Viticulturist** George Kefford **Est.** 1977
Dozens 1800 **Vyds** 4ha

Melbourne solicitor George Kefford, with wife Jacky, runs Merricks Estate as a weekend and holiday enterprise. It produces distinctive, spicy, cool-climate shiraz, which has accumulated an impressive array of show trophies and gold medals. The fully mature vineyard and skilled contract winemaking by Simon Black are producing top class wines.

🍷🍷🍷🍷🍷 **Chardonnay 2022, Mornington Peninsula** When you have plump white stone fruit, tangy citrus, creamy fluffy lees, a dab of cedary oak and invigorating acidity all in one glass, it makes for a very enjoyable chardonnay. This is that and more. Supple and juicy across the palate with a lingering finish. Screw cap. 13.5% alc. RATING 95 DRINK 2023-2030 $45 JF ✪

🍷🍷🍷🍷 **Thompson's Lane Rosé 2022, Mornington Peninsula** RATING 90 DRINK 2022-2023 $26 JF

Pinot Noir 2018, Mornington Peninsula RATING 90 DRINK 2022-2026 $45 JF

Merriworth ★★★★★

63 Merriworth Road, Tea Tree, Tas 7017 (postal) **Region** Southern Tasmania
T 0406 657 774 **www**.merriworth.com.au **Open** Not **Winemaker** Anna Pooley, Justin Bubb **Viticulturist** Mark McNamara **Est.** 2017 **Dozens** 600 **Vyds** 2ha

It was their love of pinot noir that lured Mark McNamara and Kirralee Hatch to Tasmania after several years studying viticulture and winemaking on the Australian mainland. In '17 they purchased the 2ha Third Child vineyard and renamed it Merriworth. Planted by local John Skinner in '01 on a hillside overlooking the Jordan River at Tea Tree in the Coal River Valley, the site is home to 9 clones of pinot noir and 3 of riesling, planted on river flats of cracking clay soil and shallow, eroded slopes over dolerite rock. The brand is currently devoted exclusively to riesling and pinot noir from this site. Vibrant, young wines are made with accuracy and precision by Anna Pooley and Justin Bubb.

🍷🍷🍷🍷🍷 **Estate Riesling 2022, Tasmania** A scintillating riesling that shows characters of pristine lemon, lime and green apple fruits coiled around crystalline acidity. Focused and precise, it has impressive velocity and clarity on the palate with the lightest phenolic tweak of texture. It races off with a trail of white flowers, crushed stone, marzipan and lemon zest. It's a beauty. Screw cap. 12.5% alc. RATING 95 DRINK 2023-2028 $31 DB ✪

mesh ★★★★★

40 Eden Valley Road Angaston SA 5353 (postal) **Region** Eden Valley
T (08) 8561 3200 **www**.meshwine.com **Open** Not **Winemaker** Robert Hill-Smith, Jeffrey Grosset **Est.** 2002 **Dozens** 2000 **Vyds** 12ha

Mesh is the profound yet unlikely weaving together of the skills, knowledge and ideas of 2 names arguably more obsessive about South Australian riesling than any other: Robert Hill-Smith (5th-generation custodian of Yalumba) and Clare Valley legend Jeffrey Grosset. Their simple mandate is to champion Eden Valley riesling in a single wine. Fruit is sourced from 2 vineyards planted in '44 and '82 at 425m elevation. The result is as legendary as its story anticipates, though unfairly (yet perhaps inevitably) never seems to enjoy quite the limelight enjoyed by Hill-Smith and Grosset's own rieslings.

🍷🍷🍷🍷 **Riesling 2022, Eden Valley** Pale straw with aromas of freshly squeezed lime, juicy white peach and green apple with hints of Christmas lily, orange blossom, wet river stones and grapefruit pith. Tight focused and pithy in texture with a wonderful line of vivid porcelain acidity and some serious velocity of the focused exit. Screw cap. 12.5% alc. **RATING** 95 **DRINK** 2023-2029 $35 DB ✪
Classic Release Riesling 2017, Eden Valley We wine hacks constantly harp on about riesling being undervalued, but when you try a wine like this you'll get it. Lime, green apple and grapefruit with underlying soft spice, wildflowers, stone and dried hay. Calm yet still with mineral focus, clarity and velocity, stunning length of flavour and toasty, limey complexity. Very nice indeed. Screw cap. 12.5% alc. **RATING** 95 **DRINK** 2023-2033 $40 DB ✪

Metala ★★★★★

Lake Plains Road, Langhorne Creek, SA 5255 **Region** Langhorne Creek
T (08) 8537 3182 **www**.metala.com.au **Open** By appt **Winemaker** Jim Urlwin
Viticulturist Guy Adams **Est.** 1998 **Dozens** 25 000 **Vyds** 225ha

The wheel has turned full circle at Metala. It began its journey back in 1882 when William Formby purchased Metala Estate; vines were first planted in 1891. In 1962, Metala Shiraz Cabernet Sauvignon won the inaugural Jimmy Watson Trophy. In '66, Wolf Blass made the first vintage of his Yellow Label, based on shiraz and malbec from Langhorne Creek. As each vintage passed, volume soared, as did Grey Label (the first vintage '67, 100% Langhorne Creek cabernet sauvignon and shiraz). I'm not suggesting Metala was the largest supplier of grapes to Blass: clearly, it wasn't. But it became part of a huge cauldron of wine through the '70s and '80s as Australia moved to one of the world's 5 largest exporters (by value). Metala was a brand that had been swallowed by Saltram, itself thrown away as an autumn leaf. In '81, 5th-generation Guy Adams began serious attempts to unify the brand name, the 225ha of vines and the surrounding farmland. In '22, a long struggle saw TWE finally agree to terms for its divestment. In the same year, the Brothers in Arms brand, also owned by the Adams family, became part of Metala.

🍷🍷🍷🍷 **William Formby Shiraz 2021, Langhorne Creek** Elegance and balance are the keywords for a wine of beauty that words can't do justice to. Hard to reconcile with the '18, which surely is sweet. Screw cap. 14.5% alc. **RATING** 96 **DRINK** 2023-2043 $80 JH
Brothers In Arms Shiraz 2021, Langhorne Creek The '21 vintage has resulted in excellent colour, bouquet and palate. It really is an attractive medium- to full-bodied shiraz, and has a very long future for those with the long term in the mind's eye. Screw cap. 14.5% alc. **RATING** 95 **DRINK** 2025-2046 $55 JH

🍷🍷🍷🍷 **Shiraz Cabernet 2021, Langhorne Creek** **RATING** 93 **DRINK** 2023-2035 $20 JH ✪
Cabernet Sauvignon 2021, Langhorne Creek **RATING** 92 **DRINK** 2023-2038 $20 JH ✪
Brothers In Arms Cabernet Sauvignon 2020, Langhorne Creek **RATING** 92 **DRINK** 2023-2038 $45 JH
Shiraz 2022, Langhorne Creek **RATING** 90 **DRINK** 2023-2025 $20 JH ✪
Brothers In Arms Cabernet Sauvignon 2021, Langhorne Creek **RATING** 90 **DRINK** 2028-2033 $55 JH
William Formby Cabernet Sauvignon 2018, Langhorne Creek **RATING** 90 **DRINK** 2023-2026 $80 JH

Mewstone Wines ★★★★★

11 Flowerpot Jetty Road, Flowerpot, Tas 7162 **Region** Southern Tasmania
T 0439 367 653 **www**.mewstonewines.com.au **Open** Fri–Sun 10–4 **Winemaker** Jonathan
Hughes **Viticulturist** Luke Andree **Est.** 2011 **Dozens** 7000 **Vyds** 3.6ha

Brothers Matthew and Jonathan (Jonny) Hughes established Mewstone vineyard on the
banks of the D'Entrecasteaux Channel in the tiny hamlet of Flowerpot in '11. Jonny is the
winemaker; he studied winemaking in NZ before working in Langhorne Creek, Central
Otago, Mornington Peninsula, Barolo, Hunter Valley and Okanagan Valley in British
Columbia. Heading home to Tasmania, Jonny spent 7 years as the assistant winemaker at
Moorilla Estate. With the vineyard established to produce the single-site Mewstone wines, the
brothers have embarked on a 2nd label, Hughes & Hughes, which focuses on Tasmania as a
whole. Quality grapes are purchased from other local vineyards, and small-batch production
means he can put maximum effort in.

Ⓨ Ⓨ Ⓨ Ⓨ Ⓨ **Pinot Noir 2021, Tasmania** This is in every sense an exceptionally rich and
concentrated pinot, with excellent colour and layered spice, black cherry and
plum fruit in the style of high-quality Vosne-Romanée. Spices and classy tannins
carry the wine through to its compelling finish. Screw cap. 13.2% alc. **RATING** 97
DRINK 2023–2041 $70 JH ✪

Ⓨ Ⓨ Ⓨ Ⓨ Ⓨ **Hughes & Hughes Chardonnay 2021, Tasmania** It's sourced from vineyards
in the north west, Derwent and Coal River Valleys. The immediately complex
bouquet leads into a vibrantly crisp palate with a particularly satisfying finish
nourished by vibrato acidity. Grew and grew each time revisited. Value plus.
554 dozen made. Screw cap. 13.2% alc. **RATING** 96 **DRINK** 2023–2031 $37 JH ✪

Hughes & Hughes Pied de Cuve Pinot Noir 2021, Tasmania From the
Tinderbox vineyard in the D'Entrecasteaux Channel district. The spicy, savoury
overtones to the bouquet replay on the palate along with perfumed berries,
spices, and a fresh finish and aftertaste; its lightness of foot isn't a play on words.
Screw cap. 12.5% alc. **RATING** 95 **DRINK** 2023–2031 $50 JH ✪

Hughes & Hughes Lees Aged Chardonnay 2021, Tasmania From the
Clarence House vineyard in the Coal River Valley. Imposing complexity from the
first whiff to the last sip, flinty acidity strumming the base notes of the funky palate.
129 dozen made. Screw cap. 13.7% alc. **RATING** 95 **DRINK** 2023–2026 $50 JH ✪

Ⓨ Ⓨ Ⓨ Ⓨ Ⓨ **Chardonnay 2021, Tasmania RATING** 93 **DRINK** 2023–2027 $70 DB
Riesling 2021, Tasmania RATING 92 **DRINK** 2023–2030 $55 JH
Hughes & Hughes Milk Vat Pinot Noir 2021, Tasmania RATING 90
DRINK 2023–2026 $50 DB

Michael Hall Wines ★★★★★

103 Langmeil Road, Tanunda, SA 5352 **Region** Mount Lofty Ranges
T 0448 911 835 **www**.michaelhallwines.com **Open** Fri–Sat 11–5 or by appt
Winemaker Michael Hall **Est.** 2008 **Dozens** 2500

Michael Hall was once a jewellery valuer for Sotheby's in Switzerland. He came to Australia
in '01 to pursue winemaking – a lifelong interest – and undertook the wine science degree at
CSU, graduating as dux in '05. His vintage work in Australia and France is a veritable who's
who of producers: in Australia with Cullen, Giaconda, Henschke, Shaw + Smith, Coldstream
Hills and Veritas; in France with Domaine Leflaive, Meo-Camuzet, Vieux Telegraphe and
Trevallon. His wines are as impressive as his experience suggests they should be.

Ⓨ Ⓨ Ⓨ Ⓨ Ⓨ **Sauvignon Blanc 2022, Adelaide Hills** Arguably the finest sauvignon of the
region, as tightly embedded amid a latticework of quality oak as it is free-flowing
and creamy following barrel fermentation and time on lees. Nettle and hedgerow
segue to mirabelle plum and yellow fruits, all jettisoned to compelling length by a
juicy skein of acidity. A sense of immaculate poise, tension and layered complexity.
Excellent wine. Screw cap. 13.5% alc. **RATING** 95 **DRINK** 2023–2032 $38 NG ✪

Mount Torrens Syrah 2021, Adelaide Hills While I can sense the stems, there is such depth of fruit and long-limbed grape tannins that I have no doubt the verdancy will be absorbed in time. Ferrous, bloody, olive pasted and laden with smoky, spiced meats. A very good wine in an embryonic phase. Put this away for 5–8 years. Screw cap. 14.4% alc. RATING 95 DRINK 2024-2032 $60 NG

Stonewell Road Shiraz 2021, Barossa Valley Sporting an impressive array of super-ripe black fruits and cassis, there is a real inky, earthy intensity to this wine's form. Dark moody spice, clove and tobacco leaf, graphite and licorice and dark chocolate, they're all there in spades, with dense tannin support and a classic Stonewell fruit flow on the finish. Screw cap. 14.4% alc. RATING 95 DRINK 2023-2033 $60 DB

Lenswood Pinot Noir 2021, Adelaide Hills Pointed aromas of wild strawberry, damson plum and heather. An undercarriage of sous bois, campfire, rhubarb and root spice. Sappy and taut, the tannins form a sinuous arc across the palate, etching it with a glimpse of fruit, while a firmness suggests that halcyon times are still to come. Screw cap. 13.4% alc. RATING 95 DRINK 2024-2034 $60 NG

Piccadilly Chardonnay 2021, Adelaide Hills A fine nose of toasted hazelnut, nougat, crème brûlée, nectarine, lemon curd and ginger crystals. The long finish expansive, immensely fresh and driven by tensile acidity and a leesy, polenta-like generosity. Screw cap. 13% alc. RATING 94 DRINK 2024-2031 $55 NG

ŶŶŶŶŶ **Sang de Pigeon Shiraz 2021, Barossa Valley** RATING 93 DRINK 2023-2030 $32 DB ✪
Flaxman's Valley Syrah 2021, Eden Valley RATING 93 DRINK 2023-2030 $60 DB
Sang de Pigeon Shiraz 2020, Barossa Valley RATING 93 DRINK 2023-2028 $32 DB ✪
Greenock Roussanne 2022, Barossa Valley RATING 92 DRINK 2023-2027 $45 DB
Sang de Pigeon Pinot Noir 2021, Adelaide Hills RATING 92 DRINK 2022-2027 $32 NG

Mike Press Wines ★★★★

PO Box 224, Lobethal, SA 5241 **Region** Adelaide Hills
T (08) 8389 5546 **www.mikepresswines.com.au** **Open** Not **Winemaker** Mike Press **Viticulturist** James Press **Est.** 1998 **Dozens** 20000 **Vyds** 22ha
Mike and Judy Press established their Kenton Valley Vineyards in '98, when they purchased 34ha of land in the Adelaide Hills at an elevation of 500m. They planted mainstream cool-climate varieties (merlot, shiraz, cabernet sauvignon, sauvignon blanc, chardonnay and pinot noir) intending to sell the grapes to other wine producers. Even an illustrious 43-year career in the wine industry did not prepare Mike for the downturn in grape prices that followed, leading to the development of the Mike Press wine label. They produce high-quality sauvignon blanc, chardonnay, rose, pinot noir, merlot, shiraz, cabernet merlot and cabernet sauvignon, which are sold at mouth-wateringly low prices.

ŶŶŶŶŶ **Single Vineyard Shiraz 2021, Adelaide Hills** A wine that is at odds with its generous alcohol. It's medium- to full-bodied with a freshness contributed by its relatively open weave. The bouquet, too, is part of that freshness. Above all else, it is the variety speaking loud and clear in a vintage to be remembered for years to come. Screw cap. 14.8% alc. RATING 94 DRINK 2023-2041 $15 JH ✪

ŶŶŶŶŶ **Single Vineyard Pinot Noir Rosé 2022, Adelaide Hills** RATING 92 DRINK 2023-2023 $13 JH ✪
Jimmy's Block Single Vineyard Shiraz 2021, Adelaide Hills RATING 92 DRINK 2023-2041 $18 JH ✪
Single Vineyard Chardonnay 2022, Adelaide Hills RATING 90 DRINK 2023-2023 $13 JH ✪

Miles from Nowhere   ★★★★★

PO Box 128, Burswood, WA 6100 **Region** Margaret River
T (08) 9264 7800 **www**.milesfromnowhere.com.au **Open** Not **Winemaker** Frederique
Perrin, Julian Scott **Viticulturist** Ivan Pagano **Est.** 2007 **Dozens** 40 000 **Vyds** 100h
Miles from Nowhere is owned by Franklin and Heather Tate. After working with his parents
to establish Evans & Tate from '87–05, Franklin returned to the Margaret River in '07.
The Miles from Nowhere name comes from the long journey Franklin's ancestors made
over 100 years ago from Eastern Europe to Australia. The plantings include petit verdot,
chardonnay, shiraz, sauvignon blanc, semillon, viognier, cabernet sauvignon and merlot.

ΨΨΨΨΨ **Origin of Now Shiraz 2021, Margaret River** This is a solid offering. Dark
plums, baking spices and fresh herbs with a spray of pomegranate molasses. It's full
bodied with shapely and textural tannins. Lots to like, other than the 2kg bottle.
Cork. 14.5% alc. **RATING** 95 **DRINK** 2023–2031 $89 JF
Origin of Now Cabernet Sauvignon 2021, Margaret River From the
weighty bottle to the wine within, this is big and expansive across the full-bodied
palate. Yet, there's a plushness, too, a generosity of flavour from cassis, blackberry
pie and a lovely array of spices – warm and exotic. Some heft to the tannins, yet
refreshment throughout. Cork. 14.5% alc. **RATING** 95 **DRINK** 2023–2033 $89 JF

ΨΨΨΨ♀ **Origin of Now Chardonnay 2021, Margaret River RATING** 92
DRINK 2023–2028 $89 JF
Best Blocks Cabernet Sauvignon 2020, Margaret River RATING 92
DRINK 2023–2030 $22 JF ✪
Rosé 2022, Margaret River RATING 90 **DRINK** 2022–2023 $15 JF ✪
Best Blocks Shiraz 2020, Margaret River RATING 90 **DRINK** 2022–2028
$22 JF ✪

Millbrook Winery   ★★★★★

Old Chestnut Lane, Jarrahdale, WA 6124 **Region** Perth Hills
T (08) 9525 5796 **www**.millbrook.wine **Open** Thurs–Mon 10–5 **Winemaker** Emma
Gillespie **Viticulturist** John Fogarty **Est.** 1996 **Dozens** 10 000 **Vyds** 8ha
Millbrook is situated in the historic town of Jarrahdale, southeast of Perth. Located at the
picturesque Chestnut Farm, the property backs on to the Serpentine River and is nestled
among jarrah forests. Chestnut Farm dates back to the 19th century, when the original
owner planted an orchard and grapevines in 1865, providing fruit to the local timber-millers
in Jarrahdale. In 1996 Chestnut Farm and Millbrook Winery were bought by Peter and
Lee Fogarty, marking the family's first entry into the wine business. Together with their
children John, Mark and Anna they planted the vineyard. In '01 a state-of-the-art winery was
completed, including a restaurant. In addition to the 8ha estate, Millbrook draws on vineyards
in prime locations across WA for its Regional Range.

ΨΨΨΨΨ **Limited Release Chardonnay 2021, Western Australia** Squeaky and
tightly wound, pent up with green apple, grapefruit juice and kiwifruit fruit
characters and dosed with lavish woody spices. It feels complex with its layers of
flavour, intensity and a general sense of energy. A detailed, complex and nuanced
chardonnay that's not quite ready to roll yet, but give it time. Screw cap. 14% alc.
RATING 94 **DRINK** 2024–2035 $50 MB

ΨΨΨΨ♀ **Estate Viognier 2022, Perth Hills RATING** 93 **DRINK** 2023–2028 $40 MB
Regional Range Verdejo 2022, Margaret River RATING 90
DRINK 2022–2024 $25 JF ✪

Millon Wines   ★★★★

48 George Street, Williamstown, SA 5351 (postal) **Region** Eden Valley
T (08) 8524 6691 **www**.millonwines.com.au **Open** Not **Winemaker** Angus Wardlaw
Est. 2013 **Dozens** 20 000 **Vyds** 84ha

Millon Wines has 2 vineyards: one in the Eden Valley, the 2nd in Clare Valley. Winemaker Angus Wardlaw, with a degree in wine science from CSU and experience in the Clare Valley as winemaker at Kirrihill Wines, 'believes the Eden Valley is the future of the Barossa' (see separate entry for his family business, Brothers at War). He makes the Millon wines with a minimalist approach.

Reserve Shiraz 2020, Barossa Deep blood plum, black cherry and blackberry fruits flecked with amaro herbs, baking spices, turned earth, cocoa powder, graphite, chocolate and crème de cassis. The fruit presence is black and broody with some blackberry pastille tones, tight, fine tannin and light amaro and clove notes on the finish. Screw cap. 14% alc. RATING 92 DRINK 2023-2030 $55 DB
The Impressionist Riesling 2022, Eden Valley There is some excellent value to be had here. Eden Valley riesling from the strong '22 vintage singing true to regional form with bright, freshly squeezed lime notes and hints of orange blossom, crushed stone, grapefruit sorbet and lemon curd. Some lovely briny acidity driving things along and a suggestion of umami right at the tail end. Nice! Screw cap. 12% alc. RATING 91 DRINK 2023-2026 $18 DB ✪

Miners Ridge
★★★★☆

135 Westgate Rd, Armstrong, Vic 3377 **Region** Grampians
T 0438 039 727 **www**.minersridge.com.au **Open** By appt **Winemaker** Adam Richardson **Viticulturist** Andrew Toomey **Est.** 1998 **Dozens** 450 **Vyds** 17ha
Andrew and Katrina Toomey established Miners Ridge Wines after many years growing grapes in the Great Western region for other wineries. They decided to take small parcels of their finest fruit and craft a range of wines to reflect their 17ha vineyard site at Armstrong, enlisting experienced local winemaker Adam Richardson (ATR Wines) as their contract winemaker. Their vineyard, nestled on a gentle ridge in the foothills of Victoria's Grampians, takes its name from Chinese gold miners who worked the area's goldfields in the mid–1800s.

A.T. Shiraz 2021, Grampians Seriously peppery and seriously good. Black cherry, licorice and plum characters come rolled in sweet, woodsy, peppery spice, soy and fragrant herb notes tagging along for the ride. The length is sound and satisfying but the excitement here is all about the flavour profile. This is a beautiful wine. Screw cap. 14.5% alc. RATING 95 DRINK 2024-2034 $40 CM ✪
Merino Block Riesling 2022, Grampians 25g/L RS leaves a soft, mellifluous riesling with very good fruit intensity and length. This is where sheer deliciousness meets the 'world of fine wine' quality. It's all apples and limes and, apart from anything else, drinking it is a great pleasure. Screw cap. 13% alc. RATING 94 DRINK 2023-2033 $25 CM ✪

Cabernet Sauvignon 2021, Grampians RATING 92 DRINK 2024-2032 $25 CM ✪
Viognier 2021, Grampians RATING 92 DRINK 2023-2028 $28 CM ✪
Chardonnay 2022, Grampians RATING 91 DRINK 2023-2028 $28 CM ✪

Ministry of Clouds
★★★★★

765 Chapel Hill Road, McLaren Vale, SA 5171 **Region** McLaren Vale
T 0417 864 615 **www**.ministryofclouds.com.au **Open** By appt **Winemaker** Julian Forwood, Bernice Ong, Chris Parsons **Viticulturist** Richard Leask **Est.** 2012
Dozens 5000 **Vyds** 9.6ha
These wines have always been good, but today the best expressions are defined by McLaren Vale, rather than too much external dabbling: detailed wines that are long of limb and vibrant of fruit, dappled with savoury tannins and saline freshness. Clare Valley riesling and Tassie chardonnay are the outliers, dangling from the belt of the Vale's older vines and upper reaches, exciting new varieties including picpoul, mencia and a fringe of cooler Adelaide Hills material. Tim Geddes long made the wines, yet today the team is a triumvirate, with former Wedgetail Estate maker Chris Parsons joining the fray at the new winery in '22. Julian and Bernice craft this and shape that, while Chris is the technical raft. A firm understanding of

what varieties grow best where exemplified by 3 new clones of tempranillo, 2 of which are ex-Vega Sicilia. More poignant, one is from their warmer Toro property Pintia. Stay tuned!

🍷🍷🍷🍷 **Riesling 2022, Clare Valley** Obviously dodged most of the rain: this has an exceptionally rich, layered and complex palate, acidity piercing the veil of citrus fruit on the lingering finish and aftertaste. Screw cap. 12.3% alc. **RATING** 96 **DRINK** 2023–2042 $32 JH ✪

Chardonnay 2021, Tasmania Hand picked, whole-bunch pressed to used French barriques for fermentation and 9 months on lees. This is the usual approach, focusing on the purity and length of the grapefruit-driven fruit and lowering the cost of production. It's as clean as a whistle. Screw cap. 12.9% alc. **RATING** 96 **DRINK** 2023–2029 $48 JH ✪

Single Vineyard Blewitt Springs Shiraz 2020, McLaren Vale Sourced from dry-grown vines planted in 1960 by Patritti. A brilliant crimson-purple hue, a bouquet of white and red flowers and a palate that radiates the outcome of growing grenache in Blewitt Springs. All class. Screw cap. 14.5% alc. **RATING** 95 **DRINK** 2023–2035 $65 JH

Onkaparinga Rocks Single Vineyard Shiraz 2020, McLaren Vale Whole-berry fermentation; hand plunged daily, basket pressed to new and used French puncheons. Shiraz with speed wheels on, oscillating between spicy/savoury fruit on the one hand and red and black cherry fruits on the other. Screw cap. 14.5% alc. **RATING** 95 **DRINK** 2023–2033 $65 JH

Kintsugi 2020, McLaren Vale Kintsugi is the ancient Japanese art repairing broken pottery using a glue of gold-laced lacquer. Ministry explains the process as a case where the whole is greater than the sum of its parts, here blending grenache, mataro, shiraz and carignan. It's light- to medium-bodied, but fragrant and juicy. Screw cap. 14.5% alc. **RATING** 94 **DRINK** 2023–2030 $85 JH

Mr Barval Fine Wines   ★★★★☆

7087 Caves Road, Margaret River, WA 6285 **Region** Margaret River
T 0407 726 077 **www.**mrbarval.com **Open** 7 days 11–5 **Winemaker** Robert Gherardi
Est. 2015 **Dozens** 1300

Robert Gherardi was born with wine in his blood. As a small boy he'd go to Margaret River to pick grapes with 3 generations of his extended Italian family. Nonetheless, his first degree was in marine science and biotechnology; while completing the course he worked in an independent wine store in Perth. Having tasted his way around the world in the bottle, at age 25 he enrolled in the full oenology and viticulture degree. This led to employment at Moss Wood for 4 years, then Brown Hill Estate as assistant winemaker and finally to Cullen for 3 years. Vanya Cullen encouraged him to travel to Barolo and work with Elio Altare. This included moving to Barolo with his wife and children to experience the 4 full seasons of viticulture and winemaking. He returns to Italy each year for his boutique travel business, with customised tours of Barolo, Valtellina and further north.

🍷🍷🍷🍷 **Riesria Cabernet Sauvignon 2020, Margaret River** Given that this spends 2 years in barrel (and there's obviously some new oak in the mix) and settles for a year in bottle before release, its approachability is commendable. The colour is excellent, the rather subtle fruit soft, the spices just the right amount and the tannins shapely, ripe and textural. Yes, easy to drink now or a few years hence. Screw cap. 14.4% alc. **RATING** 95 **DRINK** 2023–2033 $90 JF

🍷🍷🍷🍷 **Mistral 2022, Margaret River** **RATING** 93 **DRINK** 2023–2029 $33 JF ✪
Riserva Chardonnay 2021, Margaret River **RATING** 93 **DRINK** 2023–2028 $120 JF
Cabernet Malbec 2020, Margaret River **RATING** 93 **DRINK** 2023–2030 $40 JF
Giro di Nebbiolo 2022, Margaret River **RATING** 92 **DRINK** 2023–2028 $75 JF
Prima Alba 2022, Margaret River **RATING** 92 **DRINK** 2023–2027 $33 JF

Mr Hugh Wines

1018 Murrindindi Road, Murrindindi, Vic 3717 (postal) **Region** Upper Goulburn
T 0438 305 314 **www**.mrhughwine.com **Open** Not **Winemaker** Hugh Cuthbertson
Est. 1979 **Dozens** 90 000 **Vyds** 70ha

Hugh Cuthbertson has had a long and high-profile wine career that led him to take over his parents' Murrindindi Vineyards, creating Yarradindi Wines in '15. The Mr Hugh fortified wines are crafted from a solera system started in the 1880s by Melbourne wine merchant W.J. Seabrook. The overarching Yarradini brand was reinvented as Mr Hugh Wines in '23.

ŸŸŸŸŸ **Sipping Bliss Aperitif NV, Australia** A dark, nutty Apera of tremendous flavour intensity and complexity. So inviting, intoxicatingly so, with a basis of old material bringing forth burnt toffee aromas with dried fruits, gingerbread, bitter almond, oolong tea and vanilla while younger material brings freshness and lift. Simply stunning. 375mL. Screw cap. 18% alc. **RATING** 96 $50 JP ✪
Sipping Bliss Digestif NV, Australia Hard to believe fortified styles are losing ground in Australia when they can be as good as this. Old age plays a role here, how refreshing, with a basis of aged material that is intensely sweet and luscious in nutty rancio characters, caramel toffee, dried fruits, chocolate panforte and coffee grounds. So good. 500ml. Screw cap. 18% alc. **RATING** 95 $50 JP ✪

ŸŸŸŸŸ **The Blarney Rock Cabernet Sauvignon 2021, Coonawarra** **RATING** 92 **DRINK** 2023-2033 $45 JP

Mr Mick

7 Dominic Street, Clare, SA 5453 **Region** Clare Valley
T (08) 8842 2555 **www**.mrmick.com.au **Open** 7 days 10–4.30 **Winemaker** Tim Adams, Brett Schutz **Est.** 2011 **Dozens** 30 000 **Vyds** 195ha

This is the venture of Tim Adams and wife Pam Goldsack. The name was chosen to honour KH (Mick) Knappstein, a legend in the Clare Valley and the broader Australian wine community. Tim worked at Leasingham Wines with Mick from '75–86, and knew him well. When Tim and Pam acquired the Leasingham winery in Jan '11, together with its historic buildings, it brought the wheel full circle. Various commentators have used Mick's great one-liner: 'There are only two types of people in the world: those who were born in Clare, and those who wish they had been'.

ŸŸŸŸŸ **Tempranillo 2019, Clare Valley** There's a lot of tempranillo for your dollar here. Dark cherry, woody spices and warm hazelnut characters with a flicker of salted licorice, it manages varietal character while having mellowed into a plush, lush red wine. A bit of complexity seals the deal. Best drunk in the next year or so. Screw cap. 13% alc. **RATING** 91 **DRINK** 2022-2024 $17 MB ✪

🍇 Mr Murphy Wine Co

17 Greenhills Flaxley Rd, Macclesfield, SA 5153 **Region** Adelaide Hills
T 0437 213 355 **www**.mrmurphywineco.com.au **Open** By appt **Winemaker** Josh Amos-Winfield **Est.** 2021 **Dozens** 430 **Vyds** 1ha

Mr Murphy is an addition to the festoon of pulpy, sessionable wine styles found in every wine bar around the country. The wines are crafted with varying degrees of carbonic effect to achieve bright florals, effusive primary fruit and a soft structural latticework. The style of the wines and their irreverent labelling reflect trends in the market and maker Josh Amos-Winfield's commercial nous. Josh managed pubs and cellar doors in a previous life, roles that provided insight into what was going down as opposed to what was not. He returned to university as a mature-aged student to learn his craft. Most fruit is purchased, with the Adelaide Hills in focus.

ŸŸŸŸŸ **Lagrein 2021, Langhorne Creek** I have only tasted 3 lagrein wines from Australia. Two impressed me more than virtually any other wine hewn of recently introduced varieties. That includes tempranillo and even sangiovese. A gorgeous deep, glossy purple. Dark, lustrous fruits sluiced with alpine herbs teleporting me to the Alto Adige. Screw cap. 14% alc. **RATING** 92 **DRINK** 2022–2025 $27 NG

Syrah 2021, Adelaide Hills A sleek and savoury wine, albeit virtually devoid of any tannin. Smoked meat, whole-bunch derived iodine and spice, lilac and sassafras. Classy. A welcome restraint and demure savouriness, too. Mid-weighted of feel, suitably fresh and of decent length. Yet a wine without tannin is a tough proposition when it comes to a second glass. Screw cap. 14% alc. **RATING** 91 **DRINK** 2022–2028 $40 NG

Tempranillo 2021, Adelaide Hills A gently extracted expression layering a core of sweet cherry with a swathe of dried herbs, anise, mulberry leaf and a dab of vanillin oak. In all, an easy-drinking, everyday sort of wine. Screw cap. 13.5% alc. **RATING** 90 **DRINK** 2022–2025 $30 NG

Mr Riggs Wine Company ★★★★★

169 Douglas Gully Road, McLaren Flat, SA 5171 (postal) **Region** McLaren Vale
T 1300 946 326 **www**.mrriggs.com.au **Open** Not **Winemaker** Ben Riggs **Est.** 2001
Dozens 28 000 **Vyds** 12ha

With over 25 years of winemaking experience, Ben Riggs is well established under his own banner. Ben sources the best fruit from individual vineyards in McLaren Vale, Clare Valley, Adelaide Hills, Langhorne Creek, Coonawarra and from his own Piebald Gully Vineyard (shiraz and viognier). Each wine expresses the essence of not only the vineyard but also the region's terroir. The vision of the Mr Riggs brand is unpretentious and personal: 'To make the wines I love to drink'.

The Chap 2017, McLaren Vale Coonawarra Don't try to persuade me that these uber bottles, with their wax seals, etc., are user friendly. They aren't. This is a blend of McLaren Vale shiraz and Coonawarra cabernet sauvignon, the percentages not given. The cool vintage right across the southeastern corner of Australia wasn't easy for later ripening varieties. Diam. 14.5% alc. **RATING** 94 **DRINK** 2023–2027 $100 JH

Mr Brightside Eurotrash 2021, Adelaide Hills **RATING** 92 **DRINK** 2023–2026 $22 NG ✪
JFR Shiraz 2020, McLaren Vale **RATING** 92 **DRINK** 2022–2035 $50 NG
Burnt Block Shiraz 2020, McLaren Vale **RATING** 92 **DRINK** 2022–2035 $50 NG
The Magnet Grenache 2021, McLaren Vale **RATING** 91 **DRINK** 2022–2026 $30 NG
Watervale Riesling 2022, Clare Valley **RATING** 90 **DRINK** 2023–2026 $25 JH ✪
Sanjo Sangiovese 2021, Adelaide Hills **RATING** 90 **DRINK** 2022–2025 $30 NG
Piebald Syrah 2021, Adelaide Hills **RATING** 90 **DRINK** 2022–2025 $30 NG
Montepulciano d'Adelaide 2021 **RATING** 90 **DRINK** 2022–2027 $30 NG
The Bolter Cabernet Sauvignon 2021, McLaren Vale **RATING** 90 **DRINK** 2023–2038 $25 NG ✪

Mistletoe Wines ★★★★★

410a Bridgman Road, Wattle Ponds, NSW 2330 (postal) **Region** Hunter Valley
T (02) 4998 7770 **www**.mistletoewines.com.au **Open** Not **Winemaker** Scott Stephens
Viticulturist Liz Riley **Est.** 1989 **Dozens** 5000

Mistletoe Wines can trace its history back to 1909 when a vineyard was planted on what was then called Mistletoe Farm. Ken and Gwen Sloan purchased the Pokolbin property in '89 and created a family business spanning 3 generations, with son Robert tending the vines and daughter Cassandra running the cellar door with Gwen and granddaughter Natane. In '22 the Sloan family sold the property and Ken and Gwen are selling the remaining stock at bargain prices, via their website. The quality and consistency of these wines are irreproachable.

Museum Release Reserve Semillon 2009, Hunter Valley Pale green gold. Fourteen years young, fresh and vibrant, the faces of citrus led by Meyer lemon

and lemongrass, before a burnish of honey is painted by an artist. Sheer bliss.
Screw cap. 10.6% alc. RATING 98 DRINK 2023–2039 $35 JH ✪

Home Vineyard Shiraz 2021, Hunter Valley The flavours are complex, with
plum, spice, leather and Hunter earth, the balance flawless, the length prodigious.
I have tasted many Hunter shiraz wines aged between 30 and 50 years, and have
no doubt whatsoever this will cruise through the 50 year barrier. Screw cap.
13% alc. RATING 97 DRINK 2023–2073 $25 JH ✪ ♥

🍷🍷🍷🍷🍷 **Reserve Semillon 2021, Hunter Valley** An exception to Mistletoe's estage-
grown base, this is made from semillon grown on the Trevena vineyard. Classic
Hunter style: intensity, focus, purity, length; the fruit flavour headed by lemon/
lemongrass/lime, crisp acidity tying the parcel up. Screw cap. 11.4% alc.
RATING 96 DRINK 2023–2043 $20 JH ✪

Reserve Shiraz 2021, Hunter Valley Polished saddle leather, blackberry,
licorice, and Hunter earth and spice. The colour is superb, the power beyond the
scope of the majority of high-class Hunter shiraz wines. Screw cap. 13.5% alc.
RATING 95 DRINK 2025–2045 $35 JH ✪

🍷🍷🍷🍷🍷 **Home Vineyard Semillon 2021, Hunter Valley** RATING 93 DRINK 2023–2031
$16 JH ✪

Hunter Shiraz 2021, Hunter Valley RATING 91 DRINK 2023–2027 $18 JH ✪

Mitchell   ★★★★☆

246 Hughes Park Road, Sevenhill via Clare, SA 5453 **Region** Clare Valley
T (08) 8843 4258 **www.mitchellwines.com Open** 7 days 11–5 **Winemaker** Simon
Pringle **Viticulturist** Angus Mitchell **Est.** 1975 **Dozens** 10000 **Vyds** 70ha
One of the stalwarts of the Clare Valley, established by Jane and Andrew Mitchell, producing
long-lived rieslings and cabernet sauvignons in classic regional style. The range now also
includes semillon, grenache and shiraz. A lovely old stone apple shed is the cellar door and
upper section of the upgraded winery. Children Angus and Edwina are now working in the
business, heralding generational changes. Over the years the Mitchells have established or
acquired 70ha of vineyards on 4 excellent sites, some vines over 60 years old; all are managed
organically, with biodynamic composts used for over a decade.

🍷🍷🍷🍷🍷 **McNicol Riesling 2013, Clare Valley** Powerful, it could be said, and
ludicrously well priced. A soft, supple and mellifluous wine of honeyed
characters, ripe apple, juicy lime, toast and truffle. It's all happening. A high note
of amontillado in perfume and palate, too. Lovely. Gentle oxidative notes build
immense complexity and vitality. It's almost like a stellar matured chardonnay,
but for that wonderful streak of briny acidity. A full-flavoured, concentrated
and wonderful wine of power and presence. Unique, yet so Clare. Screw cap.
11.8% alc. RATING 96 DRINK 2022–2027 $45 MB ✪

🍷🍷🍷🍷🍷 **Sparkling Peppertree Shiraz NV, Clare Valley** RATING 93 $45 MB
Alcatraz Vineyard Riesling 2022, Clare Valley RATING 93 DRINK 2022–2028
$20 MB ✪
Watervale Riesling 2022, Clare Valley RATING 93 DRINK 2022–2030
$22 MB ✪
Pinot Gris 2022, Clare Valley RATING 92 DRINK 2022–2024 $25 MB ✪

Mitchell Harris Wines   ★★★★★

38 Doveton Street North, Ballarat, Vic 3350 **Region** Pyrenees
T (03) 5331 8931 **www.mitchellharris.com.au Open** Tue 3–9, Wed–Thurs 12–9, Fri–
Sat 12–late **Winemaker** John Harris **Est.** 2008 **Dozens** 1800 **Vyds** 0.5ha
Mitchell Harris Wines is a partnership between Alicia and Craig Mitchell and Shannyn and
John Harris. John, the winemaker, began his career at Brown Brothers, then spent 8 years as
winemaker at Domaine Chandon in the Yarra Valley, cramming in Northern Hemisphere
vintages in California and Oregon. The Mitchell and Harris families grew up in the Ballarat

area and have an affinity for the Macedon and Pyrenees regions. While the total make is not large, a lot of thought has gone into the creation of each of the wines, which are sourced from the Pyrenees, Ballarat and Macedon regions. Wines can be tasted at Mitchell Harris' atmospheric namesake wine bar in the heart of Ballarat.

🍷🍷🍷🍷🍷 **Sabre 2019, Macedon Ranges Pyrenees Ballarat** 68/32% chardonnay/ pinot noir. One sip and you know that you're in high-class territory. This is powerful, fresh and complex at once, its bready, heady, toasty flavours served racy and refreshing. Apples, grilled peaches, strawberries and lees; there's a lot going on here (it's a meal of a wine), and yet it remains festive and free-flowing. Diam. 12.2% alc. **RATING** 95 **DRINK** 2024–2028 $50 CM ✪ ♥

Sauvignon Blanc Fumé 2022, Pyrenees Smoky bacon notes work beautifully with the intense, passionfruit-like, lychee-laced fruit flavours here. This is a wine that impresses from the first sip. It's textural, it has excellent concentration of flavour, and it finishes the job with authority. It's excellent. Screw cap. 13.2% alc. **RATING** 95 **DRINK** 2024–2029 $30 CM ✪ ♥

Sabre Rosé 2019, Macedon Ranges Pyrenees Ballarat Chardonnay/pinot noir. The trick is to deliver complexity within a fresh-faced context, and that's what this wine does so well. It's both refreshing and engaging. Strawberry, roasted nuts, redcurrant and citrus flavours put on a fine dance, abundant with twirls, zips and flavour. Diam. 12% alc. **RATING** 94 **DRINK** 2023–2026 $60 CM

🍷🍷🍷🍷🍷 **Pinot Meunier & Sangiovese Rosé 2022, Pyrenees RATING** 93 **DRINK** 2023–2027 $30 CM ✪

Shiraz 2021, Pyrenees RATING 92 **DRINK** 2023–2030 $35 CM
Cabernet Sauvignon 2021, Pyrenees RATING 92 **DRINK** 2024–2032 $35 CM
Wightwick Vineyard Pinot Noir 2022, Ballarat RATING 90 **DRINK** 2025–2031 $45 CM

Mitchelton

 ★★★★★

Mitchellstown via Nagambie, Vic 3608 **Region** Nagambie Lakes
T (03) 5736 2222 **www.**mitchelton.com.au **Open** 7 days 10–5 **Winemaker** Natalie Cleghorn **Viticulturist** John Armstrong **Est.** 1969 **Dozens** 35 000 **Vyds** 139ha
Mitchelton was founded by Ross Shelmerdine, named after the explorer Thomas Mitchell, who passed by here. Ross had a splendid vision for the striking winery, restaurant, now-iconic observation tower and surrounding vineyards. Owned by Gerry Ryan OAM (founder of Jayco) since '12, Mitchelton is a destination in its own right, with music concerts hosting such varied luminaries as Dame Kiri Te Kanawa and Jimmy Barnes; a hotel and spa also opened in '18. Mitchelton has estate vineyards in both Nagambie and Heathcote and purchases fruit from growers across Victoria.

🍷🍷🍷🍷🍷 **Preece Grenache Rosé 2022, Nagambie Lakes** A delicate tea-rose hue introduces a smashing young rosé with a host of summer berries and raspberries in a starring role. The palate is lithe, clean and juicy with the raciest of acidity to close. Top quality for the price. Screw cap. 12.5% alc. **RATING** 92 **DRINK** 2022–2024 $22 JP ✪

Shiraz 2021, Nagambie Lakes A top year and a top shiraz, plush in Nagambie Lakes' ripe fruits and earthy, medium-bodied style. Finely tuned, subtly executed and varietally exact. Anise, brambly blackberries, cinnamon, baked earth and woody spices aplenty. Enjoyable drinking at a fair price. Screw cap. 14.3% alc. **RATING** 92 **DRINK** 2022–2027 $28 JP ✪

Roussanne 2022, Nagambie Lakes Having promoted marsanne for decades, Mitchelton is now turning its attention to marsanne's blending partner, roussanne. It shares some similarities, but expect more herbals, less florals. Here, acacia, watercress, quince, apple and just a lick of ginger. Tight across the palate with some well-handled phenolic grip. Nicely textural, too. Screw cap. 12% alc. **RATING** 91 **DRINK** 2022–2025 $28 JP ✪

Blackwood Park Riesling 2022, Nagambie Lakes A full-on citrus fest with splashes of Tahitian lime, lemon sorbet zestiness, and pithy ruby grapefruit bite with a signature citrus blossom scent. The '22 boasts a little more palate texture than usual, toning down the usual exuberance, but racy acidity is still a signature. Screw cap. 12.1% alc. **RATING** 91 **DRINK** 2022–2028 $28 JP ✪

Chardonnay 2021, Nagambie Lakes Bountiful in white stone fruit, grapefruit, lemon zest, toasted almond and spice. A softly textured mid-palate with an attractive biscuity oak influence. Taut and lively. Screw cap. 13.5% alc. **RATING** 91 **DRINK** 2022–2025 $28 JP ✪

Mitolo Wines

141 McMurtrie Road, McLaren Vale, SA 5171 **Region** McLaren Vale
T (08) 8323 9304 **www**.mitolowines.com.au **Open** 7 days 10–5 **Winemaker** Luke Mallaby **Est.** 1999 **Dozens** 40 000

Mitolo had a meteoric rise once Frank Mitolo decided to turn a winemaking hobby into a business. In '00 he took the plunge into the commercial end of the business, inviting Ben Glaetzer to make the wines. Split between the Jester range and single-vineyard wines, Mitolo began life as a red wine–dominant brand but now produces a range of varietals. In November '17 Mitolo opened their $3 million tasting room, restaurant and event space with a flourish. Luke Mallaby joined Mitolo in '21, after 20+ years of winemaking, most recently at Rosemount Estates.

🍷🍷🍷🍷🍷 **Masso Montepulciano 2021, McLaren Vale** Arguably the finest wine at this address. Beautifully crafted, promoting its floral freshness with gentle extraction and ample whole berries. Embraces the variety's sinuous, ferruginous tannins, sans perceivable new oak nor forfeit of power. In essence, not too much messing about. Very good drinking. Screw cap. 14.5% alc. **RATING** 96 **DRINK** 2022–2030 $42 NG ✪

Ourea Sagrantino 2020, McLaren Vale Sagrantino can produce wines of power, breadth, uncanny freshness and ferocious tannins. This variety bodes well for Australia, and the changing climate. A fine example. Think sage, mint, thyme, rosemary, salami and desiccated black cherry strung across a ferrous carapace. Screw cap. 14.5% alc. **RATING** 95 **DRINK** 2022–2032 $42 NG ✪

Cinquecento Sangiovese 2020, McLaren Vale Exemplary sangiovese. This is an apogee of modern styling, without any forfeit of varietal personality, be it the frisk of tannins or flirt of freshness. Dried red cherry, lilac and anise brushed with thyme, sage and mint. The tannins, expansive, spindly and so refined. The oak, present yet an adjunct to the greater mould. Damn! Exceptional. Screw cap. 14.5% alc. **RATING** 95 **DRINK** 2022–2029 $42 NG ✪

Marsican Shiraz 2019, McLaren Vale A morass of dark fruits, molten and almost llicorella of pungency, across a landscape saturated with lavender, five-spice, licorice strap and mace. The oak, positioned well. The fruit, capable of handling almost anything thrown at it. Long and forceful. Southern Rhône of feel, without the tannic mettle. This has some way to go. Cork. 14.8% alc. **RATING** 95 **DRINK** 2022–2038 $250 NG

Savitar Shiraz 2019, McLaren Vale A regional stalwart, in the classicist mould. Coffee beans, vanilla, cedar and dark fruit allusions. Raspberry bonbon sweetness expands with air, sousing the finish. A bit hard to get past the oak at this stage, but time will surely imbue the benefit of the doubt. Screw cap. 14.5% alc. **RATING** 94 **DRINK** 2022–2035 $105 NG

G.A.M. Shiraz 2019, McLaren Vale A rich wine that plies a pulpy jubilance laden with blackcurrant, blueberry, anise and baking spices alongside a bracken density doused with coffee grind and cocoa nibs. The result is a confluence of freshness, svelte tannins, a well-positioned curb of oak and a nourishing finish. Screw cap. 14.5% alc. **RATING** 94 **DRINK** 2022–2032 $69 NG

🍷🍷🍷🍷 **Angela Shiraz 2020, McLaren Vale RATING** 93 **DRINK** 2022–2030 $42 NG
Jester Malbec 2021, McLaren Vale RATING 91 **DRINK** 2022–2026 $27 NG ✪
la Spiaggia Sparkling Glera 2022, McLaren Vale RATING 90 **DRINK** 2022–2024 $32 NG

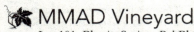 MMAD Vineyard

Lot 101, Blewitt Springs Rd Blewitt Springs, SA 5171 (postal) **Region** McLaren Vale
T (08) 7089 3389 **www**.mmadvineyard.com **Open** Not **Winemaker** Adam Wadewitz,
Martin Shaw **Viticulturist** Murray Leake, Ben Jonas **Est.** 2021 **Vyds** 14ha

MMAD Vineyard is the venture of 2 Masters of Wine and 2 highly regarded winemakers
with many years of fine wine experience. The label is derived from the first letter of each
of their names: Martin Shaw, Michael Hill Smith, Adam Wadewitz and David LeMire. The
first 2 founded and own the Adelaide Hills-based Shaw + Smith in '89, while Adam and
David are now co-CEOs at Shaw + Smith, Adam chief winemaker and David head of sales
and marketing. In early '21 they found an outstanding Blewitt Springs property with 3ha of
1939-planted grenache, 5.4ha of shiraz, the oldest planted in '41, and 3ha of chenin blanc,
the oldest planted in '64. Their aim is to continuously improve soil and vine health while
promoting plant and insect diversity.

ŸŸŸŸŸ **Blewitt Springs Grenache 2021, McLaren Vale** The clarity of the wine
matches its freshness. The highly fragrant blend of cherry and plum drives a very
long, fine and elegant palate. Screw cap. 14% alc. **RATING** 97 **DRINK** 2023–2032
$75 JH ✪

Blewitt Springs Shiraz 2021, McLaren Vale Deep but bright colour
announces a wine of tremendous presence, the whole-bunch component
(15–20%), 15 days on skins, 33% in concrete vessels, the balance in stainless
steel and used oak. A magical combination of techniques to produce blackberry,
licorice and dark chocolate flavours, the tannins so fine they are almost silky.
Screw cap. 13.5% alc. **RATING** 97 **DRINK** 2023–2041 $75 JH ✪

ŸŸŸŸŸ **Blewitt Springs Chenin Blanc 2021, McLaren Vale** Half whole-bunch
pressed to used French puncheons for fermentation, the balance crushed into
tulip-shaped concrete vessels before maturation in used French puncheons. The
blend of components gives rise to textured, layered citrus peel flavours sewn
together by a shaft of glistening acidity. Major surprise. Screw cap. 12.5% alc.
RATING 95 **DRINK** 2023–2036 $48 JH ✪

Monak Wine Co

5691 Sturt Highway, Monak, NSW 2738 **Region** Murray Darling
T 0418 570 064 **www**.monakwineco.com.au **Open** Fri–Sat 10–6 or by appt
Winemaker Cindy Heley **Viticulturist** Paul Heley **Est.** 2020

Monak Wine Co. is a relatively new addition to the Murray Darling wine scene but the
woman behind it has been making wine in the region for more than 25 years. Owner and
winemaker Cindy Heley works with local winegrowers and also grows 'hard-to-source
varieties'. Her passion lies in the soil and the people of the Murray Darling and she is a strong
advocate for highlighting its untapped potential, especially with alternative varieties that thrive
in the region's warm, dry conditions. Production is focused on small-batch winemaking; the
first vintage in '20 crushed just 20t of grapes.

ŸŸŸŸŸ **Mon Cinq Grenache Rosé 2021, Murray Darling** Delicious wine. Both
dry and raspberried at once, almost into blackcurrant bud territory, with floral
and anise overtones. Succulent. Pale in colour but bright with complex flavour.
Screw cap. 12.5% alc. **RATING** 92 **DRINK** 2023–2025 $25 CM ✪

Montague Estate

325 Tom Cullity Drive, Margaret River WA 6280 **Region** Margaret River
T (08) 9755 6995 **www**.montagueestate.com.au **Open** Wed–Sun 11–5
Winemaker Jonathan Mettam **Viticulturist** Tim Quinlan **Est.** 2020 **Dozens** 3475
Vyds 25ha

Montague Estate is located in Wilyabrup on what was previously the old Heydon Estate
vineyard, and prior to that, Arlewood. The vineyard is planted to a little over 8ha of
chardonnay, 4ha of mataro, 3.2ha of grenache, 2.6ha of shiraz, 1.8ha of cabernet sauvignon

and smaller amounts of cabernet franc, petit verdot, merlot, malbec, viognier, albariño and semillon. Tim Quinlan has been looking after the vines there since Heydon Estate days.

ΨΨΨΨ♀ **Shiraz 2021, Margaret River** A sweetly accented, spiced and supple wine that starts off with lovely aromatics, a mix of florals, fruit and warm earth. The palate fleshes out to full bodied with plentiful tannins, richly layered with flavour, a touch rustic and a good drink. Screw cap. 13.8% alc. **RATING** 92 **DRINK** 2022–2030 $42 JF

Cabernet Franc 2021, Margaret River It's on the riper end of the spectrum and seems to have a fair whack of new oak in the mix. Despite the aforementioned, there's good fruit underneath. Lovely bramble, currants and cassis dusted with cocoa and baking spices. Full bodied with ripe, teetering on powerful tannins bolstered by the oak which pinches the finish. Add some hearty fare and all will be better. Screw cap. 14.8% alc. **RATING** 92 **DRINK** 2023–2030 $45 JF

Dextra 2021, Margaret River 57/29/14% merlot/cabernet franc/petit verdot. Each fermented separately and aged 13 months in French and Hungarian hogsheads (15% new) before blending. It's come together well with spiced red berries to the fore, woodsy spices and oak tannins adding some shape to the palate. Screw cap. 13.8% alc. **RATING** 91 **DRINK** 2022–2027 $45 JF

Cabernet Sauvignon 2021, Margaret River It's soft and appealing, not complex but quite delicious with hints of cassis and currants, cigar box and dried herbs plus florals. The tannins seem light on and lightly textural. A wine for today rather than the long haul. Screw cap. 13.5% alc. **RATING** 91 **DRINK** 2022–2026 $45 JF

Aurum Blanc de Blanc 2020, Margaret River Mid-gold and deep, toasty, ripe and full bodied with baked quince and cinnamon. It's a touch advanced. I was expecting more life and vitality, but it has appeal. Just don't delay the opening. Diam. 13.2% alc. **RATING** 90 **DRINK** 2022–2023 $52 JF

Semillon 2022, Margaret River Deceptive in its restraint at first, but acidity kicks in taking the citrus, hay and lime flavours along for a ride. Tight, flinty and zesty with some texture while remaining pure and long. Screw cap. 11.8% alc. **RATING** 90 **DRINK** 2023–2030 $42 JF

Montalto ★★★★★

33 Shoreham Road, Red Hill South, Vic 3937 **Region** Mornington Peninsula **T** (03) 5989 8412 **www.**montalto.com.au **Open** 7 days 11–5 **Winemaker** Simon Black **Viticulturist** Dan Prior **Est.** 1998 **Dozens** 12000 **Vyds** 47ha

John Mitchell and family established Montalto in '98, but the core of the vineyard goes back to '86. It is planted to pinot noir, chardonnay, pinot gris, riesling, shiraz, tempranillo and sauvignon blanc. Intensive vineyard work opens up the canopy, with yields of 3.7–6.1t/ha. Wines are released in 3 ranges: the flagship Single Vineyard, Montalto Estate wines and Pennon Hill. Montalto leases several external vineyards that span the Peninsula, giving vastly greater diversity of pinot noir sources and greater insurance against weather extremes. There is also a broad range of clones adding to that diversity. Montalto has hit new heights with its wines from these blocks.

ΨΨΨΨΨ **The Eleven Chardonnay 2021, Mornington Peninsula** From 11 rows of clone P58 (ex-Penfolds) planted in '86 on the home vineyard. Elegant and delicious, with every aspect handled by winemaker Simon Black with the touch of a master. Grapefruit, lemon and white peach varietal fruit expression. Screw cap. 13% alc. **RATING** 96 **DRINK** 2023–2036 $90 JH

Estate Syrah 2021, Mornington Peninsula A very impressive cool-grown shiraz. On one hand is fragrance and freshness, on the other is texture, structure and depth. Its primary fruit is black cherry infused with sparkles of spice and crushed black pepper. The balance needed to carry its multi-decade life span is there in spades. Screw cap. 13.5% alc. **RATING** 96 **DRINK** 2023–2045 $55 JH ✪

Tuerong Chardonnay 2021, Mornington Peninsula Glorious chardonnay; rich and complex, strongly reminiscent of premier cru Meursault, with deep-seated succulence matched by precisely calibrated acidity that frees up the finish and long aftertaste. Screw cap. 13% alc. **RATING** 96 **DRINK** 2023–2036 $75 JH ✪

Tuerong Syrah 2021, Mornington Peninsula Outrageously smooth, stylish and elegant. Beautiful ripe, juicy fruit layered with spices and fresh herbs with a touch of menthol all flood the medium-bodied palate. From there, tannins as fine as silk and a refreshing spray of acidity take this wine to a long finish. Screw cap. 13.5% alc. **RATING** 96 **DRINK** 2022–2033 $75 JF ✪

Estate Rosé 2022, Mornington Peninsula Now, this is my style of rosé. Delicate flavours of rosehip, cranberries and spiced cherries. The palate is full of tangy acidity, cleansing all the way through, but there's a slip of texture adding to the pleasure of drinking this dry, lovely wine. Screw cap. 13.5% alc. **RATING** 95 **DRINK** 2022–2025 $45 JF ✪

Estate Chardonnay 2021, Mornington Peninsula Whole-bunch pressed direct to French oak (28% new), wild-yeast fermented and 100% mlf. The complex, faintly and deliberately funky bouquet takes on another dimension on the long, tantalising palate. It requires attention, but repays the taster in gold. Screw cap. 13% alc. **RATING** 95 **DRINK** 2023–2031 $55 JH

Estate Pinot Gris 2022, Mornington Peninsula Surprisingly reticent for a pinot gris from this region and producer. Still very good with pear and cream, just enough to coat the palate, plus ginger flower and spice. A pleasant pop of lemony acidity, enjoyable even if it tapers on the finish. Minor quibble. Screw cap. 13.5% alc. **RATING** 94 **DRINK** 2022–2026 $45 JF

North One Pinot Noir 2021, Mornington Peninsula By a considerable margin, the richest of the '21 Montalto pinot noir releases, although the fruit expression is in the same spectrum of savoury, spicy and challenging. Screw cap. 13.5% alc. **RATING** 94 **DRINK** 2023–2031 $90 JH

♀♀♀♀♀ **Merricks Pinot Noir 2021, Mornington Peninsula** **RATING** 93 **DRINK** 2023–2027 $75 JH
Estate Pinot Noir 2021, Mornington Peninsula **RATING** 93 **DRINK** 2023–2028 $55 JH
Tuerong Pinot Noir 2021, Mornington Peninsula **RATING** 91 **DRINK** 2023–2029 $75 JH
Main Ridge Pinot Noir 2021, Mornington Peninsula **RATING** 91 **DRINK** 2023–2027 $75 JH

Monterra   ★★★★

RSD 1436 Meadows Road, Willunga, SA 5172 (postal) **Region** McLaren Vale
T 0428 581 177 **www**.monterrawines.com.au **Open** Not **Winemaker** Daniel Zuzulo
Est. 2014 **Dozens** 20 000 **Vyds** 15ha

Another venture by Canadian-born and raised (but long-term McLaren Vale resident) Norm Doole, here in partnership with Mike Farmilo and Nick Whiteway. The trio also own and run Colab and Bloom (see separate entry), both wineries falling under the banner of Field Day Wine Co. Fruit is sourced from small vineyards in the Adelaide Hills, McLaren Vale, Barossa Valley and Fleurieu Peninsula.

♀♀♀♀♀ **Reserve Shiraz 2021, McLaren Vale** A well-polished regional archetype for those who appreciate heft, lavish yet well-placed oak and oodles of blue fruits, anise, violet and Christmas cake flavours trailing long. Screw cap. 14.4% alc. **RATING** 91 **DRINK** 2022–2032 $45 NG

Reserve Shiraz 2021, Barossa Valley Aromas of juicy plum, boysenberry and mulberry fruits. A hint of baking spices, red licorice, barbecued meats, dark chocolate and an array of purple floral tones. Juicy and plummy with a meaty edge, powdery tannins and a ferrous twang to the acid profile, with some red cherry notes that swoop in as the wine fades away. Screw cap. 14.5% alc. **RATING** 91 **DRINK** 2023–2027 $45 DB

Moores Hill Estate

3343 West Tamar Highway, Sidmouth, Tas 7270 **Region** Northern Tasmania
T (03) 6394 7649 **www**.mooreshill.com.au **Open** 7 days 11–5 **Winemaker** James
Oliver **Viticulturist** Constance Olivier **Est.** 1997 **Dozens** 4000 **Vyds** 5.6ha
Moores Hill Estate vineyard consists of pinot noir, riesling, pinot gris and chardonnay, with a
very small amount of cabernet sauvignon and merlot. The vines are located on a northeast-
facing hillside, 5km from the Tamar River and 30km from Bass Strait. Moores Hill became
Tasmania's first 100% solar-powered winery in '17, the wines all made onsite. In '22, James
and Constance took ownership from Julian Allport and Fiona Weller. James, who holds a
Bachelor of Viticulture and Oenology from the University of Adelaide, is keen on pinot noir,
with vintages in Geelong, Mornington, Oregon, Burgundy and Germany under his belt.
He spent 2 years at Yering Station (as assistant winemaker then winemaker) prior to Moores
Hill. Constance is from France and earned her Master of Oenology in Dijon, Burgundy. Her
first vintage in Australia was at Yering Station in '19, followed by time in the vineyard with
Andrew Marks at Gembrook and in the winery with Simon Steele at Medhurst.

🍷🍷🍷🍷 **Riesling 2022, Tasmania** I don't know if describing a wine's acidity as ripe and
long is 'correct,' but that is what we have here. Porcelain-like and vivid, lemon and
lime fruits stretched taut over its frame, with hints of crushed quartz, white flowers
and marzipan adding to the enjoyment. The finish is pure, precise and true with a
tubular palate shape that lingers persistently. Lovely drinking. Screw cap. 12% alc.
RATING 95 **DRINK** 2023–2028 $35 DB ✪

🍷🍷🍷🍷 **Pinot Noir 2021, Tasmania RATING** 93 **DRINK** 2023–2028 $40 DB
Blanc de Blancs NV, Tasmania RATING 92 $45 DB
Pinot Noir 2022, Tasmania RATING 92 **DRINK** 2023–2029 $40 DB

Moorilla Estate

655 Main Road, Berriedale, Tas 7011 **Region** Southern Tasmania
T (03) 6277 9960 **www**.moorilla.com.au **Open** Fri–Mon 12–5 **Winemaker** Conor
van der Reest **Viticulturist** Peter Mueller (south) and Jesse Graffam (north) **Est.** 1958
Dozens 11 000 **Vyds** 17.7ha
Moorilla Estate was the 2nd winery to be established in Tasmania in the 20th century, Jean
Miguet's La Provence beating it to the punch by 2 years. However, through much of the
history of Moorilla Estate, it was the most important winery in the state. Magnificently
situated on a mini-isthmus reaching into the Derwent River, it has always been a must-
visit for wine lovers and tourists – much more so since the establishment of Mona, David
Walsh's wildly eccentric ancient and contemporary art museum. The combination of winery,
underground museum, above-ground sculpture park, cellar door, wine bar and 2 restaurants
(The Source and Faro) makes for one seriously fun cultural precinct. Production is around
160t/year, sourced entirely from the vineyards around Moorilla and its St Matthias vineyard
(Tamar Valley).

🍷🍷🍷🍷 **Cloth Label Red 2017, Tasmania** Pinot noir/shiraz/cabernet sauvignon/
cabernet franc and a squirt of riesling. It's a complex little thing. Sapid morello
cherry, juicy plum and redcurrant fruits infused with sweet spice, tobacco, pressed
flowers, roasting game, amaro, polished leather and earth. Gentle red fruits with
a mineral cadence and an elegant, spiced sour cherry finish. Screw cap. 13% alc.
RATING 95 **DRINK** 2023–2028 $65 DB
Cloth Label St Matthias Vineyard White 2017, Tasmania Pinot gris/
gewürztraminer/chardonnay/sauvignon blanc/riesling (plus a pinch of pinot
noir). It makes for a deeply coloured and enchanting wine with plenty of texture
and sapid mineral twang. Citrus, tropical fruits, crushed stone, dried honey, rose
petals, soft spice, yellow plum, dried hay, wildflowers, chicken stock, lemon
curd and whey. Complex, calm and steely. Screw cap. 13.2% alc. **RATING** 95
DRINK 2023–2027 $75 DB
Muse St Matthias Vineyard Syrah 2017, Tasmania Aromas of dark plum
and black cherry fruits with hints of black pepper, leather, tobacco, dark spice,

olive tapenade, cedar and some violet and stone fruit top notes. Nicely poised on the palate, a meaty edge cruises in and the lasting impression is of a harmonious wine with a fine, granitic tannin structure, mineral-rich acidity lending drive and frame. Screw cap. 13.7% alc. RATING 95 DRINK 2023–2033 $56 DB

 PPPPP Extra Brut St Matthias Vineyard 2017, Tasmania RATING 93
DRINK 2023–2033 $52 DB
Praxis St Matthias Vineyard Chardonnay Musque 2022, Tasmania
RATING 93 DRINK 2023–2026 $26 DB ✪
Muse St Matthias Vineyard Sauvignon 2019, Tasmania RATING 93
DRINK 2023–2026 $34 DB ✪
Muse Pinot Noir 2017, Tasmania RATING 93 DRINK 2023–2029 $56 DB
Extra Brut St Matthias Vineyard Rosè 2017, Tasmania RATING 92
DRINK 2023–2030 $52 DB
Muse St Matthias Vineyard Chardonnay 2019, Tasmania RATING 92
DRINK 2023–2027 $44 DB
Praxis St Matthias Vineyard Pinot Noir 2020, Tasmania RATING 91
DRINK 2023–2027 $33 DB

Moorooduc Estate   ★★★★★

501 Derril Road, Moorooduc, Vic 3936 **Region** Mornington Peninsula
T (03) 5971 8506 **www.**moorooducestate.com.au **Open** 7 days 11–5 **Winemaker** Dr Richard McIntyre, Jeremy Magyar **Viticulturist** Peninsula Vine Care **Est.** 1983
Dozens 6000 **Vyds** 14ha
Richard McIntyre has taken Moorooduc Estate to new heights, mastering wild-fermentation, revamping grape sourcing and leasing additional Mornington Peninsula vineyards to increase production from 1500 to 6000 cases annually. Daughter Kate McIntyre MW joined the business full-time in '10. The single-vineyard Robinson Pinot Noir and Chardonnay, Garden Vineyard Pinot Noir and McIntyre Shiraz are priced a little below the flagship The Moorooduc McIntyre Chardonnay and Pinot Noir.

PPPPP McIntyre Vineyard Chardonnay 2021, Mornington Peninsula Chardonnay can age gracefully (providing the stars have aligned) yet I often wonder, why bother when it tastes this good right now? In the mix, citrus and white stone fruit, funky sulphides and mouth-watering acidity, leesy texture and just enough oak spice to add a bit more deliciousness. Screw cap. 13.2% alc. RATING 96 DRINK 2023–2030 $85 JF
Robinson Vineyard Chardonnay 2021, Mornington Peninsula As elegant as a Givenchy evening gown. All silky and fine – this is as pure, long and textural as they come. Yes, flavours satisfy from nougat, white nectarine and Meyer lemon with a layer of luscious lees, but all that sits behind how this wine feels. And it feels good. Moreish with juicy acidity a feature in '21. Screw cap. 12.8% alc. RATING 96 DRINK 2023–2031 $65 JF ✪
Pinot Gris On Skins 2022, Mornington Peninsula It won't be everyone's cup of gris but I love this wine. It has flavour, body, phenolics and an all-around yumminess. Look, sometimes that's the right word to pop out. This is tangy with chinotto, barberries, peach fuzz, ripe and unripe pears, and the thread of tannins is woven in neatly. It's savoury with a slip of fruit sweetness. Screw cap. 13% alc. RATING 95 DRINK 2023–2027 $40 JF ✪
The Moorooduc McIntyre Pinot Noir 2021, Mornington Peninsula There's a gentle persuasion, a slight tension between the supple tannins and gossamer-like acidity that gives this definition yet still stays refined. The light hue belies the flavours of cherries and pips, sumac, chinotto and mandarin peel. Very even across the palate. Very easy to drink. A smashing wine. Screw cap. 13% alc. RATING 95 DRINK 2023–2031 $85 JF
Robinson Vineyard Pinot Noir 2021, Mornington Peninsula Incredibly perfumed, fine and detailed. Lots of exotic spices on the go with sweet rhubarb

and red cherries, it smells of autumn. Filigree tannins are laced through the fine acidity, which leads this gently through to a finish that feels, of all things, calm. My new Zen wine. Screw cap. 13% alc. RATING 95 DRINK 2023-2030 $65 JF
McIntyre Vineyard Shiraz 2021, Mornington Peninsula Moorooduc Estate is holding back this savoury, complex wine until early 2024. The aromas are so enticing, all floral and inky with a perfumed punch. Medium bodied and awash with dark plums, celery root, blood orange and a distinct ferrous character. The coarse sand-like tannins will meld into the wine given time and a key attribute is the wine's savouriness. Screw cap. 13% alc. RATING 95 DRINK 2024-2034 $65 JF
Garden Vineyard Pinot Noir 2021, Mornington Peninsula Of all the '21 Moorooduc Estate pinots, this has the most structure. Not surprising given that it is 100% whole-bunch fermented. Plenty of twiggy, woodsy tones infusing the dark spiced cherries and red plums, leafy freshness with chinotto and radicchio, smoky, woody char too. Lots going on and fans of the style will be stoked. Screw cap. 13.4% alc. RATING 95 DRINK 2023-2033 $65 JF
Pinot Gris 2021, Mornington Peninsula A cared-for pinot gris, indeed a proper gris should have texture, flavour, depth and an insatiable desire to drink it. Thank goodness for Moorooduc Estate, as it offers all that and more: lusciousness across the palate, varietal flavours, creamy lees and a certain tang and vivacity. Screw cap. 14% alc. RATING 94 DRINK 2022-2028 $40 JF ✪
Pinot Noir 2021, Mornington Peninsula Now, this has come together beautifully and appears so gentle and refined. Subtle aromas of spiced cherries and autumnal leaves, sumac and woodsy spices. The palate is shy of medium-bodied with fine, lacy tannins, a core of sweet-ish fruit and a savoury overlay. It's compelling and totally enticing, so it's a shame this is not out now – boo hoo! In 2024 apparently, but worth following up. Screw cap. 13.5% alc. RATING 94 DRINK 2024-2028 $40 JF ✪

🍷🍷🍷🍷 Chardonnay 2021, Mornington Peninsula RATING 92 DRINK 2022-2027 $40 JF

Morambro Creek Wines ★★★★

Riddoch Highway, Padthaway, SA 5271 (postal) **Region** Padthaway
T (08) 8723 1065 **www**.morambrocreek.com.au **Open** Not **Winemaker** Ben Riggs
Est. 1994 **Dozens** 30 000 **Vyds** 178.5ha
The Bryson family has been involved in agriculture for more than a century, moving to Padthaway in 1955 as farmers and graziers. From the '90s they have progressively established large plantings of shiraz (88.5ha), cabernet sauvignon (47.5ha), chardonnay (34.5ha) and sauvignon blanc (8ha). The Morambro Creek and Mt Monster wines have been consistent winners of wine show medals.

🍷🍷🍷🍷 Jip Jip Rocks Cabernet Sauvignon 2020, Padthaway There's a bit of grunt to the tannin here, which works a treat with the generosity of the fruit. Plum, mint and floral characters put on a full-bodied show before (slightly less convincing) woodsy/twiggy/herbal characters appear on the finish. The star is that upfront flavour. It's complex and delicious at once. Screw cap. 14.5% alc. RATING 92 DRINK 2023-2029 $25 CM ✪
Shiraz 2020, Padthaway If you're on the hunt for intense flavour, look no further. This really serves it up to you. Blackberry, licorice and leather flavours come coated in vanilla cream and mint. It feels a little round-shouldered, but it's by no means short. Indeed, this is satisfying from go to whoa, and is both harmonious and smooth. Screw cap. 14.5% alc. RATING 92 DRINK 2023-2030 $40 CM
Chardonnay 2021, Padthaway Pear and nectarine flavours flow easily through the palate. This is an attractive wine, well flavoured without being excessively so, easily accessible without being overly simple. Butter and toast flavours whisper about the edges, which will please many. It's an easy wine to like. Screw cap. 13% alc. RATING 91 DRINK 2022-2026 $40 CM

Jip Jip Rocks Shiraz Cabernet 2021, Padthaway Dark berried flavour, served straight up. This takes plum jam and blackcurrant characters and infuses them with cloves and toast, the effect both straightforward and effective. One sip and you just want to nestle into it like a cat into a fluffy blanket. Screw cap. 14.5% alc. **RATING** 91 **DRINK** 2022-2027 $25 CM ✪

Jip Jip Rocks Shiraz 2021, Padthaway This wine has a flavour that I call 'liquid toast'. It tastes of luscious, ripe, juicy plum, but there's also a toasted element, and it slips straight through the wine. There are clove flavours and eucalyptus notes also, but think plums on toast, juicy and satisfying, and you're on the right track. One glass very quickly becomes two. Screw cap. 14.5% alc. **RATING** 91 **DRINK** 2022-2028 $25 CM ✪

Mordrelle Wines   ★★★★★

411 River Road, Hahndorf, SA 5243 **Region** Adelaide Hills
T 0448 928 513 **www.mordrellewines.com.au Open** By appt **Winemaker** Martin Moran **Viticulturist** Martin Moran **Est.** 2010 **Dozens** 2500

Based in Hahndorf in the Adelaide Hills, Mordrelle Wines is owned by Martin Moran with wife Michelle and her family, David and Jane Dreckow. The Mordrelle portfolio sources fruit from their own small vineyard in the nearby village of Mylor, plus sauvignon blanc, grüner veltliner, chardonnay and pinot noir from other Adelaide Hills locations and barbera, malbec, tempranillo, cabernet and shiraz from Langhorne Creek. Martin has also worked on viticulture research projects in Langhorne Creek and (tapping into his Argentinian roots) has made malbec from there as well as a regional trophy-winning barbera and other varieties. Mordrelle's labels are created from original artworks painted by Jose Luis Moran, Martin's late father.

♟♟♟♟♟ **Malbec Lagrein Cabernet Sauvignon Shiraz 2021, Langhorne Creek** The malbec in this blend is a clonal selection imported from Argentina. The wine more than lives up to the promise of the colour and the pure fragrance of the clone. High-class tannins and utterly delicious fruits; a dangerous wine, so silky is the mouthfeel and flavours ranging through red, black and blue fruits. Celestial value. Screw cap. 13.8% alc. **RATING** 97 **DRINK** 2025-2035 $35 JH ✪ ♥

The Gaucho Limited Edition Reserva Malbec 2020, Langhorne Creek The sultry bouquet provides the starting gun for a wine of utterly exceptional character, reminiscent of the 'black wine' of the Cahors region of France. The silky tannins are the key to a wine of hypnotic texture/structure that flows serenely along the plum-infused palate. Diam. 14% alc. **RATING** 97 **DRINK** 2023-2040 $80 JH ✪

♟♟♟♟♟ **Basket Press Tempranillo 2021, Langhorne Creek** This is a powerful wine, tempranillo flourishing in the regional water-cooled environment, underscored by the great vintage. Excellent deep colour, and spent 18 months in oak giving the tannins time to soften and resolve their profile. It has layers of cherry fruit, but there's no excessive extraction, the basket press the key. Screw cap. 14% alc. **RATING** 96 **DRINK** 2025-2036 $35 JH ✪

The Gaucho Malbec 2021, Langhorne Creek A malbec of outstanding depth, texture and structure. The magic of the wine stems from the rivulet of acidity that flows throughout the long palate. It results in black fruits that draw you back to the spices, dark chocolate and impeccable management of tannins. Screw cap. 13.5% alc. **RATING** 96 **DRINK** 2025-2035 $35 JH ✪

Basket Press Shiraz 2021, Langhorne Creek Good depth to the colour, and a complex bouquet with spice, blackberry and black cherries driving the palate. Fine tannins and nuances of oak add to the appeal of this medium-bodied, focused wine. Screw cap. 14.5% alc. **RATING** 96 **DRINK** 2025-2035 $45 JH ✪

Basket Press Barbera 2020, Langhorne Creek It seems this wine was sourced from the only vineyard of barbera in Langhorne Creek; an evocative burst of warm spices and licorice, the savoury palate pushing forest berries to the centre, ample acidity underpinning the finish and aftertaste. Screw cap. 14% alc. **RATING** 96 **DRINK** 2023-2035 $35 JH ✪

Basket Press Cabernet Sauvignon 2019, Langhorne Creek Good colour; fragrant cassis/redcurrant bouquet, also a touch of choc mint. A smooth, velvety palate – striking. Fine-spun tannins attest to the skilled vinification. Screw cap. 14.5% alc. RATING 96 DRINK 2023–2039 $96 JH

Cellar Release The Gaucho Basket Press Malbec 2017, Langhorne Creek The very cool '17 vintage, accompanied by rain at times, delayed picking until the end of March, but the grapes ripened without a problem. Certainly, has savoury inputs to a medium-bodied wine, but the juicy plum and spice fruit holds sway. Elegance is also a key to this delicious wine. Screw cap. 13.5% alc. RATING 96 DRINK 2023–2037 $50 JH ✪

Limited Release Basket Press Pinot Noir 2021, Adelaide Hills Is this not the benchmark for Hills pinot? It is by far the best example that I have tasted. Carnal. Dense. Savoury. Autumnal. Meaty. Mushroom dashi, dark cherry, sous bois and a ferrous earthen marrow. Great stuff. Mid-weighted, intense of flavour and so fresh. The last of a dying breed, perhaps. Get in while the going is good! Screw cap. 13% alc. RATING 95 DRINK 2022–2030 $50 NG ✪

Blanc de Blancs Reserva Chardonnay 2016, Adelaide Hills It is easy to draw an analogous synergy between this – an idiosyncratic sort of wine in the scape of fizz from the Hills – and grower champagne. The rust of autumn leaves, almond croissants, mandarin peel and ginger glaze. An effervescent finish of energy and class following five years on lees. Crown. 12% alc. RATING 94 DRINK 2022–2028 $50 NG

♟♟♟♟♀ **Basket Press Pinot Noir 2021, Lenswood** RATING 93 DRINK 2022–2030 $40 NG

Blanc de Blancs 2010, Adelaide Hills RATING 93 DRINK 2022–2026 $150 NG

Clone 1654 Basket Press Syrah 2018, Adelaide Hills RATING 92 DRINK 2022–2027 $40 NG

Clone 1125 Syrah 2019, Adelaide Hills RATING 91 DRINK 2022–2025 $40 NG

Morgan Simpson ★★★☆

PO Box 39, Kensington Park, SA 5068 **Region** McLaren Vale
T 0417 843 118 **www**.morgansimpson.com.au **Open** Not **Winemaker** Richard Simpson **Viticulturist** Mark Gilbert **Est.** 1998 **Dozens** 1200 **Vyds** 17.1ha
Morgan Simpson was founded by SA businessman George Morgan (since retired) and winemaker Richard Simpson, who is a graduate of CSU. The grapes are sourced from the Clos Robert Vineyard, planted to shiraz (9ha), cabernet sauvignon (3.5ha), mourvèdre (2.5ha) and chardonnay (2.1ha), established by Robert Allen Simpson in '72. Most of the grapes are sold, the remainder used to provide the reasonably priced, drinkable wines for which Morgan Simpson has become well known.

♟♟♟♟♀ **Basket Press Shiraz 2020, McLaren Vale** There is a lot to like here. The fruit flows mellifluously without shrill acidity or brittle oak. The oak that is there, mocha/bourbon American, is nestled well in the context of style. Riffs on sassafras, maraschino cherry, cinnamon and saturated dark fruits. A bit soupy. A swathe of sooty tannins provides direction and a sense of tension. In all, intriguing, far from jammy and well worth a whiff. Screw cap. 16.6% alc. RATING 90 DRINK 2022–2030 $24 NG ✪

Morningside Vineyard ★★★☆

665 Middle Tea Tree Road, Tea Tree, Tas 7017 **Region** Southern Tasmania
T (03) 6268 1748 **Open** By appt **Winemaker** Samantha Connew **Viticulturist** Mark Hoey **Est.** 1980 **Dozens** 600 **Vyds** 2.8ha
The name 'Morningside' was given to the old property on which the vineyard stands because it gets the morning sun; the property on the other side of the valley was known as Eveningside. Established in 1980 by Peter and Brenda Bosworth, Morningside was acquired

by the Melick and Hall families (owners of the adjacent Pressing Matters vineyard) in '19. Consistent with the observation of the early settlers, the Morningside grapes achieve full maturity with good colour and varietal flavour.

ŸŸŸŸ♀ **Pinot Noir 2020, Tasmania** This is a tightly framed pinot that will be ravishing with a a few more years yet before its release. A touch of floral spicy exoticism delivers a flourish to the bouquet and palate. The finish is bony and taut, thanks equally to tense, cool season acidity and firm, fine fruit tannins. A spell in oak might have well aided its evolution. Screw cap. 13.5% alc. **RATING** 90 **DRINK** 2027-2032 $38 TS

Morris   ★★★★★

Mia Mia Road, Rutherglen, Vic 3685 **Region** Rutherglen
T (02) 6026 7303 **www.**morriswines.com **Open** 7 days 10–4 **Winemaker** David Morris
Est. 1859 **Dozens** 36 000 **Vyds** 60ha
One of the greatest of the fortified winemakers, ranking an eyelash behind Chambers Rosewood. Morris has changed the labelling system for its sublime fortified wines with a higher-than-average entry point for the (Classic) Muscat; Topaque and the ultra-premium wines are being released under the Old Premium (Rare) label. The art of these wines lies in the blending of very old and much younger material. These Rutherglen fortified wines have no equivalent in any other part of the world (with the honourable exception of Seppeltsfield in the Barossa Valley). In '16 Casella Family Brands acquired Morris after decades of uninterested ownership by Pernod Ricard.

ŸŸŸŸŸ **Old Premium Rare Muscat NV, Rutherglen** An average age of 20 years; its one-of-a-kind solera going back generations. That kind of history is a joy to behold, not to mention taste. The darkest walnut brown-amber hue glistens in the glass. Pours slow-motion thick with enticing wood-aged characters of Christmas pudding, fig, raisin, coffee bean, caramel … the list goes on. A seamless entity of great beauty lifted and enhanced by clean, bright spirit. 500ml. Screw cap. 17% alc. **RATING** 98 $120 JP ✪
Old Premium Rare Topaque NV, Rutherglen That colour! Olive to black-burnished walnut with great viscosity. The aroma could inspire Omar Khayyam: concentrated soused raisins, roasted almonds, toffee, mocha, burnt butter and malt. Extraordinary complexity and length and yet so fresh. Magical. 500ml. Screw cap. 17.5% alc. **RATING** 98 $120 JP ✪
Cellar Reserve Grand Topaque NV, Rutherglen Dried fruits, butterscotch, malt biscuits, toffee, roasted nuts and orange peel. It's sweet, yes, but here's where the art of the blender comes into play. It floats smoothly and cleanly, dispensing the most complex of flavours with the greatest of ease. What a treat! 500ml. Screw cap. 17.3% alc. **RATING** 97 $80 JP ✪
Cellar Reserve Grand Muscat NV, Rutherglen Lush, rich and deeply intense. Moves in slow motion with nutty walnut aromas, spice, leather and signature butterscotch. So complex to taste, that's the blender's art on show. Leaves nothing behind as it fills the mouth with concentrated flavour. An international-quality superstar on our doorstep. 500ml. Screw cap. 17.3% alc. **RATING** 97 $80 JP ✪

ŸŸŸŸŸ **Cellar Reserve Grand Tawny NV, Rutherglen** David Morris selected some older parcels (40–50yo) to include in this delightful, elegant tawny. Wine blending prowess is at the heart of this fortified, refinement too. A bouquet of grilled nuts, coffee caramels, dried fruits and dusty walnut with intriguing, aromatic, spellbinding rancio character to the core. Memorable drinking. 500ml. Screw cap. 500ml. 19% alc. **RATING** 96 $80 JP
Classic Topaque NV, Rutherglen Hard to beat on price and flavour. Draws on an impressive solera of past vintages to bring the complexity of age and the freshness of youth to the glass. The rich scent of honey, malt, raisin, orange peel and toasted nuts introduces a warm, sweet mouthful of pleasure. Consistency plus, as always. 500ml. Screw cap. 17.5% alc. **RATING** 94 $25 JP ✪

Classic Muscat NV, Rutherglen Amber in colour with a nose that's sweet, floral, honeyed and utterly compelling. With an average age of 3–5 years, you get the obvious grapeyness of youth combined with a dash of Morris magic. Turkish delight, fruitcake, vanilla, nougat and toffee. Runs long, smooth, clean and fresh. 500ml. Screw cap. 17.5% alc. **RATING** 94 $25 JP ✪

 Old Premium Rare Tawny NV, Rutherglen **RATING** 93 $120 JP
Bin 158 Durif 2018, Rutherglen **RATING** 91 **DRINK** 2022-2033 $27 JP ✪

Mosquito Hill Wines ★★★★

18 Trinity Street, College Park, SA 5069 (postal) **Region** Southern Fleurieu
T 0411 661 149 **www.**mosquitohillwines.com.au **Open** Not **Winemaker** Glyn Jamieson, Daniel Franklin **Est.** 1996 **Dozens** 2000 **Vyds** 4ha
This is the venture of Glyn Jamieson, who also happens to be Professor of Surgery of the University of Adelaide. His interest in wine dates back decades, and in '94 he commenced the part-time (distance) winemaking degree at CSU: he says that while he never failed an exam, it did take him 11 years to complete the course. A year in France led him to Burgundy, hence the planting of chardonnay, pinot blanc and savagnin on the slopes of Mt Jagged on the Magpies Song vineyard and pinot noir on the Hawthorns vineyard. He built a small winery for the first vintage in '11.

🍷🍷🍷🍷🍷 Emeritus Chardonnay 2018, Southern Fleurieu Grilled peach, burnt butter, nectarine and cedar characters put on a fine display here. There's a richness to this chardonnay; it's an archetype of its variety. It's also a wine of length, and boasts more than a little finesse through the finish. It makes no false moves, and makes plenty of good ones. Screw cap. 12.5% alc. **RATING** 94 **DRINK** 2023-2027 $31 CM ✪

🍷🍷🍷🍷🍷 Brut Blanc de Blancs Méthode Traditionnelle 2017, Fleurieu **RATING** 92 **DRINK** 2023-2025 $38 CM
Emeritus Pinot Noir 2018, Southern Fleurieu **RATING** 90 **DRINK** 2023-2027 $31 CM

Moss Brothers ★★★★

351 Herdigan Road, Wandering, WA 6308 (postal) **Region** Margaret River
T 0402 275 269 **www.**mossbrotherswines.com.au **Open** Not **Winemaker** Rory Parks
Est. 1984 **Dozens** 7000 **Vyds** 16.03ha
This is the reincarnation of the Moss Brothers brand, though not its vineyards, which were acquired by Amelia Park in '15. It is a parallel business to Trove Estate. Paul Byron and Ralph Dunning are the major forces in both ventures, both with extensive whole-of-business expertise across Australia.

 Wild Garden Organic 2022, Margaret River An expressive floral and citrusy nose with some quince, lime juice and slate-like texture. There's enough spice, texture and vibrant acidity to warrant another glass. Screw cap. 13.5% alc. **RATING** 91 **DRINK** 2023-2026 $30 JF
Fidium Cabernet Sauvignon 2021, Margaret River There's so much flavour, density and richness to this wine it's hard to know where to start. At first, lots of cedary oak and menthol then bursts of blackberries, cassis and bitter chocolate infused with cinnamon and cloves across a full-bodied palate. Rather blocky tannins for the variety, raspy on the finish though time should help there. Screw cap. 14.5% alc. **RATING** 90 **DRINK** 2023-2032 $40 JF

Moss Wood ★★★★★

926 Metricup Road, Wilyabrup, WA 6284 **Region** Margaret River
T (08) 9755 6266 **www.**mosswood.com.au **Open** By appt **Winemaker** Clare Mugford, Keith Mugford **Est.** 1969 **Dozens** 11 000 **Vyds** 18.14ha

Widely regarded as one of the best wineries in the region, producing glorious chardonnay, power-laden semillon and elegant cabernet sauvignon that lives for decades. Moss Wood also owns RibbonVale Estate, the wines treated as vineyard-designated within the Moss Wood umbrella.

ΨΨΨΨΨ **Semillon 2022, Margaret River** The depth and flesh on this wine at such a young age makes it immediately accessible, but it will last quite some distance too. Today it's refreshing with upfront fruit, all lemon and white nectarines, lemongrass, some orange peel and grapefruit pith. Powerful yet equally compelling. Screw cap. 14.5% alc. **RATING** 95 **DRINK** 2022-2035 $48 JF ✪
Ribbon Vale Elsa 2021, Margaret River A wine to be reckoned with as it stands firm in structure and flavour. Expect lemongrass, nettle, lime curd and woodsy spices via well-integrated oak. It's all about style, and stylish as a result. Supple, with some phenolic grip adding to its complexity and depth. Impressive. Screw cap. 13.5% alc. **RATING** 95 **DRINK** 2022-2032 $80 JF

Mt Bera Vineyards   ★★★★☆

198c Torrens Valley Road, Gumeracha, SA 5233 **Region** Adelaide Hills
T (08) 8189 6030 **www**.mtberavineyards.com.au **Open** Fri–Sun 11–4, Mon–Thurs by appt **Winemaker** Greg Horner, Katrina Horner **Viticulturist** Greg Horner, Katrina Horner **Est.** 1997 **Dozens** 5000 **Vyds** 17ha
In '08, Greg and Katrina Horner (plus 4 kids and a growing collection of animals) purchased Mt Bera from Louise Warner. Greg and Katrina grew up on farms, and the 75ha property, with its homestead built in the 1880s, was irresistible. The property is located in a sanctuary overlooking the Torrens Valley out to Adelaide, 45 mins' drive away. Vines are planted in varying micro-climates around the property, facilitating a diverse range of varieties, and are managed according to organic/biodynamic principles.

ΨΨΨΨΨ **Boundless Horizons Grüner Veltliner 2018, Adelaide Hills** A fine adaptation, highlighting the inner beauty of grüner veltliner in shades of tropical white peach, green melon, citrus and apple. Not to mention fruit blossom, which casts a lovely aromatic overlay to the wine. Light on its feet but there are hidden depths here, texture, too, not to mention extended ageing ability. Elegance in a glass. Screw cap. 13.8% alc. **RATING** 95 **DRINK** 2022-2028 $60 JP

ΨΨΨΨΨ **Gruvee Grüner Veltliner 2018, Adelaide Hills RATING** 92 **DRINK** 2022-2026 $30 JP ✪
Boundless Horizons Merlot 2013, Adelaide Hills RATING 92
DRINK 2022-2028 $60 JP
Amphitheatre Shiraz Blaufränkisch 2019, Adelaide Hills RATING 91
DRINK 2022-2025 $30 JP
Dream Catcher Sauvignon Blanc 2020, Adelaide Hills RATING 90
DRINK 2022-2025 $30 JP
Running with the Cows Tempranillo 2018, Adelaide Hills RATING 90
DRINK 2022-2026 $30 JP

Mount Eyre Vineyards   ★★★★★

173 Gillards Road, Pokolbin, NSW 2320 **Region** Hunter Valley
T 0438 683 973 **www**.mounteyre.com **Open** At Garden Cellars, Hunter Valley Gardens
Winemaker Michael McManus, Andrew Spinaze, Mark Richardson **Viticulturist** Neil Grosser **Est.** 1970 **Dozens** 3000 **Vyds** 34ha
This is the venture of 2 families whose involvement in wine extends back several centuries in an unbroken line: the Tsironis family in the Peleponnese, Greece; and the Iannuzzi family in Vallo della Lucania, Italy. Their largest vineyard is at Broke, with a smaller vineyard at Pokolbin. The 3 principal varieties planted are chardonnay, shiraz and semillon, with smaller amounts of merlot, chambourcin, verdelho, fiano and nero d'Avola.

ŸŸŸŸŸ **Honeytree Semillon 2022, Hunter Valley** A beautifully made semillon. Lemon rules the roost, glittering acidity taking the flavours to all corners of the mouth. The quality of the fruit is awesome. Screw cap. 11% alc. **RATING** 96 **DRINK** 2023-2033 $33 JH ✪

Honeytree Fiano 2022, Hunter Valley Yet another example of fiano that is well suited to the broad sweep of Australia's wine regions. An immediate attribute is its colour – or absence thereof. This is quickly followed by its scented bouquet, the fresh ginger accents of the palate lead nashi pear to a crisp, crunchy finish. Screw cap. 12.5% alc. **RATING** 95 **DRINK** 2023-2030 $38 JH ✪

ŸŸŸŸ♀ **Monkey Place Creek Rosé 2022, Hunter Valley RATING** 90 **DRINK** 2023-2023 $23 JH ✪

Mount Horrocks

The Old Railway Station, Curling Street, Auburn, SA 5451 **Region** Clare Valley **T** (08) 8849 2243 **www**.mounthorrocks.com **Open** W'ends & public hols 10–5 **Winemaker** Stephanie Toole **Est.** 1982 **Dozens** 2500 **Vyds** 9.4ha
Owner/winemaker Stephanie Toole has never deviated from the pursuit of excellence in the vineyard and winery. She has 2 vineyard sites in the Clare Valley, certified organic since '14 and biodynamic since '20. The attention to detail and refusal to cut corners is obvious in all her wines. The cellar door is in the renovated old Auburn railway station.

ŸŸŸŸŸ **Watervale Riesling 2022, Clare Valley** Very much on song with its white flower, apple- and lime-blossom aromas. While it isn't the least uncertain in the mouth, it grows rapidly on the back palate and finish, with palpable structure to its lime-drenched flavours and acidity. Screw cap. 13% alc. **RATING** 96 **DRINK** 2023-2035 $39 JH ✪

Semillon 2022, Clare Valley Offers a hallmark acid profile with the softness of lemon, ginger and a pleasing wet herbal detail. This release is perhaps a bit more minerally, with a pumice-like aspect to the texture. It's a wonderful drink, attractive in its refreshment factor but offering further potential over years. Good stuff. Screw cap. 13.5% alc. **RATING** 94 **DRINK** 2023-2040 $40 MB ✪ ♥

Alexander Vineyard Shiraz 2021, Clare Valley Lush and rich with dark berry fruitiness with a support act of tobacco, clove and cinnamon, a flicker of choc-mint in the mix. Scents are more fruit-driven, the palate showing the glue of fine but prominent woody oak with spice as the overarching theme. That being said, it has pleasure in impressive concentration, the palate-staining intensity a feat. Screw cap. 14% alc. **RATING** 94 **DRINK** 2023-2040 $52 MB

ŸŸŸŸ♀ **Cabernet Sauvignon 2021, Clare Valley RATING** 93 **DRINK** 2023-2036 $62 MB

Nero d'Avola 2021, Clare Valley RATING 92 **DRINK** 2022-2027 $44 MB
Cordon Cut Riesling 2022, Clare Valley RATING 90 **DRINK** 2022-2030 $44 MB

Mt Jagged Wines

3191 Victor Harbor Road, Mt Jagged, SA 5211 **Region** Southern Fleurieu **T** (08) 8554 9520 **www**.mtjaggedwines.com.au **Open** Thurs–Sun 10–5 **Winemaker** Simon Parker **Est.** 1989 **Dozens** 1000 **Vyds** 25ha
Mt Jagged's vineyard was established with close-planted semillon, chardonnay, merlot, cabernet sauvignon and shiraz. The vineyard sits at 350m above sea level on a diversity of soils, ranging from ironstone/clay for the red varieties to sandy loam/clay for the whites. The cool climate vineyard (elevation and proximity to the ocean) produces fresh, crisp, zingy white wines and medium-bodied savoury reds of complexity and depth. In '13 the property was purchased by Tod and Suzanne Warmer.

ŸŸŸŸ♀ **Wishing Well Shiraz 2016, Barossa Valley** This was tasted as a 7yo wine and yet it feels both fresh and unyielding. Indeed, oak hasn't fully integrated yet and may never properly do so. It's thick with cedar and cream though it also boasts a good body of blackberried fruit flavour, along with coal, resin, mint and polished leather. Assertive tannin is bigger than the wine itself. A long life ahead, cork permitting. Cork. 14.5% alc. RATING 93 DRINK 2026–2040 $299 CM

Mount Langi Ghiran Vineyards ★★★★★

80 Vine Road, Bayindeen, Vic 3375 **Region** Grampians
T (03) 5359 4400 **www**.langi.com.au **Open** 7 days 10–5 **Winemaker** Adam Louder, Liz Ladhams **Viticulturist** Damien Sheehan **Est.** 1969 **Dozens** 45 000 **Vyds** 70ha
Mount Langi Ghiran produces outstanding shiraz, crammed with flavour and vinosity, that has long pointed the way for cool-climate examples of the variety. New shiraz plantings are propagated in Mount Langi Ghiran's nursery from the Old Block, planted in '69 with a pre-phylloxera clone. The business was acquired by the Rathbone family group (owners of Yering Station and Xanadu) in '02. Winemaker Adam Louder, born and bred in the Grampians, joined in '16, having previously worked in Bordeaux and Napa Valley, as well as at sister winery Xanadu. The quality of wine here is exemplary.

ΨΨΨΨΨ **Cliff Edge Cabernet Sauvignon Merlot 2021, Grampians** It's hard to imagine a more perfectly structured wine. It has both fruit and oak flavour in good measure, too, but the curl of tannin and the deft line of acidity is really quite something. Cedar-like oak seems slightly too heavy, combined as it is with medium-weight (at most) blue and black berried fruits. But time will set things right, and then we'll have a beautiful wine on our hands. Screw cap. 14.5% alc. RATING 94 DRINK 2026–2036 $35 CM ✪
Cliff Edge Shiraz 2021, Grampians Everything here feels exact, and exacting. Red cherried fruit, black pepper notes, integrated cedar oak and drifts of assorted florals, all of which hone to a long, peppery finish. It's mid-weight at most and it's all it needs to be. This is the kind of wine that gives elegance its good name. Screw cap. 14.5% alc. RATING 94 DRINK 2024–2035 $35 CM ✪

ΨΨΨΨΩ **Billi Billi Shiraz 2021, Grampians** Heathcote RATING 93 DRINK 2023–2028 $20 CM ✪
Mast Shiraz 2020, Grampians RATING 93 DRINK 2024–2034 $90 CM
Cliff Edge Riesling 2022, Grampians RATING 91 DRINK 2023–2030 $25 CM ✪
Cliff Edge Barbera 2021, Grampians RATING 91 DRINK 2023–2027 $35 CM
Billi Billi Rosé 2022, Grampians RATING 90 DRINK 2023–2025 $20 CM ✪

Mt Lofty Ranges Vineyard ★★★★★

Harris Road, Lenswood, SA 5240 **Region** Lenswood
T (08) 8389 8339 **www**.mtloftyrangesvineyard.com.au **Open** Fri–Sun & public hols 11–5
Winemaker Peter Leske **Est.** 1992 **Dozens** 3000 **Vyds** 4.6ha
Mt Lofty Ranges is owned and operated by Sharon Pearson and Garry Sweeney. Nestled high in the Lenswood subregion of the Adelaide Hills at an elevation of 500m, the very steep north-facing vineyard (pinot noir, sauvignon blanc, chardonnay and riesling) is pruned and picked by hand. The soil is sandy clay loam with a rock base of white quartz and ironstone, and irrigation is kept to a minimum to allow the wines to display vintage characteristics.

ΨΨΨΨΨ **S&G Shiraz 2021, Adelaide Hills** Tightly furled blue- and black-fruit allusions, pepper grind, clove and gamey saucisson. Mid-weighted, yet wild and forceful and brimming with personality. A wine with soul and an indelible sense of place. The gritty phalanx of charcoal tannins, astringent and purposeful, is what makes this wine so savoury, complex and absolutely delicious. Screw cap. 13.5% alc. RATING 95 DRINK 2022–2032 $85 NG

ΨΨΨΨΩ **S&G Chardonnay 2021, Lenswood** RATING 93 DRINK 2022–2030 $85 NG
Down the Road Gewürztraminer 2022, Lenswood RATING 92 DRINK 2022–2026 $30 NG ✪

Aspire Fumé Blanc 2022, Lenswood RATING 92 DRINK 2022-2026
$30 NG ✪
Old Apple Block Chardonnay 2021, Lenswood RATING 92
DRINK 2022-2030 $35 NG
Old Cherry Block Sauvignon Blanc 2022, Lenswood RATING 91
DRINK 2022-2024 $25 NG ✪
Old Gum Block Shiraz 2021, Adelaide Hills RATING 91 DRINK 2022-2028
$35 NG

Mount Majura Vineyard ★★★★★

88 Lime Kiln Road, Majura, ACT 2609 **Region** Canberra District
T (02) 6262 3070 **www**.mountmajura.com.au **Open** 7 days 10–5 **Winemaker** Dr Frank
van de Loo **Viticulturist** Emily White **Est.** 1988 **Dozens** 5000 **Vyds** 12.7ha
Vines were first planted in 1988 by Dinny Killen on a site on her family property that had
been especially recommended by Dr Edgar Riek; its attractions were red soil of volcanic
origin over limestone, with reasonably steep east and northeast slopes providing an element of
frost protection. The tiny vineyard has been significantly expanded since it was purchased in
'99. Blocks of pinot noir and chardonnay have been joined by pinot gris, shiraz, tempranillo,
riesling, graciano, mondeuse and touriga nacional. One of the star performers of the
Canberra District.

🍷🍷🍷🍷🍷 **The Silurian Late Disgorged Chardonnay Pinot Noir 2010, Canberra
District** What a difference 11 years on lees makes. Disgorged July '22 and a mere
900 bottles allocated. This is excellent. Gently aromatic with lemon blossom and
the merest hint of toasty aged complexity. The palate is crazily alive: vibrant,
juicy and bright with a delicious oyster shell/saline character plus plenty of fine
bead. The all-important acidity is showing no signs of waning. Diam. 11.5% alc.
RATING 95 DRINK 2022-2026 $70 JF
Riesling 2022, Canberra District You'd call this pristine. Maybe racy, steely
and dry. Yet it's not harsh or hard with the flavours building, and they are
intriguing: mint, eucalyptus, pepper, lemon oil and aniseed. There's texture, it's
slippery, juicy and very satisfying, what with the invigorating acidity expanding
the finish. Screw cap. 11.5% alc. RATING 95 DRINK 2022-2032 $34 JF ✪

Mount Mary ★★★★★

Coldstream West Road, Lilydale, Vic 3140 (postal) **Region** Yarra Valley
T (03) 9739 1761 **www**.mountmary.com.au **Open** Not **Winemaker** Sam Middleton
Est. 1971 **Dozens** 4500 **Vyds** 18ha
Mount Mary was one of the foremost pioneers of the Yarra Valley after 50 years without
viticultural activity. From the outset they produced wines of rare finesse and purity. The late
founder, Dr John Middleton, practised near-obsessive attention to detail long before that
phrase slid into oenological vernacular. He relentlessly strove for perfection and all 4 of the
wines in the original Mount Mary portfolio achieved just that (within the context of each
vintage). Charming grandson Sam Middleton is equally dedicated, assuming the winemaker
mantle in '11. In '08 Mount Mary commenced a detailed program of vine improvement, in
particular assessing the implications of progressively moving towards a 100% grafted vineyard
to provide immunity from phylloxera and a move to sustainable organic viticulture.

🍷🍷🍷🍷🍷 **Quintet 2021, Yarra Valley** 45/30/17/6/2% cabernet sauvignon/merlot/
cabernet franc/malbec/petit verdot. A saturated purple-red hue. Aromas of
blackberries, blackcurrants, dark cherry skins and crushed violets. A whisper
of pencil-shaving oak. An elegant, concentrated, pure and structured wine
that will become even more special with time. Cork. 13.3% alc. RATING 98
DRINK 2023-2040 $205 PR ✪ ♥
Triolet 2021, Yarra Valley 65/25/10% sauvignon blanc/semillon/muscadelle.
A stunning Triolet with its aromas of greengages, white nectarine, Meyer lemon,
lemongrass and jasmine. There's a hint of sandalwood coming from the oak.
Seductive, powerful and restrained. Slippery, chalky textured, tightly wound and

very long, this is going to be a great and long-lived wine. In a league of its own. Screw cap. 12.8% alc. **RATING** 98 **DRINK** 2022-2032 $120 PR ✪ ♥

Pinot Noir 2021, Yarra Valley A bright crimson red. Perfumed and seductive even at this early stage. Aromas of wild red berries, gentle spice, dark rose and bracken. Concentrated and structured with very fine, sinewy and savoury tannins. A brilliant, non-mainstream Yarra Valley pinot that's been built to go the distance. Cork. 13.3% alc. **RATING** 97 **DRINK** 2022-2035 $205 PR

ᵀᵀᵀᵀᵀ **Chardonnay 2021, Yarra Valley** A light, bright gold with green tinges. Seductive with its bouquet of melon, fresh fig, yellow peach, chamomile and a little lemongrass. A savoury nuance, too. On the palate, which is powerful, densely packed and structured, you'll find some grapefruit pith and hazelnut. Finishes extremely long, saline and gently grippy. Screw cap. 13.2% alc. **RATING** 96 **DRINK** 2022-2030 $125 PR

ᵀᵀᵀᵀᵀ **Marli Russell by Mount Mary RP2 2021, Yarra Valley RATING** 93 **DRINK** 2022-2027 $55 PR
Marli Russell by Mount Mary RP1 2021, Yarra Valley RATING 92 **DRINK** 2022-2026 $45 PR

Mount Monument Vineyard ★★★★☆

1399 Romsey Road, Romsey, Vic 3434 **Region** Macedon Ranges
T 0410 545 646 **www**.mountmonument.com.au **Open** Fri 11–8, Sat–Sun 11–4
Winemaker Ben Rankin **Est.** 2008 **Dozens** 800 **Vyds** 2.3ha
Mount Monument nestles into the shoulder of Mount Macedon, one of Australia's coolest wine regions. At 600m the volcanic silica soils are host to the chardonnay, pinot noir and riesling planted in '96 (prior to its acquisition by Nonda Katsalidis) as well as newer plantings of pinot noir, riesling and nebbiolo added in '20 and '21. The vineyard is managed with minimal chemical intervention, and utilises organic and biodynamic inputs.

ᵀᵀᵀᵀᵀ **Shiraz 2021, Heathcote** Such a temperate and refined shiraz. So much so, it's hard to put down. Best not to then, otherwise you'll miss out on the florals, the spice, the tantalising fruit. The palate is surprisingly pared back, just shy of fuller bodied, the tannins supple and there's an elegance across the palate. Smart and very delicious. Screw cap. 14% alc. **RATING** 95 **DRINK** 2022-2031 $40 JF ✪

ᵀᵀᵀᵀᵀ **Chardonnay 2020, Macedon Ranges RATING** 93 **DRINK** 2022-2029 $60 JF
Riesling 2021, Macedon Ranges RATING 92 **DRINK** 2022-2028 $50 JF
Pinot Noir 2020, Macedon Ranges RATING 90 **DRINK** 2023-2032 $60 JF

Mount Pleasant ★★★★★

401 Marrowbone Road, Pokolbin, NSW 2320 **Region** Hunter Valley
T (02) 4998 7505 **www**.mountpleasantwines.com.au **Open** Thurs–Mon 10–5
Winemaker Adrian Sparks, Jaden Hall **Viticulturist** Belinda Kelly, Nicholas Cooper
Est. 1921 **Vyds** 85.8ha
While the vaunted history of craftsmanship here is indisputable, the reds have ebbed from the reductive tension championed by former chief winemaker Jim Chatto, to a more relaxed expression under new maker Adrian Sparks. Sparks seems to have a predilection for mid-weighted, lower-alcohol styles of red, not dissimilar to the great Hunter River Burgundies crafted by Maurice O'Shea. This is a style that is as aspirational today as it was revered then, gleaned from a polyglot of historical vineyards, variable geologies and stylistic patinas, including expressions of the Old Paddock and Rosehill vineyards. The whites, too, feel less austere. Their fealty to the regional pedigree of steely, long-lived semillon, however, is clear.

ᵀᵀᵀᵀᵀ **1921 Vines Old Paddock Vineyard Shiraz 2021, Hunter Valley** Maurice O'Shea didn't waste time in planting the Old Paddock, with its slope and bright volcanic soil. It is a wine of overt structure and texture from ripe tannins, the fruit spectrum dark, the length impressive. It evolves as it sits on the tasting table, opening more doors as the perfume brings spice, licorice and game/charcuterie into play. Screw cap. 13.5% alc. **RATING** 98 **DRINK** 2031–2061 $140 JH ✪

1880 Vines Old Hill Vineyard Shiraz 2021, Hunter Valley Aromas of fresh earth and leather are matched by red berry and plum fruits, all replayed on the medium-bodied palate. It's the overall juicy freshness and elegance that define this wine and its terroir. Screw cap. 13.5% alc. **RATING** 98 **DRINK** 2031–2056 $140 JH ✪

Lovedale Semillon 2022, Hunter Valley An early release to members only; commercially available in 2027. It fills the mouth with a harmonious blend of citrus, pear and hallmark acidity that will provide a 30-year future, by that time it'll be redolent of lightly browned toast, honey and citrus marmalade. Screw cap. 11% alc. **RATING** 97 **DRINK** 2023–2052 $55 JH ✪

Rosehill Vineyard Shiraz 2021, Hunter Valley This has a lighter, brighter colour than that of its siblings, and is lighter bodied and fresh, red fruits to the centre. It's also more immediately approachable, its fruits, tannin and acidity all symbiotically balanced. Yet, it will coast through the next 30 years without blinking. Screw cap. 14% alc. **RATING** 97 **DRINK** 2026–2051 $55 JH ✪

Mountain D Full Bodied Dry Red 2021, Hunter Valley Maurice O'Shea first used the Mountain A (light bodied), Mountain B (medium bodied) and Mountain C (full bodied) terminology in 1937. They were wines of quality and longevity – as here, a perfumed bouquet reflecting a 5-day cold soak and 10 days on skins. Matured for 12 months in new French oak, the quality of the dark fruits absorbing the oak, the tannins silky. A great wine. Screw cap. 14% alc. **RATING** 97 **DRINK** 2025–2055 $80 JH ✪

O.P. & O.H. Single Vineyard Shiraz 2021, Hunter Valley Curious labelling, as the Old Paddock and Old Hill vineyards are 500m apart and quite distinct. The French oak (25% new) is more obvious than that of its siblings, but it's easily carried by the mouth-watering acidity of its red and black cherry/berry fruits. Screw cap. 14% alc. **RATING** 97 **DRINK** 2031–2056 $55 JH ✪

♟♟♟♟♟ **Estate Grown Semillon 2022, Hunter Valley** No frills in the vinification: cool-fermented for 14 days in stainless-steel tanks with cultivated yeast. Spent 2 months on lees before clarification and bottling. The fruit profile is the expected lime/lemon flavours, not so much the slinky acidity which makes it very much a now or later proposition – an outright bargain. Screw cap. 11% alc. **RATING** 95 **DRINK** 2023–2037 $25 JH ✪

Single Vineyard Old Hill Pinot Noir 2021, Hunter Valley This wine has been handled with kid gloves: hand picked and destemmed, 10% retained as whole bunches. Open fermented with thrice daily plunging, 8 days on skins, 8 months in French puncheons. The colour is excellent, and the abundant red fruits and superfine tannins are as good as they come. This challenges the idea that the Hunter is too hot for pinot noir. Screw cap. 13.5% alc. **RATING** 95 **DRINK** 2023–2041 $55 JH

Estate Grown Shiraz 2018, Hunter Valley A testament to a great vintage, balance and sensitivity. 10 days on skins, gentle plunging and pumping over, matured for 12 months in oak (10% new). The bouquet is highly expressive, with red and purple fruits to the fore and right on cue, fine-spun earthy tannins. The ultimate drink now or decades to come. Screw cap. 14% alc. **RATING** 95 **DRINK** 2023–2043 $30 JH ✪

Philip Shiraz 2018, Hunter Valley Always a major part of the annual Mount Pleasant production, and for some years of modest quality and deep discounts. The quantity made these days is far less, most surprising given its estate origins and its quality – a classic medium-bodied, finely balanced wine proudly flying the flag for Mount Pleasant and Hunter Valley shiraz. The great vintage was its own reward. Screw cap. 14% alc. **RATING** 95 **DRINK** 2023–2043 $30 JH ✪

Elizabeth Semillon 2017, Hunter Valley An aged release. All the grapes are estate grown, far distant from Elizabeth's heyday. Ah, what a drop-dead beauty, with the poise of a ballerina, feet barely touching the ground. The first stage of honey and toast just commenced, with 4–5 stages still to follow. Screw cap. 11% alc. **RATING** 95 **DRINK** 2023–2037 $30 JH ✪

Mount Henry Shiraz Pinot Noir 2021, Hunter Valley Created by Maurice O'Shea in 1944. The 2 varieties were separately vinified: the dominant shiraz with cultured yeast, the pinot noir wild fermented. The pinot finished its fermentation in new French puncheons, the shiraz tank fermented and the components blended after 7 months. The shiraz is all-seeing, the pinot noir demurely peeping through the depth of the tannins and oak. It's still to settle down, but will slowly reveal its origins. Screw cap. 13.5% alc. **RATING** 94 **DRINK** 2029–2049 $40 JH ✪

ȲȲȲȲȲ **Estate Grown Chardonnay 2021, Hunter Valley RATING** 93 **DRINK** 2023–2026 $25 JH ✪
Estate Grown Fiano 2021, Hunter Valley RATING 93 **DRINK** 2023–2030 $30 JH ✪
Estate Grown Rosé 2022, Hunter Valley RATING 90 **DRINK** 2023–2025 $25 JH ✪
Estate Grown Tempranillo Touriga 2021, Hunter Valley RATING 90 **DRINK** 2024–2029 $30 JH

Mount Stapylton Wines ★★★☆

1212 Northern Grampians Road, Laharum, Vic 3401 **Region** Grampians **T** 0429 838 233 **www.**mountstapyltonwines.com.au **Open** By appt **Winemaker** Leigh Clarnette **Viticulturist** Robert Staehr **Est.** 2002 **Dozens** 300 **Vyds** 1.5ha
Mount Stapylton's vineyard is planted on the historic Goonwinnow Homestead farming property at Laharum, on the northwest side of the Grampians, in front of Mt Stapylton. In '17 the vineyard lease was purchased from founder Howard Staehr by the Staehr family and is now being run as an addition to their mixed farming enterprise.

ȲȲȲȲȲ **Shiraz 2020, Grampians** Generously fruited and textured. There are trademark spice notes here, as much roasted spice as out-and-out pepper, but in any case they play second fiddle to the plushness of the cherry and plum flavoured fruit. This is a mid-weight wine with a pillowy softness; the flavours just seem to nestle into your mouth, on their way through. It's a wine that will please many. Screw cap. 14% alc. **RATING** 91 **DRINK** 2023–2030 $33 CM

Mount Terrible ★★★★★

289 Licola Road, Jamieson, Vic 3723 **Region** Central Victoria **T** 0429 406 037 **www.**mountterriblewines.com.au **Open** By appt **Winemaker** John Eason **Est.** 2001 **Dozens** 350 **Vyds** 2ha
John Eason and wife Janene Ridley began the long, slow (and at times very painful) business of establishing their vineyard just north of Mt Terrible in 1992 – hence the choice of name. In '01 they planted 2ha of pinot noir on a gently sloping, north-facing river terrace adjacent to the Jamieson River. DIY trials persuaded John to have the first commercial vintage in '06 contract-made. He has since made the wines himself in a fireproof winery built on top of an underground wine cellar. John has a sense of humour second to none, but must wonder what he has done to provoke the weather gods, alternating in their provision of fire, storm and tempest. Subsequent vintages have provided some well earned relief.

ȲȲȲȲȲ **Chardonnay 2022, Central Victoria** With purity, focus and length, this inaugural release is a triumph. It has all the indicia of cool-grown chardonnay, starting quietly but accelerating continuously to the intense, classic white peach and grapefruit duo on the long palate and lingering, fresh aftertaste. 45 dozen made. Screw cap. 12.7% alc. **RATING** 97 **DRINK** 2023–2037 $45 JH ✪

ȲȲȲȲȲ **Pinot Noir Rosé 2022, Central Victoria** Light but vivid hue. Strawberry/ raspberry aromas: purity for short. This has real presence, real pinot fruit, made from the ground up. Its mouthfeel and texture are also admirable. And don't be scared of keeping some bottles for a year or 2. Screw cap. 13% alc. **RATING** 94 **DRINK** 2023–2027 $25 JH ✪

Mount Trio Vineyard ★★★★

2534 Porongurup Road, Mount Barker WA 6324 **Region** Porongurup
T (08) 9853 1136 **www**.mounttriowines.com.au **Open** By appt **Winemaker** Gavin
Berry, Andrew Vesey, Caitlin Gazey **Est.** 1989 **Dozens** 3500 **Vyds** 8.5ha
Mount Trio was established by Gavin Berry and wife Gill Graham (plus business partners)
shortly after they moved to the Mount Barker area in late '88, Gavin to take up the position of
chief winemaker at Plantagenet, which he held until '04, when he and partners acquired the
now very successful and much larger West Cape Howe. The 8.5ha vineyard is now entirely
planted to pinot noir, riesling and chardonnay, with other varietals sourced from Mt Barker,
Great Southern and Frankland River.

🍷🍷🍷🍷🍷 **Rosé Sangiovese 2022, Great Southern** Very pale, light and dry. A
refreshing, cherry-imbued wine of vibrancy but gentle savouriness in tow. Scents
of that red cherry, pomegranate juice and faint cashew – similarly the palate
follows through. It's lively, delicious, moreish and just the right amount of detail
and drinkability. Screw cap. 13% alc. **RATING** 93 **DRINK** 2023–2025 $18 MB ✪
Riesling 2022, Porongurup Great drinking here with a fruitiness that feels
ultra-appealing set among higher-tension acidity and lashings of citrus blossom
floral characters. Scents of orange, lemon blossom, ripe apple and papaya. The
palate delivers more mandarin-like citrus with red apple, juicy lime and some
light, steely notes. Not particularly tense or complex, but very delicious in its
gulpable way. Screw cap. 11.5% alc. **RATING** 92 **DRINK** 2023–2028 $23 MB ✪
Home Block Pinot Noir 2021, Porongurup From a best-barrel selection.
Succulent and supple, quite ripe and rich in red cherry fruit character licked by
kirsch and woody spices, but in that a potent yet silky textural flow and a good
deal of drinkability. Feels perfumed and quite pretty and has some grip and tumble
of dustiness, but the gist is a structured, serious pinot. Screw cap. 14.5% alc.
RATING 92 **DRINK** 2023–2028 $35 MB

Mountadam Vineyards ★★★★★

High Eden Road, Eden Valley, SA 5235 **Region** Eden Valley
T 0427 089 836 **www**.mountadam.com.au **Open** By appt **Winemaker** Caitlin Brown
Viticulturist Caitlin Brown **Est.** 1972 **Dozens** 30 000 **Vyds** 148ha
Founded by the late David Wynn for winemaker son Adam, Mountadam was (somewhat
surprisingly) purchased by Möet Hennessy Wine Estates in '00. In '05, Mountadam returned
to family ownership when it was purchased by David and Jenni Brown from Adelaide. David
and Jenni have worked to bring the original Mountadam property back together with the
purchase of Mountadam Farm in '07 and the High Eden vineyard from TWE in '15, thus
reassembling all of the land originally purchased by David Wynn.

🍷🍷🍷🍷🍷 **Milton Cabernet Sauvignon 2021, High Eden** Packed with bramble-edged
blackberry, blackcurrant and black cherry fruits. Hints of brown spice, violets, briar,
licorice, cedar, sage and vanilla bean. There's a lovely density with great tension
between that High Eden mineral line and the ripe black fruits with fine, granite-
dust tannins. The alcohol is high but it handles it well and that fruit weight is
impressive. Screw cap. 15.5% alc. **RATING** 95 **DRINK** 2023–2035 $40 DB ✪
Cabernet Sauvignon 2021, Eden Valley The fruit purity on display is really
something and there is a balance here, despite the higher alcohol level. Ripe
blackberry and blackcurrant fruits with hints of briar, dried citrus blossom, roast
capsicum, fine spice and cedar all come into play with fine, self-assured tannins
and lacy acidity finishing long and bright. Screw cap. 15.5% alc. **RATING** 95
DRINK 2023–2035 $35 DB ✪
Estate Chardonnay 2021, Eden Valley Pale straw with pristine white
peach, nectarine, fig and citrus fruits with underlying hints of soft spice, cashew
oak, white flowers and crushed quartz. A slink of texture on the palate with
crème fraîche notes, a crystalline acid line providing clarity and drive and a
long finish with excellent length of flavour. Screw cap. 13.5% alc. **RATING** 94
DRINK 2023–2030 $40 DB ✪

🍷🍷🍷🍷 Chardonnay 2021, Eden Valley RATING 93 DRINK 2023–2028 $28 DB ✪
Riesling 2022, Eden Valley RATING 92 DRINK 2023–2028 $28 DB ✪
Gewürztraminer 2022, Eden Valley RATING 92 DRINK 2023–2027 $28 DB ✪
Patriarch Shiraz 2021, Eden Valley RATING 92 DRINK 2023–2033 $45 DB
Five-Fifty Shiraz 2020, Barossa RATING 91 DRINK 2023–2028 $20 DB ✪
Five-Fifty Cabernet Sauvignon 2020, Barossa RATING 91 DRINK 2023–2027 $20 DB ✪
Five-Fifty Shiraz 2021, Barossa RATING 90 DRINK 2023–2027 $20 DB ✪
Five-Fifty Cabernet Sauvignon 2021, Barossa RATING 90 DRINK 2023–2029 $20 DB ✪
Shiraz 2021, Eden Valley RATING 90 DRINK 2023–2030 $35 DB

Mulline ★★★★★

131 Lumbs Road, Sutherlands Creek, Vic 3331 **Region** Geelong
T 0402 409 292 **www**.mulline.com **Open** First w/end of the month 11–4
Winemaker Ben Mullen **Est.** 2019 **Dozens** 4000
This is the venture of Ben Mullen and business partner Ben Hine, the derivation of the winery name self-evident. Ben Mullen grew up in the Barossa Valley and studied oenology at the University of Adelaide, graduating in '12. His journey thereafter was in the purple, working at Yarra Yering, Oakridge, Torbreck and Leeuwin Estate, Domaine Dujac in Burgundy in '13 (lighting a fire for pinot noir and chardonnay), Craggy Range in NZ ('15), coming back to Geelong as winemaker for Clyde Park in '17–18. Ben Hine is also from SA working in hospitality for many years before obtaining his law degree. There is a range of single-vineyard wines at the top, backed by the Geelong region range (and no wines from elsewhere).

🍷🍷🍷🍷🍷 Single Vineyard Sutherlands Creek Pinot Noir 2022, Geelong A bright cherry red. The most perfumed of this year's single-vineyard pinots from Mulline. It will also be the most long-lived. Delicate with aromas of wild strawberry, redcurrant, pomegranate, peony and a hint of dried herbs. Equally detailed on the elegant, fine-boned and long palate. Screw cap. 12.5% alc. RATING 97 DRINK 2022–2028 $60 PR ✪
Single Vineyard Bannockburn Syrah 2022, Geelong A deep, bright crimson. Aromas of blackcurrant pastilles, damson plums, aromatic brown spices, a little garrigue and graphite. This rich, energetic, medium-bodied and structured wine is still a pup. You'll find silky and persistent tannins on the long finish, but it'll need another 2–3 years to fully hit its straps. Screw cap. 13.5% alc. RATING 97 DRINK 2023–2030 $60 PR ✪ ♥

🍷🍷🍷🍷🍷 Single Vineyard Portarlington Pinot Noir 2022, Geelong Aromas of wild strawberries and kirsch sit alongside whole-bunch derived notes of white pepper and dried mountain herbs. Concentrated and balanced, this flows nicely across the palate with its silky tannins and bright, juicy, acidity. Screw cap. 13% alc. RATING 96 DRINK 2022–2026 $60 PR ✪
Single Vineyard Sutherlands Creek Chardonnay 2022, Geelong A bright green gold. Opens with aromas of white nectarine and peach, lemon verbena and grapefruit pith before revealing attractive savoury, nutty notes. There's real drive and persistence on the palate, too, which culminates in a long, mineral and chalky finish. Excellent. Screw cap. 12.5% alc. RATING 96 DRINK 2023–2028 $60 PR ✪
Single Vineyard Curlewis Fumé Blanc 2022, Geelong A straw gold with green tinges. With its scents of orange and lemon pith, blackcurrant, curry leaves and fennel seeds, this is not your average sauvignon blanc. Just as good on the textured, saline palate, which closes with a touch of grip from the skin-contact derived phenolics that give the wine structure and length. Impressive stuff. Screw cap. 12.5% alc. RATING 95 DRINK 2023–2027 $60 PR
Single Vineyard Sutherlands Creek Shiraz Viognier 2022, Geelong Bright crimson purple. Aromatic with spiced blackberries and raspberry coulis and unmistakable apricot-infused, viognier scents. A hedonistic, balanced and delicious mouthful from the get-go. Screw cap. 13% alc. RATING 95 DRINK 2023–2027 $60 PR

Single Vineyard Drysdale Pinot Noir 2022, Geelong The most immediate of this year's single-vineyard pinots from Mulline. Redolent of strawberries and raspberries, a gentle spice and floral notes. Opulent and fleshy, with fine, velvety tannins. Screw cap. 13% alc. RATING 95 DRINK 2023–2026 $60 PR

Sauvignon Blanc 2022, Geelong A light bright green gold. Aromas of green mango skin, lemon sorbet and orange blossom with some floral green herb notes. The palate is bright and gently textured, and this very well-put-together wine finishes long and precise. Screw cap. 12.5% alc. RATING 95 DRINK 2023–2027 $30 PR ✪

Single Vineyard Portarlington Syrah 2022, Geelong A deep crimson purple. Perfumed with red and blue fruits, violets, spices, some green olive tapenade and a little ponzu. Concentrated yet not remotely heavy, the tannins are velvety and textured. An excellent new addition to the range. 75 dozen made. Screw cap. 13.5% alc. RATING 95 DRINK 2023–2030 $60 PR

Single Vineyard Portarlington Chardonnay 2022, Geelong Aromas of orchard fruits, citrus and some light oyster shell scents add to the wine's complexity. On the palate, the phenolics give the wine focus on the long, chalky finish. My score may prove to be conservative if this continues to blossom in the bottle. Screw cap. 13% alc. RATING 94 DRINK 2023–2027 $60 PR

🍷🍷🍷🍷🍷 **Syrah 2022, Geelong** RATING 93 DRINK 2022–2027 $35 PR ✪
Single Vineyard Sutherlands Creek Fumé Blanc 2022, Geelong RATING 93 DRINK 2023–2027 $60 PR
Single Vineyard Curlewis Riesling 2022, Geelong RATING 91 DRINK 2023–2028 $40 PR
Nouveau 2022, Geelong RATING 90 DRINK 2023–2024 $32 JH

Murdoch Hill ★★★★★

260 Mappinga Road, Woodside, SA 5244 **Region** Adelaide Hills
T (08) 7200 5018 **www**.murdochhill.com.au **Open** 7 days 11–4 **Winemaker** Michael Downer **Est.** 1998 **Dozens** 10 000 **Vyds** 25.4ha
A little over 17ha of vines have been established on the undulating, gum tree–studded countryside of Charlie and Julie Downer's 80yo Erika property, 4km east of Oakbank. The varieties planted are sauvignon blanc, shiraz, cabernet sauvignon, cabernet franc and chardonnay; a further 8.3ha in Lenswood is planted to chardonnay and pinot noir. Son Michael is winemaker, with a bachelor of oenology degree from the University of Adelaide.

🍷🍷🍷🍷🍷 **The Landau Single Vineyard Oakbank Syrah 2021, Adelaide Hills** Shiraz of the Year. Score awarded by the Halliday tasting panel at the annual Awards judging. NG writes: This is one of the finest Australian shiraz/syrah wines I have come across in a long time. So finely tuned, aromatic and fresh it makes my head spin. Violet, iodine, purple fruit persuasions and a swathe of the most beautiful, shapely tannins, like pinions of savoury enforcement riddling olive and smoked meat across the mid-weighted palate. Clearly fruit comes off a site as beautiful as the hands that crafted this wine. Screw cap. 13.5% alc. RATING 99 DRINK 2022–2030 $51 PD ❤

🍷🍷🍷🍷🍷 **Orion Oakbank Syrah 2021, Adelaide Hills** Has excellent colour grading to a vivid purple-crimson rim. The bouquet and palate sing lustily from the same page, with black fruits, spices, dark chocolate, licorice and sandalwood. It's built for the long haul. Screw cap. 13.5% alc. RATING 96 DRINK 2023–2041 $85 JH

The Tilbury Chardonnay 2021, Adelaide Hills An immediately attractive wine with fresh, vibrant varietal fruit in the grapefruit/white peach spectrum. Oak is a minor contributor, acidity an important driver to the finish and aftertaste. All up purity. Screw cap. 13% alc. RATING 95 DRINK 2023–2036 $51 JH

🍷🍷🍷🍷🍷 **Red Blend 2021, Adelaide Hills** RATING 92 DRINK 2022–2025 $28 NG ✪
The Rocket Limited Release Chardonnay 2021, Adelaide Hills RATING 92 DRINK 2023–2030 $85 JH
Syrah 2021, Adelaide Hills RATING 92 DRINK 2022–2027 $28 NG ✪

Chardonnay 2022, Adelaide Hills RATING 91 DRINK 2022–2026 $36 NG
The Sulky Riesling 2022, Adelaide Hills RATING 91 DRINK 2022–2028
$36 NG

Murray Street Vineyards

37 Murray Street, Greenock, SA 5360 **Region** Barossa Valley
T (08) 8562 8373 **www**.murraystreet.com.au **Open** 7 days 10–5 **Winemaker** Ben
Perkins **Est.** 2001 **Dozens** 20 000 **Vyds** 120ha
Murray Street Vineyards has established itself as a producer of exceptionally good wines,
ranging from the top-tier Icon wines to the newly released Artisan range, launched in '22.
The 120ha of estate vines are located in the Barossa's western ridge, in Greenock (80ha) where
winemaker Ben Perkins grew up, and in Gomersal (40ha).

🍷🍷🍷🍷🍷 **Icon Aria 2020, Barossa Valley** A lovely rich blend of 90/10% shiraz/mataro.
The fruit is all plum and macerated summer berry tones with plenty of chocolate,
leather, spice and meaty nuance. It feels very composed and calm with that
subregional ferrous note and a real meaty flex to the lingering finish. Diam.
14.4% alc. RATING 95 DRINK 2023–2035 $125 DB
Icon Per Se 2020, Barossa Valley A deep, inky blend of 88/6/5/1% cabernet
sauvignon/malbec/cabernet franc/merlot showing rich cassis-like fruits with
underlying hints of cigar box, ground spice, cinnamon, undergrowth, dried herbs,
graphite and light jasmine top notes. There is a meaty, ferrous edge to the fruit
on the palate, tight-grained tannin and a lingering savoury-edged finish. Diam.
14.5% alc. RATING 94 DRINK 2023–2035 $125 DB
Greenock Estate Shiraz 2020, Barossa Valley Impressively coloured and
sporting deep, juicy plum, blue and boysenberry fruits underscored with hints
of baking spices, cedar, pepper, dark chocolate, pressed purple flowers, grilled
figs and ferrous earth. Excellent fruit weight and purity with a powdery tannin
framework and some ironstone heft to the plummy fruit depth on the finish.
Diam. 14.4% alc. RATING 94 DRINK 2023–2033 $60 DB

🍷🍷🍷🍷🍷 **Artisan Rosé 2022, Barossa Valley** RATING 92 DRINK 2023–2025 $25 DB ✪
Artisan Cabernet Sauvignon 2020, Barossa Valley RATING 92
DRINK 2023–2029 $35 DB
Artisan Cabernet Shiraz 2020, Barossa Valley RATING 92 DRINK 2023–2028
$35 DB
Artisan Shiraz 2020, Barossa Valley RATING 91 DRINK 2023–2028 $35 DB
Artisan Grenache Mataro Shiraz 2020, Barossa Valley RATING 91
DRINK 2023–2026 $35 DB
Artisan Semillon 2022, Barossa Valley RATING 90 DRINK 2023–2027
$25 DB ✪

Murrumbateman Winery

131 McIntosh Circuit, Murrumbateman, NSW 2582 **Region** Canberra District
T 0432 826 454 **www**.murrumbatemanwinery.com.au **Open** 7 days 10–5
Winemaker Bobbie Makin **Viticulturist** Bobbie Makin **Est.** 1973 **Dozens** 3500
Vyds 4ha
Draws upon 4ha of estate-grown sauvignon blanc and shiraz. It also incorporates an à la carte
restaurant and function room, together with picnic and barbecue areas.

🍷🍷🍷🍷🍷 **Four Barrel Shiraz 2021, Canberra District** With a chargrilled steak, this
wine would work a treat. On its own, it's ripe and plump with lots of herbal
infusions. Thankfully the richness of fruit tends to keep green accents at bay. Full
bodied with cedary sweet oak and lots of spices in the mix including a flutter of
pepper. Screw cap. 13.5% alc. RATING 90 DRINK 2023–2031 $60 JF

MyattsField Vineyards

Union Road, Carmel Valley, WA 6076 **Region** Perth Hills
T (08) 9293 5567 **www**.myattsfield.com.au **Open** Fri–Sun and public hols 11–5
Winemaker Josh Davenport, Rachael Davenport, Josh Uren **Est.** 1997 **Dozens** 4000
Vyds 4.5ha
MyattsField Vineyards is owned by Josh and Rachael Davenport. Both have oenology degrees
and domestic and Flying Winemaker experience, especially Rachael. In '06 they decided
they would prefer to work for themselves. They left their employment, building a winery
in time for the '07 vintage. Their vineyards include verdelho, mourvèdre, touriga, and durif
alongside shiraz, cabernet sauvignon, merlot and petit verdot. They also purchase small parcels
of grapes.

Vermentino 2022, Perth Hills This is light, fresh and delicate. Refreshing, no
doubt. Expect cucumber in tonic water, lemon sorbet and dried pear characters
found in both the bouquet and palate. The texture is gently chalky and puckering,
ultimately giving a good reset with each sip. Good extension of flavour, too.
Screw cap. 11% alc. **RATING** 93 **DRINK** 2023–2025 $25 MB ✪
Rosé 2022, Perth Hills Mourvèdre/sangiovese/viognier. Light and lean with
accents of sour cherry, cranberry drink and lychee with a dusting of piquant
cinnamon spice. It feels dry and savoury as a style, pale and pretty in its delicate
fruitiness with high drinkability as a calling card. Vibrant and energetic, too.
Some quiet complexity here and pleasing overall. Screw cap. 12% alc. **RATING** 91
DRINK 2023–2025 $25 MB ✪
Durif 2021, Perth Hills Inky and rich, thick-set, broad and concentrated.
Verging on port characters, stewed forest berries, preserved plum, choc-licorice,
cola and kirsch all in fine fettle and extremely overt. Tannins wrap around chunky,
ripe fruit, sweet spice, more cola, brandy-soaked dried fruits and nuts. Huge. It
does it all pretty darn well, too, not one for the faint-hearted, but enthusiasts will
be well served. Screw cap. 15.8% alc. **RATING** 90 **DRINK** 2023–2028 $30 MB

Naked Run Wines

8305 Horrocks Righway, Sevenhill, SA 5453 (postal) **Region** Clare Valley
T 0408 807 655 **www**.nakedrunwines.com.au **Open** Not **Winemaker** Steve Baraglia
Viticulturist Bradley Currie **Est.** 2005 **Dozens** 1500 **Vyds** 20ha
Naked Run is the virtual winery of Jayme Wood, Bradley Currie and Steven Baraglia; their
skills ranging from viticulture through to production, and also to the all-important sales and
marketing (and not to be confused with Naked Wines). Riesling and shiraz are sourced from
Clare Valley, grenache from Barossa and Clare valleys, among other varietals.

Place in Time Sevenhill Riesling 2018, Clare Valley A mature-release
riesling. Rich scents of honey, toffee, lemon curd and apricot with hints of
pleasing kerosene. A pool of honeycomb, lemon, ginger and butterscotch, cool,
limey acidity keeping everything fresh. Delicious, is the message. This feels right
in the zone, complex, interesting, and good to get stuck into now. Screw cap.
11.5% alc. **RATING** 94 **DRINK** 2022–2025 $45 MB

The Aldo Barossa Valley Grenache 2021, Clare Valley **RATING** 91
DRINK 2022–2028 $25 MB ✪
Hill 5 Shiraz Cabernet 2021, Clare Valley **RATING** 90 **DRINK** 2022–2027
$25 MB ✪

Nannup Estate

Lot 25 Perks Road, Nannup, WA 6275 (postal) **Region** Blackwood Valley
T (08) 9756 2005 **www**.nannupestate.com.au **Open** Not **Winemaker** Ryan Aggiss
(contract) **Viticulturist** Mark Blizard **Est.** 2017 **Dozens** 5000 **Vyds** 14.43ha
Nannup Estate is owned by Mark Blizard and family. The vineyard sits high on the granite
ridges of the Blackwood River escarpment. The first 6ha of vines were planted in '98, with

subsequent plantings in '00 and '06. The vineyard now comprises almost 14.5ha of cabernet sauvignon, merlot, chardonnay, tempranillo and malbec.

ΨΨΨΨΨ **Rolling Hills Malbec 2021, Blackwood Valley** Soft and fleshy malbec with hallmark perfume of ripe plum, dark chocolate, fig and date notes with prominent seasoning of clove, cinnamon and Asian five-spice. Thick set on the palate, well stained, juicy and rich with more of the same from the bouquet in characters. Finishes choc-minty and plush. It's a strong showing for the variety. Screw cap. 14.5% alc. **RATING** 93 **DRINK** 2023–2028 $38 MB

Rolling Hills Cabernet Sauvignon 2021, Blackwood Valley Medium weight red of juicy blackcurrants, cassis, choc nut elements and a suggestion of eucalyptus between the aromas and flavours. While ostensibly bright and fresh to taste an overlay of fine, silty tannins lend structure and definition and draw the wine to a cool finish with each sip. Well judged and balanced expression. Screw cap. 14% alc. **RATING** 92 **DRINK** 2023–2030 $38 MB

Narkoojee ★★★★★

220 Francis Road, Glengarry North, Vic 3854 **Region** Gippsland
T (03) 5192 4257 **www**.narkoojee.com **Open** 7 days 10.30–4.30 **Winemaker** Axel Friend **Viticulturist** Axel Friend **Est.** 1980 **Dozens** 5000 **Vyds** 13.8ha
Narkoojee, originally a dairy farm owned by the Friend family, is near the old gold-mining town of Walhalla and looks out over the Strzelecki Ranges. The wines are produced from the estate vineyards, with chardonnay accounting for half the total. Former lecturer in civil engineering and extremely successful amateur winemaker Harry Friend changed horses in '94 to take joint control of the vineyard and winery with son Axel, and they haven't missed a beat since; their skills show through in all the wines.

ΨΨΨΨΨ **Reserve Pinot Noir 2021, Gippsland** The Reserve is pretty spick at the moment, full of chinotto and blood orange, with requisite cherry pip flavours with some fresh herbs. The palate is quite refined, accommodating tangy acidity and fine tannins; it's also moreish and appealing in every way. Screw cap. 13.5% alc. **RATING** 95 **DRINK** 2023–2031 $46 JF ✪

Valerie Pinot Noir 2021, Gippsland Dark cherries abound, and so too Middle Eastern spices and a slight tamarind character adding lovely complexity. Medium bodied, the palate very even with velvety tannins and there's a gentleness and calmness even. And then, a burst of sweet fruit and tangy acidity to close. Screw cap. 13.5% alc. **RATING** 95 **DRINK** 2023–2031 $67 JF

Chairman's Selection Peter's Pinot Noir 2021, Gippsland Assuming this is a one-off as its made in honour of outgoing chairman Peter Sheehan and a mere 270 bottles were produced. Morello cherries, ripe black cherries, menthol and cranberry tang, woodsy spices with the oak well knitted into this wine. Medium bodied with raw silk tannins, expressive and distinctly Narkoojee. Screw cap. 13.5% alc. **RATING** 95 **DRINK** 2023–2031 $150 JF

ΨΨΨΨΨ **Four Generations Merlot 2021, Gippsland** **RATING** 93 **DRINK** 2022–2030 $46 JF

Reserve Chardonnay 2021, Gippsland **RATING** 93 **DRINK** 2023–2030 $46 JF

Pinot Noir 2021, Gippsland **RATING** 92 **DRINK** 2023–2029 $31 JF

Reserve Maxwell Cabernet 2021, Gippsland **RATING** 92 **DRINK** 2024–2034 $46 JF

The Harry Shiraz 2021, Gippsland **RATING** 92 **DRINK** 2024–2031 $150 JF

Valerie Shiraz 2021, Gippsland **RATING** 92 **DRINK** 2023–2033 $67 JF

Lily Grace Chardonnay 2021, Gippsland **RATING** 92 **DRINK** 2023–2028 $31 JF

Valerie Chardonnay 2021, Gippsland **RATING** 90 **DRINK** 2023–2030 $67 JF

Valerie Viognier 2021, Gippsland **RATING** 90 **DRINK** 2023–2027 $67 JF

Isaac Reserve Shiraz 2021, Gippsland **RATING** 90 **DRINK** 2024–2033 $46 JF

Nashdale Lane Wines

125 Nashdale Lane, Nashdale, NSW 2800 **Region** Orange
T 0458 127 333 **www**.nashdalelane.com **Open** 7 days 11–5 **Winemaker** Nick Segger
Tanya Segger **Viticulturist** Nick Segger, Tanya Segger **Est.** 2001 **Dozens** 6000 **Vyds** 18ha
Nashdale Lane began as a dream following Nick and Tanya Segger's brief working holiday on
a tiny vineyard in Tuscany in '91, setting in motion a long search for a suitable patch of their
own. The dream became reality in '01 with the purchase of an 18yo vineyard in Orange.
At first the winemaking was contracted out, but these days Nick and Tanya are hands-on in
both the winery and cellar door, the latter set up in a refurbished apple packing shed on the
property. The organically managed vineyard is planted to chardonnay, shiraz, pinot gris and
sauvignon blanc, with smaller amounts of riesling, pinot noir, tempranillo and arneis. An old
apple shed has been converted to a cellar door and visitors to Nashdale Lane can stay in luxury
cabins set among the vines.

Legacy Chardonnay 2021, Orange Powdery talc and white nectarine, white
rose, acacia blossom and candied lemon rind. Dried apple and pear with almond
croissant. There's a gentleness to the flow of this wine with plenty of flavour
weight and a lovely biscuity finish. Elegant. Screw cap. 13% alc. **RATING** 92
DRINK 2022–2028 $60 SW
Pinot Gris 2022, Orange Honeydew, lemon, ruby grapefruit peel, nashi pear
and rosewater. A leisurely shape and weight with lemon pith and a chalky texture.
A gris with a little more complexity that still achieves a pleasant, crowd-pleasing
style. Screw cap. 12.5% alc. **RATING** 91 **DRINK** 2022–2026 $30 SW
Medium Dry Riesling 2022, Orange A late-picked style with 12g/L of RS.
Pink Lady apple skin, grapefruit citrus and lemon gum oil. Perky acidity for a
medium-dry style and the additional sugar is well integrated, making for a more
generous fruit weight. Screw cap. 12.5% alc. **RATING** 90 **DRINK** 2022–2028
$40 SW
Riesling 2021, Orange Lime juice, Red Delicious apple and pear flesh.
Linear and juicy with a slippery mouthfeel and nice natural acidity. Puckering
and finishes bone dry. An aromatic and bright cool-climate riesling. Screw cap.
11.5% alc. **RATING** 90 **DRINK** 2022–2028 $50 SW
Arneis 2021, Orange Greengage plum, white pear, jasmine blossom and
lemonade icy poles. Green almonds, cucumber and margarita salt. A balanced
example of arneis that achieves that slinky texture and ease of flow. Screw cap.
13% alc. **RATING** 90 **DRINK** 2022–2025 $40 SW
The Social Rouge Shiraz Sangiovese NV, Orange Morello cherries,
raspberry tea, mulberry and sweet nutmeg with gum nut, dark chocolate and
vanilla pod. Oak is dominant, but so too is a sappy tea tree leaf note. The wine
invokes Aussie bushland and summer holidays camping around a fire while leaning
into its vintage conditions. Appreciative nod. Screw cap. 14.1% alc. **RATING** 90
DRINK 2022–2026 $35 SW

Neldner Road

119 Neldner Road, Marananga, SA 5355 **Region** Barossa Valley
T (08) 8524 4465 **www**.neldnerroad.com.au **Open** By appt **Winemaker** Dave Powell
Viticulturist Dave Powell **Est.** 2014 **Dozens** 8000 **Vyds** 30ha
Neldner Road is the winemaking home of the tour-de-force that is Dave Powell
(ex-Rockford, ex-Torbreck, ex-Powell & Son). Dave is known for many things, rich and
authoritative wines among them, but his main and enduring claim is as a champion of unique
vines and vineyards in the Barossa and Eden valleys. Few have placed a higher value on the
old vine grenache, mataro and shiraz of these regions as he has, or over a long period of time.
Neldner Road will continue to champion these varieties and vineyards both to the home
market and to the world beyond.

ŸŸŸŸŸ **Herrmann Shiraz 2019, Barossa Valley** A voluptuous wine with lots of length. It offers so much warm flavour, all blackberry and black licorice, with toast, cedar and hay notes rising through the back half of the wine. There are mint notes, too, but the thing here is that blackness and depth to all that meaty, Barossa dirt-strewn fruit behind. Screw cap. 15% alc. RATING 96 DRINK 2023–2035 $150 CM

Loechal Shiraz 2019, Eden Valley There's certainly a lot of oak flavour here but it's seductive oak and it works. Indeed the aromatics on this wine are amazing. Flavours are wild with florals, bright with blue and red berried fruit, grainy tannin, woodsy smoke and resiny cedar. Tremendous presence and concentration, without being in any way baked; it feels picked at the perfect moment. Screw cap. 14.5% alc. RATING 96 DRINK 2023–2035 $150 CM

Chatterton's Shiraz 2018, Barossa Valley Eden Valley 'This is my RunRig,' Dave Powell says. It's a phenomenal wine. It's a wall of flavour, and a wall of tannin, and it has length that goes on and on. Hay, cedar, gritty earth, sweet plum, dense blackberry and tar, and then meats and woodsmoke through the finish. The roll of tannin here, inked with graphite, is something else. It's a monster but it's so well shaped. Screw cap. 14.5% alc. RATING 96 DRINK 2023–2035 $275 CM

Powell & Son Kraehe Shiraz 2017, Barossa Valley A wine of meat and mineral with dried herbs along with asphalt and a flood of plum. It's more floral than you'd expect, given that it's Barossa and not Eden, but it also brings bass notes, and plenty of them. Of all the wines in the Powell/Neldner line-up, this needs a few years to shake off its grumble. Cork. 14.5% alc. RATING 96 DRINK 2026–2040 $750 CM

Kleinig Mataro 2017, Barossa Valley Incredible tannin structure. Ultrafine, but with grain and assertion. The tannin doesn't hold the wine up, if anything it simply enables it, this despite the fact that the fruit is both mid-weight and measured. This is a fantastic wine. Complex, rigid and lengthy. Screw cap. 14.5% alc. RATING 96 DRINK 2022–2035 $275 CM ♥

Powell & Son Steinert Flaxman's Valley Shiraz 2017, Eden Valley This is from the same vineyard as Rockford's Flaxman shiraz. It's a wine that is both powerful and refined. It's meaty and it's floral and it's lifted, but there are depths to the pools of plum and spread to the growls of graphite. Presence, it has plenty. This just loads the palate up and holds you there, but it also has length and plenty of it. Cork. 14.5% alc. RATING 96 DRINK 2023–2036 $750 CM

Powell & Son Brennecke Grenache 2017, Barossa Valley Bit more oak here. Some development, too. Mushrooms, raspberries, woodsmoke and sweet earth. Choc-orange overtones. Beautiful tannin structure, but velvety with it, like strings of gum. This was grown on a 100+yo vineyard and while it has the concentration you'd expect, it's the pure seductiveness of it that really grabs you. Screw cap. 14.5% alc. RATING 95 DRINK 2022–2032 $275 CM

Marsanne 2021, Barossa Valley Wonderful intensity. Stone fruit and melon characters, in a floral context. Almonds and smoke. So much richness, body, grip and length. White wine for red wine lovers, if you will. Grown on sandy soils. Aged in oak. Tiny volume. Lovely. Screw cap. 14% alc. RATING 94 DRINK 2023–2027 $50 CM

Powell & Son Barossa & Eden Shiraz 2019, Barossa Valley Eden Valley Dark chocolate and blackberry flavours come lifted with florals – it tastes exactly as you would expect (and hope) of these regions combined. Bright but deep, structured but juicy, the fruit flavours tumbling, joyously, over themselves through the finish. Screw cap. 14.5% alc. RATING 94 DRINK 2022–2030 $50 CM

ŸŸŸŸŸ **Steinert Riesling 2022, Eden Valley** RATING 93 DRINK 2023–2033 $30 CM ✪

Powell & Son Shiraz 2019, Barossa Valley RATING 93 DRINK 2022–2029 $30 CM ✪

Powell & Son Grenache Shiraz Mataro 2018, Barossa Valley RATING 93 DRINK 2022–2028 $50 CM

New Era Vineyards

PO Box 391, Woodside SA 5244 **Region** Adelaide Hills
T 0413 544 246 **www**.neweravineyards.com.au **Open** Not **Winemaker** Bob Baxter,
Iain Baxter **Viticulturist** Bob Baxter, Iain Baxter **Est.** 1988 **Dozens** 1500 **Vyds** 15ha
The New Era vineyard is situated over a gold reef that was mined until '40, when all
recoverable gold had been extracted. The vineyard now includes shiraz, pinot noir, cabernet
sauvignon, tempranillo, merlot, saperavi, sangiovese, touriga nacional, nebbiolo, nero d'Avola
and chardonnay. Much of the production is sold to other winemakers in the region. The small
amount of wine made has been the subject of favourable reviews.

Lagrein 2021, Limestone Coast A raft of bolshy tannins and aromas
so beautifully and incongruously alpine that the whole equation makes me
smile. This is delicious! Spruce, purple fruits, lilac, thistle and mountain amaro
soused with herbs from somewhere higher up. A faint whiff of tea tree gives its
origins away, yet this is a full-weighted wine of considerable character and class.
Screw cap. 14% alc. **RATING** 93 **DRINK** 2022–2026 $30 NG ✪

Sangiovese 2021, Adelaide Hills Good sangiovese here, embellishing the
region's proclivity for sweet cherry fruit with a bristle of briar, a belt of licorice
and a smattering of dried herbs, imparting a welt of savouriness to the spread of
tannins that direct the finish. A mid-weighted, delicious and thoroughly versatile
wine. Screw cap. 14% alc. **RATING** 91 **DRINK** 2022–2026 $30 NG

The Colours Grüner Veltliner 2022, Adelaide Hills A febrile nerve of
talc, cumquat, apricot pith and rosewater. This has little to do with grüner in
my playbook, but it is a delicious light- to mid-weighted expression of marginal
energy. Screw cap. 13% alc. **RATING** 90 **DRINK** 2022–2025 $27 NG

Nick Haselgrove Wines

13 Blewitt Springs Road, McLaren Flat, SA 5171 **Region** McLaren Vale
T (08) 8383 0886 **www**.nhwines.com.au **Open** 7 days 10–3 by appt **Winemaker** Nick
Haselgrove **Est.** 1981 **Dozens** 12 000 **Vyds** 12ha
After various sales, amalgamations and disposals of particular brands, 3rd-generation winemaker
Nick Haselgrove owns The Old Faithful (the flagship), Blackbilly, Clarence Hill and James
Haselgrove labels.

James Haselgrove Futures Shiraz 2020, McLaren Vale A free-flow of red
and black fruits muddled with anise, camphor and clove. A clamp of sweet mocha
and bourbon-scented oak provides a modicum of tension. Old-school gear done
well. The oak, integral to the flavour profile as it is to the structural latticework,
nicely integrated into the fray. Screw cap. 14.5% alc. **RATING** 93 **DRINK** 2022–2033
$75 NG

The Old Faithful Shiraz 2018, McLaren Vale The seasoning of the oak, green
and medicinal, the first impression. Crushed black fruits, tea tree, clove, anise and
mint. Full bodied and impressionable, the finish is peppery, throaty and defined by
brittle oak tannins. Patience may well be the virtue that this wine requires. Diam.
14.5% alc. **RATING** 93 **DRINK** 2023–2038 $70 NG

Tir Na N'og Old Vines Grenache 2021, McLaren Vale Smoky barrel-
ferment aromas shuffle to raspberry bonbon, rosewater and purple pastille.
A big wine. Soupy and sweet across the mid-palate before the oak corrals the
excess. This will have its fans, but in an era of fibrous, transparent and electric
expressions of grenache, this is a sole survivor. Screw cap. 14% alc. **RATING** 92
DRINK 2022–2027 $45 NG

Nick O'Leary Wines

149 Brooklands Road, Wallaroo, NSW 2618 **Region** Canberra District
T (02) 6230 2745 **www**.nickolearywines.com.au **Open** By appt **Winemaker** Nick
O'Leary **Viticulturist** Nick O'Leary **Est.** 2007 **Dozens** 17 000 **Vyds** 12ha

At the ripe old age of 28, Nick O'Leary had been in the wine industry for over a decade, working variously in retail, wholesale, viticulture and winemaking. Two years earlier he had laid the foundation for Nick O'Leary Wines, purchasing shiraz from local vignerons. His wines have had extraordinarily consistent success in local wine shows and competitions since the first vintages, and have built on that early success in spectacular fashion.

ŢŢŢŢŢ **White Rocks Riesling 2022, Canberra District** Quite breathtaking and ethereal. It has power and definition but everything is seamless: the citrus flavours, mandarin and lemon with pops of finger lime, the talc-like acidity and the refinement. All on show. A joyous drink as much as a classy one. Screw cap. 12% alc. RATING 97 DRINK 2023–2035 $40 JF ✪ ♥
Bolaro Shiraz 2021, Canberra District The most savoury shiraz in the range even if the heady, floral aromatics and deep blood plum and cherry fruit might indicate otherwise at first. Pepper, tamarind, cedary and toasty oak seamlessly integrated as the ferruginous character pops up. Medium bodied and beautifully ripe with shaped tannins and excellent persistence. Screw cap. 13.5% alc. RATING 97 DRINK 2023–2035 $58 JF ✪ ♥

ŢŢŢŢŢ **Heywood Shiraz 2022, Canberra District** If I had to pick one region for its shiraz, Canberra District has my heart. The aromatics, the quality fruit, the plush palate, everything just comes together to produce a fine-boned red. Heywood is no exception. Dark fruit, spicy, cedary oak just a bit player, the shapely detailed tannins, the fine acidity and the overall feel of this wine are all remarkable. Screw cap. 13.5% alc. RATING 96 DRINK 2023–2035 $37 JF ✪
Heywood Riesling 2022, Canberra District Fruit off the Heywood home block and it delivers the goods. Purity of flavour, subtle texture, superfine acidity and a lingering finish. Nothing harsh here, just beautiful riesling from a region that excels in growing it and a winemaker who intrinsically understands its nuances. Screw cap. 12% alc. RATING 96 DRINK 2023–2033 $37 JF ✪
Riesling 2022, Canberra District A tip-top go-to wine. It has all you want from a riesling: citrus flavours, spice, some texture yet racy acidity, length and line with a bit of 'oh yeah, that's good'. There's succulence and moreish quality. Love it. Screw cap. 12% alc. RATING 95 DRINK 2023–2033 $25 JF ✪
Shiraz 2021, Canberra District This is the style of shiraz I want to drink. The aromatic and juicy one; the spicy and lightly fruited one; the compelling and just fabulous one. Very even across the palate, with velvety, plush tannins, and beautifully composed. Screw cap. 13.5% alc. RATING 95 DRINK 2023–2033 $30 JF ✪

Night Harvest   ★★★☆

PO Box 921, Busselton, WA 6280 **Region** Margaret River
T (08) 9755 1521 **www.**nightharvest.com.au **Open** Not **Winemaker** Bruce Dukes, Ben Rector, Simon Ding **Viticulturist** Andy Ferreira **Est.** 2005 **Dozens** 2000 **Vyds** 300ha
Andy and Mandy Ferreira arrived in Margaret River in 1986 as newly married young migrants. They were involved in the establishment of about 300ha of Margaret River vineyards, many of which they continue to manage today (Brash vineyard and Passel Estate are among the estates that fall into this category). As their fortunes grew, they purchased their own property and produced their first wines in '05.

ŢŢŢŢŢ **John George Cabernet Sauvignon 2020, Margaret River** Allowing the regional flavours to star is always the right move with this variety and this place. While there's an oak overlay, cassis, mulberries and choc-mint eventually rise to the top. Full bodied with raspy tannins and lemony acidity. Screw cap. 14% alc. RATING 90 DRINK 2023–2033 $40 JF

Nightfall Wines

PO Box 18 Coonawarra, SA 5263 **Region** Coonawarra
T 0488 771 046 **www**.nightfallwines.com.au **Open** Not **Winemaker** Sam Brand,
Peter Weinberg **Viticulturist** Trent Brand **Est.** 2016 **Dozens** 800 **Vyds** 4ha
One prime site in Coonawarra, boasting terra rossa soil over a base of limestone and growing
3 classic varieties: cabernet sauvignon, cabernet franc and merlot. The aim – which thus far
is unswervingly high – is to express this vineyard site, via the wines, with the same kind of
clarity as the stars in the night sky above. It sounds like a stretch until you taste the wines that,
at least so far, have proven revelatory.

Merlot 2019, Coonawarra It's a medium-weight wine but the finesse of tannin
and length through the finish make a serious impression. Tobacco, sweet plum,
spearmint and mulberry flavours glide persuasively throughout, tannin etching its
way into the frame from the mid-palate onwards, but not at the expense of the
flavour, which continues to sail on. Wow. This is very good. Diam. 14.5% alc.
RATING 95 DRINK 2025–2035 $120 CM
Cabernet Franc 2019, Coonawarra This is a wine of elegant length. It's not
big or even overtly complex, yet it's not simple, it feels sophisticated and it sings
sweet and long through the finish. It tastes of grasses and summer berries, field
flowers and the memory of twigs. It's both as delicious and as finely tuned as it
sounds. Diam. 14.5% alc. RATING 95 DRINK 2024–2034 $120 CM
Leo Cabernet Sauvignon 2019, Coonawarra It's a satiny wine. It's built on
cedar, blackcurrant, pure raspberry and woodsmoke. While it's medium-weight
at most and fresh with acidity, it still manages to cruise through the mouth
as if it owns the place. It's delicious. It's classy. Diam. 14.5% alc. RATING 94
DRINK 2023–2034 $120 CM
Draco Cabernet Sauvignon 2019, Coonawarra A flood of blackcurrant,
a curl of cedar, subtle tobacco-like notes and general rounds of mint and
woodsmoke. Of all the Nightfall wines this pushes the envelope the most, in
the way the flavours billow out to the edges, bringing alcohol warmth into the
mix. The net result is beautiful. Diam. 15% alc. RATING 94 DRINK 2026–2040
$250 CM

Dry Red 2019, Coonawarra RATING 93 DRINK 2023–2032 $50 CM

Nikola Estate

148 Dale Road, Middle Swan, WA 6056 **Region** Swan Valley
T (08) 9374 8050 **www**.nikolaestate.com.au **Open** Thurs–Sun 10–5
Winemaker Damian Hutton, Marcello Fabretti **Viticulturist** Matty Trent **Est.** 2019
Vyds 56ha
While the Nikola brand may be new to the Swan Valley, the Yukich family behind it is
anything but. In 2019, Houghton Estate in the Swan Valley (vineyards, historic cellar door and
the winemaking facility) was purchased by brothers Graeme and Kim Yukich (3rd generation)
from the private equity Carlyle Group, forming what is now the Nikola Estate. Winemaker
Damian Hutton has moved from a long history at Millbrook (Fogarty Group) to assume the
mantle at Nikola. Looking further back in time, the first acquisition of Houghton property
by the Yukich family occurred in 1989 (45ha sold to Mark Yukich, 2nd generation) which
precipitated the formation of Oakover Wines in the '90s. Prior to that, the Yukich Brothers
wine company was formed in '53 by Nikola Yukich.

Gallery Series The Impressionist Arneis 2022, Geographe Delicious,
tightly wound expression with lots of flint, sea spray and ozone in perfume over
green apple and nashi pear fruitiness. The palate is grippy, chewy and spiked with
clove spice, delivering more of that flinty mineral character, a briny tang to acidity
and additional nashi pear (indeed strong here). This works the mojo of arneis well.
Screw cap. 14.6% alc. RATING 93 DRINK 2022–2025 $50 MB
Regional Chardonnay 2021, Margaret River A soft, pulpy chardonnay
with pleasing cool acidity among peaches and cream, pink grapefruit and sea

spray characters. Gently seasoned with cinnamon and woody spices. A fine, talc-like minerally finish, too. It's lush, freshening and lively, yet delivers layers of flavour and a decent sense of concentration. Screw cap. 13.2% alc. **RATING** 93 **DRINK** 2022-2030 $50 MB

Gallery Series The Symbolist Red Blend 2022, Swan Valley Perth Hills 39/19/14/11/9/4/4% tempranillo/mencia/grenache/arinto/malbec/shiraz/ montepulciano. A thirst-slaking red of vibrancy and crunch. Red cherry, raspberry, white pepper, mint and eucalyptus with faint game meat and woody spice. It's loose-knit, but that crispness resets the palate. It feels unadorned and pure, shows quiet complexity and has an easy-drinking appeal. Screw cap. 13.3% alc. **RATING** 92 **DRINK** 2022-2025 $35 MB

Regional Cabernet 2021, Margaret River How lovely. This is all blueberry and cassis in perfume with licorice, cedar and saltbush chiming in. The palate is set at a gracious medium weight, feels refreshing with its minerally acidity and tightens gently in a web of fine, silty tannins. Flavours slip from cassis to red berry fruits with dried herbs, sweet earth, choc-truffle and peppery spice. So very pleasing. Screw cap. 13.5% alc. **RATING** 91 **DRINK** 2022-2030 $50 MB

Gallery Range: The Modernist Tempranillo Shiraz Grenache 2021, Western Australia This is delicious and moreish, a soft melange of black cherry, cola, dark chocolate, clove, blood orange and grunty cinnamon and tobacco elements. Scents and flavours roll around in sync. The palate is all slosh and subsequent pucker with layers of fruit, spice and savouriness. Screw cap. 14.6% alc. **RATING** 91 **DRINK** 2022-2028 $50 MB

Nillumbik Estate   ★★★★

195 Clintons Road, Smiths Gully, Vic 3760 **Region** Yarra Valley
T 0488 440 058 **www**.nillumbikestate.com.au **Open** Fri–Sun 12–5 **Winemaker** John Tregambe **Est.** 2001 **Dozens** 1250 **Vyds** 1.6ha
In establishing Nillumbik Estate, John and Chanmali Tregambe shared the multi-generational winemaking experience of John's parents, Italian immigrants who arrived in Australia in the 1950s. The estate plantings of pinot noir are supplemented by cabernet sauvignon, chardonnay, shiraz and nebbiolo purchased from Sunbury, Heathcote and the King Valley.

Old Earth Shiraz 2018, Heathcote A deep-ish cherry-brick red. An old-school Heathcote shiraz with ripe blackberry and dark plum fruits, licorice, marzipan and vanillin from oak that hasn't yet fully integrated. Equally ripe and plush on the palate, there's no shortage of flavour but, to the wine's credit, it finishes moderately long with gently grippy tannins giving structure and focus. Screw cap. 13% alc. **RATING** 91 **DRINK** 2022-2027 $55 PR

Matteo Nebbiolo 2017, King Valley A light, bright brick colour. This has attractive and varietal aromas of cherries, leather, blood oranges and some spice that lead onto a palate with good depth and lovely mouthfeel. The tannins are fine and ameliorating in harmony with the fruit, and while this is in its perfect drinking window right now, it will still look good for a few years. Screw cap. 13% alc. **RATING** 91 **DRINK** 2022-2027 $40 PR

The Back Block Petit Verdot 2018, King Valley A deep cherry red. Dark fruits, menthol, cedar and bay leaf scents lead onto the palate, which is sweetly fruited and robust. At 4 years old, this fleshy yet quite firmly structured red is just coming into its own. Screw cap. 13% alc. **RATING** 90 **DRINK** 2022-2027 $50 PR

919 Wines

39 Hodges Road, Glossop, SA 5344 **Region** Riverland
T 0408 855 272 **www**.919wines.com.au **Open** Wed–Sun & public hols 10–5 & by appt
Winemaker Eric Semmler **Viticulturist** Eric Semmler **Est.** 2000 **Dozens** 2500 **Vyds** 15ha
Eric and Jenny Semmler have a special interest in fortified wines. Eric made fortified wines for Hardys and worked at Brown Brothers. Jenny has worked for Strathbogie Vineyards, Pennyweight Wines and St Huberts. They have planted micro-quantities of varieties

for fortified wines: palomino, durif, tempranillo, muscat à petits grains, tinta cão, shiraz, tokay and touriga nacional, and some of that fruit is used for single vareital wines with big personalities. They use minimal water application, deliberately reducing the crop levels, and are certified organic.

🍷🍷🍷🍷 **Reserve Touriga Nacional Tempranillo 2022, Riverland** This is a medium-weight wine with a tonne of character. It's both sweet and sour, almost balsamic-like, with candied cherry highlights, florals and dusty spice notes. It's a wine that's been built on a backbone of acidity and is refreshing as a result, but its nuanced flavours are hung on that sure, straight line and shine attractively throughout. Screw cap. 14% alc. **RATING** 92 **DRINK** 2023–2028 $40 CM
Reserve Durif 2021, Riverland Full-throttle red wine with coffee cream, toast, baked plum and ferrous characters flooding the palate. It's warm with alcohol and thick with both fruit and oak flavours; not subtle but it sure packs a punch. Screw cap. 15% alc. **RATING** 92 **DRINK** 2024–2030 $45 CM

Nintingbool ★★★★
56 Wongerer Lane, Smythes Creek, Vic 3351 (postal) **Region** Ballarat
T 0429 424 399 **www**.nintingbool.com.au **Open** Not **Winemaker** Peter Bothe
Est. 1998 **Dozens** 600 **Vyds** 2ha
Peter and Jill Bothe purchased the Nintingbool property in 1982 and built their home in '84, using bluestone dating back to the gold rush. They established an extensive Australian native garden and home orchard but in '98 diversified by planting pinot noir, with a further planting the following year lifting the total to 2ha, with small volumes of shiraz, pinot grigio and chardonnay sourced from around the region.

🍷🍷🍷🍷 **Pinot Grigio 2022, Ballarat** You get pear and candied citrus flavour, you get a bit more texture than usual, and you get straight-up appeal. It feels a bit more 'gris' than 'grigio' in that it's edging towards fullness rather than freshness, but that's not a negative. The price puts the equation in the buyer's favour, too. Screw cap. 12.9% alc. **RATING** 91 **DRINK** 2023–2025 $23 CM ✪
Shiraz 2020, Ballarat Exceptionally meaty and smoky, which if you're of a certain bent isn't a bad thing. Indeed for many it's a positive. There are black cherry, salted caramel and licorice characters here too, along with roasted woodsy spices. It's an interesting wine. Characterful. The opposite of cookie cutter. Screw cap. 14.1% alc. **RATING** 90 **DRINK** 2023–2028 $27 CM

Nocton Vineyard ★★★★
373 Colebrook Road, Richmond, Tas 7025 **Region** Southern Tasmania
T (03) 6260 2688 **www**.noctonwine.com.au **Open** 7 days 10–4 **Winemaker** Alain Rousseau **Viticulturist** Alex Van Driel **Est.** 1998 **Dozens** 12500 **Vyds** 36ha
Nocton Vineyard is the reincarnation of Nocton Park. The 34ha were planted in '99 and are predominately planted to pinot noir, chardonnay, merlot, chenin blanc and sauvignon blanc. Wines are released under the labels Nocton Vineyard and Willow Reserve Series. The quality across both labels is very good.

🍷🍷🍷🍷 **Willow Pinot Noir 2017, Tasmania** Cherry red in the glass with notes of wild strawberry and red cherry. Scattered hints of leaf litter, mushroom risotto, turned earth, French-oak spice and game meats. A dark overtone on the nose lifts on the palate to show pleasing complexity, fruit purity, a fine acid drive and a lingering finish. Screw cap. 13.5% alc. **RATING** 93 **DRINK** 2023–2028 $55 DB
Estate Pinot Noir 2021, Tasmania Bright red and dark-cherry fruits, with deeper tones of dark plum. Set on a bed of fine spice, forest floor, berry compote and light, earthy notes. Fine, lacy acidity provides propulsion for a wine that finishes long, pure and moreish. Screw cap. 13.9% alc. **RATING** 91 **DRINK** 2023–2026 $36 DB

Nocturne Wines

185 Sheoak Dr, Yallingup, WA 6282 (postal) **Region** Margaret River
T 0477 829 844 **www**.nocturnewines.com.au **Open** Not **Winemaker** Julian
Langworthy **Est.** 2007 **Dozens** 1300 **Vyds** 8ha

Nocturne Wines creates consistently high-quality, limited-quantity wines, which explore Margaret River's subregions and vineyards. Nocturne started as the side hustle that has evolved into a fully fledged (and sought after) brand. In '16, Julian Langworthy purchased the Sheoak vineyard in Yallingup (a former Jimmy Watson–producing vineyard, for the Harvey River Bridge Estate Cabernet 2010), with its 4ha of mature cabernet sauvignon vines. These vines are now the backbone of Nocturne's Sheoak Single Vineyard Cabernet, and the very essence of the single-vineyard wine.

Sheoak Single Vineyard Cabernet Sauvignon 2021, Margaret River
Such a purity to this wine – the mulberries and cassis intermingling with cooling acidity, menthol and cedary oak plus the fineness throughout. Fuller bodied but precise as the tannins are charming with the texture of fine sandpaper. While it offers plenty of enjoyment now, it's still in a shy stage given its youth. This will continue to age gracefully. Screw cap. 13.5% alc. **RATING** 96 **DRINK** 2024–2040 $60 JF ✪

Forrest Single Vineyard Chardonnay 2021, Margaret River Complex, detailed and fabulous. It flirts with grapefruit, lemon and finger lime, heady florals and it adds ginger and woodsy spices, too. It's creamy and textural but mainly, it's refreshing and detailed with a fine line of acidity teasing this to a long, pure finish. Screw cap. 13% alc. **RATING** 96 **DRINK** 2023–2032 $60 JF ✪

Carbunup SR Sangiovese Tempranillo 2022, Margaret River This has the Langworthy trademark rose-gold blush and texture. It comes together beautifully. Fragrant with florals, red licorice, grated ginger and a tinge of red berries. The palate is perfectly modulated between the super-refreshing acidity and its creamy texture. Screw cap. 12.5% alc. **RATING** 95 **DRINK** 2022–2024 $35 JF ✪

Treeton SR Chardonnay 2021, Margaret River At first sip, this just takes off, it's so racy. Lots of lemon and grapefruit tang with some cooling fresh herbs and a dab of lime curd. It's tight, linear, flinty and funky, ultra-refreshing and so enjoyable. Screw cap. 13% alc. **RATING** 95 **DRINK** 2022–2031 $35 JF ✪

Yallingup SR Cabernets 2021, Margaret River **RATING** 93 **DRINK** 2023–2036 $35 JF ✪

North Run

Harvest Food & Wine, 55 View Street, Bendigo, Vic 3550 **Region** Bendigo
T 0434 365 504 **www**.northrunwine.com.au **Open** Tues–Sat 8–4 **Winemaker** Lincoln
Riley and Tobias Ansteed **Est.** 2014 **Dozens** 650 **Vyds** 1ha

Lincoln Riley has had a successful career as a sommelier and winemaker, starting in '08 with Foster e Rocco in the winemaking sphere. In the same year he received the Judy Hirst Award for Best Wine List and Australian Sommelier of the Year, in '09 winning *The Age Good Food Guide* accolade as Sommelier of the Year. He finished as head sommelier of Stokehouse in '14, moving back to Central Victoria and, with partner Marsha Busse, purchased their Harcourt property in the same year. They have planted equal quantities of shiraz and nebbiolo on close spacing, and currently run their cellar door from their eatery Harvest Food and Wine in View St, Bendigo.

Fleur Rosé Harcourt North 2021, Bendigo A pale copper bronze; this is refreshingly dry and savoury. There's a slip of texture, crunchy, lemony-acidity and try stopping at one glass on a hot day. Screw cap. 13.5% alc. **RATING** 91 **DRINK** 2022–2024 $30 JF

Norton Estate

758 Plush Hannans Road, Lower Norton, Vic 3401 **Region** Western Victoria
T (03) 5384 8235 **www**.nortonestate.com.au **Open** Sat 11–5, Sun 11–4
Winemaker Best's Wines **Est.** 1997 **Dozens** 1200 **Vyds** 5.66ha
In '96 the Spence family purchased a rundown farm at Lower Norton and planted vines on
the elevated, frost-free buckshot rises. The surprising success of the initial planting of shiraz
prompted further plantings of shiraz, cabernet sauvignon and sauvignon blanc. The vineyard
is halfway between the Grampians and Mt Arapiles, 6km northwest of the Grampians
region, and has to be content with the Western Victoria zone, but the wines show regional
Grampians character and style.

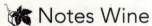 **Wendy's Block Shiraz 2021, Western Victoria** Cedar oak makes its presence
felt, being the first and last thing you notice. But the cherry fruit and sweet spice
notes are ripe, well formed and attractive. The silken nature of the mouthfeel
makes for a pretty sexy drinking experience. This is a medium-weight wine,
done very well. Screw cap. 13.5% alc. **RATING** 94 **DRINK** 2025–2035 $65 CM
Arapiles Run Shiraz 2021, Western Victoria Beautifully balanced. Not in
any way a blockbuster but what it lacks in overt power it makes up for with
finesse, elegance and length. Cherry flavours, red and black, with plum, clove,
sandalwood and bacon-y oak. It feels polished and convincing from start to finish,
with the integration of oak the only piece of the puzzle yet to fall properly into
place. It will. Screw cap. 13.5% alc. **RATING** 94 **DRINK** 2024–2035 $38 CM ✪
Rockface Shiraz 2021, Western Victoria There's delicious sweet fruit here,
pure and abundant, but then there's a coating of savouriness around it, and some
dark choc notes, too. The net effect is wonderful. Plums, raspberries, saltbush
and smoked spice flavours all do their best to charm your socks off. Screw cap.
13.5% alc. **RATING** 94 **DRINK** 2023–2032 $25 CM ✪

 Cabernet Sauvignon 2021, Western Victoria RATING 93 **DRINK** 2024–2031
$25 CM ✪
Sauvignon Blanc 2022, Western Victoria RATING 91 **DRINK** 2023–2026
$25 CM ✪

Notes Wine ★★★★☆

1–3 St Huberts Road, Coldstream, Vic 3770 **Region** Yarra Valley
T (03) 5960 7096 **www**.noteswine.com.au **Open** 7 days, 10–5 **Winemaker** Tom
Shanahan **Viticulturist** Larry Sadler **Est.** 2022 **Dozens** 4000
Notes is a Treasury Wine Estates (TWE) brand made by winemaker Tom Shanahan. Multi-
regional blends are common in this range, such as riesling from Tasmania and the Eden Valley,
syrah from the Grampians and Heathcote, though most pointedly this is where TWE tries to
get in on the 'natural' wine action, with a natural rosé and an obligatory pét-nat. Currently
available at Hubert Estate.

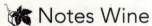 **Spirited Viognier NV, McLaren Vale** A refined nose of apricot kernel,
rosewater, musk, treacle and spiced date. Tamarind freshness tows length.
Dense, yet tightly furled for a fortified. Sweet and expansive, yet paradoxically
compact and restrained. This is really very good. Vinolok. 17.5% alc. **RATING** 96
$45 NG ✪

 Grüner Veltliner 2021, Henty RATING 92 **DRINK** 2023–2027 $30 CM ✪
Riesling 2021, Tasmania Eden Valley RATING 91 **DRINK** 2023–2026 $30 DB

Nova Vita Wines ★★★★

11 Woodlands Road, Kenton Valley, SA 5235 (postal) **Region** Adelaide Hills
T (08) 8356 0454 **www**.novavitawines.com **Open** Not **Winemaker** Mark Kozned
Est. 2005 **Dozens** 20 000 **Vyds** 49ha
Mark and Jo Kozned's 30ha Woodlands Ridge vineyard is planted to chardonnay, sauvignon
blanc, pinot gris and shiraz. They subsequently established the Tunnel Hill vineyard,

with 19ha planted to pinot noir, shiraz, cabernet sauvignon, sauvignon blanc, semillon, verdelho, merlot and sangiovese. The name Nova Vita reflects the beginning of the Kozned's new life, the firebird on the label coming from their Russian ancestry – it is a Russian myth that only a happy or lucky person may see the bird or hear its song.

Firebird Chardonnay 2021, Adelaide Hills Fine aromas of truffled curd, white fig and mirabelle plum. Some cinnamon-spiced oak frames a mid-palate, cashew creamy and nourishing. This is a very good chardonnay, still embryonic, as delicious as it is. I'd love to taste this in a few years once it fills out. Screw cap. 12.5% alc. **RATING** 93 **DRINK** 2022-2028 $40 NG

Firebird Cabernet Sauvignon 2019, Adelaide Hills This is a lovely cabernet. Mid-weighted, savoury and fresh. Gratifying scents of bouquet garni, dried tobacco, tomato leaf, pencil shavings, graphite and currant. The tannins, a lithe foil of tension compressing the fruit as much as promoting it. An easygoing finish of poise and unpretentious confidence. Luncheon claret sort of gear. Screw cap. 14.5% alc. **RATING** 93 **DRINK** 2022-2027 $40 NG

Firebird Rosé 2022, Adelaide Hills All pinot. Tangerine, blossom and a 'je ne sais quoi' drift of punch, pucker and succulence, finishing dry and oh-so fresh. Delicious rosé. Screw cap. 13% alc. **RATING** 92 **DRINK** 2022-2023 $25 NG ✪

Firebird Pinot Noir 2021, Adelaide Hills Among the better pinots tasted from the region, suffusing buoyant red fruits and sap with a healthy burr of sous bois, porcini dashi and root spice. Measured, intense of flavour and delicious to drink. Screw cap. 13.5% alc. **RATING** 92 **DRINK** 2022-2028 $40 NG

Firebird The Blend 2019, Adelaide Hills Cabernet, shiraz and merlot serve an easy-drinking, everyday sort of savoury red with a whiff of class. This is sitting pretty. Reminiscent of something delicate and floral from the Loire. Mid-weighted and savoury. A sinuous tannic line carries crushed redcurrant, tomato leaf, rolled sage and bay leaf, while the natural-feeling acidity tows impressive length. I'd be happy with this as my house wine. Screw cap. 14% alc. **RATING** 92 **DRINK** 2022-2026 $25 NG ✪

Project K The GTR 2021, Adelaide Hills A lovely drift into a nether of tamarind, rosehip, turmeric, roasted almond and veal stock all nourishing a core of generosity. This is amber wine done well. Nothing brittle, hard or out of focus. Just a free flow of gris, traminer and riesling, co-fermented. Screw cap. 12% alc. **RATING** 91 **DRINK** 2022-2024 $40 NG

Project K The SPN Shiraz Pinot Noir 2021, Adelaide Hills A punchy, mid-weighted wine promoting effusiveness of fruit, a burst of sappy energy and plenty of crunch in a contemporary, semi-carbonic vein. Florals, red and purple berries, dried herbs and a slink of sweetness across the finish. Screw cap. 13.5% alc. **RATING** 90 **DRINK** 2022-2024 $40 NG

Reserve Shiraz 2019, Adelaide Hills A gritty, smoky and meaty shiraz, mid-weighted and immensely savoury. There is not a great deal of flair here, but there is girth and a raft of finely tuned tannins, both grape and oak. Umami warmth across the mid-palate. A good addition to the backyard asado in support of an Argentine victory and all that is good in the world. Screw cap. 13.5% alc. **RATING** 90 **DRINK** 2022-2028 $40 NG

Nugan Estate   ★★★★

580 Kidman Way, Wilbriggie, NSW 2680 **Region** Riverina
T (02) 9362 9993 **www.**nuganestate.com.au **Open** Mon–Fri 9–4 **Winemaker** Daren Owers **Est.** 1999 **Dozens** 300 000

Nugan Estate has been in the energetic hands of Matthew Nugan since his mother Michelle Nugan retired in '13. Wines are made at the family's Spanish-styled home base in Riverina, the design reflecting the family heritage (in 1938, Alfredo and Annelise Nugan fled their home in Alcira, Spain and migrated to Australia). Fruit is sourced from Riverina, King Valley, Coonawarra, Langhorne Creek and McLaren Vale.

♀♀♀♀♀ **Cookooathama Limited Release Botrytis Semillon 2020, Riverina** Glacé
pineapple, apricot and tinned peaches. Sweet green figs, lemon curd and treacle
tart. Lusciously sweet but not overt. Balanced by persistent acidity, cumquat
marmalade and lemon skin. Screw cap. 11% alc. **RATING** 92 **DRINK** 2022-2026
$24 SW ✪

Alcira Vineyard Cabernet Sauvignon 2020, Coonawarra This is a dry,
structural cabernet with blackcurrant, spearmint and mulberry flavours topped
with coffee-cream oak. There's quite a deal of tannin here, almost more than
the fruit can deal with, but as the wine breathes both tobacco and fruit flavours
rush up to save the day. This is a good release. Screw cap. 14.5% alc. **RATING** 91
DRINK 2023-2030 $26 CM ✪

Alfredo Dried Grape Shiraz 2020, South Eastern Australia Inspired by a
northern Italian practice, this displays cherry jam, raspberry tarts and blackberry
preserves with black pepper-studded salumi, dried olives and rosemary. Firm
angular tannins balance the richness of fruit and alcohol and the wine finishes
surprisingly dry and fresh. Screw cap. 14.5% alc. **RATING** 91 **DRINK** 2022-2026
$28 SW ✪

Manuka Grove Vineyard Durif 2019, Riverina Baked blackberry pie,
raspberry compote, mulberry and clove. Prunes and black figs. Tightly packed
fruit with firm tannins and enticing acidity. The array of black, red and hints
of blue fruit is well supported by acidity that carries the flavours while enabling
the richness and depth you'd expect from Riverina durif. A well-made wine.
Screw cap. 14.5% alc. **RATING** 91 **DRINK** 2022-2026 $26 SW ✪

Cookooathama Limited Release Botrytis Semillon 2019, Riverina
Caramelised pineapple, apricot pie, mango flesh and honeycomb. Daffodils and
lemon meringue pie. The wine is lusciously sweet and syrupy on the palate
with hints of brandy oranges and a touch of nutmeg and vanilla pod on the
finish. A weighty sticky with plenty of oomph. Screw cap. 11% alc. **RATING** 90
DRINK 2022-2025 $27 SW

Nuova Scuola Wines   ★★★☆

167 Tipperary Road, Redgate, Qld 4605 **Region** South Burnett
T 0408 850 595 **www**.nuovascuola.com.au **Open** 7 days, 10–5 by appt
Winemaker Sarah Boyce, Stefano Radici **Viticulturist** Sarah Boyce, Stefano Radici
Est. 2017 **Dozens** 500 **Vyds** 2.5ha
Winemakers Sarah Boyce and Stefano Radici met in NZ in '09, fell in love and haven't
looked back. They have been working side by side in many different wineries in many parts
of the world including Italy, France, Canada, the US, NZ, Mexico and – of course – Australia.
Queensland's South Burnett has its limitations, but they believe the climate is ideal for Iberian
and Italian varieties. In '21 the duo purchased a vineyard with plantings of viognier, verdelho,
tempranillo, shiraz and sangiovese. The property also houses the cellar door.

♀♀♀♀♀ **La Maria Field Blend Series 2022, Murray Darling South Burnett** 80/20%
fernão pires/verdelho. Attractive golden colour. Zippy, slippery and textural white
of high drinkability and good X-factor. Scents of candle wax, lemon curd, ginger
and apricot, flavours similarly set with medium-weight concentration and a cool
line of briny acidity at its core. A fun time to be had. Clever. Screw cap. 12% alc.
RATING 92 **DRINK** 2022-2026 $23 MB ✪

O'Leary Walker Wines   ★★★★★

7093 Horrocks Highway, Leasingham, SA 5452 **Region** Clare Valley
T 1300 342 569 **www**.olearywalkerwines.com **Open** Mon–Sat 10–4, Sun & public hols
11–4 **Winemaker** David O'Leary, Nick Walker, Jack Walker, Luke Broadbent **Est.** 2000
Dozens 20 000 **Vyds** 45ha
David O'Leary and Nick Walker together had more than 30 years' winemaking experience
with some of the biggest Australian wine groups when they took the plunge and established

their own winery and label in '00. Certified organic since '13, Clare Valley vineyards focus on riesling, shiraz and cabernet sauvignon, while Adelaide Hills sites are planted to chardonnay, cabernet sauvignon, pinot noir, shiraz, sauvignon blanc and merlot. The 4th generation of Walker winemakers is now on board, with Nick's son Jack working at the Leasingham winery.

🍷🍷🍷🍷🍷 **Polish Hill River Riesling 2022, Clare Valley** Tense and detailed. It's waxy in texture, concentrated with lemon-lime flavours, zinged with tight, bright grapefruit acidity and soaked in crushed granite and quartz-like coolness. It extends beautifully, finishes vivid, crystalline and mouth-watering. Very well done. Pristine, energetic and complex expression. Screw cap. 11.5% alc. RATING 94 DRINK 2022–2035 $30 MB ✪

🍷🍷🍷🍷🍷 **Grüner Veltliner 2022, Clare Valley** RATING 93 DRINK 2022–2026 $35 MB ✪
Seasonal Release Grenache 2021, Clare Valley RATING 93 DRINK 2022–2030 $28 MB ✪
Polish Hill River Armagh Shiraz 2020, Clare Valley RATING 93 DRINK 2022–2030 $35 MB ✪
Watervale Riesling 2022, Clare Valley RATING 92 DRINK 2022–2028 $25 MB ✪
Nero d'Avola 2019, Clare Valley RATING 92 DRINK 2022–2026 $28 MB ✪
Seasonal Release Pinotage 2021, Clare Valley RATING 90 DRINK 2022–2026 $30 MB

Oakdene ★★★★★

255 Grubb Road, Wallington, Vic 3221 **Region** Geelong
T (03) 5256 3886 **www.**oakdene.com.au **Open** 7 days 10–4 **Winemaker** Robin Brockett, Marcus Holt **Viticulturist** Andrew Butler **Est.** 2001 **Dozens** 8000 **Vyds** 32ha
Bernard and Elizabeth Hooley purchased Oakdene in '01. Bernard focused on planting the vineyard (shiraz, pinot gris, sauvignon blanc, pinot noir, chardonnay, merlot, cabernet franc and cabernet sauvignon) while Elizabeth worked to restore the 1920s homestead. Much of the wine is sold through the award-winning Oakdene Restaurant and cellar door. The quality is exemplary, as is the consistency of that quality; Robin Brockett's skills are on full display.

🍷🍷🍷🍷🍷 **Kristen Sparkling Blanc de Blancs 2018, Geelong** 100% chardonnay and aged on lees for 38 months before being disgorged; 2g/L dosage. Plenty going on here with its bouquet of lemon, pink grapefruit, subtle brioche and a touch of oyster shell. The palate is dry and even, finishing chalky textured and long. Diam. 11.9% alc. RATING 95 DRINK 2022–2027 $38 PR ✪
William Single Vineyard Bellarine Peninsula Shiraz 2021, Geelong A bright, medium crimson-ruby red. Complex with aromas of red and blue fruits, white and black pepper and well-handled floral, spicy whole bunch characters. Medium bodied, this has both good depth and structure and while it's approachable now (with food), it's totally worth putting a few bottles away. Screw cap. 13.1% alc. RATING 95 DRINK 2023–2029 $43 PR ✪
Peta's Single Vineyard Bellarine Peninsula Pinot Noir 2021, Geelong A small percentage of whole bunches in the ferment, matured in French barriques (some new) for 12 months. Attractive wine, with good varietal expression and length, spicy cherry to the fore. Ready now. Screw cap. 12.8% alc. RATING 94 DRINK 2023–2030 $43 JH

🍷🍷🍷🍷🍷 **Bellarine Peninsula Rosé 2022, Geelong** RATING 92 DRINK 2022–2024 $24 PR ✪
Bellarine Peninsula Chardonnay 2021, Geelong RATING 92 DRINK 2023–2030 $26 JH ✪
Ly Ly Single Vineyard Bellarine Peninsula Pinot Gris 2021, Geelong RATING 92 DRINK 2022–2026 $28 PR ✪
Bellarine Peninsula Pinot Noir 2021, Geelong RATING 92 DRINK 2023–2026 $26 JH ✪

Field Blend 2022, Geelong RATING 91 DRINK 2022-2025 $24 PR ✪
Liz's Single Vineyard Bellarine Peninsula Chardonnay 2021, Geelong
RATING 91 DRINK 2023-2026 $38 JH
Bellarine Peninsula Shiraz 2021, Geelong RATING 90 DRINK 2022-2027
$24 PR ✪
Bernard's Single Vineyard Bellarine Peninsula Cabernets 2021, Geelong
RATING 90 DRINK 2022-2027 $30 PR

Oakridge Wines

864 Maroondah Highway, Coldstream, Vic 3770 **Region** Yarra Valley
T (03) 9738 9900 **www.**oakridgewines.com.au **Open** 7 days 10–5 **Winemaker** David
Bicknell **Viticulturist** Steve Faulkner **Est.** 1978 **Dozens** 33 000 **Vyds** 60ha
Winemaker David Bicknell has long proved his worth as an extremely talented winemaker. At
the top of the Oakridge brand tier is 864, all Yarra Valley vineyard selections, only released in
the best years (chardonnay, pinot noir, syrah, cabernet sauvignon); next is the Vineyard Series
(the chardonnay, pinot noir and sauvignon blanc come from the cooler Upper Yarra Valley;
the shiraz and cabernet sauvignon from the Lower Yarra). The estate vineyards are Oakridge,
Hazeldene and Henk vineyards. In early '21, the brand was sold to Paragon Wine Estates,
which is part of the Woolworths-owned Endeavour Group. Oakridge Wines is the *Halliday
Wine Companion 2024* Best Value Winery.

🍷🍷🍷🍷🍷 **864 Single Block Release Close Planted Block Oakridge Vineyard Syrah
2021, Yarra Valley** The superb colour is no surprise, nor is the perfume and
sheer elegance of the wine in the mouth. Black cherries, black peppercorns and
spices have quicksilver energy and speed. It will live for decades thanks to its
perfect balance. Screw cap. 13.9% alc. RATING 98 DRINK 2023-2051 $96 JH ✪
**864 Single Block Release Aqueduct Block Henk Vineyard Pinot Noir
2021, Yarra Valley** Wonderful fruit purity and complexity here with its scents
of white strawberries, crushed rose petals and patchouli. The effortless medium-
bodied palate has a real sense of elegance with persistent, silky tannins in perfect
harmony with the fruit. A superb wine. Screw cap. 13.4% alc. RATING 98
DRINK 2023-2031 $98 PR ✪
**864 Single Block Release Drive Block Funder & Diamond Vineyard
Chardonnay 2021, Yarra Valley** A bright, pale green gold. Another truly
great, albeit restrained, release, with piercing aromas of white nectarines, nashi,
pink grapefruit, white flowers and crushed stone. Simultaneously concentrated
and elegant, the pure, mineral-inflected and chalky palate is painfully long. Still
just a baby, this might just be the best and possibly the most long-lived Oakridge
864 Chardonnay yet. Screw cap. 13.5% alc. RATING 98 DRINK 2022-2032
$98 PR ✪ ♥
**864 Single Block Release Winery Block Oakridge Vineyard Cabernet
Sauvignon 2021, Yarra Valley** A dense, powerful and structured wine. On the
nose there's a core of perfectly ripened black fruits, crushed violets, dark chocolate
and graphite. The medium bodied, firmly structured and persistent palate is
equally good, and anyone fortunate enough to still have a bottle 10–15 years will
be well rewarded. Screw cap. 13.8% alc. RATING 97 DRINK 2023-2032 $98 PR ✪
Vineyard Series Willowlake Chardonnay 2021, Yarra Valley Scents of ripe
stone fruits, a little yellow plum even and a hint of oyster shell. There's wonderful
depth and intensity on the mid-palate and the wine finishes taut, saline and long.
While you'll no doubt enjoy drinking this now, it's worth giving this some time
to open up. For a single-vineyard Yarra Valley chardonnay of this quality, this is a
real bargain. Screw cap. 13.2% alc. RATING 97 DRINK 2022-2028 $48 PR ✪
Original Vineyard Cabernet Sauvignon 2021, Yarra Valley A bright,
medium deep crimson purple. Fragrant with aromas of cassis, violets, hawthorn
and cedar. Fine boned, elegant and concentrated with an old-vine creaminess on
the mid-palate. While the wine's very fine-grained and gently chewy tannins will
ensure this can be cellared for 10+ years, no one who opens a bottle along the

way will be disappointed. Screw cap. 13.7% alc. RATING 97 DRINK 2023–2037 $90 PR ✪

Vineyard Series Willowlake Pinot Noir 2021, Yarra Valley The Willowlake vineyard was one of the first to venture to the Upper Yarra. Balance is the key word for this beautiful pinot, the red cherry/berry fragrance is mirrored by the palate, where delicate but clear savoury notes of spice are woven through the red fruit palate and aftertaste. Screw cap. 13.2% alc. RATING 97 DRINK 2023–2035 $45 JH ✪

ⓎⓎⓎⓎⓎ **Vineyard Series Hyde Park Shiraz 2021, Yarra Valley** While Oakridge has been taking fruit from the Hyde Park vineyard for some time, this is the first Vineyard Series release. A saturated and bright crimson purple. Aromas of dark fruits, bramble, Asian spices and dark chocolate. Inky and concentrated with ripe, persistent tannins, this can be approached now, but those who put some in the cellar should be well rewarded. Screw cap. 14.2% alc. RATING 96 DRINK 2022–2028 $48 PR ✪

Vineyard Series Henk Chardonnay 2021, Yarra Valley The Upper Yarra, on red volcanic soils, produces taut wines of extreme length. Here citrus, white stone fruit and green apple are bolstered by natural acidity. Winemaker David Bicknell makes the difficult seem easy. Screw cap. 13.3% alc. RATING 96 DRINK 2023–2036 $45 JH ✪

Vineyard Series Henk Pinot Noir 2021, Yarra Valley From the '08-planted Henk vineyard at Woori Yallock. A bright, medium cherry red. Ripe and lifted with dark fruits, rose petals and spice. Even better on the palate, which is sumptuous yet fine with satiny tannins rounding out an impressive wine. Screw cap. 13.2% alc. RATING 96 DRINK 2022–2029 $48 PR ✪

Horst Riesling 2022, Yarra Valley Made in honour of Horst 'Jim' Zitzlaff, who founded Oakridge. Fermented in old oak, 18 g/L RS. A very bright green gold. Restrained with citrus, apple, nectarine and honeysuckle scents. Such is the interplay between the fruit, sugar and acid, you barely notice the sweetness on the palate. A zesty mouthful that's textured, balanced, refreshing and long. Only 70 dozen made. Screw cap. 11% alc. RATING 95 DRINK 2022–2032 $45 PR ✪

Sauvignon 2021, Yarra Valley A blend of 90/10% sauvignon blanc/semillon. With its appetising aromas of ripe pear, quince and lemon, this is more white Bordeaux in style than Loire Valley, while the dry, flinty medium-bodied palate has good weight and tension. Screw cap. 12.2% alc. RATING 95 DRINK 2022–2027 $35 PR ✪

Vineyard Series Hazeldene Pinot Noir 2021, Yarra Valley Exhibiting an array of spices including cardamom and nutmeg pods with red fruits and pomegranate, this floral, compact, medium-bodied and structured wine is precise and long. Screw cap. 13.2% alc. RATING 95 DRINK 2023–2027 $48 PR ✪

Vineyard Series Barkala Cabernet Sauvignon 2021, Yarra Valley Perfectly ripened cabernet fruit exhibiting aromas of dark cherry, violets, a little bramble and some complexing bell pepper. Medium bodied and compact, the fruit has swallowed up the oak and while it's a touch firm once it fleshes out a little (and it will) this should provide considerable pleasure for a decade or so. Screw cap. 13.6% alc. RATING 95 DRINK 2022–2031 $48 PR ✪

Pinot Noir 2021, Yarra Valley Whole-berry and whole-bunch fermented, 9 months on lees. This approach guarantees complexity, and when you add the impact of the '21 vintage, the only question is, how much do you have to spend? Its texture and structure are impeccable, the varietal fruit enhanced by the vinification, the length and finish likewise. Screw cap. 13.2% alc. RATING 95 DRINK 2023–2036 $30 JH ✪

ⓎⓎⓎⓎⓎ **Garden Gris 2022, Yarra Valley** RATING 93 DRINK 2022–2027 $35 PR ✪
Hyde Park Cabernet Sauvignon 2021, Yarra Valley RATING 93 DRINK 2022–2027 $48 PR
Meunier 2022, Yarra Valley RATING 92 DRINK 2023–2027 $35 PR

Oakway Estate

575 Farley Road, Donnybrook, WA 6239 **Region** Geographe
T (08) 9731 7141 **www**.oakwayestate.com.au **Open** W'ends 11–5 **Winemaker** Tony
Davies **Viticulturist** Wayne and Ria Hammond **Est.** 1997 **Dozens** 1000 **Vyds** 2ha
Ria and Wayne Hammond run a vineyard, cattle and sustainable blue-gum plantation in
undulating country on the Capel River in the southwest of WA. The grapes are grown
on light gravel and loam soils that provide good drainage, giving even sun exposure to the
fruit and minimising the effects of frost. The vineyard is planted to shiraz, merlot, cabernet
sauvignon, nero d'Avola, malbec, muscat, sauvignon blanc, vermentino and chardonnay.

Los Ninos Single Vineyard Malbec 2021, Geographe Plush and juicy with
scents of dark plum, violets, black jelly beans and clove. Great texture, soft but
with a sheath of fine, silty tannins, a slosh of amaro-tinged acidity under plummy
fruit, cola notes and more of that black jelly bean piquancy/sweetness. It does
the dictionary definition of malbec well, delivering a lush, easy drinking and yet
somewhat layered version. Screw cap. 14.9% alc. **RATING** 90 **DRINK** 2022–2028
$28 MB

Il Siciliano Single Vineyard Nero d'Avola 2021, Geographe This is a
lustier expression of nero, higher in alcohol than most. Scents of warm, stewed
berries, cherry cola, cinnamon and clove. The palate is soft and squishy with
some fine, gravelly tannins lending some shape. Big flavours of warm forest
berry compote, cola, dark chocolate and clove – a bit breathy through the
finish. Despite the elevated booze, the wine has mojo, just expect a fuller
flavoured, bombastic and more potent nero. Screw cap. 15.1% alc. **RATING** 90
DRINK 2022–2026 $28 MB

Oates Ends

22 Carpenter Road, Wilyabrup, WA 6280 **Region** Margaret River
T 0401 303 144 **www**.oatesends.com.au **Open** By appt **Winemaker** Cath Oates
Viticulturist Russ Oates **Est.** 1999 **Dozens** 2000 **Vyds** 11ha
Cath Oates returned home to Margaret River after an international winemaking career
spanning 15 years. The wines are made from the family Wilagri vineyard, planted in
'99 and now owned and managed by viticulturist brother Russ Oates. Oates Ends is the
culmination of both of their respective experience and wine philosophies. The vineyard is
run on sustainable farming principles (Cath is also chair of AGW's Sustainability Advisory
Committee). Sheep are a big part of the vineyard program with winter mowing a given and
they are increasingly being relied upon for leaf plucking during the growing season.

The G.W.B Sauvignon Blanc Semillon 2022, Margaret River GWB could
be great white blend or great white bite, as the label mentions winemaker Cath
Oates' close encounter with a white shark. Lots of detail in the wine, which is
fermented in barrel with 6 months on lees and some mlf. A good thing as the
acidity is racy and tangy; lots of lemon and spice, lime curd and kiwi fruit. Lightly
textural and tangy to the end. A good drink here. Screw cap. 12% alc. **RATING** 93
DRINK 2023–2027 $28 JF ✪

Chardonnay 2022, Margaret River This lovely chardonnay has richness and
depth, full of stone fruit and grapefruit with ginger spice and honeycomb. Plus,
layering on the full palate from cashew-like lees and a general creaminess with
oak playing its part yet neatly integrated. The tangy acidity keeps this even and
refreshing all the way through. Screw cap. 13% alc. **RATING** 93 **DRINK** 2023–2033
$60 JF

Cabernet Sauvignon 2020, Margaret River A leafy tomato fragrance,
menthol and alpine herbs. The more usual attributes of black olives, cassis and
mulberries appear, a little tart with a whiff of bay leaves and Aussie bush. Medium
weighted and juicy with the cedary oak adding to the mouthcoating tannins and
flavour. It's refreshing in a way, even if it will last some distance. Lots of acidity
in the mix and just a slight greenness to the finish, but food will temper that.
Screw cap. 13.5% alc. **RATING** 91 **DRINK** 2025–2035 $60 JF

Ocean Eight Vineyard & Winery   ★★★★★

271 Tucks Road, Shoreham, Vic 3916 **Region** Mornington Peninsula
T (03) 5989 6471 **www.**oceaneight.com.au **Open** Thurs–Sat 11–5, Sun 11–3
Winemaker Michael Aylward **Viticulturist** Luke O'Connor **Est.** 2004 **Dozens** 6000
Vyds 16ha
Chris, Gail and Michael Aylward were involved in the establishment of the Kooyong vineyard and winery, and after selling Kooyong in '03, retained their 6ha pinot gris vineyard at Shoreham. After careful investigation, they purchased another property, where they have now planted 7ha of pinot noir and 3ha of chardonnay. A small winery has been set up, and the focus will always be on estate-grown grapes.

Pinot Gris 2022, Mornington Peninsula Ocean Eight hangs its vinous hat on pinot gris and for good reason. Not a voluptuous wine but it has layers of flavour: fresh and spiced poached pears, some creamy lees and honeycomb with refreshing citrus tones. Lovely texture, with a slip of phenolics adding to its shape plus there's succulence and light acidity throughout. Gris done good. Screw cap. 13.5% alc. **RATING** 95 **DRINK** 2023–2028 $42 JF ✪

Verve Chardonnay 2021, Mornington Peninsula This is slinky and fine, moreish and mouth-watering. It's very good. While there's a citrus riff, mainly lemon, this is savoury and all about texture. Linear, yet the palate comes bolstered by some creamy, nutty lees and lemon curd flavour and the talc-like acidity dances along. Screw cap. 12.5% alc. **RATING** 95 **DRINK** 2023–2031 $60 JF

Aylward By Ocean Eight Chardonnay 2020, Mornington Peninsula
It's been a while between drinks with Ocean Eight, so it's very pleasing to have this bang-on chardy to hand. It's layered, detailed and refined with grapefruit, white peach, dried figs and ginger spice. The palate expands with cashew-like lees flavour while lemon sorbet acidity just reins everything into submission. Screw cap. 13.5% alc. **RATING** 95 **DRINK** 2023–2030 $80 JF

Aylward By Ocean Eight Pinot Noir 2021, Mornington Peninsula
RATING 93 **DRINK** 2024–2033 $100 JF
Pinot Noir 2021, Mornington Peninsula RATING 90 **DRINK** 2023–2028 $60 JF

Old Plains   ★★★★

71 High Street, Grange, SA 5023 (postal) **Region** Adelaide Plains
T 0407 605 601 **www.**oldplains.com **Open** Not **Winemaker** Domenic Torzi, Tim Freeland **Viticulturist** Dom Torzi **Est.** 2003 **Dozens** 4000 **Vyds** 12ha
Old Plains is a partnership between Tim Freeland and Domenic Torzi, who have acquired some of the last remaining small parcels of old-vine shiraz, grenache and cabernet sauvignon in the Adelaide Plains region. Wines made from these vines are sold under the Old Plains label. Unique circumstances led to the creation of the Longhop label, fruit now being sourced from various regions.

Alluvium Old Vine Cabernet Shiraz 2021, Adelaide Plains A savoury, full-bodied expression founded on a structural refinement that other cultivars fail to provide in these hot parts. A sluice of evergreen tannins framed by a morass of palate-staining currant and herbs, a mulch of plenitude and uncanny sophistication. A very good drink. Screw cap. 14.5% alc. **RATING** 94 **DRINK** 2022–2035 $40 NG ✪

Power of One Old Vine Shiraz 2021, Adelaide Plains RATING 93
DRINK 2022–2030 $40 NG
Terreno Old Vine Grenache 2021, Adelaide Plains RATING 93
DRINK 2022–2030 $25 NG ✪
Longhop Cabernet Sauvignon 2021, Adelaide Plains RATING 92
DRINK 2022–2032 $20 NG ✪
Longhop Angaston Merlot 2021, Barossa Valley RATING 91
DRINK 2022–2025 $25 NG ✪

Raven Riesling 2021, Adelaide Hills **RATING** 91 **DRINK** 2022-2032 $25 NG
Longhop Old Vine Shiraz 2021, Adelaide Plains **RATING** 90
DRINK 2022-2027 $25 NG ✪

Olive Hills Estate   ★★★★

3221 Murray Valley Highway, Rutherglen, Vic 3685 **Region** Rutherglen
T 0438 561 331 **www**.olivehills.com.au **Open** 7 days 10–4 **Winemaker** Ross Perry,
Harry Perry **Viticulturist** Ross Perry, Joe Perry **Est.** 1999 **Dozens** 2000 **Vyds** 15ha
The Perry family brought a historic piece of Rutherglen wine history back to life when they
purchased the neglected Olive Hills mansion and 202ha of land in '97. The site, including
vineyards, had first been developed in 1886, but fell to ruin over time. Ross and Kay Perry
bought the heritage-listed house and land and set about returning it to its former glory,
including vineyards and wine production. Ross had studied winemaking at Charles Sturt
University, while Kay had experience in marketing and sales. Their sons, Harry and Joe, have
also embraced the life, with Harry studying winemaking, and Joe planning future studies
in viticulture.

🍷🍷🍷🍷🍷 du Cluse 2018, Rutherglen 15 varieties – from cabernet sauvignon to
sangiovese, touriga, durif and viognier – go into this delightful melange. Brings a
Euro-style sense of savoury and brooding to Aussie-style generosity. Allspice, clove,
leather, baked earth, cassis, bramble, chocolate and tar. A lively 5yo that's juicy,
smooth and very drinkable. Love the vein of gentle savouriness that infiltrates the
ripe, generous fruit. Screw cap. 14.5% alc. **RATING** 92 **DRINK** 2023-2027 $49 JP
Sangiovese Nebbiolo 2022, Rutherglen Not your everyday red blend, but
clearly there is a plan. One grape is generous and sweet-fruited, while the other
offers lovely aromatics and a firm tannin structure. The 2 work surprisingly well,
bringing red cherry, dried cranberry, rose, anise and peppery aromas and flavours.
It's firm in tannin structure now, but nevertheless, it's easy to enjoy. Screw cap.
13.4% alc. **RATING** 90 **DRINK** 2023-2028 $35 JP
Ode To Bordeaux 2022, Rutherglen Cabernet sauvignon/malbec/petit
verdot/cabernet franc. A bold, full-bodied red in deep, dark purple hues. Lives
large in the glass with expansive aromas covering undergrowth, herbs, cassis,
Dutch licorice, earth and toast. Time in French hogsheads has delivered some
fine tannins, woodsy oak characters and warmth. And speaking of warmth,
there is a touch of alcohol heat to close. Screw cap. 15.7% alc. **RATING** 90
DRINK 2023-2030 $49 JP

Oliver's Taranga Vineyards   ★★★★★

246 Seaview Road, McLaren Vale, SA 5171 **Region** McLaren Vale
T (08) 8323 8498 **www**.oliverstaranga.com **Open** 7 days 10–4 **Winemaker** Corrina
Wright **Viticulturist** Don Oliver **Est.** 1839 **Dozens** 10 000 **Vyds** 90ha
William and Elizabeth Oliver arrived from Scotland in 1839 to settle in McLaren Vale.
Six generations later, members of the family are still living on the Whitehill and Taranga
farms. The Taranga property has 15 varieties planted (the lion's share to shiraz, grenache and
fiano, with lesser quantities of cabernet, touriga, mataro, sagrantino, tempranillo, mencia,
vermentino and white frontignac). Corrina Wright (the Oliver family's first winemaker)
makes the wines.

🍷🍷🍷🍷🍷 RW Reserve Grenache 2021, McLaren Vale Possibly the finest wine I've
tasted from this address. A brilliant vintage accentuating the sleight of hand.
Cranberry, lilac, rosehip and kirsch are woven across a detailed tannic quilt,
pulled taut by juicy acidity. A drape of dried lavender and thyme mitigates any
fruit sweetness. A delicious wine, if not a bit oak-sweet, of composure and real
succulence. Screw cap. 14.5% alc. **RATING** 95 **DRINK** 2023-2030 $75 NG

🍷🍷🍷🍷🍷 Small Batch Sagrantino 2021, McLaren Vale **RATING** 93 **DRINK** 2022-2032
$55 NG
HJ Shiraz 2020, McLaren Vale **RATING** 93 **DRINK** 2023-2033 $75 NG

Small Batch Grenache 2022, McLaren Vale RATING 92 DRINK 2022-2026
$32 NG
Chica Mencia Rosé 2022, McLaren Vale RATING 92 DRINK 2023-2024
$27 NG ✪
Small Batch Vermentino 2022, McLaren Vale RATING 92 DRINK 2022-2025
$27 NG ✪
Small Batch Mencia 2022, McLaren Vale RATING 92 DRINK 2022-2026
$35 NG
DJ Cabernet Sauvignon 2020, McLaren Vale RATING 92 DRINK 2023-2035
$75 NG
Small Batch Brioni's Blend 2022, McLaren Vale RATING 91
DRINK 2022-2025 $35 NG
Corrina's Small Batch Cabernet Shiraz 2021, McLaren Vale RATING 91
DRINK 2022-2028 $40 NG
Fiano 2022, McLaren Vale RATING 90 DRINK 2022-2025 $27 NG
Shiraz 2021, McLaren Vale RATING 90 DRINK 2022-2026 $30 NG

Orbis Wines   ★★★☆

307 Hunt Road, McLaren Vale, SA 5171 **Region** McLaren Vale
T 0466 986 318 **www**.orbiswines.com.au **Open** By appt **Winemaker** Lauren Langfield
Viticulturist Richard Leask **Est.** 2018 **Dozens** 2000 **Vyds** 27ha
Orbis Wines hail from a site of 32ha at an elevation of 150m, planted in the '60–70s. The old-vine shiraz was recently complemented with tempranillo, while grenache, albariño, montepulciano, nero d'Avola and fiano will soon be coming on stream, making for a Mediterranean potpourri. Owners Brad Moyes and Kendall Grey's fervent belief that these varieties will define McLaren Vale's future (as much as shape its present) underlies a holistic culture in the truest sense: regenerative farming, recycled timber, solar power, polyculture in the vineyard, the abolishment of heavy machinery and the negation of foil capsules and screw caps, are some of their efforts in the name of bona fide sustainability, carbon neutrality and the promotion of biodiversity. The overarching style is one of mid-weighted freshness, poise and giddy drinkability.

🍷🍷🍷🍷🍷 **Trousseau 2022, McLaren Vale** A lightweight, effusively flavoured red sitting in that zone between rosato and 'thrills with a chill' sort of gear. There's delicacy and inherent beauty as dried rose petals, sandalwood, clove, strawberry and white pepper infuse a waft of salinity, sewing the attack to the long, broadening finish. Lovely wine. Cork. 12.8% alc. RATING 92 DRINK 2023-2025 $37 NG

Orlando   ★★★★★

Barossa Valley Way, Rowland Flat, SA 5352 (postal) **Region** Barossa Valley
T (08) 8131 2400 **www**.orlandowines.com **Open** Not **Winemaker** Tim Pelquest-Hunt
Est. 1847 **Dozens** 10 000 **Vyds** 14ha
Orlando is the parent who has been separated from its child, Jacob's Creek (see separate entry). While Orlando is over 170 years old, Jacob's Creek is little more than 45 years old. For what are doubtless marketing reasons, Orlando aided and abetted the separation, but the average consumer is unlikely to understand the logic and, if truth be known, is unlikely to care.

🍷🍷🍷🍷🍷 **Steingarten Riesling 2022, Eden Valley** A picture of fruit purity, velocity and precision, pure and limey with a crushed quartz backbone and a crystalline line of acidity zipping things along. Great drinking now, but it will age beautifully. Screw cap. 11% alc. RATING 96 DRINK 2023-2038 $50 DB ✪
Lawson's Shiraz 2020, Padthaway Vanillin oak hits you straight up but the power of the fruit behind it is impressive. There's a grain to this wine, a patter of pink peppercorns in among the wealth of plum-drenched fruit, an impression that serious claims on quality are being made. Given the power here, and the persistence, and the balance, it's easy to be swept along by it all. Screw cap. 14% alc. RATING 95 DRINK 2024-2034 $70 CM

Printz Shed Barossa Valle Shiraz 2021, Barossa Deep magenta–crimson with a distinct violet note that floats above the pure satsuma plum, blueberry and boysenberry fruits. Hints of baking spices, dark chocolate, plum concentrate, licorice, pan juices, olive tapenade and wildflowers. Superfine, compact sandy tannins and a bright line of acidity mean the wine never feels heavy or overdone, just pure, juicy and jammed full of Barossaness. Screw cap. 14% alc. **RATING** 94 **DRINK** 2023–2033 $35 DB ✪

Jacaranda Ridge Cabernet Sauvignon 2019, Coonawarra Classic flavours of blackcurrant, tobacco, leather and malt come tipped with both dust and mint. It's not a massive wine but it has very good power, and certainly enough to carry the swagger of tannin. Screw cap. 14% alc. **RATING** 94 **DRINK** 2023–2032 $70 CM

🍷🍷🍷🍷🍷 **Bangalow Lane Cabernet Sauvignon 2021, Barossa RATING** 93 **DRINK** 2023–2033 $35 DB ✪

Ossa Wines

100 Crossins Road, Swansea, Tas 7190 (postal) **Region** Tasmania
T 0447 404 469 **www**.ossa.wine **Open** Not **Winemaker** Liam McElhinney
Viticulturist Jay Dillon **Est.** 2021 **Dozens** 850 **Vyds** 20ha
Rod and Cecile Roberts retained the best consultants in the state when their 20ha Ossa vineyard was planted and the first wines made. Tasmanian Vintners is a custom crush and ferment facility providing birth-to-bottle care. Their desire for sustainability resulted in an entirely solar-powered structure; removing noxious plant species; fencing wildlife zones; and cleaning waterways. The vineyard wasn't in bearing in '20, so they sourced small parcels of chardonnay, pinot noir and sparkling, and the first wine ex the estate Belbrook vineyard was chardonnay '21. All of which made the 2020 Pinot Noir, winning Best Wine at the Australian Pinot Noir Challenge '21 (and a second trophy for Best Tasmanian Wine) akin to a fairy tale.

🍷🍷🍷🍷🍷 **Syrah 2021, Tasmania** Dark and red plum fruits layered with dark spices, violets, white pepper, vanilla, roasting meats and some gingery spice cut across the field of vision. There's a plushness and grace here that will impress many, pitch-perfect ripeness and sustain and a sense that when it comes to syrah, Tasmania has just gone up a class. Superb. Screw cap. 13.8% alc. **RATING** 96 **DRINK** 2023–2035 $120 DB

Pinot Noir 2021, Tasmania Ripe red and black cherries, raspberry flan, sous bois, layers of spice, pressed flowers, rhubarb, tobacco and light gamey nuance. The initial attack of fruit here is amazing … seemingly fruit sweet before morphing savoury in a slow fade of complex, fine tannin. This is an absolute pleasure to drink. Screw cap. 13.8% alc. **RATING** 96 **DRINK** 2023–2033 $120 DB

Chardonnay 2021, Tasmania Flush with stone and citrus fruits, sheathed in soft spice along with hints of almond blossom, crushed stone, a whiff of struck flint and a touch of oyster shell. Excellent tension and clarity with a tautly stretched canvas of fruit, crystalline acidity and a softly spiced exit showing ample power, drive and grace. Screw cap. 13% alc. **RATING** 94 **DRINK** 2023–2028 $90 DB

🍷🍷🍷🍷🍷 **Méthode Traditionnelle 2017, Tasmania RATING** 92 **DRINK** 2023–2028 $90 DB

Grüner Veltliner 2022, Tasmania RATING 92 **DRINK** 2023–2026 $60 DB

Otherness

38 Murray Street, Angaston, SA 5353 **Region** Barossa Valley
T (08) 8563 6595 **www**.otherness.com.au **Open** Thurs–Sat 11–10, Sun–Mon 11–5
Winemaker Ian Hongell, Neil Pike, Steve Baraglia, John Hughes, Marco Cirillo, Craig Stansborough, Alex MacClelland, Dan Standish **Est.** 2015 **Dozens** 800
Otherness is an exciting collaboration between South Australian winemakers and musician, restauranteur and wine man Grant Dickson. Well loved for his eclectic wine list in his

former life at the Barossa's beloved FermentAsian, Dickson is intimately connected with the surrounding wine regions and their makers. Each cuvée is crafted by a different winemaker, representing a who's-who list of local producers. Unusually and significantly for a contract-making arrangement, each maker is declared and celebrated on the label. The cellar door doubles as a hip wine bar and bottle shop.

ŶŶŶŶŶ **Urth Riesling 2021, Clare Valley** Pale in the glass with a tinge of green, the wine displays inviting aromas of fresh lime, green apple and grapefruit with citrus blossom top notes, crushed stone and some curd, soft spice and crème fraîche tones courtesy of the barrel ferment portion. Focused and limey with a slink of texture and a beautiful sapid acidity. Made by Grant Dickson. Screw cap. 11.8% alc. **RATING** 95 **DRINK** 2023-2033 $35 DB ✪

Skuld Riesling 2021, Eden Valley Freshly squeezed lime juice leaps from the glass with hints of Christmas lily, crushed quartz, lemon curd and citrus blossom. Expressive with a swell of juicy lime and grapefruit reigned in by a seam of crystalline acidity. Finishes pure with a driven, tubular palate shape and dots of cream and curd on a core of pure lime. Made by Ian Hongell. Screw cap. 11.3% alc. **RATING** 95 **DRINK** 2023-2030 $35 DB ✪

Fratres Cabernet Franc 2022, Barossa Valley A bouncy, leafy-edged cabernet franc that tingles with fruit purity and easy-drinking vibes. Plums, exotic spice, flowers, a touch of briar and just a whiff of charcuterie make for good drinking times with a sapid minerally cadence and a superfine, powdery tannin frame. Good stuff. Made by Alex MacClelland. Cork. 14.4% alc. **RATING** 94 **DRINK** 2023-2028 $55 DB ♥

Urth Riesling 2022, Clare Valley Pale straw in the glass with aromas of freshly squeezed lime juice, grapefruit and crunchy green apple. Hints of crushed stone, light lemon curd tones, jasmine, citrus blossom and lime sorbet. Some textural flesh and an expansive bloom of fresh lime and blossom riding on rails of sapid, mineral-laden acidity. Made by Grant Dickson. Screw cap. 12% alc. **RATING** 94 **DRINK** 2023-2030 $35 DB ✪

Skuld Riesling 2022, Eden Valley Pale with green flashes in the glass and aromas of freshly squeezed lime, grapefruit, Bickford's lime cordial, Christmas lily, orange blossom and crushed quartz. Some nice texture on the palate with dots of lemon curd and crème fraîche, fine lacy acidity that provides ample tension and propulsion as the wine scoots to a precise limey finish. Made by Ian Hongell. Screw cap. 11.5% alc. **RATING** 94 **DRINK** 2023-2030 $35 DB ✪

ŶŶŶŶŶ **Harmonica Aglianico Montepulciano 2021, Barossa RATING** 93 **DRINK** 2023-2029 $55 DB

440 Cabernet Sauvignon 2019, Barossa Valley RATING 92 **DRINK** 2023-2030 $55 DB

Ottelia   ★★★★

2280 V&A Lane, Coonawarra, SA 5263 **Region** Coonawarra
T 0409 836 298 **www.**ottelia.com.au **Open** 7 days 10–4 **Winemaker** John Innes
Est. 2001 **Dozens** 8000 **Vyds** 9ha

John and Melissa Innes moved to Coonawarra intending, in John's words, to 'stay a little while'. The first sign of a change of heart was the purchase of a property ringed by red gums and with a natural wetland dotted with Ottelia ovalifolia, a native water lily. They still live in the house they built there. John worked as winemaker at Rymill Coonawarra while Melissa established a restaurant. After 20 years, John left Rymill to focus on consultancy work throughout the Limestone Coast and to establish and run Ottelia. The tasting room and rather flash restaurant are at 5 Memorial Drive, Coonawarra.

ŶŶŶŶŶ **Riesling 2022, Mount Gambier** Both elegant and intense. Lime jelly and lemon sorbet characters meet slate and grapefruit pulp. It feels measured and long, and while there is ample fruit intensity here, in riesling terms, it remains all about the finish, which is mouth-wateringly long. Screw cap. 11% alc. **RATING** 94 **DRINK** 2023-2035 $30 CM ✪

Chardonnay 2022, Mount Gambier This is direct and linear in general, but the flavour profile itself is charming. White peach and citrus with blossomy aspects bordering on honeysuckle. It all flows evenly through the palate, indeed harmoniously, before pushing out through the extended finish. Screw cap. 12.7% alc. RATING 94 DRINK 2024–2032 $32 CM ✪

ŶŶŶŶŶ **Shiraz 2021, Coonawarra** RATING 92 DRINK 2023–2032 $28 CM ✪
Sangiovese 2021, Limestone Coast RATING 92 DRINK 2023–2027 $28 CM ✪
Pinot Gris 2022, Limestone Coast RATING 91 DRINK 2023–2025 $27 CM ✪
Sauvignon Blanc 2022, Mount Gambier RATING 91 DRINK 2023–2027 $27 CM ✪

Ouse River Wines   ★★★★

PO Box 40, Ouse, Tas 7140 **Region** Tasmania
T (03) 6287 1309 **www.ouseriverwines.com.au Open** Not **Winemaker** Peter Dredge, Nick Glaetzer **Est.** 2002 **Dozens** 240 **Vyds** 19ha
Ouse River Wines is one of the most interesting developments in Tasmania. Bernard and Margaret Brain own a 1000ha property north of Ouse at the top end of the Derwent Valley. They run 9 enterprises on the property, including the vineyard that is the furthest inland in Tasmania. It has a continental climate and a diurnal temperature range during ripening of 7°C more than the areas surrounding Hobart. The first planting of 1ha in late '02 was followed by 1ha planted each year until '06; further plantings over the years resulted in a total of 6.55ha of pinot noir, 10.25ha of chardonnay and 1ha of riesling. The pinot has been used by House of Arras from the second vintage and in every vintage since.

ŶŶŶŶŶ **Pinot Noir 2021, Tasmania** Mid-ruby with characters of wild cherries and macerated strawberries layered with exotic spice, hints of leaf litter, shiitake broth, pressed flowers, Chinese barbecue shop, dried tangerine rind and earth. Sour cherry flows in on the palate, the acid line is tight and prominent and the finish shows plenty of gamey nuance and chutzpah. Screw cap. 13.5% alc. RATING 92 DRINK 2023–2028 $50 DB
Chardonnay 2021, Tasmania Tales of white peach, grapefruit and roasted hazelnuts along with tones of soft spice, white flowers, lemon curd, stone, oatmeal and nougat. The aromas transpose neatly over to the palate, which shows some slinky texture and a glorious line of briny acid driving things along. Screw cap. 13.5% alc. RATING 92 DRINK 2023–2027 $55 DB
Pinot Noir 2020, Tasmania Mid-ruby in the glass with notes of macerated dark and red cherries, mushroom, hanging game, exotic spice, dried orange rind, washed-rind cheese and earth. There are plenty of plum and cherry fruits on the palate, tight and fine gravel-dust tannins and lots of spice, sour cherry and earthy nuance on the lingering finish. Screw cap. 13.5% alc. RATING 92 DRINK 2023–2028 $50 DB

Paisley Wines   ★★★★

158 Hurns Road, Angaston, SA 5353 (postal) **Region** Barossa Valley
T 0491 377 737 **www.paisleywines.com.au Open** Not **Winemaker** Derek Fitzgerald
Est. 2017 **Dozens** 1800 **Vyds** 5ha
Derek Fitzgerald made wines for nearly 20 years in WA, Langhorne Creek and the Barossa Valley before gentle persuasion by wife Kirsten led to the decision to make wine on their own account. The varieties produced are classic Barossa: grenache, mataro and shiraz. Derek has winkled out some small parcels of grapes from long-proven vineyards up to 70 years old.

ŶŶŶŶŶ **Cashmere Riesling 2022, Eden Valley** Pale straw in the glass with classic regional characters of freshly squeezed limes, Bickford's lime cordial along with hints of crushed stone, Christmas lily, frangipani, lemon zest and some struck stone notes. Mouth-filling and pure of fruit with great acid drive, this is a worthy follow to the '21 vintage. Screw cap. 12.5% alc. RATING 92 DRINK 2023–2027 $30 DB ✪

Silk Shiraz 2020, Barossa Valley Deeply coloured with aromas of liquored plums, blackberry, licorice, vanilla, dark chocolate, earth, a splash of eucalyptus and a waft of purple flowers. Fruit-pure and energetic with nervy acidity and a plush tide of macerated plums, cassis and spice on the finish. Screw cap. 14.5% alc. RATING 92 DRINK 2023-2028 $30 DB ✪

Clurichaun Single Vineyard Mataro 2020, Barossa Valley There's a lovely floral edge here, all wispy jasmine and frangipani top notes, before the wine flexes with characters of amaro-flecked plum and blackberry fruits, deep, dark spice and hints of garrigue, roasting meats, leather, earth and scattered herbs. Some serious depth with an almost tarry edge to the dark and black fruits, tight compact tannin and bright acidity provide frame and drive. Screw cap. 15% alc. RATING 92 DRINK 2023-2030 $48 DB

Boombox Shiraz 2020, Barossa This immediately leaps out of the glass with aromas of damson plums, black cherries and mulberry fruits cut with fruitcake, licorice, blackberry jam, choc-mint and a whiff of oak spice. Mouth-filling and slinky with ripe dark and black fruits, baking spices and a dollop of creamy oak with a tight, fine tannin frame and sprightly acidity. Screw cap. 14.7% alc. RATING 91 DRINK 2023-2027 $25 DB ✪

Amplifier Chardonnay 2022, Padthaway Pale straw with characters of citrus, melon and white peach with hints of soft spice, clotted cream, white flowers, nougat and stone. Notes of poached pears and light herbal tones flow in on the palate, which shows some nice creamy texture and blossom top notes, slippery and supple with fine acid drive and a finish redolent in stone fruits and spice. Screw cap. 13% alc. RATING 90 DRINK 2023-2026 $25 DB ✪

Linen Fiano 2022, Adelaide Hills Aromas of white peach, nectarine, grilled pineapple and citrus. Hints of white flowers, vanilla beans, pine nuts, dried herbs and a waft of lanolin. There is a pithy, textural aspect to the palate shape while a briny acid line provides drive and gets the salivary glands working. Screw cap. 13% alc. RATING 90 DRINK 2023-2025 $30 DB

Velvet Grenache 2021, Barossa Valley Light crimson in the glass with bright raspberry, red plum and cranberry fruit notes supported by hints of exotic spice, gingerbread, watermelon, strawberry cream, earth and a liminal nudge of amaro herbs. Light, detailed, chalky of tannin and definitely easy to drink, you could safely pop this in the fridge should the weather dictate such matters. Screw cap. 15% alc. RATING 90 DRINK 2023-2025 $30 DB

Turntable GSM 2020, Barossa Valley A well-weighted, fruit-pure blend that ticks a lot of boxes. Crimson in the glass with aromas of juicy satsuma plum, cherry and macerated berry fruits that mesh with layers of fine spice, ginger cake, earth and licorice. The finish is dark fruited and savoury with plenty of fine, sandy tannin support and a briny, spicy trail as it fades. Screw cap. 14.7% alc. RATING 90 DRINK 2023-2025 $25 DB ✪

Palmer Wines   ★★★★

1271 Caves Road, Dunsborough, WA 6281 **Region** Margaret River
T (08) 9756 7024 **www.**palmerwines.com.au **Open** Thurs–Mon 10–5.30
Winemaker Mark Warren, Bruce Dukes, Clive Otto **Est.** 1977 **Dozens** 6000
Vyds 51.39ha

Steve and Helen Palmer have mature plantings of cabernet sauvignon, sauvignon blanc, shiraz, merlot, chardonnay and semillon, with smaller amounts of malbec and cabernet franc. Recent vintages have had major success in WA and national wine shows.

🍷🍷🍷🍷🍷 **Cabernet Sauvignon 2020, Margaret River** At first, there's a coolness and calm stemming from the fine flavours of cassis and mulberries, the florals and a touch of menthol and Aussie bush. Refreshing acidity, too, and all that goes a long way to temper the full-bodied palate, wave of cedary oak and the determined tannins: massive, ripe and raspy, in time they will yield. The best years are ahead of it. Screw cap. 14.6% alc. RATING 93 DRINK 2026-2038 $35 JF ✪

Malbec 2020, Margaret River If you were expecting a wallflower, leave now. This is jam-packed with flavour: fleshy ripe black plums, blackcurrants doused in cocoa plus warm woodsy spices. The French oak is impacting the flavour – cedary and sweet and the tannins, a touch raspy and expanding them further. Plenty of refreshing acidity and just needs more time to gel or hearty fare in the meantime. Screw cap. 14% alc. **RATING** 91 **DRINK** 2024–2033 $35 JF

The Grandee Cabernets 2020, Margaret River 40/30/24/6% cabernet sauvignon/malbec/merlot/cabernet franc. You'll meet a centurion guard of tannins first. They won't budge, only time will do that. Behind them, dark fruit saturates the palate, woodsy, spicy cedary oak, too. Structured and formidable, but come back to this in a few years. Screw cap. 14.2% alc. **RATING** 90 **DRINK** 2024–2035 $42 JF

Paracombe Wines

294b Paracombe Road, Paracombe, SA 5132 **Region** Adelaide Hills
T (08) 8380 5058 **www.paracombewines.com Open** By appt **Winemaker** Paul Drogemuller **Viticulturist** Paul Drogemuller **Est.** 1983 **Dozens** 20000 **Vyds** 41.8ha
Paul and Kathy Drogemuller established Paracombe Wines in the wake of the devastating Ash Wednesday bushfires. The winery is located high on a plateau at Paracombe, looking out over the Mount Lofty Ranges, and the vineyard is run with minimal irrigation and hand pruning to keep yields low. The wines are made onsite.

🍷🍷🍷🍷🍷 **Cabernet Sauvignon 2018, Adelaide Hills** Bottle age has bestowed this with additional layers of nourishing and rewarding complexity. Red and black currants are muddled with dried herbs, cedar and graphite. Yet the mid-palate is the star, a soupçon of beef bouillon, tapenade and dried porcini-derived umami. Lovely drinking. The finish may be on the wane. Just. Yet very good it is. Screw cap. 14.2% alc. **RATING** 95 **DRINK** 2022–2027 $27 NG ✪ ♥

Cabernet Franc 2019, Adelaide Hills There are so many cuvées made at this address that it is hard to keep up. Styles and quality, too, are often peripatetic. But there are moments of glory, particularly with cabernet franc. The tannins, nervy from start to finish, corralling allspice, mint, redcurrant, pimento and dried sage. Immensely savoury and perfectly weighted. The track record of ageability, too, is brilliant. Screw cap. 13.5% alc. **RATING** 94 **DRINK** 2022–2032 $32 NG ✪ ♥

🍷🍷🍷🍷🍷 **Pecorino 2022, Adelaide Hills RATING** 91 **DRINK** 2022–2025 $28 NG ✪
Pinot Noir 2022, Adelaide Hills RATING 90 **DRINK** 2022–2025 $25 NG ✪
V5 Grüner Veltliner 2021, Adelaide Hills RATING 90 **DRINK** 2022–2025 $25 NG ✪

Paralian Wines

8 Caffrey Crescent, Port Willunga, SA 5173 **Region** McLaren Vale
T 0413 308 730 **www.paralian.com.au Open** By appt **Winemaker** Skye Salter, Charlie Seppelt **Est.** 2018 **Dozens** 1000
Charlie Seppelt and Skye Salter have covered many miles and worked in many places since they met in '08 working the vintage at Hardys Tintara in McLaren Vale. By the time they established Paralian Wines in '18 they had accumulated 46 vintages between them, working for others. The name is a noun for someone who lives by the sea. Charlie's first exposure to McLaren Vale was as a vintage casual at d'Arenberg and it was vinous love at first sight. He and Skye headed off overseas, a high point undertaking vintage in Burgundy. He headed back to Australia, she went on to the Languedoc, seemingly ideal, but found it as depressing as Burgundy had been inspirational. They agreed McLaren Vale, and in particular Blewitt Springs, was the place they wanted to make grenache and shiraz with high fragrance and brightness. No fining or additions are used other than SO_2 and little requirement for new oak.

🍷🍷🍷🍷🍷 **Springs Hill Vineyard Shiraz 2022, McLaren Vale** A lustrous crimson. Fine, detailed and succulent boasting riffs on blueberry, white pepper, lilac, nori and cardamom across seams of svelte, sandy tannins. This is a glorious shiraz, with the pulp and verve of berries, tannins finding a glorious confluence of freshness, lilt and effortless length. Crozes-Hermitage from the Vale. Screw cap. 14% alc. **RATING** 96 **DRINK** 2023–2030 $48 NG ✪

Marmont Vineyard Grenache 2022, McLaren Vale Lilac, juniper, orange peel, cranberry and that inimitable scent of sour cherry liqueur. Lifted purple florals. Broad of spread and jittery of energy. Wonderful transparency, juxtaposed against a Mediterranean sweetness of fruit. Just a bit green, attesting to the whole clusters (20%) in the ferment. A little time will allow it to gel. Screw cap. 14% alc. **RATING** 95 **DRINK** 2023–2030 $48 NG ✪

Bowyer Ridge Vineyard Chardonnay 2022, Adelaide Hills A thrilling mid-weighted chardonnay. Think almond meal, corn kernel, citrus zest and allusions of glazed quince and toasted hazelnut barrelling long. The oak is beautifully embedded and while I've made this sound powerful, it has a latent, sophisticated and subdued energy that builds across the glass. The best Paralian chardonnay I've tasted yet. Superlative. Screw cap. 13% alc. **RATING** 95 **DRINK** 2023–2033 $55 NG

🍷🍷🍷🍷🍷 **Springs Hill Cabernet Sauvignon 2022, McLaren Vale RATING** 93 **DRINK** 2024–2035 $70 NG

Blewitt Springs Grenache Shiraz 2022, McLaren Vale RATING 92 **DRINK** 2023–2027 $40 NG

Paringa Estate ★★★★★

44 Paringa Road, Red Hill South, Vic 3937 **Region** Mornington Peninsula
T (03) 5989 2669 **www.**paringaestate.com.au **Open** 7 days 11–5 **Winemaker** Lindsay McCall, Jamie McCall **Est.** 1985 **Dozens** 21 000 **Vyds** 36ha
Teacher-turned-winemaker Lindsay McCall has an absolutely exceptional gift for winemaking across a range of styles, immensely complex pinot noir and shiraz leading the way. The wines have an unmatched level of success in the wine shows and competitions that Paringa Estate is able to enter, the limitation being the relatively small production of the top wines in the portfolio. Son Jamie joined the winemaking team in '12, after completing winemaking and viticulture at the University of Adelaide. He was put in charge of winemaking at Paringa Estate in '17 following 5 home vintages and one in Oregon, focusing on pinot noir.

🍷🍷🍷🍷🍷 **The Paringa Single Vineyard Chardonnay 2021, Mornington Peninsula** The high acid year has favoured the suite of chardonnays, resulting in a finely tuned and tighter than usual The Paringa Chardonnay. No shrinking violet though – packed with stone fruit, grapefruit and Meyer lemon and a powder puff of spices, honeycomb and malt. Savoury, long and detailed, even lipsmacking. Classy stuff. Screw cap. 13.5% alc. **RATING** 96 **DRINK** 2023–2031 $80 JF

The Paringa Single Vineyard Pinot Noir 2021, Mornington Peninsula The Paringa has a reputation for being a powerful pinot noir, no doubt about it, but sometimes, a vintage offers up this wine with comparatively more restraint and vibrancy thanks to acidity. It's rich and detailed, full of dark cherries, blood orange, amaro and a smoky, twiggy character. Full bodied with densely packed tannins a little raspy but detailed and juicy. Should cellar very well. Screw cap. 13.5% alc. **RATING** 96 **DRINK** 2024–2035 $100 JF

Estate Rosé 2022, Mornington Peninsula This ticks all my rosé boxes. As in, it's a bronze-pastel pink hue, fragrant with ginger flowers and roses, dry yet flavoursome and full of texture. There's cleansing acidity throughout and it freshens up the palate preparing it for the next sip. Screw cap. 13.5% alc. **RATING** 95 **DRINK** 2022–2025 $29 JF ✪

Estate Chardonnay 2021, Mornington Peninsula This is altogether racy and superfine – no mlf, so in its own way it feels lighter, certainly against flagship The Paringa. Still plenty of flavour and texture via monthly lees stirring in French oak puncheons. The finish is long and persistent, and as usual, it has that savoury, moreish factor. Screw cap. 13% alc. **RATING** 95 **DRINK** 2022–2031 $50 JF ✪

Robinson Vineyard Pinot Noir 2021, Mornington Peninsula Swooning stuff with rosehip, cherries, baking spices, blood orange and glacé citrus too; complex and detailed with forest floor and general autumnal aromas. The just shy of full-bodied palate is still settling with the tannins and acidity jostling for pole position. Give this breathing space or more time in bottle. Screw cap. 13% alc. RATING 95 DRINK 2024–2036 $80 JF

Estate Pinot Noir 2021, Mornington Peninsula Not a shy and retiring wine, but by golly this is good. Full of forest floor and menthol aromas, flavours of dark cherries, rhubarb, chinotto and blood orange with lots of refreshing acidity but also plenty of tannins. Fuller bodied, firm and forceful yet the fruit is sweetly flavoured across the palate. There's a lot going on in this wine. Screw cap. 13% alc. RATING 95 DRINK 2023–2033 $70 JF

🍷🍷🍷🍷🍷 **Peninsula Chardonnay 2022, Mornington Peninsula** RATING 93 DRINK 2023–2030 $30 JF ✪

Estate Pinot Gris 2022, Mornington Peninsula RATING 93 DRINK 2022–2025 $28 JF ✪

Estate Shiraz 2021, Mornington Peninsula RATING 93 DRINK 2024–2034 $50 JF

The Paringa Single Vineyard Shiraz 2021, Mornington Peninsula RATING 92 DRINK 2024–2036 $80 JF

Estate Riesling 2022, Mornington Peninsula RATING 90 DRINK 2023–2027 $28 JF

Peninsula Pinot Noir 2021, Mornington Peninsula RATING 90 DRINK 2023–2029 $34 JF

Peninsula Shiraz 2021, Mornington Peninsula RATING 90 DRINK 2023–2033 $30 JF

Parker Coonawarra Estate   ★★★★★

15688 Riddoch Highway, Penola, SA 5263 **Region** Coonawarra
T (08) 8737 3525 **www**.parkercoonawarraestate.com.au **Open** 7 days 10–4
Winemaker James Lienert, Andrew Hardy, Keeda Zilm **Est.** 1985 **Dozens** 30 000
Vyds 20ha

Parker Coonawarra Estate is at the southern end of Coonawarra, on rich terra rossa soil over limestone. Cabernet sauvignon is the dominant variety (17.45ha), with minor plantings of merlot and petit verdot. It is now part of The Usual Suspects Collective, which also owns Hesketh Wine Company, St John's Road, Vickery Wines and Ox Hardy. Production has risen substantially since the change of ownership.

🍷🍷🍷🍷🍷 **95 Block 2020, Coonawarra** This cabernet/petit verdot stands like a bouncer at the door of a nightclub, sinew and muscle and brawn, black t-shirt and all. It offers dense blackcurrant-driven fruit, big bones of tannin, rippled mouthfeel and complexity in the form of ash, woodsmoke and tobacco characters. One thing is for certain: this wine walks the talk, delivering the kind of rock-solid complexity, structure and fruit that will see it age (beautifully) over the long term. Screw cap. 14.5% alc. RATING 97 DRINK 2028–2051 $65 CM ✪ ♥

First Growth 2019, Coonawarra Cabernet sauvignon The spread of flavour here is elite. It's the way the flavours expand as they roll through the mouth, the finish vastly more voluminous than the start. It shows textbook cabernet sauvignon characters of blackcurrant, bay leaf and tobacco, and while there are oak influences in the form of cedar, chocolate and dark, sweet coffee, they are folded into the fruit with the deftest of touch. And then there are the tannins. These have a sweetness of their own, and an authority, and yet they are a masterclass in integration. Stand back. This wine has its sights set firmly on the future. Screw cap. 14.5% alc. RATING 97 DRINK 2030–2050 $110 CM

🍷🍷🍷🍷🍷 **Kidman Block 2021, Coonawarra** This shiraz really flexes its muscles. Strong currant-driven fruit (black and red) comes lashed with caramel, cedar, vanilla and woodsmoke, though it's the thick ropes of tannin that amps up the general feeling of seriousness. This isn't a wine to mess with. It has balance, herb notes, ripe fruit and, most importantly, a noteworthy extra kick of flavour through the finish. Screw cap. 14% alc. RATING 96 DRINK 2027–2046 $65 CM ✪

🍷🍷🍷🍷♀ **Terra Rossa Cabernet Sauvignon 2021, Coonawarra** RATING 93
DRINK 2025–2035 $34 CM ✪
Terra Rossa Shiraz 2021, Coonawarra RATING 93 DRINK 2024–2035
$34 CM ✪
Terra Rossa Merlot 2021, Coonawarra RATING 93 DRINK 2024–2031
$34 CM ✪
S.B.W. King Kong Fumé Blanc 2022, Mount Gambier RATING 92
DRINK 2024–2027 $28 CM ✪

Passel Estate

655 Ellen Brook Road, Cowaramup, WA 6284 **Region** Margaret River
T (08) 9717 6241 **www**.passelestate.com **Open** 7 days 10.30–5 **Winemaker** Bruce
Dukes **Viticulturist** Andy Ferreira **Est.** 1994 **Dozens** 1500 **Vyds** 6.7ha
Wendy and Barry Stimpson were born in England and South Africa respectively and, during
numerous visits to Margaret River over the years, fell in love with the region's environment.
They made Margaret River home in '05 and in '11 purchased and expanded the vineyard,
which is planted to shiraz, cabernet sauvignon and chardonnay.

🍷🍷🍷🍷♀ **Cabernet Sauvignon 2018, Margaret River** This is ready to enjoy now.
Expect cassis, blackberries, mocha, black olives and leafy/menthol freshness.
Medium bodied, there's a softening to the palate with slightly pomace-like tannins
and an appealing coolness. Screw cap. 14% alc. RATING 91 DRINK 2022–2026
$46 JF
Chardonnay 2020, Margaret River Yellow gold. A big waft of vanilla oak
hits first followed by woodsy spices. The palate is in 2 parts: melon, stone fruit,
buttered toast and lime giving an impression of richness yet a tight line of acidity
keeping everything reined in. Screw cap. 12.5% alc. RATING 90 DRINK 2023–2029
$45 JF
Lot 71 Reserve Cabernet Sauvignon 2017, Margaret River Showing a
fair amount of development yet still reveals plenty of varietal attributes of bramble
berries, cassis and mocha. The oak (matured in French barriques, 58% new, for
18 months) has meshed although plenty of woodsy, cedary character adds to the
tannin structure. Screw cap. 14% alc. RATING 90 DRINK 2022–2027 $96 JF

Passing Clouds

30 Roddas Lane, Musk, Vic 3461 **Region** Macedon Ranges
T (03) 5348 5550 **www**.passingclouds.com.au **Open** 7 days 10–5 **Winemaker** Cameron
Leith **Est.** 1974 **Dozens** 5500 **Vyds** 5ha
Graeme Leith and son Cameron undertook a monumental change when they moved the
entire operation that started way back in '74 in Bendigo to its new location at Musk, near
Daylesford. The vines at Bendigo had been disabled by ongoing drought and all manner of
pestilence, and it was no longer feasible to continue the business there. However, they still
have a foot in the Bendigo region courtesy of their friends, the Adams at Rheola. Graeme
has now left the winemaking in the hands of Cameron, instead using his formidable skills as a
writer. In '18, a dedicated train stop was established at the Passing Clouds cellar door.

🍷🍷🍷🍷🍷 **Pinot Noir 2022, Macedon Ranges** I'm a sucker for Macedon pinot noir and
this wine makes me happy. It's gentle, pretty, fine and long. It's not weighty, in
fact, it's lighter framed, but the florals, cherry accents, spice, fresh herbs and supple
tannins count for much. It's a wine to enjoy for today rather than cellar. It really is
gorgeous. Screw cap. 12.4% alc. RATING 95 DRINK 2022–2028 $29 JF ✪
Rheola Shiraz 2021, Bendigo A new wine? I'd like to know more (or
anything) about it as it's my pick of the 4 straight shiraz offerings this vintage.
Deep and rich with fruit matched to the savoury tones. Supple, sweet tannins
work across the full-bodied palate, there's a vitality, a freshness, an evenness that
makes this delicious. Screw cap. 14.5% alc. RATING 95 DRINK 2023–2035 $53 JF
Viognier 2022, Bendigo This is a power-packed number. It has so much fruit
impact now, there's a strong case for hopping into it straight away. If you do,

you'll find the varietal apricot fruit, spice and more to fill the mouth. Screw cap. 13% alc. RATING 94 DRINK 2023–2026 $38 JH ✪

Serpentine Shiraz 2021, Bendigo Bendigo shiraz can pack a powerful punch. Yet it has these gloriously rich qualities, too – the dark fruit, the hint of Aussie bush and a minerally sensation to the acidity. Expect blackberry jam and plum compote, pepper and sweet baking spices, river mint and tamarind. The full-bodied palate is layered with ripe fruit, plush tannins and cedary oak. It comes together well. Screw cap. 14.8% alc. RATING 94 DRINK 2024–2034 $58 JF

Graeme's Shiraz Cabernet 2021, Bendigo I have a soft spot for this wine – it's Aussie as, smelling of the Bendigo bush. Rich, robust with dark fruit and warming spices, some roasted meat, too (or was that the leg of lamb in my oven?), and plush tannins. Full bodied with a certain caress across the palate. BTW, it did go well with the lamb. Screw cap. 14.5% alc. RATING 94 DRINK 2024–2043 $34 JF ✪

Estate Pinot Noir 2021, Macedon Ranges Deeply coloured and structured, yet restrained with fruit flavours a whisper of cranberries, cherries and pips. Fresh herbs, menthol and cedary oak impart tannins. Everything falls into place nicely. Screw cap. 12.5% alc. RATING 94 DRINK 2023–2031 $53 JF

♟♟♟♟♀ **Rosé 2022, Macedon Ranges** RATING 92 DRINK 2022–2025 $34 JF
Riesling 2022, Macedon Ranges RATING 92 DRINK 2022–2027 $34 JF
The Angel 2021, Bendigo RATING 92 DRINK 2024–2034 $58 JF
Daylesford Sparkling Chardonnay NV, Macedon Ranges RATING 90 $68 JF
Kilmore Pinot Noir 2022, Port Phillip RATING 90 DRINK 2022–2028 $34 JF
Riesling 2022, Bendigo RATING 90 DRINK 2022–2026 $34 JF

Patina ★★★★★

109 Summerhill Lane, Orange, NSW 2800 **Region** Orange
T 0414 736 342 **www**.patinawines.com.au **Open** By appt **Winemaker** Gerald Naef, Nadja Wallington, Steve Mobbs **Viticulturist** Gerald Naef **Est.** 1999
Dozens Vyds 2.8ha

Gerald Naef's childhood home in sunny Lodi, California, was surrounded by the vast vineyard and winery operations of Gallo and Robert Mondavi. It would be hard to imagine a more different environment than that provided by Orange, where their cool-climate vineyard now sits at 930m elevation. Gerald and wife Angie moved to Australia in '81; Gerald was pursuing a career in agriculture and they established a farm in northwest NSW. In '95 they moved the family to Orange and by '99 had planted their first vineyard, with a winery following in '07. Steve Mobbs has been involved in the winemaking since '17 and wines from the '22 vintage are made by Steve and Nadja Wallington at ChaLou.

♟♟♟♟♟ **Reserve Chardonnay 2021, Orange** A bouquet of spiced baked apples, peach skin, candied ginger and shortbread. Nougat, praline and lemon oil. This wine is beguiling in its aromatics and takes a left turn on the palate to roasted nuts and pools of texture. Laden with detail and flows effortlessly. It's no wonder it has a cult following. Amaro bitters and five-spice on the finish. The flavours go on and on. Screw cap. 12.6% alc. RATING 96 DRINK 2022–2032 $75 SW ✪ ♥

Scandalous Riesling 2022, Orange A fitting name for such a delicious wine. Tangerine, lime skin, honeysuckle and blossom nectar. An off-dry style that exudes class, with sugar sweetness executed like a perfect quenelle of lime sorbet. Screw cap. 12.3% alc. RATING 95 DRINK 2022–2035 $28 SW ✪

Rosé 2021, Orange Pinot noir, merlot and chardonnay in this begonia-pink rosé. Rainier cherries, pink grapefruit oil and galangal root. A textured crunch of Pink Lady apples followed by strawberries and cream and cherry tomato savoury tones. Layered and complex, this is supreme rosé made with commitment. Screw cap. 12.6% alc. RATING 95 DRINK 2022–2030 $25 SW ✪ ♥

Chardonnay 2021, Orange Papaya, muskmelon and golden peach flesh. Danish custard pastries, honeycomb and ground ginger. Baked clay and roasted pine nuts. A generously weighted chardonnay with toast and creamy notes maintaining ripe orchard fruits and dancing acidity. A natural flow and honest wine. Screw cap. 13.1% alc. RATING 95 DRINK 2022–2028 $40 SW ✪

Pinot Noir 2019, Orange Red rhubarb stalks, bleeding pomegranate seeds, fennel seeds and cured meats. Strawberry leaf and dried oregano. There is a sultry nature to the fruit with blood orange zest, amaro bitters and cassia bark. Chewing tobacco and allspice. A stand-out for its savoury flavours. Succulent and rugged, this is a magical wine that speaks of well-loved earth and a sense of place. Screw cap. 13.4% alc. RATING 95 DRINK 2022–2027 $45 SW ✪

Jezza 2018, Orange Merlot/cabernet franc/cabernet sauvignon/petit verdot. Mulberries, Davidson plum, blackcurrant and lingonberries. This wine feels otherworldly in its extreme depth of savoury umami and filagree of texture. Volatility blows off with a stiff decant and the wine opens up with black bean, porcini, li hing mui (Chinese dried plums) and autumn leaves. Powdered coriander and cumin linger. A unique tasting experience. Screw cap. 14.7% alc. RATING 95 DRINK 2022–2028 $65 SW

Patrick of Coonawarra ★★★★

Cnr Ravenswood Lane/Riddoch Highway, Coonawarra, SA 5263 **Region** Coonawarra
T (08) 8737 3687 **www.patrickofcoonawarra.com.au Open** 7 days 10–5
Winemaker Luke Tocaciu **Est.** 2004 **Dozens** 5000 **Vyds** 93.5ha
Patrick Tocaciu (who died in 2013) was a district veteran, with prior careers at Heathfield Ridge Winery and Hollick Wines. Wrattonbully plantings (almost 55ha) cover all the major varieties, while in Coonawarra the low-yielding Home Block (cabernet sauvignon) is supplemented by a 2nd vineyard of 17.5ha of cabernet and smaller amounts of riesling and sauvignon blanc. Son Luke, with a degree in oenology from the University of Adelaide and vintage experience in Australia and the US, has taken over in the winery.

🍷🍷🍷🍷🍷 **Block 5 Aged Riesling 2015, Coonawarra** In its drinking prime. Lime, honey, dust, wax and tangerine characters burst persuasively through the palate and on through the finish. Medium in intensity but it makes the most of its every turn. Delightful. Screw cap. 11% alc. RATING 93 DRINK 2022–2027 $45 CM

Joanna Shiraz 2017, Wrattonbully Soft, creamy, custard-like oak sits atop medium-weight red-berried fruit, like a cherry pie in liquid form, like a bed made of marshmallows and roses. Oak, slightly minty, is prominent here, but so too is seduction. Screw cap. 14% alc. RATING 92 DRINK 2024–2030 $50 CM

Patrick Sullivan Wines ★★★★★

146 Peterson Road, Ellinbank, Vic 3821 (postal) **Region** Gippsland
T 0439 729 780 **www.patricksullivan.com.au Open** Not **Winemaker** Patrick Sullivan
Est. 2011 **Dozens** 2000 **Vyds** 10ha
Patrick Sullivan is the 'been everywhere, done everything' man, planting vines at age 15 and heading to London 3 years later. Viticulture studies followed, coupled with working at Vina di Anna, a winery in Sicily, thereafter appointed international wine buyer for Vina di Anna's owner, a London-based wine distribution business. Back in Australia, he became increasingly interested in Gippsland and the Baw Baw Shire in particular; winemaker Bill Downie was his guide both there and thereafter in the Yarra Valley. His beliefs and practices took shape over this time, notably sustainability/biodynamics and ultra-close spacing of 7000 vines/ha. In '14 he and wife Megan purchased the 69ha property now called Tumblestone Farm, sitting on red volcanic soil over sandstone at the base of the Strzelecki Ranges. They live on the farm with their 2 young children and have planted pinot noir and chardonnay. In the meantime he works with chardonnay from the Millstream, Bullswamp and Ada River vineyards.

🍷🍷🍷🍷🍷 **Ada River Chardonnay 2022, Gippsland** Without ego, just matter of fact, Patrick Sullivan says, 'This is the best wine I've made to date.' Why? The balance of acid, fruit, texture and tension. No argument, young man. This is something else. Electrifying, pure and long. It couples power and elegance, detail and delight, flavour and finesse. Citrus, white stone fruit, flinty, funky sulphides, electrifying acidity. Mesmerising. Diam. 13.5% alc. RATING 97 DRINK 2023–2033 $88 JF ✪ ♥

ΨΨΨΨΨ **Bull Swamp Chardonnay 2022, Gippsland** Pure, refined and breathtaking. While it has all the mouth-watering flavours one craves in a chardonnay, it's the palate, again, that seals the deal. Long, detailed hints of lees just to extend it with popping finger lime acidity. He captures the purity of the site, teases out its essence and bottles it. Screw cap. 13.5% alc. RATING 96 DRINK 2023-2033 $88 JF

Ada River Pinot Noir 2022, Gippsland This is a beauty, quite savoury with such an even palate thanks to supple tannins. Tangy and juicy full of macerated cherries and blood orange, zest, and layers of spices with fine acidity. It feels quite ethereal. Diam. 13.5% alc. RATING 95 DRINK 2023-2033 $88 JF

Woori Yallock Chardonnay 2022, Yarra Valley Fans of richer, more voluptuous styles of chardonnay made with great precision, this is for you. An orchard grove of fruit flavours with tangy citrus, then the layering of texture starts – ginger cream, hazelnut/almond lees and cedary, spicy, sweet oak. Powerful, savoury with moreish sulphides and really, there's a lot to take in and a lot to enjoy. Diam. 13.5% alc. RATING 95 DRINK 2023-2031 $70 JF

Black Sands Chardonnay 2022, Henty This is the most approachable and open-knit of the 4 chardonnays. Luscious, in a way, with stone fruit and citrus, a super-creamy mid-palate with light leesy/nutty nuances and a hint of lemon curd. The palate expands with flavour and acidity drives it long. Diam. 13.5% alc. RATING 94 DRINK 2023-2031 $50 JF

Patritti Wines ★★★★★

13–23 Clacton Road, Dover Gardens, SA 5048 **Region** Adelaide
T (08) 8296 8261 **www.**patritti.com.au **Open** Mon–Sat 9–5 (7 days Dec)
Winemaker James Mungall, Ben Heide **Est.** 1926 **Dozens** 190 000 **Vyds** 16ha
A family-owned and -run business founded by Giovanni Patritti. Today it has 3 vineyard locations with a mix of old and new plantings. The most historic are patches of grenache (1.3ha), shiraz (0.4ha), muscat gordo (0.5ha), and pedro ximénez and palomino (0.25ha combined), all held by a long-term lease from the City of Marion, the oldest vines planted 1906. Today they are encircled by businesses of all kinds, residential housing and scattered remnants of vineyards which are actively protected by most residents and local planning boards.

ΨΨΨΨΨ **Lavoro Grenache 2021, McLaren Vale** Bright, clear colour. Rich, ripe and juicy, red fruits to the lead, but neatly trimmed by notes of spice and pepper. Screw cap. 14.5% alc. RATING 95 DRINK 2023-2031 $25 JH ✪

JPB Single Vineyard Shiraz 2020, McLaren Vale The depth of colour verges outright on black, both the wine in the bottle and the glass bottle itself. Its flavour (blackberry and cherry), texture and structure all come from another era, arguably fitting given this wine's dedication to founder Giovanni Patritti. Cork. 14% alc. RATING 95 DRINK 2023-2043 $65 JH

Blewitt Springs Estate Shiraz Cabernet 2018, McLaren Vale A rich, powerful and rewarding wine that builds a warming gravitas from its attack of soy, beef bouillon, stringy menthol oak scents and macerated cherry. Best, the mid-palate's gumption suggests lower yields than other wines at this address. The finish is long and effortless. Cork. 14.5% alc. RATING 94 DRINK 2022-2035 $150 NG

ΨΨΨΨ **Marion Tawny Grenache NV, Adelaide** RATING 93 $40 NG
Rare Topaque NV, Barossa Valley RATING 93 $40 NG
Lot Three Single Vineyard Shiraz 2020, McLaren Vale RATING 92 DRINK 2022-2030 $40 NG
Vermentino 2021, Adelaide Hills RATING 91 DRINK 2022-2024 $28 NG ✪
Section 181 Single Vineyard Grenache 2020, McLaren Vale RATING 90 DRINK 2022-2028 $40 NG
Saperavi 2019, Barossa Valley RATING 90 DRINK 2022-2028 $28 NG

Paul Conti Wines

529 Wanneroo Road, Woodvale, WA 6026 **Region** Greater Perth
T (08) 9409 9160 **www.paulcontiwines.com.au Open** Tues–Sat 11–5 **Winemaker** Jason
Conti **Viticulturist** Paul Conti **Est.** 1948 **Dozens** 4000 **Vyds** 11ha

Third-generation winemaker Jason Conti has assumed control of winemaking, although
father Paul (who succeeded his own father in 1968) remains involved in the business. Over
the years Paul challenged and redefined industry perceptions and standards. The challenge for
Jason is to achieve the same degree of success in a relentlessly and increasingly competitive
market environment, and he is doing just that. There are 4 estate vineyards; 3 in Greater
Perth, in Carabooda (chenin blanc), at the homestead property in Woodvale (nero d'Avola),
and in Mariginiup (shiraz), and one in Wilyabrup in Margaret River (planted to chardonnay,
sauvignon blanc, muscat à petit grains, malbec, cabernet sauvignon and shiraz).

Mariginiup Shiraz 2021, Greater Perth A bold and lusty shiraz, deeply
concentrated and palate-staining to an extreme. In all that, a relative balance,
though there are quibbles about booze-related breathiness on the palate and
overzealous wood seasoning over the ripe, potent fruit characters. Dark chocolate,
salted licorice, tar, ripe plum and cola in both bouquet and palate. Big and
beefy, done well, would be the message overall. Screw cap. 15% alc. **RATING** 93
DRINK 2022-2030 $30 MB ✪

Nero d'Avola 2020, Western Australia Inky and rich with dark cherry,
cola and salted licorice characters. Robust and thick set, it's a potent mouthful
of gummy, textured nero with amplified varietal character. This will satisfy
those seeking some oomph from the variety, or a jolly, juicy, dark-fruited and
sweet-spiced red. Well done, in its way. Screw cap. 14.5% alc. **RATING** 90
DRINK 2022-2026 $22 MB ✪

Cabernet Sauvignon 2020, Margaret River A full-figured expression, plush
with inky cassis and lifted with bay leaf, white pepper and herb and spice notes.
The palate neatly echoes the bouquet in its various characters. It's generous in
flavour, with a smudge of mocha-powder tannin supported by succulent, saline
acidity. A brooding, beefy cabernet with youth and vigour on its side. Screw cap.
14.5% alc. **RATING** 90 **DRINK** 2022-2030 $26 MB

Paul Nelson Wines

14 Roberts Road, Denmark, WA 6333 **Region** Denmark
T 0406 495 066 **www.paulnelsonwines.com.au Open** By appt **Winemaker** Paul Nelson
Est. 2009 **Dozens** 3500 **Vyds** 11ha

Paul Nelson started making wine with one foot in the Swan Valley and the other in the
Great Southern while completing a bachelor's degree in viticulture and oenology at Curtin
University. He then worked successively at Houghton in the Swan Valley, Goundrey in Mount
Barker, Santa Ynez in California, and South Africa (for 4 vintages), hemisphere-hopping to
the Rheinhessen, 3 vintages in Cyprus, then moving to a large Indian winemaker in Mumbai
before returning to work for Houghton. He moved on from Houghton and (in partnership
with wife Bianca) now makes small quantities of table wines from 2 of the oldest vineyards
in Great Southern, the lauded Karriview vineyard in Denmark and the Bouverie vineyard in
Mount Barker. The duo also have a winemaking project in Piemonte, Italy.

Loam Syrah 2022, Frankland River Exquisite wine. An exercise in precision as
much as it is in power. Peppers, roasted cherries, sweet cedar, diced twigs and boxes
of spices. It tastes important. It makes you concentrate. There's a silken aspect to
the tannin but there's a graininess there too; it feels both analog and digital. There
are also undergrowth notes here, soil-like, as if ripe, squishy berries have been
dug up from the ground and tossed straight into wood. Wow. Diam. 13.5% alc.
RATING 97 **DRINK** 2024-2038 $95 CM ✪

Karriview Pinot Noir 2022, Great Southern Complexity writ large. Cherry-
plum flavours with the added verve of strawberry and cranberry run headlong
into game and sweet, twiggy spice notes. There's energy, there are floral notes,

there's earth and there's a spread of dry, meaty, grippy tannin. It's like a tree full of lights and bells; it's all lit up, and with every swirl the flavours and scents do chime. Screw cap. 13% alc. RATING 95 DRINK 2024-2034 $69 CM

ŸŸŸŸ♀ **Le Viandier Sangiovese Mourvèdre Rosé 2022, Mount Barker Frankland River** RATING 93 DRINK 2023-2026 $33 CM ✪
Loam Riesling 2021, Mount Barker RATING 93 DRINK 2023-2028 $65 CM
Le Viandier Pinot Nero Syrah 2022, Mount Barker RATING 92 DRINK 2023-2027 $33 CM
Loam Pinot Noir 2022, Denmark RATING 92 DRINK 2025-2032 $150 CM
P.N Shiraz 2022, Mount Barker RATING 90 DRINK 2023-2028 $30 CM

Paul Osicka

Majors Creek Vineyard at Graytown, Vic 3608 **Region** Heathcote
T (03) 5794 9235 **www.**paulosickawines.com.au **Open** By appt **Winemaker** Simon Osicka **Viticulturist** Alison Phillips **Est.** 1955 **Vyds** 13ha
The Osicka family arrived from Czechoslovakia in the early 1950s. Vignerons in their own country, their vineyard in Australia was the first new venture in central and southern Victoria for over half a century. With the return of Simon Osicka to the family business, there have been substantial changes. Simon held senior winemaking positions at Houghton, Leasingham, and as group red winemaker for Constellation Wines Australia, interleaved with vintages in Italy, Canada, Germany and France, working at the prestigious Domaine Jean-Louis Chave for the '10 vintage. The fermentation of the red wines has changed from static to open fermenters and French oak has replaced American. Extensive retrellising of the 65yo estate plantings is now complete. Paul Osicka, Simon's father, passed away in '19 after 50 vintages and over 60 years of involvement in the vineyards.

ŸŸŸŸŸ **Osicka Selection Tooboorac Shiraz 2021, Heathcote** A single-vineyard wine from the southern part of Heathcote. This sings a different song to the standard Osicka Selection Heathcote Shiraz, with red and blue fruits held in a filmy web of savoury tannins. It is finely wrought and has perfect balance, the fruit seeing the tannins off on the finish. Screw cap. 14.5% alc. RATING 96 DRINK 2023-2046 $33 JH ✪
Majors Creek Vineyard Grenache 2021, Heathcote This is a serious play at grenache. It has character, it has flavour, it has that something extra. Raspberry and smoked meat characters meet fragrant herbs and juicy redcurrant. There's a firmness to the tannin, excellent length, and an all-round impression that we have something serious, and excellent, on our hands. Screw cap. 13.5% alc. RATING 95 DRINK 2023-2031 $38 CM ✪ ♥
Moormbool Shiraz 2021, Heathcote Arguably the most elegant wine in the Paul Osicka line-up. This is driven by plum, black cherry and redcurrant flavours, but it's the inflections of twiggy spice, dried herbs and smoked cedar notes that stamp its class. There's a choc-mint character, but it's so gentle and so well integrated that it's barely noticed, though its effect is felt. This is a medium-weight wine that's been made and grown very, very well. Screw cap. 14.5% alc. RATING 95 DRINK 2024-2032 $60 CM
Majors Creek Vineyard Shiraz 2021, Heathcote Solid flavour here and yet it all seems so respectable, and so well managed. Cool mint, ripe plums, crushed violets and assorted woodsy spice notes have this in a fine, flavoursome shape. The texture is velvety and tannin rolls and curls its way through the back half of the wine, keeping everything in line. Screw cap. 14.5% alc. RATING 95 DRINK 2024-2035 $38 CM ✪
Osicka Selection Shiraz 2021, Heathcote Fruit from 3 Heathcote vineyards: 2 east facing on red Cambrian soils, the 3rd on decomposed granite south of the town. A black-fruited palate sprinkled with spices and ripe tannins unfolds as the wine runs long to an impressive finish. Screw cap. 14.5% alc. RATING 95 DRINK 2023-2041 $28 JH ✪

Osicka Selection Colbinabbin Cabernet Sauvignon 2021, Heathcote
Sourced from a vineyard on the eastern slope of Mount Camel. Matured in
French oak (20% new) for 14 months. It includes 3% shiraz ex the same vineyard.
This is a strikingly different style to its shiraz siblings, with sweet cassis fruit,
cedary oak and polished tannins. Drink this and cellar those shiraz releases.
Screw cap. 14.5% alc. RATING 95 DRINK 2023–2036 $33 JH ✪

Majors Creek Vineyard Cabernet Sauvignon 2021, Heathcote Dusty
overtones signal the variety but from there it's all dense, dark, well-managed fruit
flavour. It tastes of blackberries and blackcurrants with clove, toast and tar flavours
rumbling through. There's not a lot of tannin here but there's enough, melted
straight into the fruit, to give the wine shape. This is a red wine with a big,
warm heart. Screw cap. 14.5% alc. RATING 94 DRINK 2024–2035 $38 CM ✪

ℙℙℙℙℙ **Riesling 2022, Heathcote** RATING 93 DRINK 2023–2032 $30 CM ✪

Paulett Wines ★★★★

752 Jolly Way, Polish Hill River, SA 5453 **Region** Clare Valley
T (08) 8843 4328 **www.paulettwines.com.au Open** 7 days 10–5 **Winemaker** Neil
Paulett, Jarrad Steele **Viticulturist** Matthew Paulett **Est.** 1983 **Dozens** 35 000
Vyds 79.5ha
The Paulett story is a saga of Australian perseverance, commencing with the 1982 purchase of
a property with 1ha of vines and a house, promptly destroyed by the terrible Ash Wednesday
bushfires the following year. Son Matthew joined Neil and Alison Paulett as a partner in the
business some years ago; he is responsible for viticulture. The winery and cellar door have
wonderful views over the Polish Hill River region, the memories of the bushfires long gone.

ℙℙℙℙℙ **Polish Hill River Riesling 2022, Clare Valley** A tightly wound, classic Clare
expression. It's nervy and ultra-refreshing, crisp and very dry. Scents of lemongrass,
lime juice and green apple with flavours similarly echoing the bouquet.
Concentrated but still flinty and lighter in weight. Mouth-watering and intense,
it's a pristine and very direct offering, mainlining the quintessential, regional style.
Screw cap. 12% alc. RATING 94 DRINK 2022–2040 $38 MB ✪
Organic Riesling 2022, Clare Valley Spot-on with distinct, lemon-lime
citrus characters, a touch of blackberry and a rustle of minty herbal lift. Tightly
wound and yet with an inherent juiciness, excellent persistence of flavour and a
sizzling, briny mineral vein, too. Compact, racy, refreshing. Screw cap. 12.5% alc.
RATING 94 DRINK 2023–2035 $40 MB ✪

ℙℙℙℙℙ **Shiraz 2020, Clare Valley** RATING 93 DRINK 2022–2030 $35 MB ✪
Riesling 2022, Clare Valley RATING 92 DRINK 2022–2030 $28 MB ✪
109 Reserve Cabernet Sauvignon 2020, Clare Valley RATING 92
DRINK 2024–2035 $120 MB
Polish Hill River Aged Release Riesling 2018, Clare Valley RATING 92
DRINK 2022–2026 $75 MB

Paulmara Estates ★★★★

144 Seppeltsfield Rd, Nuriootpa, SA 5355 **Region** Barossa Valley
T 0417 895 138 **www.paulmara.com.au Open** By appt **Winemaker** Jason Barrette
Viticulturist Paul Georgiadis **Est.** 1999 **Dozens** 650 **Vyds** 13ha
Born to an immigrant Greek family, Paul Georgiadis grew up in Waikerie, where his
family had vineyards and orchards. He became the whirlwind grower-relations manager
for Southcorp, and one of the best-known faces in the Barossa Valley. Paul and wife Mara
established a vineyard in '95, currently planted to shiraz, sangiovese, mataro, nero d'Avola
and cabernet sauvignon. A second vineyard of old-vine cabernet and shiraz (up to 50yo) was
purchased in '11.

ℙℙℙℙℙ **Aretî Marananga Shiraz 2020, Barossa Valley** Deep, impenetrable crimson
in the glass with notes of opulent blackberry, cassis, kirsch and black cherry with

hints of fruitcake spice, licorice, rum and raisin chocolate, vanilla, cedar and earth. Substantial gravel dust tannins here and impressive fruit depth and flow as the wine exits in a black, spicy tide. Cork. 14.5% alc. RATING 94 DRINK 2023–2033 $240 DB

ŢŢŢŢ♀ **Cabernet Sauvignon 2020, Barossa Valley** RATING 90 DRINK 2023–2027 $30 DB

Paxton ★★★★☆

68 Wheaton Road, McLaren Vale, SA 5171 **Region** McLaren Vale
T (08) 8323 9131 **www.**paxtonwines.com **Open** 7 days 10–5 **Winemaker** Ashleigh Seymour, Kate Goodman (Consultant) **Viticulturist** David Paxton **Est.** 1979
Dozens 32 000 **Vyds** 147.5ha

David Paxton is one of Australia's most respected viticulturists, with a career spanning 45+ years. He started his successful premium grower business in 1979 and has been involved with planting and managing some of the most prestigious vineyards in McLaren Vale, Barossa Valley, Yarra Valley, Margaret River and Adelaide Hills. There are 7 vineyards in the family holdings in McLaren Vale: Thomas Block (28ha), Jones Block (22ha), Quandong Farm (18ha), Landcross Farm (2ha), Maslin Beach (3.5ha), Gateway (55ha) and 19th (12ha). All are certified organic and biodynamic. The vineyards hold some of the region's oldest vines, including EJ shiraz, established in 1887. Paxton's principal focus is on premium shiraz, grenache and cabernet, though the winery also crafts wines from alternative varieties such as tempranillo, graciano and sangiovese with great success. The cellar door sits on Landcross Farm, a historic 1860s sheep farm in the original village consisting of limestone houses, shearing shed and a pop-up wine bar.

ŢŢŢŢŢ **EJ Shiraz 2020, McLaren Vale** It's a remarkably elegant and graceful shiraz, blackberry and plum are pacemakers, the oak a trifle obvious, but the tannins are fine. The overall length and balance are excellent. Screw cap. 14.5% alc. RATING 95 DRINK 2025–2045 $100 JH
Mataro 2021, McLaren Vale Scintillating aromas of beef stock, pepper-crusted salami and barbecue. Carnal, wild and impressively savoury, this is a full-weighted wine for those who detest facile sweet fruit. An armoury of majestic tannins ploughs the field for a long, briny finish. An excellent expression. Screw cap. 14% alc. RATING 94 DRINK 2023–2030 $35 NG ✪

ŢŢŢŢ♀ **Graciano 2022, McLaren Vale** RATING 93 DRINK 2023–2026 $30 NG ✪
EJ Shiraz 2021, McLaren Vale RATING 93 DRINK 2023–2035 $100 NG
Sangiovese 2022, McLaren Vale RATING 92 DRINK 2023–2026 $35 NG
Jones Block Single Vineyard Shiraz 2020, McLaren Vale RATING 92 DRINK 2022–2030 $45 NG
Baterista Shiraz 2019, McLaren Vale RATING 92 DRINK 2022–2035 $75 NG

Payne's Rise ★★★★★

10 Paynes Road, Seville, Vic 3139 **Region** Yarra Valley
T (03) 5964 2504 **www.**paynesrise.com.au **Open** Thurs–Sun 11–5 **Winemaker** Franco D'Anna (Contract) **Viticulturist** Tim Cullen **Est.** 1998 **Dozens** 2000 **Vyds** 5ha

Tim and Narelle Cullen have progressively established 5ha of cabernet sauvignon, shiraz, pinot noir, chardonnay and sauvignon blanc. They carry out all the vineyard work (Tim is also a viticulturist for a local agribusiness) and are planting new clones and rootstocks with an eye to the future. Narelle is responsible for sales and marketing. A cellar door and restaurant extension have been added, expanding the original 1860s homestead of the region's first settler, Thomas Payne.

ŢŢŢŢŢ **Brody's Block Pinot Noir / Syrah 2022, Yarra Valley** Vivid crimson, this is bursting with ripe yet fresh aromas of blackcurrants, raspberries, lifted spice and a dusting of dark cocoa powder. Lively and fleshy, this vibrant, medium-bodied and flavourful wine finishes with chewy, persistent tannins. A delicious wine. Screw cap. 13% alc. RATING 95 DRINK 2022–2027 $39 PR ✪

Chardonnay 2022, Yarra Valley Bright green gold. Aromas of white nectarines, freshly picked apricots and a little spice and vanillin from the oak, which, I should add, has already been swallowed up by the fruit. The palate is generous yet balanced and restrained and the finish is long and satisfying. Screw cap. 12.5% alc. **RATING** 95 **DRINK** 2022–2028 $35 PR ✪

Mr Jed Pinot Noir 2021, Yarra Valley A light ruby red. With its aromas of red fruits, sweet spices and a hint of lavender and incense stick, there's a lot going on here. Fine, textured and mouth-filling, this has both good acidity and persistent, gently grippy tannins. Screw cap. 13% alc. **RATING** 94 **DRINK** 2022–2025 $39 PR ✪

▼▼▼▼ **Mr Jed Pinot Noir 2022, Yarra Valley RATING** 93 **DRINK** 2022–2028 $39 PR

Peccavi Wines

1121 Wildwood Road, Yallingup Siding, WA 6282 **Region** Margaret River
T 0404 619 861 **www**.peccavi-wines.com **Open** By appt **Winemaker** Bruce Dukes, Remi Guise, Jeremy Muller, Stuart Watson **Viticulturist** Colin Bell **Est.** 1996
Dozens 6000 **Vyds** 16.5ha

Jeremy Muller spent years searching New and Old World wine regions (even looking at the sites of ancient Roman vineyards in England), but did not find what he was looking for until one holiday in Margaret River. There he found a vineyard in Yallingup that was for sale and he did not hesitate. He quickly put together an impressive contract winemaking team and appointed Colin Bell as viticulturist. The wines are released under 2 labels: Peccavi for 100% estate-grown fruit (all hand-picked) and No Regrets for wines with contract-grown grapes and estate material. The quality of the wines is very good, reflecting the skills and experience of the winemaking team.

▼▼▼▼▼ **The Estate Cabernet Sauvignon 2020, Margaret River** The Estate wines are certainly no wallflowers, although I do wonder if 2 years in oak seems too much. The fruit is good. Very good. It is encased in sweet, cedary, slippery oak that adds a lovely texture, but lots of wood flavouring, too. Time might settle the matter. Until then, decant to consider its savouriness, power and regional thumbprint. Screw cap. 13.5% alc. **RATING** 95 **DRINK** 2024–2040 $150 JF

The Estate Merlot 2020, Margaret River At first, it comes across as rich, ripe and full bodied with drying tannins on the finish, more oak-derived than fruit. But appealing savouriness soon comes to the fore: smoky, cigar box, spiced red fruit dipped in chocolate plus sumac. Tannins have power and texture like hazelnut skins. It's certainly a structured merlot with a fan base. Screw cap. 14% alc. **RATING** 95 **DRINK** 2024–2034 $150 JF

▼▼▼▼ **Chardonnay 2021, Margaret River RATING** 93 **DRINK** 2023–2031 $65 JF
Old Block Cabernet Sauvignon 2020, Margaret River RATING 92 **DRINK** 2023–2038 $75 JF
No Regrets Cabernet Merlot 2021, Margaret River RATING 90 **DRINK** 2022–2028 $26 JF
Cabernet Sauvignon 2019, Margaret River RATING 90 **DRINK** 2024–2032 $75 JF

Penfolds

30 Tanunda Road, Nuriootpa, SA 5355 P16 **Region** Barossa Valley
T (08) 8568 8408 **www**.penfolds.com **Open** 7 days 10–5 **Winemaker** Peter Gago **Est.** 1844

Penfolds is the star in the crown of Treasury Wine Estates (TWE) but its history predates the formation of TWE by close on 170 years. Its shape has changed in terms of its vineyards, its management, its passing parade of great winemakers and its wines. There is no other single winery brand in the New or the Old World with the depth and breadth of Penfolds. Retail prices range from less than $20 to $1000 for Grange, which is the cornerstone, produced every year, albeit with the volume determined by the quality of the vintage, not by cash flow. There is now a range of regional wines of single varieties and the Bin Range of wines that includes both regional blends and (in some instances) varietal blends. Penfolds is a red wine producer at heart, but its Yattarna and Reserve Bin A chardonnays are the quality equal of anything the company produces.

ΨΨΨΨΨ **Yattarna Bin 144 Chardonnay 2020, Tasmania Adelaide Hills** The 18 months in bottle is celebrated by a wonderful bouquet surging with a burst of spice, char, smoke and grapefruit. The palate is a masterful display of mouth-watering precision and freshness, yet with the complexity of a great chardonnay. Screw cap. 12.5% alc. RATING 98 DRINK 2023-2040 $175 JH

Reserve Bin A Chardonnay 2021, Adelaide Hills This wastes no time in establishing its extreme quality and complexity. It is a complete wine, with power, focus and length welded together and white peach and pink grapefruit allied with a shaft of cleansing acidity. Hard to resist right now. Screw cap. 12.5% alc. RATING 97 DRINK 2023-2036 $125 JH

Magill Estate Shiraz 2020, Adelaide Penfolds continues the move toward an unequivocal single-vineyard stamp for this wine. Black fruits (cherry and blackberry) in a bracket of oak, savoury tannins and, most importantly, fresh acidity and a toothsome 7g/L RS. Its lifespan? Indefinite, but as it's finished with a cork, cellaring conditions are important. Cork. 14.5% alc. RATING 97 DRINK 2025-2045 $150 JH

RWT Bin 798 Shiraz 2020, Barossa Valley When you see a wine with this depth of colour, grading to a brilliant crimson rim, you know all is well. The deliberate use of French oak was a decision made when planning the birth of RWT with its inaugural '97 vintage, and in tasting through Penfolds' array of red wines, it stands out. It's a brilliant trifecta of intense fruit, balanced tannins, and that classy oak. Cork. 14.5% alc. RATING 97 DRINK 2025-2050 $200 JH

Bin 169 Cabernet Sauvignon 2019, Coonawarra The excellent quality of the '19 Coonawarra vintage comes through in this classic cool-climate cabernet sauvignon. Cassis/blackcurrant is the driver, and persistent but fine and savoury tannins the engine for long distance travel. A wine for generational pleasure. Cork. 14.5% alc. RATING 97 DRINK 2025-2050 $300 JH

ΨΨΨΨΨ **Bin 407 Cabernet Sauvignon 2020, South Australia** Sourced from McLaren Vale, Coonawarra, Padthaway and Wrattonbully. An unambiguously good cabernet in the mainstream of Penfolds' vast knowledge of South Australia's hot (meaning good) spots for the variety. It's a polished, well-balanced expression. Cork. 14.5% alc. RATING 96 DRINK 2023-2042 $120 JH

Bin 150 Marananga Shiraz 2020, Barossa Valley From the heart of the Barossa Valley, and – as usual – proud of it. The deep colour stains the glass as the wine is swirled. A fusion of dark chocolate, dark berries, leather and cedar oak. Dialled up, not down, yet it achieves without heat on a full-bodied palate that is not confronted by tannins. A very good example of the style. Cork. 14.5% alc. RATING 95 DRINK 2025-2045 $100 JH

Bin 389 Cabernet Shiraz 2020, South Australia A 51/49% blend of cabernet sauvignon and shiraz from McLaren Vale, Barossa Valley and Padthway. This is big, bold, beautiful and quintessentially Australian. It makes no apologies for its wealth of black fruits, almost succulent tannins, and vanillin oak. Cork. 14.5% alc. RATING 95 DRINK 2025-2040 $100 JH

Grange Bin 95 2018, South Australia Fruit sourced from the Barossa Valley, McLaren Vale and Clare Valley. It's unclear whether Penfolds' assessment of 'Instantly, an assault of piercing VA [volatile acidity]', is in reference to a passing phase or to the deliberate retention of VA, but it's part of Grange. For me, persistent black shoe polish marks the bouquet of this wine. It'll be at least another 8 years before it calms down. There's so much screaming for attention it's distracting, and senses of proportion are lost. Cork. 14.5% alc. RATING 95 DRINK 2030-2050 $1000 JH

Bin 51 Riesling 2022, Eden Valley A highly floral bouquet spanning citrus blossom and rose petals. A fresh and bright palate has the expected length and balance, promising much for the future. Screw cap. 11.5% alc. **RATING** 94 **DRINK** 2023-2042 $40 JH ✪

Bin 311 Chardonnay 2021, Adelaide Hills Tasmania No room for the usual Tumbarumba component in this chardonnay. There's nothing lacking in a delicious palate following a tightly furled bouquet. It simply needs another couple of years for its promise to be realised. Screw cap. 12.5% alc. **RATING** 94 **DRINK** 2023-2028 $50 JH

Bin 28 Shiraz 2020, South Australia An improbably fluid wine that has entirely unexpected elements of grace. All the components of fruit, oak, tannins and acidity – the last particularly important – are in synergistic union. No blowing of trumpets here. Cork. 14.5% alc. **RATING** 94 **DRINK** 2023-2035 $50 JH

🍷🍷🍷🍷♀ **Bin 128 Shiraz 2020, Coonawarra RATING** 93 **DRINK** 2023-2040 $60 JH
Bin 23 Pinot Noir 2021, Tasmania RATING 92 **DRINK** 2023-2027 $50 JH
St Henri Shiraz 2019, South Australia RATING 91 **DRINK** 2025-2030 $135 JH
Bin 138 Shiraz Grenache Mataro 2020, Barossa Valley RATING 90 **DRINK** 2023-2032 $60 JH

Penley Estate   ★★★★★

McLeans Road, Coonawarra, SA 5263 (postal) **Region** Coonawarra
T (08) 7078 1853 **www.**penley.com.au **Open** Not **Winemaker** Kate Goodman, Lauren Hansen **Viticulturist** Hans Loder **Est.** 1988 **Dozens** 45000 **Vyds** 84ha
In 1988 Kym, Ang and Bec Tolley joined forces to buy a block of land in Coonawarra – Penley Estate was underway, the amalgamation of a 5th generation wine family Penfold and Tolley. In '15 Ang and Bec took full ownership of the company, appointing Kate Goodman as winemaker. Viticulturist and geologist Hans Loder adopts progressive initiatives in the vineyard. Kate Goodman is the *Halliday Wine Companion 2024* Winemaker of the Year.

🍷🍷🍷🍷🍷 **Eos Shiraz Cabernet Sauvignon 2021, Coonawarra** Olives, herbs, blackcurrant and cedar. The flavours are one thing but it's the flow, the command, and the authoritative push of the finish. This is top-shelf gear. Bacon-esque oak adds a final flourish to a beautifully pitched (and structured) red wine. Screw cap. 14.5% alc. **RATING** 96 **DRINK** 2026-2044 $100 CM ♥

Helios Cabernet Sauvignon 2021, Coonawarra This wine is characterised by its strong arms of tannin and force of ripe fruit, though it also feels completely in balance and, indeed, as if it's been finessed into ideal position. Everything just feels right. Blackcurrant, mint, boysenberry, florals and smoky/spicy oak, all tucked neatly into one another. It's a standout wine. Screw cap. 14.5% alc. **RATING** 96 **DRINK** 2027-2050 $150 CM

Steyning Cabernet Sauvignon 2021, Coonawarra The fruit is in full bloom and the tannin is firm and substantial. It still manages to have plenty of length. Blackcurrant, gum leaf, cedar and violets, with peppercorns and plums filling it out. There's more than a little 'wow' to this. It feels fresh too, in a good way. It's excellent. Screw cap. 14.5% alc. **RATING** 96 **DRINK** 2026-2042 $75 CM ✪

Steyning Cabernet Sauvignon 2020, Coonawarra There's great boldness to the fruit profile here, but what really sets this wine apart is its combination of freshness, substance and structure. Commanding firmness offers a beautiful mix of boysenberry and blackcurrant, all finished by a delicious smattering of choc-mint. Its balance, length and overall styling are all spot on. In short, it stacks up from every angle. Screw cap. 14.5% alc. **RATING** 96 **DRINK** 2026-2040 $75 CM ✪

Eos Cabernet Shiraz 2020, Coonawarra Quality, pure and commanding. This is what Coonawarra is all about. Elegance, complexity and power all in one, matched to a tannin profile that feels uncompromised. Sweet tobacco, blackcurrant, spearmint, plum and cedar flavours put on a gala performance. It sure is tannic but, then, the fruit is up to it. Wonderful wine, with a huge future ahead of it. Screw cap. 14.5% alc. **RATING** 96 **DRINK** 2027-2045 $100 CM

Chertsey Cabernet Blend 2021, Coonawarra Medium weight in the best of ways, complex throughout, textbook structure and noteworthy length.

Blackcurrant, peppercorns, dust and cedar with mint highlights. The web of tannin, combined with the juiciness of the fruit, is exemplary. Penley Estate is on great form. Screw cap. 14.5% alc. **RATING** 95 **DRINK** 2026-2044 $75 CM

Chertsey Cabernet Blend 2020, Coonawarra This is such a clean, neat, elegant red wine, and yet it also has obvious (read: impressive) power. It tastes of blackberry and pencil, fragrant herbs and toast, redcurrant and cedar. Its tannin, which is assertive, sits like a sheet in the wine, pulled tight, the fruit flavours nestled in around it. It feels commanding and sure, with the brightest of futures ahead. Screw cap. 14.5% alc. **RATING** 95 **DRINK** 2026-2040 $75 CM

Project E Cabernet Sauvignon 2021, Coonawarra A strict wine with noteworthy length and no shortage, despite its slender feel, of fruit power. It makes you re-evaluate the ways and wonders of wine. Plum and blackcurrant flavours merge with dried herbs, resin, root vegetables and hay. Tannin is fine grained, stringy, and assertive at once. Everything lingers. Screw cap. 14% alc. **RATING** 94 **DRINK** 2026-2038 $50 CM

Blewitt Springs Shiraz 2021, McLaren Vale Pure and clear in the glass with bright and juicy raspberry, violet, choc-mint and port-wine jelly flavours slowly drifting into darker, more blackberried pools. It smells like Black Forest cake and tastes a little of it too, though the finish is controlled and dry. It's drinking well already though there's certainly no hurry. Screw cap. 14% alc. **RATING** 94 **DRINK** 2023-2033 $45 CM

♥♥♥♥♡ **Francis Cabernet Franc 2022, Coonawarra** **RATING** 93 **DRINK** 2023-2029 $30 CM ✪

Project E Cabernet Sauvignon 2022, Coonawarra **RATING** 93 **DRINK** 2023-2030 $50 CM

Preservative Free Cabernet Sauvignon 2022, Coonawarra **RATING** 93 **DRINK** 2022-2027 $30 CM ✪

Clarendon Cabernet Sauvignon 2021, McLaren Vale **RATING** 92 **DRINK** 2024-2033 $45 CM

Hyland Shiraz 2021, Coonawarra **RATING** 92 **DRINK** 2023-2030 $30 CM ✪

Phoenix Cabernet Sauvignon 2021, Coonawarra **RATING** 91 **DRINK** 2023-2028 $20 CM ✪

Pinot Noir 2021, Yarra Valley **RATING** 90 **DRINK** 2023-2028 $45 CM

Penna Lane Wines   ★★★★

Lot 51 Penna Lane, Penwortham via Clare, SA 5453 **Region** Clare Valley **T** 0403 462 431 www.pennalanewines.com.au **Open** Fri–Sun 11–5 **Winemaker** Peter Treloar, Steve Baraglia **Est.** 1998 **Dozens** 4500 **Vyds** 4.37ha

Penna Lane is located in the beautiful Skilly Valley, 10km south of Clare. The estate vineyard (shiraz, cabernet sauvignon and semillon) is planted at an elevation of 450m, which allows a long, slow ripening period, usually resulting in wines with intense varietal fruit flavours.

♥♥♥♥♡ **Watervale Riesling 2022, Clare Valley** Straightforward expression with plenty of joy and verve. A big hit of the sweet lime in the snout, whiffs of green apple, a sniff of talc and lemon essence with faint gingery notes, too. The palate is awash with limey sweetness and piquant tang. It's all flesh, juice and suppleness underpinned with a sloshy tang of citrus. A zesty number, with high drinkability. Screw cap. 12.5% alc. **RATING** 93 **DRINK** 2022-2030 $33 MB ✪

Pepper Tree Wines   ★★★★★

86 Halls Road, Pokolbin, NSW 2320 **Region** Hunter Valley **T** (02) 4909 7100 www.peppertreewines.com.au **Open** Mon–Fri 9–5, w'ends 9.30–5 **Winemaker** Jim Chatto (consultant) **Est.** 1991 **Dozens** 50 000 **Vyds** 172.1ha

Pepper Tree is owned by former geologist and oil explorer Dr John Davis. It sources the majority of its Hunter Valley fruit from its Davis Family Tallavera Grove vineyard at Mt View, but also has premium vineyards at Orange (Carillion vineyard), Coonawarra (Calcare vineyard) and Wrattonbully (Stonefields vineyard). Jim Chatto's appointment as consultant winemaker (effective from the '23 vintage) is the second time that Chatto has had ultimate responsibility for the wines, previously '07–14. By chance, the '23 vintage represents the 10th anniversary of the blissful '13 wines made under his direction.

ŸŸŸŸŸ **Museum Release Limited Release Tallawanta Single Vineyard Semillon 2013, Hunter Valley** Semillon of the Year. The Tallawanta vineyard is best known for sublime shiraz with a 50-year life span, but if the vintage was very good – as in this case – semillon is nipping at its heels. The detail, the balance, the length, the aftertaste … all perfect. Screw cap. 11.5% alc. **RATING** 99 **DRINK** 2023-2053 $130 JH ✪ ♥

Museum Release Tallawanta Single Heritage Vineyard Shiraz 2013, Hunter Valley The only tangible difference between this and the Museum Release Coquun Reserve is $20. The vineyard and the vinification are identical, this is just a little more elegant, the Coquun a little more powerful. Screw cap. 14.5% alc. **RATING** 98 **DRINK** 2032-2053 $160 JH

Museum Release Single Vineyard Reserve Coquun Shiraz 2013, Hunter Valley From the famous Tallawanta vineyard planted 1920 with typical sandy loam. Deeply coloured. Lovely shiraz, as befits this great vineyard. Gloriously complex and textured. Ripe tannins are at the core of the wine. Screw cap. 14.5% alc. **RATING** 98 **DRINK** 2023-2053 $140 JH ✪

Stone Mountain Single Vineyard Premium Reserve Riesling 2022, Orange Spectacular appearance – whiter than white. A floral-scented bouquet is a promising start, but it's on the palate that the trap shuts as you have to avoid dribbling so intense and pure is it. Breaks just about every preconception imaginable. Extraordinary wine. Screw cap. 12% alc. **RATING** 97 **DRINK** 2023-2037 $55 JH ✪

Museum Release Block 21A Single Vineyard Reserve Cabernet Sauvignon 2013, Wrattonbully From an unusual small block that has demonstrated its ability to produce brighter, fresher red fruits that are highly floral in nature. This is indeed a delicious, seductive cabernet that is a pleasure to drink. Its cassis heart has just the right amount of tannin and oak support. Screw cap. 14% alc. **RATING** 97 **DRINK** 2028-2033 $110 JH

Museum Release Alluvius Single Vineyard Reserve Semillon 2013, Hunter Valley Glorious 10yo wine, the purity is almost painful so intense is it, finesse on the highest scale, lemon zest, Granny Smith apple; acidity perfect. Screw cap. 10.7% alc. **RATING** 97 **DRINK** 2023-2048 $90 JH ✪

Museum Release Limited Release Tallavera Single Vineyard Shiraz 2013, Hunter Valley Matured in French puncheons (35% new) for 14 months. Marries elegance, textured complexity and freshness even though 10 years old. Savoury, spicy and immensely satisfying. Screw cap. 13.8% alc. **RATING** 97 **DRINK** 2023-2043 $100 JH ✪

ŸŸŸŸŸ **Single Vineyard Alluvius Semillon 2022, Hunter Valley** The fruit comes from the Casuarina vineyard with the sandy soil that is scattered through Pokolbin. Meyer lemon and a tightly woven strand of lime make an immediate impact, heretically suggesting this could be mistaken for a 1yo riesling. Either way, it is a compelling wine. Screw cap. 10.5% alc. **RATING** 96 **DRINK** 2023-2042 $55 JH ✪

Venus Block Single Vineyard Premium Reserve Chardonnay 2021, Orange Colour still to come, at present water-white. Creeps up on the palate with a hammer blow of grapefruits (yellow and pink), gritty acidity, Granny Smith apple and white peach all there. Screw cap. 13.8% alc. **RATING** 96 **DRINK** 2023-2036 $55 JH ✪

Museum Release Venus Block Single Vineyard Reserve Chardonnay 2013, Orange Matured in French puncheons (30% new) for 8 months. A very complex bouquet of funk and toast; the palate willowy and slender yet intense. Orange's cool climate is different from all other regions. Screw cap. 13% alc. **RATING** 96 **DRINK** 2023-2038 $90 JH

Museum Release 8R Single Vineyard Reserve Merlot 2013, Wrattonbully 8R is a recently introduced merlot clone; I think this wine makes a strong case for its quality. Texture and structure are impressive, blackcurrant and earth/black olive jumping the cabernet sauvignon fence, French oak adding its voice. Screw cap. 14% alc. **RATING** 95 **DRINK** 2023–2048 $100 JH

Museum Release Single Vineyard Reserve Elderslee Road Cabernet Sauvignon 2013, Wrattonbully Matured for 20 months in French oak (40% new). Complex wine trades mint and fruit pastille, juicy, then fine but persistent tannins. Screw cap. 14.2% alc. **RATING** 95 **DRINK** 2025–2035 $80 JH

Museum Release Single Vineyard Strandlines Reserve Cabernet Shiraz 2013, Wrattonbully Matured 17 months in French oak. Stacked with fruits of red and purple, and a sheen of dark chocolate on the bouquet and palate alike. Screw cap. 14.2% alc. **RATING** 95 **DRINK** 2023–2033 $100 JH

Limited Release BDX-4 Cabernet Sauvignon Merlot Malbec Petit Verdot 2020, Wrattonbully Matured 18 months in barrel. It's a medium- to full-bodied wine with exemplary balance and a long finish, its cellaring potential measured in decades. Screw cap. 14.2% alc. **RATING** 94 **DRINK** 2025–2045 $40 JH ✪

ȲȲȲȲȲ **Premium Reserve Single Vineyard Elderslee Road Cabernet Sauvignon 2020, Wrattonbully RATING** 93 **DRINK** 2023–2031 $55 JH
Museum Release The Gravels Single Vineyard Reserve Shiraz Viognier 2013, Wrattonbully RATING 92 **DRINK** 2023–2025 $100 JH

PepperGreen Estate   ★★★☆

13 Market Place, Berrima, NSW 2577 **Region** Southern Highlands
T (02) 48771070 **www.**peppergreenestate.com.au **Open** Mon, Wed–Fri 10–5; w'ends 9–5 **Winemaker** Balog Brothers (Contract) Kiri Irving (Contract) **Viticulturist** Ben Brazenor **Est.** 2016 **Dozens** 3750 **Vyds** 16ha
Established in 2016 in the bucolic Southern Highlands town of Berrima, PepperGreen Estate's proprietary vineyard is tucked away in nearby Canyonleigh at 750m elevation, complete with olive oil processing and a high-quality tasting room that serves modern cuisine. Pinot noir, shiraz, riesling and chardonnay are all grown on the estate's holdings as the owners endeavour to appropriate ideal grape varieties to the region's cool climate.

ȲȲȲȲȲ **Cabernet Sauvignon Merlot 2019, Orange** Blackcurrant meets mulberry and raspberry leaf. A touch of sage leaf and wild thyme is nicely balanced with nutmeg, powdered cardamom and sweet vanilla pods. Oak shows itself with wood varnish and drip coffee notes, but the plushness of merlot fruit manages to shine through. A well-balanced blend showcasing both varieties and drinking very well now. Screw cap. 14% alc. **RATING** 90 **DRINK** 2022–2028 $35 SW

Pepperjack   ★★★★

Saltram, Murray Street, Angaston, SA 5353 **Region** Barossa Valley
T (08) 8561 0200 **www.**saltramwines.com.au **Open** 7 days 10–5 **Winemaker** Richard Mattner **Est.** 1996
Pepperjack Wines first hit the scene in 1998 with a release of the esteemed '96 vintage and they have been a name on wine lovers' lips ever since. Today, the brand is part of Treasury Wine Estates' portfolio and the wines (made at Saltram) remain true to their roots, with flavoursome releases that sing of the Barossa. The range has expanded in recent years, adding to the shiraz and cabernet sauvignon that so many wine drinkers cut their teeth on. Provides excellent value across the board. Wines can be tasted at Saltram cellar door.

ȲȲȲȲȲ **The Rare Find Shiraz 2021, Barossa Valley** Deep magenta/crimson with a surprising violet-flecked aromatic profile and plenty of ripe plum and blackberry fruits along with hints of spicy oak, fruitcake, chocolate bullets, cedar, cassis and earth. There is a nice fruit intensity and weight here, dark and distinctly Barossan, with a tight, sandy tannin architecture and a finish that speaks clearly of its roots. Screw cap. 14.5% alc. **RATING** 93 **DRINK** 2023-2033 $50 DB

The Rare Find Shiraz 2020, Barossa Valley An impressive and voluptuous display with lovely dark plum and berry fruits, baking spice notes, purple floral tones, dark chocolate, violets and judicious oak use. There's an impressive plush fruit flow on the palate, superfine ripe tannins and a lovely weight and texture to its form. Screw cap. 14.5% alc. **RATING** 93 **DRINK** 2023-2031 $50 DB

Porterhouse Graded Shiraz 2021, Langhorne Creek Being a carnivore, I would love to see this come packaged with a steak, but that could be asking too much. Vibrant magenta in hue with slurpy aromas of macerated plums, blueberry and boysenberry cut with spice, purple floral tones, rum and raisin chocolate and licorice. Pure plummy fruit with a very upbeat feel and fine, chalky tannin. Screw cap. 14.5% alc. **RATING** 92 **DRINK** 2023-2028 $35 DB

Scotch Fillet Graded Shiraz 2021, McLaren Vale While the name leaves little to the imagination, there is appeal should one's universe move outside of the meaty realm. Expect a polished, large-framed wine of abundant florals, blue and dark fruit flavours, a lashing of oak for restraint and an underbelly of aniseed. Not a great deal of personality, but for the risk-averse looking for a powerful wine sans flaws, perhaps this is the ticket. Screw cap. 14.5% alc. **RATING** 91 **DRINK** 2022-2030 $35 NG

Cabernet Sauvignon 2021, Barossa Valley A rich and satisfying Barossa Valley cabernet sauvignon. Plentiful blackberry and cassis notes set on a base of dark spice with hints of mint, dried herbs and earth. Packed full of varietal flavour with a curtain of chalky tannin and a plush, dark-fruited exit. Always excellent value. Screw cap. 14.5% alc. **RATING** 91 **DRINK** 2023-2026 $25 DB ✪

Sauvignon Blanc 2022, Tasmania Limestone Coast Just a touch of barrel ferment complexity. Pale straw with a green flourish and bright, punchy aromas of gooseberry and citrus fruits with a splash of nettle, lychee, clotted cream and zesty grapefruit notes. Possessing a swift acid cadence and a chalky, savoury swagger as it fades off crisp and clean. Very impressive. Screw cap. 12.5% alc. **RATING** 90 **DRINK** 2022-2024 $25 DB ✪

Petaluma ★★★★★

254 Pfeiffer Road, Woodside, SA 5244 **Region** Adelaide Hills
T (08) 8339 9390 **www**.petaluma.com.au **Open** 7 days 10–5 **Winemaker** Ben Thoman
Viticulturist Mike Harms **Est.** 1976 **Dozens** 130 000 **Vyds** 240ha
The Petaluma range has been expanded beyond the core group of Croser sparkling, Clare Valley Riesling, Piccadilly Valley Chardonnay and Coonawarra Merlot. Newer arrivals of note include Adelaide Hills Viognier and Shiraz. The plantings in the Clare Valley, Coonawarra and Adelaide Hills provide a more than sufficient source of estate-grown grapes for the wines. In '17 Petaluma (along with all wine brands owned by Lion Nathan) was acquired by Accolade.

🍷🍷🍷🍷🍷 **Chardonnay 2021, Piccadilly Valley** The pale, green-gold colour is a fine start. A fruit blossom-filled bouquet verges on outright perfume. The palate sleek and long, with fruit-sweet pink grapefruit and Granny Smith apple highlighted by partial mlf. Screw cap. 13.5% alc. **RATING** 96 **DRINK** 2023-2030 $54 JH ✪

Tiers Chardonnay 2019, Piccadilly Valley When the back label says 'This has inherited a resilience and breeding which will allow it to develop the complexity with finesse, achieved only by a few of the world's great chardonnays' it's a hard bar to leap over. This wine can't quite do it, but it's a high-class package, with great balance, precision and length. Screw cap. 14% alc. **RATING** 96 **DRINK** 2023-2029 $140 JH

Tiers Chardonnay 2021, Piccadilly Valley This is a very good contemporary chardonnay. It plays a slightly terse reductive hand to corral the stone-fruit allusions while a pungent mineral authority crackles across the finish. This melds with bright acidity to carry good length. Some lees-derived nougatine, creamed hazelnut and truffle placate the tensile feel while layering a juicy finale. Screw cap. 13.5% alc. **RATING** 95 **DRINK** 2023–2033 $140 NG

🍷🍷🍷🍷♀ **Croser Late Disgorged 2010, Adelaide Hills** **RATING** 93 **DRINK** 2023–2032 $67 NG

Hanlin Hill Riesling 2022, Clare Valley **RATING** 93 **DRINK** 2023–2032 $36 MB

Evans Vineyard 2018, Coonawarra **RATING** 93 **DRINK** 2023–2032 $77 CM

Croser Vintage Pinot Noir Chardonnay 2019, Adelaide Hills **RATING** 91 **DRINK** 2023–2032 $48 NG

Peter Drayton Wines ★★★★★

Ironbark Hill Vineyard, 694 Hermitage Road, Pokolbin, NSW 2321 **Region** Hunter Valley **T** (02) 6574 7085 **www**.pdwines.com.au **Open** 7 days 10–5 **Winemaker** Peter Drayton, Jeremy O'Brien, Grant Richardson **Viticulturist** Peter Drayton, Jeremy O'Brien, Grant Richardson **Est.** 2001 **Dozens** 21 000 **Vyds** 14ha

Owned by Peter and Leesa Drayton. The estate plantings include shiraz, chardonnay, semillon, cabernet sauvignon, tempranillo, merlot, verdelho and tyrian. Peter is a commercial/industrial builder, so constructing the cellar door was a busman's holiday. The cellar door is shared with Ironbark Hill Brewing Co, which is brewed onsite.

🍷🍷🍷🍷 **Anomaly Barbera 2022, Hunter Valley** I must say it's very attractive, with rich red and black fruits, including raspberry, and nicely weighted tannin. I'm happy to be a champion for this wine. Screw cap. 13.5% alc. **RATING** 95 **DRINK** 2023–2032 $36 JH ✪

Museum Release Premium Release Semillon 2013, Hunter Valley There's something about the bouquet I don't get, could it be botrytis? Regardless, the palate is delicious, with ripe citrus notes and a hint of guava, acidity as it should be. These 10+yo semillons should be national treasures. Screw cap. 11% alc. **RATING** 95 **DRINK** 2025–2028 $45 JH ✪

🍷🍷🍷🍷♀ **Anomaly Montepulciano 2022, Hunter Valley** **RATING** 93 **DRINK** 2023–2032 $36 JH

Anomaly Vermentino 2022, Hunter Valley **RATING** 93 **DRINK** 2023–2027 $30 JH ✪

Anomaly Shiraz Touriga 2022, Hunter Valley **RATING** 90 **DRINK** 2023–2037 $36 JH

Wildstreak Rosé 2022, Hunter Valley **RATING** 90 **DRINK** 2023–2025 $30 JH

Peter Lehmann ★★★★★

Para Road, Tanunda, SA 5352 **Region** Barossa Valley **T** (08) 8565 9555 **www**.peterlehmannwines.com **Open** By appt **Winemaker** Nigel Westblade, Brett Schutz, Andrew Cockram, Lauren Hutton **Viticulturist** Jade Rogge **Est.** 1979 **Dozens** 300 000 **Vyds** 1100ha

The seemingly indestructible Peter Lehmann (the person) died in June 2013, laying the seeds for what became the last step in the sale of the minority Lehmann family ownership in the company. The Hess Group of California had acquired control in '03 (leaving part of the capital with the Lehmann family) but a decade later it became apparent that Hess wished to quit its holding. Various suitors put their case forward but Margaret Lehmann (Peter's widow) wanted ongoing family, not corporate, ownership. Casella thus was able to make the successful bid in November '14, followed by the acquisition of Brand's Laira in December '15.

🍷🍷🍷🍷 **The Barossan Grenache 2021** Clear, bright hue. Fragrant and flowery bouquet, the palate one of purity to its basket of red fruits and berries. Delicious wine – if the day is warm, don't hesitate to give it a light chill. Screw cap. 14.5% alc. **RATING** 96 **DRINK** 2023–2029 $25 JH ✪

Margaret Semillon 2016, Barossa This wine is showing beautifully, as always. It sits pale straw in the glass, characters of drying hay overlaying pithy lemon fruits with hints of clotted cream, white flowers, washed rind cheese, crushed stone, lemon curd, beeswax, nougat and a light wash of stone fruit. Endlessly complex, the Margaret semillon is consistently one of the finest examples of the variety in the land. Screw cap. 11% alc. RATING 96 DRINK 2023–2035 $45 DB ✪ ♥

Mentor 2019, Barossa This cabernet sauvignon has a bright aromatic profile, no doubt from a wee bit of malbec lift, with pure blackberry, blueberry and cassis notes meshing seamlessly with hints of fine spice, earth, licorice, cedar and scattered herbs. Support comes in the way of fine, sandy tannins and the wine shows plenty of drive and fruit purity. Great value. Screw cap. 14.5% alc. RATING 95 DRINK 2023–2033 $45 DB ✪

8 Songs Shiraz 2019, Barossa An impressive release from a low-yielding vintage with more purity and grace than fruit heft and power. It sports a beautiful bright colour and is packed with ripe satsuma plum, boysenberry and blueberry notes, quite perfumed with hints of violets, chocolate, fine spice and earth, with compact gypsum-like tannin support and composed, wonderfully balanced finish. Screw cap. 14.5% alc. RATING 95 DRINK 2023–2033 $45 DB ✪

🍷🍷🍷🍷 **H&V Cabernet Sauvignon 2021, Barossa Valley** RATING 92 DRINK 2023–2027 $25 DB ✪

The Bond Grenache 2021, Barossa RATING 91 DRINK 2023–2027 $25 DB ✪

Black Queen Sparkling Shiraz 2017, Barossa RATING 90 DRINK 2023–2026 $42 DB

H&V Riesling 2022, Eden Valley RATING 90 DRINK 2023–2027 $25 DB ✪

Petrichor Wines ★★★★

40A Negara Crescent, Goodwood, Tas 7010 **Region** Tasmania
T 0405 365 717 **www**.petrichorwines.com.au **Open** By appt **Winemaker** Kate Akmentins, Tim Hodgkinson **Viticulturist** Kate Akmentins, Tim Hodgkinson **Est.** 2018 **Dozens** 130 **Vyds** 1.8ha

Petrichor is the scent of rain on dry soil. Kate Akmentins and Tim Hodgkinson visited Tasmania in '06 and decided it was where their future lay. Three daughters, including twins, arrived, leading to the acceleration of their plans. In mid '14 they decamped from Sydney, 3 years later purchasing a 10ha property at Tea Tree in the Coal River Valley, with a north-facing slope and sunshine all day. One decision they made early on was to farm biodynamically, with close-planting (1m x 1m) of pinot noir, syrah, gamay and grüner veltliner. Their first vintage from the biodynamically farmed vineyard will be from '23, with parcels of carefully selected fruit purchased from other Tea Tree vineyards until this time.

🍷🍷🍷🍷 **Single Vineyard Coal River Valley Pinot Noir 2021, Tasmania** Aromas of dark cherry, redcurrant, wild strawberry and raspberry tones. Hints of exotic spice and amaro herbs, rhubarb, morello cherries, sous bois and lighter tones of game and tobacco. Airy with a detailed, diaphanous palate shape, gentle powdery tannin and a shimmering acid cadence, the wine fades with a sweep of sour cherry and spice. Diam. 13% alc. RATING 93 DRINK 2023–2030 $65 DB

Petronio ★★★★

Cambus Rd Yering, Vic 3770 (postal) **Region** Yarra Valley
T (03) 9842 1822 **www**.petroniowines.com.au **Open** Not **Winemaker** Maximilian Petronio **Est.** 2005 **Dozens** 1500

Max Petronio started his winemaking career with Rob Dolan at Yarra Ridge in '95, going on to Yering Farm as an assistant winemaker from '01–05, working alongside Alan Johns in both the vineyard and winery. Petronio Wines, which have always been made at Yering Farm and will continue to be, was launched in '05. Max is focused on making single-vineyard wines and working with a range of growers in the Yarra Valley, Pyrenees, King Valley, Nagambie Lakes and the Strathbogie Ranges.

🍷🍷🍷🍷 **By Maximilian Pinot Noir 2021, Yarra Valley** Light garnet, this attractive and forward wine has scents of red fruits, underbrush and a touch of spice. Delicate yet persistent on the palate with very fine tannins and bright acidity. Should fill out nicely over the next couple of years. Screw cap. 13% alc. **RATING** 91 **DRINK** 2022-2026 $33 PR

By Maximilian Shiraz 2020, Yarra Valley A medium–deep cherry red. Perfumed with ripe raspberries, violets and some allspice and incense notes from 100% whole bunches. Medium bodied, the palate is already supple, silky and reasonably long. I'd be drinking (and enjoying) this wine now and over the next 2–3 years. Screw cap. 14% alc. **RATING** 91 **DRINK** 2022-2025 $28 PR ✪

By Maximilian Shiraz 2021, Pyrenees Grown on the Malakoff vineyard. Matured in a combination of French and American 300L barrels, 20% new. Sweet plum and vanilla custard flavours with clove, earth and mint as highlights. Alcohol warmth detracts from the finish but the flavour profile in general is most enjoyable. Screw cap. 15% alc. **RATING** 90 **DRINK** 2023-2029 $35 CM

Pewsey Vale Vineyard ★★★★★

Eden Valley Road, Eden Valley, SA 5353 **Region** Eden Valley
T (08) 8561 3200 **www.**pewseyvale.com **Open** By appt **Winemaker** Louisa Rose
Est. 1847 **Dozens** 20 000 **Vyds** 65ha

Pewsey Vale was a famous vineyard established in 1847 by Joseph Gilbert. It was appropriate that when the Hill-Smith family began the renaissance of the Eden Valley plantings in 1961, it should do so by purchasing Pewsey Vale and establishing 50ha of riesling. In '77 the riesling also finally benefited from being the first wine to be bottled with a Stelvin screw cap. While public reaction forced the abandonment of the initiative for almost 20 years, Pewsey Vale never lost faith in the technical advantages of the closure. A quick taste (or better, a share of a bottle) of Contours Riesling will tell you why.

🍷🍷🍷🍷🍷 **10 Years Cellar Aged The Contours Museum Reserve Single Vineyard Estate Riesling 2013, Eden Valley** Light straw in the glass with aromas of dried hay, Bickford's lime cordial, almond blossom, brioche, cultured butter, crushed quartz, pecans and the lightest whiff of marzipan. The palate endlessly complex and sustained with a porcelain acidity. Contours, you beautiful little wine. An absolute belter of a museum release. Screw cap. 12% alc. **RATING** 97 **DRINK** 2023-2033 $50 DB ✪ ♥

🍷🍷🍷🍷🍷 **1961 Block Single Vineyard Estate Riesling 2022, Eden Valley** Pristine characters of freshly squeezed lime and lemon fruits with a blast of crunchy green apple and hints of crushed quartz, Christmas lily and lighter wafts of marzipan and petrichor. Detailed and precise, the fruit rides on rails of minerally acidity, setting a cracking pace across the palate before finishing pure and true. Great stuff. Screw cap. 12.5% alc. **RATING** 95 **DRINK** 2023-2033 $26 DB ✪

1961 Block Single Vineyard Estate Riesling 2021, Eden Valley The vineyard is on skeletal soil; the wine wild-yeast fermented. The bouquet brings talc, citrus blossom and a herbal whisper, the palate reflecting those characters, plus acidity. Screw cap. 12% alc. **RATING** 95 **DRINK** 2023-2036 $35 JH ✪

Contours 5YR Riesling 2017, Eden Valley Museum release. Light straw in the glass with aromas of Bickfords' lime cordial, Christmas lily, orange blossom, almond paste, wildflowers, drying grass and crushed quartz. Long and pure with some soft spice notes joining in on the palate and a focused finish that sails off slowly into the distance. Screw cap. 12.5% alc. **RATING** 94 **DRINK** 2023-2030 $40 DB ✪

🍷🍷🍷🍷🍷 **Single Vineyard Estate Riesling 2022, Eden Valley RATING** 93 **DRINK** 2023-2029 $26 DB ✪

Lighter Riesling 2022, Eden Valley RATING 91 **DRINK** 2023-2025 $26 DB ✪

Lighter Riesling 2021, Eden Valley RATING 91 **DRINK** 2023-2026 $26 JH ✪

Pfeiffer Wines ★★★★★

167 Distillery Road, Wahgunyah, Vic 3687 **Region** Rutherglen
T (02) 6033 2805 **www.pfeifferwines.com.au Open** Mon–Sat 9–5, Sun 10–5
Winemaker Jen Pfeiffer, Chris Pfeiffer **Viticulturist** Paul Heard, Mick Patford
Est. 1984 **Dozens** 20000 **Vyds** 33ha

Family-owned and -run, Pfeiffer Wines occupies one of the historic wineries (built in 1885) that abound in North East Victoria, which is worth a visit on this score alone. In 2012 Chris Pfeiffer was awarded an Order of Australia Medal (OAM) for his services to the wine industry. Both hitherto and into the future, Pfeiffer's Muscats, Topaques and other fortified wines are a key part of the business. The arrival of daughter Jen, by a somewhat circuitous and initially unplanned route, has dramatically lifted the quality of the table wines, led by the reds. Chris Pfeiffer celebrated his 50th vintage in '23, having well and truly set the scene for supremely gifted daughter Jen to assume the chief winemaking role.

ΨΨΨΨΨ **Rare Topaque NV, Rutherglen** Winemaker/blender Jen Pfeiffer is celebrated as a master of her art. Here, she combines complex raisined sweetness with an almost delicate touch, eliciting a fineness of detail in addition to the expected richness. There's raisin, roasted nuts, malt, sweet tea with honey, burnt butter and a citrus peel delicacy that brings an almost floral moment on the way to the long finish. Delicious, harmonious. 500ml. Screw cap. 17.5% alc. **RATING** 97 $130 JP

Rare Muscat NV, Rutherglen The average age of Pfeiffer's Rare muscat is 25 years, with fruit blended from the best parcels of the best vintages. It speaks of history as well as the winemaker's blending skills, with super-concentrated aromas and exquisite complexity of flavour presented in detail, fresh and alive. Which is in itself an art, with 303g/L RS. A rare winemaking skill indeed. 500ml. Screw cap. 17.5% alc. **RATING** 97 $130 JP

ΨΨΨΨΨ **Winemakers Selection Shiraz 2021, Great Western** Lights up the senses with the prettiest, most arresting aromatic intensity. Black pepper, blackberry, cassis, briar, anise and fruitcake spices. This is one instance where the alcohol does not reflect the contents which, while generous, are far from hot or lacking in structure. Quite the opposite. Tannins are in balance as the wine glides smoothly with fruit and spice-filled energy across the tongue. Screw cap. 15.2% alc. **RATING** 96 **DRINK** 2023-2032 $35 JP ✪

Rare Tawny NV, Rutherglen This is one impressive Rare tawny. It comprises a mix of Portuguese and French grapes and sports an average age of 25 years. It's super-impressive in complexity with barrel age delivering an intense concentration of flavour that's layered and raisiny rich with an aged, nutty rancio character that lasts and lasts. And it's all delivered fresh, clean and long. Do yourself a favour … 500ml. Screw cap. 20% alc. **RATING** 96 $95 JP

Grand Muscat NV, Rutherglen The burnished walnut colour helps translate what follows: a rich world of deep, raisiny muscat fruit, nutty rancio aged characters of malt, plum pudding and luscious honeyed sweetness in a wonderfully evocative, concentrated muscat essence. The winemaker has brilliantly brought aged muscat characters to life through the judicious blending of age and youth with fresh spirit. Bravo. 500ml. Screw cap. 17.5% alc. **RATING** 96 $85 JP

Grand Topaque NV, Rutherglen Tasting a Grand Topaque is not only a joy but a privilege, a reminder of the generations of winemakers who laid down parcels of fruit in barrel to get to this point. Take a big sniff, let the senses fill with the scent of panforte, raisin, burnt butter, roasted nuts and toffee. Flows sweet, layered and so lingeringly long. 500ml. Screw cap. 17.5% alc. **RATING** 96 $85 JP

Seriously Nutty Medium Dry Apera NV, Rutherglen Seriously nutty in name, in deed and so delicious. A brilliant, old gold colour that glistens in the glass. The wood-aged fino produces vanillin and nutty hazelnut aromas with candied peel and salted caramel toffee. A light sweetness mixes with apricot, honey, nougat and toasty notes towards an acid-taut, austere, and long-lasting finish. 500ml. Screw cap. 21.5% alc. **RATING** 95 $50 JP ✪

Seriously Fine Pale Dry Apera NV, Rutherglen Fresh, bright and dry with saline crunch and savoury flor nuance. Almond, green apple, preserved lemon, green olive and sea spray aromas. That mineral saltiness and tang teases the tastebuds and jolts the palate. The perfect aperitif. Serve chilled. 500ml. Screw cap. 16% alc. RATING 95 $29 JP ✪

Classic Topaque NV, Rutherglen Whoa! The step up from entry-level Rutherglen topaque to Classic topaque is stunning. The amber colour runs deeper, the perfume becomes more concentrated, and the overall effect is a rich, complex infusion of fruit plus oak plus fortifying spirit. Salted caramel, honey cake, dried fruits, smoky lapsang souchong tea with a luscious, silky textured follow on. All that and freshened up perfectly with a clean, bright spirit. 500ml. Screw cap. 17.5% alc. RATING 95 $35 JP ✪

Classic Muscat NV, Rutherglen The 'Classic' designation is where we start to see what a little age and development can bring to muscat. Flavours run deeper, complexity grows, and the degree of lusciousness makes itself better known. They are all here, smoothly and confidently so, in crushed raisin, dried fruit, malt extract, toffee and walnut. Runs smooth, sweet and, importantly, lingers long. 500ml. Screw cap. 17.5% alc. RATING 95 $35 JP ✪

ⵧⵧⵧⵧⵧ **The Piper 2021, Rutherglen** RATING 92 DRINK 2023-2032 $50 JP
Classic Tawny NV, Rutherglen RATING 92 $25 JP ✪
Marsanne 2022, Rutherglen RATING 91 DRINK 2023-2027 $23 JP ✪
Durif 2021, Rutherglen RATING 91 DRINK 2023-2033 $35 JP
Muscat NV, Rutherglen RATING 91 $25 JP ✪
Seriously Pink Apera NV, Rutherglen RATING 91 $20 JP ✪
Topaque NV, Rutherglen RATING 91 $25 JP ✪
Carlyle Shiraz 2021, Victoria RATING 90 DRINK 2023-2027 $20 JP ✪
Tempranillo 2021, North East Victoria RATING 90 DRINK 2023-2027 $28 JP

Phaedrus Estate ★★★★

220 Mornington-Tyabb Road, Moorooduc, Vic 3933 **Region** Mornington Peninsula **T** (03) 5978 8134 **www.phaedrus.com.au Open** W'ends & public hols 11–5 **Winemaker** Ewan Campbell, Maitena Zantvoort **Viticulturist** Ewan Campbell, Maitena Zantvoort **Est.** 1997 **Dozens** 3000 **Vyds** 2.5ha

Since Maitena Zantvoort and Ewan Campbell established Phaedrus Estate, they have gained a reputation for producing premium cool-climate wines. Their winemaking philosophy brings art and science together to produce wines showing regional and varietal character with minimal winemaking interference. The vineyard includes 1ha of pinot noir and 0.5ha each of pinot gris, chardonnay and shiraz.

ⵧⵧⵧⵧⵧ **Fumé Blanc Sauvignon Blanc 2022, Mornington Peninsula** Lots of texture, lots of flavour, so there's a lot to like. The fruit is not in the tropical vein, it's more peaches and lemon with wafts of flint, smoky sulphides and woodsy spices with zesty acidity. Most of all, it's savoury and thoroughly appealing. More, please. Screw cap. 12.5% alc. RATING 93 DRINK 2022-2027 $28 JF ✪

Fiano 2022, Mornington Peninsula While the aromas are ephemeral, one whiff and they're gone, the palate really sings. Some white stone fruit, powdered ginger and a touch of honeycomb appear alongside lemony saline acidity. There is texture, too, fleshing out the palate with a smidge of phenolics. Really good drinking here, folks. A neat alternative to Mornington Peninsula staples. Screw cap. 12.5% alc. RATING 92 DRINK 2022-2026 $28 JF ✪

Chardonnay 2022, Mornington Peninsula There's always a ripe white peach character to this, no matter the vintage, and here it comes doused in ginger spice, creamed honey and some leesy nuttiness. Fleshy and ripe across the palate with a slip of fruit sweetness kept fresh by lemony acidity. An all-around, easy-to-drink chardonnay. Screw cap. 13% alc. RATING 91 DRINK 2022-2027 $28 JF ✪

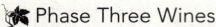

Phase Three Wines

157 Craneford Road, Flaxman Valley, SA 5235 **Region** Barossa
T 0414 860 693 **www**.phasethreewines.com.au **Open** By appt **Winemaker** Ben Kelley,
Sabina Kelley **Viticulturist** Ben Kelley, Sabina Kelley **Est.** 2019 **Dozens** 250 **Vyds** 2ha
Ben and Sabina Kelley's Phase Three Wines is a vibrant new addition to the Barossa wine
landscape. The duo relocated to the Eden Valley from NSW, purchasing a 15ha property and
planting 3 small vineyards for their estate wines. The current releases, from grapes sourced
from some of the Barossa's most sought-after growers (Hoffmann in Ebenezer; and Mattschoss,
Bartholomaeus and Walker in the Eden Valley), are beautifully packaged, traditionally shaped
regional wines of vibrancy and verve, which sets the tone nicely for the future.

Dero Shiraz Pinot Noir 2021, Barossa A Barossa shiraz/pinot? Yes, please!
The aromatic pinot component flexes its muscles here with cherry and forest-floor
tones before the shiraz powers in on the palate with plum and earth notes, turning
up the volume on fruit depth and intensity. Textured and quite powerful on the
palate with bright acidity and fine tannin support. Impressive. Diam. 14.4% alc.
RATING 93 **DRINK** 2023–2030 $45 DB

Philip Shaw Wines

100 Shiralee Road, Orange, NSW 2800 **Region** Orange
T (02) 6362 0710 **www**.philipshaw.com.au **Open** 7 days 11–5 **Winemaker** Daniel Shaw
Est. 1989 **Dozens** 25 000 **Vyds** 66ha
Philip Shaw, former chief winemaker of Rosemount Estate and then Southcorp, first became
interested in the Orange region in 1985. In '88 he purchased the Koomooloo vineyard
and began extensive plantings. The varieties include shiraz, merlot, pinot noir, sauvignon
blanc, cabernet franc, cabernet sauvignon, chardonnay and viognier and the vineyard is in
conversion to organic. Philip has handed the reins to sons Daniel and Damian to concentrate
on his HOOSEGG wines.

No.10 Méthode Traditionnelle Chardonnay 2010, Orange Disgorged
in '20 with 4g/L dosage. Baked apples, lemon oil, pie crust and crushed peanut
shell. Oyster mushroom and fine sandstone threaded throughout. Acidity
continues to ferry the fruit along as the wealth of autolytic characters takes centre
stage. Sourdough starter, hazelnut skin, gingerbread and pancake batter. It's a
symphony of flavours, textures and resonating tunes. Beautiful. Cork. 14% alc.
RATING 95 **DRINK** 2022–2026 $75 SW ♥
No. 89 Shiraz 2019, Orange Blackcurrants, raspberry and cherry pie. Soft
licorice, caraway seeds, clove studs, moist potting soil, prune and undergrowth.
Deeply nuanced with salted licorice with black olive brine. The wine's acidity
directs the palate and the finish is supple with a touch of black pepper. Intrigue
and pedigree. Screw cap. 14% alc. **RATING** 95 **DRINK** 2022–2028 $60 SW
Small Batch Cabernet Sauvignon Shiraz Merlot 2017, Orange A
welcome bundle of perfectly ripe blackcurrant, black cherries and plums.
Tobacco leaf, cedar and five-spice. Bitter dark chocolate leads to granite and dried
mushroom. Tannins are fine and silty and lasting flavours of cocoa and clove. This
is built for the long haul with a well-structured base and expertly timed harvest.
Screw cap. 13.5% alc. **RATING** 95 **DRINK** 2022–2028 $65 SW
No. 8 Pinot Noir 2021, Orange Lingonberries, redcurrant and strawberry
leaves. The bunchy component adds a sappy, ripe mulberry leafiness and orange
bitters on the palate. It's a wine that is designed and crafted from knowledge. Will
cellar well. The oak just slightly clips the pureness of the fruit. Screw cap. 13% alc.
RATING 94 **DRINK** 2022–2028 $45 SW

Small Batch Riesling 2022, Orange RATING 93 **DRINK** 2022–2028 $35 SW ✪
Small Batch Cabernet Sauvignon 2013, Orange RATING 93
DRINK 2022–2028 $65 SW
The Gardener Pinot Gris 2022, Orange RATING 92 **DRINK** 2022–2026
$25 SW ✪

No. 19 Sauvignon Blanc 2022, Orange RATING 92 DRINK 2022-2026 $30 SW
The Wire Walker Pinot Noir 2022, Orange RATING 92 DRINK 2022-2026 $25 SW ✪
No. 19 Sauvignon Blanc 2021, Orange RATING 92 DRINK 2022-2026 $30 SW ✪
The Conductor Merlot 2019, Orange RATING 92 DRINK 2022-2028 $25 SW ✪
The Architect Chardonnay 2022, Orange RATING 91 DRINK 2022-2028 $25 SW ✪
The Idiot Shiraz 2021, Orange RATING 91 DRINK 2022-2026 $25 SW ✪
Pink Billy Saignée 2021, Orange RATING 90 DRINK 2022-2025 $30 SW

Piano Piano ★★★★

852 Beechworth–Wangaratta Road, Everton Upper, Vic 3678 **Region** Beechworth
T (03) 5727 0382 **www.**pianopiano.com.au **Open** By appt **Winemaker** Marc Scalzo
Est. 2001 **Dozens** 1500 **Vyds** 4.6ha

'Piano piano' means 'slowly slowly' in Italian, and this is how Marc Scalzo and wife Lisa Hernan have approached the development of their business. Marc has a degree in oenology from CSU, many years' practical experience as a winemaker with Brown Brothers and vintage experience with Giaconda, John Gehrig and in NZ with Seresin Estate and Delegat's. In 1997 they planted 2.6ha of merlot, cabernet sauvignon, tempranillo and touriga nacional on their Brangie vineyard in the King Valley; they followed up with 1.2ha of chardonnay ('06) and 0.8ha of shiraz ('08) on their Beechworth property.

🍷🍷🍷🍷🍷 **Henry's Block Shiraz 2019, Beechworth** Employs a relatively modest 10% whole bunches and the effect is immediate and hugely positive, especially on the fragrance. Dark-fruited expression of plums, berries, black cherries, graphite and spice oh–so lifted and buoyant. The palate is svelte and lively with fine, ripe tannins. Will evolve nicely in the bottle over time, if you let it. Screw cap. 13.2% alc. RATING 93 DRINK 2023-2027 $45 JP

Sophie's Block Chardonnay 2021, Beechworth The 100% barrel fermentation is immediately apparent from the scent of almond meal and vanilla to the warm, textural palate. In between, the drinker gets to explore stone fruits, nougat, spice, almond nuttiness and generous flavours against a lanolin-smooth backdrop. Ready to enjoy right now. Screw cap. 13% alc. RATING 92 DRINK 2022-2027 $45 JP

Pinot Grigio 2022, Alpine Valleys Beechworth Top drinking at a low price boasting the kind of understated subtlety that grigio does so well. Layers of apple, citrus and green pear move in unison, together with a touch of almond-skin bite that adds that little something extra. Smooth, clean, refreshing. Screw cap. 12.8% alc. RATING 91 DRINK 2022-2025 $20 JP ✪

Pierrepoint Wines ★★★★

271 Pierrepoint Road, Tarrington, Vic 3300 **Region** Henty
T 0439 476 198 **www.**pierrepointwines.com.au **Open** Most days 11–6
Winemaker Owen Latta (Contract) **Viticulturist** Andrew Lacey, Jennifer Lacey
Est. 1997 **Dozens** 550 **Vyds** 5.5ha

Pierrepoint was established by Andrew and Jennifer Lacey on the foothills of Mt Pierrepoint, at an elevation of 200m. The predominantly red buckshot soils of the vineyard are derived from ancient volcanic basalt, rich in minerals. Two hectares each of pinot noir and pinot gris and 1.5ha of chardonnay are planted on an ideal north-facing slope. Owen Latta took over the winemaking from the '21 vintage.

🍷🍷🍷🍷🍷 **Alexandra Chardonnay 2021, Henty** Glowing yellow in colour but fresh (and rich) on the palate. This is an intriguing wine. It tastes of popcorn and grilled peach, sweet peas and cedar, and then honeysuckle and lime through the finish. All the while it feels zippy enough, before finishing long. Screw cap. 12.5% alc. **RATING** 94 **DRINK** 2023-2028 $40 CM ✪

Nicks Pick Pinot Gris 2021, Henty RATING 93 DRINK 2022-2025 $30 CM ✪
Pinot Noir 2021, Henty RATING 92 DRINK 2024-2030 $40 CM
Sparkling Pinot Gris 2019, Henty RATING 91 DRINK 2022-2025 $40 CM
Lacey Dessert Pinot Gris 2019, Henty RATING 90 DRINK 2022-2025 $30 CM

Pierro   ★★★★★

Caves Road, Wilyabrup via Cowaramup, WA 6284 **Region** Margaret River
T (08) 9755 6220 **www.pierro.com.au Open** 7 days 10–5 **Winemaker** Dr Michael Peterkin **Est.** 1979 **Dozens** 10 000 **Vyds** 7.85ha
Dr Michael Peterkin is another of the legion of Margaret River medical practitioner-vignerons; for good measure, he married into the Cullen family. Pierro is renowned for its stylish white wines, which often exhibit tremendous complexity; the chardonnay can be monumental in its weight and texture. That said, its red wines from good vintages can be every bit as good.

Chardonnay 2021, Margaret River As usual, this is rich and ripe, voluptuous even, but it curves back with the firm thread of acidity restraining it. Full of lemon-lime bitters, stone fruit and honeydew, ginger spice and lots of creamy lees filling out the palate. Then wham! The acidity says stop. Screw cap. 13.5% alc.
RATING 96 **DRINK** 2022-2029 $110 JF
VR Cabernet Sauvignon 2018, Margaret River The oak is seamlessly integrated into the body of the wine. And true to Pierro style, it's medium weighted. Yes, some woodsy spices and cedary notes but merely a seasoning. There's a five-spice character, fresh tobacco, mocha and cassis – complex and detailed. The palate is finely tuned to the finish. Screw cap. 14% alc. **RATING** 96 **DRINK** 2022-2038 $132 JF
VR Chardonnay 2019, Margaret River A style that is reminiscent of a soliloquy, delivered confidently, as this stands alone, stylistically unconcerned with all others around it. Pristine fruit bathed in vanillin, cedary oak, ginger spice and clotted cream. The palate has depth, somewhat expansive yet it follows a linear path of acidity. It's complex, detailed and stamped Pierro. Screw cap. 13.5% alc.
RATING 95 **DRINK** 2023-2028 $132 JF
L.T.Cf. Cabernet Sauvignon Merlot 2019, Margaret River Ethereal, lighter framed and a lovely drink. Full of raspberry leaves, just-ripe blackberries, pops of spice and the distinct Margaret River fragrance – it's a native bush character and very pleasing. Lithe tannins and a gentleness across the palate make this ready to enjoy now. Screw cap. 14% alc. **RATING** 95 **DRINK** 2022-2030 $50 JF ✪
Reserve Cabernet Sauvignon Merlot 2019, Margaret River A beautifully modulated wine highlighting the fineness and elegance of the Pierro style. Never showy or loud. They are distinctive. All the best regional and varietal components are neatly combined and flow across the just medium-bodied palate. It's fragrant, the tannins are fine yet shapely and the pomegranate-like acidity keeps the length going. Screw cap. 14% alc. **RATING** 95 **DRINK** 2022-2034 $99 JF

L.T.C. Semillon Sauvignon Blanc 2022, Margaret River RATING 92 DRINK 2023-2028 $42 JF

Pike & Joyce   ★★★★★

730 Mawson Road, Lenswood, SA 5240 **Region** Adelaide Hills
T (08) 8389 8102 **www.pikeandjoyce.com.au Open** 7 days 11–4 **Winemaker** Steve Baraglia, Andrew Kenny **Est.** 1998 **Dozens** 5000 **Vyds** 18.5ha
This is a partnership between the Pike family (of Clare Valley fame) and the Joyce family, related to Andrew Pike's wife, Cathy. The Joyce family have been orchardists at Lenswood for over 100 years and also have extensive operations in the Riverland. Together with Andrew

they have established a vineyard planted to sauvignon blanc (5.9ha), pinot noir (5.73ha), pinot gris (3.22ha), chardonnay (3.18ha) and semillon (0.47ha). The wines are made at the Pikes' Clare Valley winery.

🍷🍷🍷🍷🍷 **W.J.J. Reserve Pinot Noir 2022, Adelaide Hills** A mid-weighted weld of clonal rivets, bolstered with some whole-bunch briar and refined oak cladding. This is very good and a varietal beacon among the few left in the Adelaide Hills. White pepper and bunchy dill, yet not obtuse. Darker cherry carnal delights layered below. Savoury, dense and of considerable torque this drives long and it will, no doubt, age very well across the mid-term. Latent, explosive and plenty in store. Screw cap. 13.5% alc. **RATING** 94 **DRINK** 2023-2030 $65 NG

🍷🍷🍷🍷🍷 **Clonal Selection MV6 Pinot Noir 2022, Adelaide Hills** **RATING** 93 **DRINK** 2023-2030 $50 NG
Sirocco Chardonnay 2022, Adelaide Hills **RATING** 93 **DRINK** 2023-2030 $32 NG ✪
Clonal Selection 114 Pinot Noir 2022, Adelaide Hills **RATING** 92 **DRINK** 2023-2028 $50 NG
W.J.J. Reserve Pinot Noir 2021, Adelaide Hills **RATING** 92 **DRINK** 2022-2030 $65 NG
Épice Gewürztraminer 2022, Adelaide Hills **RATING** 91 **DRINK** 2022-2024 $30 NG
Clonal Selection 777 Pinot Noir 2022, Adelaide Hills **RATING** 91 **DRINK** 2023-2026 $50 NG
Céder Riesling 2022, Adelaide Hills **RATING** 91 **DRINK** 2022-2028 $30 NG
L'optimiste Shiraz 2021, Adelaide Hills **RATING** 91 **DRINK** 2022-2026 $40 NG
Sirocco Chardonnay 2021, Adelaide Hills **RATING** 91 **DRINK** 2022-2026 $32 NG
Innesti Nebbiolo 2021, Adelaide Hills **RATING** 91 **DRINK** 2022-2027 $40 NG

Pikes
★★★★★

233 Polish Hill River Road, Sevenhill, SA 5453 **Region** Clare Valley
T (08) 8843 4370 **www**.pikeswines.com.au **Open** 7 days 10–4 **Winemaker** Steve Baraglia, Andrew Kenny **Viticulturist** Andrew Pike **Est.** 1984 **Dozens** 50 000 **Vyds** 130ha

Pikes is a family affair, established in the 1980s by Andrew, Neil and Cathy Pike with support from their parents Merle and Edgar. A generation on, Neil Pike has retired after 35 years as chief winemaker and Andrew's sons Jamie and Alister have come on board (Jamie to oversee sales and marketing, Alister to run the craft brewery that opened in '14). Riesling inevitably makes up half of all plantings; shiraz, cabernet, sangiovese, pinot grigio and tempranillo dominate the other half. Pikes' flagship wines are the Merle Riesling and EWP Shiraz, named after Merle and Edgar, and only made in exceptional vintages. Winner of the People's Choice Award in 2022 and 2023.

🍷🍷🍷🍷🍷 **The Merle Riesling 2017, Clare Valley** A mature release with loads of vim and vigour, it almost looks like a young wine! That said, calling cards of crème brûlée, honeycomb and toast are creeping in, lending complexity and detail to the zesty lime, green apple and pink grapefruit freshness. Texture is succulent, the finish zingy, clean and bright. This is complex, layered, intriguing and straight up delicious. Bravo. Screw cap. 12% alc. **RATING** 96 **DRINK** 2022-2035 $70 MB ✪
The Merle Riesling 2022, Clare Valley Complex and potent, precise and exceptional in its carriage of flavour and the detail within. It's very aromatic, redolent of fresh lime, green apple, ozone, ginger, jasmine and thyme. Flavours are similar but set within a very fresh feeling, chalky textured rapier thrust of tart lime, pink grapefruit and tangerine fruitiness, offset with very minerally, briny tang. An epic wine. Screw cap. 11.5% alc. **RATING** 95 **DRINK** 2022-2040 $55 MB

The Hill Block Cabernet 2021, Clare Valley Beautiful aromatics starring blueberry, violet floral lift, a sniff of cassis, dried rosemary and dark chocolate. Supple on the palate with lush cassis and plum fruit characters squished through a sheath of light, suede tannin and gently spiked with dried herb and black peppery spice. Flavours linger with bright, cassis fruit and more of the spice, gently. Satisfying expression, refined, restrained, but vibrant. It's very good. Screw cap. 13.5% alc. RATING 94 DRINK 2023–2035 $75 MB

The E.W.P. Shiraz 2021, Clare Valley There's a levity and freshness in this wine that seems almost an anomaly in the Clare Valley. It's elegant, refined, pure of fruit, savoury in a way and cinched with a web of silky yet puckering tannins. Plenty of aromatics too, sweet spice, clove, raspberry, brambles and turned earth in the mix. Great length and persistence of flavours too. A refined shiraz. Screw cap. 13.5% alc. RATING 94 DRINK 2023–2036 $75 MB

ŸŸŸŸŸ **Olga Emmie Riesling 2022, Clare Valley** RATING 93 DRINK 2022–2029 $27 MB ✪

Traditionale Riesling 2022, Clare Valley RATING 93 DRINK 2022–2037 $27 MB ✪

Il Premio Sangiovese 2021, Clare Valley RATING 93 DRINK 2023–2030 $75 MB

Los Companeros Shiraz Tempranillo 2020, Clare Valley RATING 92 DRINK 2022–2027 $25 MB ✪

Luccio Sangiovese 2021, Clare Valley RATING 91 DRINK 2022–2027 $25 MB ✪

Luccio Albariño 2022, Clare Valley RATING 90 DRINK 2022–2024 $25 MB ✪

Homage Cabernet Malbec 2021, Clare Valley RATING 90 DRINK 2023–2028 $28 MB

The Dogwalk Cabernets 2020, Clare Valley RATING 90 DRINK 2022–2028 $25 MB ✪

Pindarie ★★★★

946 Rosedale Road, Gomersal, SA 5352 **Region** Barossa Valley
T (08) 8524 9019 **www.**pindarie.com.au **Open** 7 days 11–5 **Winemaker** Peter Leske
Viticulturist Wendy Allan **Est.** 2005 **Vyds** 36ha
Owners Tony Brooks and Wendy Allan met at Roseworthy College in 1985. Tony was the 6th generation of farmers in SA and WA, and was studying agriculture; NZ-born Wendy was studying viticulture. On graduation Tony worked overseas managing sheep feedlots; Wendy worked for the next 12 years with Penfolds, working her way up to become a senior viticulturist. She also found time to study viticulture in California, Israel, Italy, Germany, France, Portugal, Spain and Chile, working vintages and assessing vineyards for wine projects.

ŸŸŸŸŸ **Western Ridge Shiraz 2021, Barossa Valley** Deep crimson with notes of blackberry, cassis and plum on a bed of baking spices, licorice, olive tapenade, dark chocolate and earth. Toothsome and sinewy with an array of ripe black berry fruits, tight sandy tannins and an energetic line holding its alcohol well and providing great drinking from a strong vintage. Screw cap. 15% alc. RATING 92 DRINK 2023–2028 $30 DB ✪

Schoff's Hill Cabernet Sauvignon 2021, Barossa Valley Deep crimson with characters of blackberry, blackcurrants and black cherries underscored by hints of baking spices, licorice, drying grass, dried herbs, turned earth and lighter tones of capsicum and tomato leaf. Mouth-filling with a crème de cassis-like palate presence, tight chalky tannins and pleasing acid drive. Finishes black fruited and rich. Screw cap. 14% alc. RATING 91 DRINK 2023–2028 $38 DB

Small Block Montepulciano 2021, Barossa Valley Bright crimson in the glass with a purple edge. Characters of ripe blood plum, black cherries and boysenberry with hints of purple flowers, earth, spice, liquored fruits and a reductive, struck flint note. Bright acidity pushes the lush fruit along and chalky tannin provides ample grip as the wine fades off in a mist of macerated black fruits and spice. Screw cap. 14% alc. RATING 90 DRINK 2023–2028 $32 DB

Pine Drive Vineyards ★★★★

PO Box 1138, Nuriootpa, SA 5355 **Region** Barossa Valley
T 0404 029 412 www.pinedrivevineyards.com **Open** Not **Winemaker** Joanne Irvine
Viticulturist Matthew Grayson **Est.** 1962 **Dozens** 100 **Vyds** 8.5ha
Pine Drive Vineyards is a fledgling wine label established by Matthew Grayson and Bernadette
Stewart, a Queenslander and a Canadian, who met in Qatar and whose mutual love of wine
saw them relocate to the Barossa Valley, purchasing a property in between the northern
subregions of Moppa and Ebenezer. Their 8.5ha of shiraz vines, some planted in 1964, lie on
the famous rolling Moppa sand dunes that Max Schubert was fond of when he crafted the
early vintages of Grange Hermitage. This is a young winery and one to watch.

🍷🍷🍷🍷 **The Pine Drive Shiraz 2021, Barossa Valley** Deep magenta with lifted fruit
aromas of satsuma plum, chocolate, olive tapenade, brown spice, dried citrus rind
and earth. There's a real purity and intensity to the deep plum and black fruits
on the palate, rich and inviting with spice and light floral top notes. Some nice
billowing tannin architecture, too, with a rich, harmonious fruit flow and a supple,
slinky finish. Screw cap. 14.5% alc. **RATING** 94 **DRINK** 2023–2030 $32 DB ✪

🍷🍷🍷🍷 **The Stella Grenache 2021, Barossa Valley RATING** 91 **DRINK** 2023–2027
$22 DB ✪

Pipan Steel ★★★★★

583 Carrolls Road, Mudgegonga, Vic 3737 **Region** Alpine Valleys
T 0418 679 885 www.pipansteelwines.com.au **Open** By appt **Winemaker** Paula
Pipan, Daniel Balzer **Viticulturist** Radley Steel, Paula Pipan **Est.** 2008 **Dozens** 230
Vyds 0.4ha
For Paula Pipan and Radley Steel, it's been a long journey in search of a dream, of bringing
their girls up in the country on a vineyard. The vineyard would not be planted to just
any grape variety, it had to be nebbiolo. Their search for suitable land took them to the
Hunter Valley, Margaret River, Italy and ended on a hillside of decomposed granite soil in
Mudgegonga in North East Victoria in the foothills of the Australian Alps. And so Pipan
Steel was born. Under the sponsorship of Tyrrell's Wines winemaker Andrew Spinaze, Paula
was accepted into the wine degree at Charles Sturt University. Radley, a sports medicine
practitioner, moved his practice to North East Victoria and became the viticulturist. Three
nebbiolo clones were sourced from Gruppo Matura in Italy and planted in east-west oriented
rows down the hillside, which drops from 410m to 390m. Each clone is vinified separately,
and each wine spends time in large, seasoned French oak for 2 years and then another 2 years
in bottle before release.

🍷🍷🍷🍷 **IX Nebbiolo 2018, Alpine Valleys** Clone IX boasts everything you love
about nebbiolo: the lifted, dark rose petal and red-fruited fragrance, followed by
arrestingly beautiful flavours. Striking rose, hibiscus, cherry, redcurrant, pepper and
cola scents with gentle, earthy undertones. Sets the scene for a nebbiolo that flows
effortlessly, joyously, supple in tannin, balanced and fresh. Close your eyes and
enjoy its romance. Screw cap. 14% alc. **RATING** 96 **DRINK** 2023–2033 $50 JP ✪
Tesoro Nebbiolo 2018, Alpine Valleys A blend of three clones: 41/35/24%
VII/IX/X. Air please! Tesoro loves a swish or 3 of air, or a full decant. Florals
and savoury earthy notes bring this dark-fruited beauty to life. The palate remains
taut, enjoying the waiting game. Tied together tightly at this stage by clone
VII, with its well-defined astringent tannins. Allow time for the other clones to
make their presence felt. It will be worth it. Screw cap. 13.8% alc. **RATING** 95
DRINK 2023–2033 $60 JP

🍷🍷🍷🍷 **VII Nebbiolo 2018, Alpine Valleys RATING** 93 **DRINK** 2023–2033 $50 JP
X Nebbiolo 2018, Alpine Valleys RATING 93 **DRINK** 2023–2031 $50 JP

Pipers Brook Vineyard ★★★★★

1216 Pipers Brook Road, Pipers Brook, Tas 7254 **Region** Tasmania
T (03) 6382 7555 **www.kreglingerwineestates.com Open** By appt **Winemaker** Luke
Whittle **Viticulturist** Luciano Caravia **Est.** 1974 **Dozens** 70 000 **Vyds** 176.51ha
The Pipers Brook empire has almost 200ha of vineyard supporting the Ninth Island, Pipers
Brook and Kreglinger labels with the major focus, of course, being on Pipers Brook.
Fastidious viticulture and a passionate winemaking team along with immaculate packaging
and enterprising marketing create a potent and effective blend. Pipers Brook operates a cellar
door at the winery and is owned by Belgian-owned sheepskin business Kreglinger.

ΨΨΨΨΨ **Riesling 2022, Tasmania** Vivid lemon, grapefruit and crunchy red apple fruit
notes with hints of struck river stones, citrus blossom, lime juice and a suggestion
of fennel further back. There is a wicked sense of tension and velocity to this,
with a mineral acid line providing a brisk cadence, the lemon-lime fruit shooting
across the palate with impressive focus and steely resolve, finishing with a slow
fade. Yes! Screw cap. 13% alc. **RATING** 96 **DRINK** 2023-2030 $35 DB ✪
Kreglinger Brut Rosé NV, Tasmania The palest of salmon flushes in the
glass with a fine, lovely bead. Pure redcurrant and red cherry notes with hints
of raspberry pastry, crushed stone and light red blossom hints. Tight and focused
with impressive drive and fruit purity, excellent tension and a crystalline sense
of place. Superb-value drinking. Diam. 12.5% alc. **RATING** 95 $40 DB ✪
Rosé 2022, Tasmania Aromas of crunchy red cherry, redcurrant, wild strawberry
and raspberry. Some morello cherry swoops in on the palate, which shows hints
of wildflowers, mountain herbs, gentle spice, berry cream and lighter red licorice
tones. It's all framed by a shimmering scaffold of mineral-laden acidity that provides
both velocity and a perfect canvas for the pristine red fruits. A distinctly serious
pinot noir rosé. Screw cap. 13.5% alc. **RATING** 94 **DRINK** 2023-2026 $50 DB

ΨΨΨΨ **Pinot Noir 2021, Tasmania RATING** 93 **DRINK** 2023-2027 $50 DB
Chardonnay 2021, Tasmania RATING 93 **DRINK** 2023-2026 $45 DB
Kreglinger Brut NV, Tasmania RATING 92 $35 DB
Sauvignon Blanc 2022, Tasmania RATING 92 **DRINK** 2023-2025 $35 DB
Pinot Meunier 2021, Tasmania RATING 91 **DRINK** 2023-2026 $45 DB

Pirathon ★★★★

979 Light Pass Road, Vine Vale, SA 5352 **Region** Barossa Valley
T **www.**pirathon.com **Open** By appt **Winemaker** Julian Bermingham
Viticulturist Paul Aworth **Est.** 2005 **Dozens** 9000 **Vyds** 22ha
Pirathon primarily focuses on full-bodied Barossa Valley shiraz from the northwestern districts
of Greenock (contract-grown) and Maranaga (estate-grown). They also own Gaelic Cemetery
Vineyard in the Clare Valley (see separate entry). A new 480T winery was completed in '21.

ΨΨΨΨ **Gold Shiraz 2020, Barossa Valley** Deep, saturated magenta with punchy
aromas of super-ripe blackberry, blood plum and boysenberry fruits with hints of
dark chocolate, chocolate bullets, violets, liqueur cherries, clove, star anise, cedar
and vanilla bean. Rich, slurpingly opulent fruit, slightly broody and ironstone-
studded with thick, fine tannin heft and a crème de cassis and kirsch flow on the
finish. Screw cap. 14.5% alc. **RATING** 92 **DRINK** 2023-2033 $100 DB
Silver Shiraz 2020, Barossa Valley Deep magenta with aromas of black cherry,
satsuma plum and blackberry fruits underscored with hints of baking spices,
cedar, licorice, olive tapenade, clove and dark chocolate. Sinewy coal dust tannin
heft and a real kirsch-like flow on the exit. Screw cap. 14.5% alc. **RATING** 90
DRINK 2023-2028 $28 DB
Bronze Shiraz 2020, Barossa Valley Magenta-splashed crimson in the glass
with bright aromas of juicy plum, macerated summer berry fruits and hints of
baking spices, licorice, orange blossom, dark chocolate and earth. Plenty of ripe
fruit depth, bright acid drive and a tide of cassis-like fruit as the wine fades away.
Screw cap. 14.5% alc. **RATING** 90 **DRINK** 2023-2028 $28 DB

Pirie Tasmania

1a Waldhorn Drive, Rosevears, Tas 7277 **Region** Northern Tasmania
T (03) 6335 5480 **www**.tamarridge.com.au/pirie **Open** 7 days 10–5 **Winemaker** Tom
Wallace **Est.** 2004 **Vyds** 82.9ha

Pioneer of Northern Tasmanian viticulture, when Dr Andrew Pirie first established Piper's
Brook Vineyard in 1974, Northern Tasmania was considered too cold to sustain viticulture.
His success silenced the critics, and he subsequently founded Ninth Island and Pirie. While
no longer associated with the brand, the name remains in honour of its founder. Pirie is today
the premium sparkling brand of the Brown Family Wine Group, sourced from Northern
Tasmania and ably crafted by Tom Wallace.

Late Disgorged Chardonnay Pinot Noir 2011, Tasmania Aged for 10 years
on lees before disgorgement in '22. Light straw with a fine, energetic bead and
mousse. Aromas of green apple, citrus fruits and redcurrants with hints of fresh
brioche, soft spice, oyster shell, tarte Tatin, white flowers, pastry and crushed
stone. A picture of precision with racy cadence and plenty of tension gently
pulling in the expansive biscuity autolysis characters, finishing long and pure with
a lovely mineral focus. Diam. 12% alc. **RATING** 96 **DRINK** 2023-2035 $145 DB
Vintage Chardonnay Pinot Noir 2019, Tasmania A blend of 52/48%
chardonnay/pinot noir; 3 years on lees before disgorgement and dosage. Fresh
and mealy with clearly defined apple and citrus fruit and plenty of autolytic
complexity in the way of fresh brioche and pastry notes. Pure and driven with
expansive citrus, sourdough and citrus zest notes with a long, lively mineral
cadence. Diam. 12% alc. **RATING** 95 **DRINK** 2023-2030 $50 DB ✪
Traditional Method NV, Tasmania A 55/45% blend of chardonnay and pinot
noir sourced from the Tamar Valley with small amounts from earlier vintages
matured in used French oak. Second fermentation in bottle with two years on
lees prior to disgorgement. It's as fresh as a daisy, the palate long, the finish and
aftertaste nodding their heads in agreement. Diam. 12% alc. **RATING** 94 $35 JH ✪

Pirramimma

Johnston Road, McLaren Vale, SA 5171 **Region** McLaren Vale
T (08) 8323 8205 **www**.pirramimma.com.au **Open** Mon–Fri 9.30–4.30, w'ends &
public hols 11–5 **Winemaker** Geoff Johnston **Viticulturist** Andrew Johnston **Est.** 1892
Dozens 50 000 **Vyds** 91.5ha

A long-established family-owned company with outstanding vineyard resources, which it is
using to full effect. A series of intense old-vine varietals includes semillon, sauvignon blanc,
chardonnay, shiraz, grenache, cabernet sauvignon and petit verdot, all fashioned without
over-embellishment. Wines are released in several ranges: Ironstone, White Label, Stock's
Hill, Heritage and 1892, as well as the icon wines War Horse and ACJ.

French Oak Chardonnay 2021, Adelaide Hills McLaren Vale A
chardonnay for those seeking a full-flavoured salve amid a wave of linear styles.
Not that there is anything fat or overtly rich about this. Far from it! The wine is,
however, a vessel of pleasure first and foremost. The oak, while palpable with its
cedar-vanilla edge, is far better embedded than in recent years past. Loads of stone
and tropical fruit persuasions, with just enough tension for length and intrigue.
Screw cap. 13.5% alc. **RATING** 91 **DRINK** 2023-2028 $35 NG
Low Trellis Ironstone Shiraz 2019, McLaren Vale Mottled bricking edges
allude to gentle bottle age. Old-school malty aromas of Ovaltine, camphor and
sweet vanilla. Tamarind, clove, cigar and cinnamon follow. The palate is full,
cushy and avuncular, like walking into your childhood room after decades away.
A wine ready to drink, but not short of charm. Screw cap. 14.5% alc. **RATING** 90
DRINK 2023-2028 $70 NG

Pizzini

★★★★★

175 King Valley Road, Whitfield, Vic 3768 **Region** King Valley
T (03) 5729 8278 **www.pizzini.com.au Open** 7 days 10–5 **Winemaker** Joel Pizzini
Viticulturist David Morgan **Est.** 1978 **Dozens** 90 000 **Vyds** 80ha

The Pizzini family have been grapegrowers in the King Valley for over 40 years. Originally much of the then riesling, chardonnay and cabernet sauvignon grape production was sold, but since the late '90s the focus has been on winemaking, particularly from Italian varieties. Pizzini's success has enabled an increase in vineyard holdings to 80ha, with 30ha of sangiovese, 20ha of pinot grigio, 13ha of prosecco, 2.5ha each of brachetto, arneis and verduzzo, 2ha each of nebbiolo and colorino and 0.5ha of teroldego.

🍷🍷🍷🍷🍷 **Coronamento Nebbiolo 2018, King Valley** A nebbiolo of both power and grace. Aromas of rose, potpourri, anise and white pepper. They meld with cherry liqueur, cranberry, balsamic, woodsmoke, earth, cured meats and vanilla pod, to name a few of the complex ingredients on the palate. Savoury tannins are artfully integrated. It's drawn together tight and oh my, it's a beauty. Give it time. Screw cap. 13.8% alc. **RATING** 96 **DRINK** 2023-2033 $141 JP
Nebbiolo 2018, King Valley Pizzini understands nebbiolo better than many, bringing that mix of power, floral beauty, immediate drinkability and ageing potential. Fragrant in rose petal, anise, fennel seed, bracken and spice with dark cherries. Explores further, deeper, on the palate reaching into pockets of savouriness and oak, drawn firmly together with cherry-pip dry tannins and trademark acidity. Bring out the Italian cheeses and enjoy. Screw cap. 13.8% alc. **RATING** 95 **DRINK** 2023-2033 $55 JP
Nebbiolo 2017, King Valley The light hue is crystal clear, the bouquet perfumed, rose petals and spice to the fore, the palate fresh and lively without excess tannin. A top place to acquaint those who haven't previously encountered nebbiolo. Screw cap. 13.3% alc. **RATING** 95 **DRINK** 2023-2037 $55 JH
Per gli Angeli 2013, King Valley A 'vin santo' style, trebbiano is air-dried, pressed and matured for 5 years in small oak barrels. The style combines luscious sweetness with a delicate, savoury almond-led twist. Is it worth it? You bet. Maple syrup, quince paste, burnt orange, hazelnut, dried fruits, candied cumquat. Luscious, sticky, balanced and nutty with a bitter almond skin bite to close. 375ml. Screw cap. 13.2% alc. **RATING** 95 **DRINK** 2023-2025 $125 JP
Il Barone 2021, King Valley Beechworth Cabernet sauvignon/shiraz/sangiovese/nebbiolo/teroldego. Savoury, ripe and juicy and slightly chaotic with French and Italian varieties going head to head. Aromas of ripe black and red fruits, cassis and plum, chocolate, leafy dry Aussie bush, dried herbs and a touch of spice. Steady, reliable tannins steer the ship, carrying deep-concentrated flavour within a medium-bodied, nicely textural framework. Screw cap. 13.9% alc. **RATING** 94 **DRINK** 2023-2034 $55 JP
Rubacuori Sangiovese 2018, King Valley A convergence of cultures emerges in the glass, of Italian-style savouriness and rusticity with Australian sun-filled, rich and generous fruit. There's so much going on here, complexity defined in layers of black fruits, spice, licorice, autumnal undergrowth, tilled soil and leather. All are delivered confidently on cherry-pip dry, lasting tannins. Screw cap. 13.8% alc. **RATING** 94 **DRINK** 2023-2029 $141 JP

🍷🍷🍷🍷🍷 **Riesling 2022, King Valley RATING** 93 **DRINK** 2023-2030 $24 JP ✪
Forza di Ferro Sangiovese 2021, King Valley RATING 93 **DRINK** 2023-2035 $55 JP
Pinot Grigio 2022, King Valley RATING 92 **DRINK** 2023-2025 $24 JP ✪
Moscato 2022, King Valley RATING 91 **DRINK** 2023-2027 $24 JP ✪
Il Soffio Prosecco Rosé NV, King Valley RATING 91 $28 JP ✪
Rosetta Sangiovese Nebbiolo Rosé 2022, King Valley RATING 91 **DRINK** 2023-2025 $24 JP ✪
Nonna Gisella Sangiovese 2022, King Valley RATING 91 **DRINK** 2023-2027 $25 JP ✪
Prosecco NV, King Valley RATING 90 $23 JP ✪

Place of Changing Winds ★★★★★

Waterloo Flat Road, Bullengarook, Vic 3437 **Region** Macedon Ranges
T 1300 942 662 **www**.placeofchangingwinds.com.au **Open** By appt **Winemaker** Remi
Jacquemain, Robert Walters, Tom Trewin **Viticulturist** Remi Jacquemain, Robert
Walters, Tom Trewin **Est.** 2012 **Dozens** 1000 **Vyds** 3.1ha

This extraordinary high-density vineyard is slotted between Mount Macedon and Mount
Bullengarook. It's the brainchild of the committed and obsessive Robert Walters, the founder
of importer Bibendum, boasting a dazzling array of boutique wine luminaries in its portfolio.
Through his many connections and much research comes Place of Changing Winds,
known as Warekilla in the local Wurundjeri language. It's a rocky site at 500m elevation,
surrounded by forest. The whole farm covers 33ha but vines comprise just 3.1 ha, planted
to 44000 vines. A high-density site of pinot noir and chardonnay, ranging from 12500 to
33000 vines/ha: there is nothing like this in Australia, or even in Burgundy (where 10000
vines is deemed high density). No expense has been spared and the level of detail is nothing
short of extraordinary. Robert also sources syrah and marsanne from Heathcote, through a
long-term relationship with a grower at Colbinabbin. The glorious Larderdark Macedon
Ranges Chardonnay 2021 was sold out well in advance of this year's publication, its tasting
note can be found at www.winecompanion.com.au. Best New Winery 2022.

ΨΨΨΨΨ **High Density Pinot Noir 2021, Macedon Ranges** This has great clarity and
depth of colour, and an extra layer of richness, initially with the essence of dark
berries, switching to red berries minutes later, the mouthfeel supple and smooth.
Diam. 13.8% alc. **RATING** 98 **DRINK** 2023–2043 $185 JH

Between Two Mountains Pinot Noir 2021, Macedon Ranges An
exotically perfumed bouquet, partly from the inclusion of 1/3 whole bunches in
the ferment and 18 months maturation in used Stockinger barrels. The power
and length of the wine are extraordinary, and the 'drink to' date should prove
conservative. Diam. 13.7% alc. **RATING** 98 **DRINK** 2023–2040 $115 JH ✪ ♥

ΨΨΨΨΨ **Colbinabbin Vineyard Syrah 2020, Heathcote** This is a beautiful and elegant
syrah that says 'cool climate' rather than Heathcote, partly thanks to a cooler
growing season. It's heady, floral and light, full of red fruits, exotic spices and
cracked white pepper with pomegranate tang to the acidity. Only just medium
bodied, but it packs in lots of flavour and complexity with silky tannins and
superb length. Diam. 13% alc. **RATING** 96 **DRINK** 2022–2035 $49 JF ✪

PLAN B! WINES ★★★★

Freshwater Drive, Margaret River, WA 6285 (postal) **Region** Various
T 0413 759 030 **www**.planbwines.com **Open** Not **Winemaker** Vanessa Carson
Est. 2003 **Dozens** 35 000 **Vyds** 40ha

Plan B is owned and run by wine consultant Terry Chellappah 'between rocking the bass
guitar and researching bars'. He says he is better at one than the other. Plan B has been notably
successful, with significant increases in production. Winemaker Vanessa Carson has made
wine in Margaret River and Frankland Valley, as well as in Italy and France.

ΨΨΨΨΨ **The Next Hundred Years Riesling 2022, Great Southern** It's an intense and
textural expression, complex, layered and premium of feel. Quince and preserved
lemon scents with whiffs of ginger and flinty minerality. Similar to taste, with
a pink grapefruit tang washed over the lot. Acidity is ultra perky, so too a slick
of appealing, nutty savouriness. A compelling rendition of riesling. Screw cap.
12.5% alc. **RATING** 94 **DRINK** 2023–2030 $42 MB

ΨΨΨΨΨ **The King Chardonnay 2022, Margaret River RATING** 93 **DRINK** 2022–2030
$33 JF ✪

Frespañol Shiraz 2021, Frankland River RATING 93 **DRINK** 2022–2030
$25 MB ✪

OD Riesling 2022, Great Southern RATING 92 **DRINK** 2023–2025 $25 JH ✪

The Next Hundred Years Syrah 2021, Great Southern RATING 92
DRINK 2024–2035 $40 MB

Plantagenet Wines   ★★★★★

45 Albany Highway, Mount Barker, WA 6324 **Region** Mount Barker
T (08) 6243 3913 **www.**plantagenetwines.com **Open** 7 days 10.3–4.30 **Winemaker**
Mike Garland **Viticulturist** Tom Wisdom **Est.** 1968 **Dozens** 25 000 **Vyds** 21ha
Plantagenet was established by founder Tony Smith with the planting of 5 vineyards; Bouverie
in 1968, Wyjup in '71, Crystal Brook in '88, Rocky Horror in '99, and Rosetta in '01. These
vineyards remain the cornerstones of the substantial production. At the top of the tree are the
Icon wines, made only in exceptional vintages; the Wyjup Collection is the top tier produced
annually. The Pantagenet range is named after regions ruled by the Plantagenet kings in the
12th–15th centuries.

Wyjup Collection Chardonnay 2021, Mount Barker Lush, toasty and
rich. A decadent chardonnay with hallmark power and presence. Graceful glide
in texture with layers of spice, ripe fruit, judicious oak seasoning and general
chardonnay lavishness. All of this fits together superbly. It's not a classy wine,
but it has pedigree and wears its heft well, finishing fresh, tight and spicy. Lots
of perfume, lots of flavour, all so well done. Screw cap. 13% alc. **RATING** 93
DRINK 2022–2030 $70 MB
Wyjup Collection Malbec 2021, Mount Barker It ticks the boxes of malbec
expectations, with bold perfume, big flavour, soupy plush texture, velvety tannins
and a spectrum of plummy, spicy, herbal fruit in the mix. Very even, smooth and
rolling long, this feels pedigree in its way and delivers a sumptuous and seamless
experience. A premium malbec indeed. Screw cap. 14% alc. **RATING** 93
DRINK 2022–2032 $70 MB
Wyjup Collection Cabernet Sauvignon 2020, Mount Barker A
concentrated, flamboyant expression with an inky intensity of ripe blackberries,
cassis, lavender and chewy, dusty clove/oaky spice. It's a mouthful alright, palate-
staining and big. In all that, consistency and evenness, and despite the lusty wood
handling, it all sits nicely in the dense fruit character of the wine. Brassy, done
well. Screw cap. 14% alc. **RATING** 93 **DRINK** 2022–2035 $80 MB
Wyjup Collection Riesling 2022, Mount Barker A delicious and easy-
drinking riesling with acid low-key and fruitiness to the fore. Lots of ripe, green
apple juice, quince and nectarine with some faint minty elements. Decent
concentration here, albeit the wine feels gentle and missing a little energy, but a
really charming drink all up. Complexity in minerally elements and textural detail
to boot. Screw cap. 12% alc. **RATING** 92 **DRINK** 2022–2030 $45 MB
York Chardonnay 2021, Great Southern Buttery and golden, syrupy and
plush. A richer, fuller-flavoured style for enthusiasts of such, and done quite well
with balanced oak seasoning, intensity of ripe fruit, and cool acidity underlying.
Geez, it's a mouthful, but those seeking old-school, good-school chardonnay styles
will be well served here. Good length and a sense of quiet complexity, too. Kudos.
Screw cap. 13.2% alc. **RATING** 92 **DRINK** 2022–2029 $40 MB
Wyjup Collection Shiraz 2020, Mount Barker A dark, inky, brooding
shiraz lavished with ripe plum, licorice, saltbush, meat drippings and clove/
cedar wood seasoning. Scents and flavours repeat similarly, with bold aromas
followed by pronounced and distinct flavours. Soft texture, supple tannins.
The finish is a bit shorter than hoped, with espresso/coffee ground flavours a
letdown in an otherwise rich and moreish red. Screw cap. 13.5% alc. **RATING** 90
DRINK 2022–2035 $80 MB

Pt. Leo Estate   ★★★★☆

3649 Frankston-Flinders Road, Merricks, Vic 3916 **Region** Mornington Peninsula
T (03) 5989 9011 **www.**ptleoestate.com.au **Open** 7 days 11–5 **Winemaker** Tod Dexter
(Consultant) **Est.** 2006 **Dozens** 600 **Vyds** 20ha
Pt. Leo Estate is owned by one of Australia's wealthiest families, headed by octogenarian
John Gandel and wife Pauline. They have donated countless millions of dollars to charity,
and 30 years ago they purchased 20ha of land on the wild side of the Mornington Peninsula,

building several houses for the exclusive use of family. Over the ensuing years they added parcels of land, created a lake at the entrance of the property, and in '06 planted a 20ha vineyard. It is now also the site of a 16ha sculpture park featuring works by international and Australian artists. A cellar door and restaurant opened in October '17 and the fine dining restaurant, Laura, opened in March '18. A third space, the Wine Terrace, has since been added. Ainslie Lubbock (ex Attica and The Royal Mail Hotel) oversees service alongside head sommelier Amy Oliver (ex Cutler + Co, Rockpool) and culinary director Joseph Espuga.

Rosé 2022, Mornington Peninsula Admiring the garden art at Pt. Leo Estate with a glass of this refreshing rosé is a rather lovely way to spend an afternoon. Made from pinot noir so it has crisp acidity, a flutter of red fruits with a dab of spice. A slip of texture, too. Screw cap. 13% alc. **RATING** 92 **DRINK** 2023–2024 $39 JF

Pinot Noir 2020, Mornington Peninsula Mid-ruby hue; lots of flavour from dark cherries and oak spice to bresaola and dried herbs. The palate unfurls with supple tannins and refreshing acidity. Screw cap. 13.5% alc. **RATING** 92 **DRINK** 2023–2029 $49 JF

Chardonnay 2020, Mornington Peninsula Plush ripe stone fruit and citrus, lovely creamy lees and cedary oak in the mix, but all as one and curtailed by tangy acidity and decent length. Screw cap. 13.5% alc. **RATING** 92 **DRINK** 2023–2028 $48 JF

Shiraz 2019, Mornington Peninsula Dark as the night sky with a shot of purple. Dense and very rich with an abundance of fruit, oak and tannins. An attractive plush palate, ripe and expansive. You'd have this with a juicy steak. Screw cap. 14% alc. **RATING** 92 **DRINK** 2023–2030 $50 JF

Ponting ★★★★☆

169 Douglas Gully Road, Blewitt Spings SA 5171 (postal) **Region** McLaren Vale
T 0439 479 758 **www**.pontingwines.com.au **Open** Not **Winemaker** Ben Riggs
Est. 2020 **Dozens** 9500

The Ponting label falls under the aegis of Three Kings Wine Merchants, a collaboration between winemaker Ben Riggs and the former Australian cricket captain, Ricky Ponting. A tensile chardonnay and a pinot noir, hewn of cooler-climate Tasmanian fruit as an homage to the cricketing Taswegian's involvement, are exceptions to the South Australian sourcing pervasive across the lineup: an Adelaide Hills Sauvignon Blanc, a McLaren Vale Shiraz, a Langhorne Creek Cabernet and at the pointy end, the Ponting 366 cuvée.

366 Shiraz Cabernet Sauvignon 2019, McLaren Vale Coonawarra With a bottle this heavy, one has a good idea of what to expect: power, bombast and polish. Yet it is all pulled off with considerable aplomb. The oak, judiciously toasted, imparts a whiff of cedar and a rivet of tannin behind which crème de cassis, dried sage, bay leaf, green olive and graphite are welded to a long finish by admirable grape tannins. The overall impression is savoury, nicely stylised and highly ageable. A classy wine. Screw cap. 14.5% alc. **RATING** 95 **DRINK** 2024–2035 $117 NG

127 Shiraz 2020, Barossa Valley RATING 92 **DRINK** 2023–2028 $38 DB
Mowbray Boy Pinot Noir 2021, Tasmania RATING 91 **DRINK** 2023–2027 $38 DB

Pooles Rock ★★★★★

576 De Beyers Road, Pokolbin, NSW 2320 **Region** Hunter Valley
T (02) 4993 3688 **www**.poolesrock.com.au **Open** 7 days 10–5 **Winemaker** Xanthe Hatcher **Est.** 1988 **Vyds** 14.6ha

Pooles Rock was founded, together with the Cockfighter's Ghost brand, in '88 by the late David Clarke OAM, and acquired by the Agnew family in '11 (who also own the neighbouring Audrey Wilkinson). Pooles Rock sources fruit from a number of wine regions, although its essential operations are based in the lower Hunter. Over time, the emphasis has become one of site-specific iterations across 3 tiers: Single Vineyard (proprietary Hunter fruit), Premiere (externally sourced fruit from as far afield as South Australia and Tasmania) and Museum Releases (aged wines, incorporating all sources). The style is one of optimal ripeness, plump palate weight and precise structural latticework.

🍷🍷🍷🍷🍷 **Cellar Release Post Office Shiraz 2014, Hunter Valley** Sourced from the 100yo estate Post Office plantings. 2014 has always been regarded as a great shiraz vintage in the Hunter, this wine also adding its praises to the skies. Beautiful colour, a limpid crimson; what the bouquet says, the palate does: the full monty of red, purple and black flavours, the fruit profile still bright and clear, the length impeccable. Screw cap. 14% alc. RATING 97 DRINK 2023–2034 $180 JH
Cellar Release Post Office Shiraz 2011, Hunter Valley Oh my, this is magnificently luscious and improbably young. Further years/decades will introduce new and different aromas and flavours. Take a winner's ticket at Tattslotto, and methodically enjoy it year on year, judging not for quality, but for pleasure. Screw cap. 13.2% alc. RATING 97 DRINK 2023–2041 $180 JH

🍷🍷🍷🍷🍷 **Single Barrel Chardonnay 2022, Hunter Valley** This was borne of the realisation that, during the classification of all the barrels, 1 puncheon (different each year) would stand out as the most complete. This vintage was tough, but the wine emerged unscathed, with length and finesse to its flavour kit. Screw cap. 12.5% alc. RATING 96 DRINK 2024–2029 $65 JH ✪
Premiere Chardonnay 2022, Hunter Valley Whole-bunch pressed, directly transferred to French puncheons (40% new); a barrel selection was made with deliberate mlf; then matured 9 months with fortnightly bâtonnage. As complex as they come, but has retained focus and freshness. Screw cap. 12.5% alc. RATING 95 DRINK 2023–2028 $45 JH ✪
Soldier Settler Semillon 2022, Hunter Valley From the Soldier Settler vineyard in the Broke Fordwich subregion, which (obliquely) has some of the vines planted in 1918 by the soldiers from World War I. This has an already-apparent lick of the honey its Premiere sibling may develop with 5 years' maturation in bottle. Screw cap. 12.5% alc. RATING 95 DRINK 2023–2038 $45 JH ✪
Cellar Release Semillon 2009, Hunter Valley This wine won an impressive array of gold medals and trophies in '09 and '10. What was Pooles Rock's flagship release has prospered since then, gleaming green–gold, now with honey and buttered toast flavours and crackling acidity. It still has its best in front of it. Screw cap. 10.7% alc. RATING 95 DRINK 2023–2025 $75 JH
Premiere Semillon 2022, Hunter Valley Both this and its Soldier Settler sibling come from the Soldier Settler vineyard, albeit Premiere includes some parcels from the Pokolbin subregion. The labels are similar and there's only a $5 price difference between them. But there's honey absent from this wine. Screw cap. 12.5% alc. RATING 94 DRINK 2023–2033 $40 JH ✪

🍷🍷🍷🍷🍷 **Centenary Block Shiraz 2021, Hunter Valley** RATING 93 DRINK 2026–2035 $120 NG
Post Office Shiraz 2021, Hunter Valley RATING 91 DRINK 2022–2030 $45 NG

Pooley Wines   ★★★★★

Butcher's Hill Vineyard, 1431 Richmond Road, Richmond, Tas 7025 **Region** Tasmania **T** (03) 6260 2895 **www.pooleywines.com.au Open** 7 days 10–5 **Winemaker** Anna Pooley, Justin Bubb **Viticulturist** Steven Ferguson **Est.** 1985 **Dozens** 9000 **Vyds** 18ha Pooley Wines is a glowing exemplar of a boutique Tasmanian family estate. Three generations of the family have been involved in its development, with the little hands of the 4th generation now starting to get involved. The heart of production has historically been the glorious Campania vineyard of Cooinda Vale (after which the brand was originally named), planted to 12ha of chardonnay, pinot noir, riesling and pinot grigio, with new plantings currently underway. In '03, the family planted pinot noir and pinot grigio (and more recently chardonnay, riesling and syrah, bringing plantings to 6ha) at Belmont vineyard near Richmond, renamed Butcher's Hill. A cellar door was established in the heritage-listed sandstone barn and coach house of the distinguished 1830s convict-built Georgian home, standing in pride of place on the heritage property. Wine quality has risen to dramatic effect, no small feat while doubling production, since the return to Tasmania of Anna Pooley and husband Justin Bubb to establish the winemaking arm of the estate in '12. Pooley's riesling, pinot noir and chardonnay now rank among Tasmania's finest. Conversion to organic viticulture is currently underway, with a goal of achieving certification by 2026.

Jack Denis Pooley Pinot Noir 2021, Tasmania Deep ruby with aromas of wild strawberries and cherries layered with fine spice and hints of sous bois, leaf litter, mushroom broth, almond blossom, polished leather, earth and light game notes. All restraint and grace, the flow and tension across the palate in check, tannins gentle and fine with a swell of umami before the wine sails away, all fruit purity and complex, savoury characters. Very impressive. Screw cap. 13.2% alc. **RATING** 97 **DRINK** 2023-2035 $175 DB

Butcher's Hill Riesling 2022, Tasmania Pristine fruit and unwavering precision equals a beautiful wine. Green apple and lime fruits, wildflowers, crushed stone and grapefruit pith with liminal glimpses of lemon curd. It sports a wicked tubular palate shape of pure citrus fruits and rides on mineral-laden rails of acidity, all focus, velocity and detail. Tremendous length of flavour and sustain here. Screw cap. 13.2% alc. **RATING** 96 **DRINK** 2023-2035 $70 DB ✪

Cooinda Vale Riesling 2022, Tasmania Pristine lime, green apple and lemon fruit notes with underlying hints of crème fraîche, citrus blossom, grapefruit pith and crushed stone. Savoury and pure with a crystalline acid presence and a distinct umami note on the finish as the lime and lemon fruits sail off into the distance. Fantastic stuff. Screw cap. 12.2% alc. **RATING** 96 **DRINK** 2023-2035 $70 DB ✪

Cooinda Vale Rosé Pinot Noir 2021, Tasmania Mid-crimson with aromas of black and red cherries, redcurrant and macerated strawberries layered with spice, amaro, pressed flowers, shiitake broth and lighter notes of leaf litter and roasting game. Beautifully poised on the palate, energetic yet with a sense of calm and grace. Just a lovely composition, finishing spicy, complex and red-fruited with plenty of sustain and savoury flow. Screw cap. 13.3% alc. **RATING** 96 **DRINK** 2023-2033 $75 DB ✪

Butcher's Hill Oronsay Pinot Noir 2021, Tasmania Butchers Hill shows great elegance and purity with a savoury line across the palate. Cherry and a touch of redcurrant with dried citrus rind, fine spice, amaro herbs, light game, tobacco, pastis and gentle purple florals with chalky tannin and a minerally line. Nothing out of place and a sense of umami on the stony exit. Screw cap. 13% alc. **RATING** 96 **DRINK** 2023-2038 $125 DB

Cooinda Vale Oronsay Pinot Noir 2021, Tasmania A beautifully composed wine with elegant tones of dark cherry, wild strawberry, kirsch, cedar, sous bois, amaro herbs, earth, shiitake broth and light game and dried meat notes. Restrained and nicely poised with sultry spiced dark fruits, gentle powdery tannin and an umami-rich acid line. Very comfortable in its own skin and gorgeous drinking. Screw cap. 13.2% alc. **RATING** 96 **DRINK** 2023-2040 $125 DB

Cooinda Vale Chardonnay 2021, Tasmania A picture of purity, length and detail with pristine stone and citrus fruits sheathed in gentle spice with notes of white flowers, toasted nuts, almond paste, grapefruit pith, oyster shell and lemon zest. There is a shimmering clarity to the palate, long and true with just a hint of oatmeal and a long finish. A captivating, graceful wine with a pitch-perfect composition. Screw cap. 13.1% alc. **RATING** 96 **DRINK** 2023-2030 $75 DB ✪

Butcher's Hill Pinot Noir 2021, Tasmania Aromas of wild strawberry and dark cherry fruits and hints of fine spice, white truffle, dried orange rind, purple flowers, sous bois and softly spoken oak. There's a neat transposition of aromas over to the palate. Finely honed and showing plenty of detail, compact, powdery tannins and a lovely swelling tide of red fruit, spice and undergrowth on the sustained finish. Screw cap. 13.5% alc. **RATING** 96 **DRINK** 2023-2033 $75 DB ✪

Butcher's Hill Chardonnay 2021, Tasmania White peach, nectarine and lemon with hints of clotted cream, river stone, vanillin oak, oatmeal, nougat, lemon curd and almond blossom. Good mid-palate weight, too, swelling with creamy notes and roasted hazelnuts before sailing off on rails of fine, lacy acidity leaving a wake of soft spice, stone fruits and meal. Long of finish and beautiful drinking. Screw cap. 13.4% alc. RATING 95 DRINK 2023–2030 $65 DB

Riesling 2021, Tasmania Barely detectable RS has been deliberately retained here, balancing the acidity that provides finely structured Granny Smith apple and lime juice flavours that unfold in waves through to the lingering finish and aftertaste. Screw cap. 12.8% alc. RATING 95 DRINK 2023–2031 $42 JH ✪

J.R.D. Syrah 2021, Tasmania I've decided I'm all-in on Tasmanian syrah. Here, blueberry, boysenberry and dark plum fruit tones are backed up by hints of exotic spice, dried citrus rind, black pepper, violets, tobacco, charcuterie, cocoa powder and stone. Superfine and powdery milk chocolate tannins, lovely tension, an interplay between acid and fruit and a long savoury exit that shows restraint and grace. Screw cap. 13.7% alc. RATING 95 DRINK 2023–2040 $120 DB

Butcher's Hill Cane Cut Riesling 2022, Tasmania Light straw with notes of candied lime, poached pear, apricot nectar, dried honey, lemon curd, citrus blossom, light marmalade and stone. It weighs in at 143g/L of RS, but that wicked acidity tempers the wine and it shows no cloying, racing clean as a whistle across the palate leaving a wake of candied citrus fruits, blossom and sweetened lime juice. Screw cap. 9% alc. RATING 94 DRINK 2023–2033 $45 DB ♥

🍷🍷🍷🍷🍷 **Pinot Grigio 2022, Tasmania** RATING 92 DRINK 2023–2027 $45 DB

Poonawatta   ★★★★★

1227 Eden Valley Road, Flaxman Valley, SA 5235 **Region** Eden Valley
T 0448 031 880 **www.poonawatta.com.au Open** Wed–Mon 11–4.30
Winemaker Andrew Holt, Christa Deans, Harry Mantzarapis **Viticulturist** Andrew Holt **Est.** 1880 **Dozens** 1800 **Vyds** 4ha

The Poonawatta story is complex, stemming from 0.8ha of shiraz planted in 1880. When Andrew Holt's parents purchased the Poonawatta property, the vineyard had suffered decades of neglect and the slow process of restoration began. While that was underway, the strongest canes available from the winter pruning of the block were slowly and progressively dug into the stony soil, establishing the Cuttings Block over 7 years, and the yield is even lower than that of the 1880 Block. The riesling is produced from a separate vineyard planted by the Holts in the '70s. Grenache was planted in '19.

🍷🍷🍷🍷🍷 **The Eden Riesling 2022, Eden Valley** Pale straw in the glass and smelling crisp and pure with juicy limes, orange blossom, crushed quartz and light marzipan notes. Swift and true, it sets a brisk pace across the palate thanks to sizzling acidity and great clarity, finishing with and a blast of freshly squeezed limes and green apple. Screw cap. 12% alc. RATING 93 DRINK 2023–2028 $35 DB ✪

Trois Shiraz 2020, Eden Valley There's a lovely depth of fruit here with super-ripe blackberry, dark plum and boysenberry notes on a bed of fine spice, purple floral tones, turned earth with lighter tones of sage and mountain herbs. Super-tight tannin and plenty of structure and latent power on display as the wine fades with oodles of spicy black fruits and gentle cedary nuance. Screw cap. 14% alc. RATING 93 DRINK 2023–2030 $48 DB

The Cuttings Shiraz 2019, Eden Valley Deep crimson in the glass with notes of rich blackberry pastille, dark plum and cassis on a bed of compact spice, dark chocolate, licorice and a fair lick of cedary oak. Sits in medium-bodied territory with a bright line and compact, drippy granitic tannins that lead to a mouth-puckering finish. Screw cap. 14.5% alc. RATING 91 DRINK 2023–2030 $60 DB

Poppelvej

185 Almond Grove Road, Willunga South, SA 5172 **Region** McLaren Vale
T 0431 432 570 **www.**poppelvej.com **Open** By appt **Winemaker** Uffe Deichmann
Est. 2016 **Dozens** 3500

Poppelvej is the name of the street where Uffe Deichmann grew up. It is a benevolent confluence of Danish winemaker with an inquisitive mind, Adelaide Hills and McLaren Vale fruit and minimalist handling. The culture here is one of early picking for freshness, zero additions (other than minimal sulphur dioxide for psychological reassurance) and little messing about. The wines are neither fined nor filtered, firmly in the natural camp and for those accustomed to conventional winemaking, potentially challenging. Yet the modus here is one of textural detail and imminent drinkability.

Sort Sol Cabernet Franc 2021, McLaren Vale This is delicious. Mid-weighted, highly aromatic and almost balletic, such is its energy and trajectory of flavours. Licorice root, blackcurrant, tomato leaf, mint and chilli. While there is an obvious carbonic effect manifest in purple pastille and floral notes, there are admirable tannins, too. A nourishing experience of considerable intrigue. Diam. 12.5% alc. **RATING** 92 **DRINK** 2023-2027 $32 NG

Ceased to Exist Syrah 2020, McLaren Vale This is a richly flavoured and textural experience. Brooding dark fruits, woodsy and dank and brimming with porcini and Bovril, expand across a back palate bulwarked by oak tannins and a spurt of balsamic freshness. The finish is firm and a little drying, yet the wine's concentration and intensity handle it well. Diam. 14% alc. **RATING** 92 **DRINK** 2022-2028 $40 NG

Ego Friendly Arneis 2022, McLaren Vale A gingery, lemon squash sort of affair with the jittery cadence and shimmering energy of a skin-inflected, minimalist approach. This is a lovely wine; please, drink in huge draughts with a broad smile. Diam. 13% alc. **RATING** 91 **DRINK** 2023-2025 $34 NG

Dead Ohio Sky Mouvèdre Rosé 2022, McLaren Vale A dazzling interpretation of mourvèdre as a pallid, onion-skinned rosé. An intensity belying the light-ish weight. The effortless flow from attack to finish is embellished with a natural palate of bamboo reed, tangerine chutney and quince paste, rather than anything forced. It makes for compelling, mellifluous drinking. Nothing complex, mind you. But deliciousness in spades. Diam. 12.5% alc. **RATING** 91 **DRINK** 2023-2024 $30 NG

Dancing in the Doldrums Pinot Meunier 2022, Adelaide Hills Light bodied, edgy and brimming with red-fruit allusions, crushed clove, cardamom, tamarind and other scents that transport one to the souk. This expands nicely across a jittery scale of whole-bunch tannins and a spark of volatility, as is the wont here. Delicious wine, best on the cooler side. Diam. 12% alc. **RATING** 91 **DRINK** 2023-2024 $34 NG

Rookie Grenache 2022, McLaren Vale Sits somewhere between rosato and a light red, best drunk on the cooler side. Wild fermented and foot stomped. Frisky, edgy and desirable with riffs on cherry amaro, bergamot, fecund strawberry and mint. Gentle tannic compression and a whirl of volatility for verve and lift. Diam. 12% alc. **RATING** 90 **DRINK** 2023-2024 $34 NG

Port Phillip Estate

263 Red Hill Road, Red Hill, Vic 3937 **Region** Mornington Peninsula
T (03) 5989 4444 **www.**portphillipestate.com.au **Open** 7 days 11–5 **Winemaker** Tim Perrin **Viticulturist** Stuart Marshall **Est.** 1987 **Dozens** 7000 **Vyds** 21.04ha

Port Phillip Estate's wines are made at sibling winery Kooyong, but they have their own personality. If anything, the impressive cellar door – featuring both brands, restaurant and luxury accommodation – at Port Phillip Estate makes it the show pony. While single-site chardonnay and pinot noir take centre stage, lately shiraz and more experimental styles, by conservative Mornington Peninsula standards, have impressed. Tim Perrin, who spent 7 years at Oakridge in the Yarra Valley, took over as chief winemaker at the start of '23 and is charged with crafting both Kooyong and Port Phillip Estate wines.

ϘϘϘϘϘ **Red Hill Chardonnay 2021, Mornington Peninsula** Rhetorically speaking, could any more flint and funk go into this wine? It's so good. Savoury, tangy and alive with a light tannic pull on the finish. In between, citrus, white peach and lots of warming spices with mouth-watering acidity. There's a lot going on with this, great now and will garner more complexity in time. Screw cap. 13.5% alc. **RATING** 95 **DRINK** 2023-2031 $36 JF ✪
Morillon Single Block Chardonnay 2021, Mornington Peninsula Gosh, this is looking mighty good. It's the seductive sulphides, not too much, just the flinty, smoky, minerally aspect; embarrassingly, salivating. Tight but not mean as there's enough fruit to carry all the elements, including really creamy lees, refreshing acidity and the well-integrated oak. One of the best to date. Screw cap. 13.5% alc. **RATING** 95 **DRINK** 2023-2031 $55 JF
Tuerong Shiraz 2021, Mornington Peninsula At first, the reduction clipped the palate and I went yeah, nah. Waited for it to unfurl in the glass and went yeah, yeah. Fantastic dark purple colour with lots of pepper, aniseed and baking spices infusing the black plums. It feels cool and cooling, medium bodied with lovely fine emery-board tannins and ultra-refreshing. Oh yeah. Screw cap. 13% alc. **RATING** 95 **DRINK** 2023-2031 $40 JF ✪
Balnarring Chardonnay 2021, Mornington Peninsula This and its Red Hill sibling are more or less made the same, so the sense of place comes to the fore. More generosity with the fruit profile here with baked apple, Meyer lemon and ripe white stone fruit, the acidity softer and more giving. The palate fleshes out with cedary oak and spices, lipsmacking sulphides and citrusy acidity. Immediately approachable. Screw cap. 13.5% alc. **RATING** 94 **DRINK** 2023-2029 $36 JF ✪

ϘϘϘϘϙ **Salasso Rosé 2022, Mornington Peninsula** **RATING** 93 **DRINK** 2022-2024 $27 JF ✪
Quartier Pinot Noir 2022, Mornington Peninsula **RATING** 91 **DRINK** 2023-2026 $32 JF
Balnarring Pinot Noir 2021, Mornington Peninsula **RATING** 91 **DRINK** 2023-2028 $40 JF
Red Hill Pinot Noir 2021, Mornington Peninsula **RATING** 90 **DRINK** 2022-2027 $40 JF
Morillon Single Block Pinot Noir 2021, Mornington Peninsula **RATING** 90 **DRINK** 2023-2029 $60 JF

Portsea Estate   ★★★★☆

183 Hotham Road, Portsea, Vic 3944 **Region** Mornington Peninsula
T 0439 029 646 **www.**portseaestate.com **Open** By appt **Winemaker** Matt Lugge, Will Ross **Viticulturist** Matt Lugge **Est.** 2000 **Dozens** 3500 **Vyds** 4ha
Portsea Estate belongs to noted filmmaker Warwick Ross, whose highly rated '13 film *Red Obsession* took an inside look at China's fascination for the greatest wines of Bordeaux. The first 7 vintages were made at Paringa Estate by Lindsay McCall, before an onsite winery was built at Portsea Estate. More recently the business acquired 10ha in Main Ridge, planted to pinot noir, pinot gris and chardonnay. It also runs a native plant nursery on the property, with 1500 olive trees for olive oil production and honey from 20 hives. Matt Lugge succeeded Tim Elphick as winemaker in '21; he is assisted by Warwick's son Will, who is also partner and general manager.

ϘϘϘϘϘ **Brut Vintage Méthode Traditionnelle 2018, Mornington Peninsula** 70/30% chardonnay/pinot noir; 45 months on lees, disgorged Jul '22 with 4g/L dosage. Now, this is terrific and delicious. A lovely straw hue with heady aromas of toasted brioche, lemon tart and frangipane, fresh citrus flavours and a touch of apple. This has a fine bead and plenty of lively acidity, complexity and excellent length. Bravo. Diam. 12.5% alc. **RATING** 95 **DRINK** 2023-2026 $52 JF

ŶŶŶŶŶ Main Ridge Block Pinot Noir 2022, Mornington Peninsula RATING 93
DRINK 2023–2031 $52 JF
Main Ridge Block Reserve Chardonnay 2022, Mornington Peninsula
RATING 93 DRINK 2023–2030 $52 JF
Portsea Block Pinot Noir 2022, Mornington Peninsula RATING 93
DRINK 2023–2029 $52 JF
Portsea Block Chardonnay 2022, Mornington Peninsula RATING 92
DRINK 2023–2030 $52 JF
Main Ridge Block Chardonnay 2022, Mornington Peninsula RATING 90
DRINK 2023–2028 $52 JF

Precious Little Wine

Peninsula Providore, 2250 Bull Creek Rd, Tooperang, SA 5255 **Region** South Australia
T 0417 212 514 **www**.preciouslittlewine.com.au **Open** First w'end of month 11–4
Winemaker Marty O' Flaherty **Viticulturist** Adam Smith **Est.** 2016 **Dozens** 600
Precious Little is the side project of mates Marty O'Flaherty and Adam Smith. Ex-chef Marty
is winemaker for Atkins Family and Fox Gordon Wines, having cut his winemaking teeth
at Zilzie in Victoria before working across South Australia and as far afield as Piedmont.
Adam, Clare Valley born and bred, has 20 years of experience as an independent viticultural
consultant and a grower liaison officer, now enjoying the challenge of seeking out exciting
parcels for Marty to transform into small-batch wines. Current sourcing is from growers in
the Barossa Valley, Langhorne Creek, Adelaide Hills and Clare Valley. Wines can be tasted
at the nearby Peninsula Providore.

ŶŶŶŶŶ Marananga Nero d'Avola 2021, Barossa Valley Crimson in the glass with
notes of super-ripe plum, blueberry and boysenberry cut with fine spice, purple
florals, sarsaparilla, earth and softly spoken oak. Plenty to like here with a pure
fruit profile, tight, powdery tannin and a brisk acid cadence. Screw cap. 14% alc.
RATING 92 DRINK 2023–2028 $30 DB ✪

Pressing Matters

665 Middle Tea Tree Road, Tea Tree, Tas 7017 **Region** Southern Tasmania
T 0474 380 109 **www**.pressingmatters.com.au **Open** Thurs–Sun 10–4 or by appt
Winemaker Samantha Connew **Viticulturist** Mark Hoey **Est.** 2002 **Dozens** 3000
Vyds 12ha
Greg Melick is a busy bloke – senior counsel, wine show judge and 52 years as Major General
in the Australian Defence Force, but lucky for us, he managed to establish Pressing Matters
in '06, just outside the beautiful township of Richmond in the Coal River Valley. Pressing
Matters' 7ha of estate vineyards are an equal split between riesling and pinot noir and the
acquisition of the Morningside vineyard in '19 has expanded the range. These days, rockstar
Tassie winemaker Samantha Connew is onboard and the wines, already some of the most
highly awarded in Tasmania, continue to go from strength to strength.

ŶŶŶŶŶ Cuvée C Pinot Noir 2021, Tasmania Coal River Valley pinot noir. Plush and
inviting plum and black cherry fruits with hints of hanging game meats, exotic
spices, leaf litter, shiitake mushrooms, shoyu and Chinese barbecue shop. Lovely
fruit presence and fruit/acid tension here, with a finish that trails off persistently
with gamey, spiced cherry notes and a large serving of class. Screw cap. 13.8% alc.
RATING 95 DRINK 2023–2030 $150 DB
Pinot Noir 2021, Tasmania Coal River Valley pinot noir. Dark red in the glass
with aromas of black cherry and dark plum dotted with spices, Chinese roast
duck, mushroom broth, rhubarb, leaf litter, dried herbs and soy. Lovely ripe cherry
fruits on the palate with a nice sapid line of minerally acidity hitting all the right
notes of fruit tension, gamey complexity and effortless drinkability. Screw cap.
13.8% alc. RATING 94 DRINK 2023–2028 $75 DB

ŶŶŶŶŶ Morningside Vineyard Chardonnay 2021, Tasmania RATING 90
DRINK 2023–2026 $45 DB

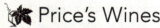 ## Price's Wines

14 Gurney Road, Rose Park, SA 5067 (postal) **Region** McLaren Vale
T 0438 808 874 **www.priceswine.com Open** Not **Winemaker** Matt Koch, Sam Price
Viticulturist Nick Price, Troy Eliker **Est.** 2012 **Dozens** 1200 **Vyds** 16ha

Price's Wines is a story of a man with a hankering to return to the land. Nick Price grew up on a farm on South Australia's Eyre Peninsula. A decade ago he returned – to McLaren Vale, anyway, where he purchased a site on red, ferrous clay over a limestone substrata. Fruit is sourced from the Price's Wines estate and from McLaren Vale vineyards farther afield, to craft a suite of single-vineyard offerings as a sort of negotiant-type dynamic. The wines are robust and distinctly old-school, despite the contemporary livery.

Block 5 Cabernet Sauvignon 2022, McLaren Vale Varietal fealty ticked: currant, bay leaf and olive. Structural firmament, intact, with nothing aggressive or shrill. Finish, of solid length and poise. A rich wine, plenty regional and assertively varietal. The aura is savoury and appetising. Screw cap. 14.5% alc. **RATING** 91 **DRINK** 2022-2030 $45 NG

Block 3 Reserve Shiraz 2021, McLaren Vale An aspirational sort of wine. Some purple pastilles and florals. Feels excessive now, but should gel. While there is little inherently wrong, it is smothered with oak at this stage and the acidity is shrill. Screw cap. 14.7% alc. **RATING** 90 **DRINK** 2022-2033 $60 NG

Primo Estate

McMurtrie Road, McLaren Vale, SA 5171 **Region** McLaren Vale
T (08) 8323 6800 **www.primoestate.com.au Open** 7 days 11–4 **Winemaker** Joe Grilli
Viticulturist Joe Grilli **Est.** 1979 **Dozens** 10000 **Vyds** 16ha

Joe Grilli has always produced innovative and excellent wines. The biennial release of the Joseph Sparkling Red (in its tall Italian glass bottle) is eagerly awaited, the wine immediately selling out. The vineyard is planted to cabernet sauvignon, shiraz, nebbiolo, sangiovese, nero d'Avola and pinot grigio. Also highly regarded are the extra virgin olive oils.

Joseph The Fronti NV, McLaren Vale I always dig this mellifluous delve into fortified's smooth, torrefied patina of walnut husk, honeycomb, ginger crystals, raisins and polished mahogany. The meld of spirit and fruit, impeccable, drinking like a quasi-PX from Jerez. Screw cap. 16.5% alc. **RATING** 97 $33 NG ✪

Joseph Nebbiolo 2020, McLaren Vale Here is a wine that improves each vintage. A coarse punctation of mocha tannins at present, but there is plenty to like. Floral, with darker fruit allusions accented with thyme, mint, polished leather and soot. Exceptional weight, sap and mineral crunch and oak tannins across the finish. Time will settle things into a smoother gear, yet this could rise to one of the country's best. Screw cap. 13% alc. **RATING** 94 **DRINK** 2024-2035 $90 NG

Joseph Moda Cabernet Sauvignon Merlot 2020, McLaren Vale
RATING 93 **DRINK** 2024-2040 $90 NG

Joseph Sparkling Red NV, McLaren Vale RATING 92 $90 NG

Zamberlan Cabernet Sauvignon Sangiovese 2021, McLaren Vale
RATING 90 **DRINK** 2022-2030 $40 NG

Principia ★★★★★

139 Main Creek Road, Red Hill, Vic 3937 **Region** Mornington Peninsula
T (03) 5931 0010 **www.principiawines.com.au Open** By appt **Winemaker** Darrin Gaffy **Viticulturist** Darrin Gaffy **Est.** 1995 **Dozens** 750 **Vyds** 3.5ha

Darrin Gaffy's guiding philosophy for Principia is minimal interference, thus the vines (3ha of pinot noir and 0.5ha of chardonnay) are not irrigated and yields are restricted to 3.75t/ha or less. All wine movements are by gravity or by gas pressure, which in turn means there is no filtration, and both primary and secondary fermentation are by wild yeast. 'Principia' comes from the word 'beginnings' in Latin.

♟♟♟♟♟ **Altior Pinot Noir 2021, Mornington Peninsula** No Altior was made in '20, so welcome back. At 40% new French oak, it is pared back from previous vintages and all the better for it. A mass of dark cherries and plums, licorice-infused rhubarb, cedary spices and more besides. Full bodied and finely tuned yet rich and replete with supple tannins and a long thread of acidity tying everything up neatly. Screw cap. 14% alc. **RATING** 96 **DRINK** 2023-2035 $70 JF ✪

Kindred Hill Pinot Noir 2021, Mornington Peninsula Beautiful definition across the Principia pinots, this is the most savoury yet still excellent fruit in the mix. Rhubarb, dark cherries, blood orange and chinotto with heady aromas of damp forest floor and baking spices. Fuller bodied with shapely, velvety tannins and fine acidity all add to the wine's terrific length. Best of all, this is so delicious. Classy wine. Screw cap. 14.2% alc. **RATING** 96 **DRINK** 2023-2033 $70 JF ✪

Chardonnay 2021, Mornington Peninsula Yep. This tastes good. Really good. It's a chorus of chardonnay flavours all lemon and grapefruit, zest and a whiff of sexy sulphides before the palate teases with more. Superfine and long with fine acidity, the right amount of lees and a flutter of spicy oak. Satisfaction guaranteed. Screw cap. 14% alc. **RATING** 96 **DRINK** 2022-2031 $50 JF ✪

Pinot Noir 2021, Mornington Peninsula It's packed with flavour yet not a big wine as the vibrant acidity takes centre stage. The chorus is all spiced red cherries, charred radicchio, amaro and blood orange, so it's mouth-watering and refreshing at the same time. Just medium bodied, tannins are silky fine and the acidity drives this to a resounding finish. Moreish to the last drop. Screw cap. 13.7% alc. **RATING** 95 **DRINK** 2022-2031 $50 JF ✪

Printhie Wines ★★★★★

208 Nancarrow Lane, Nashdale, NSW 2800 **Region** Orange
T (02) 6366 8422 **www**.printhiewines.com.au **Open** Fri–Sat 10–5, Sun–Thurs 11–4
Winemaker Drew Tuckwell **Viticulturist** Dave Swift **Est.** 1996 **Dozens** 20 000
Vyds 33ha

Owned by the Swift family. Brothers Edward and David took over from their parents Jim and Ruth Swift in the early '00s. Together the family have clocked up almost 20 years of commercial wine production and the vineyards are now reaching a good level of maturity at 25 years. The 33ha of estate vineyards are planted between 630–1070m elevation, including Orange's highest vineyard at 1070m. Winemaker Drew Tuckwell has been at Printhie since '07 and has over 20 years of winemaking experience in Australia and Europe.

♟♟♟♟♟ **Swift Vintage Brut 2015, Orange** Chardonnay/pinot noir; 2.25g/L dosage, tiraged Sep '15 and disgorged Aug '22. Yellow peach, juicy mango, lemon butter and sourdough. Ripe nectarines, Pink Lady apples, whipped cream and lemon sorbet. Fruit reigns supreme with extended lees ageing adding biscuit and cashew notes. A triumph. Cork. 12% alc. **RATING** 96 **DRINK** 2022-2030 $65 SW ✪

Swift Cuvée Brut #10 NV, Orange Chardonnay/pinot noir; 4.5g/L dosage, 75 months on lees, disgorged Feb '22. Turned apples, glacé pears, Anzac biscuits and warmed lemon curd. Puckering and ever-present chardonnay acidity with white nectarine and a blush crab apple mid-palate. The lower dosage sits well with the fruit presence and biscuity yeast notes. Delightful drinking now but will age gracefully. Cork. 12% alc. **RATING** 96 $50 SW ✪

Swift Cuvée Brut #11 NV, Orange Chardonnay/pinot noir; 5g/L dosage, 68 months on lees, disgorged August '22. Aromas of alpine strawberries, white peach and casaba melon. Lemon pith, chalkboard dust and crushed limestone. Honeysuckle, pear nectar and shortbread. The dosage sits a little on the outskirts but with enough fruit weight for balance. Cork. 12% alc. **RATING** 95 $50 SW ✪

Super-Duper Chardonnay 2019, Orange Finger limes, crushed limestone, lemon curd and sheep's whey. Equally a wine that delights and allures. Energy that leaps from the glass and complexities that have you peering deeper. The top-quality oak has settled and succulent acidity rolls on and on. Screw cap. 12.8% alc. **RATING** 95 **DRINK** 2023-2032 $85 SW

Swift Vintage Brut 2014, Orange Chardonnay/pinot noir; 6.0g/L dosage, tiraged Aug '14 and disgorged Dec '21. Braeburn apples, Corella pear, musk, strawberries and yellow peach skin. A wave of lemon curd, warmed butter, roasted almond praline, vanilla, quince and hints of yellow florals. A generous palate with the dosage adding to the ripe fruit weight. Drinking very well now. Cork. 12% alc. RATING 94 DRINK 2022–2028 $65 SW

ŶŶŶŶŶ Topography Chardonnay 2022, Orange RATING 93 DRINK 2023–2028 $38 SW
Super-Duper Syrah 2019, Orange RATING 93 DRINK 2022–2030 $85 SW
Swift Rosé Brut #09 NV, Orange RATING 92 $50 SW
Topography Pinot Gris 2022, Orange RATING 92 DRINK 2023–2026 $30 SW ✪
Snow Line Three Pinots Rosé 2022, Orange RATING 92 DRINK 2022–2024 $30 SW ✪
Mountain Range Pinot Gris 2022, Orange RATING 92 DRINK 2023–2025 $24 SW ✪
Topography Shiraz 2021, Orange RATING 92 DRINK 2022–2028 $38 SW
Mountain Range Sauvignon Blanc 2022, Orange RATING 91 DRINK 2023–2025 $24 SW ✪
Mountain Range Chardonnay 2022, Orange RATING 90 DRINK 2023–2028 $24 SW ✪
Topography Cabernet Sauvignon 2021, Orange RATING 90 DRINK 2022–2030 $38 SW
Mountain Range Cabernet Sauvignon 2021, Orange RATING 90 DRINK 2022–2030 $24 SW ✪

Project Wine   ★★★☆

83 Pioneer Road, Angas Plains, SA 5255 (postal) **Region** South Australia
T (08) 8537 0600 **www**.projectwine.com.au **Open** Not **Winemaker** Peter Pollard
Est. 2001 **Dozens** 155 000
Originally designed as a contract winemaking facility, Project Wine has developed a sales and distribution arm that has rapidly developed markets both domestic and overseas. Located in Langhorne Creek, it sources fruit from most key SA wine regions, including McLaren Vale, Barossa Valley and Adelaide Hills. The diversity of grape sourcing allows the winery to produce a wide range of products under the Drop Zone, Tail Spin, Pioneer Road, Parson's Paddock and Bird's Eye View labels.

ŶŶŶŶŶ Drop Zone Reserve Malbec 2021, Fleurieu Grown on 12yo vines and matured in a combination of seasoned American and French oak barrels for 9 months. The fruit has largely shrugged off its oak and presents as fresh and eager to please. That's a good start. Clove, black cherry, violet and redcurrant characters run through to a gently savoury, toasty conclusion. Screw cap. 14.5% alc. RATING 90 DRINK 2023–2028 $32 CM

Protero   ★★★★

60 Olivers Road, McLaren Vale SA 5171 **Region** Adelaide Hills
T (08) 8323 8000 **www**.pannell.com.au **Open** By appt **Winemaker** Stephen Pannell
Viticulturist Stephen Pannell **Est.** 1999 **Dozens** 5000 **Vyds** 15.2ha
Stephen and Fiona Pannell first discovered the nebbiolo growing outside Gumeracha in the northern Adelaide Hills in '04 – it had been planted by Rose and Frank Baldasso in '99. The vineyard, on a western-facing slope, is home to 5 clones of nebbiolo that Stephen has worked with since '05. Surrounded by native bush, twice in 20 years the vineyard has been surrounded by fire and twice it has survived (including a week after the Pannells bought the property in Dec '19). They have since removed chardonnay, pinot noir, merlot and viognier from the vineyard and planted barbera, dolcetto, gewürztraminer, pinot gris and riesling. Nebbiolo remains a passion.

ΨΨΨΨΨ **Gumeracha Nebbiolo 2021, Adelaide Hills** A wine crafted in a beautiful fashion, espousing fruit while forfeiting none of the structural spindle and vitality that makes nebbiolo compact, savoury and so delicious. Satsuma and damson plum, red cherry and dried thyme segue to a burst of rosewater across the mid-palate before the pull of sinew and clatter of tannic bone, the signature of variety and style. Screw cap. 14% alc. **RATING** 93 **DRINK** 2022–2028 $45 NG

Gumeracha Barbera 2020, Adelaide Hills A delicious rendition of barbera. Mid-weighted and punchy, with a core of blackberry, sweet dark cherry, anise and violet cascading across a long, jittery finish. Barbera's vibrancy is on full display, with an auspicious touch of oak toning and directing all the energy. Very good drinking. Screw cap. 14.5% alc. **RATING** 93 **DRINK** 2022–2026 $38 NG

Pinots Grigio Bianco Nero 2022, Adelaide Hills 82/10/8% pinot grigio/pinot blanc/pinot nero. This is delicious. A wash of freshly crushed golden apple, nashi pear granita and lemon balm, the fruit sweetness gaining intensity across a rivulet of chewiness and a skein of succulent freshness. Screw cap. 13% alc. **RATING** 92 **DRINK** 2022–2024 $28 NG ✪

Aromatico 2022, Adelaide Hills Given the canny blend of gewürztraminer, riesling and sauvignon blanc, this is a mellifluous drift of Turkish delight, grape spice and citrus verbena tucked within a gentle carapace of talc, skinsy pickup and soft salty freshness. A drink-now sort of proposition. Delicious. Screw cap. 13% alc. **RATING** 90 **DRINK** 2022–2024 $28 NG

Provenance Wines

100 Lower Paper Mills Road, Fyansford, Vic 3221 **Region** Geelong
T (03) 5222 3422 **www**.provenancewines.com.au **Open** 7 days 11–5 summer, Thurs–Mon 11–5 winter **Winemaker** Scott Ireland, Sam Vogel **Viticulturist** Blake Tahapehi **Est.** 1996 **Dozens** 7000 **Vyds** 20ha

When Scott Ireland and partner Jen Lilburn established Provenance Wines, they knew it wouldn't be easy starting a winery with limited capital and no fixed abode. The one thing the business had was Scott's 20+ years' experience operating contract wine services in the Hunter Valley, Barossa, Coonawarra, Mudgee, Clare Valley, Yarra Valley and Tasmania. He says he met so many dedicated small winemakers that he was hooked for life. In '04 Scott moved to Austins & Co as winemaker while continuing to grow the Provenance business, developing key relationships with growers in Geelong, the ultra-cool Macedon, Ballarat and Henty. In '16 Sam Vogel, Scott's long-term assistant winemaker, stepped up to join the business as a partner and they took a long-term lease of 25% of the Fyansford Paper Mill, refurbishing the heritage-listed 1870s local bluestone buildings.

ΨΨΨΨΨ **Shiraz 2021, Geelong** An exquisitely beautiful wine. Complex by nature, svelte by design, seductive in its own way. Musk, black pepper, blueberry and ripe plum flavours roll across the palate in an even wave, inspiring pleasure at every step. You have to admire the oak here – it's so perfectly judged, it's the perfect seasoning. But then everything about this wine is deft, in the best of ways. Screw cap. 14% alc. **RATING** 96 **DRINK** 2023–2032 $36 CM ✪

Chardonnay 2021, Geelong What a beautiful chardonnay. The combination of grapefruit and nougat flavours here is delicious, to say the least, and the white peach and chalk notes through the finish only build on that. It's also both lengthy and elegant; it's a top-notch wine. Screw cap. 13% alc. **RATING** 95 **DRINK** 2023–2029 $55 CM

Chardonnay 2021, Henty Crushed fennel, cracked wheat, grapefruit, pure peach and nectarine knitted together with nougat and smoked cedar wood. What a combination of flavours. There's texture here, too, along with spice notes and some crackle to the pop of fruit. It's also a little bit brooding, but for sheer quality this wine has it all going on. Screw cap. 12.8% alc. **RATING** 95 **DRINK** 2024–2031 $55 CM

Pinot Gris 2022, Henty This is well refined and crafted but it's also punchy, and in that context it's a beauty. Pear, honeysuckle, sherbet and red apple characters put on a textural, generous, delicious show, both energetic and lingering. Yes please. Screw cap. 12.8% alc. **RATING** 94 **DRINK** 2023-2026 **$33** CM ✪

Golden Plains Chardonnay 2021, Victoria Fruit from Ballarat, Henty and Geelong. This is pretty swish. Nougat, lime, yellow peach and pineapple flavours mingle with honeysuckle and custard powder-like notes. It's fresh, flavoursome and direct at once, boasting quite serious length through the finish. Screw cap. 12.8% alc. **RATING** 94 **DRINK** 2024-2030 **$35** CM ✪

Golden Plains Pinot Noir 2021, Victoria Fruit from Ballarat, Geelong and Henty. This is a delight for the senses. Sweet cherry and plum flavours mingle with sweet/woodsy spice notes, all very well in itself, but all this is then elevated by a sweet-sour, undergrowth-like aspect that really draws you in – and keeps you there. Screw cap. 13.2% alc. **RATING** 94 **DRINK** 2023-2028 **$35** CM ✪

Pinot Noir 2021, Henty This is a more substantial wine than you would expect of a pinot noir from Henty. Not a bad thing, just an observation. It's built on macerated cherry and rhubarb flavours with brighter strawberry-like notes and generous splashes of fragrant herbs and floral notes. There's a lot going on, in other words, all of it impressive. It will be fascinating to watch this wine develop. Screw cap. 13% alc. **RATING** 94 **DRINK** 2024-2032 **$55** CM

Chardonnay 2021, Ballarat There's a strength to this wine both in the mouthfeel and in the flavour. Green pineapple, leatherwood honey, melon and ripe peach flavours come folded with vanilla and nougat. It's full in body but the acid line is assertive. It will be a joy to watch this wine grow over the coming years. Screw cap. 12.8% alc. **RATING** 94 **DRINK** 2024-2032 **$55** CM

Pinot Noir 2021, Macedon Ranges This is a particularly autumnal pinot noir. It's all undergrowth and earth, tobacco leaf and complex cherry, with roasted nut and fragrant herb characters in the mix too. All these flavours are rolling out logically and well, already, but it has all the traits to go to another level again with an extra handful of years under its belt. Screw cap. 12.8% alc. **RATING** 94 **DRINK** 2024-2034 **$55** CM

Pinot Noir 2021, Ballarat A fragrant wine with cherry, plum and nasturtium notes blending gradually into cedar and woodsmoke. It's sinewy and long, with twiggy spice notes pulling through the cranberried juiciness of the palate. This has cellar-worthiness written all over it, thanks to its length, tannin and overall savoury feel. Screw cap. 13.5% alc. **RATING** 94 **DRINK** 2025-2033 **$55** CM

♟♟♟♟♟ **Pinot Noir 2021, Geelong RATING** 93 **DRINK** 2025-3031 **$55** CM
Riesling 2022, Henty RATING 92 **DRINK** 2023-2029 **$33** CM

Punch   ★★★★☆

10 Scott Street, St Andrews, Vic 3761 **Region** Yarra Valley
T 0424 074 234 **www**.punched.com.au **Open** W'ends 12–5 **Winemaker** James Lance
Viticulturist James Lance **Est.** 2004 **Dozens** 1800 **Vyds** 3.45ha
In the wake of Graeme Rathbone taking over the brand (but not the real estate) of Diamond Valley, James and wife Claire leased the vineyard from James' parents David and Catherine Lance, including the 0.25ha block of close-planted pinot noir. In all, Punch has 2.25ha of pinot noir, 0.8ha of chardonnay and 0.4ha of cabernet sauvignon.

♟♟♟♟♟ **Lance's Vineyard Pinot Noir 2020, Yarra Valley** Extremely low yields in '20 make this the only Punch red for the vintage. A medium bright garnet. Gorgeous aromatics. Ripe raspberries and cherries intermingle with Asian spices and potpourri. Layered with sinewy yet fine tannins, there's real persistence on the palate and it's the sort of wine that you'd be pleased to have kept some 8–10 years from now. Screw cap. 13% alc. **RATING** 97 **DRINK** 2022-2030 **$59** PR ✪

♟♟♟♟♟ **Lance's Vineyard Chardonnay 2020, Yarra Valley RATING** 92 **DRINK** 2022-2028 **$46** PR

Punt Road

10 St Huberts Road, Coldstream, Vic 3770 **Region** Yarra Valley
T (03) 9739 0666 **www.**puntroadwines.com.au **Open** 7 days 10–5 **Winemaker** Tim
Shand, Jarrod Johnston, Travis Bush **Viticulturist** Barry Potts **Est.** 1987 **Dozens** 20 000
Vyds 60ha

Punt Road is owned by the Napoleone family, 3rd-generation fruit growers in the Yarra
Valley. Their vineyard in Coldstream is one of the most historic sites in Victoria, first planted
to vines by Swiss immigrant Hubert De Castella in 1860. The Napoleone Vineyard was
established on the property in 1987. Tim Shand, chief winemaker since '14, established a
reputation for the consistent quality of all the Punt Road wines. Jarrod Johnston takes over the
winemaking reins from the '23 vintage. The 2 main ranges are Punt Road and Airlie Bank,
plus a small production of single-vineyard 'Block' wines, only available at the cellar door and
made only in the best vintages.

Napoleone Vineyard Block 3 Cabernet Sauvignon 2021, Yarra Valley
A deep crimson red. Gorgeous aromatics of red and black fruits, violets, cedar
and a dusting of black cocoa powder. This is simultaneously concentrated,
elegant and textured and while already a pleasure to drink, those perfectly
judged, fine-grained tannins will ensure a long life ahead. Screw cap. 13.4% alc.
RATING 97 **DRINK** 2022–2035 $95 PR ✪ ♥

Napoleone Vineyard Block 4 Chardonnay 2021, Yarra Valley A very
bright green gold. Pure fruited from the first whiff with its mix of stone fruits,
pink grapefruit and white flowers, while the oak is barely perceptible. Equally
harmonious on the palate, this has real drive and persistence all within a very
fine, elegant framework. Screw cap. 12.5% alc. **RATING** 96 **DRINK** 2023–2028
$50 PR ✪

**Napoleone Vineyard Block 11 Cabernet Sauvignon 2021, Yarra
Valley** A medium deep and bright ruby red. Darker fruited than the '20, you'll
find scents of cassis, black plums, lavender and cedar on the suave and nicely
concentrated bouquet. Layered, concentrated and elegant, the tannins are so
creamy and plush that they almost melt in the mouth. Screw cap. 13.4% alc.
RATING 96 **DRINK** 2023–2030 $95 PR

JMN Block 18 Gamay 2022, Yarra Valley Bright ruby red. With its aromas
of crushed raspberries, red cherries, pink peppercorns and mountain herbs, this
is another very good gamay from the team at Punt Road. Really crunchy fruited
and energetic on the palate, this ready-to-drink and moreish wine finishes long
and succulent. Screw cap. 13% alc. **RATING** 95 **DRINK** 2022–2027 $32 PR ✪

Napoleone Vineyard Block 1 Pinot Noir 2021, Yarra Valley Bright ruby
crimson. A touch closed when I tasted this in Jan '23, this didn't need a lot of air
to reveal aromas of red cherries, redcurrants and rose petals – the fruit has totally
swallowed up the wood. The compact palate is very well balanced, too. Screw cap.
12.5% alc. **RATING** 94 **DRINK** 2022–2031 $50 PR

Airlie Bank Garden Red 2022, Yarra Valley RATING 93 **DRINK** 2023–2026
$24 PR ✪

Airlie Bank Pinot Noir 2022, Yarra Valley RATING 91 **DRINK** 2022–2027
$24 PR ✪

Napoleone Vineyard Pinot Noir 2022, Yarra Valley RATING 91
DRINK 2023–2026 $32 PR

Napoleone Vineyard Chardonnay 2022, Yarra Valley RATING 91
DRINK 2023–2025 $28 PR ✪

Napoleone Vineyard Block 13 Malbec 2021, Yarra Valley RATING 91
DRINK 2023–2028 $50 PR

Airlie Bank Gris Fermented On Skins 2022, Yarra Valley RATING 90
DRINK 2022–2024 $24 PR ✪

Purple Hands Wines

24 Vine Vale Road, Tanunda, SA 5352 **Region** Barossa Valley
T 0401 988 185 **www.purplehandswines.com.au Open** 7 days 10–5 **Winemaker** Craig
Stansborough **Viticulturist** Craig Stansborough, Jordan Zerk **Est.** 2006 **Dozens** 5000
Vyds 14ha
The finely honed, contemporary Barossa wines of Purple Hands are borne out of a
partnership between Mark Slade and winemaker Craig Stansborough. Their home estate,
the Stansborough vineyard, lies in the far south of the Barossa Valley and is planted with
shiraz, montepulciano and aglianico. They also source grenache from the Zerk vineyard and
cabernet sauvignon from the Woodlands vineyard, both near Lyndoch. The range includes
pinot blanc, pinot gris and several red blends. Purple Hands captures the purity and elegance
that is possible when the raw materials are in good hands.

Planta Circa Ancestor Vine Cabernet Sauvignon 2021, Barossa Valley
Not a peep of herbaceousness in this wine, which is, in my humble opinion, what
makes Barossa Valley cabernet sauvignon so wonderful. Deep, super-ripe black
fruits, baking spices, cedary oak nuance, vanilla, licorice, grippy granitic tannins,
bright acidity and a lovely flow of blackberry and cassis. Very impressive. Diam.
14.5% alc. **RATING** 95 **DRINK** 2023–2035 $80 DB

Grenache 2021, Barossa Valley There is no doubt that Barossa grenache is on
a roll at the moment, and here is a great example at an excellent price. Showing
impressive fruit purity and spicy whole bunch lift, it sits at the lighter end of
medium bodied. Sashays across the palate with a great cadence leaving a plume of
juicy plum, raspberry, gingerbread and spice in its wake, finishing with a savoury
swish. It's a ripper. Screw cap. 14% alc. **RATING** 94 **DRINK** 2023–2028 $30 DB ✪

Mataro Grenache Shiraz 2021, Barossa Valley RATING 93 **DRINK** 2023–2027
$30 DB ✪
Planta Circa Ancestor Vine Shiraz 2021, Barossa Valley RATING 93
DRINK 2023–2028 $80 DB
After Five Wine Co. Aglianico 2021, Barossa Valley RATING 92
DRINK 2023–2027 $35 DB
After Five Wine Co. Montepulciano 2021, Barossa Valley RATING 92
DRINK 2023–2028 $35 DB
After Five Wine Co. Primitivo 2021, Barossa Valley RATING 92
DRINK 2023–2027 $35 DB
Shiraz 2021, Barossa Valley RATING 92 **DRINK** 2023–2027 $35 DB
Colours of the South Pinot Blanc 2022, Barossa Valley RATING 91
DRINK 2023–2025 $28 DB ✪
After Five Wine Co. Single Vineyard Serata 2021, Barossa Valley
RATING 91 **DRINK** 2023–2027 $45 DB
Colours of the South Pinot Blanc 2021, Barossa Valley RATING 91
DRINK 2023–2024 $28 DB ✪
Colours of the South Mourvèdre 2021, Barossa Valley RATING 91
DRINK 2023–2027 $28 DB ✪
After Five Wine Co. Single Vineyard Shiraz 2021, Barossa Valley
RATING 91 **DRINK** 2023–2028 $45 DB
After Five Wine Co Shiraz Primitivo 2021, Barossa Valley RATING 90
DRINK 2023–2026 $35 DB
After Five Wine Co. Montepulciano 2020, Barossa Valley RATING 90
DRINK 2023–2026 $35 DB

Pyren Vineyard

Glenlofty-Warrenmang Road, Warrenmang, Vic 3478 (postal) **Region** Pyrenees
T (03) 5467 2352 **www.pyrenvineyard.com Open** Not **Winemaker** Leighton Joy
Viticulturist Graeme Miles **Est.** 1999 **Dozens** 10 000 **Vyds** 28.3ha

Established by the Joy family, Pyren is run by owner/winemaker Leighton Joy. The 28ha property on the slopes of the Warrenmang Valley, near Moonambel, is planted to shiraz, cabernet sauvignon, sauvignon blanc, cabernet franc, gamay, malbec and petit verdot.

Reserve Syrah 2021, Pyrenees An exquisite wine. It takes woodsy spice notes and delivers them overflowing with fresh, ripe, juicy berries, blue and black and red. It throws pepper into flowers, mezcal into cedar, and pops licorice sticks into the berried flow of it all. This is both a fastidious wine and a joyous one. It's worth celebrating. Diam. 14% alc. **RATING** 97 **DRINK** 2023-2033 $60 CM ✪ ♥

Soliloquy Of Chaos Shiraz 2020, Pyrenees Ultra-seductive and yet simultaneously complex. This is a wonderful wine. The freshness of boysenberry, cherries and plums then cedar wood and twiggy spice aplenty. It's seamless, the tannin structure is intricate, it has the mettle to age and the spread to run. This is why we love wine. Diam. 14% alc. **RATING** 96 **DRINK** 2025-2037 $50 CM ✪

Reserve Cabernet 2021, Pyrenees There's both a sweetness and a fullness to the blue and red-berried fruit here, which plays beautifully with the smokiness of the oak and the leafy/twiggy tobacco-like characters that come as part of the varietal territory. This is complex, stern and easygoing all at once; it's both characterful and enchanting, courtesy of the sheer array of flavours. Diam. 14% alc. **RATING** 95 **DRINK** 2023-2033 $60 CM

Earthscape Shiraz 2021, Pyrenees There's an elegance to this release. It's a shiraz that feels modern. It's driven by cherry-plum flavours with smoked cedar and mint top notes, but it gets meatier, juicier and more complex, with roasted nut and woodsy spice notes in the mix. It's in a good place now, but it's on its way to somewhere better. The tannin is a particular highlight. Screw cap. 14% alc. **RATING** 94 **DRINK** 2025-2035 $35 CM ✪

Union 2021, Pyrenees 67/21/10/2% cabernet franc/petit verdot/cabernet sauvignon/shiraz. It's certainly been made to age, but the juicy, balanced, mouth-watering quality here is quite striking. This feels as though it's been painted in watercolours and, given that the fruit flavours are ripe, that's a very good thing. A fine, filigreed, berry-and-spice wine. Diam. 13% alc. **RATING** 94 **DRINK** 2025-2035 $60 CM

Earthscape Franc 2021, Pyrenees **RATING** 93 **DRINK** 2023-2030 $40 CM
Earthscape Malbec 2021, Pyrenees **RATING** 92 **DRINK** 2023-2027 $40 CM

Quarisa Wines ★★★☆

743 Slopes Road, Tharbogang, NSW 2680 (postal) **Region** South Australia **T** (02) 6963 6222 **www**.quarisa.com.au **Open** Not **Winemaker** John Quarisa **Est.** 2005 John Quarisa has had a distinguished winemaking career spanning over 20 years, working for some of Australia's largest wineries including McWilliam's, Casella and Nugan Estate. John and Josephine Quarisa have set up a very successful family business using grapes from various parts of NSW and SA, made in leased space. Production has risen in leaps and bounds, doubtless sustained by the exceptional value for money provided by the wines.

Treasures Cabernet Sauvignon 2020, Coonawarra Blackcurrant, smoked tobacco and bay leaf characters put on a well-flavoured show. Mint and lemon fresh notes provide the highlights. The tannin here is slightly more drying than it needs to be, but the fruit continues to romp juicily through. Screw cap. 14.5% alc. **RATING** 90 **DRINK** 2023-2028 $20 CM ✪

Quartz Hill ★★★★

65 Lillicur West Road, Lamplough, Vic 3352 **Region** Pyrenees **T** (03) 5465 3670 **www**.quartzhillwines.com.au **Open** By appt **Winemaker** Darrin Gaffy, Owen Latta, Peter McLean, Alex McLean **Viticulturist** Shane Mead **Est.** 1995 **Dozens** 600 **Vyds** 4.15ha

Quartz Hill was established in 1995, with Shane and Michelle Mead relocating from Melbourne to run their vineyard in '99. After growing grapes for other wine labels for many years, the first Quartz Hill wine came onto the market in '09. Winemaking is a family effort, with brother Darrin Gaffy from Principia on the Mornington Peninsula (see separate entry) as winemaker. Grenache and touriga have been added to the shiraz, viognier and mencia plantings. The cellar door and winery opened in '21.

ΨΨΨΨΨ **Viognier 2020, Pyrenees** If viognier is on your radar then this is a good one to jump at. It offers a body of stone fruit–driven flavour, with associated floral characters, but it's also zippy with citrus. In other words, it's fresh, juicy and flavoursome at once. There's a subtle chalkiness to the finish too – another positive. Screw cap. 13.5% alc. RATING 92 DRINK 2022-2026 $25 CM ✪
Viognier 2018, Pyrenees Heavy (French) oak characters, but there's enough fruit weight to support it. Indeed there's a lot of wine here. Stone fruit, coconut, cedar, pine and sweet spice flavours combine to pretty dramatic effect. It all flows, it all feels fresh. Screw cap. 13.5% alc. RATING 92 DRINK 2023-2027 $32 CM
Syrah 2019, Pyrenees A spicy, biodynamically grown shiraz with plenty of fruit in support. White and black pepper, twig-like notes, boysenberry and sweet plum flavours swing persuasively through the palate, before clove-infused tannin pulls through the finish. It still feels super-fresh and it has many years ahead of it. This is a neat, compact, savoury-styled expression. Screw cap. 13.8% alc. RATING 91 DRINK 2023-2032 $42 CM

Quattro Mano   ★★★☆

PO Box 189, Hahndorf, SA 5245 **Region** Barossa Valley
T 0430 647 470 **www**.quattromano.com.au **Open** By appt **Winemaker** Anthony Carapetis, Christopher Taylor, Philippe Morin **Est.** 2006 **Dozens** 2500 **Vyds** 3.8ha
Anthony Carapetis, Philippe Morin and Chris Taylor have collective experience of over 50 years working in various facets of the wine industry, Philippe as a leading sommelier for over 25 years, and presently as founder and director of French Oak Cooperage, Anthony and Chris as winemakers. They produce an eclectic range of wines, tempranillo the cornerstone. It's an impressive, albeit small, business.

ΨΨΨΨΨ **La Reto Tempranillo 2021, Barossa Valley** Bright crimson with dark cherry and boysenberry fruit notes along with hints of baking spices, violets, cola, earth and licorice. There is a nicely spiced plum flow of fruit on the palate, bright acidity and a medium-length finish flush with spice and berry fruits. Screw cap. 14% alc. RATING 91 DRINK 2023-2028 $28 DB ✪

Quealy Winemakers   ★★★★★

62 Bittern-Dromana Road, Balnarring, Vic 3926 **Region** Mornington Peninsula
T (03) 5983 2483 **www**.quealy.com.au **Open** 7 days 9–5 **Winemaker** Kathleen Quealy, Tom McCarthy **Viticulturist** Lucas Blanck, Kevin McCarthy **Est.** 1982 **Dozens** 8000 **Vyds** 8ha
Kathleen Quealy and Kevin McCarthy were among the early waves of winemakers on the Mornington Peninsula. They challenged the status quo – most publicly by introducing Mornington Peninsula pinot gris/grigio (with great success). Behind this was improvement and diversification in site selection, plus viticulture and winemaking techniques that allowed their business to grow significantly. The estate plantings are 2ha each of pinot noir, pinot gris and friulano, as well as smaller plots of riesling, chardonnay, malvasia istriana and moscato giallo. Their leased vineyards are established on what Kathleen and Kevin consider to be premium sites for pinot gris and pinot noir. These are now single-vineyard wines: Musk Creek, Campbell & Christine and the newer Tussie Mussie vineyard. Son Tom stepped up as head winemaker in '19. Lucas Blanck manages the certified organic estate vineyards; the leased vineyards are moving towards 100% organic management.

ΨΨΨΨΨ **Tussie Mussie Pinot Gris 2022, Mornington Peninsula** Intensely flavoured with stone fruit, poached apple and pears drizzled with lemon honey and powdered ginger. Luscious on the palate but not weighty, it's all about texture with creaminess throughout. The flavours linger long and the finish, too. Screw cap. 13.6% alc. **RATING** 95 **DRINK** 2023–2027 $35 JF ✪

Feri Maris Single Block Pinot Grigio 2022, Mornington Peninsula A finely tuned, racy yet lightly textural offering. Sliced pears and honey, lemon juice and ginger spice, crunchy nashi pear and lively acidity throughout. Screw cap. 12.8% alc. **RATING** 95 **DRINK** 2023–2028 $40 JF ✪

Musk Creek Pinot Noir 2021, Mornington Peninsula Always intriguing, often complex with a lot going on from the distinct twiggy, whole-bunch aromas and flavours adding sapidity to cherry plum with hints of mint and wafts of damp earth. There's rhubarb, blood orange, woodsy spices and some cedary/charry oak. Lots of layers and detail with lithe tannins and mouth-watering acidity to close. Screw cap. 12.6% alc. **RATING** 95 **DRINK** 2023–2031 $48 JF ✪

Seventeen Rows Pinot Noir 2021, Mornington Peninsula The most structured offering in the Quealy stable – the tannins are textural with seemingly more fruit weight. Hints of rhubarb, dark cherries, mocha and dried herbs plus cedar oak. The palate doesn't quite flesh out, even if it is medium bodied, as the acidity is keeping everything reined in, bar the slightly bitter, charred radicchio character on the finish, which adds to the mouthfeel and pleasure of drinking. Screw cap. 12.6% alc. **RATING** 95 **DRINK** 2024–2033 $75 JF

Lina Lool Amber 2021, Mornington Peninsula When malvasia, moscato giallo, friulano, riesling and ribolla gialla get together for a party lasting 146 days on skins, Lina Lool arrives. I love this wine. Swooning aromas and flavours of lychee, musk, pink grapefruit with peach-fuzz tannins all chewy and textural. It's a savoury, dry wine with lemon salt, preserved lemon flavours and Japanese pickled ginger. Diam. 12.6% alc. **RATING** 95 **DRINK** 2022–2026 $35 JF ✪

Turbul Friulano 2021, Mornington Peninsula What a difference a vintage makes. 2021 has been kind to friulano and the result is lovely, textural, chewy tannins from extended skin-contact and talc-like acidity perfectly in sync with the array of flavours. There's baked quince, grilled almonds and ginger, lemon rind and celery. It's savoury, complex and fabulous. Diam. 13% alc. **RATING** 95 **DRINK** 2022–2028 $40 JF ✪

Musk Creek Pinot Gris 2022, Mornington Peninsula Has the most colour of the gris releases, and is also the richest with baked pears, lemon butter and lime cream. It's a serious style, full bodied with peach-fuzz texture, slightly sticky phenolics and a little bitter on the finish. Screw cap. 13.8% alc. **RATING** 94 **DRINK** 2023–2027 $40 JF ✪

KKO1 Pinot Noir 2021, Mornington Peninsula Somewhat deceptive at first, appearing all light and bright with its pale ruby hue. Then it starts to build. Some meaty reduction adding savouriness, the palate expands to take in cherry flavours, oak spices, poached rhubarb with lemon juice and a compelling poppy fruit character. Tannins feel lacy and fine with acidity upfront and holding the fort. Screw cap. 12.4% alc. **RATING** 94 **DRINK** 2024–2031 $45 JF

🍷🍷🍷🍷🍷 **Halarah Main Ridge Pinot Gris 2022, Mornington Peninsula** **RATING** 92 **DRINK** 2023–2027 $35 JF

Balnarring Vineyard Pinot Grigio 2022, Mornington Peninsula **RATING** 92 **DRINK** 2023–2028 $35 JF

Campbell & Christine Pinot Noir 2021, Mornington Peninsula **RATING** 92 **DRINK** 2024–2031 $48 JF

Quiet Mutiny   ★★★★

10 Elaine Cresecent, West Hobart, Tas, 7000 (postal) **Region** Tasmania
T 0410 552 317 **www**.quietmutiny.wine **Open** Not **Winemaker** Greer Carland
Est. 2017 **Dozens** 400
Owner and winemaker Greer Carland grew up on the Laurel Bank family property, learning to prune vines at an early age. She completed her oenology degree at the University of Adelaide in '00 and, after a few years of international vintages in Chile, France and the US

and a short stint in WA, she returned to Tasmania in '04. For the next 12 years she worked with Julian Alcorso at Winemaking Tasmania (now Tasmanian Vintners), also making the Laurel Bank wines. In '16 she left to focus on making the family wines at Laurel Bank and to start her own label. The name Quiet Mutiny is a reference to Australia's first female pirate. She intends to secure land and establish a vineyard for Quiet Mutiny with her viticulturist husband Paul Smart.

🍷🍷🍷🍷 **Charlotte's Elusion Rosé 2022, Tasmania** Pinot meunier from Tasmania's East Coast forms the base of this snappy little rosé. Light salmon with a slight coppery hue. Fragrant with tones of redcurrant, red cherry and raspberry fruits with underlying hints of pressed flowers, crushed stone, red berry cream, wildflowers and herbs. Gentle, fresh and moreish with some nice briny acidity for a sapid, lipsmacking twang and a lovely swell of red and citrus fruits on the finish. Screw cap. 12.7% alc. **RATING** 92 **DRINK** 2023–2026 $35 DB
Venus Rising Pinot Noir 2021, Tasmania Bright red cherry, plum and strawberry fruits mesh with hints of pithy undergrowth and souk-like spice. Finishes toothsome with a light sheen of funk, gentle tannin support, ample bright-fruit drive and a whole bunch of inherent drinkability. Diam. 13.5% alc. **RATING** 91 **DRINK** 2022–2028 $52 DB
Charlotte's Elusion Riesling 2022, Tasmania An expressive and expansive riesling that shows ripe lime, green apple and grapefruit notes with hints of white flowers, stone, soft spice, crème fraîche and some lighter, more exotic guava and papaya notes speaking softly in the background. There is a nice dry, savoury palate shape with a swish of lemon curd and bright apple fruits on the finish. Screw cap. 12.9% alc. **RATING** 90 **DRINK** 2023–2027 $40 DB

Quin Wines   ★★★★★

785 Seppeltsfield Road, Seppeltsfield SA 5355 (postal) **Region** Barossa Valley
T 0407 363 842 **www**.quinwines.com.au **Open** Not **Winemaker** Andrew Quin
Est. 2018 **Dozens** 500 **Vyds** 7.2ha
The story of Quin Wines and of Andrew and Skye Quin all happened so logically, and quickly, you have to draw breath for a moment. Andrew and Skye met at high school in Melbourne, and travelled the world before settling in the Barossa Valley. Andrew's journey started in his grandmother's garden as a young boy, which led to the study of horticulture and, eventually, viticulture and winemaking. After consolidating his knowledge at wineries in Victoria and Sonoma, California, he mixed travel and work in the French Languedoc region. After his return to Australia, a chance visit to Hentley Farm in '08 led to his appointment as chief winemaker for the relatively newly minted brand. It was the '14 purchase of the 7.2ha Cambourne vineyard that allows him to have fun, winning a slew of trophies at the Barossa Wine Show.

🍷🍷🍷🍷 **Shiraz 2020, Eden Valley** Satsuma plum, blueberry and boysenberry fruit tones are joined by hints of fine spice, sage, violets, softly spoken vanillin oak and earth. The fruit darkens on the palate, tensing before fanning out on the finish with a cascade of dusty, granitic tannin and plenty of Eden Valley drive. Lovely. Screw cap. 14.5% alc. **RATING** 95 **DRINK** 2023–2033 $55 DB
Shiraz 2020, Barossa Valley Deep magenta hue with characters of super-juicy plum and macerated summer berry fruits underlined with hints of baking spices, dark chocolate, jasmine, ironstone and earth. The fruit density and bright acidity are bang-on while fine, sandy tannins provide ample support for the cellar. Screw cap. 14.5% alc. **RATING** 95 **DRINK** 2023–2035 $55 DB
Riesling 2022, Eden Valley Pale in the glass with a flash of green. Bright aromas of freshly squeezed lime juice, Bickford's lime cordial, grapefruit and green apple alongside hints of Christmas lily, crushed quartz, jasmine, orange blossom, freshly cut fennel and marzipan. Precise and sapid, showing plenty of vitality and drive as it races across the palate with a saline, minerally acidity as its pulse. Screw cap. 11.5% alc. **RATING** 94 **DRINK** 2023–2028 $28 DB
Mataro 2021, Barossa Valley A cracking example of a straight mataro, a variety that is too often blended away. Packed with spicy, earthen characters and a swell of violet-flecked red and dark berry fruits with plenty of blueberry lift.

Medium bodied with trademark mataro tannin flex and a very appealing spicy red-fruited finish. Screw cap. 14% alc. **RATING** 94 **DRINK** 2023-2030 $55 DB
Grenache 2021, Barossa Valley Fruit tones of red plum, cherry and raspberry with hints of wild strawberries, gingerbread, violets, earth, red licorice and just a whiff of pipe tobacco. There's plenty of space on the palate and a cascade of fine, sandy tannin tumbles through the red and dark plummy fruit, which tends savoury and pure on the sustained finish. Screw cap. 14% alc. **RATING** 94 **DRINK** 2023-2030 $55 DB

🍷🍷🍷🍷 **Nebbiolo 2021, Pyrenees RATING** 93 **DRINK** 2023-2033 $55 DB
Mataro Rosé 2022, Barossa Valley RATING 92 **DRINK** 2023-2026 $25 DB ✪

R. Paulazzo

852 Oakes Road, Yoogali, NSW 2680 (postal) **Region** Riverina
T 0412 696 002 **www.rpaulazzo.com.au Open** Not **Winemaker** Rob Paulazzo
Est. 2013 **Vyds** 12ha
Rob Paulazzo covered a lot of ground before establishing his eponymous Riverina business. In Australia he worked for McWilliam's and Orlando, in NZ for Giesen. He also completed 4 vintages in Burgundy, plus vintages in Tuscany, the Napa Valley and Niagara Peninsula (Canada). In addition to the family's vineyard, Rob also sources fruit from Hilltops, Tumbarumba, Orange and Canberra District.

🍷🍷🍷🍷 **F-1833 Botrytis Semillon 2019, Riverina** Quince paste, stewed peach, dandelion and marigold blooms. Apricot danish, vanilla bean and orange marmalade. With persimmon and tangerine citrus on the palate, the wine is well-balanced with luscious sweetness and orange oils. Excellent for the price. Screw cap. 11% alc. **RATING** 95 **DRINK** 2022-2026 $28 SW ✪

🍷🍷🍷🍷 **S-3011 Cabernet Sauvignon 2019, Hilltops RATING** 92 **DRINK** 2022-2030 $30 SW ✪
Reserve Pinot Noir 2021, Tumbarumba RATING 91 **DRINK** 2022-2028 $35 SW
G-0501 Shiraz 2019, Hilltops RATING 90 **DRINK** 2022-2028 $30 SW

Rahona Valley

3/48 Collins Road, Dromana **Region** Mornington Peninsula
T (03) 5989 2254 **www.rahonavalley.com.au Open** Sat–Sun 12–5 **Winemaker** Natalie Fryar, Alisdair Park **Est.** 2014 **Dozens** 2000 **Vyds** 13.2ha
Toby Pieters and Dianne Gardiner made a 'vine change' to Rahona Valley in '14, moving from an inner-city suburb of Melbourne to Red Hill and purchasing one of the smallest commercial vineyards in the region. They have since expanded into Mornington Peninsula and now also work with growers in Tasmania.

🍷🍷🍷🍷 **Abel Pinot Gris 2022, Tasmania** This is how gris should be: textural, luscious without being too blousy, flavoursome with poached pears, topped with creamed honey, ginger powder and white pepper. It's savoury though, with creamy lees in the mix while well-handled phenolics add shape and a little grip to the finish. Gorgeous. Screw cap. 12.5% alc. **RATING** 95 **DRINK** 2023-2028 $30 JF ✪
Sauvignon Blanc 2022, Mornington Peninsula The Peninsula is chardonnay and pinot noir territory. This refreshing lively drink proves that's not exclusively so. It's more citrus dominated with lemon, limes and pink grapefruit with the merest hint of sugar snap peas and feijoa. The palate is racy and juicy, and the slip of texture adds to the pleasure of drinking it. Screw cap. 12.5% alc. **RATING** 95 **DRINK** 2023-2025 $25 JF ✪

🍷🍷🍷🍷 **Trinity 2022, Mornington Peninsula RATING** 92 **DRINK** 2022-2024 $35 JF
Pinot Shiraz 2021, Mornington Peninsula Heathcote RATING 92 **DRINK** 2022-2028 $38 JF
Rosé 2022, Mornington Peninsula RATING 90 **DRINK** 2022-2025 $29 JF

Raidis Estate

147 Church Street, Penola, SA 5277 **Region** Coonawarra
T (08) 8737 2966 **www.raidis.com.au Open** Thurs–Sun 12–6 **Winemaker** Steven
Raidis **Est.** 2006 **Dozens** 6000 **Vyds** 24.29ha
The Raidis family has lived and worked in Coonawarra for over 40 years. Chris Raidis was
only 3 years old when he arrived in Australia with his parents, who were market gardeners
in Greece before coming here. In '94 he planted just under 5ha of cabernet sauvignon; son
Steven significantly expanded the vineyard in '03 with sauvignon blanc, riesling, pinot gris,
merlot and shiraz. The cellar door was opened by then Deputy Prime Minister Julia Gillard
in '09, an impressive example of pulling power.

🍷🍷🍷🍷🍷 **PG Project Oak Pinot Gris 2021, Coonawarra** This really does lay down the
law. It's dry, pebbly, smoky-in-a-good-way, sheeted with nectarine and punchy
through the finish. It's more about mouth perfume than it is about overt fragrance,
nothing wrong with that, but the poise and presence of the palate are where it's at
anyway. Screw cap. 13% alc. **RATING** 94 **DRINK** 2023–2027 $40 CM ✪

🍷🍷🍷🍷🍷 **The Trip 2015, Coonawarra RATING** 93 **DRINK** 2023–2032 $100 CM
The Kid Riesling 2022, Coonawarra RATING 92 **DRINK** 2023–2031
$24 CM ✪
Cheeky Goat Pinot Gris 2022, Coonawarra RATING 92 **DRINK** 2023–2026
$26 CM ✪
Billy Cabernet Sauvignon 2019, Coonawarra RATING 92 **DRINK** 2025–2032
$35 CM
Wild Goat Shiraz 2021, Coonawarra RATING 91 **DRINK** 2024–2031 $35 CM
The Kelpie Sauvignon Blanc 2022, Coonawarra RATING 90
DRINK 2023–2027 $24 CM ✪
Mama Goat Merlot 2021, Coonawarra RATING 90 **DRINK** 2024–2028
$35 CM

Rare Hare

166 Balnarring Rd, Merricks North, Vic 3926 **Region** Mornington Peninsula
T (03) 5931 2500 **www.rarehare.com.au Open** 7 days 11–5 **Winemaker** Geraldine
McFaul **Viticulturist** Anthony Davenport **Est.** 2014 **Dozens** 4000 **Vyds** 11ha
Rare Hare was Willow Creek Vineyard, rebranded in early '23. Louis Li took over the
Willow Creek business in '13; coming from a family of hotel developers, with an artistic
background and a love of design, he had grand plans. Today, his vision has been realised in
the Jackalope hotel, its stylish restaurant Doot Doot Doot, a cocktail bar and art installations.
There's also the Rare Hare cellar door and eatery. Winemaker Geraldine McFaul continues
to craft excellent cool-climate wines, particularly chardonnay and pinot noir, with the 11ha
site renamed LL vineyard in recognition of its owner. She's also sourcing special parcels of
single-vineyard fruit to complement the range.

🍷🍷🍷🍷🍷 **RJ & CJ Vineyard Shiraz 2021, Pyrenees** This is possibly the most elegant
shiraz I've tasted from fruit off Robert and Cameron John's Malakoff Estate site.
It's also enjoyable for its savouriness rather than sweet fruit. It's spicy, meaty and
peppery with a judicious cedary oak influence. It's medium bodied with textural,
almost grainy tannins and plenty of detail, yet it's a delicious drink. That's the
important bit. Screw cap. 14% alc. **RATING** 95 **DRINK** 2023–2031 $50 JF ✪
LL Vineyard Chardonnay 2021, Mornington Peninsula This is lovely. A
symphony of citrus, from lemon to grapefruit and a hint of preserved lime, nicely
spiced with ginger powder and extra flavour from creamy lees and a smidge of
sulphides, you know, flinty and funky. It has body but is finely tuned, elegant and
lifted by refreshing acidity. Screw cap. 13% alc. **RATING** 95 **DRINK** 2023–2031
$50 JF ✪
DL Vineyard Pinot Noir 2021, Mornington Peninsula DL is David Lloyd,
former owner of Eldridge Estate ('21 was his penultimate vintage). It is the prettiest
of the trio of Rare Hare's single-vineyard pinots, with a flush of sweet-ish red

cherries, warm earth and florals plus Moroccan mint. The palate is subtle, lighter framed with lacy tannins and a line of acidity tying everything together neatly. Lovely wine. Screw cap. 13.5% alc. **RATING** 95 **DRINK** 2023–2029 $50 JF ✪

🍷🍷🍷🍷🍷 **HR & RM Vineyard Pinot Noir 2021, Mornington Peninsula RATING** 93 **DRINK** 2023–2033 $50 JF
LL Vineyard Pinot Noir 2021, Mornington Peninsula RATING 93 **DRINK** 2023–2031 $50 JF
Pinot Noir 2022, Mornington Peninsula RATING 91 **DRINK** 2022–2024 $35 JF

Ravenscroft Vineyard ★★★★

274 Spring Creek Road, Stanthorpe, Qld 4380 **Region** Granite Belt
T (07) 4683 3252 **www**.ravenscroftvineyard.com **Open** Fri–Sun 10–4.30
Winemaker Mark Ravenscroft, Caitlin Hawkes Roberts, Nick Roberts
Viticulturist Mark Ravenscroft, Caitlin Hawkes Roberts, Nick Roberts **Est.** 2002
Dozens 1000 **Vyds** 1.5ha
Mark Ravenscroft was born in South Africa and studied oenology there. He moved to Australia in the early '90s, and in '94 became an Australian citizen. His wines come from estate plantings of verdelho, pinotage and albariño, supplemented by contract-grown grapes from other vineyards in the region. The wines are made onsite.

🍷🍷🍷🍷🍷 **Vermentino 2022, Murray Darling** Bright and refreshing with a fine, chalky pucker and a good sense of intensity with minerally charm. The palate is almost brisk with its fresh-fruit vibrancy and saline-acid cut, albeit there are quince and nashi pear flavours to help out. The perfume is floral, with more of that pear showing a light dusting of sweet spice. Feels true to the variety, and it's very good. Screw cap. 13.4% alc. **RATING** 93 **DRINK** 2022–2026 $38 MB
Skin Contact Fiano 2022, Murray Darling A squeaky textured, lighter expression of skin-contact white wine. Pear skin scents, touches of honeycomb, cinnamon spice and ginger to sniff on. Flavours again show pear skin, a splash of green apple, cinnamon and strong gingery spice notes. It does well to balance refreshment and textural detail. It's a cleverly made, great drinking wine. Screw cap. 13.6% alc. **RATING** 93 **DRINK** 2022–2027 $45 MB
Reserve Chardonnay 2021, Granite Belt A quietly complex, medium-weight chardonnay with strong mineral elements, judicious wood seasoning and a bright, stone-fruit-meets-citrus-fruit profile. The perfume is welcoming, gentle and fresh, the flavours a little richer but well-judged with oak handling lending toasty cinnamon spice notes. A flinty, saline-mineral element delivers additional complexity. Screw cap. 13% alc. **RATING** 93 **DRINK** 2022–2030 $54 MB
Wild Ferment Rosé 2022, Granite Belt Predominantly sangiovese, blended with verdelho and vermentino. This is a well-pitched rosé in a savoury and very dry vogue. Scents of cranberry drink, raspberry and guava. Flavours are similarly oriented around red berries and gentle tropical fruits, a cool, blood orange tang to finish. It's refreshing, textural and just that little bit interesting, too. Well done. Screw cap. 12% alc. **RATING** 92 **DRINK** 2022–2024 $34 MB
Tempranillo 2021, Granite Belt A refreshing, medium-bodied expression with hallmark sour cherry, sweet spice, sarsaparilla, anise and clove scents and flavours. Compact and reserved, there's a refinement to the wine and a sense of control and poise. Among the tension and finesse it still retains a refreshment factor. Very well balanced. A delightful rendition of tempranillo here. Screw cap. 13% alc. **RATING** 92 **DRINK** 2022–2028 $40 MB
Verdelho 2022, Granite Belt A zesty, fruity, light and tight white wine. Lean expressions of tropical fruits in bouquet and palate, with fine chalky mineral notes, a little pleasing saline character in the mix, and a good extension of flavours overall. Great to see a more understated, skinsy, puckering and vibrant rendition of the variety. Screw cap. 12% alc. **RATING** 90 **DRINK** 2022–2025 $40 MB

Ravensworth

312 Patemans Lane, Murrumbateman, ACT 2582 **Region** Canberra District
T (02) 6226 8368 **www**.ravensworthwines.com.au **Open** By appt in Sept
Winemaker Bryan Martin **Viticulturist** Bryan Martin **Est.** 2000 **Dozens** 8000 **Vyds** 3.4ha
Ravensworth is led by innovative winemaker Bryan Martin, his wife Jocelyn, plus his brother
David. Bryan takes an organic approach, eschewing chemicals, preventing soil compaction
and allowing the vines to thrive in what he describes as 'natural forestry principles'. The
vineyard comprises 26 varietals, mostly shiraz, riesling and sangiovese with marsanne,
roussanne and viognier plus recent plantings of gamay, chardonnay, savagnin, ribolla gialla and
nebbiolo. He also sources fruit for Ravensworth's other labels including the Regional range.
In '20, a winery and cellar were completed, the latter made with straw bales, and filled
with large-format oak, Italian amphorae, ceramic eggs and concrete vessels: all expressing Bryan's
desire to experiment and craft minimum-intervention wines with texture. A 2nd generation
has come on board with son Lewis starting his wine science studies at CSU in '22.

Regional Sangiovese 2022, Hilltops This represents the 20th vintage for
Bryan Martin's sangiovese. I reckon he has the knack now. There's a lovely
fragrance and such delightful fruit in this, all red cherries and barberries with
splashes of blood orange and amaro. Tannins are spot-on, all textural, shapely
and mouthcoating, while the juicy acidity seals the deal. Screw cap. 13% alc.
RATING 95 **DRINK** 2023–2030 $32 JF ✪

Regional Tinto 2022, Hilltops Tempranillo/mataro/grenache. Tinto is one of
those wines you pour, smell, drink and say 'that's delicious', immediately going in
search of food to match. When you do, continue enjoying the savoury characters
as much as the juicy tangy fruit, grainy tannins, texture and vibrant acidity.
Screw cap. 13.5% alc. **RATING** 95 **DRINK** 2023–2027 $32 JF ✪

Regional Riesling 2022, Canberra District As always, natural acidity is key
and there's no shortage here. Expect florals and lemon blossom especially, with
citrus flavours shaking it up with ginger spice, lemon balm and Kanzi apple.
There's a line of fine tannins also giving this more mouthfeel. Bravo to a riesling
that expresses all that without losing its essence. Screw cap. 12% alc. **RATING** 95
DRINK 2022–2032 $30 JF ✪

Regional Barbera Nebbiolo 2022, Hilltops Nebbiolo's acidity and tannins
offset the juicy fruit of barbera. A core of sweet and sour cherries, amaro and
bitter herbs, woodsy spices and charred radicchio. It's tangy, supple and juicy with
grainy tannins. And dare I say it is very Italianate in outlook. Love it. Screw cap.
13.3% alc. **RATING** 95 **DRINK** 2023–2028 $32 JF ✪

The Grainery 2021, Canberra District It has all the texture and detail
marsanne, viognier and roussanne bring via winemaking, yet a finer rendition
this vintage. A lovely balance of stone fruit, quince, Japanese pickled ginger and
a raft of warm spices. Slippery, light phenolics, a millefeuille of creamy lees and a
savoury overlay make this a tip-top tipple. It shines more with food. Screw cap.
12.5% alc. **RATING** 95 **DRINK** 2023–2028 $50 JF ✪

Estate Shiraz Viognier 2021, Canberra District Shiraz with a 4% glug of
viognier, co-fermented, and gee it adds a lot to the palate, plumping it out, and
aromatically, adding some florals. Although in unison, this is lovely, peppery, spicy,
tangy and savoury. Medium bodied, fine acidity, silty tannins and moreish to the
last drop. Screw cap. 13.5% alc. **RATING** 95 **DRINK** 2023–2031 $52 JF

Regional Pinot Gris 2022, Hilltops An excellent skin-contact/amber wine
with an attractive copper-cherry hue. Fragrant with florals, Mediterranean
herbs and loads of spices from ginger powder to star anise. It has this gorgeous
watermelon/Campari flavour, plus pink grapefruit with some wilted radicchio,
bitter herbs and plenty of chewy phenolics. It's also refreshing. Screw cap.
12.5% alc. **RATING** 94 **DRINK** 2022–2027 $30 JF ✪

Regional Fiano & Trebbiano 2022, Canberra District This is savoury,
textural and phenolic. Good white phenolics though, which add shape, mouthfeel
and detail throughout. Lots going on with preserved lemon, salted limes and a raft

of spices, ginger and coriander especially. Very dry and very appealing, with food though, please. Screw cap. 12.7% alc. **RATING** 94 **DRINK** 2023–2027 $30 JF ✪

🍷🍷🍷🍷🍷 **Neighbourly Chardonnay 2021, Tumbarumba Margaret River** **RATING** 93 **DRINK** 2022–2028 $30 JF ✪
Neighbourly Bianco 2021, Hilltops Swan Valley Canberra District **RATING** 93 **DRINK** 2022–2026 $29 JF ✪
Neighbourly Rosso 2021, Hilltops Canberra District **RATING** 93 **DRINK** 2023–2027 $27 JF ✪
Neighbourly Shiraz 2021, Hilltops Margaret River Canberra District **RATING** 92 **DRINK** 2023–2029 $30 JF ✪
Velo Rosé 2021, Canberra District **RATING** 91 **DRINK** 2022–2030 $45 JF
Estate Sangiovese 2021, Canberra District **RATING** 91 **DRINK** 2023–2028 $45 JF
Charlie-Foxtrot Gamay Noir 2022, Tumbarumba Canberra District **RATING** 90 **DRINK** 2023–2026 $38 JF

Red Edge ★★★★

54 Golden Gully Road, Heathcote, Vic 3523 **Region** Heathcote
T 0407 422 067 **www**.rededgewine.com.au **Open** By appt Mon–Fri 9–5, Sat 10–4.30
Winemaker Peter Dredge, Will Dredge **Viticulturist** Peter Dredge **Est.** 1971
Dozens 1500 **Vyds** 14ha
Red Edge's vineyard dates back to 1971 and the renaissance of the Victorian wine industry. In the early '80s it produced the wonderful wines of Flynn & Williams, and was rehabilitated by Peter and Judy Dredge, producing 2 quite lovely wines in their inaugural vintage and continuing that form in succeeding years.

🍷🍷🍷🍷🍷 **71 Block Shiraz 2018, Heathcote** Leather, sweet blackberry and woodsmoke flavours present as complex, mellifluous and direct. Essentially, it's a gutsy red that's easy to like. There's a churn of well-massaged tannin through the finish, but this is really all about flavour, gently developed, and a good amount of it. Screw cap. 14.6% alc. **RATING** 93 **DRINK** 2022–2028 $70 CM
Rosé 2021, Heathcote The pale copper colour of this wine belies its heightened fragrance and flavour. It really does serve its deliciousness straight at you. Florals, candied citrus, leather, red berry and orange notes do some pretty persuasive talking. The finish is perhaps slightly too dry, but gee, this is good drinking. Screw cap. 12.5% alc. **RATING** 91 **DRINK** 2023–2025 $25 CM ✪
Shiraz 2018, Heathcote Bold fruit flavour, straight down the line. Blackberry, plum and red cherry with sweet spice and cedar-wood notes happily married therein. There's some alcohol warmth here but it has the flavour to go with it. Mint and game-like notes add some play around the edges. Screw cap. 14.5% alc. **RATING** 91 **DRINK** 2022–2027 $40 CM
Cabernet Sauvignon 2018, Heathcote A dusty, fluid, juicy cabernet that's true to its variety and yet, also a unique expression. It's more boysenberry than blackcurrant, more dust than tobacco, more red berry than dark. It still manages good form on the finish and, in the context that it is showing some signs of development, is pretty much already in its drinking prime now. Screw cap. 14.2% alc. **RATING** 91 **DRINK** 2022–2027 $25 CM ✪

Redbank ★★★★

1597 Snow Road, Milawa, Vic 3678 **Region** King Valley
T (08) 8561 3200 **www**.redbankwines.com **Open** 7 days 10–5 **Winemaker** Dave Whyte **Viticulturist** Michael Murtagh **Est.** 2005 **Dozens** 33 000 **Vyds** 20ha
The Redbank brand was for decades the umbrella for Neill and Sally Robb's Sally's Paddock. The brand was aquired by Hill-Smith Family Vineyards in '05, leaving the Robbs with the winery, surrounding vineyard and the Sally's Paddock label. Local winegrowers – the Ross, Judd and Murtagh families – purchased the brand in Aug '18 and have launched a

new cellar door venture under the umbrella of Milawa Providore. Redbank purchases grapes locally from the King Valley and Whitlands as well as further afield.

ŸŸŸŸ♈ **Prosecco NV, King Valley** Bring out the peaches and enjoy this vibrant sparkling. Catches the prosecco personality so well in pear, citrus and apple with a chalky lemon texture. Lightly savoury, too. Crown. 11% alc. **RATING** 91 $25 JP ✪
Sunday Morning Prosecco Rosé NV, King Valley A blend of prosecco with quite a splash of grenache for that lively pink colour and an infusion of summer berries. Prosecco brings the lemony crispness, grenache brings a touch of confection and a delightful punnet of fresh strawberry and raspberry scents and flavours. Perfect Sunday morning patio pairing. Cork. 12.5% alc. **RATING** 90 $25 JP ✪

RedHeads Wine

258 Angaston Road, Angaston, SA 5353 **Region** South Australia
T (08) 8562 2888 www.redheadswine.com **Open** Thurs–Sun 11–5 **Winemaker** Alex Trescowthick, Darren Harvey **Est.** 2003 **Dozens** 25 000 **Vyds** 8ha
RedHeads was established by Tony Laithwaite in McLaren Vale and has since moved to the Barossa Valley. The aim was to allow winemakers working under corporate banners to produce small-batch wines. The team 'liberates' premium parcels of grapes from large companies 'a few rows at a time, to give them the special treatment they deserve and to form wines of true individuality and character.'

ŸŸŸŸ♈ **Esule Cabernet Sauvignon Cabernet Franc 2020, McLaren Vale** Deeply coloured with leafy-edged black berry fruits dusted with dark spices, amaro herbs, sarsaparilla, tobacco, earth, cedar and crème de cassis. I'm a sucker for these plushly fruited, leafy-edged wines with their tight, sandy tannins and impressive fruit density while retaining a sense of 'crunch' in their line. Hello, lamb roast! Screw cap. 14.5% alc. **RATING** 93 **DRINK** 2023-2028 $65 DB
Dogs of the Barossa Shiraz 2020, Barossa Valley Deep and saturated in colour, here's a wine for those who seek power and black-fruited horsepower. Blackberry jam, black cherry and dark plum fruits, clove, sarsaparilla, Bounty bars, warm earth, cola, rum and raisin chocolate and Dutch salted licorice. Broody, flexing and thick-shouldered with grippy coal-dust tannins. One for those seeking power over poise. Screw cap. 14.5% alc. **RATING** 92 **DRINK** 2023-2028 $65 DB
Whip-Hand Cabernet Sauvignon 2020, Barossa Deep, impenetrable crimson in hue with characters of ripe black berry fruits with hints of cloves, five-spice, vanillin oak, iodine, eucalyptus, roasting meats, earth and crème de cassis. Rich, opulent and thickly proportioned with dense, compact tannins and a roll of crème de cassis-like fruit on the finish. Cork. 14.5% alc. **RATING** 91 **DRINK** 2023-2028 $65 DB

Redman

14830 Riddoch Highway, Coonawarra, SA 5263 **Region** Coonawarra
T (08) 8736 3331 www.redman.com.au **Open** Mon–Fri 9–5, w'ends 11–4
Winemaker Bruce Redman, Daniel Redman **Viticulturist** Malcolm Redman, Michael Redman **Est.** 1966 **Dozens** 18 000 **Vyds** 34ha
Redman has been making wine in Coonawarra for over 110 years – and Coonawarra cabernet for 50 years. Brothers Bruce (winemaker) and Mal (general manager) and Bruce's sons Dan (winemaker and marketer) and Mike (assistant winemaker and cellar hand), represent the 4th and 5th generations of the family business. Their flagship wine is The Redman, a blend of the best barrels of cabernet sauvignon, shiraz and (sometimes) merlot, made only in exceptional years.

ŸŸŸŸŸ **The Redman 2019, Coonawarra** Made from what Redman describes as 'the best of the best [of its] cabernet and shiraz'. It's assertively tannic but not to the point of imbalance. Indeed it's an intriguing wine, sinewy at heart but with fruit flavour that builds and builds as it breathes. Resin, redcurrant and mint flavours teem with cedar and polished leather. It's by no means a big wine, but its charms are significant. Screw cap. 13.5% alc. **RATING** 95 **DRINK** 2025-2038 $80 CM

🍷🍷🍷🍷 **The Last Row Limited Release Shiraz 2020, Coonawarra RATING** 91 **DRINK** 2023-2031 $30 CM
Shiraz 2020, Coonawarra RATING 91 **DRINK** 2023-2030 $23 CM ✪

Reillys Wines   ★★★★

Cnr Leasingham Road/Hill Street, Mintaro, SA 5415 **Region** Clare Valley
T (08) 8843 9013 **www**.reillyswines.com.au **Open** 7 days 10–4 **Winemaker** Justin Ardill **Viticulturist** Rob Smyth **Est.** 1994 **Dozens** 25 000 **Vyds** 115ha
Established in '93 by Justin and Julie Ardill. Justin hand made the first vintage in '94 on the verandah of the heritage-listed Reillys Cottage – built in 1856 by Irish shoemaker Hugh Reilly – which today serves as their cellar door and restaurant. Justin continues to use the same traditional winemaking techniques of prolonged open fermentation, hand plunging and barrel maturation. The wines are made from estate vineyards (the oldest planted in 1919).

🍷🍷🍷🍷 **Watervale Riesling 2022, Clare Valley** Easy-drinking riesling here. Limey fresh, a squirt of green apple and a bit of peppery spice in the mix with some lemony notes, too. Feels quite light on in concentration, but should deliver the requisite zing for the acid hounds. Cool and clean overall. An understated version of the regional staple, in a way. Screw cap. 12.5% alc. **RATING** 90 **DRINK** 2023-2029 $32 MB

Renzaglia Wines   ★★★★

38 Bosworth Falls Road, O'Connell, NSW 2795 **Region** Central Ranges
T (02) 6337 5756 **www**.renzagliawines.com.au **Open** By appt **Winemaker** Mark Renzaglia, Sam Renzaglia **Viticulturist** Mark Renzaglia, Sandy Dengate **Est.** 1997 **Dozens** 2500 **Vyds** 6ha
The Renzaglia family's history in grape growing dates back to 1982 in Alto Pass, Illinois, when the Renzaglias were among the first to plant vines in what was then a dry county (in which the sale of alcohol was banned). Second-generation Mark Renzaglia was drawn to Australia by his now wife Sandy and, taking a leaf out of their ancestors' book, they planted their first vineyard in '97 in O'Connell Valley of NSW, the very first to do so. Sons Sam and Paul have since joined the family business and in that time Renzaglia Wines has expanded the range to include modern representations under the di Renzo label as well as their thoughtful and classically framed Renzaglia range.

🍷🍷🍷🍷 **Shiraz 2021, Orange** A perfumed example of cool-climate shiraz with blackberries, dried blueberries and juniper. Underlying notes of Kalamata olives, freshly picked thyme, dried fennel and cardamom pods. The palate is juicy, with acidity that rolls in waves and carries the spice along for the ride. Soft and supple tannins round out an elegant drink. Screw cap. 13.1% alc. **RATING** 93 **DRINK** 2022-2032 $38 SW
di Renzo Cabernets 2021, Orange Notes of blackberries and pencil shavings showcase this wine's cabernet sauvignon, cabernet franc make-up. Elderberry and licorice root are followed by cigar box and coffee grinds. A muscular frame shows firm tannins with hints of nettle and black pepper spice. The acidity, which lifts the palate, is key here. An intriguing blend. Screw cap. 13.4% alc. **RATING** 91 **DRINK** 2022-2032 $32 SW
Bella Luna Chardonnay 2021, Central Ranges Makrut lime leaves, lemon oil and yellow peaches greet the nose with cashew butter and apple strudel coming through. A textured palate with melted butter, baked apples and almond praline finishes savoury and decadent. A rich style for the die-hard chardonnay fans. Screw cap. 12% alc. **RATING** 90 **DRINK** 2022-2038 $60 SW
Bella Luna Cabernet Sauvignon Merlot 2021, Central Ranges A heady blend of redcurrants, ripe raspberries, cherry and coconut comes to the forefront. Sweet chewing tobacco and spiced cola lingers on the nose. The merlot shines

through with a distinct weight in the mid-palate and rounded, plush tannins. A cuddly drink that shows why these 2 varieties get along so well. Screw cap. 12.7% alc. **RATING** 90 **DRINK** 2022–2038 $60 SW

Reschke Wines ★★★★★

7089 Riddoch Highway, Padthaway, SA 5271 (postal) **Region** Coonawarra
T (08) 8239 0500 **www**.reschke.com.au **Open** Not **Winemaker** Ben Wurst **Est.** 1998
Dozens 25 000 **Vyds** 155ha
The Reschke family have been landowners in Coonawarra for over 100 years, with a large holding that is part terra rossa, part woodland. Cabernet sauvignon (with 120ha) takes the lion's share of the plantings, with merlot, shiraz and petit verdot making up the balance. In '20, Reschke was purchased by Coonawarra-based CW Wines.

♟♟♟♟♟ Vitulus Shiraz 2021, Coonawarra This is as seamless as they come and yet it has grain, it has texture. Saturated plum and licorice flavours come infused with mint, roasted cedar, woodsy spice and florals. It's pretty and it's powerful, and it has good extension through the finish. This is a wine that will please a lot of red wine drinkers. Screw cap. 14.5% alc. **RATING** 95 **DRINK** 2024–2034 $30 CM ❂
Bos Cabernet Sauvignon 2015, Coonawarra It's both developed and beautiful. The spread of tannin here is really something, matched as it is to leather, red berries, complex spice and undergrowth characters. This is what it's all about. Violet and tobacco characters add yet more to the show, as do subtle dark chocolate notes. Screw cap. 14.5% alc. **RATING** 95 **DRINK** 2023–2029 $45 CM ❂
Empyrean Cabernet Sauvignon 2014, Coonawarra Bold and slightly beefy but with lots of charm. This is the beauty of cellaring; it can soften the edges and allow a wine's inner beauty to shine through. Violet, chocolate and cedar characters lift from curranty/leathery fruit. Velvety tannin rolls through the back half of the wine, adding a sense of command. Screw cap. 14.5% alc. **RATING** 94 **DRINK** 2023–2030 $150 CM

♟♟♟♟♀ Bull Trader Cabernet Sauvignon 2020, Coonawarra **RATING** 93 **DRINK** 2023–2032 $20 CM ❂
Vitulus Cabernet Sauvignon 2020, Coonawarra **RATING** 93 **DRINK** 2025–2035 $30 CM ❂
R-Series Rosé 2022, Limestone Coast **RATING** 92 **DRINK** 2023–2025 $20 CM ❂
Bull Trader Shiraz 2021, Coonawarra **RATING** 92 **DRINK** 2023–2029 $25 CM ❂
Bull Trader Cabernet Sauvignon Merlot 2020, Coonawarra **RATING** 92 **DRINK** 2023–2030 $25 CM ❂
Bull Trader Merlot 2021, Coonawarra **RATING** 91 **DRINK** 2023–2027 $25 CM ❂
Empyrean Cabernet Sauvignon 2016, Coonawarra **RATING** 91 **DRINK** 2023–2027 $150 CM
R-Series Sauvignon Blanc 2022, Limestone Coast **RATING** 90 **DRINK** 2023–2026 $20 CM ❂

Ricca Terra ★★★★

PO Box 305, Angaston, SA 5353 **Region** Riverland
T 0411 370 057 **www**.riccaterra.com.au **Open** By appt **Winemaker** Ashley Ratcliff
Viticulturist Ashley Ratcliff **Est.** 2017 **Dozens** 12 000 **Vyds** 80ha
Ricca Terra is the venture of Ashley and Holly Ratcliff. Ashley began his journey in wine in '92 when he joined Orlando as a viticulturist, thereafter moving to Yalumba where he remained until '16. During this time he obtained a bachelor of applied science, a master's degree in marketing and became a graduate of the AWRI sensory evaluation course. In his 15 years with Yalumba he was winery manager for the vast Riverland winery and technical manager (viticulture). He was the recipient of 4 major state and federal industry awards, all focusing on viticulture in drought-prone regions. So when he and Holly purchased an 8ha

vineyard in the Riverland it presented the opportunity to plant varieties pushing the envelope, such as the rare ancient Balkan variety slankamenka bela. There are now 80ha of varieties, mainly selected for the climate and grown with smart viticultural practices. Ricca Terra means rich earth in Italian.

Vermentino 2022, Riverland Red and green apple flavours slosh refreshingly through lime, lemonade and gunmetal. There's some texture here, some grip, in a juicy context. This could easily be dismissed as a fruit bomb, such is the intensity of flavour, but the truth is that it has very good length and feels engaging from start to finish. Screw cap. 12.5% alc. **RATING** 93 **DRINK** 2023-2026 $27 CM ✪

Skin Contact White Field Blend 2022, Riverland Trebbiano/greco. It's grippy but not excessively so – the real joy is the flavour, which is both intense and interesting. Grapefruit, yellow apples, citrus and wild, fragrant herb notes. A hay-like aspect too but then, every time you put your nose/mouth near this you notice something different. There's a lot going on in the context of a neat package. Screw cap. 14% alc. **RATING** 93 **DRINK** 2023-2026 $30 CM ✪

Arinto 2022, Riverland You have to admire the combination of texture and flavour. This is a fluid, silty wine with assorted citrus, grapefruit and stone fruit flavours shooting persuasively throughout. It's absolutely worth a run. Screw cap. 13.5% alc. **RATING** 93 **DRINK** 2023-2026 $30 CM ✪

Juicy June 2022, Riverland Negroamaro/grenache. Light in colour and flavour, in a positive way. It's a juicy, refreshing style of red, able to be chilled but not compulsorily so, with earth, dark chocolate, chicory and sweet earth/herb notes stepping their way through the palate. The finish is dry, spicy, sheeted with fine-grained tannin and satisfying. Screw cap. 12.8% alc. **RATING** 92 **DRINK** 2023-2027 $23 CM ✪

Fiano 2022, Riverland The pleasing thing here is that you get pulpy fruit, both pure and intense, but you also get texture, and some chalk-like savouriness too. It's a many-trick pony. Grapefruit, nectarine and nashi pear flavours cruise appealingly through the palate, charming as they pass. Screw cap. 13.3% alc. **RATING** 92 **DRINK** 2023-2025 $27 CM ✪

Terra do Rio White Field Blend 2022, Riverland Blend of arinto, greco and albariño. There's just enough bite and just enough softness to give this genuine appeal. Grapefruit pulp, lemon rind, nectarine and gooseberry characters get some good fruit-driven revs going, though it's got a charisma above and beyond that makes you stop and take notice. Screw cap. 13.8% alc. **RATING** 92 **DRINK** 2023-2026 $25 CM ✪

Bronco Buster 2022, Riverland Blend of vermentino and fiano. It's a fruity white wine done so well. Fruit salad with flashes of brine, lime and hay. All the flavours march confidently, and tastily, through the palate. Much enjoyment to be had here. Screw cap. 13% alc. **RATING** 91 **DRINK** 2023-2026 $23 CM ✪

Small Batch Nero d'Avola 2022, Riverland Purple in colour and with good general depth, but in a bright, energetic context. Violets, star anise, boysenberry and blueberry flavours come crackled with spice and dried leaves. More complex than your average nero. Dry to finish. It's a good drink. Screw cap. 13.8% alc. **RATING** 91 **DRINK** 2023-2027 $27 CM ✪

Soldiers' Land Grenache 2022, Riverland From 91yo vines, this throws raspberry and blueberry jube flavours straight out at you and it does so in fine style. Woodsy spice notes add to the attractiveness of the picture. No problems here, it's delicious. Screw cap. 14.7% alc. **RATING** 91 **DRINK** 2023-2027 $30 CM

Colour of Calmness Rosé 2022, Riverland Made with sangiovese and negroamaro. Pale pink crimson in the glass and racy on the palate. Watermelon, brine, strawberry and fennel characters rollick through a juicy, refreshing palate. Strawberry is the dominant flavour here. It works nicely. Screw cap. 12.6% alc. **RATING** 90 **DRINK** 2023-2025 $23 CM ✪

Soldiers' Land Riesling 2022, Riverland Fragrant and lively. There's a slip of sweetness to the lime- and apple-driven fruit profile, it finishes dry, slightly grippy and convincing. This is fun to drink but it's more than that; there's quality to the fruit. Screw cap. 11.7% alc. **RATING** 90 **DRINK** 2023-2027 $27 CM

Soldiers' Land Shiraz 2022, Riverland Very little sign of oak (read: none) and indeed it smells a little 'tanky', but the fruit flavours here are open, ripe, and generous. Sweet raspberry, tilled earth, prune and flashes of sweet/fragrant herbs. It's easy to like. Screw cap. 14.8% alc. RATING 90 DRINK 2023-2027 $30 CM

22 Degree Halo Riesling, Zibibbo & Doradillo 2022, Riverland Light, textural, herbal and all-round pleasant. Sophisticated in a light-bodied way. Crushed fennel, citrus and tonic-water characters keep you both refreshed and interested. Screw cap. 12% alc. RATING 90 DRINK 2023-2025 $20 CM ✪

22 Degree Halo Rosé 2022, Riverland Blend of grenache, mataro and sangiovese. Cranberry, watermelon and raspberry flavours are served fleshy, ripe and dry. There's a lingering savouriness to this but it's not at the expense of fruit. It's pretty tidy. Screw cap. 12.8% alc. RATING 90 DRINK 2023-2025 $20 CM ✪

Terra do Rio Red Field Blend 2021, Riverland Blend of sousão, tinta cão and touriga nacional. It's a free-flowing, unencumbered wine until the finish, where it turns (attractively) stringy and dry. There's little or no oak evident here, a fact that suits the fruit perfectly. It's a food wine with a bit of juiciness, and a bit of character. Gunmetal, cherries, saltbush; those kinds of notes. It works. Screw cap. 13.9% alc. RATING 90 DRINK 2023-2027 $25 CM ✪

Broken Forklift NV, Riverland Made using zibibbo, vermentino and muscat grapes. Rose tea in colour, intensely sweet, toffeed, honeyed, all burnt apples and sugared nuts but with candied citrus and orange peel characters. In short it's pretty damn delicious. 375ml. Screw cap. 17.5% alc. RATING 90 $40 CM

Richard Hamilton ★★★☆

439 Main Road, McLaren Vale, SA 5171 **Region** McLaren Vale
T (08) 8323 8830 **www.richardhamiltonwines.com Open** Mon–Fri 10–5, w'ends & public hols 11–5 **Winemaker** Paul Gordon, Greg Foster **Viticulturist** Lee Harding
Est. 1972 **Dozens** 25 000 **Vyds** 40.46ha
Richard Hamilton has outstanding estate vineyards, some of great age, all fully mature. An experienced and skilled winemaking team has allowed the full potential of those vineyards to be realised. The quality, style and consistency of both red and white wines has reached a new level; being able to keep only the best parcels for the Richard Hamilton brand is an enormous advantage.

🍷🍷🍷🍷 **Hamilton Centurion Old Vine Shiraz 2020, McLaren Vale** Hewn of old, dry-grown vines, an original 1892 planting. Lilac, red and dark cherry, some mace, cardamom and a twang of tangy acidity melded to French oak latticework. There is weight, persistence and oomph, if not a great deal of finesse to the structural elements. Screw cap. 14.5% alc. RATING 91 DRINK 2023-2035 $80 NG

Ridgemill Estate ★★★★

218 Donges Road, Severnlea, Qld 4380 **Region** Granite Belt
T (07) 4683 5211 **www.ridgemillestate.com Open** Fri–Mon 10–5, Sun 10–3
Winemaker Martin Cooper, Peter McGlashan **Est.** 1998 **Dozens** 900 **Vyds** 2.1ha
Martin Cooper acquired what was then known as Emerald Hill Winery in '04. In '05 he reshaped the vineyards – which now have plantings of chardonnay, tempranillo, shiraz, merlot, cabernet sauvignon, saperavi, verdelho and viognier – setting a course down the alternative variety road. There is a quite spectacular winery and cellar door facility, and self-contained cabins in the vineyard.

🍷🍷🍷🍷🍷 **Riesling 2021, Granite Belt** This is a high-tensile, energetic and tightly wound riesling. It's fragrant with lemon-lime citrus characters, whiffs of flinty minerality and lightly dashed with scents of jasmine and talc. The palate is brisk and refreshing, compact, minerally and licked with green apple juice and tart lime. A fantastic expression, mouth-watering and zesty while concentrated, detailed and fresh. Bravo. Screw cap. 12% alc. RATING 94 DRINK 2022-2035 $30 MB ✪

Y Y Y Y Y **WYP Chardonnay 2021, Granite Belt** RATING 93 DRINK 2022–2032 $40 MB
The Spaniard Tempranillo 2021, Hilltops RATING 93 DRINK 2022–2027
$40 MB
Pressings Pinot Grigio Verdelho 2022, Granite Belt RATING 92
DRINK 2024–2030 $35 MB

RidgeView Wines

273 Sweetwater Road, Pokolbin, NSW 2320 **Region** Hunter Valley
T (02) 6574 7332 **www.**ridgeview.com.au **Open** Wed–Sun 10–5 **Winemaker** Darren
Scott, Gary MacLean, Mark Woods, Scott Comyns **Viticulturist** Darren Scott **Est.** 3000
Dozens 3000 **Vyds** 15ha
RidgeView is an insider's secret, brimming with a solid suite of wines and some exceptional
aged releases and older cellar stock. The address also boasts the funkiest retro label in all of the
Hunter Valley. In '20 RidgeView purchased a neighbouring property, Eagle's Nest, planted
to chardonnay, sangiovese, verdelho and shiraz. A new winery is slated for completion in '23.
This will complement the established restaurant and its holistic culture of wines, local produce
and herbs, all grown at the estate.

Y Y Y Y Y **Impressions Single Vineyard Reserve Semillon 2019, Hunter Valley**
From 50yo vines on the sandy flats of Brokenback vineyard. Still in the first
phase of development with citrus pith and zest, highlighted by the silvery notes
of refreshing acidity. On a journey that will take a decade to reach the finish line.
Screw cap. 11% alc. RATING 95 DRINK 2023–2029 $45 JH ✪
Museum Release Impressions Reserve Semillon 2009, Hunter Valley
The pale straw-green hue could be that of a 1 or 2yo wine; the invitingly fresh
palate sending the same message of the enduring magic of the product of variety,
place and age. Just so good; the vintage was perfect, rated 10/10. Screw cap.
10.8% alc. RATING 95 DRINK 2023–2029 $75 JH
**Museum Release Impressions Single Vineyard Chardonnay 2017,
Hunter Valley** 50% matured in new and 1yo French oak, barrel fermented and
held on lees for 8 months. The gleaming green hue promises good things; this
wine delivers very fine and intense grapefruit and brioche flavours on the long
palate. Screw cap. 13.5% alc. RATING 94 DRINK 2023–2027 $40 JH ✪

Y Y Y Y Y **Impressions Single Vineyard Chardonnay 2020, Hunter Valley** RATING 91
DRINK 2023–2025 $35 JH

Rieslingfreak

103 Langmeil Road, Tanunda, SA 5352 **Region** Clare Valley
T 0400 102 025 **www.**rieslingfreak.com **Open** Mon–Sat 10–4 **Winemaker** John
Hughes, Belinda Hughes **Viticulturist** Richard Hughes **Est.** 2009 **Dozens** 7500
Vyds 40ha
Rieslingfreak sits at the apex of riesling producers, a dedicated specialist with one of the finest
winemakers of the variety. John Hughes established Rieslingfreak in '09 and now produces
some 11 distinct releases per year, with fruit sourced from the Eden and Clare valleys. The
exacting nature of the project is writ large in precise, evocative white wines that vibrate with
purity and tension, built not only for early consumption but long-haul cellaring. Hughes'
commitment to the variety is unswerving with incremental increases in quality seemingly
coming each year. From dry styles to wines of varying sweetness levels, this is the definitive
riesling project in Australia.

Y Y Y Y Y **No. 2 Riesling 2022, Clare Valley** Laser-like and inwardly concentrated,
ultra-zesty and supremely mouth-watering. A highly structured riesling of detail
and strong minerality. Opens with an understated bouquet delivering lemony
freshness and jasmine floral lift, the palate offering tart lime, flinty mineral
licks and zesty grapefruit juice piquancy. The texture is impressive, too, chalky,
puckering and very, very dry. Scintillating stuff! Screw cap. 10% alc. RATING 96
DRINK 2022–2035 $37 MB ✪

No. 1 Riesling 2020, Clare Valley The deep colour is healthy, the wine protected by piercing linear acidity that is the framework of the wine. The finish leaves a mouth-watering film in all corners of the mouth. Screw cap. 11.5% alc. RATING 96 DRINK 2023-2040 $110 JH

No. 8 Riesling 2022, Clare Valley A medium-sweet style that's superbly balanced. Set on a knife's edge of sweet fruit, waxy texture and cool acidity, the wine has concentration and inherent freshness all wrapped up. Scents of ripe lime, sweet apple juice, green melon and honeysuckle, with flavours similarly oriented. Gently sweet, for sure, but with a ticklish tang and lively fizz of acidity. What a drink! Screw cap. 7% alc. RATING 96 DRINK 2022-2030 $37 MB ✪ ♥

No. 12 Riesling 2022, Eden Valley A savoury riesling, stony, dry and highlighted with gentle cashew savouriness and briny acidity. Complex, individual and distinct with a perfume of green apple, frangipani, sea spray and cashew. Flavours echo this character list. The wine is a little loose-knit in the nicest sense and bolstered with that attractive briny, minerally acid profile. It's an excellent offering. Screw cap. 12% alc. RATING 95 DRINK 2022-2030 $37 MB ✪

No. 10 Riesling 2022, Clare Valley Eden Valley Concentrated and relatively rich, albeit swashbuckling in its filigree of tart acidity and chalky, chewy phenolic grip. The perfume is ripe apple, lime, quince and green mango with faint, alpine herb lift. Flavours run riot between brown lime, ginger, green apple and some truffley, savoury elements with the texture quite juicy and the finish tingly with flinty mineral elements. Potent, powerful and layered, this is a riesling of great presence. Screw cap. 11.5% alc. RATING 94 DRINK 2022-2035 $45 MB

No. 3 Riesling 2022, Clare Valley Stacked with lime, green apple and lashed with zingy acidity and juicy in its general verve and appeal. Scents of lime, tangerine and green mango, with flavour similar albeit driven with a rapier thrust of tingly, stony, minerally acidity. The finish trails off with a brilliant, effusive, fine and strongly minerally character. Classic stuff at an elevated level. Screw cap. 11% alc. RATING 94 DRINK 2022-2035 $27 MB ✪

No. 6 Riesling 2017, Clare Valley No. 6 is released after 5 years bottle age. A bright, light straw green, and it will continue developing for a minimum of 10 years. This wine has bracing acidity, yet there's detail that gives balance. Screw cap. 10.5% alc. RATING 94 DRINK 2023-2037 $60 JH

🍷🍷🍷🍷 **No. 4 Riesling 2022, Eden Valley** RATING 93 DRINK 2022-2032 $27 MB ✪

RIKARD Wines ★★★★☆

279 Old Canobolas Road, Nashdale, NSW 2800 **Region** Orange
T 0481 871 683 **www**.rikardwines.com.au **Open** Fri–Mon 11–5 (closed during vintage) **Winemaker** William Rikard-Bell **Viticulturist** William Rikard-Bell **Est.** 2015 **Dozens** 2700 **Vyds** 5ha

William Rikard-Bell's first job as winemaker was at Canobolas Smith in Orange. After interludes in Bordeaux, Mudgee and the Hunter, he returned to Orange and purchased a 10ha block on Mt Canobolas with his wife Kimberley. They have planted 5000 pinot noir and chardonnay vines at 1050m above sea level. More chardonnay and pinot will be planted in the future, and possibly some riesling. The vines are close planted, with narrow rows and a low cordon height. The grapes are hand picked, the small-batch wines made using traditional Old World techniques. A winery and bottling line was completed in '20.

🍷🍷🍷🍷🍷 **Black Label Riesling 2022, Orange** Apple blossom, grapefruit zest, honeysuckle and nashi pear. Lemongrass and chervil. There is an almost sieve-like texture across the palate and an element of orange sherbet. Toasted Marcona almonds linger and the wine is succulent and dry. Plenty of energy and electricity. Screw cap. 12.3% alc. RATING 95 DRINK 2022-2030 $60 SW

🍷🍷🍷🍷 **Merlot/Malbec 2021, Orange** RATING 93 DRINK 2022-2028 $50 SW
Black Label Pinot Noir 2021, Orange RATING 93 DRINK 2022-2032 $75 SW
Chardonnay 2021, Orange RATING 92 DRINK 2022-2028 $40 SW
Shiraz 2021, Orange RATING 92 DRINK 2022-2026 $60 SW

Riesling 2022, Orange RATING 91 DRINK 2022-2032 $35 SW
Pinot Noir 2021, Orange RATING 90 DRINK 2022-2026 $45 SW

Riposte Wines ★★★★★

PO Box 256, Lobethal, SA 5241 **Region** Adelaide Hills
T 0423 014 489 **www**.ripostewines.com.au **Open** Not **Winemaker** Tim Knappstein
Est. 2006 **Dozens** 14 000

Tim Knappstein is a 3rd-generation vigneron, his winemaking lineage dating back to 1893 in the Clare Valley. He made his first wines at the family's Stanley Wine Company and established his own wine company in the Clare Valley in 1976. After the sale of that company in '81, Tim relocated to Lenswood in the Adelaide Hills to make cool-climate wines led by pinot noir and chardonnay. His quest has now been achieved with consistently excellent wines reflected in the winery's 5-star rating since the '12 Wine Companion.

The Scimitar Single Vineyard Riesling 2022, Clare Valley A riesling that flies a flag of detail and considerable refinement, manifesting as a jet stream of Rose's lime juice, quince paste and jasmine notes all gliding on a tail of juicy acidity and a lick of sweetness. Vim, vigour and admirable succulence. Screw cap. 11.5% alc. RATING 92 DRINK 2022-2030 $26 NG ✪

The Stiletto Pinot Gris 2022, Adelaide Hills This winery offers tremendous value across its range, which is founded on fine fruit sourcing and sensible craftsmanship. Nashi pear, toffee apple and scents of pastis reverberate from nose to mid-weighted palate, flowing across a chewy mid-palate of thrumming intensity to an effortless finish. Screw cap. 12.5% alc. RATING 92 DRINK 2022-2024 $24 NG ✪

The Katana Single Vineyard Chardonnay 2021, Adelaide Hills Bright, vivacious and refined, this punches well above its weight. Riffs on glazed quince, white peach, fig and nougat. Creamy at the core, yet tensile at the seams, with a fold of vanillin oak corseting the flavours while directing them long. Sophisticated drinking. Screw cap. 13% alc. RATING 92 DRINK 2022-2028 $28 NG ✪

The Sabre Pinot Noir 2021, Adelaide Hills A strongly regional pinot with a streak of rhubarb, tinderbox and pickled cherry. A curb of sandalwood tannins and a carnal whiff of autumnal leaves offsetting the inherently sweet fruit with a waft of welcome savouriness. Mid-weighted, open-knit and ready to drink. Screw cap. 13.5% alc. RATING 91 DRINK 2022-2027 $38 NG

The Cutlass Single Vineyard Shiraz 2021, Adelaide Hills A savoury, mid-weighted shiraz with distinctive cool-climate elements as much as warmer ones. Bing cherry, peppercorn, clove and a potpourri of Indian spices are lifted by iodine and purple floral scents. There is flesh as much as sinew. Good drinking. Screw cap. 14% alc. RATING 91 DRINK 2022-2028 $28 NG ✪

Risky Business Wines ★★★★☆

PO Box 6015, East Perth, WA 6892 **Region** Various
T 0457 482 957 **www**.riskybusinesswines.com.au **Open** Not **Winemaker** Gavin Berry, Warren Proft **Viticulturist** Rob Quenby **Est.** 2013 **Dozens** 8900

The name Risky Business is decidedly tongue-in-cheek because the partnership headed by Rob Quenby has neatly side-stepped any semblance of risk. The grapes come from vineyards in Great Southern and Margaret River in WA and King Valley in Vic, the latter added in '18 for prosecco, pinot grigio and sangiovese. Since the batches of wine are small, the partnership is able to select grapes specifically suited to the wine style and price. So there is no capital tied up in vineyards, nor in a winery – the wines are contract-made.

Prosecco NV, King Valley There's an enviable consistency to Risky Business' prosecco style. It's seen here from the bright, just-cut green apple and citrus summery scents through to the utterly delicious lemon sorbet crunch and bubbly zing on the palate. And dry … prosecco looks so good when it's dry and clean-cut. Crown. 10% alc. RATING 95 $25 JP ✪

Tempranillo 2021, Frankland River RATING 91 DRINK 2022-2028 $28 JF ✪
Luxe Riesling 2022, Mount Barker RATING 90 DRINK 2022-2028 $25 JF ✪

RiverBank Estate

126 Hamersley Road, Caversham, WA 6055 **Region** Swan Valley
T (08) 9377 1805 **www.riverbankestate.com.au Open** Wed–Sun 10–4 **Winemaker** Troy
Overstone **Est.** 1982 **Dozens** 4500 **Vyds** 12ha

RiverBank Estate was first planted on the fertile banks of the Swan River in '82 and has
grown to encompass 12ha of mature, low-yielding vines (18 varieties), the wines made onsite.
The property was purchased by the Lembo family in '17 and has been rebranded into 3 wine
ranges: On The Run, Rebellious and Eric Anthony.

🍷🍷🍷🍷🍷 **Eric Anthony Zinfandel 2022, Swan Valley** Unfined and unfiltered. It's a
lush but well-judged expression of zinfandel, playing to the variety's best assets of
judicious ripeness, dusty, cinching tannins and bright acidity. This is a charming
red imbued with lusty, sweet and exotic spice, pleasing woody elements, dark
cherry and ripe plum notes and a distinct panforte choc-nuttiness through and
through. Even, balanced and long, too. Pleasure central. Screw cap. 14.5% alc.
RATING 94 **DRINK** 2023-2030 $35 MB ✪

🍷🍷🍷🍷 **Rebellious Grenache 2022, Swan Valley RATING** 90 **DRINK** 2023-2028
$25 MB ✪

Riversdale Estate

222 Denholms Road, Cambridge, Tas 7170 **Region** Southern Tasmania
T (03) 6248 5555 **www.riversdaleestate.com.au Open** Thurs–Sun 10–5
Winemaker Jasper Marais **Viticulturist** Rainier Roberts, Ian Roberts **Est.** 1991
Dozens 9000 **Vyds** 37ha

Ian Roberts purchased the Riversdale property in 1980 while a university student. The
unique feature of the property is its frontage to the Pittwater waterfront, which acts as a
buffer against frost and also moderates the climate during the ripening phase. It is a large
property with 37ha of vines and one of the largest olive groves in Tasmania. The estate also
includes luxury French Provincial-style cottages overlooking the vines, a French bistro, an
orangery (where high tea is served) and a cellar door. Wine quality is consistently good and
can be outstanding.

🍷🍷🍷🍷🍷 **Crater Chardonnay 2021, Tasmania** Light straw in the glass with inviting
characters of juicy peach, nectarine, grapefruit and grilled figs. Tight acidity
frames the ripe fruit nicely on a backdrop of dreamy, nutty French oak, vanillin
and nougat. A subtle squeak of phenolics adds texture as the wine fades slowly
with memories of stone fruit and oatmeal. Screw cap. 13.5% alc. **RATING** 94
DRINK 2023-2029 $75 DB
Centaurus Pinot Noir 2021, Tasmania There is aromatic power and
complexity here, with impressive fruit depth and grace. Laden with complex
spice and hints of forest floor, some game meat facets and a lick of judicious
French oak with a Burgundian flow on the palate. Tannin and acid poised just so,
and a sveltely fruited finish with a savoury flick of its tail. Screw cap. 13.5% alc.
RATING 94 **DRINK** 2026-2032 $75 DB

🍷🍷🍷🍷 **Chardonnay 2021, Tasmania RATING** 92 **DRINK** 2023-2026 $45 DB
Pinot Noir 2021, Tasmania RATING 90 **DRINK** 2023-2027 $45 DB

🍇 Rivulet

RMB 100, Swansea, Tasmania 7190 **Region** Tasmania
T 0404 845 854 **www.rivuletwine.com Open** Not **Winemaker** Keira O'Brien
Est. 2018 **Dozens** 500

After growing up in North East Victoria and working vintages in McLaren Vale and the Yarra
and Hunter valleys, winemaker Keira O'Brien felt the pull of Tasmania, working 5 years at
Tasmanian Vintners before starting her own wine label, Rivulet Wines, in '19. The packaging
is inviting and the wines are delicious and thoughtfully composed. An exciting newcomer
from the Apple Isle.

🍷🍷🍷🍷♀ **Priory Pinot Noir 2021, Tasmania** Bright cherry in colour with tones of wild strawberry, redcurrant and red cherry on a bed of fine spice, light game notes, forest floor, shiitake mushroom and fine French oak. Airy on the palate with a fine line of acidity and pure, spicy cherry fruits flitting around. Finishes pure and endearing. Screw cap. 13.5% alc. **RATING** 93 **DRINK** 2023–2029 $50 DB

Burnside Pinot Noir 2021, Tasmania Bright cherry red with notes of spiced cherry, red plum and wild strawberry. Underlined with soft spice, purple flowers, earth, red licorice and gentle oak nuance. Purely fruited, with just the merest hint of forest floor, fine-grained tannins in support and bright acidity pushing forward to a medium-length finish that's flush with spicy cherry and red fruit. Screw cap. 13.5% alc. **RATING** 93 **DRINK** 2023–2029 $50 DB

Forestier Chardonnay 2021, Tasmania Light straw in hue with notes of white peach, Meyer lemon, ginger cake, lightly spiced French oak, white flowers and crushed stone. Fragrant and pure fruited in the mouth with bright acidity and a lovely textural pithiness on the finish. Screw cap. 12.8% alc. **RATING** 92 **DRINK** 2023–2028 $50 DB

Pinot Noir 2021, Tasmania Bright raspberry, red plum and red cherry fruits with hints of five-spice, purple flowers, cherry clafoutis and judicious French-oak spice. Finely poised, pure drinking with bright acidity and a lovely calm composition. Screw cap. 13.5% alc. **RATING** 91 **DRINK** 2023–2026 $38 DB

Rob Dolan Wines   ★★★★☆

21–23 Delaneys Road, South Warrandyte, Vic 3134 **Region** Yarra Valley
T (03) 9876 5885 **www**.robdolanwines.com.au **Open** 7 days 10–5 **Winemaker**
Rob Dolan, Adrian Santolin **Viticulturist** Maris Feldgen **Est.** 2010 **Dozens** 30 000
Vyds 25ha
Rob Dolan has been making wine in the Yarra Valley for over 30 years and knows its every nook and cranny. In '11 he was able to purchase the Hardys Yarra Burn winery at an enticing price. It is singularly well equipped and, in addition to making the excellent Rob Dolan wines there, he conducts an extensive contract winemaking business. Business is booming, production having doubled, with exports driving much of the increase.

🍷🍷🍷🍷🍷 **Signature Series Chardonnay 2020, Yarra Valley** A luminous green gold. Reticent at first, this blossomed in the glass to reveal aromas of ripened nectarines and white peaches, grilled cashews and attractive (not overdone) reductive, struck-match notes. Gently textured, this silky and persistent wine is tightly structured and while it's totally enjoyable now, there's little doubt time in bottle will see it improve further. Screw cap. 13.5% alc. **RATING** 96 **DRINK** 2022–2028 $80 PR

🍷🍷🍷🍷♀ **Black Label Pinot Noir 2021, Yarra Valley RATING** 93 **DRINK** 2022–2026 $28 PR ✪

White Label Pinot Noir 2021, Yarra Valley RATING 92 **DRINK** 2022–2027 $40 PR

Rob Hall Wines   ★★★★★

157 Pine Avenue, Healesville, Vic 3777 (postal) **Region** Yarra Valley
T 0448 224 003 **www**.robhallwine.com.au **Open** Not **Winemaker** Rob Hall **Est.** 2013
Dozens 2000 **Vyds** 3ha
Rob Hall has had considerable experience in making Yarra Valley chardonnay and pinot noir, previously at Mount Mary, and thereafter at Kellybrook. His business took several steps forward in '15. First, he acquired the 3ha vineyard on the property where he grew up. It was planted in '96 by his parents (in particular, mother Harriet, hence Harriet's vineyard). Next he leased the Limbic winery at Pakenham Upper. It has an underground barrel room, making it ideal for maturation, and also enabling much cellar work to be conducted using gravity. It is well equipped with a sorting table, Bucher crusher/destemmer, and a Bucher press.

🍷🍷🍷🍷🍷 **Harriet's Vineyard Blanc de Noir 2019, Yarra Valley** Disgorged in '22 with zero dosage. Bright, pale gold with green tinges. Small red fruits, red apples, some freshly baked goods and a little leatherwood honey can be found in this subtle and delicate sparkling. The palate is bone dry, chalky and very gently textured. It's also long, well balanced and drinking well right now. Cork. 11.5% alc. **RATING** 96 **DRINK** 2023–2026 $55 PR ✪

Cabernets 2022, Yarra Valley Cabernet sauvignon with a tiny amount of malbec. Aromas of dark cherries, blackberries, crushed violets and just a soupçon of cedar. Medium bodied, this is both creamily textured and structured with ripe, fine-grained tannins ensuring that, as approachable as this is now, it will age well, too. That it's so fairly priced is a bonus. Indeed, I gave it an extra point for that. Screw cap. 13.5% alc. **RATING** 96 **DRINK** 2022–2028 $30 PR ✪

Nenagh Park Vineyard Pinot Noir 2022, Yarra Valley Bright ruby crimson. A pure fruited wine centred around perfectly ripened strawberries and raspberries with scents of peony and allspice. It's deceptive on the palate in that while it's light on its feet and quite delicious, it's also structured with a little orange peel and spice on the long finish. Terrific from beginning to end. Screw cap. 13.5% alc. **RATING** 96 **DRINK** 2023–2030 $50 PR ✪

Gladysdale Pinot Noir 2022, Yarra Valley Bright ruby red. Lifted and perfumed with aromas of red fruits, tangelo, pink peppercorns and some delicate floral notes. Elegant and supple with super-silky tannins before finishing energetic and long. Screw cap. 13.5% alc. **RATING** 96 **DRINK** 2023–2029 $50 PR ✪

Harriet's Vineyard Chardonnay 2022, Yarra Valley A bright green gold. Subtle and complex with its bouquet of just-picked white nectarines, lightly grilled nuts, lemongrass and a little sea spray. Fills out nicely on the mid-palate and there's a touch of grip on the finish keeping the wine focused and long. Screw cap. 13% alc. **RATING** 95 **DRINK** 2023–2028 $45 PR ✪

Harriet's Vineyard Pinot Noir 2022, Yarra Valley A medium crimson ruby. Aromas of strawberries, satsuma plums, lightly poached rhubarb and a little potpourri. Still quite tightly wound, there's a lovely core of red and black fruits on entry before the compact and sturdy tannins kick in on the finish. Screw cap. 13.5% alc. **RATING** 95 **DRINK** 2023–2030 $50 PR ✪

Pinot Noir 2022, Yarra Valley A light ruby red. Fragrant and floral with wild strawberries, spiced cherries and a gentle dusting of aromatic spices. The palate is resolved and harmonious for such a young wine and builds nicely with supple yet persistent tannins kicking in on the finish. One of the best value Yarra pinots I've tasted recently. Screw cap. 13.5% alc. **RATING** 94 **DRINK** 2023–2029 $33 PR ✪

🍷🍷🍷🍷 **Chardonnay 2022, Yarra Valley** **RATING** 93 **DRINK** 2023–2026 $30 PR ✪

Robert Channon Wines ★★★☆

32 Bradley Lane, Amiens, Qld 4352 **Region** Granite Belt
T (07) 4683 3260 **www**.robertchannonwines.com **Open** Mon, Tues & Fri 11–4, w'ends 10–5 **Winemaker** Paola Cabezas, Ash Smith, Robert Channon **Viticulturist** Clark Strudwick **Est.** 1998 **Dozens** 2500 **Vyds** 8ha

Peggy and Robert Channon have established verdelho, chardonnay, pinot gris, shiraz, cabernet sauvignon and pinot noir under permanent bird protection netting. The initial cost of installing permanent netting is high but in the long term it is well worth it: it excludes birds and protects the grapes against hail damage. Also, there is no pressure to pick the grapes before they are fully ripe.

🍷🍷🍷🍷 **Pinot Gris 2022, Granite Belt** This plays its cards right as a gris: slippery in texture, fuller flavoured and a little savoury. Scents of nashi pear, cinnamon spice, marzipan and orange blossom. The palate glides along on that slick of ripe pear, and shows sweet-almond savouriness to finish. Ticking lots of boxes. Screw cap. 11% alc. **RATING** 90 **DRINK** 2022–2024 $30 MB

Robert Oatley Vineyards ★★★★★

Craigmoor Road, Mudgee, NSW 2850 **Region** Mudgee
T (02) 9433 3255 **www**.robertoatley.com.au **www**.craigmoor.com.au **Open** Thurs–Mon
from 11am **Winemaker** Larry Cherubino **Est.** 2006 **Vyds** 155ha
Robert Oatley Vineyards, founded by the late Robert (Bob) Oatley AO BEM, is a family-
owned winery led by his eldest son Sandy Oatley who, with his father, brother and sister,
planted the first Oatley vineyards in the late 1960s. The Robert Oatley brand has a trio
of labels producing wines from Margaret River, Great Southern and McLaren Vale: the
Signature Series, particular vineyard sites with Finisterre, and the best of the best barrels under
The Pennant. Previously based in Margaret River, the cellar door is now in Mudgee, where
the family also produces wines for Mudgee labels Montrose and Craigmoor.

ŸŸŸŸŸ **The Pennant Shiraz 2018, McLaren Vale** There is a lather of toasty, high-
quality oak. But at this early stage, it is to be expected. Behind this lies ample
Indian spice, blue and black fruits, licorice and soaring violet riffs compressed
into a vortex of tension by quality tannins. Screw cap. 13.5% alc. **RATING** 95
DRINK 2022-2032 $105 NG

ŸŸŸŸŸ **Robert Oatley Finisterre Grenache 2022, McLaren Vale** **RATING** 91
DRINK 2022-2028 $40 NG
Robert Oatley Signature Series Shiraz 2020, McLaren Vale **RATING** 91
DRINK 2022-2029 $24 NG ✪
Robert Oatley Finisterre Chardonnay 2020, Margaret River **RATING** 91
DRINK 2022-2026 $40 JF

Robert Stein Vineyard

Pipeclay Lane, Mudgee, NSW 2850 **Region** Mudgee
T (02) 6373 3991 **www**.robertstein.com.au **Open** 7 days 10–4.30 **Winemaker** Jacob
Stein, Lisa Bray **Viticulturist** Matthew Bailey **Est.** 1976 **Dozens** 20000 **Vyds** 19.5ha
Robert (Bob) Stein established this vineyard in the 1970s, although the family history
stretches back to Bob's great-great-grandfather, Johann Stein, brought to Australia in 1838
by the Macarthur family to supervise the planting of the Camden Park vineyard. Three
generations on, Bob's grandson Jacob is chief winemaker. Jacob returned to the family
business after various vintages around the globe, including in Germany's Rheingau and
Rheinhessen, where his passion for riesling was ignited. The estate Wallenstein vineyard was
certified organic in '90; other vineyards are run according to organic principles. The winery
was certified organic in '20.

ŸŸŸŸŸ **Half Dry RS 15 Riesling 2022, Orange** Lemon sorbet, delicate white florals,
green melon and celeriac. A tug of war between perfect fruit sweetness and
cool climate, natural acidity. Then there is its underground lair of texture and
framework. A joy of a wine crafted with the utmost care. Screw cap. 11% alc.
RATING 96 **DRINK** 2022-2032 $50 SW ✪ ♥
Reserve Riesling 2022, Mudgee Lime and lemon bath salts, elderflower jelly,
crushed pumice, celery heart and white pepper. A swathe of texture across the
palate. Concentrated and dense fruit weight with a multifaceted construction.
Built for the long haul but equally drinking so well now. Screw cap. 11% alc.
RATING 96 **DRINK** 2022-2035 $60 SW ✪ ♥
The Kinnear 2019, Mudgee 97/3% shiraz/cabernet sauvignon. The Kinnear
was the ship that sailed Johann Stein to Australia and is the flagship wine.
Hibiscus, red tulip, black cherries, Assam tea leaves and clove studs. The wine
is intoxicating and yet modish in restraint. Silky tannins with buoyant acidity.
A class act. Screw cap. 14% alc. **RATING** 96 **DRINK** 2022-2030 $97 SW ♥
Dry Riesling 2022, Mudgee Zested lime, Jazz apples and acacia blossoms.
Powerful and weighted with a pithy pomelo grip and an apple and citrus-loaded
mid-palate. A star of the region. Delightful. Screw cap. 11% alc. **RATING** 95
DRINK 2022-2030 $40 SW ✪

Reserve Cabernet Sauvignon 2019, Mudgee Red cherries, blackberries and blood plum skin. Adzuki bean, mocha, powdered cinnamon and brown mushroom. Tanned leather and fine powdery tannins persist. A twinge of sappy clove and bay leaf. A wine that fits snugly into its sleeping bag of oak. Fine and long flavour length. Classy. Screw cap. 14% alc. RATING 95 DRINK 2022-2030 $80 SW ❤

ŶŶŶŶŶ **Blühen Dry Rosé 2022, Mudgee** RATING 93 DRINK 2022-2027 $38 SW
Blühen Shiraz Riesling 2022, Mudgee RATING 93 DRINK 2022-2026 $44 SW
Third Generation Chardonnay 2021, Mudgee RATING 92 DRINK 2022-2028 $35 SW
Gewürztraminer 2022, Mudgee RATING 91 DRINK 2022-2025 $35 SW
Cabernet Sauvignon 2021, Mudgee RATING 91 DRINK 2022-2030 $40 SW
Blühen Montepulciano 2022, Mudgee RATING 90 DRINK 2022-2028 $44 SW

Robin Brockett Wines ★★★★☆

43 Woodville St, Drysdale, Vic 3222 (postal) **Region** Geelong
T 0418 112 221 **www.robinbrockettwines.com Open** Not **Winemaker** Robin Brockett
Est. 2013 **Dozens** 400
Robin Brockett is chief winemaker at Scotchmans Hill, a position he has held for over 30 years, making consistently very good wines through the ebbs and flows of climate. In '13 he took the first steps towards the realisation of a 35-year dream of making and selling wines under his own label. He put in place an agreement to buy grapes from the Fenwick (2ha) and Swinburn (1ha) vineyards, and in '13 made the first wines. Robin is one of the most experienced winemakers in the Geelong region.

ŶŶŶŶŶ **Swinburn Vineyard Bellarine Peninsula Pinot Noir 2021, Geelong** Poised with its core of raspberries, crushed black cherries, lifted florals and spice. Light-to medium-bodied but not lacking in intensity, this energetic wine finishes with balanced, crunchy tannins and bright acidity. A beautifully put-together wine and one that will blossom nicely. 80 dozen made. Screw cap. 13% alc. RATING 95 DRINK 2023-2030 $42 PR ✪

ŶŶŶŶŶ **Heyward Vineyard Bellarine Peninsula Chardonnay 2021, Geelong** RATING 93 DRINK 2022-2027 $42 PR
Fenwick Vineyard Bellarine Peninsula Pinot Noir 2021, Geelong RATING 93 DRINK 2023-2027 $42 PR
Swinburn Vineyard Bellarine Peninsula Pinot Noir 2020, Geelong RATING 90 DRINK 2022-2026 $32 PR

Rochford Wines ★★★★★

878-880 Maroondah Highway, Coldstream, Vic 3770 **Region** Yarra Valley
T (03) 5957 3333 **www.rochfordwines.com.au Open** 7 days 9–5 **Winemaker** Kaspar Hermann **Viticulturist** John Evans **Est.** 1988 **Dozens** 27 000 **Vyds** 26ha
This Yarra Valley property was purchased by Helmut Konecsny in '02; he had already established a reputation for pinot noir and chardonnay from the family-owned Romsey Park Vineyard in the Macedon Ranges (sold in '10). Since '10, Helmut has focused on his Yarra Valley winery and vineyards. In addition to the cellar door, the property has 2 restaurants, a retail shop and an expansive natural amphitheatre and observation tower.

ŶŶŶŶŶ **Premier Single Vineyard Chardonnay 2021, Yarra Valley** Stone and orchard fruits with some delicate spice and marine scents. Even better on the palate. There's a gentle creaminess yet the wine is tightly coiled with good inner energy. There's a little orange pith on the long, balanced finish. Good stuff and worth cellaring. Screw cap. 13% alc. RATING 96 DRINK 2022-2028 $100 PR
Premier Single Vineyard Pinot Noir 2021, Yarra Valley A light, bright crimson. Full of boysenberries, raspberries and warm spices such as cinnamon and clove. Seamless and smooth with fine, very persistent tannins which augur well for the future. Screw cap. 13% alc. RATING 96 DRINK 2023-2031 $100 PR

Isabella's Single Vineyard Cabernet Sauvignon 2021, Yarra Valley A very bright magenta. Redolent of blackcurrants and blackberries with violets, pencil block shavings and a soupçon of licorice root. Concentrated with firm yet noble cabernet tannins. Very persistent. A class act. Screw cap. 13.8% alc. **RATING** 96 **DRINK** 2023-2032 $80 PR

Terre Single Vineyard Chardonnay 2021, Yarra Valley A very bright green gold. Cool fruited with aromas of stone fruits and citrus along with a hint of white pepper. Silky in texture and taut, this finishes saline and long. Screw cap. 12.5% alc. **RATING** 95 **DRINK** 2023-2028 $60 PR

Isabella's Single Vineyard Chardonnay 2021, Yarra Valley A very bright green gold. Gently vanillin with ripe stone fruits, a little orange blossom and some spice. Textured on the palate with a gentle saline edge giving the wine balance and length. A wine to enjoy in the short- to medium-term. Screw cap. 13% alc. **RATING** 94 **DRINK** 2022-2026 $75 PR

Terre Single Vineyard Pinot Noir 2021, Yarra Valley A light, bright ruby red. Highly perfumed and herbal inflected with its aromas of redcurrants, damson plums, rosemary and spices. Fine-boned and silky, the tannins are harmonious. Fleshes out nicely on the mid-palate. Very drinkable now and over the next few years. Screw cap. 13.4% alc. **RATING** 94 **DRINK** 2022-2028 $70 PR

ΨΨΨΨΨ **Estate Syrah 2021, Yarra Valley RATING** 93 **DRINK** 2022-2028 $33 PR ✪
Dans les Bois Single Vineyard Chardonnay 2021, Yarra Valley RATING 93 **DRINK** 2022-2027 $49 PR
L'Enfant Unique Single Vineyard Pinot Noir 2021, Yarra Valley RATING 93 **DRINK** 2024-2029 $85 PR
Dans les Bois Single Vineyard Pinot Noir 2021, Yarra Valley RATING 93 **DRINK** 2024-2031 $50 PR
Estate Chardonnay 2021, Yarra Valley RATING 92 **DRINK** 2023-2024 $38 PR
Estate Pinot Noir 2021, Yarra Valley RATING 91 **DRINK** 2022-2025 $38 PR

Rockcliffe   ★★★★

18 Hamilton Road, Denmark, WA 6333 **Region** Great Southern
T 0419 848 195 **www**.rockcliffe.com.au **Open** 7 days 11–5, or by appt
Winemaker Elysia Harrison, Mike Garland, Neil Miles **Viticulturist** Elysia Harrison, Mike Garland, Neil Miles **Est.** 1990 **Dozens** 30 000 **Vyds** 11ha
The Rockcliffe winery and vineyard business, formerly known as Matilda's Estate, is owned by citizen of the world Steve Hall. The wine ranges echo local surf place names, headed by Rockcliffe itself but extending to Third Reef and Quarram Rocks. Over the years, Rockcliffe has won more than its fair share of trophies and gold and silver medals in wine shows.

ΨΨΨΨΨ **Single Site Cabernet Sauvignon 2020, Great Southern** A medium-weight, detailed expression of cabernet sauvignon. A bold perfume of cassis, sea spray, dark chocolate and a herbal sage leaf character. Succulent texture, depth and concentration to taste, but a lift and freshness from both gravelly mineral notes and cool acidity. Flows beautifully and builds with a fine, chocolate-powder tannin pucker. A serious wine with immediate appeal, but a long future ahead of it, too. Screw cap. 14.5% alc. **RATING** 94 **DRINK** 2022-2035 $60 MB

ΨΨΨΨΨ **Single Site Malbec 2021, Great Southern RATING** 93 **DRINK** 2022-2028 $45 MB
Single Site Chardonnay 2021, Great Southern RATING 93 **DRINK** 2022-2030 $60 MB
Nautica Chardonnay 2021, Great Southern RATING 93 **DRINK** 2024-2030 $100 MB
Nautica Shiraz 2021, Great Southern RATING 93 **DRINK** 2023-2033 $100 MB
Single Site Riesling 2022, Great Southern RATING 92 **DRINK** 2023-2033 $35 MB
Single Site Pinot Noir 2021, Great Southern RATING 92 **DRINK** 2022-2029 $60 MB

Single Site Mourvèdre 2021, Great Southern RATING 90 DRINK 2024–2027
$45 MB
Single Site Cabernet Sauvignon 2021, Frankland River RATING 90
DRINK 2025–2035 $60 MB
Single Site Shiraz 2021, Frankland River RATING 90 DRINK 2025–2035
$60 MB

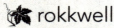 rokkwell   ★★★★

PO Box 2, Ballandean, Qld 4382 **Region** Granite Belt
T 0416 851 545 **www**.rokkwell.com.au **Open** Not **Winemaker** Dawn Walker
Viticulturist Dawn Walker **Est.** 2019 **Dozens Vyds** 1.6ha
Based in Ballandean in Queensland's Granite Belt, rokkwell is a fledgling producer, with
winemaker Dawn Walker having spent time under the guidance of Ridgemill Estate's
esteemed winemaker Peter McGlashan. She moved to the region in '19 as part of her
vocational pursuit, studying a bachelor of wine science through the University of Southern
Queensland. Since '21, Dawn and family have focused on the home estate and vineyards,
with varieties including chardonnay, nebbiolo and sauvignon blanc alongside newer plantings
of nero d'Avola and arneis.

🍷🍷🍷🍷 **Rosé Nebbiolo 2022, Granite Belt** Textural indeed. A finely tuned rosé
that manages savouriness, attractive fruit character and a bone-dry chalky finish.
Scents of tart cherries, white pepper and faint hazelnut. Flavours are in a similar
vogue, lightly juicy and then whipped to tension with fine, puckering tannin.
Very refreshing all up, good detail and generally a fine expression of the style.
Screw cap. 12.6% alc. **RATING** 93 **DRINK** 2022–2024 $30 MB ✪
Chardonnay 2022, Granite Belt An unoaked chardonnay. Fleshy, juicy and
generous in style. Aromas of rockmelon, pawpaw and kiwifruit with flavours more
aligned with stone fruits, a touch of honey butter in there too. It's round and soft
but finds an undertow of refreshing acidity. Old-school, good-school. Screw cap.
12% alc. **RATING** 90 **DRINK** 2022–2025 $30 MB

 Rongo Wines   ★★★★

PO Box 1034, Ashwood VIC 3147 **Region** Yarra Valley
T 0410 735 397 **www**.rongowines.com **Open** Not **Winemaker** Ray Chen, Josh Liu
Est. 2021 **Dozens** 450
Rongo Wines is a joint project between friends Ray Chen and Josh Liu. The pair met while
working in Napa Valley and have worked in wine all over the world, from China and America
to New Zealand, France and Australia. Their academic credentials are equally impressive.
They both studied winemaking and viticulture at Lincoln University (NZ) and UC Davis
(California), and studied for their masters at Cornell University (New York) and Adelaide
University. Rongo is a project that works around their day jobs. Ray is product innovation
manager at Endeavour Group and Josh is assistant winemaker at Stuart Wines, Heathcote.
They source fruit from growers with sustainable practices and produce the wine in rented
winery space, operating out of an outer Melbourne suburb with barrel storage and cellar.

🍷🍷🍷🍷 **Rhapsody Orange Blend 2022, Strathbogie Ranges** A blend of riesling,
shiraz and chardonnay. Reveals a lovely delicacy of flavour and texture in red
apple, pear and yellow peach. Acidity is well tuned to aid the textural flow. An
amber wine of style and grace. Cork. 12.5% alc. **RATING** 91 **DRINK** 2023–2027
$32 JP
Reflection Riesling 2022, Strathbogie Ranges A charming, spicy, textural
wine, which plays to the attributes of Strathbogie Ranges riesling. That spiciness,
nicely interpreted and highlighted with a touch of sweetness, enjoys a starring role
on a palate bright in citrus blossom, lime pith and apple with a lemon butteriness.
Not to mention a smoothness that opens up all manner of food-matching ideas.
Screw cap. 12.5% alc. **RATING** 91 **DRINK** 2023–2028 $32 JP

Ros Ritchie Wines

Magnolia House, 190 Mount Buller Road, Mansfield, 3722 **Region** Upper Goulburn
T 0448 900 541 **www**.rosritchiewines.com **Open** Fri 5–8, w'ends & public hols 11–4
Winemaker Ros Ritchie **Est.** 2008 **Dozens** 2000 **Vyds** 7ha
Ros Ritchie was winemaker at the Ritchie family's Delatite winery from '81–06, but moved on to establish her own winery with husband John in '08 on a vineyard near Mansfield. They became shareholders in Barwite Vineyards in '12 (planted to chardonnay, pinot noir, riesling, pinot gris and shiraz) and in '14 established their new winery there. Apart from gewürztraminer (grown at Dead Man's Hill vineyard), they work with local growers, foremost the Barwite, McFadden, Timbertop and Baxendale vineyards, the last planted by the very experienced viticulturist Jim Baxendale (and wife Ruth) high above the King River Valley. All vineyards are managed with minimal spray regimes. The cellar door is located at the historic Magnolia House at Mansfield.

ŸŸŸŸŸ **Barwite Vineyard Riesling 2022, Upper Goulburn** A wine that encapsulates the grace and beauty of High Country riesling. The scent is like spring air, with apple and citrus blossoms all steely and fresh. Gently opening up at this early stage, but there is much more to uncover: lime juice, green apple, grapefruit, a hint of honeysuckle and talc-like minerality. Racy and focused. Screw cap. 12% alc. **RATING** 95 **DRINK** 2022-2032 $28 JP ✪

ŸŸŸŸŸ **Barwite Vineyard Pinot Grigio 2022, Upper Goulburn RATING** 92 **DRINK** 2022-2025 $25 JP ✪
Dead Man's Hill Vineyard Gewürztraminer 2022, Upper Goulburn RATING 91 **DRINK** 2022-2026 $28 JP ✪
Timbertop Vineyard Nebbiolo Rosé 2022, Upper Goulburn RATING 91 **DRINK** 2022-2025 $25 JP ✪
Sandy Creek Vineyard Vermentino 2022, Upper Goulburn RATING 90 **DRINK** 2022-2025 $28 JP

Rosabrook Margaret River Wines

1390 Rosa Brook Road, Rosabrook WA 6285 (postal) **Region** Margaret River
T (08) 9368 4555 **www**.rosabrook.com.au **Open** Not **Winemaker** Severine Logan
Viticulturist Murray Edmonds **Est.** 1980 **Dozens** 12000 **Vyds** 25ha
The original Rosabrook estate vineyards were established between '84 and '96. In later years Rosabrook relocated to a more eastern part of the Margaret River wine region. Warm days and cool nights, influenced by the ocean, result in slow, mild ripening conditions.

ŸŸŸŸŸ **Single Vineyard Estate Cabernet Sauvignon 2019, Margaret River** Violets, blueberries and mulberries, the whiff of gum leaves and dried herbs. An elegance across the medium-bodied palate plumped up by juicy, ripe fruit and sweet yet grainy tannins. Woodsy spices and toasty mocha oak in the mix and there's a slightly bitter, charred radicchio character on the finish, adding to the more savoury parts of this very good wine. Screw cap. 14% alc. **RATING** 93 **DRINK** 2023-2033 $45 JF
Single Vineyard Estate Chardonnay 2020, Margaret River Wafts of lavender, lemon blossom and popcorn with stone fruit and citrus on the palate. With layers of creamy lees and sweet cedary oak, it comes across as fleshy, ripe and interesting. Screw cap. 13% alc. **RATING** 91 **DRINK** 2023-2029 $45 JF

Rosby

122 Strikes Lane, Mudgee, NSW 2850 **Region** Mudgee
T 0419 429 918 **www**.rosby.com.au **Open** Thurs–Mon 10–4 **Winemaker** Tim Stevens, James Manners **Viticulturist** Gerald Norton-Knight **Est.** 1993 **Dozens** 1800 **Vyds** 8ha
Gerald and Kay Norton-Knight have shiraz and cabernet sauvignon established on a truly unique site in Mudgee. Many vignerons like to think that their vineyard has special qualities, but in this instance the belief is well based. The vineyard is situated in a small valley with

unusual red basalt over a quartz gravel structure, encouraging deep root growth, making the use of water far less critical than normal. Tim Stevens of Huntington Estate has purchased some of the ample production and makes the Rosby wines. A cellar door has recently been completed at Rosby and there is an art gallery and sculpture garden onsite, too.

Chardonnay 2022, Mudgee White nectarine and golden apple aromas with subtle almond nougat and crème fraîche. Hints of cashew and vanilla suggest restrained oak use, which allows the fruit to shine. A well-rounded chardonnay with poise. Screw cap. 11% alc. **RATING** 92 **DRINK** 2022-2030 $35 SW

Reserve Cabernet Sauvignon 2021, Mudgee The world of red and black fruits collide. Black plums, red raspberry, hibiscus and thistle. Sweet ripe mulberries, chewing tobacco and dark chocolate – the fruit is riper still on the mid-palate. Prune puree, dragonfruit and Cherry Ripe. Tannins are chewy and firm with nicely framed oak presence and a slick lick of acidity. A smart-looking wine. Screw cap. 14.4% alc. **RATING** 91 **DRINK** 2023-2028 $50 SW

Sangiovese 2022, Mudgee Ripe pomegranate, raspberry and blood plums with traces of gingerbread spices like nutmeg, ground ginger and cinnamon. Baked red earth is followed by button mushrooms. Lively acidity and fine tannins, this is a variety well suited to its place and showcasing moderate weight and body. Screw cap. 12.7% alc. **RATING** 90 **DRINK** 2022-2032 $35 SW

Reserve Shiraz 2021, Mudgee Blackberry, blackcurrant, blood plums and Assam tea leaves with distinct clove, black peppercorns and sweet figs. The palate is velvety and luxurious. Specks of vanilla and coffee grinds are telltale signs of quality French oak. More lifting acidity would help the flavour line, but this is still an assured shiraz to be enjoyed by a wide range of palates. Screw cap. 14.2% alc. **RATING** 90 **DRINK** 2023-2027 $50 SW

Rosenthal Wines ★★★★

24 Rockford Street, Denmark, WA 6333 (postal) **Region** Great Southern
T 0432 312 918 **www**.rosenthalwines.com.au **Open** Not **Winemaker** Luke Eckersley, Coby Ladwig **Est.** 2001 **Dozens** 35 000 **Vyds** 40ha
The original Rosenthal vineyard (Springfield Park) was established in 1997 just north of Manjimup by Dr John Rosenthal. In '12 Coby Ladwig and Luke Eckersley acquired the business and relocated it to Denmark, Great Southern. Both have a sound knowledge of vineyards throughout the southwest of WA. The fruit for Rosenthal wines is sourced from their leased vineyard in Mount Barker, plus growers in Frankland River and Pemberton.

Richings Cabernet Sauvignon 2021, Frankland River A dark and brooding medium-bodied red. Scents of clove, cinnamon, tree bark and ripe plum with minty highlights and a whiff of sea spray. Dark cherry, ripe plum, milk chocolate, cola and pencil shaving oak seasoning. Firm in texture, tightly wound, mouth-watering with acidity and strict with sandy tannin. A serious expression. Screw cap. 14.5% alc. **RATING** 94 **DRINK** 2026-2040 $60 MB

Richings Riesling 2022, Mount Barker RATING 93 **DRINK** 2023-2035 $35 MB

Collector Cabernet Sauvignon 2021, Mount Barker RATING 93 **DRINK** 2025-2040 $90 MB

Richings Shiraz 2021, Frankland River RATING 93 **DRINK** 2023-2035 $60 MB

Collector Chardonnay 2021, Mount Barker RATING 92 **DRINK** 2023-2029 $90 MB

The Marker Cabernet Sauvignon 2021, Frankland River RATING 90 **DRINK** 2023-2033 $40 MB

Rosily Vineyard

871 Yelverton Road, Wilyabrup, WA 6284 **Region** Margaret River
T (08) 9755 6336 **www**.rosily.com.au **Open** Sat 11–5, or by appt **Winemaker** Mike
Lemmes **Viticulturist** Jarod Bawden **Est.** 1994 **Dozens** 5000 **Vyds** 12.2ha
Ken Allan and Mick Scott acquired the Rosily Vineyard site in 1994 and the vineyard was
planted over 3 years to sauvignon blanc, semillon, chardonnay, cabernet sauvignon, merlot,
shiraz, grenache and cabernet franc. The first crops were sold to other makers in the region,
but by '99 Rosily had built a 120t capacity winery. It has gone from strength to strength, all
of its estate-grown grapes being vinified under the Rosily Vineyard label, the wines often
over-delivering for their prices. The vineyard was certified organic (ACO) in '17.

Gros Ventre Grenache Shiraz Rosé 2022, Margaret River A lovely pink
blush draws the eye to the glass while flavours of spiced watermelon, redcurrants
and Meyer lemon excite the palate. Crunchy acidity and a slip of talc-like
texture all add to the appeal of this refreshing, cheery rosé. Screw cap. 12.5% alc.
RATING 92 **DRINK** 2022-2024 $24 JF ✪

Reserve Chardonnay 2021, Margaret River A mid-gold hue. This is no
wallflower on the flavour front. Rich, voluptuous and full of ripe stone fruit,
toasted malt, preserved ginger and loads of sweet vanillin toasty oak. Thankfully,
there's plenty of acidity keeping the palate rather tight. As with all things in life,
this is better with food. Screw cap. 13% alc. **RATING** 91 **DRINK** 2022-2030 $60 JF

Semillon Sauvignon Blanc 2022, Margaret River Plenty of energy and
drive with this varietal duo working in unison. Finger limes, crushed makrut
lime leaves, lemon balm and Chinese gooseberries lead the flavour profile.
There's texture and depth and all in all, it's a stylish wine. Screw cap. 12.5% alc.
RATING 90 **DRINK** 2022-2025 $24 JF ✪

Reserve Cabernet Sauvignon 2020, Margaret River The full-on aromas
come as strong as the flood of flavours immediately following. No shortage of
mulberries, cassis, dried herbs, wafts of charcuterie and just-varnished wood.
The palate is weighty, densely packed with fruit and a mouthful of burly tannins.
Either give this more time in the cellar or serve it with appropriate food.
Screw cap. 14% alc. **RATING** 90 **DRINK** 2024-2034 $60 JF

Ross Hill Wines

134 Wallace Lane, Orange, NSW 2800 **Region** Orange
T (02) 6365 3223 **www**.rosshillwines.com.au **Open** 7 days 10.30–4.30
Winemaker Luke Steele **Viticulturist** Peter Robson **Est.** 1994 **Dozens** 25 000
Vyds 20.7ha
Peter and Terri Robson planted chardonnay, merlot, sauvignon blanc, cabernet franc,
cabernet sauvignon and pinot noir on north-facing slopes of the Griffin Road vineyard
in '94. In '07 their son James and his wife Chrissy joined the business and the Wallace Lane
vineyard (pinot noir, sauvignon blanc and pinot gris) was planted. The vines are now mature
and the winery was certified carbon neutral in '13. The Barrel & Larder School of Wine and
Food (WSET Levels 1 and 2) operates from the extended cellar door.

Pinnacle Series Griffin Road Vineyard Cabernet Franc 2021, Orange
A show-stopping '21 cabernet franc setting new style trends for the variety.
Sweet elderberry, acai and tonka bean. Exotic purple flowers, vanilla bean and
patchouli. The palate is lithe with a silken texture and a long cola-spiced finish.
Superb acidity and finely woven silty tannins. Screw cap. 13.8% alc. **RATING** 96
DRINK 2022-2035 $50 SW ✪

Eastern View Chardonnay 2021, Orange The first release of the top-tier
chardonnay from Ross Hill. Yellow baked apples, yellow peach and candied lemon
zest. Brioche fresh from the oven, roasted cashews and brown butter biscuits. Built
for the long haul with pinpoint acidity and undulating waves of texture. The nutty
toffee nuances will only get better with cellaring. Screw cap. 13% alc. **RATING** 95
DRINK 2022-2035 $95 SW

Pinnacle Series Chardonnay 2021, Orange White peaches in syrup, lemon balm and talc. A cracked marble/stony character leads to a sparkler flint aroma. The palate is equal parts power and a deft touch of grace. Buttery pastry, peaches and cream. Oak frames the fruit superbly. A hazelnut skin finish continues for long moments. Everything you want in quality chardonnay. Screw cap. 12.9% alc. RATING 95 DRINK 2022-2035 $40 SW ✪

The Griffin 2019, Orange Unusually, merlot dominates the blend this vintage, with stewed plums, black cherry and orange rind followed by brambles, blackcurrants and olive skin. Fine cabernet tannins ensure longevity, and the wine is astute, yet plush. Red raspberry and sumac spice unfurl towards the end of the palate. Screw cap. 13.8% alc. RATING 95 DRINK 2022-2038 $95 SW

🍷🍷🍷🍷♀ **Pinnacle Series Griffin Road Vineyard Cabernet Sauvignon 2021, Orange** RATING 93 DRINK 2022-2038 $50 SW
Pinnacle Series Pinot Gris 2022, Orange RATING 92 DRINK 2022-2030 $30 SW ✪
Jack Shiraz 2021, Orange RATING 92 DRINK 2022-2032 $30 SW ✪
Maya Chardonnay 2022, Orange RATING 91 DRINK 2022-2032 $25 SW ✪
Isabelle Cabernet Sauvignon Merlot Cabernet Franc Malbec Petit Verdot 2021, Orange RATING 91 DRINK 2022-2030 $30 SW
Monacle Lighter in Alcohol Pinot Grigio 2022, Orange RATING 90 DRINK 2022-2025 $30 SW
Tom Cabernet Sauvignon 2021, Orange RATING 90 DRINK 2022-2035 $30 SW

Rouleur ★★★★★

80 Laurens Street, North Melbourne, Vic 3051 **Region** Various
T 0419 100 929 **www.**rouleurwine.com **Open** By appt **Winemaker** Matt East
Est. 2015 **Dozens** 2500
Owner Matt East's interest in wine began while growing up in the Yarra Valley and watching his father plant a vineyard in Coldstream. From '99–15 his day job was in sales and marketing, culminating in his appointment in '11 as national sales manager for Wirra Wirra (which he had joined in '08). Following his retirement from that position, he set in motion the wheels of Rouleur. He lives in Melbourne, with the Yarra in easy striking distance for sourcing fruit and making wine (at Yering Farm in Coldstream). He also makes wines from McLaren Vale. Back in Melbourne he has transformed a dilapidated milk bar in North Melbourne into his inner-city cellar door.

🍷🍷🍷🍷🍷 **Pinot Gris et al 2022, Yarra Valley** 90/7/3% pinot gris/gewürztraminer/ chardonnay. A glorious onion skin hue mottled with pink. At once vibrant aromas of lychee, pickled cumquat, nashi pear, ginger and tamarind, yet by the same token, subtle and demur and embedded into the structural course of pucker and salty freshness. This is a delicious wine, defined by flavour, texture and a languid linger, hanging around and beckoning the next sip. Screw cap. 12.7% alc. RATING 95 DRINK 2022-2026 $36 NG ✪ ♥

Arlo's Pinot Noir 2021, Upper Yarra Valley A welt of tamarind, clove, Campari and mezcal-soused tannins. The latter edgy in the bunchy way, serving as a restraining order for punchy red fruits. Just the right amount of everything: verve, structure and fruit. Below, a carnal burr of autumnal mulch and game. Delicious! Diam. 13.2% alc. RATING 95 DRINK 2022-2028 $47 NG ✪

Issy's Chardonnay 2021, Upper Yarra Valley Incandescent white peach and nectarine riffs beam from the glass. The mid-palate: almond meal, dried porcini, tatami straw and cereal. A skein of juicy acidity drags impressive length while the judicious oak framework buffers excess. I'd bury this for five years to flesh it out. A tensile idiom. Lean, bright and detailed. Diam. 13.1% alc. RATING 94 DRINK 2022-2030 $47 NG

🍷🍷🍷🍷♀ **Strawberry Fields Pinot Meunier 2022, King Valley** RATING 93 DRINK 2022-2025 $35 NG ✪
Shiraz 2021, McLaren Vale RATING 93 DRINK 2022-2027 $35 NG ✪

Rowlee

19 Lake Canobolas Road, Nashdale, NSW 2800 **Region** Orange
T (02) 6365 3047 **www**.rowleewines.com.au **Open** Wed–Sat 10–5 **Winemaker** Nicole
Samodol, James Manny **Viticulturist** Nicole Samodol, James Manny **Est.** 2001
Dozens 7000 **Vyds** 8ha

Rowlee's vineyard (arneis, chardonnay, gewürztraminer, nebbiolo, pinot gris, pinot noir, riesling and sauvignon blanc) was planted over 20 years ago by Nik and Deonne Samodol in the high-altitude (950m) cool climate of Orange. Their daughter, Nicole Samodol, and her partner James Manny 'combine European wine growing heritage with New World practices' to make the wines in 3 ranges: Rowlee, Single Vineyard and R-Series.

Single Vineyard Riesling 2022, Orange Mexican orange blossom, pink grapefruit, quince and custard apple. Delivers layers of texture, like delicate hand-spun yarn. A chew of lees, an angle of tannin and overall lustrous flow. An ancient rocky minerality on the finish. A hint of alcohol only just peeks through. Instead, enjoy its exotic perfume and journey over the palate. Screw cap. 13% alc. **RATING** 95 **DRINK** 2022–2030 $35 SW ✪

R-Series Chardonnay 2021, Orange A rarified bottling of the best barrels from an exceptional vintage. Crunchy green apple, white peach, pomelo pith and chalk shavings. Piercing acidity and popcorn kernel notes round out the finish. Vibrating on a high note, this wine extrudes energy and spirit. Screw cap. 12.6% alc. **RATING** 94 **DRINK** 2023–2028 $75 SW

Single Vineyard Fumé Blanc 2022, Orange RATING 93 **DRINK** 2023–2026 $35 SW ✪
Single Vineyard Pinot Gris 2022, Orange RATING 92 **DRINK** 2023–2026 $38 SW
R-Series Nebbiolo 2019, Orange RATING 92 **DRINK** 2023–2032 $110 SW
Single Vineyard Gewürztraminer 2022, Orange RATING 91 **DRINK** 2023–2026 $35 SW
Single Vineyard Arneis 2022, Orange RATING 90 **DRINK** 2023–2025 $38 SW

Rudderless Wines

Victory Hotel, Main South Road, Sellicks Hill, SA 5174 **Region** McLaren Vale
T (08) 8556 3083 **www**.rudderlesswines.com.au **Open** 7 days Mon–Sat 10–late,
Sun 11–late **Winemaker** Peter Fraser, Shelley Torresan **Viticulturist** Jock Harvey
Est. 2004 **Dozens** 550 **Vyds** 2ha

Rudderless is owned by Doug Govan of McLaren Vale's Victory Hotel (c. 1858.) The vineyard was planted on 2 levels (in 1999 and 2003) to a complex mix of shiraz, graciano, grenache, malbec, mataro and viognier. It surrounds the hotel, which is situated in the foothills of the Southern Willunga Escarpment as it falls into the sea. The wines are mostly sold through the Victory Hotel, where the laid-back Doug keeps a low profile.

Sellicks Hill Mataro 2021, McLaren Vale This is by far the best wine of the suite, the barrique influence almost discouraged by the sheer tenacity of fruit melding effortlessly with the tannic guile of mataro. Dark-fruit allusions are found in anise, peppered charcuterie, ironstone and blood. This is exceptional. Screw cap. 13.8% alc. **RATING** 94 **DRINK** 2023–2032 $35 NG ✪

Sellicks Hill Shiraz 2021, McLaren Vale RATING 92 **DRINK** 2023–2030 $35 NG
Sir George Shiraz Malbec 2021, McLaren Vale RATING 92 **DRINK** 2023–2032 $50 NG
Sellicks Hill Grenache 2021, McLaren Vale RATING 91 **DRINK** 2023–2028 $35 NG
Sellicks Hill Malbec 2021, McLaren Vale RATING 91 **DRINK** 2023–2032 $35 NG

Running With Bulls

40 Eden Valley Road, Angaston SA 5353 (postal) **Region** Barossa Valley
T (08) 8561 3200 www.runningwithbulls.com.au **Open** Not **Winemaker** Sam Wigan
Est. 2008 **Dozens** 19 000

Running With Bulls is the Hill-Smith Family's foray into value- and flavour-packed, Spanish-inspired wines under the helmsmanship of winemaker Sam Wigan. These 'alternative' varieties are well suited to the Barossa Valley. Running With Bulls have consistently released excellent wines every year – full of character and inherent drinkability while remaining strong to their Barossa roots. Think contemporary riffs on tempranillo and garnacha (grenache) and you are on the right track. They suggest their red wines, with their light tannin loads, can be enjoyed in the warmer months.

ΨΨΨΨΩ **Albariño 2022, Barossa** Pale straw in the glass with characters of crisp green apple, nashi pear and Meyer lemon along with hints of white flowers, crushed quartz, freshly cut fennel, marzipan and oyster shell. Crisp, dry and refreshing, this is just delicious drinking all around and would be a perfect picnic wine. Screw cap. 12% alc. **RATING** 92 **DRINK** 2023-2025 $31 DB

Russell & Suitor

1866 Pipers River Road, Lower Turners Marsh, Tas 7267 (postal) **Region** Riverland
T 0400 684 654 www.russellandsuitor.com.au **Open** Not **Winemaker** Alex Russell
Viticulturist Alex Russell **Est.** 2019 **Dozens** 6000 **Vyds** 14.43ha

Winemaker and owner Alex Russell is based in Tasmania's Pipers River, where he produces the cool-climate varieties of chardonnay, pinot noir, riesling and sauvignon blanc, under the label Russell & Suitor. He also has a significant focus on alternative varieties under his Alejandro, Franca's Vineyard and Plums & Roses labels (saperavi, durif, vermentino, lagrein, arneis, nero d'Avola, montepulciano, etc), making an extensive range of wines out of his Renmark property in South Australia. Russell began his winemaking career at Angove, Zilzie and the Riverland Vine Improvement Committee nursery in the early '00s.

ΨΨΨΨΩ **Son of a Bull Riesling Pinot Gris Gewürztraminer 2022, Tasmania** It's great to see these Euro-style blends on the local wine scene – varieties that pull in the same direction and provide focus, texture and, more often than not, fascinating drinking. Pale straw, green apple, nashi pear and citrus fruits, a touch of guava and lychee, some soft spice and struck match complexity with a wave of white flowers and white pepper. Textural, mouth-filling and good drinking. Ausgezeichnet! Screw cap. 12.5% alc. **RATING** 92 **DRINK** 2023-2026 $29 DB ✪
Son of a Bull Riesling 2022, Tasmania Pale straw in the glass with aromas of lime cordial, grapefruit juice and green apple with hints of lemon sherbet, orange blossom, crushed stone, soft spice and light tones of marzipan. The fruit is pure and endearing and some clotted cream and dried herb notes flow in on the palate. There's some slinky texture and the cadence and exit flow long and sapid. Screw cap. 12% alc. **RATING** 90 **DRINK** 2023-2026 $29 DB

Rymill Coonawarra

110 Clayfield Road, Glenroy, SA 5277 **Region** Coonawarra
T (08) 8736 5001 www.rymill.com.au **Open** 7 days 10–5 **Winemaker** Lewis White
Viticulturist Martin Wirper **Est.** 1974 **Dozens** 25 000 **Vyds** 140ha

The Rymills are descendants of John Riddoch and have long owned some of the finest Coonawarra soil, upon which they have grown grapes since the '70s. In '16 the Rymill family sold the business, but the management, vineyard and winery teams remained in place, with new capital financing improvements in the vineyards and cellar. The winery building also houses the cellar door with viewing platforms over the winery.

ΨΨΨΨΨ **Pioneers Petit Verdot 2022, Coonawarra** Berried fruit flavours, ripe and sound, come adorned with just enough roasted spice, florals and smoked cedar additions. This is a red wine in a very good place. It feels even-handed, ripe,

generous and yet well contained. No hesitation. Screw cap. 14.2% alc. **RATING** 94
DRINK 2023-2030 $25 CM

♥♥♥♥♀ **Classic Release Cabernet Sauvignon 2020, Coonawarra** RATING 93
DRINK 2024-2035 $32 CM ✪
Classic Release Shiraz 2020, Coonawarra RATING 92 **DRINK** 2024-2032
$32 CM
The Dark Horse Cabernet Sauvignon 2020, Coonawarra RATING 91
DRINK 2023-2029 $25 CM ✪
The Dark Horse Shiraz 2021, Coonawarra RATING 90 **DRINK** 2023-2029
$27 CM

Saddler's Creek   ★★★★

Marrowbone Road, Pokolbin, NSW 2320 **Region** Hunter Valley
T (02) 4991 1770 **www**.saddlerscreek.com **Open** 7 days 10–5 **Winemaker** Brett
Woodward, Sam Rumpit **Viticulturist** Brett Woodward, Sam Rumpit **Est.** 1990
Dozens 8000 **Vyds** 8ha
Saddler's Creek is a boutique winery that is little known outside the Hunter Valley, but has
built a loyal following of dedicated supporters. It came onto the scene over 25 years ago with
some rich, bold wines, and maintains this style today. Fruit is sourced from the Hunter Valley
and Langhorne Creek, with occasional forays into other premium regions.

♥♥♥♥♥ **Winemaker's Craft Single Suitcase Barbera 2021, Adelaide Hills** The
bouquet has a richly perfumed bouquet that quickly transcends expectations,
and the palate continues the theme with its juicy/soft mouthfeel. Screw cap.
14.5% alc. **RATING** 94 **DRINK** 2023-2030 $45 JH
Winemaker's Craft Single Suitcase Sagrantino 2021, Adelaide Hills
Sagrantino imposes itself on the unwary in no time, with no soft landing, and a
tannin broadside to close. The very engaging and insightful back label suggests
the wine is 'best enjoyed with hearty slow cooked meals' and the wine as 'rich
and savoury, with generous fruit and substantial tannins.' Screw cap. 15.8% alc.
RATING 94 **DRINK** 2025-2030 $45 JH
Rare Muscat NV, Riverina Rutherglen The olive-green colour of the rim,
and walnut brown of the centre, tells all immediately: this has been cleverly
sourced from the Riverina and Rutherglen, and is, of course, extremely complex
and luscious. 375ml. Screw cap. 17.7% alc. **RATING** 94 $40 JH

♥♥♥♥♀ **Botrytis Semillon 2019, Riverina** RATING 93 **DRINK** 2023-2030 $40 JH
Ryan's Reserve Stephanie's Vineyard Chardonnay 2021, Hunter Valley
RATING 91 **DRINK** 2023-2033 $40 JH
Ryan's Reserve Sylvia Semillon 2021, Hunter Valley RATING 90
DRINK 2023-2025 $40 JH

Sailor Seeks Horse   ★★★★★

Port Cygnet Winery, 60 Lymington Road, Cygnet, Tas 7112 **Region** Southern Tasmania
T 0418 471120 **www**.sailorseekshorse.com.au **Open** By appt **Winemaker** Paul
Lipscombe, Gilli Lipscombe **Est.** 2010 **Dozens** 1000 **Vyds** 8ha
While I (James) was given comprehensive information about Paul and Gilli Lipscombe and
their vineyard, I am none the wiser about the highly unusual and very catchy name. The
story began in '05 when they resigned from their (unspecified) jobs in London, did a vintage
in Languedoc and then headed to Margaret River to study oenology and viticulture. They
worked in large, small, biodynamic, conventional, minimum- and maximum-intervention
vineyards and wineries – Woodlands, Xanadu, Beaux Freres, Chehalem and Mt Difficulty, all
household names. By '10 they were in Tasmania working for Julian Alcorso's Winemaking
Tasmania (now Tasmanian Vintners) and found a derelict vineyard that had never cropped,
having been abandoned not long after being planted in '05. It was in the Huon Valley,
precisely where they had aimed to begin – the coolest district in Tasmania.

🍷🍷🍷🍷🍷 **Huldufolk Pinot Noir 2021, Tasmania** The interplay of fruit and acid, the dance of amaro herbs and spice, the jostle between sweet and sour. On any given day these battles and romances can be different, such is the game. This wine reveals all of those complex relationships like a well-choreographed dance. Screw cap. 12% alc. **RATING** 96 **DRINK** 2023–2033 $110 DB

Huldufolk Chardonnay 2021, Tasmania To my eyes, Sailor Seeks Horse wines seem to be made in a very considered and thoughtful fashion. The '21 Huldufolk is a cracker. Pristine white peach, nectarine and citrus fruits, scattered tones of flint, oatmeal and crushed river stone. Softly spiced, with everything in frame and focus, composition just so, a shimmering line of acidity providing illumination and tension. Screw cap. 13% alc. **RATING** 96 **DRINK** 2023–2030 $110 DB ♥

Huon Valley Chardonnay 2021, Tasmania White peach and lemon finely etched with lacy acidity and river stone and softly spiced with notes of lemon curd and blossom. Pure and driven with a spine of crystalline, sapid acidity providing velocity and pulse, flavours fading with memories of citrus, spice and stone. Beautiful drinking. Screw cap. 12.2% alc. **RATING** 96 **DRINK** 2023–2029 $65 DB ✪

Huon Valley Pinot Noir 2021, Tasmania A Huon Valley–sourced wine displaying a sheen of amaro and spice. There is a wild, perfumed edge akin to a siren's call pour moi. A complex whirling dervish of raspberry, bramble, game, roast chestnuts, souk-like spices, cherry clafoutis, turned earth and crushed stone with a vivid mineral cadence and a distinct voice of site and vision. Screw cap. 13.2% alc. **RATING** 95 **DRINK** 2023–2030 $65 DB

Saint & Scholar ★★★★

3174 Barossa Valley Way, Nuriootpa, SA 5355 **Region** Adelaide Hills
T (08) 8388 7777 www.saintandscholar.com.au **Open** Fri–Sun 11–5
Winemaker Stephen Dew, Tim Dolan **Viticulturist** Nigel Van Der Zande **Est.** 2017
Dozens 18 000 **Vyds** 50ha

Owned by Ed Peter, Dirk Wiedmann and Reid Bosward, Saint & Scholar is substantial for a relative newcomer, with 50ha of shiraz, pinot noir, pinot gris, chardonnay and sauvignon blanc. Winemaker Stephen Dew is the Saint, Reid Bosward (winemaker at Kaesler) was the Scholar. Reid handed over the winemaking reins to third-generation Barossa winemaker Tim Dolan in '22.

🍷🍷🍷🍷🍷 **The Masters Series Chardonnay 2021, Adelaide Hills** This is a decadent chardonnay despite its tensile feel. Flavour so intense that one cannot recognise the low-ish alcohol. No obvious single note, however, but a confluence of oak, lees and stone fruits. A creamy core that never obfuscates the energy from bristling attack to long, resinous finish, growing in fruit sweetness with air. Very good. Screw cap. 12.5% alc. **RATING** 94 **DRINK** 2023–2030 $80 NG

🍷🍷🍷🍷🍷 **Holier Than Boz Chardonnay 2021, Adelaide Hills RATING** 93 **DRINK** 2023–2028 $40 NG

Dewy's Nectar Sauvignon Blanc 2021, Adelaide Hills RATING 92 **DRINK** 2023–2028 $40 NG

St Anne's Vineyards ★★★★

Cnr Perricoota Road/24 Lane, Moama, NSW 2731 **Region** Perricoota
T (03) 5480 0099 www.stanneswinery.com.au **Open** 7 days 9–5 **Winemaker** Trent Eacott, Richard McLean **Est.** 1972 **Dozens** 20 000 **Vyds** 182ha

The McLean family has a multi-pronged grapegrowing and winemaking business with 182ha of vines on the Murray River. All the mainstream varieties are grown, the lion's share to chardonnay, shiraz, cabernet sauvignon and merlot. There is also a very small planting at Myrniong in the Pentland Hills, a 50-minute drive from the heart of Melbourne, where the main cellar door is situated. There are 4 other cellar doors: Moama (Cnr Perricoota Road and 24 Lane), Lorne (150 Mount Joy Parade), Echuca (53 Murray Esplanade) and Bendigo (3 Belvoir Park Road).

ΨΨΨΨΩ **Grenache 2022, Heathcote** Raspberried fruit flavour with inlays of sweet spice. There's some alcohol warmth here but it remains juicy and flowing. This is an enjoyable wine to drink. Fennel and smoky reductive notes on the finish add both tightness and complexity. It's light-ish but it works all the angles well. Screw cap. 14% alc. **RATING** 91 **DRINK** 2023–2027 $24 CM ✪

Tatalia Shiraz 2021, Heathcote A bloom of vanillin oak sits slightly separate from the wealth of warm, cherry-plum fruit. Undergrowth, game, floral and tar characters all contribute too. It's not subtle but it sure packs a punch. Screw cap. 15% alc. **RATING** 90 **DRINK** 2024–2032 $36 CM

St Brioc Wines

PO Box 867, McLaren Vale, SA 5171 **Region** McLaren Vale
T 0400 585 395 **www.**stbriocwineco.com.au **Open** Not **Winemaker** Mark Wenk
Est. 2008 **Dozens** 500

St Brioc Wines started as a collaboration between sisters Jo Madigan and Trish Wenk and their families; winemaker Matt Wenk (of Smidge Wines, see separate entry) came on board a decade later. The name comes from the property where the girls spent their early years, further supported by the Celtic symbol dedicated to St Brioc, the Inchbrayok Cross that provided the inspiration for the logo and label.

ΨΨΨΨΩ **Fiano 2022, McLaren Vale** A tight, sandy and pungently mineral fiano with no shortage of ripe fruit flavours, despite an earlier picking window. Pickled quince, ginger, tamarind, raw almond, pistachio and aniseed all careen long and effortlessly. This address is one of consummate craftsmanship and stellar value. Screw cap. 12.5% alc. **RATING** 93 **DRINK** 2022–2026 $28 NG ✪

St Huberts

Cnr Maroondah Highway/St Huberts Road, Coldstream, Vic 3770 **Region** Yarra Valley
T (03) 5960 7096 **www.**sthuberts.com.au **Open** 7 days 10–5 **Winemaker** Greg Jarratt
Est. 1966 **Vyds** 20.49ha

The St Huberts of today has a rich 19th-century history, not least in its success at the 1881 Melbourne International Exhibition, which featured every type of agricultural and industrial product. The wine section alone attracted 711 entries. The Emperor of Germany offered a Grand Prize, a silver gilt epergne, for the most meritorious exhibit in the show. A St Huberts wine won the wine section, then competed against objects as diverse as felt hats and steam engines to win the Emperor's Prize, featured on its label for decades thereafter. Like other Yarra Valley wineries, it dropped from sight at the start of the 20th century, was reborn in 1966 and, after several changes of ownership, became part of what today is TWE. The wines are made at Coldstream Hills but have their own, very different, focus.

ΨΨΨΨΨ **Reserve Cabernet Sauvignon 2021, Yarra Valley** An impressively deep ruby red. Sleek and seductive with aromas of perfectly ripened cassis, a touch of crushed violets and just a little cedar/tobacco from the already well-integrated oak. The palate is medium bodied and lithe, closing with firm yet very fine tannins. Screw cap. 13.5% alc. **RATING** 96 **DRINK** 2024–2032 $80 PR

ΨΨΨΨΩ **Sparkling Rosé 2016, Yarra Valley RATING** 93 **DRINK** 2022–2027 $55 PR
Pinot Blanc 2022, Mornington Peninsula RATING 92 **DRINK** 2022–2024 $40 PR
Pinot Noir NV, Yarra Valley RATING 92 **DRINK** 2023–2027 $50 PR
Chardonnay 2021, Yarra Valley RATING 91 **DRINK** 2022–2025 $50 PR
Cabernet Merlot 2021, Yarra Valley RATING 91 **DRINK** 2022–2025 $40 PR

St Hugo

2141 Barossa Valley Way, Rowland Flat, SA 5352 **Region** Barossa Valley
T 1300 162 992 **www.**sthugo.com **Open** Fri–Mon 10.30–4.30 **Winemaker** Peter Munro **Est.** 1983 **Dozens** 50 000 **Vyds** 57ha

This is a stand-alone business within the giant bosom of Pernod Ricard, focused on the premium and ultra-premium end of the market, thus differentiating it from Jacob's Creek. There is a restaurant with kitchen garden, and self-catering accomodation is available in a 19th-century stone cottage.

Black Shiraz Cabernet 2018, Barossa Coonawarra Barossa shiraz and Coonawarra cabernet sauvignon of unknown proportions. Deep crimson with aromas of blackberry and black cherry sheathed in cedar and oak spice with hints of licorice, violets, tobacco leaf and chocolate. This wine will cellar magnificently, with savoury, ripe, granitic tannins cascading through the pure black fruits to composure and grace on the long finish. Cork. 14.5% alc. RATING 96 DRINK 2023-2038 $140 DB

Koch Shiraz 2018, Barossa Valley Deep crimson with intense chocolatey blackberry and black cherry fruits cut with hints of baking spices, graphite, pressed flowers, cedar and crushed stone. Excellent concentration with stunning fruit density and balance throughout its length, the chalky cut of chocolate tannins providing gentle support and finishing long with a sweep of spice, cassis and kirsch. Superb stuff. Cork. 14.5% alc. RATING 96 DRINK 2023-2043 $80 DB

Riesling 2022, Eden Valley Freshly squeezed lime, crushed quartz and Christmas lily straight up. Hints of bath salts and orange blossom flitter further in the background and I love the way this wine coils, the tension between fruit and acidity clearly evident, before it sizzles across the palate showing great drive and just a hint of phenolic texture, finishing dry, minerally true and with an ache of umami. Screw cap. 11.5% alc. RATING 95 DRINK 2023-2033 $40 DB ✪

Cabernet Sauvignon 2020, Coonawarra A very good St Hugo. There's a decent amount of oak but it feels in check – the fruit is so juicy that the oak helps to keep it bedded. It's a mulberried, curranty, minty release with eucalyptus top notes, apple-like acidity, and excellent spread to the tannin. The chalkiness of the finish, inlaid with juicy fruit, is the key. It's not a massive release, but it's lengthy. Screw cap. 14% alc. RATING 95 DRINK 2027-2042 $58 CM

Vetus Purum Shiraz 2020, Barossa Famous name and famously cellar-worthy, if you can keep your hands off it long enough. There is a distinct framework of fine, ripe sandy tannin from which the pure dark berry and plum fruit hang dusted with spice and violets, dark chocolate and earthen tones appearing last. A classic style from a strong vintage. Screw cap. 14.5% alc. RATING 95 DRINK 2023-2035 $58 DB

Single Vineyard Fabal Shiraz 2019, Barossa Valley This sits true to its northern Barossa roots with dense blackberry, black cherry and dark plum fruits that have inky tension to their form. Layers of baking spices, licorice, cedar, crème de cassis, earth, roasted nuts, vanillin oak and brandied fruits. There is a firmness and sinewy shape to the tannins, begging for time in the cellar and with that, you should be in for quite a treat indeed. Cork. 14.5% alc. RATING 95 DRINK 2023-2038 $80 DB

Single Vineyard Flint Cabernet Sauvignon 2019, Coonawarra It's not necessarily a big wine but it has that extra kick of flavour through the finish. It will age like a champion. It offers blackcurrant, black olives, boysenberry and mint flavours with a smooth, creamy vanillin aspect to the texture. Dry tobacco characters add top notes but it's the slow, rolling churn of tannin through the flavour-laden finish that defines and distinguishes. Screw cap. 14.5% alc. RATING 95 DRINK 2026-2040 $80 CM

Vetus Purum Cabernet Sauvignon 2018, Coonawarra Elegant cabernet with blackcurrant and tobacco as the main drivers, though with smoked cedar and mint notes rippling through. Everything about this wine feels calm and confident as if it's in no real hurry to impress. It has length, complexity and charm all on its side. Screw cap. 14% alc. RATING 95 DRINK 2027-2043 $240 CM

Single Vineyard Southern Valley Shiraz 2016, Barossa Valley I have a sneaking suspicion that this excellent '16 release will keep on truckin' in the cellar for many years. That's not to say its lush red and dark berry and plum fruits aren't delicious now – all flecked with cedar and oak spice, violets and chocolate, they make an alluring package. But that granitic tannin structure is built for the long haul. Cork. 14% alc. **RATING** 95 **DRINK** 2023-2043 $80 DB

Cabernet Shiraz 2020, Barossa Valley Coonawarra Bright crimson in the glass with vivacious aromas of ripe satsuma plum, black cherry and blackberry fruits supported by a hint of oak spice, violets, licorice, cedar, dried herbs, earth and dark chocolate. There is a nice sense of energy to the fruit here, which acts as a fulcrum for the tight, fine tannin and bright acidity, poised nicely with some great sustain on the finish. Screw cap. 14.5% alc. **RATING** 94 **DRINK** 2023-2033 $58 DB

 Semillon 2022, Barossa Valley RATING 93 **DRINK** 2023-2033 $40 DB
Grenache Shiraz Mataro 2022, Barossa RATING 93 **DRINK** 2023-2033 $58 DB
Chardonnay 2022, Eden Valley RATING 93 **DRINK** 2023-2028 $40 DB

St Johns Wine ★★★★

Unit 3, 2 Smeaton Way, Rockingham WA 6168 **Region** Western Australia
T 08 9528 5001 **www.stjohnswine.com Open** By appt **Winemaker** Kyle Huizenga
Est. 1997 **Dozens** 50 000 **Vyds** 100ha
St Johns Wine was established in 1997 with their first vineyards in the Blackwood Valley (50ha), followed in '98 by the St Johns Brook vineyard in Yelverton (30ha). A 1200t winery with temperature-controlled wine storage was built in '04. The wines are released under the St Johns Brook, Optimus, Tweed River, Round Puzzle and Crush labels. Although there is no cellar door, appointments can be made to taste the wines at the Rockingham office.

 Round Puzzle Vermentino 2021, Blackwood Valley Texture is built into this via 8 months of ageing in used oak, and it's worked a treat. It still retains lemon balm, mandarin and a slip of lemony saline acidity across the palate. It's refreshing and crisp to finish. The price is a sticking point. Screw cap. 13% alc. **RATING** 91 **DRINK** 2022-2025 $40 JF

The Terraces Optimus Chardonnay 2021, Margaret River A mid-gold hue. Lots of winemaking artefact: vanillin toasty oak, lees all creamy and nutty with sticky phenolics. The palate is tight yet lively thanks to the acidity, though more fruit ripeness would flesh it out. This seems to miss the mark as a flagship wine. Screw cap. 12.5% alc. **RATING** 90 **DRINK** 2024-2029 $100 JF

Round Puzzle Cabernet Malbec 2020, Margaret River All in all, this comes together well showing cassis, blackberries and dark plums with a kitchen cupboard full of spices included. Leafy with cooling menthol, which appeals, and the full-bodied palate is at once flushed with tangy and tart fruit and firm tannins. Screw cap. 14.5% alc. **RATING** 90 **DRINK** 2024-2034 $40 JF

St Leonards Vineyard ★★★★

St Leonards Road, Wahgunyah, Vic 3687 **Region** Rutherglen
T 1800 021 621 **www.stleonardswine.com.au Open** W'ends 9–5 **Winemaker** Nick Brown **Viticulturist** Will Stephen **Est.** 1860 **Dozens** 3500 **Vyds** 12ha
An old favourite, with a range of premium wines cleverly marketed through an attractive cellar door at the historic winery on the banks of the Murray. It is run by Eliza Brown (director), sister Angela (sales & marketing director) and brother Nick (winemaker/director). They are perhaps better known as the trio who fulfil the same roles at All Saints Estate.

Wahgunyah Shiraz 2021, Rutherglen The flagship wine sourced from old-vine shiraz. Strikes a chord with complexity of fruit, velvet-like density, lingering finish and elegance. Crammed with dark plum and black cherry fruits, oak spice, licorice and baked earth, replete with soft tannins. Can be broached now, later or both. Screw cap. 14.3% alc. **RATING** 93 **DRINK** 2023-2031 $85 JP

Hip Sip Muscat NV, Rutherglen A highly successful attempt to engage with a younger audience, Hip Sip is an entry-level Muscat that is sweet, grapey and oh-so enjoyable. Maturation is not extensive, allowing the full fruit charm to be revealed in attractive florals, Turkish delight, dried fruits and peel and sticky treacle. Bright, clean and fresh. 375ml. Screw cap. 17.5% alc. RATING 92 $22 JP ✪

Cabernet Franc 2022, Rutherglen One of the few believers in letting cabernet franc fly solo, and it's always a pleasure to enjoy. Black pepper calls out from the glass with red plum, cherry, red licorice and thyme. A fruit-forward style that gives full voice to black and red berries, pepper and herbs with a dash of earthiness and leather filling out the palate. A firm tannin presence brings good line and length. Screw cap. 13.4% alc. RATING 91 DRINK 2023–2026 $35 JP

Pilot Project Marsie 2022, Rutherglen 75/25% marsanne/muscat. The amber/cloudy rosé colour indicates skin contact with the scent of muscat's lifted florals and marsanne's honeysuckle to the fore. Lovely texture and mouthfeel here with the subtle, gentle influence of pear, apple and quince. Chill and enjoy. Cork. 13% alc. RATING 91 DRINK 2023–2025 $32 JP

Hip Sip Tawny NV, Rutherglen Hip sip indeed with its smart packaging and easy drinking introduction to a fortified tawny bursting in dried fruits, fresh cracked walnuts, Ferrero Rocher chocolate and nutty toffee. Lingers nicely. Clean, dry finish. Screw cap. 18% alc. RATING 90 $22 JP ✪

Salo Wines   ★★★★★

28 Dorothy Street, Healesville, Vic 3777 (postal) **Region** Yarra Valley
T (03) 5962 5331 www.salowines.com.au **Open** Not **Winemaker** Steve Flamsteed, Dave Mackintosh **Est.** 2008 **Dozens** 250
Business partners Steve Flamsteed and Dave Mackintosh say that Salo means dirty and a little uncouth, which with the Australian sense of humour, can be a term of endearment. They wish to keep their wines a little dirty by using hands-off, minimal winemaking except for a few strange techniques to make more gritty, textured wines.

🍷🍷🍷🍷 **Chardonnay 2022, Yarra Valley** Salo only makes one Yarra wine, and the '22 is another ripper. From a low-yielding vintage, this is slightly more powerful than the '21 and here you'll find aromas of white nectarines, lemon oil and spice with some marine scents. Intense and richly textured on the palate and balanced by the wine's vibrant acidity and a touch of grip on the finish. Screw cap. 13% alc. RATING 96 DRINK 2023–2029 $50 PR ✪

Salomon Estate   ★★★★☆

Braeside Road, Finniss, SA 5255 **Region** Southern Fleurieu
T 0417 808 243 www.salomonwines.com **Open** By appt **Winemaker** Bert Salomon, Simon White **Viticulturist** Simon White **Est.** 1997 **Dozens** 7000 **Vyds** 12.1ha
Bert Salomon is an Austrian winemaker with a long-established family winery in the Kremstal region, not far from Vienna. He became acquainted with Australia during his time with import company Schlumberger in Vienna; he was the first to import Australian wines (Penfolds) into Austria, in the mid-1980s, and later became head of the Austrian Wine Bureau. He was so taken by Adelaide that he moved his family there for the first few months of each year, setting in place an Australian red winemaking venture. He retired from the Bureau and is now a full-time travelling winemaker, running the family winery in the Northern Hemisphere vintage and overseeing the making of the Salomon Estate wines.

🍷🍷🍷🍷 **Wildflower Peninsula Syrah-V 2019, Fleurieu** Shiraz co-fermented with 6% viognier. The colour is excellent, the bouquet likewise with sultry black fruits that are mimicked by the palate. Dark chocolate and licorice also emerge. Screw cap. 14% alc. RATING 94 DRINK 2023–2039 $30 JH ✪

Saltram   ★★★★★

Murray Street, Angaston, SA 5353 **Region** Barossa Valley
T (08) 8561 0200 www.saltramwines.com.au **Open** 7 days 10–5 **Winemaker** Alex MacKenzie **Est.** 1859 **Dozens** 60 000 **Vyds** 60ha

Established in 1859, Saltram is one of the grand old Barossa marques with a rich history, Thomas Hardy having introduced the wines to the London market in the late 1800s. Some famous winemakers have tread the boards there over the years – Fred Ludlow, Bryan Dolan, Peter Lehmann and Nigel Dolan. The estate has been revitalised under Shavaughn Wells and current winemaker Alex MacKenzie and the portfolio includes many highlights from the stellar Saltram No. 1 through to the value-packed Pepperjack range (see separate entry).

ŸŸŸŸŸ **Mr Pickwick's Limited Release Particular Tawny NV, Barossa Valley**
This was my first tawny crush some 30 years ago and to be honest, I've still got the hots for it. Complex with characters of baking spices, red and dark berry fruits, mahogany, candied orange peel, roasting walnuts, salted caramel, toffee apple and dark liquor chocolates. Sweet and inviting with light rancio tones on the palate, it is the kind of wine that you can sip all night. Cork. 19% alc. RATING 96 $75 DB ✪
The Journal Centenarian Old Vine Shiraz 2017, Barossa Sourced from a single 1901-planted vineyard. The tight granitic tannins and fine acidity of the Eden Valley frame this wine nicely, the fruit within plush yet elegant, packed with notes of spice, sage, earth, licorice and violets. There is a sense of elegance and power here. Screw cap. 14% alc. RATING 95 DRINK 2023-2035 $180 DB

ŸŸŸŸ♀ **Mamre Brook Riesling 2022, Eden Valley** RATING 92 DRINK 2023-2028 $25 DB ✪
Winemaker's Selection Old Vine Grenache 2021, Barossa Valley RATING 92 DRINK 2023-2027 $35 DB
Mamre Brook Shiraz 2020, Barossa RATING 92 DRINK 2023-2029 $38 DB
Limited Release Winemaker's Selection Single Vineyard Fiano 2022, Barossa Valley RATING 91 DRINK 2023-2024 $25 DB ✪
1859 Shiraz 2022, Barossa RATING 90 DRINK 2023-2027 $21 DB ✪

Samson Tall   ★★★★

219 Strout Road, McLaren Vale, SA 5171 **Region** McLaren Vale
T 0488 214 680 **www**.samsontall.com.au **Open** 7 days 11–5 **Winemaker** Paul Wilson, Heather Budich **Est.** 2018 **Dozens** 2500
Paul Wilson and Heather Budich purchase grapes from local growers, making the wine in a small winery on their property. The cellar door is a small church built in 1854, the winery and church (with a small historic cemetery) surrounded by gardens and a vineyard. Paul has learned his craft well; all of the wines are well made and the grapes well chosen.

ŸŸŸŸŸ **Hatwell Vineyard Grenache 2021, McLaren Vale** Venerable old Blewitt Springs bush vines, fermented wild under the aegis of whole-berry carbonic maceration, together with a righteous 30 days on skins. Creosote, kirsch and mint, with a bow of eucalyptus-clad astringency drying the finish. Lots to love. Time will tell. Screw cap. 14.5% alc. RATING 94 DRINK 2022-2030 $60 NG

ŸŸŸŸ♀ **Cinsault Mataro Rosé 2022, McLaren Vale** RATING 93 DRINK 2022-2025 $27 NG ✪
Grenache Rosé 2022, McLaren Vale RATING 93 DRINK 2022-2024 $27 NG ✪
Shiraz 2021, McLaren Vale RATING 93 DRINK 2022-2027 $32 NG ✪
Grenache 2021, McLaren Vale RATING 93 DRINK 2022-2028 $32 NG ✪
Tempranillo 2021, McLaren Vale RATING 93 DRINK 2022-2030 $32 NG ✪
Grenache Blanc Picpoul 2022, McLaren Vale RATING 91 DRINK 2022-2026 $27 NG ✪

Sandalford   ★★★★★

3210 West Swan Road, Caversham, WA 6055 **Region** Swan Valley
T (08) 9374 9374 **www**.sandalford.com **Open** 7 days 10–5 **Winemaker** Ross Pamment
Viticulturist Ben Maher **Est.** 1840 **Dozens** 60 000 **Vyds** 106.5ha

Sandalford is one of Australia's oldest and largest privately owned wineries. In '70 it moved beyond its original Swan Valley base, purchasing a substantial property in Margaret River that is now the main source of its premium grapes. Wines are released under the 1840 (Swan Valley), Element, Winemakers, Margaret River and Estate Reserve ranges with Prendiville Reserve at the top.

ΨΨΨΨΨ **1840 Cabernet Merlot 2020, Swan Valley** This smells like the right stuff. Regal scents of mahogany, new leather, cassis and lavender. Flavours ruffle and pump with dark cherry, cassis, dark chocolate, clove and cinnamon spice with light eucalyptus notes. The wine sits thick and rich on the palate then teeters into a shimmy of graphite-laced minerally tannin pucker with clove spice lingering. Screw cap. 14% alc. RATING 93 DRINK 2023-2035 $50 MB

Prendiville Reserve Cabernet Sauvignon 2020, Margaret River If any more stuffing from fruit to oak is packed into this wine, the bottle would shatter! Powerful stuff here. Structured and full bodied with plentiful tannins but also a core of ripe mulberries and blackberries, which add juiciness and freshness throughout. Screw cap. 14% alc. RATING 93 DRINK 2024-2038 $130 JF

1840 Chenin Blanc 2022, Swan Valley This wine is a treat. Chenin 101 with lime, green apple, briny minerality and an almost quinine/tonic water-pleasing bitterness. It feels tight and compact but dense in flavour, and while offering a certain richness there's that saline acidity tightening the wine and drawing it long. Screw cap. 12.5% alc. RATING 92 DRINK 2023-2030 $30 MB ✪

Prendiville Reserve Shiraz 2020, Margaret River The oak is cedary, sweet and dominating. However, the richness of the fruit is managing to hold it at bay. Concentrated with plums, baking spices and fruitcake, an attractive floral lift comes by and firm tannins are holding fort across the full-bodied palate. Obviously in its infancy and time will help knit everything together. Screw cap. 14.5% alc. RATING 92 DRINK 2024-2032 $130 JF

1840 Rosé 2022, Swan Valley Grenache fermented in stainless steel with time on lees. Pale pink hue. A gently perfumed red flower, red berry bouquet and a crisp, clean and dry palate providing more of the same. It's good. Screw cap. 12.5% alc. RATING 90 DRINK 2023-2023 $28 JH

Estate Reserve Sauvignon Blanc Semillon 2022, Margaret River Citrus and feijoa, kiwi fruit and passionfruit pith come to play with texture a defining feature. Slippery with a succulence across the palate and flavours all bound by fine acidity. Refreshing as a spring day, and that's part of its appeal. Screw cap. 12.5% alc. RATING 90 DRINK 2022-2025 $28 JF

Estate Reserve Wilyabrup Vineyard Chardonnay 2021, Margaret River At this early stage, it's a wine in parts: the citrus flavours, the lemony acidity, the cedary oak and the texture haven't coalesced. Time should sort that all out. Screw cap. 12.5% alc. RATING 90 DRINK 2024-2031 $50 JF

Sandhurst Ridge   ★★★★

156 Forest Drive, Marong, Vic 3515 **Region** Bendigo
T (03) 5435 2534 **www.**sandhurstridge.com.au **Open** 7 days 11–5 **Winemaker** Paul Greblo **Viticulturist** Paul Greblo **Est.** 1990 **Dozens** 3000 **Vyds** 7.3ha
Brothers Paul and George Greblo began Sandhurst Ridge in 1990, planting the first 2ha of shiraz and cabernet sauvignon. Plantings have increased to over 7ha, principally cabernet and shiraz but also a little merlot, nebbiolo and sauvignon blanc. As the business has grown, the Greblos supplemented their crush with grapes grown in the region; today the brand is owned by Paul Greblo and Karen Sorensen.

ΨΨΨΨΨ **Reserve Shiraz 2021, Bendigo** Sleek and elegant, this is what the term Reserve is for. Deep purple in hue. Offers a world of bramble, black fruits, briar, saltbush and baking spices underpinned by fine-knit tannins. Oak offers support, but not overtly so. Restraint is its middle name but it's in the service of delivering a fully integrated, beautifully expressed and finely delivered Bendigo shiraz. Screw cap. 14.3% alc. RATING 93 DRINK 2022-2031 $50 JP

Shiraz 2021, Bendigo The Greblo brothers have a family history of winemaking in Italy. There are hints of it here with the firmness of savoury tannins and dry, astringent finish. In between, you'll find generous black fruits, sour cherry, baking spices, dark chocolate and anise. Oak is in tune with the fruit, so too those firm tannins in place for the ageing process ahead. Screw cap. 14.7% alc. **RATING** 91 **DRINK** 2022-2030 $32 JP

Rosé 2022, Bendigo A blend of nebbiolo, cabernet sauvignon and sauvignon blanc. Dressed in bright pomegranate hues, it's quite a standout colour-wise. On the palate, a flavoursome mix of red berries, spice and dusty earthiness against a textural background. Aromas of rose, red cherry, blackcurrant leaf and potpourri. Tasty drinking. Screw cap. 12.5% alc. **RATING** 90 **DRINK** 2022-2027 $22 JP ✪

Fringe Shiraz 2021, Bendigo Soft, young, sweet fruited and ready to go. Further ageing isn't out of the question, but there is immediate appeal here with a chorus line of black and red fruits singing in harmony with plenty of upfront spiciness and well-struck oak. A clean, tannic set of heels completes this well-priced shiraz. Screw cap. 14% alc. **RATING** 90 **DRINK** 2022-2026 $24 JP ✪

Sanguine Estate

77 Shurans Lane, Heathcote, Vic 3523 **Region** Heathcote
T (03) 5433 3111 **www.**sanguinewines.com.au **Open** W'ends & public hols 10–5
Winemaker Mark Hunter **Viticulturist** Mark Hunter **Est.** 1997 **Dozens** 15 000
Vyds 28ha
The Hunter family – parents Linda and Tony, their children Mark and Jodi and their respective partners Melissa and Brett – have 21.5ha of shiraz and a 'fruit salad block' of chardonnay, viognier, verdelho, merlot, tempranillo, petit verdot, lagrein, nebbiolo, grenache, cabernet sauvignon and cabernet franc. Low-yielding vines and the magic of the Heathcote region have produced shiraz of exceptional intensity. With the ever-expanding vineyard, Mark has become full-time vigneron and winemaker, and Jodi has taken over from her father as CEO and general manager.

🍷🍷🍷🍷🍷 **D'Orsa Shiraz 2019, Heathcote** Cedar oak shows keenly but sits in perfect harmony with the fresh depth of the plum-driven fruit. Mint and floral aspects add brightness to a toasty, dark-fruited show, and boysenberry characters and the general juiciness add vibrancy. Energy, depth and a rock-solid tannin structure; it's not a bad combination. Screw cap. 14.9% alc. **RATING** 95 **DRINK** 2026-2040 $70 CM

Tempranillo 2021, Heathcote Medium-weight red wine with more than its fair share of charm. It offers berried flavours with inlays of fragrant herbs, but it's the quiet insistence of the finish, the general juiciness and, as unsexy as it sounds, the balance of it that takes the enjoyment factor up a level. Screw cap. 14% alc. **RATING** 94 **DRINK** 2023-2031 $30 CM ✪

Robo's Mob Shiraz 2020, Heathcote There's both viognier and whole bunches in this hearty Heathcote shiraz. Plum, violet, cedar, licorice and smoked clove characters put on a sweet, ripe, bold display, every box ticked, every corner of your mouth covered. This is a full-bodied red wine, done well. Screw cap. 14.8% alc. **RATING** 94 **DRINK** 2024-2034 $33 CM ✪

🍷🍷🍷🍷🍷 **Cabernets 2021, Heathcote RATING** 93 **DRINK** 2024-2032 $25 CM ✪
Wine Club Shiraz 2020, Heathcote RATING 93 **DRINK** 2023-2033 $30 CM ✪
Inception Shiraz 2020, Heathcote RATING 93 **DRINK** 2024-2033 $43 CM
Progeny Shiraz 2021, Heathcote RATING 91 **DRINK** 2023-2027 $25 CM ✪
Music Festival Shiraz 2021, Heathcote RATING 91 **DRINK** 2023-2028 $35 CM

Santa & D'Sas

2 Pincott Street, Newtown, Vic 3220 (postal) **Region** Various
T 0417 384272 **www**.santandsas.com.au **Open** Not **Winemaker** Andrew Santarossa,
Matthew Di Sciascio **Est.** 2014 **Dozens** 9000
Santa & D'Sas is a collaboration between the Santarossa and Di Sciascio families. Andrew
Santarossa and Matthew Di Sciascio met while studying for a bachelor of applied science
(wine science). Wines released under the Valentino label (fiano, sangiovese and shiraz) are
dedicated to Matthew's father, the 'ish' range walks its own path.

🍷🍷🍷🍷 **Prosecco NV, King Valley** Captures the effortless, bubbly energy and joie de
vivre of the grape so well. Purity of expression in lemon sherbet, quince, green
apple and grapefruit aromas. RS at 8.5g/L brings with it a good depth of flavour
and creamy texture, with a surge of tangy acidity to close. Crown. 11% alc.
RATING 94 $24 JP ✪

🍷🍷🍷🍷 **...ish Fiano 2022, King Valley** **RATING** 91 **DRINK** 2023–2027 $25 JP ✪
...ish Prosecco 2022, King Valley **RATING** 90 **DRINK** 2023–2026 $25 JP ✪

Santolin Wines

c/- 21-23 Delaneys Road, South Warrandyte, Vic 3134 (postal) **Region** Yarra Valley
T 0402 278 464 **www**.santolinwines.com.au **Open** Not **Winemaker** Adrian Santolin
Est. 2012 **Dozens** 1000
Adrian Santolin grew up in Griffith, NSW, and has worked in the wine industry since
he was 15. He moved to the Yarra Valley in '07 with wife Rebecca, who has worked in
marketing roles at various wineries. Adrian's love of pinot noir led him to work at wineries
such as Wedgetail Estate, Rochford, De Bortoli, Sticks and Rob Dolan Wines. In '12 his
dream came true when he was able to buy 2t of pinot noir from the Syme-on-Yarra vineyard,
increasing production in '13 to 4t, split between chardonnay and pinot noir. The newer Cosa
Nostra range is dedicated to 'interesting' Italian blends, grapes sourced from around Victoria.

🍷🍷🍷🍷 **Cosa Nostra Fiano 2021, Heathcote** Some colour pickup, but no oak
mentioned in dispatches. What is present is the textural, layered flavour mat of
fiano, with citrus zest/peel and a fresh, crisp finish. 400 dozen made. Screw cap.
13.5% alc. **RATING** 92 **DRINK** 2023–2025 $25 JH ✪
Cosa Nostra Il Capo 2019, Heathcote A 90/10% blend of nero d'Avola
and negroamaro; vibrant crimson-purple showing no signs of age. Meaty and
fleshy with spiced plums and soft tannins. Screw cap. 13.4% alc. **RATING** 91
DRINK 2023–2029 $29 JH

Sapling Yard Wines

50 Molonglo St, Bungendore, NSW 2622 **Region** Canberra District
T 0410 770 894 **www**.saplingyard.com.au **Open** Sat 11–4, Sun by appt
Winemaker Carla Rodeghiero, Malcolm Burdett **Est.** 2008 **Dozens** 1800 **Vyds** 1.2ha
Carla Rodegheiro and Andrew Bennett work full-time in the pharmaceutical clinical research
and building industries respectively. Carla started out as a microbiologist working as a locum
in hospitals in Australia and London. While in London, she also worked evenings in a wine
bar in Carnaby Street where she tasted a 1993 Mount Langi Ghiran Shiraz and vowed to
one day make a wine of similar remarkable quality. In '97 she began a wine science degree
at CSU, completing the last residential term in '04 (with 9-week-old daughter Mia in tow),
having worked vintages in the Hunter Valley, Orange, Macedon Ranges and Willamette
Valley, Oregon. In '08 Carla and Andrew planted a 1.2ha vineyard at Braidwood to pinot
noir, riesling, pinot blanc and tempranillo but they also continue to source their best grapes
from the Canberra District.

🍷🍷🍷🍷 **Canberra Shiraz Viognier 2021, Canberra District** An enticing dark purple-
garnet hue and lots of aromatics as in pepper and wintergreen with a lovely floral
lift. What's pleasing is the savouriness across the medium-bodied palate – yes there
are flavours of dark plums and blueberries but more in the background, cedary

oak and spices, too. Refreshing acidity to the end and the tannins are shapely if a little austere, so match with food or cellar for a few years. Screw cap. 13.2% alc. **RATING** 91 **DRINK** 2023–2031 $38 JF

Braidwood Riesling 2022, Canberra District Nervy and energetic plus tightly coiled thanks to the bracing yet talcy acidity. Delicate citrus blossom, wet stones and waxy aromas with a smidge of lemon-lime and mandarin flavours to the fore. More time in bottle will bolster the palate in absence of fruit ripeness. It's dry and races to the finish. Screw cap. 10.5% alc. **RATING** 90 **DRINK** 2023–2030 $38 JF

Savaterre

929 Beechworth-Wangaratta Road, Everton Upper, Vic 3678 **Region** Beechworth **T** (03) 5727 0551 **www**.savaterre.com **Open** By appt **Winemaker** Keppell Smith **Est.** 1996 **Dozens** 2500 **Vyds** 8ha
Keppell Smith embarked on a career in wine in 1996, studying winemaking at CSU and (at a practical level) with Phillip Jones at Bass Phillip. He has established 8ha of chardonnay and pinot noir (close-planted at 7500 vines/ha), shiraz and sagrantino on the 40ha Savaterre property, at an elevation of 440m. Organic principles govern the viticulture and the winemaking techniques look to the Old World.

Pinot Noir 2019, Beechworth Savaterre continues its top pinot run with another stunner, featuring fine aromatics drenched in Australian bush scents, pepper, tomato leaf, cherry and undergrowth. Offers a compelling wine with a vein of bitter herbs running long and an Italian amaro bite that brings an engaging savouriness. Clean, brisk, youthful and not even close to its prime. Screw cap. 13.5% alc. **RATING** 97 **DRINK** 2023–2031 $80 JP ✪

Chardonnay 2021, Beechworth A chardonnay of both power and elegance, persistence and concentration. A mineral laciness joins with stone fruits in pure white peach and nectarine, Meyer lemon, biscuit and spice to produce a honeyed, textural palate of well-defined chardonnay character. Oak is nicely melded to the whole. Tasted before release and exuding youthful energy, this is definitely going to be a keeper. Screw cap. 13.5% alc. **RATING** 95 **DRINK** 2023–2033 $95 JP

Shiraz 2019, Beechworth Good structure here with stems playing their part to lay groundwork for a lifted, aromatic, neatly spiced – not to mention, complex – young shiraz. The perfume is inviting in ripe black cherry, bracken, woodsy spices, a splash of pepper and leafy undergrowth. Velvet-like density, fleshy texture and runs long. Screw cap. 13.5% alc. **RATING** 95 **DRINK** 2023–2035 $80 JP

Save Our Souls

121 Yarragon South Rd, Yarragon, Vic 3823 (postal) **Region** Various **T** 0418 856 669 **www**.saveoursouls.com.au **Open** Not **Winemaker** Jason Searle, William Downie **Est.** 2009 **Dozens** 3000
This cleverly named business (an evolution of the previous name, Souled Out) is owned by winemakers Jason Searle and William Downie. After many years of friendship they decided to make wines from suitable Victorian regions at affordable prices, that upheld a sense of place more than convention.

Pinot Noir 2020, Mornington Peninsula This just-right pinot certainly put me in a good frame of mind. It's gentle, although neat acidity is the main driver as tannins are supple and fine. Juicy with macerated cherries spiced with chinotto, star anise and menthol filling out the lighter-framed palate with some charred radicchio on the finish. Drink now and stop worrying. Screw cap. 13.2% alc. **RATING** 91 **DRINK** 2022–2026 $32 JF

Pinot Noir 2021, Mornington Peninsula Fresh and vibrant, a little flirty and uncomplicated. I reckon that equals a delicious drink. It's a lighter-framed offering with spicy and tangy cherries, supple tannins and a squirt of finger lime acidity. Screw cap. 12.9% alc. **RATING** 90 **DRINK** 2023–2027 $32 JF

Savina Lane Wines

90 Savina Lane, Severnlea, Qld 4380 **Region** Granite Belt
T (07) 4683 5377 **www.**savinalanewines.com.au **Open** Wed–Sat 10–5 **Est.** 2012
Dozens 800 **Vyds** 3.5ha

Brad and Cheryl Hutchings established Savina Lane Wines in 2012 by extending and rehabilitating an existing, much older vineyard. The cellar door includes an underground cellar providing year-round stable temperatures. As well as multiple trophies for the '12 Old Vine Shiraz (ex 40yo dry grown vines), Savina Lane has had conspicuous success with various of its alternative varieties, which include fiano, petit manseng, tempranillo, graciano and montepulciano.

ŶŶŶŶŶ **Reserve Old Vine Shiraz 2017, Granite Belt** The bouquet is all stewed berries, ripe plum, dark chocolate and even whiffs of young port. Potent start. The palate is chewy, glistening with al dente tannins and the slick of concentrated ripe and stewed dark berries, brown spice and a dash of white pepper. It feels well judged in its seasoning, weight and balance, but is phasing into secondary stewed and savoury characters. Finishes just a little dry, dusty and firm. Has some mojo. Screw cap. 13.3% alc. **RATING** 91 **DRINK** 2022–2025 $130 MB
Quintessence Fiano 2021, Granite Belt Slippery, savoury-edged white wine with Meyer lemon, chamomile tea, juniper and ginger scents gently flecked with cashew and macadamia nut creaminess. Fleshy in the palate with a good sense of concentration, but also lift and pucker from tingly, tart acidity. It all feels very fiano 101, perhaps a bit more complex with that nutty savouriness floating through the wine, and in that very pleasing. Screw cap. 13.8% alc. **RATING** 90 **DRINK** 2022–2024 $37 MB

SC Pannell

60 Olivers Road, McLaren Vale, SA 5171 **Region** McLaren Vale
T (08) 8323 8000 **www.**pannell.com.au **Open** 7 days 11–4 **Winemaker** Stephen Pannell **Viticulturist** Stephen Pannell **Est.** 2004 **Dozens** 18 000 **Vyds** 9ha

The only surprising piece of background is that it took (an admittedly still reasonably youthful) Steve Pannell and wife Fiona so long to cut from Constellation/Hardys and establish their own winemaking and consulting business. Steve radiates intensity and his extended experience has resulted in wines of the highest quality, right from the first vintage. The Pannells have 2 vineyards in McLaren Vale, the first planted in 1891 with a precious 3.6ha of shiraz. The future for the Pannells is limitless, the icon status of the label already well established.

ŶŶŶŶŶ **Smart Clarendon Grenache 2021, McLaren Vale** Perhaps the finest vestige of old-vine grenache in the country, the Smart vineyard is elevated, cool and ferrous. Pannell seems to care little about the eucalyptus inflections that mark his wines, presumably part of the terroir. I'll go with it. Bloodstone, tomato leaf, pickled ume, sour cherry and cardamom teem long. A wine of paradoxical beauty and older-school sensibilities. Screw cap. 13.5% alc. **RATING** 95 **DRINK** 2023–2032 $75 NG
Field Street Shiraz 2021, McLaren Vale This is a gorgeous wine of such imminent and visceral pleasure that it is hard to put down. Poise, freshness and danger, the calling cards. Blueberry, seaweed, cinnamon, tamarind, pomegranate and turmeric. The Indian potpourri of exotica with a carnal burr of tannin to the finish. Long and seamless. Just great to drink! Screw cap. 14% alc. **RATING** 94 **DRINK** 2022–2028 $32 NG ✪

ŶŶŶŶŶ **Old McDonald Grenache 2021, McLaren Vale** **RATING** 93 **DRINK** 2023–2030 $75 NG
Aglianico 2021, McLaren Vale **RATING** 93 **DRINK** 2023–2030 $45 NG
Merrivale Shiraz 2021, McLaren Vale **RATING** 92 **DRINK** 2022–2029 $45 NG
Basso Garnacha 2021, McLaren Vale **RATING** 92 **DRINK** 2022–2028 $30 NG ✪

NO220 Grenache 2022, McLaren Vale RATING 91 DRINK 2022–2025 $40 NG
Grenache Shiraz Touriga 2020, McLaren Vale RATING 91 DRINK 2023–2030
$32 NG
Dead End Tempranillo 2021, McLaren Vale RATING 90 DRINK 2023–2027
$32 NG

Scarborough Wine Co ★★★★★

179 Gillards Road, Pokolbin, NSW 2320 **Region** Hunter Valley
T (02) 4998 7563 **www.**scarboroughwine.com.au **Open** Thurs–Mon 10–5
Winemaker Ian Scarborough, Jerome Scarborough **Viticulturist** Liz Riley, Jerome
Scarborough **Est.** 1985 **Dozens** 25000 **Vyds** 47ha
Ian Scarborough honed his winemaking skills during his years as a consultant, and has
brought all those skills to his own label. The Scarborough family acquired a portion of the
old Lindemans Sunshine vineyard (after it lay fallow for 30 years) and have planted it with
semillon and chardonnay.

ŸŸŸŸŸ The Obsessive The Cottage Vineyard Semillon 2022, Hunter Valley
The Cottage vineyard has sandy, almost talc soils. Hand picked, whole-bunch
pressed with 450L/t of free-run juice, which is is strikingly low (700L is typical
total extraction). Full of lemon, pear and honeysuckle fruit resulting in an elegant
wine with gentle acidity, which means you don't have to wait for this. Screw cap.
10% alc. RATING 95 DRINK 2023–2033 $35 JH ✪
The Obsessive Gillards Road Vineyard Chardonnay 2020, Hunter
Valley Estate-grown fruit was crushed, destemmed and pressed, fermentation of
free-run juice was initiated in tank then transferred to new French oak barrels
for completion; matured in those barrels for 15 months with lees stirring. It's a
complex wine, with a stone-fruit, fig and nutty flavour wheel, the balance and
length faultless. Screw cap. 13.2% alc. RATING 95 DRINK 2023–2030 $45 JH ✪

ŸŸŸŸŸ Yellow Label Chardonnay 2020, Hunter Valley RATING 93
DRINK 2023–2029 $28 JH ✪

Scarpantoni Estate ★★★☆

Scarpantoni Drive, McLaren Flat, SA 5171 **Region** McLaren Vale
T (08) 8383 0186 **www.**scarpantoniwines.com **Open** Mon–Fri 9–5, w'ends & public
hols 11.30–4.30 **Winemaker** Michael and Filippo Scarpantoni, David Fleming **Est.** 1979
Dozens 37000 **Vyds** 40ha
Scarpantoni has come a long way since Domenico Scarpantoni purchased his first vineyard
in 1958. He worked for Thomas Hardy at its Tintara winery, then as vineyard manager for
Seaview Wines and soon became one of the largest private grapegrowers in the region. The
winery was built in '79 with help from sons Michael and Filippo, who continue to manage
the company.

ŸŸŸŸŸ Nero d'Avola 2022, McLaren Vale This is good. A burly, more traditional
style, strongly evocative of a great many wines in Sicily, nero's spiritual home.
A wave of dusty tannins corrals blood plum, baked terracotta, apricot and
bergamot accents. A trail of freshness draws length. Satisfying. Screw cap.
14.5% alc. RATING 90 DRINK 2023–2026 $26 NG

Schild Estate Wines ★★★★☆

1095 Barossa Valley Way, Lyndoch, SA 5351 (postal) **Region** Barossa Valley
T (08) 8524 5560 **www.**schildestate.com.au **Open** Not **Winemaker** Ben Wurst
Viticulturist Michael Schild **Est.** 1998 **Dozens** 40000 **Vyds** 134ha
Ed Schild is a Barossa Valley grapegrower who first planted a small vineyard at Rowland
Flat in 1952, steadily increasing his vineyard holdings over the next 50 years to their present
level. The flagship wine is made from 170+yo shiraz vines on the Moorooroo vineyard. In
Apr '23, the Schild brand and inventory was sold to CW Wines and the winery facility to

Atlas Wines. Son Michael has taken over the grapegrowing side of the business, with Ed moving towards retirement.

ŢŢŢŢŢ **Moorooroo Shiraz 2020, Barossa Valley** Always an impressive wine, this release shows a deep crimson colour and fruit on the damson plum, boysenberry, blueberry and black cherry spectrum. Hints of dark chocolate, baking spices, purple flowers, blackberry pastille and earth. Dense, rich and pure with an excellent fine-tannin frame, bright acidity and plenty of power as it sails off into the distance. Cork. 14.5% alc. RATING 95 DRINK 2023–2035 $199 DB

ŢŢŢŢŢ **Prämie Shiraz 2020, Barossa Valley** RATING 93 DRINK 2023–2030 $55 DB
Ben Schild Angus Brae Vineyard Shiraz 2020, Barossa Valley RATING 91 DRINK 2023–2027 $40 DB
Shiraz 2020, Barossa Valley RATING 90 DRINK 2023–2026 $26 DB

Schoolhouse Wines   ★★★★

4 Nelson Street, Stepney, SA 50969 **Region** Coonawarra
T (08) 8362 6135 **www.cwwines.com Open** Mon–Fri 9–5 **Winemaker** Ben Wurst
Est. 2020 **Dozens** 5000

Schoolhouse is the top brand of the large wine enterprise CW Wines, a business with a host of local and SA labels. Coonawarra shiraz and cabernet sauvignon are Schoolhouse's mainstays, with a Limestone Coast sauvignon blanc featuring in the 2nd tier Headmaster range. The wines are crafted by Ben Wurst, who has worked in the region for close to 20 years.

ŢŢŢŢŢ **Block A2 Shiraz 2021, Coonawarra** There's a flow to this wine. You might even call it smooth. It tastes of sweet red berries, plums and redcurrant, with smoked clove notes, mint and cedarwood. Oak is lavishly applied but the fruit is up to it. Everything here feels substantial but at no point does it feel overdone. Screw cap. 14.5% alc. RATING 93 DRINK 2025–2035 $30 CM ✪
Cabernet Sauvignon 2020, Coonawarra Blackcurrant and gumleaf flavours come with a bit of grain, a bit of character. Toast and vanilla flavours add more positives to the show. This feels both sweet-fruited and complex, a run of grippy tannin adding to the overall solid feel. This will mature well. Screw cap. 14.5% alc. RATING 93 DRINK 2025–2033 $80 CM
Block C1 Cabernet Sauvignon 2020, Coonawarra Cedar oak on pure blackcurrant, with a boysenberry juiciness keeping it all fresh. Oak and fruit are sitting slightly separate for now but time should bring them together. Tannin here is present but not dangerous; it's just firm enough. For the oak and fruit here there's an inherent elegance to this wine. Screw cap. 14.5% alc. RATING 93 DRINK 2026–2035 $30 CM ✪
Block D1 Merlot 2019, Coonawarra Plum and mulberry flavours come wrapped in cedar and woodsmoke. It's not a big wine but there's good volume here, and the texture to go with it. Tannin is slightly blocky but the length is decent, the aftertaste all coffee grounds and berries. Screw cap. 14.5% alc. RATING 91 DRINK 2025–2033 $70 CM

Schubert Estate   ★★★★☆

261 Roennfeldt Rd, Marananga , SA 5355 **Region** Barossa Valley
T 0423 054 086 **www.schubertestate.com Open** Wed–Sun 10–5 **Winemaker** Matt Reynolds **Est.** 2000 **Dozens** 4200 **Vyds** 14ha

Founders Steve and Cecilia Schubert sold their business to Mrs Sofia Yang and Mrs Lin Tan in '19. It was agreed that the Schuberts would guide the new owners as they came to grips with running a small but ultra-successful high-end wine business. They continued making the Goose-yard Block and the Gander on premises, with larger-scale production moving 5km down the road to Schubert's 'sister' winery, Hare's Chase, in '20 with the construction of a winery, warehouse and lab. In '23, a refurbished homestead on the grounds was made available for short stays, along with an onsite tasting room that replaces the now-closed Adelaide city cellar door.

🍷🍷🍷🍷🍷 **The Gander Reserve Shiraz 2017, Barossa Valley** Schubert Estate's flagship shiraz offering is a monolithic powerhouse. What it lacks in grace it more than makes up for with sheer black-fruited grunt and ferruginous western Barossa architecture, all dark soy, rum and raisin chocolate, Dutch blackstrap licorice and dark, turned earth. If you're after a big bugger, this rich, muscular wine should be on your radar. Cork. 15% alc. RATING 95 DRINK 2023-2033 $258 DB

The Sentinel Single Vineyard Shiraz 2019, Barossa Valley Deep crimson with fruit characters of cassis, blackberry and black cherry studded with hints of fruitcake spice, blackberry jam, cedar, vanillin oak, earth, licorice and rum and raisin chocolate. There is a weighty crème de cassis flow to the fruit on the palate with powdery tannin support and a rolling swell of cassis and spice on the persistent finish. Cork. 15% alc. RATING 94 DRINK 2023-2033 $100 DB

Goose-yard Block Shiraz 2019, Barossa Valley I remember trying this wine for the first time many moons ago and being blown away by its concentration and distinct expression of the western Barossa. It's still an impressive wine with rich, concentrated cassis and black fruits, dark moody spice notes, confident, sappy-edged oak and a flexing dark chocolate tannin profile. Distinctive and bold right to the last drop. Cork. 15.5% alc. RATING 94 DRINK 2023-2033 $160 DB

🍷🍷🍷🍷🍷 **The Lone Goose Shiraz 2019, Barossa Valley** RATING 93 DRINK 2023-2030 $100 DB

The Gosling Single Vineyard Shiraz 2019, Barossa Valley RATING 92 DRINK 2023-2030 $50 DB

Schwarz Wine Company

★★★★☆

PO Box 779, Tanunda, SA 5352 **Region** Barossa Valley
T 0417 881 923 **www.**schwarzwineco.com.au **Open** 7 days 11-5 at Artisans of Barossa, 24 Vine Vale Road, Tanunda, SA 5352 **Winemaker** Jason Schwarz **Est.** 2001 **Dozens** 3500

The economical name is appropriate for a business that started with 1t of grapes in 2001. Shiraz was purchased from Jason Schwarz's parents' 1968-planted vineyard in Bethany, the following year half a tonne of grenache was added, once again purchased from the parents. In '05, grape sale agreements with another (larger) winery were terminated, freeing up 1.8ha of shiraz and 0.8ha of grenache. From this point on things moved more quickly: in '06 Jason formed a partnership (Biscay Road Vintners) with Peter Schell of Spinifex, giving them total control over production.

🍷🍷🍷🍷🍷 **Meta Mataro 2022, Barossa Valley** Vibrant, purple magenta in the glass with aromas of blueberry, satsuma plum and mulberry set on a base of exotic spice, pressed flowers, turned earth, roasting meats, amaro and just the right dial setting on the mataro 'garrigue'. Bottom line, it's a pure-fruited, exotic little number with a savoury flow, lovely billowing tannins and an air of effortless drinkability. Screw cap. 14.2% alc. RATING 95 DRINK 2023-2039 $40 DB ✪

Meta Grenache 2022, Barossa Valley Red and dark plum and cherry fruits are joined by hints of raspberry coulis, red licorice, earth, dried citrus rind and orange blossom infused with ginger spice. Light on the tannin and a twang of sapid acidity, sour-cherry style on the exit. Good fun drinking and don't be afraid to pop it in the fridge. Screw cap. 14% alc. RATING 94 DRINK 2023-2027 $40 DB ✪

Nitschke Block Single Vineyard Shiraz 2021, Barossa Valley An initial blast of ripe macerated plum and cassis characters backed up by hints of olive tapenade, violets, cedar, amaro herbs, earth, licorice, vanilla, baking spices and chocolate-dipped cherries. Broody and resonant on the palate with a deep, dark fruit presence, layers of spice and fine, powdery tannin and a sustained cassis-like finish. Screw cap. 14.5% alc. RATING 94 DRINK 2023-2033 $50 DB

🍷🍷🍷🍷🍷 **Chenin Blanc 2022, Barossa Valley** RATING 93 DRINK 2023-2026 $28 DB ✪

Thiele Road Single Vineyard Grenache 2022, Barossa Valley RATING 93 DRINK 2023-2029 $50 DB

Meta Grenache Blanc 2022, Barossa Valley RATING 92 DRINK 2023–2026
$40 DB
Meta Shiraz 2021, Barossa RATING 92 DRINK 2023–2027 $40 DB
Rosé 2022, Barossa Valley RATING 91 DRINK 2023–2026 $28 DB ✪

Scion ★★★★

74 Slaughterhouse Road, Rutherglen, Vic 3685 **Region** Rutherglen
T (02) 6032 8844 **www.**scionwine.com.au **Open** Mon–Sat 10–5, Sun 10–4
Winemaker Rowly Milhinch **Est.** 2002 **Dozens** 4000 **Vyds** 4.85ha
Self-taught winemaker Rowly Milhinch is a descendant of GF Morris, one of Rutherglen's
most renowned vignerons of the mid-19th century. Rowly aspires to make contemporary
wines 'guided by a creative interpretation of traditional Rutherglen varietals, durif a specialty'.
The wines are made from the estate Linlithgow vineyard and the revitalised 1.48ha Terravinia
vineyard managed by Rowly.

♥♥♥♥♀ **After Dark Durif 2021, Rutherglen** Takes durif to the next level, revealing its
great suitability as a semisweet fortified. The grape is certainly versatile. Deep, inky
purple hues. Intense, penetrating aromas in shades of blueberry, blackberry, plum,
lavender, vanilla, dusty cocoa, dark chocolate and cinnamon. Great concentration
and depth of flavour. Warms the soul. 500ml. Screw cap. 17.8% alc. RATING 93
DRINK 2023–2028 $35 JP ✪
Viognier 2021, Rutherglen Rowly Milhinch doesn't do mainstream or
predictable. His viognier explores the 'other' side to the grape, the finer side,
the more delicate and potentially more interesting side. Light lemon colour.
Citrus cues light up the aroma: Meyer lemon, grapefruit and lime, with lifted
spring florals and honeysuckle. The citrus/floral beat continues on the palate,
bright and fresh and emphatic. Delicious. Screw cap. 13.3% alc. RATING 92
DRINK 2023–2027 $42 JP

Scorpo Wines ★★★★★

23 Old Bittern-Dromana Road, Merricks North, Vic 3926 **Region** Mornington Peninsula
T (03) 5989 7697 **www.**scorpowines.com **Open** By appt **Winemaker** Paul Scorpo
Est. 1997 **Dozens** 6000 **Vyds** 17.3ha
Paul Scorpo has a background as a horticulturist/landscape architect, working on major
projects ranging from private gardens to golf courses in Australia, Europe and Asia. His family
has a love of food, wine and gardens, all of which led to them buying a derelict apple and
cherry orchard on gentle rolling hills between Port Phillip and Western Port bays. They have
established pinot noir (10.4ha), pinot gris and chardonnay (3.2ha each) and shiraz (0.5ha).

♥♥♥♥♥ **Old Cherry Orchard 10K Single Vineyard Pinot Noir 2021, Mornington
Peninsula** This is up there as one of the finest Peninsula pinots this vintage. It's
beautiful and stately at the same time. Deep flavours of cherries and pips, blood
orange and Angostura bitters, mint and spicy oak just mingling in the background.
Persuasive tannins, textural and lithe join up with refreshing acidity to ensure the
finish is long and satisfying. Yep, a humdinger. Screw cap. 13.6% alc. RATING 97
DRINK 2024–2034 $90 JF ✪

♥♥♥♥♥ **Eocene Single Vineyard Chardonnay 2021, Mornington Peninsula** Don't
be fooled by the fine acidity, the length of this wine and its precision. It has plenty
of punch with quality fruit, spicy oak and lovely nutty, leesy flavours. It's just that
everything is packaged up so well and the result? Harmony. Screw cap. 12.5% alc.
RATING 96 DRINK 2022–2031 $75 JF ✪
Eocene High Density Vineyard Pinot Noir 2021, Mornington Peninsula
At first, it comes across as powerful with some meaty reduction, a little charry
and tannins holding sway. Then it shifts, unfurls and becomes far more revealing.
There's a gloss and smoothness across the palate with black cherries, savoury spices
and herbs and a smidge of radicchio. Yes, it has structure but it is also seductive.
Screw cap. 13.6% alc. RATING 96 DRINK 2023–2033 $90 JF

Noirien Pinot Noir 2022, Mornington Peninsula It's in a happy place, offering perfectly juicy and ripe cherries and rhubarb dusted in Middle Eastern spices plus chinotto. Tangy pomegranate acidity teases the supple tannins to a lingering finish. Nice one. Screw cap. 13% alc. RATING 95 DRINK 2023-2032 $35 JF ✪

Bestia Pinot Grigio Tradizionale 2021, Mornington Peninsula A gorgeous coppery/orange hue and packed with texture and flavour. Lovely fruit sweetness coming through with pops of finger lime and blood orange, a little smoky with wafts of potpourri and chinotto plus fine phenolics – the right amount of chew, grip and savouriness. Refreshing, but a wine that needs food (and don't we all). Screw cap. 13.3% alc. RATING 95 DRINK 2022-2027 $45 JF ✪

Estate Chardonnay 2021, Mornington Peninsula One of my go-to Peninsula chardonnays for its quality, complexity and flavour profile. This is rather racy with its moreish acidity but it's also layered with fruit, creamy, roasted cashew lees and some white miso. Added palate weight thanks to a pull of phenolics, which add to the mouthfeel. And this does feel good. Screw cap. 12.9% alc. RATING 95 DRINK 2022-2031 $55 JF

ŸŸŸŸŸ **Aubaine Chardonnay 2022, Mornington Peninsula** RATING 93 DRINK 2022-2028 $35 JF ✪

Estate Pinot Noir 2020, Mornington Peninsula RATING 93 DRINK 2023-2030 $55 JF

Estate Pinot Gris 2021, Mornington Peninsula RATING 91 DRINK 2023-2026 $35 JF

Scotchmans Hill   ★★★★★

190 Scotchmans Road, Drysdale, Vic 3222 **Region** Geelong **T** (03) 5251 3176 **www**.scotchmans.com.au **Open** 7 days 11.30–4 **Winemaker** Robin Brockett, Marcus Holt **Est.** 1982 **Dozens** 50 000 **Vyds** 80ha

Scotchmans Hill has been a consistent producer of well-made wines under the stewardship of long-term winemaker Robin Brockett and assistant Marcus Holt. The wines are released under the Scotchmans Hill, Cornelius, Jack & Jill and Swan Bay labels. A change of ownership in '14 resulted in significant vineyard investment.

ŸŸŸŸŸ **Cornelius Sutton Vineyard Bellarine Peninsula Chardonnay 2020, Geelong** Ripe yellow nectarines, jasmine, orange oil and subtle vanillin from the impeccably handled oak. This is both expansive and tightly wound on the palate, which is no mean feat. There's citrus, lemongrass and lime finishing long and grapefruit pithy. A lovely wine from beginning to end. Screw cap. 13% alc. RATING 97 DRINK 2023-2028 $75 PR ✪ ♥

ŸŸŸŸŸ **Bellarine Peninsula Shiraz 2021, Geelong** An excellent and bright crimson-purple hue. Ripe red fruits, cocoa nibs, white pepper and a hint of violets in the bouquet, while the medium-bodied palate exudes charm. It's well weighted and structured, too, with very fine and persistent tannins. Screw cap. 14.5% alc. RATING 96 DRINK 2023-2031 $45 PR ✪

Bellarine Peninsula Pinot Noir 2021, Geelong The bright, clear colour sends a signal promptly picked up by the perfumed (roses et al) bouquet and elegant palate. Here the savoury notes from whole bunches (15%) provide the texture to underpin the red cherry and rhubarb fruits at its heart. Screw cap. 13% alc. RATING 96 DRINK 2023-2036 $45 JH ✪

Cornelius Airds Vineyard Bellarine Peninsula Chardonnay 2020, Geelong From a vineyard planted in 1988. A subtle and complex wine. Bright, green-gold hue. Aromas of lemon and grapefruit with just-ripened white nectarines and a hint of jasmine. A fine line of acidity runs through, suggesting that, as good as this is now, it will be even better in a couple of years. 150 dozen made. Screw cap. 13% alc. RATING 96 DRINK 2023-2030 $75 PR ✪

Bellarine Peninsula Chardonnay 2021, Geelong Whole-bunch pressed to barrel, wild-yeast fermentation, lees stirred monthly, matured in new and used French barriques for 12 months. A mouth-filling, rich and creamy palate is striking, but does allow grapefruit to make a limited appearance on the complex, satisfying finish. Screw cap. 13% alc. **RATING** 95 **DRINK** 2023–2029 $45 JH ✪

Cornelius Kincardine Vineyard Bellarine Peninsula Chardonnay 2020, Geelong Tangerine and rockmelon fruit aromas with hints of jasmine and subtle vanilla spice. The gently creamy, textured and nutty palate finishes long with fresh stone fruits and a hint of grapefruit pith. 150 dozen made. Screw cap. 13% alc. **RATING** 95 **DRINK** 2023–2027 $75 PR

Cornelius Spray Farm Vineyard Bellarine Peninsula Syrah 2020, Geelong A very bright crimson. The pick of this year's Scotchmans Hill single-vineyard syrah releases, there's plenty going on here. Red fruits, floral notes and some whole-bunch derived sage and thyme notes can all be found in this purple-fruited, medium-bodied, fine-boned and detailed wine. Screw cap. 14% alc. **RATING** 95 **DRINK** 2023–2030 $75 PR

Cornelius Kirkcaldy Vineyard Bellarine Peninsula Pinot Noir 2020, Geelong Lifted and perfumed with aromas of dark, sour cherries, coriander seeds and Asian spices. Good depth of fruit on the palate, too. This is concentrated, energetic and detailed, with long, silky yet gently chewy tannins rounding out a wine that can be cellared with confidence. Screw cap. 13.5% alc. **RATING** 95 **DRINK** 2023–2031 $72 PR

Bellarine Peninsula Sauvignon Blanc 2022, Geelong A bright green gold, this is simply bursting with intense blackcurrant leaf, citrus and succulent herbs while the equally energetic palate is gently textured, flavoursome and refreshing. A textbook example of cool-climate sauvignon blanc and just the ticket for seafood and salads. Screw cap. 13% alc. **RATING** 94 **DRINK** 2022–2025 $30 PR ✪

Swan Bay Bellarine Peninsula Pinot Noir 2021, Geelong Made by the Scotchmans Hill team as a second label, its design emphasising its role. Do not be fooled: this has all the texture, length and balance of a seriously good pinot, a flamenco dance of red fruits and spices. Screw cap. 13% alc. **RATING** 94 **DRINK** 2023–2025 $27 JH ✪

Bellarine Peninsula Shiraz 2020, Geelong It has a studied elegance that's the mark of winemaker Robin Brockett. Cherries (red and black) and blood plum provide the fruit flavour, finely strung tannins the texture and structure. He made the best of a very difficult vintage. Screw cap. 14% alc. **RATING** 94 **DRINK** 2023–2030 $45 JH

🍷🍷🍷🍷🍷 **Cornelius Airds Vineyard Bellarine Peninsula Blanc de Blanc 2018, Geelong** **RATING** 93 **DRINK** 2022–2026 $60 PR

Bellarine Peninsula Riesling 2022, Geelong **RATING** 93 **DRINK** 2022–2032 $35 PR ✪

Swan Bay Bellarine Peninsula Chardonnay 2021, Geelong **RATING** 93 **DRINK** 2023–2029 $27 JH ✪

Cornelius Single Vineyard Bellarine Peninsula Pinot Gris 2021, Geelong **RATING** 93 **DRINK** 2022–2025 $38 PR

Cornelius Norfolk Vineyard Bellarine Peninsula Pinot Noir 2020, Geelong **RATING** 93 **DRINK** 2023–2027 $72 PR

Cornelius Strathallan Vineyard Bellarine Peninsula Syrah 2020, Geelong **RATING** 92 **DRINK** 2023–2029 $75 PR

Cornelius Armitage Vineyard Bellarine Peninsula Pinot Noir 2020, Geelong **RATING** 92 **DRINK** 2023–2027 $72 PR

Cornelius Single Vineyard Bellarine Peninsula Sauvignon 2021, Geelong **RATING** 91 **DRINK** 2022–2026 $35 PR

Jack & Jill Bellarine Peninsula Pinot Gris 2021, Geelong **RATING** 90 **DRINK** 2022–2025 $30 PR

Seabrook Wines

1122 Light Pass Road, Tanunda, SA 5352 **Region** Barossa Valley
T (08) 8563 0368 **www**.seabrookwines.com.au **Open** Thurs–Mon 11–5
Winemaker Hamish Seabrook **Est.** 2004 **Dozens** 3000 **Vyds** 10.1ha

Hamish Seabrook is the youngest generation of a proud Melbourne wine family once involved in wholesale and retail distribution and as leading show judges of their respective generations. Hamish, too, is a wine show judge but was the first to venture into winemaking, working with Best's and Brown Brothers in Victoria before moving to SA with wife Joanne. In '08 Hamish set up his own winery on the family property in Vine Vale, having previously made the wines at Dorrien Estate and elsewhere. Here they have shiraz (4.4ha), cabernet sauvignon (3.9ha) and mataro (1.8ha), and also continue to source small amounts of shiraz from the Barossa, Langhorne Creek and the Grampians.

The Merchant Shiraz 2020, Barossa Valley A powerful, broody shiraz that shows impressive fruit density. Blackberry, cassis and dark chocolate–dipped cherries are studded with hints of clove, five-spice, Cherry Ripe, cedar, turned earth, licorice and graphite. Compact, tightly packed tannins and a rich, concentrated flow of fruit on the finish. Screw cap. 14.5% alc. **RATING** 95 **DRINK** 2023-2033 $40 DB ✪

The Chairman Shiraz 2019, Great Western Plum, blueberry and dried summer berry fruits with a hint of fine spice, a touch of black pepper and roasting meats, violets and light licorice and cedar tones. Milk chocolate tannins and bright acidity frame the fruit nicely and there is a real sense of composure as the wine sails away. Screw cap. 14.5% alc. **RATING** 95 **DRINK** 2023-2030 $50 DB ✪

The Merchant Shiraz 2019, Barossa Valley There's density to the aromas here with ripe blood plum, blackberry, crème de cassis, licorice, dark chocolate, baking spices, violets and a lick of oak-derived coconut and cedar. Cascading, tightly packed tannins give structure and there is bright acidity and cadence, yet the wine remains concentrated, intense and long of finish. Screw cap. 14.5% alc. **RATING** 94 **DRINK** 2023-2030 $40 DB ✪

Tiger Moth Marshall Montepulciano 2021, Adelaide Hills **RATING** 90 **DRINK** 2023-2027 $29 DB

Lineage Shiraz 2020, Barossa Valley **RATING** 90 **DRINK** 2023-2026 $22 DB ✪

Seize The Day

★★★★

27 Gerald Roberts Road Seppeltsfield, SA 5355 **Region** Barossa Valley
T 0412 455 553 **www**.seizetheday.net.au **Open** By appt **Winemaker** Contract
Est. 2003 **Dozens** 1200 **Vyds** 4ha

Established in '99 by Peter Milhinch and Sharyn Rogers, Seize The Day (formerly Milhinch Wines) is planted to 10ha of shiraz and cabernet sauvignon near Greenock Creek, which flows through the property. At the foot of the vineyard is a restored 1860s German settlers cottage offering luxury accommodation. The winery and surrounding property were sold to Bosotum Winery in 2019 who contract Angus Smibert (of Whistle Post Wines, Coonawarra) to oversee operations. The Seize the Day phrase on the wine labels pays homage to founder Peter Milhinch's journey through adversity, 'Carpe Diem – we never know what tomorrow may bring!'

Classic Shiraz 2020, Barossa Valley Aromas of juicy satsuma plum, blackberry and boysenberry fruits with hints of baking spices, dark chocolate, vanillin oak, cassis, olive tapenade and roasting meats. There is some really nice broody depth to the fruit here with classic ironstone Seppeltsfield tannin grip and a finish that lingers persistently with loads of cassis, spice and earthy tones. Cork. 14.5% alc. **RATING** 92 **DRINK** 2023-2033 $45 DB

Seize The Day Shiraz 2020, Barossa Valley A bright, plummy western Barossa shiraz. Deeply coloured with aromas of ripe blood plum, boysenberry and dark cherry fruits cut with hints of baking spices, chocolate, citrus blossom, olive tapenade and roasting meats. Ferrous-edged sandy tannins and an expansive, spiced plum finish wrap things up nicely. Cork. 14.5% alc. **RATING** 91 **DRINK** 2023-2030 $50 DB

Cabernet Sauvignon 2020, Barossa Valley Blackberry, blackcurrant and black cherry fruits. Hints of baking spices, licorice, blackberry pastille, tobacco, cedar, ironstone and earth. There is some sinew and muscle, with fine, sandy tannin support and a finish that is backed with spiced blackberry and black cherry. Cork. 14% alc. **RATING** 90 **DRINK** 2023-2030 $40 DB

Shiraz Cabernet 2020, Barossa Valley A deeply fruited and structured affair, with plush blackberry, dark plum and black cherry fruits loaded with hints of licorice, oak spice, dark chocolate and earthy tones. The tannins are superfine and provide ample structure and form, finishing long with crème de cassis notes and spice. Cork. 14% alc. **RATING** 90 **DRINK** 2023-2030 $42 DB

Semitone ★★★☆

Ingliston Road, Ballan, Vic 3342 (postal) **Region** Victoria
T 0400 514 613 **Open** Not **Winemaker** David Garner **Est.** 2017 **Dozens** 300
It all started with 0.5t of Pyrenees cabernet sauvignon back in '17, hence the name Semitone. What started off as a curiosity and passion for winemaking, coupled with opportunity and shadowing of a number Victorian winemakers, teacher-come-amateur-winemaker David Garner is now in his 5th vintage of making ultra-small batches of wine from predominantly (at this stage) Western Victorian vineyards in the Pyrenees, Geelong and Grampians regions. Production grew to 1t/year in the subsequent vintages, culminating in a 3t production from the amazing '21 vintage in Vic, in time for the first commercial release.

 Shiraz 2021, Pyrenees Attractive deep, solid purple-red hues to this young red – very Pyrenees. It captures both a youthful liveliness and sound fruit-tannin base for a rewarding future. The lifted scent of turned earth, Aussie bush notes, bramble and bay leaf melds beautifully with the wild red berries and anise spice. Maturation in French oak and pliant tannins bring a seamless integration throughout. Screw cap. 14.5% alc. **RATING** 91 **DRINK** 2022-2026 $28 JP ✪

Semprevino ★★★★

271 Kangarilla Road, McLaren Vale, SA 5171 (postal) **Region** McLaren Vale
T 0417 142 110 **www.**semprevino.com.au **Open** Not **Winemaker** Russell Schroder
Est. 2006 **Dozens** 800
Semprevino is the venture of Russell Schroder and Simon Doak, who became close friends while at Monash University in the early 1990s – studying mechanical engineering and science respectively. Russell is the prime mover, who, after working for CRA/Rio Tinto for 5 years, left on a 4-month trip to Western Europe and became captivated by the life of a vigneron. Returning to Australia, he enrolled in part-time wine science at CSU, obtaining his wine science degree in 2005. Between '03 and '06 he worked vintages in Italy and Victoria, coming under the wing of Stephen Pannell at Tinlins (where the Semprevino wines are made).

 Shiraz 2021, McLaren Vale Archetypal Vale shiraz. Warm of feel. Redolent of crushed blackberry and Australian scrub, the waft of eucalyptus strong. Licorice blackstrap, iodine, lilac and a smear of tapenade across the finish, a tad hot. A bite of oak to conclude. Screw cap. 14.6% alc. **RATING** 91 **DRINK** 2022-2030 $35 NG

Sangiovese Cabernet 2021, Adelaide A full-weighted wine that remains light on its feet. Sangiovese imparts frisk and edge, galvanising the smaller cabernet component (20%) into a meld of succulent red and dark fruits, alongside a fibrous spindle of herbal grape tannins, a curb of oak and a waft of anise. Solid drinking. Screw cap. 14.3% alc. **RATING** 90 **DRINK** 2022-2028 $45 NG

Seppelt

36 Cemetery Road, Great Western, Vic 3377 **Region** Great Western
T (03) 5361 2239 **www**.seppelt.com.au **Open** 7 days 10–5 **Winemaker** Adam Carnaby,
Clare Dry **Est.** 1851 **Vyds** 648ha

Seppelt was once Australia's foremost sparkling wine producer and a pioneer of superb small-volume red wines. The latter, under winemaker Colin Preece from the 1930s–60s, is probably most relevant to the Seppelt we know today. Colin's reds were ostensibly Great Western–sourced, but – as the laws of the time allowed – were often regional, varietal and vintage blends. He'd be like a kid in a lolly shop if he'd had today's viticultural resources to draw on, and would have been quick to recognise the current winemakers and viticulturists for the supreme quality of today's portfolio, too. In '16, Ararat businessman Danial Ahchow leased the cellar door from current owner TWE, saving it from closure. Winemaker Clare Dry took over from Adam Carnaby from the '21 vintage. Grapes are sourced from Great Western and wines are made in the Barossa.

Drumborg Vineyard Riesling 2022, Henty Has the brilliance and purity of a perfectly cut diamond, the low yield (flowering problems due to unstable weather) adding to the gentle insistence of the lime juice, Granny Smith apple and lemon flavours. The acidity is a silken web of an unseen orb spider. Screw cap. 11% alc. **RATING** 97 **DRINK** 2023–2037 $40 JH ✪

Salinger Vintage Cuvée Méthode Traditionnelle 2017, Henty A 52/42/6% blend of pinot noir, chardonnay and pinot meunier that trumpets the ultra-cool region. The vintage was wet and cool, but disease-free. The wine has developed yet more intensity to its Meyer lemon fruit base, the length of the palate exceptional. Bargain of the year. Cork. 10.5% alc. **RATING** 96 **DRINK** 2023–2026 $30 JH ✪

St Peters Shiraz 2021, Grampians The flavour profile is as you'd expect, all cherry plum with inflections of pepper, smoked meat, cedar and assorted woodsy herbs, but it has some extra air in its tyres from there, namely a plumpness to its mid-palate, a velvety curl to its tannin and above average length. It remains true to its established style but there's a power and complexity that really puts it up there. Screw cap. 14.5% alc. **RATING** 96 **DRINK** 2026–2045 $80 CM

Drumborg Vineyard Pinot Noir 2021, Henty A masterclass in not judging pinot noir by the depth of its colour, here only a little deeper than its pinot meunier sibling. And there's more in the mouth, initially hesitant then majestically expanding on the finish. The rainbow of berry aromas surging from the glass. Screw cap. 13% alc. **RATING** 96 **DRINK** 2023–2033 $45 JH ✪

Drumborg Vineyard Pinot Meunier 2021, Henty Pinot meunier is so easily hurt in the vinification process, seeking more colour, more body, but none of that has impinged on this perfumed wine. Violets, red and blue scents are folded into a gently spicy/savoury palate, whole bunches in the ferment just so. Screw cap. 13.5% alc. **RATING** 95 **DRINK** 2023–2030 $36 JH ✪

Drumborg Vineyard Chardonnay 2021, Henty The complex flowery, scented and powdery bouquet slips alongside the intense and equally complex palate. Winemaker Clare Dry has nailed a wine that allows delicacy and intensity equal time, stone fruit and grapefruit ditto. Will reveal more and more over the next 5 years. Screw cap. 13% alc. **RATING** 95 **DRINK** 2023–2032 $40 JH ✪

Grüner Veltliner 2022, Henty RATING 93 **DRINK** 2023–2027 $27 CM ✪
Chalambar Shiraz 2021, Grampians Heathcote RATING 93
DRINK 2026–2046 $27 JH ✪
Pierlot Brut Cuvée NV, Henty RATING 92 $30 CM ✪
Jaluka Chardonnay 2021, Henty RATING 92 **DRINK** 2023–2025 $27 JH ✪

Seppeltsfield

730 Seppeltsfield Road, Seppeltsfield, SA 5355 **Region** Barossa Valley
T (08) 8568 6200 **www**.seppeltsfield.com.au **Open** 7 days 10.30–5 **Winemaker** Fiona
Donald, Charlie Seppelt, Matthew Pick **Viticulturist** Kingsley Fuller **Est.** 1851
Dozens 8000 **Vyds** 1500ha

The historic Seppeltsfield property and its bounty of old fortified wines was established by
the Seppelt family in 1851. Later acquired by Foster's Group (now Treasury Wine Estates),
Seppeltsfield returned to private ownership in '07 with Warren Randall now owning in excess
of 90% of its capital. Warren, former sparkling winemaker for Seppelt Great Western in the
1980s, has led a revival of Seppeltsfield, gradually restoring the heritage-listed property. The
estate's 1888 gravity cellar is back in full operation and a tourism village has been established.
Warren has also slowly pieced together the largest premium, privately owned vineyard holding
in the Barossa – enabling Seppeltsfield to complement its treasure trove of fortifieds with table
wine releases. The 100 Year Old Paras have no parallel anywhere else in the world and the
conjunction of 100 years of devoted stewardship (think former cellarmaster James Godfrey)
and have had an outcome that can never, ever, be duplicated.

100 Year Old Para Vintage Tawny 1923, Barossa Valley The wine is every
bit as awesome as its predecessors, the intensity and the flavours lingering in the
mouth for a seemingly endless time. Its acidity has none of the edgy cuts that can
sometimes need a spice-laden biscuit or chocolate to tame the acidity. 100 points?
Of course. It is the one and only wine whose history, past, present and future
demand it and is deservedly the inaugural inductee to the James Halliday Hall of
Fame: WIne. 100ml. Cork. 21.3% alc. **RATING** 100 $1650 JH ♥

Para 21 Year Old Tawny 2002, South Australia Seppeltsfield is a national
treasure. A tawny with 21 years under its belt here. The usual head-spinningly
complex array of aromas and flavours that make us flip our lids for this stuff.
Candied citrus fruits, fruitcake spices, mahogany, brandy snaps, toffee, rancio,
candied nuts, layers of spice and comforting whiffs of warm, woody tones and
leather. Viscous, unctuous and wildly complex, reaching a crescendo before slowly
fading at a glacial pace with amazing length and freshness. Wonderful. Screw cap.
20% alc. **RATING** 97 **DRINK** 2023-2053 $105 DB ♥

No. EC3 Tinta Cão Tinta Amarela Touriga 2021, Barossa The vibrant,
striking crimson-purple hue introduces a wine that accompanied me up to dinner
on the day it was tasted. The bouquet is intensely floral, with rosehip, cherry
blossom and Eastern spices, the palate gloriously juicy yet with a mouth-watering,
savoury spine. Screw cap. 13.5% alc. **RATING** 96 **DRINK** 2023-2030 $50 JH ✪

The Southing Shiraz 2020, Barossa Deep, bright crimson through to the
rim. Evocative bouquet of spiced plum and cedar aromas without any overripe
notes, then a full-bodied palate that dares to have elegance and balance. Screw cap.
15.1% alc. **RATING** 96 **DRINK** 2030-2045 $85 JH

Para Rare Tawny NV, South Australia Deep tawny in the glass with flashes of
amber and mahogany. Brandy-soaked fruitcake, raisin essence, deeply layered spice
and roasted nuts. Toffee apple, rancio, polished leather, salted caramel and candied
citrus. Complex, vital and complete with an incredibly long finish that builds
before trailing off in slow motion with memories of liquored fruits and complex
spice. Screw cap. 20.2% alc. **RATING** 96 $90 DB

The Westing Shiraz 2021, Barossa Deep crimson to the rim of the glass
and aromas of blackberry, black cherry and satsuma plum fruits. There is a slight
ferrous edge here with hints of salted licorice, violets, olive tapenade, veal jus,
dried citrus rind and roasting meats. Full bodied with compact, chocolatey
tannins and a tide of black fruits and baking spices on the powerful finish.
Screw cap. 14% alc. **RATING** 95 **DRINK** 2023-2038 $85 DB

Great Terraced Vineyard Grenache 2021, Barossa The bright, clear hue
sets the tone for a wine of absolute purity, both of place and variety. Raspberry
leads the way, studded with spices and a dusting of white pepper. Screw cap.
14.5% alc. **RATING** 95 **DRINK** 2023-2037 $85 JH

The Southing Shiraz 2021, Barossa Intense macerated plums, black cherry and blueberry fruits with hints of licorice, brown spice, violets, dark chocolate, purple flowers, sage and coal dust. Velvety with crushed granite tannins and hints of milk chocolate joining the deep plum and cassis-like fruit on the finish. Plenty of depth and power, but the acidity carries it nicely with a long plum finish. Screw cap. 14% alc. RATING 95 DRINK 2023–2038 $85 DB

Para Grand Tawny NV, South Australia Heady aromas of raisin essence, fruitcake, caramelised citrus rind, rancio and brandied fruits. Long and incredibly complex, yet with a seam of freshness as it slides across the palate leaving a wake of caramel, citrus rind, toffee apple, raisins and liquored fruits with a finish that just keeps going. Screw cap. 20.9% alc. RATING 95 $40 DB ✪

Grenache 2022, Barossa Juicy plum, blueberry and cranberry fruits cut with exotic spices, orange blossom, gingerbread, cola, pomegranate and earth. Juicy and glossy, slinking its way across the palate leaving a trail of gingery spice and ripe plummy fruit. A fine example of contemporary Barossa grenache that speaks to drinkability. Screw cap. 14% alc. RATING 94 DRINK 2023–2028 $30 DB ✪

No. EC4 Cabernet Sauvignon Shiraz 2021, Barossa Deeply coloured with glossy, pure-fruited vibes, it displays ripe cassis and bramble berry and plum fruits, hints of brown spice, dried herbs, licorice, cedar, vanilla bean, pressed flowers and earth. Tight-grained, fine tannins flex on the palate, which is full bodied, self-assured and flows with rich cassis and plum fruits and a gentle wash of herbs and spice. Screw cap. 14.4% alc. RATING 94 DRINK 2023–2035 $50 DB

The Westing Shiraz 2020, Barossa Fresh earth and black fruits intermingle on the bouquet; the palate is firm and distinctly savoury, with fine tannins and mouth-watering acidity joining to shape the lingering finish of the wine. Screw cap. 14.9% alc. RATING 94 DRINK 2025–2035 $85 JH

♟♟♟♟♙ **Watervale Riesling 2022, Clare Valley** RATING 93 DRINK 2023–2033 $30 DB ✪
Touriga 2022, Barossa RATING 93 DRINK 2023–2025 $30 DB ✪
Nero d'Avola 2022, Barossa RATING 92 DRINK 2023–2026 $30 DB ✪
The Northing Shiraz 2021, Barossa RATING 92 DRINK 2023–2035 $85 DB
Grenache Rosé 2022, Barossa RATING 91 DRINK 2023–2025 $30 DB

Serafino Wines   ★★★★★

Kangarilla Road, McLaren Vale, SA 5171 **Region** McLaren Vale
T (08) 8323 0157 **www.**serafino.com.au **Open** Mon–Fri 10–4.30, w'ends & public hols 10–4.30 **Winemaker** Michelle Heagney **Viticulturist** Andrew Godfrey **Est.** 2000 **Dozens** 30 000 **Vyds** 121ha
After the sale of Maglieri Wines to Beringer Blass in 1998, Maglieri founder Serafino (Steve) Maglieri acquired the McLarens on the Lake complex originally established by Andrew Garrett. The operation draws upon over 120ha of shiraz, cabernet sauvignon, chardonnay, merlot, semillon, barbera, nebbiolo, sangiovese, and grenache; part of the grape production is sold. Steve was awarded a Member of the Order of Australia in '18.

♟♟♟♟♟ **Tawny NV, McLaren Vale** A trove of walnut husk, mahogany, molasses, varnish and Chinese medicine cabinet. Fortifieds such as these serve as a vestige of the past as much as an immense pleasure for the present. Rich and throaty, with the spirit embedded nicely into the fray. Cork. 18.5% alc. RATING 94 $40 NG ✪

♟♟♟♟♙ **Shiraz 2021, McLaren Vale** RATING 92 DRINK 2022–2028 $28 NG ✪
Cabernet Sauvignon 2021, McLaren Vale RATING 92 DRINK 2022–2030 $28 NG ✪
Bellissimo Barbera 2022, McLaren Vale RATING 91 DRINK 2022–2025 $25 NG ✪
Sharktooth Wild Ferment Chardonnay 2020, Adelaide Hills RATING 91 DRINK 2022–2026 $40 NG
Bellissimo Tempranillo 2022, McLaren Vale RATING 90 DRINK 2022–2027 $25 NG ✪

Serengale Vineyard

1168 Beechworth-Wangaratta Road, Everton Upper, Vic 3678 **Region** Beechworth
T 0428 585 348 **www.serengalebeechworth.com.au Open** By appt **Winemaker** Gayle
Taylor **Viticulturist** Serena Abbinga, Gayle Taylor **Est.** 1999 **Dozens** 1000 **Vyds** 7ha

Gayle Taylor and Serena Abbinga established their business in '99. Gayle had worked in the
wine industry for over 20 years, while Serena was seeking to return to North East Victoria
after many years in inner-city Melbourne. A 3-year search culminated in the acquisition of
a 24ha property in the Everton Hills. In the early years they concentrated on planting the
7ha vineyard, with 2.6ha of merlot, 1.2ha chardonnay, 1ha each of cabernet sauvignon,
shiraz and pinot gris, and 0.2ha of prosecco. In '15 the winery was completed, and the first
vintage made.

Merlot Cabernet 2019, Beechworth A striking merlot-dominant wine of
great integrity and class. Masterfully showcasing the floral beauty of merlot –
violet, rose petal – with the wild herbal interplay of the other – fennel, sage, bay
leaf. Plum and black cherry fruits are lifted and concentrated with fine, velvety
tannins tying everything together. Four years old and there's so much vinous life
still to enjoy. Screw cap. 13.9% alc. **RATING** 96 **DRINK** 2023–2032 $42 JP ✪ ♥

Pinot Gris 2021, Beechworth RATING 90 **DRINK** 2023–2026 $39 JP

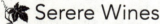 Serere Wines

3, 62–64 Marshall Street, Dapto, NSW 2530 (postal) **Region** North East Victoria
T 0421 066 601 **www.sererewines.com.au Open** Not **Winemaker** Joe Warren
Est. 2018 **Dozens** 600

A chef, working across Australia and beyond, falls out of love with shift work and in love
with wine. He returns to school, studies viticulture and oenology and starts afresh with a new
career in wine. It's not a familiar path, but one that has placed Joe Warren in good stead.
Four years working in wineries in North East Victoria and time spent in McLaren Vale, the
Granite Belt and the Grampians gave him a solid basis to go out on his own, and Serere was
born in '18. He and partner Bec Noonan set up Serere using grapes from the Beechworth
and surrounding regions, working with growers who grew the varieties they were passionate
about: chardonnay, roussanne, viognier, shiraz and pinot meunier. And the Serere name, Latin
for bound, interwoven and entwined? The name aligned with their view of wine, something
that is not merely a product for consumption, but a journey and experience of connections.

Whitlands High Plateau Pinot Meunier 2021, King Valley Bright cherry
red hues. And then that scent! Wildflowers, lavender, musky spice, red cherry,
mulberry, twig and leaf succinctly capture the complex beauty of the grape. An
accomplished wine fine in tannin and already revealing a budding complexity.
Screw cap. 12.8% alc. **RATING** 93 **DRINK** 2023–2028 $42 JP

Roussanne 2021, Beechworth Cuttings were taken from Giaconda for this
wine. Aspires to take roussanne to that next level as a stand-alone variety, one
that is rich and complex. Confident winemaking on display. Buttery yellow in
hue with full-on scents of citrus blossom, honeysuckle, baked apple, quince and
peach. Smooth beeswax mouthfeel runs long, delivering complexity along the
way. Impressive all around. 80 dozen produced. Screw cap. 13.6% alc. **RATING** 93
DRINK 2023–2028 $54 JP

Shiraz Viognier 2021, Beechworth Florals, ripe red fruits, baking spices and
autumnal earthy notes with just a light dusting of pepper bring this charming,
medium-bodied young red to vivid life. Well-integrated oak completes a highly
attractive vinous picture. Won't mind some further ageing, either. Screw cap.
14% alc. **RATING** 92 **DRINK** 2023–2028 $56 JP

Whitlands Chardonnay 2021, King Valley Captures the regional chardonnay
signature beautifully with a zesty, streamlined, citrus-flowing wine. Delicate
perfume in apple blossom and grapefruit, lemon sorbet and white nectarine.
Strikes a mix of nougat, almond meal and stone fruits on the palate with bright,

crunchy acidity courtesy of one of the highest vineyards in the state. Lipsmacking good. Screw cap. 12.8% alc. **RATING** 92 **DRINK** 2023-2028 $46 JP
Syrah 2021, Beechworth The herbal edge that 100% whole bunches bring to this wine is nicely countered by the plummy, soft influence of carbonic maceration. All up, this wine sits pretty nicely within what some like to define as syrah – it's not too heavy and there's a strong inner core of black, red fruits and spice with more besides. Screw cap. 13.2% alc. **RATING** 91 **DRINK** 2023-2028 $46 JP

Serrat ★★★★★

115 Simpsons Lane, Yarra Glen, Vic 3775 (postal) **Region** Yarra Valley
T (03) 9730 1439 **www**.serrat.com.au **Open** Not **Winemaker** Tom Carson, Kate Thurgood **Viticulturist** Kate Thurgood **Est.** 2001 **Dozens** 1000 **Vyds** 3.5ha
Serrat is the family business of Tom Carson (after a 12-year reign at Yering Station, now running Yabby Lake and Heathcote Estate for the Kirby family) and wife Nadège. They have close planted (at 6600 vines/ha) 1.4ha of pinot noir, 0.77ha of shiraz, 0.4ha of chardonnay, 0.3ha of grenache, 0.28ha of nebbiolo, 0.12ha of grenache blanc, 0.8ha each of malbec and mataro and 0.6ha of viognier. As well as being a consummate winemaker, Tom has one of the best palates in Australia and a deep understanding of the fine wines of the world, which he and Nadège drink at every opportunity (when they aren't drinking Serrat).

🍷🍷🍷🍷🍷 **Shiraz Viognier 2022, Yarra Valley** A saturated purple hue. Saturated and intense on the nose, too. Concentrated yet balanced, you'll find aromas of blue and dark fruits, violets, incense and sweet spices such as clove and cinnamon. A gorgeous mouthful, this is powerful and structured but without any sense of heaviness. Australian shiraz viognier doesn't get much better than this. It's a steal at this price, too. Screw cap. 13.5% alc. **RATING** 98 **DRINK** 2022-2035 $50 PR ✪
Pinot Noir 2022, Yarra Valley Darkly fruited with ripe raspberries, cherry skins, crushed violets, sandalwood and fennel seeds. You barely notice the whole bunches. The subtly creamy and detailed palate gets better the longer it sits in the glass, and I love how this wine is built to age yet still drinking well in its youth. Screw cap. 13% alc. **RATING** 97 **DRINK** 2022-2031 $50 PR ✪

🍷🍷🍷🍷🍷 **Grenache Noir 2022, Yarra Valley** With its perfumed aromas of spiced raspberries, preserved rhubarb and 'herbes de Provence' this is another delightful grenache from Serrat. Light to medium bodied, fine, chalky tannins and bright acidity round out a wine that you'll struggle to keep your hands off. Screw cap. 14% alc. **RATING** 96 **DRINK** 2022-2022 $50 PR ✪ ♥
Other Terroir Pinot Noir 2022, Yarra Valley A bright ruby crimson. Nicely detailed, this brightly fruited wine has aromas of red cherries and redcurrants with hints of violets and subtle spice. The light- to medium-bodied and impeccably balanced palate makes for a wine that is approachable now but has both the depth and structure to reward up to 10 years in the cellar. Screw cap. 13.5% alc. **RATING** 96 **DRINK** 2022-2031 $42 PR ✪
Chardonnay 2022, Yarra Valley A bright green gold. White stone fruits, rockmelon, orange blossom, a hint of jasmine and very subtle oak can all be found in this very complex and subtle wine. On the palate, this has a gentle creaminess balanced by a crystalline acidity. A little more open and softer than last year's version but equally as good. Screw cap. 13.5% alc. **RATING** 96 **DRINK** 2022-2029 $50 PR ✪
Fourre-Tout 2022, Yarra Valley 59/20/17/4% barbera/nebbiolo/malbec/pinot noir. A deep crimson purple. This has a riotous amalgam of black cherries, blueberries and blackcurrants together with violets, musk and a hint of bay leaf. Juicy and delicious, this is the ideal bistro wine that would go down a treat with everything from charcuterie to a big bowl of spaghetti or lamb cutlets. The perfect hump day wine! Screw cap. 13.5% alc. **RATING** 95 **DRINK** 2022-2029 $35 PR ✪

Settlers Rise

Maleny Manor, 894 Landsborough-Maleny Road, Maleny, Qld 4552 (postal)
Region Queensland
T (07) 5478 5558 **www.**settlersrise.com.au **Open** Not **Winemaker** Peter Scudamore-Smith MW (Contract) **Est.** 1998 **Dozens** 3000 **Vyds** 7ha
After a change of ownership in 2007, Settlers Rise has closed its Montville site and moved its operations to Maleny Manor (a luxurious wedding and accommodation function centre). One ha of chambourcin has been established at the property, and another 6ha vineyard is leased.

Terroirs Of The Aged Reserve Chardonnay 2012, Granite Belt A full-experience chardonnay with ripe apricot, coconut and vanilla cream characters, lemon curd, sweet lime and a fine dusting of clove in scents and flavours. Luxurious with a keen sense of underlying vitality. Delivering some nutty, fig/date savoury secondary elements with a quiet, briny freshness within. Really lovely drinking, but best done with a good chill and soon. Screw cap. 13% alc. **RATING** 93 **DRINK** 2022–2025 $95 MB

Terroirs Of The Aged Reserve Chardonnay 2010, Granite Belt A mature release wine. It's rich and round, hugely concentrated in honey-butter toast perfume and shows similar flavours with a good dusting of cinnamon sugar, licks of wheatgerm and the last skerrick of limey acidity lending gentle freshness. It's such an opulent wine in its current incarnation, and will suit those seeking heft and oomph. Screw cap. 12.5% alc. **RATING** 91 **DRINK** 2022–2025 $95 MB

Sevenhill Cellars

111c College Road, Sevenhill, SA 5453 **Region** Clare Valley
T (08) 8843 5900 **www.**sevenhill.com.au **Open** 7 days 10–5 **Winemaker** Will Shields
Viticulturist Craig Richards **Est.** 1851 **Dozens** 25 000 **Vyds** 96ha
One of the historical treasures of Australia, the oft-photographed stone wine cellars are the oldest in the Clare Valley and winemaking has been an enterprise within this Jesuit province since 1851. All the wines reflect the estate-grown grapes from old vines. In recent years, Sevenhill Cellars has increased its vineyard holdings from 74ha to 96ha.

St Ignatius 2019, Clare Valley 52/28/14/6% cabernet sauvignon/merlot/malbec/cabernet franc. The colour and bouquet open up with plenty on show, but it's the full-bodied palate that sweeps all before it, the oak particularly feisty and the black fruits complex and commanding. Screw cap. 14% alc. **RATING** 95 **DRINK** 2023–2035 $50 JH ✪

Brother John May Reserve Release Shiraz 2019, Clare Valley A formidable shiraz. So deep, so dark, so potent and yet, stellar balance. Dark cherry, mocha and espresso characters among ripe plum, choc-orange, brined black olive and leafy, minty elements. Rich, satiny, very concentrated and finishes way into the distance. Finds an even keel between ripeness, spice, wood seasoning and freshness. Screw cap. 14% alc. **RATING** 95 **DRINK** 2023–2040 $150 MB

27 Miles Riesling 2022, Clare Valley It's very citrusy, tart and refreshing. High in floral, citrus and flinty perfume. The palate is really tight, with shy juiciness coming into play too. Fruity sweetness? Barely there, but apparent. It's a very acid-driven style. Drink now? Sure, but this one really is for the cellar to let it relax and unwind. Screw cap. 10.5% alc. **RATING** 94 **DRINK** 2024–2040 $50 MB

Inigo Barbera 2021, Clare Valley Vivid crimson-purple hue. Another example of winemaker Will Shields' intelligence and dexterity. Ultra-fragrant red berries sweep through the long, light- to medium-bodied palate, giving this the character (being texture and structure) of grenache or pinot noir. Screw cap. 12.5% alc. **RATING** 94 **DRINK** 2023–2028 $28 JH ✪

Open Range Grenache 2021, Clare Valley Lots of white pepper and aromatic green herb elements overlaid on ripe cherry, cassis and game meat characters – the bouquet and palate reverberate these notes succinctly. Definitively a bigger, bolder expression of grenache, but done with aplomb. Screw cap. 14.5% alc. RATING 94 DRINK 2024–2035 $80 MB

St Ignatius 2020, Clare Valley Cabernet sauvignon, merlot, malbec and cabernet franc all play a hand here. Silky smooth, finely tuned with graphite-laced tannins, concentrated and inky but with a fresh finish. It's fragrant, too, with loads of dark berry, violets, tobacco and pencil shavings to sniff on. Drinking well now (though needs a big decant), but a future prospect for the patient among us. Screw cap. 14% alc. RATING 94 DRINK 2024–2045 $50 MB

Inigo Cabernet Sauvignon 2020, Clare Valley 87/8/3/2% cabernet sauvignon/ruby cabernet/cabernet franc/shiraz. An unexpectedly fragrant and fresh wine. Red berry and blackberry flavours shape the medium–bodied palate. Screw cap. 14.5% alc. RATING 94 DRINK 2023–2035 $28 JH ✪

Vaulted Cellar Shiraz 2020, Clare Valley Ripe plum, dried cranberry, truffle, licorice and a fine dusting of bitter cocoa powder over the top. Thick and round, soft and long, there's great potency to taste, palate-staining qualities, sweet fruit, spice and a nutty finish. Feels high-class, with power and grace. Screw cap. 14% alc. RATING 94 DRINK 2022–2035 $50 MB

🍷🍷🍷🍷 **Inigo Riesling 2022, Clare Valley** RATING 93 DRINK 2023–2032 $25 JH ✪
Spire's Lament Viognier 2021, Clare Valley RATING 93 DRINK 2023–2028 $45 JH

Seville Estate   ★★★★★

65 Linwood Road, Seville, Vic 3139 **Region** Yarra Valley
T (03) 5964 2622 **www**.sevilleestate.com.au **Open** 7 days 10–5 **Winemaker** Dylan McMahon **Est.** 1972 **Dozens** 8000 **Vyds** 12ha

Seville Estate was founded by Dr Peter and Margaret McMahon in 1972. After several changes of ownership, Yiping Wang purchased the property in early '17. Yiping's supportive yet hands-off approach has allowed winemaker and general manager Dylan McMahon (grandson of founder Peter McMahon) to steer the ship. The estate has expanded to encompass the neighbouring vineyard and property (formerly Ainsworth Estate). This extra land has allowed for replanting original vine material grafted onto rootstock to preserve the original '72 clones and safeguard the future of this unique property. Seville Estate also has luxury accommodation with the original homestead and 3 self-contained apartments.

🍷🍷🍷🍷 **Chardonnay 2022, Yarra Valley** A very bright green gold. There's a lot packed into this concentrated yet supremely balanced and structured wine. Pure and saline, you'll find aromas of white pear, early-picked nectarine, lime pith and wet stone scents. Almost painful in its intensity, this finishes very long with good grip and a fine vein of acidity. A glorious wine destined for a very long life. Screw cap. 12.8% alc. RATING 98 DRINK 2022–2028 $80 PR ✪ ♥

Pinot Noir 2022, Yarra Valley Due to low crops, this is the estate's only 2022 pinot noir. A deep ruby crimson. There's an understated subtlety on the bouquet with its aromas of black cherry and raspberries, star anise and a little freshly churned earth. On the palate, this is tightly wound and there's an old-vine creaminess to its texture. The tannins are lingering but discreet. Screw cap. 13.2% alc. RATING 97 DRINK 2022–2035 $80 PR ✪

Dr McMahon Pinot Noir 2021, Yarra Valley From the original pinot noir vines planted in '72. A light, bright ruby garnet. Very perfumed, the whole bunches and the oak have been swallowed up by the fruit. Little red strawberries, peony, licorice root, spice and a little tobacco on the bouquet. Delicate yet powerful and structured, this is a fascinating wine that will take time for the winemaker's influence to submerge. 50 dozen made. Screw cap. 13% alc. RATING 97 DRINK 2023–2035 $200 PR

Old Vine Reserve Shiraz 2021, Yarra Valley From a single site at Seville Estate planted in '72. With its aromas of dark cherry and blackberries, graphite and warm spice, this has a backward, Cornas-like vibe. Powerful yet silken textured with persistent yet fine tannins. A touch closed today, this has all the components to turn into something special over the next 10–15 years. Screw cap. 13.5% alc. **RATING** 97 **DRINK** 2023-2035 $95 PR ✪

Dr McMahon Shiraz 2020, Yarra Valley A bright, medium crimson. Aromas of small red fruits, licorice root, graphite and pink peppercorns, while the new oak is beginning to integrate with the wine. There's an old-vine intensity on the palate with the silkiest of tannins. It will take time for the hand of the winemaker to submerge into the wine, and for those with the patience and the pockets, it will be fascinating to follow its evolution. 50 dozen made. Screw cap. 13% alc. **RATING** 97 **DRINK** 2023-2040 $200 PR

ΨΨΨΨΨ **Single Vineyard Series Gembrook Chardonnay 2022, Yarra Valley** A bright green gold. Seductively scented with aromas of ripe nashi pear, lemon, chamomile flower and a little oyster shell. This has good fruit concentration on the palate, it's balanced by the wine's tensile acidity and long, chalky finish. More approachable as a young wine than the '21 but will provide considerable pleasure for some time. Screw cap. 12.5% alc. **RATING** 96 **DRINK** 2023-2029 $45 PR ✪

Shiraz 2021, Yarra Valley A gorgeous crimson purple. Seductive and perfumed. Aromas of red fruits, cardamom and green peppercorn. Some freshly hung meat. Medium bodied, with good depth and sweet spices, this is framed by persistent yet silky tannins. Screw cap. 13.5% alc. **RATING** 96 **DRINK** 2022-2030 $60 PR ✪

Riesling 2022, Yarra Valley A small crop has produced a wonderfully aromatic wine with gardenias, ripe citrus, grapefruit pith, delicate chamomile and spice. Slatey textured, there's good grip on the long, gentle finish. Beautifully balanced and structured without being austere. Drink now or let this slowly unfurl over the next decade or so. Screw cap. 12% alc. **RATING** 95 **DRINK** 2022-2028 $40 PR ✪

Singe Vineyard Series Woori Yallock Pinot Noir 2022, Yarra Valley Vibrant cherry red. Bursting at the seams with bright red and black fruits, spice and just the right amount of whole-bunch-influenced dried flowers and herbs. Ripe and slippery on the palate, this can totally be enjoyed now but there are also enough fine-grained tannins for it to age gracefully over the short- to medium-term. Screw cap. 13% alc. **RATING** 94 **DRINK** 2023-2027 $45 PR

ΨΨΨΨΨ **Blanc de Blancs 2018, Yarra Valley** **RATING** 93 **DRINK** 2022-2027 $60 PR
Old Vine Reserve Cabernet Sauvignon 2021, Yarra Valley **RATING** 93 **DRINK** 2022-2035 $95 PR
Single Vineyard Series Three Reds Cabernet Malbec Merlot 2021, Yarra Valley **RATING** 92 **DRINK** 2022-2028 $45 PR

Sfera Wines by Wirrega Vineyards ★★★★

PO Box 94, Mundulla, SA 5270 **Region** Limestone Coast
T (08) 8743 4167 **www**.sferawines.com.au **Open** By appt **Winemaker** Shane Harris **Viticulturist** Jeff Flint **Est.** 1993 **Dozens** 8000 **Vyds** 164ha
In '93, Scott Collett, Rocco Melino, Roger Oakeshott, Grant Tilbrook, John Younger and Guido Zuccoli – a group that holds an awesome amount of knowledge about every aspect of the wine industry – formed a partnership to develop this large vineyard which, until '13, was content to stick to supplying grapes for some of the partners' own enterprises and to businesses as large as Pernod Ricard. Rocco and Guido have since passed on, with Guido's daughter Lynne and Simon and Karina Spier joining the partnership.

ΨΨΨΨΨ **Rosso 2021, Limestone Coast** Blend of dolcetto, shiraz, lagrein and tempranillo; co-fermented with 10% whole bunches. It feels jolly and simple at first, with raspberry and eucalyptus driving, but as it moves through the palate it turns darker and more serious, in a good way, eventually finishing with a delicious burst of licorice-like flavour. This is both tasty and energetic at once. It works a treat as a result. Screw cap. 13.5% alc. **RATING** 92 **DRINK** 2023-2027 $27 CM ✪

Montepulciano 2021, Limestone Coast It basically presents sweet, red-berried flavour but then inflections of saltbush, balsamic, iodine and tonic-like herbs add that bit extra. This is a ripe, mid-weight, well-balanced red with enough going on to make you want a second or third glass. Screw cap. 14.5% alc. RATING 91 DRINK 2023–2027 $20 CM ✪

Shadowfax Winery

K Road, Werribee, Vic 3030 **Region** Port Phillip
T (03) 9731 4420 **www**.shadowfax.com.au **Open** Wed–Mon 11–5 **Winemaker** Alister Timms **Viticulturist** Ko Hironaka **Est.** 1998 **Dozens** 10 000 **Vyds** 28ha

Once an offspring of Werribee Park, Shadowfax is now very much its own master. It has 10ha of mature vineyards at Werribee; plus 5ha of close-planted pinot noir, 5ha of chardonnay and 2ha of pinot gris at the Little Hampton vineyard in Macedon; and 3ha of pinot noir, 2ha of chardonnay and 1ha of gewürztraminer elsewhere in Macedon. Alister Timms, with degrees in science (University of Melbourne) and oenology (University of Adelaide) became chief winemaker in '17 (replacing long-serving winemaker Matt Harrop).

🍷🍷🍷🍷🍷 **Minnow Carignan Grenache Mataro 2022, Port Phillip** What's a super-delicious, good value yet compelling red? Minnow. The 3 varieties work in harmony, offering flavours of spiced cherries and dark plums, although it is savoury with some charcuterie and an attractive ferrous character. Flavours sway across a mid-weighted palate, fine tannins and some sandy texture that the acidity keeps flowing. Screw cap. 13% alc. RATING 95 DRINK 2023–2028 $32 JF ✪
Pinot Gris 2022, Macedon Ranges As gris as it gets with its symphony of pears ranging from fresh and poached to a pear-drop essence. Luscious and rich with clotted cream and lemony flavours throughout, and no shortage of spices plus neat phenolics. Rather delicious on its own or with food. Screw cap. 13% alc. RATING 95 DRINK 2023–2028 $34 JF ✪
Pinot Noir 2021, Macedon Ranges A savoury, spicy, stemmy undertow takes its time in allowing red cherry and plum fruits full access, but with several returns to the glass the fruits hold sway on the bouquet and palate, the other components satisfied with the complexity they bring on the finish. Chalk and cheese to the '20. Screw cap. 13% alc. RATING 95 DRINK 2023–2031 $40 JH ✪
Midhill Chardonnay 2021, Macedon Ranges A classy chardonnay strutting its cool-climate credentials with aplomb. Flinty, fine and pure; long and persistent across the palate. It teases out citrus, woodsy spices and lemon curd flavours yet sits comfortably in a savoury zone. It's moreish and irresistible in equal measure. Screw cap. 13% alc. RATING 95 DRINK 2022–2031 $70 JF
Minnow Roussanne 2022, Port Phillip A fan of roussanne? Oh yeah! Brimming with white and yellow peaches, river mint and honeycomb and butterscotch and yet, it has this savoury and creamy overlay. White miso and ginger spice, lots of texture, slippery phenolics and excellent length. Screw cap. 13% alc. RATING 94 DRINK 2023–2027 $32 JF ✪
Straws Lane Pinot Noir 2021, Macedon Ranges It's awash with wild strawberries, poached rhubarb, blood orange and zest plus cool alpine herbs and radicchio. Mid-weighted with sinewy tannins and while the acidity is refreshing it needs to settle into the wine. It will in time, and this will be something special as result. Screw cap. 13% alc. RATING 94 DRINK 2025–2035 $70 JF
K Road Shiraz 2021, Port Phillip An impressive rendition from a cooler vintage, though the oak needs time to settle. Yet within, bramble berries and plums are drenched in baking spices, pepper, woodsmoke and a touch of meaty reduction. Full bodied, with firm/raspy tannins yet buoyant thanks to bright and tangy acidity. It's savoury, complex and will last some distance. Screw cap. 14% alc. RATING 94 DRINK 2024–2036 $70 JF

🍷🍷🍷🍷🍷 **Chardonnay 2021, Macedon Ranges** RATING 93 DRINK 2022–2028 $45 JF
Little Hampton Pinot Noir 2021, Macedon Ranges RATING 91 DRINK 2025–2035 $70 JF
Minnow Viognier 2022, Pyrenees RATING 90 DRINK 2023–2025 $32 JF

Shaw + Smith

136 Jones Road, Balhannah, SA 5242 **Region** Adelaide Hills
T (08) 8398 0500 **www**.shawandsmith.com **Open** 7 days 11–5 **Winemaker** Adam
Wadewitz, Martin Shaw **Viticulturist** Murray Leake **Est.** 1989 **Vyds** 62ha

Cousins Martin Shaw and Michael Hill Smith MW already had unbeatable experience
when they founded Shaw + Smith as a virtual winery in '89. In '99, Martin and Michael
purchased the 36ha Balhannah property, building the superbly designed winery and planting
more sauvignon blanc, shiraz, pinot noir and riesling. The 20ha Lenswood vineyard,
10km northwest of the winery, is mainly planted to chardonnay and pinot noir, as is a high-
density vineyard in the Piccadilly Valley.

♟♟♟♟♟ M3 Chardonnay 2021, Adelaide Hills The '21 M3 release sees a price rise,
which the makers clearly consider fitting for a wine celebrated as one of the best
chardonnays in the country. It's also an outstanding vintage. Quietly, it wields its
magic. Its youthful exuberance is tightly wound, with whispers of green apple,
grapefruit, lemon peel and almond, firming and rising through the wine. Acidity
drives and energises the pristine fruit with oak a gentle accompaniment. Fine and
elegant now. An outstanding future is writ large. Screw cap. 13% alc. **RATING** 97
DRINK 2022-2031 $55 JP ✪

♟♟♟♟♟ Lenswood Vineyard Chardonnay 2021, Adelaide Hills Transparent and
tensile with an additional nuance of flavour, vibrato and mineral cohesion etched
into the firmament of complexity each year. White peach, toasted hazelnut,
jasmine and nougatine teem long. The oak, nestled beautifully, serves as a framing
backdrop rather than the centrepiece. A wine of precision, intense flavours and
immense class. Screw cap. 13% alc. **RATING** 96 **DRINK** 2023-2032 $95 NG

Riesling 2022, Adelaide Hills Freshness and chew, here, with texture and
complexity from whole bunches. Super-intense of flavour. A lather of lime
blossom, green apple slushy and jasmine cascade along a chalky beam of acidity.
Long and pliant. Very impressive, auguring for an extremely bright future. Screw
cap. 12.5% alc. **RATING** 95 **DRINK** 2022-2037 $36 NG ✪

Balhannah Vineyard Shiraz 2020, Adelaide Hills A headily aromatic shiraz
with notes of lavender and green olive and an underbelly of verdant herb and
mezcal. Damson plum, red cherry, violet and sarsaparilla trail across a raft of
peppery tannins, a bit drying due to the low-yielding year. A whiff of iodine,
peat and smoked meat lingers. This will benefit from some patience. Screw cap.
14% alc. **RATING** 95 **DRINK** 2023-2032 $95 NG

Shiraz 2021, Adelaide Hills Leaner, lighter and fresher than what I recall from
prior vintages. Satsuma plum, lilac, Bing cherry, star anise and clove meld with
white pepper, cedar and vanillin-framed tannins that drive proceedings long. Savvy
bunch and oak assemblage confer poise and authority. Classy, while needing time
to shed the oak cladding. Screw cap. 13.5% alc. **RATING** 94 **DRINK** 2023-2032
$55 NG

♟♟♟♟♀ Sauvignon Blanc 2022, Adelaide Hills RATING 93 **DRINK** 2022-2024
$31 NG ✪

M3 Chardonnay 2022, Adelaide Hills RATING 93 **DRINK** 2023-2031
$55 NG

Pinot Noir 2022, Adelaide Hills RATING 93 **DRINK** 2023-2029 $55 NG

Lenswood Vineyard Pinot Noir 2021, Adelaide Hills RATING 93
DRINK 2023-2029 $95 NG

Shepherd's Hut

★★★★

PO Box 194, Darlington, WA 6070 **Region** Porongurup
T (08) 9299 6700 **www**.shepherdshutwines.com.au **Open** Not **Winemaker** Rob Diletti
Viticulturist Laura Wishart **Est.** 1996 **Dozens** 1200 **Vyds** 18ha

Shepherd's Hut wines is named after an 1850s stone hut found in ruins on an adjacent property
to the vineyard. In the mid-90s, founder Dr Michael Wishart (and family) restored the hut,

which still features honey-coloured Mount Barker stone, all the while establishing riesling, chardonnay, sauvignon blanc, shiraz and cabernet sauvignon. Most of the grapes are sold to other makers in the region, but those retained make high quality wine at mouth-watering prices thanks to the skill of winemaker Rob Diletti.

♥♥♥♥♀ **Riesling 2022, Porongurup** A tightly wound, pristine riesling. Citrus dominates the bouquet with whiffs of lemon blossom and ozone. The palate is full but tight, a little juicy but very dry and electric. Finishes long, cool and crisp. A touch of fruitiness emerges, mixed tropicals or similar, but the main deal is vibrant citrus fruits spiked with a fine, talc-like minerally feel. Screw cap. 11.6% alc. **RATING** 93 **DRINK** 2024–2035 $29 MB ✪

Riesling 2021, Porongurup A bright and juicy expression leaning heavily into the green apple and lime juice zone. It's heavily aromatic, pretty with that lime the dominant feature, flickers of sage leaf, a bit of sea spray, too. The palate is very refreshing, crisp and threaded through with lemony, zesty acidity. It finishes long and vibrant. A ripping drink. Screw cap. 11.3% alc. **RATING** 93 **DRINK** 2022–2030 $29 MB ✪

Pinot Noir 2021, Porongurup A bright and juicy pinot noir with easy appeal. Very cherry, lots of raspberry and woody spices in perfume with a bit of graphite smokiness in the mix. The palate is similar in terms of characters, sweet upfront and finishes twiggy and sooty/earthy to close. Medium weight, vibrant and almost crisp in texture. A feel-good red. Screw cap. 13.5% alc. **RATING** 90 **DRINK** 2022–2030 $35 MB

Sherrah Wines ★★★★

148 McMurtrie Rd, McLaren Vale SA 5171 **Region** McLaren Vale **T** 0429 123 383 **www**.sherrahwines.com.au **Open** Fri–Mon 11–5 **Winemaker** Alex Sherrah **Viticulturist** Ben Lacey **Est.** 2016 **Dozens** 4000

Alex Sherrah's career started with a bachelor of science in organic chemistry and pharmacology, leading him to travel the world, to return home broke and in need of a job. Time spent as a cellar rat at Tatachilla and a graduate diploma in oenology at Waite University were followed by a job at Kendall Jackson's Napa Valley crown jewel, Cardinale, making ultra-premium Bordeaux-blend wines. Stints at Knappstein and O'Leary Walker followed, punctuated by vintages in Burgundy and Austria. At the end of '11 he moved to McLaren Vale and Coriole, where he became senior winemaker in '12, remaining there for 6 years, before moving on to head up winemaking at Haselgrove, his present day job. I (James) cannot help but pass on some of his words of wisdom (and I'm not being sarcastic): 'Wine to me is not about tasting blackcurrant and cigar box but how the wine "feels" to drink. I believe in balance, a great wine should have no sharp edges, it should have beautiful smooth curves from front to back.' Small wonder he makes such wonderful wines.

♥♥♥♥♀ **Preservative Free Grenache 2022, McLaren Vale** This effusive grenache is a brilliant, lipsmacking incantation of joy. A good portion of stems, carbonically infused with giddy scents of patchouli, salumi, orange verbena, turmeric and cardamom. A herbal slake of tannins imparts imminent drinkability. Screw cap. 14% alc. **RATING** 92 **DRINK** 2022–2024 $25 NG ✪

Pétillant-Naturel 2022, McLaren Vale Fiano/chenin blend. A nourishing turbidity to the hue. This is delicious, performing the visceral task required of a pét-nat: be frothy, effusive, palpably dry, entertain a little and be sufficiently poised to drink in large draughts. Lemonade mixed with tonic and soused with tangerine bitters. Crown. 12.5% alc. **RATING** 92 **DRINK** 2022–2024 $35 NG

Skin Party Fiano 2022, McLaren Vale Aromas of pickled peach, ginger chutney, lime pickle and dried hay. The texture is beautifully handled, promoting a plump deliciousness, rather than a barrage of phenolics as this idiom can too often fall into. A well-crafted and highly versatile wine for the contemporary table. Screw cap. 12.5% alc. **RATING** 90 **DRINK** 2023–2026 $30 NG

Shut the Gate Wines

Clare Valley 8453 Main North Rd, Clare, SA 5453 | Snowy Mountains Berridale,
39 Jindabyne Rd, Berridale, NSW 2628 **Region** Clare Valley
T (08) 8843 4114 | **Winemaker** 0488 243 200 **www.shutthegate.com.au Open** Clare
Valley, 7 days 10–4.30, Snowy Mountains, 7 days 10–6 **Winemaker** Richard Woods,
Rasa Fabian **Viticulturist** Aaron Ackland **Est.** 2013 **Dozens** 6000 **Vyds** 6.3ha
Shut the Gate is the venture of Richard Woods and Rasa Fabian, which took shape after
5 years' involvement in the rebranding of Crabtree Watervale Wines, followed by 18 months
of juggling consultancy roles. During this time Richard and Rasa set the foundations for
Shut the Gate. The engine room of the business is the Clare Valley, where with considerable
care the wines are made and the grapes for many of the wines are sourced.

Estate Grown Riesling 2022, Clare Valley A powerful yet compact expression
of precision and steely acid spine. Scents of lime, grapefruit, bath salts and sage.
Flavours in a tightly wound frame of chalky acidity, briny tang and lemon-on-
green-apple fruitiness. Whoosh! Set your palates to stunned for the acid bomb.
It's refreshing and done well in its style. Screw cap. 12% alc. **RATING** 93
DRINK 2022-2033 $35 MB ✪

For Freedom Polish Hill River Riesling 2022, Clare Valley A very
approachable style with lots of intensity, drive and invigorating acidity. It's strong in
the lemon-lime department and big on zingy, grapefruity freshness. So concentrated,
deeply flavoured, almost rich but for the zesty acidity. Excellent length and
persistence, too. Impressive for its power and presence. This one should win a few
hearts! Screw cap. 12% alc. **RATING** 93 **DRINK** 2022-2035 $29 MB ✪

For Freedom Gewürztraminer 2022, Clare Valley A volley of jasmine,
frangipani, lychee and rosewater then shows a faint hand of yeasty, sourdough-like
savouriness to sniff on. The palate is similarly set, slippery but finds a nice chisel
of chalky chew and finishes refreshing and clean. A masterclass in well-balanced
varietal expression, gifting us ideal summer drinking or a match for spicy dishes.
Screw cap. 12% alc. **RATING** 92 **DRINK** 2022-2026 $29 MB ✪

For Freedom Single Site Barbera 2021, Wrattonbully On the one hand
this medium-bodied wine is meaty, on the other hand it's floral and minty, and
in-between there's a run of juicy, red berried fruit flavour. It's not dense or heavy
but it's a pretty tasty little number nonetheless. Drink this while it's young and
frisky. Screw cap. 14% alc. **RATING** 92 **DRINK** 2023-2027 $32 CM

Blossom 24GRS Riesling 2022, Clare Valley As the name suggests, this one
holds 24g/L RS. Candied lime, crystallised ginger, lychee and kiwifruit in scents
and flavours. Supple, slurpy texture, bright acidity under it all and a general sense
of come-hither drinkability. Intensity and freshness work hand-in-hand. A lively,
relatively simple wine, but does the trick as a sweeter expression. Screw cap.
11.5% alc. **RATING** 90 **DRINK** 2022-2030 $25 MB ✪

For Love Watervale Riesling 2022, Clare Valley It's a light-on, floral and
steely expression, understated and delicate in approach. Scents of jasmine, lemon,
green apple and ozone. Flavours set to lemon, pink grapefruit and flinty minerality
with a very screechy, high-toned acid theme. The refreshment factor is high!
Screw cap. 12% alc. **RATING** 90 **DRINK** 2022-2030 $29 MB

Shy Susan Wines

Billy Button Wines, 11 Camp Street, Bright, Vic 3741 **Region** Tasmania
T 0434 635 510 **www.shysusanwines.com.au Open** 7 days 11–6 **Winemaker** Glenn
James **Est.** 2015 **Dozens** 300
Shy Susan (Tetratheca gunnii) is a critically endangered wildflower endemic to a tiny part
of Tasmania. Her survival depends completely on a little native bee, who alone is capable of
pollination. Their fate is forever entwined. Glenn James worked with Tasmanian fruit for
nearly 2 decades before producing the unique Shy Susan range from some of Tasmania's most
exciting vineyards. Glenn relocated to the Alpine Valleys in '20; that vintage was wiped out
by bushfires and '21 is his first vintage produced from the Alpine Valleys. Partner Jo Marsh is

the owner and winemaker of Billy Button Wines (see separate entry) and Shy Susan shares its Bright and Myrtleford cellar doors.

ŸŸŸŸŸ **Pinot Noir 2021, Alpine Valleys** A stunning, fully expressive pinot that should draw attention to the quality now to be found in the high, cool Alpine Valleys. Terrific dark red cherry hues. A purity of clean pinot aromas: cherry, cranberry, rosehip, red licorice and allspice with just a smidge of vanillin oak. Boasts texture, succulence and a degree of tannin edginess that smacks the lips and works the tastebuds. Screw cap. 14% alc. **RATING** 95 **DRINK** 2023-2031 $65 JP

ŸŸŸŸŸ **Blanc de Blancs 2016, Tasmania** **RATING** 93 **DRINK** 2023-2028 $75 JP
Chardonnay 2021, Alpine Valleys **RATING** 91 **DRINK** 2022-2027 $55 JP

Sidewood Estate ★★★★★

6 River Road Hahndorf, SA 5125 **Region** Adelaide Hills
T (08) 8388 1673 **www.**sidewood.com.au **Open** 7 days 11–5 **Winemaker** Darryl Catlin
Viticulturist Mark Vella **Est.** 2004 **Vyds** 90ha
Sidewood Estate is owned by Owen and Cassandra Inglis who operate it as a winery and cidery. Situated in the Onkaparinga Valley, the vines weather the cool climate of the Adelaide Hills. Significant expenditure on regeneration of the vineyards was already well underway when Sidewood invested over $12 million in the winery, increasing capacity from 500t to 2000t each vintage and implementing sustainable improvements including 100kW solar panels, water treatment works and insulation for the winery. The expansion includes new bottling and canning facilities capable of handling 6 million bottles of wine and cider annually. A multimillion-dollar restaurant, cellar door and cidery opened in '20. Wines are released under the Sidewood Estate, Stablemate and Mappinga labels.

ŸŸŸŸŸ **Owen's Chardonnay 2021, Adelaide Hills** A beautiful wine of pristine fruit and faultless winemaking. There is tension and power to its white peach, nectarine and grapefruit, yet there's also delicacy. Its gold medal at the 2022 Sydney Royal Wine Show should be the first of many. 300 dozen made. Screw cap. 12.5% alc. **RATING** 97 **DRINK** 2023-2036 $50 JH ✪

ŸŸŸŸŸ **Pinot Noir 2021, Adelaide Hills** Sidewood consistently over-delivers with its immaculately made wines. The perfumed red flower bouquet opens another door to the complex, layered palate, with savoury wild red berries and spice to close. Screw cap. 13% alc. **RATING** 96 **DRINK** 2023-2036 $35 JH ✪
Shiraz 2021, Adelaide Hills The bouquet is expressive and multifaceted, with pepper, licorice and spice decorating the black fruits, dark chocolate and earth on the medium-bodied palate. Its balance is flawless. Exceptional value. Screw cap. 14.5% alc. **RATING** 96 **DRINK** 2023-2046 $26 JH ✪
Sauvignon Blanc 2022, Adelaide Hills Distinct nettle on the bouquet catches attention until the delicious palate takes over, grapefruit leading the way, supported by gooseberry and a hint of passionfruit. The finish is crisp and lipsmacking. Screw cap. 12% alc. **RATING** 95 **DRINK** 2023-2024 $22 JH ✪
Mappinga Chardonnay 2021, Adelaide Hills The bells and whistles have been thrown at this, yet the result is delicious. White fig, cantaloupe and nectarine densely packed within a carapace of vanillin pod oak and juicy acidity, all shimmering across the textural scape and dragging the flavours long, crunchy and succulent. Screw cap. 12.5% alc. **RATING** 95 **DRINK** 2022-2032 $38 NG ✪
Mappinga Fumé Blanc 2021, Adelaide Hills This is special, gleaning inspiration from top sancerre with the resinous flaxen hue and gingery oak-inflected framework. Yet there is so much stuffing that the wine can almost handle it. Riffs on apricot chutney, glazed quince, gooseberry and yellow plum, with the oak palpable across the meandering, complex and pulsating finish. Screw cap. 12.5% alc. **RATING** 94 **DRINK** 2023-2027 $38 NG ✪

ŸŸŸŸŸ **Pinot Noir 2022, Adelaide Hills** **RATING** 93 **DRINK** 2023-2028 $35 NG ✪
Oberlin Pinot Noir 2022, Adelaide Hills **RATING** 93 **DRINK** 2023-2030 $45 NG

Abel Pinot Noir 2022, Adelaide Hills RATING 93 DRINK 2023-2030 $45 NG
Oberlin Pinot Noir 2021, Adelaide Hills RATING 93 DRINK 2022-2028 $45 NG
Mappinga Shiraz 2021, Adelaide Hills RATING 93 DRINK 2022-2031 $65 NG
Abel Pinot Noir 2021, Adelaide Hills RATING 93 DRINK 2022-2030 $45 NG
Ironstone Barrels The Tyre Fitter Syrah 2020, Adelaide Hills RATING 93 DRINK 2023-2027 $50 NG
Rosé 2022, Adelaide Hills RATING 92 DRINK 2022-2023 $24 NG ✪
777 Pinot Noir 2022, Adelaide Hills RATING 92 DRINK 2023-2026 $45 NG
Pinot Blanc 2021, Adelaide Hills RATING 92 DRINK 2022-2026 $25 NG ✪
Chardonnay 2021, Adelaide Hills RATING 92 DRINK 2023-2029 $25 NG ✪
Ironstone Barrels The Tyre Fitter Syrah 2021, Adelaide Hills RATING 92 DRINK 2022-2030 $50 NG
Ironstone Barrels The Old China Hand Syrah 2021, Adelaide Hills RATING 91 DRINK 2022-2028 $50 NG
777 Pinot Noir 2021, Adelaide Hills RATING 90 DRINK 2022-2030 $45 NG

Sieber Wines   ★★★★

82 Sieber Road, Tanunda South, SA 5352 **Region** Barossa Valley
T (08) 8562 8038 www.sieberwines.com **Open** 7 days 11–4 **Winemaker** Tony
Carapetis **Viticulturist** Ben Sieber **Est.** 1999 **Dozens** 9500 **Vyds** 50ha
Richard and Val Sieber are the 3rd generation to run Redlands, the family property,
traditionally a cropping/grazing farm. They have diversified into viticulture with shiraz
occupying the lion's share, the remainder split between viognier, grenache and mourvèdre.
The vineyard has since grown from 14 to 50ha on the home farm, with a small family-run
chardonnay vineyard in Margaret River a recent addition.

🍷🍷🍷🍷🍷 **Chardonnay 2022, Margaret River** Pale straw in the glass with characters
of peach, nectarine, fig and citrus fruits dotted with clotted cream, soft spice,
cashewy oak and oyster shell. Crisp and moreish with bright fruit and acidity and
a peachy finish. Screw cap. 13.5% alc. **RATING** 90 **DRINK** 2023-2028 $30 DB
GSM 2021, Barossa Valley Plenty of plush plum and berry fruits on display
here with nice ginger spice lift, citrus blossom, licorice, roasting meats, redcurrant
jelly and turned earth. With bright morello cherry fruit flow, sandy tannin and
an upbeat line, it makes for a great bistro wine. Screw cap. 14.9% alc. **RATING** 90
DRINK 2023-2028 $20 DB ✪

Sieger Estate Wines   ★★★☆

777 Light Pass Road, Tanunda, SA 5352 **Region** Barossa Valley
T 403683067 www.siegerestate.com **Open** Thurs–Sun 11–4.30 **Winemaker** Degang
Lui, Jo Irvine (consultant) **Viticulturist** Steve Kurtz **Est.** 2016 **Dozens** 3000 **Vyds** 8ha
Sieger Estate was founded by Degang Liu in '16 with an initial purchase of 16ha planted with
4ha of cabernet sauvignon. A further purchase of a 4ha plot of shiraz came in '18, and more
expansion still to Victoria's Heathcote in '19. The wines are for the most part 'traditional'
Barossa with rich, resonant fruit, a fair lick of spicy oak and compact tannin structures built for
the cellar and those seeking regional truth. Wines are primarily aimed at the export market,
but nevertheless make a welcome addition to the local wine scene.

🍷🍷🍷🍷🍷 **Frederick Organic Montepulciano 2021, Barossa Valley** A purple-hued,
delightfully perfumed release. It retains a spacious, nimble mouthfeel while
showing ripe plum, cherry and raspberry fruits with hints of orange blossom,
exotic spice, cola and red licorice. Light on the tannin with a juicy palate shape,
it finishes dry and moreish. Screw cap. 14% alc. **RATING** 91 **DRINK** 2023-2026
$50 DB

Silent Noise

44 Hamilton Road, McLaren Flat, SA 5171 **Region** McLaren Vale
T (08) 8383 0533 **www**.silentnoisewine.com.au **Open** Mon–Fri 9–4.30, w'ends &
public hols 11–4 **Winemaker** Charlie O'Brien **Est.** 2016 **Dozens** 2000 **Vyds** 0.2ha
Charlie O'Brien is the son of Helen and Kevin O'Brien, founders of Kangarilla Road. As a
small child (a photo on the website says it all) he revelled in the noise of vintage, the 'silent
noise' that of the wine when bottled. Since leaving school at the end of '16 he worked
vintages at Gemtree and Yangarra Estate in McLaren Vale, Pikes in the Clare Valley, Pike
& Joyce in the Adelaide Hills, Moss Wood in Margaret River, as well as Paul Mas in the
Languedoc and Château Haut-Bailly in Bordeaux. The world is his oyster.

FO Shiraz 2022, McLaren Vale Exuberant florals, purple fruits and dill pickles.
A mid-weighted jangle along some white pepper freshness, with herbal tannins
corralling, verdant and edgy, a legacy of the whole-bunch inclusion. Screw cap.
14% alc. **RATING** 90 **DRINK** 2023–2026 $35 NG

Silkman Wines

c/– The Small Winemakers Centre, McDonalds Road, Pokolbin, NSW 2320
Region Hunter Valley
T 0414 800 256 **www**.silkmanwines.com.au **Open** 7 days 10–5 **Winemaker** Shaun
Silkman, Liz Silkman **Est.** 2013 **Dozens** 4000
Winemaking couple Shaun and Liz Silkman (one-time dux of the Len Evans Tutorial)
were both born and raised in the Hunter Valley. They both worked many vintages (both
in Australia and abroad) before joining forces at First Creek Wines. This gives them the
opportunity to make small quantities of the 3 classic varieties of the Hunter Valley: semillon,
chardonnay and shiraz. Unsurprisingly, the wines have been of outstanding quality.

Reserve Semillon 2022, Hunter Valley An utterly exceptional 1yo semillon
with so much going for it. It's hard to imagine how it will be 20 years hence
as citrus in all its forms does battle with crunchy acidity. Screw cap. 10.7% alc.
RATING 97 **DRINK** 2023–2035 $50 JH ✪

Single Vineyard Blackberry Semillon 2022, Hunter Valley Aromas of
French pastry disappear the moment the raw power of the grapefruit and Meyer
lemon, bathed in minerally acidity, enter the mouth. There's a long story here,
culminating in the Silkmans taking over the running and custodianship of the
vineyard. Screw cap. 10.7% alc. **RATING** 96 **DRINK** 2023–2043 $50 JH ✪

SILK Chardonnay 2021, Hunter Valley The wine is fruit, not oak, driven.
Silkman Wines say they're looking for a leaner, lighter Hunter Valley style. This
certainly pressed the button on the judges at the Hunter Valley Wine Show '22,
winning 2 trophies, led by Best Chardonnay of Show. Screw cap. 12.4% alc.
RATING 96 **DRINK** 2023–2028 $80 JH

Reserve Shiraz 2021, Hunter Valley Good colour; the bouquet suggests
there's more richness/ripeness in this wine, and the palate – to a degree –
confirms that there is indeed a rich vein of red and black fruits to be mined by the
consumer at a time and place of their choosing. Screw cap. 13.2% alc. **RATING** 96
DRINK 2025–2035 $50 JH ✪

Museum Release Reserve Semillon 2017, Hunter Valley Another take on
these glorious mature semillons, all with many years of life to come on the high
road; in the midst of all this intensity, this has a line of delicacy that counter-
intuitively polishes all elements of the wine. Screw cap. 11% alc. **RATING** 96
DRINK 2023–2038 $50 JH ✪

Reserve Chardonnay 2021, Hunter Valley The bouquet is still relatively
closed, allowing talc to raise its hand, and a whisper of citrus blossom. The
structure of the wine is impeccable, it's length a given. Screw cap. 12.5% alc.
RATING 95 **DRINK** 2023–2030 $50 JH ✪

**Museum Release Single Vineyard Blackberry Semillon 2017, Hunter
Valley** The fragrance of the bouquet is a call to arms, and the palate obliges with

custard apple, lemon curd and sultry spices, the overall balance bringing calm just when needed. Screw cap. 10.6% alc. RATING 95 DRINK 2023-2038 $50 JH

🍷🍷🍷🍷 Shiraz Pinot Noir 2021, Hunter Valley RATING 92 DRINK 2023-2030 $30 JH ❂
Shiraz 2021, Hunter Valley RATING 92 DRINK 2023-2032 $30 JH ❂

Silkwood Estate   ★★★☆

2280 Channybearup Road, Pemberton, WA 6260 **Region** Pemberton
T (08) 9776 1584 www.silkwoodestate.com.au **Open** Fri–Mon & public hols 10–4
Winemaker Michael Ng **Viticulturist** Joel Stefanetti **Est.** 1998 **Dozens** 20000 **Vyds** 25ha
Silkwood Wines has been owned by the Bowman family since '04. The vineyard is patrolled by a large flock of guinea fowl, eliminating most insect pests and reducing the use of chemicals. In '05 the adjoining vineyard was purchased, lifting the estate plantings to 25ha, which include shiraz, cabernet sauvignon, merlot, sauvignon blanc, chardonnay, pinot noir, riesling and zinfandel.

🍷🍷🍷🍷 The Walcott Riesling 2022, Pemberton A tasty number driven by acidity and steely in its nature. Zingy lime juice, a big squeeze of grapefruit juice and some light, talc-like mineral characters all bound in a laser-like thrust across the palate. Perfume is a little mute but more of the citrus stuff going on. Refreshing as. Screw cap. 12.5% alc. RATING 92 DRINK 2023-2035 $28 MB ❂

Silver Lining   ★★★☆

60 Gleneagles Road, Mount Osmond, SA 5064 (postal) **Region** Adelaide Hills
T 0438 736 052 www.silverliningwine.com.au **Open** Not **Winemaker** Leigh Ratzmer, Marty Edwards **Viticulturist** Vitiworks, Simon Tolley **Est.** 2020 **Dozens** 1200
The name alone says a lot about the positive and life-affirming attitude of Marty Edwards, whose love of the Adelaide Hills was nurtured by his family's pioneering involvement with The Lane Vineyard in Hahndorf. They have all left that business now but after being diagnosed with Parkinson's Disease in '12, Marty decided he still had a lot more to give. He focused on his health and young family, but couldn't give up his passion for Hills vineyards and wines. Silver Lining Wines was the result, with proceeds going to Parkinson's Disease research with the aim of helping others on the same challenging journey as this inspiring vigneron.

🍷🍷🍷🍷 Pinot Noir 2022, Adelaide Hills Ample flavour and bags of personality equip this mid-weighted pinot with riffs on sassafras, bracken, dark cherry, black olive tapenade and a skittish framework of edgy tannins that corral and compress any excess. Screw cap. 13% alc. RATING 91 DRINK 2022-2026 $32 NG

Silver Spoon Estate   ★★★★

503 Heathcote-Rochester Road, Heathcote, Mount Camel, Vic 3523 **Region** Heathcote
T 0412 868 236 www.silverspoonestate.com.au **Open** Fri–Sun 10.30–5 **Winemaker** Peter Young **Viticulturist** Peter Young **Est.** 2008 **Dozens** 2000 **Vyds** 22ha
When Peter and Tracie Young purchased an existing shiraz vineyard (planted around '99) on the top of the Mt Camel Range in '08, they did not waste any time. They immediately planted a second vineyard, constructed a small winery and in '13 acquired a neighbouring vineyard. The estate name comes from the Silver Spoon fault line that delineates the Cambrian volcanic rock from the old silver mines on the property. Peter became familiar with vineyards when working in the '70s as a geologist in the Hunter Valley and subsequently completed the master of wine technology and viticulture degree at the University of Melbourne. A new cellar door opened in '21.

🍷🍷🍷🍷 East Meets West Shiraz 2020, Heathcote There's a lot to like about this shiraz. It has very good depth, the flavours feel open for business, it has complex spice notes tucked within and it finishes with both well-massaged tannin and an all-round sense of balance. It's an impressive result from a not-so-easy vintage. Screw cap. 14.6% alc. RATING 94 DRINK 2023-2032 $31 CM ❂

🍷🍷🍷🍷🍷 **The Ensemble Shiraz Viognier 2020, Heathcote** RATING 92
DRINK 2023–2029 $35 CM
The Quartz Mourvèdre Grenache Rosé 2022, Heathcote RATING 91
DRINK 2022–2024 $27 CM ✪
Cambrian White Viognier 2022, Heathcote RATING 90 DRINK 2022–2025
$31 CM

Silverwaters Vineyard ★★★★☆

PO Box 41, San Remo, Vic 3925 **Region** Gippsland
T (03) 5678 5230 **www**.silverwatersvineyard.com.au **Open** Not **Winemaker** Rick
Lacey **Viticulturist** Hercules van der Walt **Est.** 1995 **Dozens** 670 **Vyds** 2.8ha
Hercules van der Walt grew up in South Africa on a cattle farm and his wife Emily grew up
in Melbourne. They met backpacking in Europe and the rest is history. Except the city was
not his thing and the country, not hers. What to do? A chance drive to Phillip Island and a
For Sale sign on the Silverwaters vineyard solved the problem. Country and close enough
to the city. Credit to them, locals told them how important the vineyard was and what a
shame it would be to lose that heritage – a site approaching its 30th year. It could have been
grubbed, but they decided to become vignerons. Hercules keeps a full-time job as a wind
turbine technician yet works the vineyard too; Emily has left her university administration job
to concentrate on the brand. As of '23, local Rick Lacey of Purple Hen fame oversees the
wines and a new cellar door is expected to open soon. It bodes well.

🍷🍷🍷🍷🍷 **Single Vineyard Chardonnay 2021, Gippsland** Damn. Here's another
chardonnay I kept tasting and tasting because it was so good, realising I'd snuck
in quite a few sips along the way. It was nearly dinner time. Lovely purity to this,
refined and delicious with succulence throughout. Reined in by fine acidity yet
nougatine and fluffy creamy lees bolster the palate alongside lemon/briny flavours.
Impressive. Screw cap. 12.8% alc. RATING 95 DRINK 2023–2031 $38 JF ✪

🍷🍷🍷🍷🍷 **Single Vineyard Pinot Noir 2021, Gippsland** RATING 93 DRINK 2023–2033
$43 JF
Single Vineyard Shiraz 2021, Gippsland RATING 92 DRINK 2024–2034 $45 JF

Sinapius ★★★★★

4232 Bridport Road, Pipers Brook, Tas 7254 **Region** Northern Tasmania
T 0418 998 665 **www**.sinapius.com.au **Open** Mon–Fri 11–5, w'ends 12–5
Winemaker Linda Morice **Est.** 2005 **Dozens** 2000 **Vyds** 4.3ha
Vaughn Dell and Linda Morice purchased the former Golders vineyard in '05 (planted in '94).
More recent vineyard plantings include 14 clones of pinot noir and 11 clones of chardonnay,
as well as small amounts of grüner veltliner, pinot gris, pinot blanc, gewürztraminer, riesling
and gamay. The vineyard is close-planted, the density up to a backbreaking 11 110 vines/
ha, with the fruiting wire 40cm above the ground. The wines are made with a minimalist
approach: natural ferments, basket pressing, extended lees ageing and minimal fining and
filtration. Tragically, Vaughn died suddenly, days after celebrating his 39th birthday, in May
'20. Australia has lost a winemaker of ultimate skill and vision shared by a small handful of
others.

🍷🍷🍷🍷🍷 **Single Vineyard Close Planted Grüner Veltliner 2021, Tasmania**
Fascinating. Austria, here we come. The already full colour announces a grüner
full of spice and white pepper on the bouquet, preparing you for a hammer blow
of flavour on the palate. Instead, it ripples with refreshing mineral notes, before
perfect varietal fruit comes back on the finish. Screw cap. 13% alc. RATING 96
DRINK 2023–2029 $38 JH ✪
Esmé 2021, Tasmania Estate-grown gamay. Not fined or filtered, with the
only addition of minimal SO$_2$ at bottling. Bright, clear crimson. A wildflower and
violet-perfumed bouquet floats out of the glass with minimal agitation, adding
spicy, sultry notes of plum on the finely balanced palate. Screw cap. 12% alc.
RATING 96 DRINK 2023–2030 $38 JH ✪

Singlefile Wines

90 Walter Road, Denmark, WA 6333 **Region** Great Southern
T 1300 885 807 **www**.singlefilewines.com **Open** 7 days 11–5 **Winemaker** Mike
Garland, Coby Ladwig, Patrick Corbett **Est.** 2007 **Dozens** 10 000 **Vyds** 3.75ha
In '07, former geologist Phil Snowden and wife Viv bought an established vineyard (planted
in '89) in the beautiful Denmark subregion, pulling out the old shiraz and merlot vines and
keeping (and planting) more chardonnay. They also kept Larry Cherubino (as a consultant)
to set up partnerships with established vineyards in Frankland River, Porongurup, Denmark,
Pemberton and Margaret River. The consistency of the quality of the Singlefile wines is
outstanding, as is their value for money.

Single Vineyard Shiraz 2021, Frankland River This is a seriously good,
cool-grown shiraz. Its deep, bright colour hops in early, as it were, to claim the
crown, but there's more to come for what is a complex, medium-bodied wine.
The bouquet has spicy, woody, earthy notes followed by a fruit-dominant palate,
with tangy red and black berries to the fore. Screw cap. 14.2% alc. **RATING** 96
DRINK 2023-2036 $39 JH ✪
The Vivienne Chardonnay 2020, Denmark Gleaming straw-green. A very
complex and immediately striking bouquet, with grapefruit at all points along the
way, the palate persuasive with its silver lining of cashew and acidity. Screw cap.
12.6% alc. **RATING** 96 **DRINK** 2023-2030 $100 JH
The Philip Adrian Cabernet Sauvignon 2019, Frankland River Cedar,
cigar box, bay leaf and savoury-edged cassis aromas and flavours hunt in a pack,
and have so tamed the tannins they've become silky, an unusual situation to say
the least. But that doesn't mean the wine won't cellar well. Screw cap. 14.2% alc.
RATING 96 **DRINK** 2023-2044 $100 JH
The Pamela Riesling 2022, Porongurup Generous in colour with a full ramp
of citrus and passionfruit lifted on the finish by lingering, lime-infused, acidity.
Screw cap. 11.4% alc. **RATING** 95 **DRINK** 2023-2030 $45 JH ✪

Chardonnay 2021, Great Southern RATING 92 **DRINK** 2023-2030 $30 JH ✪
Single Vineyard Cabernet Sauvignon 2020, Frankland River RATING 92
DRINK 2023-2035 $39 JH

Sir Paz Estate

54 Parker Road, Wandin East, Vic 3139 **Region** Yarra Valley
T (03) 5964 2339 **www**.sirpaz.com **Open** Fri–Sun 10.30–5 **Winemaker** Adrian
Santolin **Est.** 1997 **Dozens** 5500 **Vyds** 22ha
The Zapris family emigrated from Greece a generation ago, bringing with them a family
tradition of winemaking. They established Sir Paz Estate in '97, planting just under 6ha of
shiraz; the 1st release of '01 scored an emphatic gold medal at the Victorian Wines Show
'03 as the highest-scored entry. This success led to further plantings, today including shiraz,
merlot, chardonnay and sauvignon blanc, producing both still and sparkling wines.

Eden Blanc de Blanc 2019, Yarra Valley 100% chardonnay that spent
18 months on lees, bottled with 8.5g/L dosage. Bright green gold. Light on its
feet with aromas of lemon peel, white pear and gentle brioche notes. Dry, crisp
and well balanced on the palate, this fresh, aperitif-style sparkling is refreshing and
very drinkable. Diam. 12% alc. **RATING** 91 **DRINK** 2022-2025 $60 PR
Shiraz 2019, Yarra Valley Deep ruby. Darkly fruited, there are warm spices
together with some oak-derived cedar and vanilla pod scents. The palate is plushly
fruited with ripe, soft tannins rounding out a wine to enjoy now and over the
next 3–4 years. Screw cap. 14% alc. **RATING** 91 **DRINK** 2022-2027 $45 PR
Sparkling Shiraz 2019, Yarra Valley A bright ruby red. With small red berries,
spice and a little licorice on the nose, the wine's gentle sweetness on the palate
is balanced by fine tannins and crisp acidity. This would work well, after dinner,
with soft cheeses. Diam. 14% alc. **RATING** 90 **DRINK** 2022-2027 $60 PR

Merlot 2019, Yarra Valley While the oak is still evident, there's an abundance of blackberries, blood plums, juniper and clove. Medium bodied, there's some flesh on the front of the palate before finishing with fine yet slightly drying tannins. Have this with food now or wait another 2–3 years for those tannins to soften. Screw cap. 14% alc. **RATING** 90 **DRINK** 2022–2027 $45 PR

Sirromet Wines   ★★★★

850 Mount Cotton Road, Mount Cotton, Qld 4165 **Region** Granite Belt
T (07) 3206 2999 **www**.sirromet.com **Open** 7 days 10–4.30 **Winemaker** Jessica Ferguson, Glen Eaton **Viticulturist** Phil O'Real **Est.** 2000 **Dozens** 55 000 **Vyds** 30ha
What was once an ambitious venture is today Qld's largest winery. The founding Morris family commissioned a leading architect to design the state-of-the-art winery, the state's best viticultural consultant to plant 3 major vineyards (in the Granite Belt) and skilled winemaker Adam Chapman to make the wine. It also has a 200-seat restaurant firmly aimed at the tourist market, taking full advantage of its location between Brisbane and the Gold Coast. In recent years, the focus has shifted to emerging varieties such as vermentino, fiano, pecorino, montepulciano and aglianico in an attempt to mitigate the warmer temperatures and lower rainfall of climate change. Jessica Ferguson has overseen the winemaking since '21.

🍷🍷🍷🍷 **Granit Nebbiolo 2019, Granite Belt** Pale garnet colour. Sappy and savoury red of sour cherry, woody spices, pepper, stewed tomato and dried herb characters. It's sleek and tightly wound, gentle and fresh yet showing some development in malty spice and dried cranberry characters. Tannins weave their magic in a light sheath and acidity is tinged with an amaro-like tang. Screw cap. 12.3% alc. **RATING** 93 **DRINK** 2023–2030 $30 MB ✪
The Edward Cabernet Shiraz 2019, Granite Belt Lots to go off in the perfume: game meat, lavender, raspberry, truffle and brambly, mixed herbs. The palate is chewy and dense but finds levity in briny mineral characters and a good deal of woody spice seasons the flavours, yet the balance feels judicious and the lower alcohol works a charm for finesse and freshness. Screw cap. 12.8% alc. **RATING** 93 **DRINK** 2024–2036 $49 MB
Granit Fiano 2021, Riverland This does the variety justice. It's got scents of tart pear, lemon ginger tea and cashews. Flavours are similarly oriented, albeit with a layer of pleasing, bitter herbs in the mix. Vibrant, lively, easy-drinking style with quiet complexity on hand. It feels contemporary, too. Nice one. Screw cap. 12.7% alc. **RATING** 91 **DRINK** 2022–2024 $26 MB ✪

Sister's Run   ★★★★

PO Box 148, McLaren Vale, SA 5171 **Region** South Australia
T (08) 8323 8979 **www**.sistersrun.com.au **Open** Not **Winemaker** Elena Brooks **Est.** 2001
Sister's Run is now part of the Brooks family empire, the highly experienced Elena Brooks making the wines. The Stiletto and Boot on the label are those of Elena, and the motto 'The truth is in the vineyard, but the proof is in the glass' is, one would guess, the work of marketer extraordinaire husband Zar Brooks.

🍷🍷🍷🍷 **Bethlehem Block Gomersal Cabernet Sauvignon 2020, Barossa** Blackberry, black cherry and blackcurrant along with dried hay, licorice, dark chocolate, pipe tobacco and a touch of tomato leaf. Some light blackcurrant pastille and cassis notes on the palate, sandy tannins tugging at the roof of the mouth and a bright line of acidity as the wine fades with memories of black fruits, spice and licorice. Screw cap. 14% alc. **RATING** 92 **DRINK** 2023–2028 $23 DB ✪
St Petri's Riesling 2021, Barossa Valley Pale straw with aromas of freshly squeezed lime, grapefruit and green apple with hints of orange blossom, custard apple, mineral salts, lemongrass and crushed stone. Just a peek of clotted cream on the palate, which is savoury in shape with a mineral line finishing dry with a sweep of Meyer lemon, lime and blossom. Screw cap. 11% alc. **RATING** 91 **DRINK** 2023–2027 $20 DB ✪

Calvary Hill Lyndoch Shiraz 2020, Barossa Deep crimson with lifted aromas of satsuma plum, cassis and boysenberry fruits with hints of dark chocolate, sage, baking spices, teacake, olive tapenade, earth and licorice. Blackberry and black cherry join on the palate along with graphite and roasting meats before the wine compacts and sails off leaving a cassis-like wake. Screw cap. 14.5% alc. **RATING** 91 **DRINK** 2023–2028 $23 DB ✪

Old Testament Cabernet Sauvignon 2020, Coonawarra Not only does it offer a mouthful of fruit-driven flavour but it delivers it in soft-hearted style. This is a wine that slips down easily. Plum-driven flavours with top notes of mint. One glass isn't enough. Screw cap. 14% alc. **RATING** 91 **DRINK** 2023–2028 $23 CM ✪

Epiphany Shiraz 2020, McLaren Vale A richly flavoured wine that is extremely attractive for the price. Scents of damson plum, blueberry and satsuma plum with red, sour fleshiness piercing the mid-palate and providing lift. Supple and round with a lilt of acidity and a crease of oak tannin across the lingering, easygoing finish. Screw cap. 14.5% alc. **RATING** 91 **DRINK** 2022–2027 $23 NG ✪

Sittella Wines ★★★★★

100 Barrett Street, Herne Hill, WA 6056 **Region** Swan Valley
T (08) 9296 2600 **www**.sittella.com.au **Open** Tues–Sun & public hols 11–4
Winemaker Yuri Berns **Est.** 1993 **Dozens** 15 000 **Vyds** 25ha
Simon and Maaike Berns acquired a 7ha block (with 5ha of vines) at Herne Hill, making the first wine in '98 and opening a most attractive cellar door facility. They also own the Buckshot Ridge vineyard in Margaret River. Plantings in Margaret River have increased with new clones of cabernet sauvignon, cabernet franc, P95 chardonnay and malbec. New clones of tempranillo and touriga nacional have also been added to the Swan Valley plantings.

🍷🍷🍷🍷🍷 **Grand Prestige Late Disgorged 2010, Pemberton** Sparkling Wine of the Year. Score awarded by the Halliday tasting panel at the annual Awards judging. MB writes: Very toasty scents laced with sea spray, dried apple, fig, cinnamon and nougat. The palate is set similarly with characters of more toast and cinnamon with licks of honey in the mix, yet a piercing line of saline acidity makes its mark, too. Creamy mouthfeel on top of that and a salted nut finish lingers. Quite a profound wine on hand. Cork. 12.5% alc. **RATING** 97 **DRINK** 2023–2027 $125 PD ♥

🍷🍷🍷🍷🍷 **Solera Pedro Ximénez NV, Swan Valley** Rich, sticky and luscious, but lifts on a freshness of clean spirit and cool acidity. Lots of dried fruit, candied nuts, clove, cinnamon spice between the bouquet and palate. The drinkability here is the charm: there's a sense of vitality and lift, with fine tannins and the finish a chew of woody spice. Very good. Screw cap. 18.5% alc. **RATING** 94 $50 MB

🍷🍷🍷🍷♀ **Marie Christien Lugten Grand Vintage 2017, Pemberton RATING** 93 **DRINK** 2023–2030 $55 MB

Grand Vintage Blanc de Blancs 2017, Pemberton RATING 93 **DRINK** 2023–2028 $55 MB

Albariño 2022, Swan Valley RATING 93 **DRINK** 2023–2025 $25 MB ✪

Solera Liqueur Verdelho NV, Swan Valley RATING 93 **DRINK** 2022–2025 $80 MB

Grand Vintage Rosé 2017, Pemberton RATING 92 **DRINK** 2023–2030 $55 MB

Avant-Garde Dry Rosé 2022, Swan Valley RATING 92 **DRINK** 2023–2025 $25 MB ✪

Six Acres ★★★★

20 Ferndale Road, Silvan, Vic 3795 **Region** Yarra Valley
T 0408 991 741 **www**.sixacreswines.com.au **Open** By appt **Winemaker** Ralph Zuccaro
Viticulturist Ralph Zuccaro **Est.** 1999 **Dozens** 800 **Vyds** 1.64ha
Nestled in the southern hills of the Yarra Valley, Six Acres boutique winery and vineyard is owned and worked by the Zuccaro family. Planted in '99 by Ralph and Lesley Zuccaro, the

vineyard (pinot noir, cabernet sauvignon and merlot) is dry grown on deep red volcanic soil, with yields kept low to encourage balance and concentration within the grapes. Currently biologically farmed, the family's goal is to move towards organic/sustainable grapegrowing. The small size of the property means that the whole family is involved in the minimal intervention winemaking process.

ŸŸŸŸŸ Silvan Block Cabernet Sauvignon 2019, Yarra Valley A light–medium ruby red. With its aromas of blackcurrants, peony, cedar and herbs, this is at the more fragrant and delicate end of the cabernet spectrum. On the palate, this medium-bodied wine has real depth and substance, but those chewy, fine-grained and persistent tannins mean another 5–7 years are needed for it to fulfil its potential. Screw cap. 13.5% alc. **RATING** 95 **DRINK** 2023–2030 $49 PR

ŸŸŸŸŸ Spectrum Syrah 2021, Yarra Valley RATING 92 **DRINK** 2023–2027 $24 PR ☺

Skillogalee   ★★★★

Trevarrick Road, Sevenhill via Clare, SA 5453 **Region** Clare Valley
T (08) 8843 4311 **www**.skillogalee.com.au **Open** 7 days 9.30–5 **Winemaker** Kerri Thompson **Viticulturist** Brendan Pudney **Est.** 1989 **Dozens** 15 000 **Vyds** 51ha
David and Diana Palmer established Skillogalee in '89. In '02, the Palmers purchased next-door neighbour Waninga vineyard with 30ha of 30yo vines, allowing an increase in production without any change in quality or style. David and Diana retired in '21, selling Skillogalee to the Clausen family. Talented winemaker Kerri Thompson (Wines by KT), who has long consulted to the Palmer family while making her own wines at Skillogalee, took over the winemaking from the '22 vintage.

ŸŸŸŸŸ Trevarrick Riesling 2022, Clare Valley It's tense and fresh feeling with a pleasing juiciness and accessibility in its youth. Scents of lime, talc, Parisian almonds and frangipani with flavours keenly set to lime, green apple and more of the talc-like mineral character. It flows beautifully, finishes with some pleasing puckering dryness and generally delivers a very well-balanced and energetic expression. Screw cap. 12.5% alc. **RATING** 94 **DRINK** 2023–2040 $55 MB
Trevarrick Shiraz 2021, Clare Valley Big, bold scents of dark chocolate, ripe cherry, raspberry coulis and hazelnuts. Nice start. Effortless in the palate despite some concentration and ripe fruit flavours. Touches of vanilla cream and cinnamon spice. Very even and flows beautifully through a long, sweet finish. Tannins are soft and grip gently through each sip. Well done, here. Screw cap. 14% alc. **RATING** 94 **DRINK** 2023–2035 $75 MB

ŸŸŸŸŸ Small Batch Grenache 2022, Clare Valley RATING 93 **DRINK** 2023–2030 $55 MB
Small Batch Malbec 2022, Clare Valley RATING 93 **DRINK** 2023–2030 $55 MB
Trevarrick Single Contour Cabernet Sauvignon 2021, Clare Valley RATING 93 **DRINK** 2023–2037 $75 MB
Cabernet Sauvignon 2021, Clare Valley RATING 92 **DRINK** 2023–2030 $35 MB
Small Batch Cabernet Franc 2022, Clare Valley RATING 91 **DRINK** 2023–2026 $40 MB

Slow Wine Co   ★★★★

24 Victoria Street, Millthorpe, NSW 2798 **Region** Orange
T 412667455 **www**.slowwineco.com.au **Open** Fri–Sun 11–5, Mon–Thurs 11–3
Winemaker Will Rikard-Bell **Viticulturist** Tim Essen **Est.** 1990 **Dozens** 1500 **Vyds** 12ha
Terrey and Barbie Johnson (and family) raise beef cattle on a property at the southern end of Orange. Seeking to diversify, the Johnsons planted a vineyard at an elevation of 960m, one of the coolest in the region. The plantings began in '90 with chardonnay and cabernet sauvignon, the latter since grafted or removed because the climate is simply too cool.

About 60% of grapes are sold to various other producers making Orange-designated wines. In '13 the brand evolved from Bantry Grove to Slow Wine Co, for which a steadily increasing portion of the grapes is retained.

🍷🍷🍷🍷🍷 **Pinot Noir 2016, Orange** A stellar vintage in Orange is reflected in this charming aged-release pinot noir. Pomegranate molasses, red cherry cordial, raspberry leaf and wet tobacco. Blackcurrant, clove and tonka bean follow with hints of rosemary stem and creeping ivy vine. Peppered salami and cinnamon spice come through with sappy and juicy fruit quality and pillowy tannins. Screw cap. 13.4% alc. RATING 93 DRINK 2023–2028 $45 SW

Tribus Pinot Gris Riesling Gewürztraminer 2022, Orange Pear nectar, grated apple and lime cordial. Lychee and mangosteen. It's the palate that drives this wine with slinky acidity, almond meal graininess and shaved fennel. A kaleidoscope of fruits is backed by careful winemaking and appreciation for the assemblage. Screw cap. 12.5% alc. RATING 92 DRINK 2022–2026 $25 SW ✪

Pinot Noir 2021, Orange Pomegranate juice, rhubarb and black cherry skin. There is a rousing melange of dried herbs in this wine. Ripped thyme, marjoram and crushed rosemary with wet coffee grounds and cured meat notes. A wine of equal savoury elements and sappy red and black fruit. Screw cap. 13.3% alc. RATING 92 DRINK 2023–2028 $35 SW

Merlot 2018, Orange Blood plums, blackberry and stewed mulberries with mocha, tobacco and chai spices. Earthy tones of potting soil and wood ear mushroom come through and tannins are pillowy but ever-present. A touch of amaro bitterness on the finish. A steal at the price. Screw cap. 13.2% alc. RATING 92 DRINK 2023–2026 $30 SW ✪

Family Reserve Pinot Noir 2017, Orange Brambly wild raspberries and alpine strawberries stewed over campfire embers with nettles, dried leaves and paperbark. It's an outdoor experience of aromas. Soft tannins and perky acidity that rolls on a humming tune. Tannins have mellowed but still stand upright. Amaro bitters and a cola spice finish. Drinking very well now. Screw cap. 13.2% alc. RATING 92 DRINK 2022–2026 $60 SW

Riesling 2022, Orange Acacia and linden florals, calamansi lime juice, green apple flesh and fresh rain. Fennel and crisp celery. Salt flakes and sandstone. A fine-boned wine. Screw cap. 12.3% alc. RATING 91 DRINK 2022–2028 $25 SW ✪

Family Reserve Chardonnay 2019, Orange Buttered sourdough, caramelised apples and lemon balm. This has plenty of orchard fruits compacted into its taut framework. The tightwire acidity, creamy mlf and nutty praline finish make for intriguing components of a full-bodied wine. Grated nutmeg, puff pastry and sandalwood linger on the finish. Screw cap. 12.8% alc. RATING 91 DRINK 2022–2028 $50 SW

Sauvignon Blanc 2021, Orange Pineapple core, mango flesh, pickled limes and ginger. Pinenut, sunflowers and lemon verbena. A cresting wave of tropical flavours, slippery acidity and a weighty mid-palate. Nutmeg and ground ginger spice. Yellow boiled lollies and significant fruit sugars. It's overt but seductive. Screw cap. 13.8% alc. RATING 90 DRINK 2022–2026 $29 SW

Chardonnay 2019, Orange Pomelo and yellow blossoms, lime peel and honey cakes. There is a suppleness to the acidity and a touch of allspice on the finish. Screw cap. 13% alc. RATING 90 DRINK 2023–2026 $32 SW

Small Gully Wines
★★★☆

Roennfeldt Road, Marananga, SA 5355 **Region** Barossa Valley
T 0403 472 332 **www.**smallgullywines.com.au **Open** By appt **Winemaker** Stephen Black, Joe Black **Viticulturist** Charlie Black **Est.** 1999 **Vyds** 66ha

Small Gully was founded by grapegrowers Robert Bader and Darren Zimmerman and winemaker Stephen Black (ex Barossa Valley Wine Estates). The trio built a winery on Darren's Marananga property in '02, situated in a 'small gully' on Roennfeldt Road. Darren and Robert have established superb low-yielding shiraz vineyards, while small parcels of grenache, mourvèdre and cabernet sauvignon are also acquired from local growers. Stephen's sons, Joe and Charlie, focused on winemaking and viticulture respectively, are the 2nd generation to work with the label.

🍷🍷🍷🍷 **Mr Black's Concoction Old Fashioned Tawny NV, Barossa Valley** Deep tawny with a flash of mahogany and notes of raisins, polished leather, fruitcake, roasted nuts and lighter tones of mahogany. Sweet raisin fruit notes with light rancio nuance, a nice seam of freshness and a finish that lingers with memories of fruitcake and leather. Screw cap. 18% alc. **RATING** 92 $50 DB

Small Island Wines

4 Spark Drive Cambridge, Tas 7004 (postal) **Region** Southern Tasmania
T 0414 896 930 **www**.smallislandwines.com **Open** Not **Winemaker** James Broinowski
Est. 2015 **Dozens** 750 **Vyds** 4ha

Tasmanian-born James Broinowski completed his bachelor of viticulture and oenology at the University of Adelaide in '13. He was faced with the same problem as many other graduates wanting to strike out on their own: cash. While others in his predicament may have found the same solution, his was the first wine venture to successfully seek crowdfunding. The first year, he bought enough pinot noir from Glengarry in Tasmania's north to make 2100 bottles of pinot noir (which won a gold medal at the Royal International Hobart Wine Show '16) and 200 bottles of rosé. The following year he was able to buy pinot from the highly rated Gala Estate on the East Coast, as well as a repeat order from Glengarry. In '19, James added Saltwater River vineyard on the Tasmania Peninsula to his roster of premium single sites. The quality of the wines is seriously good, too.

🍷🍷🍷🍷 **Black Label Pinot Noir 2021, Tasmania** Red fruits are dusted with complex whole-bunch ferment tones of souk-like spices, hanging game meats, shiitake, shoyu, amaro herbs, Campari and purple flowers. Great, gamey, complex drinking. Screw cap. 13.5% alc. **RATING** 93 **DRINK** 2023-2027 $45 DB
Glengarry P82 Pinot Noir 2021, Tasmania Lightly coloured with punchy whole-bunch characters of struck flint and souk-like spices that hover over the ripe red cherry, redcurrant and raspberry fruits. Spacious and airy on the palate with a gamey, flinty and amaro herby form along with a touch of sour cherry and a whole bucket load of funk in the trunk. I dig it! Screw cap. 13.5% alc. **RATING** 93 **DRINK** 2023-2027 $49 DB
Saltwater River MV6 Pinot Noir 2021, Tasmania Light crimson with sexy-smelling red and dark cherry fruits cut with hints of exotic spice, earth, leaf litter, mushrooms, purple flowers and game meats. Gamey notes flow on the palate also, along with amaro herbs and Chinese barbecue characters. Complex drinking with a silky tannin frame and bright minerally drive. Screw cap. 13.5% alc. **RATING** 93 **DRINK** 2023-2029 $90 DB
Single Vineyard Glengarry P91 Pinot Noir 2021, Tasmania Aromas of bunchy red fruits with hints of exotic spice, leaf litter, Chinese barbecue, struck flint and pressed purple flowers. Light and airy with spicy red cherry fruits along with a gamey, exotically spiced fruit flow, gentle tannin and bright minerally acid line. Screw cap. 13.5% alc. **RATING** 92 **DRINK** 2023-2026 $49 DB
Cabernet Franc 2021, Tasmania Light, diaphanous red in the glass with aromas of redcurrant, red plum, blackcurrant and mulberry supported by hints of fine spice, red licorice, light, leafy tones, roasting meats, pressed purple flowers and warm earth. Sporting a spacious palate shape, superfine, gravelly tannins and a sapid acid pulse, there is a lot to like here. Pop it in the fridge to take the edge off if needed. Screw cap. 13.5% alc. **RATING** 92 **DRINK** 2023-2025 $49 DB
Riesling 2022, Tasmania Riesling from the Derwent Valley. Characters of green apple, lemon and melon with hints of rosewater, crushed stone, soft spice, guava and almond blossom. A swell of texture is checked by tight, minerally acidity and the wine tails away with lovely tension and floral-flecked citrus purity. Screw cap. 12.9% alc. **RATING** 91 **DRINK** 2023-2028 $35 DB
Saltwater River Hoyle's Cut Pinot Noir 2021, Tasmania Spiced red and dark cherry fruits on a bed of exotic spices, pressed purple flowers, mushroom

broth, rhubarb, struck flint, Chinese roast duck and star anise. There is an enchanting exotic edge to the wine with some light amaro and hanging game notes coming through. Finishes with nervy acidity and wild-eyed cherry fruit. Screw cap. 13.5% alc. **RATING** 91 **DRINK** 2023-2028 $90 DB

Saltwater River Chardonnay 2021, Tasmania Showing plenty of ripe white peach and nectarine with hints of soft spice, clotted cream, white flowers, vanilla bean, almond paste and nougat. Tight and sapid on the palate with stone fruit and greengage tones, lemon curd and tarte Tatin with lipsmacking, minerally intensity on the finish. Screw cap. 13% alc. **RATING** 91 **DRINK** 2023-2026 $36 DB

Small Victories Wine Co ★★★★

3–5 Tanunda Road, Nuriootpa, SA, 5355 **Region** Barossa Valley
T (08) 8568 7877 **www.**smallvictorieswine.com **Open** Fri–Mon 11–4 **Winemaker** Julie Ashmead **Est.** 2021
Sisters-in-law Jules and Bec Ashmead work at Elderton as winemaker (Jules) and production/logistics (Bec). The decision to create Small Victories came about after the constant search for wines that were interesting and a little different. In the end, they made their own, sourcing fruit from Elderton (shiraz, grenache, mataro and carignan) and from growers in the Adelaide Hills and Ricca Terra in the Riverland. The wines are made at Elderton. Sales from the wines support 2 local charities, Variety and Trees For Life. The label has a strong focus on sustainability, including environmentally friendly packaging, lightweight bottles and recycled cardboard cartons.

⚑⚑⚑⚑⚑ **Vermentino 2022, Riverland** You'd be hard pressed to find a more aromatic white wine. This really does throw a garden of flowers and fruits at you. Sloshy red apple, pear and talc, slate and the buds of currants. It has a textural, stony dryness to it as well, almost quartz-like, which is quite an achievement given the billow of fruit. It's a gorgeous wine to drink, by any standards. Screw cap. 12.8% alc. **RATING** 94 **DRINK** 2023-2027 $28 CM ✪
Old Vine Grenache 2022, Barossa Valley This wine put a smile on my face with its bouncy aromas and flavours of raspberry, mulberry, red plum and nectarine fruits cut with a hint of Asian five-spice, musk, gingerbread, cola, citrus blossom, dried citrus rind and earth. Light, savoury and slurpy, enjoy this while it is young as it is all about exuberance and fun. Screw cap. 14.5% alc. **RATING** 94 **DRINK** 2023-2026 $28 DB ✪

⚑⚑⚑⚑⚑ **Rosé 2022, Barossa Valley Riverland RATING** 93 **DRINK** 2023-2026 $28 CM ✪
Shiraz 2022, Eden Valley RATING 93 **DRINK** 2023-2029 $28 DB ✪
Sangiovese 2022, Adelaide Hills RATING 91 **DRINK** 2022-2026 $28 NG ✪
Pinot Gris 2022, Adelaide Hills RATING 91 **DRINK** 2023-2026 $28 NG ✪

Smalltown Vineyards ★★★☆

28 Jenke Road, Marananga, SA, 5355 (postal) **Region** Barossa Valley
T 0411 861 604 **www.**btpvintners.com.au **Open** Not **Winemaker** Tom White
Viticulturist Tom White **Est.** 2011 **Dozens** 8000 **Vyds** 8ha
Smalltown produces a range of funkily labelled wines from vineyard sources across the Barossa and Eden valleys. Originally an export label partnership between Boutinot (UK) and Rolf Binder, the brand was subsequently purchased by Tom White from the Curator Wine Company, who now makes the wines and sells both to export markets and domestically through Vinous Solutions. Solid, well-priced bistro-style wines are the order of the day from the classic varieties across the region.

⚑⚑⚑⚑⚑ **Rag & Bone Riesling 2022, Eden Valley** This is a great follow up to the very impressive '21 release, again there is wonderful aromatic detail and clarity with super-pure freshly squeezed lime juice, green apple and grapefruit with hints of Christmas lily, orange blossom, crushed quartz and almond paste. Vivid, detailed and crisp with lovely acid drive and a lipsmacking finish. Screw cap. 12% alc. **RATING** 92 **DRINK** 2023-2030 $30 DB ✪

Smeaton Estate

Level 1, 206 Greenhill Road, Eastwood, SA 5063 (postal) **Region** Adelaide Hills
T 0429 109 537 **www**.smeaton.estate **Open** Not **Winemaker** Con Moshos
Viticulturist John Smeaton **Est.** 1996 **Dozens** 450 **Vyds** 25ha
Janice and John Smeaton planted their Martin Hill vineyard to shiraz (6.5ha), sauvignon blanc (5.2ha), semillon (4.5ha), chardonnay (4ha), merlot (2.9ha), riesling (1.3ha) and pinot gris (0.6ha). They intended to sell the grapes, but a '17 partnership with winemaker Con Moshos, an Adelaide Hills veteran with longstanding close ties to Brian Croser, got them started on riesling. That worked out rather well, and the estate range has since expanded to sauvignon blanc and merlot.

🍷🍷🍷🍷🍷 **The Minx Sauvignon Blanc 2020, Adelaide Hills** Textural, persuasive and fresh, without being overly tweaked and shrill. Baked quince, crystallised ginger, golden apple and the faintest whiff of greengage. A mid-weighted sauvignon that's layered, poised, a little soapy and strident through the mouth. Solid drinking. Screw cap. 13% alc. **RATING** 91 **DRINK** 2022-2024 $24 NG ✪

Smidge Wines

150 Tatachilla Road, McLaren Vale, SA 5171 **Region** McLaren Vale
T 0419 839 964 **www**.smidgewines.com **Open** 2nd w'end of each month, 12–5
Winemaker Matt Wenk **Est.** 2004 **Dozens** 8000 **Vyds** 4.1ha
Smidge Wines is owned by Matt Wenk and wife Trish Callaghan. It was for many years an out-of-hours occupation for Matt; his day job was as winemaker for Two Hands Wines (and Sandow's End). In '13 Matt retired from Two Hands; this meant the Smidge wines could no longer be made at Two Hands and the winemaking operations have been moved to McLaren Vale, where Smidge is currently leasing a small winery. Smidge owns the vineyard in Willunga that provides the grapes for all the cabernet sauvignon releases and some of the McLaren Vale shiraz. The vision is to build a modern customised facility on the Willunga property in the not-too-distant future.

🍷🍷🍷🍷🍷 **Pedra Branca Saperavi 2021, McLaren Vale** Opaque. Mighty, yet so fresh, glorious and long that this stereotype-shattering wine is riveting. The extraction is beautifully controlled, promoting freshness without vacuity, structure and herbal intrigue sans dryness. Glorious chewy tannins. Dill pickle, purple and blue fruits, aniseed and a bouquet of purple flowers at the finale. Screw cap. 14% alc. **RATING** 95 **DRINK** 2022-2032 $45 NG ✪

🍷🍷🍷🍷🍷 **il Piano Fiano 2022, McLaren Vale RATING** 93 **DRINK** 2022-2027 $28 NG ✪
Uno Momento Montepulciano 2020, McLaren Vale RATING 93 **DRINK** 2022-2030 $38 NG
Houdini Cabernet Sauvignon 2018, McLaren Vale RATING 93 **DRINK** 2022-2030 $38 NG
Houdini Shiraz 2019, McLaren Vale RATING 92 **DRINK** 2022-2027 $28 NG ✪
Houdini Sauvignon Blanc 2022, Adelaide Hills RATING 90 **DRINK** 2022-2024 $28 NG
Adamo Shiraz 2020, Barossa Valley RATING 90 **DRINK** 2023-2030 $38 NG

Smith & Hooper

Caves Edward Road, Naracoorte, SA 5271 **Region** Wrattonbully
T (08) 8561 3200 **www**.smithandhooper.com **Open** By appt **Winemaker** Heather Fraser **Est.** 1994 **Dozens** 15 000 **Vyds** 62ha
Smith & Hooper can be viewed as simply one of many brands within the Hill-Smith family financial/corporate structures. However, it is estate-based, with cabernet sauvignon and merlot planted on the Hooper vineyard in '94; and cabernet sauvignon and merlot planted on the Smith Vineyard in '98. Spread across both vineyards are 9ha of trial varieties.

🍷🍷🍷🍷🍷 **Pinot Grigio 2022, Wrattonbully** The flavour profile is all pear, preserved lemon, grapefruit and apple blossom, attractive in itself, but it's the intensity that makes you take notice. This is fruity, floral and satisfying to drink. Screw cap. 13.5% alc. **RATING** 91 **DRINK** 2023–2025 $19 CM ✪

Cabernet Sauvignon Merlot 2021, Wrattonbully Both the flavours and the fragrances rush up to greet you. Blackcurrant, eucalyptus, smoked tobacco, blueberry and black licorice, with cedar oak in support. There's a clear sweetness to the profile here, and softness, but then there are savoury/herbal notes as a counterpoint. It drinks easily and well. Screw cap. 13.5% alc. **RATING** 91 **DRINK** 2023–2030 $21 CM ✪

Snake + Herring ★★★★★

3763 Caves Road, Wilyabrup, WA 6284 **Region** Margaret River
T 0427 881 871 **www.**snakeandherring.com.au **Open** 7 days 11–5 summer, 11–4 winter
Winemaker Tony Davis **Est.** 2010 **Dozens** 12 000
Tony (Snake) Davis and Redmond (Herring) Sweeny both started university degrees before finding that they were utterly unsuited to their respective courses. Having stumbled across Margaret River, Tony's life changed forever; he enrolled at the University of Adelaide, thereafter doing vintages in the Eden Valley, Oregon, Beaujolais and Tasmania, before 3 years at Plantagenet, next Brown Brothers, then a senior winemaking role at Yalumba, a 6-year stint designing Millbrook Winery in the Perth Hills and 4 years with Howard Park in Margaret River. Redmond's circuitous course included a chartered accountancy degree and employment with an international accounting firm in Busselton, and the subsequent establishment of Forester Estate in '01, in partnership with Kevin McKay. Back on home turf he is the marketing and financial controller of Snake + Herring.

🍷🍷🍷🍷🍷 **The Distance Chardonnay 2022, Margaret River** This arrived unannounced with no details and lots of curiosity. It is awesome. It has power and poise. Ripe fruit and a savoury carapace. It has definition and detail. An amalgamation of white stone fruit, Meyer lemon and smoky sulphides with some chicken stock (usually lees derived) and the oak is seamlessly integrated, adding a smidge of spice. A superb drink no matter how it came to be, but I might die wondering. Screw cap. 13% alc. **RATING** 96 **DRINK** 2023–2033 $70 JF ✪

Corduroy Karridale Chardonnay 2022, Margaret River Fine, long and pure with gossamer-like acidity threaded through the lemon, lime and white nectarine flavours. It comes lightly spiced and lightly textured with some delicate leesy accents. Savoury, too, and mouth-watering with the right amount of tension to delight and even more pleasure to come in time. Screw cap. 12.5% alc. **RATING** 95 **DRINK** 2023–2032 $48 JF ✪

Bizarre Love Triangle Pinot Gris Gewürztraminer Riesling 2022, Great Southern Nothing bizarre about this tryst, it's out in the open with heady aromatics of roses, musk, ginger and lemon balm. Pears and lemons, quince paste and lemon cream add to the thrilling palate, which is also racy with almost powder-puff acidity. Refreshing and such a good drink. Screw cap. 12.5% alc. **RATING** 95 **DRINK** 2022–2030 $28 JF ✪

🍷🍷🍷🍷🍷 **Sabotage Riesling 2022, Great Southern** **RATING** 92 **DRINK** 2022–2028 $27 JF ✪

At First Sight Grenache 2021, Great Southern **RATING** 92 **DRINK** 2022–2027 $27 JF ✪

Solum Wines ★★★★☆

193 Seventh Avenue, Rosebud, Vic 3939 (postal) **Region** Mornington Peninsula
T 0413 050 417 **www.**solumwines.com.au **Open** Not **Winemaker** Ryan Horaczko
Viticulturist Ryan Horaczko **Est.** 2019 **Dozens** 175 **Vyds** 0.8ha
Ryan Horaczko's foray into wine began while working at his father's burgeoning booze shop. As it turned out, he had a knack for tasting and started to get more serious before travel took him to some of the world's great wine regions. He enrolled in the bachelor of agriculture and technology – viticulture and winemaking at Melbourne Polytechnic in '17. There he met

chardonnay and pinot noir specialist Darrin Gaffy, from Principia winery. The rest is history. Ryan now works part-time at Principia. While he loves syrah, sourcing some from Quartz Hill in the Pyrenees, co-owned by Darrin's sister, he lives on the Peninsula and has taken on a lease of a 0.8ha vineyard.

🍷🍷🍷🍷🍷 **Chardonnay 2021, Mornington Peninsula** Fruit off 2 sites – Balnarring and Merricks North, and this comes up trumps as a rich yet lithe, juicy wine. Neatly layered with stone fruit, citrus and spice, sweet-ish cedary oak and creamy lees. There's an intriguing and appealing lemony-saline character and a savoury edge, then just when it starts to feel luscious, tangy acidity comes in to keep it on a linear path. Screw cap. 13.3% alc. **RATING** 95 **DRINK** 2022-2030 $35 JF ☻

🍷🍷🍷🍷🍷 **Syrah 2021, Pyrenees RATING** 93 **DRINK** 2023-2033 $35 JF ☻

 # Somos ★★★★

333 Foggo Road, McLaren Flat, SA 5171 **Region** South Australia
T 0430 613 966 **www.**somoswines.com **Open** Mon–Thurs by appt, Fri–Sun 11–4
Winemaker Mauricio Ruiz Cantú, Ben Caldwell **Est.** 2013 **Dozens** 5000
Somos means 'we are' in Spanish, suggestive of the close bond partners Ben Caldwell and Mauricio Ruiz Cantú, who is from Mexico, formed while studying oenology and viticulture at the University of Adelaide. Upon graduating in '13, they created a successful export brand called Juguette aimed at the Mexican market. The gist is small-batch Australian classics, largely hewn of old vines. This 'kept the light on for years … [but] it wasn't what we were going home and frothing over', to quote Mauricio. Thus, Somos was born. The modus-operandi: to quench the thirst with fresh, climate-appropriate varieties grown in the Adelaide Hills and McLaren Vale. As Somos grew, the decision was made to work only with organic and/or biodynamically certified growers, or at the very least, those growers that are part of the Sustainable Winegrowing Australia initiative. The philosophy in the winery is similar, with minimal additions and less-intrusive winemaking. Expect lots of carbonic maceration, judicious use of skin contact and ersatz field blends.

🍷🍷🍷🍷🍷 **Los Melones Dinámicos Viognier 2021, McLaren Vale** Mandarin peel, ginger, chutney, tamarind, kombucha, cumquat, apricot and dried tatami straw are cleaved from sandy phenolics alloyed with viognier's oiliness for a long slide of flavour. A very intense, highly textural, idiosyncratic behemoth. Certified biodynamic. Diam. 13.9% alc. **RATING** 93 **DRINK** 2022-2024 $33 NG ☻

Pinot Meunier 2022, Adelaide Hills This is crafted beautifully. Scents of tamarind, clove, mango peel and turmeric. Lightweight, carbonic-floral and glimpsing whole-bunch green, without ever straying into the garden bed. A thread of acidity is strung taut about a spindle of diaphanous tannins. In all, transparent and edgy. Thrills with a chill sort of ease, as much as intellectual rigour. Diam. 12% alc. **RATING** 92 **DRINK** 2022-2024 $33 NG

Mencia 2021, Adelaide Hills Mencia is performing well here. Think cool-climate syrah with greater levity, florals and whole-bunch spiky astringency. This barely nudges mid-weight, yet forfeits no flavour or presence. Iodine, blueberry, lilac and a sachet of lavender, clove, fennel seed and lapsang souchong is strewn across the pushy finish. Diam. 12.5% alc. **RATING** 92 **DRINK** 2022-2025 $33 NG

Biodynamically Farmed Aglianico 2021, McLaren Vale A variety of tannic fortitude, high acidity and dark fruits tamed by semi-carbonic fermentation. A betrayal of varietal character? Personally, I think so. Yet the deliciousness cannot be denied. A whiff of dried tobacco and pepper-crusted salami, intact. Yet the mid-palate, round and red fruited, is a mindless swish. Some gentle tannic tension at the finish. Procork. 12.9% alc. **RATING** 92 **DRINK** 2022-2025 $38 NG

Cabernet Franc 2021, McLaren Vale A mid-weighed expression, successfully melding florals and pulpy pastilles with a fine structural lattice of lithe, leafy tannins. Aromas of damson plum, pickled cherry, ume, root spices, tomato leaf and menthol jitter long, with the well-positioned oak a mere signpost. This is delicious drinking. Diam. 13.7% alc. **RATING** 91 **DRINK** 2022-2027 $38 NG

Sons of Eden

Penrice Road, Angaston, SA 5353 **Region** Barossa Valley
T (08) 8564 2363 **www.sonsofeden.com Open** 7 days 11–6 **Winemaker** Corey Ryan,
Simon Cowham **Viticulturist** Simon Cowham **Est.** 2000 **Dozens** 9000 **Vyds** 60ha
Corey Ryan and Simon Cowham both learnt and refined their skills in the Eden
Valley. Corey is a trained oenologist with over 20 vintages under his belt, having cut his teeth
as a winemaker at Henschke. Thereafter he worked for Rouge Homme and Penfolds in
Coonawarra, backed up by winemaking stints in the Rhône Valley and in NZ for Villa Maria
Estates. Simon has had a similarly international career covering such diverse organisations as
Oddbins, UK, and the Winemakers' Federation of Australia. Switching from the business
side to grapegrowing when he qualified as a viticulturist, he worked for Yalumba as technical
manager of the Heggies and Pewsey Vale vineyards. With these backgrounds, it comes as no
surprise to find that the estate-grown wines are of outstanding quality.

🍷🍷🍷🍷🍷 **Zephyrus Shiraz 2020, Barossa** Open fermented and hand plunged, each
fermenter with a portion of whole bunches (10–35%). Matured for 12 months
in French hogsheads (35% new). A delicious shiraz, with a juicy mouthfeel,
partly due to whole bunches that also invest attractive spicy notes on the finish.
Screw cap. 14.5% alc. **RATING** 96 **DRINK** 2023–2035 $48 JH ❂

Freya Riesling 2022, Eden Valley Opens with a perfumed bouquet of white
flowers and citrus blossoms, the palate tracking with exemplary analysis and purity.
Its lime/lemon flavour baseline gives it presence now and into the distant future.
Screw cap. 12.5% alc. **RATING** 95 **DRINK** 2023–2042 $25 JH ❂

Marschall Shiraz 2021, Barossa Valley From 6 vineyards in 6 districts,
with a wide range of fermentation techniques, though all with skin contact
for 15-20 days, including 5-day cold soak. Matured in new and used French
hogsheads for 14 months. A smooth and supple medium-bodied wine is the
result, with plum and blackberry fruits, integrated oak and tannins. Value-plus.
Screw cap. 14.5% alc. **RATING** 95 **DRINK** 2023–2036 $29 JH ❂

Romulus Old Vine Shiraz 2020, Barossa Valley Blackberry, satsuma plum
and red cherry fruit notes mesh with an array of fine spices and hints of pressed
flowers, licorice, dark chocolate and earth. Lovely balance and fruit purity, with
the pull of gentle sandy tannin and plenty of drive from the bright acidity. A great
contemporary Barossa shiraz. Screw cap. 14.5% alc. **RATING** 95 **DRINK** 2023–2035
$80 DB

Autumnus Shiraz 2018, Eden Valley The flexing stature of the flagship Sons
of Eden wine is quite something. Packed to the rafters with opulent blackberry,
blackcurrant, black cherry and blood plums cut with deep dark spice, blackcurrant
pastille, turned earth, sage, pressed flowers, licorice, cedar and fairly voluminous
oak nuance. If you seek a sleek, plush shiraz this may be just the ticket. Cork.
14.5% alc. **RATING** 95 **DRINK** 2023–2038 $350 DB

Kennedy GSM 2021, Barossa Valley The 22nd release of this particular blend.
And it's a good 'un! Bright, perfumed and detailed with super-pure plummy fruit,
layers of spice, earth, florals, gingerbread and roasting meat goodness. Driven by
a vivid line of lacy acidity and framed with powdery tannin, it seems like it is a
good place and will provide great drinking over the medium term. Screw cap.
14.5% alc. **RATING** 94 **DRINK** 2023–2030 $30 DB ❂

🍷🍷🍷🍷🍷 **Eurus Cabernet Sauvignon 2021, Eden Valley RATING** 93 **DRINK** 2023–2030
$80 DB

Remus Old Vine Shiraz 2020, Eden Valley RATING 93 **DRINK** 2023–2030
$80 DB

Sorby Adams Wines

759 Light Pass Road, Angaston, SA 5353 **Region** Eden Valley
T (08) 8564 2435 **www.sorbyadamswines.com Open** By appt **Winemaker** Simon Sorby
Adams **Viticulturist** Simon Sorby Adams **Est.** 2004 **Dozens** 15 000 **Vyds** 15ha

In '92, Simon Sorby Adams purchased a 3.2ha vineyard that had been planted by Pastor Franz Julius Lehmann (none other than Peter Lehmann's father) in 1932. Simon added 0.25ha of viognier, which, as one might expect, is used in a shiraz viognier blend. Most recent plantings are of shiraz, riesling, cabernet sauvignon and traminer. Simon also purchased the Jellicoe vineyard at Mt McKenzie in '06.

ΨΨΨΨΨ **Jellicoe Riesling 2022, Eden Valley** Pale straw with green flashes and a beautiful nose of freshly squeezed lime, crunchy green apple, Christmas lily, crushed quartz, marzipan and white flowers. Notes of lemon zest and a touch of grapefruit pith texture on the palate, which shows a pristine tubular palate shape and great drive from the minerally acid line. Focused, true and just lovely to drink. Screw cap. 11.5% alc. **RATING** 95 **DRINK** 2023–2035 $35 DB ✪

ΨΨΨΨΨ **The Thing Shiraz 2018, Barossa RATING** 92 **DRINK** 2023–2033 $150 DB
Margret Pinot Gris 2022, Eden Valley RATING 91 **DRINK** 2023–2026 $35 DB
Jazz Pinot Rosé 2022, Eden Valley RATING 91 **DRINK** 2023–2026 $35 DB

Soul Growers

218 Murray Street, Tanunda, SA 5352 **Region** Barossa Valley
T (08) 8523 2691 **www**.soulgrowers.com **Open** By appt **Winemaker** Paul Heinicke, Stuart Bourne **Est.** 1998 **Dozens** 10 000 **Vyds** 4.85ha

Friends and partners Paul Heinicke, Stuart Bourne (ex Château Tanunda) and Tom Fotheringham (sales and marketing, ex Penfolds) first met while all working at Barossa Valley Estate. Soul Growers source from multi-generational family growers (26 in total) in Moppa, Ebenezer, Kalimna, Vine Vale, Eden Valley and Nuriootpa with pocket-handkerchief vineyard blocks of mataro at Nuriootpa and grenache at Krondorf.

ΨΨΨΨΨ **Hampel Single Vineyard Shiraz 2021, Barossa Valley** Super-plush satsuma plum and blackberry fruits underscored by hints of baking spices, cedar, crème de cassis, violets, roasting meats, olive tapenade, chocolate bullets and earth. A core of deep northern Barossa black fruits on the palate with chocolate-dipped cherry overtones, fine chocolatey tannins and a crashing swell of cassis fruit on the long finish. Impressive. Cork. 14.5% alc. **RATING** 96 **DRINK** 2023–2040 $160 DB
Hoffmann Single Vineyard Shiraz 2021, Barossa Valley Opulent blackberry, black cherry and satsuma plum fruits with layers of dark spice, clove, cinnamon and star anise, rum and raisin, salted licorice, cedar, Cherry Ripe, blueberry pie and a whiff of coconut and fruitcake. There's a deep, thundering cassis fruit flow, compact, silty tannins and loads of kirsch and liquored cherries on the finish. The oak is fairly percussive at this stage, but the fruit can certainly handle it. Cork. 14.5% alc. **RATING** 95 **DRINK** 2023–2040 $160 DB
El Mejor 2021, Barossa Valley Cabernet sauvignon/mourvèdre/shiraz. An intensely concentrated aromatic profile and fruit flow. It borders on moody with graphite-dusted blackberry and black cherry fruits, blackcurrant pastille and dried herbs courtesy of the cabernet sauvignon, earth, meats and spice from the mourvèdre and the rich, soulful plum and dark chocolate tones of shiraz. Fine, sandy tannin with a strong black fruit presence on the finish. Cork. 14% alc. **RATING** 94 **DRINK** 2023–2038 $160 DB

ΨΨΨΨΨ **Equilibrium GSM 2021, Barossa Valley RATING** 93 **DRINK** 2023–2029 $35 DB ✪
Slow Grown Shiraz 2020, Barossa Valley RATING 93 **DRINK** 2023–2029 $60 DB
Slow Grown Shiraz 2021, Barossa Valley RATING 92 **DRINK** 2023–2030 $60 DB
Provident Valley Shiraz 2021, Barossa RATING 91 **DRINK** 2023–2028 $35 DB
Persistence Grenache 2021, Barossa Valley RATING 91 **DRINK** 2023–2026 $60 DB

Cellar Dweller Cabernet Sauvignon 2021, Barossa RATING 91
DRINK 2023-2030 $60 DB
Single Vineyard Graciano 2020, Barossa Valley RATING 91 DRINK 2023-2026
$35 DB
Persistence Grenache 2022, Barossa Valley RATING 90 DRINK 2023-2028
$60 DB

SOUMAH
★★★★★

18 Hexham Road, Gruyere, Vic 3770 **Region** Yarra Valley
T (03) 5962 4716 **www**.soumah.com.au **Open** 7 days 10–5 **Winemaker** Scott
McCarthy **Viticulturist** Lucas Hoorn **Est.** 1997 **Dozens** 12000 **Vyds** 19.47ha
Unravelling the story behind the exotically named SOUMAH and its strikingly labelled
Savarro (reminiscent of 19th-century baroque design) was a voyage of discovery. SOUMAH
is in fact an abbreviation of South of Maroondah (Highway); Savarro is an alternative name
for savagnin. This is the venture of Brett Butcher, who has international experience in the
hospitality industry as CEO of the Langham Group and a long involvement in retailing wines
to restaurants in many countries. The many varieties planted have been clonally selected and
grafted onto rootstock with the long-term future in mind, although some of the sauvignon
blanc has been grafted over to bracchetto.

ΨΨΨΨ Equilibrio Single Vineyard Pinot Noir 2021, Yarra Valley An attractive
light ruby red. Elegant and perfumed, this opens with aromas of wild strawberries,
redcurrants, blood orange and floral notes. Poised and silky in the mouth, this
really is quite persistent and beautifully balanced. A very good effort from go to
whoa. Screw cap. 13.5% alc. RATING 96 DRINK 2023-2028 $80 PR
Equilibrio Single Vineyard Viognier 2021, Yarra Valley Complex aromas
of apricots, white peaches and plums with some orange blossom and honey
notes. The palate is powerful yet restrained. Textured, well balanced and finishes
long with a refreshing orange pith bitterness at the end. Seriously good viognier.
Screw cap. 14% alc. RATING 95 DRINK 2022-2026 $80 PR

ΨΨΨΨ Hexham Vineyard Savarro 2021, Yarra Valley RATING 93 DRINK 2023-2025
$29 PR ✪
U. Ngumby Single Vineyard Pinot Noir 2021, Yarra Valley RATING 93
DRINK 2023-2027 $45 PR
Hexham Single Vineyard Syrah 2021, Yarra Valley RATING 93
DRINK 2023-2029 $40 PR
Wild Savagnin No. 2 Savagnin NV, Yarra Valley RATING 93
DRINK 2023-2027 $80 PR
The Butcher Thomas Hendy Cut Syrah Cabernet Sauvignon Nebbiolo
2021, Yarra Valley RATING 92 DRINK 2023-2028 $50 PR
Equilibrio Single Vineyard Chardonnay 2021, Yarra Valley RATING 92
DRINK 2023-2026 $80 PR
U. Ngumby Single Vineyard Chardonnay 2021, Yarra Valley RATING 92
DRINK 2023-2026 $45 PR
Ai Fiori Single Vineyard Rosato 2022, Yarra Valley RATING 91
DRINK 2023-2025 $28 PR ✪
Hexham Single Vineyard Pinot Grigio 2022, Yarra Valley RATING 91
DRINK 2022-2024 $28 PR ✪
Hexham Single Vineyard Pinot Noir 2021, Yarra Valley RATING 91
DRINK 2022-2028 $45 PR
Hexham Single Vineyard Pinot Noir Syrah 2021, Yarra Valley RATING 90
DRINK 2023-2026 $35 PR
Hexham Single Vineyard Viognier 2021, Yarra Valley RATING 90
DRINK 2023-2024 $35 PR

Southern Light Vineyards

50 Long Gully Rd, Healesville, Vic 3777 (postal) **Region** Mornington Peninsula
T 0414 909 075 **www**.southernlightvineyards.com.au **Open** Not **Winemaker** Anthony
Fikkers **Est.** 2021 **Dozens** 600 **Vyds** 6ha

Joval Wines has been a major player in the wine import/distribution scene for decades and
lately has bought several Yarra Valley labels outright. It was only a matter of time before it
added a winery to expand the range, including a new label. Enter Southern Lights Vineyards.
Previously known as Long Gully Estate, an established winery with vineyards, it is the new
home to Joval Wine's suite of cool-climate vineyards from the Mornington Peninsula and
Yarra Valley. Serious inroads being undertaken comprise of new plantings and thoughtful
viticulture alongside a commitment to quality. Eye-catching labels, too.

Ghostgum Vineyard Pinot Noir 2021, Mornington Peninsula The
wine's good, the colour less so (some browning to the rim). Lots of punchy,
whole-bunch characters; somewhat overt and it'll be polarising as a style. I like
it with its peppery and spicy aromas and while sweet-fruited, by and large, it's
savoury. Dark cherries, autumnal damp earth, chinotto and blood orange with
an attractive amaro twist. The palate is surprisingly light, tannins ethereal yet in
the background, with lots of acidity driving this. Diam. 13.5% alc. **RATING** 92
DRINK 2023–2032 $85 JF
Ghostgum Vineyard Chardonnay 2021, Mornington Peninsula There's
plenty to like with its melon, citrus and ginger blossom with creamy lees and oak
spices adding to the palate weight. Yet it is simple, soft and pleasant, lacking the
X-factor for a wine at this price. Diam. 13% alc. **RATING** 91 **DRINK** 2023–2028
$75 JF

Spence

760 Burnside Road, Murgheboluc, Vic 3221 **Region** Geelong
T (03) 5265 1181 **www**.spencewines.com.au **Open** 1st Sun each month 11–5, or
by appt **Winemaker** Peter Spence, Scott Ireland **Est.** 1997 **Dozens** 1300 **Vyds** 3.2ha

Peter and Anne Spence were sufficiently inspired by an extended European holiday – which
included living on a family vineyard in Provence – to purchase a small property and establish
a vineyard and winery. They have planted 3.2ha on a north-facing slope in a valley 7km south
of Bannockburn, the lion's share to 3 clones of shiraz (1.83ha), the remainder to chardonnay,
pinot noir and viognier. The vineyard attained full organic status in '08, since then using only
biodynamic practices.

Pinot Noir 2021, Geelong Another very good '21 release from Spence.
Ripe red fruits and pomegranate intermingle with some spice and a little damp
earth. Medium bodied, the palate is fleshy while the tannins give the wine grip
and focus. That it's well priced is a bonus. Screw cap. 13.5% alc. **RATING** 94
DRINK 2023–2028 $35 PR ✪
Viognier 2021, Geelong Fermented and matured in amphora. A very bright
green gold. Totally convincing from the get-go with aromas of white peach and
apricot, honeysuckle and spice. Equally good on the palate, this has richness and
texture that scream viognier, but tension and length, too. If you like the northern
Rhône variety, this is well worth seeking out. Screw cap. 13.2% alc. **RATING** 94
DRINK 2022–2027 $35 PR ✪

Chardonnay 2021, Geelong RATING 93 **DRINK** 2022–2029 $35 PR ✪
Shiraz 2021, Geelong RATING 92 **DRINK** 2023–2026 $35 PR

Spikey Bridge Vineyard

194 Relbia Rd, Relbia, Tas 7258 (postal) **Region** Northern Tasmania
T 0412 478 841 **www**.spikeybridge.com.au **Open** Not **Winemaker** Jeremy Dineen
Est. 2017 **Dozens** 2500 **Vyds** 10ha

The wines from Tamar Valley's Spikey Bridge Vineyard are a team effort, with Ros and Martin Rees joined by Katie and Jeremy Dineen. Jeremy, a highly respected leader in the Tasmanian wine industry, handles the winemaking. There are two labels: Broad Arrow provides value and pure drinking; the Spikey Bridge pinot noir is the top wine in the portfolio. With this team onboard, it is definitely a Tasmanian winery you want to keep on your radar.

ᵀᵀᵀᵀᵀ **Pinot Noir 2018, Tasmania** Bright, detailed red and dark cherry fruits underlined with fine baking spices, leaf litter, game meats, purple floral notes, raspberry flan and light oak-spice nuance. Aromas of pressed flowers and rose petals joining the party, a sprinkle of alpine herbs too, finishing tight and bright with a long, persistent flow of red fruits and spice. Screw cap. 13.9% alc. **RATING** 94 **DRINK** 2023-2028 $80 DB

ᵀᵀᵀᵀᵀ **Broad Arrow Pinot Noir 2021, Tasmania** **RATING** 90 **DRINK** 2023-2026 $29 DB

Spinifex

★★★★★

46 Nuraip Road, Light Pass, SA 5355 **Region** Barossa Valley
T (08) 8564 2059 **www**.spinifexwines.com.au **Open** By appt **Winemaker** Peter Schell
Viticulturist Peter Schell **Est.** 2001 **Dozens** 6000 **Vyds** 13ha

Peter Schell and Magali Gely are a husband-and-wife team from NZ who came to Australia in the early '90s to study oenology and marketing at Roseworthy College. They have spent 4 vintages making wine in France, mainly in the south where Magali's family were vignerons for generations near Montpellier. The focus at Spinifex is the red varieties that dominate in the south of France: mataro (a synonym for mourvèdre), grenache, shiraz and cinsault. The wines are made in open fermenters, basket pressed, with partial wild (indigenous) fermentation and relatively long post-ferment maceration. A new cellar door is set to open in June '23.

ᵀᵀᵀᵀᵀ **Sol Solice Grenache 2022, Barossa** Plenty of vibrant, aromatic fruit with juicy red plum, cranberry and mulberry fruits sheathed in gingery spice and hints of cola, earth, dried citrus rind, teacake, orange blossom, raspberry coulis and redcurrant paste. Firm, chalky tannin grip and a lively, mineral-laden wine finishing juicy – just a pure, joyous rendition. Screw cap. 14.3% alc. **RATING** 97 **DRINK** 2023-2033 $60 DB ✪ ♥

La Maline 2021, Eden Valley A shiraz/viognier blend with distinctly northern Rhône sensibilities. The fruit purity and depth scream of its antipodean roots, but the sense of mineral energy, tight granitic tannins and earthy amaro and spice-speckled aspects are a nod to Côte-Rôtie. The wine is graceful but has a real sense of latent power, a wonderfully pure depth of plum and dark fruits and a long, detailed finish. Great vintage, too. Screw cap. 14.2% alc. **RATING** 97 **DRINK** 2023-2040 $80 DB ✪

ᵀᵀᵀᵀᵀ **Indigene 2021, Barossa Valley** 52/48% shiraz/mataro. A harmonious and plushly fruited wine with incredible colour to boot. It's all satsuma plum and boysenberry with hints of garrigue and exotic spice, blueberry and dried cranberry, a touch of struck flint and purple florals. The tannin ramps up on the palate, firm yet ripe and long, and there is sapidity and frame to the acidity. Amazingly pure fruit and a gentle wisp of complexing reductive characters and spice. Screw cap. 14.3% alc. **RATING** 96 **DRINK** 2023-2038 $70 DB ✪

Moppa Vineyard Shiraz 2021, Barossa Valley A super-saturated, magenta-edged crimson. Aromas of ripe blueberry, satsuma plum and boysenberry fruit notes. Hints of spices, sandalwood, dark chocolate and citrus blossom. Plush and opulent with a mineral-laden line and melt-in-the-mouth tannins, it's a wine of great harmony and quality. Screw cap. 14.2% alc. **RATING** 96 **DRINK** 2023-2040 $60 DB ✪

Single Vineyard Moppa Shiraz 2020, Barossa Valley Deep crimson purple in the glass with aromas of satsuma plum, blackberry and boysenberry with hints of fine baking spices, licorice, earth, crème de cassis, sandalwood, leather, vanilla bean and wafts of cedar. Deep and resonant on the palate with a frame of firm, fine sandy tannin upon which the fruit is stretched like a canvas. Screw cap. 14.5% alc. RATING 96 DRINK 2023-2038 $60 DB ✪

Esprit 2021, Barossa Valley 41/35/21/3% mataro/cinsault/grenache/shiraz. Ripe blueberry and juicy plum notes over layered spices and hints of pressed purple flowers, cherry compote, hazelnuts, dried cranberries and roasting meats with a waft of tobacco and mace further back. Pure and savoury with the finest of tannins and a sense of composure, all the components pulling in the same direction. Just flat-out great drinking. Screw cap. 14% alc. RATING 95 DRINK 2023-2028 $35 DB ✪

Bête Noir Shiraz 2021, Barossa Sports a super-saturated, magenta-splashed hue with aromas of bright plum, black cherry and blueberry fruits cut with hints of violets, ironstone, dark chocolate, smoked meats, cherry confit and earth. There's a ferrous edge to the tight tannins and an acid line that propels the pure fruit briskly across the palate, finishing elegant yet opulent shiraz. Screw cap. 14.5% alc. RATING 95 DRINK 2023-2038 $48 DB ✪

Rosé 2022, Barossa Valley 52/30/16/2% grenache/mataro/shiraz/cinsault. Light salmon in the glass with aromas of nectarine, raspberry and grapefruit plus hints of redcurrant jelly, white flowers, crushed stone and maybe a touch of lanolin. Sapid and fine with a shimmering acid line, savoury palate shape and an endearing lipsmacking briny finish that begs another glass. Screw cap. 12.5% alc. RATING 94 DRINK 2023-2026 $28 DB ✪

Single Vineyard Grenache 2021, Barossa Valley Brilliant crimson in the glass with flashes of purple and notes of juicy plum, raspberry, red cherry and blueberry with hints of fine spice, gingerbread, purple florals, red licorice, earth, cola and lighter tobacco tones. Plenty of space and detail with fine, compact gypsum-like tannins and a brisk acid cadence, finishing savoury, balanced and spice-laden. Screw cap. 14.5% alc. RATING 94 DRINK 2023-2029 $45 DB

🍷🍷🍷🍷🍷 La Cigale 2021, Barossa Valley RATING 92 DRINK 2023-2027 $28 DB ✪

Spring Spur ★★★☆

52 Fredas Lane, Tawonga, Vic 3697 (postal) **Region** Alpine Valleys
T (03) 5754 4849 **www**.springspurwine.com.au **Open** Not **Winemaker** Alex Phillips
Est. 2017 **Dozens** 80
South African-born winemaker Alex Phillips graduated from the University of Stellenbosch in '13, where she was named best academic student: viticulture and oenology and took home the award for best agricultural science student, too. After mentoring under Adam Mason at Mulderbosch Vineyards in Stellenbosch, Alex found her feet as assistant winemaker at Billy Button Wines in the Alpine Valleys (see separate entry). It was here she met her fiancé, Lin. The pair live on Spring Spur — a working horse property in the Kiewa Valley, where Alex brings Spring Spur wines to life.

🍷🍷🍷🍷🍷 Vermentino 2022, King Valley This Sardinian white grape variety is enjoying its new home in the King Valley. It brings out a saline, almond-skin earthiness that suits its savoury nature. Combine that with a tight citrus and apple flavour, a smidge of honeysuckle aromatics and a dry, almost austere finish. This '22 rocks. Screw cap. 12% alc. RATING 90 DRINK 2023-2026 $32 JP

Spring Vale Vineyards ★★★★

130 Spring Vale Road, Cranbrook, Tas 7190 **Region** East Coast Tasmania
T (03) 6257 8208 **www**.springvalewines.com **Open** 7 days 11–4 **Winemaker** Matt
Wood **Viticulturist** Tim Lyne **Est.** 1986 **Dozens** 15 000 **Vyds** 32.5ha
Lyn and Rodney Lyne have progressively established pinot noir (19ha), chardonnay (4ha), pinots gris and meunier (3ha each), syrah (2ha), sauvignon blanc (1ha) and gewürztraminer (0.5ha) since '86. The nearby Melrose vineyard was purchased in 2007. Son Tim, armed with a degree in viticulture and a MBA, is now general manager and viticulturist.

🍷🍷🍷🍷 **Rosé 2022, Tasmania** Pale salmon pink with aromas of ruby red grapefruit, raspberry, redcurrant and watermelon with hints of soft spice, pressed flowers, berry cream, stone, dried herbs and a whiff of red licorice in the distance. There's some nice texture, bright saline acidity and a wash of lightly spiced red and citrus fruits on the finish. Screw cap. 12.5% alc. **RATING** 92 **DRINK** 2023–2026 $32 DB

Melrose Pinot Noir 2022, Tasmania Delicate in the glass, the colour of watered-down Ribena with aromas of redcurrant, red cherry and raspberry fruits cut with exotic spice and pressed purple flowers with light mushroomy and gamey facets. It seems overly spacious and light but I think that is the whole point. I dig it! Screw cap. 13.5% alc. **RATING** 90 **DRINK** 2023–2026 $32 DB

Springs Road Wines ★★★★☆

761 Playford Highway, Cygnet River, Kangaroo Island, SA 5233 **Region** Kangaroo Island **T** 0499 918 448 **www**.springsroad.com.au **Open** 7 days 12–5 Oct–Apr, Wed–Mon 12–4 May–Sept **Winemaker** Joch Bosworth, Scott McIntosh **Viticulturist** Joch Bosworth **Est.** 1994 **Dozens** 4000 **Vyds** 11ha

Springs Road runs east–west across the northern part of Kangaroo Island. The Springs Road vineyards were established in '94 on a small sheep property about 7km west of Kingscote and are now owned and operated by Joch Bosworth and Louise Hemsley-Smith from Battle of Bosworth in McLaren Vale (see separate entry). Small quantities of chardonnay, shiraz, cabernet sauvignon and a cabernet sauvignon shiraz blend are made from the very low-yielding 20yo vines. The vineyards have been managed organically since Louise and Joch took over in '16, and are awaiting certification.

🍷🍷🍷🍷🍷 **Terre Napoléon Shiraz 2021, Kangaroo Island** Fresh, complex and well-structured, yet with straight-out drinkability left intact. This is the kind of savoury-styled wine that you really do want to hook into, within the bounds of price and general alcohol responsibility of course. Black pepper, twiggy spice, cloves and prime cuts of juicy black cherries and plums. Beautiful. Screw cap. 14% alc. **RATING** 96 **DRINK** 2023–2033 $80 CM

Little Island Rosé 2022, Kangaroo Island McLaren Vale A dry style, well made and presented. Spiced strawberry and cherry flavours all juicy and appealing before a textural, well-honed, satisfying finish. It doesn't put a foot wrong. Screw cap. 13% alc. **RATING** 94 **DRINK** 2022–2024 $25 CM ✪

🍷🍷🍷🍷🍷 **Chardonnay 2022, Kangaroo Island RATING** 93 **DRINK** 2022–2027 $35 CM ✪

Squitchy Lane Vineyard ★★★★★

Medhurst Road, Coldstream, Vic 3770 **Region** Yarra Valley **T** (03) 5964 9114 **www**.squitchylane.com.au **Open** Fri–Sun 11–5 **Winemaker** Medhurst Wines **Est.** 1982 **Dozens** 1500 **Vyds** 5.75ha

Mike Fitzpatrick acquired a taste for fine wine while a Rhodes scholar at Oxford University in the '70s. Returning to Australia he guided Carlton Football Club to 2 premierships as captain, then established Melbourne-based finance company Squitchy Lane Holdings. The wines of Mount Mary inspired him to look for his own vineyard and in '96 he found a vineyard of sauvignon blanc, chardonnay, pinot noir, merlot, cabernet franc and cabernet sauvignon, planted in '82, just around the corner from Coldstream Hills and Yarra Yering.

🍷🍷🍷🍷🍷 **SQL Sauvignon Blanc 2019, Yarra Valley** A bright green-gold, this smells of exotic passionfruit and guava complemented by some vanilla and toast from well-handled and well-integrated oak. Textured, grippy, balanced and long, this is an absolutely delicious example of cool-climate, barrel-fermented sauvignon blanc. 115 dozen made. Screw cap. 13% alc. **RATING** 96 **DRINK** 2022–2026 $32 PR ✪

Cabernet Sauvignon Cabernet Franc Merlot 2019, Yarra Valley A medium, bright crimson red. Not a big wine, this is both elegant and concentrated. Dark plums, blackberries, blackcurrant leaf, star anise and some cedar from impeccably handled oak lead onto the medium-bodied palate, which has good depth before finishing with perfectly handled persistent tannins. Screw cap. 13.5% alc. **RATING** 96 **DRINK** 2023-2029 $34 PR ✪

The Key Single Vineyard Chardonnay 2019, Yarra Valley A bright, lemony green-gold hue. Opens with ripe nectarine, a little white peach and some jasmine. Even better on the palate, which is refined with a little grip giving the wine structure on the long, satisfying finish. Screw cap. 13% alc. **RATING** 94 **DRINK** 2022-2028 $58 PR

Stage Door Wine Co ★★★★

22 Whibley Street, Henley Beach, SA 5022 (postal) **Region** Eden Valley
T 0400 991 968 **www**.stagedoorwineco.com.au **Open** Not **Winemaker** Phil Lehmann **Viticulturist** Dan Falkenberg **Est.** 2013 **Dozens** 3000 **Vyds** 32.3ha
Stage Door Wine Co is owned by Graeme Thredgold, a successful musician who changed tack to the liquor industry in the early '90s. He started out in sales with Lion Nathan and SA brewing before venturing into the world of wine as national sales manager for Andrew Garrett in '98. Around '00 he moved on to the more fertile pasture of Tucker Seabrook as state sales manager for SA. Further roles with Barossa Valley Estate and as general manager of Chain of Ponds Wines added to an impressive career in sales and marketing, before he made his final move – to general manager of Eden Hall Wines, which is owned by his sister and brother-in-law, Mardi and David Hall. Grapes are sourced mainly from the family vineyard, plus contract-grown fruit.

🍷🍷🍷🍷🍷 **Riesling 2022, Eden Valley** A little more Christmas lily and freshly squeezed lime, instead of orange blossom, when compared to its '21 sibling. This release seems to have a little more detail and clarity to boot; running on rails of crystalline acidity and displaying a real sense of green apple crunch on the crisp, dry finish. Pretty delicious. Screw cap. 12.9% alc. **RATING** 92 **DRINK** 2023-2028 $25 DB ✪

GSM 2021, Barossa Valley Bright magenta with purple tones. Super-ripe red plum, macerated berry fruits, mulberry and sour cherry on the nose, with hints of clove, cola, pressed flowers, red licorice and berry cream. The wine sports a spacious mouthfeel, a superb chalky tannin profile and is juicy, bouncy and irresistibly easy to drink. Screw cap. 13% alc. **RATING** 92 **DRINK** 2023-2026 $25 DB ✪

Headliner Cabernet Sauvignon 2020, Eden Valley Crimson in the glass with notes of herb-flecked blackberry, blackcurrant and black cherry fruits with hints of baking spices, sage, dried herbs, earth, purple flowers and dark chocolate. A nice balance between the plushness of fruit and structure, with a slight herbal, musky edge to the fruit, crushed-stone tannins and a finish that teeters on the edge of savoury. Screw cap. 14.8% alc. **RATING** 91 **DRINK** 2023-2028 $50 DB

Grüner Veltliner 2022, Eden Valley Light straw in the glass with notes of green apple, lemon, lime and yellow plum with hints of white pepper, crushed quartz, frangipani, Chinese gooseberry, soft spice and guava. Fine, lacy acidity, a touch of lemon curd texture and dry with apple and citrus fruits on the exit. Screw cap. 12.5% alc. **RATING** 90 **DRINK** 2023-2026 $25 DB ✪

Riesling 2021, Eden Valley Pale straw with green flashes and notes of Bickford's lime cordial, orange blossom, green apple, lemon zest, dried mandarin rind, crushed stone and lemon curd. These characters transpose to the palate, which shows plenty of focus, drive and pure lime and green apple fruit. Screw cap. 11% alc. **RATING** 90 **DRINK** 2023-2028 $25 DB ✪

Staniford Wine Co ★★★★

20 Jackson Street, Mount Barker, WA 6324 **Region** Great Southern
T 0405 157 687 **www**.stanifordwineco.com.au **Open** By appt **Winemaker** Michael Staniford **Est.** 2010 **Dozens** 500
Michael Staniford has been making wine in Great Southern since '95, principally as senior winemaker for Alkoomi at Frankland River, with additional experience as a contract maker for other wineries. The business is built around single-vineyard wines; in particular

a chardonnay from a 25+yo vineyard in Albany and a cabernet sauvignon from a 20+yo vineyard in Mount Barker. The quality of these 2 wines is every bit as one would expect.

❦❦❦❦❦ **Reserve Chardonnay 2019, Great Southern** It's a rich and lush chardonnay. Heady scents of ripe rockmelon and nectarine with caramel, sea spray, sugared almond and honey. The palate is slick and round, smooth and toasty with more rockmelon and nectarine, gentle limey acidity, more candied nuts and some honey to finish. In its style, done well. Screw cap. 14% alc. **RATING** 94 **DRINK** 2023-2027 $45 MB

Reserve Cabernet Sauvignon 2018, Great Southern Predominantly cabernet sauvignon with seasoning of merlot/cabernet franc/petit verdot. Mellow, supple red splashed with ripe plum, dark chocolate, mahogany and new leather with succulent, fine tannins tightening the wine gently. Feels regal and elegant, well balanced and generous but with a sense of freshness, too. In great form. Diam. 14% alc. **RATING** 94 **DRINK** 2023-2035 $45 MB

Stanton & Killeen Wines

440 Jacks Road, Murray Valley Highway, Rutherglen, Vic 3685 **Region** Rutherglen **T** (02) 6032 9457 **www**.stantonandkilleen.com.au **Open** Mon–Sat 9–5, Sun & public hols 10–5 **Winemaker** Adriaan Foot **Viticulturist** Ben Rose **Est.** 1875 **Dozens** 15 000 **Vyds** 34ha

In '20, Stanton & Killeen celebrated its 145th anniversary. The business is owned and run by 7th-generation vigneron Natasha Killeen and her mother and CEO, Wendy Killeen. Fortifieds are a strong focus for the winery with around half of its production dedicated to this style. Their vineyards comprise 14 varieties, including 7 Portuguese cultivars used for both fortified and table wine production. A vineyard rejuvenation program has been implemented since '14, focusing on sustainable and environmentally friendly practices. South African winemaker Adriaan Foot joined in Jan '23.

❦❦❦❦❦ **Rare Muscat NV, Rutherglen** Base wines for this Rare Muscat were laid down by the legendary Jack Stanton in the 1960s. A wine to savour, such is the level of immense concentration. Plum pudding, treacle, raisin, licorice, chocolate and walnut intertwine immaculately with an aged nuttiness to close. Rich, sweet and powerful. 375ml. Screw cap. 18.5% alc. **RATING** 97 $145 JP

❦❦❦❦❦ **Grand Muscat NV, Rutherglen** Burnished walnut in hue and blessed with a symmetry of sweet lusciousness and clean spirit. Layer after layer of dark malt biscuit, raisin, fig, prune, walnut, roasted nuts and butterscotch toffee across a silken, supple palate texture. Melt in the mouth stuff. 500ml. Screw cap. 18.5% alc. **RATING** 96 $105 JP

Rare Topaque NV, Rutherglen Rare in name and deed with aged material the basis for an extraordinary wine experience. Walnut-brown amber hues. Malt, burnt toffee and raisin fruitcake aromas with the added depth of complex nutty rancio. Rich, luscious flavours fill the senses with a vein of sweet, cold tea bringing freshness across the palate. Stays with you for a long, long time. 375ml. Screw cap. 18.5% alc. **RATING** 96 $145 JP

Fortitude Durif 2021, Rutherglen Fortitude is dedicated to the late Norman Killeen, who understood the spicier, more elegant side of durif well. Deep, dark, dense and still a little reticent to give away too much yet, but, it's bringing blue fruits, blackberries, a rosemary herbal interplay and a brightness of spice with just a tantalising glimpse of toasty, woodsy oak all rolled up smoothly in even-handed tannins. Screw cap. 14.9% alc. **RATING** 95 **DRINK** 2023-2034 $40 JP ✪

Jack's Block Shiraz 2021, Rutherglen Stanton & Killeen has a history of balancing fleshy, robust, warm-climate shiraz on the one hand, and elegance on the other. While the '21 Jack's Block is notably high-ish in alcohol, it is not immediately obvious. What is obvious are the ripe, sweet blackberries, plums, blackstrap licorice and world of baking and woodsy spice that comes your way. And all are nicely kept in place by ripe tannins and smart oak handling. Classy. Screw cap. 14.9% alc. **RATING** 95 **DRINK** 2023-2035 $50 JP ✪

Grand Topaque NV, Rutherglen This degree of topaque complexity and age reflects both extended barrel age and the winemaker's blending skills at a high level. The result is a luscious deep dive into a rich intensity of plum pudding, orange peel, malt extract, coffee/mocha espresso shot and roasted almond in both depth and concentration of flavour. The finish lasts and lasts and lasts. 500ml. Screw cap. 18.5% alc. RATING 95 $105 JP

Alvarinho 2022, Rutherglen RATING 93 DRINK 2023–2029 $30 JP ✪
Classic Muscat NV, Rutherglen RATING 93 $40 JP
Classic Topaque NV, Rutherglen RATING 92 $40 JP
Shiraz Durif 2021, Rutherglen RATING 91 DRINK 2023–2027 $25 JP ✪
Terra Mãe Tinta Blend 2021, Rutherglen RATING 91 DRINK 2023–2028 $32 JP
Muscat NV, Rutherglen RATING 91 $25 JP ✪
Méthode Traditionnelle Tempranillo 2021, Rutherglen RATING 90 DRINK 2023–2023 $40 JP
Arinto 2022, Rutherglen RATING 90 DRINK 2023–2026 $30 JP
Topaque NV, Rutherglen RATING 90 $25 JP ✪

Stargazer Wine

37 Rosewood Lane, Tea Tree, Tas 7017 **Region** Tasmania
T 0408 173 335 www.stargazerwine.com.au **Open** By appt **Winemaker** Samantha Connew **Viticulturist** Samantha Connew, Bryn Williams **Est.** 2012 **Dozens** 2500 **Vyds** 5ha

Samantha Connew obtained a Postgraduate Diploma of Oenology and Viticulture from Lincoln University, Canterbury, NZ, before moving to Australia. Here she undertook the Advanced Wine Assessment course at the Australian Wine Research Institute in '00, was chosen as a scholar at the '02 Len Evans Tutorial, won the George Mackey Award for the best wine exported from Australia in '04 and was awarded International Red Winemaker of the Year at the International Wine Challenge, London in '07. After a highly successful and lengthy position as chief winemaker at Wirra Wirra, Sam moved to Tasmania (via the Hunter Valley) to make the first wines for her own business, something she said she would never do. The emotive name (and label) is in part a tribute to Abel Tasman, the first European to sight Tasmania before proceeding to the South Island of NZ, navigating by the stars.

Palisander Vineyard Riesling 2021, Tasmania Notes of white peach, nectarine, soft spice, lemon curd, orange blossom, marzipan and crushed stone. There is a slightly exotic edge to the fruit on the palate, perhaps a waft of guava and incoming rain, all on a crystalline kinetic acid framework that's both precise and welcoming. Impressive clarity and detail, as with all of Sam Connew's wines. Screw cap. 12.7% alc. RATING 97 DRINK 2023–2030 $45 DB ✪ ♥
Palisander Vineyard Pinot Noir 2021, Tasmania Perfectly poised and walking confidently on a line of funk and fruit purity. Bright red cherry, strawberry, poached rhubarb and pomegranate with layers of exotic spice, mushroom broth and a waft of amaro-esque herbs. Long of finish, with fine tannins and a complex vapour trail that leaves a mesmerizing wake. It's looking terrific. Diam. 12.8% alc. RATING 97 DRINK 2022–2032 $55 DB ✪ ♥

Tupelo 2022, Tasmania 37/34/22/7% pinot gris/riesling/pinot blanc/ gewürztraminer. Supple and heady with skin-contact textural slinkiness, a sapid, briny sense of umami and a whole lot of joyful imbibement within. Nothing out of place, everybody in tune and playing the same song, it makes for a captivating drink. A stunning white blend. Screw cap. 12.2% alc. RATING 96 DRINK 2023–2027 $35 DB ✪
Coal River Valley Riesling 2022, Tasmania There's almost a Germanic feel to this wine with its pristine white peach, lime juice and green apple crunch, along with hints of beeswax, almond blossom, makrut lime, Epsom salts and sea spray. Precise and focused with crystalline acidity and pitch-perfect tension as it saunters the ridgeline of fruit sweetness and acidity finishing dry with impressive

detail, clarity and drive. Astounding value. Screw cap. 11.8% alc. **RATING** 96 **DRINK** 2023–2030 $35 DB ✪

Rada Pinot Meunier Pinot Noir 2022, Tasmania Light, airy ruby in the glass, it's immediately a very pretty and complex-smelling wine. Aromas of redcurrant and cranberry, exotic spices, pressed purple flowers, amaro herbs, rhubarb and dried tangerine peel draw you into the glass. Spacious and precise with a diaphanous fruit presence and wisps of gamey complexity as it makes its endearing journey across the palate. Just lovely. Screw cap. 13% alc. **RATING** 94 **DRINK** 2023–2027 $35 DB ✪

Chardonnay 2021, Tasmania Bright, detailed white peach and citrus fruits with just a hint of orange blossom, marzipan, grapefruit, crushed stone, lemon barley and gentle oak spice. Composed, pure and detailed with a swift acid cadence and a lovely wash of bright, peachy fruit and spice on the exit. Screw cap. 13.5% alc. **RATING** 94 **DRINK** 2023–2028 $65 DB

Steels Creek Estate

1 Sewell Road, Steels Creek, Vic 3775 **Region** Yarra Valley
T (03) 5965 2448 www.steelscreekestate.com.au **Open** Sat–Mon & public hols 10–6
Winemaker Simon Peirce **Viticulturist** Simon Peirce **Est.** 1981 **Dozens** 400 **Vyds** 1.7ha
The Steels Creek vineyard (chardonnay, shiraz, cabernet sauvignon, cabernet franc and colombard), family-operated since 1981, is located in the picturesque Steels Creek Valley. All the wines are made onsite by winemaker and owner Simon Peirce.

🍷🍷🍷🍷🍷 **Single Vineyard Cabernet Sauvignon 2021, Yarra Valley** A medium and bright crimson ruby. Aromas of cassis, blackberries, cedar and a waft of crushed violets. Medium to full bodied, this is nicely concentrated with fine and persistent tannins perfectly integrated. Very well balanced, this will reward those wanting to put a few bottles of this well-priced single-vineyard Yarra cabernet in their cellar. Agglomerate. 13% alc. **RATING** 95 **DRINK** 2023–2030 $40 PR ✪

🍷🍷🍷🍷🍷 **Cabernet Franc 2021, Yarra Valley RATING** 92 **DRINK** 2023–2028 $36 PR
Single Vineyard Shiraz 2021, Yarra Valley RATING 91 **DRINK** 2023–2030 $40 PR

Stefano Lubiana

60 Rowbottoms Road, Granton, Tas 7030 **Region** Southern Tasmania
T (03) 6263 7457 www.slw.com.au **Open** Wed–Sun 11–4 **Winemaker** Steve Lubiana
Est. 1990 **Vyds** 26ha
Monique and Steve Lubiana moved from the inland of Australia to the banks of the Derwent River in 1990 to pursue Steve's dream of making high quality sparkling wine. The sloping site allowed them to build a gravity-fed winery and his whole winemaking approach since that time has been based on attention to detail within a biodynamic environment. The first sparkling wines were made in '93 from the initial plantings of chardonnay and pinot noir. Over the years they have added riesling, sauvignon blanc, pinot gris and merlot. The Italian-inspired Osteria restaurant is based on their own biodynamically grown produce, free-range meats are from local farmers and the seafood is wild-caught. In '16 the Lubianas purchased the Panorama vineyard, first planted in '74, in the Huon Valley.

🍷🍷🍷🍷🍷 **Grande Vintage 2011, Tasmania** 50/50% chardonnay/pinot noir. Pale in the glass with a fine, energetic bead and mousse. Aromas of crunchy green apple, nashi pear and citrus fruits with hints of brioche, mushroom, white flowers, flint, toast, almond paste, roast chestnuts and meal. Long, savoury and true with mineral drive and toasty complexity, finishing very long with a saline, acid cadence. Wonderful drinking. Diam. 12.5% alc. **RATING** 96 **DRINK** 2023–2033 $86 DB
Late Disgorged 2008, Tasmania 60/40% chardonnay/pinot noir. Pale straw with a vibrant, energetic bead and mousse. Aromas of green apple and crunchy red fruits dotted with tones of soft spice, clotted cream, fresh brioche, white

flowers, crushed stone, dried shiitake and light lemon curd notes. Complex creamy notes abound on the palate and the finish is long, with lemon and fresh pastry notes for days. Diam. 12.5% alc. RATING 96 DRINK 2023–2033 $90 DB

La Roccia Pinot Noir 2021, Tasmania Another Lubiana single-block wine that wows with complexity and a vivid line. Mid-ruby in the glass with wild cherry fruits speckled with amaro herbs and exotic spices, dried tangerine rind, Chinese barbecue, shiitake, rhubarb and turned earth. Chewy tannin support and a vivid acid line provide tension and cadence, finishing long, true and pure. Cork. 13.5% alc. RATING 96 DRINK 2023–2033 $93 DB

Il Giardino Pinot Noir 2021, Tasmania A wildly expressive pinot noir. Mid-ruby in the glass with characters of wild cherries and strawberries, jasmine, leaf litter, Peking duck, exotic spices, amaro, mushroom risotto, dried citrus rind and turned earth. Sleek and savoury with a pitch-perfect composition fading slowly off into the distance with an array of wild berries, spice and game notes. Cork. 13.5% alc. RATING 95 DRINK 2023–2033 $93 DB

Sasso Pinot Noir 2021, Tasmania Striking for its complex aromatic depth. The fruit is pure and true: all red and dark cherry and red plums set on a bed of exotic spices with hints of leaf litter, Chinese barbecue, shiitake broth, pressed purple flowers and earth. Plenty of fruit depth and amaro–edged complexity with tight, grainy tannins, a touch of game and a long finish with driving sour cherry acidity. Lovely stuff. Cork. 13.5% alc. RATING 95 DRINK 2023–2030 $129 DB

Pinot Noir 2021, Tasmania Aromas of spiced red and dark cherries and raspberry top notes. Hints of exotic spices, jasmine, mushroom broth, sous bois, hanging game and earth. Mouth-filling and pure with everything you could ask from a Tasmanian pinot, finishing long, pure, savoury, complex and poised beautifully. Screw cap. 13% alc. RATING 95 DRINK 2023–2030 $70 DB

Estate Chardonnay 2021, Tasmania Wonderfully pure and taut with ripe white peach, grapefruit and lemon fruits stretched on a canvas of stone and soft spice. Hints of nougat, almond blossom, toasted hazelnuts, crème fraîche, softly spoken French oak and a dab of oatmeal and flint. Clarity and tension are both bang on and the wine glides onwards with great balance. Screw cap. 13% alc. RATING 95 DRINK 2023–2028 $70 DB

Riesling 2022, Tasmania Pale straw in the glass, the wine is all fresh lime and green apple crunch with hints of crushed stone, white flowers, makrut lime and a whiff of fennel. There is just a squeak of phenolic texture before the wine coils and zooms off thanks to a bright line of sherbety acidity leaving a wake of almond blossom, apple and lime as it retreats. Screw cap. 12.5% alc. RATING 94 DRINK 2023–2028 $40 DB ✪

Ruscello Pinot Noir 2021, Tasmania There is a touch more aromatic richness here compared to the other single-vineyard offerings along with a touch of sour cherry. Interestingly, the tannin profile is akin to gravel dust, providing gentle support, and the wine fades with an array of exotic spices, red fruits and sous bois notes. Cork. 13.5% alc. RATING 94 DRINK 2023–2030 $93 DB

🍷🍷🍷🍷🍷 **Primavera Pinot Noir 2021, Tasmania** RATING 92 DRINK 2023–2028 $40 DB
Pinot Gris 2022, Tasmania RATING 91 DRINK 2023–2026 $45 DB
Grüner Veltliner 2022, Tasmania RATING 91 DRINK 2023–2026 $41 DB

Stella Bella Wines ★★★★★

205 Rosabrook Road, Margaret River, WA 6285 **Region** Margaret River
T (08) 9758 8611 **www**.stellabella.com.au **Open** 7 days 10–5 **Winemaker** Luke Jolliffe
Viticulturist James Hayward **Est.** 1996 **Dozens** 40 000 **Vyds** 55.7ha
This enormously successful winemaking business produces wines of true regional expression with fruit sourced from the central and southern parts of Margaret River. The company owns and operates 6 vineyards, and also purchases fruit from small contract growers. Substantial quantities of wine covering all styles and pricepoints make this an important producer for Margaret River.

ŶŶŶŶŶ **Luminosa Chardonnay 2021, Margaret River** This vintage is up there as one of the finest to date, the pared-back winemaking allowing the excellent fruit to take center stage but not entirely on its own. This is flinty, funky, yet oh-so-fine. Brimming with grapefruit, beautifully balanced oak adding spice and depth. This lingers long, leaving a lasting impression. Surprisingly approachable now, but will last some distance. Screw cap. 13% alc. RATING 97 DRINK 2022–2032 $100 JF

ŶŶŶŶŶ **Suckfizzle Chardonnay 2021, Margaret River** Tightly focused with smokin' sulphides, grapefruit and spice. Mouth-watering acidity drives the palate, which is detailed and complex but all of that aside, and most importantly, it's a fabulous drink. According to the back label, 'Suckfizzle Chardonnay says kiss my arse.' Each to their own. Screw cap. 13.1% alc. RATING 96 DRINK 2022–2031 $90 JF
Luminosa Cabernet Sauvignon 2020, Margaret River A beautifully composed wine with everything in balance. It feels light yet is medium bodied with elegant silky tannins, supple and sweet fruit and a long, gentle finish. Impressive. Screw cap. 13.5% alc. RATING 96 DRINK 2023–2038 $110 JF
Suckfizzle Cabernet Sauvignon 2020, Margaret River Everything a Margaret River cabernet sauvignon should be: medium bodied, elegant, long and pure. Wafts of violets, mulberries and blueberries all spiced up with French oak adding flavour as much as tannins that end up textural and fine. Screw cap. 14.3% alc. RATING 95 DRINK 2023–2038 $70 JF

ŶŶŶŶŶ **Suckfizzle Sauvignon Blanc Semillon 2021, Margaret River** RATING 93 DRINK 2023–2031 $50 JF
Otro Vino Pinot Gris 2022, Margaret River RATING 92 DRINK 2022–2025 $27 JF ✪
Otro Vino Rosé 2022, Margaret River RATING 92 DRINK 2022–2023 $27 JF ✪
Otro Vino The Italian Sangiovese 2022, Margaret River RATING 92 DRINK 2022–2027 $35 JF
Shiraz 2021, Margaret River RATING 92 DRINK 2023–2033 $38 JF
Cabernet Sauvignon 2020, Margaret River RATING 92 DRINK 2022–2025 $38 JF
Sauvignon Blanc 2022, Margaret River RATING 90 DRINK 2022–2026 $27 JF
Semilon Sauvignon Blanc 2022, Margaret River RATING 90 DRINK 2022–2025 $27 JF
Otro Vino Chardonnay 2021, Margaret River RATING 90 DRINK 2022–2026 $27 JF
Chardonnay 2021, Margaret River RATING 90 DRINK 2023–2030 $38 JF
Skuttlebutt Cabernet Sauvignon Shiraz 2020, Margaret River RATING 90 DRINK 2022–2025 $20 JF ✪

Steve Wiblin's Erin Eyes   ★★★★

58 Old Road, Leasingham, SA 5452 (postal) **Region** Clare Valley
T 0418 845 120 **www**.erineyes.com.au **Open** Not **Winemaker** Steve Wiblin **Est.** 2009
Dozens 2500

Steve Wiblin became a winemaker after encouragement from his mentor at Tooheys Brewery who had a love of fine wine. Because Tooheys owned Wynns and Seaview, the change in career from beer to wine was easy. Steve moved from the world of big wineries to small when he co-founded Neagles Rock in '97. In '09 he left Neagles Rock and established Erin Eyes explaining, 'In 1842 my English convict forebear John Wiblin gazed into a pair of Erin eyes. That gaze changed our family make-up and history forever. In the Irish-influenced Clare Valley, what else would I call my wines but Erin Eyes?'

ŶŶŶŶŶ **Pride of Erin Single Vineyard Reserve Riesling 2022, Clare Valley** A zesty, herbal riesling of concentrated flavour profile and racy, tightly packed texture. Scents of lemon blossom, green apple and talc. Limey and zingy in the palate, a lick of blackcurrant and some flinty elements in the mix. Quite a detailed riesling with good extension of flavour, too. Feels apt for the region in its compact and racy way. Screw cap. 11.5% alc. RATING 93 DRINK 2022–2034 $40 MB

Stilvi

PO Box 116, Dromana, Vic 3936 **Region** Mornington Peninsula
T 0408 811 072 **www**.stilviwines.com.au **Open** By appt **Winemaker** Tim Elphick
Est. 2020 **Dozens** 600

Tim Elphick calls Stilvi his Peninsula passion project. That is, small-batch winemaking, both modern and ancient techniques from skin contact to clay vessels, all in a bid to create interesting wine and conversation. It's early days, with Tim sourcing fruit from various sites, mostly pinot gris, with pinot noir and chardonnay soon to be added. After 11 years as winemaker at Portsea Estate, he quit in '21 to concentrate on Stilvi, which means 'shimmering light' or 'shine' in Greek. As it turns out, one of his favourite Greek rock bands, Pyx Lax, released an album called *Stilvi* in '98. The wine is a delightful collaboration with his teenage daughter Kalypso, who designed the labels.

🍷🍷🍷🍷🍷 **Jungle Freak Single Vineyard Pinot Gris 2022, Mornington Peninsula**
Three weeks on skins have allowed not just a lovely blush of copper to infuse the wine but loads of fragrance and texture, too. Heady with white blossom, ginger flower and powdered ginger with the well-modulated palate ebbing and flowing with flavour: ripe pears, baked apple pie and some fine chewy tannins to stretch out the palate. This is a beauty. Screw cap. 12.5% alc. **RATING** 95 **DRINK** 2023–2030 $35 JF ✪

🍷🍷🍷🍷🍷 **Kalypso Field Blend 2022, Mornington Peninsula RATING** 91
DRINK 2023–2026 $38 JF

Stockman's Ridge Wines

21 Boree Lane, Lidster, NSW 2800 **Region** Orange
T (02) 6365 6212 **www**.stockmansridge.com.au **Open** Mon 12–5, Fri 11–5, Sat 11–8, Sun 11–5 **Winemaker** Will Rickard-Bell **Viticulturist** Jonathan Hambrook **Est.** 2002
Dozens 2500 **Vyds** 5ha

Stockman's Ridge is a handy operation in Orange, providing a swag of well-crafted wines from the usual cadre of varieties. The dark horses are the grüner veltliner and zinfandel, grown at circa 800m elevation. The 'groovy grüner' (as American sommeliers called it in the late '90s when its fashionability rose to a crescendo) is pungent and fresh, an easy hop, skip and a jump for riesling drinkers. Live music happens on weekends and accommodation is available at the onsite Swagman Homestead.

🍷🍷🍷🍷🍷 **Outlaw Grüner Veltliner 2022, Orange** Nashi pear, lime pith and powdered chalk on the nose with white nectarine flesh, celery heart and a touch of sea spray. The saline element is a nice complement to the bright fruit weight. A wine showing promise. Screw cap. 11.5% alc. **RATING** 92 **DRINK** 2023–2026 $35 SW

Stoke Wines

98 Sneyd Road, Mount Jagged, SA 5211 **Region** Kangaroo Island
T 0407 389 130 **www**.stokewines.au **www**.guroowine.com.au **Open** Summer weekends
Winemaker Nick Dugmore, Rebecca Dugmore **Est.** 2016 **Dozens** 600 **Vyds** 4.2ha

Stoke Wines belongs to wife-and-husband team Rebecca and Nick Dugmore. Nick's love affair with Kangaroo Island began on a surf trip around Australia in '08. Kangaroo Island was the first stop, the rest of the itinerary is still awaiting completion. A 4.2ha vineyard near Stokes Bay is farmed regeneratively, wines are made on the mainland at Mount Jagged. The Guroo project is a rolling guest winemaker series that pairs a varietal 'guru' with the same fruit for 3 consecutive vintages. The inaugural Guroo was Charlotte Hardy of Charlotte Dalton Wines (from '19); Stephen George of Ashton Hills and Wendouree was the second winemaker to join the project in '21, with Sue Bell of Bellwether Wines in the Coonawarra coming onboard in '22. Steve Crawford of Frederick Stevenson Wines (Barossa/Adelaide Hills) is up next, his first vintage will be '23.

🍷🍷🍷🍷🍷 **Guroo Cabernet Sauvignon 2021, Kangaroo Island** It's a strange marriage that has a totally splendid outcome: Stephen George, a master winemaker of pinot noir, making a come-hither, diaphanous cabernet sauvignon that can sensibly be enjoyed tonight or in 5 years time – the sooner, the better. Screw cap. 13.5% alc. RATING 92 DRINK 2023–2028 $50 JH

Guroo Pinot Noir 2022, Kangaroo Island Guest winemaker Stephen George puts a stamp of authenticity on the wine. The result is a pretty pinot, with cherry and plum aromas and flavours. It's a curious matter that Kangaroo Island hasn't been home to more makers of pinot. Screw cap. 13% alc. RATING 91 DRINK 2023–2028 $50 JH

Guroo Syrah 2021, Kangaroo Island Made by Charlotte Dalton. Medium bodied-plus, but has good line, length and balance to the supple, fruit-driven wine. The flavours have the imprint of the high-quality vintage, with softly spiced plum fruit and easygoing tannins and oak. Screw cap. 13.5% alc. RATING 91 DRINK 2023–2033 $50 JH

Stomp Wines ★★★★★

504 Wilderness Road, Lovedale, NSW 2325 **Region** Hunter Valley
T 0409 774 280 **www**.stompwines.com.au **Open** Thurs–Mon 10–5
Winemaker Michael McManus **Est.** 2004 **Dozens** 15 000
After a seeming lifetime in the food and beverage industry, Michael and Meredith McManus moved to full-time winemaking. They set up Stomp Winemaking, a contract winemaker designed to keep small and larger parcels of grapes separate through the fermentation and maturation process, thus meeting the needs of boutique wine producers in the Hunter Valley. The addition of their own Stomp label is a small but important part of their business.

Limited Release Shiraz 2021, Hunter Valley An attractive wine, the oak and fruit fused together on a medium-bodied palate. Good line, length and balance. Screw cap. 13.5% alc. RATING 95 DRINK 2023–2033 $70 JH

Museum Release Limited Release Shiraz 2017, Hunter Valley This has slimmed down since first tasted as a new release in March '19, the tannins absorbed, its fruit line and finish excellent. Retains its best features from the prior tasting. Screw cap. 14.5% alc. RATING 95 DRINK 2023–2035 $70 JH

Limited Release Fiano 2022, Hunter Valley No-frills winemaking gives fiano the chance to express itself without enhancements such as oak. It has texture and structure all of its own, the aroma and flavour pitched between that of riesling and chardonnay. It presses my button every time I taste it. Screw cap. 12.5% alc. RATING 94 DRINK 2023–2028 $28 JH ✪

Semillon 2022, Hunter Valley RATING 93 DRINK 2023–2043 $28 JH ✪
Chardonnay 2022, Hunter Valley RATING 90 DRINK 2023–2026 $28 JH

Stoney Rise ★★★★☆

96 Hendersons Lane, Gravelly Beach, Tas 7276 **Region** Northern Tasmania
T (03) 6394 3678 **www**.stoneyrise.com **Open** Thurs–Mon 10–5 **Winemaker** Joe Holyman **Est.** 2000 **Dozens** 2000 **Vyds** 7.2ha
The Holyman family had been involved in vineyards in Tasmania for 20 years, but Joe Holyman's career in the wine industry – first as a sales rep, then as a wine buyer and more recently working in wineries in NZ, Portugal, France, Mount Benson and Coonawarra – gave him an exceptionally broad-based understanding of wine. In '04 Joe and wife Lou purchased the former Rotherhythe vineyard, which had been established in '86, and set about restoring it to its former glory. There are 2 ranges: the Stoney Rise wines, focusing on fruit and early drinkability; and the Holyman wines – with more structure, more new oak and the best grapes, here the focus is on length and potential longevity. In '21, the duo opened a new tasting room/wine bar onsite, designed by local studio Cumulus.

Holyman Pinot Noir 2021, Tasmania Joe Holyman isn't going to put anything other than statutory stuff on the back label – certainly no vinification clues – and he doesn't provide the information voluntarily. This is a very enjoyable pinot, red and black cherries riding high, whole bunches not obvious. A very good vintage. Screw cap. 12% alc. RATING 95 DRINK 2023-2031 $60 JH

Chardonnay 2022, Tasmania There is precision and oodles of interest with some funky marzipan and parmesan-rind notes that flitter above the keenly honed lemon and grapefruit tones. Just a whiff of some struck flint in there, too. Clarity and tension via a crystalline acid profile, and there is a hint of curds and whey before the wine focuses and zips off with memories of softly spiced citrus fruits. Very nice. Screw cap. 11.5% alc. RATING 94 DRINK 2023-2027 $32 DB ✪

Grüner Veltliner 2022, Tasmania Grüner veltliner of sizzling, sapid focus and drive. Pale straw in the glass with green flashes and notes of crunchy green apples and citrus dusted with hints of crushed stone, white pepper, petrichor, spent yeast, dried herbs and white flowers. There's a searing acid structure here that provides a super-crisp, saliva-inducing ride with a dry, savoury finish. Yeah! Screw cap. 11.5% alc. RATING 94 DRINK 2023-2025 $32 DB ✪

Pinot Noir 2021, Tasmania The bouquet is attractive and right on the money varietally, with spicy/savoury/stemmy nuances looking, says winemaker Joe Holyman (via the wine's back label), for a haggis dim sim to share it with. Screw cap. 12% alc. RATING 94 DRINK 2023-2032 $32 JH ✪

Holyman Chardonnay 2021, Tasmania This has what it takes. It's relatively light bodied with excellent length and drive, the varietal fruit expression largely in the citrus arena, but also encompassing stone fruit. The barrel-fermented oak inputs are negligible, the acidity also balanced. Screw cap. 12.5% alc. RATING 94 DRINK 2023-2031 $60 JH

Holyman Project X Pinot Noir 2019, Tasmania A very good vintage. Typical Tasmanian clarity and retention of primary colour. It handles the new oak well, but there's a faint whisper of green to the otherwise elegant and long palate. Screw cap. 12% alc. RATING 94 DRINK 2023-2034 $90 JH

🍷🍷🍷🍷♀ **Savagnin 2022, Tasmania** RATING 93 DRINK 2023-2026 $40 DB
No Clothes Gris Friulano 2022, Tasmania RATING 90 DRINK 2023-2025 $32 DB

Stonier Wines ★★★★★

Cnr Thompson's Lane/Frankston-Flinders Road, Merricks, Vic 3916
Region Mornington Peninsula
T (03) 5989 8300 **www.**stonier.com.au **Open** 7 days 11–5 **Winemaker** Justin Purser
Viticulturist Tim Brown, Alex McLean **Est.** 1978 **Dozens** 15 000 **Vyds** 40ha
This may be one of the most senior wineries on the Mornington Peninsula but that does not stop it from moving with the times. It has embarked on a serious sustainability program that touches on all aspects of its operations. It is one of the few wineries in Australia to measure its carbon footprint in detail, using the officially recognised system of the Winemaker's Federation of Australia. It is steadily reducing its consumption of electricity; it uses rainwater, collected from the winery roof; it has created a balanced ecosystem in the vineyard by strategic planting of cover crops and reduction of sprays; and it has reduced its need to irrigate. Justin Purser took over as head winemaker in '22. Later that same year, Stonier was purchased from Accolade by Circe Wines, owned by 3 local families.

🍷🍷🍷🍷🍷 **Reserve Pinot Noir 2022, Mornington Peninsula** As expected given it's a reserve, there's more depth and detail with cherry-picked fruit off the best vineyards around Merricks and Red Hill. The 40% whole bunches in the ferment have added a lift to the already heady aromas of autumn leaves damp from rain, dark cherries, woodsy spices and cedary oak. The palate is fuller-bodied, plush with ripe, velvety tannins, textural, too, and the finish lingers and lingers. Screw cap. 13.5% alc. RATING 96 DRINK 2023-2035 $70 JF ✪

KBS Vineyard Chardonnay 2022, Mornington Peninsula There's a generosity to the Stonier chardonnays and it's on show here. Quince and white peach infused with lemon juice and zest, lemon curd and nutty/creamy lees flavours then warm spices and oak come into play. There's a lot going on flavour-wise, yet everything is neatly in place with the palate supple and smooth and the finish long and convincing. Screw cap. 13.5% alc. RATING 95 DRINK 2023–2031 $70 JF

Pinot Noir 2022, Mornington Peninsula Upfront cherries and pips, lightly spiced with blood orange and zest with wafts of forest floor and savoury oak. Sweet fruit, supple tannins and uplifting acidity glide across the palate. It tastes so good. Screw cap. 13.5% alc. RATING 95 DRINK 2023–2032 $40 JF ✪

Reserve Chardonnay 2022, Mornington Peninsula Detail, complexity and deliciousness in equal measure. Expect stone fruit mingling with citrus, creamy lees with spicy oak and the acidity keeping the palate finely tuned. Fleshy, fuller-bodied and luscious yet it feels quite effortless and is satisfying through to the long finish. Screw cap. 13.5% alc. RATING 95 DRINK 2023–2030 $70 JF

Gainsborough Park Vineyard Chardonnay 2022, Mornington Peninsula Gosh, heady aromas do tease with florals, ginger-infused green tea and exotic spices, from cinnamon and star anise to cardamom. Then the palate, with its siren call of stone fruit, citrus and oak spices, seduces. There's succulence throughout, layers of flavour and the result is a satisfying wine. Screw cap. 13% alc. RATING 95 DRINK 2023–2032 $70 JF

🍷🍷🍷🍷 Chardonnay 2022, Mornington Peninsula RATING 93 DRINK 2023–2030 $40 JF

W-WB Pinot Noir 2022, Mornington Peninsula RATING 91 DRINK 2024–2030 $70 JF

Stormflower Vineyard   ★★★★☆

3503 Caves Road, Wilyabrup, WA 6280 **Region** Margaret River
T 0421 867 488 **www**.stormflower.com.au **Open** 7 days 11–5 **Winemaker** Joel Page
Viticulturist Joel Page **Est.** 2007 **Dozens** 2800 **Vyds** 10ha

Stormflower Vineyard was founded by David Martin, Howard Cearns and Nic Trimboli, 3 friends better known as co-founders of Little Creatures Brewery in Fremantle. They thought the location of the vineyard (planted in the mid '90s) was ideal for producing high-quality wines. They pulled out one-third of the vines planted in the wrong way, in the wrong place, leaving almost 10ha of cabernet sauvignon, shiraz, chardonnay, sauvignon blanc, semillon and chenin blanc in place. Now the sole owner, David Martin is the driving force in the vineyard, with a family background in agriculture. The vineyard, certified organic in '16, is managed using natural soil biology and organic compost. A new winery was completed just in time for the '20 vintage, with all wines now made onsite.

🍷🍷🍷🍷🍷 **Wilyabrup Chardonnay 2022, Margaret River** The combination of stone fruit and citrus flavours, the lemon curd and cashew-like lees, the sweet cedary oak, the hint of sulphides and slip of texture on the finish all add up to a delicious wine. The palate fleshes out but is curtailed by fine acidity, which also extends the length. Screw cap. 13.7% alc. RATING 95 DRINK 2023–2030 $50 JF ✪

Wilyabrup Sauvignon Blanc 2022, Margaret River A terrific wine that goes down a savoury route with a focus on the palate. It tastes of some complex barrel fermentation – the creamy lees, the nuttiness, the lovely texture. There's a nod to tropical fruit, but it's all in the background with lively acidity ensuring it lingers. Screw cap. 13.6% alc. RATING 94 DRINK 2022–2026 $30 JF ✪

🍷🍷🍷🍷 **Wilyabrup Semillon Sauvignon Blanc 2022, Margaret River** RATING 93 DRINK 2022–2024 $30 JF ✪

Wilyabrup Cabernet Sauvignon 2020, Margaret River RATING 90 DRINK 2024–2030 $65 JF

Wilyabrup Shiraz 2020, Margaret River RATING 90 DRINK 2023–2027 $40 JF

Studley Park Vineyard ★★★☆

5 Garden Terrace, Kew, Vic 3101 (postal) **Region** Port Phillip
T (03) 9852 8483 **www**.studleypark.com.au **Open** Not **Winemaker** Llew Knight
(Contract) **Est.** 1994 **Dozens** 500 **Vyds** 0.5ha

Geoff Pryor's Studley Park Vineyard is one of Melbourne's best-kept secrets. It is on a bend
of the Yarra River barely 4km from the Melbourne CBD, on a 0.5ha block once planted to
vines, but for a century used for market gardening, then replanted with cabernet sauvignon.
Immediately across the river is the epicentre of Melbourne's light industrial development,
while on the northern and eastern boundaries are suburban residential blocks.

🍷🍷🍷🍷♀ **Rosé 2022, Port Phillip** A luminous salmon pink. A ripe rosé with aromas of
cranberries, pomegranates, orange pith and spice. Drier (and better for it) and
more textured than the previous vintage, I like the balance between the fruit and
the wine's bright acidity. A lovely effort from one of Melbourne's most unusual
vineyards. Screw cap. 12.5% alc. **RATING** 92 **DRINK** 2022–2025 $20 PR ✪

SubRosa ★★★★☆

PO Box 181, Ararat, Vic 3377 **Region** Various
T 0478 072 259 **www**.subrosawine.com **Open** Not **Winemaker** Adam Louder
Est. 2013 **Dozens** 400

SubRosa was created by 2 high-performing partners in life and in this exceptional new
winery. Adam Louder had completed 31 vintages in the Grampians, Pyrenees, Margaret
River, Bordeaux and the Napa Valley, most with famous names. He met Gold Coast–born
partner Nancy Panter in the Napa Valley in '11 while she was working on projects that
included the Olympic Games, FIFA World Cup and NFL. After the '12 London Olympics,
she and Adam moved between the US and Australia, returning permanently to Australia in
'15, having laid the ground work for SubRosa in '13.

🍷🍷🍷🍷🍷 **Viognier 2021, Grampians** A rich, viscous expression of this variety and an
excellent one, too. This is a powerful white wine. Grilled stone fruit and wild
flings of spice meet toast, butterscotch and quartz. Length, power and dare – this
wine has it all. Screw cap. 14.5% alc. **RATING** 95 **DRINK** 2024–2028 $48 CM ✪
Shiraz 2019, Grampians Pyrenees This floods the palate with sweet, ripe,
plum, although mint, florals, cedar and smoked spice notes are swept along with
it. It's as accomplished as it is seductive, the finesse of its tannin yet another quality
marker. Screw cap. 14.5% alc. **RATING** 94 **DRINK** 2023–2031 $35 CM ✪

🍷🍷🍷🍷♀ **Malakoff Estate Shiraz 2019, Pyrenees RATING** 93 **DRINK** 2024–2032
$48 CM
Nebbiolo 2019, Pyrenees RATING 92 **DRINK** 2023–2030 $48 CM

Surveyors Hill Vineyards ★★★★

215 Brooklands Road, Wallaroo, NSW 2618 **Region** Canberra District
T (02) 6230 2046 **www**.surveyorshill.com.au **Open** W'ends & public hols 11.30–3
Winemaker Brian Sinclair, Greg Gallagher **Est.** 1996 **Vyds** 10ha

Surveyors Hill Vineyards is on the slopes of the eponymous hill, at 550m–680m above sea
level. It is an ancient volcano, producing granite-derived, coarse-structured (and hence well
drained) sandy soils of low fertility. This has to be the ultimate patchwork-quilt vineyard with
1ha each of chardonnay, shiraz and viognier; 0.5ha each of roussanne, marsanne, aglianico,
nero d'Avola, mourvèdre, grenache, muscadelle, moscato giallo, cabernet franc, riesling,
semillon, sauvignon blanc, touriga nacional and cabernet sauvignon.

🍷🍷🍷🍷♀ **Cabernet Franc 2019, Canberra District** This works. Fragrant with florals,
spice and red fruits, just enough to know it's cab franc. The palate works off
medium-bodied with supple, attractive, shapely and ripe tannins. There's a
gentleness to this and it's appealing as a result. Screw cap. 14.5% alc. **RATING** 91
DRINK 2022–2027 $30 JF

Tinto Garnacha Graciano Tempranillo 2019, Canberra District A savoury and enjoyable blend. A light mix of red fruits and spice, a slight trace of charred radicchio with supple tannins and refreshing throughout. Screw cap. 14% alc. **RATING** 91 **DRINK** 2022–2026 $24 JF ✪

Sussex Squire Wines   ★★★★

293–295 Spring Gully Road, Gillentown, SA 5453 **Region** Clare Valley
T 0458 141 169 **www**.sussexsquire.com.au **Open** 7 days 11–4 **Winemaker** Daniel
Wilson, Mark Bollen **Viticulturist** Mark Bollen **Est.** 2014 **Dozens** 1200 **Vyds** 7.5ha
Fourth-generation farmers Mark and Skye Bollen purchased 5ha of '98-planted shiraz in the
Clare Valley in '14. It's now dry-grown and organically managed, while 0.5ha each of nero
d'Avola, sangiovese, mataro, grenache and malbec have also been added. A flock of Black
Suffolk sheep roam the vineyard during winter to provide natural weed control and fertilise
the soil.

🍷🍷🍷🍷🍷 **Thomas Block Single Vineyard Shiraz 2021, Clare Valley** Thick set,
            rich and dark fruited, dusted liberally with woody spice and layering in dark
            mocha and earthy savouriness. It's a heady, potent expression, dry and firm with
            a zing of tangy acidity to finish. It feels bold, upfront and potent. A chunky
            expression of intensity and depth. Decant to drink now or hold on a spell.
            Screw cap. 14.2% alc. **RATING** 90 **DRINK** 2024–2035 $40 MB
            **JRS The Sussex Squire Barrel Selection Cabernet Sauvignon 2019,
            Clare Valley** Big and bold, lavished with spicy, cedary oak, thick-set and broad-
            shouldered. Tastes and smells like booze-soaked berries, milk chocolate, kirsch
            and prunes. It's a rollicking ride. Heft, girth and density are the calling cards,
            shame about the adjunct lemony tang to finish. For enthusiasts of bold, muscular
            reds. Screw cap. 14.5% alc. **RATING** 90 **DRINK** 2022–2030 $80 MB

Susuro   ★★★★

134/5 Hall St, Port Melbourne, Vic 3207 **Region** Various
T (03) 9646 1862 **www**.susuro.com.au **Open** Thurs–Fri 4–8, Sat–Sun 12–6
Winemaker Nikki Palun **Est.** 2014 **Dozens** 2500
Nikki Palun grew up in a family of backyard winemakers. She had a career in music first, then
entered the wine industry as export manager at De Bortoli and went on to study winemaking
at Charles Sturt University. In '14, she started the Octtava and Susuro wine labels; Susuro
specialises in Italian grape varieties and 'maturing in as many different vessels as possible' to
increase complexity and texture. Nikki is a graduate of the Australian wine industry's Future
Leaders Program, has served as a Wine Victoria board member, and has been involved in
the Victorian Government wine ministerial advisory committee. Her wines can be tasted at
Susuro's urban cellar door in Port Melbourne.

🍷🍷🍷🍷🍷 **Octtava Piano Chardonnay 2021, Mornington Peninsula** It's not the most
            complex, yet it's certainly made with care and attention. Enough citrus, woodsy
            spices and some toasty oak, not a lot just a seasoning with roasted cashew-like
            lees. The palate is lighter framed with tangy, mouth-watering acidity. Screw cap.
            13% alc. **RATING** 93 **DRINK** 2023–2029 $49 JF
            Nebbiolo 2021, Pyrenees Dried roses, juicy cherries, earth notes, sweet spices,
            and a general woody undergrowth element. There's lots going on here but the
            momentum is never compromised. This is the kind of light- to mid-weight wine
            you want at your table, good food all around, all the juices flowing. Screw cap.
            13.5% alc. **RATING** 93 **DRINK** 2023–2028 $39 CM
            Octtava Piano Pinot Noir 2021, Mornington Peninsula There's a vitality
            and refreshment quality to this thanks to its savoury tones with chinotto,
            Angostura bitters and warming spices. Yes, cherries and pips, too, with some
            herbal accents and plenty of upfront acidity. Tannins are light and textural, the
            palate the same with a smidge of poached rhubarb on the finish. Screw cap.
            13.5% alc. **RATING** 91 **DRINK** 2023–2030 $49 JF

Octtava Piano Chardonnay 2020, Mornington Peninsula A subtle, almost pared-back style with light layers of citrus, mostly a lemon-grapefruit combo, and gently spiced. The palate is tight but not lean as there are nutty, leesy flavours coming through alongside some butterscotch, spicy oak and lemony acidity. Screw cap. 13% alc. RATING 91 DRINK 2022-2028 $49 JF

Vermentino 2021, McLaren Vale Pink ginger, banana lolly, citrus blossom and talc characters putting on a show with a difference. It's dry and lively but both the texture and the flavour profile put it out there on its own, in a positive way. Screw cap. 11.9% alc. RATING 90 DRINK 2023-2026 $39 CM

Sutton Grange Winery   ★★★★★

Carnochans Road, Sutton Grange, Vic 3448 **Region** Bendigo
T (03) 8672 1478 **www.**suttongrange.com.au **Open** W'ends 11–5 **Winemaker** Chris Smailes **Est.** 1998 **Dozens** 6000 **Vyds** 12ha
Sutton Grange, a 400ha property, in the foothills of Leanganook near Harcourt, combines a horse training facility with grape growing and winemaking. This multi-functional enterprise was acquired in '96 by Peter Sidwell, a Melbourne businessman with horse racing and breeding interests. The wine side of the business dates back to '98 and a chance lunch at the property with modern-day Bendigo wine pioneer Stuart Anderson (founder of Balgownie) and local winemaker Alec Epis. Vines went in soon after, with Stuart Anderson's Burgundy-born son-in-law, Gilles Lapalus, installed as winemaker in '01. He introduced biodynamics to the property and planted Italian varieties suited to a changing climate. The experienced wine-making hand of Melanie Chester (ex Seppelt) from '15 took the Sutton Grange name to greater heights. In '22 Mel passed the baton to Chris Smailes (ex Blue Pyrenees Estate).

♥♥♥♥♥ **Fairbank Rosé 2022, Central Victoria** Rosé of the Year. Score awarded by the Halliday tasting panel at the annual Awards judging. JP writes: Shiraz/cabernet sauvignon/sangiovese. Chris Smailes delivers on his first vintage release. Attractive tea rose hues. Gentle, lifted aromas of raspberry, wild strawberry and lively spice. Love the smoothness, the inviting spice, the bright red berries and clean acid crunch to taste. And so, so versatile. Screw cap. 13% alc. RATING 97 DRINK 2023-2025 $35 PD ✪ ♥

Estate Viognier 2021, Bendigo Viognier walking an ever-so-fine line between generous and over-the-top richness. It's beautifully managed as it slips and slides between yellow peach, nectarine, citrus and apricot pip, emerging clean and bright with a briskness of acidity and firm structure. Nails the style. Screw cap. 13% alc. RATING 96 DRINK 2021-2027 $50 JP ✪ ♥

Estate Fiano 2021, Bendigo An exploration of fiano that is warm, unctuous and rich. Brings a heady perfume of stewed quince, spiced apple, nougat and nectarine. Contains a deep well of flavour with background spices and lemon curd smoothness. Love the lick of tangy acidity to close. A new chapter begins for the variety. Screw cap. 12.5% alc. RATING 95 DRINK 2022-2026 $50 JP ✪

♥♥♥♥♡ **Fairbank Ancestrale Sparkling Rosé 2022, Central Victoria** RATING 90 DRINK 2023-2027 $40 JP

Fairbank Field Blend 2022, Central Victoria RATING 90 DRINK 2023-2025 $35 JP

Sweetwater Wines   ★★★★☆

Hungerford Hill, 2450 Broke Road, Pokolbin, NSW 2320 **Region** Hunter Valley
T (02) 4998 7666 **www.**sweetwaterwines.com.au **Open** 7 days 10–5 **Winemaker** Bryan Currie **Est.** 1998 **Vyds** 16ha
Sweetwater Wines is a single-vineyard winery making semillon, shiraz and cabernet sauvignon, all stored in a temperature-controlled underground wine cellar that is part of the very large ornate house and separate guest accommodation built on the property. The reason for the seemingly unusual focus on cabernet sauvignon is the famed red volcanic soil over

limestone. Bryan Currie has made the wines since '16, and the wines can be tasted at the nearby Hungerford Hill cellar door.

ŸŸŸŸŸ **Single Estate Shiraz Cabernet 2021, Hunter Valley** This ticks all the boxes, and does so with generosity of luscious black cherry and plum fruits. I doubt I would pick its Hunter Valley origin if served blind, which is not a veiled criticism of this wine. Screw cap. 14% alc. RATING 95 DRINK 2023–2046 $65 JH

ŸŸŸŸŸ **Single Estate Shiraz 2021, Hunter Valley** RATING 91 DRINK 2023–2027 $65 JH

Swinging Bridge   ★★★★★

701 The Escort Way, Orange, NSW 2800 **Region** Orange
T 0447 416 295 **www.swingingbridge.com.au Open** 7 days 10–4 **Winemaker** Tom Ward **Viticulturist** Tom Ward **Est.** 1995 **Vyds** 6ha

Swinging Bridge Estate was established in '95 by the Ward and Payten families. In '08, having been involved from the start, Tom and Georgie Ward took the helm and have since evolved Swinging Bridge into a premium supplier of cool-climate wines from Orange. The label had its founding in Canowindra with initial plantings of chardonnay and shiraz. It's named after the historic wooden pedestrian bridge that traverses the Belubula River at the foot of the vineyard. Tom and Georgie searched for a number of years for the perfect place to call home in Orange, both for their family and Swinging Bridge. Tom's pursuit of premium grapes resulted in a number of wines made from grapes grown on Peter and Lee Hedberg's Hill Park vineyard (planted in 1998), which is now the permanent home of Swinging Bridge. Tom and Georgie were able to realise their move when this outstanding property became available.

ŸŸŸŸŸ **by Tom Ward Hill Park Pinot Noir 2022, Orange** Pomegranate, hibiscus and red raspberry. Pink peppercorn-crusted pastrami, wild baby tomatoes and baked clay. The palate weight is sturdy but ethereal with a sour cherry note followed by a density of flavour that continues long. An interplay between succulent acidity, fine tannins and exquisite cool-climate fruit. Marvelous. Screw cap. 13% alc. RATING 96 DRINK 2022–2038 $90 SW

by Tom Ward Mrs Payten Chardonnay 2022, Orange Another smashing Mrs Payten, here in its purest form with the added vibrancy of a cool year. Grapefruit sorbet, lemon sherbet and crushed white rock. The wine slithers over the palate and flicks its tail of acidity at whiplash speed. What is left are the flavours of buttercream icing and almond meal. Electric intensity and a memorable wine. Screw cap. 12.7% alc. RATING 95 DRINK 2022–2035 $35 SW ✪

by Tom Ward M.A.W. Pinot Noir 2022, Orange A stellar example of carefully handled fruit and apparent effortless winemaking. Bilberries, cranberries and hibiscus are studded with cloves, Tahitian vanilla bean and dried rose petals. Weathered sandstone and autumn leaves show up on the palate. The wine glides gracefully into taut, interwoven tannins and is almost brazen in its purity. Screw cap. 13.1% alc. RATING 95 DRINK 2022–2035 $35 SW ✪

by Tom Ward Hill Park Chardonnay 2021, Orange Bright pineapple slices, white peach and yellow apple. A flinty reduction complemented by lemon rinds, marigold blooms and toasted popcorn kernels. The palate is leesy with a lactose creaminess and the acidity is powerful and undulating. Delivers potency of force in a graceful manner, showing why Orange is in the driver's seat of cool-climate chardonnay. Screw cap. 12.9% alc. RATING 95 DRINK 2022–2035 $80 SW

by Tom Ward Caldwell Lane Block A Chardonnay 2021, Orange Tangerine skin, bergamot tea and yellow peach skin drift from the glass with a wild energy of honeysuckle, lemon oil and sandstone. Waves of lingering acidity, a nut butter creaminess and a touch of phenolic grip make for a chardonnay of charisma and charm. A well-balanced wine with purity of fruit at its heart. Screw cap. 12.4% alc. RATING 95 DRINK 2022–2035 $65 SW

by Tom Ward Hill Park Chardonnay 2017, Orange Museum release. Ripe yellow peaches, mango skin and papaya are supported by churned butter, roasted chestnuts and crème caramel. Flavour is compacted on the palate, with persistent acidity yielding to the roasted and toasted marvels of a Parisian bakery. Drinking very well now, but still has plenty of potential for development. Screw cap. 13% alc. RATING 95 DRINK 2022–2032 $85 SW

 by Tom Ward Caldwell Lane Pinot Noir 2022, Orange RATING 93 DRINK 2022–2035 $65 SW
by Tom Ward #009 Gamay 2022, Orange RATING 92 DRINK 2022–2032 $35 SW
by Tom Ward #008 Cabernet Franc Shiraz 2021, Orange RATING 92 DRINK 2022–2038 $35 SW
by Tom Ward #006 Tempinot 2021, Orange RATING 91 DRINK 2022–2038 $35 SW
by Tom Ward #003 Amber 2022, Orange RATING 90 DRINK 2022–2030 $35 SW
Shiraz 2021, Orange RATING 90 DRINK 2022–2032 $25 SW ✪

Swings & Roundabouts ★★★★

2807 Caves Road, Yallingup, WA 6232 **Region** Margaret River
T (08) 9756 6640 **www**.swings.com.au **Open** 7 days 10–5 **Winemaker** Brian Fletcher
Est. 2004 **Dozens** 10 000 **Vyds** 5ha
The Swings & Roundabouts name comes from the expression used to encapsulate the eternal balancing act between the various aspects of grape and wine production. Swings aims to balance the serious side with a touch of fun. The wines are released under the Swings & Roundabouts and Backyard Stories labels. The arrival of Brian Fletcher as winemaker has underwritten the quality of the wines. He has never been far from the wine headlines, with over 35 years of experience making wine all over the world.

 Backyard Stories Cabernet Sauvignon 2021, Margaret River There's a feeling that this wants to let loose but just can't right now. It's too young, too tight. There's a regional expression of mulberries, leafy freshness and blueberries with wafts of warm earth and grainy tannins. It's a good wine but its best days are ahead of it, so come back to this in a couple of years. Screw cap. 14% alc. RATING 93 DRINK 2024–2034 $55 JF
Backyard Stories Chardonnay 2022, Margaret River There must be an oak lover at work because there's plenty in this. It adds vanilla pod and sweet cedary flavours to the mix, perhaps needed to bolster the palate that plays tight with the acidity. Lots of stone fruit, grapefruit and lemon with layers of clotted cream. It finishes high and dry; lots to enjoy here. Screw cap. 12.5% alc. RATING 91 DRINK 2023–2032 $50 JF
Sparkling Rosé Méthode Traditionnelle 2021, Margaret River A pale copper hue and smelling of strawberries and shortbread, florals and spice. It's refreshing and lively and while not complex, it's a good glass of fizz. Diam. 12% alc. RATING 90 DRINK 2022–2024 $60 JF
Backyard Stories Pinot Noir 2022, Mount Barker There's a distinct and really earthy aroma here, a bit like tempranillo in a way, with loads of Middle Eastern spices and goji berries. A mix of dried and macerated cherries, sinewy tannins and lots of upfront acidity yet it has appeal for a refreshing, 'drink now' wine. Screw cap. 14% alc. RATING 90 DRINK 2023–2028 $45 JF

Swinney ★★★★★

325 Frankland-Kojonup Road, Frankland River, WA 6396 (postal) **Region** Frankland River
T (08) 9200 4483 **www**.swinney.com.au **Open** Not **Winemaker** Rob Mann
Viticulturist Rhys Thomas **Est.** 1998 **Dozens** 2500 **Vyds** 160ha
The Swinney family (currently parents Graham and Kaye, and son and daughter Matt and Janelle) has resided on their 2500ha property since 1922. In the '90s they decided to diversify and now have 160ha of vines across 4 vineyards, including the Powderbark Ridge vineyard in Frankland River (planted in '98, purchased in partnership with former Hardys winemaker

Peter Dawson). The lion's share goes to shiraz (67ha) and cabernet sauvignon (48ha), followed by riesling, semillon, pinot gris, gewürztraminer, viognier, vermentino and malbec. They also pushed the envelope by establishing grenache, tempranillo and mourvèdre as bush vines, a rarity in this part of the world.

ΨΨΨΨΨ **Farvie Mourvèdre 2021, Frankland River** Highly aromatic with game meat, dried cherry, white pepper, alpine herbs and violets. Supple on the palate, more game meat here, too, and cherries dark and vibrant. A dusting of fine clove and cinnamon, a faint lick of mint. Tannins a silty web that grows gently into a chew. This hits the matrix of quality fruit and adroit winemaking – the resulting wine is excellent. Screw cap. 14% alc. **RATING** 96 **DRINK** 2022-2032 $150 MB ❤

Syrah 2021, Frankland River An impressive wine from the first whiff through to the long, swooping finish. Fine but persistent tannins bookend the palate, and the feel and fruit flavours are mouth-watering and lingering, yet despite all this, the wine is only medium-bodied. Screw cap. 14% alc. **RATING** 95 **DRINK** 2023-2036 $46 JH ✪

Grenache 2021, Frankland River This new found love affair between Frankland River and grenache isn't a one night stand. The wine has elegance with a capital E, its blend of strawberry, rhubarb and pomegranate wrapped in gossamer tannins. Screw cap. 14% alc. **RATING** 95 **DRINK** 2023-2029 $46 JH ✪

Farvie Syrah 2021, Frankland River Succulent, medium-bodied red of suede texture, red berry fruit, crushed granite minerality and spice. Super-fragrant with all that garam masala perfume lavishly dusted on raspberry and cranberry fruitiness. The palate flows beautifully and long while tannins thread tension and grip. Refined and definitively 'syrah' over shiraz. Screw cap. 14% alc. **RATING** 95 **DRINK** 2023-2035 $150 MB ❤

Mourvèdre 2021, Frankland River On the face of it, Frankland River is too cool to produce quality mourvèdre, but this is a most attractive wine. The aromas and fruit flavours are of sour and black cherries, backed by the finest tannins. It's light- to medium-bodied, and has very good length. Screw cap. 14% alc. **RATING** 94 **DRINK** 2023-2031 $46 JH

ΨΨΨΨΨ **Mencia 2021, Frankland River RATING** 93 **DRINK** 2023-2028 $46 MB
Riesling 2022, Frankland River RATING 92 **DRINK** 2023-2025 $37 JH

Symphonia Wines ★★★☆

1699 Boggy Creek Road, Myrrhee, Vic 3732 **Region** King Valley
T 0418 682 277 **www**.symphoniafinewines.com.au **Open** By appt **Winemaker** Lilian Carter **Est.** 1998 **Dozens** 1500 **Vyds** 28ha
Peter Read and his family are veterans of the King Valley, commencing the development of their vineyard in 1981. After extensive trips to Western and Eastern Europe, Peter embarked on an ambitious project to trial a series of grape varieties little known in this country. Current owners Peter and Suzanne Evans are committed to continuing Peter Read's pioneering legacy.

ΨΨΨΨΨ **Pinot Grigio 2022, King Valley** Immediately, resolutely varietal, brimming with grigio green apple, lemon, quince, nectarine and a distinctive dusty acacia-honeysuckle floral character. Moves fast with brisk acidity keeping a focused, tight line. Love the lick of lemon tang to close. Mouth-wateringly good. Screw cap. 13% alc. **RATING** 91 **DRINK** 2022-2025 $28 JP ✪

Symphony Hill Wines ★★★★☆

2017 Eukey Road, Ballandean, Qld 4382 **Region** Granite Belt
T (07) 4684 1388 **www**.symphonyhill.com.au **Open** 7 days 10–4 **Winemaker** Abraham de Klerk **Viticulturist** Abraham de Klerk **Est.** 1999 **Dozens** 6000 **Vyds** 3.5ha
Ewen Macpherson purchased an old table-grape and orchard property in '96. A partnership with his parents, Bob and Jill Macpherson, led to development of the vineyard while Ewen completed his bachelor of applied science in viticulture ('03). The vineyard (now much expanded) was established using state-of-the-art technology.

ŸŸŸŸŸ **Amphora Nero d'Avola 2020, Riverland** Is this the highest-priced Riverland wine in history? Pure, vibrant and imbued with strong nero d'Avola DNA in red cherry, peppery, woody spice and a blood orange character that adds pleasing bitterness and sweetness at once. Texture is impossibly silky, graphite tannins superfine and gently cinching, the length is stellar and the wine feels complex and detailed overall. Screw cap. 13.3% alc. RATING 95 DRINK 2022-2026 $250 MB ♥
Organic Reserve Lagrein 2020, Granite Belt A thunderous red of concentration, power, richness and ripe fruit characters. Intense bouquet of ripe plum, dark chocolate, salted licorice and malt with a faint lift of mint and eucalyptus. The palate is firm with chewy tannins, brooding ripe plum, more salted licorice and dark chocolate notes with clove and game meat chiming in. In all that muscular flex, excellent balance. Well done. Screw cap. 14.9% alc. RATING 94 DRINK 2024-2035 $65 MB
Reserve Shiraz 2020, Barossa Valley Rich, potent and thick set in a full-bodied frame. It's massive in volume, with perfume a fog of ripe plum, dark chocolate, Christmas pudding and vanilla cola. Flavours follow similarly with vanilla icing layered over dark berries, stewed plums, sarsaparilla and dark chocolate. So smooth and velvety with supple tannins and cool acidity underneath all that opulence. In all the heft, good balance here, and wine of commanding presence. Screw cap. 14.9% alc. RATING 94 DRINK 2024-2035 $150 MB

ŸŸŸŸ♀ **Reserve Verdelho 2022, Granite Belt** RATING 93 DRINK 2023-2026 $45 MB
Albariño 2022, Granite Belt RATING 93 DRINK 2022-2026 $65 MB
Reserve Saperavi 2020, Murray Darling RATING 93 DRINK 2022-2030 $65 MB
Reserve Durif 2020, Riverland RATING 93 DRINK 2022-2035 $95 MB
Cabernet Sauvignon Shiraz NV, Riverland RATING 92 DRINK 2022-2028 $45 MB
Prieto Picudo 2020, Riverland RATING 91 DRINK 2022-2025 $45 MB
Fiano 2022, Murray Darling RATING 90 DRINK 2022-2025 $45 MB

Syrahmi   ★★★★★

2370 Lancefield-Tooborac Road, Tooborac, Vic 3523 **Region** Heathcote
T 0407 057 471 **www**.syrahmi.com.au **Open** By appt **Winemaker** Adam Foster
Viticulturist Adam Foster **Est.** 2004 **Dozens** 3000 **Vyds** 0.8ha
Adam Foster worked as a chef in Victoria and London before moving to the front of house and becoming increasingly interested in wine. He then worked as a cellar hand with a who's who in Australia and France, including Torbreck, Chapoutier, Mitchelton, Domaine Ogier, Heathcote Winery, Jasper Hill and Domaine Pierre Gaillard. He became convinced that the Cambrian soils of Heathcote could produce the best possible shiraz, and since '04 has purchased grapes from the region. In '17, 0.8ha of shiraz (3 clones) were planted at 8888 vines/ha at Tooborac, with a winery completed in time for the '19 vintage.

ŸŸŸŸŸ **La La Shiraz 2017, Heathcote** Released as a 6yo wine. Concentrated, complex and terrifically long. All smoked meat and ripe plum, red cherry and undergrowth. There's a mesmerising floral aspect, neither pretty nor green but somewhere in between – as if you're walking through a dark garden where wild exotics grow. That's the kind of place this wine leads you to. 696 bottles made. Screw cap. 13.6% alc. RATING 97 DRINK 2023-2033 $200 CM

ŸŸŸŸŸ **Garden of Earthly Delights Pinot Noir 2021, Macedon Ranges** Pure, clean and powerful. Forest berries and sweet spice, twigs, mint and cedar. It's one of those wines that lays its credentials down from the outset and never lets up. It's expressive but it's also brooding, it winks at you as it bunkers down. You can drink this now or later but preferably later, as it will mature well. Screw cap. 12.8% alc. RATING 95 DRINK 2023-2033 $60 CM
Demi Shiraz 2021, Heathcote Beautiful wine. Plum pie and roasted nuts, trails of woodsmoke and undergrowth, leather and a whisper of truffle. It's complex,

fluid, medium in weight and confident in the way it traverses its complex terrain. It will mature well but, there's really no need to wait – it's joyous right now. Screw cap. 13.6% alc. **RATING** 95 **DRINK** 2023–2032 $29 CM ✪

Garden of Earthly Delights Chardonnay 2021, Macedon Ranges
Lemon curd, wheat, honeydew melon and assorted floral notes work in with earth, bran and cedar. If you called it kaleidoscopic you wouldn't be exaggerating. It's not thick with flavour (it's relatively lean), but everything here both spreads and gathers. It's quite grippy too, picking up on the wine's inherent presence. Screw cap. 11.8% alc. **RATING** 94 **DRINK** 2023–2030 $55 CM

Angus Shiraz 2019, Heathcote This is meaty, spicy, floral and no doubt more, its plum-shot heart surrounded by all manner of goings on. Floral notes sit high in the wine, as do smoked meat characters and sweet cedar. It's a hell of a ride but, most importantly, it's a convincing one. Screw cap. 13.5% alc. **RATING** 94 **DRINK** 2023–2030 $60 CM

🍷🍷🍷🍷♀ **Garden of Earthly Delights Blanc 2022, Heathcote RATING** 91 **DRINK** 2023–2028 $40 CM

Grenache 2020, Heathcote RATING 91 **DRINK** 2023–2028 $45 CM

Tahbilk ★★★★★

254 O'Neils Road, Tabilk, Vic 3608 **Region** Nagambie Lakes
T (03) 5794 2555 **www.tahbilk.com.au Open** Mon–Fri 9–5, Sat–Sun 10–5
Winemaker Alister Purbrick, Joanne Nash, Alan George, Brendan Freeman **Est.** 1860
Dozens 120 000 **Vyds** 221.5ha

For 5 generations, the Purbrick family have tended vines and protected the delicate watering holes and landscape of their property outside Nagambie. The winery should be visited at least once by every wine-conscious Australian. It produces marsanne and a range of reds made very much as they were by the late, great Eric Purbrick. The family has moved fast in securing a more sustainable future, re-establishing natural wetlands, revegetating 160ha of land with indigenous trees and plants and beginning the journey to converting its vineyards to organic. Tahbilk was first accredited as a carbon-neutral winery in '13. A founding member of Australia's First Families of Wine.

🍷🍷🍷🍷🍷 **1860 Vines Shiraz 2019, Nagambie Lakes** Complexity rules with a depth of dark fruit intensity lifted by aromatic spices with signature Tahbilk earthiness, undergrowth and a splash of savouriness. That core of delightful spice, including Asian five-spice and cassia bark, is an essential part of these old shiraz vines. They mesh with well-measured oak on the palate and finely textured tannins, bringing a sustained flavour and length. That's a wow! Screw cap. 14% alc. **RATING** 97 **DRINK** 2023–2045 $360 JP ♥

Very Rare Tawny NV, South Australia What a precious piece of winemaking history here, originally a fortified sourced from the Barossa and McLaren Vale, made and then aged, blended at the famous Seabrook Wine Merchants in Melbourne. After time in a Yarra Valley winery, the barrels came up for auction in '20 and here is the result: a gloriously decadent fortified, 80 years in the making, but still so fresh and vital. Sticky date pudding, molasses, raisin, and a flash of nutty rancio before an ever-lasting sweet intensity, impressively long and satisfying, finally brings this delicious wine to a close. All 10 barrels were bought by Tahbilk and will be slowly released over time. 500ml. Screw cap. 18.5% alc. **RATING** 97 $110 JP

🍷🍷🍷🍷🍷 **Eric Stevens Purbrick Cabernet Sauvignon 2019, Nagambie Lakes**
Varietal potency, depth and structure. Unashamedly medium bodied, as per the Tahbilk way, the ESP arrives fragrant in dark fruits, briar, earth and dried herbs with rosemary, sage and a lifted leafiness. Maintains a firm line of tannin across the palate, something to see it through a decade or more in bottle. It's good for it. Love the emerging complexity of spiced oak and dusty cacao. A real treat for the senses. Screw cap. 14% alc. **RATING** 96 **DRINK** 2023–2036 $74 JP ✪ ♥

Marsanne 2022, Nagambie Lakes A concentrated, fully expressive young marsanne. Citrus blossom, honeysuckle, green almond, Meyer lemon and pear aromas lead into a wine with all the ingredients for developing complexity. The varietal trademarks are lining up nicely, led by lemon-bright acidity, spring floral and citrus flavours with potential plus for further ageing. Screw cap. 13% alc. RATING 95 DRINK 2022-2035 $22 JP ❂

Grenache Mourvèdre Rosé 2022, Nagambie Lakes Sports the prettiest musk-pink colour, but don't assume this is sweet or lightweight. It's anything but. Fresh, crunchy acidity provides the basis of striking fruit intensity: cherry, cranberry, acacia, pepper, spice. A light spray of juicy sweet fruit brings succulence and length. Seriously good rosé, whatever the occasion. Screw cap. 12.5% alc. RATING 95 DRINK 2022-2027 $22 JP ❂

Eric Stevens Purbrick Shiraz 2019, Nagambie Lakes An artful display of Central Victorian shiraz. It talks of the earth and native bush scents, black fruits, brown spice and anise both gentle and lifted. The palate is refined with layers of ripe blackberries, plum, bay leaf, dried herbs, dark chocolate and anise sustained by vanillin oak and fine tannins. A keeper, if you can wait. Screw cap. 14% alc. RATING 95 DRINK 2023-2036 $74 JP

Museum Release Marsanne 2017, Nagambie Lakes A long-time champion of marsanne, Tahbilk celebrates both its youthful energy and its aged beauty. Here we see the latter in all of its timeless allure, maintaining the honeysuckle, citrus, appley brightness of its youth while starting to build on its earlier promise of beeswax smooth texture with a developing gentle toastiness. Another stunning museum release. Screw cap. 12% alc. RATING 95 DRINK 2023-2032 $28 JP ❂

1927 Vines Marsanne 2017, Nagambie Lakes The equivalent of a bottle-aged Hunter semillon, albeit with marsanne. It's ground-breaking in style, showcasing the grape in a different light. Herbals and florals on the bouquet, penetrating and lifted. Picked early, it's bracing and crunchy against a background of quince, green apple, grilled grapefruit and lemon zest. Still young and coiled tight, give it time. Screw cap. 10.5% alc. RATING 95 DRINK 2023-2032 $48 JP ❂

Old Vines Cabernet Shiraz 2019, Nagambie Lakes The style remains 'Tahbilk traditional' in its approach. Super-ripe blackberries offer the base upon which layers of spice, anise, earth, briar, leaf, leather and woodsy oak mingle and meld against a background of warm, cedary oak. Early days for this wine. Screw cap. 14.5% alc. RATING 94 DRINK 2023-2034 $48 JP ♥

🍷🍷🍷🍷 **Viognier 2022, Nagambie Lakes** RATING 93 DRINK 2022-2028 $22 JP ❂
Shiraz 2020, Nagambie Lakes RATING 93 DRINK 2023-2028 $27 JP ❂
Cabernet Sauvignon 2020, Nagambie Lakes RATING 92 DRINK 2023-2028 $27 JP ❂
Pinot Gris 2022, Nagambie Lakes RATING 90 DRINK 2022-2027 $22 JP ❂
Riesling 2022, Nagambie Lakes RATING 90 DRINK 2022-2028 $22 JP ❂

Talisman Wines   ★★★★

Wheelman Road, Wellington Mill, WA 6236 **Region** Geographe
T 0401 559 266 **www.**talismanwines.com.au **Open** By appt **Winemaker** Peter Stanlake **Viticulturist** Victor Bertola **Est.** 2009 **Dozens** 3000 **Vyds** 9ha
Kim Robinson and wife Jenny began the development of their vineyard in 2000 and now have cabernet, shiraz, malbec, zinfandel, chardonnay, riesling and sauvignon blanc. Kim says that 'after 8 frustrating years of selling grapes to Evans & Tate and Wolf Blass, we decided to optimise the vineyard and attempt to make quality wines'. The measure of their success has been consistent gold-medal performance (and some trophies) at the Geographe Wine Show. They say this could not have been achieved without the assistance of vineyard manager Victor Bertola and winemaker Peter Stanlake.

🍷🍷🍷🍷 **Ferguson Valley Riesling 2022, Geographe** Aromatic, all citrus and green apple, touches of talc and whiffs of sea spray. The palate follows on lemon-limey, a squish of pulpy pink grapefruit and a stony, minerally finish. It's tight and refreshing but loose-knit enough to be approachable now. A striking riesling with easy appeal. Screw cap. 11.7% alc. RATING 94 DRINK 2023–2034 $25 MB ✪

Ferguson Valley Zinfandel 2020, Geographe Well-judged zinfandel showing the fuller flex of the variety with a judicious balance of acidity, fine, chewy tannin and meritorious alcohol levels. Dark plum, cola, dark chocolate, salted licorice and woody spices to the max, all finding a neat measure in perfume and palate. It's even fresh through the finish. It feels like it drinks well now, but cellaring should reward. Screw cap. 14.6% alc. RATING 94 DRINK 2023–2035 $45 MB

🍷🍷🍷🍷 **Ferguson Valley Merlot 2021, Geographe** RATING 93 DRINK 2023–2032 $30 MB ✪
Arida Rosé 2022, Geographe RATING 90 DRINK 2023–2025 $25 MB ✪

Tallis Wine

195 Major Plains Road, Dookie, Vic 3646 **Region** Goulburn Valley
T 0408 211 661 **www**.talliswine.com.au **Open** Thurs–Sun 11–5 **Winemaker** Richard Tallis, Victor Nash **Viticulturist** Richard Tallis, Ben Rose **Est.** 1997 **Dozens** 2000 **Vyds** 24.75ha

Fourth-generation farmers Richard and Alice Tallis planted their vineyard on the red volcanic loam soils of their traditional farming property, bringing back viticulture to the Dookie area after its absence for almost 100 years. (In the late 1800s Dookie flourished with expansive vineyards, and at its peak produced one-third of Victoria's wine.) Tallis uses a 'tread lightly' approach in the vineyard, avoiding sprays and using mulching and composting, with minimum intervention in the winery. In May '23, the cellar door became 'Rye at Tallis', a wine bar/event space run by a local team.

🍷🍷🍷🍷 **The Silent Showman Cabernet Sauvignon 2021, Goulburn Valley**
Generous in ripe black fruits, clove, cinnamon – plenty of woodsy spice all around – and earth. Brings varietal cabernet leafiness to the supple palate. Solid tannins sweep along bringing cassis, chocolate and spice through the finish. Not short on flavour or style. Screw cap. 14.6% alc. RATING 93 DRINK 2023–2032 $45 JP

The Silent Showman Shiraz 2021, Goulburn Valley Deep, dark and dense in purple-garnet hues. The scent of well-toasted, smoky oak hangs over the bouquet teeming with black fruits, licorice, baked earth and spice. Delivers a generous and warm oak-spiced richness of flavour and tannin depth, with just a hint of alcohol heat to close. Living large and looking for a barbecued steak for company. Screw cap. 14.8% alc. RATING 92 DRINK 2023–2034 $45 JP

Taltarni ★★★★★

339 Taltarni Road, Moonambel, Vic 3478 **Region** Pyrenees
T (03) 5459 7900 **www**.taltarni.com.au **Open** Wed–Sun 11–5 **Winemaker** Robert Heywood, Ben Howell **Viticulturist** Barry Morris **Est.** 1969 **Dozens** 45 000 **Vyds** 74ha
The Goelet family, founders of Clos du Val (Napa Valley), Domaine de Nizas (Languedoc) and Clover Hill (see separate entry) purchased Taltarni in '72 concluding an ambitious search for their first Australian site. Taltarni is the larger of the 2 Australian ventures, its estate vineyards of great value and underpinning the substantial annual production. Insectariums are established in permanent vegetation corridors, each containing around 2000 native plants that provide a pollen and nectar source for the beneficial insects, reducing the need for chemicals and other controls of the vineyards. Taltarni celebrated 45 years of winemaking in '22.

🍷🍷🍷🍷 **The Patron Cabernet Shiraz 2017, Pyrenees** Ex 50yo estate vines from the best blocks. Adventurous winemaking has paid off, with a medium to full body notable for its balance and length. Cedary notes suggest new oak, but either way, the gambit worked. Only 116 dozen bottles made. Cork. 13.5% alc. RATING 96 DRINK 2023–2042 $125 JH

⟡⟡⟡⟡⟡ Shiraz 2020, Heathcote RATING 93 DRINK 2023-2033 $35 CM ✪
Blanc de Blancs 2018, Pyrenees RATING 92 DRINK 2023-2029 $33 CM
Chardonnay Pinot Noir Pinot Meunier Brut 2017, Pyrenees RATING 91
DRINK 2023-2025 $28 CM ✪
Shiraz Viognier 2020, Pyrenees RATING 91 DRINK 2022-2030 $28 CM ✪
Cuvée Rosé NV, Victoria RATING 90 $25 CM ✪

Tamar Ridge   ★★★★☆

1a Waldhorn Drive, Rosevears, Tas 7277 **Region** Northern Tasmania
T (03) 6330 0300 **www.**tamarridge.com.au **Open** 7 days 10–4 **Winemaker** Tom Wallace,
Anthony De Amicis **Est.** 1994 **Dozens** 14000 **Vyds** 130ha
Since the Brown Family Wine Group (then Brown Brothers) acquired Tamar Ridge and its
sister brands of Pirie and Devil's Corner in '10, it has tactically honed each of the 3 labels to
increasingly play to its strengths. For Tamar Ridge, this means a strategic focus on pinot noir,
sourced from its magnificent and substantial Kayena vineyard, tucked into a fold of the Tamar
River in the north of the Tamar Valley. Single Vineyard and experimental Research Series
pinot noirs are exciting indicators of the direction of evolution of the brand under talented
winemaker Tom Wallace.

⟡⟡⟡⟡⟡ Pinot Noir 2021, Tasmania Whole bunches are part of the story, access to
Tamar Ridge's 130ha of estate vineyards is another. The strong colour easily
achieved, the powerful and complex bouquet bringing blood and satsuma plum
aromas to the fore. Balance is achieved by a savoury/foresty twist to the finish.
Screw cap. 13% alc. RATING 95 DRINK 2023-2036 $34 JH ✪

⟡⟡⟡⟡⟡ Research Series Kayena Vineyard Pinot Noir 2021, Tasmania RATING 93
DRINK 2023-2039 $55 DB
Pinot Noir 2020, Tasmania RATING 91 DRINK 2023-2028 $34 TS

Tambo Estate   ★★★★

96 Pages Road, Tambo Upper, Vic 3885 **Region** Gippsland
T 0418 100 953 **www.**tambowine.com.au **Open** Thurs–Sun 11–5 **Winemaker** Alastair
Butt **Viticulturist** Bill Williams **Est.** 1994 **Dozens** 1924 **Vyds** 5.11ha
Bill and Pam Williams returned to Australia in the early '90s after 7 years overseas, and began
the search for a property which met the specific requirements for high-quality table wines
established by Dr John Gladstones in his masterwork *Viticulture and Environment*. They chose
a property in the foothills of the Victorian Alps on the inland side of the Gippsland Lakes,
with predominantly sheltered, north-facing slopes. They planted a little over 5ha: 3.4ha to
chardonnay, as well as a little cabernet sauvignon, pinot noir and sauvignon blanc. They are
mightily pleased to have secured the services of Alastair Butt (ex Seville Estate).

⟡⟡⟡⟡⟡ Nebbiolo Rosé 2021, Pyrenees An attractive pale bronze hue. A refreshing
style yet it comes with savoury flavours and texture, too. Cranberries sprinkled
with nutmeg and woodsy spices, and the 4 months spent in used oak have added a
slip of creaminess. Screw cap. 13.8% alc. RATING 93 DRINK 2022-2024 $29 JF ✪
Merrill Chardonnay 2021, Gippsland A linear style with all manner of citrus
inputs – lemon juice and zest and blossom plus a smidge of sulphides adding to
the attraction. Quite heady, actually. The palate is reined in by fine acidity with
some texture thanks to creamed honey and nutty, moreish lees flavours. Screw cap.
13.1% alc. RATING 92 DRINK 2022-2030 $29 JF ✪
Merrill Aged Release Chardonnay 2011, Gippsland This aged release is
showing well starting with its pale–medium gold hue. There's still a flutter of stone
fruit and citrus matched to the aged characters: toastiness and clotted cream plus
honeycomb. Some phenolic grip to the finish and best enjoyed now. Screw cap.
13.1% alc. RATING 90 DRINK 2022-2024 $33 JF

Tapanappa ★★★★★

15 Spring Gully Road, Piccadilly, SA 5151 **Region** Piccadilly Valley
T (08) 7324 5301 **www.tapanappa.com.au Open** 7 days 11–4 **Winemaker** Brian Croser
Est. 2002 **Dozens** 2500 **Vyds** 16.7ha

Tapanappa was founded by Brian and Ann Croser in 2002. The word Tapanappa is derived from the local Aboriginal language that translates to 'stick to the path'. Through Tapanappa, Brian is continuing a career-long mission of producing unique 'wines of terroir' – matching the climate, soil and geology to the right varieties from Tapanappa's 3 distinguished sites in SA. Wines are made from the Whalebone vineyard at Wrattonbully (planted to cabernet sauvignon, shiraz and merlot in '74), the Tiers vineyard in the Adelaide Hills' Piccadilly Valley (chardonnay) and the Foggy Hill vineyard on the southern tip of the Fleurieu Peninsula (pinot noir). The winery and cellar door are located in the heart of the Piccadilly Valley.

ŸŸŸŸŸ **Tiers Vineyard Chardonnay 2022, Piccadilly Valley** This is resinous and latent with multitudinous layers of flavour compressed by classy oak and juicy acidity. I like the way the fruit is subdued in a quasi-burgundian fashion, with power packed behind. It will come. And it does. With air. Raw almond, hazelnut, quinine and Japanese radish. The barest hint of stone fruit. A long, saline linger. Give this time, for it is among the country's greats. Screw cap. 13.8% alc. **RATING** 97 **DRINK** 2024–2034 $110 NG ♥

ŸŸŸŸŸ **Tiers Vineyard 1.5m Chardonnay 2022, Piccadilly Valley** An incredibly intense chardonnay, mid-weighted and tightly furled. The edges are as chewy as they are sleek, with a parry of freshness melding with a thrust of oak, effortlessly subsumed by the sheer palate-staining extract. White peach, nectarine, peat and truffle. A creamy generosity, febrile energy and kaleidoscopic complexity, all in one. Excellent. Screw cap. 13.5% alc. **RATING** 96 **DRINK** 2023–2032 $59 NG ✪

Definitus Foggy Hill Pinot Noir 2021, Fleurieu This is an outstanding release. The combination of attractive strawberry and spice characters with firm tannins and exceptional length is enough to get any pinot lover's heart racing. The flavours here really do soar on and on. Assertive tannin feels totally uncompromised, in the best of ways. A champion wine, tailor-made for a 5–10 year stint in the cellar. Screw cap. 12.5% alc. **RATING** 96 **DRINK** 2025–2035 $90 CM ♥

Whalebone Vineyard Merlot Cabernet Franc 2019, Wrattonbully The volume of fruit here matched to the sure swagger of tannin speaks in no uncertain terms of the quality on offer. This is absolutely top echelon. Blackcurrant, bay leaves, cedarwood, beetroot and kirsch flavours drum captivatingly through the palate and on through the long, but highly structured, finish. Screw cap. 14.2% alc. **RATING** 96 **DRINK** 2026–2044 $90 CM ♥

Foggy Hill Vineyard Pinot Noir 2022, Fleurieu It was a cool vintage but there's plenty of weight to this release. There are ample twiggy spice notes or variations thereof, which is interesting given that the grapes were completely destemmed. Mace, green but fragrant herbs, and plum notes that come via both sweet and sour cherries. There's the gloss of smoky, cedar oak here, too, but it's immaculately well integrated. Another point of note is the tannin, which is both fine and tight. Another excellent wine. Cork. 14% alc. **RATING** 95 **DRINK** 2025–2035 $55 CM

Foggy Hill Vineyard Pinot Noir 2021, Fleurieu A pretty pinot with a cherry and plum duo that provide the heart of both bouquet and palate. It's a base for the spices and rose petals that will appear over the next 2–3 years, in the meantime the juicy mouthfeel of the palate will do the work. Screw cap. 12.5% alc. **RATING** 95 **DRINK** 2023–2036 $55 JH

Whalebone Vineyard Cabernet Shiraz 2019, Wrattonbully The effect of shiraz on this blend is significant. It's a wine threaded with herbal, tobacco-like graphite and mint notes, and structurally it feels very cabernet too, in that the tannin has a strictness to it. But then the mid-palate is awash with shiraz's plush, sweet, plum–driven fruit. In other words this is a textbook example of this blend: cabernet builds the foundation, and shiraz adds the cuddles. Cork. 14.2% alc. RATING 95 DRINK 2025–2037 $55 CM

Clone 114 Pinot Noir 2021, Adelaide Hills The winemaker calls '21 a 'model' vintage, deciding to keep the 114 clone pinot separate to show its floral delicacy. Unrestrained, expressive aromatics in strawberry, red cherry, dried flowers and musk. Firm on the palate, tight and coiled, with cherry-pip tannins keeping things firmly in place. It's well placed for a long future. Screw cap. 12.5% alc. RATING 94 DRINK 2022–2031 $55 JP

♟♟♟♟♀ **Single Vineyard Riesling 2022, Eden Valley** RATING 93 DRINK 2022–2032 $35 NG

Chardonnay 2022, Piccadilly Valley RATING 93 DRINK 2023–2029 $49 NG

Whalebone Vineyard Blend 2020, Wrattonbully RATING 93 DRINK 2022–2036 $90 JP

Single Vineyard Riesling 2020, Eden Valley RATING 91 DRINK 2023–2030 $35 JH

Tar & Roses ★★★★★

61 Vickers Lane, Nagambie, Vic 3608 **Region** Nagambie Lakes
T (03) 5794 1811 **www.**tarandroses.com.au **Open** 1st w'end each month 10–4
Winemaker Narelle King **Est.** 2006 **Dozens** 40 000

Tar & Roses produces wines inspired by the classic Mediterranean varietals and was named after the signature characteristics of nebbiolo. The name also ties back to the winemaking team behind the venture, the legendary Don Lewis and his winemaking partner Narelle King. Narelle is carrying on the Tar & Roses tradition after Don's passing in '17.

♟♟♟♟♟ **Lewis Riesling 2022, Central Victoria** A wine named for star riesling maker Don Lewis that lives up to the name in both fruit concentration and class. At once delicate and floral but with a solid core of pure, intense lime and citrus. A pitch-perfect riesling embracing a touch of savoury lemongrass, a pinch of spice and a brisk sherbety tingle set to some racy acidity. Age will be kind to it. Screw cap. 12.5% alc. RATING 96 DRINK 2022–2032 $26 JP ✪ ♥

The Fog Nebbiolo 2021, Heathcote Unfurls slowly, as nebbiolo can do so brilliantly, releasing lifted, generous aromatics. Rose petals, red licorice, pepper, cranberry, cherry and woodsmoke aromas mingle. Lovely balance on display in lifted fruit, savoury, earthy tannins and a long finish. Reveals assured confidence and poise with a grape that can be notoriously difficult to work with. Screw cap. 14.6% alc. RATING 95 DRINK 2023–2031 $55 JP

Pinot Grigio 2022, Central Victoria King Valley Tar & Roses promotes the grape's natural blush colour. No filtration here. Fragrant in stone fruit, red apple and citrus scents with a flash of spiced pear. Subtle but highly effective. Hits the mark on the palate both flavour- and texture-wise, with a clean, brisk finish of bright acidity. Screw cap. 13.8% alc. RATING 94 DRINK 2022–2025 $24 JP ✪

Tempranillo 2021, Central Victoria Shimmering in deep purple with lifted and intense aromas of earth, bay leaf, black cherry, licorice and rosemary. A wine of some poise and class which belies the pricepoint. Succulent fruit holds the key to its charm, enhanced by a touch of savouriness and guided by ripe, cherry tannins. No reason not to open now, but it can also take time in bottle. Screw cap. 14.5% alc. RATING 94 DRINK 2022–2029 $27 JP ✪

♟♟♟♟♀ **Shiraz 2020, Heathcote** RATING 92 DRINK 2022–2028 $24 JP ✪

Pinot Noir 2021, Mornington Peninsula RATING 91 DRINK 2022–2025 $44 JP

Prosecco NV, Central Victoria RATING 90 $24 JP ✪

Rosé Mediterraneo 2022, Central Victoria RATING 90 DRINK 2022–2026 $24 JP ✪

Chardonnay 2021, Mornington Peninsula RATING 90 DRINK 2022–2025 $40 JP

TarraWarra Estate

311 Healesville-Yarra Glen Road, Yarra Glen, Vic 3775 **Region** Yarra Valley
T (03) 5957 3510 **www.**tarrawarra.com.au **Open** Tues–Sun 11–5 **Winemaker** Clare
Halloran, Adam McCallum **Viticulturist** Stuart Sissins **Est.** 1983 **Dozens** 9000 **Vyds** 28ha
TarraWarra is, and always has been, one of the top-tier wineries in the Yarra Valley. Founded
by Marc Besen AC and wife Eva Besen AO, it has operated on the basis that quality is
paramount, cost a secondary concern. The creation of the TarraWarra Museum of Art
(twma.com.au) in a purpose-built building provides another reason to visit. Changes in the
vineyard include the planting of shiraz and merlot, and in the winery, the creation of a 4-tier
range: the deluxe MDB label made in tiny quantities and only when the vintage permits; the
single-vineyard range; the Reserve range; and the 100% estate-grown varietal range.

Barbera 2021, Yarra Valley This is every bit as good, if not better, than last
year's iteration. You'll find an attractive amalgam of dark cherries, plum, violets
and mountain herbs on the nose, while the palate is ripe, plush and well balanced
by the wine's grippy, perfectly judged tannins. I'd be drinking this at around 16°C.
Screw cap. 14% alc. **RATING** 95 **DRINK** 2022–2028 $35 PR ♻
Reserve Chardonnay 2021, Yarra Valley A deep-ish and bright green gold.
Another classic rich but balanced chardonnay from TarraWarra. Aromas of ripe
stone fruits, lemon confit, honey and a little fresh vanilla bean. Textured with
a gentle creaminess and good tension to close. Screw cap. 13% alc. **RATING** 95
DRINK 2022–2026 $55 PR
Reserve Pinot Noir 2021, Yarra Valley A medium ruby crimson. Redolent
of wild strawberries, subtle floral notes and Asian spices. It's all there on the palate,
too, with excellent depth and persistence and sinewy, gently chewy tannins.
Screw cap. 13.5% alc. **RATING** 95 **DRINK** 2022–2031 $70 PR

Pinot Noir 2021, Yarra Valley **RATING** 93 **DRINK** 2023–2028 $35 PR ♻
Chardonnay 2021, Yarra Valley **RATING** 92 **DRINK** 2022–2026 $30 PR ♻

Tarrawatta

102 Stott Highway, Angaston, SA 5353 (postal) **Region** Eden Valley
T 0447 117 762 **www.**tarrawattawine.com.au **Open** Not **Winemaker** Craig Isbel
Viticulturist Nick Radford **Est.** 2017 **Dozens** 1700 **Vyds** 9.3ha
Tarrawatta's inaugural shiraz and grenache immediately secured its place among the who's who
of the Barossa, making this one of the most exciting newcomers in the '22 edition. Devoted
exclusively to red wines, fruit is currently sourced entirely from the estate Ambervale vineyard
in the northern Eden Valley. First planted in the mid 1800s, today the site boasts mostly dry-
grown shiraz, cabernet sauvignon and a little grenache, with vines dating from 1968. A 2nd
site is earmarked for planting. Nick Radford oversees the vineyards and management of the
estate, with Izway's Craig Isbel taking care of winemaking. The estate is owned by the Goldin
Group, alongside Sloan Estate in the Napa and three Bordeaux châteaux, including Château
Le Bon Pasteur in Pomerol.

Ambervale Shiraz 2020, Eden Valley Deep magenta in colour, this is a
deeply resonant, powerful rendition of Eden Valley shiraz packed with plush black
and dark plum, blackberry and blueberry fruit notes. Dredged with spice, sage,
tobacco leaf, violets, roasting meat and earth. Excellent fruit purity and density
with latent power to burn and yet, a sense of grace as it sails off. A great example.
Cork. 14.8% alc. **RATING** 96 **DRINK** 2023–2035 $52 DB ♻
Godswalk 2019, Eden Valley Rich aromas of blackberry, blueberry, blood
plum and cassis with hints of tobacco, pickled walnuts, cedar, dried herbs, violets,
baking spices, licorice, dark chocolate, sage and earth. It's a big wine relying on
muscle and horsepower rather than grace … and that might just be exactly what
you are after. If so, this is a pretty impressively proportioned wine of great purity.
Shiraz/cabernet sauvignon. Screw cap. 14.9% alc. **RATING** 94 **DRINK** 2023–2035
$250 DB

Ambervale Cabernet Sauvignon 2020, Eden Valley **RATING** 90
DRINK 2023–2028 $52 DB

Taschini

5 Memorial Drive, Coonawarra, SA 5263 **Region** Coonawarra
T 0400 576 410 **www**.taschini.com.au **Open** Mon–Thurs 10–4 **Winemaker** Matilda
Innes **Est.** 2020 **Dozens** 500

It was only a matter of time before Matilda Innes would be lured into winemaking. Her
parents Melissa and John are Limestone Coast legends, vignerons and foodies behind the
Ottelia label and Fodder restaurant/cellar door in Coonawarra. But Taschini has its own
identity. Matilda says: 'This is about making lots of fun, little wine projects and not so much
about being the 2nd generation at Ottelia.' This means sourcing small parcels of fruit to make
wines with personality and difference. Having a strong hospitality background has helped
shaped her view. Before returning home to Coonawarra in '17 with partner Paul Stone (the
chef now on the pans at Fodder) Matilda honed her skills at top-notch Melbourne restaurants.
More wines are coming onboard, which is exciting. Matilda credits a local Italian lady for
suggesting the cute name: Taschini means little pockets.

ΨΨΨΨΨ Skinsy Chardonnay Sauvignon Blanc 2022, Mount Gambier It's certainly
a bit 'out there' with its textural grippiness and smoky overtones, but the truth
is that this is a fine wine, well made and flavoured. Lemongrass, gunmetal, apple
and passionfruit flavours put on a dry-but-delicious show, an attractive smokiness
lingering. Screw cap. 11.9% alc. **RATING** 92 **DRINK** 2023-2026 $32 CM
Bunchy Cabernet Sauvignon 2022, Coonawarra Pure blackcurrant, lashings
of red roses and tips of violet. This has some X-factor. It's dry, tannic, sinewy
and generous at once, all in a super-fresh, mouth-watering, light-bodied context.
Screw cap. 12.9% alc. **RATING** 92 **DRINK** 2023-2026 $32 CM

Taylors

89A Winery Road, Auburn, SA 5451 **Region** Clare Valley
T 1800 804 295 **www**.taylorswines.com.au **Open** Mon–Fri 9–5, w'ends 10–4
Winemaker Mitchell Taylor, Adam Eggins, Phillip Reschke, Chad Bowman, Thomas
Darmody **Viticulturist** Syd Kyloh **Est.** 1969 **Dozens** 250000 **Vyds** 400ha

Taylors has been a significant family-owned producer since Bill Taylor Sr, together with his
2 sons, Bill and John, purchased their Clare Valley property in '69. Few producers manage
to combine such substantial production volumes with such an impressive haul of wine
show medals and trophies, as Taylors routinely manages. Wine style is unerringly traditional
and generally punches at or above its weight across all price levels. A founding member of
Australia's First Families of Wine.

ΨΨΨΨΨ St Andrews Riesling 2022, Clare Valley The wine opens with lemon
blossom, tangerine, mint and green apple. Lovely start. The palate is a rush of
green lime, mandarin, flinty mineral elements and minty herbal lift. It's a juicy
number stacked with minerally characters and very refreshing in its pronounced
acid profile. The overall feel is a wine of easy drinking and loose-knit nature,
the latter a quibble about tension and drive. A strong release, overall. Screw cap.
11.5% alc. **RATING** 93 **DRINK** 2022-2035 $37 MB
The Visionary 2018, Clare Valley An ultra-premium release cabernet.
Concentrated, smooth, sweet-fruited and hearty, fine tannins tightening things
nicely as the wine finishes fresh and bright. Polished and elegant in its make-up,
albeit acidity does poke out through the finish. Lots of lovely things to see in
this wine, but perhaps best drunk in a few years for it to fully form and flourish.
Screw cap. 14.5% alc. **RATING** 92 **DRINK** 2025-2040 $200 MB
Masterstroke Cabernet Shiraz 2018, Clare Valley Inky, rich, toasty and
concentrated with lashings of stewed plum, cherry cola, licorice, new leather
and grainy, woody spices. A cedary overlay, with pencil shavings and toast
leaning heavily into the dark fruit profile. In that, it seems to work quite nicely
in its potent way. The heft of the varieties, the richness, the booze all seem to
sop up the cedary elements. An old-school kinda style, but nails the brief on that.
Screw cap. 14% alc. **RATING** 92 **DRINK** 2022-2035 $60 MB

St Andrews Chardonnay 2021, Clare Valley It's rich, soft and generously seasoned in a full-flavoured style. Opens with ripe apple, stone fruits, melon and a cinnamon/clove oak overlay with whiffs of honeyed toast. Flavours roll around all mellow, toasty and supple, yet the underlying course of acidity is bright and refreshing, too. Sweeter, riper expression yes, but this should please those seeking bolder chardonnay. Screw cap. 13.5% alc. **RATING** 91 **DRINK** 2022-2030 $37 MB

Estate Label Riesling 2022, Clare Valley Adelaide Hills Sweet lime cordial, a little crunch of green apple, some yeasty floral lift – the bouquet on song. Tastes neat and tidy, refreshing, limey/green appley and finishes mouth-watering and with a puff of talc-like minerality. Nicely done in an easy-drinking style. Screw cap. 12% alc. **RATING** 90 **DRINK** 2022-2027 $22 MB ✪

The Pioneer Shiraz 2018, Clare Valley A polished expression of shiraz. Rich and ripe plum, salted licorice, cola, vanilla and lavender scents and flavours. Seamless in texture – glossy, slick and concentrated, but lifts on some orange juice freshness to finish long and smooth. It doesn't feel particularly complex or deep, but has great mouthfeel, persistence and pleasing perfume. Screw cap. 14.5% alc. **RATING** 90 **DRINK** 2022-2035 $200 MB

Tellurian   ★★★★★

408 Tranter Road, Toolleen, Vic 3551 **Region** Heathcote
T 0417 440 533 www.tellurianwines.com.au **Open** W'ends 11–4.30, or by appt
Winemaker Tobias Ansted **Viticulturist** Tim Brown **Est.** 2002 **Dozens** 7000 **Vyds** 32ha
The vineyard is situated on the western side of Mt Camel at Toolleen, on the red Cambrian soil that has made Heathcote one of the foremost regions in Australia for the production of shiraz (Tellurian means 'of the earth'). Viticultural consultant Tim Brown not only supervises the certified organic Tellurian estate plantings, but also works closely with the growers of grapes purchased under contract for Tellurian. Further plantings on the Tellurian property in '11 introduced small parcels of grenache, mourvèdre, carignan, nero d'Avola, marsanne, viognier, fiano, riesling and grenache gris to the 20ha of shiraz.

♇♇♇♇♇ **Grenache 2022, Heathcote** This is a beautiful grenache. It's gutsy in varietal terms but it's complex, measured and moreish. Smoked meats, plums, raspberries, nuts and assorted exotic spice notes come drifted with florals. One sip and you know that you're onto something special. There's a good deal of dry, velvety tannin here too but the flow of fruit remains uninterrupted; always a good sign. Screw cap. 14% alc. **RATING** 95 **DRINK** 2024-2032 $40 CM ✪

Block 3 BLR Shiraz 2021, Heathcote Plum, clove, cedar and sweet spice characters put on a flamboyant – and downright delicious – display. Tannin is fine and grainy, length is juicy and sustained. Everything is in alignment here. Screw cap. 14.6% alc. **RATING** 95 **DRINK** 2024-2036 $50 CM ✪

Tranter Shiraz 2021, Heathcote Such velvety mouthfeel. Plum, redcurrant, clove and mint flavours take the veneer of cedarwood and run with it. This is a hand-in-glove seamless red wine, simultaneously sophisticated and effortless. Screw cap. 14.6% alc. **RATING** 94 **DRINK** 2025-2035 $45 CM

♇♇♇♇♀ **EVO Shiraz 2021, Heathcote RATING** 93 **DRINK** 2023-2031 $35 CM ✪
Marsanne 2022, Heathcote RATING 92 **DRINK** 2024-2030 $35 CM
GSM 2021, Heathcote RATING 92 **DRINK** 2024-2030 $31 CM

Tempus Two Wines   ★★★★

Cnr Broke Road/McDonalds Road, Pokolbin, NSW 2321 **Region** Hunter Valley
T (02) 4993 3999 www.tempustwo.com.au **Open** 7 days 10–5 **Winemaker** Andrew Duff **Est.** 1997 **Dozens** 55 000 **Vyds** 120ha
Tempus Two is a mix of Latin (Tempus means time) and English. It has been a major success story: production was just 6000 dozen in 1997 with sales increasing by over 140% by the early 2020s. Its cellar door and restaurant complex (including the Oishii Japanese restaurant) are situated in a striking building. The design polarises opinion; I (James) like it.

🍷🍷🍷🍷🍷 **Pewter Semillon 2022, Hunter Valley** Using a dumpy bottle shape reminiscent of an 18th century fortified wine is not a happy match for an elegant, crisp style. The bottle will deter from long-term cellaring. At least the screw cap means if all else fails it can be matured standing up, and allow determined Hunter semillon tragics to say 'not before 2027.' Screw cap. 10.5% alc. **RATING** 94 **DRINK** 2023-2030 $40 JH ✪

🍷🍷🍷🍷🍷 **Copper Semillon 2022, Hunter Valley RATING** 93 **DRINK** 2028-2035 $30 JH ✪
Copper Shiraz 2021, Barossa Valley Hunter Valley RATING 92 **DRINK** 2023-2028 $35 DB
Copper Wilde Chardonnay 2021, Hunter Valley RATING 91 **DRINK** 2023-2026 $30 JH
Pewter Shiraz 2021, Barossa Valley RATING 90 **DRINK** 2023-2028 $45 DB

Ten Minutes by Tractor ★★★★★

1333 Mornington-Flinders Road, Main Ridge, Vic 3928 **Region** Mornington Peninsula **T** (03) 5989 6455 **www.**tenminutesbytractor.com.au **Open** 7 days 11–5 **Winemaker** Imogen Dillon, Martin Spedding **Viticulturist** Fabiano Frangi **Est.** 1997 **Dozens** 12000 **Vyds** 38.3ha

Ten Minutes by Tractor is owned by Martin and Karen Spedding. It was established in 1997 with 3 Main Ridge vineyards – McCutcheon, Judd and Wallis – all located within a 10-minute tractor ride from each other. Three vineyards have been added since: a high-density vineyard at the cellar door and restaurant site (organically certified in '04), the Coolart Road vineyard in the north of the Peninsula, and the Main Ridge Spedding vineyard, a high-density pinot noir vineyard planted in '16. The wines are released in 3 ranges: 10X, made from estate-managed vineyards on the Mornington Peninsula; Estate, a reserve level blend; and Single Vineyard, from the best performing vineyard sites, usually a single block. In February '18, a fire destroyed the main storage facility at the cellar door and restaurant site, with over 16000 bottles of wine lost (including a treasured collection acquired across 20 years for the restaurant cellar). The site was rebuilt, including a new private dining room and underground cellar for the restaurant, as well as a private cellar door tasting room and wine gallery.

🍷🍷🍷🍷🍷 **Mills Chardonnay 2021, Mornington Peninsula** Fruit from Merricks that usually makes its way into the Estate range, but is good enough to stand alone this vintage. It's exceptionally good. Interesting aromas and flavours, quite chalk-like or limestoney, with oyster shell, lemon, grapefruit and pith with a juicy palate. There's succulence, texture and a fine layer of umami lees. Refreshing all the way through. Screw cap. 13.5% alc. **RATING** 95 **DRINK** 2023-2031 $82 JF
McCutcheon Chardonnay 2021, Mornington Peninsula This has substance and depth and is rather enticing. Expect lemon and grapefruit, rind and pith, too. Tangy and juicy with oak spices adding another layer of complexity. Tight across the palate thanks to the acidity, although there's texture and length. Moreish, savoury and very good. Screw cap. 13.5% alc. **RATING** 95 **DRINK** 2023-2031 $82 JF
Estate Chardonnay 2021, Mornington Peninsula Fine acidity is the keystone in the range, and across the Peninsula generally, in the '21 chardonnay vintage. This is a blend of different sites and winemaking and very much the sum of its parts. Citrus and stone fruit, ginger spice and nougatine, cedary/toasty oak and white miso lees come neatly packaged and held together by cooling acidity. Screw cap. 13% alc. **RATING** 95 **DRINK** 2022-2030 $49 JF ✪
Coolart Road Pinot Noir 2021, Mornington Peninsula The most complete single-site pinot in the range, it's still tight and uploaded with acidity but all the other elements are there to play a part. The silky tannins, the dark fruits and spice, the warm earth and undergrowth aromas. A more elegant style as a result. Screw cap. 13% alc. **RATING** 95 **DRINK** 2023-2031 $86 JF

ⵉⵉⵉⵉⵡ **10X Pinot Noir 2022**, Mornington Peninsula RATING 93 DRINK 2023–2029 $37 JF
Up The Hill Estate Pinot Noir 2021, Mornington Peninsula RATING 93 DRINK 2024–2031 $54 JF
Down The Hill Estate Pinot Noir 2021, Mornington Peninsula RATING 93 DRINK 2024–2033 $54 JF
Judd Chardonnay 2021, Mornington Peninsula RATING 93 DRINK 2023–2029 $82 JF
10X Pinot Noir 2021, Mornington Peninsula RATING 93 DRINK 2022–2028 $35 JF ✪
10X Barrel Fermented Sauvignon Blanc 2021, Mornington Peninsula RATING 92 DRINK 2022–2024 $34 JF
10X Chardonnay 2022, Mornington Peninsula RATING 91 DRINK 2023–2028 $34 JF
10X Chardonnay 2021, Mornington Peninsula RATING 91 DRINK 2022–2026 $35 JF
10X Rosé 2021, Mornington Peninsula RATING 91 DRINK 2022–2023 $34 JF
10X Pinot Gris 2021, Mornington Peninsula RATING 90 DRINK 2022–2024 $35 JF
McCutcheon Pinot Noir 2021, Mornington Peninsula RATING 90 DRINK 2023–2031 $86 JF
Judd Pinot Noir 2021, Mornington Peninsula RATING 90 DRINK 2024–2031 $86 JF

Tenafeate Creek Wines ★★★★

1071 Gawler–One Tree Hill Road, One Tree Hill, SA 5114 **Region** Mount Lofty Ranges **T** (08) 8280 7715 **www**.tcw.com.au **Open** Fri–Sun & public hols 11–5
Winemaker Larry Costa, Michael Costa **Est.** 2002 **Dozens** 3000 **Vyds** 1ha
Larry Costa, a former hairdresser, embarked on winemaking as a hobby in '02. The property, with its 1ha of shiraz, cabernet sauvignon and merlot, is situated on the rolling countryside of One Tree Hill in the Mount Lofty Ranges. The business grew rapidly, with grenache, nebbiolo, sangiovese, petit verdot, chardonnay, semillon and sauvignon blanc purchased to supplement the estate-grown grapes. Michael Costa, Larry's son (with 18 vintages under his belt, mainly in the Barossa Valley, with Flying Winemaker stints in southern Italy and Provence), joined his father as co-owner of the business.

ⵉⵉⵉⵉⵡ **One Tree Hill Basket Press Cabernet Sauvignon Merlot 2021**, Adelaide Hills Currant, sage, mint and juniper. The oak, embedded nicely within the fray. There is weight, flow, sap and punch to this, resulting in varietal marrow melded to sensitive winemaking and high-quality fruit. The structural lattice is on the softer side, facilitating earlier enjoyment. Nothing wrong with that. Screw cap. 14.5% alc. RATING 92 DRINK 2022–2030 $35 NG
Dry Grown Merlot 2021, Adelaide Hills This is a sensitively crafted, pulpy, energetic and immensely enjoyable merlot. And no, that is not an oxymoron! Full-weighted, yet frisky. Lilac, anise and damson the calling cards. Prosaic, perhaps, yet poised, fresh and eminently gulpable. Screw cap. 14.5% alc. RATING 91 DRINK 2022–2027 $35 NG
Purple Haze Shiraz 2022, Adelaide Hills Fun gear. A glossy vermilion. Grapey. Violet, anise, boysenberry and rosewater. The tannins are a bit stern, but fun drinking amid the mindless torpor demanded by a neighbourhood barbecue party. Screw cap. 14.5% alc. RATING 90 DRINK 2022–2025 $38 NG
One Tree Hill Basket Press Durif 2021, Mount Lofty Ranges Purple-People-Eater opaque. Glossy. Violet, with creosote and blue fruits so ripe. The tannins a reinforcement of sanity, restraint and a certain poise, despite the alcohol heat. A brooding, brutish thing with loads of fun tucked between the tannic seams. Screw cap. 16% alc. RATING 90 DRINK 2022–2032 $35 NG

One Tree Hill Basket Press Shiraz 2020, Mount Lofty Ranges A very hot year in these parts, made clear by the skinsy, tannic burl. Malt, bitter chocolate, dark and blue fruits and molten kirsch. A drying finish that needs placation, yet there is ample personality, grunt force and a level of poise that makes reaching for the next glass easier. Screw cap. 15% alc. **RATING** 90 **DRINK** 2022–2030 $40 NG

Terindah Estate

90 McAdams Lane, Bellarine, Vic 3223 **Region** Geelong
T (03) 5251 5536 **www**.terindahestate.com **Open** 7 days 10–4 **Winemaker** Robin Brockett **Est.** 2003 **Dozens** 3000 **Vyds** 5.6ha
Retired quantity surveyor Peter Slattery bought the 48ha property in '01, intending to plant the vineyard, make wine and develop a restaurant. He has achieved all of this (with help from others, of course), planting shiraz, pinot noir, pinot gris, picolit, chardonnay and zinfandel. Picolit is most interesting: it is a highly regarded grape in northern Italy, where it makes small quantities of high-quality sweet wine. It has proven very temperamental here, as in Italy, with very unreliable fruit set. In the meantime, he makes classic wines of very high quality from classic grape varieties.

Single Vineyard Bellarine Peninsula Shiraz 2021, Geelong A gorgeous crimson red, this is attractive from the outset with aromas of red and black fruits, fennel seeds, cracked black pepper, violets and just a little cedar from the well-handled oak. Medium bodied, balanced and persistent, the tannins are really fine and long. A beautifully put-together wine and one that should age gracefully, too. Screw cap. 13.5% alc. **RATING** 95 **DRINK** 2023–2029 $44 PR ✪

Single Vineyard Bellarine Peninsula Rosé 2022, Geelong RATING 90 **DRINK** 2022–2024 $32 PR

Terrason Wines

105/202 Beavers Road Northcote, Vic 3070 (postal) **Region** Victoria
T 0450 840 578 **www**.terrasonwines.com **Open** Not **Winemaker** Marc Lunt
Viticulturist Philip Abela, John Darling **Est.** 2016 **Dozens** 1000
The brainchild of Marc Lunt and Leanne Westell, Terrason Wines is many things. Since '16, it has been sourcing grapes from King Valley and Yarra Valley growers, making small amounts of wine from the kind of grapes they wish to explore: chardonnay, aligoté, gamay and pinot noir. All wines are made with minimal input. Marc and Leanne are also importers of French wine; again, choosing the kinds of wines that appeal to them, organic and made with minimal intervention. With both their French and Australian wines, the couple aims to adhere to a sustainable wine growing and honest winemaking philosophy. 'Our wines don't masquerade as something they are not, we aim for the terroir to speak for itself,' says Marc. Marc has made wine in Australia and in France where he spent a decade training and working harvests in Burgundy and Bordeaux.

Macclesfield Chardonnay 2022, Yarra Valley A little richer than Terrason's Swallowfield Chardonnay, the bouquet is fragrant with mirabelle plum, honeysuckle, white flowers and a hint of sea spray. Persistent and chalky textured on the palate, this is well-balanced and complex. Screw cap. 13% alc. **RATING** 95 **DRINK** 2023–2028 $45 PR ✪
Swallowfield Pinot Noir 2022, Yarra Valley Light, bright crimson purple. A straight-up gorgeous bouquet with spiced strawberries, red cherries, violets, white pepper and just the right amount of whole-bunch derived mountain herbs. Gently creamy, this lithe and energetic wine has bright acidity and finely chiselled tannins. Screw cap. 13.5% alc. **RATING** 95 **DRINK** 2023–2029 $45 PR ✪

Swallowfield Chardonnay 2022, Yarra Valley RATING 93 **DRINK** 2023–2027 $45 PR

Terre à Terre ★★★★★

15 Spring Gully Rd, Piccadilly SA 5151 **Region** Piccadilly Valley
T 0400 700 447 **www.**terreaterre.com.au **Open** At Tapanappa, Wed–Sun 11–4
Winemaker Xavier Bizot **Viticulturist** Xavier Bizot **Est.** 2008 **Dozens** 4000 **Vyds** 20ha
It would be hard to imagine 2 better-credentialled owners than Xavier Bizot (son of the
late Christian Bizot of Bollinger fame) and wife Lucy Croser (daughter of Brian and Ann
Croser). 'Terre à terre' is a French expression meaning down to earth. The close-planted
vineyard is on a limestone ridge, adjacent to Tapanappa's Whalebone vineyard. The vineyard
area has increased, leading to increased production (the plantings include cabernet sauvignon,
sauvignon blanc, cabernet franc and shiraz). Wines are released under the Terre à Terre, Down
to Earth, Sacrebleu and Daosa labels.

ŸŸŸŸŸ **Crayères Vineyard Cabernet Sauvignon Shiraz 2020, Wrattonbully**
Intensity of flavour is very good, but it's the tannin and the associated length that
really sets it apart. Blue, black and red-berried fruits, pencil shavings, gum leaf
and cocoa notes push persuasively through the palate, rolls of tannin then pressing
from the back palate on. A terrific release that will cellar like an absolute charm.
Screw cap. 14% alc. **RATING** 96 **DRINK** 2026–2040 $50 CM ✪

Crayères Vineyard Sauvignon Blanc 2022, Wrattonbully Both fermented
and aged in oak. There's a softness to the mouthfeel but there's also plenty of
drive and cut. This certainly covers the bases. Candied citrus, grapefruit pulp,
green pineapple and herb notes team to delicious, not to mention sophisticated,
effect here. The length of the finish is excellent too. Fantastic wine. Screw cap.
13.5% alc. **RATING** 95 **DRINK** 2024–2032 $50 CM ✪

Crayères Vineyard Cabernet Franc 2020, Wrattonbully Boasts the
prettiness of florals, the attraction of juicy fruit, and the sure-footed feel imparted
by ultrafine-grained tannin. This is one of those medium-weight red wines that
has an insistence, an impression of authority. At this low price, that's quite a feat.
Complexity and length, in this context, go without saying. A stand-out wine.
Screw cap. 13.8% alc. **RATING** 95 **DRINK** 2024–2036 $32 CM ✪

Daosa Blanc de Blancs 2018, Piccadilly Valley Scents of glazed quince, citrus
marmalade, shiitake, oak-derived acacia, almond meal and toasted brioche. A wine
of indelible precision as much as latent power, building across a long finish draped
with some perceivable sweetness. Diam. 12% alc. **RATING** 95 **DRINK** 2022–2030
$90 NG

ŸŸŸŸ¥ **Down to Earth Sauvignon Blanc 2022, Wrattonbully** **RATING** 92
DRINK 2023–2026 $32 CM

Téssera Wines ★★★★

McCallum Court, Strathalbyn, SA 5255 (postal) **Region** Adelaide Hills
T 0403 716 785 **www.**tesserawines.com.au **Open** Not **Winemaker** Peter Leske, Phil
Christiansen **Viticulturist** Jed Hicks, Arthur Loulakis, Ross McMurtrie **Est.** 2015
Dozens 1552
Téssera Wines started life in 2015 sourcing grapes from its local area around Strathalbyn on
the Fleurieu Peninsula. The word 'tessera' means 'four' in Greek and refers to the 4 close
friends who founded the company. As sales have increased, sourcing of grapes has broadened
to include McLaren Vale and the Adelaide Hills. Red wines are made by Phil Christiansen
in McLaren Vale, whites by Peter Leske. The company focuses on small-batch, quality wines
that remain true to the varietal integrity of the grapes sourced.

ŸŸŸŸ¥ **Chaste Shiraz 2020, McLaren Vale** Shiraz suits the tannic clip of American
oak. Fun! Dark, brooding and carnal. Star anise, Chinese medicine cabinet, clove
and oodles of palate-staining dark fruits. Despite the heat and rather obvious
power, the wine remains compact and relatively poised while driving long.
Screw cap. 14.6% alc. **RATING** 92 **DRINK** 2022–2032 $32 NG

Stompa Sauvignon Blanc 2022, Adelaide Hills Lightweight and textural,
rather than brittle, sweet-sour and tropical. While relatively prosaic, there is

a waxy lanolin-like feel, accents of quince, preserved Moroccan lemon and curry leaf giving a whiff of sophistication. Screw cap. 12.5% alc. **RATING** 90 **DRINK** 2022-2024 $28 NG

The Good Oil Shiraz Cabernet 2020, McLaren Vale A burly wine cast in American wood – a hark back to a tradition. Dark-fruit allusions, a belt of licorice, soy, hoisin, liniment and mocha-vanilla. There is heft in spades. Not necessarily much finesse, but that is probably not the point here. Personality, on the other hand, is. Screw cap. 14.5% alc. **RATING** 90 **DRINK** 2022-2030 $32 NG

Teusner

95 Samuel Road, Nuriootpa, SA 5355 **Region** Barossa Valley
T (08) 8562 4147 **www**.teusner.com.au **Open** By appt **Winemaker** Kym Teusner
Est. 2001 **Dozens** 30 000 **Vyds** 120ha
Teusner is a partnership between former Torbreck winemaker Kym Teusner and Javier Moll, and is typical of the new wave of winemakers determined to protect very old, low-yielding, dry-grown Barossa vines. The winery approach is based on lees ageing, little racking, no fining or filtration and no new American oak. As each year passes, the consistency, quality (and range) of the wines increases; there must be an end point, but it's not easy to guess when, or even if, it will be reached.

🍷🍷🍷🍷🍷 **MC Sparkling Shiraz Late Disgorgement 2005, Barossa Valley** Crimson with an energetic bead and mousse, the wine shows complex characters of plum, cherry and black fruits with polished leather notes coming into play. Still plenty of layered spice, earth, licorice and charcuterie facets. Super-fresh in the mouth with a nice red plum flourish and vivid acid cadence with meaty notes on the exit. Lovely drinking. Crown. 14.5% alc. **RATING** 95 **DRINK** 2023-2028 $90 DB

Big Jim Shiraz 2021, Barossa Valley Deep crimson and packed with plump, ripe satsuma plum and macerated summer berry fruits. Hints of baking spices, dark chocolate, earth, chocolate bullets, violets, olive tapenade, softly spoken cedar tones and vanilla. Plush and pure with bright acid drive and a fan of spicy dark and black berry fruits on the exit. Screw cap. 14.5% alc. **RATING** 95 **DRINK** 2023-2033 $70 DB

Joshua 2022, Barossa Valley A blend of grenache, mataro and shiraz unencumbered by artifact with pure, spicy plummy fruits, ginger spice and citrus blossom. Savoury, bright and spacious with a blast of sour morello cherry on the finish. It's still hitting the spot. Screw cap. 14.5% alc. **RATING** 94 **DRINK** 2023-2031 $37 DB ✪

Avatar 2021, Barossa Valley Grenache/mataro/shiraz. Packed full of ripe plummy fruit and dredged with spices, purple floral notes, licorice, earth and lighter dried orange rind and turned earth. A meaty facet flows in on the palate, which shows a lovely fruit depth, tight, compact tannins and a swell of spice and dark fruit on the exit. Screw cap. 14.5% alc. **RATING** 94 **DRINK** 2023-2028 $45 DB

Albert Shiraz 2019, Barossa Valley Deep crimson in the glass with plenty of rich blackberry, dark plum, black cherry and a lift of mulberry. Full-bodied with a sprightly seam of freshness, tightly packed gravelly tannins and a finish that fans out nicely with spiced plums, dark chocolate and softly spoken oak. Screw cap. 14.5% alc. **RATING** 94 **DRINK** 2023-2033 $70 DB

🍷🍷🍷🍷 **The Dog Strangler 2021, Barossa Valley RATING** 93 **DRINK** 2023-2030 $37 DB

The Wark Family Shiraz 2021, Barossa Valley RATING 93 **DRINK** 2023-2030 $32 DB ✪

The Empress Riesling 2022, Eden Valley RATING 92 **DRINK** 2023-2028 $30 DB ✪

Bilmore Shiraz 2021, Barossa Valley RATING 92 **DRINK** 2023-2028 $30 DB ✪

The Independent Shiraz Mataro 2021, Barossa Valley RATING 92
DRINK 2023–2029 $30 DB ✪
The Gentleman Cabernet Sauvignon 2021, Barossa RATING 92
DRINK 2023–2030 $30 DB ✪
The Riebke Shiraz 2020, Barossa Valley RATING 92 DRINK 2023–2028
$30 DB ✪

Thalia ★★★★

680 Main Road, Berriedale, Tas 7011 (postal) **Region** Tasmania
T 08 9282 5417 **www**.thalia.wine **Open** Not **Winemaker** Liam McElhinney
Viticulturist John Fogarty, Christian De Camps, Fred Peacock **Est.** 2021 **Dozens** 2000
Vyds 3ha
Thalia is the entry-level non-vintage brand of the Fogarty Wine Group's Tasmanian sparkling
operation, sister label to its more premium Lowestoft brand. Pinot noir takes the lead in
each blend, supported largely by chardonnay, sourced from across the length and breadth of
Tasmania, with a Reserve Cuvée hailing exclusively from a cool, coastal site on the Tasman
Peninsula. A serious newcomer to the Tasmanian sparkling set, crafting cuvées of this calibre
is no simple undertaking.

🍷🍷🍷🍷🍷 **Rosé NV, Tasmania** The palest of blushes in the glass with aromas of red apple,
cranberry and raspberry along with hints of tarte Tatin, biscuity spice, roasted
cashews, lemon butter, white flowers and stone. There is lovely red-fruited
richness and a swell of biscuity complexity that's reeled in by crystalline acidity
for a sustained finish. Diam. 12.5% alc. RATING 94 $55 DB

🍷🍷🍷🍷🍷 **Reserve Cuvée NV, Tasmania** RATING 93 $65 DB

The Happy Winemaker ★★★★★

16 Maddern Street, Black Hill, Vic 3350 (postal) **Region** Victoria
T 0431 252 015 **www**.thehappywinemaker.com.au **Open** Not **Winemaker** Jean-Paul
Trijsburg **Est.** 2015 **Dozens** 700 **Vyds** 1ha
Jean-Paul Trijsburg graduated with an agronomy degree from the Wageningen University
in the Netherlands and followed this with a joint MSc in viticulture and oenology in
Montpellier, France and Geisenheim, Germany. In between degrees he headed to Burgundy
in '07, which left him with a love of all things French, but he went on to work in wineries
in Pomerol, the Rheingau, Rioja, Chile and South Africa. Since '12, he has called Australia
home, having worked for Hanging Rock Winery in the Macedon Ranges and Lethbridge
Wines in Geelong. Today, he farms a small pinot noir vineyard in the Ballarat region, with
additional sourcing from Heathcote, Bendigo and Ballarat.

🍷🍷🍷🍷🍷 **Carménère by Jean-Paul 2021, Heathcote** It's all twigs and spices, boulders
and earth, with forest and winter berry characters coming at pace. It charges
through like a fury of nutshells, undergrowth and moss. It's not for everyone –
rage of this kind never is. But geez, as a drink, it's a ride to remember. Screw cap.
13.3% alc. RATING 95 DRINK 2022–2029 $32 CM ✪
Syrah by Jean-Paul 2021, Sunbury A beautiful style of red. Savoury to its
back teeth, but with juicy red-berried fruit running the length of it. Hazelnuts
and cherries, boysenberries and twiggy spices, flashes of cedar and mint. This is
perfectly polished. Indeed it's enough to make you think that we have a new star
in our midst. Screw cap. 13.2% alc. RATING 95 DRINK 2023–2033 $30 CM ✪
Pinot Gris by Jean-Paul 2022, Bendigo Personality plus. Quartz, pear and
apple flavours crunch their way through the palate. There's both dramatic flavour
and dramatic dryness at play here. The price of admission seems more than
reasonable. It's a controlled explosion of flavour, in the most positive of ways.
Screw cap. 12.5% alc. RATING 94 DRINK 2023–2026 $27 CM ✪ ♥
Riesling by Jean-Paul 2022, Bendigo The intensity of flavour here is
remarkable. Lime, apple and lemon sorbet notes burst convincingly onto the palate
and out through the finish. There's a lot of acidity and a lot of flavour, a little fruit

sweetness, too. For all that, it also feels long and linear. This is a riesling to make you sit up and take notice. Screw cap. 12.5% alc. RATING 94 DRINK 2024–2032 $27 CM ✪

Pinot Noir by Jean-Paul 2021, Ballarat First and foremost, this pinot noir is dry and sturdy, though there's also more than enough fruit, spice and overall flavour. Reduction and cedar oak are put to positive effect, though both are applied with restraint. The defining feature of this wine is its fruit-backward nature, which should mean that its best drinking years are ahead rather than now. Screw cap. 12.6% alc. RATING 94 DRINK 2024–2033 $37 CM ✪

🍷🍷🍷🍷🍷 **Grenache Blanc de Noir by Jean-Paul 2022, Heathcote** RATING 93 DRINK 2023–2028 $30 CM ✪
Mistelle Blanc NV, Victoria RATING 93 $40 CM
Nebbiolo by Jean Paul 2021, Strathbogie Ranges RATING 90 DRINK 2024–2030 $32 CM

The Islander Estate Vineyards ★★★★★

78 Gum Creek Road, Cygnet River, SA 5223 **Region** Kangaroo Island
T (08) 8553 9008 **www**.iev.com.au **Open** Thurs–Tues 12–5 **Winemaker** Jacques Lurton, Yale Norris **Viticulturist** Jacques Lurton, Yale Norris **Est.** 2000 **Dozens** 8000 **Vyds** 11ha

Established by one of the most famous Flying Winemakers in the world, Bordeaux-born and -trained and part-time Australian resident Jacques Lurton. The close-planted vineyard is principally planted to cabernet franc, shiraz and sangiovese, with lesser amounts of grenache, malbec, semillon and viognier. The wines are made and bottled at the onsite winery in true estate style. The property was ravaged by the terrible bushfire that devastated many (not all) parts of the island in January '20. It consumed the entire vineyard and its infrastructure, the house, the laboratory and the office, which became the sacrificial lamb slowing the fire sufficiently to allow the protection of the winery and its stock of bottled wine, and the wines still in barrel and tank. Long-time friend and business partner Yale Norris cut back every vine down to 20cm, hoping that shoots would appear. With great fortune, 70% of the vineyard recovered, and harvest began again from their estate vineyard in '23.

🍷🍷🍷🍷🍷 **Sangiovese 2021, South Australia** Very good colour. Fragrant bouquet and a complex, medium-bodied palate with cherry all-sorts: red, black and spiced. Overall a very good wine. Finely milled tannins the icing on the cake. Screw cap. 14% alc. RATING 95 DRINK 2023–2033 $35 JH ✪
Sem Sauv Blanc 2021, South Australia The semillon was fermented in new French puncheons, the sauvignon blanc tank fermented. Matured for 12 months in barrel and tank, no mlf. Awash with flavour, ranging from citrus to exotic tropical notes. Screw cap. 13% alc. RATING 95 DRINK 2023–2026 $35 JH ✪
The Rosé 2022, Kangaroo Island Ultra-pale partridge eye. Jacques Lurton had primary responsibility for this wine, underlining the skilled balance between wild strawberries and forest nuances sneaking up to a mouth-cleansing finish. Ideal for Chinese cuisine. Screw cap. 13% alc. RATING 94 DRINK 2023–2034 $35 JH ✪

🍷🍷🍷🍷🍷 **Sauvignon Blanc 2022, Kangaroo Island** RATING 92 DRINK 2023–2024 $35 JH
The White Chardonnay 2021, South Australia RATING 92 DRINK 2023–2029 $28 JH ✪

The King's Creed ★★★★

169 Douglas Gully Road, Blewitt Spings SA 5171 (postal) **Region** McLaren Vale
T 0439 479 758 **www**.threekingswinemerchants.com.au **Open** Not **Winemaker** Ben Riggs **Est.** 2020

The King's Creed label falls under the aegis of Three Kings Wine Merchants, a collaboration between winemaker Ben Riggs, former Wallaby Nathan Sharpe and ex-LVMH marketeer, David Krenich. The wines are marked with salubrious oak and plenty of extract at the pointy end of the hierarchy.

♥♥♥♥♀ Rosé 2022, Fleurieu Raspberry and cranberry with edges of snow peas and spice. It's both generous and neat at the same time. It's a dry, mouth-watering style but there's plenty of juicy flavour here, and those herbal edges give it something extra. Screw cap. 13% alc. RATING 91 DRINK 2023-2024 $25 CM ✪
Pinot Grigio 2022, Adelaide Hills Hand picked and cool-fermented in tank with a small portion matured in oak. Solid grigio, mid-weighted, nicely chewy and brimming with notes of lanolin, quince paste and spiced apple. Screw cap. 13% alc. RATING 90 DRINK 2022-2024 $25 NG ✪
Shiraz 2020, McLaren Vale Ample satisfaction for those in search of full-bodied, hot-climate shiraz with a modicum of class. Kirsch, blue-fruit allusions, aniseed and florals all flowing long and effortlessly to a warm, throaty finish. Screw cap. 14.5% alc. RATING 90 DRINK 2022-2028 $25 NG ✪

The Lake House Denmark ★★★★

106 Turner Road, Denmark, WA 6333 **Region** Denmark
T (08) 9848 2444 **www.lakehousedenmark.com.au Open** 7 days 10–5
Winemaker Harewood Estate (James Kellie) **Est.** 1995 **Dozens** 8000 **Vyds** 5.2ha
Garry Capelli and Leanne Rogers purchased the property in '05 and restructured the vineyard to grow varieties suited to the climate – chardonnay, pinot noir, semillon and sauvignon blanc – incorporating biodynamic principles. They also manage a couple of small family-owned vineyards in Frankland River and Mount Barker with a similar ethos. The combined cellar door, restaurant and gourmet food emporium is a popular destination.

♥♥♥♥♥ Premium Reserve Single Vineyard Cabernet Sauvignon 2020, Frankland River A mellow, elegant and deeply flavoured medium-bodied cabernet. Delivers succulent texture with fine, firm tannin structure. An impressive red wine imbued with plummy fruit, mixed brown spice character, pleasing earthiness and herbal bay leaf characters. Understated power and great balance are inherent. Screw cap. 14.5% alc. RATING 94 DRINK 2022-2040 $59 MB

♥♥♥♥♀ Merum Reserve Single Vineyard Riesling 2022, Porongurup RATING 93 DRINK 2022-2030 $39 MB
Premium Reserve Single Vineyard Riesling 2022, Porongurup RATING 92 DRINK 2022-2027 $39 MB
Premium Reserve Sauvignon Blanc Semillon 2022, Denmark RATING 90 DRINK 2023-2028 $39 MB
Merum Semillon Sauvignon Blanc 2022, Denmark RATING 90 DRINK 2023-2027 $39 MB
Merum Reserve Shiraz 2020, Frankland River RATING 90 DRINK 2022-2028 $42 MB

The Lane Vineyard ★★★★★

5 Ravenswood Lane, Balhannah, SA 5244 **Region** Adelaide Hills
T (08) 8388 1250 **www.thelane.com.au Open** 7 days 10–5 **Winemaker** Turon White
Viticulturist Jared Stringer **Est.** 1993 **Dozens** 25 000 **Vyds** 75ha
The Lane Vineyard is one of the Adelaide Hills' elite wine tourism attractions, with a cellar door and restaurant that offers focused tastings by region and style, with endless views. Established by the Edwards family in '93, it was aquired by the UK's Vestey Group in '12, following their establishment of Coombe Farm in the Yarra Valley. Four distinct tiers of single-vineyard wines are produced at The Lane: the entry-level Lane series from the Adelaide Hills, the Provenance range from in and around the Adelaide Hills and the top-tier Estate and Heritage ranges from their Hahndorf estate vines.

♥♥♥♥♥ Heritage Shiraz Viognier 2020, Adelaide Hills White pepper, clove and green olive meld with blueberry, salumi, star anise, sumac, lilac and a skein of iodine freshness. Tannic astringency confers a savoury welt while evincing authority, despite the regional sweetness. Precise and persistent. Screw cap. 14% alc. RATING 96 DRINK 2022-2030 $120 NG

Gathering Sauvignon Blanc Semillon 2021, Adelaide Hills A sophisticated wine of restraint, filigreed freshness, detail, impeccably nestled oak and impressive precision. Barrel fermented and aged with substantial time on lees. Lemongrass, tonic, barley sugar, quince, nettle and cantaloupe, with a gingery spice trailing long. This will be fascinating to drink over a mid-term ageing trajectory. Screw cap. 13.5% alc, RATING 95 DRINK 2022–2030 $40 NG ✪

Estate Cuvée Blanc de Blancs 2018, Adelaide Hills A drier sparkling than the regional norm. A core of creamed cashew and nougat, some barrel work imparting textural breadth and acacia notes across a waft of mandarin peel, marmalade and ginger. Wonderful intensity on show. A bit shins and elbows-edgy. I'd like to taste this again in a few years, as its future bodes very well indeed. Diam. 12.5% alc. RATING 94 DRINK 2022–2030 $70 NG

Gathering Sauvignon Blanc Semillon 2022, Adelaide Hills Very good thanks to the quality of fruit and maturation in barrel conferring a stone-fruited pungency and mineral trajectory to the greengage, guava and nettle undertones. Mid-weighted and powerful, with juiciness growing in steam across the long finish. This is a very sophisticated bordeaux blend. Screw cap. 13% alc. RATING 94 DRINK 2023–2028 $45 NG

Heritage Chardonnay 2021, Adelaide Hills Lean and steely, with a riff of lime curd, nougat and pungent mineral attesting to extended lees work. There is a whiff of nectarine and pear nectar, but it needs time to liberate itself from a reductive carapace. When it does so, I expect good things. Screw cap. 12.8% alc. RATING 94 DRINK 2023–2032 $100 NG

🍷🍷🍷🍷🍷 **Provenance Pinot Noir 2022, Adelaide Hills** RATING 93 DRINK 2023–2030 $55 NG

Provenance Cabernet Franc 2022, Adelaide Hills RATING 93 DRINK 2023–2028 $45 NG

Beginning Chardonnay 2021, Adelaide Hills RATING 93 DRINK 2022–2030 $50 NG

LDR 2022, Adelaide Hills RATING 92 DRINK 2023–2028 $30 NG ✪

Provenance Tempranillo 2022, Adelaide Hills RATING 92 DRINK 2023–2030 $45 NG

Provenance Gamay 2022, Adelaide Hills RATING 92 DRINK 2023–2028 $55 NG

Shiraz 2021, Adelaide Hills RATING 92 DRINK 2022–2028 $30 NG

Reunion Shiraz 2020, Adelaide Hills RATING 92 DRINK 2022–2028 $65 NG

Pinot Noir 2022, Adelaide Hills RATING 91 DRINK 2023–2030 $30 NG

Provenance Pinot Blanc 2022, Adelaide Hills RATING 91 DRINK 2022–2025 $35 NG

The Other Wine Co ★★★★

136 Jones Road, Balhannah, SA 5242 **Region** South Australia
T (08) 8398 0500 **www**.theotherwineco.com **Open** At Shaw + Smith **Winemaker** Matt Large **Viticulturist** Murray Leake **Est.** 2015 **Dozens** 5000
This is the venture of Michael Hill Smith and Martin Shaw, established in the shadow of Shaw + Smith but with an entirely different focus and separate marketing. The name reflects the wines, which are intended for casual consumption; the whole focus being freshness combined with seductive mouthfeel.

🍷🍷🍷🍷🍷 **Pinot Gris 2022, Adelaide Hills** This is excellent gris. A thrust of nashi pear granita and preserved lemon is met with a parry of quinine bitterness and chewy phenolics, impeccably managed on the side of intrigue. The finish is long, compact and immensely juicy. Stellar value and sumptuous drinking, all at a very fair price. Screw cap. 13% alc. RATING 93 DRINK 2022–2026 $26 NG ✪

Ricca Terra Farms Arinto 2022, Riverland The back label of a bottle of wine is rarely a place for good or reliable reading, but this wine describes itself as 'savoury, saline and textural,' and it has to be acknowledged that this is the perfect summary. It's grippy, dry and different, too, thanks to its flavour/texture profile, and these descriptors combined make it a wine worth seeking out. Screw cap. 13% alc. **RATING** 92 **DRINK** 2022–2025 $26 CM ✪

Grenache 2021, Adelaide Hills A mid-ruby hue segues to scents of bergamot, cranberry, kirsch, cocoa nib and a waft of scrubby menthol. The tannins, a sandy splay across the mouth, pull the saliva in readiness for the next glass. There is a succulence, sappiness and grippy structural latticework to this, making for very good drinking. Screw cap. 14% alc. **RATING** 92 **DRINK** 2022–2026 $27 NG ✪

No. 1 Savagnin 2021, Fleurieu The inaugural release of this Jura-inspired expression, the influence of flor clear from the first whiff. Think cheesecloth, chamomile and aged parmesan with a backdrop of peat. Notes of lemon peel, pickled cumquat and tangerine rise above. Saline and chalky, with that malty, whisky-like overtone lingering long. Clearly a cuvée to follow into the future. Screw cap. 13.5% alc. **RATING** 92 **DRINK** 2023–2030 $28 NG ✪

The Pawn Wine Co.

10 Banksia Road, Macclesfield, SA 5153 (postal) **Region** South Australia
T 0438 373 247 **www**.thepawn.com.au **Open** Not **Winemaker** Tom Keelan
Viticulturist Tom Keelan **Est.** 2002 **Dozens** 10 000 **Vyds** 35ha
The Pawn Wine Co. began as a partnership between Tom Keelan and Rebecca Willson (Bremerton Wines) and David and Vanessa Blows. Tom was for some time manager of Longview Vineyards at Macclesfield in the Adelaide Hills, and consulted to the neighbouring vineyard, owned by David and Vanessa. In '17 Tom and Rebecca purchased David and Vanessa's share, but David still supplies grapes to the Pawn Wine Co., and Tom works very closely with David and his 3 sons to produce food-friendly wines that reflect their origins.

🍷🍷🍷🍷🍷 **Fiano 2022, Langhorne Creek** Wild-yeast fermented; orange blossom, distinct melon and almonds, but then a funky/feral mouthfeel. It's a wine of courage. Screw cap. 12% alc. **RATING** 94 **DRINK** 2023–2029 $22 JH ✪

🍷🍷🍷🍷🍷 **Shiraz 2021, Adelaide Hills** **RATING** 91 **DRINK** 2022–2028 $40 NG

The Story Wines

170 Riverend Road, Bangholme, Vic 3175 **Region** Grampians
T 0411 697 912 **www**.thestory.com.au **Open** By appt **Winemaker** Rory Lane
Viticulturist Andrew Toomey, Tim Morris, Rory Lane **Est.** 2004 **Dozens** 2500 **Vyds** 6ha
Before becoming a winemaker, Rory Lane was on an academic path, earning himself a degree in Greek literature. He says that after completing his degree and 'desperately wanting to delay an entry into the real world, I stumbled across a postgraduate wine technology and marketing course, where I soon became hooked on … the wondrous connection between land, human and liquid'. Vintages in Australia and Oregon germinated the seed and he zeroed in on the Grampians, where he purchases small parcels of high-quality grapes. He makes the wines in a small factory where he has assembled a basket press, a few open fermenters, a mono pump and some decent French oak. A cellar door is due to open late '23 or early '24.

🍷🍷🍷🍷🍷 **R. Lane Vintners Westgate Vineyard Syrah 2021, Grampians** This is a stellar red wine. It's so glossy, so svelte, so well flavoured and so well formed. It pushes cherry and plum flavours through peanut and sweet spice, though there are myriad herb and nut characters here, not to mention peppers. It's both an elegant wine and a powerful one, and its velvety mouthfeel makes it a joy to drink. Screw cap. 13.5% alc. **RATING** 96 **DRINK** 2025–2040 $75 CM ✪

Super G Grenache Syrah Mourvèdre 2022, Grampians It's not heavy but it's so wild with spice and so generally captivating that it's hard to put it down. This is a cracker of a wine. Red and blue berried fruit flavours, black pepper notes, a mezcal aspect and flings of roasted nuts. It's ripe and robust, in a mid-weight way, but the real key here is that it's aflame with roasted spice/pepper notes. Screw cap. 14% alc. **RATING** 95 **DRINK** 2024–2034 $34 CM ✪

Marsanne Roussanne Viognier 2020, Grampians This is both seriously structured and seriously flavoured. Talk about presence. It's both nutty and fresh, a little positively reductive, too, with stone fruit, chestnut, sweet hay and bacon-like characters pushing persuasively throughout. It has some grip, a lot of punch, and excellent length. Watch this space; it will continue to evolve from here. Screw cap. 13% alc. **RATING** 95 **DRINK** 2025-2032 $34 CM ✪

Whitlands Close Planted Riesling 2022, King Valley 7 g/L RS. It sits pale in the glass, smells delicate on the nose, and is then intense on the palate, but soft. This is a gorgeous style of wine. It offers lemon, makrut lime and chalk notes with the most delicious burst of flavour-carrying acidity through the finish. Screw cap. 11.5% alc. **RATING** 94 **DRINK** 2024-2035 $35 CM ✪

Moyston Hills Syrah 2021, Grampians Rory Lane calls this wine syrah because of its 'proper' syrah spice and perfume. It certainly projects plenty of the spicy stuff – pepper, fennel seed, bay leaf, rosemary – but there's more to laud. Works a fine-textured tannin riff through dark cherry, plum and dusty cacao, finishing with a lasting, gentle savouriness. Dances rather than glides. Delicious. Screw cap. 14% alc. **RATING** 94 **DRINK** 2022-2030 $40 JP ✪

🍷🍷🍷🍷🍷 **Skin Contact Marsanne Roussanne Viognier 2021, Grampians** **RATING** 92 **DRINK** 2023-2027 $42 CM

The Thief?

117A Murray Street, Tanunda, SA 5352 **Region** Barossa Valley
T 0439 823 251 **www**.thethiefwines.com.au **Open** Wed–Thurs 2–6, Fri 2–late, or by appt
Winemaker Natasha Mooney **Est.** 2016 **Dozens** 1500 **Vyds** 10ha
The Thief? is 1 of 2 side projects for the well-known and highly talented Natasha Mooney, who is a winemaker by day for some of SA's larger wineries. While her other side project, La Bise, focuses on bought-in fruit, The Thief? is produced from Natasha's own vines, planted to shiraz and cabernet in the '90s. She purchased the Barossa vineyard in '16 and is in the process of converting it to organic/biodynamic status. The name is a nod to Natasha's great-great-grandfather John Mooney, who was wrongly accused of stealing a cow.

🍷🍷🍷🍷🍷 **Shiraz 2021, Barossa Valley** Deep crimson in the glass with notes of juicy satsuma plum and summer berry fruits, violets, baking spices, licorice, earth and roasting meats. Svelte and rich with impressive density and flow on the palate and finishing with a swoop of spicy plum fruits. Screw cap. 14% alc. **RATING** 90 **DRINK** 2023-2029 $33 DB

Old Vine Shiraz Cabernet 2021, Barossa Valley Deep, purple-splashed magenta with notes of blackberry, blood plum and boysenberry fruits with plenty of baking spices, cedar, vanilla pod, licorice, violets and dark chocolatey notes. Tight, compact and toothsome on the palate with graphite and dark/black fruits, grainy tannin heft and a decent dash of cedar and clove finishing dry with puckering tannins. Screw cap. 14% alc. **RATING** 90 **DRINK** 2023-2028 $55 DB

The Wanderer

2850 Launching Place Road, Gembrook, Vic 3783 **Region** Yarra Valley
T 0415 529 639 **www**.wandererwines.com **Open** By appt **Winemaker** Andrew Marks
Est. 2005 **Dozens** 500
The Wanderer wines are a series of single-vineyard wines made by Andrew Marks, winemaker and viticulturalist at Gembrook Hill Vineyard. Andrew spent 6 years as a winemaker with Penfolds before returning to Gembrook Hill in '05. He has worked numerous vintages in France and Spain including Etienne Sauzet in Puligny Montrachet in '06 and more recently over 10 vintages in the Costa Brava, Spain. Andrew seeks to achieve the best expression of his vineyards through minimal handling in the winery.

🍷🍷🍷🍷🍷 **Chardonnay 2021, Upper Yarra Valley** Bright green gold. A subtle wine that reveals itself slowly. Scents of stone fruits, citrus, jasmine and orange blossom lead onto the palate which has a gentle creaminess together with a very fine vein of acidity. The finish is layered and long. Lovely stuff. Diam. 12.5% alc. **RATING** 96 **DRINK** 2023-2027 $35 PR ✪

Pinot Noir 2021, Yarra Valley A light, bright crimson. Fragrant and pretty with aromas of small red fruits, pomegranate, peony and a hint of pink peppercorns. Fills out nicely on the palate, the texture of the wine belying the colour. Persistent, finishing with subtle, fine, savoury tannins. Diam. 13% alc. **RATING** 95 **DRINK** 2022-2028 $35 PR ✪

The Willows Vineyard   ★★★★☆

310 Light Pass Road, Light Pass, SA 5355 **Region** Barossa Valley
T (08) 8562 1080 **www.thewillowsvineyard.com.au Open** Wed–Mon 10.30–4.30
Winemaker Peter Scholz, Jack Scholz **Viticulturist** Peter Scholz, Jack Scholz **Est.** 1989
Dozens 6000 **Vyds** 42.74ha

The Scholz family has been growing grapes for generations, and they have over 40ha of vineyards, including vines planted in 1936. Father-and-son winemaking team Peter and Jack make rich, ripe, velvety wines, some marketed with some bottle age.

🍷🍷🍷🍷🍷 **G Seven Shiraz 2021, Barossa Valley** Inviting aromas of plums and black cherries lined with deep spice, cassis, licorice, dark chocolate, violets and blueberry strudel. There's almost a liquored blackberry character on the palate, but there is still crunch and verve to the wine's form with fine, silky tannins and a bright acid pulse. Screw cap. 14.4% alc. **RATING** 95 **DRINK** 2023-2029 $45 DB ✪

Bonesetter Shiraz 2020, Barossa Valley Plenty of black-fruited depth, oak and spicy, dark chocolate. There's a lot packed into this bottle, but it finishes savoury and balanced with ripe, sandy tannins. It could be from nowhere else except the Barossa. And I love that. Screw cap. 14.9% alc. **RATING** 94 **DRINK** 2023-2036 $75 DB

🍷🍷🍷🍷🍷 **G Seven Mataro 2022, Barossa Valley RATING** 93 **DRINK** 2023-2033 $35 DB ✪

The Doctor Sparkling Red NV, McLaren Vale RATING 92 $45 DB
Old Vine Semillon 2022, Barossa Valley RATING 92 **DRINK** 2023-2033 $22 DB ✪
Riesling 2022, Barossa Valley RATING 92 **DRINK** 2023-2028 $20 DB ✪
G Seven Grenache 2022, Barossa Valley RATING 92 **DRINK** 2023-2030 $35 DB
Shiraz 2020, Barossa Valley RATING 91 **DRINK** 2023-2029 $35 DB

Thick as Thieves Wines   ★★★★☆

355 Healesville - Koo Wee Rup Road, Badger Creek, Vic 3777 **Region** Yarra Valley
T 0417 184 690 **www.tatwines.com.au Open** By appt **Winemaker** Syd Bradford
Viticulturist Syd Bradford **Est.** 2009 **Dozens** 2000 **Vyds** 2ha

A growing interest in good food and wine might have come to nothing had it not been for Pfeiffer Wines giving Syd Bradford a vintage job in '03. In that year he enrolled in the wine science course at CSU; he then moved to the Yarra Valley in '05, gaining experience at a number of wineries including Coldstream Hills. Syd was desperate to have a go at crafting his own 'babies'. In '09 he came across a small parcel of arneis from the Hoddles Creek area, and Thick as Thieves was born. The techniques used to make his babies could only come from someone who has spent a long time observing and thinking about what he might do if he were calling the shots.

🍷🍷🍷🍷🍷 **Limited Release Syrah 2022, Yarra Valley** A deep and gorgeous crimson purple. Darkly fruited, you'll find aromas of potpourri, exotic spices and a little olive tapenade on the nose. A little licorice root and some violets, too. Medium bodied and beautifully balanced, this finishes long with chewy, fine tannins and very bright acidity. As good a Thick as Thieves wine as I can remember tasting. Screw cap. 12.8% alc. **RATING** 96 **DRINK** 2022-2028 $45 PR ✪

Purple Prose Gamay 2022, King Valley A very bright, medium crimson red. Perfumed with its aromas of morello cherries, wild strawberries, violets and white pepper. Bright and flavoursome in the mouth, there are enough gently grippy tannins to suggest that it should age well in the short- to medium-term. Good stuff. Screw cap. 12.2% alc. RATING 94 DRINK 2022-2027 $38 PR ✪

🍷🍷🍷🍷🍷 **The Aloof Alpaca Arneis 2022, Yarra Valley** RATING 93 DRINK 2022-2028 $27 PR ✪
Plump Pinot Noir 2022, Yarra Valley RATING 93 DRINK 2024-2032 $38 PR
Driftwood Gamay Pinot Noir 2022, King Valley Yarra Valley RATING 90 DRINK 2022-2025 $35 PR

Thicker Than Water

86 McMurtrie Rd, McLaren Vale, SA 5171 **Region** McLaren Vale
T (08) 8323 7940 **www**.thickerthanwaterwines.com.au **Open** 10–5 Mon–Fri, w'ends 11–5 **Winemaker** Campbell Greer **Viticulturist** Chalk Hill Viticulture **Est.** 1999 **Dozens** 3700 **Vyds** 8.9ha
Thicker Than Water (previously McLaren Vale III Associates) is a very successful boutique winery owned by Mary and John Greer and Reg Wymond. An impressive portfolio of estate-grown wines allows them control over quality and consistency, and thus success in Australian and international wine shows. The cellar door opened in January '23.

🍷🍷🍷🍷🍷 **Squid Ink Shiraz 2020, McLaren Vale** This is an exceptionally crafted shiraz of a rich and burly omnipresence. Certainly more contemporary. Blue fruit coulis, anise, white pepper and nori accents drive through a curtain of oak, setting the trail for impressive ageability. Screw cap. 14.5% alc. RATING 95 DRINK 2023-2035 $65 NG
Giant Squid Ink Shiraz 2020, McLaren Vale An older-school, full-bodied wine that is nevertheless considerably fresher and finer-boned than in recent memory. Aromas of cedar, campfire, hoisin, clove, anise, creased leather, sweet earth and soy. Well-applied mocha oak serves as a restraint as much as a signpost of good length. There is plenty of charm on display, encouraging one to simply give in and sip. Screw cap. 14.5% alc. RATING 94 DRINK 2022-2030 $180 NG

🍷🍷🍷🍷🍷 **Legacy Shiraz 2021, McLaren Vale** RATING 93 DRINK 2022-2035 $120 NG
Paralarva Shiraz 2022, McLaren Vale RATING 92 DRINK 2022-2028 $45 NG

Thistledown Wines ★★★★★

c/- Revenir, Peacock Road North, Lenswood, SA 5240 (postal) **Region** South Australia
T 0424 472 831 **www**.thistledownwines.com **Open** Not **Winemaker** Giles Cooke MW **Est.** 2010 **Dozens** 10 000
Thistledown is a conflation of wisdom, foresight and strident confidence; an assemblage of talent, superb old-vine sites and remarkable wines that have established a firmament at the top of the grenache totem in this country. Giles Cooke and Fergal Tynan – each a master of wine, historian and lover of the world's finest grenache – became tired of international stereotypes of Australian wine. With vast experience respectively making and selling wines from Spain, they began to carve out a niche defined by filigreed precision, thirst-slaking tannins and crunchy red fruit elements. These are small-batch micro-ferments handled in the right vessels and extracted with aplomb. They unravel as exquisite expressions to be sure.

🍷🍷🍷🍷🍷 **This Charming Man Single Vineyard Clarendon Grenache 2022, McLaren Vale** Ironstone imparts a ferrous bite to pithy sour cherry, cranberry, campfire, pomegranate, tamarind and sandalwood notes with a grind of white pepper across a lattice of pin bone tannins, curtailing sweetness while promoting stunning length. Superb! Transparent and brimming like a mini Rayas. Among Australia's very greatest reds in my opinion. Screw cap. 14% alc. RATING 97 DRINK 2023-2031 $80 NG ✪ ♥

🍷🍷🍷🍷🍷 **The Vagabond Old Vine Blewitt Springs Grenache 2022, McLaren Vale**
Brilliant! Like a slinky, before release over the top step, as riffs on persimmon,
Seville orange, rosehip, pomegranate and impeccably ripe cherry clafoutis unwind
and expand with a rattle. Long, with gorgeous tannins. World class. Screw cap.
14.5% alc. RATING 96 DRINK 2022–2030 $60 NG ✪

**Sands of Time Single Vineyard Blewitt Springs Grenache 2022,
McLaren Vale** Lifted and fresh and laden with sweet, succulent red fruits, tangerine
zest, musk, kirsch, rosewater and lilac. This is a brilliant, flamboyant grenache, if
not a little sweet across the diaphanous tannic seams. It is a treat to witness the rise
of grenache, the flag bearer of the most exciting chapter of Australian wine to date.
Screw cap. 14.5% alc. RATING 96 DRINK 2023–2030 $95 NG

Walking with Kings Roussanne Grenache Blanc 2022, McLaren Vale
Tatami straw, lemon drop, quinine, pickled stone fruits and ginger. Long and
drawn out with chewy tannins and a waft of maritime freshness. Soft, mind you,
but perfectly positioned. A mid-weighted wine of textural tapestry, poise and
verve. Screw cap. 13.5% alc. RATING 95 DRINK 2023–2028 $60 NG

Bachelor's Block Ebenezer Shiraz 2021, Barossa Valley A savoury tour
de force of black olive, tar, blood, clove, aniseed, mace and a ferrous underbelly
of ironstone echoing the site. The mid-palate slips into the girth of Barossa,
imparting sweet purple fruits and weight. It is always easy, of course, to want
less of what is on offer, yet the thrum of energy here delivers length, welcome
restraint and serious complexity. The nose alone is worth the price! Diam.
14.5% alc. RATING 95 DRINK 2022–2032 $95 NG

She's Electric Old Vine Single Vineyard Grenache 2022, McLaren Vale
Damson plum and Marasca cherry. Anise, thyme, menthol and lavender. A
tad drying. A delicious wine of an expansive mid-palate, intensity of fruit and
prodigious length, yet without the translucent pinosité and levity – despite the
alcohol and oomph – that marks the very best examples of grenache from the
Vale. Screw cap. 14.5% alc. RATING 94 DRINK 2022–2032 $70 NG

Thorny Devil Old Vine Grenache 2022, McLaren Vale Savoury, the
signature. Varying degrees of whole bunches. A number of picking windows,
too, to embellish freshness and enough weight. I'd be hard-pressed to find a
better wine than this for the price. Kirsch, ume, cranberry, bergamot with
pixelated tannin, sandy of feel, directing length. Screw cap. 14% alc. RATING 94
DRINK 2022–2028 $36 NG ✪

Where Eagles Dare Mattschoss Vineyard Shiraz 2021, Eden Valley
A lather of lilac, lavender and licorice defines a sumptuous nose. Purple fruits and
rosewater, the palate, with a creep of tannin growing in gravitas across the back
end as the wine opens. This is a delicious, full-weighted expression of considerable
class and detail. Top of the totem in the region. The sole caveat, the burn across
the throaty finish. Diam. 14.5% alc. RATING 94 DRINK 2022–2032 $95 NG

Where Eagles Dare Mattschoss Vineyard Shiraz 2020, Eden Valley
This is dense, compact and tense enough to promote graceful ageing. A large-
framed and clearly warm–climate wine, yet the tannins are refined and saliva-
inducing. In its infancy, cedar and mocha oak, bitter chocolate, iodine, black
olive tapenade, anise and blue- to darker-fruit allusions with a whiff of violet and
charcuterie riffs. Very good. Screw cap. 14.5% alc. RATING 94 DRINK 2022–2032
$80 NG

🍷🍷🍷🍷🍷 **Great Escape Chardonnay 2022, Eden Valley** RATING 93 DRINK 2022–2028
$34 NG ✪

Fool on the Hill Mattschoss Vineyard Grenache 2022, Eden Valley
RATING 93 DRINK 2023–2029 $95 NG

The Distant Light Grenache Shiraz 2020, Barossa Valley RATING 93
DRINK 2022–2032 $75 NG

Gorgeous Grenache Blanc 2022, South Australia RATING 92
DRINK 2022–2026 $26 NG ✪

Cloud Cuckoo Land Fiano Zibibbo 2022, Riverland RATING 92
DRINK 2022–2024 $24 NG ✪
Gorgeous Grenache 2022, South Australia RATING 90 DRINK 2022–2024
$26 NG
Gorgeous Shiraz 2022, South Australia RATING 90 DRINK 2022–2025
$26 NG
Cloud Cuckoo Land Nero d'Avola Montepulciano Aglianico 2022,
Riverland RATING 90 DRINK 2022–2026 $24 NG ✪

Thomas St Vincent

PO Box 633, McLaren Vale, SA 5171 **Region** McLaren Vale
T 0438 605 694 **www.thomasstvincent.com Open** Not **Winemaker** Gary Thomas
Est. 2016 **Dozens** 240
Among the more exciting suites of wine to pass across my tasting bench in years, Thomas
St Vincent wines are hugely influenced by the greatest wines of the Rhône and Provence.
I (Ned) don't say that lightly. Winemaker Gary Thomas has tasted a trove of the greatest
wines in the world, including Rayas – and it shows. These wines suggest a craftsperson deeply
versed in the philosophy of terroir as much as the pragmatic mechanics of winemaking. This
is the sturm und drang of the Alpilles, the Dentelles and the Pyrenees, washed onto the
foreshores of the Gulf of Saint Vincent and delivered intuitively to the glass.

ΨΨΨΨΨ **Blewitt Springs Provencale Rouge 2020, Fleurieu** A southern Rhône-
style blend of 65% mourvèdre and small portions of cinsault, carignan, grenache,
morrastel and counoise. Smoked meats, camphor and succulent red fruits doused
in thyme and lavender. Excellent wine at a ridiculous price. Atypically Australian
in the most beautiful way. Screw cap. 14.5% alc. **RATING** 96 **DRINK** 2022–2032
$39 NG ✪ ♥
Blewitt Springs Septentrionale Rouge 2020, Fleurieu Shiraz, with a
touch of cabernet sauvignon. There is a drive here to make herb-doused wines
that glimpse fruit, as opposed to being saturated with it. This is delicious. Smoked
meat, sapid sour cherry, dried thyme, lavender, rosemary, sage and a smear of olive
encased in the most effortless, savoury guise. Mercifully, no eucalyptus. This would
be very hard to discern in a blind line-up of Provençal greats. Diam. 14.5% alc.
RATING 95 **DRINK** 2022–2030 $39 NG ✪ ♥

Thomas Wines

28 Mistletoe Lane, Pokolbin, NSW 2320 **Region** Hunter Valley
T (02) 4998 7134 **www.thomaswines.com.au Open** 7 days 10–5 **Winemaker** Andrew
Thomas **Viticulturist** Andrew Thomas **Est.** 1997 **Dozens** 12 000 **Vyds** 6ha
Andrew Thomas moved to the Hunter Valley from McLaren Vale to join the winemaking
team at Tyrrell's Wines. After 13 years, he left to continue the development of his own
label. He makes single-vineyard wines, underlining the subtle differences between the
various subregions of the Hunter. The major part of the production comes from long-term
arrangements with growers of old-vine semillon and shiraz. The acquisition of Braemore
vineyard in '17 was significant, giving Thomas Wines a long-term supply of grapes from one
of the Hunter Valley's most distinguished semillon sites. Andrew's eldest son Daniel stepped
into the role of assistant winemaker in '20.

ΨΨΨΨΨ **Kiss Limited Release Shiraz 2021, Hunter Valley** Lovely hue and depth,
the bouquet full of plum and blackberry verging on outright perfume, the
palate taking no prisoners with its power and purity, the aftertaste long lasting.
Sheer class, and not afraid to flaunt its wares. Screw cap. 13.7% alc. **RATING** 97
DRINK 2033–2043 $95 JH ✪
Braemore Cellar Reserve Semillon 2017, Hunter Valley Light quartz green,
due for release September '23. A seriously delicious semillon, makrut lime to the
fore, then polished acidity, balance, line, length and purity. Screw cap. 10.9% alc.
RATING 97 **DRINK** 2023–2027 $70 JH ✪

TTTTT **Two of a Kind Shiraz 2021, Hunter Valley McLaren Vale** The fruit from each region was fermented separately, then blended before maturing 16 months in French hogsheads. A fascinating blend, with major synergy, as each component takes centre stage, but the dusty/chocolate/fine/savoury notes prevail. This is a mighty $25 wine. Screw cap. 13.7% alc. **RATING** 96 **DRINK** 2033-2053 $25 JH ✪

Elenay Barrel Selection Shiraz 2021, Hunter Valley Excellent colour, with a savoury/spicy edge to the fruit. Its palate drives the core with purple and black fruits before a return of some savoury notes to the finish. Aspires to and achieves elegance. Screw cap. 14% alc. **RATING** 96 **DRINK** 2023-2043 $65 JH ✪

Braemore Individual Vineyard Semillon 2022, Hunter Valley The striking bouquet with tantalising aromas of lemongrass, wild herbs and spice translates into a beautifully shaped wine with the line and length of classic semillon, its endpoint far, far distant. Screw cap. 10.8% alc. **RATING** 95 **DRINK** 2023-2047 $38 JH ✪

The O.C. Individual Vineyard Semillon 2022, Hunter Valley 'The O.C.' denotes the Oakey Creek vineyard and its sandy soil that's so ideal for semillon. Here the fruit spectrum is yellow rather than lime, the overall minerally aromas smartly giving way to a complex matrix with an emphatic full stop to the finish. Screw cap. 11% alc. **RATING** 95 **DRINK** 2023-2030 $30 JH ✪

The Dam Block Individual Vineyard Shiraz 2021, Hunter Valley The grapes come from a tiny 0.8ha block just across the edge of the lake. There's no question about the strong textural play on the palate and bouquet of the wine, which offers a convincing replay of the '21 Kiss Limited Release, particularly earthy nuances. Screw cap. 13% alc. **RATING** 95 **DRINK** 2025-2040 $45 JH ✪

Synergy Vineyard Selection Shiraz 2021, Hunter Valley This wine was made by blending a large number of barrels that didn't have the quality needed for Single Vineyard status. It's a most attractive wine, at the lighter end of medium bodied, and there's a rush of spice, tannins and blackberry on the finish. It won the trophy for Best 1yo Shiraz at the Hunter Valley Wine Show '22. Exceptional value. Screw cap. 13.5% alc. **RATING** 95 **DRINK** 2023-2035 $25 JH ✪

Museum Release Kiss Limited Release Shiraz 2017, Hunter Valley It's not hard to see why the price is $100 for this vintage of Kiss (the flagship release ex the best shiraz available; keep it simple stupid). The extract of tannins is a highlight of this wine – balanced and integrated. Patience will be rewarded for decades to come. Screw cap. 14.5% alc. **RATING** 95 **DRINK** 2027-2037 $100 JH

Synergy Vineyard Selection Semillon 2022, Hunter Valley The synergy comes from various old-vine sources. The outcome is a wine of purity, precision and length. Yet it's also complex, with the ability to engage each and every taste bud in the mouth with citrus, acid and a hint of grass. Screw cap. 11.5% alc. **RATING** 94 **DRINK** 2023-2042 $23 JH ✪

Sweetwater Individual Vineyard Shiraz 2021, Hunter Valley Any red wine of the '21 vintage is by definition better than any offering from '20, with no more than a handful of Hunter Valley shiraz wines that dared to make the point. This is a wine with a 20+ year future, firm, earthy black fruits not requiring a 'thank god' finish. Screw cap. 14.2% alc. **RATING** 94 **DRINK** 2023-2044 $35 JH ✪

TTTTⱲ **Vat 32 Vineyard Selection Semillon Chardonnay 2022, Hunter Valley** **RATING** 93 **DRINK** 2032-2050 $35 JH ✪

Belford Individual Vineyard Shiraz 2021, Hunter Valley RATING 93 **DRINK** 2025-2035 $35 JH ✪

Thompson Estate   ★★★★★

Tom Cullity Drive, Wilyabrup, WA 6284 **Region** Margaret River
T (08) 9755 6406 **www.**thompsonestate.com **Open** 7 days 10.30–4.30 **Winemaker** Paul Dixon **Est.** 1994 **Dozens** 10 000 **Vyds** 38ha

Cardiologist Peter Thompson planted the first vines at Thompson Estate in '97, inspired by his and his family's shareholdings in the Pierro and Fire Gully vineyards and by visits to many of the world's premium wine regions. Two more vineyards (both planted in '97) have been purchased, varieties include cabernet sauvignon, cabernet franc, merlot, chardonnay, sauvignon blanc, semillon, pinot noir and malbec.

ΨΨΨΨΨ **The Specialist Cabernet Sauvignon 2019, Margaret River** The love affair between Margaret River and cabernet sauvignon is seemingly indissoluble. The bouquet is fragrant and flowery, the medium-bodied palate supple and juicy, cassis to the fore, but backed by finely balanced, ripe tannins. There's oak present, but you don't notice it. Screw cap. 14% alc. RATING 97 DRINK 2023–2040 $90 JH ✪

ΨΨΨΨΨ **The Specialist Cabernet Sauvignon 2020, Margaret River** Drink now or cellar? Either way, both are worthy choices. Today it has an abundance of varietal flavour, tantalisingly so, and a structured framework of firm but lovely tannins, lots of cedary oak adding flavour and wood tannins. A lot to consider, so pour another glass and do just that. Screw cap. 14.3% alc. RATING 96 DRINK 2024–2040 $90 JF
Four Chambers Pinot Noir Rosé 2022, Margaret River The light copper-pink hue entices, so too aromas and flavours of rose petals, shiso and fresh raspberries both ripe and a little tart. There's a snip of texture and yet lively acidity takes the palate for a smooth ride. Very enjoyable and refreshing to the last drop. Screw cap. 13% alc. RATING 95 DRINK 2022–2025 $25 JF ✪
Small Batch Malbec 2021, Margaret River Malbec, when grown well and made equally so, blends excellent plum fruits with distinct savoury nuances of crushed rock and squid ink. True. They're in this juicy number. Firm tannins across a fuller-bodied palate but plenty of refreshing acidity, too. Screw cap. 14.5% alc. RATING 95 DRINK 2023–2033 $35 JF ✪
Cabernet Sauvignon 2020, Margaret River This reminds me of a wine that, many moons ago, I gave to a friend to try. The response was, 'I feel sophisticated drinking this.' I feel the same way now. Classy cabernet aromas and flavours, a finely tuned palate, super-refreshing with the oak well tucked in. It delights at every turn. Screw cap. 14.3% alc. RATING 95 DRINK 2024–2035 $50 JF ✪
Chardonnay 2021, Margaret River Margaret River is a big region with diverse climate parameters and chardonnay has an enduring capacity to respond to the winemaker's baton. Wilyabrup is the heart of the region, producing chardonnays with great complexity of white stone fruit, citrusy acidity, and cashew for good measure. Screw cap. 13.3% alc. RATING 94 DRINK 2023–2031 $50 JH

ΨΨΨΨΨ **The Specialist Chardonnay 2021, Margaret River** RATING 93 DRINK 2024–2031 $80 JF
Four Chambers Sauvignon Blanc 2022, Margaret River RATING 90 DRINK 2022–2025 $25 JF ✪

Thorn-Clarke Wines   ★★★★★

266 Gawler Park Road, Angaston, SA 5353 **Region** Barossa Valley
T (08) 8564 3036 **www.thornclarkewines.com.au Open** Fri–Sun 10–5
Winemaker Peter Kelly **Viticulturist** Steve Fiebiger **Est.** 1987 **Dozens** 90 000
Vyds 222ha
Established by David and Cheryl Clarke (née Thorn), and son Sam, Thorn-Clarke is one of the largest family-owned estate-based businesses in the Barossa. Their winery is close to the border between the Barossa and Eden valleys and 3 of their 4 vineyards are in the Eden Valley: the Mt Crawford vineyard is at the southern end of the Eden Valley, while the Milton Park and Sandpiper vineyards are further north in the Eden Valley. The 4th vineyard is at St Kitts, at the northern end of the Barossa Ranges. In all 4 vineyards careful soil mapping has resulted in matching of variety and site, with all the major varieties represented.

ΨΨΨΨΨ **William Randell Shiraz 2019, Barossa** One of the icon wines in the Thorn-Clarke quiver and always a deep-coloured, powerful affair. Packed with blackberry, red plum and black cherry fruits with hints of baking spices, licorice, dark chocolate, cedar, pipe tobacco and earth. It holds that alcohol in on the palate, which features fine, sandy tannin support and some feisty morello cherry notes on the finish. Cork. 14.9% alc. RATING 94 DRINK 2023–2035 $70 DB

ŶŶŶŶ♀ Single Vineyard Selection Hoffmann DV Ebenezer Rd Mataro 2021, Barossa Valley RATING 93 DRINK 2023–2033 $45 DB
Single Vineyard Selection Nuriootpa Sands East Block Grenache 2021, Barossa Valley RATING 93 DRINK 2023–2028 $40 DB
Bona Fide Single Vineyard St Kitts Cabernet Sauvignon 2019, Barossa Valley RATING 93 DRINK 2023–2030 $60 DB
Ron Thorn Single Vineyard Shiraz 2018, Barossa RATING 93 DRINK 2023–2033 $110 DB
Varietal Collection Chardonnay 2022, Eden Valley RATING 92 DRINK 2023–2026 $30 DB ✪
Single Vineyard St Kitts Canyon Block Shiraz 2021, Barossa Valley RATING 92 DRINK 2023–2033 $45 DB
Single Vineyard Milton Park Sandpiper Petit Verdot 2021, Barossa RATING 92 DRINK 2023–2033 $45 DB
Shotfire GSM 2020, Barossa Valley RATING 92 DRINK 2023–2028 $35 DB
Sandpiper Riesling 2022, Eden Valley RATING 91 DRINK 2023–2027 $25 DB ✪
Shotfire Quartage 2020, Barossa RATING 91 DRINK 2023–2030 $35 DB
Sandpiper Rosé 2022, Barossa Valley RATING 90 DRINK 2023–2025 $25 DB ✪
Bona Fide Graciano Shiraz 2021, Barossa RATING 90 DRINK 2023–2028 $60 DB

Thousand Candles ★★★★★

159 Killara Road, Gruyere, Vic 3770 **Region** Yarra Valley
T 0413 655 389 **www**.thousandcandles.com.au **Open** By appt **Winemaker** Stuart Proud, Tim Holmes **Viticulturist** Stuart Proud, Cameron Joyce **Est.** 2010 **Dozens** 3500 **Vyds** 25ha

What is now called the Thousand Candles vineyard was originally known as Killara Estate, which was planted in 1995. The property is a dramatic one, plunging from a height of several hundred metres above the Yarra River down to its flood plains. After an interesting launch of wines that had no variety/s specified on the labels (original winemaker Bill Downie said that he wished to be free to use whatever single or varietal blend best reflected the site and vintage), the vineyard is now producing superb pinot noirs and more than useful shiraz, an ex post facto salute to the vision of Bill.

ŶŶŶŶŶ **Gathering Field Shiraz Malbec 2021, Yarra Valley** A gorgeous bright crimson purple. I've not come across this shiraz/malbec blend before but from what was a great vintage in the Yarra Valley, this totally works. Dark plums, blackberries, smoked meats and black pepper aromas abound. The stylish palate is concentrated and very well balanced with ripe, fine-grained tannins. Screw cap. 13% alc. RATING 96 DRINK 2022–2030 $35 PR ✪ ♥
Single Vineyard Pinot Noir 2021, Yarra Valley Bright crimson red. A gently textured wine that was made with respect for the fruit and has real persistence and finesse. There's lovely purity to the aromas of red cherries, small, wild strawberries, violets and spice. The whole bunches are barely perceptible, and velvety, quite firm and persistent tannins are in complete harmony with the wine, too. Diam. 13% alc. RATING 96 DRINK 2023–2028 $65 PR ✪
Gathering Field Shiraz 2021, Yarra Valley This opens with aromas of blackcurrant pastilles, boysenberries, black pepper, floral notes and a little charcuterie. The medium-bodied, youthful and very well-balanced palate finishes with gently chewy, very fine-grained tannins and a little spice. Screw cap. 13% alc. RATING 96 DRINK 2022–2030 $35 PR ✪
Gathering Field Pinot Noir 2021, Yarra Valley A bright, medium ruby red. Perfumed and redolent of strawberries, raspberries, flowers and gentle spice. It's equally impressive on the well-delineated, nicely concentrated and suave palate. The quantity and quality of the tannins are spot on too. Screw cap. 13% alc. RATING 95 DRINK 2023–2029 $35 PR ✪

Single Vineyard Cabernet Sauvignon 2021, Yarra Valley A medium and bright crimson ruby. This is the essence of good cool-climate cabernet sauvignon. Aromas of cherries, blackcurrants, violets and a little bell pepper, the oak discreet. The palate is nicely weighted, with medium-bodied fruit of good intensity and superfine, persistent tannins. Diam. 13.5% alc. RATING 95 DRINK 2022–2030 $65 PR

ɸɸɸɸɸ **Gathering Field Red Blend 2021, Yarra Valley** RATING 91 DRINK 2023–2028 $35 PR
Gathering Field Pinot Shiraz 2021, Yarra Valley RATING 90 DRINK 2022–2025 $35 PR

Three Dark Horses ★★★★

307 Schuller Road, Blewitt Springs, SA 5171 (postal) **Region** McLaren Vale **T** 0405 294 500 **www**.3dh.com.au **Open** Not **Winemaker** Matt Broomhead **Viticulturist** Matt Broomhead **Est.** 2009 **Dozens** 5000 **Vyds** 8.9ha
Three Dark Horses is the project of former Coriole winemaker Matt Broomhead. After vintages in southern Italy and the Rhône Valley, he returned to McLaren Vale in late '09 and, with his father Alan, buys quality grapes, thanks to the many years of experience they both have in the region. The 3rd dark horse is Matt's grandfather, a vintage regular. Shiraz, cabernet, touriga nacional and grenache are planted and the shiraz vines planted in '64 have been successfully reworked. Part of the vineyard is sand soil–based interspersed with ironstone, a highly desirable mix for shiraz and cabernet sauvignon.

ɸɸɸɸɸ **Grenache Touriga 2022, McLaren Vale** A lightning rod of energy, soaring florals and pulpy blue fruits underlying grenache's more hedonistic tendencies. Some bramble from whole bunches imbues savouriness. It is a rich and throaty wine, yet fresh, effusive of fruit, detailed of structural latticework and impressively long. Screw cap. 14.5% alc. RATING 93 DRINK 2023–2028 $30 NG ✪
Grenache 2021, McLaren Vale There is a lot to like here: molten raspberry, root spice, dank camphor accents and a potpourri of herbs the underbelly, though sweetness of fruit teems on and on. Delicious, yet in need of grape tannin and a salve of savouriness. Screw cap. 14.5% alc. RATING 90 DRINK 2023–2028 $30 NG

3 Drops ★★★★★

PO Box 1828, Applecross, WA 6953 **Region** Mount Barker
T 0417 172 603 **www**.3drops.com **Open** Not **Winemaker** Robert Diletti (Contract)
Est. 1998 **Dozens** 3500 **Vyds** 20.5ha
3 Drops is the name of the Bradbury family vineyard at Mount Barker. The name reflects wine, olive oil and water – all of which come from the substantial property. The vineyard is planted to riesling, sauvignon blanc, semillon, chardonnay, cabernet sauvignon, merlot, shiraz and cabernet franc, and irrigated by a large wetland on the property. 3 Drops also owns the 14.7ha Patterson vineyard, planted in '82 to pinot noir, chardonnay and shiraz.

ɸɸɸɸɸ **Pinot Noir 2021, Great Southern** This establishes its quality and variety from the first sip, the texture and structure with greater depth and forest floor complexity than most others from the Great Southern. There's a beating pulse to the wine that will capture attention for years to come. Screw cap. 13.5% alc. RATING 96 DRINK 2023–2035 $32 JH ✪
Riesling 2022, Great Southern The bouquet is gently floral – citrus and apple blossom – but there's nothing gentle about the palate, which is intense and very persistent thanks to its rapier-like acidity and overall purity. Screw cap. 12.5% alc. RATING 95 DRINK 2023–2037 $27 JH ✪
Cabernets 2021, Great Southern A blend of 70/30% cabernet sauvignon/ malbec picked 6 weeks apart, which left no choice but separate fermentation and maturation, the parcels blended just prior to bottling after 15 months in French oak (25% new). The colour is superb, but why? Juicy overtones of cassis, ditto. Normally a blend of similar bordeaux reds doesn't enhance the wine as

much as it does (say) with shiraz and viognier. Screw cap. 14% alc. **RATING** 95 **DRINK** 2023–2036 $29 JH ✪

Chardonnay 2021, Great Southern Fruit from 40yo vines on the Patterson vineyard; wild-yeast initiated fermentation in French oak (25% new); cultured yeast added halfway through to ensure no sugar remained unfermented. The wine was left in barrel on yeast lees until bottling in Feb '22. The complexity of the grapefruit-accented fruit might escape attention on the first taste, but not the second. Screw cap. 13% alc. **RATING** 95 **DRINK** 2023–2031 $32 JH ✪

Shiraz 2020, Great Southern Bright colour; spice, licorice and blackberry join hands on the palate, tannins locking them together, TA joining in the chorus. Lovely wine. Screw cap. 13.5% alc. **RATING** 95 **DRINK** 2023–2035 $29 JH ✪

Rosé 2022, Great Southern A blend of 85/15% cabernet franc/merlot. A bright, clear light crimson. A tactile wine with a spicy/savoury underlying base that is juicy to the point of downright mouth-watering. There's almost no cuisine able to march over the top of this long palate. Screw cap. 13% alc. **RATING** 94 **DRINK** 2023–2025 $27 JH ✪

Merlot 2021, Great Southern Merlot can seem too soft, needing cabernet sauvignon to give it structure. This has no such need. It's fresh and bright, red fruits joining blue and black, the trio soaking up their 25% new French oak with panache. Screw cap. 14.5% alc. **RATING** 94 **DRINK** 2023–2031 $29 JH ✪

🍷🍷🍷🍷 **Sauvignon Blanc 2022, Great Southern RATING** 92 **DRINK** 2023–2025 $25 JH ✪

Three Elms   ★★★★

82 Riversdale Road, Frankland River, WA 6396 (postal) **Region** Frankland River
T 0458 877 734 **www.**threeelms.com.au **Open** Not **Winemaker** Laura Hallett
Est. 2017 **Dozens** 8000 **Vyds** 44ha

This venture is succession planning at its best. Merv and Judy Lange had a 1200ha wool and grain farm when, in 1971, they decided to plant a few vines and Alkoomi was born. By '14, Alkoomi was one of James Halliday's Top 100 Australian Wineries with 104ha of estate vineyards and annual production of 60000 dozen. Four years earlier (in '10) they had handed ownership to daughter Sandy and husband Rod Hallett, who had been an integral part of the business for many years as they raised their daughters Emily, Laura and Molly. In '17 Three Elms was established, its name taking the first letter of the name of each daughter. Laura obtained a bachelor of agribusiness, majoring in viticulture, from Curtin University in '15. Her sisters both work in the business (admin/marketing) and are part of Three Elms' management group.

🍷🍷🍷🍷 **Timbertops Riesling 2021, Frankland River** Zingy, zesty, expressive riesling. Scents of ozone, lime, green apple and honeysuckle. The palate is delicate and pure feeling, with more of the apple and lime of the bouquet and a faint trickle of saline minerality. Very refreshing, fine and vibrant. Screw cap. 11.6% alc. **RATING** 93 **DRINK** 2022–2030 $30 MB ✪

Timbertops Gewürztraminer 2021, Frankland River Scents of rosewater, lychee and apricot with a sprinkle of bay leaf herbal piquancy. Flavours are of a similar ilk with a pleasingly greasy texture, a cool cut of acidity entrenched through the wine. Very well balanced overall, set to medium weight and delivering refreshment factor and drinkability. Thai takeaway, get set. Screw cap. 13.5% alc. **RATING** 92 **DRINK** 2022–2028 $30 MB ✪

Timbertops Cabernet Franc 2020, Frankland River Mellow and medium weight, dark fruited but with requisite cab franc nuance of green herb and regional eucalyptus characters. Quite bright and vibrant with blood orange acidity leaping through the mulberry and boysenberry fruit, clove and brambly greenery to taste. It's fragrant, too, evocative of brambles and sweet earthiness. Such pleasing drinking here. Screw cap. 12.8% alc. **RATING** 92 **DRINK** 2022–2027 $30 MB ✪

Tillie J ★★★★☆

305 68B Gadd Street, Northcote, Vic 3070 (postal) **Region** Yarra Valley
T 0428 554 311 **www**.tilliejwines.com.au **Open** Not **Winemaker** Natillie Johnston
Viticulturist Natillie Johnston **Est.** 2019 **Dozens** 350

Natillie (Tillie) Johnston began her career in '12, one of the vintage crew at Coldstream Hills, and says her love for pinot noir began there. She then spent 4 of the next 8 years drifting between the Northern and Southern hemispheres working for an all-star cast of wineries: Leeuwin Estate, Brokenwood, Cristom (Oregon), Keller (Rheinhessen), Framingham (Marlborough) and Yarra Yering. Since then, she's been assistant winemaker at Giant Steps to Steve Flamsteed and Jess Clark. In '19 she took the opportunity to buy 2t of grapes from Helen's Hill of whatever variety she chose, which was, of course, pinot noir. The range has since expanded to Yarra Valley chardonnay, with a Langhorne Creek grenache in the mix, too.

🍷🍷🍷🍷🍷 Pinot Noir 2022, Yarra Valley Bright crimson-purple, this leaps out of the glass with its primary scented bouquet redolent of dark cherries, damson plums and a little wild strawberry together with floral and spicy notes. Concentrated, bright and youthful on the palate, the tannins are taut and persistent and this quite delicious wine should drink well for at least a decade. Very well done. Screw cap. 12.5% alc. **RATING** 95 **DRINK** 2022–2030 $75 PR

🍷🍷🍷🍷🍷 Project 5255 Grenache 2022, Langhorne Creek **RATING** 93 **DRINK** 2022–2025 $35 PR ✪
Anna's Rosé Grenache Mataro Carignan 2022, Yarra Valley **RATING** 92 **DRINK** 2022–2025 $28 PR ✪
Chardonnay 2022, Yarra Valley **RATING** 92 **DRINK** 2022–2027 $45 PR

Tim Adams ★★★★

156 Warenda Road, Clare, SA 5453 **Region** Clare Valley
T (08) 8842 2429 **www**.timadamswines.com.au **Open** 7 days 10–4.30 **Winemaker** Tim Adams, Brett Schutz **Viticulturist** Mick Plumridge **Est.** 1986 **Dozens** 60 000
Vyds 195ha

Tim Adams and partner Pam Goldsack preside over a highly successful business. Having expanded the range of estate plantings with tempranillo, pinot gris and viognier, in '09 the business took a giant step forward with the acquisition of the 80ha Leasingham Rogers vineyard from CWA, followed in '11 by the purchase of the Leasingham winery and winemaking equipment (for less than replacement cost). The winery is now a major contract winemaking facility for the region.

🍷🍷🍷🍷🍷 Aberfeldy Shiraz 2018, Clare Valley Tim Adams' famed premium release is impressive for its volume, concentration and power. It finds balance, even with its big, chunky status. Dark cherry, mocha and vanilla-cola scented and flavoured, with the palate draped in sweet cinnamon/clove woody tannins that lend grip and pucker. Very rich, very potent, sweet and ultra-ripe at heart. Cellar long. Screw cap. 14.9% alc. **RATING** 94 **DRINK** 2025–2040 $65 MB

🍷🍷🍷🍷🍷 Schaefer Shiraz 2018, Clare Valley **RATING** 93 **DRINK** 2023–2036 $40 MB
Pinot Gris 2022, Clare Valley **RATING** 92 **DRINK** 2022–2024 $24 MB ✪
Riesling 2022, Clare Valley **RATING** 92 **DRINK** 2022–2035 $24 MB ✪
Shiraz 2019, Clare Valley **RATING** 92 **DRINK** 2022–2035 $26 MB ✪

Tim Gramp Wines ★★★★

1033 Mintaro Road, Watervale, SA 5452 **Region** Clare Valley
T (08) 8843 0199 **www**.timgrampwines.com.au **Open** W'ends 12–4 **Winemaker** Tim Gramp **Viticulturist** Tim Gramp **Est.** 1990 **Dozens** 6000 **Vyds** 16ha
Tim Gramp has quietly built up a very successful business, and by keeping overheads to a minimum, provides good wines at modest prices. Over the years, estate vineyards (shiraz, riesling, cabernet sauvignon, grenache and tempranillo) have been expanded significantly.

🍷🍷🍷🍷🍷 **Watervale Riesling 2022, Clare Valley** Tight, racy, lean and cool. A pure expression with lemon and lime juice tang, grapefruit and light gingery elements with faint talc/floral lift. The palate is zingy, crisp and crackles with citrusy freshness and briny minerality. Good stuff right here. Screw cap. 12.5% alc.
RATING 93 **DRINK** 2022-2035 $23 MB ✪

Basket Pressed Watervale Cabernet Sauvignon 2018, Clare Valley
Slick with satiny tannins, imbued with blueberry and mulberry fruit characters, seasoned with clove and cigar box savoury elements and generally looking a bit claret-like. It's pitched perfectly between all its elements and drinkability is high. A gem here. Screw cap. 14.5% alc. **RATING** 93 **DRINK** 2022-2035 $24 MB ✪

Tim McNeil Wines

71 Springvale Road, Watervale, SA 5452 **Region** Clare Valley
T (08) 8843 0040 **www.**timmcneilwines.com.au **Open** Fri–Sun & public hols 11–5
Winemaker Tim McNeil **Est.** 2004 **Dozens** 1500 **Vyds** 2ha
When Tim and Cass McNeil established Tim McNeil Wines, Tim had long since given up his teaching career, graduating with a degree in oenology from Adelaide University in '99. He then spent 11 years honing his craft at important wineries in the Barossa and Clare valleys. In '10 Tim McNeil Wines became his full-time job. The McNeils' 16ha property at Watervale includes mature dry-grown riesling. The cellar door overlooks the riesling vineyard, with panoramic views of Watervale and beyond.

🍷🍷🍷🍷🍷 **Watervale Riesling 2022, Clare Valley** This is refreshing and bright. A highly drinkable expression of the regional staple imbued with lime and green apple scents (hints of blackcurrant?), flavours of lime, ginger, nectarine and a pulse of pink grapefruity acidity through it all. Texture is juicy but finds cut and thrust with chewiness and that rapier thrust of cool acid. Delightful drink, well balanced and judged. Screw cap. 12.5% alc. **RATING** 93 **DRINK** 2022-2035 $25 MB ✪

Tinklers Vineyard

Pokolbin Mountains Road, Pokolbin, NSW 2320 **Region** Hunter Valley
T (02) 4998 7435 **www.**tinklers.com.au **Open** 7 days 10–5 **Winemaker** Usher Tinkler
Est. 1946 **Dozens** 7000 **Vyds** 41ha
Three generations of the Tinkler family have been involved with the property since 1942. Originally a beef and dairy farm, vines have been both pulled out and replanted at various stages and part of the adjoining 80+yo Ben Ean vineyard has been acquired. Plantings include semillon (14ha), shiraz (11.5ha), chardonnay (6.5ha) and smaller areas of merlot, muscat and viognier. The majority of the grape production is sold to McWilliam's and Tyrrell's. Usher was chief winemaker at Pooles Rock and Cockfighter's Ghost for over 8 years, before taking on full-time responsibility at Tinklers. See also Usher Tinkler Wines.

🍷🍷🍷🍷🍷 **Poppys Chardonnay 2022, Hunter Valley** A well-above-average Hunter chardonnay with a subset of grapefruit and passionfruit aromas carrying on through the neatly framed palate and its fresh aftertaste. Screw cap. 12.5% alc.
RATING 95 **DRINK** 2023-2033 $45 JH ✪

U and I Shiraz 2021, Hunter Valley From the oldest vines, planted 1948. Bright crimson; from nose to tail different from and better than its Old Vines sibling; attractive medium-bodied shiraz. Screw cap. 13.5% alc. **RATING** 95
DRINK 2023-2033 $65 JH

School Block Semillon 2022, Hunter Valley The vines are planted on sandy gravel soils, and in 1887 was the site of the first Pokolbin school. A pattern of juicy, lemon flavoured, wines running across Pokolbin is emerging; the development over the next 2-3 years will be interesting. Screw cap. 11% alc.
RATING 94 **DRINK** 2023-2028 $25 JH ✪

🍷🍷🍷🍷🍷 **Hill Chardonnay 2022, Hunter Valley RATING** 93 **DRINK** 2023-2032 $25 JH ✪
Old Vines Planted 1948 Shiraz 2021, Hunter Valley RATING 91
DRINK 2023-2030 $45 JH

Tokar Estate

6 Maddens Lane, Coldstream, Vic 3770 **Region** Yarra Valley
T (03) 5964 9585 **www**.tokarestate.com.au **Open** 7 days 10.30–5 **Winemaker** Martin
Siebert **Est.** 1996 **Dozens** 5000 **Vyds** 12ha

Leon Tokar, a very successful businessman, and wife Rita dreamed of a weekender and hobby
farm and it was largely by chance that in 1995 they found a scruffy paddock fronting onto
Maddens Lane. By the end of the day they had signed a contract to buy the property. The
Tokars wasted no time and by '99, had planted their 12ha vineyard and built a Mediterranean-
inspired cellar door and restaurant. Martin Siebert has been winemaker for many years,
making consistently good wines and, with son Daniel Tokar as general manager, has full
responsibility for the day-to-day management of the business.

Coldstream Vineyard Cabernet Sauvignon 2021, Yarra Valley An inviting
crimson-ruby red. Opens with a ripe core of black cherries with some cedar,
hedgerow and a hint of rose petals. Layered and rich on the palate, the tannins
are firm but balanced and the wine beautifully put together. A lovely effort.
Screw cap. 14% alc. **RATING** 96 **DRINK** 2023–2034 $70 PR ✪
Coldstream Vineyard Shiraz 2021, Yarra Valley An alluring and bright
crimson purple. Instantly appealing on the nose, too, with aromas of red and black
fruits, spices and cedary oak. The ripe, medium- to full-bodied palate is balanced,
while very persistent tannins round out the wine. Screw cap. 14% alc. **RATING** 95
DRINK 2023–2032 $70 PR

Pinot Noir 2021, Yarra Valley RATING 93 **DRINK** 2023–2029 $35 PR ✪
Tempranillo 2021, Yarra Valley RATING 92 **DRINK** 2023–2028 $35 PR
Rosé 2022, Yarra Valley RATING 90 **DRINK** 2023–2024 $30 PR
Chardonnay 2021, Yarra Valley RATING 90 **DRINK** 2023–2026 $35 PR

Tolpuddle Vineyard

37 Back Tea Tree Road, Richmond, Tas, 7025 **Region** Southern Tasmania
T (08) 8155 6003 **www**.tolpuddlevineyard.com **Open** At Shaw + Smith
Winemaker Adam Wadewitz, Martin Shaw **Viticulturist** Carlos Souris, Murray Leake
Est. 1988 **Dozens** 2800 **Vyds** 28ha

If ever a winery was born with blue blood in its veins, Tolpuddle would have to be it. The
vineyard was established in 1988 on a continuous downhill slope facing northeast; in '06 it
won the inaugural Tasmanian Vineyard of the Year Award. Michael Hill Smith MW and
Martin Shaw are joint managing directors. David LeMire looks after sales and marketing;
Adam Wadewitz, one of Australia's brightest winemaking talents, is senior winemaker.
Vineyard manager Carlos Souris loses nothing in comparison, with over 30 years of
grapegrowing in Tasmania under his belt and an absolutely fearless approach to making a
great vineyard even greater.

Chardonnay 2021, Tasmania Wonderfully ripe and focused white peach,
nectarine and citrus notes dotted with clotted cream, soft spice, struck match,
crushed stone, almond paste, white flowers and cashew-like oak. The finish is
long and true, framed by a porcelain acidity that provides a killer cadence. This
release cements Tolpuddle's place in the upper echelon of Australian chardonnay
producers. Screw cap. 13% alc. **RATING** 98 **DRINK** 2023–2029 $96 DB ✪ ♥

Pinot Noir 2021, Tasmania Perfumed strawberry and raspberry notes with
some dark cherry and boysenberry in the bass. Hints of Asian five-spice, rhubarb,
sous bois and rain falling on turned earth, just a whiff of struck flint in the
distance. The whole-bunch component is beautifully judged, the palate shape
sleek with ample tension and grace, gentle tannins weighing in. Seamless drinking
now but will reward those with patience. Screw cap. 13.5% alc. **RATING** 96
DRINK 2023–2035 $96 DB

Tomich Wines

87 King William Road, Unley, SA 5061 **Region** Adelaide Hills
T (08) 8299 7500 **www.tomich.com.au Open** By appt **Winemaker** Randal Tomich
Viticulturist Randal Tomich **Est.** 2002 **Dozens** 40 000 **Vyds** 85ha
Patriarch John Tomich was born on a vineyard near Mildura, where he learned the skills
and knowledge required for premium grape growing. After a career as an ENT specialist, he
completed postgraduate studies in winemaking at the University of Adelaide in 2002. His
son Randal is a cutting from the old vine (metaphorically speaking), having invented new
equipment and techniques for tending the family's vineyard in the Adelaide Hills, resulting in a
60% saving in time and fuel costs. Third-generation Jack Tomich has since joined the team, too.

🍷🍷🍷🍷 **Icon 1777 Pinot Noir 2021, Adelaide Hills** A bastion of stellar value, this
address is also capable of fine-tuned expressions, transparent and complex, boasting
fealty to exceptional sources. In this instance, the proprietary Woodside vineyard.
Pickled cherry, ume, root spice and shiitake dashi. A twine of woodsy tannins
parcels it up. Integrated freshness delivers it long. Exceptional pinot. Screw cap.
13.5% alc. **RATING** 95 **DRINK** 2022–2030 $65 NG

🍷🍷🍷🍷 **Cabernet Sauvignon 2021, Coonawarra RATING** 92 **DRINK** 2022–2030
$22 NG ✪
Woodside Vineyard Chardonnay 2021, Adelaide Hills RATING 91
DRINK 2022–2026 $25 NG ✪
Woodside Vineyard Pinot Noir 2021, Adelaide Hills RATING 91
DRINK 2022–2026 $35 NG
Shiraz 2020, McLaren Vale RATING 91 **DRINK** 2022–2028 $22 NG ✪
Woodside Vineyard Sauvignon Blanc 2022, Adelaide Hills RATING 90
DRINK 2023–2025 $25 NG ✪

Toolangi

878–880 Maroondah Hwy, Coldstream, Vic 3770 **Region** Yarra Valley
T (03) 5957 3388 **www.toolangi.com Open** Sat 11–5, Sun 11–4 **Winemaker** Kaspar
Hermann **Est.** 1995 **Dozens** 7500 **Vyds** 14ha
Helmut Konecsny, owner of Rochford Wines, purchased Toolangi in '18 and immediately
started ringing in the changes. Apart from new-look packaging, Helmut and his team set
about upgrading the vineyard and introducing new winemaking practices. Wines are available
at Rochford Wines.

🍷🍷🍷🍷 **F Block Chardonnay 2021, Yarra Valley** A bright green-gold hue. Aromas
of ripe white peach, acacia, wet stone and a little discreet toast from already
integrated oak. Mineral, textured and slippery, the palate is both structured and
very well balanced. Finishes long and, as good as this is now, those that have
the patience to lay some down for 2–5 years will be well rewarded. Screw cap.
13.5% alc. **RATING** 97 **DRINK** 2022–2029 $100 PR

🍷🍷🍷🍷 **Pauls Lane Chardonnay 2021, Yarra Valley** A bright, deep-ish green gold.
Enticing aromas of lightly spiced apples and stone fruits with hints of mint and
pink grapefruit. Generous and giving on the front palate, I like how this fine-
boned wine finishes taut and long. A stylish wine that should age gracefully.
Screw cap. 13.4% alc. **RATING** 95 **DRINK** 2023–2031 $44 PR ✪
D Block Shiraz 2021, Yarra Valley Vibrant crimson purple. Loads of spice here
and mountain herbs to go with the dark fruits and savoury nuance. Medium to
full bodied, there's an attractive fleshiness balanced by the wine's ripe, chewy and
slow-building tannins and bright acidity. It would approachable now with food,
but a little patience might be the order of the day. Screw cap. 13% alc. **RATING** 94
DRINK 2024–2032 $100 PR

🍷🍷🍷🍷 **E Block Pinot Noir 2021, Yarra Valley RATING** 92 **DRINK** 2024–2030 $100 PR
Pinot Noir 2021, Yarra Valley RATING 92 **DRINK** 2022–2024 $30 PR ✪
Chardonnay 2021, Yarra Valley RATING 91 **DRINK** 2022–2024 $30 PR

Toorak Winery ★★★★

Vineyard 279 Toorak Road, Leeton, NSW 2705 **Region** Riverina
T (02) 6953 2333 **www**.toorakwines.com.au **Open** Mon–Fri 10–5, w'ends by appt
Winemaker Robert Bruno, Martin Wozniak **Est.** 1965 **Dozens** 200 000 **Vyds** 145ha
A traditional, long-established Riverina producer. Production has increased significantly, utilising substantial estate plantings and grapes purchased from growers in the Riverina and elsewhere. Wines are released under the Willandra Estate, Willandra Leeton Selection and Toorak Road labels. There has been a shift in emphasis away from bulk and buyers-own-brand sales and towards improving quality of Toorak's own brands.

🍷🍷🍷🍷🍷 **Toorak Road Cabernet Sauvignon 2021, Gundagai** Concentrated blackberries and black cherries are supported by soft licorice, crushed black pepper and star anise. Grainy tannins show a thoughtful use of oak and a good kick of fresh acidity keeps the wine upbeat and age worthy. Screw cap. 13.5% alc. **RATING** 91 **DRINK** 2022-2035 $18 SW ✪

Toorak Road Sauvignon Blanc 2021, Tumbarumba Ripe orchard fruits, peach halves, lemon curd and gunflint. Underneath sit roasted macadamia nuts, oat biscuits and almond meal. A rich palate to match the aroma intensity, the acidity is slinky and the backbone of new oak stands up to greet it. A steal for the price. Screw cap. 12.7% alc. **RATING** 90 **DRINK** 2022-2032 $22 SW ✪

Toorak Road Durif 2021, Riverina Speaks of lingonberries, stewed mulberries and black olives. Fresh sage leaf and bitter chocolate shavings lead to a wet tar character. The wine is inky and compressed with blue fruit highlights, the palate surprisingly fresh with acidity lifting the mid-palate. A durif of class and a great price, to boot. Screw cap. 13.5% alc. **RATING** 90 **DRINK** 2022-2032 $15 SW ✪

Topper's Mountain Wines ★★★★★

13420 Guyra Road, Tingha, NSW 2369 **Region** New England
T 0411 880 580 **www**.toppers.com.au **Open** Sun 11–4 **Winemaker** Jan Taborsky
Viticulturist Mark Kirkby **Est.** 2000 **Dozens** 1200 **Vyds** 10ha
Topper's Mountain is an innovative producer primarily focused on alternative varieties. Planting began in '00 with 15 rows each of 28 different varieties and clones, the intention being to find those that held the most promise. In the main, the team have found success with Italian and Iberian varieties such as nebbiolo and touriga, but it is the manseng that really sings. This high-acid botrytis-resistant white variety from southwest France was originally thought to be petit manseng when first planted, but DNA testing in '20 found it to be actually gros manseng.

🍷🍷🍷🍷🍷 **Manseng 2022, New England** Gros manseng. Dried mango, ripe pineapple and golden apple skin. Hints of tangerine and preserved lemon. Pineapple bitters and iced tea. The peaks of acidity are balanced by troughs of texture, which makes for a joyous wine to explore. Screw cap. 13.5% alc. **RATING** 95 **DRINK** 2022-2030 $35 SW ✪ ♥

Manseng 2021, New England Eclectic aromas of candied orange rind, apricot, dried pineapple, honeysuckle blossom, ginger root and chamomile tea. Baked clay and tangerine are alive on the palate, with thrilling acidity and a toasted kernel character that lingers. Alluring and full of charisma, this is a wine of great energy. Screw cap. 13% alc. **RATING** 95 **DRINK** 2022-2032 $35 SW ✪

Hill of Dreams 2021, New England A skinsy sauvignon blanc/verdejo/grüner veltliner field blend. There are pools of depth to the aromas, with notes of preserved lime and green mango skins, fenugreek and fennel pods. Dry and more saline on the palate, the wine tells the story of hard-working vines and early picking. A journey from start to finish. Screw cap. 12% alc. **RATING** 94 **DRINK** 2022-2038 $40 SW ✪

🍷🍷🍷🍷🍷 **Gewürztraminer 2021, New England** **RATING** 93 **DRINK** 2022-2032 $35 SW ✪

Viognier 2021, New England **RATING** 93 **DRINK** 2022-2030 $45 SW

Gewürztraminer 2022, New England RATING 92 DRINK 2022–2026 $35 SW
Nebbiolo 2017, New England RATING 91 DRINK 2022–2028 $47 SW

Torbreck Vintners

348 Roennfeldt Road, Marananga, SA 5352 **Region** Barossa Valley
T (08) 8562 4155 **www**.torbreck.com **Open** 7 days 10–5 by appt **Winemaker** Ian
Hongell, Scott McDonald **Viticulturist** Nigel Blieschke **Est.** 1994 **Dozens** 70 000
Vyds 112ha

Torbreck Vintners was already one of Australia's best-known producers of high-quality red
wine when, in '13, wealthy Californian entrepreneur and vintner Peter Kight (of Quivira
Vineyards) acquired 100% ownership of the business. Talented winemaker Ian Hongell joined
the team in '16. Shiraz (and other Rhône varieties) is the focus, led by The Laird, RunRig,
The Factor and Descendant. Wines are unfined and unfiltered.

🍷🍷🍷🍷🍷 The Laird 2018, Barossa Valley 100% shiraz. Head-spinning cassis, kirsch and
macerated plums with hints of cedar, vanilla, tobacco, dark chocolate, licorice,
garrigue, bay leaf, sarsaparilla, cola, turned earth, graphite and pressed flowers.
Retains a sense of elegance and place with restrained power. It's a muscular,
prodigiously structured wine with a minerally edge and deep Barossan soul.
Cork. 15.5% alc. **RATING** 98 **DRINK** 2023–2048 $800 DB ❤
RunRig 2020, Barossa Valley Torbreck's shiraz/viognier blend is a Barossa
icon wine. The '20 is in fine form with intense blackberry, plum and cherry
fruits framed by deep spice, cedar, vanillin oak, star anise, dark chocolate, roasting
meats, crème de cassis and earth. Long, ripe granitic tannins cascade through the
opulent black fruits and the wine's architecture suggests that it will have long and
distinguished cellaring potential. Cork. 15.5% alc. **RATING** 97 **DRINK** 2023–2045
$300 DB

🍷🍷🍷🍷🍷 The Factor 2020, Barossa Valley 100% shiraz. An inky, graphite–led
intensity of fruit and a sense of purity. Compression, too, with deep satsuma
plum, blackberry and black cherry fruits initially feeling compact and tight before
exploding onto the palate with substantial tannin heft and layers of dark spice,
cedar, licorice and dark chocolate. While you could happily tuck into this tonight,
it will cellar like a champion. Cork. 15% alc. **RATING** 96 **DRINK** 2023–2043
$150 DB
Les Amis Grenache 2020, Barossa Valley I'm a big fan of this wine. It's got
a cruisey, loose–knit and savoury vibe: detailed raspberry, mulberry and red plum
shades and a gorgeous array of gingery spice, red licorice, star anise, sarsparilla,
cola, Chinese barbecue and earth. This openness is juxtaposed by a cascade of
chalky tannin and a mineral–rich focus, a spiced plume of red fruits on the exit.
Cork. 15% alc. **RATING** 96 **DRINK** 2023–2035 $200 DB
The Pict 2020, Barossa Valley Torbreck seems to squeeze out every last bit
of the exotic spice and meaty, earthy goodness that mataro has to offer. Textured,
supple yet structured with cascading dark plum and berry fruits, clove, pressed
flowers, star anise, cardamom, barbecued meats, hoisin, licorice, charcuterie and
turned earth. Superfine chalky tannins capture the attention and then retreat
into the fruit. It's savoury and meaty and really, really delicious. Cork. 15% alc.
RATING 95 **DRINK** 2023–2035 $80 DB
Hillside Vineyard Grenache 2020, Barossa Valley There is a bit more space
to this grenache, a sense of light and perhaps the volume on the floral top notes
has been turned up a notch. The tannin profile is different, too, and sports a fine,
sandy, kinetic feel on the palate finishing with oodles of spice and gentle red plum
and raspberry fruits with a real sense of savoury intrigue as the wine fades slowly
away. Cork. 15% alc. **RATING** 95 **DRINK** 2023–2035 $80 DB
The Steading 2021, Barossa Valley Grenache/shiraz/mataro from 40–150yo
vines. Fragrant with lifted blueberry, dark plum and punchy cranberry fruit
characters with hints of frangipani, gingerbread, cherry clafoutis, Chinese
barbecue, earth and blueberry pie. Bright with vivid acidity and powdery tannin,

it cuts a super-spicy savoury line and represents the Torbreck style with aplomb. Screw cap. 15% alc. **RATING** 94 **DRINK** 2023–2033 $40 DB ✪

Kyloe 2021, Barossa Valley Deep magenta in colour with some reduction, not unusual for mataro, that dissipates with time in the glass. Meaty, exotically-spiced dark plum and blackberry fruits cut with hints of smoked, cured meats, olive tapenade, purple flowers, struck flint and earth. A sense of compression and tension on the palate with velvety fruit, tight acidity and compact, powdery tannins. Finishes long with the characteristic wild mataro spice. Screw cap. 14.5% alc. **RATING** 94 **DRINK** 2023–2030 $32 DB ✪

The Struie 2021, Barossa Valley There's a graphite edge to the wine's aromatic profile, some sage and bay leaf notes above the deep blackberry and black cherry fruit tones. Hints of crème de cassis, spice box, licorice, chocolate and earth make their presence felt with tight, granitic tannins and inky fruit depth. It's a concentrated shiraz, yet retains some nice elegance and mineral drive, despite all the fruit power on display. Cork. 15% alc. **RATING** 94 **DRINK** 2023–2038 $55 DB

The Gask 2021, Eden Valley 100% shiraz. Aromas of crème de cassis, blueberry and mulberry fruits cut with hints of baking spices, sage, graphite, licorice and lighter tones of choc-mint and garrigue. Eden Valley elegance and slatey tannin grip are on display but with a fruit depth and power that could only come from Torbreck. Finishes long and deeply fruited with an intense tide of cassis and dark spice. Cork. 15% alc. **RATING** 94 **DRINK** 2023–2035 $80 DB

Descendant 2020, Barossa Valley Shiraz/viognier. Aromas of macerated satsuma plums, mulberry and blueberry pie with a blast of Asian five-spice, violets, earth, stone fruit, tobacco and licorice. Pillowy tannins bloom from the pure fruit and for all the wine's latent horsepower, there is a sense of brightness, despite the plushness and fruit depth. Screw cap. 15% alc. **RATING** 94 **DRINK** 2023–2038 $150 DB

🍷🍷🍷🍷 **Cuvée Juveniles 2021, Barossa Valley** **RATING** 93 **DRINK** 2023–2029 $29 DB ✪

The Growers' Cut Shiraz 2020, Barossa Valley **RATING** 93 **DRINK** 2023–2035 $80 DB

Woodcutter's Shiraz 2021, Barossa Valley **RATING** 92 **DRINK** 2023–2029 $29 DB ✪

Hillside Vineyard Shiraz Roussanne 2021, Barossa Valley **RATING** 92 **DRINK** 2023–2029 $32 DB

Woodcutter's Rosé 2022, Barossa Valley **RATING** 91 **DRINK** 2023–2026 $25 DB ✪

Cuvée Juveniles Blanc 2022, Barossa Valley **RATING** 91 **DRINK** 2023–2026 $29 DB

Trait Wines ★★★★★

256 Carters Road, Burnside, WA 6285 **Region** Margaret River
T 0438 808 678 **www.**traitwines.com **Open** By appt **Winemaker** Theo Truyts
Viticulturist Theo Truyts **Est.** 2019 **Dozens** 500 **Vyds** 2.7ha

Vigneron Theo Truyts (originally from Lesotho in Southern Africa) and his wife Clare Trythall (born in Japan to English and Welsh parents, grew up in Singapore and went on to become an ER doctor) purchased their '98-planted Margaret River vineyard in '19. After grafting a substantial block of sauvignon blanc to chardonnay, the majority of the vineyard is now chardonnay with the remainder made up of sauvignon blanc, semillon and chenin blanc. They also source chenin blanc and grenache from bush vines in Geographe.

🍷🍷🍷🍷 **Chardonnay 2021, Margaret River** Gosh, these Trait wines are super. While oak makes an impact here – the wine is in barrel for 11 months, adding a slippery texture and lots of woodsy spices – the fruit handles it. It's also the long line of acidity that pulls all the flavours into line and keeps this thrillingly good. Classy stuff. Screw cap. 13% alc. **RATING** 96 **DRINK** 2022–2031 $89 JF

Chenin Blanc 2022, Margaret River One taste of this whet-the-appetite chenin and you immediately want to stop working and take it out to lunch. As I did. It's refined and superfine, kicking off on a citrus riff with barely ripe pears. Lemon saline-like acidity drives this to such a long finish but along the way, a touch of persimmon tannins gives some pull and shape. There goes my work day. Screw cap. 13.1% alc. RATING 95 DRINK 2022–2029 $33 JF ✪

Pen-y-Bryn Chardonnay 2022, Margaret River This comes across as racy, pure and linear. Grapefruit pith and lemon zest with pure natural acidity teasing out the palate. The oak is completely obliterated by the fruit and, aside from the creamy lees, this is all about refinement. Just dips a little on the finish but a minor quibble. Screw cap. 13.3% alc. RATING 95 DRINK 2022–2032 $53 JF

Sauvignon Blanc 2022, Margaret River Perky and bright. But don't be alarmed. This is full of electrifying acidity and flavours. Tangy citrus as in pomelo, quinine/tonic water with lemon barley flavours, fresh basil and pleasing lemon curd are more a textural component from time on lees in barrel. I'm wide awake and taking notice. Screw cap. 13.2% alc. RATING 95 DRINK 2023–2030 $33 JF ✪

♟♟♟♟♟ **Field Blend 2022, Margaret River** RATING 92 DRINK 2022–2028 $33 JF
Grenache 2022, Frankland River RATING 90 DRINK 2022–2030 $39 JF

Trentham Estate ★★★★

6531 Sturt Highway, Trentham Cliffs, NSW 2738 **Region** Murray Darling
T (03) 5024 8888 **www**.trenthamestate.com.au **Open** 7 days 10–5 **Winemaker** Anthony Murphy, Steve Yang **Viticulturist** Pat Murphy **Est.** 1988 **Dozens** 60 000 **Vyds** 35.89ha
Remarkably consistent tasting notes across all wine styles from all vintages attest to the expertise of ex-Mildara winemaker Anthony Murphy, a well-known and highly regarded producer. The estate vineyards are on the Murray Darling. With an eye to the future, but also to broadening the range of the wines on offer, Trentham Estate is selectively buying grapes from other regions with a track record for the chosen varieties. Trentham Estate celebrated its 35th anniversary in '23.

♟♟♟♟♟ **Reserve Blanc de Blanc NV, Tasmania** The intensity of flavour here is a bit special. Turkish delight, blackcurrant and musk drive through brown bread and citrus. Length is very good, as is presence. It's unsubtle, perhaps, but it's worth the asking price and then some. Cork. 12% alc. RATING 93 $28 CM ✪

Cellar Reserve Verdejo 2022, Murray Darling There's plenty to keep you interested here. It's a dry style with enticing floral notes, citrus, a musk-like aspect and drives of chalk and nectarine. There's a textural element too, like grape skins, especially through the back half. Everything works well here. Screw cap. 12% alc. RATING 92 DRINK 2023–2026 $28 CM ✪

Reserve Pinot Noir 2021, Yarra Valley This is a savoury wine at heart, full of snapped twig and sweet spice notes, but then the run of sweet-sour red-black cherry fruit is convincing in itself as well; it covers the bases. It's juicy, it has an appropriate rumble of tannin, and it pushes cleanly (if a touch reductively) and well through the finish. Varietal character is writ large here; always a good thing. Screw cap. 13.5% alc. RATING 92 DRINK 2024–2029 $28 CM ✪

Reserve Shiraz 2020, Heathcote The palate is awash with cherry plum, clove, mint and crème caramel flavours. There's a bit of heft to this wine but it remains easy to enjoy. Grippy tannin and lots of well-managed fruit; it's a handy combination. Screw cap. 14.5% alc. RATING 92 DRINK 2024–2032 $28 CM ✪

The Family Sangiovese Rosé 2022, Murray Darling Spicy, savoury and fruity all at once. This definitely kicks some goals. Cherries and woodsy spice notes come delivered in a light-but-textural package. This is a most enjoyable drink. Screw cap. 12.5% alc. RATING 90 DRINK 2023–2024 $18 CM ✪

Trevelen Farm

506 Weir Road, Cranbrook, WA 6321 **Region** Great Southern
T 0418 361 052 **www.trevelenfarm.com.au Open** 7 days 10–4.30 **Winemaker** James
Kellie **Est.** 1993 **Dozens** 3000 **Vyds** 6.5ha

In '08, John and Katie Sprigg passed ownership of their 1300ha wool, meat and grain
producing farm to son Ben and wife Louise. However, they kept control of the 6.5ha of
sauvignon blanc, riesling, chardonnay, cabernet sauvignon and merlot planted in '93. When
demand requires, they increase production by purchasing grapes from growers in Frankland
River. Riesling remains the centrepiece of the range.

Katie's Kiss Riesling 2022, Great Southern A distinctly sweeter and more
cloying style, but the acidity does a good job of balance and freshness. Scents of
preserved lemon, sweet lime, ginger and honey, flavours orientated to candied
mixed citrus, mandarin, light honey and a touch of talc-like minerality. It's
pleasing and simple, but the little puff of drying texture elevates things. The
balance, albeit orientated to sweeter fruit characters, is well done. Screw cap.
11.5% alc. **RATING** 90 **DRINK** 2023–2026 $18 MB ✪

Trifon Estate Wines

PO Box 258, Murchison, Vic 3610 **Region** Various
T (03) 9432 9811 **www.trifonestatewines.com.au Open** Not **Winemaker** Glenn
Eberbach, Amelie Mornex **Viticulturist** Sam Gallo, Ben Rose (consultant) **Est.** 1998
Dozens 90 000 **Vyds** 312ha

Trifon Estate has flown under the radar since it was established in '18. Since then, 312ha of
vines have been planted to 16 varieties, the lion's share to shiraz and cabernet (47ha and 42ha,
respectively), followed by malbec (38.7ha), chardonnay (23.7ha), sauvignon blanc (18ha),
pinot grigio (10.44ha) and merlot (8.10ha), with smaller amounts of petit verdot, durif,
tempranillo, sangiovese and riesling, traminer, semillon, marsanne and viognier.

Lagoon View Winemakers Selection Cabernet Sauvignon 2015,
Goulburn Valley A release by magnum, high in ripe fruit, medium in body
and ready to go. A touch of mint introduces black cherry, cassis, roasting
herbs, savoury earth and chocolatey notes. Fills the mouth with warmth and
concentrated flavour, punctured by sturdy tannins. Screw cap. 14.5% alc.
RATING 92 **DRINK** 2023–2029 $60 JP
Lagoon View Winemakers Selection Shiraz 2014, Goulburn Valley
Available only by magnum, this 9yo shiraz is drinking well right now. The
immediacy of youth has been overtaken by maturity in black fruit flavours
retaining great spice, a regional Aussie bush element that is so Goulburn Valley
and background woody notes that bring that added touch of complexity.
Screw cap. 14.1% alc. **RATING** 91 **DRINK** 2023–2026 $60 JP
Lagoon View Sparkling Cuvée Chardonnay 2022, Goulburn Valley
A young, engaging chardonnay-based Charmat method sparkling with plenty
of energy and zest. Brings a sense of its location with spring blossom and
honeysuckle aromas. Fresh citrus, stone fruits and apple nicely braced by tangy
acidity. Cork. 12.5% alc. **RATING** 90 **DRINK** 2023–2023 $24 JP ✪

tripe.Iscariot

20 McDowell Road, Witchcliffe, WA 6286 (postal) **Region** Margaret River
T 0414 817 808 **www.tripeiscariot.com Open** Not **Winemaker** Remi Guise **Est.** 2013
Dozens 800

This has to be the most way-out winery name of the century. It prompted me (James) to
email South African–born and trained winemaker/owner Remi Guise asking to explain
its derivation and/or meaning. He courteously responded with a reference to Judas as 'the
greatest black sheep of all time', and a non-specific explanation of 'tripe' as 'challenging in
style'. He added, 'I hope this sheds some light, or dark, on the brand.' The wines provide a
better answer, managing to successfully harness highly unusual techniques at various points

of their elevage. His day job as winemaker at Naturaliste Vintners, the large Margaret River contract winemaking venture of Bruce Dukes, provides the technical grounding, allowing him to throw the 'how to' manual out of the window when the urge arises.

Brawn Chardonnay 2021, Margaret River A wine like this could easily make you fall in love – with Margaret River and chardonnay from there. Understandable. It's the latent power of such beautiful fruit, all Gingin clone. Lemon verbena, pink grapefruit, juicy green apples kissed by oak spices and indeed the oak seamlessly integrated. The palate is pure and long, lightly textured, minerally and mouth-watering. What a wine. Screw cap. 12.8% alc. **RATING** 96 **DRINK** 2022–2031 $42 JF ✪

Aspic Grenache Rosé 2022, Margaret River Such a joy to drink with its combo of red berries, red licorice and a smattering of woodsy spices. Best of all, it's savoury, textural and slightly creamy with a snip of tannins adding more shape. It finishes dry-ish but oh-so-long thanks to its refreshing acidity. Screw cap. 12.8% alc. **RATING** 95 **DRINK** 2022–2025 $32 JF ✪

Cock's Foot Madrigal Muscat d'Alexandrie 2021, Margaret River Apparently, there are only 12 rows of muscat, a heady variety, in Margaret River. They're 45 years old, so Remi Guise has his hands on them. Partial skin contact, partial oak fermentation, partial stainless steel, no sulphur. The resulting wine is floral, dry, textural, refreshing, delicate and full of lemon verbena, musk, lychees and dried pears. Lovely. Screw cap. 12.4% alc. **RATING** 95 **DRINK** 2022–2026 $32 JF ✪

Stygian Bloom Cabernet Sauvignon 2021, Margaret River Stygian Bloom, surely the lead singer of a goth rock band. OK, it is a very distinct, powerful red. Everything has come together brilliantly but what's unusual are the fine, plentiful sandpaper-like tannins that give this shape and detail. Full bodied and full of dark fruit, nori, cedar, black licorice and warm earth. Screw cap. 13.8% alc. **RATING** 95 **DRINK** 2024–2038 $62 JF

Kroos Chenin Blanc 2020, Margaret River Always a delight to try chenin blanc from this producer. It's wonderfully fleshy and ripe with poached quince and lemon curd, red apple skins and a lemon-ginger herbal infusion. And yet, it's not a big wine, as fine acidity gently leads this to a persistent finish. Complex and compelling. Screw cap. 12.8% alc. **RATING** 95 **DRINK** 2022–2030 $42 JF ✪

Absolution Karridale Chenin Blanc 2021, Margaret River As fragrant as a bouquet of spring flowers, with loads of lemon and lime blossom. There's a lightness of touch to this refreshing wine that's led by red apple, citrus and an appealing aspirin/lemon character, which lends itself to a delicate, phenolic texture, even if finishes a tad short. But it's also nutty, savoury and a lovely drink. Screw cap. 13% alc. **RATING** 94 **DRINK** 2022–2027 $32 JF ✪

Cloisonné Grenache Noir Grenache 2021, Margaret River **RATING** 93 **DRINK** 2022–2028 $32 JF ✪

Trofeo Estate

★★★★★

85 Harrisons Road, Dromana, Vic 3936 **Region** Mornington Peninsula
T (03) 5981 8688 **www.trofeoestate.com** **Open** 7 days 10–5 **Winemaker** Richard Darby **Est.** 2012 **Dozens** 7500 **Vyds** 18.5ha
This property has had a chequered history, from failed passionfruit farm in the 1930s to a vineyard planted by the Seppelt family in the '40s and later acquired by leading Melbourne wine retailer and wine judge, the late Doug Seabrook. The vines were destroyed in a bushfire in '67 and not replanted until '98. From there, it passed through several hands and various stages of neglect until the latest owner, Jim Manolios, developed the property as a restaurant, vineyard and winery with pinot noir, chardonnay, pinot gris, shiraz and cabernet sauvignon grown using organic and biodynamic principles. All Trofeo Estate wines are matured in terracotta amphorae imported from Chianti, Italy.

Amphora Terracotta Rosé 2022, Mornington Peninsula An attractive pale bronze hue with lovely texture, some volume and depth. It has a whisper of watermelon, roses, lemon balm and the merest hint of creaminess yet is dry

and refreshing in equal measure. I could drink this all day. Screw cap. 12.5% alc.
RATING 95 DRINK 2022–2024 $32 JF ✪

ESC Pinot Gris Terracotta Amphora Wine 2021, Mornington Peninsula
This has a copper blush and wonderful, heady aromas of ginger flower, blood
orange, freshly sliced ginger and pickled watermelon rind. The palate is juicy,
succulent and grippy from the tannins, which is why this needs to be partnered
with food. Screw cap. 12.3% alc. RATING 95 DRINK 2023–2028 $34 JF ✪

**The Chosen Few Aged In Terracotta Amphorae Pinot Noir 2021,
Mornington Peninsula** Trofeo produces interesting, often compelling wine
and the way terracotta interacts with it is fascinating: no brutish oak to be found.
There's more depth of flavour here, although it's by no means a big wine, with
feathery light tannins and fine acidity with a delightful mix of varietal characters.
The palate is plush and extends long to finish on a high. Diam. 13.4% alc.
RATING 95 DRINK 2022–2030 $58 JF

The Chosen Few Chardonnay 2021, Mornington Peninsula There's an
extra level of flavour and complexity as this is essentially an amphora selection – the
ones with the X-factor, I guess, go into the final blend. Stone fruit, citrus, some
flintiness, a light spray of creamy lees and super-bright acidity. This is linear and
pure. Impressive drink. Cork. 13.5% alc. RATING 95 DRINK 2022–2031 $49 JF ✪

🍷🍷🍷🍷🍷 **ESC Pinot Noir Terracotta Amphora Wine 2021, Mornington Peninsula**
RATING 93 DRINK 2022–2028 $34 JF ✪

**Aged In Terracotta Amphorae Single Block Pinot Noir 2021,
Mornington Peninsula** RATING 93 DRINK 2022–2028 $49 JF

Aged in Terracotta Chardonnay 2021, Mornington Peninsula RATING 93
DRINK 2022–2028 $34 JF ✪

Aged in Terracotta Amphorae Pinot Gris 2022, Mornington Peninsula
RATING 92 DRINK 2023–2027 $32 JF

Aged in Terracotta Amphorae Pinot Noir 2021, Mornington Peninsula
RATING 92 DRINK 2022–2028 $36 JF

Blanc de Noir 2019, Mornington Peninsula RATING 92 DRINK 2023–2025
$58 JF

**The Chosen Few Aged In Terracotta Amphorae Cabernet Sauvignon
2020, Mornington Peninsula** RATING 90 DRINK 2024–2030 $46 JF

**The Chosen Few Aged In Terracotta Amphorae Shiraz 2020,
Mornington Peninsula** RATING 90 DRINK 2023–2028 $46 JF

Tscharke   ★★★★★

376 Seppeltsfield Road, Marananga, SA 5360 **Region** Barossa Valley
T 0438 628 178 **www**.tscharke.com.au **Open** Thurs–Mon 10–5 **Winemaker** Damien
Tscharke **Est.** 2001 **Dozens** 5000 **Vyds** 28ha

Damien Tscharke grew up in the Barossa Valley among the vineyards at Seppeltsfield and
Marananga. Wines under the Tscharke label are estate-grown and have catchy, snappy names,
followed by a Single Vineyard range. Top shelf is the Gnadenfrei collection, including a
white and 2 red blends, named for the vineyard where grenache, grenache blanc, shiraz and
mourvèdre are sourced. The estate is certified organic.

🍷🍷🍷🍷🍷 **Gnadenfrei Red I GSM 2021, Barossa Valley** Pure notes of juicy plum,
cranberry and raspberry coulis dotted with Asian spices, pressed flowers, sous bois,
gingerbread and earth. The tannins simmer away with a sense of latent power and
the fruit purity and flow are spot-on as the wine floats off to an extended encore.
Terrific stuff. Screw cap. 14.5% alc. RATING 96 DRINK 2023–2035 $140 DB

Stone Well Single Vineyard Grenache 2021, Barossa Valley Ripe plum,
raspberry and cranberries set on a canvas of gingery spice, red licorice, earth, cola
and purple flowers. There is a lovely flow of spiced, plummy fruit on the palate
that's pure and true. Superfine sandy tannins and a bright yet stony line of acidity
drive the wine forward. This will take a light chill if the weather dictates such
actions. Screw cap. 15% alc. RATING 95 DRINK 2023–2028 $45 DB ✪

Gnadenfrei Red II Mourvèdre Shiraz Grenache 2021, Barossa Valley
We're at the pointy end of the Tscharke offering here. Notes of plum and blackberry cut through with spice, chocolate, violets, roasting meats, herbs and warm earth. Impressive fruit weight and purity here, a tight, compact tannin framework and shimmering acidity that propels the wine forward to a bright, spicy red/dark fruited finish. Screw cap. 14% alc. RATING 95 DRINK 2023-2030 $140 DB
Gnadenfrei White Grenache Blanc 2021, Barossa Valley It gladdens my heart to see examples of grenache blanc, and this one is a beauty. Notes of clotted cream and curd from lees work among white peach, pear and citrus notes. Hints of soft spice, white flowers, white tea and almond paste. A lovely, textural wine with a vital, lemony acid tail and a white-fruited, creamy flow on the exit. Great stuff. Screw cap. 13.5% alc. RATING 95 DRINK 2023-2026 $90 DB
Stone Well Single Vineyard Shiraz 2021, Barossa Valley Fragrant and lifted with oodles of bunchy spice fluttering above plum, black cherry and blackberry fruits. Asian spices, maybe a waft of washed rind cheese and amaro herbs with licorice, chocolate, earth and purple floral notes. Spacious and pure on the palate with grippy kinetic tannins and a distinctly moreish vibe. Screw cap. 14% alc. RATING 94 DRINK 2023-2028 $45 DB
Elements Mourvèdre Shiraz Grenache 2021, Barossa Valley A translucent crimson in the glass hints at the wine's spacious, airy mouthfeel, with red cherry, raspberry and plum notes framed by spice, florals and bright, briny acidity. The tannin is there for support and fades back into the fruit, the wine exiting with a savoury palate shape and a vapour trail of ginger-spiced red fruits. Screw cap. 14% alc. RATING 94 DRINK 2023-2028 $28 DB ☻

🍷🍷🍷🍷 **A Thing of Beauty Grenache 2021, Barossa Valley** RATING 93 DRINK 2023-2026 $28 DB ☻
Grenache Rosé 2022, Barossa Valley RATING 92 DRINK 2023-2026 $24 DB ☻
Shiraz Shiraz Shiraz 2021, Barossa Valley RATING 92 DRINK 2023-2028 $24 DB ☻
Gnadenfrei North Single Vineyard Shiraz 2021, Barossa Valley RATING 92 DRINK 2023-2027 $45 DB

Turkey Flat   ★★★★★

67 Bethany Road, Tanunda, SA 5352 **Region** Barossa Valley
T (08) 8563 2851 **www.turkeyflat.com.au** **Open** 7 days 11–5 **Winemaker** James Adams
Est. 1990 **Dozens** 20 000 **Vyds** 47.83ha
The establishment date of Turkey Flat is given as 1990 but it might equally have been 1870 (or thereabouts), when the Schulz family purchased the Turkey Flat vineyard; or 1847, when the vineyard was first planted to the very old shiraz that still grows there today and the 8ha of equally old grenache. Plantings now comprise shiraz (24ha), grenache (10.5ha), cabernet sauvignon (5.9ha), mourvèdre (3.7ha) and smaller plantings of marsanne, viognier and dolcetto. The business is run by sole proprietor Christie Schulz.

🍷🍷🍷🍷🍷 **Grenache 2021, Barossa Valley** The estate vines are mostly over 100 years old. Bright, clear colour announces a perfumed red flower and fruit bouquet, the palate adding some purple fruit and gently savoury notes for the finish. Screw cap. 13.8% alc. RATING 96 DRINK 2023-2035 $45 JH ☻
Rosé 2022, Barossa Valley Pale salmon pink. Grenache leads mataro by the nose (pun regretted) in what is one of Australia's best rosés, year in, year out. It's dry, but has spice and red berry fruits to spare, and won't be found lacking wherever and whenever you choose to enjoy it. Screw cap. 12.5% alc. RATING 94 DRINK 2023-2023 $25 JH ☻
Mataro 2021, Barossa Valley Dry grown; matured for 8 months in French puncheons. Elegant, medium bodied, fragrant spicy and savoury aromas and flavours with fine-spun tannins on a long finish. Screw cap. 13.8% alc. RATING 94 DRINK 2023-2036 $40 JH ☻

🍷🍷🍷🍷 **White 2022, Barossa Valley** RATING 92 DRINK 2023-2027 $25 DB ☻

Turners Crossing Vineyard

747 Old Bridgewater-Serpentine Road, Serpentine, Vic 3517 (postal) **Region** Bendigo
T 0434 169 747 **www**.turnerscrossing.com.au **Open** Not **Winemaker** Adam Marks,
Rob Ellis, Cameron Leith **Est.** 1999 **Dozens** 4000 **Vyds** 42ha

This outstanding, mature vineyard was named to remember the original landholder, Thomas
Turner. During the Gold Rush period European settlers in the area started to plant vineyards,
trusting that Bendigo's terroir would reveal itself as a suitable site on which to grow grapes.
And they were right to be so confident. Its alluvial composition of rich limestone soils and
Mediterranean climate make it a happy home for viticulture in particular. Turners Crossing
vineyard now spans 42ha of mature vines, with shiraz, cabernet sauvignon, viognier and
picolit (a rare white Italian variety).

Viognier 2021, Bendigo Made under contract by Rob Ellis at Hanging Rock
Winery in a forward, ripe and decidedly tropical-fruited approach, this viognier
will appeal to many. Honeyed citrus, orange blossom, peach and melon aromas.
The palate is slippery and soft with some additional biscuity, nougat flavours and
oh-so textural. A good example of a fuller-bodied style. Screw cap. 14% alc.
RATING 91 **DRINK** 2023-2030 $40 JP

Turon Wines

1760 Lobethal Road, Lobethal, SA 5241 **Region** Adelaide Hills
www.turonwines.com.au **Open** By appt **Winemaker** Turon White **Est.** 2013 **Vyds** 1ha

This is the impressive venture of Turon and Alex White. Working for several small wineries
while studying at university, Turon realised the potential of the ever-varying site climates
within the Adelaide Hills. His overseas winemaking experience while completing his degree
was appropriately lateral, with vintages in Oregon and Hungary. Out of this came a highly
detailed minimal-intervention, lo-fi approach to winemaking. The pair built a small winery in
Lenswood in '17 and planted a low-yielding, high-density vineyard in '20, which is managed
with biodynamic and organic principles in mind. The 1ha under vine is all pinot noir at this
stage, specifically Abel, Pommard, MV6 and 777 clones.

Hills Series Chardonnay 2022, Adelaide Hills An effortless, poised and
beautifully weighted chardonnay. Textural, bumptious in a way, yet chiselled
across the taut finish. Fine scents of spiced pear, nectarine, ginger, truffle and
tatami straw. The trajectory of flavour, a crescendo. This is excellent for the
money. Screw cap. 13.5% alc. **RATING** 93 **DRINK** 2023-2030 $35 NG ✪

Pinot Gris 2022, Adelaide Hills Gris doesn't get much better than this in
Australia, a textural composition of chewy pear skin and ginger-doused acidity,
compressing lemon squash, nashi, spiced apple and quince. A mid-weighted
wine of flair and ease all at once. Very good. Screw cap. 12.5% alc. **RATING** 93
DRINK 2023-2027 $25 NG ✪

Hills Series Gamay 2022, Adelaide Hills This is good. The feel is effusive,
the weight attractive and the vibe one of joyous drinkability. The bone of herbal
tannin, too, suggests that mid-term ageing is not out of the question. Red fruits,
dried thyme and chinotto. I'd put money on this to develop in a positive fashion.
Screw cap. 13.4% alc. **RATING** 92 **DRINK** 2023-2028 $38 NG

Balhannah Single Vineyard Syrah 2020, Adelaide Hills Good wine.
Excellent aromas. Think charcuterie, clove, molten licorice, blue fruits and
menthol, with some gentle oak tannins desperately trying to tuck in the seams
of sweetness, expanding well across the belt line. A final hurrah of raspberry
bonbon and spice. A hot year, handled well. Screw cap. 13% alc. **RATING** 92
DRINK 2022-2030 $45 NG

Lenswood Single Vineyard Chardonnay 2021, Adelaide Hills This requires
a good waft of air to unravel. Flinty, match struck and pungently mineral, in that
contemporary domestic guise, at least to kick off with. Lean of feel. Flecks of
lemon balm, lime curd and nectarine skitter across a leesy oatmeal palate. There
is plenty to like. But disjointed for now. Patience should be a virtue. Screw cap.
13% alc. **RATING** 91 **DRINK** 2022-2030 $45 NG

Two Hands Wines ★★★★★

273 Neldner Road, Marananga, SA 5355 **Region** Barossa Valley
T (08) 8562 4566 **www**.twohandswines.com **Open** 7 days 11–5 **Winemaker** Richard
Langford **Viticulturist** Travis Coombe **Est.** 1999 **Dozens** 55 000 **Vyds** 40ha
The 'hands' in question were originally those of founders Michael Twelftree and Richard
Mintz. Grapes are sourced from the Barossa Valley (where the business has 40ha of shiraz),
McLaren Vale, Clare Valley, Eden Valley, the Adelaide Hills and Heathcote. The emphasis
is on sweet fruit and soft tannin structure, all signifying the precise marketing strategy of
what is a very successful business. In '15, Two Hands embarked on an extensive planting
program using vines propagated from a number of vineyards (including Prouse Eden Valley,
Wendouree 1893, Kaelser Alte Reben, Penfolds Modbury, Kays Block 6, Kalimna 3C), as
well as a high-density 1.4ha clos (a walled vineyard) with bush vines trained to stakes, known
as echalas, in the style of terraced vineyards in the northern Rhône Valley.

♀♀♀♀♀ Twelftree Chaffeys Road Seaview Grenache 2021, McLaren Vale An
exceptional grenache by virtue of its transparency, chiffon-like tannin and salty
freshness. Best, though, is the mandala of souk-like aromas and their reverberations
across a long, seamless finish. No paucity of grip, either. Think tamarind, pickled
orange rind, chutney and succulent red berries. Delicious. Screw cap. 14.5% alc.
RATING 96 **DRINK** 2022–2030 $45 NG ✪

Twelftree Adams Road Blewitt Springs Grenache 2021, McLaren Vale
This is transparent, diaphanous and the archetype of the oft-used comparison with
pinot noir, sans any drying influence of eucalyptus. Dried thyme, fennel, spiced
cherry and amaro. Long, lithe and filigreed. Elegance is as much the signature
as the intensity of flavour. Sumptuous wine of regional pedigree. Screw cap.
14.5% alc. **RATING** 96 **DRINK** 2022–2029 $45 NG ✪

Twelftree Schuller Blewitt Springs Grenache 2020, McLaren Vale
Distinctively red fruit-centric incorporating sour cherry, raspberry and cranberry
riffs. Rosehip tea, Seville orange, peony and lavender, to boot. A waft of menthol
across a long dance, punctuated by a burr of sandy, pixelated tannins. A bright,
ethereal wine marked by a giddy drinkability. Screw cap. 14.1% alc. **RATING** 96
DRINK 2022–2028 $45 NG ✪

Harriet's Garden Shiraz 2021, Adelaide Hills This is good. Pointed aromas
of green peppercorn, dill, green olive, charcuterie, blueberry, clove and iodine. A
little wild, immensely energetic and highly savoury, skittering amid rivets of finely
wrought tannin. The oak, a bit stringy. Good length, all the same. An impressive
wine that is mid-weighted of feel, vital and boasts the depth that marks the upper
tier of this address. Screw cap. 14% alc. **RATING** 95 **DRINK** 2024–2032 $65 NG

Lily's Garden Shiraz 2021, McLaren Vale Fruitcake and baking spices, clove,
star anise and boysenberry. The palate expands admirably, absorbing the kit of
oak that tends to a feel of older-school astringency on other cuvées. The finish,
pulsing, saline and long, shedding the obvious sweetness with air as the tannins
grow in stature and grasp the wine's scruff, imparting a confident augur of age-
worthiness. Diam. 14.5% alc. **RATING** 95 **DRINK** 2023–2035 $65 NG

Fields of Joy Shiraz 2021, Clare Valley Floral and pulpy initially, with a
seriousness imparted by classy French oak and impeccably extracted tannins.
Boysenberry lifted by scents of violet and amped by clove, cardamom and star
anise as rivets of complexity unravel. A sluice of kirsch marks the finish. Punchy
length. A wine of power as much as refinement. Bravo! Screw cap. 14.5% alc.
RATING 95 **DRINK** 2022–2035 $60 NG

Yacca Block Single Vineyard Menglers Hill Shiraz 2020, Eden Valley
There is a distinct ferrous quality to the aromatic profile of this wine with an
ironstone and graphite-sheathed core of blackberry, black cherry and dark plum
fruit underscored with notes of baking spices, licorice and dark chocolate oak.
For all its sinew and flex, there is some space to its palate shape with tight granitic
tannin support and a mineral-laden seam of acidity providing ample propulsion on
the finish. Diam. 14.4% alc. **RATING** 95 **DRINK** 2023–2025 $125 DB

Twelftree Adam's Road Blewitt Springs Grenache 2020, McLaren Vale
Creamy and floral. Modern and slick. Purple fruit, anise, tapenade, dried nori and charcuterie scents. A smart, hedonic display of that diplomatic point between northern Rhône aspirations and Aussie heft and polish. The tannins, taut and refined, a mark of class amid the barrage of extract and fruit. Classy for the style. Screw cap. 14.5% alc. RATING 95 DRINK 2022–2030 $45 NG ✪

Twelftree Seaview Willunga Grenache Mourvèdre 2020, McLaren Vale
I love this blend. Perhaps the wine I enjoy most of the suite, at least for immediate pleasure. Mourvèdre, an unsung hero slaying the sweetness of shiraz fruit in its path with a sabre of ferrous, olive-crusted tannins, all smoked charcuterie-chunky. Twelftree likes the combination of tank and used puncheons, his wont with all eponymous cuvées. A delicious wine. Screw cap. 14.3% alc. RATING 95 DRINK 2022–2028 $35 NG ✪

Twelftree Chaffeys Road Seaview Grenache 2020, McLaren Vale
More purple fruit-centric with lilac lift segueing to blueberry, plum, lavender and a sluice of iodine reduction. Considerable girth across the mid-palate, but the tannins are assertive, compressing the fruit into a sense of tension and propulsion. I like this. It lacks the ethereal lilt of the Blewitt cuvée, but it is compact, ferrous and hewn of a savoury bone. Screw cap. 14.4% alc. RATING 95 DRINK 2022–2029 $45 NG ✪

Sexy Beast Cabernet Sauvignon 2021, McLaren Vale McLaren Vale's ocean-modulated climate has long since been noted for the quality of its cabernet sauvignons. This great vintage has created a cabernet with its midpoint of luscious full-bodied wines at one extreme, and savoury tannins on the other. Screw cap. 14.4% alc. RATING 94 DRINK 2023–2041 $32 JH ✪

Dave's Block Single Vineyard Blythmans Road Blewitt Springs Shiraz 2020, McLaren Vale A capacious behemoth, spreading glycerol across the cheeks while staining the palate with flavours of crushed clove, licorice strap, crème de myrtille, raspberry and nori. An ethereal ebb between sheer power and an uncanny lightness of being. Cedar oak rims corral and compress the fray, the absence of grape tannins notable. A highly polished, ebullient and very Australian style. Diam. 14% alc. RATING 94 DRINK 2023–2032 $125 NG

Coach House Block Single Vineyard Greenock Shiraz 2020, Barossa Valley There is a bright, ferrous undertone to this wine though red fruits and violets come through with increased volume on the nose along with roasting meats, mocha, espresso and light tobacco hints in the distance. Bright acid drive, chalky tannin architecture and a sense of space despite its latent western Barossa horsepower. Diam. 14.5% alc. RATING 94 DRINK 2023–2035 $125 DB

🍷🍷🍷🍷🍷 **Max's Garden Shiraz 2021, Heathcote** RATING 93 DRINK 2024–2036 $65 CM

Bella's Garden Shiraz 2021, Barossa Valley RATING 93 DRINK 2023–2033 $65 DB

Twelftree Schuller Blewitt Springs Grenache 2021, McLaren Vale RATING 93 DRINK 2022–2029 $45 NG

Twelftree Vinegrove Road Grenache 2020, Barossa Valley RATING 93 DRINK 2022–2028 $45 NG

Brave Faces Grenache Mourvèdre Shiraz 2022, Barossa Valley RATING 92 DRINK 2023–2030 $32 DB

Samantha's Garden Shiraz 2021, Clare Valley RATING 92 DRINK 2024–2032 $65 NG

Charlie's Garden Shiraz 2021, Eden Valley RATING 92 DRINK 2023–2033 $65 DB

Twelftree Vinegrove Road Grenache 2021, McLaren Vale RATING 92 DRINK 2022–2028 $45 NG

Ares Shiraz 2019, Barossa Valley RATING 92 DRINK 2023–2034 $200 JH

2 Mates   ★★★☆

160 Main Road, McLaren Vale, SA 5171 (postal) **Region** McLaren Vale
T 0411 111 198 **www.2mates.com.au Open** Not **Winemaker** Mark Venable,
David Minear **Viticulturist** Ben Glaetzer **Est.** 2005 **Dozens** 250 **Vyds** 20ha
The 2 mates are Mark Venable and David Minear, who say, 'Over a big drink in a small bar
in Italy a few years back, we talked about making "our perfect Australian shiraz". When we
got back, we decided to have a go.' The wine ('05) was duly made and won a silver medal at
the Decanter World Wine Awards in London, in some exalted company.

ŸŸŸŸ♀ **Balancing Act Shiraz 2021, McLaren Vale** A powerful wine, high in alcoholic
octane as it steamrolls across the mouth, pummelling the gums with extract.
Mercifully, the oak is well handled, allowing riffs on dark fruits, liniment, anise
and lilac to shine. Well made for the idiom. Will have plenty of fans to be sure.
Screw cap. 14.9% alc. **RATING** 91 **DRINK** 2022-2028 **$35** NG

Tyrrell's Wines   ★★★★★

1838 Broke Road, Pokolbin, NSW 2321 **Region** Hunter Valley
T (02) 4993 7000 **www.tyrrells.com.au Open** 7 days 9–4 by appt **Winemaker** Andrew
Spinaze, Mark Richardson, Chris Tyrrell **Viticulturist** Andrew Pengilly **Est.** 1858
Dozens 150 000 **Vyds** 150ha
One of the most successful family wineries, a humble operation for the first 110 years of
its life that has grown out of all recognition over the past 45 years. Vat 1 Semillon is one
of the most dominant wines in the Australian show system and Vat 47 Chardonnay is one of
the pacesetters for this variety. Its estate plantings include over 100ha in the Hunter Valley
and 26ha in Heathcote. In '17 Tyrrell's purchased the 13.5ha Stevens Old Hillside vineyard
on Marrowbone Road; 6.11ha are planted to shiraz, including a 1.1ha block planted in 1867,
the balance planted in 1963, notably to shiraz and semillon. There are 11 blocks of vines older
than 100 years in the Hunter Valley and the Tyrrell family owns 7 of those blocks. A founding
member of Australia's First Families of Wine.

ŸŸŸŸŸ **Old Patch Shiraz 2021, Hunter Valley** The vines were planted in 1867 and
are the oldest in New South Wales. The beautiful colour caused my antennae
to wave furiously, and I wasn't misled. The grapes/vines were given no special
treatment: hand-picked and sorted in the vineyard, bucket-by-bucket, not
crushed, only whole berries and bunches. Sheer perfection, and the ultimate
example of a medium-bodied shiraz achieved without a skerrick of new oak.
Screw cap. 13% alc. **RATING** 99 **DRINK** 2023-2071 **$180** JH ✪ ♥
Vat 1 Winemaker's Selection Semillon 2022, Hunter Valley An iconic –
arguably the most iconic of all – Hunter semillon. The flowery, meadow grass
and lemon blossom bouquet was followed by a superbly elegant yet intense palate
that I refused to spit out. At last, Hunter semillon is being recognised by its price.
Screw cap. 11% alc. **RATING** 98 **DRINK** 2023-2047 **$105** JH ✪ ♥
Johnno's Shiraz 2021, Hunter Valley The vines were planted in 1908 on
sandy soil. The colour is on par with its peers, but from that point on, it's on its
own. The bouquet is earthy, in the style of the region at large. There's spice also
in play on a complex matrix, and the fruit reveals itself after much swirling and
fiddling. The palate has quite wonderful red fruits studded with spices that cast a
net over me. Screw cap. 13% alc. **RATING** 98 **DRINK** 2023-2061 **$180** JH
HVD Chardonnay 2022, Hunter Valley Vines were planted 1908 on what is
believed to be the oldest-producing chardonnay vineyard in Australia, and likely
the world. No special treatment, thus 85/15% 1–4yo/new French barriques.
Extraordinary focus and intensity in this great wine: white peach, Granny Smith
apple, and mouth-watering, persistent acidity. Screw cap. 13% alc. **RATING** 97
DRINK 2023-2030 **$100** JH ✪
8 Acres Shiraz 2021, Hunter Valley Vines planted in 1892. Cherries take
control of the bouquet, the medium-bodied palate nodding in agreement, but
bringing more, much more, to the party via a luscious assemblage of red and

purple fruits. Whole bunches and berries have contributed, tannins making it clear that their presence is not a mere sinecure. The wine is a thing of beauty. Screw cap. 13.3% alc. **RATING** 97 **DRINK** 2023–2041 $180 JH

Single Vineyard Belford Chardonnay 2021, Hunter Valley The vineyard is the northernmost of the estate vineyards, planted on light, almost talc-like sandy soils. It is unlike peers thanks to its multilayered, tangy fruit with a hint of blood orange (both skin and flesh). Outstanding value. Screw cap. 12.5% alc. **RATING** 97 **DRINK** 2023–2035 $45 JH ✪

♟♟♟♟♟ **Vat 9 Winemaker's Selection Shiraz 2021, Hunter Valley** Created in 1962 by the late Murray Tyrrell. The wine overflows with lively, spicy fruits that dance in the mouth as the oak joins in the savoury core, reflecting the maturation in 'mostly newer' oak for the usual 14 months. There also appears to be some whole bunches involved. Screw cap. 13.5% alc. **RATING** 96 **DRINK** 2023–2046 $150 JH

Single Vineyard NVC Shiraz 2021, Hunter Valley The vineyard was planted in 1921 and the wine matured in a 3yo Stockinger cask for 14 months. It is well into medium-bodied territory, filling the mouth with plum and blackberry fruit underpinned by suede tannins. Its purity and balance are impeccable. Screw cap. 13% alc. **RATING** 96 **DRINK** 2023–2051 $70 JH ✪

Old Hillside Vineyard Shiraz 2021, Hunter Valley The vineyard was planted back in 1950 on a steep, east-facing slope. Its vinification is no different from its siblings, but the colour is a deep crimson, and the velvet and silk palate is in the top-flight echelon where spitting out any part of each taste is nigh on impossible. Screw cap. 13.5% alc. **RATING** 96 **DRINK** 2025–2055 $80 JH

Estate Grown Chardonnay 2022, Hunter Valley From dry-grown vines planted in 1984 and 2003 in the HVD vineyard. While the bouquet is relatively quiet, the palate is amazing. It borders luscious, not common with 1yo chardonnay. The fruit rainbow has yellow peach at its centre, vibrant citrusy acidity driving the back palate and a lingering finish. Screw cap. 13.3% alc. **RATING** 95 **DRINK** 2023–2029 $40 JH ✪

Single Vineyard Mother's Shiraz 2021, Hunter Valley 'Mother's' stands for mother vines. It was planted in 2010 with cuttings taken from 4 Acres, Johnno's and Old Patch vineyards, ensuring the best shiraz clones are preserved. Its upbringing shines through with its flawless array of red and purple fruits on a palate of striking clarity and poise. Drink whenever the mood takes you. Screw cap. 13% alc. **RATING** 95 **DRINK** 2023–2043 $65 JH

4 Acres Shiraz 2021, Hunter Valley The vines were planted 1879 on deep red clay soils over limestone, and it is the oldest block on the Tyrrell's Ashmans property. Bright, clear crimson hue. Cherry blossom perfume fills the bouquet, the palate opening with red and black cherries, moving through to a gently savoury finish. It's where you find the tannins a Burgundian vigneron would applaud. Screw cap. 13% alc. **RATING** 95 **DRINK** 2023–2033 $180 JH

Special Release Fiano 2022, Hunter Valley The back label neatly compresses the raison d'être for fiano (and specifically this wine): 'The wine has intense varietal characteristics with aromas of pear and spice. The palate is perfectly balanced between fruit intensity and textural elements ...' It is that tension that makes fiano so interesting and so well balanced with almost all foods. Screw cap. 11.5% alc. **RATING** 94 **DRINK** 2023–2025 $30 JH ✪

Shiraz 2021, Hunter Valley Man alive. This may well have had some help with bits 'n' pieces from the old vines. I don't know how else such elegance and poise in a medium-bodied style could be made in a challenging vintage with too much rain and not enough sunshine for all but the old boys. Screw cap. 13.5% alc. **RATING** 94 **DRINK** 2023–2036 $26 JH ✪

♟♟♟♟♟ **Vat 63 Winemaker's Selection Chardonnay Semillon 2022, Hunter Valley** **RATING** 93 **DRINK** 2023–2038 $60 JH

Vat 8 Winemaker's Selection Shiraz Cabernet 2021, Hunter Valley McLaren Vale **RATING** 93 **DRINK** 2025–2040 $100 JH

Lunatiq Shiraz 2021, Heathcote **RATING** 92 **DRINK** 2023–2036 $35 JH

Chardonnay 2022, Hunter Valley RATING 91 DRINK 2023–2025 $26 JH
Special Release Shiraz Pinot Noir 2022, Hunter Valley RATING 91
DRINK 2023–2037 $35 JH
Estate Grown Shiraz 2021, Hunter Valley RATING 91 DRINK 2023–2036
$40 JH
Semillon 2022, Hunter Valley RATING 90 DRINK 2023–2025 $25 JH

Ulithorne   ★★★★

85 Kays Road, Blewitt Springs, SA 5171 **Region** McLaren Vale
T 0409 963 223 **www.ulithorne.com.au Open** By appt **Winemaker** Peter Flewellyn
Est. 1971 **Dozens** 2500 **Vyds** 7.2ha
Ulithorne produces small quantities of red wines from selected parcels of grapes from its estate
vineyard in McLaren Vale, planted in 1950 by Bob Whiting. The small-batch, high-quality
wines are influenced by Ulithorne's associate Laurence Feraud, owner of Domaine du Pegau
of Châteauneuf-du-Pape. The business was sold to CW Wines in Dec '20.

🍷🍷🍷🍷🍷 **Frux Frugis Shiraz 2019, McLaren Vale** A full-throttle expression pulled off
with aplomb. Old-vine vinosity, very clear and impressive. The thrust of kirsch,
licorice strap, star anise, clove and black cherry is parried by well-appointed
oak, chewy grape skin tannins and juicy acidity underlying the morass. As far as
wines of this ilk go, this is good. Cork. 14.5% alc. **RATING** 93 **DRINK** 2023–2032
$120 NG
Prospera Shiraz 2021, McLaren Vale Barrel-fermented aromas of smoked
meats and vanilla curd are toasty and intoxicating. Spice and dark plum, mosey
amid the morass. Clove, pepper and cardamom spruik a spicy finish. A throaty,
nourishing wine of appeal. Screw cap. 14.5% alc. **RATING** 92 **DRINK** 2023–2032
$50 NG
Meracus Grenache 2020, McLaren Vale Very good grenache, synergistic
with the warmer and saturated darker fruit tones of the southern Rhône, than the
Vale's regional trend toward a balletic straddle of ripeness and red fruits. A little
more freshness would be nice. Attractive riffs on sandalwood, campfire, dried rose
and blood plum. Screw cap. 14.5% alc. **RATING** 91 **DRINK** 2023–2027 $50 NG
Paternus Cabernet Shiraz 2020, Coonawarra McLaren Vale A multi-
regional blend, with the cabernet drawn from the terra rossa soils of Coonawarra.
Rich, yet compact and surprisingly fresh for such an aspirational style. The cedary
oak supports are embedded nicely into the density. Redcurrant, clove and mint
mingle with a smoky barrel-ferment aroma of bacon and vanilla splayed across a
finish underlain by dill and notes of hedgerow. Screw cap. 14.5% alc. **RATING** 91
DRINK 2023–2027 $80 NG
Epoch Rosé 2022, McLaren Vale Good rosé, presumably grenache-driven.
A gentle coral hue segues to cranberry, tangerine and dried thyme sensations,
with a twirl of perky freshness and gentle phenolic rails corralling the fruit. Good
crunchy intensity and a finish on the better side of dryness. Screw cap. 13% alc.
RATING 90 **DRINK** 2023–2024 $25 NG

🍇 Ulster Park Wines   ★★★☆

11 Main North Road, Auburn, SA 5451 **Region** Clare Valley
T 0437 913 148 **www.ulsterparkwines.com.au Open** Fri–Sun 1–5 **Winemaker** Kevin
Mitchell **Viticulturist** Michael Smith **Est.** 2000 **Dozens** 500 **Vyds** 4ha
Some call it the 'Paris end' of the Clare Valley, while others know it as the parish of Auburn.
Ulster Park Wines is a staple in this hamlet and is definitively known for the regional red grape
hero, shiraz. The farm's past life was as a dairy farm of repute, now owned and run by the
Smith family across two generations. The vines were first planted by the Smiths in 1988 with
the flagship shiraz, Matriarch, first released in '04. Pinot gris has joined shiraz in the vineyards
alongside, while a rosé and sparkling wine are easy bedfellows in the simple portfolio. Shiraz
really is the focal point, though, with varied iterations released each year to celebrate the full
potential of the variety and a reflection of traditional expressions from Clare Valley.

ŶŶŶŶŶ **Matriarch Shiraz 2018, Clare Valley** Full bodied but revelling in a lift and freshness, this is all mulberry, bright kirsch and choc-orange scents and flavours with slippery texture and a vibrant, juicy finish. While not overly complex, there's a compelling drinkability to the wine, a joyful feel and bounciness in texture and fruit characters. Easy drinking. Good times. Screw cap. 14.5% alc. **RATING** 90 **DRINK** 2022–2030 $45 MB

Ulupna Winery ★★★★

159 Crawfords Road, Strathmerton, Vic 3641 **Region** Goulburn Valley
T (03) 9533 8831 **www**.ulupnawinery.com.au **Open** By appt **Winemaker** Vio Buga, Viviana Ferrari **Est.** 1999 **Dozens** 35 000 **Vyds** 22ha
Ulupna started out as a retirement activity for Nick and Kathy Bogdan. The vineyard on the banks of the Murray River is planted to shiraz (50%), cabernet sauvignon (30%) and chardonnay (20%); the plantings allowing for expansion in the years ahead. The wines are made under the direction of Vio Buga, who also designed and planted the vineyard.

ŶŶŶŶŶ **Royal Phoenix Single Vineyard Shiraz 2020, Goulburn Valley** Boasts Central Victorian generosity and ripeness but carries it well, including the high alcohol content, to deliver a wine that rolls out smoothly. Delivers a wealth of dark plum and berry flavours rich in spice, anise, toasty oak and supported by smooth, fine-grained tannins. Nicely balanced and ready to be enjoyed or aged further. Your call. Screw cap. 15% alc. **RATING** 92 **DRINK** 2023–2028 $55 JP
"U" Shiraz 2019, Goulburn Valley A wine to mark 20 years of Ulupna. A celebratory wine big on flavour and impact. Fragrant and complex in ripe, plum-scented fruits, blackberries, baked earth, chocolate and a world of warm spice. At its core lies a solid, sweet-fruited centre, fleshy in texture and sturdy in tannins. Cork. 15% alc. **RATING** 92 **DRINK** 2023–2033 $180 JP
Shiraz 2020, Goulburn Valley Works a strong line in savouriness from the outset against a background of ripe, earthy, dark berries, plums and licorice spiciness. Roasted meat juices and smokehouse flavours contribute added interest. The higher alcohol and ripe tannins produce sweeping warmth and texture. Solid winter fare. Screw cap. 15% alc. **RATING** 90 **DRINK** 2023–2030 $32 JP

UMAMU Estate ★★★★☆

PO Box 1269, Margaret River, WA 6285 **Region** Margaret River
T (08) 9757 5058 **www**.umamuestate.com **Open** Not **Winemaker** Bruce Dukes, Glenn Goodall **Viticulturist** Colin Bell, AHA Viticulture **Est.** 2005 **Dozens** 500 **Vyds** 16.4ha
Chief executive Charmaine Saw explains, 'An upbringing in both eastern and western cultures, graduating in natural science, training as a chef combined with a passion for the arts and experience as a management consultant have all contributed to my building the business creatively yet professionally.' The palindrome 'UMAMU', says Charmaine, is inspired by balance and contentment. In practical terms, this means a sustainable approach to viticulture and a deep respect for the terroir. The plantings, dating back to '78, include cabernet sauvignon, chardonnay, shiraz, semillon, sauvignon blanc, merlot and cabernet franc.

ŶŶŶŶŶ **Ann's Cabernet Sauvignon 2019, Margaret River** I want to know more about Ann, whose name graces the label that says cabernet is one of her favourite varieties. Clearly, the woman has good taste. It's beautifully proportioned with quality fruit rising to the top all mulberries and blackberries doused in cedar, spice and all things nice. The palate reaffirms the joy of a medium-bodied wine with such slinky, velvety tannins. Cheers, Ann. Screw cap. 13.8% alc. **RATING** 95 **DRINK** 2022–2037 $60 JF

ŶŶŶŶŶ **MacAnn Cabernets 2019, Margaret River RATING** 93 **DRINK** 2022–2034 $38 JF

Usher Tinkler Wines

97 McDonalds Road, Pokolbin, NSW 2320 **Region** Hunter Valley
T 02 4998 7069 **www**.ushertinklerwines.com **Open** 7 days 10–5 **Winemaker** Usher
Tinkler **Est.** 2014 **Dozens** 10 000 **Vyds** 22ha

Usher Tinkler is the progeny of 3 generations of Hunter farmers, setting out on his own
after first making wine (of sorts) in the family bathtub. His nemesis: boring wines. Set in
the original Pokolbin church built in 1905, the Tinkler tasting room is as iconoclastic as it is
brimming with a sense of place, much like his wines. The Usher Tinkler Reserve wines meld
the Hunter's proclivity for bright fruit and its shiraz wines' earthen terracotta accent, with
quality oak and stridently extracted structural latticework. They age well.

Reserve Chardonnay 2022, Hunter Valley A big bottle and an out-there
label are the obvious points of distinction for this wine compared to the Tinklers
Vineyard releases. The bouquet is tantalising, the palate brisk and minerally.
Screw cap. 12.5% alc. **RATING** 95 **DRINK** 2023-2032 $60 JH

Utopos ★★★★★

PO Box 764, Tanunda, SA 5352 **Region** Barossa Valley
T 0409 351 166 **www**.utopos.com.au **Open** Not **Winemaker** Kym Teusner **Est.** 2015
Dozens 1500 **Vyds** 20ha

The fates were kind when Neil Panuja, a friend of Kym Teusner's from 'the big smoke', said
he had the wish (and the cash) to get into fine-wine production and asked that Kym keep
an eye out for something special. Shortly thereafter a vineyard that Kym had coveted from
his beginnings in the Barossa Valley came onto the market. The 20ha site was duly acquired,
Kym investing in a small share that he couldn't really afford but had to have. The vineyard
is on Roenfeldt Road at one of the highest points of the boundary between Greenock and
Marananga. The depleted stoney soils consistently produce low yields of high-quality grapes
that loudly proclaim their origin. The X-factor is the site-driven savoury balance that Kym
says he always longs for. The name they have given the business is the root word of Utopia.
Everything is just so right: great vineyard, great winemaker, great story, great packaging.

(E)Utopos Shiraz 2018, Barossa Valley Sourced from 1974-planted blocks.
A deep, impressive wine that shows excellent fruit purity and density in the way
of blackberry, satsuma plum and black cherry. Layers of spice, dark chocolate,
graphite and roasting meats add complexity and the tannin/acid architecture is
well suited to cellaring. Long, sustained and a picture of grace and latent power.
Cork. 14.5% alc. **RATING** 96 **DRINK** 2023-2040 $250 DB
Shiraz 2021, Barossa Valley Impressive plummy depth and purity with hints
of fine spice, graphite, ironstone, licorice, dark chocolate, vanilla and softly spoken
French oak. Fine sandy tannins lend ample support, and there is clarity to the
wine despite the rich fruit weight. Finishes long, pure and true to its western
Barossa roots. Cork. 14.5% alc. **RATING** 95 **DRINK** 2023-2038 $85 DB
Cabernet Sauvignon 2021, Barossa Valley Bright blackberry and red cherry
fruits of impressive purity are framed by hints of fine spice, licorice, tobacco
leaf, cedar and earth. Some blackcurrant pastille notes flow in on the palate,
which shows substantial, fine tannin grip and a bright cadence lending sustain
to the finish. Impressive now but will cellar nicely. Cork. 14.5% alc. **RATING** 95
DRINK 2023-2038 $85 DB
Mataro Shiraz Grenache 2021, Barossa Valley Juicy and bright with pure
dark plum and blueberry notes framed by spice, earth, roasting meats, pressed
flowers, ginger cake and licorice. For the fruit depth, there is quite a sprightly gait
with fine tannin acting in support. Cork. 14.5% alc. **RATING** 94 **DRINK** 2023-2033
$85 DB

Cabernet Shiraz 2021, Barossa Valley **RATING** 92 **DRINK** 2023-2025 $85 DB

Utter Wines ★★★★

2427 Maroondah Highway, Buxton, Vic 3711 **Region** Upper Goulburn
T 0411 550 519 **www.**riverhousewineandtruffles.com.au **Open** By appt
Winemaker Adrian Utter, Robert Utter **Viticulturist** Adrian Utter **Est.** 2012
Dozens 500 **Vyds** 2ha

Agronomist and viticulturist Adrian Utter and his father, Robert, farm a family property at Buxton in the Acheron River Valley. Initial plantings of grape vines have expanded slowly to just under 2ha of high-density vines, with further gradual expansion planned. The Utters believe the high continentality of the mountain valley, with cool nights and warm days, allows longer ripening, preserving the vibrancy of the fruit. Sustainability guides vineyard practices, promoting biodiversity and maintaining plant health. The complete process from planting to bottling is performed by Adrian and Robert. The farm also supports a productive truffiere (Buxton Black Truffles) and beef cattle production.

ŸŸŸŸ♀ **Syrah 2021, Upper Goulburn** An arresting cool-climate syrah alive and bouncing in the prettiest florals and peppery energy. Layered in between are blueberries, dark fruits, woodsy spices, earth and well-tended oak, detailed throughout in firm, fine tannins. Diam. 13.6% alc. **RATING** 93 **DRINK** 2023-2026 $40 JP

Pinot Noir 2021, Upper Goulburn Delicate scents of just-picked strawberries, red cherries, dried flowers, musk and anise. Attractive florals are key to this young pinot, together with a juicy, red-berried palate and chalky tannin presence. Basks in a warm, textural glow, rolling smoothly off the tongue. Diam. 13.5% alc. **RATING** 90 **DRINK** 2023-2027 $40 JP

Valhalla Wines ★★★★★

163 All Saints Road, Wahgunyah, Vic 3687 (postal) **Region** Beechworth
T 0429 330 280 **www.**valhallawines.com.au **Open** Not **Winemaker** Anton Therkildsen
Viticulturist Anton Therkildsen **Est.** 2001 **Dozens** 1400

Anton Therkildsen and wife Antoinette Del Popolo planted their first vineyard in Rutherglen in '02 to shiraz and durif, purchasing viognier, marsanne, grenache and mourvèdre from local growers. Anton uses traditional winemaking methods, making and cellaring the wines in their straw-bale winery. Sustainable viticulture practices are used, with minimal use of sprays and annual planting of cover crops between the rows. Rainwater harvesting, recycled packaging, a worm farm and the composting of grape skins and stalks complete the picture. Operations have since moved to Beechworth and all fruit is purchased from trusted growers throughout North East Victoria.

ŸŸŸŸŸ **Reserve Durif 2021, Rutherglen** A wine of poise, engaging charm AND cellaring potential. Blueberry, cherry, plum, lavender, rosemary and hazelnut. Expansive and finely edged on the palate with an inviting core of lifted aromatics, fruit, chocolate and a touch of savouriness. Grape tannins are in control, but not aggressively so. It's a subtle difference that allows drinkability now and later. Best of both worlds. Screw cap. 14.2% alc. **RATING** 95 **DRINK** 2022-2032 $40 JP

Reserve Chardonnay 2019, Alpine Valleys Shows a confident winemaking hand for a chardonnay of some elegance. Pale yellow and bright. Grapefruit, stone fruit, nougat and preserved lemon perfume is lifted and inviting. What follows offers plenty of flavour, leesy almond meal texture and overall complexity. Stays with you on a long finish. Nicely detailed throughout with a bright future ahead. Screw cap. 12.6% alc. **RATING** 95 **DRINK** 2022-2030 $35 JP ✪

Riesling 2018, King Valley An arousing scent of concentrated lime with lemon butter and delicate floral aromatics ushers in this complex, but incredibly youthful, 4yo riesling. Crisp, dry and tangy, the palate shows hints of toast with green apple and citrus. Chalky in texture and tight in lemony acidity with fabulous focus and drive. Screw cap. 12.6% alc. **RATING** 95 **DRINK** 2022-2030 $25 JP ✪

Reserve Tempranillo 2021, Alpine Valleys Tempranillo thrives in the Alpine Valleys and this is an excellent, well-priced example. Dark in colour and personality with a deep, spiced black cherry/plum fragrance with forest undergrowth, herbs and bay leaf. A subtle hand with oak gives full and lasting expression to the fruit and well-handled acid/tannin interplay. Well balanced. More, please! Screw cap. 13.7% alc. **RATING** 94 **DRINK** 2022-2028 $30 JP ✪

🍷🍷🍷🍷 Tempranillo 2022, Alpine Valleys **RATING** 92 **DRINK** 2022-2024 $28 JP ✪

Vanguardist Wines

121A Radford Road, Seppeltsfield, SA 5355 **Region** Barossa Valley
T 0487 193 053 **www**.vanguardistwines.com **Open** By appt **Winemaker** Michael John Corbett **Viticulturist** Michael John Corbett **Est.** 2014 **Dozens** 2000 **Vyds** 7.5ha
Vanguardist Wines' maker Michael John Corbett draws on established sources across South Australia to craft a delicious swag of Mediterranean-inspired wines of textural intrigue. A card of neutral wood, ambient ferments and plenty of whole-bunch is dealt with a deft hand. The results, often compelling. Corbett's opus is grenache, specifically Blewitt Springs grenache, hewn of the region's low-yielding elevated old vineyards. His ripeness barometer challenges notions of what is optimal, flirting with marginal levels of alcohol on the lower side. Quantities are small, selling out fast.

🍷🍷🍷🍷 Grenache 2021, McLaren Vale A smorgasbord of optimally ripe kirsch, dried rose, tamarind, turmeric and Seville orange peel. A spindle of nebbiolo-esque tannins, always the signature. The finish, a long plume licked with mint and a waft of tea tree oil. Intense, detailed, a bit gritty, heady of personality and absolutely delicious. Diam. 14.3% alc. **RATING** 96 **DRINK** 2022-2028 $65 NG ✪
Grenache Mourvèdre Rosé 2022, McLaren Vale A pallid coral, flecked with onion-skin edges. Gorgeous. Tangerine, cumquat and freshly lain tatami straw. The acidity, dutiful. A mid-weighed, fresh and immensely savoury rosé that leans on a chewy rail of phenolics and a swirl of white miso lees work doused with raw almond and orange oil. A quinine bite to conclude a delicious experience. Diam. 12.7% alc. **RATING** 95 **DRINK** 2022-2024 $45 NG ✪ ♥
Blewitt Springs Mourvèdre 2021, McLaren Vale This is very good, edging into a glimmer of near-perfect ripeness. Succulent, all the same. Beef bouillon, a smear of green olive, mulberry, clove, white pepper and multitudinous spices. Not as flamboyant as the grenache, nor as intriguing as the rosé, but there is an understated cool and plenty of class. Screw cap. 13.6% alc. **RATING** 94 **DRINK** 2022-2028 $55 NG

Varney Wines

62 Victor Harbor Road, Old Noarlunga, SA 5168 **Region** McLaren Vale
T 0450 414 570 **www**.varneywines.com.au **Open** Thurs–Mon 11–5 **Winemaker** Alan Varney **Est.** 2017 **Dozens** 1500
Alan Varney's Australian career (based on an oenology degree from the University of Melbourne) grew out of a vintage stint with d'Arenberg into an 11-year employment, much of it as senior winemaker. He says that this period meant he came to be friends with many of the best local growers in McLaren Vale, the Adelaide Hills and Langhorne Creek. He is a brilliant winemaker, saying, 'I am not afraid to step out of the box and go with my intuition … I only use old seasoned oak with no fining or filtration.' His ability to draw the varietal heart of each wine he makes with the majority of alcohol levels between 12% and 14% is extraordinary. The unspoken question is whether he will increase the small amounts of each wine he makes; my (James') guess is not by much.

🍷🍷🍷🍷 Vint Mencia 2022, McLaren Vale Think cool-climate syrah in a more savoury, mellifluous guise, smattered with dried thyme, fennel and peppery tannins, a twine of attractive astringency. A sphere of blue-fruited succulence expands across a fullish girth with energy, drive, length and immense joy. Great drinking! Screw cap. 14% alc. **RATING** 95 **DRINK** 2022-2027 $35 NG ✪
Fiano 2021, Langhorne Creek The best release of fiano to date at this address, successfully melding scents of stone fruit, marzipan and anise, with lees-derived

truffled inflections and white miso spread. Taut and compact, yet by the same token, expansive, textural and really intense of flavour. Long. A salubrious wine, with the vanillin framework of quality oak used to superb effect. Screw cap. 12.4% alc. **RATING** 95 **DRINK** 2022–2027 $30 NG ✪

Grenache 2022, McLaren Vale Cherry pie, pomegranate, persimmon, kirsch and a broad slake of star anise, dried thyme and lavender. Alan Varney understands the need for tannin, the pinion of compression and the inherent tension that comes with it, as much as the bulwark against fruit sweetness. A rather fine wine at a very fair price. Screw cap. 14.6% alc. **RATING** 94 **DRINK** 2023–2030 $36 NG ✪

🍷🍷🍷🍷 **GSM 2021, McLaren Vale RATING** 93 **DRINK** 2022–2028 $35 NG ✪
Fiano 2022, Langhorne Creek RATING 92 **DRINK** 2023–2029 $30 NG ✪
Chardonnay 2022, Adelaide Hills RATING 92 **DRINK** 2023–2028 $34 NG
Entrada Rosé of Grenache 2022, McLaren Vale RATING 91
DRINK 2022–2023 $27 NG ✪

Vasse Felix

Cnr Tom Cullity Drive/Caves Road, Cowaramup, WA 6284 **Region** Margaret River **T** (08) 9756 5000 **www.**vassefelix.com.au **Open** 7 days 10–5 **Winemaker** Virginia Willcock **Viticulturist** Bart Molony **Est.** 1967 **Dozens** 150 000 **Vyds** 330ha
Vasse Felix is Margaret River's founding wine estate, established by regional pioneer Dr Tom Cullity. Owned and operated by the Holmes à Court family since '87, Paul Holmes à Court has brought the focus to Margaret River's key varieties of cabernet sauvignon and chardonnay. Chief winemaker Virginia Willcock has energised the winemaking and viticultural team with her no-nonsense approach and fierce commitment to quality. Vasse Felix has 3 scrupulously managed vineyards throughout Margaret River that contribute all but a small part of the annual production. Wines include the Tom Cullity (cabernet blend) and Heytesbury Chardonnay under the Icon collection. Other wines fall under the Premier, Filius and Classic collections.

🍷🍷🍷🍷🍷 **Heytesbury Chardonnay 2021, Margaret River** Excellent fruit and a second-to-none level of detail. This is an evocative wine. Funky sulphides rockin' it while a gossamer thread of acidity holds everything in line – the citrus flavours, the texture, the wine totally enveloping the oak and, while it's a powerhouse of flavour, there's a purity to this. It's such a contrast. How does it achieve that? Screw cap. 13% alc. **RATING** 98 **DRINK** 2023–2033 $110 JF ✪ ♥

Tom Cullity Cabernet Sauvignon Malbec 2019, Margaret River Trepidation over tasting a flagship wine so young lasted a nanosecond before turning to 'oh my, this is awesome'. In this seductive youthful stage, it's fragrant with florals from violets to lavender, blueberries and bramble all wonderfully savoury with lots of warming spices. The palate offers charm, detail and excellent structure with velveteen tannins and a fine acid line to a long, long finish. Screw cap. 14.5% alc. **RATING** 98 **DRINK** 2024–2040 $190 JF ♥

🍷🍷🍷🍷🍷 **DHJ1 Single Plot Chardonnay 2021, Margaret River** This new chardonnay was accompanied by a note saying Virginia Willcock and her team 'were blown away by the jasmine florals, oyster-like salinity and a logic-defying limestone minerality.' Well, who am I to argue? It's also linear, fine and long, a pure style without any new oak, only excellent fruit and Usain Bolt-like acidity yet all wound up to create a savoury style. Funky, flinty and fabulous, too. Screw cap. 12.5% alc. **RATING** 96 **DRINK** 2022–2031 $75 JF ✪

Cabernet Sauvignon 2020, Margaret River A marker of great cabernet is being seduced by the aromas and flavours, which need to be in harmony, and let's not forget beautiful tannins matched to fine acidity. Does this fall into that class? Too right it does. Varietal flavours are pitch-perfect and not quite understated, this is cabernet after all, and the result is a certain elegance and class. A gorgeous rendition. Screw cap. 14.5% alc. **RATING** 96 **DRINK** 2023–2040 $55 JF ✪

Sauvignon Blanc 2021, Margaret River Serious sauv blanc that's seriously good, but not as you know it. Wild fermentation in oak with some skin contact creates a structured, savoury wine with an absence of overt tropical flavours. Instead, phenolics add shape and mouthfeel while textural talc-like acidity ensures this remains refreshing. It is complex, flavoursome and moreish. Screw cap. 12.5% alc. RATING 95 DRINK 2022-2028 $33 JF ✪

Syrah 2021, Margaret River Not the easiest vintage in Margaret River, but you wouldn't know it with this buoyant yet savoury offering. It's highlighting the exuberance of youth with its poppy dark fruits all spiced and tarted up with cranberry juice flavour. As it opens in the glass more layers are revealed, the texture of fine sandy tannins and lots of them, there's a stony quality in a positive way as this is still tight. Savoury, complex and appealing. Screw cap. 14% alc. RATING 94 DRINK 2022-2033 $37 JF ✪

 Chardonnay 2021, Margaret River RATING 93 DRINK 2023-2031 $45 JF
Filius Shiraz 2021, Margaret River RATING 93 DRINK 2022-2031 $29 JF ✪
Filius Sauvignon Blanc Semillon 2020, Margaret River RATING 92 DRINK 2022-2032 $29 JF ✪
Filius Sauvignon Blanc Semillon 2022, Margaret River RATING 91 DRINK 2022-2027 $29 JF
Classic Dry Red 2021, Margaret River RATING 91 DRINK 2022-2028 $20 JF ✪
Classic Dry White 2022, Margaret River RATING 90 DRINK 2022-2024 $20 JF ✪
Filius Chardonnay 2021, Margaret River RATING 90 DRINK 2022-2028 $29 JF

Vella Wines   ★★★★

147B Sheoak Hill Road, Mount Torrens, SA 5244 (postal) **Region** Adelaide Hills
T 0499 998 484 **www.vellawines.com.au** **Open** Not **Winemaker** Henry Borchardt,
Franco D'Anna, Darryl Catlin **Viticulturist** Mark Vella **Est.** 2013 **Dozens** 1200
Vyds 10ha

Mark Vella began in Orange, NSW, at Bloodwood Estate in '95. Over the following 28 years, he plied his trade as a viticulturist in Orange, the Hunter Valley and now (and permanently) the Adelaide Hills. Mark also manages vineyards throughout the Adelaide Hills via his vineyard management company Vitiworks, pinpointing outstanding parcels of fruit for the Vella brand. He also supplies contracted fruit to over 60 leading wine producers in SA. Henry Borchardt and Darryl Catlin make the chardonnay, gamay and pinot blanc blend and Franco D'Anna makes the pinot noir.

 Harvest Widow Chardonnay 2020, Adelaide Hills Mid-weighted and taut, yet with enough stone fruit riffs strung across a chalky, oak-inflected chord. A core of creamed cashew and nougatine provides nourishment before a long stream of flavour, uncluttered and pure, comprises the impressive finish. Screw cap. 13% alc. RATING 94 DRINK 2022-2030 $32 NG ✪

Gambler Gamay 2020, Adelaide Hills RATING 93 DRINK 2022-2025 $35 NG ✪
Troublemaker Pinot Blanc Pinot Gris Gewürztraminer 2019, Adelaide Hills RATING 90 DRINK 2022-2025 $25 NG ✪

Vélo Wines   ★★★★

755 West Tamar Highway, Legana, Tas 7277 **Region** Northern Tasmania
T (03) 6330 3677 **www.velowines.com.au** **Open** 7 days 10–4 **Winemaker** Micheal
Wilson, Winemaking Tasmania (now Tasmanian Vintners) **Est.** 1966 **Dozens** 3000
Vyds 1.4ha

The 0.9ha of cabernet sauvignon (apparently Tasmania's oldest) and 0.5ha of pinot noir of Tamar Valley's Legana vineyard were planted in 1966 by wine pioneer Graham Wiltshire. Viticulturist (and Olympic cyclist) Micheal Wilson and his wife Mary Wilson purchased the Legana vineyard in '11, painstakingly rehabilitating the almost 50yo vines. Shiraz, sauvignon blanc, riesling, pinot gris and chardonnay have since been planted. The estate changed hands again in '17 and it's now under the ownership of trio Ken Hudson, Peter Bond and David Vautin. A modern new cellar door shares its real estate with Timbre Restaurant, a hyper-sustainable offering from chef Matt Adams.

ŸŸŸŸ♀ **Legana Estate Riesling 2022, Tasmania** Aromas of freshly squeezed lime, lemon and grapefruit juice with a burst of crisp green apple. Hints of crushed stone, white flowers, marzipan and a suggestion of bath salts off in the distance. A well of sherbety texture on the palate, appearing pure and crystalline with just a suggestion of RS as it walks the ridgeline of acid/sugar. It's a lovely, detailed wine and a great drink. Screw cap. 11.3% alc. **RATING** 92 **DRINK** 2023-2026 $32 DB

Legana Estate Cabernet Sauvignon 2021, Tasmania Aromas of leafy blackcurrant and blackberry fruits with hints of redcurrant, earth, licorice, tomato leaf, capsicum, blackcurrant pastille and cedar. Espresso and tobacco notes flow in on the palate, which shows ripe, herbal-flecked crème de cassis-like fruit, a dense, compact tannin structure and a sustained finish featuring rich fruits and tomato leaf herbaceousness. Screw cap. 13.5% alc. **RATING** 92 **DRINK** 2023-2030 $36 DB

Legana Estate Pinot Noir 2022, Tasmania Spiced red plum and cherry fruits cut with fine spice and hints of macerated strawberries, sous bois, red licorice and earth. Bright ripe plum and cherry fruits on the palate, quite fruit-sweet and instantly appealing with bright acid drive and a light, chalky tannin grip. Screw cap. 13.5% alc. **RATING** 91 **DRINK** 2023-2028 $38 DB

Legana Estate Sauvignon Blanc 2022, Tasmania A brisk, stony sauvignon blanc. Bright aromas of gooseberry, green apple, peach and citrus fruits. Hints of white flowers, wild herbs, marzipan, crushed stone and a waft of freshly cut fennel. Plenty of natural acid drive and a lovely sense of clarity and detail to its form; finishes crisp and shimmering with endearing herb-dusted citrus and stone fruits. Screw cap. 12% alc. **RATING** 91 **DRINK** 2023-2025 $30 DB

Legana Estate Pinot Noir 2021, Tasmania Bright cherry red in hue with notes of red plum, macerated strawberries and red and dark cherry. Soft spice and leaf-litter notes lie on an understory that shows fine acidity, a brisk cadence, light tannins and a wash of pure cherry fruits on the exit. Screw cap. 13.5% alc. **RATING** 91 **DRINK** 2023-2028 $38 DB

Vickery ★★★★★

7 Belvidere Road, Nuriootpa, SA 5355 (postal) **Region** Clare Valley
T (08) 8362 8622 **www**.vickerywines.com.au **Open** Not **Winemaker** John Vickery, Keeda Zilm **Est.** 2014 **Dozens** 10 000 **Vyds** 18ha

With more than 50 years' experience, John Vickery was the uncrowned but absolute monarch of riesling makers in Australia until, in his semi-retirement, he passed the mantle on to Jeffrey Grosset. Vickery, his most recent riesling venture, began in conjunction with Phil Lehmann, with wine marketer Jonathon Hesketh in the background. Respected winemaker Zeeda Kilm (ex-O'Leary Walker) has since taken over the winemaking, working alongside John. Vickery is a member of The Usual Suspects collective of producers.

ŸŸŸŸŸ **Riesling 2022, Eden Valley** A picture of purity, precision and velocity with tight, limey fruit cut with high tones of Christmas lily, crushed quartz, orange blossom and river stone. Tight, vivid acidity has the wine riding on rails and setting a brisk cadence with uber-pure lime fruits powering through to the finish. It's quite lovely. Screw cap. 12% alc. **RATING** 95 **DRINK** 2023-2030 $24 DB ✪

The Reserve Zander Quarry Block Riesling 2019, Eden Valley Straw in the glass with aromas of Bickford's lime cordial, green apple, drying hay, marzipan, crushed quartz, pressed white flowers and river stone. Beginning to take on some toasty characters and finishing long, complex and dry with a flinty exit. Lovely drinking. Screw cap. 12% alc. **RATING** 95 **DRINK** 2023-2030 $34 DB ✪

ŸŸŸŸ♀ **Watervale Riesling 2021, Clare Valley** **RATING** 92 **DRINK** 2023-2028 $23 DB ✪

Victory Point Wines ★★★★★

92 Holben Road, Cowaramup, WA 6284 **Region** Margaret River
T 0417 954 655 **www**.victorypointwines.com **Open** Wed–Sun 11–4 **Winemaker** Mark
Messenger (Contract) **Viticulturist** Colin Bell **Est.** 1997 **Dozens** 2500 **Vyds** 13.7ha
Judith and Gary Berson have set their sights high. They established their vineyard without
irrigation, emulating those of the Margaret River pioneers (including Moss Wood). The
fully mature plantings comprise 4.2ha of chardonnay and 0.4ha of pinot noir; the remainder
Bordeaux varieties with cabernet sauvignon (6.2ha), cabernet franc (0.5ha), malbec (1.7ha)
and petit verdot (0.7ha). The cellar door overlooks the 20+yo vineyard.

♟♟♟♟♟ **Malbec 2021, Margaret River** A wonderful purple-black hue. Exceptional
varietal flavours at play; violets, black plums and cherries with a waft of warm
earth and dark chocolate. It's full bodied, rich and ripe with plentiful tannins
plumped by cedary sweet oak. A well-composed wine. Screw cap. 14.5% alc.
RATING 95 **DRINK** 2023–2030 $35 JF ✪

Chardonnay 2020, Margaret River If you like your chardonnay rich and full
bodied with plenty of flavour, here's one to satisfy. Loads of ripe peaches, melon
doused in lemon curd and cream, nutty/leesy flavours, too, with the oak adding
spices and sweetness. It's not blousy though, as there's tight acidity and some
moreish sulphides adding another layer of complexity and depth. It's also delicious.
Screw cap. 13.5% alc. **RATING** 95 **DRINK** 2023–2030 $55 JF

Cabernet Sauvignon 2020, Margaret River An elegant, pitch-perfect
cabernet brimming with regional flavours. It's a whorl of cassis, mulberries, some
woodsy spices and eucalyptus all in place. But the keystone, its lovely fine tannins
and length. Screw cap. 13.5% alc. **RATING** 95 **DRINK** 2023–2035 $55 JF

The Mallee Root 2020, Margaret River 57/43% cabernet sauvignon/
malbec. For the price and quality, this is excellent. It's drinking beautifully now,
it's supple, sweetly fruited, spicy, savoury and compact. Yet there's depth and
length with textural tannins adding another layer. Screw cap. 14% alc. **RATING** 94
DRINK 2023–2032 $29 JF ✪

♟♟♟♟♀ **Rosé 2022, Margaret River RATING** 92 **DRINK** 2022–2023 $30 JF ✪
Pinot Noir 2021, Margaret River RATING 90 **DRINK** 2023–2026 $65 JF

🍇 View Wine ★★★★

Sancerre Estate, 60 Zambelli Road, Ballandean, Qld 4382 **Region** Granite Belt
T 0428 777 166 **www**.viewwine.au **Open** Fri–Sun 11–3 **Winemaker** Brad Allan,
Stacey Allan **Viticulturist** Brad Allan, Stacey Allan **Est.** 2013 **Dozens** 800 **Vyds** 4ha
Brad and Stacey Allan acquired what was then Smith's vineyard in '13, renaming the property
Sancerre Estate and creating the new View Wines label. The husband-and-wife team oversee
all aspects of View Wines' vineyard and winemaking, with the benefit of some assistance
from Bent Road's Robert Richter (co-owner and viticulturist), Andrew Scott (assistant
winemaker) and Glen Robert (co-owner and winemaker) along the way. The property is
primarily planted to regional staples of sauvignon blanc and shiraz but perhaps their most
exciting wines are the dry wines produced from gros manseng and alvarinho.

♟♟♟♟♟ **Alvarinho 2021, Granite Belt** Savoury-edged with waxy texture, medium-
weight and strongly aromatic. There's quince, preserved lemon, tonic water
and strong gingery spice on the palate and a bouquet of gentle oatmeal and
cashew savouriness subtly lingering. Quite a powerful style, but with excellent
balance. A striking wine. Screw cap. 13.2% alc. **RATING** 94 **DRINK** 2022–2025
$38 MB ✪ ♥

♟♟♟♟♀ **Gros Manseng 2021, Granite Belt RATING** 92 **DRINK** 2022–2026 $30 MB ✪
Shiraz 2021, Granite Belt RATING 92 **DRINK** 2022–2030 $40 MB
Barrel Ferment Sauvignon Blanc 2021, Granite Belt RATING 92
DRINK 2022–2028 $36 MB

Vigna Bottin

192 Main Road, Willunga SA 5172 **Region** McLaren Vale
T 0484 254 994 www.vignabottin.com.au **Open** Thurs 11–4, Fri 11–4 and 5.30–9.30,
w'ends 11–5, Mon 11–4 **Winemaker** Paolo Bottin **Viticulturist** Paolo Bottin **Est.** 2006
Dozens 2700 **Vyds** 15.22ha

The Bottin family migrated to Australia in 1954 from Treviso in northern Italy, where they
were grapegrowers. The family began growing grapes in McLaren Vale in '70, focusing
on selling mainstream varieties to wineries in the region. When son Paolo and wife Maria
made a trip back to Italy in '98, they were inspired to do more, and, says Paolo, 'My love
for barbera and sangiovese was sealed during a vintage in Pavia. I came straight home to
plant both varieties in our family plot. My father was finally happy!' The focus remains on
Mediterranean varieties and Italian hospitality.

Montepulciano 2021, McLaren Vale A very good inaugural release.
Montepulciano's ferrous tannic gravel, dried tobacco, mineral pungency and
robust black fruits flow long across a plane of perceivable oak and bouillon. The
tannins, ripples of sinew from attack to gritty finish, are particularly impressive,
placating fruit sweetness while marking this muscular wine with a noble Italianate
aura. Screw cap. 14.5% alc. **RATING** 95 **DRINK** 2023–2030 $40 NG ✪

Fiano 2022, McLaren Vale RATING 93 **DRINK** 2023–2027 $29 NG ✪
Barbera 2020, McLaren Vale RATING 93 **DRINK** 2023–2026 $45 NG
Sangiovese 2020, McLaren Vale RATING 93 **DRINK** 2022–2026 $35 NG ✪
Nero d'Avola 2020, McLaren Vale RATING 92 **DRINK** 2023–2027 $40 NG
Compare's Shiraz 2020, McLaren Vale RATING 92 **DRINK** 2022–2031
$29 NG ✪

Vignerons Schmölzer & Brown

39 Thorley Road, Stanley, Vic 3747 **Region** Beechworth
T 0411 053 487 www.vsandb.com.au **Open** By appt **Winemaker** Tessa Brown, Jeremy
Schmölzer **Viticulturist** Tessa Brown **Est.** 2014 **Dozens** 2500 **Vyds** 2ha

Winemaker/viticulturist Tessa Brown graduated from CSU with a degree in viticulture in
the late '90s and undertook postgraduate winemaking studies at the University of Adelaide
in the mid-'00s. Her self-description of being 'reasonably peripatetic' covers her winemaking
in Orange in '99 and also in Canberra, SA, Strathbogie Ranges, Rioja and Central Otago
before joining Kooyong and Port Phillip Estate in '08. In '09 Mark Walpole showed Tessa and
architect partner Jeremy Schmölzer a property that he described as 'the jewel in the crown of
Beechworth'. When it came onto the market in '12, they were in a position to jump. The
property (named Thorley) was 20ha and cleared; they planted chardonnay, shiraz, riesling and
nebbiolo. By sheer chance, just across the road was a tiny vineyard, a bit over 0.4ha, with
dry-grown pinot and chardonnay around 20 years old. When they realised it was not being
managed for production, they struck up a working relationship with the owners, getting the
vineyard into shape and making their first (very good) Brunnen wines in '14. The Obstgarten
wines come from a small, high-altitude riesling vineyard in the King Valley.

Brunnen Pinot Noir 2021, Beechworth A serious statement about the ability
of Beechworth to make quality pinot, making drinkers sit up and take notice.
Tightly layered and complex in red cherry fruit, fragrant bergamot, violet, earth
and bramble. Knits together tightly and perfectly on the palate, running the
distance, going deeper and deeper through to the finish. impressive. Screw cap.
13% alc. **RATING** 96 **DRINK** 2023–2031 $55 JP ✪
Obstgarten T Riesling 2022, King Valley Spring blossoms and white flowers
meet super-fragrant lemon and lime zest aromas. Sherbety brisk throughout with
real zing to the acidity, the palate showcases a dry, distinctly cool-climate riesling
of class. Great focus and drive thanks to striking acidity. Deserves, needs, further
bottle ageing. Screw cap. 11% alc. **RATING** 95 **DRINK** 2023–2033 $37 JP ✪
Thorley Syrah 2021, Beechworth An elegant, cool-climate syrah of a lively,
enduring spiciness and charm. Here's a vintage that offers a wealth of the region's

pepper and spice with ripe, dark plums, black cherry, toasty oak and an intriguing whisper of savoury, smoked meats. Rolls across the tongue aided by fine-cut tannins. Depth and grace. Diam. 13% alc. **RATING** 95 **DRINK** 2023-2033 $55 JP

Obstgarten K Riesling 2021, King Valley With 38g/L RS, this is the producer's take on a modern, German-style Kabinett riesling with striking King Valley acidity keeping beat. Complex jasmine, alpine wild flowers, white pepper, lime, nashi pear and apple aromas. As fresh as the alpine air, bristling in clean acidity with lilting sweetness and spice against a citrus, apple and pear background. Don't over-chill. Screw cap. 9.5% alc. **RATING** 95 **DRINK** 2023-2031 $39 JP ✪ ♥

Thorley Chardonnay 2021, Beechworth Made with the intention to age, Thorley can be shy in its youth. The '21 is certainly coiled, taut and, yes, quiet. But, the groundwork is there for something special. A delicate scent of citrus, grapefruit, nectarine and pear. The palate is in the peach and nectarine spectrum, gently spiced and a little buttery. Composed and linear, it offers up a racy acid drive, something to build a future on. Diam. 12.5% alc. **RATING** 94 **DRINK** 2023-2031 $55 JP

🍷🍷🍷🍷🍷 **Thorley Riesling 2021, Beechworth** **RATING** 93 **DRINK** 2023-2031 $55 JP
Obstgarten Riesling Selection 2021, Beechworth **RATING** 93 **DRINK** 2023-2027 $44 JP
Brunnen Chardonnay 2021, Beechworth **RATING** 92 **DRINK** 2023-2028 $55 JP
Pret-a-Blanc 2022, King Valley **RATING** 91 **DRINK** 2023-2026 $31 JP
Pret-a-Rouge 2021, Beechworth **RATING** 91 **DRINK** 2023-2025 $31 JP

Vinaceous Wines   ★★★★

49 Bennett Street, East Perth, WA 6004 (postal) **Region** Western Australia
T (08) 9221 4666 **www.**vinaceous.com.au **Open** Not **Winemaker** Gavin Berry, Michael Kerrigan **Est.** 2007 **Dozens** 8000
This somewhat quirky venture was the baby of wine marketer Nick Stacy, Michael Kerrigan (winemaker/partner Hay Shed Hill) and Gavin Berry (winemaker/partner West Cape Howe). Nick Stacy separated from the business in '20 (John Waldron, managing partner of Risky Business Wines, has since stepped in), taking the Reverend V and Clandestine Vineyards brands with him. Fruit is primarily sourced from Margaret River and Great Southern. The wines are of seriously good quality and equally good value.

🍷🍷🍷🍷🍷 **Crafted By Hand Rosé 2022, Margaret River** Yep, this easily ticks the 'wine for summer' box. Aside from the refreshment factor, there's detail, too. A whisper of red fruits, watermelon flesh and rind, with an attractive textural palate and just right with juicy, tangy acidity all the way. Screw cap. 13% alc. **RATING** 92 **DRINK** 2022-2024 $28 JF ✪

Voodoo Moon Malbec 2021, Frankland River An alluring fuller-bodied red, all thanks to the variety and region. Fragrant with violets, wet stones and earth; laden with dark fruits, especially blackberries, licorice and a dusting of cocoa powder. The tannins are ripe and textural, and the palate extends and holds length thanks to the acidity. There's a lot to enjoy, so do so. Screw cap. 14.5% alc. **RATING** 92 **DRINK** 2022-2028 $25 JF ✪

Pétillant Naturel 2022, King Valley The introduction of gewürztraminer to this pinot grigio/arneis blend adds an interesting lick of passionfruit and spice. Pale lemon and cloudy, there's a touch of the tropical alongside scents of apple, citrus and honeysuckle. It pops up on the palate, bringing with it a summery mix of grapefruit skin, lemon sorbet and spiced apple. Dry and dusty to close. Crown. 12.5% alc. **RATING** 91 **DRINK** 2022-2026 $30 JP

Snake Charmer Shiraz 2021, Frankland River There's certainly a charm to Frankland River shiraz – it's the quality and power of the fruit. This pops with freshness and juiciness then adds some meaty, inky flavours. There's a touch of oak sweetness across the mid-weight palate, yet it finishes clean and fresh. Screw cap. 14% alc. **RATING** 90 **DRINK** 2022-2027 $25 JF ✪

Red Right Hand Shiraz Grenache Tempranillo 2020, Margaret River
No need to overthink what's in the glass, other than that this comes in bright
and juicy, with a core of good fruit dabbed with licorice and mint. Tangy and
refreshing with just enough tannins to ensure this goes down well at your mate's
barbecue. Screw cap. 14.5% alc. **RATING** 90 **DRINK** 2022–2026 $22 JF ✪

Vindana Wines   ★★★★★

PO Box 705, Lyndoch, SA 5351 **Region** Barossa Valley
T 0437 175 437 **www**.vindanawines.com.au **Open** Not **Winemaker** Scott Higginson
Est. 1968 **Dozens** 350 **Vyds** 1ha
Scott Higginson is a 7th-generation vigneron, whose family history starts in 1846 on the
banks of Jacobs Creek and continues there for 111 years until an ill-fated decision to sell
and move to the Riverland where a series of moves to protect growers from collapses in the
market turned sour. Scott returned to the Barossa Valley, completing the wine marketing
degree at Roseworthy Agricultural College and adding extensive work with medium to
large wineries. In '13 he purchased a housing block at Lyndoch with enough room for 1ha
of vines. He also purchases small parcels of premium fruit, making wine on a minimum-
intervention basis. With a couple of 8th-generation feet on the ground, some very good
wines materialised overnight.

🍷🍷🍷🍷🍷 **Keeper of the Stones Limited Release Grenache 2022, Barossa Valley**
Super-spicy damson plum, boysenberry and blueberry fruits with underlying hints
of gingerbread, pressed purple flowers, citrus blossom, sarsaparilla, cola, Turkish
delight, rose petals and earth. A plush and immensely floral grenache that gives
off a Cherry Ripe vibe with tight tannin and bright acidity. It's quite delicious.
Screw cap. 15% alc. **RATING** 95 **DRINK** 2023–2033 $35 DB ✪
Keeper of the Stones Limited Release Shiraz 2021, Barossa Valley Inky
crimson in the glass with characters of macerated satsuma plum, black cherry
compote and blackberry fruits with underlying hints of earth, dark chocolate–
dipped cherries, aniseed, Christmas spices, tapenade, purple flowers and softly
spoken oak. Full bodied and concentrated with a tight grainy tannin architecture,
a seam of fresh acidity and a rolling swell of lush cassis and kirsch-like fruit on the
finish. Screw cap. 14% alc. **RATING** 95 **DRINK** 2023–2036 $39 DB ✪
Keeper of the Stars Cabernet Sauvignon 2021, Barossa Valley Bright
blackberry, blackcurrants and black cherry compote with hints of brown
spice, pastis, brandied fruits, fruitcake, earth, violets, sage and kirsch. Plenty of
concentration, fine tannin support, bright acidity and a thick flow of cassis and
kirsch on the finish. A very impressive cabernet sauvignon, plush and intense yet
shows finesse. Screw cap. 13% alc. **RATING** 95 **DRINK** 2023–2038 $39 DB ✪

Vinea Marson   ★★★★☆

411 Heathcote-Rochester Road, Heathcote, Vic 3523 **Region** Heathcote
T 0430 312 165 **www**.vineamarson.com **Open** Sat–Sun 11–5 **Winemaker** Mario
Marson **Viticulturist** Mario Marson **Est.** 2000 **Dozens** 2500 **Vyds** 7.12ha
Owner-winemaker Mario Marson spent many years as the winemaker/viticulturist with
the late Dr John Middleton at the celebrated Mount Mary. Mario has over 35 years of
experience in Australia and overseas, having undertaken vintages at Isole e Olena in Tuscany
and Piedmont and at Domaine de la Pousse d'Or in Burgundy, where he was inspired to
emulate the multi-clonal wines favoured by these producers, pioneered in Australia by John
Middleton. In '99 he and his wife, Helen, purchased the Vinea Marson property on the
eastern slopes of the Mt Camel Range. They have planted shiraz and viognier, plus Italian
varieties of sangiovese, nebbiolo, barbera and refosco dal peduncolo. Marson also sources
northeastern Italian varietals from Porepunkah in the Alpine Valleys.

🍷🍷🍷🍷🍷 **Rosato 2021, Heathcote** Bright, berried, textural and persistent. Indeed there's
a lovely savoury side to this as well. Strawberry jelly, hay, orange blossom and
sweet spice notes combine to beautiful drinking effect here. The moreish-ness is
off the charts. Screw cap. 13.5% alc. **RATING** 95 **DRINK** 2022–2025 $28 CM ✪ ❤

🍷🍷🍷🍷 Col Fondo Prosecco 2021, Alpine Valleys RATING 91 DRINK 2023–2026
$34 CM
Friulano #10 2019, Alpine Valleys RATING 90 DRINK 2023–2025 $32 CM

Vinifera Wines ★★★★

194 Henry Lawson Drive, Mudgee, NSW 2850 **Region** Mudgee
T (02) 6372 2461 **www.**viniferawines.com.au **Open** Sun–Fri 11–4, Sat 10–5
Winemaker Lisa Bray, Jacob Stein **Viticulturist** Paul Stig **Est.** 1994 **Dozens** 1200
Vyds 11ha
Having lived in Mudgee for 15 years, Tony McKendry (a regional medical superintendent)
and wife Debbie succumbed to the lure of winemaking; they planted their small (then 1.5ha)
vineyard in '95. In Debbie's words, 'Tony, in his spare 2 minutes per day, also decided to
start wine science at CSU in 1992'. She continues, 'He's trying to live 27 hours per day
(plus we have 4 kids!). He fell to pieces when he was involved in a severe car smash in 1997.
Two months in hospital stopped his full-time medical work, and the winery dreams became
inevitable'. Financial compensation finally came through and the small winery was built. The
now-expanded vineyard includes 3.25ha each of chardonnay and cabernet sauvignon, 1.5ha
of tempranillo and 1ha each of semillon, grenache and graciano.

🍷🍷🍷🍷🍷 Reserve Chardonnay 2022, Mudgee Chalkboard dust meets white grapefruit
pith, lemon sorbet, shortbread and scallop shell. Elegant white jasmine flowers and
orchard apple. The wine is luscious and full bodied with electric acidity. A finely
crafted chardonnay with good mlf creaminess and plenty of energy. A steal at the
price. Screw cap. 13.5% alc. RATING 95 DRINK 2023–2028 $35 SW ✪

🍷🍷🍷🍷 Easter Semillon 2022, Mudgee RATING 92 DRINK 2022–2028 $30 SW ✪

Vino Intrepido ★★★★☆

22 Compton Street, Reservoir, Vic, 3078 (postal) **Region** Various
T 0488 479 999 **www.**vinointrepido.com **Open** Not **Winemaker** James Scarcebrook
Est. 2016 **Dozens** 850
Before the grape crush took hold, James Scarcebrook started out in wine retail, working his
way from cellar door assistant to marketing coordinator at Domaine Chandon in the Yarra
Valley and most recently in sales with leading importers. A love of Italian varieties had been
cemented earlier when he took off overseas for 16 months in '11 after finishing a master of
wine business at Adelaide University. Then in '16, a small parcel of Heathcote sangiovese
morphed into the inaugural Vino Intrepido. Dedicated solely to Italian varieties with fruit
sourced mostly from Victorian growers, the range has expanded to include vermentino,
friulano, fiano, nero d'Avola and nebbiolo amongst others.

🍷🍷🍷🍷🍷 Sting Like A Bee Fiano 2022, Mornington Peninsula As soon as I stuck my
nose in the glass to take in all the aromas, I knew I'd enjoy this rich wine. White
blossom, lavender and creamed honey with powdered ginger jump out, and then
the palate builds an extra layer of texture and creaminess. Neat phenolics also add
depth while fine acidity gives an impression of lightness. Nice one. Screw cap.
12.5% alc. RATING 95 DRINK 2022–2024 $37 JF ✪

🍷🍷🍷🍷 Grey Matter Ramato Pinot Grigio 2022, Nagambie Lakes RATING 91
DRINK 2022–2025 $30 JP
Spanna In The Works Nebbiolo 2021, Pyrenees RATING 91
DRINK 2024–2030 $43 CM
Sacred & Profane Sagrantino 2021, Heathcote RATING 91
DRINK 2023–2028 $35 CM
Dulcet Tones Dolcetto 2021, Macedon Ranges RATING 90
DRINK 2022–2024 $35 JF

Vino Volta

184 Anzac Road, Mount Hawthorn, WA 6016 **Region** Swan Valley
T 0427 614 610 **www**.vinovolta.com.au **Open** By appt **Winemaker** Garth Cliff
Est. 2019 **Dozens** 2800 **Vyds** 7ha

Garth Cliff was winemaker at Houghton in the Swan Valley for 10 years prior to starting
Vino Volta with his partner Kristen McGann in Jan '19. Vino Volta largely (although not
exclusively) focuses on chenin blanc (they make 3 styles) and grenache from the Valley.
Chenin blanc is in a revival phase currently, much of it thanks to Cliff, culminating in the
inaugural nationwide Chenin Blanc Challenge in 2020, held in the Swan Valley. Together
they have also started their own wine import portfolio called Wine Terroirists, calling on
McGann's long experience in the trade. Cliff is an active (in every sense) member of the Swan
Valley Winemakers Association and a tireless proponent for the region.

ŸŸŸŸŸ **Love Sick Puppy Dolcetto 2022, Geographe** Here's a dolcetto to rewrite all
preconceptions of the variety. For starters, it has an X-factor, but it also has polish
and a quiet insistence, herb notes, licorice root and a cherry-and-rose aspect – a la
nebbiolo. It's fascinating. It's delicious. It's absolutely worth hunting down. Screw
cap. 14% alc. **RATING** 94 **DRINK** 2023–2027 $32 CM ✪

ŸŸŸŸŸ **La Chingadera 2021, Margaret River Geographe Swan Valley RATING** 93
DRINK 2023–2028 $35 CM ✪
**Different Skins Frontignac Gewürztraminer 2022, Swan Valley Perth
Hills RATING** 91 **DRINK** 2023–2027 $35 CM

Vintage Longbottom

15 Spring Gully Road, Piccadilly, SA 5151 (postal) **Region** Piccadilly Valley
T (08) 8132 1048 **www**.vintagelongbottom.com **Open** Not **Winemaker** Matt Wenk
Est. 1998 **Dozens** 48 000 **Vyds** 94.9ha

Kim Longbottom has moved her wine business from Padthaway to the Adelaide Hills'
Piccadilly Valley, where Tapanappa has taken on the responsibility of making 3 tiers of wines.
At the top is Magnus Shiraz from Clarendon and Blewitt Springs; the middle is the H Range
from the McLaren Vale floor districts; and there is a sparkling range from the Adelaide
Hills. Her daughter Margo brings experience in fashion, digital marketing and business
administration.

ŸŸŸŸŸ **H Pinot Noir Syrah 2021, Adelaide Hills** This is delicious drinking.
Lightweight, herbal and vital. A hark back to a long Australian tradition of
embellishing pinot's grace and levity with the more palpable tannis of syrah.
Damson plum, sweet morello cherry, root spice and a thread of white pepper-
doused acidity promoting freshness and pointed length. Another glass, please!
Screw cap. 13.3% alc. **RATING** 93 **DRINK** 2022–2026 $28 NG ✪
Henry's Drive Shiraz 2021, McLaren Vale Things seem to have lightened
up here recently. For the better. While there is still oomph and drive, the fruit
is of a redder complexion, fresher, sapid and of juicy tannic sinew. The oak, far
better integrated. There is intrigue and appeal. Damson plum, violet, kelp and
a compote of red fruits muddled with star anise. The acidity is shrill, but that is
picking straws. Screw cap. 14.6% alc. **RATING** 92 **DRINK** 2022–2030 $40 NG
H Sauvignon Blanc 2021, Adelaide Hills Considerably better than the
regional norm, with a herbal cadence over a tropical one. Savoury, lightweighted,
dry and brisk. Reminiscent of the Loire. Perhaps a bit too brisk, such is the
singeing level of acidity. Yet sugar snap peas, nettle, greengage and a hint
of guava careen long. Good sauvignon. Screw cap. 12.4% alc. **RATING** 90
DRINK 2023–2024 $28 NG

Vinteloper ★★★★

Lot 100 – 68 Chambers Road, Hay Valley, SA 5252 **Region** Adelaide Hills
T 0491 334 795 **www**.vinteloper.com.au **Open** Thurs–Sun 11–5 **Winemaker** David
Bowley **Viticulturist** David Bowley **Est.** 2008 **Dozens** 7500 **Vyds** 10ha
In David Bowley's words, 'Vinteloper is a winery started by a guy who decided, on instinct,
to skip through his own daisy fields.' Vineyards and wineries had permeated David's mind
before he left school, so it was inevitable that he would obtain his oenology degree at Adelaide
University (in '02). After several years training in both Australia and France, he founded
Vinteloper in '08. Wife Sharon draws the unique labels. Vinteloper continues to handcraft
wines styled with a light touch and upbeat aromatics.

ΨΨΨΨ♀ **Watervale Riesling 2022, Clare Valley** A crushed orchard fruit blend in a
glass. A delicate framework of juicy acidity, a gentle skinniness and some hibiscus
and makrut lime lift for levity. Talc, sure. But the schtick here is one of immense
pleasure, rather than hardness. A lovely, lithe, long and imminently impressionable
slipstream. Great wine for the money! Screw cap. 11% alc. **RATING** 92
DRINK 2022-2028 $32 NG
Pinot Gris 2022, Adelaide Hills Subtle. Immaculate poise between an orchard
spread of fruit accents, chewy seams and a sluice of gentle freshness towing
impressive length. Screw cap. 13.2% alc. **RATING** 91 **DRINK** 2022-2025 $32 NG

Voyager Estate ★★★★★

41 Stevens Road, Margaret River, WA 6285 **Region** Margaret River
T (08) 9757 6354 **www**.voyagerestate.com.au **Open** Wed–Sun 10–5 **Winemaker** Travis
Lemm **Viticulturist** Glen Ryan **Est.** 1978 **Dozens** 40 000 **Vyds** 112ha
Voyager Estate is located on Stevens Road in the Boodjidup Valley, which is emerging as
hallowed ground (Leeuwin, the western neighbour, Xanadu's Stevens Road vineyard and
the vineyards of Voyager Estate complete the trinity of prestige in this neck of the woods).
The estate was established in '78 by viticulturist Peter Gherardi, and later purchased and
expanded by Michael Wright in '91. Michael's daughter, Alexandra Burt, has been at the
helm since '05. As of '23, the vineyard and winery are certified organic and there is extensive
clonal and varietal experimentation in the estate vineyards. The grounds are well known for
their immaculate year-round grooming, as is the lavish, high-ceiling tasting room, home to
an award-winning restaurant.

ΨΨΨΨΨ **MJW Chardonnay 2021, Margaret River** Often a powerhouse of a wine, but
this vintage, it's not too big, not too light, just right. The palate is refined and feels
effortless as the citrus flavours mingle with grilled-almond lees, clotted cream and
some oak spice offering savoury nuances. There's certainly texture, but the fine
line of acidity just reins in everything as the finish lingers. It feels cool and calm.
Screw cap. 13% alc. **RATING** 96 **DRINK** 2023-2033 $120 JF
The Modern Cabernet Sauvignon 2021, Margaret River It has all the
varietal appeal of Margaret River: its shapely tannins, supple and ever-so-slightly
grainy and its savouriness. Very little oak impact other than a complementary
light seasoning of cedary spices. Decant or let this beauty breathe in the glass.
Screw cap. 14.5% alc. **RATING** 95 **DRINK** 2023-2035 $50 JF ✪
Broadvale Block 6 Chardonnay 2021, Margaret River There's subtlety,
delicacy and energy within this stylish wine. It comes across as a little reserved
with lemon blossom, a lemony saline character plus ruby grapefruit, but it opens
up to reveal more. With tangy acidity and a hint of nutty lees, the spicy oak
flavour is a seasoning rather than a dominating attribute. Screw cap. 12% alc.
RATING 95 **DRINK** 2022-2031 $65 JF
Cabernet Sauvignon 2019, Margaret River There's such a distinct Voyager
Estate character to this wine, largely because the fruit comes off the estate
vineyard. It's heady with tobacco leaf, nori, dried herbs, mulberries and cassis.
It's savoury and supple and the tannins feel mellow and shapely, there's depth,
complexity and length. It's captivating now but will reward the patient more so.
Screw cap. 14% alc. **RATING** 95 **DRINK** 2023-2039 $95 JF

⟁⟁⟁⟁♀ **Chardonnay 2021, Margaret River** RATING 93 DRINK 2023-2026 $55 JH
Project U11 Syrah 2021, Margaret River RATING 93 DRINK 2022-2031
$55 JF
Shiraz 2021, Margaret River RATING 93 DRINK 2022-2031 $38 JF
Sauvignon Blanc Semillon 2022, Margaret River RATING 92
DRINK 2022-2027 $26 JF ✪
The Modern Cabernet Sauvignon 2020, Margaret River RATING 92
DRINK 2023-2035 $50 JH
Chenin Blanc 2022, Margaret River RATING 90 DRINK 2022-2027 $25 JF ✪
Coastal Cabernet Sauvignon 2021, Margaret River RATING 90
DRINK 2023-2033 $30 JF

Walter ★★★★

179 Tinja Lane, Mudgee, NSW 2850 **Region** Mudgee
T 0419 251 208 **www**.walterwines.com.au **Open** Thurs–Mon 10–5 **Winemaker** Lisa
Bray (Contract) **Est.** 1994 **Dozens** 2000 **Vyds** 20ha
Lynn and Paul Walter had been keen observers of Mudgee and its wines for 15 years before
deciding to take the plunge and plant a 20ha vineyard. It was the mid-'90s and all the portents
were good. As competition increased and prices for grapes decreased, they realised that their
original business plan of simply being growers was not going to be financially viable, even
though they thought the downturn would prove to be a temporary one.

⟁⟁⟁⟁♀ **Federation Hill Sparkling Shiraz 2019, Mudgee** Black peppercorn,
concentrated cherry and red raspberry greet the nose with a background of olive
tapenade, clove and nutmeg spice. The richly dense fruit is complemented by a
savoury element of tamari almonds and cola spices. Luscious in its traditional style,
but built with svelte tannins and balanced peaks of acidity. A fine sparkling shiraz
indeed. Crown. 13.5% alc. RATING 93 DRINK 2022-2030 $44 SW
Federation Hill Reserve Shiraz 2018, Mudgee Black cherry tea,
huckleberry and cocoa nibs open to tanned leather and tobacco leaves. Coils of
black and red berries unpinned by potting soil and cracked peppercorn. The '18
is drinking beautifully with soft tannins and waves of acidity. Screw cap. 13.8% alc.
RATING 92 DRINK 2022-2030 $33 SW
Federation Hill Shiraz 2021, Mudgee Opens with an array of blackberries,
plum skin and picked blueberries with a mocha-coffee spice. Ripe blackberry
compote interwoven with soft licorice exhibits a sumptuous mouthfeel. Driving
acidity lifts the wine while silky tannins make for a classic and graceful style of
shiraz. Screw cap. 14% alc. RATING 91 DRINK 2022-2032 $33 SW
Federation Hill Chardonnay 2022, Mudgee Lime sherbet, green apple
curls and crunchy white peach. A touch of flinty reduction peaks interest. The
wine displays vanilla frozen yoghurt creaminess and young almonds, which
complements the freshness of the fruit. There is an element of restraint and effort
of poise. A second glass for a second look, this is chardonnay to spend some time
with. Screw cap. 12.5% alc. RATING 90 DRINK 2023-2028 $30 SW

Wantirna Estate ★★★★★

10 Bushy Park Lane, Wantirna South, Vic 3152 (postal) **Region** Yarra Valley
T (03) 9801 2367 **www**.wantirnaestate.com.au **Open** Not **Winemaker** Maryann Egan,
Reg Egan **Est.** 1963 **Dozens** 700 **Vyds** 4.2ha
Reg and Tina Egan were among the early movers in the rebirth of the Yarra Valley. The
vineyard surrounds the house they live in, which also incorporates the winery. These days
Reg describes himself as the interfering winemaker but in the early years he did everything,
dashing from his legal practice to the winery to check on the ferments. Today much of the
winemaking responsibility has been transferred to daughter Maryann, who has a degree in
wine science from CSU. Both have honed their practical skills among the small domaines
and châteaux of Burgundy and Bordeaux, inspired by single-vineyard, terroir-driven wines.
Maryann was also winemaker for many years in Domaine Chandon's infancy.

🍷🍷🍷🍷🍷 **Isabella Chardonnay 2021, Yarra Valley** A complex wine with hints of jasmine, aromas of fresh apricots, a touch of orange blossom and some almond meal. Textured and structured, there's an old-vine creaminess to this classic 'old world' styled and totally lovely wine that, despite its richness, finishes fine and very long. Screw cap. 13% alc. RATING 97 DRINK 2022-2028 $90 PR ✪

Lily Pinot Noir 2020, Yarra Valley Made from 45–55yo vines, and it shows! A gorgeous wine from the outset, this is seductive and perfumed with aromas of red fruits intermingled with violets, jasmine and a little forest floor just starting to emerge. A subtle touch of wood-derived sweet spice, too. As good on the palate as it is an essay in elegance. No one who manages to get their hands on a bottle will be disappointed. Screw cap. 13.5% alc. RATING 97 DRINK 2022-2030 $90 PR ✪

🍷🍷🍷🍷🍷 **Amelia Cabernet Sauvignon Merlot 2020, Yarra Valley** Only 2 barrels were made of this classic, cool-climate Yarra cabernet. Gently perfumed, with aromas of new-season cherries, lilac and a little cigar box already starting to emerge. The medium-bodied, bordeaux-like palate is supported by lively acidity and fine, gravelly tannins. Give this time to open up if you're drinking it now, and for those putting some down, this should age effortlessly over the next 5–15 years. Screw cap. 13% alc. RATING 95 DRINK 2022-2032 $90 PR

Warramate ★★★★☆

27 Maddens Lane, Gruyere, Vic 3770 (postal) **Region** Yarra Valley
T (03) 5964 9267 **www**.warramatewines.com.au **Open** At Yarra Yering 7 days 10–5
Winemaker Sarah Crowe **Est.** 1970 **Dozens** 3000 **Vyds** 6.6ha
A long-established and perfectly situated winery reaping the full benefits of its 50yo vines; recent plantings have increased production. All the wines are well made, the shiraz providing further proof of the suitability of the variety to the region. In '11 Warramate was purchased by the partnership that owns the adjoining Yarra Yering; the Warramate brand is kept as a separate operation, using the existing vineyards.

🍷🍷🍷🍷🍷 **Syrah 2021, Yarra Valley** A medium, bright crimson red. Primary red fruits, violets and some whole-bunch derived spice. A lovely burst of flavour on the juicy, balanced and open-knit palate. Quite delicious now, but balanced and structured enough to cellar for at least 5–7 years, too. Screw cap. 13.5% alc. RATING 95 DRINK 2022-2026 $38 PR ✪

Cabernet Merlot Malbec 2021, Yarra Valley A deep-ish crimson red. Another successful, vibrant fruit-driven red from Warramate. Aromas of freshly picked cherries and a hint of bell pepper and cedar lead onto the medium-bodied, quite delicious and fine-boned palate. Screw cap. 13.5% alc. RATING 94 DRINK 2022-2028 $38 PR ✪

🍷🍷🍷🍷🍷 **Pinot Noir 2022, Yarra Valley** RATING 93 DRINK 2022-2028 $38 PR
Marsanne Roussanne 2021, Yarra Valley RATING 92 DRINK 2022-2026 $38 PR
Chardonnay 2021, Yarra Valley RATING 91 DRINK 2022-2026 $38 PR

Warramunda Estate ★★★★★

860 Maroondah Highway, Coldstream, Vic 3770 **Region** Yarra Valley
T 0412 694 394 **www**.warramundaestate.com.au **Open** Fri–Sun 11–4
Winemaker Robert Zak-Magdziarz **Viticulturist** Dan Sergeant **Est.** 1998
Dozens 6000 **Vyds** 25.2ha
The Magdziarz family acquired Warramunda from the Vogt family in '07, producing their first vintage in '13. They have built on the existing solid foundations with a deep respect for the surrounding landscape and a vision for terroir-driven wines. Viticulture follows biodynamic principles, vines are unirrigated and wines are all naturally fermented with wild yeast. Second label Liv Zak (named for daughter Olivia, studying viticulture, winemaking and business at CSU) was launched in '15.

ΨΨΨΨΨ **Liv Zak Malbec 2021, Yarra Valley** A saturated crimson purple. This is both concentrated and perfumed. Aromas of blackberries, dark cherry and plums sit alongside a little cedar and mountain herbs. Medium to full bodied, this powerful and balanced wine manages to be both plush and structured, which means that while it can be enjoyed now, it also has excellent ageing potential. A superb straight malbec. Screw cap. 14% alc. **RATING** 97 **DRINK** 2022-2028 $45 PR ✪

ΨΨΨΨΨ **Coldstream Pinot Noir 2021, Yarra Valley** An open and attractive nose with crushed raspberries, cranberries and a touch of violet. While this well-weighted and balanced wine is already a pleasure to drink, there are more than enough fine-grained tannins and bright acidity to suggest this will only keep getting better. Screw cap. 13% alc. **RATING** 95 **DRINK** 2022-2028 $55 PR

ΨΨΨΨΨ **Coldstream Merlot 2021, Yarra Valley RATING** 93 **DRINK** 2022-2029 $45 PR
Late Harvest Fortified Viognier 2015, Yarra Valley RATING 90
DRINK 2022-2028 $60 PR

Water Wheel

Bridgewater-Raywood Road, Bridgewater-on-Loddon, Vic 3516 **Region** Bendigo
T (03) 5437 3060 **www**.waterwheelwine.com **Open** Mon–Fri 9–5, w'ends 12–4
Winemaker Bill Trevaskis, Amy Cumming **Est.** 1972 **Dozens** 35 000 **Vyds** 136ha
Peter Cumming, with more than 2 decades of winemaking under his belt, has quietly built on the reputation of Water Wheel year by year. The winery is owned by the Cumming family, which has farmed in the Bendigo region for more than 50 years, with horticulture and viticulture special areas of interest. Over half the vineyard area is planted to shiraz (75ha), followed by chardonnay and sauvignon blanc (15ha each), cabernet sauvignon and malbec (10ha each) and smaller plantings of petit verdot, semillon, roussanne and grenache. Water Wheel continues to make wines that over-deliver at their modest prices.

ΨΨΨΨΨ **Viognier 2021, Bendigo** Aims for a degree of complexity courtesy of barrel fermentation, and the result is a full-bodied, textural viognier that flows effortlessly. Apricots, honeysuckle and peach offer an enticing group of flavours. A lovely, smooth palate texture and clean acid drive top this hedonistic wine experience. Screw cap. 13.4% alc. **RATING** 92 **DRINK** 2022-2026 $24 JP ✪

Waterton Hall Wines

61 Waterton Hall Road, Rowella, Tas 7270 **Region** Northern Tasmania
T 0417 834 781 **www**.watertonhall.com.au **Open** By appt **Winemaker** Tasmanian
Vintners **Est.** 2006 **Dozens** 1800 **Vyds** 10.1ha
The homestead that today is the home of Waterton Hall Wines was built in the 1850s. Originally a private residence, it was modified extensively in 1901 by neo-gothic architect Alexander North and ultimately passed into the ownership of the Catholic church from 1949–96. In '02 it was purchased by Jennifer Baird and Peter Cameron and in '15 passed into the family ownership of 'one architect, one farmer, one interior designer, one finance director and one labradoodle'. Their real names are David and Susan Shannon, John Carter and Belinda Evans (the dog's name is Bert.) Susan and John are sister and brother.

ΨΨΨΨΨ **Chardonnay 2022, Tasmania** The first release of this Tamar Valley chardonnay. Lifted aromas of white peach, nectarine and citrus fruits cut with soft spice, white flowers, crushed stone, suggestions of oatmeal, oyster shell and softly spoken cashew oak. Citrus, stone fruits and a touch of yellow plum and custard apple on the palate, again soft spice and some honeysuckle notes with a tight lemon curd finish. Screw cap. 13% alc. **RATING** 91 **DRINK** 2023-2027 $38 DB

Watkins ★★★★

59 Grants Gully Road, Chandlers Hill, SA, 5159 **Region** Langhorne Creek
T 0422 418 845 **www**.watkins.wine **Open** Fri–Sat 11–6, Sun 11–5 **Winemaker** Sam
Watkins **Viticulturist** David Watkins **Est.** 2019 **Dozens** 6500 **Vyds** 150ha
Sibling trio Ben, Sam and Jo Watkins, under the guidance of parents David and Ros Watkins,
established Watkins as a new label based at their Chandlers Hill winery and cellar door in the
Adelaide Hills. They are tapping into their well-established estate vineyards there and in
Langhorne Creek: both regions' vines are maritime influenced, with afternoon sea breezes
tempering summer ripening temperatures. The top-of-the-ridge cellar door overlooks rolling
hillside vines on one side and St Vincent Gulf on the other. Winemaker Sam Watkins has
worked in the Napa Valley and Porto, as well as Orange, Coonawarra, Barossa and McLaren
Vale. Brother Ben is commercial director, and sister Jo is brand director and cellar door manager.

🍷🍷🍷🍷🍷 **Chilled Light Red 2022, Langhorne Creek** Grenache/sangiovese blend. A
most attractive light-bodied dry red with savoury tannins and spices giving texture
and structure to the vivid raspberry and red cherry fruit. A wine that sings for joy.
Screw cap. 13.5% alc. **RATING** 94 **DRINK** 2023-2024 $26 JH ✪
Macclesfield Chardonnay 2021, Adelaide Hills This is a streamlined wine
with flavour bursting from its seams. Poached white peach, cinnamon stick, white
fig, nougat and a hint of brûlée are played with a diplomatic hand, somewhere
between taut and tensile, bumptious and generous. Reminds me of something
from the Mâconnais. Texturally chewy, moreish and persuasive. Very good
drinking. Screw cap. 12.5% alc. **RATING** 94 **DRINK** 2022-2030 $50 NG

🍷🍷🍷🍷🍷 **Chardonnay 2021, Langhorne Creek RATING** 93 **DRINK** 2023-2029 $24 JH ✪
Symmetry G.S.M. 2021, Langhorne Creek RATING 91 **DRINK** 2023-2026
$26 JH ✪
Grenache Rosé 2022, Langhorne Creek RATING 90 **DRINK** 2023-2024
$24 JH ✪
Wavemaker Merlot 2021, Langhorne Creek RATING 90 **DRINK** 2023-2027
$26 JH

Watson Family Wines ★★★☆

3948 Caves Road, Wilyabrup, WA 6280 **Region** Margaret River
T (08) 9755 6226 **www**.watsonfamilywines.com.au **Open** 7 days 10–5 **Winemaker** Stuart
Watson **Viticulturist** Jaden McLean **Est.** 1973 **Dozens** 1000 **Vyds** 2ha
Watson Family Wines is owned and operated by the Watson Family of Woodlands Wines
(est. 1973) in Margaret River. The Watson Family Wines are an affordable (sub $30) set
of Margaret River varietals, focusing on shiraz, cabernet merlot, chardonnay and semillon
sauvignon blanc; they also make a nebbiolo.

🍷🍷🍷🍷🍷 **Sauvignon Blanc Semillon 2019, Margaret River** This is super-tight and
lean. There's a slight green edge with capsicum and jalapeño, but also salted
lemon and Mediterranean herbs. It lingers, remains refreshing and is good value.
Screw cap. 12% alc. **RATING** 90 **DRINK** 2022-2024 $21 JF ✪

Weathercraft Wine ★★★★

1242 Beechworth-Wangaratta Road, Everton Upper, Vic 3678 **Region** Beechworth
T (03) 5727 0518 **www**.weathercraft.com.au **Open** By appt **Winemaker** Raquel Jones
Viticulturist Raquel Jones **Est.** 1998 **Dozens** 1800 **Vyds** 4ha
In 2016, Raquel and Hugh Jones discovered a vineyard 10min out of Beechworth,
neighbouring the likes of Giaconda and Castagna. It had an immaculate 20yo vineyard of
shiraz, planted in '98, with fruit sold to Yalumba (for a single-vineyard shiraz) as well as
to smaller producers. Raquel and Hugh retained some of the shiraz and have since added
tempranillo, albariño, grenache and monastrell, a nod to Raquel's Spanish heritage. Biological
farming and soil health is a priority for them and the preference is for traditional, low-
intervention winemaking, including the use of amphora.

ΨΨΨΨΨ **Chardonnay 2021, Beechworth** A wine of some stature courtesy of a fine-edged structure, discreet oak and built-in, citrus-defined complexity. There's a youthful energy in the scent and flavours focusing on lemon, lime, nectarine, and white peach, together with a gentle mealy nuttiness. Very much in the evolution phase, but worth broaching now for the utter juiciness and joy of fruit. Screw cap. 13% alc. RATING 94 DRINK 2023–2027 $41 JP

ΨΨΨΨΫ **Whole Bunch Rosé Shiraz 2022, Beechworth** RATING 92 DRINK 2022–2024 $32 JP
Albariño 2022, Beechworth RATING 90 DRINK 2022–2025 $41 JP
Tempranillo 2021, Beechworth RATING 90 DRINK 2023–2025 $38 JP

Welland ★★★★

Welland Road, Nuriootpa, SA 5355 **Region** Barossa Valley
T 0438 335 510 **www.**wellandwines.com **Open** By appt **Winemaker** Ben Chapam **Viticulturist** Amanda Mader **Est.** 2017 **Dozens** 5000 **Vyds** 1.7ha
Surrounded by the sprawling northern expanse of the township of Nuriootpa and destined to be sold for development, the 1923-planted Welland shiraz vineyard was rescued in '17 by a group of friends led by Ben and Madeleine Chapman. The neglected vineyard of 30 rows was resurrected in '19 with new trellising, irrigation and replanting. Fruit from the site is supplemented from other vineyards around the Barossa and Eden valleys.

ΨΨΨΨΫ **Old Hands Cabernet Sauvignon 2021, Barossa** Deep crimson with aromas of blackberry and dark plum fruits with hints of brown spice, roasting meats, roast capsicum, purple flowers, earth, licorice, sage, violets and cedar. Bright, lifted blackcurrant notes on the palate with a snappy acid line, powdery tannin grip and a lovely sense of balance and grace. Screw cap. 14.5% alc. RATING 93 DRINK 2023–2035 $70 DB
Valley & Valley Cabernet Sauvignon 2022, Barossa Bright crimson with dark plum and macerated summer berry fruits. Hints of licorice, sage, espresso, cedar, red plum, violets and vague herb and undergrowth tones. Medium bodied and chalky in tannin with a nice red plummy edge to the darker berry fruits and an energetic, bright passage across the palate. Screw cap. 14.5% alc. RATING 90 DRINK 2023–2029 $30 DB

Wellington & Wolfe ★★★★★

3 Balfour Place, Launceston, Tas 7250 (postal) **Region** Tasmania
T 0474 425 527 **www.**wellingtonwolfe.com **Open** Not **Winemaker** Hugh McCullough **Est.** 2017 **Dozens** 250
There are many routes to winemaking, and a master's degree in modern history from Scotland is among the more unusual. Hugh McCullough came to love wine through hospitality work ultimately culminating in a master's in viticulture and oenology, focusing on sparkling and aromatic wine production. Vintages in Oregon, Washington, the Barossa and Tasmania followed, finally settling in Launceston with his partner, winemaker Natalie Fryar (Bellebonne), establishing Wellington & Wolfe in '17. The aromatic expression, depth of flavour and racy acidity of Tasmanian riesling are his first love; 2nd label Wolfe at the Door was introduced in '20 to showcase the 'supporting' varietals. Production is tiny and fruit is sourced from growers in Pipers River and the Tamar Valley. A talented newcomer to watch.

ΨΨΨΨΨ **Riesling 2022, Tasmania** A lovely Tamar Valley riesling that is crisp, perfumed and decidedly easy to drink. Pale straw with aromas of fresh lime, lemon and green apple characters with hints of jasmine, crushed stone, marzipan and almond blossom. There is a great sense of clarity, the porcelain acidity acting as a spotlight for the fruit and providing a vivid pulse finishing in a blast of citrus and blossom. Screw cap. 12% alc. RATING 95 DRINK 2023–2029 $39 DB ✪
Eylandt Off Dry Riesling 2022, Tasmania Pale straw with aromas of juicy white peach, grapefruit and lime underscored by hints of clotted cream, crushed river stone, orange blossom and lighter whiffs of lemon curd and struck match.

There is just a tickle of phenolic texture and the interplay and tension between fruit and acid is a beautiful thing. Sails focused, fine and laden with minerals and pure peachy fruit. Screw cap. 8.5% alc. RATING 95 DRINK 2023–2029 $50 DB ✪

ᵀᵀᵀᵀ♀ **Wolfe at the Door Pinot Noir 2022, Tasmania** RATING 90 DRINK 2023–2028 $32 DB

West Cape Howe Wines ★★★★★

Lot 14923 Muir Highway, Mount Barker, WA 6324 **Region** Mount Barker
T (08) 9892 1444 **www.**westcapehowewines.com.au **Open** Mon–Fri 10–5, w'ends 11–4
Winemaker Gavin Berry, Stephen Craig, Mike Webster **Viticulturist** Rob Quenby
Est. 1997 **Dozens** 60 000 **Vyds** 310ha
West Cape Howe is owned by a partnership of 4 WA families, including those of Gavin Berry and Rob Quenby. Grapes are sourced from estate vineyards in Mount Barker and Frankland River. The Langton vineyard (Mount Barker) has 100ha planted to cabernet sauvignon, shiraz, riesling, sauvignon blanc, chardonnay and semillon; the Russell Road vineyard (Frankland River) has 210ha. West Cape Howe also sources select parcels of fruit from valued contract growers.

ᵀᵀᵀᵀᵀ **Riesling 2022, Porongurup** This has a floral and citrus blossom-filled bouquet and a palate that is at once delicate and mouth-coating. The resolution of the paradox is the purity of Porongurup's fruit, its minerally acidity a driving force. Screw cap. 11.5% alc. RATING 96 DRINK 2023–2032 $30 JH ✪
King Billy Shiraz 2017, Mount Barker This the best wine of this not-often-seen label's '17 vintage, which was a great year for shiraz. The past 5 years have seen the wine open up, coasting along with cedar and spice threaded through the blackberry and cherry fruit. Silky tannins bring closure. 150 dozen made. Screw cap. 14.5% alc. RATING 96 DRINK 2023–2037 $50 JH ✪
Sauvignon Blanc 2022, Mount Barker The fruit comes from the mature 30yo Langton vineyard, with no tricks in the ferment. The wine has that group of sauvignon blanc flavours covering tropical, herbal, and gooseberry. Bright acidity with an edge of citrus provides an extra degree of length. Screw cap. 12.5% alc. RATING 94 DRINK 2023–2023 $22 JH ✪

ᵀᵀᵀᵀ♀ **Riesling 2022, Mount Barker** RATING 92 DRINK 2023–2030 $22 JH ✪

Whispering Brook ★★★★★

Rodd Street, Broke, NSW 2330 **Region** Hunter Valley
T (02) 9818 4126 **www.**whispering-brook.com **Open** Thurs–Sun 10.30–5 and by appt
Winemaker Susan Frazier, Adam Bell **Viticulturist** Adam Bell, Neil Grosser **Est.** 2000
Dozens 1100 **Vyds** 3ha
It took some time for partners Susan Frazier and Adam Bell to find the property on which they established their vineyard over 20 years ago. It has a combination of terra rossa loam soils on which the reds are planted, and sandy flats for the white grapes. A trip to Portugal in '07 inspired the planting of Portuguese varieties, including touriga and arinto, alongside Hunter staples, shiraz and semillon. The partners have also established an olive grove and accommodation in the large house set in the vineyard, offering vineyard and winery tours.

ᵀᵀᵀᵀᵀ **Vintage Release Single Vineyard Limited Release Semillon 2017, Hunter Valley** It is intense and has prodigious length, all the stars aligned with magnificent growing conditions. The colour is still pale green quartz, and with its pH of 3.17 and TA of 6g/L could easily coast by its 50th birthday. Screw cap. 12% alc. RATING 98 DRINK 2023–2037 $68 JH ✪
Vintage Release Limited Release Chardonnay 2017, Hunter Valley The colour – pale straw-green – is a useful introduction (and promise of future longevity), but it's the grapefruit and Granny Smith apple that hit the taste buds with the first sip, and the overall cohesion (even the acidity) of a chardonnay that steps around 95% of its cohort. Screw cap. 13% alc. RATING 97 DRINK 2023–2033 $60 JH ✪

ƎƎƎƎƎ **Single Vineyard Limited Release Semillon 2022, Hunter Valley** It's full of promise, tightly focused and perfectly balanced, the fruit already giving a glimpse of its future array of citrus zest, Granny Smith apple and a slash of snow peas and wild herbs. Screw cap 11% alc. **RATING** 96 **DRINK** 2023–2042 $35 JH ✪

Vintage Release Single Vineyard Shiraz 2017, Hunter Valley Initially docile in the mouth then picked up the pace, and tannins give the wine a very firm handshake not soon forgotten. Screw cap. 14.5% alc. **RATING** 95 **DRINK** 2027–2047 $100 JH

Single Vineyard Limited Release Arinto 2022, Hunter Valley Whispering Brook seems to have the ability to add a measure of power not matched by most other makers of a given variety. Most would think for an effectively unknown variety it's asking too much, but this has essence of grapefruit flavours. Screw cap. 13% alc. **RATING** 94 **DRINK** 2025–2035 $40 JH ✪

Whistler Wines ★★★★

241 Seppeltsfield Road, Stone Well, SA 5352 **Region** Barossa Valley
T (08) 8562 4942 www.whistlerwines.com **Open** 7 days 10.30–5 **Winemaker** Michael J Corbett, Adam Hay **Viticulturist** Sam Pfeiffer **Est.** 1997 **Dozens** 9500 **Vyds** 15ha
With 4 generations of grape-growing under their belts, the Pfeiffer family estate was purchased by Martin and Sally Pfeiffer in the early 1980s while Martin ran the Penfolds vineyards. They gradually planted Kalimna 3C cuttings from the famous 'Grange' vineyards and bottled their first wine from the '97 vintage. Whistler Wines launched with brothers Martin and Chris at the helm. The next generation, brothers Josh and Sam Pfeiffer, came on board in '13, introducing new wine styles and sustainable vineyard practices. Today, Martin and Sally have retired and Sam runs the ship with Michael J Corbett in charge of the winemaking, striking a nice balance of traditional Barossan styles and contemporary new-wave regional vibrancy.

ƎƎƎƎƎ **Estate Shiraz 2021, Barossa Valley** Deep magenta with purple splashes. Plenty of opulence and fruit depth within; ripe juicy blood plum, blackberry and boysenberry with baking spices, jasmine, dark chocolate, licorice, espresso, vanilla bean and a waft of black pepper and turned earth. Compact, chalky tannins and a savoury yet deeply fruited exit that shows plenty of detail and vivacity. Diam. 14.3% alc. **RATING** 94 **DRINK** 2023–2033 $60 DB

Estate Shiraz Cabernet 2021, Barossa Valley Bright, vibrant magenta–crimson hue. Notes of plum, blackberry, boysenberry and blueberry with hints of baking spices, licorice, dark chocolate and lighter tones of jasmine, dried herbs, tobacco and pepper. Fresh and lively with an impressive flow of plums and spice, tight, sandy tannins and a finish that shows nice sustain. Diam. 14% alc. **RATING** 94 **DRINK** 2023–2030 $50 DB

ƎƎƎƎ♀ **Divergent S.M.G. 2022, Barossa Valley RATING** 93 **DRINK** 2023–2026 $25 DB ✪
MJC Grenache 2021, Barossa Valley RATING 93 **DRINK** 2023–2028 $80 DB
Double Back Grenache 2022, Barossa Valley RATING 92 **DRINK** 2023–2026 $40 DB
Atypical Shiraz 2021, Barossa Valley RATING 92 **DRINK** 2023–2025 $30 DB ✪
Shiver 2021, Barossa Valley RATING 92 **DRINK** 2023–2026 $40 DB
Estate Cabernet Sauvignon 2021, Barossa Valley RATING 92 **DRINK** 2023–2030 $50 DB
Yonda Riesling 2022, Barossa Valley RATING 91 **DRINK** 2023–2027 $25 DB ✪

Whistling Eagle Vineyard ★★★★☆

2769 Heathcote-Rochester Road, Colbinabbin, Vic 3559 **Region** Heathcote
T (03) 5432 9319 www.whistlingeagle.com **Open** By appt **Winemaker** Ian Rathjen
Viticulturist Ian Rathjen **Est.** 1995 **Dozens** 950 **Vyds** 40ha
This is a remarkable story. Owners Ian and Lynn Rathjen are farmers living and working on the now famous Cambrian red soil of Heathcote. Henning Rathjen was lured from his birthplace in Schleswig Holstein by the gold rush, but soon decided farming provided a more

secure future. In 1858 he made his way to the Colbinabbin Range, and exclaimed, 'We have struck paradise.' Among other things, he planted a vineyard in the 1860s, expanding it in the wake of demand for the wine. He died in 1912, and the vineyards disappeared before being replanted in '95, with 40ha of immaculately tended vines. The core wine is shiraz, with intermittent releases of sangiovese, viognier, cabernet sauvignon and semillon.

🍷🍷🍷🍷 **Eagles Blood Shiraz 2019, Heathcote** It brings on the silk and also the refinement. This is neat, crisp and flavoursome at once. Roasted plum and redcurrants, a lick of boysenberry and then a spread of earth and woodsy spice notes. Nothing over the top here; it feels immaculate. Time will bring greater complexity. Screw cap. 14.5% alc. RATING 95 DRINK 2025–2040 $60 CM

🍷🍷🍷🍷 **GSM 2021, Heathcote** RATING 93 DRINK 2023–2030 $30 CM ✪
Sangiovese 2021, Heathcote RATING 91 DRINK 2023–2026 $30 CM

Wicks Estate Wines ★★★★☆

21 Franklin Street, Adelaide, SA 5000 (postal) **Region** Adelaide Hills
T (08) 8212 0004 **www.wicksestate.com.au Open** Not **Winemaker** Adam Carnaby
Viticulturist Tim Wicks **Est.** 2000 **Dozens** 30 000 **Vyds** 54ha
Tim and Simon Wicks had a long-term involvement with orchard and nursery operations at Highbury in the Adelaide Hills prior to purchasing their property at Woodside in '99. They planted fractionally less than 54ha of sauvignon blanc, shiraz, chardonnay, pinot noir, cabernet sauvignon, tempranillo and riesling.

🍷🍷🍷🍷 **C.J. Wicks Shiraz 2021, Adelaide Hills** Bright aromatics, snappy freshness and considerable detail, with depth, clarity of blue-fruit allusions and spicy complexity on show. Whiffs of cardamom, star anise, dill and mezcal suggestive, too, of some whole bunches in the fray. A backbone of fibrous tannins runs out the impressive finish. Screw cap. 14% alc. RATING 94 DRINK 2022–2029 $45 NG

🍷🍷🍷🍷 **C.J. Wicks Chardonnay 2022, Adelaide Hills** RATING 92 DRINK 2023–2030 $45 NG
Shiraz 2021, Adelaide Hills RATING 92 DRINK 2022–2027 $25 NG ✪
Pamela Chardonnay Pinot Noir 2016, Adelaide Hills RATING 91 DRINK 2022–2025 $30 NG
Night Owl Shiraz 2021, Adelaide Hills RATING 91 DRINK 2023–2038 $35 NG
C.J. Wicks Pinot Noir 2022, Adelaide Hills RATING 90 DRINK 2023–2028 $45 NG
C.J. Wicks Pinot Noir 2021, Adelaide Hills RATING 90 DRINK 2022–2027 $45 NG

🍇 Wild Fire Wines ★★★★

55 Hazelwood Road, East Warburton, 3799 Vic (postal) **Region** Victoria
T 0438 002 299 **www.wildfirewines.com.au Open** Not **Winemaker** Peter Newman **Est.** 2017
Three semi-retired friends with a life-long interest in wine took it further, as so often happens. Peter Newman, a vigneron in the Otway Ranges, found pieces of molten metal (the result of the 1983 Ash Wednesday bushfires) in the Otways' soil, which inspired the name. Geoff Shenfield took over the sourcing of fruit and supplies. John Harry was already growing vines and making wine off his Iona vineyard in East Warburton, which then became the brand's home. The estate vineyard sits at 370m elevation and grows chardonnay, pinot noir and shiraz; fruit is also sourced from around Victoria. Growth is steady, but the intention is to remain small. 'Yeah, I know, what the hell was I thinking?' says Geoff Shensfield, as surprised as any that their small project keeps on growing.

🍷🍷🍷🍷 **The Summit Shiraz 2020, Grampians** The Summit label represents Wild Fire's super-premium wines. Lashings of cherry, red berries and briar, with a lilting blackberry/sweet pastille note that springs from the glass. The word delicious comes to mind, with a palate that is both finely detailed, balanced and yet so juicy and fresh. Wild berries to the fore, with anise, a touch of bitter chocolate and dried herbs. Ripe tannins travel easily in tune. Elegant and charming. Screw cap. 14% alc. **RATING** 94 **DRINK** 2022-2030 $75 JP

🍷🍷🍷🍷♀ Chardonnay 2021, Upper Yarra Valley **RATING** 92 **DRINK** 2022-2031 $33 JP
Pinot Noir 2019, Upper Yarra Valley **RATING** 92 **DRINK** 2022-2032 $29 JP ✪
Riesling 2021, Grampians **RATING** 90 **DRINK** 2022-2030 $27 JP

Willem Kurt Wines ★★★★

365 Buckland Gap Road, Beechworth, Vic 3747 **Region** Beechworth
T 0428 400 522 **www.willemkurtwines.com.au Open** By appt **Winemaker** Daniel Balzer **Viticulturist** Daniel Balzer **Est.** 2014 **Dozens** 600 **Vyds** 2.6ha
This is the venture of Daniel Balzer and Marije van Epenhuijsen; he with a German background, and she Dutch. The name of the winery is drawn from the middle names of their two children: Willem (Dutch) and Kurt (German). Daniel began working first at Yarra Ridge (including a vintage in Germany) before moving to Gapsted Wines in '03, then completing his bachelor of wine science at CSU the following year. Many years were given over to contract winemaking for smaller producers before Daniel and Marije began making wine for their own brand. They planted their own vineyard in '17 to shiraz, chardonnay, vermentino and more recently, sangiovese. Wines have been solely from estate fruit since '22; a new cellar door will open in '23.

🍷🍷🍷🍷🍷 Chardonnay 2021, Beechworth The essence of Beechworth chardonnay, beautifully captured. The granitic soils produce an effortless natural balance with a stone-like mineral tang. It's here in spades, joining nectarine, lime, ruby grapefruit, almond macaroon and nougat laced in a subtle oak spice. Fabulous concentration of fruit on display, smooth and textural, too. Runs long and delicious. Screw cap. 12.6% alc. **RATING** 95 **DRINK** 2023-2031 $42 JP ✪

🍷🍷🍷🍷♀ Vermentino 2022, Beechworth **RATING** 91 **DRINK** 2023-2025 $32 JP

William Downie ★★★★★

121 Yarragon South Road, Yarragon, Vic 3823 (postal) **Region** Gippsland
T 03 5634 2216 **www.williamdownie.com.au Open** Not **Winemaker** William Downie
Viticulturist William Downie **Est.** 2003 **Dozens** 5000 **Vyds** 6ha
One wine rules William Downie: pinot noir. Stints in Burgundy and De Bortoli in the Yarra Valley during the early '00s have contributed to his respect and love for the variety. However, he always believed Gippsland to be the place in Australia where it can really shine. Bill and wife Rachel Needoba moved to their Yarragon property, Guendulain Farm, in '07 and set about planting a high-density vineyard, 10 000 vines per ha. Today, the site covers 2ha. He leases 4ha including Bull Swamp and Camp Hill all made at a Warrigal winery. Not quite a one-man show, as Kevin Collett and Charlie Brindle work alongside him in the vineyards. And why pinot noir? 'So I don't have to talk about pinot noir,' William says. 'It's about the differences between the wines that make them interesting.' Given he is one of the most talented and thoughtful winemakers, there's plenty to consider.

🍷🍷🍷🍷🍷 Camp Hill Pinot Noir 2022, Gippsland Oh, Bill Downie. It's been far too long between drinks. And you come back with this superfine, textural and captivating offering. It has an ethereal quality yet density of flavour, all dark fruit, warming spices, complex, floral and alive. Raw silk tannins swooshing like George Constanza's pants (a *Seinfeld* reference, check it out on YouTube) across the medium-bodied palate. Diam. 12% alc. **RATING** 96 **DRINK** 2023-2035 $100 JF
Bull Swamp Pinot Noir 2022, Gippsland At first, this seemed a bit feral and funky, but it's more about autumn with wafts of mushrooms, truffles and really fragrant, healthy compost. Pops of ironstone infiltrate the red cherry accents, some blood orange tang and zest. Quite tight and lean with finely honed tannins and life-affirming acidity, as in, it pulses with energy. Diam. 12% alc. **RATING** 95 **DRINK** 2023-2032 $100 JF

Willoughby Park

678 South Coast Highway, Denmark, WA 6333 **Region** Great Southern
T (08) 9848 1555 **www**.willoughbypark.com.au **Open** Thurs–Sun 11–5
Winemaker Elysia Harrison **Est.** 2010 **Dozens** 13 000 **Vyds** 19ha
Bob Fowler, who comes from a rural background and had always hankered for a farming life,
stumbled across the opportunity to achieve this in early '10. Together with wife Marilyn, he
purchased the former West Cape Howe winery and surrounding vineyard when West Cape
Howe moved to the larger Goundrey winery. In '11 Willoughby Park purchased the Kalgan
River vineyard and business name, and winemaking operations have been transferred to
Willoughby Park. There are 3 labels: the Kalgan River and Ironrock single-vineyard ranges,
and Willoughby Park and the Great Southern brand for estate and purchased grapes.

Ironrock Chardonnay 2021, Great Southern This has power and grace. A
cavalcade of stone fruits, green apple, citrus, cinnamon spice and creamy, nougat-
like sweetness and savouriness in bouquet and palate. A lightly creamy texture
stretching luxuriously to a cool, bright, and slightly saline nutty finish. There's
a distinct sense of pedigree and polished winemaking here. Kudos. Screw cap.
13.5% alc. **RATING** 93 **DRINK** 2022–2030 $40 MB
Ironrock Riesling 2022, Great Southern A dictionary definition of Great
Southern riesling, it's steely, refreshing and electric with acidity. Jasmine, lemon,
lime and warm slate/flinty minerally aromas. Flavours are citrusy, with pulpy
grapefruit juice and tart, lemony zing the dominant forces. Expect talc-like
minerally puffs and a bit of mandarin sorbet, sweet-and-sour zestiness. Nicely
done, all up. Screw cap. 12% alc. **RATING** 91 **DRINK** 2022–2030 $35 MB
Kalgan River Cabernet Sauvignon 2021, Albany Scents of cassis, bay leaf,
faint cedar and black olive. Flavours are darker fruited, and the wine feels lightly
juicy and refreshing with briny acidity. Layers of woody spice, piquant black
olive and bay leaf. It rolls along with easy appeal, a sense of restraint and finishes
long and succulent. Drink a few now and lose a few in the cellar. Charming stuff.
Screw cap. 14.5% alc. **RATING** 91 **DRINK** 2022–2033 $32 MB

Willow Bridge Estate ★★★★★

178 Gardin Court Drive, Dardanup, WA 6236 **Region** Geographe
T (08) 9728 0055 **www**.willowbridge.com.au **Open** 7 days 10.30–4.30
Winemaker Kim Horton **Viticulturist** Robbie O'Leary, Ant Davenport **Est.** 1997
Dozens 25 000 **Vyds** 59ha
Jeff and Vicky Dewar established Willow Bridge Estate after acquiring a spectacular
180ha hillside property in the Ferguson Valley. Chardonnay, semillon, sauvignon blanc,
shiraz and cabernet sauvignon were planted, with merlot, tempranillo, chenin blanc and
viognier following. Many of its wines offer exceptional value for money. Kim Horton, with
25 years of winemaking in WA, believes that wines are made in the vineyard; the better the
understanding of the vineyard and its unique characteristics, the better the wines reflect
the soil and the climate.

Gravel Pit Shiraz 2021, Geographe Matured in fine-grain French oak
(35% new). Deeply coloured; a wine that always comes out on top, making light
of vintage variation. Thanks to its balance, it's utterly pleasurable to savour the oak,
the generosity of its black fruits, its ripe tannins and its notes of spices and pepper
spun throughout. Screw cap. 14.5% alc. **RATING** 96 **DRINK** 2023–2036 $30 JH ✪

Bookends Fumé Sauvignon Blanc Semillon 2022, Geographe **RATING** 93
DRINK 2023–2035 $30 MB ✪
G1-10 Chardonnay 2022, Geographe **RATING** 93 **DRINK** 2023–2030
$35 MB ✪
Solana 2021, Geographe **RATING** 93 **DRINK** 2022–2029 $35 MB ✪
Coat of Arms Cabernet Sauvignon 2021, Geographe **RATING** 93
DRINK 2023–2035 $35 MB ✪
Dragonfly Sauvignon Blanc Semillon 2022, Geographe **RATING** 91
DRINK 2023–2024 $22 JH ✪

Wills Domain

Cnr Abbeys Farm Road/Brash Road, Yallingup, WA 6281 **Region** Margaret River
T (08) 9755 2327 **www.**willsdomain.com.au **Open** 7 days 10–5 **Winemaker** Richard
Rowe **Est.** 1985 **Dozens** 20 000 **Vyds** 20ha

When the Haunold family purchased the original Wills Domain vineyard in '00, they were
adding another chapter to a family history of winemaking stretching back to 1383 in what
is now Austria. Their Yallingup vineyard is planted to shiraz, semillon, cabernet sauvignon,
sauvignon blanc, chardonnay, merlot, petit verdot, malbec, cabernet franc and viognier. The
onsite restaurant has won numerous accolades.

🍷🍷🍷🍷🍷 **Eightfold Semillon 2022, Margaret River** While there's some sweetness
on the palate (oak or fruit?), this is so appealing with intriguing flavours. Flinty,
spicy, lemongrass and Meyer lemon, makrut lime and honeydew. There's creamed
honey and clotted cream texture with soft acidity. Nice one. Screw cap. 12.5% alc.
RATING 93 **DRINK** 2023–2029 $45 JF

Paladin Hill Shiraz 2021, Margaret River What a colour – the darkest purple
with a shot of ruby, and intense aromas and flavours of ripe fruit, licorice, star
anise and cedary, sweet oak. It's voluptuous with fleshy, ripe tannins filling out
the palate. Screw cap. 14% alc. **RATING** 92 **DRINK** 2023–2033 $85 JF

Eightfold Chardonnay 2022, Margaret River Gentle and even with soft
acidity melding with stone fruit, poached apples and spice. Welcoming creamy
lees across the palate and oak neatly in place. Screw cap. 13% alc. **RATING** 91
DRINK 2023–2030 $45 JF

Eightfold Cabernet Sauvignon 2021, Margaret River At first, this doesn't
seem very cabernet-esque, though some airing helps. Yet the medium–bodied
palate has sweet cassis, squid ink, baking spices plus firm yet textural tannins.
There is malbec in this, and it adds a dollop of juicy fruit and savouriness.
Screw cap. 13.5% alc. **RATING** 91 **DRINK** 2023–2031 $45 JF

Paladin Hill Chardonnay 2022, Margaret River There's a lot going on,
from ripe fruit to winemaking. Cedary sweet oak infuses the citrus and stone fruit,
fleshy, and rich yet some detail with creamy lees and pulsating acidity. Not a show
pony but no wallflower either. Screw cap. 13% alc. **RATING** 90 **DRINK** 2023–2028
$85 JF

Eightfold Shiraz 2021, Margaret River Deeply coloured – the black-red
of Chanel Rouge Noir – while flavours are rich from ripe plums and stewed
cherries to lashings of woodsy spices. Full–bodied with cedary oak and a whiff of
woodsmoke, it's a voluptuous style, and lots to like with firm tannins yet a slight
green edge to them. Screw cap. 13.5% alc. **RATING** 90 **DRINK** 2023–2029 $45 JF

Paladin Hill Matrix Cabernet Sauvignon 2021, Margaret River It's
unclear if this is a straight cabernet sauvignon, although varietal flavours are
strong: mulberries, cassis, menthol and bay leaf. Deep, full bodied and a lot of
winemaking artefact, namely the impact of cedary oak, sweet and spicy yet a little
bitter on the finish. More time to mellow is a good thing so come back to this in
a couple of years. Screw cap. 14% alc. **RATING** 90 **DRINK** 2024–2036 $110 JF

Willunga 100 Wines

PO Box 2239, McLaren Vale, SA 5171 **Region** McLaren Vale
T 0417 401 856 **www.**willunga100.com **Open** Not **Winemaker** Renae Hirsch,
Skye Salter **Est.** 2005 **Dozens** 9500 **Vyds** 19ha

Established by David Gleave MW and John Ratcliffe in '05, Willunga 100 focuses on the
diverse districts within McLaren Vale and dry-grown bush-vine grenache. Winemaker Renae
Hirsch took over from Skye Salter in '23. Grapes are sourced from single sites across McLaren
Vale, including viticulturist Sue Trott's Trott vineyard, in addition to Willunga's own 19h site
in Blewitt Springs – majority grenache with a plot of 80yo shiraz vines.

🍷🍷🍷🍷🍷 **Smart Vineyard Clarendon Grenache 2022, McLaren Vale** Thirst-slaking
tannins bridge the attack and a chewy, ferrous finish, the framework in which

blood plum, bergamot, kirsch, dried thyme and lilac carouse. I'd like a bit more stuffing to this; more mid-palate density. Yet there is plenty of energy suffused with nourishing tannins and drinkability in spades. Lots to like. Screw cap. 14.5% alc. RATING 92 DRINK 2023–2028 $55 NG

Trott Vineyard Blewitt Springs Grenache 2022, McLaren Vale There is a great deal of attention paid here to tannin management, which I appreciate. After all, the tamarind, raspberry liqueur, cardamom and Moroccan basement scents need some sort of savoury, sinewy placation. This, mid-weighted of feel yet dense and dutifully fresh, manages it with aplomb. Screw cap. 14.5% alc. RATING 92 DRINK 2023–2028 $55 NG

Shiraz Viognier 2021, McLaren Vale Floral, streamlined and pixelated with spicy detail. Lilac, kelp, blueberry, charcuterie and a smear of tapenade across a thread of peppery acidity and lithe, dutifully astringent tannins. The oak, a little obtuse. Full, yet deft on its feet, endowing poise and effortless drinkability. Screw cap. 14.5% alc. RATING 92 DRINK 2023–2030 $28 NG ✪

Shiraz Grenache 2022, McLaren Vale This transparent, bright and effusively flavoured grenache offers exceptional value. The caveat, perhaps, is the eucalyptus that dries out the finish slightly. Otherwise, kirsch, Seville orange, purple pastille, thyme and briar. A regalia of tannic detail and chewy nourishment at the finish. Screw cap. 14.5% alc. RATING 90 DRINK 2023–2026 $28 NG

Cabernet Shiraz 2021, McLaren Vale There is a verdant edginess to this, irrespective of the weight, as if portions have been intentionally picked on the lighter side of the ripening spectrum. Good drinking all the same. Pickled plum, mint, thyme and tomato leaf. A dill- to mezcal-edge to the tannic frisk across the finish. Screw cap. 14.5% alc. RATING 90 DRINK 2023–2027 $28 NG

Wilson Vineyard   ★★★★

Polish Hill River, Sevenhill via Clare, SA 5453 **Region** Clare Valley
T (08) 8822 4050 **www.**wilsonvineyard.com.au **Open** W'ends 10–4 **Winemaker** Daniel Wilson **Est.** 1974 **Dozens** 3000 **Vyds** 11.9ha
In '09 the winery and general operations were passed on to son Daniel Wilson, the 2nd generation. Daniel, a graduate of CSU, spent 3 years in the Barossa with some of Australia's largest winemakers before returning to Clare in '03. Parents John and Pat Wilson still contribute in a limited way, content to watch developments in the business they created. Daniel continues to follow John's beliefs about keeping quality high, often at the expense of volume, and rather than talk about it, believes the proof is in the bottle.

🍷🍷🍷🍷 **DJW Polish Hill River Riesling 2022, Clare Valley** Potent and energetic with lime juice, green apple and pulpy, grapefruit zestiness. Scents and flavours similar, with a puff of talc in the palate and light and zingy acidity cooling and tightening. Very refreshing is the message, in an understated and pure way. Lovely in the glass. Screw cap. 12% alc. RATING 93 DRINK 2022–2036 $25 MB ✪

Polish Hill River Riesling 2022, Clare Valley This has fruit in spades, with loads of fresh, almost-sweet citrus, perky green apple characters and a bit of anise and mandarin sorbet in the mix. Fresh, bold and bright with frisky acidity and excellent persistence. It's a real thirst-slaker here, simple in a way but great for its vitality and drinkability. Kudos. Screw cap. 12.5% alc. RATING 92 DRINK 2022–2030 $30 MB ✪

Special Blend Shiraz Cabernet 2017, Clare Valley Strong and evocative scents of rich stewed plum, mahogany, old leather, cola, dried violets and espresso. The palate has some gloss and then finishes powdery dry, feels full-weighted and in the early days of benign decay. Flavours of stewed plum, roast beetroot, garam masala and a gentle, ferrous-iron earthiness to finish. It's in a pleasant place. Screw cap. 14.5% alc. RATING 90 DRINK 2022–2027 $36 MB

Windance Wines

2764 Caves Road, Yallingup, WA 6282 **Region** Margaret River
T (08) 9755 2293 **www**.windance.com.au **Open** 7 days 10–5 **Winemaker** Tyke
Wheatley **Viticulturist** Tyke Wheatley **Est.** 1998 **Dozens** 4500 **Vyds** 9ha
Drew and Rosemary Brent-White founded this family business, situated 5km south of
Yallingup. Cabernet sauvignon, shiraz, sauvignon blanc, chardonnay, merlot, malbec, semillon
and grenache have been established. The vineyard is certified biodynamic. Daughter Billie and
husband Tyke Wheatley now own the business: Billie, a qualified accountant, manages the
business and the cellar door; and Tyke (with winemaking experience at Picardy, Happs and
Burgundy) has taken over the winemaking and manages the vineyard.

Glen Valley Chardonnay 2021, Margaret River At first the core is tight and
lean, all citrusy with perky acidity and some flinty notes. Then richer flavours
come in with a mix of warm spices, ginger flower, vanillin oak and creamy lees.
It's not too weighty as it backs off from being overly rich and oaky as the finish
lingers long. Screw cap. 12.5% alc. **RATING** 95 **DRINK** 2023–2030 $42 JF ✪

Wild Things Amphora Cabernet Sauvignon 2021, Margaret River
RATING 93 **DRINK** 2024–2036 $55 JF
Cabernet Sauvignon 2021, Margaret River RATING 92 **DRINK** 2024–2034
$34 JF
Cabernet Merlot 2201, Margaret River RATING 91 **DRINK** 2023–2033
$26 JF ✪
Shiraz 2021, Margaret River RATING 91 **DRINK** 2022–2031 $30 JF
Glen Valley Riesling 2022, Mount Barker RATING 90 **DRINK** 2022–2030 $30 JF

Windows Estate

4 Quininup Road, Yallingup, WA 6282 **Region** Margaret River
T (08) 9756 6655 **www**.windowsestate.com **Open** 7 days 10–5 **Winemaker** Chris
Davies **Viticulturist** Chris Davies **Est.** 1999 **Dozens** 2000 **Vyds** 7ha
Chris Davies planted the dry-farmed Windows Estate vineyard (cabernet sauvignon, merlot,
malbec, petit verdot, syrah, chenin blanc, chardonnay, semillon and sauvignon blanc) in '96,
at the tender age of 19. A trained viticulturist, he has tended the vines ever since, gaining
organic certification in '19. Initially selling his fruit to other winemakers, Chris began making
his own wines in '06. As vigneron, he has had considerable show success for consistently
outstanding wines.

Petit Lot Chardonnay 2021, Margaret River Dry-grown blocks with varying
soils and clonal selections. Hand picked, barrel and clay egg fermentation, matured
for 11 months in French oak (50% new). Its impact is immediate and intense,
yet there's also precision in what will be a gloriously complex maturity in 5 or so
years. Screw cap. 12% alc. **RATING** 97 **DRINK** 2023–2036 $64 JH ✪
Petit Lot Basket Pressed Syrah 2019, Margaret River Low-yielding, dry-
grown vines from a block with a portion of viognier. Brilliantly fresh in colour,
aroma and flavour. A juicy, light- to medium-bodied palate with red fruit to the
fore, superfine tannins bringing up the rear. Screw cap. 13.5% alc. **RATING** 97
DRINK 2023–2039 $42 JH ✪

Petit Lot La Terre 2021, Margaret River Hand-picked sauvignon blanc
fermented in clay eggs and barrel, a small portion on skins; 70% matured in
used French barriques, 30% in clay eggs. A wine of tremendous complexity
and intensity, reaching a high point on the finish of the palate with lemon
zest and electrifying acidity. Great packaging. Screw cap. 12% alc. **RATING** 96
DRINK 2023–2030 $39 JH ✪
Petit Lot Chenin Blanc 2021, Margaret River Oh yeah, this is good. Really
good. Think dried pears and poached quince, lemon curd and ginger powder,
lime zest plus woodsy spices. It's savoury and creamy yet almost invigorating
thanks to the sorbet-like acidity. It's also complex, detailed and a delight to drink.
Screw cap. 12.5% alc. **RATING** 96 **DRINK** 2022–2030 $39 JF ✪

Petit Lot Basket Pressed Malbec 2019, Margaret River A confident wine, but it's not brash. Malbec as it should be with a core of excellent fruit, structured and detailed. Not a fruit bomb though, as it's layered with savouriness, oak spice and lots of detail. Full bodied and blessed with ripe, shapely tannins and a certain refreshment. Screw cap. 14.5% alc. RATING 95 DRINK 2022–2030 $55 JF

La Fenêtre Cabernet Sauvignon 2017, Margaret River Cassis and 100% new oak come together to provide a wine of quality. The bouquet is fragrant, and the one caveat is that the tannins need a few more years to fully resolve. Screw cap. 14% alc. RATING 95 DRINK 2023–2042 $85 JH

Petit Lot Basket Pressed Cabernet Sauvignon 2019, Margaret River Cabernet from a dry-grown, low-yielding home block. Hand picked, open fermented with 30 days on skins and matured in French oak (40% new) for 18 months. It's clearly a block that produces such substantial tannins that even 30 days doesn't result in full agglomeration. Screw cap. 14% alc. RATING 94 DRINK 2023–2038 $64 JH

🍷🍷🍷🍷 **Petit Lot Semillon 2021, Margaret River** RATING 90 DRINK 2023–2030 $39 JF

Wine Unplugged ★★★★☆

2020 Upton Road, Upton Hill, Vic 3664 (postal) **Region** Victoria
T 0432 021 668 **www.wineunplugged.com.au** **Open** Not **Winemaker** Callie Jemmeson
Est. 2010 **Dozens** 5000

Callie Jemmeson believes that winemaking doesn't have to have barriers: what it does need is quality, focus and a destination. With a strong emphasis on vineyard selection and a gentle approach to their small-batch winemaking, the wines are a true reflection of site. The wines are released under the Pacha Mama and Cloak & Dagger labels.

🍷🍷🍷🍷 **Pacha Mama Pinot Noir 2021, Yarra Valley** A light, bright cherry red. This fragrant wine is redolent with red fruits, rose petals and a little spice. Equally good on the medium-bodied, silky and persistent palate, there is much joy to be had now, but anyone with a few bottles left in the cellar in 3-5 years will be amply rewarded. Screw cap. 12.6% alc. RATING 95 DRINK 2022–2028 $34 PR ✪

Pacha Mama Touriga Nacional 2022, Pyrenees The herbal nuances, the flush of fruit, the inflections of red licorice and smoked rubber. This is a dry, complex, sinewy red wine with a high interest factor, not to mention quality. The dry, tannic, mouth-watering nature of this will make it an excellent dining partner. Screw cap. 13.1% alc. RATING 94 DRINK 2024–2030 $38 CM ✪

🍷🍷🍷🍷 **Cloak & Dagger Prosecco 2022, Central Victoria** RATING 92 DRINK 2023–2026 $27 JP ✪

Cloak & Dagger The Dagger Pinot Grigio 2022, North East Victoria RATING 92 DRINK 2022–2025 $28 JP ✪

Pacha Mama Pinot Gris 2022, North East Victoria RATING 92 DRINK 2022–2027 $29 JP ✪

Pacha Mama Grenache 2022, Pyrenees RATING 92 DRINK 2023–2028 $38 CM

Pacha Mama Golden Hour Nouveau Shiraz 2022, Heathcote RATING 91 DRINK 2023–2027 $28 CM ✪

Pacha Mama Shiraz 2020, Heathcote RATING 91 DRINK 2023–2028 $30 CM

Wine x Sam ★★★★☆

69-71 Anzac Avenue, Seymour, Vic 3660 **Region** Central Victoria
T 03 57 990 437 **www.winebysam.com.au** **Open** Fri–Sun 9–4 **Winemaker** Sam Plunkett, Mark Hickin **Est.** 2012 **Dozens** 70000 **Vyds** 8ha

The Plunkett family helped pioneer grape growing in the Strathbogie Ranges, planting the first vines there in 1968. In the mid-2000s, Plunkett Wines went into partnership with the Fowles family and many wine awards and accolades followed. That business arrangement dissolved in '11 and Sam Plunkett and his wife, Bronwyn Dunwoodie, began exploring new opportunities including an opening to make wine at Elgo Estate. Online wine retailer Naked Wines placed its first order and Wine x Sam took off. In addition to their own vineyards, the couple have access to 53ha of Plunkett family vines and source fruit from growers in the Strathbogie Ranges (Booroola), Heathcote (Tait Hamilton) and Central Victoria (Gentle Annie).

🍷🍷🍷🍷🍷 **The Victorian Riesling 2022, Upper Goulburn** Combines zesty freshness, delicious acidity with real weight and developing texture across the mid-palate. A lick of sugar softens the edges. Lemon sherbet, green apple, grapefruit zest and background musk bring the delicacy of cool-climate fruit to the glass. It's hard to decide whether to drink now or later. Why not do both? Screw cap. 11.5% alc. RATING 95 DRINK 2022-2032 $24 JP ✪

🍷🍷🍷🍷🍷 **The Victorian Prosecco 2022, Central Victoria** RATING 92 DRINK 2022-2026 $24 JP ✪
The Victorian Primitivo 2021, Strathbogie Ranges RATING 92 DRINK 2022-2028 $24 JP ✪
Stardust & Muscle Pinot Noir 2021, Alpine Valleys Upper Goulburn RATING 92 DRINK 2022-2028 $32 JP
The Victorian Shiraz 2021, Heathcote RATING 90 DRINK 2022-2026 $24 JP ✪
Stardust & Muscle Chardonnay 2021, Strathbogie Ranges RATING 90 DRINK 2022-2031 $32 JP

Wines by KT ★★★★☆

20 Main North Road, Watervale, SA 5452 **Region** Clare Valley
T 0419 855 500 **www.**winesbykt.com **Open** Thus–Mon 11–4 **Winemaker** Kerri Thompson **Est.** 2006 **Dozens** 4500 **Vyds** 9ha

KT is winemaker Kerri Thompson. Kerri graduated with a degree in oenology from Roseworthy Agricultural College in '93, and thereafter made wine in McLaren Vale, Tuscany, Beaujolais and the Clare Valley, becoming well known as the Leasingham winemaker in the Clare Valley. She resigned from Leasingham in '06 after 8 years at the helm and established Wines by KT, sourcing grapes from Clare Valley growers with a focus on minimal-intervention grapegrowing.

🍷🍷🍷🍷🍷 **Peglidis Vineyard Watervale Riesling 2022, Clare Valley** This is precise and racy, so intense in its piercing zing across the palate. Scents are lime on green apple, fragrant talc, frangipani and grapefruit pith, flavours similar with a rapier-like thrust through the mouth. Brilliant, crystalline expression with so much freshness and vitality on its side. This drinks with vigour and a high-refreshment factor now, but will mellow gracefully over a very, very long time. A top-quality marque. Screw cap. 12% alc. RATING 95 DRINK 2022-2040 $38 MB ✪
Melva Wild Ferment Riesling 2022, Clare Valley A textural feast, chewy and savoury, scents of green apple, gin, alpine herbs and preserved lemon. Flavours are set among the grip and pucker of talc-like texture. It tastes like apple juice shot through tonic water with a strong squeeze of lime. It's flavoursome, fuller than expected and a little breathy with nutty savouriness all working coherently. Screw cap. 12% alc. RATING 94 DRINK 2022-2028 $34 MB ✪

🍷🍷🍷🍷🍷 **5452 Watervale Riesling 2022, Clare Valley** RATING 93 DRINK 2022-2030 $29 MB ✪
Cabernet Franc 2021, Clare Valley RATING 93 DRINK 2022-2028 $34 MB ✪
Tinta 2021, Clare Valley RATING 92 DRINK 2022-2025 $34 MB
Pinot Gris 2022, Clare Valley RATING 91 DRINK 2023-2028 $34 MB

Wines of Merritt

PO Box 1122, Margaret River, WA 6285 **Region** Margaret River
T 0438 284 561 **www**.winesofmerritt.com.au **Open** Not **Winemaker** Nick James-Martin **Est.** 2017 **Dozens** 20

Wines of Merritt is the project of Nick and Sarah James-Martin. Nick grew up in the Riverland, spending his early working life in some of Adelaide's better restaurants, helping his family establish a vineyard in McLaren Vale. Two years working for *WINE Magazine* in London facilitated wine travel through France, Spain, Portugal and Italy. He then studied wine marketing and oenology at the University of Adelaide and worked at Rosemount, Vasse Felix and Stella Bella, plus overseas vintages in Hawke's Bay, NZ, and Languedoc, France. Sarah is a hospitality professional; prior to moving to Margaret River she ran the acclaimed Salopian Inn in McLaren Vale and worked for other wineries in the region. Merritt is the family name of Nick's great-grandparents.

ΨΨΨΨΨ **Single Vineyard Small Batch Chenin Blanc 2021, Margaret River** Such a classy wine with flavours of lemon verbena and lemon barley water spiced with ginger powder and lime zest, crunchy pears and quince, too. It's refreshing thanks to its lemon sorbet-like acidity, yet there's texture with some nutty, creamy lees influence and a distinct wet stone note. It's tight, refined and dry, which I love. Screw cap. 12.3% alc. **RATING** 95 **DRINK** 2022–2027 $40 JF ✪
Single Vineyard Small Batch Cabernet Sauvignon 2021, Margaret River Give this time to unfurl as it's a terrific drink when allowed to do so. It then reveals requisite regional characters of mulberries, warm earth with wafts of menthol and dried spices. It comes across as medium bodied with supple, ripe tannins, licorice, new leather and some pomegranate tartness to the acidity that keeps this lively and refreshing. Screw cap. 13.4% alc. **RATING** 94 **DRINK** 2022–2035 $40 JF ✪

ΨΨΨΨΨ **Rosé 2021, Margaret River RATING** 92 **DRINK** 2022–2023 $28 JF ✪
Blanc 2021, Margaret River RATING 91 **DRINK** 2022–2025 $28 JF ✪
Single Vineyard Small Batch Syrah 2021, Margaret River RATING 90 **DRINK** 2022–2028 $40 JF

Winmark Wines

229 Wollombi Rd, Broke NSW 2330 **Region** Hunter Valley
T 02 9997 5373 **www**.winmarkwines.com.au **Open** 7 days 10–5 **Winemaker** Xanthe Hatcher, John Belsham (consultant) **Viticulturist** Liz Riley **Est.** 2016 **Dozens** 3100 **Vyds** 11ha

Karin Adcock is a Danish-born and -educated entrepreneur with the gift of making the difficult seem easy. Scandinavian design of things large or small, utilitarian or simply decorative gave her a head start in Australia. In '16 she purchased what was then Poole's Rock, assembling teams of experts to rejuvenate the 11ha vineyard and embark on a long-term program for the whole property. The property has expanded since and is complemented by artworks, antiques and artefacts, notably sculptures, collected by Adcock from around the world. Buildings on the property have also been converted into residences large and small for tourists who stay overnight. Needless to say, Winmark's wine is part and parcel of the business. Consultant John Belsham, a New Zealander, has an impeccable track record of 35 years of experience with a focus on chardonnay and dealing with the uncertainties of working in a climate that can change for the worse in a matter of hours.

ΨΨΨΨΨ **7 2 Chardonnay 2021, Hunter Valley** From the oldest vines on the estate vineyard. By some distance the best of the 4 Winmark chardonnays tasted, reflecting the guiding hand of consultant John Belsham. Screw cap. 13% alc. **RATING** 96 **DRINK** 2023–2031 $89 JH
Single Vineyard Reserve Chardonnay 2021, Hunter Valley Pressed to French oak for fermentation and 11 months' maturation with extended lees contact. As with all the Winmark wines, there is attention to detail: here, and with its sibling 7 2 Chardonnay 2021, oak does play a significant role, joining

the white peach and cashew on the long palate. Screw cap. 13% alc. RATING 95
DRINK 2023–2029 $55 JH

♥♥♥♥♀ Chardonnay 2021, Hunter Valley RATING 92 DRINK 2023–2027 $37 JH
Rusty's Run Chardonnay 2022, Hunter Valley RATING 91 DRINK 2023–2028
$32 JH

Wirra Wirra Vineyards ★★★★★

255 Strout Road, McLaren Vale, SA 5171 **Region** McLaren Vale
T (08) 8323 8414 **www**.wirrawirra.com **Open** Mon–Sat 10–5, Sun & public hols 11–5
Winemaker Emma Wood, Tom Ravech, Kelly Wellington, Grace Wang **Viticulturist**
Anton Groffen **Est.** 1894 **Dozens** 140 000 **Vyds** 21.5ha
Wirra Wirra has established a formidable reputation. The wines are of exemplary character,
quality and style; The Angelus Cabernet Sauvignon and RSW Shiraz battling each other for
supremacy, with The Absconder Grenache one to watch. Long may the battle continue under
managing director Matthew Deller MW and the winemaking team who forge along the path
of excellence first trod by the late (and much loved) Greg Trott, the pioneering founder of
modern-day Wirra Wirra. Its acquisition of Ashton Hills in '15 added a major string to its
top-quality bow; the estate vineyards are certified organic.

♥♥♥♥♥ The Absconder Grenache 2021, McLaren Vale The highest-quality
grapes are basket pressed, hand plunged and open fermented before 10 months'
maturation in French oak. The perfumed and spicy bouquet is foreplay for one of
McLaren Vale's greatest grenaches, the vintage giving fruit of stunning purity. The
flavours take in contributions of red cherry, raspberry, spice and florals. Screw cap.
14.5% alc. RATING 97 DRINK 2023–2035 $70 JH ✪

♥♥♥♥♥ Catapult Shiraz 2021, McLaren Vale The vignerons of McLaren Vale were
wildly ecstatic about the '21 vintage, and finding this wine at this price explains
their joy. It's the essence of McLaren Vale shiraz: medium- to full-bodied, laden
with black fruits of all kinds, dark chocolate, licorice and savoury, ripe tannins.
Screw cap. 14.5% alc. RATING 95 DRINK 2023–2041 $26 JH ✪
Chook Block Shiraz 2020, McLaren Vale A polished and immensely powerful
wine. Dark fruits, spice of all types, violet and molten rock is sheathed in
salubrious oak drawn tight by a belt of reductive tension. The finish is as long as
it is attractively salty, as if tapenade has been swooshed over the tongue by the last
bite of tannin. Screw cap. 14.5% alc. RATING 95 DRINK 2023–2038 $150 NG
Woodhenge Basket-Pressed Shiraz 2020, McLaren Vale Matured in a
mix of French and American barriques and hogsheads (40% new) for 18 months.
A full-bodied, dense shiraz with endless layers of black fruits, tannins and oak. If
you want a wine to save for your grandchildren, this should do nicely. Screw cap.
14.5% alc. RATING 95 DRINK 2025–2050 $40 JH ✪
RSW Shiraz 2020, McLaren Vale A big wine with a corset of reductive
restraint, imparting lilac, tapenade and furikake to a swirl of blue- and black-
fruit allusions. This is a winery on the larger side, coming to the contemporary
table and doing it very well. Tension and generosity in equal measure. Screw cap.
14.5% alc. RATING 94 DRINK 2022–2035 $70 NG
The Holy Thirst Cabernet Sauvignon Shiraz 2019, McLaren Vale This is
a slick, full-weighted wine. Heavily worked. Lots of oak, conferring accents of
coffee grind, Brylcreem and mocha. Sweet fruit emerges from the seams, tasting
like raspberry bonbon and coconut. A strap of licorice-crusted tannins a welcome
restraining device to the hedonism. Bolshy length. I'm sure that this will age well.
Screw cap. 14% alc. RATING 94 DRINK 2022–2038 $125 NG

♥♥♥♥♀ The Angelus Cabernet Sauvignon 2020, McLaren Vale RATING 93
DRINK 2022–2035 $70 NG
Amator Nouveau 2022, McLaren Vale RATING 92 DRINK 2022–2024 $35 NG
Single Vineyard Organic Tempranillo 2021, McLaren Vale RATING 92
DRINK 2022–2026 $35 NG

Amator Biodynamic Vineyards Tempranillo Touriga 2021, McLaren Vale
RATING 92 DRINK 2022–2030 $35 NG
MVCG Cabernet Sauvignon 2021, McLaren Vale RATING 91
DRINK 2022–2027 $26 NG ✪
Church Block Cabernet Sauvignon Shiraz Merlot 2021, McLaren Vale
RATING 90 DRINK 2022–2028 $25 NG ✪

Wise Wine   ★★★★★

237 Eagle Bay Road, Eagle Bay, WA 6281 **Region** Margaret River
T (08) 9755 3331 **www**.wisewine.com.au **Open** 7 days 10–5 **Winemaker** Andrew Siddell,
Matt Buchan, Larry Cherubino (Consultant) **Est.** 1986 **Dozens** 10000 **Vyds** 2.5ha
Wise Wine, headed by Perth entrepreneur Ron Wise, has been a remarkably consistent
producer of high-quality wine. The vineyard adjacent to the winery (2ha of cabernet
sauvignon and shiraz, and 0.5ha of zinfandel) in the Margaret River is supplemented by
contract-grown grapes from Margaret River, Pemberton, Manjimup and Frankland River.
The value for money of many of the wines is extraordinarily good.

ΨΨΨΨΨ Leaf Cabernet Sauvignon 2021, Margaret River An elegant style that
doesn't forfeit flavour or depth to get there. Expect cassis, mulberries, lots of
herbs, black olive and cedary oak infusing the more mid-weighted palate. Fine
tannins match the acidity to lengthen the finish. Screw cap. 14.2% alc. RATING 95
DRINK 2024–2037 $45 JF ✪

ΨΨΨΨΨ Eagle Bay Barrel Select Chardonnay 2022, Margaret River RATING 93
DRINK 2024–2032 $65 JF
Eagle Bay Barrel Select Cabernet Sauvignon 2021, Margaret River
RATING 92 DRINK 2025–2038 $75 JF
Leaf Reserve Chardonnay 2022, Margaret River RATING 90
DRINK 2023–2027 $35 JF
Leaf Fumé Blanc 2022, Margaret River RATING 90 DRINK 2023–2027 $35 JF

Witches Falls Winery   ★★★★

79 Main Western Road, Tamborine Mountain, Qld 4272 **Region** Queensland
T (07) 5545 2609 **www**.witchesfalls.com.au **Open** Sun–Fri 10–5, Sat 10–6 by appt
Winemaker Jon Heslop, Allan Windsor, Ren Dalgarno **Est.** 2004 **Dozens** 12000
Vyds 0.6ha
Witches Falls is the venture of Jon and Kim Heslop. Jon has a deep interest in experimenting
with progressive vinification methods in order to achieve exceptional and interesting results.
He has a degree in applied science (oenology) from CSU and experience working in the
Barossa and Hunter valleys, as well as at Domaine Chantal Lescure in Burgundy and with a
Napa-based winegrower. Pecorino is sourced from Witches Falls' 0.6ha of estate vines; other
fruit is sourced from growers throughout the Granite Belt and South Australia's Riverland.

ΨΨΨΨΨ Wild Ferment Saperavi 2021, Riverland A rambunctious and lavish red. It's
all forest berries, salted plum, raspberry licorice and ferrous, savoury elements
rolled into one. Lots of bright, ripe fruit perfume with dashes of minty herbs
and earthy spice. The palate a plush flow of lush fruit and spice with a faint saline
undertow and licks of sage. A fine smudge of gummy tannin to close, works a
treat. Screw cap. 14.6% alc. RATING 92 DRINK 2022–2027 $40 MB
Wild Ferment Chardonnay 2021, Granite Belt It's a sunny, golden
expression of chardonnay. Honey toast, ripe apple, peach and cream all jostling
in the big fog of perfume. The palate shows more tension than expected, green
apple, sweet peach, vanilla, faint toasty notes and chalky, minerally characters
found harmoniously and seamlessly woven. Full flavoured, generous but well
balanced, is the deal. Very pleasing indeed. Screw cap. 13% alc. RATING 92
DRINK 2022–2030 $38 MB
Wild Ferment Aglianico 2021, Riverland Slurpable and joyful red with
appropriate crunch of acidity, red fruit spectrum scents and flavours, peppery

spice, light, alpine herb and licorice elements. It's vibrant and tight, lifted and very energetic. It does aglianico well, offering a vibrant, lighter red wine. Screw cap. 13% alc. **RATING** 91 **DRINK** 2022–2027 $40 MB

Wild Ferment Negroamaro 2021, Riverland A lush, slurpy number. Dark cherry, chamomile herbal notes, cranberry tang and green olive characters between the bouquet and the palate. There's lots of character here, supple texture with a tickle of blood orange tang to the acidity and a fine grip and pucker to finish. Utter charmer. Easy to drink, refreshing red and probably better with a chill, too. Screw cap. 13.9% alc. **RATING** 91 **DRINK** 2022–2025 $40 MB

Wolf Blass ★★★★★

97 Sturt Highway, Nuriootpa, SA 5355 **Region** Barossa Valley
T (08) 8568 7311 **www**.wolfblass.com **Open** Wed–Mon 10–4.30 **Winemaker** Chris Hatcher, Steven Frost **Est.** 1966
German winemaker Wolf Blass moved to the Barossa Valley in 1961, establishing Wolf Blass Wines 5 years later. Today, Wolf Blass wines are made at all pricepoints, ranging through Red, Yellow, Gold, Brown, Grey, Black, White and Platinum labels covering every one of the main varietals, sourced from regions around South Australia. The style and range of the wines continue to subtly evolve under the leadership of chief winemaker Chris Hatcher, who has led the winemaking team (first as senior winemaker, then as chief winemaker) since '87.

ŸŸŸŸŸ **Platinum Label Shiraz 2019, Barossa Valley** Plush dollops of dark plum, blackberry and blueberry sit in medium-bodied territory on an underlayer of fine spice, dark chocolate, faint espresso and fresh-cut fennel notes. It's opulent yet graceful, sashaying across the palate with an air of elegance, a background of fine-grained tannin and a plume of fragrant oak spice enveloping the pristine fruit as the wine fades slowly. Will cellar beautifully. Screw cap. 14.5% alc. **RATING** 97 **DRINK** 2023–2042 $200 DB

Platinum Label Medlands Vineyard Shiraz 2019, Barossa Valley The concentration of flavour is significant here but it's the tannin structure and length that really get the heart racing. A bold, fantastic red wine. Sweet but fresh plums, fistfuls of earth and roasted spice, smoked cedar and peppercorns, with deli meat characters about the edges. Tannin here is a rolling river, churning and turning the wine in spirals through the finish. In the end, the flavour sings on and on, as it only does in the best of wines. Screw cap. 14.5% alc. **RATING** 97 **DRINK** 2026–2050 $200 CM

ŸŸŸŸŸ **Black Label Cabernet Shiraz Malbec 2019, Barossa Valley McLaren Vale Adelaide Hills** This is a beefy release with caramel, toast, scorched plum and dark earth flavours rumbling through the palate. The alcohol feels warm and the oak appears overt, but the fruit is intense and the finish is satisfying. Screw cap. 14.5% alc. **RATING** 95 **DRINK** 2026–2042 $130 CM

Grey Label Chardonnay 2021, Adelaide Hills Some wines make complexity looks effortless, and this is one of them. Flint, nougat, white peach and grilled nectarine characters put on an entirely convincing display, its quality franked in full by the length of the finish. Lovely wine. Screw cap. 12.5% alc. **RATING** 94 **DRINK** 2023–2029 $35 CM ✪

ŸŸŸŸŸ **Gold Label Chardonnay 2021, Adelaide Hills** **RATING** 93 **DRINK** 2023–2027 $16 CM ✪

Grey Label Cabernet Shiraz 2020, Langhorne Creek **RATING** 93 **DRINK** 2025–2035 $45 CM

Wood Park ★★★★☆

17 Milawa-Bobinawarrah Rd, Milawa, Vic 3678 **Region** King Valley
T (03) 5727 3778 **www**.woodparkwines.com.au **Open** 7 days 10–5 **Winemaker** John Stokes **Viticulturist** John Stokes **Est.** 1989 **Dozens** 12 000 **Vyds** 16ha

With a background in environmental science, John Stokes planted his first vines at Wood Park in '89 in the back paddocks of his grazing property at Bobinawarrah in the hills of the Lower King Valley, east of Milawa. The surrounding hill country has been excluded from grazing since the time of the first vine plantings. Natural regeneration, additional native plantings and 3 large dams have enhanced biodiversity. The vineyard is managed with minimal chemical use. Wood Park also sources fruit from sites in the King and Alpine Valleys, ranging from 250–800m elevation. The mix of mainstream and alternative varieties includes tempranillo, sangiovese and roussanne.

ㅇㅇㅇㅇㅇ **Premium Reserve Late Harvest Botrytis Viognier 2022, King Valley** Originally written off as unsalvageable following a severe storm, the onset of botrytis in the Wood Park viognier vines gave rise to this rare botrytised wine. Golden in hue and apricot and honey-rich in scent, it is on the palate where this excels. Excellent depth of flavour intensity and, importantly, bright, clean balancing acidity. Probably a one-off, but hopefully not. 375ml. Screw cap. 9% alc. **RATING** 93 **DRINK** 2023–2026 $38 JP

The Tuscan 2021, King Valley Cabernet sauvignon/shiraz/sangiovese/petit verdot/colorino. Delivers an evocative Italian-inspired flavour generous in wild herbs, black fruits, cherry, a little fennel seed and anise, all framed in supple, dry tannins. Takes you directly to the Italian countryside. Fab balance across the board. Screw cap. 13.5% alc. **RATING** 93 **DRINK** 2023–2028 $30 JP ✪

Chardonnay 2021, King Valley A complex chardonnay, as always from this maker. Scents of stone fruits, savoury grilled cashews, shortbread, honey and preserved lemon. Walks a fine tightrope on the palate, eliciting generosity, creaminess of texture and complexity without overstepping into blowsiness. Brings a touch of style and grace, not to mention a lasting, lingering finish to King Valley chardonnay. Screw cap. 13.5% alc. **RATING** 93 **DRINK** 2023–2031 $33 JP ✪

Pinot Noir Rosé 2022, King Valley Irresistibly pinot noir in expression, from the lively macerated cherry, raspberry, blood orange and rosehip scents to the gently dusty summer berries and talc-like palate texture. Light as a feather and so drinkable, this pale blush rosé is, to borrow a modern wine term, totally 'smashable'. Screw cap. 12.8% alc. **RATING** 92 **DRINK** 2022–2025 $27 JP ✪

Whitlands Pinot Gris 2022, King Valley Grown at 800m elevation at Whitlands and boasting a fineness of acidity, this gris shows plenty of cool-climate class. Delicate in fragrance and juicy in fruit style with just-cut apple, citrus, pear skin, white peach and a warm texture, this gris is right at home in its alpine surroundings. A touch of spice to close is a lasting memory. Screw cap. 13% alc. **RATING** 92 **DRINK** 2022–2027 $27 JP ✪

Chardonnay 2021, King Valley No shortage of flavour or texture here. Layers of white peach, nectarine, citrus, almond meal and cashews. The fragrance alone seals the deal. The palate doesn't disappoint with a notable emergence of charry, vanillin oak and complex lees-derived mealiness. Complex and tasty now, but this has time on its hands. Screw cap. 13.5% alc. **RATING** 92 **DRINK** 2022–2030 $33 JP

Reserve Tempranillo 2012, King Valley This 11yo tempranillo is a good example of the ageing ability of Wood Park's reds. It remains alive and kicking with good fruit and spice with a touch of savouriness to add interest. The deep garnet colour remains youthful and bright. Boasts complex dark berry and plum, earth, sweet leather and blackstrap licorice flavours, aided by rich, velvet-like tannins. Cork. 13.6% alc. **RATING** 91 **DRINK** 2023–2025 $65 JP

Monument Lane Roussanne 2021, King Valley A busy, intriguing white wine, each sniff bringing a new sensory discovery. Complex scents aplenty from spiced apple, quince paste and beeswax to Meyer lemon and honeysuckle. Flavours are generous, texture is warm and everything is held nicely together by a refreshing acidity. Made for early enjoyment. Screw cap. 13.5% alc. **RATING** 90 **DRINK** 2022–2025 $29 JP

Forgotten Patch Sangiovese 2021, King Valley A young sangiovese that keeps on giving, so much so, it was even better the day after opening. Shows the grape's fruit-led, relaxed side plush in black cherry fruit, dried herbs, anise and dusty earthy notes. The palate has a juicy, lithe appeal. Medium weight and fine in tannin, it rolls easily to a smooth, flavoursome finish. Screw cap. 14% alc. **RATING** 90 **DRINK** 2022-2025 $28 JP

Woodhaven Vineyard

87 Main Creek Road, Red Hill, Vic 3937 **Region** Mornington Peninsula **T** 0421 612 178 **www**.woodhavenvineyard.com.au **Open** By appt **Winemaker** Lee Ward, Neil Ward **Est.** 2003 **Dozens** 250 **Vyds** 1.6ha

Woodhaven is the tree-change venture of Lee and Neil Ward, both qualified accountants for 30 years in Melbourne. They spent 2 years looking for a suitable site on the Mornington Peninsula, ultimately finding one high on Red Hill. Bringing the venture to the point of production was a slow and, at times, frustrating business. They decided to be personally responsible for all aspects of grapegrowing and winemaking, relying on the advice readily given to them by their contemporaries at Paradigm Hill, Eldridge Estate, Myrtaceae and Main Ridge. They also decided to grow the vines biodynamically; it took 8 years to produce their first 2 barrels of wine in '10. In '13 the 0.8ha each of pinot noir and chardonnay finally produced more than 1 barrel of each wine.

Chardonnay 2021, Mornington Peninsula Woodhaven chardonnay is usually on the richer side. However, this vintage, the acidity is more pronounced and the wine's all the better for it. More citrus than stone fruit with cedary spices and some malty edges. Tangy and refreshing, lively acidity keeping everything upbeat and in place. Screw cap. 13.4% alc. **RATING** 92 **DRINK** 2022-2029 $45 JF

Pinot Noir 2020, Mornington Peninsula The colour is advanced, which is not great for a young wine, but the flavours appeal. There's a savoury edge throughout, a mix of twigs, warm earth to chinotto, sarsaparilla and bitter herbs. Hints of rhubarb and stewed cherries, a sappiness all working off a lighter framed palate. A little astringent, tangy and refreshing. Drink up. Screw cap. 13.5% alc. **RATING** 90 **DRINK** 2022-2025 $50 JF

Woodlands

3948 Caves Road, Wilyabrup, WA 6280 **Region** Margaret River **T** (08) 9755 6226 **www**.woodlandswines.com **Open** 7 days 10–5 **Winemaker** Stuart Watson **Viticulturist** Jaden McLean **Est.** 1973 **Dozens** 15 000 **Vyds** 27ha

Founders David Watson and wife Heather had spectacular success with the cabernets he made in '79 and the early '80s. Commuting from Perth while raising a family became too much and for some years the grapes from Woodlands were sold to other Margaret River producers. With the advent of sons Stuart and Andrew in '02–05 (Stuart primarily responsible for winemaking), the estate bounced back to preeminence, expanding with the purchase of the 17ha Woodlands Brook vineyard in '07. The top-end wines primarily come from the original Woodlands vineyard, where the now-certified organic vines are 50+ years old.

Ruby Jane Cabernet Sauvignon 2019, Margaret River How these Woodlands wines pack in so much flavour and concentration without feeling heavy or overwrought is astonishing. Full bodied, yes, but it's all about the layering of flavour with lavish tannins. The flavours build, intensity too, all reaching lofty heights. But this wine is far from its best – that will come in time. Worth the wait, but I do understand the urge to open one today. Screw cap. 13.5% alc. **RATING** 97 **DRINK** 2024-2049 $179 JF

Margaret 2019, Margaret River 81/11/8% cabernet sauvignon/merlot/ malbec. It's a tiptop combination as this is balanced, defined and distinct. Expect mulberries, cassis, new leather, sumac and cedary oak with baking spices on the bouquet and fuller-bodied palate. The tannins are exquisite, ripe, velvety and textural. With the exceptionally long finish, this is another wonderful, elegant Margaret. Screw cap. 13.5% alc. **RATING** 96 **DRINK** 2023-2043 $70 JF ✪

Emily Woodland Brook Vineyard 2021, Margaret River Cabernet franc and merlot are the driving force of Emily, a supple and approachable wine. The tannins are rather fine yet expand across the medium-bodied palate where a cascade of dark fruits, spice, warm earth and florals have left a mark. Don't hold back. Screw cap. 13.5% alc. **RATING** 95 **DRINK** 2024–2038 $70 JF

Clémentine Woodlands Brook Vineyard 2020, Margaret River 66/20/8/6% cabernet sauvignon/merlot/malbec/petit verdot. Complete and harmonious. The upfront fruit flavours, mainly cassis and mulberries, are tempered by lots of savoury inputs – the nutty, cedary oak, the waft of menthol, baking spices and an earthy fragrance, even a freshly whittled pencil, remember that? Medium bodied with densely packed tannins and textural if not a little raspy. Very good. Screw cap. 13.5% alc. **RATING** 95 **DRINK** 2024–2038 $49 JF ✪

Woodlands Brook Vineyard Chardonnay 2022, Margaret River For fans of richer styles of chardonnay, this one's for the taking. The plump palate is full of stone fruit, citrus and honeydew with plenty of ginger-spiced cream and nougatine. Very rich with cedary oak adding sweet spices and some phenolic grip. Screw cap. 13% alc. **RATING** 94 **DRINK** 2023–2030 $55 JF

🍷🍷🍷🍷♀ **Wilyabrup Valley Chardonnay 2022, Margaret River RATING** 93 **DRINK** 2023–2031 $38 JF

Wilyabrup Valley Cabernet Sauvignon Merlot 2020, Margaret River RATING 91 **DRINK** 2024–2036 $35 JF

Woods Crampton   ★★★★

PO Box 417, Hamilton, NSW 2303 **Region** Various
T 0417 670 655 **www**.woods-crampton.com.au **Open** Not **Winemaker** Nicholas Crampton, Aaron Woods **Est.** 2010 **Dozens** 11 000
This is one of the most impressive ventures of Nicholas Crampton (his association with McWilliam's is on a consultancy basis) and winemaking friend Aaron Woods. The 2 make the wines at the Sons of Eden winery with advice from Igor Kucic. The quality of the wines and the enticing prices have seen production soar from 1500 to 11 000 dozen, with every expectation of continued success.

🍷🍷🍷🍷🍷 **Mengler Hill Old Vine Shiraz 2021, Barossa Valley** Juicy plum, mulberry and blueberries cut through with fine spice, licorice, purple flowers, roasting meats, blueberry pastries and earth. Slinky and pure in the mouth with superfine tannins and a sprightly, super-pure mouthfeel. Tremendous value here! Screw cap. 14.5% alc. **RATING** 94 **DRINK** 2023–2029 $25 DB ✪

🍷🍷🍷🍷♀ **Light Pass Single Vineyard Shiraz 2021, Barossa Valley RATING** 92 **DRINK** 2023–2028 $25 DB ✪

Five Horses Shiraz 2021, Barossa Valley RATING 92 **DRINK** 2023–2027 $25 DB ✪

Woodvale   ★★★★

PO Box 54, Watervale, SA 5453 **Region** Clare Valley
T 0417 829 204 **www**.woodvalevintners.com.au **Open** Not **Winemaker** Kevin Mitchell **Est.** 2014 **Dozens** 3000 **Vyds** 2.8ha
Woodvale is the personal venture of Kilikanoon founder and winemaker Kevin Mitchell and his wife Kathleen Bourne. Their aim is what Kevin describes as 'modest, sustainable growth, working with the varieties that Clare does so well: riesling, shiraz, cabernet sauvignon, mataro, semillon, pinot gris, and of course, grenache'. Fruit is sourced from their own 2.8ha vineyard as well as from trusted growers in Clare Valley.

🍷🍷🍷🍷♀ **Watervale Riesling 2022, Clare Valley** Good drop this. Limey, lemony, lots of green apple crunch and a sizzle of lemongrass and ginger. Very tightly wound, acid-driven and mouth-watering. A load of floral and citrusy perfume, too. Intense and yet very refreshing. A compact, racy expression of the region's halo-white variety. Screw cap. 12.5% alc. **RATING** 93 **DRINK** 2022–2030 $27 MB ✪

Great Northern Semillon 2021, Clare Valley A textural white just shy of medium weight. Quite green in its fruit profile, scents of white pepper, cucumber, snow pea and lemon. The flavour profile lands on lemony things, more cucumber and a light, mezcal-like smoky/green element. Pleasing and refreshing though, good fleshy and yet chewy texture too. Smart wine. Screw cap. 12.5% alc. RATING 93 DRINK 2022-2030 $30 MB ✪

🍷🍷🍷🍷 **M.C.D. Grenache 2021, Clare Valley** RATING 89 DRINK 2022-2028 $30 MB

Woody Nook

506 Metricup Road, Wilyabrup, WA 6280 **Region** Margaret River
T (08) 9755 7547 **www**.woodynook.com.au **Open** 7 days 10–4.30 **Winemaker** Digby Leddin, Courtney Dunkerton **Viticulturist** Digby Leddin **Est.** 1982 **Dozens** 8000 **Vyds** 17ha

Woody Nook, with a backdrop of 24ha of majestic marri and jarrah forest, may not have the the high profile of the biggest names in Margaret River but it has had major success in wine shows over the years. Founded by Jeff and Wynn Gallagher in '78, with the first vines planted in '82, it was purchased by Peter and Jane Bailey in '00. Their investment was transformative, constructing a new winery, a gallery tasting room for larger groups and an alfresco dining area by the pond. The original vineyard remains, planted to regional stalwarts such as cabernet sauvignon, merlot and chardonnay; further plantings were added in '07, including tempranillo and graciano.

🍷🍷🍷🍷🍷 **Gallagher's Choice Cabernet Sauvignon 2019, Margaret River** This falls in the riper, richer, full-bodied camp of cabernet. There's an emphasis on blackberries and blackcurrants, with leafy freshness and no shortage of baking spices, plus a pleasing cigar box aroma. The firm tannins should melt down in time, and that's what this wine needs. Diam. 14.5% alc. RATING 93 DRINK 2024-2038 $60 JF

Single Vineyard Chardonnay 2021, Margaret River A lot going on, yet good fruit underneath. It's at once racy and tight, still shy from youth with layers of flavour, especially oak, imparting a sweetness of spice with some drying tannins. This should be more amalgamated in another year or so. Screw cap. 13.2% alc. RATING 91 DRINK 2023-2030 $40 JF

Single Vineyard Cabernet Merlot 2020, Margaret River A big, fleshy and ripe style with blackberries, mulberries and currants spiced up to the max. There's a plushness across the full-bodied palate, a certain freshness from the acidity which helps with the drying tannins and alcohol warmth on the finish. Still, there's plenty to like in the first instance. Screw cap. 14.7% alc. RATING 90 DRINK 2023-2033 $40 JF

Wynns Coonawarra Estate

77 Memorial Drive, Coonawarra, SA 5263 **Region** Coonawarra
T (08) 8736 2225 **www**.wynns.com.au **Open** 7 days 10–5 **Winemaker** Sue Hodder, Sarah Pidgeon, Chris Plummer **Viticulturist** Ben Harris **Est.** 1897

Privileged to own the longest-established vineyards in the region, first planted by John Riddoch in 1891, Wynns Coonawarra Estate still resides in the fabled triple-gabled winery that he built on Memorial Drive. Large-scale production has not prevented Wynns (an important part of TWE) from producing excellent wines covering the full price spectrum from the bargain-basement through to the deluxe. Even with steady price increases, Wynns offers extraordinary value for money and its Black Label Cabernet Sauvignon is a mainstay of many Australian cellars. Investments in rejuvenating and replanting key blocks – and skilled winemaking – have resulted in wines of far greater finesse and elegance.

🍷🍷🍷🍷🍷 **Black Label Cabernet Sauvignon 2021, Coonawarra** Such fine-grained tannin, such even-handed fruit, such a lengthy finish. This is a beautiful Black Label cabernet, elegantly medium-bodied, blessed with blackcurrant, forest berry, cool mint and cedar characters, and tempered by tobacco-like leaf notes. This will be a gorgeous drink with a few extra years on it. Screw cap. 13.4% alc. **RATING** 96 **DRINK** 2027-2046 $45 CM ✪

Glengyle Single Vineyard Cabernet Sauvignon 2021, Coonawarra It's not a monumental wine, in size terms, but it's monumentally beautiful. It makes power look easy; it takes quality in its stride. Blackcurrant and redcurrant flavours come infused with the most fragrant and beguiling of tobacco and herb characters, all of which are wrapped in a velvety over-shirt of cedary oak. It's classically styled and long; the sweetness of the fruit, matched to all those savoury herb notes, is really something to be behold, as is the length, as is the intricacy of the tannin. Screw cap. 13.6% alc. **RATING** 96 **DRINK** 2028-2048 $90 CM

John Riddoch Limited Release Cabernet Sauvignon 2020, Coonawarra The combination of both elegance and command here is quite astonishing. It tastes of blackcurrant, redcurrant, bay leaf and dried tobacco, though it's the swagger of (integrated) tannin and the gentle infusion of gravel-like notes that really take it up a gear. This is a wonderful wine. Screw cap. 13.5% alc. **RATING** 96 **DRINK** 2027-2046 $150 CM

Black Label Cabernet Sauvignon 2020, Coonawarra For decades, Wynns has been the backbone of most Australian wine collections thanks to its reliability and incredible cellaring performance. The 2020 vintage lives up to its own history beautifully. It's medium bodied, as most of the best wines are. It rolls evenly through the palate, offering blackcurrant and mint, dark olive and (whispers of) tobacco. There's a cool, alpine herb note, too. Tannin structure and length are both impeccable. Screw cap. 13.9% alc. **RATING** 95 **DRINK** 2026-2040 $45 CM ✪

V&A Lane Cabernet Shiraz 2021, Coonawarra It's classic Coonawarra in that it's red-berried and elegant, but it's also inherently complex thanks to tobacco and general leaf notes. It saves its best for the finish, where it sings both sweetly and dustily, almost as if it's rolling downhill with the wind in its hair. It's lovely. Screw cap. 12.8% alc. **RATING** 94 **DRINK** 2025-2045 $60 CM

Old Vines Shiraz 2021, Coonawarra Also known as Black Label Shiraz. This release is flush with sweet plum and clove flavours, its raspberry and nougat-cedar notes tucked neatly within. It feels simple at first but then you notice the finesse of the tannin, the way it extends as it breathes, and how intricately woven the whole picture seems. Can be enjoyed as a young wine, but its best days are ahead. Screw cap. 13.8% alc. **RATING** 94 **DRINK** 2025-2040 $45 CM

ŶŶŶŶŶ **V&A Lane Shiraz 2021, Coonawarra RATING** 93 **DRINK** 2025-2036 $60 CM
The Siding Cabernet Sauvignon 2021, Coonawarra RATING 92 **DRINK** 2024-2032 $20 CM ✪
Reframed Cabernet Franc Cabernet Sauvignon 2021, Coonawarra RATING 91 **DRINK** 2023-2026 $26 JH ✪
Shiraz 2021, Coonawarra RATING 91 **DRINK** 2023-2031 $20 CM ✪

Xanadu Wines ★★★★★

316 Boodjidup Road, Margaret River, WA 6285 **Region** Margaret River
T (08) 9758 9500 **www**.xanaduwines.com **Open** 7 days 10–5 **Winemaker** Glenn Goodall, Matt Godfrey, Steve Kyme **Viticulturist** Robert Underdown **Est.** 1977 **Dozens** 45 000 **Vyds** 82.8ha

Xanadu Wines was established in '77 by Dr John Lagan and was purchased by the Rathbone family in '05. Together with talented winemaker Glenn Goodall and his team, they have significantly improved the quality of the wines. The vineyard has been revamped via soil profiling, improved drainage, precision viticulture and reduced yields. The quality of the wines made since the acquisition of the Stevens Road vineyard in '08 has been consistently outstanding.

ŶŶŶŶŶ **Stevens Road Chardonnay 2021, Margaret River** Stevens Road doesn't play second fiddle to the Reserve Chardonnay. It's tighter, the acidity is distinctive and it feels finer but equally good. Flavours ebb and flow, one minute lemon and grapefruit the next spice and cream, oak spices, too. It is moreish, savoury and complex. This reminds me of a David Bowie concert. Xanadu chardonnay … we can be heroes, just for one day. Screw cap. 13% alc. RATING 97 DRINK 2023–2033 $90 JF ✪

Reserve Chardonnay 2021, Margaret River One taste and I'm already transported to my happy place. The palate pulses with energy, there's texture via lees, and judicious handling of oak and fruit, of course. The power and beauty of Margaret River fruit and all the refinement and detail that comes with it. The tensile yet fine acidity weaves everything together towards a super-long finish. Screw cap. 13% alc. RATING 97 DRINK 2023–2033 $120 JF ❤

Reserve Cabernet Sauvignon 2020, Margaret River This is complete, exceptional and beguiling. It's heady with mulberries, cassis and damson plum, wakame and squid ink. Medium bodied, plush and velvety across the palate thanks to sublime tannins with an outrageously long finish. This is irresistible. Screw cap. 14% alc. RATING 97 DRINK 2024–2048 $120 JF ❤

♟♟♟♟♟ **Stevens Road Cabernet Sauvignon 2020, Margaret River** 86/14% cabernet sauvignon/malbec. The inkiness of malbec and its dark cherry accents such a lovely foil to cabernet's distinct flavour. This is enticing, partly because of its heady aromatics and varietal flavours à la Margaret River, but especially the tannins. They are fine, shapely and defined. The finish is long and the wine has a bright, long future. Screw cap. 13.5% alc. RATING 96 DRINK 2024–2044 $90 JF

Vinework Syrah Nouveau 2022, Margaret River This is delicious with its cherry pop, Sichuan pepper and heady rose petal aromas. The palate is bright and juicy with just enough tannins shaping the palate, but lively acidity is definitely in the driver's seat. Chill this down, chill out and party on. My fave red wine for summer. Screw cap. 13% alc. RATING 95 DRINK 2022–2023 $30 JF ✪

Vinework Sauvignon Blanc Semillon 2022, Margaret River All in harmony with these 2 grape friends coming together with the right amount of freshness and vibrancy, yet a promise of more complexity in time. White stone fruit and lemongrass with citrus, spice and snow peas. Acidity drives this to a resounding finish. Screw cap. 13% alc. RATING 95 DRINK 2022–2030 $30 JF ✪

Vinework Chardonnay 2021, Margaret River Outrageously good for the price and quality. You'd drink this in a heartbeat given the attention to detail in its making, the moreish quality and a lot more besides. Zesty, flinty, sulphide funk, but not too much, just the right amount to weave complexity around the fruit. Refreshing and energetic but there's also texture and depth from luscious lees. Nice one. Screw cap. 12.5% alc. RATING 95 DRINK 2023–2028 $30 JF ✪

Vinework Cabernet Sauvignon 2020, Margaret River Already turns on the charm with its combo of cassis and mulberries layered with spice, dried herbs and a distinct toasted nori note. It's complete and approachable with all elements woven in smoothly. Medium bodied with fine, lithe tannins (and plenty of them) matched to a vitality and freshness throughout. Excellent for the price. Screw cap. 14% alc. RATING 95 DRINK 2022–2033 $30 JF ✪

Vinework Shiraz 2020, Margaret River Savoury and smoky with some meaty reduction. It's fuller-bodied but not weighty as the core of excellent fruit comes to the fore on the palate so, too, grainy tannins. It's a ripper red, though an extra year or so in bottle will tame the brashness of youth. If you can't wait, decant and enjoy with a chargrilled T-bone. Screw cap. 14% alc. RATING 95 DRINK 2023–2032 $30 JF ✪

Circa 77 Shiraz 2020, Margaret River A stunning deep and bright purple-red hue, matching the fruit within from plums to spiced cherries. There's an inherent brashness of youth, yet also a vibrancy as sandy tannins and crunchy acidity kick in. This deserves its place as arguably the best value shiraz in the region and beyond. Screw cap. 14.5% alc. RATING 95 DRINK 2022–2027 $20 JF ✪

Vinework Viognier 2022, Margaret River Margaret River and viognier, eh? Well, it works here. While there's a richness and depth of flavour, it's not oily or heavy, yes a slippery texture but that's attractive. Stone fruit, apricot kernel, lemon curd and baking spices with the palate moving towards full bodied. There's a zestiness with a little phenolic grip adding more shape. This is very good indeed. Screw cap. 14% alc. RATING 94 DRINK 2023–2027 $30 JF ✪

ఠఠఠఠఠ Vinework Semillon 2022, Margaret River RATING 93 DRINK 2022–2030 $30 JF ✪
Vinework Sauvignon Blanc 2022, Margaret River RATING 93 DRINK 2022–2028 $30 JF ✪
Vinework Chenin Blanc 2022, Margaret River RATING 93 DRINK 2022–2028 $30 JF ✪
Vinework Cabernet Franc 2021, Margaret River RATING 93 DRINK 2023–2028 $30 JF ✪
Vinework Shiraz Graciano 2022, Margaret River RATING 92 DRINK 2022–2024 $30 JF ✪
Vinework Chardonnay 2022, Margaret River RATING 91 DRINK 2023–2030 $30 JF

XO Wine Co ★★★★

13 Wicks Road, Kuitpo, SA 5172 (postal) **Region** Adelaide Hills
T 0402 120 680 **www**.xowineco.com.au **Open** Not **Winemaker** Greg Clack, Kate Horstmann **Est.** 2015 **Dozens** 1800
This is the busman's holiday for winemakers Greg Clack (Chain of Ponds) and Kate Horstmann (Project Wine). Evenings and spare time are devoted to XO, launched in '17 when they converted their shed into a winery. Their raison d'être revolves around small-batch, single-vineyard wines from growers in the Adelaide Hills and McLaren Vale. The initial range of grenache, barbera, chardonnay and gamay has since grown to include riesling, pinot gris and fiano, amongst others. The winemaking minimises wine movements, protecting freshness.

ఠఠఠఠఠ Small Batch Shiraz Grenache 2022, McLaren Vale A delicious and highly original take on crafting grenache, fusing semi-carbonic florals and spike from whole bunches with a landscape of muddled herbs, smoked meats, red fruits and seriously hewn tannins that echo the Rhône. Kerpow! Screw cap. 14.5% alc. RATING 94 DRINK 2022–2026 $32 NG ✪

ఠఠఠఠఠ Single Vineyard Games Night Riesling 2022, Adelaide Hills RATING 93 DRINK 2022–2029 $24 NG ✪
Skin Contact Games Night Pinot Gris 2022, Adelaide Hills RATING 92 DRINK 2022–2024 $24 NG ✪
Single Vineyard Small Batch Barbera 2022, Adelaide Hills RATING 91 DRINK 2022–2024 $32 NG
Small Batch Chardonnay 2022, Adelaide Hills RATING 91 DRINK 2022–2027 $32 NG
Small Batch Syrah 2021, Adelaide Hills RATING 91 DRINK 2022–2026 $28 NG ✪
Single Vineyard Small Batch Pinot Noir 2022, Adelaide Hills RATING 90 DRINK 2023–2028 $32 NG

Yabby Lake Vineyard ★★★★★

86–112 Tuerong Road, Tuerong, Vic 3937 **Region** Mornington Peninsula
T (03) 5974 3729 **www**.yabbylake.com **Open** 7 days 10–4 **Winemaker** Tom Carson, Chris Forge, Luke Lomax **Viticulturist** Thomas Schulz **Est.** 1998 **Dozens** 10 000 **Vyds** 50ha
This high-profile wine business was established in '98 by Robert and Mem Kirby (of Village Roadshow), who had been landowners in the Mornington Peninsula for decades. The vineyard enjoys a north-facing slope, capturing maximum sunshine while also receiving sea breezes. The main focus is on 25ha of pinot noir and 14ha of chardonnay; pinot gris and shiraz are also planted. The arrival of the hugely talented Tom Carson as group winemaker

in '08 added lustre to the winery and its wines, making the first Jimmy Watson Trophy–winning pinot noir in '14 and continuing to blitz the Australian wine show circuit with single-block pinot noirs. In Dec '22, Yabby Lake purchased a 12ha property in Tasmania's Coal River Valley, much of it already planted to pinot noir, joining the raft of mainland producers investing in the state.

ŸŸŸŸŸ **Single Block Release Block 2 Pinot Noir 2022, Mornington Peninsula**
To get this much flavour and concentration into a wine without losing any of its line and charm is a skill. Savoury, dark, bitter chocolate infusing the black cherries with toasty, cedary oak and roasted spices. Supple yet powerful with raw silk tannins weaving their way easily across the fuller-bodied palate and acidity leaving no doubt this will garner more complexity in time. Screw cap. 13.5% alc. RATING 97 DRINK 2024–2035 $125 JF

ŸŸŸŸŸ **Single Vineyard Pinot Noir 2022, Mornington Peninsula** Awash with dark cherries, blood orange and zest, Middle Eastern spices and sous bois aromas plus savoury oak. The palate is the clincher: smooth and polished with velvety tannins and fine acidity enticing it all to a long finish. Wow. Screw cap. 13.5% alc. RATING 96 DRINK 2023–2035 $75 JF ○

Single Vineyard Syrah 2022, Mornington Peninsula Concentrated, rich, deep and simply magnificent. Excellent fruit, heady aromas all spiced up, some charcuterie and florals. It works along a more savoury line and the fuller-bodied palate feels glossy and smooth, with precision tannins lightly silty and the invigorating acidity dutifully falling in place: add all that together and it makes for an outstanding wine. Screw cap. 14% alc. RATING 96 DRINK 2024–2035 $40 JF ○

Single Vineyard Chardonnay 2022, Mornington Peninsula Despite the low yields, meaning there are no single-block chardonnays this vintage, there is this exceptional wine. A perfect amalgam of stone fruit and citrus, zest and spice, savoury oak and cedar, mouth-watering acidity and creamy lees. Get it while you can. Screw cap. 13.5% alc. RATING 96 DRINK 2023–2032 $50 JF ○

Single Vineyard Pinot Noir 2021, Mornington Peninsula This has structure, detail and beauty in equal measure. Heady aromatics all florals, spiced cherries with a whiff of cedary/smoky oak. There's intensity but the medium-weighted palate is seductive with powdery tannins and lithe acidity laced throughout. It's also moreish and utterly compelling. Screw cap. 13% alc. RATING 96 DRINK 2022–2034 $70 JF ○

Single Vineyard Chardonnay 2021, Mornington Peninsula A rich and forthcoming wine. Its white peach, almond and cashew mid-palate is balanced and shaped by white grapefruit acidity, oak in play. Screw cap. 13% alc. RATING 96 DRINK 2023–2031 $48 JH ○

Winemaker's Selection Tudibaring Farm Pinot Noir 2021, Mornington Peninsula While there's a depth of flavour and complexity, this has clarity and an ethereal outlook. Laden with spice, cedary/toasty oak – just enough to add a layer of flavour, the fruit is red cherries, and in a way, this seems pretty. Then those tannins hold sway, lovely, silky tannins sashaying across the medium-bodied palate. A lovely wine. Screw cap. 13% alc. RATING 96 DRINK 2022–2033 $60 JF ○

Single Vineyard Pinot Gris 2022, Mornington Peninsula Oh, dear. A vintage representing the lowest yields in Yabby Lake's history, according to Tom Carson. Doubly a shame because this wine is exceptional. It's an exercise in refinement with a light flavouring of spiced baked pears and fresh ones mingling with some creamy lees and lots of texture without being heavy. A slight phenolic pull across the palate adds to the shape as the wine lingers long. Screw cap. 13% alc. RATING 95 DRINK 2022–2027 $36 JF ○ ♥

Winemaker's Selection Barrymore Estate Pinot Noir 2021, Mornington Peninsula Barrymore Estate is next door to Yabby Lake and shows the richness and deep flavour of fruit from this part of the Peninsula, however, there's a refinement. Plump juicy, red cherries with pomegranate and lots of exotic spices yet savoury through and through. It's only medium-bodied with supple tannins

and fine acidity, and you know what? It's rather captivating. Screw cap. 13.5% alc.
RATING 95 DRINK 2022–2033 $60 JF

Red Claw Pinot Noir 2021, Mornington Peninsula The perfumed spicy,
foresty bouquet catches attention, reinforced by the medium-bodied palate where
red cherries/berries have the depth of fruit that others lack. It will build on this
foundation through to the end of the decade. Screw cap. 13.5% alc. RATING 95
DRINK 2023–2029 $35 JH ✪

Single Vineyard Syrah 2021, Mornington Peninsula Highly fragrant with
pepper and exotic spices plus florals. The medium-bodied palate is polished and
while there's a richness of fruit flavour, this is savoury with some charcuterie notes.
The tannins are the texture of raw silk, the acidity enlivening and all leading to a
decisive finish. Screw cap. 14% alc. RATING 95 DRINK 2022–2035 $36 JF ✪

🍷🍷🍷🍷 **Red Claw Pinot Noir 2022, Mornington Peninsula** RATING 93
DRINK 2023–2028 $38 JF

Red Claw Shiraz 2021, Heathcote RATING 93 DRINK 2022–2028 $28 JF ✪

Yal Yal Estate   ★★★★

21 Yal Yal Rd, Merricks, Vic 3916 **Region** Mornington Peninsula
T 0416 112 703 **www**.yalyal.com.au **Open** Fri–Sun 10–5 **Winemaker** Rollo
Crittenden **Est.** 1997 **Dozens** 2500 **Vyds** 7ha
In '08 Liz and Simon Gillies acquired a vineyard in Merricks, planted in '97 to 1.6ha of
chardonnay and a little over 1ha of pinot noir. It has since been expanded to 7ha, devoted
equally to chardonnay and pinot noir. Pinot gris is sourced from other producers on
the Peninsula.

🍷🍷🍷🍷 **Yal Yal Rd Rosé 2022, Mornington Peninsula** A bronze-pale cherry hue with
wafts of red berries and spice. The palate is juicy and refreshing and there's texture
along the way. Screw cap. 13.5% alc. RATING 90 DRINK 2023–2024 $30 JF

Winifred Pinot Noir 2021, Mornington Peninsula There's more volume
with Winifred compared to the estate, with cedary oak bolstering the palate and
tannins. Sweet and sour cherries, barberries doused in sumac and pomegranate
juice. Tight yet bright across the palate with perky acidity in charge, making food
an essential partner. Screw cap. 12.5% alc. RATING 90 DRINK 2023–2028 $55 JF

Yalumba   ★★★★★

40 Eden Valley Road, Angaston, SA 5353 **Region** Eden Valley
T (08) 8561 3200 **www**.yalumba.com **Open** 7 days 10–4 **Winemaker** Louisa
Rose (chief), Kevin Glastonbury, Sam Wigan, Heather Fraser, Will John **Est.** 1849
Dozens 930 000 **Vyds** 180ha
Owned and run by the Hill-Smith family, Yalumba has a long commitment to quality and
great vision in its selection of vineyard sites, new varieties and brands. It has always been a
serious player at the top end of full-bodied Australian reds and was a pioneer in the use of
screw caps. It has a proud history of lateral thinking and rapid decision-making by a small
group led by Robert Hill-Smith. The synergy of the range of brands, varieties and prices is
obvious, but it received added lustre with the creation of The Caley. A founding member of
Australia's First Families of Wine.

🍷🍷🍷🍷🍷 **The Virgilius Viognier 2021, Eden Valley** Pristine stone and citrus fruits,
pitch-perfect textural components and savoury nuance. What is apparent, for
a great year, is the shimmering acidity, precision, detail and clarity; all cranked
up a notch with this release and the wine's energy and drive are spot on.
This is the best Virgilius I have seen thus far. Screw cap. 14% alc. RATING 98
DRINK 2024–2029 $50 DB ✪ ♥

The Caley Cabernet Shiraz 2018, Coonawarra Barossa Valley The Caley
has quickly established itself as a benchmark for the classic cabernet/shiraz blend.
Beautifully poised blackberry and blackcurrant lie sympatico with plum and dark

cherry. Notes of cedar and tobacco with fine spices, gentle herbal tones, dried citrus blossom, pencil case and cinnamon. Picture-perfect fruit depth, powdery mineral framework and harmony in all aspects of its composition. Cork. 14% alc. **RATING** 98 **DRINK** 2023–2053 $365 DB ♥

The Virgilius Viognier 2020, Eden Valley Pale straw in the glass with notes of apricot, lemon, grapefruit and crisp nashi pear with hints of soft spice, marzipan, white flowers and crushed quartz. In the mouth, it weaves its textural magic leaving a slinky wake across the palate, finishing dry and stony with ample acid drive and precision and a lovely sense of savoury composure and elegance. Screw cap. 14% alc. **RATING** 97 **DRINK** 2023–2028 $50 DB ✪

The Octavius Old Vine Shiraz 2018, Barossa Deep crimson with ripe blackberry, black cherry, satsuma plum and blueberry fruits cut with baking spices, vanillin oak, cedar, licorice, dark chocolate, clove and violets. Beautifully weighted and graceful with ripe tannins melting into the wine and a shimmering acidity. This will cellar beautifully, but my goodness it is lovely to drink now. Another epic Octavius release. Cork. 14.5% alc. **RATING** 97 **DRINK** 2023–2038 $150 DB

♟♟♟♟♟ **The Signature Cabernet Sauvignon Shiraz 2019, Barossa** Deep, bright crimson in the glass and densely packed with ripe blackberry, black cherry, plum and cassis fruit notes on a bed of fine spice, licorice, cedar, dark chocolate, vanillin oak and light almond blossom tones. Fine, compact and sandy tannins lending perfect structure to the pure black fruits. Pop some in your glass or the cellar. You choose. Screw cap. 14.5% alc. **RATING** 96 **DRINK** 2023–2038 $65 DB ✪

Vine Vale Grenache 2022, Barossa Valley Fragrant and great drinking with supple red cherry, dark plum and raspberry fruits cut with exotic spice, citrus blossom, Campari-esque tones, cola, gingerbread and earth. Savoury and composed with super-powdery tannins and a spicy, red-fruited exit with just a hint of roasting meats. Geez, grenache is great drinking. Screw cap. 14.5% alc. **RATING** 95 **DRINK** 2023–2033 $40 DB ✪

FDR1A Cabernet Shiraz 2018, Barossa The FDR in this wine's name stands for 'Fine Dry Red'. Eden Valley fruit for this classic cabernet/shiraz blend that shows pristine black fruit characters, layers of spice, licorice, earth and a roasting meat tone. There is a very impressive density to its fruit and the tannins melt into the wine as it rumbles off into the distance, all latent power and opulent fruit. Lovely stuff. Screw cap. 14% alc. **RATING** 95 **DRINK** 2023–2025 $50 DB ✪

The Menzies Cabernet Sauvignon 2018, Coonawarra Another beautiful release. Mint, mulberry and blackcurrant flavours drift with tobacco and forest herbs. It's a cooling cabernet but a ripe one, fluid and refreshing but firm and solid. Needs to be stashed in a cool, dark place for at least a handful of years to start showing its best. Screw cap. 14% alc. **RATING** 95 **DRINK** 2028–2038 $60 CM

The Tri-Centenary Grenache 2021, Barossa Valley A pinot-esque hue and aromas of red plum and cherry fruits on a bed of fine spices along with hints of orange rind, gingerbread, sandalwood, ironstone, purple flowers and light meaty tones. Plenty of detail and meaty nuance on the palate, too, which features a wide, fine tannin flex, bright minerally acid drive and a gentle fan of spiced red fruits. Screw cap. 14% alc. **RATING** 94 **DRINK** 2023–2030 $65 DB

The Cigar Cabernet Sauvignon 2020, Coonawarra One of the plusher expressions of cabernet that you'll encounter. Blackcurrant, black olive, spearmint and sweet, smoky, resiny cedar characters put on a lovely show here. Anise and tobacco notes complete the picture. You can't go wrong. Screw cap. 14% alc. **RATING** 94 **DRINK** 2024–2034 $35 CM ✪

Steeple Vineyard Light Pass 2018, Barossa Valley Deep bright crimson in the glass with plush blood plum, blackberry and black cherry fruit. Excellent fruit depth and concentration with hints of licorice, cedar, violets, olive tapenade, dark chocolate, tobacco, espresso and vanilla bean. Long, pure and supple with tight gypsum-like tannin and a crème de cassis and spice flow on the finish. Diam. 14% alc. **RATING** 94 **DRINK** 2023–2035 $80 DB

ŶŶŶŶ♀ **Syrah 2021, Eden Valley** RATING 92 DRINK 2023–2030 $40 DB
Samuel's Collection Bush Vine Grenache 2021, Barossa RATING 92
DRINK 2023–2028 $28 DB ✪
Samuel's Collection Bush Vine Grenache 2020, Barossa RATING 92
DRINK 2022–2025 $28 DB ✪
Samuel's Collection Roussanne 2020, Eden Valley RATING 92
DRINK 2023–2025 $28 DB ✪
Samuel's Collection Viognier 2021, Eden Valley RATING 91
DRINK 2023–2026 $28 DB ✪
Samuel's Collection Shiraz Cabernet Sauvignon 2019, Barossa
RATING 91 DRINK 2023–2027 $28 DB ✪
Samuel's Collection Roussanne 2021, Eden Valley RATING 90
DRINK 2023–2026 $28 DB
Samuel's Collection Shiraz 2021, Barossa RATING 90 DRINK 2023–2028
$28 DB

Yangarra Estate Vineyard ★★★★★

809 McLaren Flat Road, Kangarilla SA 5171 **Region** McLaren Vale
T (08) 8383 7459 **www**.yangarra.com.au **Open** Mon–Sat 11–5 **Winemaker** Peter
Fraser **Viticulturist** Michael Lane **Est.** 2000 **Dozens** 15 000 **Vyds** 87ha
In 2000, Jackson Family Wines, one of the leading premium wine producers in California,
acquired the then 172ha Eringa Park vineyard, where the oldest vines dated back to 1923.
The renamed Yangarra Estate vineyard has since moved to certified biodynamic status for its
vineyards and is exclusively devoted to varieties of the southern Rhône. Winemaker Peter
Fraser has taken Yangarra Estate to another level altogether with his innovative winemaking
and desire to explore all the possibilities of the Rhône's red and white styles. Yangarra's wines
are regularly judged to be among Australia's finest.

ŶŶŶŶŶ **Old Vine Grenache 2021, McLaren Vale** Grenache of the Year and Wine
of the Year. Score awarded by the Halliday tasting panel at the annual Awards
judging. JH writes: Bright clear though deep crimson hue; scented/perfumed,
and I'm gone for all money without even tasting it. And I haven't fooled myself.
Except why on earth is it only $45? Its red fruit sundae glistens with dew drops on
a spider's web, yet also has a savoury echo towards the finish. Screw cap. 14.5% alc.
RATING 99 DRINK 2023–2041 $45 PD ✪ ♥
GSM 2021, McLaren Vale This is a serious GSM in every way. It's very intense
and complex, but it's also seamless and composed. If this were made in the
Rhône, Robert Parker et al. would be going nuts. As it is, the price here is almost
impossible to understand. Black, red and blue berries with spices from Asia and
South America. Screw cap. 14% alc. RATING 97 DRINK 2023–2046 $35 JH ✪ ♥
Shiraz 2021, McLaren Vale It wasn't entirely a surprise that Yangarra should
have made this gorgeously succulent wine, but I couldn't help but consulting the
thesaurus to be sure 'succulent' covered the field. The entry reads: 'juicy, moist,
luscious, soft, tender, mouth-watering, appetising, flavoursome, tasty, delicious.'
Screw cap. 14% alc. RATING 97 DRINK 2023–2051 $35 JH ✪
Roux Beaute Roussanne 2021, McLaren Vale Picked on a fruit day of
the biodynamic calendar, with a portion crushed to ceramic eggs where it
remained on skins for 121 days, gleaning textural nourishment, complexity and
persuasion. The rest, in an egg sans skins. Among the greatest wines of this
country, irrespective of colour. Rooibos, lanolin, quince, pithy stone fruits and
almond croissant. A powerful, prodigiously textural wine of depth, resonance and
profound belief. Screw cap. 13% alc. RATING 97 DRINK 2023–2035 $68 NG ✪ ♥
High Sands Grenache 2020, McLaren Vale This is a wine of power reined in
by sumptuous tannins. More southern Rhône than Gredos, often the inspiration
in these parts. Darker fruits, clove and assertive tannins … those gorgeous tannins,
trailing the wine to prodigious length. Wow! Screw cap. 14.5% alc. RATING 97
DRINK 2023–2032 $300 NG

𝟀𝟀𝟀𝟀𝟀 **Ovitelli Grenache 2021, McLaren Vale** Among the finest wines in Australia, in my opinion. Blood plum, sappy raspberry, licorice root, bergamot and pepper grind. Clove, tamarind and mint. Gorgeous. Pinosité aplenty, yet beautifully extracted with skittish, long-limbed and gritty tannins corralling the fray. Tear-inducing stuff. Screw cap. 14.5% alc. RATING 96 DRINK 2023–2028 $80 NG

Hickinbotham Clarendon Grenache 2021, McLaren Vale Long, gentle extraction in amphorae gleans long-limbed tannic nourishment and a sense of pixelated freshness. While the buzz is around Blewitt Springs, Clarendon expresses a more ferrous and firm iteration. Pithy. Nobly bitter, if not a little unresolved at the finish. Cherry cola, licorice root, dried thyme, bergamot, raspberry and persimmon. Latent but very fine. Your patience will be appreciated. Screw cap. 14.5% alc. RATING 95 DRINK 2024–2031 $80 NG

Ovitelli Blanc 2021, McLaren Vale Compelling exactitude, richness and uncanny freshness. Overtones of stone fruit, Mirabelle plum and tea tree and a baritone of marzipan, truffle and pine resin. This wine marks the future in these parts, auguring real greatness. Grenache blanc/roussanne. Screw cap. 13.5% alc. RATING 95 DRINK 2022–2030 $68 NG ♥

Ironheart Shiraz 2020, McLaren Vale This is a refined wine boasting a meander of sinewy tannins, like a songline across the palate. It doesn't play any cards not dealt, the inherent freshness derived from organic principles and impeccable fruit quality, glimpsing a southern Rhône-style, despite the variety. Screw cap. 13.5% alc. RATING 95 DRINK 2023–2032 $125 NG

Roussanne 2022, McLaren Vale Often nudging the top cuvées, yet a bit more understated if not a little more effusive of its pithy, gingery stone fruit and rooibos exclamations. As reliant on a chewy rail of phenolics as obvious freshness, this is very good and strongly suggestive of great southern Rhône expressions. Screw cap. 13.5% alc. RATING 94 DRINK 2022–2028 $38 NG ✪

King's Wood Shiraz 2021, McLaren Vale There is a lighter touch to this than in past vintages, although it's still a dense, compact and richly flavoured wine. Pointed northern Rhône-like aromas of blueberry, violet, white pepper, dried nori, black olive and clove. An undercarriage of briar and hedgerow imparts a welcome savouriness. The sinewy tannic mettle suggests this will grow with stature in time. Screw cap. 13.5% alc. RATING 94 DRINK 2023–2032 $68 NG

𝟀𝟀𝟀𝟀𝟀 **Blewitt Springs Shiraz 2021, McLaren Vale** RATING 92 DRINK 2022–2030 $38 NG

Piquepoul 2022, McLaren Vale RATING 91 DRINK 2022–2025 $30 NG

Blanc 2021, McLaren Vale RATING 90 DRINK 2023–2031 $28 JH

Yarra Edge   ★★★★☆

455 Edward Road, Chirnside Park, Vic 3116 (postal) **Region** Yarra Valley
T 0428 301 517 **www.**yarraedge.com.au **Open** Not **Winemaker** Dylan McMahon
Viticulturist Lucas Hoorn **Est.** 1983 **Dozens** 3500 **Vyds** 12.73ha

Yarra Edge was established by the Bingeman family in 1983, advised and guided by John Middleton (of Mount Mary). The advice was, of course, good and Yarra Edge was always able to produce high-quality fruit if the vineyard was properly managed. From '98 the vineyard was leased, receiving minimal care until it was purchased by new owners in '13, who set about restoring it to its full glory. This has been achieved with Lucas Hoorn (formerly of Hoddles Creek Estate) as full-time vineyard manager and Dylan McMahon as contract winemaker, the wines made at Seville Estate. The quality of the wines speaks for itself.

𝟀𝟀𝟀𝟀𝟀 **Edward Single Vineyard Cabernet Sauvignon Cabernet Franc Merlot 2021, Yarra Valley** A deep, bright ruby red. Classic cabernet with its core of cassis, violets and cedar, the oak already sitting discreetly in the background. Just as good on the palate, which is both refined and concentrated with just the right amount of fine-grained, persistent tannins in support. Excellent now, this will continue to develop for years yet. A lovely effort. Screw cap. 13.4% alc. RATING 96 DRINK 2022–2032 $49 PR ✪

Premium Single Vineyard Chardonnay 2021, Yarra Valley A bright green gold. Aromas of stone fruits, spice and a gentle nuttiness can be found in this layered and nicely balanced wine. Silky textured and structured, I like the way this lingers on the finish. Screw cap. 12.8% alc. RATING 94 DRINK 2022–2026 $59 PR

ŸŸŸŸŸ **Ally Single Vineyard Cabernet Sauvignon Merlot Cabernet Franc Malbec 2021**, Yarra Valley RATING 93 DRINK 2023–2030 $59 PR
Single Vineyard Chardonnay 2021, Yarra Valley RATING 91 DRINK 2023–2027 $45 PR

Yarra Yering   ★★★★★

4 Briarty Road, Gruyere, Vic 3770 **Region** Yarra Valley
T (03) 5964 9267 **www**.yarrayering.com **Open** 7 days 10–5 **Winemaker** Sarah Crowe
Est. 1969 **Dozens** 5000 **Vyds** 40ha

In Sep '08, founder Bailey Carrodus died and in Apr '09 Yarra Yering was on the market. It was Bailey Carrodus's clear wish and expectation that any purchaser would continue to manage the vineyard and winery, and hence the wine style, in much the same way as he had done for the previous 40 years. Its acquisition by a small group of investment bankers fulfilled that wish. The low-yielding, unirrigated vineyards have always produced wines of extraordinary depth and intensity. Dry Red No. 1 is a cabernet blend; Dry Red No. 2 is a shiraz blend; Dry Red No. 3 is a blend of touriga nacional, tinta cão, tinta roriz, tinta amarela, alvarelhão and sousão. The Underhill is from a single block of shiraz planted in 1973 (from an adjacent vineyard purchased by Yarra Yering in '87). Sarah Crowe was appointed winemaker after the '13 vintage. She has made red wines of the highest imaginable quality right from the start, transitioning the range to screw caps. For good measure, she also introduced the Light Dry Red Pinot Shiraz in '14, and was named Winemaker of the Year 2017.

ŸŸŸŸŸ **Dry Red Wine No. 1 2021**, Yarra Valley 60/24/11/5% cabernet sauvignon/merlot/malbec/petit verdot, the cabernet from the original 1969-planted vineyard. A deep, bright crimson purple. Bordeaux-like with aromas of cassis, iodine, bay leaf and olive tapenade. The oak is already well integrated. Ripe, chewy tannins course through concentrated fruit, yet the overall impression is one of balance and harmony. A serious and complete cabernet. Screw cap. 13.5% alc. RATING 98 DRINK 2032–2036 $150 PR ✪

Underhill 2021, Yarra Valley A medium–deep and very bright crimson. Lifted and immediately appealing with its aromas of ripe raspberries and violets alongside a cornucopia of spices including cracked black pepper, anise and fennel seeds. A gorgeous medium-weighted, intensely flavoured and long shiraz with enough tannin to suggest patience will be rewarded. Great stuff. Screw cap. 13.5% alc. RATING 98 DRINK 2023–2035 $130 PR ✪ ♥

Carrodus Pinot Noir 2021, Yarra Valley Perfumed and savoury with red and dark fruits and some woodsy, stalk-influenced notes, too. There's an old-vine creaminess on the very well-balanced palate and ripe, persistent and velvety tannins rounding out a wine that can be confidently cellared for at least 10 years. Screw cap. 13.5% alc. RATING 97 DRINK 2022–2035 $275 PR

Pinot Noir 2021, Yarra Valley Sarah Crowe is now making pinots that stand alongside the more celebrated Yarra Yering reds. Perfumed with a bouquet of red fruits, rose petals and mountain herbs. Great depth and flow on the palate. It's deceptive, too, in that as pretty and alluring as this is now, it's also finely structured and tensile. It will be fascinating to see how this matures and unfolds. Screw cap. 13.5% alc. RATING 97 DRINK 2022–2032 $130 PR

Carrodus Cabernet Sauvignon 2021, Yarra Valley So perfumed with its aromas of dark cherry, bay leaf, cedar and some tobacco box. Lovely fruit purity here. Medium bodied with supremely fine cabernet tannins, this is the veritable iron fist in a velvet glove. Today I slightly favour the Dry Red Wine No. 1, but for anyone lucky enough to have a bottle of each 10–15 years from now it should make for a great tasting! Screw cap. 13.5% alc. RATING 97 DRINK 2024–2036 $275 PR

Carrodus Chardonnay 2021, Yarra Valley Only the second release. The Carrodus Chardonnay showing a bit more of everything than the very good Yarra Yering Chardonnay this vintage. More concentrated and structured. Saline and savoury. Real weight and texture but without any excess or heaviness. I love that touch of grip, too, on the long, chalky finish. Excellent. Screw cap. 13% alc. RATING 97 DRINK 2022–2028 $175 PR

Dry Red Wine No. 3 2021, Yarra Valley Other Red/Blend of the Year. A blend of Portuguese varieties has produced this totally gorgeous wine that's hard to put down. Exhibits a riotous array of red and black fruits, wildflowers, dried herbs, licorice root and cocoa nibs. Chewy, well-knit tannins make this wine a total joy to drink now, yet it will still be looking good 5–7 years from now. Screw cap. 13.5% alc. RATING 97 DRINK 2022–2030 $110 PR ♥

🍷🍷🍷🍷🍷 **Light Dry Red Pinot Shiraz 2022, Yarra Valley** Here you'll find dark fruits, floral notes, lifted spices and mountain herbs. There's terrific intensity and freshness, too, before finishing with firm yet fine tannins and bright acidity. It will be hard to keep your hands off this one. Those that do, however, will be well rewarded! Screw cap. 13.5% alc. RATING 96 DRINK 2023–2033 $95 PR

Agincourt Cabernet Malbec 2021, Yarra Valley A brilliant crimson purple. Aromas of cassis, blackberries, violets and a gentle whiff of cedar emanate from this beautifully put-together wine. Elegant, medium bodied and with super-supple tannins, Sarah Crowe has crafted an approachable and seductive cabernet. Screw cap. 13.5% alc. RATING 96 DRINK 2024–2032 $110 PR

Dry Red Wine No. 2 2021, Yarra Valley 96/2/1/1% shiraz/viognier/marsanne/mataro. A deep, bright crimson. A rich, ripe mouthful of wine with firm, classic, old-school Yarra Yering tannins. Dark fruits, spices and a gentle waft of cedar. An interesting contrast between this, the Underhill and the Carrodus, the No. 2 red may end up being the most long-lived of this '21 trio. Screw cap. 14% alc. RATING 96 DRINK 2024–2035 $130 PR

Carrodus Shiraz 2021, Yarra Valley Perfumed and inky, with a darker fruit profile than the Dry Red Wine No. 2 and the Underhill. Blueberry and blackberry fruits intermingle with allspice, cinnamon and mace. Compact and tightly wound, this wine has superb depth but patience will be rewarded. Screw cap. 14% alc. RATING 96 DRINK 2024–2035 $275 PR

Chardonnay 2021, Yarra Valley Brightly coloured. Complex with terrific fruit purity in the form of perfectly ripe orchard fruits and with just a hint of matchstick, too. Gentle, slatey and persistent, as good as it is now, this is also a keeper. Screw cap. 13% alc. RATING 96 DRINK 2022–2027 $130 PR

Dry White Wine No. 1 2021, Yarra Valley 75/25% semillon/chardonnay. A very bright green gold. Really bright and fresh on the nose, too, with aromas of lemon verbena, grapefruit pith and orchard fruits. Chalky, dry, long and seamless. In a word, lovely. Screw cap. 12.5% alc. RATING 96 DRINK 2022–2028 $60 PR ✪

New Territories Shiraz Touriga 2021, Yarra Valley A very bright, quite deep crimson. Attractive from the outset with its bouquet of dark fruits, iodine, licorice root and floral nuance. The svelte, medium-bodied palate impresses with its approachability and harmony. A wine in the Yarra Yering line-up that can be enjoyed with minimal cellaring. Screw cap. 13.5% alc. RATING 94 DRINK 2023–2028 $60 PR

🍷🍷🍷🍷🍷 **Sparkling Blanc de Noir 2015, Yarra Valley** RATING 93 DRINK 2022–2027 $60 PR

Yarran Wines

178 Myall Park Road, Yenda, NSW 2681 **Region** Riverina
T (02) 6968 1125 **www.**yarranwines.com.au **Open** Mon–Sat 10–5 **Winemaker** Sam Brewer **Viticulturist** Sam Brewer **Est.** 1998 **Dozens** 20 000 **Vyds** 30ha
Lorraine Brewer (and late husband John) were grape growers for over 30 years, selling the majority of their fruit. Their first vintage under the Yarran label was in '98 and each year a

little more has been made; along the way a winery with a crush capacity of 150t has been built. Son Sam worked for Southcorp and De Bortoli in Australia, and overseas (in the US and China) before returning to the family winery in '09. The estate vineyards have recently been certified organic.

A Few Words Whole Bunch Shiraz 2020, Heathcote Elevated notes of exotic purple florals, condensed blackcurrant and mulberry jam. Black olives intermingle with dark chocolate and coconut shavings. The palate is less confected, with savoury tones of roasted coffee beans and pleasantly taut acidity. An amaro-like finish will leave you reaching for more. Screw cap. 14.5% alc. **RATING** 93 **DRINK** 2022-2032 $32 SW ✪

Sauvignon Blanc 2022, Riverina An almost water-white hue with golden flecks, this '22 sauvignon blanc creeps out of the glass with subtle pineapple, custard apple, lime skin and coconut water notes. A tropical side reveals itself on the palate with mango and kiwi fruit. A richly concentrated wine with a bright lick of acidity. No herbaceous element here, just great density of fruit and freshness. Screw cap. 12.5% alc. **RATING** 90 **DRINK** 2022-2030 $16 SW ✪

A Few Words Pale Dry Rosé 2022, Riverina A dried rose-petal pink with aromas of dried Japanese plums, watermelon rind and wild strawberries. Dry and totally savoury on the palate with moderate but lingering acidity and a touch of grip, this is a crowd-pleasing wine. Screw cap. 12.5% alc. **RATING** 90 **DRINK** 2022-2025 $20 SW ✪

Pinot Grigio 2022, Riverina A delicate take on the softer style of pinot grigio. White native florals meet pear flesh and Golden Delicious apple skin. The palate is yielding and juicy, with a yearning for everyday drinking. Clean and fragrant, this is suitably priced and begs to be bought by the dozen. Screw cap. 12% alc. **RATING** 90 **DRINK** 2022-2030 $16 SW ✪

Yarrh Wines   ★★★☆

440 Greenwood Road, Murrumbateman, NSW 2582 **Region** Canberra District **T** (02) 6227 1474 **www.yarrhwines.com.au** **Open** Fri–Sun 11–5 **Winemaker** Fiona Wholohan **Viticulturist** Neil McGregor **Est.** 1997 **Dozens** 2000 **Vyds** 6ha
Fiona Wholohan and Neil McGregor are IT refugees; both now work full-time running the Yarrh Wines vineyard and making the wines. They spent 5 years moving to a hybrid organic vineyard with composting, mulching, biological controls and careful vineyard floor management. The vineyard includes cabernet sauvignon, shiraz, sauvignon blanc, riesling, pinot noir and 4 clones of sangiovese. Yarrh is a local Aboriginal word meaning 'running water' from which the district name of Yass was derived.

Riesling 2022, Canberra District Canberra riesling, there's something special about it. The way the acidity cleanses the palate without being battery acid, the way the citrus flavours and spice work gently together and the great pleasure of drinking it. Screw cap. 11.5% alc. **RATING** 91 **DRINK** 2022-2030 $30 JF

Year Wines   ★★★★

PO Box 638, Willunga, SA 5172 **Region** McLaren Vale
T 0434 970 162 **www.yearwines.com** **Open** Not **Winemaker** Luke Growden, Caleigh Hunt **Est.** 2012 **Dozens** 600
A suite of easygoing, texturally interesting, finely hewn wines crafted with minimal fussing: quality fruit, hand harvesting, wild fermentations and gentle extractive techniques. As impressive is the championing of the right varieties for the land from the layered fiano, textural grenache and smattering of ersatz field blends, these are wines that augur well for the present and even brighter for the future. The style here is one of considered immediacy, to contemplate briefly before drinking with gusto.

Grillo 2022, McLaren Vale The vines are surely young, yet the broad lines of flavour, textural exactitude and poise suggest that grillo should have been here all along. A waxy lemon skin, pear drop and ginger nose. Cedar oak, dried straw and wet woolliness buoy the flavours across the palate as maritime freshness drags them long. This is very good, reminding me of contemporary expressions of the Roussillon. Screw cap. 14% alc. **RATING** 93 **DRINK** 2023–2027 $33 NG

Noodle Juice 2022, McLaren Vale A contemporary and highly regional blend of riesling and grillo. Mid-weighted and textural, interspersing the tangerine and gingery lemon squash aromas of skin maceration with the focus and dry resolve of something approachable for the regular drinker. Pistachio, cantaloupe and lemon drop, to boot. Delicious, idiosyncratic drinking. Screw cap. 12.7% alc. **RATING** 91 **DRINK** 2023–2025 $26 NG

YEATES   ★★★☆

138 Craigmoor Road, Mudgee, NSW 2850 **Region** Mudgee
T 02 6317 2689 **www**.yeateswines.com.au **Open** Thurs–Sun 11–5 **Winemaker** Jacob Stein, Lisa Bray **Viticulturist** Sandy Yeates **Est.** 2010 **Dozens** 300 **Vyds** 11.5ha
In '10, the Yeates family purchased the Mountain Blue vineyard in Mudgee from Foster's, who in turn purchased it from Rosemount (the shiraz and cabernet were the source of Rosemount's single-vineyard Mountain Blue label). Planted in 1968, these are some of the oldest vines in Mudgee. The vineyard has been managed organically since '13 and the vines have flourished under this regimen. Riesling and albariño have since been established, too. Wines are made by Jacob Stein, of nearby Robert Stein (see separate entry).

Rosé 2022, Mudgee A 50/50% blend of tempranillo from Burrundulla Wines and shiraz off Yeates' Mountain Blue vineyard. An elegant rose gold hue with aromas of watermelon, mandarin and lilies. The palate is vibrant with red berries and cumquats, finishing with a hint of white pepper and sumac. Plenty of interest and fruit density. Screw cap. 13% alc. **RATING** 90 **DRINK** 2022–2030 $38 SW

Yelland & Papps   ★★★★☆

279 Nuraip Road, Nuriootpa, SA 5355 **Region** Barossa Valley
T 0408 628 494 **www**.yellandandpapps.com **Open** By appt **Winemaker** Michael and Susan Papps **Viticulturist** Michael Papps **Est.** 2005 **Dozens** 4000 **Vyds** 2ha
Michael and Susan Papps (née Yelland) set up this venture after their marriage in '05. It is easy for them to regard the Barossa Valley as their home because Michael has lived and worked in the wine industry in the Barossa Valley for more than 20 years. He has a rare touch, producing consistently excellent wines, but also pushing the envelope; as well as using a sustainable approach to winemaking with minimal inputs, he has not hesitated to challenge orthodox approaches to a number of aspects of conventional fermentation methods.

Single Vineyard Greenock Shiraz 2020, Barossa Valley Notes of plush satsuma plum, black cherry and summer berry fruits along with hints of baking spices, licorice, dark chocolate and spicy French oak. Impressive in its fruit depth, while retaining a sense of freshness and vitality, finishing long with a bloom of plum and blueberry fruits cut through with spice. Lovely. Screw cap. 13.4% alc. **RATING** 95 **DRINK** 2023–2033 $49 DB

Vin de Soif 2022, Barossa Valley Vin de Soif has built a solid reputation as a crowdpleaser. A bunchy, bouncy little blend of grenache, cinsault and mataro that is light and vital and provides great drinking pleasure. It's all plums and cranberries with amaro, funky exotic spice, citrus blossom, earth and light meaty tones. Just good fun drinking. Screw cap. 13.9% alc. **RATING** 94 **DRINK** 2023–2037 $32 DB

Second Take Shiraz 2021, Barossa Valley A gloriously bunchy, meaty-edged shiraz showing pure juicy plum and cherry fruits, layers of exotic spice, purple floral facets and a gamey nuance that I adore. Impressive pure fruit flow, tannin architecture and all-round zesty slurpiness. Lovely stuff. Screw cap. 13.2% alc. **RATING** 94 **DRINK** 2023–2028 $38 DB

Vin de Soif 2021, Barossa Valley It's light and breezy with pure cranberry, red plum and red cherry fruits, an array of wild-eyed exotic spices, amaro herb notes, meaty/gamey tones, red licorice, violets, citrus blossom and jasmine. Savoury, spacious and sapid, it is great drinking if you seek something light, spicy and purely fruited. Screw cap. 12.7% alc. **RATING** 94 **DRINK** 2023–2027 $32 DB ✪

 TTTTT **Single Vineyard Old Vine Grenache 2021, Barossa Valley** **RATING** 93 **DRINK** 2023–2030 $43 DB
Shiraz 2022, Barossa Valley **RATING** 92 **DRINK** 2023–2030 $32 DB
Blanc 2022, Barossa Valley **RATING** 92 **DRINK** 2023–2026 $32 DB
Second Take Mataro Cinsault 2021, Barossa Valley **RATING** 92 **DRINK** 2023–2025 $38 DB
Shiraz 2021, Barossa Valley **RATING** 92 **DRINK** 2023–2026 $32 DB
Single Vineyard Roussanne 2021, Barossa Valley **RATING** 92 **DRINK** 2023–2025 $46 DB
Vermentino 2021, Barossa Valley **RATING** 91 **DRINK** 2023–2026 $43 DB
Brumeaux Roussanne 2021, Barossa Valley **RATING** 91 **DRINK** 2023–2025 $38 DB
Second Take Grenache 2021, Barossa Valley **RATING** 90 **DRINK** 2023–2026 $38 DB

Yering Station   ★★★★★

38 Melba Highway, Yarra Glen, Vic 3775 **Region** Yarra Valley
T (03) 9730 0100 **www**.yering.com **Open** Mon–Fri 10–5 w'ends 10–6 **Winemaker** Brendan Hawker, Amanda Flynn, Darren Rathbone **Viticulturist** Rod Harrison
Est. 1988 **Dozens** 60 000 **Vyds** 112ha
The historic Yering Station (or at least the portion of the property on which the cellar door and vineyard are established) was purchased by the Rathbone family in '96; it is also the site of Yarrabank. A spectacular and very large winery was built, handling the Yarrabank sparkling and the Yering Station table wines, immediately becoming one of the focal points of the Yarra Valley – particularly as the historic Château Yering, where luxury accommodation and fine dining are available, is next door.

TTTTT **Scarlett Pinot Noir 2021, Yarra Valley** Lifted and perfumed with aromas of small red fruits, rose petals and aromatic herbs and a touch of sandalwood. More subtle and sophisticated than the Reserve Pinot 2021, this alluring and elegant wine has both delicacy and depth. The tannins are superfine and persistent, and the finish is long and ethereal. While both the label and price are a nod to Burgundy, so too is the style. Screw cap. 13.3% alc. **RATING** 97 **DRINK** 2022–2032 $250 PR
Reserve Shiraz Viognier 2021, Yarra Valley Just so fragrant with its aromas of red and blue fruits, florals, allspice and a hint of incense. This medium-bodied and beautifully poised wine caresses the palate before finishing with persistent well-knit tannins that are a good reminder that, as delicious as this is now, it's also been built to last. Screw cap. 13.7% alc. **RATING** 97 **DRINK** 2022–2032 $130 PR

TTTTT **Y28 Block Chardonnay 2021, Yarra Valley** The westerly facing Y28 block has long been a key component in Yering Station's reserve chardonnays. Refined and complex stone and orchard fruits intermingle with gentle marine scents and a little grilled cashew. Saline, tightly wound and long, but will unfurl with time. Screw cap. 13% alc. **RATING** 96 **DRINK** 2023–2028 $70 PR ✪
Carr Vineyard Shiraz 2021, Yarra Valley The inaugural release of this single vineyard wine. Complex and brooding with aromas of dark fruits, spices, incense and some cedar from the oak. Medium bodied, excellent depth, and impeccable fine-grained and persistent tannins for backbone and structure. You can open this now, but you'll thank me later if you still have a bottle 10 years from now. Screw cap. 13.6% alc. **RATING** 96 **DRINK** 2022–2032 $70 PR ✪
Reserve Chardonnay 2021, Yarra Valley An average vine age of 20 years. A bright green gold. With its aromas of white peach, tangerine oil, some toasted

hazelnuts and a little vanilla bean, this has immediate appeal. Equally engaging on the gently fleshy, impeccably balanced and very long palate. Screw cap. 13% alc. **RATING** 96 **DRINK** 2022-2028 $130 PR

Reserve Pinot Noir 2021, Yarra Valley Brendan Hawker's first beginning-to-end reserve pinot. A bright, deep-ish crimson purple. Darkly fruited and immediately seductive with its aromas of ripe raspberries, dark cherry, spice and discreet oak. There's an old-vine creaminess on the palate and you barely notice the wine's firm, velvety and persistent tannins. It's great now and it'll be great in 10 years. Screw cap. 13.5% alc. **RATING** 96 **DRINK** 2022-2032 $130 PR

Laura Barnes Pinot Noir 2021, Yarra Valley Bright crimson. A discreet bouquet with its scents of forest fruits, satsuma plum, star anise and a hint of freshly tilled earth. Even better on the palate, this has excellent depth of fruit while remaining light on its feet and delicate at the same time. No mean feat. The tannins are sophisticated and persistent, and this should age well. Screw cap. 12.9% alc. **RATING** 96 **DRINK** 2022-2031 $70 PR ✪

Reserve Cabernet Sauvignon 2021, Yarra Valley An impressive bouquet with dark cherry, blackcurrant, pencil box and violet scents. Impeccably balanced, this medium- to full-bodied and elegant wine has a good depth of fruit and excellent structure. The tannins are fine, gently chewy and persistent, and this will continue to evolve and become more complex over the next decade or so. Screw cap. 13.9% alc. **RATING** 96 **DRINK** 2022-2035 $130 PR

Y28 Block Chardonnay 2022, Yarra Valley Bright green gold. Discreet and complex with its aromas of stone fruits, jasmine, lightly toasted nuts and marine scents. Poised, persistent and tensile, it's already a pleasure to drink. Screw cap. 12.6% alc. **RATING** 95 **DRINK** 2023-2029 $70 PR

Laura Barnes Pinot Noir 2022, Yarra Valley A light, bright cherry red. With its scents of redcurrants, pomegranate, lightly spiced strawberries and a touch of rose petal, this is at the finer, more delicate end of the pinot spectrum. And while those flavours and that delicacy are duplicated on the palate, it's also got very fine, sinewy and persistent tannins. I can see this ageing beautifully. Screw cap. 12.7% alc. **RATING** 95 **DRINK** 2023-2028 $70 PR

Pinot Noir 2022, Yarra Valley Engaging scents of wild strawberries, raspberries, floral notes and a little star anise. The light- to medium-bodied palate is pure fruited and gently plush and there's a good amount of persistent, fine-grained tannins giving the wine structure and longevity. Screw cap. 13% alc. **RATING** 95 **DRINK** 2022-2029 $40 PR ✪

Chardonnay 2021, Yarra Valley There's a little struck-match character together with attractive aromas of just-picked nectarines and a hint of cashew. The palate is grapefruit pithy, gently textured and long. A very nicely put-together wine that will continue to improve over the short to medium term. Screw cap. 13% alc. **RATING** 95 **DRINK** 2022-2026 $40 PR ✪

Chardonnay 2022, Yarra Valley A touch more concentrated than the '21, this has scents of white nectarines, yellow apples and candied ginger. Vibrant and fresh on the palate, this youthful wine finishes saline and with good persistence. Screw cap. 13% alc. **RATING** 94 **DRINK** 2023-2028 $40 PR ✪

Grenache Shiraz Mourvèdre 2021, Yarra Valley Bright crimson red. An attractive combination of red fruits, a little spice and some earthier, mourvèdre-derived notes. There's a little fresh tobacco and dried herbs, too. Medium bodied and gently juicy in the mouth, fine, persistent tannins round out a wine to enjoy now and over the next 4-5 years. Screw cap. 13.8% alc. **RATING** 94 **DRINK** 2022-2028 $40 PR ✪

�♥ **Shiraz Viognier 2021, Yarra Valley RATING** 93 **DRINK** 2022-2027 $40 PR
Village Rosé 2022, Yarra Valley RATING 92 **DRINK** 2022-2024 $28 PR ✪
Village Chardonnay 2022, Yarra Valley RATING 92 **DRINK** 2022-2026 $28 PR ✪
Village Shiraz 2021, Yarra Valley RATING 91 **DRINK** 2022-2027 $28 PR ✪
Cabernet Sauvignon 2020, Yarra Valley RATING 90 **DRINK** 2022-2027 $40 PR

Yeringberg ★★★★★

810 Maroondah Highway, Coldstream, Vic 3770 **Region** Yarra Valley
T (03) 9739 0240 **www**.yeringberg.com.au **Open** By appt **Winemaker** Sandra de Pury
Viticulturist David de Pury **Est**. 1863 **Dozens** 1500 **Vyds** 12ha

A 19th century Yarra Valley pioneer, Yeringberg's renaissance began when the 3rd generation wine grower, Guill and Katherine de Pury began replanting vines in 1969, making their first commercial wine in '74. Since '08, the wines have been made by daughter Sandra while her brother, David, who has a PhD in plant physiology, manages the vineyards and Yeringberg's grass-fed lamb and cattle. Committed to the future, a new winery is in design phase and a new vine program began in '20 to mitigate against climate change and phylloxera, establishing 2 new vineyard sites on south- and east-facing slopes. The future could not be more exciting for one of the Yarra's oldest and most important producers.

♟♟♟♟♟ **Yeringberg 2021, Yarra Valley** A 58/14/14/9/5% blend of cabernet sauvignon/cabernet franc/merlot/petit verdot/malbec. From a great year, this is a fragrant and seductive Yeringberg with aromas of blackcurrants, blueberries, cherry blossom, violets and just the right amount of oak-derived cedar and pencil-shaving scents. The epitome of medium bodied, it's elegant, discreet and persistent on the palate, even at this early juncture. The fruit is perfectly framed by the wine's fine-grained and silky tannins and will mature slowly and gracefully. Screw cap. 13.5% alc. RATING 98 DRINK 2025–2035 $98 PR ✪
Marsanne Roussanne 2021, Yarra Valley Year in and year out, this wine delivers the goods. Pure fruited with stone and orchard fruits, orange blossom, fresh ginger and a touch of spice. It's mouth-filling and textured yet fresh. Finishes long and with a little apricot and fresh lime. Excellent. Screw cap. 13% alc. RATING 97 DRINK 2023–2030 $68 PR ✪

♟♟♟♟♟ **Rosé 2022, Yarra Valley** 75/25% cabernet sauvignon/shiraz. The palest of pink salmons. Gorgeous aromatics with its scents of wild strawberries, cherry skins, lavender and spring flowers. Delicate yet flavoursome in the mouth, the finish is dry and refreshing with a gentle Campari-like bitter twist. Only the second Yeringberg rosé made, and an absolute beauty! Screw cap. 13% alc. RATING 96 DRINK 2022–2025 $40 PR ✪ ♥
Pinot Noir 2021, Yarra Valley Aromatically, I can't recall a prettier Yeringberg pinot. It's got delicate new-season cherries, strawberries, rose petals and a little nutmeg spice. Gentle and sweetly fruited on entry, it's also earthy and structured with fine yet powerful tannins. Finishes long and with a touch of spice. This is destined to age well. Screw cap. 13% alc. RATING 96 DRINK 2023–2033 $98 PR
Viognier 2021, Yarra Valley Bright gold with green tinges. Richer and more opulent than last year's wine but equally compelling. A heady mix of apricots, just-ripened mangoes, orange blossom honey and a little freshly grated ginger. Voluptuous, silken textured and with excellent balance on the palate. Finishes focused and long. A hedonistic wine that's probably best enjoyed in its youth. Screw cap. 14% alc. RATING 95 DRINK 2023–2027 $45 PR ✪
Shiraz 2021, Yarra Valley Bright crimson purple. Aromas of boysenberries, dark raspberries, star anise and a gentle waft of oak-derived cedar. Medium bodied, gently plush and silken, this is already a delight. Screw cap. 14% alc. RATING 95 DRINK 2022–2030 $98 PR
Chardonnay 2021, Yarra Valley A bright green gold. Aromas of ripe yellow peach, a soupçon of freshly churned butter and toasted almonds. While creamily textured and concentrated, there's also a fine bead of acidity running through the wine. Finishes with a gentle pithiness and can be drunk with confidence now and over the next 4–6 years. Screw cap. 13% alc. RATING 94 DRINK 2022–2028 $68 PR

Yes said the seal

1251–1269 Bellarine Highway, Wallington, Vic 3221 **Region** Geelong
T (03) 5250 6577 **www.**yessaidtheseal.com.au **Open** 7 days 10–5 **Winemaker** Darren
Burke **Viticulturist** David Sharp **Est.** 2014 **Dozens** 1200 **Vyds** 8ha

This is the most recent venture of David and Lyndsay Sharp, long-term vintners on Geelong's
Bellarine Peninsula. It is situated onsite at the Flying Brick Cider Co's Cider House in
Wallington. The estate vineyard includes 3ha of pinot noir, 2ha each of chardonnay and shiraz
and 1ha of sauvignon blanc.

The Bellarine Shiraz 2021, Geelong A bright, medium crimson purple.
Opens with aromas of dark fruits, olive tapenade, black pepper and a lick of
graphite. A touch closed at present on the palate, this finishes long with fine-
grained and even tannins suggesting that as good as this is now, it will continue
to become more complex over the next 4–6 years, if not longer. Screw cap.
13.5% alc. **RATING** 95 **DRINK** 2023–2029 $50 PR ✪

The Bellarine Rosé 2022, Geelong **RATING** 92 **DRINK** 2022–2025 $38 PR

Z Wine

Shop 3, 109–111 Murray Street, Tanunda, SA 5352 **Region** Barossa Valley
T (08) 8563 3637 **www.**zwine.com.au **Open** Sun–Thurs 10–8, Fri–Sat 10–late
Winemaker Janelle Zerk **Est.** 1999 **Dozens** 10 000

Z Wine is the partnership of sisters Janelle and Kristen Zerk, whose heritage dates
back 5 generations at the Zerk vineyard in Lyndoch. Vineyard resources include growers
that supply old-vine shiraz, old bush-vine grenache and High Eden riesling. Both women
have completed degrees at the University of Adelaide (Janelle winemaking and Kristen wine
marketing). Janelle also has vintage experience in Puligny Montrachet, Tuscany and Sonoma
Valley. Wines are released under the Z Wine, Rustica and Section 3146 labels.

Hein Ancestor Vine Shiraz 2020, Barossa Valley Chocolatey red and black
fruits lie at the core of this wine, which shows an impressive array of spice, amaro,
dark chocolate and earthy tones, significant oak spice and cedary sheen, fine
tannins and a finish that bursts with plum/blackberry jam. Some excellent textural
components and serious concentration are on display here. Two barrels produced.
Diam. 14.8% alc. **RATING** 95 **DRINK** 2023–2038 $300 DB

Roman Old Vine GSM 2022, Barossa Valley Purple splashed crimson in
the glass and perfumed with juicy satsuma plums, raspberry and mulberry fruit
tones with ginger and cinnamon, violets, raspberry licorice and earth. Sprightly
acidity drives things along nicely to a savoury, spicy, red-fruited finish. Screw cap.
14.5% alc. **RATING** 94 **DRINK** 2023–2028 $45 DB

Saul Night Havest Riesling 2022, Eden Valley Pale in the glass with a slight
green flicker and inviting aromas of Bickford's lime cordial, orange blossom,
lemon zest, white peach and a waft of papaya. Quite a textural style with a swell
of citrus and peach fruit on the palate, crushed quartz and light fennel notes, too,
as it coils and powers off on rails of fine acidity, finishing dry and savoury. Screw
cap. 12.5% alc. **RATING** 94 **DRINK** 2023–2028 $35 DB ✪

Rohrlach Survivor Vine Grenache 2021, Barossa Valley Mid-crimson with
aromas of sexy ripe plum and red berry fruits cut with hints of ginger cake, red
licorice, redcurrant jelly, raspberry coulis, citrus blossom, cola and earth. At the
lighter end of medium-bodied with some lovely fruit sweetness and detail but
with a sapid edge as some sour morello cherry swoops in on the finish to join the
layers of spice. Diam. 14.5% alc. **RATING** 94 **DRINK** 2023–2033 $120 DB

Plowman Dry Grown Shiraz 2021, Barossa Valley **RATING** 93
DRINK 2023–2038 $120 DB

Hilder Ancestor Vine Mataro 2021, Barossa Valley **RATING** 93
DRINK 2023–2030 $300 DB

August Old Vine Grenache 2022, Barossa Valley RATING 92
DRINK 2023–2028 $35 DB
Rustica Grenache 2022, Barossa Valley RATING 92 DRINK 2023–2027
$25 DB ✪
Section 3146 Shiraz 2021, Barossa Valley RATING 92 DRINK 2023–2029
$35 DB
Rustica Shiraz 2020, Barossa Valley RATING 92 DRINK 2023–2027 $25 DB ✪
Feire Blanc de Blancs 2019, Eden Valley RATING 91 DRINK 2023–2030
$50 DB
Section 3146 Cabernet Sauvignon 2021, Barossa Valley RATING 91
DRINK 2023–2030 $35 DB
Nevah Chardonnay 2021, Eden Valley RATING 91 DRINK 2023–2026 $30 DB
Rustica Reserve Shiraz 2020, Barossa Valley RATING 91 DRINK 2023–2028
$35 DB
Rustica Mataro 2020, Barossa Valley RATING 91 DRINK 2023–2027 $28
DB ✪
Poole Old Vine Shiraz 2019, Barossa Valley RATING 91 DRINK 2023–2035
$120 DB
Feiern Sparkling Red NV, Barossa Valley RATING 90 $50 DB
Levarin Old Vine Bonvedro 2022, Barossa Valley RATING 90
DRINK 2023–2026 $30 DB

Zema Estate   ★★★★☆

14944 Riddoch Highway, Coonawarra, SA 5263 **Region** Coonawarra
T (08) 8736 3219 **www.zema.com.au Open** Mon–Fri 9–5, w'ends & public hols 10–4
Winemaker Joe Cory **Viticulturist** Nick Zema **Est.** 1982 **Dozens** 15 000 **Vyds** 61ha
The Zema family have always hand pruned this vineyard set in the heart of Coonawarra's terra
rossa soil. Winemaking practices are straightforward; if ever there was an example of great
wines being made in the vineyard, this is it.

♈♈♈♈♈ Family Selection Cabernet Sauvignon 2018, Coonawarra Curls of flavour-
soaked tannin. Currants with clear inlays of dry tobacco, herbs, aniseed and dust.
A general juiciness to the flow and yet it still feels as though it's a wine to be
taken seriously. All the angles and characters of this wine are positive. It's a very
good release, with an excellent future ahead. Screw cap. 14.5% alc. RATING 95
DRINK 2025–2035 $50 CM ✪
Family Selection Shiraz 2018, Coonawarra There's good substance to this
release. It's bold with ripe plum, redcurrant and boysenberry flavours, peppercorn
and toasty oak notes only add to the theme. Tannin plays a modest role but the
flavours hold good shape from start to end. A creamy aspect to the mouthfeel is
an attractive touch. Screw cap. 15% alc. RATING 94 DRINK 2024–2034 $50 CM

♈♈♈♈♉ Shiraz 2019, Coonawarra RATING 92 DRINK 2024–2032 $29 CM ✪
Cluny Cabernet Merlot 2019, Coonawarra RATING 91 DRINK 2024–2032
$26 CM ✪

Zerella Wines   ★★★★

182 Olivers Rd, McLaren Vale, SA 5171 **Region** McLaren Vale
T (08) 8323 8288 **www.zerellawines.com.au Open** Thurs–Mon 11–4 **Winemaker** Jim
Zerella **Viticulturist** Jim Zerella **Est.** 2006 **Dozens** 2500 **Vyds** 58ha
In 1950 Ercole Zerella left his native Campania in southern Italy to seek a better life in SA.
With a lifetime of farming and grapegrowing, the transition was seamless. Ercole's son Vic
followed in his father's footsteps, becoming an icon of the SA farming and wine industries. He
founded Tatachilla, where his son Jim began as a cellar hand, Jim purchased land in McLaren
Vale and, with help from family and friends, established what is now the flagship vineyard
of Zerella Wines. When Tatachilla was purchased by Lion Nathan in '00 Jim declined the
opportunity of continuing his role there and by '06 had purchased 2 more vineyards, and

become a shareholder in a 3rd. These all now come under the umbrella of Zerella Wines, with its 58ha of vines. The winemaking techniques used are thoroughly à la mode and definitely not traditional Italian.

ΨΨΨΨΨ **Oliveto Single Vineyard Mataro 2021, McLaren Vale** Reductive, before a whoosh of air liberates a ferrous brood, whiffs of damson plum, lemon verbena and thyme with a burr of smoked meat and suede across the warm finish. Loads of personality and a strong sense of place. I have long enjoyed the unpretentious aura about these wines, each year a palpable improvement on the last. Screw cap. 14% alc. **RATING** 94 **DRINK** 2023–2031 $60 NG

Single Vineyard Olivers Road Grenache 2021, McLaren Vale 'Best and fairest' sort of material. The quality of fruit, impeccable. The tannins, sandy and gritty and pixelated. Yet, amid the giddy swirl of kirsch, bergamot, lavender and dried thyme, there is something chocolatey about the oak. It's richly flavoured, precise and wonderfully fresh, all the same. Screw cap. 14.5% alc. **RATING** 94 **DRINK** 2022–2030 $60 NG

La Gita Nero d'Avola 2021, McLaren Vale Delicious, pulpy and free-flowing fresh. As good as any expression of nero I've tasted on these shores. Red and black cherry mingle with an underlying marrow of anise, lilac and spruce. Yet the calling card is one of richness, warmth and most of all, vibrancy. So light on its feet and deft of extract, this is a joy to drink. Screw cap. 14% alc. **RATING** 94 **DRINK** 2022–2026 $35 NG ✪

ΨΨΨΨ▽ **Workhorse Shiraz 2021, McLaren Vale RATING** 93 **DRINK** 2022–2029 $30 NG ✪

Packing Shed Grenache Mataro Shiraz 2021, McLaren Vale RATING 92 **DRINK** 2022–2031 $30 NG ✪

Home Block Single Vineyard Shiraz 2019, McLaren Vale RATING 92 **DRINK** 2022–2032 $60 NG

Zilzie Wines   ★★★★☆

544 Kulkyne Way, Karadoc, Vic 3496 **Region** Murray Darling – Vic
T (03) 5025 8100 **www.zilziewines.com Open** By appt **Winemaker** Jonathan Creek, Candy Jonsson **Viticulturist** Andrew Forbes, Steven Forbes **Est.** 1999 **Vyds** 700ha
The Forbes family has been farming since the early 1900s. Zilzie is currently run by Roslyn Forbes and sons Steven and Andrew, the diverse range of farming activities now solely focused on grape growing from substantial vineyards. Having established a successful business as a grower, Zilzie formed a wine company in '99 and built a winery in '00, expanding it to its current capacity of 60 000t. The wines consistently exceed expectations, given their enticing prices, that consistency driving the substantial production volume in an extremely competitive market. The business includes contract processing, winemaking and storage; the winery is certified organic.

ΨΨΨΨΨ **Platinum Edition Arinto 2022, Riverland** Piercing and long. Excellent concentration of grapefruit pulp and citrus flavours with a smoky, steely edge. This does not die wondering in any way, shape or form. It's acidic but it brings intense fruit flavour along with it. Quite a wine. Screw cap. 13% alc. **RATING** 95 **DRINK** 2024–2028 $35 CM ✪

ΨΨΨΨ▽ **Platinum Edition Grenache 2021, Barossa Valley RATING** 93 **DRINK** 2024–2032 $40 CM

Platinum Edition Fiano 2022, Adelaide Hills RATING 91 **DRINK** 2023–2025 $35 CM

Limited Edition Riesling 2021, Clare Valley RATING 91 **DRINK** 2024–2032 $70 CM

Regional Collection Shiraz 2020, Barossa Valley RATING 91 **DRINK** 2023–2028 $22 CM ✪

Limited Edition Shiraz 2021, McLaren Vale RATING 90 **DRINK** 2024–2034 $90 CM

Zitta Wines

Nitschke Road, Greenock, SA 5360 **Region** Barossa Valley
T 0419 819 414 **www**.difaziowines.com **Open** By appt **Winemaker** Angelo De Fazio
Viticulturist Angelo De Fazio **Est.** 1864 **Dozens** 4000 **Vyds** 28ha
Owner Angelo De Fazio says that all he knows about viticulture and winemaking came from
his father (and generations before him). Zitta is Italian for 'quiet', and the seeming reflection
of the letters of the name Zitta on the label is in fact nothing of the kind, turn the bottle
upside down, and you will see it is the word 'Quiet'. The Zitta vineyard dates back to 1864,
with a few vines remaining from that time, and a block planted with cuttings taken from those
vines. Shiraz dominates the plantings (24ha), the balance made up of grenache, mataro and
nero d'Avola. The property has 2 branches of Greenock Creek running through it and the
soils reflect the ancient geological history of the site.

ՔՔՔՔՔ **Single Vineyard Bernardo Greenock Shiraz 2020, Barossa Valley** Packed
with blackberry, dark plum and black cherry fruits cut with hints of baking spice,
licorice, ironstone, graphite, Cherry Ripe, cedar, tobacco and dark chocolate.
Intense, broody and showing plenty of clove and nutmeg spice with thick
cassis and kirsch fruits, chewy powdery tannins and a rich, concentrated finish.
Screw cap. 14.8% alc. **RATING** 91 **DRINK** 2023-2030 $55 DB

Zonte's Footstep

PO Box 353, McLaren Vale SA 5171 **Region** McLaren Vale
T (08) 7286 3088 **www**.zontesfootstep.com.au **Open** Mon–Thurs 11–4, Fri 11–10pm,
w'ends 11–6 **Winemaker** Brad Rey **Viticulturist** Brad Rey **Est.** 2003 **Dozens** 20 000
Vyds 214ha
Zonte's Footstep was founded by a group of winemakers and wine marketers who decided
in '03 that it was time to do their own thing in McLaren Vale. The brand produces an
extraordinary varietal range of 26 different wines using the classic northern European varieties
of shiraz, viognier, cabernet sauvignon, malbec, pinot noir, sauvignon blanc and chardonnay,
as well as the Mediterranean varieties of vermentino, pinot grigio, glera, grenache, sangiovese,
lagrein, tempranillo and montepulciano.

ՔՔՔՔՔ **Violet Beauregard Malbec 2022, Langhorne Creek** This is an impressive
picture of the indissoluble link between the fruit of malbec and Langhorne Creek.
The ideal outcome of 13.5% alcohol invests the wine with a vibrant freshness
running through the palate of blueberries and plums. Screw cap. **RATING** 95
DRINK 2025-2030 $30 JH ❂

ՔՔՔՔՔ **Rosso Cova Montepulciano 2021, McLaren Vale RATING** 91
DRINK 2022-2027 $30 NG
Lake Doctor Shiraz 2020, Langhorne Creek RATING 91 **DRINK** 2023-2033
$30 JH
Trooper Shiraz Cabernet Sauvignon 2019, Fleurieu RATING 90
DRINK 2023-2028 $28 CM

Zonzo Estate

957 Healesville-Yarra Glen Road, Yarra Glen, Vic 3775 **Region** Yarra Valley
T (03) 9730 2500 **www**.zonzo.com.au **Open** Wed–Sun 12–3 **Winemaker** Caroline
Mooney **Viticulturist** Phil Chapman **Est.** 2007 **Vyds** 15.8ha
The Zonzo brand began life as a restaurant in '07, located at the then Train Trak vineyard,
where vines were first planted back in '95. Owner Rod Micallef acquired the surrounding
property and vineyard in '15, renaming it Zonzo Estate. Winemaker Caroline Mooney has
overseen the conversion of a Lilydale warehouse into a dedicated winery, with new Swiss
cooling technology, solar power and rainwater recycling. The vineyard is growing too, with
an additional 20ha being planted in '23 to pinot noir, barbera, nebbiolo, sangiovese fiano and
pecorino. The Scoperta experimental range was launched in '21, dedicated to Italian varieties

that might better suit a future climate. Spirits and beers, produced off-site, are also part of the Zonzo range.

ŸŸŸŸ̦ **Scoperta Sagrantino 2021, Heathcote** A deep-ish cherry red. Black cherries, dried herbs, citrus zest and a touch of violets make for an appealing and perfumed bouquet. Ripe but balanced on the palate, the wine's juicy acidity and fine, gently chewy tannins will have you coming back for another sip! Screw cap. 13.5% alc. **RATING** 93 **DRINK** 2022–2026 $35 PR ✪

Shiraz 2021, Yarra Valley A light–medium bright cherry red. Lively with subtle aromas of red fruit pastille and, white and black pepper with some briary notes. Equally good on the gently persistent and even palate. Screw cap. 14% alc. **RATING** 92 **DRINK** 2022–2027 $27 PR ✪

Scoperta Sangiovese 2021, Heathcote A medium bright cherry red. Dark cherries, bramble and some floral notes are all present in this well put-together sangiovese. Just enough depth on the palate before finishing with grippy but balanced tannins and bright acidity. Screw cap. 13.5% alc. **RATING** 91 **DRINK** 2022–2027 $35 PR

Chardonnay 2021, Yarra Valley This is ripe and energetic with white peach, lemon oil, marzipan and a little vanillin from the well-handled oak. Mouth-filling and balanced, this creamy-textured wine has a hint of lemon pith on the moderately long finish. Screw cap. 13% alc. **RATING** 90 **DRINK** 2022–2026 $27 PR

Index

Wineries are arranged alphabetically under geographical
indications (see page 9), to help you find a wine or winery
if you're looking locally or on the road. If you are hoping
to visit, the following key symbols will be of assistance.

  Music events
  Cellar door sales
  Accommodation
  Food
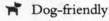 Family-friendly
  Dog-friendly

Beechworth (Vic)

Coonawarra (SA)

Currency Creek (SA)

Denmark (WA)

East Coast Tasmania

Eden Valley (SA)

Hunter Valley (NSW)

Margaret River (WA)

Orange (NSW)

Padthaway (SA)

Pemberton (WA)

Perricoota (NSW)

Perth Hills (WA)

Piccadilly Valley (SA)

Acknowledgements

The first and foremost thanks goes to you, the reader. The *Halliday Wine Companion* would not exist without the prolonged, tireless, thick-and-thin dedication of its chief author and founder, James Halliday, but all this travail would be for nothing were it not for you. We take no reader for granted; we are grateful for your support and loyalty, and regardless of whether this is your first year with this guide or your thirtieth in succession, every member of the Halliday team is determined to make your purchase of this guide worthwhile. We don't hit 'print' until we are certain that we have the Australian wine industry thoroughly covered, or until we are sure that every wine drinker's life is guaranteed to be better as a result.

Much like an iceberg though, the printed book (and the website) are the result of a great deal of beneath the surface work. We literally stop tasting for one edition and start tasting for the next the very following week. You are no doubt well aware of our tasting team – Dave Brookes, Jane Faulkner, Jeni Port, Mike Bennie, Ned Goodwin MW, Philip Rich, Shanteh Wale, James Halliday and myself – but you may not be aware of the level of sacrifice, and the level of care, every one of our tasters commits in the service of this book. The *Halliday Wine Companion* is more than just a job to all of us. Every member of the Halliday tasting panel loves wine, loves finding its secrets, and loves sharing them with you.

Every member also, more than anything, cares that the high standards of this guide, set over decades, are maintained. This comes through on every page of this book. For that, I dip my lid to James for setting the bar so high, and to the panel for being so committed to keeping this book at the top of its game. I cannot thank any of you enough.

One of the not-so-secret weapons of this guide, over a long period of time, is the calibre of people it has been able to attract to work on the guide behind-the-scenes. I'm newly returned to working on this guide but I've been associated with it on-and-off for over a decade, and over that time I know that many wheels would have fallen off on many different occasions were it not for the efforts of Beth and Jake in the Halliday office at Coldstream, both of whom have been no less than essential to this guide for many years – this edition included – as too was (the late) Paula, the latter of whom we all still miss terribly, and mention often. Beth and Jake: we love you.

But the Halliday guide has for a number of years now been headquartered at the Hardie Grant office, and here's where words really don't quite cut it. Emily Lightfoot carries the title of Tasting Manager, and all that title really does is undersell her value. Her job is to deal with thousands of wineries, a large team of tasters and suppliers, internal staff and external concerns. Every day, for the entire year, she has put her heart, soul, mind and energy, often to the detriment of her own wellbeing, into making everything run as smoothly and correctly as it possibly can, and into making this guide work. Emily Lightfoot is part of this guide's history, and forever will be.

It is common now to gloss over the assorted members of this book's production, when all of these key people of course deserve more. I can't do this though without, at the very least, singling out Nola James, who too is a rare gem, and who too has gone many miles above and beyond to ensure that this edition of the book is as readable and as correct as it can be. These key behind-the-scenes figures are heroes of this guide.

As, no doubt, are all the members of the small but mighty Hardie Grant (HGX) team, who are responsible for all elements of the *Companion*, from the book, website and magazine to the annual judging and Awards, plus myriad events and other wine-loving initiatives in between. This team, led by Jac Hardie-Grant, consists of Shana Rohn and Haydn Spurrell in marketing; Anna Webster, J'aime Cardillo and Olivia Jay in editorial; Katrina Butler in membership; George Lingard, Katie Xiao, Nicole Prioste and Claire Teisseyre in commercial, Uno de Waal in product; Glenn Moffatt in design; Christine Dixon and Sammi Gui in finance. We all play different roles; all are as essential as the other.

A special thanks here, too, to the Hardie Grant Books team; to Michael Harry, publisher; Elena Callcott, project editor; Nola James (editor, see above); Megan Ellis, typesetter; Alex Ward, designer; Ka Mo, cover artist; Kasi Collins and the rest of the Hardie Grant Books marketing team.

Tyson Stelzer, too, deserves to be acknowledged. He was the previous editor of this guide; the handover was seamless, courteous, respectful and professional, as is his renown.

But readers, this of course is not our guide, it's yours. I'm proud to acknowledge our people in this small way but it's time to pass it over to you.

Cheers,
Campbell Mattinson

This year's cover artwork was painted by Melbourne-based landscape and still life artist, Ka Mo. The painting was based on a series of images taken by James Halliday from his balcony in Coldstream.